Historic Preservation

Historic Preservation

Law and Culture

Cases and Materials

Nicholas A. Robinson

Gilbert and Sarah Kerlin Distinguished Professor of
Environmental Law Emeritus
Pace University, Elisabeth Haub School of Law

Shelby D. Green

Professor of Law
Pace University, Elisabeth Haub School of Law

Carolina Academic Press

Durham, North Carolina

ISBN 978-1-5310-0484-2
eISBN 978-1-53100-485-9
LCCN 2017957017

Carolina Academic Press, LLC
700 Kent Street
Durham, North Carolina 27701
Telephone (919) 489-7486
Fax (919) 493-5668
www.cap-press.com

Printed in the United States of America

We dedicate this casebook with gratitude in honor of Dorothy M. Miner.

Nicholas A. Robinson and Shelby D. Green

New York Preservation Archive Project

Dedication

Dorothy Marie Miner

1936–2008

Dorothy Miner taught Historic Preservation Law at the Columbia University's School of Architecture and at Pace University's School of Law, for each of the fourteen years before her death. She curated many of the materials included in this casebook. For nineteen years before her academic life, she served as the first General Counsel to the New York City Landmarks Preservation Commission. What she accomplished with and for the Landmarks Preservation Commission was extraordinary. Within weeks of her death, New York City Corporation Counsel's office honored her by rededicating its highest service award, which recognizes legal counsel serving across all the City's agencies, in her name. The State of New York coincidentally honored her the very same day. One lawyer can make all the difference.

Perpetually understaffed, the Landmarks Preservation Commission hired Dorothy to become its only staff attorney in 1975. This was a time of great uncertainty about the constitutionality of the City's Landmarks Preservation Law. State courts had divided over the legality of the landmark status conferred upon Grand Central Terminal and the case was on appeal. The New York City Real Estate Board had told Mayor Robert Wagner that the law was unconstitutional before he signed it into law in 1965. Dorothy became a key player on the City's small legal team that won the 1978 United States Supreme Court's ruling in *Penn Central Transp. Co. v. New York City*, upholding the constitutionality of New York's landmarks law. Dorothy loved the enduring quality of Justice William J. Brennan's decision. When opponents of landmarks laws railed on, she never tired of quoting Justice Sandra Day O'Connor's later ruling in 2002 that "Our polestar remains the principles set forth in *Penn Central* ..." Today, municipalities across the United States pattern their landmark procedures on those that Dorothy Miner designed in New York City. She loved to recall how Justice Brennan exclaimed, every time he walked out of Grand Central Terminal, how great it was to see the sky above the landmark terminal.

Throughout her life, Dorothy's integrity and commitment to core values was invincible, leaving no room for expedient compromising. She loved accuracy and truth, for its own sake, and had an appetite for meticulous and tireless craftsmanship in drafting legal documents replete with all their minutia and detail. She served the Landmarks Preservation Commission and a succession of Commission chairs with dedication. Self-effacing to a fault, Dorothy sought no limelight, serving both her principals and her principles ably. On April 27, 1965, after the City's Landmarks Preservation Law was adopted, the *New York Times* warned that "The past is yet to be secured for the future." Its editorial page opined that "It will take imagination, dedication, concern, citizen action, private financing and public cooperation to effect preservation under the new law." When Dorothy died on October 23, 2008, the *New York Times* hailed her as "a legal innovator." Historic preservation law thrives today, imbued with Dorothy's intellect.

Contents

List of Images

Acknowledgments

The Authors thank the Law Library of the Elisabeth Haub School of Law at Pace University, its Director, Prof. Marie Newman, and Prof. Alyssa Rosen, the Environmental Law Librarian, for their consistent and timely support. We thank the able legal staff of the National Trust for Historic Preservation for sharing its expertise. We especially commend and thank the Office of Counsel in the Landmarks Preservation Commission of the City of New York. Above all, we thank our students whose questions and insights over many years have enriched our understanding of preservation law and contributed to refining these readings.

Shelby D. Green and Nicholas A. Robinson

Historic Preservation

Law and Culture

Chapter 1

Why Protect the Historic

A. Should "Law" Protect the "Historic"?

1. Probing the Questions: Why "Preserve" Historic Cultural Patrimony?

Before exploring how America's historic preservation laws function, it is important to explore why they exist at all. This chapter examines the social and cultural foundations for caring for the creation of the past. We offer a range of questions that probe why people today decide that the structures built in the past matter. These questions illuminate themes that will recur throughout this casebook.

2. Awakening Awareness of Places Historic

What is historic? When and how will we, today, know what may be deemed *historic*? Will we know after a decade? A generation? Fifty years? Will it be a building? A place? A landscape? A structure reconstructed after a fire? A new building to replicate one from antiquity, or a wooden structure entirely rebuilt, plank-by-plank, since its first construction? And, even if we come to know these cultural possessions, why should law protect what society deems to be *historic*? Whose laws should society rely upon to do so? Should we determine that an object is a worthy subject of an "historic preservation law," should the legislation be enacted by a local government, a state, the national government, or even an international organization? How many of the same genre of historic structures need to be preserved? All architectural types? Only the most outstanding? Only those where historic events took place? And, how much of a building should be "preserved"? Can all or some of it be removed or adapted to allow new uses? If so, when or under what circumstances? Should taxpayers subsidize the preservation or adaptive reuse of historic structures? Keeping up appearances costs owners money! Will we remember why we decided to preserve a place?

Over the past 150 years, the local, state, and federal governments in the United States have grappled with these questions, and have come to agree upon how to debate and arrive at answers. This casebook explores these questions and introduces the law governing the process and substance of the laws guiding stewardship of historic cultural heritage.

The record of historic preservation law in the United States begins in a period of the nation's relative prosperity that followed the treaties of 1784 and 1794 with England, negotiated by John Jay and other founding fathers. These treaties brought a close to the revolutionary war, provided for settling war claims, fixed the nation's western border at the Mississippi River, and secured maritime trading rights. In 1803, the Louisiana Purchase extended the nation west of the Mississippi, and the Lewis and Clark Expedition returned to Washington in 1806 with accounts of the peoples and lands found westward. In 1835, Ralph Waldo Emerson began his literary career in Concord, where America's first generation of authors reflected on the young nation's brief past and mused about visionary futures. Thoreau's Walden Pond, donated to Massachusetts by the heirs of Emerson and others in 1922, is on the National Register of Historic Places. https://www.nps.gov/nr/travel/massachusetts_conservation/walden_pond.html (last visited April 5, 2017).

Different generations sought to use Walden Pond in different ways, from a recreation place of amusement to a nature refuge. Concord's literary traditions probed what it means to be a new nation. In her exploration of how America remembers and records its literary landmarks, Shelley Fisher Fishkin invokes Thoreau's writings as part of the fabric of what we learn from the Pond and why we conserve it. His writings speak to our lives still: "learning how to live in harmony with nature turns out to be both necessary for our survival and more complicated than we supposed." SHELLEY FISHER FISHKIN, WRITING AMERICA—LITERARY LANDMARKS FROM WALDEN POND TO WOUNDED KNEE 55 (2015).

The cultural instinct to set aside and save what we come to agree is historic is recurring. The first recorded legal measures to protect historic sites appears in 1850, when New York State acquired and preserved Hasbrouck House, which had served as George Washington's headquarters during the Revolutionary War (1782–83). https://parks.ny.gov/historic-sites/17/details.aspx (last visited April 5, 2017). Nearby, along the Hudson River north of West Point, he had assembled the Continental Army to be decommissioned following the successful American Revolution. Shortly thereafter, a dedicated committee of women decided to save Mount Vernon, George Washington's home in Virginia, overlooking the Potomac River. A codicil in one of his heirs' wills provided for its purchase as a public trust by Congress or the State of Virginia, if either desired to do so, and neither did. The heirs lacked income to keep up Mount Vernon. Some buildings were lost and the mansion was in severe decay. Speculators were bidding to buy the property, when in 1853, Ann Pamela Cunningham offered to raise funds to buy Washington's estate. On the eve of the Civil War until 1860, private citizens launched a nation-wide Mount Vernon crusade to raise the funds, and formed the Mount Vernon Ladies' Association of the Union, a non-governmental organization established under Virginia's laws, to hold title, and acquire George Washington's home. ELSWYTH THANE, MOUNT VERNON IS OURS (1966).

Globally, the vast majority of nations have enacted laws to protect or conserve historic monuments that commemorate or celebrate their cultural heritage. Each nation does so in a unique way, befitting its own traditions of governance and historical development. By 1895, twenty houses had been preserved as museums in the United States. By 1906, Theodore Roosevelt had signed into law the Antiquities Act of 1906, 54 U.S.C. §§320301–320303, formerly 16 U.S.C. §§431–433, which permits preservation of cultural and natural heritage on federal public lands. By 1933, concern for the "usable past" had preserved some 400 sites as house museums, and the Historic American Buildings Survey was launched by the federal government to inventory all the nation's most important historic structures. Most state legislatures enacted statutes to enable local governments to protect historic buildings and places. However, by 1966, in the wake of rapid economic growth following World War II, a report of a Special Committee on Historic Preservation under the auspices of the United States Conference of Mayors with a grant from the Ford Foundation, found that more than half the buildings listed on that Survey had been demolished. WITH HERITAGE SO RICH 191 (1966).

If no one knows a building is worth saving for its history, or an old structure becomes derelict, its demolition goes unnoticed. Even the homes of founding fathers are at risk, as is evident in the struggle to save the Locusts, the birthplace and gravesite of John Jay in Rye, New York. We describe that struggle throughout this book.

Landmarks associated with a nation's founding fathers may be obvious choices for preservation, but what about "everyday" structures from the past? When does the old ordinary, such as a neighborhood gathering place or site renowned only in local folklore, become cherished heritage and entitled to legal protection? Why does public controversy often erupt when a property owner or highway department seeks to tear down an old building that stands in the way of new architectural creations or needed transportation enhancements? Even if one old building may have some aesthetic or other merit, how many examples of obsolete and energy-inefficient construction styles does society need? How can society decide when is it appropriate for a government or public school system to spend scarce funds to protect historic assets, expenditures that may detract from the primary duty to provide education? What is the justification for requiring an owner to maintain private property to "preserve" its "historic" value?

What about religious structures? Do they serve only their religious calling, or are they part of the history and landscape of a community also? Can government require their preservation, or alternatively can public funds be invested in preserving a religious site, without there being an interference with the free exercise of religion on the one hand or aiding the parochial "establishment" of one religion over another?

What about a landscape without an extant trace of history? Should a place, with no historic structures remaining extant, be preserved because they once stood there? Should sites of prehistoric and archaeological significance be preserved, or allowed to be built upon by present generations with or without doing an archaeological dig? How should a battlefield be memorialized, as with Saratoga, Gettysburg, Antietam, Wounded Knee or the Waikiki Natatorium War Memorial in Hawaii. Re-enactors, entire corps of "soldiers" and camp followers in historic garb appear at many battlefields to create a living tableau of the past events of history. Their presence is ephemeral, but like literature they live on and reconnect today to yesterday. How should all historic sites be recalled? As Howard Mansfield muses, "This earth is no place for a house museum. Museums are fugitive. Life is fugitive. The barn is empty when we return and the horses of our youth have fled." HOWARD MANSFIELD, THE SAME AX TWICE—RESTORATION AND RENEWAL IN A THROWAWAY AGE 89 (2000). Cities, unlike preserved battlefields, are constantly evolving with each new generation. How can we promote originality and creation of new landmark buildings if we preserve "too much" of the footprint of the past?

Museums often are a refuge for historic structures that cannot be preserved in place. These are *ex situ* preservations. Are they any less worthy of note than buildings preserved in the original locations? They keep the authenticity of fabric, but lose the authenticity of place. As a last resort to monuments in harm's way, this is an essential type of preservation. The Roman Temple of Dendur, rescued from the rising waters of the Aswan High Dam in Egypt, was removed to the Metropolitan Museum of Art in New York City in 1965. Many wooden structures from across the Adirondack Mountains in New York have been removed for conservation and exhibition to the Adirondack Museum at Blue Mountain Lake, as have many New England buildings from the 1790s to 1830s been brought to Old Sturbridge Village in Massachusetts. These assemblages have saved buildings that might otherwise be lost to neglect and decay, but some criticize them as not being authentic, preferring *in situ* preservation, and decline to list moved structures on historic registers as a result. As sea level rise associated with climate change imperils landmarks situated along the coastlines, will this attitude need to change?

Even when society agrees on preserving a place, as it does in favoring cemeteries, questions emerge. Burial grounds are customarily well-maintained, but what if they are abandoned and become wards of the State? Who restores historic tombstones when families are gone? Noah Remnick, *A Historic New Jersey Cemetery Sits Neglected and Blighted*, N.Y. TIMES, March 19, 2017. https://www.nytimes.com/2017/03/19/nyregion/a-historic-new-jersey-cemetery-sits-neglected-and-blighted.html. What if a cemetery is entirely forgotten, as in the case of the African-American Burial Grounds at Foley Square in Manhattan, uncovered in 1991 while the federal General Services Administration was preparing the site for a new federal courthouse complex? What is now a National Monument was once the largest 17th and 18th century colonial era burial ground for free, indentured, and enslaved Africans. https://www.nps.gov/afbg/index.htm (last visited April 5, 2017).

At commemorative burial sites, whose memory is preserved? Under the wide sky of the Great Plains, the Sand Creek Massacre National Historic Site commemorates the assassination in 1864 of several hundred Arapaho and Cheyenne, living under a flag of truce that Abraham Lincoln had presented to the Cheyenne Chief Black Kettle the year before. Their remains and spirits are at this site. The writer Simon Ortiz (Acoma Pueblo) observes that, in order to remember, more than a place marker is needed. There should be "a National Day of Indigenous Remembrance and Survival, perhaps on November 29th, the anniversary of Sand Creek." FISHKIN, WRITING AMERICA at 165.

Historic sites do not exist in isolation. They are a part of the context of their landscapes. What is the appropriate role of historic preservation law on the inter-municipal scale? What should be the response when property owners seek to build structures that impinge on the viewshed from an historic site? Should a commercial observation tower for tourism be built on private lands overlooking the Gettysburg National Military Park? The view from the battlefield was imposed upon by a modern 307-foot tower. In 1974, local entrepreneurs erected the tower, over opposition from the state, the National Park Service and the public. They charged admission and made a profit by providing an exclusive view of the 5,800-acre battlefield. Failing to secure a state court order to remove the tower, Congress appropriated funds to take this private property by eminent domain in 2000. The tower was demolished on the 137th anniversary of the last day of the Battle of Gettysburg. Was the hyperboloid tower historic? Photographs and engineering designs record its existence. Is that enough of a record for preserving knowledge about it? *See* John Latscher, "The Taking of the Gettysburg Tower," 18 THE GEORGE WRIGHT FORUM 24 (2001), at http://www.georgewright.org/181latschar.pdf (last visited April 5, 2017). Stewardship of cultural landscapes is usually more complex than confronting a single intrusion. The Hudson River National Heritage Area, https://www.nps.gov/HURV/index.htm (last visited April 5, 2017), complements the New York State Hudson River Greenway, with its compact of local governments, which coordinate the exercise of their zoning and land use authority to conserve the Hudson River Valley landscape as a regional cultural heritage. http://www.hudsongreenway.ny.gov/Organization/GreenwayCouncil.aspx (last visited April 5, 2017). Most national heritage areas do not yet have such a coordinated federal-state-local approach to large-scale heritage stewardship.

These—and may other conundrums—constitute the focus of laws governing a society's cultural heritage. Across the United States, this body of law is known as "historic preservation law." The title is something of a misnomer. Unlike a museum, which can preserve a sculpture or other *objet d'art* within a climate controlled and secure setting, historic sites are out-of-doors, exposed to the weather and wear and tear of use. Invariably, it is costly each year to maintain, restore, and conserve historic buildings and other sites. What standards should control maintenance of such conservation? Who should decide how this is done?

What about choice of standards when a structure reflects many layers of art, architecture, and historic events? When restoring an old site that has experienced and endured changes over many decades or centuries, how should it be determined which "historic" era takes precedence? When John D. Rockefeller, Jr., saved and restored Colonial Williamsburg, Virginia, he removed all post-colonial history, including much of the historic relics from the Civil War. When is it allowable to destroy one historic asset in preference for another? Should an historic site inform today's public about only one dimension of its past, to achieve educational clarity, or is a more nuanced story to be required. When, due to fire or neglect, an historic structure is lost and it is replaced in kind, using contemporary building tools and materials, is the replica "historic"? When should an historic regulation be applied to such a structure, or to one that is entirely intact as built but which was saved by moving it to a new location? Should it be placed on a local, state or national register of historic places? When a structure is moved from its original site, has it lost its integrity? When does a change in any structure mean that it has lost all or some of its historic merit? When must, or should, the knowledge of an historic structure reside only in paintings, architectural drawings, photographs, or narratives? Can laws decide such matters?

B. Scoping Out the Study of Preservation Law

This casebook explores these questions and other related themes. It offers a study of examples of how state and local legislatures, and the courts, have pondered and resolved such issues. The chapters address the constitutional foundations for preservation law, the diverse ways that local governments have shaped preservation law, the range of federal programs, the important role of procedural assessment of parallel federal or state actions affecting historic sites, the application of laws for archaeological sites, the conservation of historic landscapes, the economics of adaptive reuse and development of historic structures, emerging issues of international law, and the implications of climate change.

The role of the federal government in cultural heritage is limited. Preservation law in America is quintessentially local. The federal Congress has enacted historic preservation laws governing properties owned by the United States, under the Property Clause of the federal Constitution, providing for recognition of historic properties on the National Register of Historic Places and as Historic Landmarks, and offering tax incentives for taxpayers who invest in maintaining registered historic places. Through the Constitution's treaty power, the United States participates in conserving historic and cultural heritage globally, as a party to the UNESCO Convention on Cultural and Natural Heritage, and other international agreements. Through the Secretary of the Interior's *Standards for the Treatment of Historic Properties*, 36 C.F.R. § 68.3, www.nps.gov/tps/standards.htm (last visited April 2, 2017), the National Park Service has played an important role in harmonizing and advancing the practices of preservation across all states. The Secretary's standards address four dimensions of the caring for historic places: a) preservation, b) rehabilitation, c) restoration, and d) reconstruction, with a set of accompanying guidelines for each.

Ultimately, except for historic places owned by the federal government, it is the local authorities across the United States that are the governmental stewards and regulators of historic assets. Most states delegate the regulatory roles to their local authorities. Even for federal sites, local governments have roles to play in protecting a federal site from external threats, through enacting buffer zones adjacent to the sites or providing public access. The capacities and expertise of local agencies is variable, and while many local governments perform well, some do poorly. Throughout the nation, the experiences of one landmark commission or historic district agency become a set of shared practices and case law emerges. Over time, myriad local decisions have produced clarity and incrementally shaped a coherent body of historic preservation law across the nation.

This casebook examines the evolution of preservation law, and the dynamics by which the law continues to be shaped. The leading role for local governments was forged when New York City adopted its Landmarks Preservation Law in 1965, and when the United States Supreme Court upheld the constitutionality of that municipal ordinance in *Penn Central Transp. Co. v. New York City,* 438 U.S. 104 (1978). This book uniquely provides the full background and case law that led to this all-important "Penn Central Case." Justice William Brennan's decision, however, does not answer the question: "what is historic"? Determining the answer to this question is left to local governments. Preservation law is fundamentally *place-based*, specific to the ordinance adopted by each local government. Decisions about "what is historic" are *site-specific,* a determination governed by the procedures specified in the local ordinance.

Is determining the historic value of a site purely contextual, or are there overarching themes and principles to be applied? How should the following sorts of questions be considered? What are the pros and cons to debate when enacting laws to protect whatever appears to be justifiably "historic"? What countervailing social perspectives or economic theories compete in the deliberative process of local governments as they seek to resolve these sorts of questions:

- What is so "historic" that laws should direct the preservation or conservation of privately owned property?
- Should landmarks be only publicly owned buildings?
- Is an original more valuable than a replica?
- What if a site lacks any historic structures, but is a place where events transpired that people remember?
- Should a prehistoric site, whose location is presumed but about which little to nothing is known, be preserved?
- When is a building "old" enough to merit protection, or is age not a necessary indicator of when landmark preservation status should govern use of private property?
- Is the owner of a private property bound to pay "extra" to preserve what the law decrees to be the historic features of a building? Is that an unfair tax or exaction of wealth?
- Is a landscape as historic as a single architectural construct?

These and other questions permeate applications of law to cultural heritage and "historic preservation." Debates over how and when to conserve heritage are found in all societies. In extreme contexts, a historic asset is lost, deemed expendable, when for those with power over its fate consider it either to be not historic and thus expendable, or even if historic, not important enough to be worthy of protection. Is such a finding purely a cost/benefit analysis? At the end of the Roman Empire, the

Goths, Vandals, and other peoples of Central Europe invaded and sacked the city of Rome. Later generations came to regard the fall of Rome as destructive of an historic classical age. When the terms vandals and vandalism entered our vocabulary, what political or ethical perspectives accompanied their adoption? What does it say about how a society regards "memory" of past artistic and architectural achievement, when it condemns, as an act of "vandalism," the demolition in 1963 of the classical Pennsylvania Station Terminal in Manhattan? http://mashable.com/2015/07/20/original-penn-station/#hk4oYOgNDPqlIs. The destruction of "Penn Station" and other major civic structures, led to the enactment of the 1965 Landmarks Preservation Law in New York City. But where government is weak or slow, vandalism remains, as when the Taliban in Afghanistan destroyed ancient relief carvings of the Buddhas of Bamiyan, Luke Harding, *Taliban Blow Apart 2,000 Years of Buddhist History*, The Guardian, March 2, 2001, https://www.theguardian.com/world/2001/mar/03/afghanistan.lukeharding, or as in 2015 and 2016 when ISIS (Daesh) in Aleppo, Syria, destroyed UNESCO World Heritage Sites (including Phoenician and Roman and early Islamic buildings and the Al-Omari Mosque dating from 720). http://whc.unesco.org/en/list/21 (last visited April 5, 2017).

When urban renewal projects in the United States in the 1950s and 1960s razed historic buildings, along with slums, or interstate highways were sited to run through urban downtown areas and again wipe out local buildings of note, many voices condemned the acts as akin to vandalism. Public reaction led to the enactment of laws like the National Historic Preservation Act of 1966, 54 U.S.C § 300101, and the National Environmental Policy Act of 1969, 42 U.S.C. § 4321, which established due process procedural rights to ensure that historic, cultural and environmental values would be considered in decision-making in development projects.

Events viewed as vandalism continue in more prosaic ways, often left to local governments to address. One high profile example from New York City is the loss of two large art deco stone *bas-relief* carvings on the 1929 façade of the Stewart & Company's department store on Fifth Avenue, a building designed by Warren & Wetmore, the same firm that designed Grand Central Terminal. Bonwit Teller, the famed department store, acquired the store in 1930 and years later Donald Trump purchased it to redevelop the site for what is now Trump Tower. The building had not received historic landmark status; subsequently, another Stewart & Company building on Fifth Avenue was accorded landmark status. http://www.nyc.gov/html/lpc/downloads/pdf/reports/402FifthAvenue.pdf (last visited April 5, 2017). As reported, "When his demolition crews moved onto Fifth Avenue to level the Bonwit Teller building, the Metropolitan Museum of Art urgently requested him to spare and salvage the *bas-relief* sculptures mounted on the front of the store. Whether the museum also volunteered to pay for the sculptures and their removal is unclear; what is irrefutable is the fact that a few days after the request, and after apparently agreeing to it, Trump impulsively told his waiting crew to go ahead and jack-hammer the pieces, and get on with the job at hand. They did, and the howl that went up from the museum, the Landmarks Preservation Commission, and a host of other civic-minded organizations no doubt exceeded even Trump's wildest expectations. The Metropolitan Museum's appraisers set the value of the two stone sculptures at $200,000. "Donald Trump Profile" Town & Country magazine (1983), http://www.townandcountrymag.com/society/money-and-power/a3478/the-trump-card/ (last visited April 1, 2017).

C. Legal Systems to Conserve the Built Environment

It is a testament to the rule of law that across America local landmarks commissions and preservation boards parse and resolve such thorny questions. The chapters of this casebook explore the pathways by which the public has endeavored to create a just system of inter-generational care for the accomplishments of civilization.

A people can take for granted and gradually lose their historic built environment without realizing the loss. There is an enthusiasm for new buildings. Yet awareness of loss can function as a "wake-up" call to balance preserving the past with creating new fashions. Public concern, at least in a democracy, stimulates calls for legislation. The first ordinances in America, in Charleston and New Orleans, emerged in this way. During the Great Depression, architects without employment were commissioned to survey and record the historic buildings across America. Yet, it was not until nearly thirty years later that it become evident that no one in American knew just how many historic structures remained, nor where they might be located. With Heritage So Rich 191–93 (1965).

Across America, the states enacted enabling statutes that allowed local governments to regulate their historic structures through local land use laws. At the federal level, Congress established a National Register of Historic Places with the enactment of the National Historic Preservation Act of 1966, 54 U.S.C. §§ 300101 *et seq*. The criteria to be applied when proposing to list structures on this Register are broad, but are capable of guiding the selection process. Experience in applying the criteria is set forth in a series of advisory memoranda issued by the Keeper of the Register. Reflect on these criteria as you debate "what is historic" in this chapter and throughout this casebook. Are these criteria specific enough to meet a due process test for regulation of private property? Would owners have sufficient notice to know if their property is "historic," and thus subject to being regulated? If not "void for vagueness," how might the process of building a record for the designation of a structure as being a landmark remedy this "vagueness" and satisfy due process of law? How well does the following language define "what is historic"? This definition has had a pervasive influence on how local landmarks commissions describe, in tangible ways, the cultural environment that they protect.

> districts, sites, buildings, structures, and objects that possess integrity of location, design, setting, materials, workmanship, feeling, and association; and
>
> (a) that are associated with events that have made a significant contribution to the broad patterns of our history; or
>
> (b) that are associated with the lives of persons significant in our past; or

(c) that embody the distinctive characteristics of a type, period, or method of construction, or that represent the work of a master, or that possesses high artistic values, or that represent a significant and distinguishable entity whose components may lack individual distinction; or

(d) that have yielded, or may be likely to yield, information important in prehistory or history.

36 C.F.R. §60.4. Is this delineation complete? What more can or should be read into it, or embraced in a state preservation law or a municipal landmarks ordinance? *See* How to Apply the National Register Criteria for Evaluation, http://www.nps.gov/nr/publications/bulletins/pdfs/nrb15.pdf (last visited April 2, 2017). How soon does (should) history begin? The National Register requires that a structure meeting these criteria be at least 50 years old. New York City's Landmarks Preservation Law requires that a structure be 30 years old, one generation. How does the passage of time provide perspective about "what is historic"? *See generally*, Nicholas A. Robinson, *Historic Preservation Law: The Metes and Bounds of a New Field*, 1 PACE L. REV. 511, 524–27 (1981).

D. Does "Memory" Inform Cultural or Legal Awareness of an Historic Site?

Why was there dismay at the "discovery" in the 1965 Conference of Mayors' Report, WITH HERITAGE SO RICH, that America had lost structures dating from the colonization of North America by Europeans? What social consciousness informs any roster of sites that belong on a local or national list of historic places? Many people have forgotten about such places, and may not miss them. It seems easy to let the structures disappear. Once gone, why bring back knowledge about them?

Human memory is a complex force. Laws about cultural heritage begin with human memories. What we recall of the past can have contemporary value. A people may preserve a place simply because of memory. In France, for example, Pierre Nora has stimulated debate over such questions through editing a magisterial set of seven volumes on places of memory (*loci memoriae),* entitled LES LIEUX DE MÉMOIRE (Places of Memory) (1984–92). In WRITING AMERICA, Shelley Fisher Fishkin emphasizes how reading authors' works in conjunction with the places that inform or inspire them, can "illuminate the complexities of the physical, social and cultural landscape that shaped their writings—and encountering landscape, in turn, can help us gain insight into the nuances and complexities of their art." WRITING AMERICA at 11.

So it is with the paintings of Yosemite National Park by Thomas Moran, Albert Bierstadt, and others, or those by Frederic Edwin Church and other Hudson River School painters of the Adirondack and Catskills New York State Forest Preserve. From 1857, these artists shared studios at the Tenth Street Studio Building at 51 West 10th Street in Manhattan. This red brick building itself was central to New York City's artists, who in 1920 bought it to save it from commercial development, but in 1956 it was razed to make space for an apartment building. Annette Blaugrund, The Tenth Street Studio—Artists-Entrepreneurs from the Hudson River School to the American Impressionists (1997). Their art and message live on, even as their studio was lost. Other studio homes, where real estate re-development pressures were less intense, such as the Florence Griswold Museum in Old Lyme, Connecticut, https://www.florencegriswoldmuseum.org (last visited November 12, 2017), the Weir Farm National Historic Site in Wilton, Connecticut, https://www.nps.gov/wefa/index.htmn, or the Thomas Cole National Historic Site, http://thomascole.org (last visited April 5, 2017), endure. All these places were preserved through citizen campaigns. The places where artists worked are part and parcel of their paintings. As Barbara Novak observes "American painters were able to make of their 'natural antiquity' a 'new order' in landscape painting, which was one answer to the difficult resolution of the problem of nature and culture." Barbara Novak, Nature And Culture—American Landscape and Painting 1825–1875 273 (1980). The link of art to living history in art continues. The Georgia O'Keefe home and studio is on the National Register of Historic Places, and inspires stewardship of landscapes of the southwestern United States. https://www.nps.gov/nr/feature/wom/1999/o'keeffe.htm (last visited April 5, 2017). Similar illustrations exist across the nation. The Brandywine River Museum of Art celebrates Horace Pippin, the African-American artist of Pennsylvania, http://www.brandywine.org/press-room/press-releases/brandywine-river-museum-art-presents-horace-pippin-way-i-see-it (last visited April 5, 2017), together with the work and art of N.C. Wyeth and others.

There is a symbiosis at work here. The paintings of American artists allow society to see and value the landscapes or places painted, and in turn to save those places and to preserve and restore their homes and studios. The same is true of music. Take for example the Appledore Hotel on the Isles of Shoals; the works of some of our greatest composers and poets who created and mastered their arts there, like Edward MacDowell, John Knowles Paine, William Mason, and Celia Thaxter, repeat the rhythms of nature that enveloped the area. Caleb Mason, The Isles of Shoals Remembered, A Legacy from America's First Musicians' and Artists' Colony (1992). These landscapes were the sites where creative genius produced contemporary industrial capacity. Human ingenuity and vision can be seen in the Slater's Mill and the Black River Valley National Historic Park in Rhode Island, https://www.nps.gov/blrv/index.htm (last visited March 30, 2017) or Paterson Great Falls National Historic Landmark in New Jersey, https://www.nps.gov/pagr/index.htm (last visited April 5, 2017), where the Industrial Revolution began in America. The preserved laboratories at Thomas Edison National Historic Park invites discovery into the mind and work of one of America's great inventors. https://www.nps.gov/edis/index.htm (last visited April 5, 2017).

A place becomes significant by association with the events and people of the place. What is historic is what we learn, remember, and value. Memory has its place. But what sort of places deserve a place in a culture's memory, whether physical or ephemeral? For Pierre Nora, such a place exists when people believe that it has "become a symbolic element of the memorial heritage of any community," (Nora 1996: XVII), or "where [cultural] memory crystallizes and secretes itself." (Nora 1989: 7). His study is for the French consciousness. In a nation of immigrants, still not at peace with indigenous tribes and communities, is there a comparable, shared culture? Or, is all memory local, in the awareness of shared experiences of those in a given place? Can we come to know and respect, and therefore value and protect, the memories and history of others not our own? Is the enormous breadth of sites on the National Register of Historic Places evidence that we already do embrace a regard for what others see as historic?

Can we envision expanding our understanding of what is historic enough to deserve the protection of the law? Beyond sustaining the built environment, should governments employ law to preserve a place devoted to a ritual or ceremony? Should we join other cultures that recognize individuals who sustain cultural traditions as being historic living laureates of historic traditions? For example, since 1950, Japan has maintained an inventory of "intangible cultural property," being the skills associated with traditional national arts and crafts. This is not like intellectual property in the western law. It is way of remembering high artistic attainment, so that the nation can consciously sustain it. Under the Law for the Protection of Cultural Properties, UNESCO, Law 214, May 30, 1950, Japan designates some individuals, or groups, as Preservers of Important Intangible Cultural Properties (informally called "Living National Treasures"). Their knowledge and skills embody the nation's rich traditions in the creation and continuation of cultural artistic heritage. These elite artisans possess techniques and skills of exceptional historic or artistic value in a performing art or traditional craft. They embody and pass on the knowledge of cultural artistic endeavors.

One such individual is Ōsaka Hiromichi, who was "recognized as a Living National Treasure for his woodwork in 1997. He honed his skills by creating replicas of historic objects from the Shōsō-in treasure house in Nara. Dating back to the eighth century, the wooden treasure house contains some 9,000 cultural artifacts, including Buddhist ceremonial objects, weapons, ornaments, documents, and scrolls. The treasures include objects from as far afield as Rome and Persia that reached Japan via the Silk Road. The influence of European and West Asian art can be clearly discerned in many of the pieces that Ōsaka was hired to recreate." *See The Creative World of Ōsaka Hiromichi, Living National Treasure,* http://www.nippon.com/en/images/i00002 (last visited April 5, 2017). The Japanese Ministry of Science, Education and Culture oversees the ancient crafts of Japan (e.g., pottery, woodworking, textiles, lacquerware, paper making, etc.).

South Korea also provides for designating a person as a "A Living National Treasure," who is able to make or perform one of the officially designated Important Intangible Cultural Properties. Once designated, these persons are granted rights to government support for the transmission of their cultural performance, and they have responsibility to show that ability and train younger students. The designation expires with his or her death.

These skills also are part of cultural stewardship of the built environment. If a historic site can only be restored and maintained using the skills of an ancient time, should the artisans who master those skills be singled out to serve? Or will a computer-generated replica do as well? We need to repair and rebuild all structures as their materials deteriorate. The Ise Shrine in Japan has been rebuilt every twenty years since 690 A.D. Worldwide, most wooden structures are constantly restored.

Should preservation laws in America learn from the Japanese or South Korean legal tradition? Is it enough to keep a place without the skills to maintain that heritage? What obligations exist, or should exist, in preservation law to act as trustees for the legacy of cultural heritage for peoples who no longer exist in a historic place? Is maintenance of museum collections sufficient? If the people of a place have vanished, and those alive today have no memory of what they thought about their monuments, should the sites nonetheless be preserved? Do we, as Pierre Nora argues, "remember" the past to differentiate it from the present, "to stop time, to block the work of forgetting," and share "a will to remember." (Nora 1989: 19). Nora has difficulty with some types of sites where memories are alien to those alive today. Nora's sites of memory exclude prehistoric and archaeological sites, since what makes them "important as sites is often precisely what ought to exclude them from being *lieux de mémoire:* the absolute absence of a will to remember and, by way of compensation, the crushing weight imposed on them by time, science, and the dreams of men." (Nora 1989: 20f.).

Is Nora correct in this assessment? Why should we not want to recreate a knowledge of a distant past via archaeology? Is it because we can never know definitively what Stone Age life was like? What archaeologists ascertain is always an approximation based on contemporary extrapolations about past lives from relics unearthed, or from extant sites such as Stonehenge. Is that re-creation of memory by archaeology more or less reliable than that of the memory of Indigenous Peoples, handed down over generations in an oral tradition? Who is the rightful stakeholder of relics of the past once rediscovered? These competing understandings of memory were pitted against each other in litigation over the fate of the Stone Age era "Kennewick Man," found preserved in the sediments of the Columbia River. *Bonnichsen v. United States*, 357 F. 3d 962 (9th Cir. 2004), discussed in Douglas Preston, *Kennewick Man Finally Freed To Share His Sucrets*, SMITHSONIAN, September 2014, available at http://www.smithsonianmag.com/history/kennewick-man-finally-freed-share-his-secrets-180952462 (last visited April 5, 2017). The hoax of the Piltdown Man is a cautionary tale, but perhaps also illustrates the public's thirst for pre-historic memories. MILES RUSSELL, THE SECRET LIFE OF CHARLES DAWSON (2013).

Should the prospect of finding the past in places where pre-historic life is revealed through archaeology be a sufficient basis for restricting the excavation or building on such sites? Are forgotten sites as important as those that ancients intended for those who came after to remember, such as the Pyramids of Giza? How does a society weigh the quest for past knowledge against allowing private developers to build new housing or shopping centers, or governments to construct new highways or schools?

When ancient civilizations in China, India, Greece or Rome acknowledged the monuments that they encountered from societies older than their own, they established cultural benchmarks, or references in time. Such sites stimulate wonder in those who behold them. Are not all civilizations still amazed at the Pharaoh's Pyramids in Egypt? Yet, as Maurice Bloch has surmised, societies routinely adapt or destroy monuments when the social importance of the past is deemed "past," and more pressing contemporary needs supplant memory. *See* M. Bloch, *The Past and the Present in the Present*, Man (N.S.) 12, 278–292 (1977). The mixed appreciation ascribed to historic sites of the past is as old as society itself. Richard Bradley, The Past in Prehistoric Societies (2002). Is it sufficient to declare that human memory links today to yesterday and projects today to the future? Is it "right" for a society to then employ law as a means to preserve the artifacts of historic memory?

E. "New" Reverence for History

Debate about how to regard the creations and events of the past is hardly new. Campaigns to save historic buildings from demolition are immediate and seen in isolation of earlier such controversies. Human awareness of time and memory seems to have evolved and became of wide social concern in the 19th century. Previously, cities would build on top of their past, often reusing building materials for new structures. Little attention was paid to protecting past developments. Much of Bath, England, sat atop ancient Roman baths that reveal an earlier era's class structures and rituals. A car parking lot was built over the battlefield where King Richard III died in battle with Henry Tudor in 1485, and where his remains were only discovered in 2012. A wooden ship sunk off of Manhattan in 1773 appeared preserved in harbor mud discovered during the excavation for the reconstruction of the World Trade Center in 2010. The reuse of sites is often guided by contemporary priorities, which have little use for what went before. In most periods of antiquity, humans focused on their present needs. In the Medieval era, Roman ruins were a quarry for new building materials. Even during the Renaissance, while rediscovering past knowledge, people focused on applying such knowledge to the present and near future. A city might preserve a site for its religious importance, but few secular structures, built in the past, were deemed important enough for a government to preserve. Buildings from the past persisted because and when they held continuing utility to present users.

George Santayana wrote in The Life of Reason 87 (1905) (Guttenberg ebook) that "those who cannot remember the past are condemned to repeat it." Crafting legal procedures for historic preservation enables us to move forward by making the physical and cultural landscapes navigable. Examining the structures and artifacts of the past helps us understand what mattered to people once, and how to build the fabric of their creativity and values into our daily lives and structures. As we adapt and reapply artifacts, our new uses are grounded and embrace historical perspective. Historic preservation can help explain past conflicts, idiosyncrasies of practices, and expressions of behavior that are distant reflections of our own humanity. Preserving buildings and landscapes enables us to make sense of otherwise unreadable texts.

In western countries, the 19th century witnessed a new ethic emerge about historic structures, and a change in perception about the role of memory in society. Historians began new inquiries, not as chroniclers like Herodotus, but as explorers and analysts of the past and its artifacts. Medieval records were translated and used to reinterpret the past. The Society of Antiquaries was founded in England (1717), and later analogues in the United States (Albany Institute of History & Art, 1791, New York, and American Antiquarian Society (1812, Wooster, Massachusetts). These institutions sought out and studied history, and restored and transmitted memories. In turn, the public began to question prevailing economic models of development, including the loss of older buildings that they valued. In England, John Ruskin (1819–1901) gave voice to such concerns, and the study of aesthetics emerged.

The vigor of public debate about the need to safeguard cultural attainments in buildings is illustrated in a fictional dialogue recounted in a 19th century English magazine, *The Studio*. These competing 19th century interests to determine the public policy are not unlike today's contending socio-economic forces that animate legal contests about preservation of historic places.

> 'I have been visiting old cities,' said the Journalist, 'and my heart is filled with sorrow at the works therein of the new men.'
>
> 'I presume,' remarked the Critic, that your pocket is filled with the copy you made out of their sins.'
>
> 'To some extent, I admit,' replied the journalist. 'We are all tradesmen, even the most artistic. But in the retirement of one's leisure moments, one may be permitted a change to consume a thought instead of selling it. And what I wanted to mourn over was the terrible sense of incongruity shown by the present generation. They never look where they are building. And so the modern iron girder-framed contract-built erection, with its veneer of terra cotta and brick, and its bedazzlement of glazed tiles and gilt iron, is remorsefully set up side by side with one of those beautiful old houses that ought—as in Belgium—be guarded and watched over by the Government.'
>
> 'You are right,' the Painter remarked; 'it is unpardonable: and another phase of the same disease is to be found in churches, especially those of importance, such as cathedrals. I mean the modern monument. Only too often is there a complete absence of sympathy, so to speak, between the memorial to some dead man of note, and its immediate surroundings. An effigy of glittering white marble on an altar tomb of imitation Italian Renaissance work does not rest peacefully with the sober grey walls of an Early English transept. It produces a sense of cheapness, very often quite undeserved.'
>
> 'Yet,' says the Lay Figure, 'there are difficulties. Would you relapse into mere imitation in order to keep your concords?'

'Or,' the Critic remarked with a pleasant smile, 'are you going to try to impose a limit of so many years, within which alone shall new buildings be allowed in a street containing old ones, or new tombs in a church that dates back more than a generation or so? You are entirely unpractical, and ought to devote yourselves to writing and painting pictures. Thinking, happily, is not an art.'

'Moreover,' the Minor Poet added, 'these things must be so. Surely the jewel loses little by the banality of its setting.'

'My idea,' retorted the Painter, 'tended rather in the direction of the banality, as you call it, of the jewel.'

'Well, replied the Minor Poet, 'everything must have a beginning. You have the new springing up side by side with the old until time blends them into harmony.'

'That is pretty—and partly true,' the Journalist mediated. But time isn't going to worry about the modern jerry-built business premises, except to clear them out at short notice, when they become obsolete, and set up others like unto them, only more so.'

'You do not think, then,' said the Lay Figure, 'that we are providing anything but public buildings for the admiration of the antiquarians and consumption of the Goths of future ages?'

'Hardly anything, I think, in our cities,' was the reply. 'The detached private houses of the suburbs is the most characteristic and most successful product of Victorian architecture. Where these are built—as to them in justice I believe they generally are—of good material, they will age and weather into very beautiful buildings—of that kind which is likely to be always popular so long as we retain the domestic qualities of the nation.'

'But what is it that you are complaining of?' interjected the Critic. 'all this is interesting. I understand the point of view of the Painter who naturally objects to new tombs in old cathedrals. But do you want to abolish the old houses in the new cities, or what?'

'Well, I admit the difficulty,' replied the Journalist. 'For one thing I would like to see all old buildings of importance registered by a Government authority as national monuments. This should make it impossible for any one to knock them about indiscriminately. I fear the new shops must be suffered sadly. There is no remedy.'

'Yet,' mediated the Lay Figure, 'there may be hardly the need for it that you think. When one visiting a foreign country for the first time, one is generally struck by the harmony—a harmony covering all styles and periods—which the architecture of a town displays when viewed as a whole. I have sometimes felt a suspicion of something of the same sort in our British cities when returning to their grateful dinginess after a long absence. We are hardly far enough away from our age to criticise it, or from our country to tell how it looks. But the old places must be looked after, and it would be a really valuable institution if we could have a Society of the Education of Deans and Chapters in Elementary Taste. The tombs they erect or allow to be erected are driving away all the ghosts.'

18 *The Studio* 74 (1899). In the cases and materials presented in subsequent chapters in this casebook, consider who emerge as the advocates for each of the interests featured by this debate from more than a century ago in *The Studio*?

F. Discussion Problems for Our Age

To explore the dimensions of what today inspires similar debates about what may be deemed "historic," this threshold chapter in the study of historic preservation law presents a handful of diverse scenarios. There are many more that could be mentioned. Memory and memorializing the past is active and on-going. Continuing debates about these places are shaping the content and outer limits of how society's laws regulate the use and stewardship of historic places. One of these scenarios will be revisited to illustrate how the debate unfolds in the different aspects of historic preservation law. This is the still on-going struggle to "preserve" and interpret the birthplace, childhood home, ancestral family seat, and burial site of one of America's founding fathers, Chief Justice John Jay. Preserving the Jay site has relied upon many, but not all, of the legal techniques provided by preservation law.

Apply your reflections on the questions raised above to debating what should be remembered as "historic" in the following problems. What role does the passage of time play? How does ignorance, or neglect, about a place affect efforts to determine if a site is "historic"? Does change all around a site make it more or less worthy of protection? What historic values should society recognize in the following scenarios?

1. Edward Hopper's Landscapes

Edward Hopper's birthplace in Nyack, New York, then in a state of neglect, was saved by a handful of citizens in 1971. Civic activists formed the Edward Hopper Landmark Preservation Foundation. The house had been boarded up, was dilapidated, and scheduled for demolition. The modest Queen Anne style building dated from 1882. Hopper's bedroom looked out onto the Hudson River. It is now preserved as the Hopper House Museum, not yet accorded landmark status. http://www.edwardhopperhouse.org (last visited April 5, 2017). When Hopper left Nyack, he and his wife, the artist Josephine Hopper, lived in New York City and Truro on Cape Cod, Massachusetts. His studio on Washington Square is in a building owned by New York University and is open for public visits. His home in Truro is privately owned and not open to the public. Neither is a designated landmark. Hopper's paintings, many of which are in the Whitney Museum of American Art, were of New York City and

New England. His landscapes and seascapes painted in and around Truro are iconic, and widely disseminated in print editions. President Barack Obama hung Hopper's painting of the Cobb Farm in Truro in his office in the White House. The original paintings are immensely valuable. What is more important, the paintings or the places he painted?

Real estate development for second homes in Truro has witnessed extensive growth for the past three decades and real estate values have risen in tandem. The Cobb farm is now a subdivision of private homes, with private access to its street and amenities. Other landscapes that Hopper painted are zones for developments. Edward and Josephine had rented Burley Cobb's house in South Truro from 1930–34, where he roamed the landscape and painted. The farms are largely gone, but local concern to save the landscapes has grown. Joyce Johnson, *Truro Struggles to Save Dwindling Landscapes*, THE CAPE CODDER, July 27, 1993.

Some of the sites Hopper painted, such as the "Highland Light, North Truro," a lighthouse commissioned by George Washington, completed in 1931, is preserved within the Cape Cod National Seashore and is listed on the National Register of Historic Places. https://www.nps.gov/nr/travel/maritime/hig.htm (last visited April 5, 2017). The Highland Light has been moved back from the Atlantic Ocean cliff to preserve it from falling into the sea, so it is not on its original location, but is nonetheless deemed historic and is preserved by the National Park Service. Hopper painted places where the Pilgrims first explored. His works conjured up the light playing across a landscape, often without people. We see landscapes through his eyes.

Most of the places that Hopper painted, like his panorama of "Cobb's Barn and Distant Houses" have been lost to development. The Mobil gas station, site of Hopper's iconic painting "Gas" (1940), a site visited by European tourists following Hopper's life, had leaking underground storage tanks and the site was remediated for pollution, rather than preserved. Its structures were lost in the 1990s. Hopper's Truro studio, which he and Josephine built in 1934, is extant, privately owned, but the view from its northern light wall of windows has changed. A very large home was built in the view shed. A group of Truro residents, "Friends of the Hopper Landscape," opposed the construction. The Town of Truro and Massachusetts state courts have ruled that this home was unlawfully constructed and the Town of Truro has ordered that it be demolished. Some real estate interests castigated the Friends as NIMBY ("not in my back yard") self-interests. The builders of the home sold it to a third party, who now seeks to reverse the demolition order. A photograph of the site accompanies the report by Ian Edwards, "Truro's Kline House Case Goes Back to Land Court," *Provincetown Banner* (Feb. 6, 2016), http://provincetown.wickedlocal.com/news/20160205/truros-kline-house-case-goes-back-to-land-court.

Artists, students of art, and collectors annually make a pilgrimage to Truro to look for Hopper's legacy and explore his landscapes. Is it enough to preserve his paintings in the Whitney Museum? His birthplace in Nyack? Should the remaining natural landscapes that Hopper painted also be listed on the National Register of Historic Places? What different considerations should attach to whether his studio is listed

Edward Hopper's *Light at Two Lights* and *Road in Maine*. Courtesy of Wikimedia Commons.

and not his landscapes? Why is Hopper's childhood home preserved and not the studio from which many masterworks emerged? If Truro does not act to preserve the Hopper landscapes, who should? Unlike the tower at Gettysburg, the loss of hill and valley to new building lots is insidious and incremental. The gradual loss of bits of the landscape views does not galvanize attention. The Truro landscape matters for ecological and aesthetic reasons. They embody culture and nature.

2. Manhattan's Colonial Dutch Street Pattern

The island of Manhattan was settled by the Dutch, who developed streets in an organic manner from the original waterfront at Pearl Street. "Streets curved to follow the lay of the land or to avoid obstacles; they might abruptly change direction altogether after someone constructed a building directly on the old street line." Mark Gelernter, A History of American Architecture; Buildings in their Cultural and Technological Context 19 (1999). The historical values in this patch-

Landmarks Preservation Commission

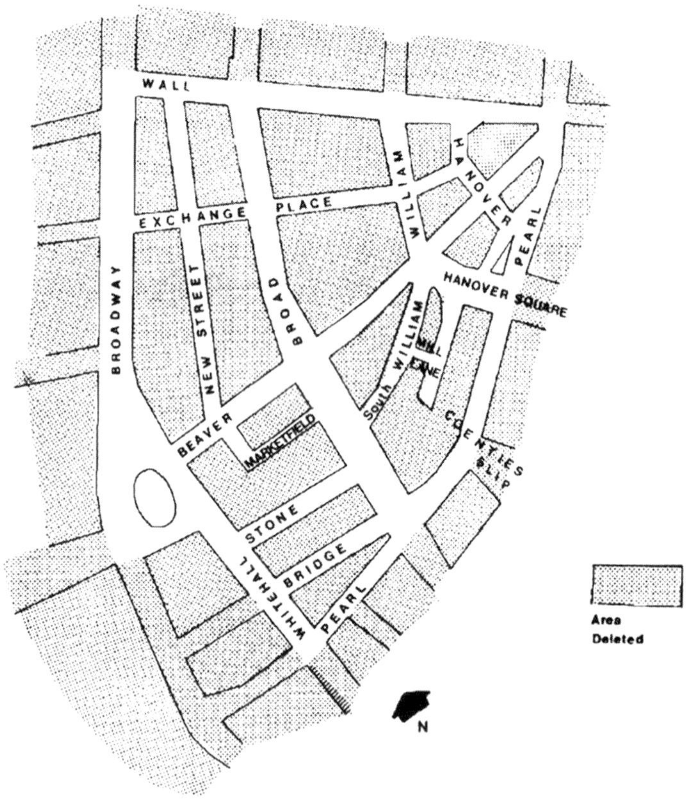

Street Plan of New Amsterdam and Colonial New York

Report of Landmarks Preservation Commission, June 14, 1983, Designation List 165, LP-1235.

work has not gone unrecognized. What can be seen in the streetscape of lower Manhattan?

New Amsterdam, on the island of Manhattan was settled by the Dutch in 1621 as a trading post and port. Street names in the settlement at the southern tip of Manhattan Island persisted after the English came in 1664 and renamed the settlement New York, and they have not changed since then, although the activities and uses long-associated with the names are long gone: Wall Street, Battery Place, Water Street, Stone Street, Beaver Street, Old Slip, Mill Lane, Cedar Street, Pine Street, Exchange Place, New Street, Broad Street, and Broadway, and the like. Where once small buildings stood, now a handful from the English era remain: Fraunces Tavern (1719), where George Washington bade farewell to his officers in 1783, and St. Paul's Chapel (where George Washington worshipped), and Trinity Church (build in 1846 on the site of the 1697 church), and City Hall. All along the small roads of one-time New Amsterdam, ever taller skyscrapers were constructed, beginning just north with the Woolworth Building on City Hall Park, the world's first skyscraper (1913). Eventually, one development sought to occupy a street, to gain a greater building lot. Did it matter?

So, what is left of the Dutch historical legacy? What links to memory can be found in lower Manhattan. Most said none. The counsel to the New York City Landmarks Preservation Commission, Dorothy Miner, and her colleagues on the small Commission staff, remembered otherwise. Comparing a Dutch map of 1660 of Nieuw Amsterdam, to later street maps, it was evident that the Dutch pathways, and later English colonial roads, remained intact. The 1660 diagram is known as the *Castello Plan,* and includes a list of people and houses drawn up by Nicasius de Sille.

In June 1983, the New York City Landmarks Preservation Commission designated as a landmark, the Street Plan of New Amsterdam, finding as follows:

> The Street Plan of New Amsterdam and Colonial New York has a special character, special historical and aesthetic interest and value as part of the development, heritage and cultural characteristics of New York City.
>
> ... Among its important qualities, the Street Plan of New Amsterdam and Colonial New York is a striking reminder of New York's colonial past and provides virtually the only above-ground physical evidence in Manhattan of the Dutch presence in New York during the 17th century; that the plan set forth by Crijn Fredericksz under assignment from the Dutch West India Company, was dictated by local geography and the need for defense; that this plan is virtually unparalleled in Colonial America; that the Castello Plan of 1660, the earliest surviving survey, based on the work of Jacques Cortelyou, reveals the presence of twelve present-day streets in their approximate current configuration; that examination of plans issued after 1660 and throughout the 18th century show very little change from the Castello Plan although pressures increased on the city's physical structure; that today this essential street pattern remains despite the disappearance of all colonial buildings; that recent archaeological excavations have shown how closely later builders have adhered to the line of the original streets although many changes have been made in grade, composition, and paving; and that the street plan of New Amsterdam and Colonial New York has accommodated change and growth for almost 360 years within its historic configuration.

* * *

Landmarks Preservation Commission, June 14, 1983, Designation List 165 LP-1235, *Street Plan Of New Amsterdam And Colonial New York*, http://s-media.nyc.gov/agencies/lpc/lp/1235.pdf at 14 (last visited April 5, 2017).

By the designation, the street design itself is a landmark structure under the New York City Landmarks Preservation Law. Today, every pedestrian along these roads knows the names of each byway and follows the directions laid out in the 17th century, even if they do not remember the Dutch. Designating the streets would preserve the remaining open space above roadways, and avert pressures from real estate interests to close roads for assembling greater area needed for ever larger buildings.

3. My Father's Ax & Re-Imagined Structures

Temples in Japan, like Russian Orthodox Churches in the countryside of Russia, or cabins in the Sierra Nevada mountains, are often made of wood. As wood ages, parts of these structures rot, weaken, and must constantly be restored and maintained in the style and with the skills of their original creation. So too is a ship like Old Ironsides, the USS Constitution. *See* https://ussconstitutionmuseum.org (last visited April 1, 2017). How should preservation laws provide for securing artists and draftsmen as experts in national heritage maintenance and restoration? Is this essential to continuing the authenticity of an historic landmark structure? When is a re-created building historic? Must it be the same building? If much of its fabric is new wood, crafted to replicate and "save" the original wooden design, is it historic? The Governor's Palace at Colonial Williamsburg, in Virginia, was built on the site as an entirely new building, the original one having been destroyed. Is it "historic"? Now that it is more than 50 years old, does it merit a listing on the National Register of Historic Places for that new reason?

Howard Mansfield in THE SAME AX, TWICE (2000), opens his book with this tale: "I know a farmer who says he has had the same ax his whole life—he only changed the handle three times and the head two times. Does he have the same ax?" Is the *act* of repairing and keeping the ax serviceable that is historic? Do we acknowledge a process when we protect the physical ax itself? How to record the skill of the farmer? James Marston Fitch, in his study HISTORIC PRESERVATION—CURATORIAL MANAGEMENT OF THE BUILT WORLD 6–11 (1990), distinguishes an original of a type (prototype) from a replica (copy of the original, sometimes by the same artist or craftsman), and a duplicate (a nearly identical copy), and facsimile (an identical copy, as in a Xerox), and a reproduction (a counterpart image). Society has the technology to reproduce original designs, so why keep the original? Is not the new variant sturdier, not have suffered from aging? Do the criteria for the National Register of Historic Places adequately capture these dimensions of what is "historic?"

When the craftsmen at Colonial Williamsburg restored the Governor's Palace, approximating the original, they had to imagine and copy features that they believed would have existed. Is this "historic"? How is this different from a provincial city in China today rebuilding old streetscapes to welcome tourism? When the State of California rebuilt the ramparts and some buildings of Fort Ross, the Russian Imperial government's southernmost seat in California, they based their work on historic paintings and sketches of the site. Is the restored Fort as "historic" as the buildings of the Spanish Presidio in San Francisco, Imperial Spain's northernmost government seat in California, which while extant are within the continuing development of this military base until conveyed to the National Park Service to be part of the Gateway Recreation Area? What about sites that are held privately? Should local governmental landmark laws determine what can and cannot be done to "restore" such sites? Is "frontier land" in Disney World purely recreational or does it offer an historic experience? Should the original Disneyland be listed on the National Register? Should it be regulated by the City of Anaheim, California, as a local landmark? In New York, "Playland," one of the first amusement parks in America, is owned by Westchester County, is listed on the National Register of Historic Places, and is subject to the historic preservation obligations that New York State laws place on governmental units that hold Historic Places. Playland has the oldest wooden roller coaster still in use. The county government complains that it is too costly to keep rebuilding Playland's old rides and buildings, and that concessionaires prefer to introduce new rides and compete with what newer amusements parks can offer. What do such arguments tell us about how the historic values of Playland are regarded? Does it make a difference that Playland is in public ownership and Disneyland is not?

4. Native Hawaiians and the Thirty Meter Telescope Atop Mauna Kea

To the native Hawaiians, Mauna Kea is sacred ground, a resting place of many of their ancestors, the point where the sky and earth meet, a temple and place of worship. To the scientists, it is a scientific marvel, the tallest summit in the world, rising more than six miles from the seabed floor and the darkest site in the world, well-suited for gazing deeper into space, to reveal knowledge of our cosmos. In 2010, the University of Hawaii applied to the Hawaiian Board of Land and Natural Resources ("BLNR") for a permit to construct an observatory in the conservation district that envelopes Mauna Kea. The telescope is called the Thirty Meter Telescope ("TMT") because the primary mirror is thirty meters wide. Already, there were thirteen telescopes on the landscape. The site is also next to a national park.

Many Native Hawaiians regarded the proposed telescope as a desecration. The right to exercise Native Hawaiian customs and traditions is explicitly protected by the state constitution (art. XII, § 7), although subject to the right of the state to regulate. But, when does the interest in the advancement of scientific knowledge outweigh the interest of Native Hawaiians in pursuing their cultural practices? To answer this question, we need to reflect on the extent to which those rights are exercised, how they might be impaired by a project, and whether the rights can be protected in these circumstances. But, in what context and what forum should any weighing take place? Is it sufficient for the land use agency, after public hearing, to decide? Or, is a "contested case hearing," in which the merits and impacts of the proposal would be considered and testimony under oath, required?

The public hearing held by the BLNR on the application to build the TMT was well-attended, by more than 200 individuals, 84 of whom spoke. A number of groups and individuals provided written comments. Several requested a contested case hearing. After a public board meeting, the BLNR voted unanimously to approve the permit, and also unanimously to hold a contested case hearing, but only after it approved the permit. At the public board meeting, attendees were asked to limit their comments to no more than five minutes. At the contested case hearing, the engineer who was engaged to develop an environmental impact statement testified that while the TMT would have only a limited increment to the cumulative impact that currently exists on Mauna Kea, the overall impact of past and present actions on the cultural, archaeological, and historic resources was "substantial, significant, and adverse" and the adverse impacts would continue. Even though granting the permit came with numerous conditions and by its terms, no construction could commence until after the contested case hearing, the decision was flawed. Holding the contested case hearing *after* the grant of the permit was not calculated to meaningfully safeguard Native Hawaiian rights. Remarkably, the BLNR findings made before and after the contested case hearing were virtually identical.

In overruling the BLNR, the Hawaii Supreme Court explained that the due process owed to Native Hawaiians as to their cultural rights and practices requires meaningful participation in any proceeding where those rights are at issue. That opportunity to be heard must be meaningful in both reality and appearance. But, where as here, the decision-maker appeared to have already decided the case, by granting the permit that threatened substantial burdens on cultural practices, prior to the contested case hearing, in which that burden would be measured, due process is denied. *Mauna Kea Anaina Hou v. Bd. Of Land & Natural Res.*, 363 P.3d 224 (Haw. 2015). On rehearing, how did the BLNR assess the weight of respective interests? Whose stories were heard? How many intrusions should be enough? Should it be relevant that there are already thirteen telescopes in the area? Is any mitigation possible? In *Kilakila 'Haleakalâ v. Bd. of Land & Natural Res.*, 382 P.3d 195 (Haw. 2016), in a plurality decision, the Hawaii Supreme Court agreed with the BLNR that given all the intrusions already present in this sacred area—thirteen other facilities on the site—the adverse impacts were long-standing, but would not be mitigated by not constructing one more telescope. In his dissent, Mr. Justice Michael Wilson spoke of the role of substantive rights in procedural decision-making, such as environmental impact assessment laws. What should be the relationship between substantive rights accorded to native Hawaiian historic, religious, or cultural values, and the judicial oversight of the administrative process? Do cultural and historic rights only exist when procedural systems afford them recognition?

5. Places Acclaimed in Literature

"Memory has [a] geography," Stuart McConnell posits in *Epilogue, The Geography of Memory*, the concluding chapter in The Memory Of The Civil War In America at 258 (2004) (Alice Fahs and Joan Waugh, eds.) The book shows how the cultural memory of the Civil War has changed over time. McConnell describes geography as "a kind of map on which individuals and societies locate past events relative to one another." Geography entails both literal and figurative dimensions involving physical and symbolic spaces, such as where monuments are erected or how cemeteries are created. Memories exist in many forms—relic collections, songs, folklore, and physical spaces—and may differ between north and south, men and women, blacks and whites, Republicans and Democrats. These myriad memories are "peacefully coexisting without much thought given in their connections," all contributing to our understanding of the Civil War as among the most tragic events in America's history.

Washington Irving is America's first author to have been acclaimed by Europeans and his fellow countrymen. His "Bracebridge Hall" helped shape many now traditional celebratory traditions of Christmas. His "Legend of Sleepy Hollow" is the hallmark of Halloween. His "Legend of Rip van Winkle" continues to be read today, and is remade in plays and movies. His home, "Sunnyside," in Irvington, New York, where he wrote his biography of George Washington and other mature works, is listed on the National Register of Historic Places, and preserved. He designed his home to emulate old Dutch and Spanish architectural styles that he admired in Europe, and romantically transported to a new home. Irving consciously designed the landscape of Sunnyside, improvising on designs he had seen in Great Britain. He launched America's traditions of landscape architecture. Set along the Hudson River, Sunnyside is a rare example of a place where today one can experience the life of an author whose literary art, and sensibilities about architecture and landscape are extant. The site was preserved by Irving's family members, and then by John D. Rockefeller, Jr., and is maintained by Historic Hudson Valley, a non-governmental organization.

But what of other landmarks? Some literary landmarks are similarly conserved, as Shelley Fisher Fishkin reveals in Writing America, her survey of sites on the National Register of Historic Places, which are home to American literature. The National Register listings, and some local landmark designations, do not always explain the connection of a site to its literary understanding or interpretation.

Take, for example, the Los Lomita, Roma, San Ygnacio and San Agustin de Laredo Historic Districts of the Lower Rio Grande Valley in Texas. The National Register lists The Old Irrigation Pump House at Hidalgo, preserved today within an area preserved as a branch of the Wild Birding Center, operated by the City of Hidalgo. http://www.cityofhidalgo.net/pumphouse.html (last visited April 5, 2017).

The Old Irrigation Pump House, part of the Louisiana-Rio Grande Canal Company Irrigation System, irrigated 40,000 acres in Hidalgo County, making possible the conversion of once arid lands into a rich source of agricultural produce and economic wealth. It operated until 1983. Through The Old Irrigation Pump House, the technological and economic geography of the site is extant. Missing is a dimension of the social history, the experiences of the migrant workers induced to work in the fields. The poet, Gloria Anzaldúa, captures memories of these historic sites. As Fishkin notes, "Hidalgo County produced more cabbages (and more onions, cantaloupes, carrots and watermelons) than any other county in Texas in the 1980s, when Anzaldúa published *Borderlands/La Frontiera*. Her family held seven generations of farm workers, and like her mother she had worked the fields when a child. Her father lived to be only 38, as she recalls "having worked himself to death." She dedicated one of the poems in that book "to those who have worked the fields." Should this memory of the farm workers be recorded as a reason for listing these sites on the National Register? Should her poem below be listed on the National Register? Is her family's history as or more important than the pumping station, listed because of its technological prowess?

> *Un mar de repollos* ("A Sea of Cabbages")
>
> "On his knees, hands swollen
> sweat flowering in his face
> his gaze on the high paths ...
> Century after century swimming
> with arthritic arms, back and forth
> circling, going around and round
> like a worm in a green sea ...
> At noon on the edge
> of the hives of cabbage
> in the fields of *ranchito* in *Tejas*
> he takes out his chile wrapped in torillas
> drinks water made hot soup by the sun.
> Sometimes he curses
> his luck, the land, the sun....
> His hands tore cabbages from their nests,
> ripping the ribbed leaves covering tenderer leaves
> encasing leaves yet more pale ...
> Century after century flailing
> unleafing himself in a sea of cabbages...."

How can designation of landmarks cope with selective memory? Is this pump house only an engineering monument and a historic structure? What significance can there be in decisions to encircle a historic industrial structure with a wildlife habitat, and not look beyond the wider circle of human cultures and their habitats and individual lives?

6. The Locusts—Birthplace of John Jay

The gathering of the diverse memories of a place and arriving at a geography that serves present generations, interprets the past, and offers guidance to mentor future behavior, is illustrated in the campaign to save and restore the place where John Jay grew up and is buried. John Jay's importance to the founding of the United States, to the governance of New York and the nation, and to the foreign affairs of America was profound. His alma mater, Columbia University (then King's College), has published seven volumes of his papers, archiving them also on the Internet. http://www.columbia.edu/cu/libraries/inside/dev/jay (last visited April 5, 2017). Yet, despite Jay's seminal role in drafting the New York State Constitution of 1777, collaborating in writing the Federalist Papers, serving as the nation's first Chief Justice, and perhaps the new nation's most important diplomat, there is no definitive biography, and his early leadership in urging the abolition of slavery is not well-celebrated. FRANK MONAGHAN, JOHN JAY: DEFENDER OF LIBERTY (1935); RICHARD B. MORRIS, JOHN JAY, THE

NATION AND THE COURT (1967). PBS NewsHour provides a biographic note entitled "What you should know about forgotten founding father John Jay." http://www.pbs.org/newshour/rundown/forgotten-founding-father/ (last visited April 5, 2017).

In 1745, John Jay's father purchased 250 acres of land along the Boston Post Road running down to Long Island Sound. It was called the "Locusts." It was part of a larger parcel, Budd's Neck, which John Budd had acquired in 1661 from Native American tribes; Budd's grandson sold the smaller parcel to Peter Jay, a merchant from New York City. Huguenots, the Jays had come from France after the Edict of Nantes in 1685. The site boasted of a great open field, which had been cleared centuries before to facilitate hunting by the indigenous people of the region. At the head of this great meadow, which is the highest elevation near the Post Road, Peter Jay built a two-story farm house. When they moved to Rye from Manhattan, Peter and Mary Jay brought John Jay as an infant, the youngest of seven children. Here John Jay grew up, attending a Huguenot school until enrolling at college in Manhattan at age 14. John's older brother, Peter, inherited the property and on his death in 1815, it passed to John Jay, who left it to his eldest son, Peter Augustus Jay. The Jay Family Cemetery was established on the grounds, and is maintained by Jay descendants. John Jay is interred there.

The original farmhouse at the Locusts had been damaged during the Revolutionary War and Peter Augustus Jay replaced the original home on its same foundation in 1837, reusing the beams, fixtures, and wood from the farmhouse to construct a Greek Revival mansion. Andrew Dolkart, an architectural historian at Columbia University, calls the new building "an extraordinary symbol of the increasing wealth and power of America during the decade of the 1830s." Douglas P. Clement, *Of (Founding) Fathers and Sons*, N.Y. TIMES, at 10. (March 15, 2016). Peter Jay's mansion and grounds remained in the Jay family until 1904. Subsequent owners, Warner van Norden, Edgar Palmer, and Zilph Devereux built a carriage house in 1907 and other structures, and designed extensive gardens, keeping the historic meadow. The estate came to be known as "Alansten." How the Jay Estate came to become the Jay Heritage Center is a case study that runs throughout this casebook, illustrating different facets of preservation law at work.

While he served as New York's second governor in 1795, Jay lived in the State's new capital, Albany. Although President John Adams asked him to return again as Chief Justice of the Supreme Court, in light of spending three decades in public service, Jay declined. His brother, then blind, was living at the Locusts in Rye, so Jay built, on family lands located in the Town of Bedford, his "Homestead," which was designed to replicate the former Jay family farmhouse in Rye. He lived there for 28 more years until his death in 1829 at age 83. He studied and advanced farming techniques, for which he was elected to the Royal Agricultural Society in London. He freed some of his slaves and supported the New York Manumission Society, advocating an end to slavery.

The Jay Homestead in Bedford remained in the Jay family until 1953. Eleanor Jay Iselin remodeled the interior of the Homestead; in 1924–26 she added a large west wing designed by Warren & Wetmore, in which to exhibit her portraits and as a place to entertain. With no Jay descendants wishing to live at the Homestead after her, Eleanor Jay Iselin was exploring its future when she died in 1953 at age 71. In 1958, Westchester County bought the house without the farmlands, and, unable to sustain the care of the historic site, conveyed it to the State of New York, which opened it to the public in 1964 as a State Historic Site. Over time, the State Parks agency restored the interior of the Homestead to reflect the 19th century period of John Jay's life there. http://johnjayhomestead.org/. Herbert Alan Johnson, JOHN JAY (State Education Department, 1976 ed.).

What does this summary of historic places in John Jay's life tell us? Other than Jay Hall at Columbia University, and the John Jay College of Criminal Justice at the City University, Jay's life in Manhattan is not recalled. A fort on Governor's Island in New York City's harbor was named after Jay, but the National Park Service pays scant attention to Jay otherwise. https://www.nps.gov/gois/learn/historyculture/fortjay.htm (last visited April 5, 2017). Jay's days in Albany largely go unnoticed. During the Bicentennial of the United States Constitution, a real estate developer was insisting on building a dense residential complex in and around the Peter Augustus Jay mansion and meadow in Rye, crowding the Jay Cemetery off into a corner. Jay's biographer, Richard B. Morris, joined a coalition of citizens urging that "to guarantee preservation, the county legislators should initiate eminent domain proceedings to preserve the entire Jay site." Richard B. Morris, *Save John Jay's Westchester Site*, N.Y. TIMES, Dec. 12, 1987 at 31. On the other hand, many citizens in Bedford, who supported the Jay Homestead, did not campaign for saving the Alansten Estate in Rye, claiming it was not John Jay's preferred home, and that Jay descendants had not preserved it. The then Secretary of the Interior, Donald P. Hodel, in his last day in office in January 1989 refused to designate Boston Post Road Historic District in Rye where the Jay Estate sits, to status as a National Historic Landmark, deferring to urgings of the real estate developer. Which of these "Jay" properties possesses an integrity of location and is sufficiently associated with John Jay's life or patterns of American history to justify finding that it is historic enough to preserve? A group of concerned Rye citizens emerged, the Jay Coalition, to protect what they believed to be historic property. How do citizens shape memory and help define the roles that different levels of government, local, state, or federal, serve to preserve John Jay's legacy?

These are the questions we ask and urge you to ponder in this legal and cultural study of historic preservation.

Support for Preservation of the Jay Estate by Notable Personages

As the public campaign of the Jay Coalition to save the Jay Estate from becoming a real estate housing project grew intense, in October of 1987, U.S. Supreme Court Justice Harry A. Blackmun made his second visit in 12 years to the Jay Estate. He paid his respects to the nation's first Chief Justice, laying a wreath on John Jay's grave. His formal remarks have been published. Harry A. Blackmun, *John Jay and the Federalist Papers*, 8 Pace L. Rev. 237 (1988), available at: http://digitalcommons.pace.edu/plr/vol8/iss2/1 (last visited April 1, 2017). Here is what he said at the site of John Jay's childhood home:

> I was impressed with the house, with the lawn, with the great trees, some of which are now gone, and with the vista down to Long Island Sound. It was a place that struck me then as symbolic of what was impressive about certain aspects of the latter part of the eighteenth century—gracious living and status, to be sure, but coupled with a sense of responsibility, particularly to government and to the art of getting together... It must be a matter of pride to be members of an old and distinguished family that contributed so much to early America, that believes in education and leadership then and now, that has sensed the merits, almost the sacredness, of family ties and of what is expected of its members in each generation. I am certain that all of us who are here today join in saluting the Jay family for its significant contributions that meant so much when this Nation that we all love was in its precarious infancy... We are grateful for John Jay's having been part of our national heritage. He was a rock to which the Nation could cling at a time when it might have drifted apart and become helpless just when rich promise lay ahead.

The visit of Justice Blackmun to Rye was well covered in the local newspapers. Tom Andersen, *Blackmun Hails Rye Preservationists*, GANNETT WESTCHESTER NEWSPAPERS, Metro, October 28, 1987, at A15.

In 1989, Chief Justice Warren E. Burger, Chairman of the Bicentennial of the United States Constitution, conveyed the unanimous support of the Commission for the preservation of the Jay Estate. "To preserve the Jay Property would be an appropriate memorial to this important Founding Father during the bicentennial period of the Constitution." Tom Anderson, U.S. Commission Backs Jay Property Preservation, THE DAILY ITEM, January 27, 1989, at 1.

Notes and Questions

1. **The value of reverence.** Justice Blackmun had been invited by the Jay Coalition and the Rye Historical Society. The Jay descendants, who are guardians of the cemetery, were present and were members of the Jay Coalition. a. What influence did Justice Blackmun's presence and words have on the county legislators contemplating acquiring the Locusts by eminent domain, or on the judges in the state courts before whom the City of Rye and the Jay Coalition and the real estate developer were appearing in repeated lawsuits? b. Was Justice Blackmun's visit and message akin to that of Jacqueline Kennedy Onassis' support for the City of New York in the campaign to save Grand Central Terminal? We turn to that pivotal campaign for historic preservation next.

G. The Book's Design

We present the major cases on the development of historic preservation law, followed up by probing questions, notes, and stories to help illuminate the subject. On a companion website (www.law.pace.edu/historic-preservation), we maintain other materials, e.g., model ordinances, guidelines, agreements, and additional literature, that will help to explain the cases and the theory of preservation.

On December 19, 2014, Congress repealed most of the laws covering historic preservation issues as originally appearing under Title 16 and recodified them under Title 54 of the U.S. Code. National Park Service and Related Programs, Pub. L. 113-287 (2014), codified as 54 U.S.C. § 300101, *et seq.* Most of the cases covered here were decided before these changes, such that the statutory references in them are to the old legislation. The cases decided after continue to use some of the shorthands from the original statute. When we introduce a topic, we use the current statutory reference, but have not changed the references in the cases.

Throughout, we make reference to a vast array of online resources with the most recent updates.

Chapter 2

Constitutional Foundations for Preservation Law: The Landmark Case of *Penn Central Transportation Company v. New York City*

A. Grand Central Terminal Landmark Designation Report

In 1965, the New York City Landmarks Preservation Law was adopted. The law provides for designation of landmarks and an application for a certificate of appropriateness when the owner wishes to make changes to the structure of the historic landmark. One of the first such landmarks to be designated was Grand Central Terminal. The designation was in response to a proposal by the owner, Penn Central Transportation Co., to significantly modify the building, demolish parts and to construct a tower where the existing structure stood.

Grand Central Terminal Landmark Designation Report

Landmarks Preservation Commission
August 2, 1967, Number 2
LP-0266

GRAND CENTRAL TERMINAL, 71-105 East 42nd Street, Borough of Manhattan,

Completed 1913; architects Reed & Stem and Warren & Westmore.

Landmark Site: Borough of Manhattan Tax Map Block 1280, Lot 1.

On May 10, 1966, the Landmarks Preservation Commission held a public hearing on the proposed designation as a Landmark of Grand Central Terminal and the proposed designation of the related Landmark Site (Item No. 19). The hearing had been duly advertised in accordance with the provisions of law. Three witnesses spoke in favor of designation. A representative of the owner also spoke. This hearing was continued to subsequent hearings of the Commission. The public hearing on Grand Central Terminal was closed January 31, 1987 (Item No. 8).

DESCRIPTION AND ANALYSIS

Grand Central Station, one of the great buildings of America, evokes a spirit that is unique in this City. It combines distinguished architecture with a brilliant engineering solution, wedded to one of the most fabulous railroad terminals of our time. Monumental in scale, this great building functions as well today as it did when built. In style it represents the best of the French Beaux Arts.

The contrast of solids and voids is a striking feature of this building. The large percentage of glass areas, to be seen in the great windows, is reminiscent of the quality of some of the best French exposition buildings, models of daring structural design in their day, which availed themselves of the latest technological knowledge of their time. The use of these windows for several levels of horizontal circulation, was in itself a daring concept. Visitors can see from the main concourse the diminutive human beings walking between the two layers of glass as they cross and recross from office to office.

The very scale of the monumental columns and the handsome sculptured details, such as the enframement of the oval windows and clock, represents a handsome and skillful combination of architectural elements to create a building overpowering in its timeless grandeur.

History of the Building

Superimposed upon the railroad empire built by the Vanderbilts, which in turn had been built upon the maritime empire of the old Commodore, was the vast network of rails soon to culminate in a new terminal destined to serve the greatest city in the country. On the shoulders of William J. Wilgus rested the staggering problem of assembling the fabulous network of electrified rails into this modern nerve center. This brilliant solution was approved to serve as the basic set of conditions for a nationwide competition among architects for the design of the terminal. The competition was won by Reed & Stem of St. Paul, Minnesota. It was their brilliant design which introduced the concept of ramps. Later Whitney Warren, of Warren & Wetmore, with the concurrence of the Vanderbilts, took over the architectural design of the terminal, as we see it today, displaying the virtuosity of his training at the Ecole des Beaux Arts in Paris.

Grand Central always has been a symbol of the City itself. Commuters, sightseers, casual visitors and City dwellers on pleasant walks go through it daily. Approximately 400,000 people a day stream through its doors, ramps and escalators. So extensive is the series of connections to nearby office buildings that many commuters can go to work without leaving the station. In 1946 Grand Central Terminal served over 65 million passengers. It boasted of 96 long-distance trains departing and 90 arriving every day. By the end of 1964, there were only 51 departures and 48 arrivals daily. Despite these dwindling numbers, the Terminal served almost 43.4 million passengers in 1964—a respectable figure for any railroad station. There are 33.7 miles of track in Grand Central and its adjoining train-yard, a total of 123 tracks—66 on the Upper Level and 57 on the Lower. On these tracks, trains carry about 140,000 paying passengers to and from Grand Central Terminal every week day, and approximately 120,000 are daily commuters.

Grand Central Depot, which preceded the present station, was opened in 1871 for the New York and Harlem Railroad and for the New Haven Railroad which once went downtown through a tunnel as far as 26th Street. After a train wreck in the smoke-filled Park Avenue tunnel in 1902, the State Legislature passed a law prohibiting steam locomotives from using the Park Avenue tracks south of the Harlem River. The law gave the two railroads until 1908 to comply with the new regulation. It was then that the railroad line had to be electrified, and the work to enlarge the station began in 1903. In 1913 the present terminal was completed in conjunction with the fabulous system of "air rights" over the tracks on which so many hotels, department houses and office buildings were subsequently built.

FINDINGS AND DESIGNATIONS

On the basis of a careful consideration of the history, the architecture and other features of this building, the Landmarks Preservation Commission finds that Grand Central Terminal has a special character, special historical and aesthetic interest and value as part of the development, heritage and cultural characteristics of New York City.

The Commission further finds that, among its important qualities, Grand Central Terminal is a magnificent example of French Beaux Arts architecture; that it is one of the great buildings of America, that it represents a creative engineering solution of a very difficult problem combined with artistic splendor; that as an American Railroad Station it is unique in quality, distinction and character; and that this building plays a significant role in the life and development of New York City.

Accordingly, pursuant to the provisions of Chapter 8-A of the Charter of the City of New York and Chapter 8-A of the Administrative Code of the City of New York, the Landmarks Preservation Commission designates as a Landmark, Grand Central Terminal, 71-105 East 42nd Street, Borough of Manhattan and designates Tax Map Block 1280, Lot 1, Borough of Manhattan, as its Landmark Site, available at http://nycnpc.org/db/bb_files/GRAND-CENTRAL.pdf (last visited January 3, 2017).

Notes and Questions

1. **Factual support for the designation.** a. Is there enough information conveyed in this ten paragraph designation to create a factual historicity of the landmark? b. Why did it only take ten paragraphs here but elsewhere it takes pages of discussion?

2. **The Vanderbilts and Grand Central Terminal.** Cornelius "Commodore" Vanderbilt (May 27, 1794–January 4, 1877) is one of the most well-known historical American figures. The patriarch of the Vanderbilt family, he built his wealth on a foundation of railroads and shipping. Starting his business with maritime travel, hence the nickname "Commodore," Cornelius purchased ferry and steamship lines until he managed to control the major shipping companies in the northeast. BARBARALEE DIAMONSTEIN, LANDMARKS: EIGHTEEN WONDERS OF THE NEW YORK WORLD 115 (1992). In the mid-1850s, around the time he turned sixty, Cornelius saw the

immense potential for profit in the railroad industry, and since he had a great deal of wealth from his shipping industry, he began to buy railroad companies. In New York alone, the Commodore bought both the New York and Harlem Railroad in 1862, the Hudson River Railroad in 1863, and the New York Central Railroad in 1867. Always an eager businessman, Cornelius saw an opportunity to rise above the competition. The Vanderbilts were in fierce competition with the Pennsylvania Railroad Company, which owned the Long Island Railroad, for riders into Manhattan and railroads to the Hudson Ferries from Philadelphia. By building a central depot for his entire group of railroad lines in the middle of Manhattan, Cornelius hoped to assert his hegemony over the New York City railways.

The Commodore commissioned the development of the Grand Central Depot, on 42nd Street and Park Avenue, as the anchor for all his north-south railroad connections to and from Manhattan. In May of 1869, Vanderbilt received permission from the State of New York to build the train station, and in September of that year, the first stone was laid; it was finished in 1871. Though Manhattan was largely uninhabited at the time, Vanderbilt knew that the city's ever growing population was soon to increasingly force people to live and work further uptown; in this way he was a visionary. In 1913, the depot was remodeled and replaced by Grand Central Terminal. A statue of Commodore Vanderbilt still stands today above 42nd Street, facing south on Park Avenue, which commemorates the Commodore's hard work and determination in building Grand Central Terminal.

3. **Grand Central Terminal's engineering feats**. The Grand Central Terminal has been described as, "the first American train station that could even begin to compare to the beautiful railway stations of Europe." DIAMONSTEIN at 117. The original building, finished in 1871, built by John B. Snook, was of the head-house type, which allowed trains to back in or out of the main building, but not drive through. It was one of the first to create a large depot for separate train lines; it even had separate waiting rooms for each of the lines. In another engineering achievement, the tracks were sunk into 4th Avenue, later known as Park Avenue, in a cut that later became a tunnel.

By the late 1890s and into the early 1900s, steam-operated trains had become a nuisance and a hazard for Grand Central Depot. Soot lined all the passageways to the trains and created quite a few accidents when it blocked signals and signs from being seen by the conductors. The situation became so dire that at the behest of the public, the New York State Legislature banned all steam-operated trains south of the Harlem River. As a final push, a need for alternative energy source to power trains, when steam engines became obsolete, spurred the remodeling of the Grand Central Depot. William J. Wilgus, vice president of the New York Central Railroad, had been examining the possibility of using electricity to power the trains. With this new idea came a plethora of other possibilities. Electrically powered trains meant that the tracks for the steam-engines no longer needed the space above them to be open for ventilation, which meant that more structures could be built above the trains. For instance, Wilgus had a plan to have all the trains run under Park Avenue on a single track until 50th Street, where they would split into two levels and enter the terminal.

Essentially, there was a design competition for companies which wanted the remodeling job. Two firms were chosen for the construction of the new terminal, Warren & Wetmore of New York City, for the design of the building, and Reed & Stem of St. Paul, Minnesota, to orchestrate the engineering.

The building's construction ran for nearly a decade, from June 1903 to February 1913. Its sheer size and beauty was not only a testament to the advances in train travel, but also an expression of the artistic talent of the contemporary community of artists. In terms of efficiency, the tracks were changed, allowing the trains to circle around underground so that they would not have to back out once inside the station to leave. Ramps were constructed, connecting all levels with the entrances and exits. The main concourse was also designed for a similar function; ensuring that passengers have easy access to information and a pleasant experience while waiting for the trains. The main concourse provided an information booth at the center, ticket windows for each separate railroad line, and baggage rooms for the passengers. Separate waiting rooms were provided for men and women, along with different amenities for both; women had a hair salon and shoe shine shop and men had a barbershop, dressing rooms, baths, and a smoking room. The lower concourse, with lower ceilings, had the same main function, but necessarily a different appearance.

Whitney Warren, of Warren & Wetmore, said that "the façade was designed to appear as if it were a gate to one of the great ancient walled cities." DIAMONSTEIN at 120. Constructed in the Beaux-Arts architectural style, huge arched windows were interspersed with Doric columns. Surrounded by sculptures of three Roman mythological gods, hand-carved out of limestone by the French sculptor Jules-Alexis Coutan, the golden clock is the crown of the terminal's façade. Inside, the massive, 60-foot high, arched windows allowed sunlight to pour into the terminal during the daytime, with five clerestory lunettes up in the 125-foot vaulted ceiling providing additional light. When night fell, the terminal was lit by large bronze chandeliers, though they no longer exist. The ceiling has a mural of the Mediterranean starry sky, with constellations of the Zodiac, taken by Warren from a painting by Paul Helleu. The ceiling's mural, restored by the Metropolitan Transportation Authority in 1998, invites the station's visitors to experience New York aesthetics at the dawn of the 20th century.

a. Does any of this remarkable history appear in the New York City Landmarks Preservation Commission designation? b. How much of this history becomes a part of the court record in the Appellate Division ruling?

4. **Beaux-Arts architecture.** The Grand Central Terminal is exemplary of the use of Beaux-Arts architecture style in the United States. Beaux-Arts architecture epitomizes the academic neoclassical architectural style that was taught at the École des Beaux-Arts in Paris. It was a reaction to romantic, picturesque, Second Empire style. MARILYN W. KLEIN & DAVID P. FOGLE, CLUES TO AMERICAN ARCHITECTURE 38 (1986). The Beaux-Arts style emphasized the mainstream examples of Imperial Roman architecture between Augustus and the Severan emperors, Italian Renaissance and French and Italian Baroque models especially, but the training could then be applied to a broader range of models. Beaux-Arts style embodies a re-emergence of grand classical archi-

tectural traditions rather than a set of motifs. Buildings of this style are "characterized by dynamic shifts in scale and form, domed central portions, facades that project and recede, and application of classical ornament." *Id.* at 39. However, there are certain features which are characteristic of Beaux-Arts architecture, including:

- **Mansard style roofs, with balustraded flat tops.**
- **Rusticated and raised first story.**
- **Romanesque arched and pedimented windows and doors.**
- **Classical motifs:** These tended to include various types of Greek columns, balustrades, pilasters, garlands, cartouches, with a prominent display of richly detailed clasps (*agraffes*) brackets and supporting consoles; references to an eclectic synthesis of historicist styles.
- **Symmetry statuary:** Sculptures—notably, bas-relief panels, figural sculptures, and sculptural groups—murals, mosaics, and other artwork, all melded together to assert a common theme of identity for the building.
- **Classical architectural details**, such as, subtle polychrome, multiple colors in one structure.

Id. at 38–39.

In the late 19th and early 20th Centuries, the Beaux-Arts style heavily influenced American architecture. John Belle & Maxinne Rhea Leighton, Grand Central: Gateway to a Million Lives 49 (2000). When American architects began to discover the École des Beaux-Arts, their Beaux-Arts style often returned to Greek models, continuing with the theme of the American Greek Revival for the early 19th century. *Id.* The style became the symbol of the City Beautiful Movement after the Columbian Exposition of 1893 in Chicago, which showed the style as beautifying civic planning. The best known architectural firm specializing in Beaux-Arts style was McKim, Mead & White, which built the original Pennsylvania Station in New York City. The first American university to institute a Beaux-Arts curriculum was the Massachusetts Institute of Technology (MIT) in 1893, when the French architect Constant-Désiré Despradelles was brought to MIT to teach. Mark Jarzombek, Designing MIT: Bosworth's New Tech (2004). In 1911, the Beaux-Arts Institute of Design was founded in New York City; its stated mission is to school architects, painters, and sculptors to work as active collaborators along the same curriculum as that taught in the École des Beaux-Arts. Donald Martin Reynolds, The Architecture of New York City: Histories and Views of Important Structures, Sites, and Symbols 224 (1984). Beaux-Arts architecture defined an era of American history and we are fortunate to still have many of the monuments to this style across the United States.

5. **Destruction of New York City's Pennsylvania Station.** The Pennsylvania Station was once one of the largest and most majestic buildings to make its way into the New York City landscape. Built by the construction firm of McKim, Mead & White for the Pennsylvania Railroad Company under president Alexander Cassatt, Pennsylvania station was also constructed in the Beaux-Arts style of architecture. When completed

in 1910, Pennsylvania Station covered an area of 8 acres, occupying two complete city blocks from Seventh Avenue to Eighth Avenue and from 31st to 33rd Streets. Pennsylvania Station was meant to be the Pennsylvania Railroad Company's equivalent to the Grand Central Terminal for railroads owned by the Vanderbilts. One of its most notable attributes was that it was one of the first rail terminals to separate arriving from departing passengers on two different concourses.

In the late 1950s, with the construction of the Interstate Highway System and airports, automobiles and airplanes became the main mode of intercity travel. Railway passenger volumes began to decline dramatically and real estate developers questioned the usefulness of such a vast railroad depot in the heart of New York City. Looking to divest itself of the high operation costs of the under-utilized railroad terminal, the Pennsylvania Railroad optioned the air rights of Pennsylvania Station. In exchange, the Pennsylvania Railroad would get a brand new, smaller, sub-street station at no cost and a 25% stake in the new Madison Square Garden complex to be built in place of the old Pennsylvania Railroad Station. The Municipal Art Society of New York, NEW PENN STATION: THE MUNICIPAL ART SOCIETY'S CAMPAIGN FOR A GRAND MOYNIHAN STATION, http://www.newpennstation.org/site/station/past (last visited April 6, 2017). The demolition of the original structure was met with mixed reviews. Although the demolition was considered justified by some as an accommodation to the changed needs of the city, it also instigated international outrage at the demolition of such a beautiful, historic structure. When the dismantling of the structure began, a New York Times editorial lamented:

> Until the first blow fell, no one was convinced that Penn Station really would be demolished, or that New York would permit this monumental act of vandalism against one of the largest and finest landmarks of its age of Roman elegance.

Editorial: Farewell to Penn Station, N.Y. TIMES, October 30, 1963.

Its destruction left a deep and lasting wound in the architectural consciousness of the city. As the editorial went on to say:

> Any city gets what it admires, will pay for, and, ultimately, deserves. Even when we had Penn Station, we couldn't afford to keep it clean. We want and deserve tin-can architecture in a tin-horn culture. And we will probably be judged not by the monuments we build but by those we have destroyed.

Id.

These words are as true today as they were back then. George Santayana's oft-misquoted maxim "those who cannot remember the past are condemned to repeat it," became very poignant in the minds of New Yorkers after Pennsylvania Station's demolition, so much so that the event is considered to have been the catalyst for the enactment of the city's first architectural preservation statutes. Though the majesty of what was once the glorious, grand Pennsylvania Station now sits half submerged in the New Jersey Meadowlands, it has served a purpose as an example of the need for historic preservation laws, without which the Grand Central Terminal and other important historical landmarks, may not be standing today. The demolition of Penn-

Penn Station c. 1910. Library of Congress, Detroit Publishing (Public Domain, Copyright 1910–1920).

sylvania Station was a heavy price to pay for future generations, but arguably without it, the Historic Preservation movement may not have had as much force, especially in New York City, and particularly when a few years later, the Grand Central Terminal was on the chopping block.

1. Denial of Certificate of Appropriateness

To change or modify a landmark, the applicable statutes and local ordinances require the owner to apply for a certificate of appropriateness. Two years to the month, after the designation of Grand Central Terminal as a historic landmark, there is a decision by the Landmarks Preservation Commission on the certificate of appropriateness.

Denial of Permit for Certificate of Appropriateness

LANDMARKS PRESERVATION COMMISSION
of
The City of New York
Parks, Recreation and Cultural Affairs Administration
August 5, 1969
CITY HALL
10:00 AM

Pursuant to the provisions of Chapter 8-A of the Administrative Code of The City of New York (Sections 207-5.0, 207-6.0 and 207-7.0) a public hearing is being held by the Landmarks Preservation Commission with respect to the following described property:

Application for Certificate of Appropriateness

BOROUGH OF MANHATTAN

69005-Block 1280, Lot I, Grand Central Terminal, 71-105 East 42nd Street (LP-0266). New multi-story office building to be erected above the roof of the Terminal (NB 69/68): alterations to station by removing stores on East 42nd Street frontage and other alterations (Alt. 1127/68).

69006-Block 1280, Lot I, Grand Central Terminal, 71-105 East 42nd Street (LP-0266). Demolition of the Terminal building from ground level up except for the Main Concourse which would be preserved and restored; new multi-story office building to be erected on the site of the Terminal (NB 69/68 as amended). Revised plans received on June 23, 1969 and August 1, 1969, make the following changes: a narrower building on its east-west axis, three stories taller, the buttresses on the southern facade have been removed, the building has been moved northward, and the south gallery of the main concourse is not preserved.

This hearing has been duly advertised and is a re-opening of the public hearing on this application held at City Hall on April 10th, 11th and 14th, 1969.

Close the hearing.

I. *BACKGROUND*

On May 10, 1966 the Landmarks Preservation Commission held a public hearing on the proposed designation as a Landmark of Grand Central Terminal and the proposed designation of the related Landmark Site. The hearing was continued to subsequent meetings of the Commission and closed January 31, 1967. On August 2, 1967, Grand Central Terminal, 71-105 East 42nd Street, Borough of Manhattan was designated as a Landmark and Tax Map Block 1280, Lot 1, Borough of Manhattan was designated as its Landmark Site (LP-0266). The designations were filed with the Board of Estimate which confirmed them on September 21, 1967 (Cal. No. 318).

On July 18, 1968 application was made to the Landmarks Preservation Commission by Penn Central Company, UGP Properties, Inc., The New York and Harlem Railroad Company and the 51st Street Realty Corporation for a Certificate of No Exterior Effect for work proposed to be done at Grand Central Terminal. The request was denied on September 20, 1968.

On January 20, 1969, the Landmarks Preservation Commission received the application of Penn Central Company, UGP Properties, Inc., The New York and Harlem

Railroad Company and the 51st Street Realty Corporation (hereinafter referred to as the applicants) for a Certificate of Appropriateness for the work that had been proposed under the application of July 18, 1968 (hereinafter referred to as Breuer I), as well as for an alternative proposal (hereinafter referred to as Breuer II).

By mutual agreement the dates of April 10th, 11th and 14th, 1969 were fixed and duly advertised for a public hearing on these matters, and May 26, 1969 was fixed as the date for the decision by the Commission on the application.

Before this date was reached, however, it was found that the land on which Breuer II was proposed to be built included land on 43rd Street running westward from Lexington Avenue on which existed a leasehold to parties other than any of the applicants. Breuer II was also found to overhang a New York City easement extending to the sky, and its supporting columns or buttresses also violated these easements. While the applicants considered whether they wished to take further steps, the date for the Commission's determination was first extended to June 9, 1969 and later to June 23, 1969. The applicants decided to revise the Breuer II plans so as to conform completely to the land which the applicants currently own. The Commission announced that it would reopen the April 1969 hearing to consider the revised plans (hereinafter referred to as Breuer II Revised). A submission of the revisions was made to the Commission on June 23, 1969 and a final and complete set of drawings was received on August 1, 1969.

By mutual agreement the date of August 5, 1969 was fixed and duly advertised for the reopened public hearing on Breuer I and Breuer II Revised. It was further agreed that, insofar as testimony was directed towards an element in which Breuer II specifically differed from Breuer II revised, all oral and written arguments received at or subsequent to the April 1969 hearing might be considered by the Commission in reaching its determination. It was agreed that the Commission's determination would be reached on or before September 9, 1969.

II. *PUBLIC HEARING*

The hearing of April 10, 11 and 14, 1969 was held as advertised. Seventy-one individuals are recorded as having testified. In the listings below, when an individual officially represented an organization this is so stated, in other cases individuals spoke for themselves, and organizational connections are given merely for identification.

The following persons spoke in favor of one or both proposals or gave their qualified approval:

> Murray Drabkin representing UGP Properties, Inc., Marcel Breuer and his partner, Herbert Beckhard, I. M. Pei, Samuel Hellenbrand, representing the Penn Central Company, Roger Starr representing the Citizens Housing and Planning Council, Edward Larrabee Barnes, Earl Fullilove representing the Building Trades Employers' Association (statement read for him), Arthur Rosenblatt, administrator for architecture and planning, The Metropolitan Museum of Art, John Baur, director of the Whitney Museum, Marian Willard Johnson, Peter Blake, editor of The Architectural Forum, Ulrich

Franzen, Ralph Gross representing the Commerce and Industry Association, Walter Wagner, editor of the Architectural Record, (article read for him), Paul Busse representing the Economic Development Council of New York City, Rolland Thompson and John O'Donoghue representing the Real Estate Board of New York.

The following persons spoke against both proposals:

Francis X. Smith, President of the City Council, Assemblyman Andrew Stein, Douglas Haskell, retired editor of The Architectural Forum, Donald H. Elliott, chairman of the New York City Planning Commission, Jaquelin Robertson representing the New York City Department of City Planning, Congressman Edward Koch, Joan Paul Carlhian representing the American Institute of Architects (the national organization), Mrs. Helmut Friedlander representing Women's City Club of New York, Arthur Holden, Mrs. Barbara Delaney, Ruth Strauss, representing the American Institute of Interiors Designers, Cornelia Van Siclen representing the Decorators Club and the Historic Landmark Society, Giorgio Cavaglieri, New York State Preservation Coordinator of the American Institute of Architects, Joseph Freitag, Charles Hughes and Fredrick Williams representing the Municipal Art Society of New York, Anne Winkler, Mrs. Eleanor Clark French, Juliet Bartlett, Basil Yurchenco representing the Architects Council of New York City (the Bronx, Brooklyn, Queens and Staten Island Chapters of the American Institute of Architects and the New York Society of Architects), Councilwoman Carol Greitzer representing herself and the Murray Hill Democratic Club, Mrs. Margot Gayle representing the Victorian Society and the Village Neighborhood Committee, Otto Teegen, Professor James Marston Fitch, School of Architecture, Columbia University, Lois Hoyt, Edwin Harris, Jr. (statement read for him), Congressman James Scheuer (statement read for him), Isabel Barringer, Gordon Roberts representing Chelsea Historic District Council, Associate Professor Adolf Placaek, librarian, Avery Architectural Library, Columbia University, Roman Heilman, Nesbitt Garmendia, Mrs. Gordon Roberts, Roger Arcara, Bronson Binger, Professor Craig Smyth, director, Institute of Fine Arts, New York University, Alice Sachs representing the Lexington Democratic Club, William Sattan, David Wallerstein representing the Committee Opposing the Demolition of Grand Central Terminal, Russell Lynes (article read for him), Charles Platt, Professor Albert Christ-Janer, dean, Art School, Pratt Institute, Eleonora Schauffler, Paul Byard, Alfred Frazer representing the New York Chapter of the Society of Architectural Historians, David Todd and George Lewis representing the New York Chapter of the American Institute of Architects, Arnold Kates, Eleanor Nadeau and Richard Fried.

The following persons took positions favoring or opposing certain aspects of the proposals or suggested modifications:

Richard Kelly and Robert Weinberg

Donald Gaynor representing Manhattan Community Planning Board No. 5 appeared and reported that a committee of the Board was presently studying the proposals.

In addition to the written copies of their statements that certain speakers left with the Commission, a number of letters, telegrams, memoranda and statements were received. If in the hand before the conclusion of the hearing, these were either read into the record or summarized by the Chairman. If received subsequent to the hearing, they were either in the Commission's office by April 30, 1969 or the date of receipt is noted.

Letters or other material in support of one or both proposals were received from the following:

> George F Mueden, Jr., Julius Nasso, Vincent Ponte and Thomas Shortman representing Local 32B, Service Employees International Union, AFL-CIO.

Supplementary material was also received from the applicants.

Letters or other material against both proposals were received from the following:

> Mrs. Walter Abel, Caroline Anderson, Wayne Andrews, Mrs. Walter Baker, Julian Bach, Jr., Mrs. James Benenson, Jr., James Biddle representing the National Trust for Historic Preservation, Mrs. C. Douglas Booth, John Booth, James Burns, Jr., Citizens Union of the City of New York (received May 13, 1969). Mrs. Arthur Cohen, Mary Coughlan, Inman Cook, Michael Deskey, Carl Feiss, Evan Frances, Professor Percivel Goodman, School of Architecture, Columbia University, Etsie Goss, Gerald Hobbins, Mrs. Robert Hoguet, Arthur Holden (received May 20, 1969), John Johansen, president, Architectural League, Mrs. F. Cliffe Johnston, Robert King, Arthur Knowles, Julian Lee, Ruth Lieb, Mrs. John Liggett, Mrs. Daniel Lindley, Rasa Lisauskas, Wriston Locklair, David Malamud, Peter Malkin, H. Robert Mandel, Stewart Manville, Judith Mara, Elizabeth Matthews, A. McVoy McIntyre, William McCracken, V. Isabellee Miller, Professor Sibyl Moholy-Nagy, School of Architecture, Pratt Institute, Lois Payne, Anne Perkins, Eugene Picket, William Platt, William Plumb, Elizabeth Pomada, Myrna Post, Joseph Roberto, university architects, New York University, Mrs. John Rolph, Edwards Rullman representing the Brooklyn Heights Association, David Saltonstall, vice-director for administration, The Brooklyn Museum, Robert Samuels, Jr., Fred Shrallow, Adele Tuch, Mrs. L. A. Van Bomel, Stuyvesant Van Veen, Phelps Warren and Mrs. Gerritt Weston.

A letter giving information about the proposals was received from Royall, Koegel Wells.

At the August 5, 1969 hearing the following persons spoke in favor of Breuer II Revised:

> Murray Drabkin, representing UGP Properties, Inc., Hebert Beckhard, and Roger Lund, representing the Penn Central Company.

The following persons spoke against Breuer II Revised:

> Joseph Freitag, chairman urban design committee of the New York Chapter of the American Institute of Interior Designers and also speaking for himself, Charles Hughes, president of the Municipal Art Society of New York, Giorgio Cavaglieri, New York State Preservation Coordinator for the American Institute of Architects, and Arthur C. Holden. Richard N. Fried and Thomas Galvin recorded their opposition without making a statement.

Letters and other material in opposition to Breuer II Revised were received from the following and were summarized by the Chairman:

> Jean Paul Carlhian, chairman of the design committee of the American Institute of Architects (the national organization), Alfred Fazer, president of the New York Chapter of the Society of Architectural Historians, Lloyd Bell, president of the New York Chapter of the American Institute of Interior Designers, Douglas Haskell and Otto Teegan. A telegram from Cornelia Van Siclen and Ruth Strauss representing the Decorators Club was received August 6, 1969, and from Ruth Sprute representing Village Neighborhood Committee Inc. and from Margot Gayle on August 8, 1969.

III. *CONSIDERATION*

Much of the testimony, both oral and written, was not directed to the criteria under which the Landmarks Preservation Commission must take its determination, but because of the wide public interest that the case had aroused, it was felt that both proponents and opponents of the proposals should be given broad latitude in expressing their views.

These background matters were of three general sorts: city planning considerations, questions of interior design control and economic problems.

Arguments against increasing the density of the office population at the heart of one of the City's most densely developed areas, questions as to the correctness of present zoning, adequacy of light and air, possible transfer of air rights to other building sites, pedestrian and vehicular circulation and underground concourse systems and their relation to rapid transit are all matters that fall within the province of the City Planning Commission and not that of the Landmarks Preservation Commission.

An offer was made by the applicants to rehabilitate the station's main concourse interior in exchange for permission to demolish the facade. The Landmarks Preservation law places on the Commission responsibility for preserving the exteriors of the City's Landmarks. The Landmarks Law gives the Commission no power over the interiors of Landmarks. The Commission therefore has no authority to approve the demolition of a designated Landmark in return for a benefit to be performed by the applicants, which would in no way serve to protect or enhance the exterior portions of the Landmark.

Since the applications were for appropriateness (under Section 207-5.0 (3) and Section 207-6.0 of chapter 8-A of the Administrative Code) and not on the ground of insufficient return (Section 207-8.0), the question of the applicant's desire for greater income cannot be a consideration in the present determination. The action of the Commission with regard to the present application is without prejudice to any submission by the applicants relating to insufficient return on the property, if they become qualified under the provisions of the Landmarks Preservation Law.

The Chairman of the City Planning Commission and a representative of the City Planning Department proposed at the hearing a series of alternatives under which the applicants would be able to transfer the unused air rights above the Grand Central Terminal to nearby sites for which certain city planning as well as economic advantages were claimed. It was stated that such a transfer would give the applicants a reasonable return without destroying or impairing the Landmark. These matters are not within the jurisdiction of the Landmarks Preservation Commission to decide. We refer to them here merely to indicate that there would appear to be other equitable alternatives open to the applicants in place of those they propose.

The responsibility of the Landmarks Preservation Commission in connection with the issuance of a certificate of appropriateness is defined in Section 207-6.0 of the Administrative Code of the City of New York. The relevant provisions, found in subdivisions (a) and (d) of this section, are as follows:

> "a. In any case where an applicant for a permit to construct, reconstruct, alter or demolish any improvement on a landmark site ... files such application with the commission together with a request for a certificate of appropriateness, and in any case where a request for a certificate of no exterior effect is denied and the applicant thereafter, pursuant to the provisions of Section 207-5.0 of this chapter, files a request for a certificate of appropriateness, the commission shall determine whether the proposed work would be appropriate for and consistent with the effectuation of the purposes of this chapter. If the commission's determination is in the affirmative on such question, it shall grant a certificate of appropriateness, and if the commission's determination is in the negative, it shall deny the applicant's request."

> "d. In making the determination referred to in subdivision (a) of this section with respect to an application for a permit to alter, reconstruct or demolish a landmark, the commission shall consider the effects of the proposed work upon the protection, enhancement, perpetuation and use of the exterior architectural features of such landmark which cause it to possess a special character or special historical or aesthetic interest or value."

Finally, the relevant "purposes of this Chapter" referred to above are stated in Section 205-1.0 as follows:

> "a. The council finds that many improvements, as herein defined, having a special character or special historical or aesthetic interest or value and many improvements representing the finest architectural products of distinct periods in the history of the city, have been uprooted, notwithstanding the feasibility of preserving and continuing the use of such improvements, and without adequate consideration of the irreplaceable loss to the people of the city of the aesthetic, cultural and historic values represented by such improvements ... It is the sense of the council that the standing of this city as a world-wide tourist

center and world capital of business, culture and government cannot be maintained or enhanced by disregarding the historical and architectural heritage of the city and by countenancing the destruction of such cultural assets."

"b. It is hereby declared as a matter of public policy that the protection, enhancement, perpetuation and use of improvements of special character or special character [sic] or special historical or aesthetic interest or value is a public necessity and is required in the interest of health, prosperity, safety and welfare of the people. The purpose of this chapter is to (a) effect and accomplish the protection, enhancement and perpetuation of such improvements … which represent or reflect elements of the city's cultural, social, economic, political and architectural history; (b) safeguard the city's historic, aesthetic and cultural heritage, as embodied and reflected in such improvements …; (d) foster civic pride in the beauty and noble accomplishments of the past; (e) protect and enhance the city's attraction to tourists and visitors and the support and stimulus to business and industry thereby provided; (f) strengthen the economy of the city; and (g) promote the use of landmarks for the education, pleasure and welfare of the people of the city."

Turning now to the application of these criteria to the matters before it, the Landmarks Preservation Commission has the responsibility of determining whether either of the two alternative proposals for altering and adding to a duly designated Landmark are appropriate. The two alternatives will be considered in turn.

BREUER I

Borough of Manhattan—Block 1280, Lot 1, Grand Central Terminal, 71-05 East 42nd Street (LP-0266). New multi-story office building to be erected above the roof of the Terminal; interior alterations to station by removing stores on East 42nd Street frontage, new escalators and public passageways leading to subway platforms and street, and related alterations

A review of the testimony reveals very little that bears on the appropriateness of the architectural design or the quality of the architectural competition.

An examination of the elevations submitted by the applicant further indicates that, in evaluating the question of appropriateness, the exterior work proposed below the level of the automobile ramp and roadway should be separately considered from the work proposed above the roof of the Terminal. While the application did not make this distinction, some proponents argued that the advantages of the street level portion of the proposal should weigh in favor of accepting the whole design. Actually, the two portions of the exterior work area about 150 feet apart and aesthetically have a totally different impact on the existing structure.

While the proposed alterations to the storefronts on the 42nd Street level do "affect and change the exterior architectural features of the Landmark" (as stated in the Commission's decision of September 20, 1968), we do not in principle find the proposed alterations inappropriate. In fact, the removal of the shops with their commercial signs and the creation of a pedestrian arcade could, in our opinion, if sensitively handled, considerably enhance the exterior of Grand Central Terminal by providing a quieter and more dignified base to support the monumental columns that rise from the ramp level. Since the suggested changes in the street level entrances would unquestionably improve pedestrian access to the Terminal and to the subway, these proposals might well be acceptable as a means of perpetuating the use of the Landmark and of protecting its main exterior architectural features.

We turn now to the multi-story office building that it is proposed to have spring [sic] through the roof of the Terminal and cantilever above the existing facades. Through the exercise of extraordinary architectural and engineering ingenuity this part of the proposal does not actually physically touch the exterior vertical surfaces of the building. This is the basis of the applicants' claim that the proposal would technically "protect" and "perpetuate" the designated features of the Landmark. On an equally technical level, it can equally well be claimed that the roof of a building forms one of its five exterior surfaces and hence is an exterior architectural feature and thus subject to the same protection as the facades.

In any event, the crucial question is whether the proposed tower would be appropriate for and consistent with the effectuation of the purposes of the Landmarks Preservation Law. Will the proposed changes adversely affect the protection, enhancement, perpetuation and use of the exterior architectural features of the Landmark in question? Will it protect and enhance any of the exterior architectural features of the Landmark which cause it to possess a special character or special historical or aesthetic interest or value? It is in regard to these all important criteria that the proponents of Breuer I are singularly silent.

The applicants claim that the Pan Am Building has already destroyed the silhouette of the south facade and that the proposed tower, with its granite facing, would either provide a better background or that one more tower could not do further damage.

New York City, unlike Paris and other world famous cities, is not rich in dramatically terminated vistas. Trinity Church at the end of Wall Street, Washington Arch at the foot of Fifth Avenue, and the RCA Building at the end of the Rockefeller Center gardens are among the few examples we have. Yet none of these have the sweep that Park Avenue still provides for the Grand Central Terminal from the south. Despite the damage that many feel the Pan Am Building has done, it can still be said that the Terminal is unique in the City in its enjoyment of such a majestic approach, either in a vehicle or on foot, as the half-mile of Park Avenue from the top of the hill at 34th Street to 42nd Street.

It is not difficult to visualize how much more detrimental Breuer I would be to the Terminal's south facade than the Pan Am Building already is. The south face of the Pan Am Building is about 375 feet back of the Terminal. The south face of Breuer I would be only 30 feet away. All the softening effects of distance (atmospheric perspective) and all the present sense of separation would be lost. The full play of sunlight and shadow on the Breuer facade would be in direct competition with the richly modeled design of the Terminal below it and nearly in the same plane.

From closer vantage points, the Pan Am Tower drops back in perspective and is largely cut off from view by the Terminal in the foreground. The great mass of the Breuer I tower right on top of the Terminal facade would offer no such relief.

The Landmarks Preservation Commission has no fixed rule against making additions to designated buildings—it all depends on how they are done and so long as they satisfy the standards of the law and do not adversely affect the protection, enhancement, perpetuation and use of the architectural features of the landmark in question. The office and reception wing added to Gracie Mansion and the school and church house added to the 12th Street side of the First Presbyterian Church are examples that harmonize in scale, material and character with the structures they adjoin. The new Watch Tower Bible and Tract Society building on Brooklyn Heights, though completely modern in idiom, respects the qualities of its surroundings and will enhance the Brooklyn Heights Historic District, as Butterfield House enhances West 12th Street, and Breuer's own Whitney Museum its Madison Avenue locale. But to balance a 55-story office tower above a flamboyant Beaux-Arts facade seems nothing more than an aesthetic joke. Quite simply, the tower would overwhelm the Terminal by its sheer mass. The "addition" would be four times as high as the existing structure and would reduce the Landmark itself to the status of a curiosity.

Landmarks cannot be divorced from their settings—particularly when the setting is a dramatic and integral part of the original concept. The Terminal, in its setting, is a great example of urban design. Such examples are not so plentiful in New York City that we can afford to lose any of the few we have. And we must preserve them in a meaningful way—which alterations and additions of such character, scale, materials and mass as will protect, enhance and perpetuate the original design rather than overwhelm it.

BREUER II REVISED

> Borough of Manhattan—Block 1280, Lot 1, Grand Central Terminal, 71-105 East 42nd Street (LP-0266). Demolition of the Terminal building from ground level up except for the Main Concourse, which would be preserved and restored; new multi-story office building to be erected on the site of the Terminal, (NB 69/68 as amended). Revised plans received June 23, 1969 and in final and complete form on August 1, 1969, make the following changes: A narrower building on its east-west axis, three stories taller, the buttresses on the southern facade have been removed, the building has been moved northward, and the south gallery of the Main Concourse is not preserved.

The total floor area of Breuer II Revised is the same as Breuer II since neither of the schemes included are under lease to others or any part of the City easement as a basis for the bulk calculations. Because of the reduction of about twenty feet in the east-west dimension of the typical tower floor and because of certain modifications in the lower stories the revised scheme has three more office floors and is 61 feet higher than the original.

The shift of the tower northward by some sixteen and a half feet has required the filling up of the south gallery portion of the interior Concourse. Thus, while the applicants have reaffirmed their commitment to restore the Concourse to the satisfaction of the Landmarks Preservation Commission, Breuer II Revised no longer has the advantage over Breuer I that the original Breuer II had. Under either of the proposals currently before the Commission (Breuer I and Breuer II Revised) only the central portion and northerly portion of the concourse interior could be restored.

The reduction in the east-west dimension of the tower has permitted the westerly face of the tower to fall behind the westerly face of the existing Terminal instead of overhanging it as the original scheme did. Breuer II Revised, however, also proposes stripping off all the present stonework from the Vanderbilt Avenue facade and replacing it with granite to match the proposed new tower. Only the stark outline of the three arched windows that light the Concourse from the west would remain.

Breuer II, (and, by implication, Breuer II Revised) was much preferred by the applicants and by most of the supporters of the application who expressed a preference between it and Breuer I.

The major arguments for tearing down a great portion of a designated Landmark and for stripping the balance of its exterior detail were: first, that the concourse interior was the only part of the building worth saving; second, that the exterior was not worth designating in the first place; third, that it cannot be seen; fourth, that it is already so compromised as no longer to be worth saving; and, fifth, that it would be better to replace it with a good building by a famous architect than to risk, as a possible future alternative, the inferior product of a lesser talent. These arguments will be considered in turn.

(1) Whatever the relative merits of the exterior and the interior of the Terminal and however much some may deplore the Commission's lack of jurisdiction over interiors, the Commission does have jurisdiction over the facades of this Landmark. We find no merit in the argument that because of its limited powers the Commission should not exercise what powers it has.

(2) Grand Central Terminal is a duly designated Landmark of the City of New York. The Landmarks Preservation Commission was established in part to remove controversies over architectural and historical merit from the private, subjective domain to the level of public policy. Designations are made after careful research, after evaluation of the particular importance—both aesthetic and historical—of each structure under consideration, and after a duly advertised public hearing. The decision to designate, according to the Landmarks Law, is made by a balanced, eleven member commission appointed by the Mayor and consisting of three architects, a realtor, a city planner or landscape architect, and historian and resident of each of the five boroughs. Furthermore, all designations are subject to review by the Board of Estimate. Confirmation of a designation by this body represents the acceptance as a public responsibility of the Landmark's preservation in accordance with the provisions of the law.

The designation report in this case, LP-0266, maintains that Grand Central Station is "one of the great buildings of America ... In style it represents the best of the French Beaux Arts ... The very scale of the monumental columns and the handsome sculptured details ... represent a handsome and skillful combination of architectural elements to create a building overpowering in its timeless grandeur." This evaluation by the Commission was confirmed and reinforced by the consensus of architectural opinion expressed at the hearing.

While several eminent architects spoke individually in favor of the Breuer II proposal, it is significant to note that some of them based their support on the premise that Grand Central Terminal would have, in any event, to be replaced. The official architectural profession, moreover, through both its national and local organizations, spoke unequivocally against the demolition or defacement of Grand Central Terminal. And this position was taken despite a frequently stated high regard for Breuer's architectural skill. The representative of the American Institute of Architects, the national organization of the architectural profession, said that the A.I.A. "voices the wish that every conceivable avenue ... be fully explored prior to any action which would permit any demolition to take place within the area now occupied by the terminal itself." This position was specifically reaffirmed in regard to Breuer II Revised by a written communication to the Commission.

(3) The view of the south facade from Park Avenue has already been discussed. The building is not only plainly, but dramatically, visible from this approach. The question of the closer views is easily settled by a walk along the south side of 42nd Street or the west side of Vanderbilt Avenue. The raised roadway, by setting the bulk of the Terminal some 50 feet back from the building line, has the effect of substantially narrowing the vertical visual angle within which the main facade can be viewed. It is true that a portion of the stylebate [*sic*] is cut off, but this effect was allowed for in the original design: the full height of the monumental columns, including their bases, is easily visible to the passing pedestrian on street level. Because of the lowered visual angle resulting from the set-back, the facade can be appreciated with considerably less neck craning than if it had been erected, as is so typical in New York, directly on the building line. The richly modeled facade gains the advantage of being dramatically illuminated by an extra wedge of daylight.

(4) & (5) The next two arguments stem from the same spirit of cynical expediency that has cost the City so much of its architectural heritage. Even if the Pan Am Building is regrettable, is this any reason to destroy the great Terminal we have? Even though a less able architect might produce a worse building than Breuer's, neither the merits or demerits of a replacement are relevant to the City's stated purpose in the Landmark Law: to "accomplish the protection, enhancement and perpetuation ... of improvements of special character or special historical or aesthetic interest or value" which the Grand Central Terminal, as a designated Landmark, is officially recognized as having.

This brings us to the heart of the matter.

If the Commission is to "consider the effects of the proposed work upon the protection, perpetuation and use of the exterior architectural features of such landmark," then to approve the demolition of a major portion of Grand Central Terminal would be in flagrant violation of the Commission's responsibility. To protect a Landmark, one does not tear it down. To perpetuate its architectural features, one does not strip them off. And this is just what Breuer II Revised proposal would do.

To approve Breuer II Revised proposal would mean the loss not only of one more fine building in addition to the many that were lost before there was a Landmarks Law to protect them. It would mean the loss of an officially designated Landmark and one that "evokes a spirit that is unique in this City." "Grand Central," as the designation report states, "always has been a symbol of the City itself."

IV. *FINDINGS*

For these reasons, and after careful consideration, the Landmarks Preservation Commission denies the application of UGP Properties, Inc., Penn Central Company, The New York and Harlem Railroad Company and the 51st Street Realty Corporation for a Certificate of Appropriateness for plans submitted to the Commission on July 18, 1968 (referred to above as Breuer I) and for plans received by the Commission on June 23, 1969 and in final and complete form on August 1, 1969 (referred to above as Breuer II Revised).

Notes and Questions

1. **The proposed addition.** a. Do you agree that there should be a prohibition on putting a tower over the landmark? b. Given the changes in the neighborhood, would this prohibition still be appropriate? c. What are the arguments for and against the Breuer Plan? d. When would post-modern architecture be compatible with Beaux-Arts architecture? When would it be appropriate to meld the two?

B. *Penn Central* New York Trial Term Decision: Judge Saypol's Decision on the Request for a Certificate of Appropriateness

Penn Central Transportation Company v. City of New York

Supreme Court of the State of New York, Trial Term, County of New York
No.14763/69 (Feb. 4, 1975)

Findings of Fact

Saypol, J. The Court hereby finds as follows:

General

1. Plaintiff Penn Central Transportation Company ("Penn Central") is a corporation organized and existing under the laws of the Commonwealth of Pennsylvania with

a general office at 466 Lexington Avenue, New York, New York. It is the successor to The New York Central Railroad Company and the Pennsylvania Railroad Company, which were merged as of February 1, 1968.

2. Penn Central was declared bankrupt on June 21, 1970 and has remained bankrupt since that time.

3. Plaintiff The New York and Harlem Railroad Company ("The New York and Harlem") is, and has been at all times relevant to this action, a corporation organized and existing under the laws of the State of New York with approximately 95% of its stock owned by the Trustees of Penn Central and with a general office at 466 Lexington Avenue, New York, New York.

4. Plaintiff The 51st Street Realty Corporation is, and has been at all times relevant to this action, and indirectly wholly-owned subsidiary corporation of Penn Central, organized and existing under the laws of the State of New York with a general office at 466 Lexington Avenue, New York, New York.

5. Plaintiff UGP Properties, Inc. ("UGP") is, and has been at all times since its formation on December 5, 1967, a corporation organized and existing under the laws of the State of New York.

6. Defendant The City of New York (the "City") is a municipal corporation of the State of New York.

7. Defendant The Landmarks Preservation Commission of the City of New York (the "Landmarks Commission") was established as a commission of the City pursuant to Local Law 46 of the City for the year 1965, which amended the Charter and the Administrative Code of the City so as to add to each of them a new Chapter 8-A.

8. Grand Central Terminal (the "Terminal") was constructed in the early 1900's and opened to the public in 1913. It is located in the Borough of Manhattan. The building faces on Forty-Second Street to its south and is bounded on the west by on its south, east and west by the Park Avenue overhead roadway. To its north, the Terminal is bounded by the Pan Am Building. It is and always has been used in the interstate and intrastate carriage of railroad passengers.

9. The Terminal is deteriorating at a substantial rate. The condition of the Terminal was such that repairs and maintenance work costing approximately $1,278,135 were necessary in June 1972.

10. The Terminal was originally intended to be a combination railroad terminal and office building. The original plan for the Terminal provided for a 20-story office tower to be constructed on top of the present Terminal and columns were built into the Terminal, which are still in place today, whose purpose is to support such a tower.

11. The land on which the Terminal stands (the "Terminal site") is designated in the Tax Map of the City as Block 1280, Lot 1, Borough of Manhattan.

12. The Terminal and the Terminal site have received partial tax exemption amounting to $11,083,489 since the early 1960's under Section 489ff of the Real Property Tax Law of the State of New York.

13. On August 2, 1967, over Penn Central's objection the Terminal was designated a Landmark and the Terminal site a Landmark site by the Landmarks Commission.

Ownership and Leasehold Interests in the Terminal Property

14. The ownership and leasehold interests in the Terminal and the Terminal site, held by the respective plaintiffs, are, and have been at all times relevant to this action, unless otherwise noted, as follows:

(a) The New York and Harlem Railroad Company owns the fee;

(b) Penn Central has a lease, expiring in the year 2,274 A.D. from The New York and Harlem Railroad Company;

(c) UGP entered into a lease, dated as of January 22, 1968, with The 51st Street Realty Corporation (the "Lease") which, at that time, had a grant of term of the Terminal [sic]and the Terminal site from Penn Central. The 51st Street Realty Corporation assigned all of its interest in the Lease, the Terminal and the Terminal site to Penn Central and The New York and Harlem on July 21, 1969.

15. The Lease was the result of arms-length negotiations and is for a term of 50 years after its commencement date with UGP having an option to renew for an additional 25 years thereafter. Under the Lease, UGP is to construct and operate a multistory office building on the southerly portion of the Terminal site.

Breuer I, II, and II Revised

16. UGP retained the architectural firm of Marcel Breuer & Associates in February, 1968, to design an office building for the Terminal site.

17. By June, 1968, Marcel Breuer & Associates completed the first schematic plans, Breuer I, for an office building with 55 office floors which would rise above the Terminal and would preserve the exterior of the Terminal.

18. On July 18, 1968, plaintiffs submitted proposed building plans for Breuer I to the Landmarks Commission and applied for a Certificate of No Exterior Effect permitting its construction. These plans were also filed with the Department of Buildings of The City of New York to obtain zoning approval. The application was denied by the Landmarks Commission on September 20, 1968.

19. Marcel Breuer & Associates following negotiations and discussions between the parties thereafter designed Breuer II, a building with 53 office floors which would have necessitated replacing part of the exterior of the Terminal.

20. On January 20, 1969, plaintiffs applied to the Landmarks Commission for a Certificate of Appropriateness, under Section 207-6.0 of the Landmarks Law, permitting construction of either Breuer I or Breuer II.

21. Because of the plaintiffs' concern that the possible adverse effect of Breuer II on the City's easement rights in the elevated roadway surrounding the perimeter of the Terminal might be used as a basis for the refusal of a permit to build Breuer II, Marcel Breuer & Associates designed Breuer II Revised which plaintiffs submitted in place of Breuer II. Breuer II Revised was substantially similar to Breuer II, except that

it would not encroach upon the elevated roadway. During the course of the proceedings, plaintiffs expressed a preference for Breuer II as revised over Breuer I.

22. Plaintiffs' application for a Certificate of Appropriateness was denied as to both Breuer I and II Revised on August 26, 1969.

23. Breuer II would be 254 feet southerly from the adjoining Pan Am Building; Breuer I and II Revised would be approximately 225 feet southerly from the Pan Am Building.

24. If Marcel Breuer & Associates had begun work on the plans for Breuer I and II Revised at the time that schematic plans for Breuer I were prepared, schematic plans for Breuer II and II Revised could have been completed by June, 1968.

Harm to Plaintiffs

25. The Terminal site is a valuable location for an office building. It is in the heart of a commercial area occupied mainly by high-rise commercial structures such as office buildings and hotels. Any of the plaintiffs' proposed structures over the Terminal site would be directly above a transportation hub of commuter, railroad and subway lines, with ready access internally by occupants of the building to such facilities.

26. In 1968 there was a favorable office rental market in favor of landlords in the Grand Central area. Rental activity for space in an office building on the Terminal site would have started on the basis of architects' plans beginning in June 1968. Construction of the building would have been completed within three to three and one-half years thereafter.

27. Plaintiffs were prepared to undertake renting and commencement of construction of an office building on the Terminal site in 1968, but were precluded from proceeding because of the defendants' refusal to permit this.

28. Diesel Construction Company, builder of the Pan Am Building, was retained in early 1968 by UGP to construct a building on the Terminal site.

29. Collins, Tuttle & Company, engaged in the sale, rental and management of real estate, was retained by UGP in December, 1967, to rent, obtain financing and as consultant for a building on the Terminal site. Collins, Tuttle & Company began a renting and financing program in early 1968. At that time Collins, Tuttle & Company solicited prospective tenants primarily to lease the space in Breuer I, principally on a single floor occupancy basis, for terms of 20 to 30 years, but these activities were halted due to defendants' denial of a Certificate of No Exterior Effect. Investors financing the building at a favorable interest rate were likewise solicited, but their participation was deferred for the same reason.

30. The total cost of Breuer I would have been $108,554,741, including construction costs of $82,344,400; Breuer II would have cost $106,541,730, of which $77,306,500 would have been construction costs; and Breuer II Revised would have cost $108,486,444, of which $79,365,000 would have been construction costs.

31. If construction of Breuer I had commenced in 1968, the City would have received substantially increased property taxes upon commencement of construction.

32. Under the Lease, Penn Central is to receive $1,000,000 per year during the construction of a building by UGP on the Terminal site. Upon completion, Penn Central is to receive an annual rent of $1.10 per square foot of net rentable space, exclusive of ground floor space, plus $400,000, plus 5% of the gross income, with a guaranteed minimum of $3,000,000 per year. Upon completion of construction, Penn Central would have received an annual rent of up to $3,738,977 from Breuer I.

33. As additional compensating to Penn Central, UGP is to pay under the Lease all taxes on the Terminal site considered as unimproved from the time UGP is permitted to construct a building. From June, 1968, through July, 1972, these taxes totaled $1,372,530. UGP is also to pay all taxes on the Terminal (the building) within the area demised to it, thereby reducing the amount of taxes that Penn Central would have to pay on the Terminal.

34. UGP expected to receive a yearly cash flow of at least $2,839,131 from Breuer I upon its completion, $3,325,620 from Breuer II and $3,181,702 from Breuer II Revised. By the end of the first five years, UGP's anticipated aggregate profit would have been $20,495,655 from Breuer I, $22,928,100 from Breuer II and $22,208,510 from Breuer II Revised.

35. Due to defendants' actions preventing plaintiffs from constructing a building on the Terminal site, Penn Central and The New York and Harlem Railroad Company have been deprived of the rent they would have received from UGP and the taxes UGP would have assumed, and UGP has been deprived of the profit if would have made from such a building.

36. For the years 1967 to 1971, the cost to Penn Central of operating the Terminal building itself, exclusive of purely railroad operations, exceeded the revenues received from concessionaires and tenants in the Terminal.

37. The net deficit to Penn Central from operating the Terminal was $1,165,470 in 1969 and $1,902,467 in 1971.

38. As of June 1, 1972, the Metropolitan Transportation Authority leased the Terminal and, together with the Connecticut Transportation Authority, receives all revenues from tenants and concessionaires in it (with the exception of any rent Penn Central would receive under its lease with UGP and has assumed all costs of operating the Terminal). Penn Central is obligated to pay these agencies $4,500,000 a year for the next five years and $2,000,000 thereafter. The Metropolitan Transportation Authority receives partial reimbursement for these costs from the City.

Transfer of Development Rights (Air Rights) Zoning Resolutions 74-79 Through 74-793

39. Zoning Resolutions 74-79 through 74-793 (the "Transfer Resolutions") contemplated compensatory relief for owners of landmarks, including long-term lessees such as UGP, for the taking caused by the designation of such properties as landmarks.

40. As originally enacted in May, 1968, the Transfer Resolutions neither provided compensation to plaintiffs nor minimized the harm suffered by plaintiffs due to the designation of the Terminal as a landmark.

41. The pertinent Transfer Resolutions as last amended in December 1969, although affording increased transfer rights from the Terminal site to other properties owned by Penn Central, do not provide compensations to plaintiffs or minimize the harm suffered by plaintiffs due to the designation of the Terminal as a landmark.

42. The property principally suggested for the transfer of development rights is the present site of the Biltmore Hotel. Development rights could not be economically transferred to the Biltmore site because:

(1) The Biltmore Hotel is and has been a profitable operation.

(2) A building on the Biltmore site could not have been profitable because (a) the ground rent required of UGP by Penn Central for a lease of the Biltmore site was $2,000,000 a year more than in the Terminal lease, and (b) there would have been increased costs of construction, financing, taxes and building operation.

(3) Rents from an office building on the Biltmore site would be significantly lower than from one on the Terminal site which is a superior location.

Declarations of Law

It is hereby concluded and declared that:

1. The Landmarks Law as applied to plaintiffs, and the actions of defendants, constitute a taking of plaintiffs' private property for public use without just compensation, in violation of the Constitution of the State of New York, Article I, Section 7.

2. The Landmarks Law as applied to plaintiffs, and the actions of defendants, deprive plaintiffs of the equal protection of the laws, in violation of the Constitution of the United States, Amendment XIV, and the Constitution of the State of New York, Article I, Section 11.

3. The Landmarks Law as applied to plaintiffs, and the actions of defendants, deprive plaintiffs of their property without due process of law, in violation of the Constitution of the United States, Amendment XIV, and the Constitution of the State of New York, Article I, Section 6.

4. There is no provision of the Landmarks Law which affords relief to the plaintiffs, with respect to the Terminal or the Terminal site against the economic hardship which they have suffered as a result of the defendants' actions under the Landmarks Law. Although Section 207-8.0 of the Landmarks Law affords such relief to landmark owners generally (including ultimately the lifting of landmark restrictions) upon a showing of economic hardship, the provisions of Section 207-8.0a(2) deny such relief to the plaintiffs, whether by way of Certificate of Appropriateness, notice to proceed or otherwise, because the Terminal and the Terminal site are partially exempted from taxation under Section 489ff of the Real Property Tax Law.

Notes and Questions

1. **New York State practice.** In New York State, the trial term court, with original jurisdiction over most cases of law and equity, is referred to as the Supreme Court, N.Y. CONST. art. VI, §7(a), in contrast to other court systems, where the Supreme

Court refers to the highest court of that state or of the federal court system. The Supreme Court's jurisdiction is constitutionally vested and cannot be statutorily limited. *Id.* When new causes of action are created, the Supreme Court automatically receives original jurisdiction. N.Y. Const. art. VI, §7 (b). The New York Supreme Court makes findings of fact which can be reviewed on appeal by the appellate court referred to as the Appellate Division. N.Y. C.P.L.R. §Intro.03[7]. The Appellate Division can reinterpret the findings of fact put forth by the Supreme Court, but cannot add new facts.

2. **Factual issues avoided.** Having read the report of the New York City Landmarks Preservation Commission about Grand Central Terminal, what facts did Judge Saypol decide not to discuss in his findings?

1. Penn Central's Interest in Grand Central Terminal: Judge Saypol's Decision on the Validity of the Designation

Penn Central Transportation Company v. The City of New York

Supreme Court of the State of New York, Trial Term, County of New York, Part XIII
Index No. 14763/69

* * *

In this January 21, 1975 ruling, Justice Saypol noted that the original designs for the Terminal provided for a twenty-story office building above the station. Penn Central never sought to build that structure. Justice Saypol found that

> Plaintiff Penn Central Transportation Company (Penn Central) controls co-plaintiff New York and Harlem Railroad which owns the fee of Grand Central Terminal located on 42nd Street in the heart of Manhattan in one of the most valuable commercial areas in the world, surrounded by multi-story office buildings and similar structures. Penn Central has a 300-year lease from New York and Harlem Railroad. Penn Central's wholly owned subsidiary, co-plaintiff 51st Street Realty Corporation, has a grant from Penn Central for a term coterminous with a lease from 51st Street Realty Corporation to co-plaintiff UGP Properties Inc., the letter under its lease undertaking to erect and operate a multi-story office building over the Terminal. When the Terminal was erected the plan and construction of its foundation contemplated the future super-imposition of twenty stories over the Terminal. * * *

Compare this presentation before Judge Saypol with the earlier 1968 findings of Special Master John VanVoorhis in the bankruptcy proceedings in federal court in Connecticut. Van Voorhis reported:

UNITED STATES DISTRICT COURT
FOR THE DISTRICT OF CONNECTICUT

In Proceedings for the Reorganization of a Railroad

In the Matter of
THE NEW YORK, NEW HAVEN AND
HARTFORD RAILROAD COMPANY, No. 30226
Debtor.

SUPPLEMENTAL REPORT OF SPECIAL MASTER RESPECTING DEBTOR'S RIGHT, TITLE OR INTEREST IN THE GRAND CENTRAL TERMINAL PROPERTIES

---

* * *

The most important development since April 19, 1965, has been the lease agreement between a Penn-Central subsidiary and a corporation known as UGP Properties, Inc. of the air rights above the Grand Central Terminal building for the construction of a proposed fifty-five story office building planned (according to a press release mentioned by Penn-Central's counsel) to have 1.9 million square feet of office space. The lease agreement is in evidence, marked BH 1, A, B, C, and provides for the payment of 1 million dollars annual rent for four years and thereafter at a $1.10 per square foot of net rentable space, exclusive of ground floor space, which may from time to time exist in the new building plus $400,000 per annum all payable monthly in advance. The term of the lease is 50 years. The tenant agrees to pay the taxes and an additional percentage rent of 5 per cent of gross income which, plus the first rent, is guaranteed to be not less than 3 million dollars per year commencing not later than four years after the commencement date of the lease. It was conceded that the plans for this proposed building, designed to float[1] ... over the Terminal building, comply with the existing regulations of the City Planning Commission and the zoning regulations. This lease was,

---

1. To provide, for places, buildings, structures, works of art, and other objects having a special character or special historical or aesthetic interest or value, special conditions or regulations, for their protection, enhancement, perpetuation [6086] or use, which may include appropriate and reasonable control of the use or appearance of the neighboring private property within public view, or both. In any such instance such measures, if adopted in the exercise of the police power, shall be reasonable and appropriate to the purpose, *or if constituting a taking of private property shall provide for a compensation which may include the limitation or remission or taxes* (emphasis supplied).... [former General City Law 920, subd, 25-a, repealed L. 1968, c. 513, §2; similar provision is now General Municipal Law §96-a, L.1968, c. 513, §3].

delivered to the tenant subject to a letter providing that if the tenant has used its best efforts "to obtain a certificate of appropriateness or notice to proceed from the Landmarks Preservation Commission* and has failed after appropriate order of the Supreme Court of the State of New York and provided, further, that there exists an outstanding designation by the Landmarks Preservation Commission of Grand Central Terminal as a landmark, Tenant and said Sublandlord shall have the right to rescind Lease and Sublease, respectively, by giving to Landlord ten days' written notice of such intention", and in exerting its 'best efforts' the tenant is required to file an application with the Landmarks Preservation Commission prior to August 1, 1968 and to bring an action or proceeding through counsel approved by the landlord against any adverse ruling by the Landmarks Preservation Commission. The landlord is given the right to rescind the lease if the tenant has not obtained this result by January 1, 1970 [extended by agreement of the parties until July 1, 1975], and upon any rescision [sic] of the lease the tenant is required to assign to the landlord its interest in any action or proceeding pending in the New York Courts relating to the application of the Landmarks Preservation Commission or relating to the designation of Grand Central Terminal as a landmark or pertaining to any rights or entities under the statute pursuant to which Grand Central Terminal is designated a landlord [landmark]. In event of adverse decision the landlord is authorized to appeal and the tenant is required to cooperate with the landlord in all matters pertaining to any such action or proceeding. When asked at the hearings whether Penn-Central had abandoned this project, the answer was unqualifiedly 'No.' Counsel for Penn-Central informed the Court on May 8, 1968, in the earlier hearings that an Article 78 proceeding [this plenary action for declaratory judgment instead] has been commenced by Central to contest the designation of Grand Central Station as a landmark, and that this suit includes a test of the constitutionality of the Landmarks Preservation Act which is subdivision 25-a of the General City Law providing that cities are empowered.

The New York City Landmarks Preservation Commission is constituted pursuant to sections 205–207 of the New York City Charter constituting Chapter 8-A added by local law No. 46, April 19, 1965. The constitutionality, in certain situations of the Landmarks Preservation Act was upheld at special term in Manhattan Club v. Landmarks Preservation Commission, 51 Misc.2d 556 and but [sic] not in Trustees of Sailors Snug Harbor v. Landmarks Preservation Commission, 58 Misc. 2d 933.** A landlord has been held entitled to test the constitutionality as applied to his property by action for a declaratory judgment. *Lutheran Church in America v. New York*, 27 App. Div. ? [sic]

---

* Pursuant to Chapter 9-A of the N.Y. City Administrative Code § 205-1.0 through 207-21.0.

** "The regulation imposes so disproportionate a burden upon the landowner that it must be set aside in this case as an unlawful taking of property without just compensation [citing cases]": Last paragraph of opinion [sic].

237. The same statute was obliquely involved in *Ncerdler* [sic] 19 N.Y.2d 78, wherein an injunction was denied to restrain the demolition of the old Metropolitan Opera House. The Court said: "It is not necessary, at this time, to enter into a discussion of the Landmarks Preservation Law or any other statute which appears to have been enacted in the exercise of the police power."

If this new project is accomplished, it appears likely to add at least $2,300,000 to the annual income of the Terminal Account. The parties stipulated that the facts stated at pages 600–05 of the transcript of the hearing held before me on May 8, 1968 are correct, and it was indicated that the rent for these air rights would be in part offset by the displacement of some stores and concessions in the Terminal building now bringing in approximately $700,000 per year. This apparently refers to stores on 42nd Street and some concessions in the waiting room entrance and on the south wall of the main rotunda of the station.

There is, of course, a precedent for this structure in the Pan-American Building located about 200 feet to the north. Whether the opposition to its construction will succeed is not presently known, but it would seem to me that the probabilities are in its favor. The Grand Central Station is not proposed to be removed.

It is doubtful that the City could insist upon its being maintained at Penn Central's expense as a memorial to the golden age of railroading. The building, as it is, is expensive to maintain, and even under the broad scope of the police power in modern times it is doubtful that it can be so constricted without there being a taking without payment of just compensation as required by the state and federal constitutions. This is particularly true in view of the similarity and close proximity to the Pan-Am Building which, it might be argued, could constitute discrimination denying the equal protection of the law. If, under a reorganization plan, all right, title and interest if [sic] New Haven in the GCT properties is to be transferred to Penn-Central, a large potential increase in the surplus revenue to be computed of the Terminal Account should result from these valuable air rights. The fairest way might be to insert a provision in the reorganization plan and purchase agreement which would require substantially more to be paid for New Haven's rights if a building is erected above the Grand Central Station.

* * * * * * * * *

Dated: July 22, 1968

Respectfully submitted,
JOHN VAN VOORHIS
Special Master

* * *

In addition to the bankruptcy determinations involving the Penn Central property interests in Grand Central Terminal, the law of historic preservation in New York was evolving. After overruling the denial of the certificate of appropriateness, Judge Saypol went on to invalidate the designation of the terminal as a landmark. He relied heavily upon *Lutheran Church in America v. New York*, cited in Judge Van Voorhis' report. The substantive challenge to the constitutionality of the Landmarks Preservation Law raised in that case was addressed by a divided Appellate Division. 42 A.D.2d 547 (rejecting the landmark designation). That decision, in turn was affirmed by the Court of Appeals, 35 N.Y. 2d 121, 316 N.E.2d 305 (N.Y. 1974).

In Lutheran Church of America, Judge Gabrielli, wrote for the majority (Judge Jason and Chief Judge Brietel, dissenting), affirming the grant of a declaratory judgment that as applied, the New York City landmark restrictions could not be sustained. Judge Gabrielli reasoned:

> It is uncontested that the existing building is totally inadequate for plaintiff's legitimate needs and must be replaced if plaintiff is to be able freely and economically to use the premises especially as it appears that adjoining structures have been integrated with plaintiff's operation. The power given the municipality to force termination of plaintiff's free use of the premises short of condemnation (which would provide compensation for plaintiff's complete loss) directly violates plaintiff's rights under the Fifth and Fourteenth Amendments to the United States Constitution, and sections 6 and 7 of article I of the New York Constitution. As in *Vernon Park Realty v. City of Mount Vernon* (307 N.Y. 493, supra) we find a situation exceeding the permissible limits of the zoning power.

35 N.Y.2d at 132, 316 N.E. 2d at 312. Judge Saypol pointed out that his findings had adequately covered elements such as economic hardship which established the unconstitutionality of the statute as applied and granted a declaratory judgment to invalidate "the designation on Constitutional grounds."

C. Appellate Division Review of *Penn Central*

Penn Central Transportation Co. v. City of New York

Supreme Court of New York, Appellate Division, First Department
50 A.D.2d 265, 377 N.Y.S.2d 20, 6 ELR 20251 (1975)

Murphy, J. Defendants have thus far been more successful, at the appellate level, in repelling a direct frontal attack on the constitutionality of the New York City Landmarks Preservation Law (Administrative Code of City of New York, ch 8-A) than in applying it to a given factual situation. *Cf. Lutheran Church in Amer. v. City of New York*, 35 N.Y.2d 121 [(N.Y. 1974)]; *Matter of Trustees of Sailors of Snug Harbor v. Platt*, 29 A.D.2d 376 [(N.Y. App. Div. 1968)]. A majority of us now feels that the time for its full implementation has arrived.

The specific issue presented in this case is whether, as applied to these plaintiffs, the city's Landmarks Preservation Law and the action of defendants thereunder with respect to certain property commonly known as the Grand Central Terminal are unconstitutional. Trial Term responded affirmatively on the grounds that plaintiffs' private property was taken for public use without just compensation and that they were deprived of due process and equal protection of the laws. We disagree.

In recent years, as we have become painfully aware that "the frontier" has been disappearing and our natural resources are rapidly being depleted, there has been an increasing national growth of interest in preserving irreplaceable buildings and sites which have historical, aesthetic or cultural significance.

These changing attitudes now acknowledge that "[urban] landmarks merit recognition as an imperiled species alongside the ocelot and the snow leopard. Over fifty per cent of the 12,000 buildings listed in the Historic American Buildings Survey, commenced by the federal government in 1933, have been razed. The threat to the remainder continues undiminished as the recent loss of Chicago's Old Stock Exchange and the precarious status of New York's Grand Central Terminal attest. If this trend is not reversed the nation at its bicentennial in 1976 will mourn the loss of an essential part of its architectural and cultural heritage rather than celebrate the visible evidence of its past." (*The Chicago Plan: Incentive Zoning and The Preservation of Urban Landmarks*, 85 Harv. L. Rev. 574–575.)

Since 1966 Congress has passed major new laws furthering historic preservation. (*See* Gray, *The Response of Federal Legislation to Historic Preservation*, 36 Law & Cont. Prob. 314.) The National Historic Preservation Act of 1966 found and declared "that the historical and cultural foundations of the Nation should be preserved as a living part of our community life and development in order to give a sense of orientation to the American people". U.S. Code, tit. 16, § 470, subd. (b).

Though "fraught with trouble" (*Lutheran Church in Amer. v. City of New York*, 35 N.Y.2d 121, 131, *supra*), the preservation of landmarks in urban areas is of special importance. Great cities have always been havens for educational and cultural activities. New York's rich history is reflective of the great deal of time, money and talent invested in building its own architectural heritage. Structures such as the Brooklyn Bridge, the Metropolitan Museum of Art, the New York Public Library and Grand Central Terminal are important and irreplaceable components of the special uniqueness of New York City. We have already witnessed the demise of the old Metropolitan Opera House (*see Matter of Keystone Assoc. v. Moerdler*, 19 N.Y.2d 78 [(N.Y. 1966)]) and the original Pennsylvania Station. Stripped of its remaining historically unique structures, New York City would be indistinguishable from any other large metropolis.

Following the evolving national trend, New York City, in 1965, provided for landmark preservation by adding chapter 8-A to its Administrative Code, pursuant to enabling legislation adopted by the State nine years earlier (former General City Law, § 20, subd. 25-a, now General Municipal Law, § 96-a). The council "declared as a matter of public policy that the protection, enhancement, perpetuation and use of improvements of special character or special historical or aesthetic interest or value is a public necessity and is required in the interest of the health, prosperity, safety and welfare of the people"; and established, as the purpose of the chapter, inter alia: "the protection, enhancement and perpetuation of such improvements and of districts which represent or reflect elements of the city's cultural, social, economic, political and architectural history", the safeguarding of "the city's historic, aesthetic and cultural heritage", the fostering of "civic pride in the beauty and noble accomplishments of the past", the protection of "the city's attractions to tourists and visitors" and the promotion of "the use of historic districts and landmarks for the education, pleasure and welfare of the people of the city." (Administrative Code, § 205-10.0.)

Briefly stated, the Landmarks Preservation Law provides for the establishment of a commission which, after a public hearing, proposes to the Board of Estimate the designation of landmark properties and historic districts. The board approves, disapproves or modifies the designation after receipt of a report from the City Planning Commission. (Administrative Code, § 207-2.0.)

Once a landmark is so designated it must be kept "in good repair" (§ 207-1.0) and any alteration, construction or demolition of an improvement on the site is regulated. (§ 207-4.0.) Comprehensive procedures are provided for changes. A landmark owner may seek a "certificate of no exterior effect" or, if there will be such exterior effect, a "certificate of appropriateness." (§§ 207-5.0–207-7.0.) There is also a procedure for seeking a certificate of appropriateness on the ground of insufficient return in the case of taxpaying commercial properties; and a similar procedure, but a different form of relief, for certain tax exempt properties used for charitable purposes. (§ 207-8.0.)

Related to the Landmarks Preservation Law are certain amendments to the New York City Zoning Resolution which permit the transfer of unused development rights over landmark properties located in certain high density areas of the city to other nearby sites. (Zoning Resolution, §§ 74-79–74-793.)

Grand Central Terminal is unquestionably one of New York City's best known buildings. Along with the Empire State Building and the Statute of Liberty, the image of its facade symbolizes New York City for millions of visitors and residents. The terminal as a whole includes a variety of architectural and engineering elements: railroad tracks and platforms; space and facilities for marshaling and handling railroad equipment; passage-ways and ramps affording access to adjacent streets, office buildings and subway stations; and concourses for the use of passengers and pedestrians passing through the terminal. The Main Concourse, probably the terminal's most striking feature, is a large room, 120 by 375 feet, with a ceiling 125 feet high at its apex.

From its formal opening to the public in 1913 (as a replacement for the "Grand Central Depot" built by Cornelius Vanderbilt in 1871) the terminal has been recognized not only for its architecture, but as a superb example of comprehensive urban design. The complete submergence of all the tracks and a double level track system not only resulted in the accommodation of more trains without the acquisition of more land, but permitted construction of revenue-producing buildings on air rights over the railroad tracks and the development of Park Avenue as one of this Nation's most prestigious residential communities. (*See* Fitch and Waite, *Grand Central Terminal and Rockefeller Center: A Historical Critical Estimate of Their Significance*, published by the New York State Parks and Recreation Division for Historic Preservation (1974).) Today, although somewhat neglected over the years, Grand Central Terminal still remains a splendid edifice and a major part of the cultural and architectural heritage of New York City.

On August 2, 1967, after a public hearing and over objection of plaintiff Penn Central Transportation Company ("Penn Central"), the Landmarks Preservation Commission proposed the designation of Grand Central Terminal as a landmark, predicated on the following findings:

> "On the basis of careful consideration of the history, the architecture and other features of this building the [Commission] finds that Grand Central Terminal has a special character, special historical and aesthetic interest and value as part of the development, heritage and cultural characteristics of New York City."
>
> "The Commission further finds that, among its important qualities, Grand Central Terminal is a magnificent example of French Beaux Arts architecture; that it is one of the great buildings of America, that it represents a creative engineering solution of a very difficult problem, combined with artistic splendor; that as an American Railroad Station it is unique in quality, distinction and character; and that this building plays a significant role in the life and development of New York City."

It is worthy of note, in such connection, that the Amtrak Improvement Act of 1974 (88 U.S. Stat 1526) in accordance with the congressional declaration that it is national policy to preserve historic sites, seeks to encourage the preservation of passenger railroad terminals of special significance and architectural quality, such as Grand Central Terminal, by authorizing the Secretary of Transportation to provide them with financial and other assistance. U.S. Code, tit. 49, § 1653.

Plaintiff Penn Central (including, for the purposes hereof, its subsidiaries, plaintiffs The New York and Harlem Railroad Company and The 51st Street Realty Corporation) is the successor to the New York Central Railroad Company and the Pennsylvania Railroad. Plaintiff UGP Properties, Inc. ("UGP"), which was incorporated after the landmark designation here in issue, is a wholly-owned subsidiary of a British company.

Penn Central's losses over the last several years brought it to insolvency and bankruptcy. In order to minimize such losses and provide offsetting revenues, it entered into a lease with UGP in January, 1968, pursuant to which UGP was to erect a tower exceeding 50 stories over the terminal. UGP undertook to pay to Penn Central $1,000,000 per year during construction and thereafter an amount that was guaranteed to equal not less than $3,000,000 annually. In addition, UGP assumed a portion of Penn Central's real estate taxes estimated at $578,500. These rental payments were to be offset in part by the elimination of approximately $700,000 to $1,000,000 in net rents presently received from concessionaires whose space would be occupied by the proposed new building. Commencing in July, 1968, plaintiffs submitted several building designs prepared by the architectural firm of Marcel Breuer & Associates to the Landmarks Commission (called Breuer I, Breuer II and Breuer II Revised) and requested an appropriate certificate (of no exterior effect or of appropriateness). Plaintiffs appear to have indicated a preference for Breuer II Revised, which would have preserved the terminal's Main Concourse, but not its famous south facade. On August 26, 1969, a certificate of appropriateness was denied.

Since Grand Central Terminal receives partial real estate tax exemption (Real Property Tax Law, §489-ff), no further administrative remedy, in the form of relief on the ground of economic hardship, was available to it. (Administrative Code, §207-8.0.) The instant action, seeking declaratory and injunctive relief from the Landmarks Law, on its face and as applied, as well as compensation for the temporary taking (between the landmark designation and its expected judicial invalidation), was commenced. The trial court severed the cause of action for damages and, as above indicated, entered judgment declaring the Landmarks Law, as applied to plaintiffs, unconstitutional and permanently enjoined defendants from acting thereunder to prevent the construction of a lawful improvement on the terminal site. For the reasons hereinbelow stated, such determination should be reversed.

Although the apparent basis for the Trial Judge's decision is the found presence of "such elements as economic hardship, lack of compensatory alternative to alleviate economic hardship, inadequacy of relief by tax rebate, etc., etc.", the rationale would seem to be stated in the penultimate paragraph of his opinion: "The point of decision here is that the authorities empowered to make the designation may do so but only at the expense of those who will ultimately have to bear the cost, the taxpayers."

Such language suggests that any regulation of private property to protect landmark values constitutes a compensable taking. Such holding would surely, as the amicus brief submitted hereon states, "eviscerate New York's Landmarks Preservation Law."

While the line between a compensable "taking" and a noncompensable "regulation" is sometimes difficult to discern, it nevertheless exists. (*See generally*, Sax, *Takings And The Police Power*, 74 Yale L. J. 36.)

In *Matter of Trustees of Sailors' Snug Harbor v. Platt* (29 A.D.2d.376, 377, *supra*) we upheld the validity of the Landmarks Preservation Law as "the right, within proper limitations, of the State to place restrictions on the use to be made by an owner of his own property for the cultural and aesthetic benefit of the community". And the Court of Appeals concluded that we were "correct in refusing to declare the entire law unconstitutional on its face." (*Lutheran Church in Amer. v. City of New York*, 35 N.Y.2d 121, 131, *supra.*)

The sole question to be decided, then, is whether plaintiffs have satisfactorily established that the law, as applied to them in this case, imposes such a burden as to constitute a compensable taking. Put another way, while the exercise of the police power to regulate the private use of property is not unlimited, it is for the one attacking such regulation in any given case to establish that the line separating valid regulation from confiscation has been breached.

In reaching such determination, consideration must be given to the importance of the regulation to the public good, the reasonableness of the regulation in achieving such end and the effect of the regulation on the economic viability of the parcel involved. (*Goldblatt v. Hempstead*, 369 U.S. 590 [(1962)].) We believe the first two requirements are met by the clearly stated purpose of the Landmarks Preservation Law and the unavailability of any reasonable alternative (short of condemnation) for the preservation of a landmark.

The remaining issue is the economic impact of the law on the particular parcel.

No claim is made that it cannot be used for its prime function—as a railroad terminal. The test to be applied is the same as in zoning cases, i.e.: have the plaintiffs demonstrated that the regulation in issue deprives them of all reasonable beneficial use of their property? (*Cf. Williams v. Town of Oyster Bay*, 32 N.Y.2d 78 [(N.Y. 1973)]; *Adamo v. Town of Babylon*, 28 N.Y.2d 982 [(N.Y. 1971)]; *Salamar Bldrs. Corp. v. Tuttle*, 29 N.Y.2d 221 [(N.Y. 1971)].)

Plaintiffs' burden, in such connection, is to establish that they are incapable of obtaining a reasonable return from Grand Central Terminal operations, not that they are not receiving it. (*Cf. Salamar Bldrs. Corp. v. Tuttle*, 29 N.Y.2d 221, *supra*; *Stevens v Town of Huntington*, 20 N.Y.2d 352 [(N.Y.1967)]; *Arverne Bay Constr. Co. v Thatcher*, 278 N.Y. 222 [(N.Y. 1938)].) In our view, such burden has not been met.

To support the claim that it is actually sustaining a loss from terminal operations, Penn Central submitted a "Statement of Revenues and Costs" for the years 1969 and 1971. These statements, which were prepared for the instant litigation, improperly attribute a considerable amount of railroad operating expenses (and some taxes) to their real estate operations. For example, the expense items included "Station Master and Staff", "Information Clerks" and "Gate Usher". Such huge cost items (for 1971) as "maintenance, repairs and service plant operation" ($1,141,679), "cleaning" ($632,753), "policing" ($438,566), "materials and supplies" ($69,692), and "utilities" ($660,710) were related to the entire terminal operation and not segregated as between the railroad and real estate portions thereof.

Moreover, and to compound the error, no rental value whatsoever was imputed to the vast space in the terminal devoted to railroad purposes. (*Cf. Matter of Seagram & Sons v. Tax Comm. of City of N. Y.*, 14 N.Y.2d 314 [(N.Y. 1964)].) Since Penn Central is in the passenger railroad business it, of necessity, must have a terminal (including trackage, platforms, concourse, waiting rooms, ramps, ticket windows and public amenities) for such service. The reasonable rental value of such space cannot properly be omitted from any meaningful analysis of the property's capacity to yield a reasonable return.

Additionally, on the record before us, plaintiffs have failed satisfactorily to show: (a) an inability to increase the terminal's commercial income by transforming vacant or underutilized space to revenue-producing use; or (b) that unused development rights over the terminal could not have been profitably transferred to one or more nearby sites (*see* New York City Zoning Resolution, §74–79 *et seq.*); or (c) that Penn Central's agreements with the Metropolitan Transportation Authority and the Connecticut Transportation Authority provide a basis for invalidating the terminal's landmark designation.

Finally, the assertion that the Landmarks Preservation Law unconstitutionally discriminates against Penn Central because, as the recipient of partial tax exemption, it is ineligible for statutory hardship relief, has already been disposed of by us. On an analogous claim in a comparable situation we hold "that this does not render the statute unconstitutional. It must be interpreted as giving power to the commission to provide relief in the situation covered by the statute, but not restricting the court from doing so in others." (*Matter of Trustees of Sailors' Snug Harbor v. Platt*, 29 A.D.2d 376, 378, *supra.*)

To summarize, in view of the nationwide "burgeoning awareness that our heritage and culture are treasured national assets" (*Maher v. City of New Orleans*, 516 F.2d 1051, 1060 [(5th Cir. 1975)]), New York City's Landmarks Preservation Law is a valid exercise of its police power. The need to preserve structures worthy of landmark status is beyond dispute; and the propriety of the landmark designation accorded Grand Central Terminal is essentially unchallenged.

The validity of the Landmarks Preservation Law, as applied to Grand Central Terminal, does not depend on a showing that the landmark parcel will be undiminished in any degree by the regulation's restrictions; only that it will not "deprive the individual property owner of 'all beneficial use of his property.'" (*Salamar Bldrs. Corp. v. Tuttle*, 29 N.Y.2d 221, 225, *supra.*)

In short, "[plaintiffs] have shown hardship but not confiscation." (*Mary Chess, Inc. v. City of Glen Cove*, 18 N.Y.2d 205, 210 [(N.Y. 1966)].) But such hardship, in the proper exercise of the city's police power, must be subordinated to the public weal, since such regulatory authority is not only "the least limitable of all the powers of government" (*Matter of Engelsher v. Jacobs*, 5 N.Y.2d 370, 373, *cert. den.* 360 U.S. 902 [(1959)]), but it "is not to be limited to guarding the physical or material interests of the citizen."

The order and judgment of Supreme Court, New York County (SAYPOL, J.) entered, respectively, on January 21, 1975 and February 4, 1975, and all findings of fact and declarations of law inconsistent herewith, should be reversed, on the law and the facts, said order, judgment and findings vacated, and judgment entered declaring that plaintiffs have failed to establish that the New York City Landmarks Preservation Law is unconstitutional as applied to them, with costs.

Notes and Questions

1. **Justice Lupiano's dissent.** Justice Lupiano dissented from the opinion in which Chief Justice Murphy and three other justices concurred. In his opinion, Justice Lupiano points out that the exposure of the Grand Central Terminal to the landmarks

law of New York City is not debated. Rather, he focused on the issue raised by Justice Murphy, "whether [the] plaintiffs have satisfactorily established that the law, as applied to them in this case, imposes such a burden as to constitute a compensable taking." 50 A.D. 2d at 275. Justice Lupiano discusses the operating deficit alleged by Penn Central because of the designation as the impetus for the takings argument. The majority concluded that Penn Central did not overcome the burden of proving an operating deficit; they point to the "Statement of Revenues and Costs" for the years 1969 and 1971, which attribute a considerable amount of railroad operating expenses to their real estate operations. *Id.* at 273. Justice Lupiano argues that this is a non-issue since the operation of the railroad station is an integral part of the real estate operations and there are many tenants and concessionaires which rely on the maintenance of the terminal to be able to carry out their business. *Id.* at 279. Furthermore, he argues, it is impossible to separate out what is a necessary expenditure for the railroad operations and what is a necessary expenditure for the real estate operations because the value of the real estate aspect of the terminal is dependent on the maintenance of the terminal itself. *Id.* at 279. "There is, therefore, a basis for claiming that the expense of operating and maintaining the building is a proper expense in ascertaining the profitability or unprofitability of its operation" for the purpose of deciding whether there has been a taking. *Id.*

Justice Lupiano then argues that the majority fails to account for the fact that the Penn Central Co. bought the terminal. The Landmarks Law itself, in determining whether there has been a taking, refers to a "reasonable return," for such purposes "[net] annual return shall be the amount by which the earned income yielded by the improvement parcel during a test year exceeds the operating expenses of such parcel during such year." *Id.* at 280, citing Admin. Code, §207-1.0, subd. v, par. (3), cl. (a). The issue here, according to Justice Lupiano, "is the application of the Landmarks Law in such manner as to deprive the terminal of such value." *Id.* at 280. If Penn Central cannot use the terminal in the way they wish, then they have been deprived of their investment-backed expectations. Considering the area at the time, it cannot be expected of them that they would buy the terminal for use as an unprofitable railroad. *Id.* at 281.

Next, Justice Lupiano asserts that the majority's position accusing the plaintiffs of failing to satisfactorily show an inability to increase the terminal's commercial income, by transferring vacant or under-utilized space to revenue-producing use, is without merit. *Id.* at 281. Penn Central has been steadfast in the attempt to increase terminal income; commercializing the building so much that this had become an issue for the landmark preservation decision. *Id.* Other attempts to increase revenue by installing a bowling alley in place of the waiting room failed of approval by the Public Service Commission and a plan for a proposed mall failed because of its infringement upon trackage. *Id.* at 281. Justice Lupiano also points out that the argument that Penn Central failed to satisfactorily show that unused development rights over the terminal could not have been profitably transferred to one or more nearby sites (*see* New York City Zoning Resolution, §74-79 *et seq.*) is unfair. *Id.* at 283. In essence, he describes the possibility of movement to another site as a flagrant exaction and usurpation of the managerial rights of the Penn Central Co. to their own property. They would furthermore be burdened by the "substantial costs that may attend the transfer of development rights because the landmark owner must submit a program for continuing maintenance of the landmark as part of his application for the special permit, the value of the development rights are less attractive." *Id.* at 284.

In concluding his dissent, Justice Lupiano states:

> plaintiffs have sustained their burden of demonstrating that the terminal site, as restricted, is incapable of producing a reasonable economic return. Concededly the operation of the terminal represents an economic hardship. Conjecture that Penn Central could have "done better" may not operate as a talisman in the resolution of this matter. It is only required that Penn Central do the best it can. The possible transfer of development rights cannot be viewed under the circumstances herein as offsetting the restrictions placed on the terminal site. The benefits to both the city and the citizenry to be derived from the designation of the terminal as a landmark are self-evident. Yet in the manner of its application as delineated above, lies the inequity of this particular case.

Id. at 284.

2. **The economic imperatives.** The Appellate Division decision in 1975 came one year after the original trial court decision. The economics of New York City at that time were in dire straits and in need of revitalization. a. Why then, despite this economic pressure, would the Appellate Division overturn the trial court's decision favoring economic development? b. Which arguments do you think were the most convincing?

3. **Questions of fact and questions of law.** The Appellate Division's decision was the last chance for the courts to make decisions on questions of fact. The highest court in New York, the New York Court of Appeals, only has appellate jurisdiction to determine questions of law. This system was inherited from the colonial period under the British, who also designated questions of fact for the lower courts and appellate review for the highest. The New York Court of Appeals is the final word in terms of determining the law of the state, including the final word on the interpretation of the state constitution. The only way that the Supreme Court of the United States can get involved is if the matter affects the United States Constitution.

D. Court of Appeals of New York *Penn Central* Decision

Penn Central Transportation Co. v. City of New York

Court of Appeals of New York
42 N.Y.2d 324, 397 N.Y.S.2d 914, 366 N.E.2d 1271,
7 ELR 20579 (1977)

Breitel, J. In broad terms, the problem in this case is determining the scope of governmental power, within the Constitution, to preserve, without resorting to eminent domain, irreplaceable landmarks deemed to be of inestimable social or cultural significance. In controversy is the constitutionality of regulation which would prohibit appellants, owner and proposed developer of the air rights above Grand Central Terminal, from constructing an office building atop the terminal.

Undisputed is the principle, rooted in the due process clause of the Constitution, that government may not, by regulation, deprive a property owner of all reasonable return on his property. There are two issues nevertheless. The first is the extent to which government, when regulating private property, must assure what is described as a reasonable return on that ingredient of property value created not so much by the efforts of the property owner, but instead by the accumulated indirect social and direct governmental investment in the physical property, its functions, and its surroundings. The second issue is whether above-the-surface development rights, transferable to adjacent sites under the city landmark ordinance, may be considered in computing return on the property when the landmark property and some of the sites to which the rights may be transferred share a common owner.

Plaintiffs, Penn Central Transportation Company and its affiliates, who have a fee interest in Grand Central Terminal, and UGP Properties, Inc., lessee of the development rights over the terminal, seek a declaration that the landmark preservation provisions of the Administrative Code of the City of New York, as applied to the terminal property, are unconstitutional. They also seek to enjoin defendants, the City of New York and the City Landmarks Preservation Commission, from enforcing those provisions against the subject property. Trial Term granted the requested relief, but a divided Appellate Division reversed and granted judgment to defendants. Plaintiffs appeal.

The order of the Appellate Division should be affirmed. Although government regulation is invalid if it denies a property owner all reasonable return, there is no constitutional imperative that the return embrace all attributes, incidental influences, or contributing external factors derived from the social complex in which the property rests. So many of these attributes are not the result of private effort or investment but of opportunities for the utilization or exploitation which an organized society offers to any private enterprise, especially to a public utility, favored by government and the public. These, too, constitute a background of massive social and governmental investment in the organized community without which the private enterprise could neither exist nor prosper. It is enough, for the limited purposes of a landmarking statute, albeit it is also essential, that the privately created ingredient of property receive a reasonable return. It is that privately created and privately managed ingredient which is the property on which the reasonable return is to be based. All else is society's contribution by the sweat of its brow and the expenditure of its funds. To that extent society is also entitled to its due.

Moreover, in this case, the challenged regulation provides Penn Central with transferable above-the-surface development rights which, because they may be attached to specific parcels of property, some already owned by Penn Central or its affiliates, may be considered as part of the owner's return on the terminal property.

Thus, the regulation does not deprive plaintiffs of property without due process of law, and should be upheld as a valid exercise of the police power.

Grand Central Terminal was formally opened to the public in 1913. Undisputed is its architectural, historical, and cultural significance (for further detail *see* opn. at App. Div., 50 A.D.2d 265, 269). On August 2, 1967, in accordance with the provisions of the New York City Administrative Code, the terminal was designated a landmark by the Landmarks Preservation Commission, and the designation was confirmed by the Board of Estimate on September 21, 1967. *See* Administrative Code of City of New York, § 207-2.0.

On July 18, 1968, plaintiffs submitted to the Landmarks Preservation Commission an application for a permit to construct the proposed office building, seeking a certificate that the work would have no exterior effect on protected architectural features. Administrative Code, § 207-5.0. The request was denied on September 20, 1968. Then plaintiffs applied to the commission for a certificate that the proposed building, even if it would have had an exterior effect, was appropriate to the site. Administrative Code, § 207-6.0. Three separate alternative proposals, each calling for erection of a substantial office building atop the terminal, were submitted. On August 26, 1969, the certificate of appropriateness was denied. Not involved, because not raised in light of the denial of a certificate of appropriateness, are the plans for the interior of the terminal. None of these administrative determinations was ever directly challenged in the courts. *Cf. Lutheran Church in Amer. v. City of New York,* 35 N.Y.2d 121, 126–128 [(N.Y. 1974)].

Instead, on October 7, 1969, plaintiffs brought this action seeking judicial invalidation of the landmark preservation provisions of the Administrative Code as applied to the terminal. Plaintiffs also sought damages for a temporary "taking" of property from the time of original designation as a landmark to the time of the requested judicial invalidation. Of course, any so-called temporary "taking" is more accurately described as a deprivation of property without due process of law. *French Investing Co. v. City of New York,* 39 N.Y.2d 587, 593–595, *app. dsmd.* 429 U.S. 990 [(1976)].

Trial court found the landmark preservation provisions, as applied, constitutionally deficient, but severed the question of damages. As noted, the Appellate Division, with two dissenters, reversed, and granted judgment to defendants.

This is not a zoning case. In many ways, the restrictions imposed on the use of the property are similar to zoning restrictions, but the purposes are different, and in determining whether regulation is reasonable, the purposes behind the regulation assume considerable significance. *Id.,* at 596. Zoning restrictions operate to advance a comprehensive community plan for the common good. Each property owner in the zone is both benefited and restricted from exploitation, presumably without discrimination, except for permitted continuing non-conforming uses. The restrictions may be designed to maintain the general character of the area, or to assure orderly development, objectives inuring to the benefit of all, which property owners acting individually would find difficult or impossible to achieve. *See, e.g., Berenson v. Town of New Castle*, 38 N.Y.2d 102, 109–110 [(N.Y. 1975)]; *Matter of 113 Hillside Ave. Corp. v. Zaino*, 27 N.Y.2d 258, 262–263 [(N.Y. 1970)].

Nor does this case involve landmark regulation of a historic district. Historic district regulation, like zoning regulation, may be designed to maintain the character, both economic and esthetic or cultural, of an area. *See Maher v. City of New Orleans*, 516 F.2d 1051, esp p 1060, *cert. den.* 426 U.S. 905 [(1976)]; *Opinion of the Justices to the Senate*, 333 Mass. 773, 778–780 [(Mass. 1955)]. The difference, generally, is that zoning does this largely by regulating construction of new buildings, while historic district regulation concentrates instead on preventing alteration or demolition of existing structures. In each case, owners although burdened by the restrictions also benefit, to some extent, from the furtherance of a general community plan.

Nor does this case partake of the principles applicable to a taking in eminent domain. As noted earlier, there is no taking for which just compensation must be paid. And it is the concept of just compensation which is so integrally related to value based on return. Instead, landmark regulation is a limitation on exploitation of property, an attribute shared with the classifications of zoning and historic districting. Yet landmark regulation is different because the burden of limitation is borne by a single owner. He may or may not benefit from that limitation but his neighbors most likely will. In contrast both an owner and his neighbors benefit to some degree and in some manner from zoning and historic districting.

Restrictions on alteration of individual landmarks are not designed to further a general community plan. Landmark restrictions are designed to prevent alteration or demolition of a single piece of property. To this extent, such restrictions resemble "discriminatory" zoning restrictions, properly condemned, affecting properties singled out in a zoning district for more restrictive or more liberal zoning limitations. *See Udell v. Haas*, 21 N.Y.2d 463, 476–478 [(N.Y. 1968)]. There is, however, a significant difference. Discriminatory zoning is condemned because there is no acceptable reason for singling out one particular parcel for different and less favorable treatment. When landmark regulation is involved, there is such a reason: the cultural, architectural, historical, or social significance attached to the affected parcel. Even when regulation is designed to achieve such an acceptable purpose, however, the landowner must be allowed a reasonable return or equivalent private use of his property. *Cf. French Investing Co. v. City of New York*, 39 N.Y.2d 587, 596, *supra*. That is, in the case of commercial property, the owner must be assured of a continued reasonable return on the property.

Reasonable return, however, is an elusive concept, incapable of easy definition. For the reasonableness of the return must be based on the value of the property, and the value of the property necessarily depends on the return permitted or available. The inevitable circularity of reasoning is obvious. *See* Berger, *The Accommodation Power in Land Use Controversies: A Reply to Professor Costonis*, 76 Colum. L. Rev. 799, 818–819 [(1976)]. In most landmark cases, however, it is acceptable to use alternative bases of valuation, assessed valuation perhaps, as a basis for determining the reasonableness of return. *See* Administrative Code, § 207-1.0, subd. (v). At best, the computation is rough and successful if it is fairly approximate. In considering reasonable return the owner's desire to expand the property physically or functionally affects the base upon which the return is to be computed. Again, there may be a circularity of cause and effect.

Grand Central Terminal is no ordinary landmark. It may be true that no property has economic value in the absence of the society around it, but how much more true it is of a railroad terminal, set amid a metropolitan population, and entirely dependent on a heavy traffic of travelers to make it an economically feasible operation. Without people Grand Central would never have been a successful railroad terminal, and without the terminal, a major transportation center, the proposed building site would be much less desirable for an office building.

Of course it may be argued that had Grand Central Terminal never been built, the area would not have developed as it has. Thus, the argument runs, construction of the terminal triggered growth of the area, and created much of the terminal property's current value. Indeed, the argument has some validity. But, in reality, it is of little moment which comes first, the terminal or the travelers. For it is the interaction of economic influences in the greatest megalopolis of the western hemisphere—the terminal initially drawing people to the area, and the society developing the area with shops, hotels, office buildings, and unmatched civil services—that has made the property so valuable. Neither factor alone accounts for the increase in the property's value; both, in tandem, have contributed to the increase.

Of primary significance, however, is that society as an organized entity, especially through its government, rather than as a mere conglomerate of individuals, has created much of the value of the terminal property. Although recent financial troubles and consequent governmental assistance make the fact more apparent, railroads have always been a franchised and regulated public utility, favored monopolies at public expense, subsidy, and with limited powers of eminent domain, without which their existence and character would not have been possible. *Cf. Ball v. New York Cent. R. R. Co.*, 229 N.Y. 33, 43 [(N.Y. 1920)]; *Schaghticoke Powder Co. v. Greenwich & Johnsonville Ry. Co.*, 183 N.Y. 306, 316 [(N.Y. 1905)]. Even in the best of times, railroads were dependent on government-granted monopolies for their rights of way, government grants for their land, and government assistance for such projects as grade crossing eliminations. Railroads were given franchises to use city streets without charge, often to the detriment of neighboring residents and often without leaving the city power to terminate the franchise. *Cf. Kellinger v. Forty-Second St. & Grand St. R. R. Co.*, 50 N.Y. 206, 210, 212 [(N.Y. 1872)]; *New York Cent. & Hudson Riv. R. R. Co. v. City of New York*, 202 N.Y. 212, 221–224 [(N.Y. 1911)]. Through the years, Penn Central and its predecessors have benefited mightily from this assistance. Today, government influence is even more pervasive, extending even to the real estate tax exemption enjoyed by Grand Central Terminal itself. Real Property Tax Law, § 489-ff.

Government has aided the terminal in less direct ways, as well. It is no accident that much of the city's mass transportation system converges on Grand Central. Numerous subways and bus routes pass through or near the terminal. Without the assistance of the city's transit system, now municipally owned and subsidized, the property, with or without a towering office structure atop it, would be of considerably decreased value. It is true that most city property benefits to some extent from public transportation, but the benefit is peculiarly concentrated and great in the area surrounding Grand Central Terminal.

Absent this heavy public governmental investment in the terminal, the railroads, and connecting transportation, it is indisputable that the terminal property would be worth but a fraction of its current economic value. Plaintiffs may not now frustrate legitimate and important social objectives by complaining, in essence, that government regulation deprives them of a return on so much of the investment made not by private interests but by the people of the city and State through their government. Instead, to prevail, plaintiffs must establish that there was no possibility of earning a reasonable return on the privately contributed ingredient of the property's value.

To put the matter another way, the massive and indistinguishable public, governmental, and private contributions to a landmark like the Grand Central Terminal are inseparably joint, and for most of its existence, made both the terminal and the railroads of which it was an integral part, a great financial success for generations of stockholders and bondholders. Their investment has long been eliminated or impaired by the recent vicissitudes of the Penn Central complex. It is exceedingly difficult but imperative, nevertheless, to sort out the merged ingredients and to assess the rights and responsibilities of owner and society. A fair return is to be accorded the owner, but society is to receive its due for its share in the making of a once great railroad. The historical, cultural, and architectural resource that remains was neither created solely by the private owner nor solely by the society in which it was permitted to evolve.

Plaintiffs contend that the terminal currently operates at a loss. Even if that be true, it is not of critical importance. What is significant, instead, is whether the property, managed efficiently, is capable of producing a reasonable return. If the courts were forced to look to the property as it is, rather than as it could be, any inadequacy of managers of property could frustrate any land use restrictions.

Perhaps of greater importance, the property may be capable of producing a reasonable return for its owners even if it can never operate at a profit. For it should be evident that plaintiffs' heavy real estate holdings in the Grand Central area, including hotels and office buildings, would lose considerable value and deprive plaintiffs of much income, were the terminal not in operation. Some of this income must, realistically, be imputed to the terminal.

The situation is analogous to that of a flagship store in a regional shopping center. The flagship store may not produce enough income to justify its construction or maintenance, but it may draw enough customers into the other, smaller stores, to make its operation worthwhile, and to extract concessions from the owners of the remainder of the center. *See G.R.F., Inc. v. Board of Assessors of County of Nassau*, 41 N.Y.2d 512, 514 [(N.Y. 1977)]. So it is with Grand Central Terminal. The terminal acts, in effect, as a magnet for Penn Central's other, more profitable, enterprises.

The discussion thus far is in accord with the teachings of *Lutheran Church in Amer. v. City of New York*, 35 N.Y.2d 121, *supra*. The Lutheran Church, owner of the landmark site, established, as plaintiffs here have not, that economic considerations did not permit maintenance of the landmark building in its existing form. *Id.,* at 132. Moreover, the Lutheran Church was a charitable institution which, over the years, did not and could not reap the same pecuniary benefits of massive governmental investment enjoyed by the railroads and Grand Central Terminal. Yet, the regulatory provisions prohibited replacement of the landmark building without any new ameliorative provisions, other than the pre-existing tax exemption to which it had always been entitled, to assure that the property remained capable of usefulness on a reasonable economic basis. The same problem was reached and discussed in *Matter of Trustees of Sailors' Snug Harbor v. Platt,* 29 A.D.2d 376, esp. p 378 [(N.Y. App. Div. 1968)]. In recognizing the invalidity of the landmark regulation as applied to Lutheran Church, however, this court, as had the court in the *Sailors' Snug Harbor* case (*supra*), declined to strike down the landmarks preservation provisions of the city administrative code. *Id.*, at 131–132. In this case, by contrast, there has been no showing that the property, owned not by a charitable enterprise but by an entity existing to make a profit, is incapable in its economic context of producing a reasonable return, even if its development is limited.

Moreover, plaintiffs have not been wholly deprived of the development rights above the terminal. Those rights have been made transferable to other parcels of land in the vicinity, at least eight of them owned by Penn Central, including the sites of the Biltmore, Commodore, Barclay, and Roosevelt Hotels.

The many defects in New York City's program for development rights transfers have been detailed elsewhere. Costonis, *The Chicago Plan: Incentive Zoning and the Preservation of Urban Landmarks*, 85 Harv. L. Rev. 574, 585–589 [(1972)]. The area to which transfer is permitted is severely limited, complex procedures are required to obtain a transfer permit, and the program, it has been said, has the unfortunate consequence of encouraging large, bulky buildings around landmarks which are dwarfed by comparison. But the possibility that a better program could have been devised does not preclude analysis and justification of the existing one in this particular application.

That several of the potential receiving parcels are encumbered by long-term leases or currently improved with suitable buildings does not make the development rights worthless. The knowledge that at some future time, when the lease term has run out or the improvements have lost their utility, a larger building could be constructed, should increase the value of the building plot, at least so long as there is a market demand for new construction. *See* Costonis, *"Fair" Compensation and the Accommodation Power: Antidotes for the Taking Impasse in Land Use Controversies*, 75 Colum. L. Rev. 1021, 1067 [(1975)].

Moreover, in this case, construction of new office buildings was at least given serious consideration on two of the available receiving parcels, the sites of the Biltmore and Roosevelt Hotels. Defendants contend that the alternative sites, and particularly the Biltmore site, are better suited for office building construction than even the terminal site. But that is beside the point. Important instead is the availability of receiving parcels, in common ownership with the landmark site, on which the development rights, or some of them, could be used. It is significant, as well, that the challenged regulation permitted splitting of the development rights among several receiving parcels, to allow optimal use of the rights.

Development rights, once transferred, may not be equivalent in value to development rights on the original site. But that, alone, does not mean that the substitution of rights amounts to a deprivation of property without due process of law. Land use regulation often diminishes the value of the property to the landowner. Constitutional standards, however, are offended only when that diminution leaves the owner with no reasonable use of the property. The situation with transferable development rights is analogous. If the substitute rights received provide reasonable compensation for a landowner forced to relinquish development rights on a landmark site, there has been no deprivation of due process. The compensation need not be the "just" compensation required in eminent domain, for there has been no attempt to take property. *See French Investing Co. v. City of New York,* 39 N.Y.2d 587, 595, *supra.*; *cf.* Costonis, *"Fair" Compensation and the Accommodation Power*, 75 Colum. L. Rev. 1021, 1061–1070.

The case at bar, like the *French* case (*supra*), fits neatly into this analysis. In *French* the development rights on the original site were quite valuable. The regulations deprived the original site of any possibility of producing a reasonable return, since only park uses were permitted on the land. And, the transferable development rights were left in legal limbo, not readily attachable to any other property, due to a lack of common ownership of the rights and a suitable site for using them. Hence, plaintiffs were deprived of property without due process of law. The regulation of Grand Central Terminal, by contrast, permitted productive use of the terminal site as it had been used for more than half a century, as a railroad terminal. In addition, the development rights were made transferable to numerous sites in the vicinity of the terminal, several owned by Penn Central, and at least one or two suitable for construction of office buildings. Since this regulation and substitution was reasonable, no due process violation resulted.

To recapitulate, a property owner is not absolutely entitled to receive a return on so much of the property's value as was created by social investment. And, even as to the privately created ingredient of the property's value, a plaintiff seeking to show that an otherwise reasonable land use regulation constitutes a deprivation of due process of law must demonstrate affirmatively that the regulation eliminates all reasonable return. *See Mary Chess, Inc. v. City of Glen Cove,* 18 N.Y.2d 205, 209–210 [(N.Y. 1966)]; *Shepard v. Village of Skaneateles,* 300 N.Y. 115, 118 [(N.Y. 1949)]. Plaintiffs in this case have failed to meet that burden. In none of their analyses do they include the benefits provided to Penn Central's varied real estate holdings by the terminal's operation. These real, albeit indirect, benefits alone might suffice to provide Penn Central with a reasonable return. But there is more. The development rights above Grand Central Terminal have been made transferable, and could be transferred to several sites owned by Penn Central and suitable for office building construction. These substitute rights are valuable, and provide significant, perhaps "fair", compensation for the loss of rights above the terminal itself. Hence, no constitutional violation has been established.

In times of easy affluence, preservation of historic landmarks through use of the eminent domain power might be desirable, or even required. But when a less expensive alternative is available, especially when a city is in financial distress, it should not be forced to choose between witnessing the demolition of its glorious past and mortgaging its hopes for the future. The landmark preservation provisions of the Administrative Code represent an effort to take a middle way. Marcus, *Mandatory Development Rights Transfer and the Taking Clause: The Case of Manhattan's Tudor City Parks*, 24 Buff. L. Rev. 77, 78, 107–110 [(1974)]. The statute needs improvement. In some cases it protects property owners inadequately. *Lutheran Church in Amer. v. City of New York*, 35 N.Y.2d 121, *supra*. But, in its generality and as applied to Grand Central Terminal, the statute does not deprive plaintiffs of due process of law.

In concluding the analysis, it is recognized that one does not pursue a path guided by ample precedent or wholly developed principles. The area is not merely difficult; it has at present viewing impenetrable densities. The last word has not only not been spoken; it has hardly been envisaged. For this case, and for the cases which may follow in its wake, deference to the unknown must be accorded. Moreover, the analysis has not been one which had been fully developed in the valuable presentations by counsel either at *nisi prius*, the Appellate Division, or in this court. In fairness then, and in order to assure that the better application of the rule be evolved, if counsel be so advised, they should be entitled to present at *nisi prius* any additional submissions which, in the light of this opinion, may usefully develop further the factors discussed. On the present record, however, the result directed by the Appellate Division is correct and in accordance with the views expressed in this opinion.

Accordingly, the order of the Appellate Division should be affirmed, with costs.

JUDGES JASEN, GABRIELLI, JONES, WACHTLER, FUCHSBERG and COOKE concur.

Order affirmed.

Notes and Questions

1. **Novel arguments.** a. Which novel argument of law did Justice Breitel insert into his decision, not present in prior decisions? b. With respect to the building of a railroad and investment in the terminal, should it make a difference if public support is to be valued in any way? c. Do you agree that *Penn Central* should be treated differently than a non-profit, like *Lutheran Church* or *Sailors' Snug Harbor*? d. Is there ever a time when the value of the property should be traced to public subsidies or grants of public land that help constitute that value? e. What is the social increment of value?

2. **The public campaign for Grand Central Terminal.** The destruction of the Pennsylvania Station in New York City had more of an impact than the Penn Central Railroad realized. So much so that when the company tried the same policy towards the Grand Central Terminal, they were met with staunch resistance. With the decline of railroad transportation in the 1950s, the Penn Central Transportation Company turned to their large tracts of land, used for railroads at the time, for development

of more economically viable commercial enterprises. The first such instance, discussed before, was that of the Pennsylvania Station, which was replaced by Madison Square Garden and a colder, more sterile Pennsylvania Station underground. When the realization of what had just happened set in, New York City pushed forth the Landmarks Preservation Law in 1965, which gained support from many local artistic and architectural groups all over the City; one such example was the Municipal Art Society ("MAS"). The hope was that never again will a Pennsylvania Station be lost.

When Penn Central came forth to get the certificate of appropriateness with their first plan for Grand Central Terminal, the New York City Landmarks Preservation Commission, under its first chairman Harmon Goldstone, vehemently rejected it. When the "aesthetic joke," as the Commission report referred to the proposal, and a second proposal a year later were rejected, Penn Central brought New York City to court, for allowing the Landmarks Preservation Law to effectuate a taking, without just compensation in violation of the state constitution. Finally, three years later, in February 1975, Judge Saypol ruled in favor of Penn Central overturning Grand Central Terminal's landmark status.

After learning that the city was not going to appeal, MAS was one of the local organizations at the forefront of the public support battle. For the original decision, MAS assembled a committee of lawyers, including United States Attorney Whitney North Seymour, Jr., to draft an amicus brief for the court. The brief said that the plan "will do irreparable harm to the architectural heritage of the city and deprive the people of New York of the extensive public benefits which derive from the continued presence of the terminal in its present form." After Judge Saypol's decision, MAS' executive director, Kent Bartwick, mounted a public campaign to save Grand Central. One of the campaign's most prominent supporters was Jacqueline Kennedy Onassis; with the support of MAS she became the face of the movement, promoting preservation, amassing national and international press coverage, and recruiting supporters and volunteers. Other notable supporters of the movement included architect Philip Johnson, founder of the Department of Architecture and Design at the Museum of Modern Art in New York City, and Brendan Gill, a prominent columnist for The New Yorker magazine. Together, this super team of historic preservation activists formed the Committee to Save Grand Central Terminal, and installed former mayor Robert Wagner as the chair of the organization. With the movement in full swing, Mrs. Onassis wrote a decisive letter to Mayor Abraham Beame, which succeeded in convincing him to allow the city to file an appeal. The Appellate Division, in December 1975, reaching a different conclusion than Judge Saypol, overruled his decision and emphasized that "the need to preserve structures worthy of landmark status is beyond dispute." This sentiment was solidified by the opinion of Justice Breitel for the New York Court of Appeals, which upheld the Landmarks Preservation Law unanimously.

The public relations campaign organized by MAS, masterminded by its new president Fred Tapert and MAS staffer Laurie Beckelman, was integral to the decision of New York Court of Appeals. Tapert had recruited the J. Walter Thompson advertising agency, who offered pro-bono assistance, to spread the good word of historic preservation. They came up with the popular slogan, "No More Bites Out of the Big Apple." MAS' efforts in enlisting a volunteer base is also quite notable: organizing rallies in front of the terminal, selling buttons and t-shirts, handing out free apples, and conducting walking tours of the station, a popular tradition that continues to this day. MAS also set up a storefront on 43rd street to function as the locus for their preservation operation. The efforts of MAS in mounting and successfully advocating for historic landmarks preservation cannot be understated. Their operations in this New York battle set the stage for the historic preservation war that was to reach to the nation's capital, acquiring national significance. *See generally* JOHN BELLE AND MAXINNE RHEA LEIGHTON, GRAND CENTRAL: GATEWAY TO A MILLION LIVES (2000).

E. *Penn Central* at the Supreme Court of the United States

1. Oral Argument Before the Court

The following oral argument is available for your listening pleasure at *Oyez.org*.[1] The archive, in addition to this oral argument, contains the Supreme Court's discussion on the oral argument. It is available in the Library of Congress and was put there by Justice Thurgood Marshall. The New York City Landmarks Preservation Commission's lawyer, Dorothy M. Miner, accompanied Leonard Koerner, who argued the case for the City. Patricia Wald appeared for the National Trust for Historic Preservation.

Penn Central Transportation Co. v. New York City

Supreme Court of the United States
Washington, D.C.
Monday, April 17, 1978

The above-entitled matter came on for argument at 10:03 o'clock a.m.

BEFORE:

WARREN E. BURGER, Chief Justice of the United States
WILLIAM J. BRENNAN, JR., Associate Justice
POTTER STEWART, Associate Justice
BYRON R. WHITE, Associate Justice
THURGOOD MARSHALL, Associate Justice
HARRY A. BLACKMUN, Associate Justice
LEWIS F. POWELL, JR., Associate Justice
WILLIAM H. REHNQUIST, Associate Justice
JOHN PAUL STEVENS, Associate Justice

---

1. Oral argument, Penn Cent. Transp. Co. v. New York City, 438 U.S. 104 (1978) (No. 77-444), *available at* http://www.oyez.org/cases/1970-1979/1977/1977_77_444.

APPEARANCES:

DANIEL M. GRIBBON, Esq., 888 Sixteenth Street, N.W., Washington, D.C. 20006; for the Appellants.

LEONARD J. KOERNER, Esq., Corporation Counsel of the City of New York, Municipal Building, New York, New York 10007; for the Appellees.

MRS. PATRICIA M. WALD, Assistant Attorney General, Office of Legislative Affairs, Department of Justice, Washington, D.C. 20530; for the United States as *amicus curiae*.

PROCEEDINGS

MR. CHIEF JUSTICE BURGER: We will hear arguments first this morning in *Penn Central Transportation Company against The City of New York*. Mr. Gribbon, you may proceed whenever you are ready.

ORAL ARGUMENT OF DANIEL M. GRIBBON, ESQ., ON BEHALF OF THE APPELLANTS

Mr. GRIBBON: Mr. Chief Justice and Justices of the Court:

Perhaps I should be intimidated legally, if not physically, by the sheer number of governments and organizations on the other side of the question presented on this appeal. There have come to the support of the appellee, the greatest city in the world, three other major cities, the nation's two largest states.

Q: When you say greatest, are you referring by population or—[Laughter]

MR. GRIBBON: I would prefer to encompass all aspects.

Q: Or weather?

MR. GRIBBON: I will still stay with greatest.

Q: Or total debt?

Mr. GRIBBON: Total tax.

Q: Tax. [Laughter]

MR. GRIBBON: It may qualify on all those scores.

Q: Mr. Gribbon, what city are you referring to? [Laughter]

MR. GRIBBON: Not Chicago. [Laughter]

In addition, twenty civic organizations, all highly respected, and finally the United States has [*sic*] had sufficient interest not only to file a brief but to participate in argument. But I am not so intimidated because the position that I put to you here on behalf of Penn Central rests on the Bill of Rights, that great charter of liberties that serves as a protection against all government, not just venal government but even the best intentioned government.

In addition, I would suggest that the unusual display of public interest here serves to emphasize a principal element in Penn Central's case; that is, the enormous public benefit which, it is claimed, will be brought about by the governmental action that we challenge.

As a result of actions taken by the New York City Landmarks Preservation Commission, pursuant to the city's landmarks law, Penn Central has been prohibited from constructing an office building over the Grand Central Terminal. That prohibition has been imposed by the city not because such a building would be unsafe or uneconomic or in violation of zoning regulations but solely to assure that all who live in New York and all who visit New York will have an unimpeded view and unrestricted enjoyment of the terminal, a structure which the commission found to be a magnificent example of French Beaux Arts architecture.

After the terminal had been designated as a landmark by a commission of eleven private citizens reporting generally to the Board of Estimate, three separate efforts were made under the guidance of the internationally known architect, Marcel Breuer, to persuade the commission, in accordance with its procedures, that an office building could be constructed without impairing the integrity of the terminal. All three were rejected. And it is now common ground among the parties that Penn Central stands effectively precluded from constructing a building over the terminal.

The record discloses that in return for the use of the air rights over the terminal, Penn Central would receive from a developer, who would bear all the risks of constructing the building, $1 million a year during construction and thereafter a minimum of $3 million a year, escalating as rental collections increased.

Q: Is there in the record anywhere a picture or a drawing, an architect's drawing or a sketch, of what this building would look like?

MR. GRIBBON: There is, Your Honor. At Record 2001. It is in Volume 4.

Q: Not in the appendix.

MR. GRIBBON: Not in the appendix, no, Your Honor. It is in the record that came up from the lower court—

Q: Thank you.

MR GRIBBON:—which is lodged, I understand.

I say, therefore, that there can be no doubt that the city's action has deprived Penn Central of something of value. While the city recognizes that Penn Central has been denied the right to construct an office building, which it is entitled to do otherwise under applicable zoning regulations, the city refuses to acknowledge that air rights constitute a form of property. It even suggests that the use of the term is something of a semantic trick. Such rights, however, have been widely used, sold, utilized for fifty years, and the Court of Appeals did not hesitate to describe the controversy as one involving air rights to the terminal.

I do not urge that the decision here should turn on whether Penn Central's loss is characterized as a property right or as a use. As the Solicitor General correctly puts it, it is the substance of the government action that controls rather than the labels that are attached to it.

Q: You do not question the right of the City of New York to take this entire property, do you?

MR. GRIBBON: No, Your Honor. The issue raised here is not, as some of the briefs here seem to suggest, whether the City of New York may validly preclude Penn Central from constructing a building. Twenty-five years ago in *Berman v. Parker* this Court in a unanimous opinion proclaimed for all that it is just as appropriate for government actions to look to things that beautify and enhance the quality of life as it is to do away with things that are unsanitary. But the issue here, simply stated, is, who is going to bear the loss or the burden that is occasioned by this substantial public benefit?

Q: Is there any doubt about how this case would have come out before the enactment of the Fourteenth Amendment?

MR. GRIBBON: I would think the same considerations are present now, Mr. Justice Rehnquist.

Q: What would you have relied on before the enactment of the Fourteenth Amendment?

MR. GRIBBON: I would think the Fifth Amendment.

Q: But *Baron v. Baltimore* said the Fifth Amendment applied only to—

MR. GRIBBON: There might have to be a little rewriting of some of the decisions there. But looking at what the Fifth Amendment has been held to do since then, I would have thought that the Fifth Amendment would provide assurance here. If it were to come up today without the Fourteenth Amendment, it is very difficult to imagine those circumstances in today's legal climate.

Q: In today's legal climate, I mean, you do not have to be that vague. Has not a case from this Court held that the Fourteenth Amendment Case does incorporate the Fifth Amendment—

MR. GRIBBON: Yes, Your Honor. And I say, I have not dealt with that, and I would not propose to do it on that basis.

Now, I would propose to address the issue that I have stated here first by examining the central premise of the different justifications that have been advanced first by the Court of Appeals and, second, by the city and its friends for imposing the full cost on Penn Central. And that premise is that where the government acts in a regulatory capacity rather than through the exercise of eminent domain, there is no need to inquire whether there has been a compensable taking.

I shall next show that the decisions of this Court interpreting the Taking Clause of the Fifth Amendment, particularly those emphasizing its high content of fairness, support the conclusion that the prohibitions imposed here do constitute a taking for which compensation is constitutionally required.

Q: You talk about the full cost. Full cost of what?

MR. GRIBBON: Of not being able to build an office building, the loss that is suffered by being prevented from developing an office building over the terminal.

Q: It has been held in a case, *Hudson*, I think it was, that a municipality could limit the height of all buildings within its borders.

MR. GRIBBON: Your Honor, I think that is true. The height limitation cases I do not believe have application here because this is very—

Q: Why not? Why is that not a taking? Excuse me.

Q: The Pan Am Building—it is not the shortest building. It is not the shortest this building.

MR. GRIBBON: No, Your Honor, it is there.

Q: It is right next door.

MR. GRIBBON: It is right next to it.

Q: Why is not—

MR. GRIBBON: It is selective, Your Honor. It does not say—

Q: The taking is just the same, selective or non-selective, is it not?

MR. GRIBBON: No. I think under the zoning case—

Q: It might be discrimination, but from the point of view of the taking, it is just exactly the same if you limit every building in the municipality to no more than fifteen stories.

MR. GRIBBON: I think the decisions indicate that the zoning, which is comprehensive and applies substantially equally to all people affected within the area, can be tolerated as a non-compensable taking on the ground that the benefits and the burdens are reasonably dispersed, not precisely.

Q: From the point of view of the property owner, the taking is precisely the same, is it not?

MR. GRIBBON: That's right. But I think the fact that other people are similarly burdened and presumably similarly benefited by the height limitation has served to justify the zoning cases, and I do not think it can serve here to justify this selective, highly particularized taking.

Q: I can understand your argument based upon discrimination of some kind. But if it has been established, as I think you concede it has, that a municipal government can limit the height of every building within its borders, why is it not, from the point of view of the property owner, just as much a taking in that case as it is in your case?

MR. GRIBBON: I think in many instances there is just as much of a taking on the property owner when that something is done by regulation as by eminent domain. But in the regulation cases where you are removing offensive uses or where in the zoning cases you are acting broadly to take care of the entire community in distributing the burdens and the benefits, it has been held not to be a taking. In terms of the English language, yes. In terms of the Constitution, I think it is just that difference.

Q: Is not the point, in the situation that you are referring to, as distinguished from that which Mr. Justice Stewart is referring to, the taking of some but not all or the taking of one but not all the others?

MR. GRIBBON: That is right. Selective. It is a height limitation for one building. All of its neighbors, including Pan Am and all of the others, can go much, much higher.

Q: This I fully understand. I still have difficulty understanding why it is not as much a taking in one case as in the other, quite apart from any argument based upon discrimination or irrationality or anything else.

MR. GRIBBON: All I can say is that the zoning cases here viewed it as being a permissible use of the regulatory power when it is done in a way—

Q: You do not try to justify it rationally. You just say that that is authority, not reason—

MR. GRIBBON: That is right. I do not know that it is not rational to say, when all the people within the area are similarly treated, nobody can have a residence or nobody can have industry. That is a permissible use of the government's power.

Q: Several wrongs do not make a right. They make just several wrongs, do they not?

MR. GRIBBON: Yes, I think that is right. But that depends on whether it is wrong to start with. The Constitution does not prevent the government from effecting necessary regulations. And every action of government has to have some kind of adverse effect on somebody. The question is where the line is going to be drawn on that adverse effect.

Q: Is there a matter of equal protection here somewhere?

MR. GRIBBON: Your Honor, we do not argue an equal protection. I think it is a solid case for a taking. The equal protection cases do not give a great deal of comfort. It perhaps is warranted for the government to pick out an historic site and say this should be preserved. We do not think it has to pick out every site, and you cannot argue as to which site is historic. And I think it is sufficient that we simply argue that when they do that, they pay for what they take for the public benefit.

Q: And the theory behind the taking—I will avoid the use of the word "taking." The limitation because it is an historic place, historic monument, is that that is for the benefit of everyone?

MR. GRIBBON: Of everybody.

Q: Yes. So, you say if it is for the benefit of everybody, everybody should pay for it.

MR. GRIBBON: Everybody should pay for it. And there is no balancing of benefits and burdens as there is the zoning cases where, as Mr. Justice and I have just been discussing, the Court has held that they are not within the taking provision.

Q: Is not part of the reasoning for the generalized use of the height regulation the notion that all of the buildings that are subject to that height regulation also derive some benefit from it in that their competitors, so to speak, cannot build above them, and each of them will have a good view from the top floor and that sort of thing?

MR. GRIBBON: Precisely, Your Honor. There is a fair distribution not only of costs but of burdens, and that therefore there in no taking.

Q: The benefits, as my Brother Rehnquist implies in his question—the theory is, I think, that the benefits are accorded to everybody in terms of light and air and so on.

MR. GRIBBON: Yes, which is not true here. We are solely burdened and unbenefited. Everybody else, not just the building but the visitors and the people that do it, are the ones that get the whole benefit out of it.

Now, the first point I wanted to make is that however the government acts, whether by eminent domain or purporting to act by government regulation, there must be inquiry into whether there is a compensable taking. Now, the Court of Appeals brushed that over. They simply recited this is government regulation and, therefore, there need be no kind of inquiry into taking. Those who support the court's action take the same view, that automatically, once you can say this is regulatory action, then there is no occasion to look to see whether there is compensation. That is the premise that underlies both the Court of Appeals decision and also the position submitted by the city here, and I think it is not supported by the Fifth Amendment itself or by the cases. The Fifth Amendment does not, by its terms, apply only to cases of eminent domain. It applies broadly. And cases in this Court have held that whatever governmental power is exercised—police power, commerce power—if there is a taking, you look to see whether the Fifth Amendment comes into play.

I suppose *Berman v. Parker*, which I mentioned earlier, stands for the proposition that the right of government to bring about changes designed, as they put it, to enhance the quality of life all comes within the police power, whether it is done under eminent domain or whether it is done through the exercise of regulatory action. And in most of the cases where there is a problem as to a taking, there has not been an exercise of eminent domain. It is government regulation which has operated in a way which may constitute a taking, even through the exercise of eminent domain has not been tried.

It is claimed here that the *Goldblatt* decision of this Court establishes a different rule, a rule that says you do not look in a case of regulation to what has been taken. You look, rather, to what is left over. That decision does contain some language with respect to the uses left to the property owner. But I do not believe it establishes anything like what the decision claimed here. The challenged regulation there prevented the sand and gravel company from continuing its operations on property that was originally rural but had become surrounded by the city of Hempstead. Far from saying, as is urged here, that valid regulatory action cannot result in a compensable taking, the Court, speaking through Mr. Justice Clark, acknowledged at the outset the basic principle on which we rest our case, saying government action in the form of regulation can be so onerous as to constitute a taking, which constitutionally requires compensation. It then found that there had been no diminution in the value of the property involved and, therefore, there was not any taking. It went on to find, despite the owner's claim that sand and gravel operations were utterly benign and unlike other things that had been barred by the exercise of the government regulation—the Court overruled him and said on safety grounds this would be upheld as a valid exercise of police power. But it did not say that as a substitute for a finding that a taking had not taken place. And I submit that that is the initial inquiry, whether a taking has taken place. And that is the inquiry that the Court of Appeals did not make and which those supporting the city would not make.

Those words, that constitutional guarantee, that property shall not be taken without compensation, incorporate an exceedingly complex constitutional concept. And though it has been with us since the beginning of the Republic, nothing approaching an all-purpose principle has been articulated from which one can discern the specific application of the concept. And this court has time and again turned down the opportunity to enunciate any such principle.

A scholar in the area recently wrote: "The judicial efforts to chart a usable test for determining when police power measures impose constitutionally compensable losses have on the whole been notably unsuccessful. With some exceptions, the decisional law is largely characterized by confusing and incompatible results, often explained in conclusionary terminology, circular reasoning, and empty rhetoric." Those are the scholar's words, not mine. But I hasten to say that I have no all-purpose test to offer the Court. And I acknowledge more than the normal humility with which one must approach such constitutional questions.

I do put to you, however, that a review of the taking cases does disclose two guidelines that may usefully be applied here in determining whether the city's action constitutes a compensable taking. When regulatory action is directed towards the elimination of offensive uses or conditions, it has been held in many cases that the resulting loss to the property owner is non-compensable because it is one that he may be properly called upon to bear for the public good. Such cases began, as you all know, with the elimination of nuisances, common nuisances, and then went on to encompass other properties and uses which, though not nuisances, were offensive to the general tenor of the community such as breweries and beer halls and livery stables.

The construction of a multistory office building in midtown Manhattan, which Penn Central is prohibited from doing, is not only permitted by the zoning laws but is actually encouraged as an efficient use of valuable land. And I submit, therefore, that the principal justification for tolerating some non-compensable diminution in property value as a result of government regulation lends no support to the city's action here.

Q: Would you be making the same argument here if all you wanted to do was replace the building with one of the same height, just that the building was inefficient and you wanted to build a new building, but you are quite willing to not go up with it, the same height? And the city said, "No, we want you to keep the old building."

MR. GRIBBON: I think if it caused us loss—and from what you say, it would cause us loss—we would be making the same argument. I think any action that we are forced to take or kept from taking that caused us a monetary loss is compensable.

Q: So, it just is not that some air space is being taken.

MR GRIBBON: In this particular case—

Q: I know, but that is not—

MR. GRIBBON: No, that is not the whole thing, no. I think it is any governmental action of this landmark designation nature.

Q: So, this would be a taking because the city would be keeping you from making more profit than you could by using the same size building.

MR. GRIBBON: I would put it because they are taking a part of our property. They are taking a part of our property right.

Q: You would make the argument even if it were conceded—which I am sure it is not—even if it were conceded that the old building was profitable in the sense that you were not losing any money on it.

MR. GRIBBON: Yes, Your Honor. If there were—

Q: If you could double what at least an accounting would show you could make by using the building, you would say they are taking part of your property?

MR. GRIBBON: I think that is a fair statement, yes.

Q: And that is your fundamental argument?

MR. GRIBBON: It is based on the notion that the reason they are doing it is to benefit the general public. And if we can show any loss under the taking cases, whether there is an expectancy of profit here or whether it is a demolition, then it should be compensable. When they take three acres out of a hundred acres of land, they do not look and say, "Well, you can do pretty well on the other ninety-seven acres." They say, "We have taken three acres, and we will give you the value of it."

And that, I submit, is precisely what we are faced with here.

Q: Mr. Gribbon, back in 1911, one plan considered was a twenty-story tower on the property, was there not?

MR. GRIBBON: Yes. Over the terminal?

Q: Yes.

MR. GRIBBON: Yes, Your Honor.

Q: Has anything along that line been suggested to the commission here at this point?

MR. GRIBBON: No, Your Honor, nothing that small has been suggested simply because it would be an inefficient utilization of land. There are no other buildings really in that area that have been built in recent days that would build only that much floor space. That is the problem in this highly prized portion of the city, to get as much floor space as is consistent with other needs. So, the answer is no, it has not been. Although I must say there is not any suggestion in the action taken by the Landmarks Commission that even that would satisfy. Nothing is going to satisfy because they want the air to roam freely over Grand Central Station.

Q: Has there been a suggestion to the contrary, the other way?

MR. GRIBBON: That twenty stories would not do?

Q: Yes.

MR. GRIBBON: No, there has not been, to my knowledge. But there has been no resilience in the Landmarks Commission, with three efforts to do this under guidance of noted people. And the answer comes back, "No, no, no." Every indication that what is wanted is the preservation of Penn Central in its pristine state, that that is the only way that the people of New York and its visitors are going to continue to enjoy this architectural monument.

Q: Suppose twenty years ago, thirty years ago, before we were as much concerned with the past as we are now, in preserving the past, you had built over Penn Central Station, without using any part of the station but just built over it a sixty or seventy story hotel and the commission now decided that that was marring the appearance, the esthetic value of this landmark and they wanted you to tear it down. I suppose there is not much doubt that you would expect compensation for that.

MR. GRIBBON: Correct, Your Honor. They could condemn it or they could regulate it, and we would be entitled to compensation. But I think the power of the city is there. And that is one of the things to be concerned about, that it is there.

Q: Are you suggesting that there is no difference in the taking aspect today in the present situation than in the one I hypothesized?

MR. GRIBBON: I do not think there should be, and I do not perceive a difference. I would have thought that would be a taking—

Q: In terms of Fifth Amendment principles.

MR. GRIBBON: I would think that would clearly have been a taking twenty years ago as well as today.

Q: Mr. Gribbon, how did Penn Central or Grand Central get that piece of land right in the middle of Park Avenue?

MR. GRIBBON: There is a long history to it. They bargained, they were pioneers—

Q: Did they receive it fair and square? [Laughter]

Did they steal it fair and square?

MR. GRIBBON: They did not steal it fair and square. They acquired it over a long period of time, and indeed that building there has done a great deal for the middle of New York. And which came first is pretty hard to say.

Q: It sure does when you drive and you have to go all the way around it. [Laughter]

MR. GRIBBON: That is what the city wants to maintain.

Q: Oh, I see.

MR. GRIBBON: They acquired it over many years from predecessor railroads largely. And it is the Grand Central Terminal now that we are talking about and not Penn Central. That is gone.

I submit that most frequently applied consideration in determining when government regulation has resulted in a compensable taking is simply stated one of fairness.

As this court observed in the *Cors* case, there is a strong element of ethics in the constitutional requirements that private property not be taken without compensation. And time and again decisions of this court have reiterated that the overriding purpose of the Fifth Amendment guarantee is to assure fairness in the impact of government upon the owners of private property. Back in 1893, Mr. Justice Brewer speaking for the court, said the Fifth Amendment prevents the public from loading upon one individual more than his just share of the burdens of government. Forty years later, Mr. Justice Brandeis, speaking for the Court: "Particular individuals may not be singled out to bear the cost of advancing the public convenience."

In 1960, the Court said the Fifth Amendment is designed to bar the government from forcing some people alone to bear the public burdens which in all fairness and justice should be borne by the public as a whole.

And just a few years ago in a decision by Mr. Justice Rehnquist I think the essence of these declarations was captured in a statement that the Fifth Amendment derives as much content from basic equitable principles of fairness as it does from technical concepts of property loss.

These two taking guidelines that I have suggested would appear to be opposite sides of the same coin. Where you are eliminating a use or a condition which is imposing a burden on other people, it is fair to permit the person who is charging that to take some expense, to take some burden, in order to eliminate the burdens on the rest of the people.

On the other hand, where the government sets out to secure an improvement or a benefit for all society, performing what has been called its entrepreneurial or its resource acquisition function, basic considerations of fairness dictate that a disproportionate share of the cost of securing that benefit not be borne or loaded on a single individual.

Significantly neither the Court of Appeals nor the city and its supporting friends have anything to say about this fairness concept, which has to be the lifeblood of the Fifth Amendment. Nothing they could say would alter the fact that the full burden of the city's action in freezing the terminal falls exclusively on Penn Central. And it is being called upon to bear a public burden which, in all fairness and justice, should be borne by the public as a whole in order to obtain the full and unimpeded enjoyment of the terminal.

I turn now to the justification that the Court of Appeals found for allowing the full cost of the terminal preservation to be borne by Penn Central. It made no inquiry into taking and simply looked to see whether Penn Central had established that it would be impossible—and that is the word of the court—for it to earn a reasonable return on the terminal without utilizing the air rights. It is our contention, of course, that whatever the remaining value of the terminal we are entitled to compensation for that part that has been taken. But even if the remaining value of the terminal is to be given the critical significance that has been accorded it by the Court, that value was erroneously ascertained. In applying what it acknowledged to be a special rule for landmark statutes, the court divided the value of property into two separate ingredients—that contributed by private efforts and that contributed by the efforts of organized society as a whole. Then without attempting to ascertain how much of the terminal's value had been contributed by private or society efforts, it concluded that Penn Central was not entitled to any compensation because it failed to establish that there was no possibility that it could not earn a reasonable return on the remaining and also unascertained privately contributed value of the terminal.

Q: As I read over the briefs filed by your brothers and sisters on the other side, my impression is that none of them really tried to defend the basic reasoning of the—that part of the reasoning of the Court of Appeals; would you agree with that?

MR. GRIBBON: I believe that is a fair statement, Mr. Justice Stewart. That is the way I read those briefs. They all back away to some degree and come forward with a further explanation of why the decision should go against Penn Central.

Q: The Court of Appeals really is a statement of Henry George's single tax, is it not?

MR. GRIBBON: Yes. But I submit it is not a statement of sound constitutional law, as many of Henry James' things were, not necessarily sound—

Q: George.

MR. GRIBBON: George. I am sorry. James would be different.

The court then went on, in addition to these two ingredients of value, to impute a great deal of income, which it did not quantify, to the terminal from other buildings in the area. And then, as if to put its position beyond all argument, the court observed that the terminal may be capable of producing a reasonable return for its owners even if it can never operate at a profit. I submit that under no circumstances can the court's view of whether Penn Central is able to earn a reasonable return on this property, absent the development rights, be accepted. I think its effort to divide property into these two segments really has no support in the authorities. And it is a principle that cannot be limited. It cannot be limited to the terminal or the landmarks. It applies to all property. It applies to a residence. It applies to a farm, to an office building. They are all valuable or not valuable, depending upon their location, depending upon social services, protection, and amenities.

If this approach were adopted, the government would be free to appropriate any property by giving only a pittance of what that property is worth on the open market.

The error in the court's opinion is perhaps further disclosed in a passage near the end where it refers to the city's financial distress and then says that in times of easy affluence, preservation of landmarks through eminent domain might be desirable or even required. Surely, however, no constitutional guarantee, particularly one based on the Fifth Amendment, should be granted or denied, depending upon the government's fiscal condition.

Q: Mr. Gribbon, down near the White House, across the street from the Hay-Adams Hotel is an historic church. I suppose it goes back well over a hundred years, does it not?

MR. GRIBBON: Saint John's?

Q: Saint John's Church. I would assume—and I think you would assume with me—that the land underlying that church is a very valuable piece of property for an office building or another hotel or what not. If that were taken—the church, which presumably has fee title to that property—began negotiations for the sale of it to the Hilton Hotel Corporation or someone to build a hotel there and some effort was made by the Congress to preserve it would be a taking, in your view, if they said, "No, you cannot tear that down and build a Hilton Hotel; you cannot do anything with it. You have got to keep it the way it is?"

MR. GRIBBON: I think it would, Your Honor. As you put the case, it seems to me, it would be a taking. And the church would be entitled to compensation on the value of that land and building.

Q: What if in that process, in that inquiry, it developed that that church was the result of many, many contributions by people, that the church corporation as such did not ever put a single dollar into it—it was all gift money—would that make any difference?

MR. GRIBBON: I do not think it would. I think whoever held the title at that point would be entitled to the compensation.

Q: They would be entitled to get the compensation for the highest and best use of that land as of today?

MR. GRIBBON: That is a phrase that has been bandied in the cases, and I am not too sure of the meaning. I think they would be willing to get what that property is worth, what the Hilton Hotel would pay for it.

Q: Presumably at the moment the highest and best use would be a hotel site.

MR. GRIBBON: If that is permitted by the generally applicable zoning law, and I take that it would be because there is a hotel across the street.

Q: And they would of course be limited to the height limit—

MR. GRIBBON: Whatever they are.

Q: —of Washington, D.C., eight hundred feet or some such.

MR. GRIBBON: The same as everybody else is limited.

What an owner has invested in a piece of property is really quite immaterial to what he gets when that property is taken. He may have an enormous investment, but he is not going to get it back if the property is not worth that. Or he may have a fully depreciated investment so that the net is zero; and yet it is the value. It is the loss to that owner. It is not really what is acquired or what the investment was but the loss to the owner which is determinative.

As we discussed earlier here in my colloquy with Mr. Justice Stewart, the city and its friends back away from the Court of Appeals' rationale and attempt to salvage this statute as being simply a form of land-use regulation or zoning. In the first place, there is not any general principle that all land use regulation or all zoning is permissible and does not constitute a taking. This Court made that clear in the leading case of *Euclid v. Ambler*. The basis on which many zoning laws have been upheld is that they represent a comprehensive regulatory program. This Court has used the term "comprehensive" in a number of recent decisions. It has not been defined. But I take it if comprehensive means anything, it means something else to the opposite of selective or highly particularized. And that is the vice of this landmark law. It is not zoning. It does not purport to be zoning. It is on top of the zoning laws. There are vast, pervasive zoning laws in the City of New York, and this fits on top of them, superimposed, and it permits highly selective and particularized actions. The designation, for example, of the public library or the Brooklyn Bridge or the Statue of Liberty as historic landmarks does not mean anything. The designation of a fine old home as an historic landmark may simply give the owner the satisfaction of putting a brass plaque on the door to that effect.

The recent designation of the Radio City Music Hall interior as a landmark was followed very quickly by efforts by the state and the city to put up about $2 million to keep the show going for another year.

But it is the unpredictable nature and the highly selective nature of what not only has been done but indeed what the law contemplates. And that is why the Court of Appeals looked at this zoning and said, "No, sir, it cannot be zoning." This really resembles discriminatory zoning, which has been condemned, and it declined to condemn it because it was historical.

Q: Mr. Gribbon, may I interrupt with a question? When does the taking take place? Supposing, with respect to the Chief Justice's example of the church, they had had no negotiations with Hilton but the Congress decided that they would designate it as an historic landmark today; they had no deal on the fire or anything like that. Would there be a taking then, or would it only take place when they could show that they had a better offer?

MR. GRIBBON: I would think it would take place at the former time.

Q: Then why do you say that putting a plaque on the door of a home is just a ceremonial act? Why would not that also be a taking?

MR. GRIBBON: I do not think it imposes any burden or loss. Indeed, it is a net gain for the owner. He does not have to do anything. He is permitted to put it on.

Q: Is he not equally forbidden to tear down the house and sell it for something else?

MR. GRIBBON: That depends on what he can later work out with the

Landmarks Commission, whether he can have additions to it which will not impair the integrity of the house, just as Penn Central attempted to do things that would not impair the terminal. The newer designation is just the start of the game.

Q: Oh, I see.

Q: Then you are assuming that the house is in a single-family occupancy zone.

MR. GRIBBON: Yes.

Q: So, it could never be anything more than basically what it is.

MR. GRIBBON: It is not burdened the way Penn Central has been burdened.

Q: Which is in a commercial zone.

MR. GRIBBON: In a commercial zone where it is precluded from doing what is permitted under the zoning law.

Under any zoning law, the people who are affected do have to deal with some restriction. But those restrictions are uniformly applied, and the affected person can move around. It can develop. It can do things within those zoning restrictions. Penn Central has no such freedom. The terminal has in effect been selected out and frozen in place. I submit that the landmarks law has thus operated as a compensable taking of its property rights which require compensation.

MR. CHIEF JUSTICE BURGER: Mr. Koerner.

ORAL ARGUMENT OF LEONARD J. KOERNER, ESQ. ON BEHALF OF THE APPELLEES

MR KOERNER: Mr. Chief Justice Burger, may it please the Court:

Appellants' argument has proceeded from the approach that the only method to regulate private property is by and through the principles of eminent domain.

Q: I do not think so. I think counsel very clearly conceded the complete validity of all the zoning legislation in New York City, at least for the purposes of this case.

MR. KOERNER: Let me just establish the perimeter of the appellants' argument.

Q: You do not contend this is a zoning case, do you?

MR. KOERNER: No. What we contend is this is another type of land-use regulation, with the very same tests enunciated by this Court for all other land-use cases, what is applied here.

Q: As applied to one particular unit?

MR. KOERNER: No. This is the nub of the case. The appellant has proceeded with the assumption that Grand Central Terminal has been singled out. That analysis might be correct if there had never been a landmarks preservation law and in response to an announcement by Penn Central that they were going to build a building on top of Grand Central Terminal, that the public reacted to it and passed a law that distinctively impacted on Penn Central.

Q: Do you contend it would be different from the case you have now?

MR. KOERNER: That is correct. That is not what is before the Court.

Q: How would it be different constitutionally?

MR. KOERNER: In this particular case we have a comprehensive land-use plan which sets out in advance the criteria for determining whether or not a building is architecturally or historically significant. The intention of the plan is to preserve all historical buildings, whether by accident they are a part of historic districts or whether they are single and outside the district.

Q: What if the five boroughs get together and said that there just is not much open space in the five boroughs, and so we are going to preserve all the open space just as it is even though it may be in private ownership. Do you think that would be constitutional?

MR. KOERNER: It would depend on the strength. You are saying without any—

Q: No, finding that there is a tremendous—

MR. KOERNER: The answer would be no, because the individual who was affected by the regulation would not be getting any return on his property, nor would he be permitted to use his property for any purpose.

Q: Supposing he was allowed to use it as open space. He could raise cattle there or have dairy farming. [Laughter]

MR. KOERNER: No, because that would not be economically productive. And we do not contend that if the appellant in this case had been able to establish that his property as restricted was not economically viable, that he would not be entitled to relief.

Q: Suppose, in my Brother Rehnquist's example, he was permitted to put a fence around it and that people, when they come and sit in the sunshine, they could pay a little fee. And he would raise enough to pay his taxes and maybe a one percent profit.

MR. KOERNER: No, that would be insufficient. The test is whether or not the property, as restricted, is economically viable. It is the same test that has been applied by this Court in other land-use cases.

Q: And it would not be enough for the landowner to say, "I may be able to make a profit here the way it is, but I could make two or three times as much if you permitted another use?"

MR. KOERNER: That is correct, that the test is not whether or not he can receive the highest and best use. There has been no taking in this case. The appellant has not had any out-of-pocket expense incurred. What he has lost is the potential to develop his property in the highest and best use.

Q: Do you not think that is a valuable right?

MR. KOERNER: Yes, but it must be balanced against the validity of the land-use regulation.

Q: Which is for the benefit of whom?

MR. KOERNER: The entire community of which the appellant is a part.

Q: But you do not think that the entire community should bear the cost of the benefits for the entire community?

MR. KOERNER: What I am saying is that the entire community should pay the appellant if the restriction denies him the right to earn a reasonable rate of return. The problem here is that everybody is trying to analogize this case to zoning. But it is a different type of land-use regulation, the promotion of which has the same effect on the community as does zoning, and that is to make the community more attractive.

Q: When you say reasonable rate of return, you sound like it is a public utility.

MR. KOERNER: No, it has traditionally been—we have not quantified it except to the extant that it has been suggested, that six percent would be reasonable. But we never got to the point in this litigation because there was a total failure of proof. The appellant was unable to show that he could not make a profit. That is precisely why we had the trial in the state court.

Q: Suppose, instead of this being owned by the Penn Central, this had been a private residence of great historic importance—Commodore Vanderbilt's house or some such thing—and the Landmarks Commission wanted to take it.

MR. KOERNER: Designate it.

Q: What kind of return do you have on a private residence, to use the measurement that you are suggesting here?

MR. KOERNER: In that case, the question is whether or not a designation would interfere with the existing use. To the extent that the owner wanted to convert the private residence to a commercial residence, then he would be entitled to show whether the property was economically viable.

Q: How about my hypothetical question to Mr. Gribbon on Saint John's Church over by the White House, by Lafayette Park. Do you think Saint John's Church could get the reasonable market value of the land, less the cost of demolition?

MR. KOERNER: No, if the designation did not interfere with the use of the church as a church. Since it is a non-profit association, it would be our position that that church could be maintained as part of an overall scheme to preserve landmarks—

Q: Even if they wanted to do what the National Presbyterian Church did, sell its downtown church for a very large office building site and move out to the outskirts where the parishioners could get to church more rapidly?

MR. KOERNER: If there was justification and they could apply to the Landmarks Commission, and that would be in a condition that would be considered by the commission.

Q: In fixing value?

MR. KOERNER: Yes. That is not involved in this particular case.

Q: Is the Landmarks Commission qualified to deal with due process?

MR. KOERNER: No. The Landmarks—

Q: Are you not giving it that business?

MR. KOERNER: No. What I am saying is that they have set up a procedure to determine which properties are historically significant. They have set up criteria—

Q: You say it is not a zoning commission.

MR. KOERNER: It is like a zoning commission to the extent that—

Q: But a minute ago you said, "Oh, no," you were not going to get into the zoning business. I thought that is what you said.

MR. KOERNER: No. What I said—

Q: Now are you going into zoning?

MR. KOERNER: No. What I am saying, that in both zoning and landmarks you have expert commissions charged with the responsibility of developing a comprehensive land-use scheme, the purpose of the scheme to benefit the community. What I am saying is that with respect to—

Q: And I assume that that commission knows how to operate a railroad terminal?

MR. KOERNER: No. The commission determines whether the railroad terminal fits under the criteria before it, that is, whether it is architecturally and historically significant.

Once it is designated, if it imposes a hardship—that is, if it denies the appellant a reasonable rate of return or makes—

Q: Who makes that determination?

MR. KOERNER: The court in this case made that determination after a lengthy trial.

Q: I am talking about the commission by itself. Do they make that determination?

MR. KOERNER: There is a procedure within—

Q: I understood that two or three times Penn Central went there, trying to work this out. Am I right?

MR. KOERNER: No. Penn Central—

Q: They did not go to it?

MR. KOERNER: No. They had applied to the commission for the right to knock down Grand Central Terminal and put up an office building. The question was whether or not that application was appropriate for the purpose of effectuating the chapter, the statute. And the Landmarks Commission properly determined that it would not be appropriate. Penn Central did not choose to litigate that issue in a court proceeding. Indeed, they have not chosen to litigate the question of whether Grand Central Terminal is a landmark. It must be assumed.

With respect to the analogy to zoning, in zoning it is reasonable to divide up areas into geographical areas. That is the reasonableness of a zoning plan. With a landmark regulation, the reasonableness depends upon the preservation purpose, and that purpose is only achieved by preserving the landmark wherever they may be in the City of New York. And it is that distinction. It is a different type of land-use regulation.

Q: The Landmark Commission can do this at any time it sees fit?

MR. KOERNER: No. There is a procedure set up where they have to have hearing. They have to make—

Q: Time wise, they could do it on a building that was eighty years old?

MR. KOERNER: Yes, that is correct. But the built-in safeguard is that if the owner of the subject property is unhappy with the designation, he can bring a special proceeding in the Supreme Court and challenge the designation on the basis of arbitrariness and capriciousness. One of the factors in considering whether there has been a deprivation of due process—

Q: I assume that is true of all state commissions.

MR. KOERNER: That is correct.

Q: So, it is nothing new, especially for this commission.

MR. KOERNER: That is precisely our point, that this is a land-use regulation that has the same effect as any other land-use regulation.

Q: What if in that proceeding the court decides that the commission was absolutely right, no one can dispute that this is a historical landmark; is that the end of it?

MR. KOERNER: No, because all that says is that the designation is proper. Whether or not the designation makes the property economically unviable is the type of issue that was reviewed by all the state courts and this Court. That is the due process claim.

Q: What standard do they use?

MR. KOERNER: Whether or not the property as restricted is being precluded of all reasonable beneficial use. I want to point out that—

Q: You mean not of all economic use but some profitable—

MR. KOERNER: That is correct. But what they do determine is what this Court has constantly reiterated, that when the police power is properly exercised—and, by the way, there is no dispute that this is a proper subject for the exercise of the police power—that the highest and maximum use is not a necessary goal, that it is presumed that that goal can be withdrawn when you exercise the police power. That is a necessary by-product.

Q: Did they set a percentage of return on initial investment like a public utility?

MR. KOERNER: No, they did not do that because in this particular case there was such a failure of proof they did not have to quantify it.

Q: You say as this case comes to us, we must judge it on the basis that Grand Central in its present use is profitable?

MR. KOERNER: Must be. And that, Your Honor, is the essence of this case, and that the appellant has ignored the lengthy trial and the two findings of the appellate court.

Q: Mr. Koerner, Grand Central is still used by the railroads for passenger service.

MR. KOERNER: That is correct.

Q: Let us assume that the Interstate Commerce Commission allowed the station to be closed for rail service on the ground that not enough people use it for that purpose and assume further that no other use of the building in its present condition is deemed feasible.

MR. KOERNER: Right.

Q: What would your position be with respect to that situation?

MR. KOERNER: Penn Central would be entitled to relief because the property as restricted was not economically viable.

Q: Is that clear from the New York law?

MR. KOERNER: Yes, it is. Yes. And I again want to emphasize the attempt by the appellant to ignore the substantial factual data presented during the trial.

Q: Is there a specific section of the New York law that deals with that situation?

MR. KOERNER: In this particular case it came under the guise of a challenge to the application as a deprivation of due process. To answer your question, it was framed in response to a due process issue raised in court. With respect to other challenges internally through the administrative process, we allow for an application for a certificate of appropriateness. That is, even to the extent of demolishing the landmark parcel if it is not economically viable.

Q: That is not in the statute.

MR. KOERNER: No, it is in the statute.

Q: It is?

MR. KOERNER: But Penn Central was a tax-exempt property, and the statute did not have this exception applicable to a tax-exempt property. So, Penn Central sued in court, and it attempted to prove in court what they could not prove before the commission.

Q: In any event—

MR. KOERNER: It is the same test.

Q: —similar to the question that my Brother Powell—if the company at any time in the future, next year or the year after that, any time it can prove that the situation has changed and that the property is no longer economically viable, it will get relief.

MR. KOERNER: That is precisely the answer. That is right.

Q: What again is the definition of being economically viable?

MR. KOERNER: It was not required to be quantified in this case. But it has traditionally meant that on his investment, he would be able to earn approximately a six percent—

Q: Like a public utility.

MR. KOERNER: Correct.

Q: Supposing that the New York Central Railroad is applying to the Railroad Rate Commission in New York for an intrastate fare change and the commission decides that you can make six percent, which we consider a reasonable rate, without a spur track of three miles, which you presently own. So, we are just going to take that three-mile spur track away from you. You will still make six percent on the total investment you have. Do you think you could do that?

MR. KOERNER: No, because I do not see the strength of the public purpose in that particular case.

Q: Supposing they want the spur track as a railroad museum to show how the 20th century used to look.

MR. KOERNER: Then again the answer to Your Honor's question is that in your application, you are singling out that particular railroad and restricting its development of its property. The entire concept of this scheme is that we are not singling out Penn Central. We are treating it like every other landmark within the City of New York. We have designated over five hundred properties. Indeed, before a designation is completed, that designation has to be approval by the City Planning Commission, which must determine whether it is consistent with the zoning plan and the master plan and whether or not any urban renewal development might interfere.

Q: Mr. Koerner, could I return for a moment to Justice Powell's question about economic viability of a demolition or something like that?

MR. KOERNER: Yes.

Q: As I understood the statute, the statutory test of whether to grant a certificate of appropriateness does not say anything at all about economic viability. Am I wrong on that?

MR. KOERNER: There are two bases for certificate of appropriateness. With respect to Penn Central, because of the tax-exempt property, you are correct, that they could not have gotten a certificate of appropriateness administratively because the economic viability question is not allowed since they were tax exempt. With respect to other commercial properties, a certificate of appropriateness can be granted.

Q: On the ground of economic—

MR. KOERNER: That is correct.

Q: What section of the statute authorizes that?

MR. KOERNER: 207—

Q: 2076.0? I do not see anything in there about economic viability.

MR. KOERNER: Can I—I just want to use my time—

Q: All right. But you do agree that with respect to the—

MR. KOERNER: Section 207-8.0.

Q: Oh, 8.0. I see. But with respect to the Grand Central, economics are totally irrelevant?

MR. KOERNER: No, because while he could not get administrative relief, we agree that if he has established his case in court that the property was not economically viable, he would have been entitled to judicial relief under the—

Q: But not under subsection—

MR. KOERNER: No, that is correct; under due process.

Q: Oh, under the Constitution. In other words, you are admitting that as applied in that situation the statute would be unconstitutional?

MR. KOERNER: If we had not had the added step that whatever deficiency was in the landmark law was corrected at trial.

Q: The landmark law, as it reads, is unconstitutional if it does not allow for some kind of remedy when there is an economic—

MR. KOERNER: That is correct. But it is not the issue in this case because Penn Central had the opportunity to establish under the very same test and failed.

Q: Mr. Koerner, I am a little confused about your references to tax exemption. What specifically is tax exempted?

MR. KOERNER: The railroad does not have to pay full city real estate taxes on the terminal. There is an exemption under the railroad law for that portion of the terminal that is used for railroad purposes so that they only pay approximately one-third the assessed valuation.

Q: Would the theory be that they are taxed in other ways or—

MR. KOERNER: It was intended to encourage them to keep up the railroad system.

Q: Does it make any difference to the constitutional issues in this case whether they were totally tax exempt or paid the full tax that everyone else pays?

MR. KOERNER: No.

Q: So, in this respect they are in the same posture as Saint John's Church?

MR. KOERNER: That is correct, with the exception that here though you can equate their business with whether or not they can make a reasonable rate of return. And one thing we have left out—my time is running out, but I want to emphasize one other factor that is quite important. We have concentrated on the restriction of Grand Central Terminal and whether that restriction imposes on them an extraordinary burden not present when other land-use regulation impacts on a parcel. What we have left out and the appellant has not commented on are the air rights. We have never contended that the transfer development rights were equal in value to what the person lost. But that is not the test. The test is whether the transfer development rights constituted a valuable asset to the appellant, that when added to his return on the railroad, which he was unable to establish, whether that satisfied even the appellant's test of fairness. And I want to briefly mention the evidence that was upheld by the two appellate courts.

Q: Mr. Koerner, before you do that, let me just understand your theory. If there is no taking here, you would not even have to give them the—

MR. KOERNER: That is correct.

Q: Then why do we have to consider?

MR. KOERNER: Because the air rights are part of the comprehensive scheme and an attempt to at least recognize that we are going to try to do everything we can—

Q: Maybe you have been more generous than the Constitution compels you to be. Why does that have any relevance at all to what we have to decide?

MR. KOERNER: Because Judge Breitel felt that the air rights—

Q: But nobody is defending his rationale.

MR. KOERNER: No. [Laughter]

To the extent that he relied on the air rights, it was appropriate to consider the air rights in the context of the whole package to determine exactly whether we have been fair.

Q: What difference does it make whether you have been fair? I do not understand your angle.

MR. KOERNER: Because the fairness concept, advocated by the appellant, goes to the concept of due process in determining value. Our plan contemplates giving the individual designee this.

Q: But your legal position is you do not have to be fair.

MR. KOERNER: No, that is not our legal position.

Q: Your position, as I understand it, is there can be a taking sometimes under this—

MR. KOERNER: That is correct. But there has not been in this particular case.

Q: That is right.

MR. KOERNER: And that the facts and circumstances of this particular case show there had not been. I will only take one more minute.

With respect to the air rights, the testimony at trial showed that the proposed builder, UPG [sic], had offered Penn Central $3.8 million a year for the right to develop air rights over the Biltmore Hotel, an eligible receiving site under the transfer development rule. Penn Central's representative testified that 3.8 was insufficient because it wanted five million. It computed the five million as follows. It was guaranteed three million if it developed the air rights above the terminal. In addition, its profit from the Biltmore was two million. So, to get the same deal that it would have had with respect to building over Grand Central Terminal, it concluded that it had to receive five million.

I urge that this is not the issue before the Court. The issue is not whether or not Penn Central was entitled to the highest and best use, the five million. The issue is whether or not the $3.8 million return, by using the Biltmore site, together with their failure to establish that the property as restricted cannot earn a reasonable rate of return, is so unfair as to really in all effects totally emasculate the land use regulation that is now under attack because in a city like New York it is unusual for all of the landmarks to be clustered in historic districts; and for the preservation purpose to be accomplished, it is necessary that the Landmark Commission be able to act wherever it finds a building of historical and architectural significance. The total plan here is a reasonable one. It is a different type of land-use regulation. But all the courts have applied the traditional rules and have properly concluded that this regulation should be sustained.

Q: Let me ask just one more question. I know you are concerned about your time. But if the transfer rights are of equal value, or substantial equal value, could we not hold that there was a taking and then on retrial they find that there was just compensation?

MR. KOERNER: No.

Q: You could go ahead with your program without any interference.

MR. KOERNER: No, because I do not think the transfer rights were of equivalent value.

Q: Oh, you concede they were not?

MR. KOERNER: It was not litigated in court. All that was litigated—

Q: For purposes of our decision, we should assume they are not?

MR. KOERNER: That is correct.

MR. CHIEF JUSTICE BURGER: Mrs. Wald.

ORAL ARGUMENT OF MRS. PATRICIA M. WALD ON BEHALF OF THE UNITED STATES AS *AMICUS CURIAE*

MRS. WALD: Mr. Chief Justice, and may it please the Court:

The United States has a vital interest in these proceedings today. Congress and the Executive have declared in many statutes that it is a national policy that quote, "historical and cultural foundations of the nation should be preserved as a living part of our community life and development in order to give our people a sense of orientation."

The Federal Government is deeply involved in historical preservation in many ways, and I will allude to them only briefly. Number one, it designates and preserves historic landmarks on its own public land. Two, it sometimes utilizes the power of eminent domain to acquire sites of national historic significance. Number three, since 1966, it maintains a National Registry of Historic Buildings which have local, state, city, and national significance, and now contains fifteen thousand such buildings.

Fourth, it provides financial aid to states and cities so that they can survey their historic preservation problems, formulate plans, and embark on preservation projects to preserve their treasures.

And, fifth, all federal agencies, pursuant to the 1966 act and to an Executive Order, who license projects or spend money on projects in any state, must take account of the need to preserve historic sites which are registered or which are eligible for registration.

Finally, there are several very specific enactments, including the National Environmental Protection Act, which requires NEPA impact statements to assess the impact of historic sites that might be affected by proposed projects.

Q: Mrs. Wald, may I just interrupt because it goes to what you are reciting now?

MRS. WALD: Yes.

Q: Has the United States ever imposed a regulation on private use of private property for historic purposes without compensating the owner?

MRS. WALD: I do not believe it has directly done so.

Q: So, it has never done anything comparable to what we have before us?

MRS. WALD: Not to my knowledge. But may I add that it does provide subsidization to local groups who embark upon some of their projects, pursuant to laws like the New York City landmark law which use a regulatory framework for preservation—

Q: Is it fair to say that the federal policy has always been that where there is a public benefit, the public shall pay?

MRS. WALD: I believe that that is an overstatement, for the following reason. Naturally the Federal Government has relied primarily upon state and local governments and their police power and their particular historic preservation laws to bring about the preservation of buildings except where those buildings are on public land.

However, we do have several instances, not for historic preservation but for other uses, which raise a similar question where the Federal Government through its regulatory powers does in fact impose restrictions upon land use which it does not compensate for by eminent domain. In the area of historic preservation, to my knowledge, you are correct, Justice Stevens, but we do not do it directly.

Q: I suppose a farmer up near Manassas is suddenly informed that the records now discover [sic???] that an important part of the Battle of Manassas was fought on his farm and, therefore, they will let him graze his cows and raise some grain but that he cannot sell it. It is just going to be preserved for the benefit of the whole people. Do you mean to suggest that they do not have to pay him the going rate per acre for that farm?

MRS. WALD: If we are referring now, as I believe you are, to the national government—

Q: Yes.

MRS. WALD: —taking such action, then right now the national government would either have to do it through eminent domain or through a state or a local government which had jurisdiction. We do not have any statutes on the books, to my knowledge, which allow us to have a national historic preservation regulatory framework such as the states and cities. That is not to say, Your Honor, and certainly we do not have the question before us today, that it would not be possible for Congress to enact such—

Q: Yes. The Chief Justice's question was a constitutional question because that is what we have in this case, not whether or not you happen to have at the moment a federal statute.

MRS. WALD: That is right. It is always very hazardous to pass on constitutional questions ahead of time.

Q: That is what we have to do in this case. [Laughter]

MRS. WALD: You are passing on a statute of course that is on the books in New York City. If the Federal Government, pursuant to a federal jurisdiction, passed such a statute, I believe that it is possible it would be constitutional.

Q: Without compensation?

MRS. WALD: Without compensation in the sense that it would be subject to the same test which we suggest constitutionally applies to state and local government. If it became so onerous to the landholder, if he could not take any beneficial uses out of his property, then it would become a taking, and it would be unconstitutional.

Q: The beneficial uses that my farmer friend up at Manassas has in mind is to leave it to his children or to sell it, as the case may be. And he can get $1,500 an acre for it in some places now. Are you suggesting the United States Government or any government could take that property without paying him the going rate?

MRS. WALD: I am not suggesting that they take it, Mr. Chief Justice. I am suggesting that a valid historical landmark statute could allow them to restrict its usage so that a particular historic framework, a particular historic use, would not be violated.

Q: If he had an offer to sell it to the supermarket, Landmark Supermarket, would that be the price? [Laughter] The Grand Central Supermarket. Would that be the price he would have to be paid?

MRS. WALD: I am sorry, I am not sure I understand your question, Justice Marshall.

Q: I am putting just one little point into the Chief Justice's plot. Now they have got the cattle and the hogs there. The Grand Central Supermarket has come to him, and they want to build a huge land mall there, and they will give him $2,500 an acre. Is that the price?

MRS. WALD: Is that the price you suggest that the government would have to pay?

Q: Yes. Yes.

MRS. WALD: I believe that the Federal Government could indeed enact a statute which would not require them to pay the price you suggest, the going rate on the market for the land, simply because they had restricted uses so as to prevent him from selling it to the supermarket.

Q: I want to get back to the hypothetical that I gave Mr. Gribbon and see what your answer is. The National Presbyterian Church, which is surely an historic place on Connecticut Avenue. Out in front of the building was the statute of John Witherspoon, one of the signers of the Declaration, I think. And they contracted to sell it for three or four million dollars. Suppose after they contracted to sell it in order to build a new church further out and had this three or four million dollar contract, the District of Columbia had said, "No, that is going to be a landmark. You cannot sell it." Now you have got the going market value fixed by a contract, an arm's length contract, with the, I think, National Broadcasters Association to put the building up there. Do you suggest the District of Columbia, under any statute, could have taken that property without paying them for it?

MRS. WALD: I do suggest that the District of Columbia could have passed a regulation which required, after designation, through a reasonable mechanism of that church as an historical site, that indeed either that site must be maintained, the church must be maintained, or if it were sold, the successor must maintain it in the church form. And I believe that a somewhat similar case—

Q: You would not say that if it were sold for $10 or whatever the buyer would pay and then he just closed down the church. You could not make him operate the church. You would not suggest that, would you?

MRS. WALD: No, I would not suggest—

Q: And the city here would indicate that if they ceased operating as a church, it would no longer be appropriate to restrict the use without compensation.

MRS. WALD: I would suggest that since the property was originally—its original use, its present use at the time it was designated, was as a church—that indeed nobody can be made obviously to operate a church if they do not want to. But I think what can be done is to restrict other uses of the property.

Q: In the Grand Central case, are you differing with your colleague that if Penn Central just shut the terminal down, that it would still be required to leave the building as it is?

MRS. WALD: Certainly I believe that the statute is valid and under the statute, if it wished to shut down the station, to cease operating, to demolish the—

Q: They cease operating and then they go in before the commission and say, "We are not making a nickel on this. Unless we can do something with it, we cannot even pay our taxes on it, reduced as they are." I thought your colleague indicated that then they could tear it down or at least if they were going to have to leave it standing, they would have to be paid for it.

MRS. WALD: I believe that the courts—although it is not in the statute in Grand Central's case—but I believe that the courts, the New York courts, in that situation, if they did not want to operate it at all, would indeed permit them to cease operating it. But I am not sure that it would permit them to go ahead and make another use of the property.

Q: The point is, in the event hypothesized by my Brother White, would the Constitution then require that compensation be paid?

MRS. WALD: I do not believe that the Constitution requires compensation be paid simply because they decided they did not want to operate it anymore as a railroad station. I believe that they would be—before a taking and compensation would be required—under existing law they would be required to find some beneficial use, to attempt to find some beneficial use that did not violate the nature of the preservation law. And I believe in fact that is what most of the cases this Court has held in the past would suggest.

For instance, in the *Goldblatt* case. The case said, candidly the ordinance completely prohibited the use, the excavation pit use, to which the property had been put before. That was completely ruled out. Yet the Court held that was not a taking because the plaintiff might well find some other uses for the property, or there had not been any showing that he could not.

There have been cases in which—the *South Terminal* case in Boston where the EPA simply said in its regulations, in its transportation plan, "You may not use a percentage of parking spaces because, if you do, it will affect the air." Clean Air Act. And the Court there held, first, that that was not a taking because, even though you could not use those spaces for parking spaces, for which they had originally been intended, you had to look around and find some other uses, less valuable—

Q: Mrs. Wald, is your test then, just applying it to the historic landmark area, if the landmark designation causes the property owner to actually lose money on the property, then it is a taking. If he can still make a reasonable return, it is not taking? Is that your test?

MRS. WALD: That is pretty much the test. I think it is a test of the past cases here. I think it is more if there is a profitable use to the property. There has been a taking—and there have been innumerable takings—

Q: Is it just one penny of profit or a reasonable return?

MRS. WALD: Certainly the cases do not tell us in the past. They leave the formula—in fact, I think—

Q: We have to decide.

MRS. WALD: —they set no set formula as a reasonable return or a beneficial use.

Q: So, you just say just a marginal profit would not be enough. It has to be a reasonable return.

MRS. WALD: I would say a reasonable return is a beneficial use.

Q: A reasonable return—how does one measure that? If it is a lot less than could be obtained by putting it to some other use, is it still reasonable?

MRS. WALD: I believe so. I believe that is exactly what all the cases have said. We do not take the test of the most profitable use. Most recently—

Q: But you do not think the test is the least profitable use either?

MRS. WALD: I certainly believe the Constitution would require the owner, if he could not use it for a particular purpose, to be able to go out and find the most profitable use consistent with the point of the regulation, namely, the preservation of the landmark.

Q: You mean you are going to make him do something with it?

MRS. WALD: No, we are going to permit him to do something with it if he wants to.

Q: What if he just wants to board it up?

MRS. WALD: If he wants to board it up and that does not in some way infringe upon the historical preservation aspect of the property, then he could do that. If the historical preservation simply says it is a beautiful church to look at from the outside and we do not care what happens, whether anybody goes in it or anything else, then we can just leave it stand there if he wants to. On the other hand, if he wants to continue to run it as a church—

Q: Who should pay the $10,000 a year insurance premiums on it and public liability in the meantime?

MRS. WALD: Well, the church may be the wrong example. But the owner continues with all of both the liabilities and the profits of ownership. But any owner has certain options about how to use his property.

Q: What profit have you got on a boarded up building?

MRS. WALD: If you boarded it up by your own choice, then—

Q: No, boarded it up because the government, from your point of view, would not let him sell it, not let them sell it.

MRS. WALD: In most of these cases, the sale—indeed, in the case instance here in the New York law, they do not forbid the sale *per se*. They only forbid the sale for a use which is restricted. So, indeed, many of the cases in which the courts have held there is no taking at a reasonable regulatory use, they point out that it leaves the option with the owner as to whether or not he wants to sell or lease it or use it for other purposes. All of these cases, if I may finish the one sentence, all of the land-use cases have pointed out that it is almost inevitable, starting with Justice Holmes back in the *Coal* case, that when the government pursues a police power for a legitimate end, it will likely end up with a diminution of value of land and the restriction of use. And unless that becomes so onerous as to move over into a taking—and where that line is drawn the courts have over the years said is very difficult—that it is a reasonable use of the police power. And I think the rule which appellant would suggest, that any time there is a loss in value of property due to a reasonably valid regulation, use of the police power, that the owner must be compensated, is indeed a radical, revolutionary rule which just simply has no foundation in the past cases of the police power or indeed in the taking cases themselves.

MR. JUSTICE BURGER: Thank you.

Do you have anything further, Mr. Gribbon?

REBUTTAL ARGUMENT OF DANIEL M. GRIBBON, ESQ., ON BEHALF OF THE APPELLANTS

MR. GRIBBON: If I may briefly, Mr. Chief Justice, I should like to answer Mr. Justice Marshall's inquiry and make clear that Penn Central did make an effort with the Landmarks Commission to obtain a certificate of appropriateness and no exterior effect. And in the Landmarks Commission there was never any attention paid to dollars. That was strictly an esthetic determination. The only time economic loss came into the picture was when the case went into court. And then instead of inquiring as to whether there was a taking and making a determination, which is not terribly complex in this case as to the value of what was taken, the courts went off on this economic inquiry into reasonable return which, as you read the Court of Appeals' opinion, we were bound to lose. There was no way to win under the way the Court of Appeals analyzed this economic problem.

Q: Mr. Gribbon, what if in passing this ordinance—was it an ordinance? What was it?

MR. GRIBBON: The landmarks law, yes, Your Honor.

Q: What if they had done their homework before they passed the ordinance and said the following landmarks are hereby designated right in the ordinance, and they did thirty of them or forty, so that you were not singled out at all. They thought they had spotted all the landmarks in town.

MR. GRIBBON: I think if the economic impact on us was the same ultimately, as it is here, the fact that they were designated in the law rather than designated by the commission would be immaterial.

Q: But you would not be singled out.

MR. GRIBBON: Well, singled out—certainly we are singled out—

Q: At least you would be one of thirty.

MR. GRIBBON: Yes. But you understand that they do not operate the same way. Among these thirty are the Statue of Liberty. And the landmarks law does not operate on it with nearly the impact it operates on us. Another one is a tree in Brooklyn. It is the way it operates to take property that we complain of here.

Q: As I heard this argument it is now the issue—as I understand your opponent, he concedes that there might be occasions and circumstances under which the operation of this ordinance did operate so as to be a taking in the constitutional sense. And you concede, with respect to the Statue of Liberty or the tree in Brooklyn, that there might be occasions when it did not so operate. And the question then is, Does it in this particular case?

MR. GRIBBON: Does it operate here?

Q: Yes.

MR. GRIBBON: And—

Q: Do you agree that we have got the case on the assumption that the station is a sustainable economic operation?

MR. GRIBBON: No, I do not think so, Your Honor, because—

Q: Did you disprove it? I thought there was the finding that it was, as they say, economically viable.

MR. GRIBBON: I say the Court of Appeals finding to that effect is totally erroneous because it is based on this concept that we need only earn a return on the privately contributed ingredients. That destroys the entire finding.

Q: Let us assume for the moment that we accept it, that it is economically viable, but nevertheless it is perfectly obvious you could make more if you build a big building on it.

MR. GRIBBON: I still say even if you accept it, the decision is wrong, and we are entitled to compensation. I do not think the fact that what we have left over is atonement for what has been taken from us.

Q: In your brief at page 17 you cite this Court's opinion in *Fuller* where you say that the government in a condemnation case cannot exclude from consideration of the jury the value that may be added by the fact that the government built a post office near the site eighty years ago. Is that substantially your argument here.

MR. GRIBBON: I think it is. I think that is a very important part of our argument. And I think that this highest and best use is something that has to be looked at very carefully, and I would ask the Court to look at the *Causby* decision here in 328, which is cited, which illustrates a number of things. In the first place, property was not taken by the government. Yet there was a loss to the property owner, and he was compensated for it. Second, his entire property was not taken. He was compensated because he was no longer able to operate a chicken farm. And it was clear that he could have operated a vegetable patch. The Court noted that. But the compensation was because he was prevented from doing that. The Court also said an expected use of a property is properly to be taken into account in making an evaluation for taking purposes.

Q: The expected use, is that what you said?

MR. GRIBBON: That is what I said, an expected use.

Q: How is that different from the highest and best potential use?

MR. GRIBBON: I am not sure how it is different. I think it makes more sense because an expected use is clearly an element of value. That is why people buy it, for what they expect to do. I think the highest and beneficial use is a term that has really outlived its usefulness, if it ever had any, because I think the cases stand for the proposition that you get compensation for what has been taken, whatever the value.

Q: Is that term obsolete when a church could show that it has a contract to sell the church and the site for $4.5 million? Does that not give some evidence of the highest and best use?

MR. GRIBBON: I would put it under terms of expected use.

Q: The highest and best use might be to sell it as a slaughterhouse for $8,000, which the zoning would prevent.

MR. GRIBBON: The zoning would prohibit, but for a legitimate use.

Q: The highest and best use always is restricted by municipal use.

MR. GRIBBON: The Solicitor General recognizes that a statute such as this landmarks law creates unusual opportunities for arbitrary action and the remedy is not in judicial review of the landmarks designation. Those who own property that is coveted for public use are rarely, if ever, going to be a majority at the polls or in law-making bodies. And the only effective discipline on government acquisition of private resources is that provided by the pocketbook. Only if the elected representatives and their designees are required to make a cost-benefit analysis and pay through the taxes what they are going to acquire from private people for public use is there any protection for private property against ever-expanding government acquisition of private resources.

Q: What if you have a regulation put down by OSHA that puts down a number of safety standards, and the owner says, "I simply cannot run the business with all those safety standards." Does that mean he has a claim of taking or is that simply a question of a regulation that forces an individual out of business like Brandeis's dissent in *Mayheimer.*

MR. GRIBBON: It may be. If the representatives have decided that those OSHA requirements are necessary to do away with them[sic???], that may be a price that the individual owner has to pay. But I suggest a difference between that where the government goes out in a resource acquisition capacity, as it is doing here, as it did in the case of the Gettysburg Battlefield many years ago, and where the government did pay eminent domain for it.

Thank you, Your Honor.

Q: In the *Causby* case the air space above a minimum safe altitude was not deemed compensable, was it?

MR. GRIBBON: Above—yes, that is right, Your Honor. It would be interference with the use. And, as I said, they could take into account an expected use, and that is actually what we are doing here, a recognizable expected use of a small building—

Q: But there it was impact on the use of the land below, on the surface.

MR. GRIBBON: On the surface. Well, yes, but I do not know that that would distinguish it. This is a recognized property use. You have to begin from the bottom and go up.

MR. CHIEF JUSTICE BURGER: Thank you, counsel. The case is submitted.

{The case was submitted at 11:27 o'clock a.m.}

Notes and Questions

1. **At issue.** a. What is the crux of the argument made by Leonard Koerner on behalf of the City of New York? b. What do you make of his concession that the air rights were not and need not be of equivalent value to the development opportunities denied?

2. Decision of the Supreme Court of the United States on the *Penn Central* Case

Penn Central Transportation Co. v. New York City

Supreme Court of the United States
438 U.S. 104, 98 S.Ct. 2646, 8 ELR 20528 (1978)

Brennan, J. The question presented is whether a city may, as part of a comprehensive program to preserve historic landmarks and historic districts, place restrictions on the development of individual historic landmarks—in addition to those imposed by applicable zoning ordinances—without effecting a "taking" requiring the payment of "just compensation." Specifically, we must decide whether the application of New York City's Landmarks Preservation Law to the parcel of land occupied by Grand Central Terminal has "taken" its owners' property in violation of the Fifth and Fourteenth Amendments.

I

A

Over the past 50 years, all 50 States and over 500 municipalities have enacted laws to encourage or require the preservation of buildings and areas with historic or aesthetic importance.[2] These nationwide legislative efforts have been precipitated by two concerns. The first is recognition that, in recent years, large numbers of historic structures, landmarks, and areas have been destroyed[3] without adequate consideration of either the values represented therein or the possibility of preserving the destroyed properties for use in economically productive ways.[4] The second is a widely shared belief that structures with special historic, cultural, or architectural significance enhance the quality of life for all. Not only do these buildings and their workmanship represent the lessons of the past and embody precious features of our heritage, they serve as examples of quality for today. "[H]istoric conservation is but one aspect of the much larger problem, basically an environmental one, of enhancing—or perhaps developing for the first time—the quality of life for people."[5]

New York City, responding to similar concerns and acting pursuant to a New York State enabling Act,[6] adopted its Landmarks Preservation Law in 1965. See N.Y.C. Admin. Code, ch. 8-A, §205-1.0 *et seq.* (1976). The city acted from the conviction

---

2. See National Trust for Historic Preservation, A Guide to State Historic Preservation Programs (1976); National Trust for Historic Preservation, Directory of Landmark and Historic District Commissions (1976). In addition to these state and municipal legislative efforts, Congress has determined that "the historical and cultural foundations of the Nation should be preserved as a living part of our community life and development in order to give a sense of orientation to the American people," National Historic Preservation Act of 1966, 80 Stat. 915, 16 U. S. C. §470 (b) (1976 ed.), and has enacted a series of measures designed to encourage preservation of sites and structures of historic, architectural, or cultural significance. See generally Gray, The Response of Federal Legislation to Historic Preservation, 36 Law & Contemp. Prob. 314 (1971).

3. Over one-half of the buildings listed in the Historic American Buildings Survey, begun by the Federal Government in 1933, have been destroyed. *See* Costonis, *The Chicago Plan: Incentive Zoning and the Preservation of Urban Landmarks*, 85 Harv. L. Rev. 574, 574 n. 1 (1972), citing Huxtable, *Bank's Building Plan Sets Off Debate on "Progress,"* N.Y. Times, Jan. 17, 1971, section 8, p. 1, col. 2.

4. *See, e. g.*, N.Y.C. Admin. Code, §205-1.0(a) (1976).

5. Gilbert, Introduction, *Precedents for the Future*, 36 Law & Contemp. Prob. 311, 312 (1971), quoting address by Robert Stipe, 1971 Conference on Preservation Law, Washington, D. C., May 1, 1971 (unpublished text, pp. 6–7).

6. *See* N.Y. Gen. Mun. Law §96-a (McKinney 1977). It declares that it is the public policy of the State of New York to preserve structures and areas with special historical or aesthetic interest or value and authorizes local governments to impose reasonable restrictions to perpetuate such structures and areas.

that "the standing of [New York City] as a world-wide tourist center and world capital of business, culture and government" would be threatened if legislation were not enacted to protect historic landmarks and neighborhoods from precipitate decisions to destroy or fundamentally alter their character. § 205-1.0(a). The city believed that comprehensive measures to safeguard desirable features of the existing urban fabric would benefit its citizens in a variety of ways: *e. g.*, fostering "civic pride in the beauty and noble accomplishments of the past"; protecting and enhancing "the city's attractions to tourists and visitors"; "support[ing] and stimul[ating] business and industry"; "strengthen[ing] the economy of the city"; and promoting "the use of historic districts, landmarks, interior landmarks and scenic landmarks for the education, pleasure and welfare of the people of the city." § 205-1.0(b).

The New York City law is typical of many urban landmark laws in that its primary method of achieving its goals is not by acquisitions of historic properties,[7] but rather by involving public entities in land-use decisions affecting these properties and providing services, standards, controls, and incentives that will encourage preservation by private owners and users.[8] While the law does place special restrictions on landmark properties as a necessary feature to the attainment of its larger objectives, the major theme of the law is to ensure the owners of any such properties both a "reasonable return" on their investments and maximum latitude to use their parcels for purposes not inconsistent with the preservation goals.

The operation of the law can be briefly summarized. The primary responsibility for administering the law is vested in the Landmarks Preservation Commission (Commission), a broad based, 11-member agency[9] assisted by a technical staff. The Commission first performs the function, critical to any landmark preservation effort, of identifying properties and areas that have "a special character or special historical or aesthetic interest or value as part of the development, heritage or cultural characteristics of the city, state or nation." § 207-1.0(n); *see* § 207-1.0(h). If the Commission determines, after giving all interested parties an opportunity to be heard, that a building or area satisfies the ordinance's criteria, it will designate a building to be a "land-

7. The consensus is that widespread public ownership of historic properties in urban settings is neither feasible nor wise. Public ownership reduces the tax base, burdens the public budget with costs of acquisitions and maintenance, and results in the preservation of public buildings as museums and similar facilities, rather than as economically productive features of the urban scene. *See* Wilson & Winkler, *The Response of State Legislation to Historic Preservation*, 36 Law & Contemp. Prob. 329, 330–331, 339–340 (1971).

8. *See* Costonis, *supra* n.2, at 580–581; Wilson & Winkler, *supra* n.6; Rankin, *Operation and Interpretation of the New York City Landmark Preservation Law*, 36 Law & Contemp. Prob. 366 (1971).

9. The ordinance creating the Commission requires that it include at least three architects, one historian qualified in the field, one city planner or landscape architect, one realtor, and at least one resident of each of the city's five boroughs. N.Y.C. Charter § 534 (1976). In addition to the ordinance's requirements concerning the composition of the Commission, there is, according to a former chairman, a "prudent tradition" that the Commission include one or two lawyers, preferably with experience in municipal government, and several laymen with no specialized qualifications other than concern for the good of the city. Goldstone, *Aesthetics in Historic Districts*, 36 Law & Contemp. Prob. 379, 384–385 (1971).

mark," § 207-1.0(n),[10] situated on a particular "landmark site," § 207-1.0(o),[11] or will designate an area to be a "historic district," § 207-1.0(h).[12] After the Commission makes a designation, New York City's Board of Estimate, after considering the relationship of the designated property "to the master plan, the zoning resolution, projected public improvements and any plans for the renewal of the area involved," § 207-2.0(g)(1), may modify or disapprove the designation, and the owner may seek judicial review of the final designation decision. Thus far, 31 historic districts and over 400 individual landmarks have been finally designated,[13] and the process is a continuing one.

Final designation as a landmark results in restrictions upon the property owner's options concerning use of the landmark site. First, the law imposes a duty upon the owner to keep the exterior features of the building "in good repair" to assure that the law's objectives not be defeated by the landmark's falling into a state of irremediable disrepair. *See* § 207-10.0(a). Second, the Commission must approve in advance any proposal to alter the exterior architectural features of the landmark or to construct any exterior improvement on the landmark site, thus ensuring that decisions concerning construction on the landmark site are made with due consideration of both the public interest in the maintenance of the structure and the landowner's interest in use of the property. *See* §§ 207-4.0 to 207-9.0.

In the event an owner wishes to alter a landmark site, three separate procedures are available through which administrative approval may be obtained. First, the owner may apply to the Commission for a "certificate of no effect on protected architectural features": that is, for an order approving the improvement or alteration on the ground that it will not change or affect any architectural feature of the landmark and will be in harmony therewith. *See* § 207-5.0. Denial of the certificate is subject to judicial review.

Second, the owner may apply to the Commission for a certificate of "appropriateness." *See* § 207-6.0. Such certificates will be granted if the Commission concludes—

---

10. "'Landmark.' Any improvement, any part of which is thirty years old or older, which has a special character or special historical or aesthetic interest or value as part of the development, heritage or cultural characteristics of the city, state or nation and which has been designated as a landmark pursuant to the provisions of this chapter." § 207-1.0(n).

11. "'Landmark site.' An improvement parcel or part thereof on which is situated a landmark and any abutting improvement parcel or part thereof used as and constituting part of the premises on which the landmark is situated, and which has been designated as a landmark site pursuant to the provisions of this chapter." § 207-1.0(o).

12. "'Historic district.' Any area which: (1) contains improvements which: (a) have a special character or special historical or aesthetic interest or value; and (b) represent one or more periods or styles of architecture typical of one or more eras in the history of the city; and (c) cause such area, by reason of such factors, to constitute a distinct section of the city; and (2) has been designated as a historic district pursuant to the provisions of this chapter." § 207-1.0(h). The Act also provides for the designation of a "scenic landmark," *see* § 207-1.0(w), and an "interior landmark." *See* § 207-1.0(m).

13. *See* Landmarks Preservation Commission of the City of New York, Landmarks and Historic Districts (1977). Although appellants are correct in noting that some of the designated landmarks are publicly owned, the vast majority are, like Grand Central Terminal, privately owned structures.

focusing upon aesthetic, historical, and architectural values—that the proposed construction on the landmark site would not unduly hinder the protection, enhancement, perpetuation, and use of the landmark. Again, denial of the certificate is subject to judicial review. Moreover, the owner who is denied either a certificate of no exterior effect or a certificate of appropriateness may submit an alternative or modified plan for approval. The final procedure-seeking a certificate of appropriateness on the ground of "insufficient return," *see* § 207-8.0—provides special mechanisms, which vary depending on whether or not the landmark enjoys a tax exemption,[14] to ensure that designation does not cause economic hardship.

Although the designation of a landmark and landmark site restricts the owner's control over the parcel, designation also enhances the economic position of the landmark owner in one significant respect. Under New York City's zoning laws, owners of real property who have not developed their property to the full extent permitted by the applicable zoning laws are allowed to transfer development rights to contiguous parcels on the same city block. *See* New York City, Zoning Resolution Art. I, ch. 2, § 12-10 (1978) (definition of "zoning lot"). A 1968 ordinance gave the owners of landmark sites additional opportunities to transfer development rights to other parcels. Subject to a restriction that the floor area of the transferee lot may not be increased by more than 20% above its authorized level, the ordinance permitted transfers from a landmark parcel to property across the street or across a street intersection. In 1969, the law governing the conditions under which transfers from landmark parcels could

---

14. If the owner of a non-tax-exempt parcel has been denied certificates of appropriateness for a proposed alteration and shows that he is not earning a reasonable return on the property in its present state, the Commission and other city agencies must assume the burden of developing a plan that will enable the landmark owner to earn a reasonable return on the landmark site. The plan may include, but need not be limited to, partial or complete tax exemption, remission of taxes, and authorizations for alterations, construction, or reconstruction appropriate for and not inconsistent with the purposes of the law. § 207-8.0(c). The owner is free to accept or reject a plan devised by the Commission and approved by the other city agencies. If he accepts the plan, he proceeds to operate the property pursuant to the plan. If he rejects the plan, the Commission may recommend that the city proceed by eminent domain to acquire a protective interest in the landmark, but if the city does not do so within a specified time period, the Commission must issue a notice allowing the property owner to proceed with the alteration or improvement as originally proposed in his application for a certificate of appropriateness. Tax-exempt structures are treated somewhat differently. They become eligible for special treatment only if four preconditions are satisfied: (1) the owner previously entered into an agreement to sell the parcel that was contingent upon the issuance of a certificate of approval; (2) the property, as it exists at the time of the request, is not capable of earning a reasonable return; (3) the structure is no longer suitable to its past or present purposes; and (4) the prospective buyer intends to alter the landmark structure. In the event the owner demonstrates that the property in its present state is not earning a reasonable return, the Commission must either find another buyer for it or allow the sale and construction to proceed. But this is not the only remedy available for owners of tax-exempt landmarks. As the case at bar illustrates, *see infra*, at 2658, if an owner files suit and establishes that he is incapable of earning a "reasonable return" on the site in its present state, he can be afforded judicial relief. Similarly, where a landmark owner who enjoys a tax exemption has demonstrated that the landmark structure, as restricted, is totally inadequate for the owner's "legitimate needs," the law has been held invalid as applied to that parcel. *See Lutheran Church v. City of New York*, 35 N.Y.2d 121, 359 N.Y.S.2d 7, 316 N.E.2d 305 ([N.Y.] 1974).

occur was liberalized, see New York City Zoning Resolutions 74-79 to 74-793, apparently to ensure that the Landmarks Law would not unduly restrict the development options of the owners of Grand Central Terminal. *See* Marcus, *Air Rights Transfers in New York City*, 36 Law & Contemp. Prob. 372, 375 (1971). The class of recipient lots was expanded to include lots "across a street and opposite to another lot or lots which except for the intervention of streets or street intersections [form] a series extending to the lot occupied by the landmark [building, provided that] all lots [are] in the same ownership." New York City Zoning Resolution 74-79 (emphasis deleted).[15] In addition, the 1969 amendment permits, in highly commercialized areas like midtown Manhattan, the transfer of all unused development rights to a single parcel. *Ibid.*

B

This case involves the application of New York City's Landmarks Preservation Law to Grand Central Terminal (Terminal). The Terminal, which is owned by the Penn Central Transportation Co. and its affiliates (Penn Central), is one of New York City's most famous buildings. Opened in 1913, it is regarded not only as providing an ingenious engineering solution to the problems presented by urban railroad stations, but also as a magnificent example of the French beaux-arts style.

The Terminal is located in midtown Manhattan. Its south facade faces 42d Street and that street's intersection with Park Avenue. At street level, the Terminal is bounded on the west by Vanderbilt Avenue, on the east by the Commodore Hotel, and on the north by the Pan-American Building. Although a 20-story office tower, to have been located above the Terminal, was part of the original design, the planned tower was never constructed.[16] The Terminal itself is an eight-story structure which Penn Central uses as a railroad station and in which it rents space not needed for railroad purposes to a variety of commercial interests. The Terminal is one of a number of properties owned by appellant Penn Central in this area of midtown Manhattan. The others include the Barclay, Biltmore, Commodore, Roosevelt, and Waldorf-Astoria Hotels, the Pan-American Building and other office buildings along Park Avenue, and the Yale Club. At least eight of these are eligible to be recipients of development rights afforded the Terminal by virtue of landmark designation.

On August 2, 1967, following a public hearing, the Commission designated the Terminal a "landmark" and designated the "city tax block" it occupies a "landmark

---

15. To obtain approval for a proposed transfer, the landmark owner must follow the following procedure. First, he must obtain the permission of the Commission which will examine the plans for the development of the transferee lot to determine whether the planned construction would be compatible with the landmark. Second, he must obtain the approbation of New York City's Planning Commission which will focus on the effects of the transfer on occupants of the buildings in the vicinity of the transferee lot and whether the landmark owner will preserve the landmark. Finally, the matter goes to the Board of Estimate, which has final authority to grant or deny the application. *See also* Costonis, *supra* n.2, at 585–586.

16. The Terminal's present foundation includes columns, which were built into it for the express purpose of supporting the proposed 20-story tower.

site."[17] The Board of Estimate confirmed this action on September 21, 1967. Although appellant Penn Central had opposed the designation before the Commission, it did not seek judicial review of the final designation decision.

On January 22, 1968, appellant Penn Central, to increase its income, entered into a renewable 50-year lease and sublease agreement with appellant UGP Properties, Inc. (UGP), a wholly owned subsidiary of Union General Properties, Ltd., a United Kingdom corporation. Under the terms of the agreement, UGP was to construct a multistory office building above the Terminal. UGP promised to pay Penn Central $1 million annually during construction and at least $3 million annually thereafter. The rentals would be offset in part by a loss of some $700,000 to $1 million in net rentals presently received from concessionaires displaced by the new building.

Appellants UGP and Penn Central then applied to the Commission for permission to construct an office building atop the Terminal. Two separate plans, both designed by architect Marcel Breuer and both apparently satisfying the terms of the applicable zoning ordinance, were submitted to the Commission for approval. The first, Breuer I, provided for the construction of a 55-story office building, to be cantilevered above the existing facade and to rest on the roof of the Terminal. The second, Breuer II Revised,[18] called for tearing down a portion of the Terminal that included the 42d Street facade, stripping off some of the remaining features of the Terminal's facade, and constructing a 53-story office building. The Commission denied a certificate of no exterior effect on September 20, 1968. Appellants then applied for a certificate of "appropriateness" as to both proposals. After four days of hearings at which over 80 witnesses testified, the Commission denied this application as to both proposals.

The Commission's reasons for rejecting certificates respecting Breuer II Revised are summarized in the following statement: "To protect a Landmark, one does not tear it down. To perpetuate its architectural features, one does not strip them off." Record 2255. Breuer I, which would have preserved the existing vertical facades of the present structure, received more sympathetic consideration. The Commission first focused on the effect that the proposed tower would have on one desirable feature created by the present structure and its surroundings: the dramatic view of the Terminal from Park Avenue South. Although appellants had contended that the Pan-American Building had already destroyed the silhouette of the south facade and that one additional tower could do no further damage and might even provide a better background for the facade, the Commission disagreed, stating that it found the ma-

17. The Commission's report stated: "Grand Central Station, one of the great buildings of America, evokes a spirit that is unique in this City. It combines distinguished architecture with a brilliant engineering solution, wedded to one of the most fabulous railroad terminals of our time. Monumental in scale, this great building functions as well today as it did when built. In style, it represents the best of the French Beaux Arts." Record 2240.

18. Appellants also submitted a plan, denominated Breuer II, to the Commission. However, because appellants learned that Breuer II would have violated existing easements, they substituted Breuer II Revised for Breuer II, and the Commission evaluated the appropriateness only of Breuer II Revised.

jestic approach from the south to be still unique in the city and that a 55-story tower atop the Terminal would be far more detrimental to its south facade than the Pan-American Building 375 feet away. Moreover, the Commission found that from closer vantage points the Pan Am Building and the other towers were largely cut off from view, which would not be the case of the mass on top of the Terminal planned under Breuer I. In conclusion, the Commission stated:

> "[We have] no fixed rule against making additions to designated buildings—it all depends on how they are done.... But to balance a 55-story office tower above a flamboyant Beaux-Arts facade seems nothing more than an aesthetic joke. Quite simply, the tower would overwhelm the Terminal by its sheer mass. The 'addition' would be four times as high as the existing structure and would reduce the Landmark itself to the status of a curiosity.
>
> "Landmarks cannot be divorced from their settings—particularly when the setting is a dramatic and integral part of the original concept. The Terminal, in its setting, is a great example of urban design. Such examples are not so plentiful in New York City that we can afford to lose any of the few we have. And we must preserve them in a meaningful way—with alterations and additions of such character, scale, materials and mass as will protect, enhance and perpetuate the original design rather than overwhelm it." *Id.*, at 2251.[19]

Appellants did not seek judicial review of the denial of either certificate. Because the Terminal site enjoyed a tax exemption,[20] remained suitable for its present and future uses, and was not the subject of a contract of sale, there were no further administrative remedies available to appellants as to the Breuer I and Breuer II Revised plans. *See* n. 13, *supra*. Further, appellants did not avail themselves of the opportunity to develop and submit other plans for the Commission's consideration and approval. Instead, appellants filed suit in New York Supreme Court, Trial Term, claiming, *inter alia*, that the application of the Landmarks Preservation Law had "taken" their property without just compensation in violation of the Fifth and Fourteenth Amendments and arbitrarily deprived them of their property without due process of law in violation of the Fourteenth Amendment. Appellants sought a declaratory judgment, injunctive relief barring the city from using the Landmarks Law to impede the construction of any structure that might otherwise lawfully be constructed on the Terminal site, and damages for the "temporary taking" that occurred between August 2, 1967, the designation date, and the date when the restrictions arising from the Landmarks Law

---

19. In discussing Breuer I, the Commission also referred to a number of instances in which it had approved additions to landmarks: "The office and reception wing added to Gracie Mansion and the school and church house added to the 12th Street side of the First Presbyterian Church are examples that harmonize in scale, material and character with the structures they adjoin. The new Watch Tower Bible and Tract Society building on Brooklyn Heights, though completely modern in idiom, respects the qualities of its surroundings and will enhance the Brooklyn Heights Historic District, as Butterfield House enhances West 12th Street, and Breuer's own Whitney Museum its Madison Avenue locale." Record 2251.

20. *See* N.Y. Real Prop. Tax Law § 489-aa *et seq.* (McKinney Supp. 1977).

would be lifted. The trial court granted the injunctive and declaratory relief, but severed the question of damages for a "temporary taking."[21]

Appellees appealed, and the New York Supreme Court, Appellate Division, reversed. 50 A.D.2d 265, 377 N.Y.S.2d 20 ([N.Y. App. Div.] 1975). The Appellate Division held that the restrictions on the development of the Terminal site were necessary to promote the legitimate public purpose of protecting landmarks and therefore that appellants could sustain their constitutional claims only by proof that the regulation deprived them of all reasonable beneficial use of the property. The Appellate Division held that the evidence appellants introduced at trial—"Statements of Revenues and Costs," purporting to show a net operating loss for the years 1969 and 1971, which were prepared for the instant litigation—had not satisfied their burden.[22] First, the court rejected the claim that these statements showed that the Terminal was operating at a loss, for in the court's view, appellants had improperly attributed some railroad operating expenses and taxes to their real estate operations and compounded that error by failing to impute any rental value to the vast space in the Terminal devoted to railroad purposes. Further, the Appellate Division concluded that appellants had failed to establish either that they were unable to increase the Terminal's commercial income by transforming vacant or underutilized space to revenue-producing use, or that the unused development rights over the Terminal could not have been profitably transferred to one or more nearby sites.[23] The Appellate Division concluded that all appellants had succeeded in showing was that they had been deprived of the property's most profitable use, and that this showing did not establish that appellants had been unconstitutionally deprived of their property.

The New York Court of Appeals affirmed. 42 N.Y.2d 324, 397 N.Y.S.2d 914, 366 N.E.2d 1271 ([N.Y.] 1977). That court summarily rejected any claim that the Landmarks Law had "taken" property without "just compensation," *id.*, at 329, 397 N.Y.S.2d, at 917, 366 N.E.2d, at 1274, indicating that there could be no "taking" since the law had not transferred control of the property to the city, but only restricted appellants' exploitation of it. In that circumstance, the Court of Appeals held that

21. Although that court suggested that any regulation of private property to protect landmark values was unconstitutional if "just compensation" were not afforded, it also appeared to rely upon its findings: first, that the cost to Penn Central of operating the Terminal building itself, exclusive of purely railroad operations, exceeded the revenues received from concessionaires and tenants in the Terminal; and second, that the special transferable development rights afforded Penn Central as an owner of a landmark site did not "provide compensation to plaintiffs or minimize the harm suffered by plaintiffs due to the designation of the Terminal as a landmark."

22. These statements appear to have reflected the costs of maintaining the exterior architectural features of the Terminal in "good repair" as required by the law. As would have been apparent in any case therefore, the existence of the duty to keep up the property was here—and will presumably always be—factored into the inquiry concerning the constitutionality of the landmark restrictions. The Appellate Division also rejected the claim that an agreement of Penn Central with the Metropolitan Transit Authority and the Connecticut Transit Authority provided a basis for invalidating the application of the Landmarks Law.

23. The record reflected that Penn Central had given serious consideration to transferring some of those rights to either the Biltmore Hotel or the Roosevelt Hotel.

appellants' attack on the law could prevail only if the law deprived appellants of their property in violation of the Due Process Clause of the Fourteenth Amendment. Whether or not there was a denial of substantive due process turned on whether the restrictions deprived Penn Central of a "reasonable return" on the "privately created and privately managed ingredient" of the Terminal. *Id.*, at 328, 397 N.Y.S.2d, at 916, 366 N.E.2d, at 1273.[24] The Court of Appeals concluded that the Landmarks Law had not effected a denial of due process because: (1) the landmark regulation permitted the same use as had been made of the Terminal for more than half a century; (2) the appellants had failed to show that they could not earn a reasonable return on their investment in the Terminal itself; (3) even if the Terminal proper could never operate at a reasonable profit some of the income from Penn Central's extensive real estate holdings in the area, which include hotels and office buildings, must realistically be imputed to the Terminal; and (4) the development rights above the Terminal, which had been made transferable to numerous sites in the vicinity of the Terminal, one or two of which were suitable for the construction of office buildings, were valuable to appellants and provided "significant, perhaps 'fair,' compensation for the loss of rights above the terminal itself." *Id.*, at 333–336, 397 N.Y.S.2d, at 922, 366 N.E.2d, at 1276–1278.

Observing that its affirmance was "[o]n the present record," and that its analysis had not been fully developed by counsel at any level of the New York judicial system, the Court of Appeals directed that counsel "should be entitled to present ... any additional submissions which, in the light of [the court's] opinion, may usefully develop further the factors discussed." *Id.*, at 337, 397 N.Y.S.2d, at 922, 366 N.E.2d, at 1279. Appellants chose not to avail themselves of this opportunity and filed a notice of appeal in this Court. We noted probable jurisdiction. 434 U.S. 983 (1977). We affirm.

II

The issues presented by appellants are (1) whether the restrictions imposed by New York City's law upon appellants' exploitation of the Terminal site effect a "taking" of appellants' property for a public use within the meaning of the Fifth Amendment, which of course is made applicable to the States through the Fourteenth Amendment, *see Chicago, B. & Q. R. Co. v. Chicago*, 166 U.S. 226, 239, 17 S.Ct. 581, 585, 41 L.Ed. 979 (1897), and, (2), if so, whether the transferable development rights afforded ap-

24. The Court of Appeals suggested that in calculating the value of the property upon which appellants were entitled to earn a reasonable return, the "publicly created" components of the value of the property—*i.e.*, those elements of its value attributable to the "efforts of organized society" or to the "social complex" in which the Terminal is located—had to be excluded. However, since the record upon which the Court of Appeals decided the case did not, as that court recognized, contain a basis for segregating the privately created from the publicly created elements of the value of the Terminal site and since the judgment of the Court of Appeals in any event rests upon bases that support our affirmance *see infra*, this page, we have no occasion to address the question whether it is permissible or feasible to separate out the "social increments" of the value of property. *See* Costonis, *The Disparity Issue: A Context for the* Grand Central Terminal *Decision*, 91 Harv. L. Rev. 402, 416–417 (1977).

pellants constitute "just compensation" within the meaning of the Fifth Amendment.[25] We need only address the question whether a "taking" has occurred.[26]

A

Before considering appellants' specific contentions, it will be useful to review the factors that have shaped the jurisprudence of the Fifth Amendment injunction "nor shall private property be taken for public use, without just compensation." The question of what constitutes a "taking" for purposes of the Fifth Amendment has proved to be a problem of considerable difficulty. While this Court has recognized that the "Fifth Amendment's guarantee ... [is] designed to bar Government from forcing some people alone to bear public burdens which, in all fairness and justice, should be borne by the public as a whole," *Armstrong v. United States*, 364 U.S. 40, 49, 80 S.Ct. 1563, 1569, 4 L.Ed.2d 1554 (1960), this Court, quite simply, has been unable to develop any "set formula" for determining when "justice and fairness" require that economic injuries caused by public action be compensated by the government, rather than remain disproportionately concentrated on a few persons. *See Goldblatt v. Hempstead*, 369 U.S. 590, 594, 82 S.Ct. 987, 990, 8 L.Ed.2d 130 (1962). Indeed, we have frequently observed that whether a particular restriction will be rendered invalid by the government's failure to pay for any losses proximately caused by it depends largely "upon the particular circumstances [in that] case." *United States v. Central Eureka Mining Co.*, 357 U.S. 155, 168, 78 S.Ct. 1097, 1104, 2 L.Ed.2d 1228 (1958); see *United States v. Caltex, Inc.*, 344 U.S. 149, 156, 73 S.Ct. 200, 203, 97 L.Ed. 157 (1952).

In engaging in these essentially ad hoc, factual inquiries, the Court's decisions have identified several factors that have particular significance. The economic impact of the regulation on the claimant and, particularly, the extent to which the regulation has interfered with distinct investment-backed expectations are, of course, relevant

25. Our statement of the issues is a distillation of four questions presented in the jurisdictional statement: "Does the social and cultural desirability of preserving historical landmarks through government regulation derogate from the constitutional requirement that just compensation be paid for private property taken for public use? "Is Penn Central entitled to no compensation for that large but unmeasurable portion of the value of its rights to construct an office building over the Grand Central Terminal that is said to have been created by the efforts of 'society as an organized entity'? "Does a finding that Penn Central has failed to establish that there is no possibility, without exercising its development rights, of earning a reasonable return on all of its remaining properties that benefit in any way from the operations of the Grand Central Terminal warrant the conclusion that no compensation need be paid for the taking of those rights? "Does the possibility accorded to Penn Central, under the landmark-preservation regulation, of realizing some value at some time by transferring the Terminal development rights to other buildings, under a procedure that is conceded to be defective, severely limited, procedurally complex and speculative, and that requires ultimate discretionary approval by governmental authorities, meet the constitutional requirements of just compensation as applied to landmarks?" Jurisdictional Statement 3–4. The first and fourth questions assume that there has been a taking and raise the problem whether, under the circumstances of this case, the transferable development rights constitute "just compensation." The second and third questions, on the other hand, are directed to the issue whether a taking has occurred.

26. As is implicit in our opinion, we do not embrace the proposition that a "taking" can never occur unless government has transferred physical control over a portion of a parcel.

considerations. *See Goldblatt v. Hempstead, supra,* 369 U.S., at 594, 82 S.Ct., at 990. So, too, is the character of the governmental action. A "taking" may more readily be found when the interference with property can be characterized as a physical invasion by government, *see, e. g., United States v. Causby,* 328 U.S. 256, 66 S.Ct. 1062, 90 L.Ed. 1206 (1946), than when interference arises from some public program adjusting the benefits and burdens of economic life to promote the common good.

"Government hardly could go on if to some extent values incident to property could not be diminished without paying for every such change in the general law," *Pennsylvania Coal Co. v. Mahon,* 260 U.S. 393, 413, 43 S.Ct. 158, 159, 67 L.Ed. 322 (1922), and this Court has accordingly recognized, in a wide variety of contexts, that government may execute laws or programs that adversely affect recognized economic values. Exercises of the taxing power are one obvious example. A second are the decisions in which this Court has dismissed "taking" challenges on the ground that, while the challenged government action caused economic harm, it did not interfere with interests that were sufficiently bound up with the reasonable expectations of the claimant to constitute "property" for Fifth Amendment purposes. *See, e.g., United States v. Willow River Power Co.,* 324 U.S. 499, 65 S.Ct. 761, 89 L.Ed. 1101 (1945) (interest in high-water level of river for runoff for tailwaters to maintain power head is not property); *United States v. Chandler-Dunbar Water Power Co.,* 229 U.S. 53, 33 S.Ct. 667, 57 L.Ed. 1063 (1913) (no property interest can exist in navigable waters); *see also Demorest v. City Bank Co.,* 321 U.S. 36, 64 S.Ct. 384, 88 L.Ed. 526 (1944); *Muhlker v. Harlem R. Co.,* 197 U.S. 544, 25 S.Ct. 522, 49 L.Ed. 872 (1905); Sax, *Takings and the Police Power,* 74 Yale L. J. 36, 61–62 (1964).

More importantly for the present case, in instances in which a state tribunal reasonably concluded that "the health, safety, morals, or general welfare" would be promoted by prohibiting particular contemplated uses of land, this Court has upheld land-use regulations that destroyed or adversely affected recognized real property interests. *See Nectow v. Cambridge,* 277 U.S. 183, 188, 48 S.Ct. 447, 448, 72 L.Ed. 842 (1928). Zoning laws are, of course, the classic example, *see Euclid v. Ambler Realty Co.,* 272 U.S. 365, 47 S.Ct. 114, 71 L.Ed. 303 (1926) (prohibition of industrial use); *Gorieb v. Fox,* 274 U.S. 603, 608, 47 S.Ct. 675, 677, 71 L.Ed. 1228 (1927) (requirement that portions of parcels be left unbuilt); *Welch v. Swasey,* 214 U.S. 91, 29 S.Ct. 567, 53 L.Ed. 923 (1909) (height restriction), which have been viewed as permissible governmental action even when prohibiting the most beneficial use of the property. *See Goldblatt v. Hempstead, supra,* 369 U.S., at 592–593, 82 S.Ct., at 988–989, and cases cited; see also *Eastlake v. Forest City Enterprises, Inc.,* 426 U.S. 668, 674, n. 8, 96 S.Ct. 2358, 2362 n. 8, 49 L.Ed.2d 132 (1976).

Zoning laws generally do not affect existing uses of real property, but "taking" challenges have also been held to be without merit in a wide variety of situations when the challenged governmental actions prohibited a beneficial use to which individual parcels had previously been devoted and thus caused substantial individualized harm. *Miller v. Schoene,* 276 U.S. 272, 48 S.Ct. 246, 72 L.Ed. 568 (1928), is illustrative. In that case, a state entomologist, acting pursuant to a state statute, ordered the claimants to cut down a large number of ornamental red cedar trees because they produced cedar rust fatal to apple trees cultivated nearby. Although the statute provided for recovery of any expense incurred in removing the cedars, and permitted claimants to use the felled trees, it did not provide compensation for the value of the standing trees or for the resulting decrease in market value of the properties as a whole. A unanimous Court held that this latter omission did not render the statute invalid. The Court held that the State might properly make "a choice between the preservation of one class of property and that of the other" and since the apple industry was important in the State involved, concluded that the State had not exceeded "its constitutional powers by deciding upon the destruction of one class of property [without compensation] in order to save another which, in the judgment of the legislature, is of greater value to the public." *Id.*, at 279, 48 S.Ct., at 247.

Again, *Hadacheck v. Sebastian*, 239 U.S. 394, 36 S.Ct. 143, 60 L.Ed. 348 (1915), upheld a law prohibiting the claimant from continuing his otherwise lawful business of operating a brickyard in a particular physical community on the ground that the legislature had reasonably concluded that the presence of the brickyard was inconsistent with neighboring uses. *See also United States v. Central Eureka Mining Co., supra* (Government order closing gold mines so that skilled miners would be available for other mining work held not a taking); *Atchison, T. & S. F. R. Co. v. Public Utilities Comm'n*, 346 U.S. 346, 74 S.Ct. 92, 98 L.Ed. 51 (1953) (railroad may be required to share cost of constructing railroad grade improvement); *Walls v. Midland Carbon Co.*, 254 U.S. 300, 41 S.Ct. 118, 65 L.Ed. 276 (1920) (law prohibiting manufacture of carbon black upheld); *Reinman v. Little Rock*, 237 U.S. 171, 35 S.Ct. 511, 59 L.Ed. 900 (1915) (law prohibiting livery stable upheld); *Mugler v. Kansas*, 123 U.S. 623, 8 S.Ct. 273, 31 L.Ed. 205 (1887) (law prohibiting liquor business upheld).

Goldblatt v. Hempstead, supra, is a recent example. There, a 1958 city safety ordinance banned any excavations below the water table and effectively prohibited the claimant from continuing a sand and gravel mining business that had been operated on the particular parcel since 1927. The Court upheld the ordinance against a "taking" challenge, although the ordinance prohibited the present and presumably most beneficial use of the property and had, like the regulations in *Miller* and *Hadacheck*, severely affected a particular owner. The Court assumed that the ordinance did not prevent the owner's reasonable use of the property since the owner made no showing of an adverse effect on the value of the land. Because the restriction served a substantial public purpose, the Court thus held no taking had occurred. It is, of course, implicit in *Goldblatt* that a use restriction on real property may constitute a "taking" if not reasonably necessary to the effectuation of a substantial public purpose, *see Nectow v. Cambridge, supra; cf. Moore v. East Cleveland*, 431 U.S. 494, 513–514, 97 S.Ct. 1932, 1943, 52 L.Ed.2d 531 (1977) (STEVENS, J., concurring), or perhaps if it has an unduly harsh impact upon the owner's use of the property.

Pennsylvania Coal Co. v. Mahon, 260 U.S. 393, 43 S.Ct. 158, 67 L.Ed. 322 (1922), is the leading case for the proposition that a state statute that substantially furthers important public policies may so frustrate distinct investment-backed expectations as to amount to a "taking." There the claimant had sold the surface rights to particular parcels of property, but expressly reserved the right to remove the coal thereunder. A Pennsylvania statute, enacted after the transactions, forbade any mining of coal that caused the subsidence of any house, unless the house was the property of the owner of the underlying coal and was more than 150 feet from the improved property of another. Because the statute made it commercially impracticable to mine the coal, *id.*, at 414, 43 S.Ct., at 159, and thus had nearly the same effect as the complete destruction of rights claimant had reserved from the owners of the surface land, see *id.*, at 414–415, 43 S.Ct., at 159–160, the Court held that the statute was invalid as effecting a "taking" without just compensation. *See also Armstrong v. United States,* 364 U.S. 40, 80 S.Ct. 1563, 4 L.Ed.2d 1554 (1960) (Government's complete destruction of a materialman's lien in certain property held a "taking"); *Hudson Water Co. v. McCarter,* 209 U.S. 349, 355, 28 S.Ct. 529, 531, 52 L.Ed. 828 (1908) (if height restriction makes property wholly useless "the rights of property ... prevail over the other public interest" and compensation is required). *See generally* Michelman, *Property, Utility, and Fairness: Comments on the Ethical Foundations of "Just Compensation" Law,* 80 Harv. L. Rev. 1165, 1229–1234 (1967).

Finally, government actions that may be characterized as acquisitions of resources to permit or facilitate uniquely public functions have often been held to constitute "takings." *United States v. Causby,* 328 U.S. 256, 66 S.Ct. 1062, 90 L.Ed. 1206 (1946), is illustrative. In holding that direct overflights above the claimant's land, that destroyed the present use of the land as a chicken farm, constituted a "taking," *Causby* emphasized that Government had not "merely destroyed property [but was] using a part of it for the flight of its planes." *Id.,* 328 U.S., at 262–263, n. 7, 66 S.Ct., at 1066. *See also Griggs v. Allegheny County,* 369 U.S. 84, 82 S.Ct. 531, 7 L.Ed.2d 585 (1962) (overflights held a taking); *Portsmouth Co. v. United States,* 260 U.S. 327, 43 S.Ct. 135, 67 L.Ed. 287 (1922) (United States military installations' repeated firing of guns over claimant's land is a taking); *United States v. Cress,* 243 U.S. 316, 37 S.Ct. 380, 61 L.Ed. 746 (1917) (repeated floodings of land caused by water project is taking); but see *YMCA v. United States,* 395 U.S. 85, 89 S.Ct. 1511, 23 L.Ed.2d 117 (1969) (damage caused to building when federal officers who were seeking to protect building were attacked by rioters held not a taking). *See generally* Michelman, *supra,* at 1226–1229; Sax, *Takings and the Police Power,* 74 Yale L. J. 36 (1964).

B

In contending that the New York City law has "taken" their property in violation of the Fifth and Fourteenth Amendments, appellants make a series of arguments, which, while tailored to the facts of this case, essentially urge that any substantial restriction imposed pursuant to a landmark law must be accompanied by just compensation if it is to be constitutional. Before considering these, we emphasize what is not in dispute. Because this Court has recognized, in a number of settings, that States and cities may enact land-use restrictions or controls to enhance the quality of life by preserving the character and desirable aesthetic features of a city, *see New Orleans v. Dukes,* 427 U.S. 297, 96 S.Ct. 2513, 49 L.Ed.2d 511 (1976); *Young v. Amer-*

ican Mini Theatres, Inc., 427 U.S. 50, 96 S.Ct. 2440, 49 L.Ed.2d 310 (1976); *Village of Belle Terre v. Boraas,* 416 U.S. 1, 9–10, 94 S.Ct. 1536, 39 L.Ed.2d 797 (1974); *Berman v. Parker,* 348 U.S. 26, 33, 75 S.Ct. 98, 102, 99 L.Ed. 27 (1954); *Welch v. Swasey,* 214 U.S., at 108, 29 S.Ct., at 571, appellants do not contest that New York City's objective of preserving structures and areas with special historic, architectural, or cultural significance is an entirely permissible governmental goal. They also do not dispute that the restrictions imposed on its parcel are appropriate means of securing the purposes of the New York City law. Finally, appellants do not challenge any of the specific factual premises of the decision below. They accept for present purposes both that the parcel of land occupied by Grand Central Terminal must, in its present state, be regarded as capable of earning a reasonable return,[27] and that the transferable development rights afforded appellants by virtue of the Terminal's designation as a landmark are valuable, even if not as valuable as the rights to construct above the Terminal. In appellants' view none of these factors derogate from their claim that New York City's law has effected a "taking."

They first observe that the airspace above the Terminal is a valuable property interest, citing *United States v. Causby, supra.* They urge that the Landmarks Law has deprived them of any gainful use of their "air rights" above the Terminal and that, irrespective of the value of the remainder of their parcel, the city has "taken" their right to this superadjacent airspace, thus entitling them to "just compensation" measured by the fair market value of these air rights.

Apart from our own disagreement with appellants characterization of the effect of the New York City law, *see infra,* at 2665, the submission that appellants may establish a "taking" simply by showing that they have been denied the ability to exploit a property interest that they heretofore had believed was available for development is quite simply untenable. Were this the rule, this Court would have erred not only in upholding laws restricting the development of air rights, *see Welch v. Swasey, supra,* but also in approving those prohibiting both the subjacent, *see Goldblatt v. Hempstead,* 369 U.S. 590, 82 S.Ct. 987, 8 L.Ed.2d 130 (1962), and the lateral, *see Gorieb v. Fox,* 274 U.S. 603, 47 S.Ct. 675, 71 L.Ed. 1228 (1927), development of particular parcels.[28] "Takings" jurisprudence does not divide a single parcel into discrete segments and

27. Both the Jurisdictional Statement 7–8, n. 7, and Brief for Appellants 8 n. 7 state that appellants are not seeking review of the New York courts' determination that Penn Central could earn a "reasonable return" on its investment in the Terminal. Although appellants suggest in their reply brief that the factual conclusions of the New York courts cannot be sustained unless we accept the rationale of the New York Court of Appeals, *see* Reply Brief for Appellants 12 n. 15, it is apparent that the findings concerning Penn Central's ability to profit from the Terminal depend in no way on the Court of Appeals' rationale.

28. These cases dispose of any contention that might be based on *Pennsylvania Coal Co. v. Mahon,* 260 U.S. 393, 43 S.Ct. 158, 67 L.Ed. 322 (1922), that full use of air rights is so bound up with the investment-backed expectations of appellants that governmental deprivation of these rights invariably—*i.e.*, irrespective of the impact of the restriction on the value of the parcel as a whole—constitutes a "taking." Similarly, *Welch, Goldblatt,* and *Gorieb* illustrate the fallacy of appellants' related contention that a "taking" must be found to have occurred whenever the land-use restriction may be characterized as imposing a "servitude" on the claimant's parcel.

attempt to determine whether rights in a particular segment have been entirely abrogated. In deciding whether a particular governmental action has effected a taking, this Court focuses rather both on the character of the action and on the nature and extent of the interference with rights in the parcel as a whole—here, the city tax block designated as the "landmark site."

Secondly, appellants, focusing on the character and impact of the New York City law, argue that it effects a "taking" because its operation has significantly diminished the value of the Terminal site. Appellants concede that the decisions sustaining other land-use regulations, which, like the New York City law, are reasonably related to the promotion of the general welfare, uniformly reject the proposition that diminution in property value, standing alone, can establish a "taking," *see Euclid v. Ambler Realty Co.,* 272 U.S. 365, 47 S.Ct. 114, 71 L.Ed. 303 (1926) (75% diminution in value caused by zoning law); *Hadacheck v. Sebastian,* 239 U.S. 394, 36 S.Ct. 143, 60 L.Ed. 348 (1915) (87 1/2 % diminution in value); *cf. Eastlake v. Forest City Enterprises, Inc.,* 426 U.S., at 674 n. 8, 96 S.Ct., at 2362 n. 8, and that the "taking" issue in these contexts is resolved by focusing on the uses the regulations permit. *See also Goldblatt v. Hempstead, supra.* Appellants, moreover, also do not dispute that a showing of diminution in property value would not establish a taking if the restriction had been imposed as a result of historic-district legislation, *see generally Maher v. New Orleans,* 516 F.2d 1051 ([5th Cir.] 1975), but appellants argue that New York City's regulation of individual landmarks is fundamentally different from zoning or from historic-district legislation because the controls imposed by New York City's law apply only to individuals who own selected properties.

Stated baldly, appellants' position appears to be that the only means of ensuring that selected owners are not singled out to endure financial hardship for no reason is to hold that any restriction imposed on individual landmarks pursuant to the New York City scheme is a "taking" requiring the payment of "just compensation." Agreement with this argument would, of course, invalidate not just New York City's law, but all comparable landmark legislation in the Nation. We find no merit in it.

It is true, as appellants emphasize, that both historic-district legislation and zoning laws regulate all properties within given physical communities whereas landmark laws apply only to selected parcels. But, contrary to appellants' suggestions, landmark laws are not like discriminatory, or "reverse spot," zoning: that is, a land-use decision which arbitrarily singles out a particular parcel for different, less favorable treatment than the neighboring ones. *See* 2 A. Rathkopf, The Law of Zoning and Planning 26-4, and n. 6 (4th ed. 1978). In contrast to discriminatory zoning, which is the antithesis of land-use control as part of some comprehensive plan, the New York City law embodies a comprehensive plan to preserve structures of historic or aesthetic interest wherever they might be found in the city,[29] and as noted, over 400 landmarks and 31 historic districts have been designated pursuant to this plan.

---

29. Although the New York Court of Appeals contrasted the New York City Landmarks Law with both zoning and historic-district legislation and stated at one point that landmark laws do not "further

Equally without merit is the related argument that the decision to designate a structure as a landmark "is inevitably arbitrary or at least subjective, because it is basically a matter of taste," Reply Brief for Appellants 22, thus unavoidably singling out individual landowners for disparate and unfair treatment. The argument has a particularly hollow ring in this case. For appellants not only did not seek judicial review of either the designation or of the denials of the certificates of appropriateness and of no exterior effect, but do not even now suggest that the Commission's decisions concerning the Terminal were in any sense arbitrary or unprincipled. But, in any event, a landmark owner has a right to judicial review of any Commission decision, and, quite simply, there is no basis whatsoever for a conclusion that courts will have any greater difficulty identifying arbitrary or discriminatory action in the context of landmark regulation than in the context of classic zoning or indeed in any other context.[30]

Next, appellants observe that New York City's law differs from zoning laws and historic-district ordinances in that the Landmarks Law does not impose identical or similar restrictions on all structures located in particular physical communities. It follows, they argue, that New York City's law is inherently incapable of producing the fair and equitable distribution of benefits and burdens of governmental action which is characteristic of zoning laws and historic-district legislation and which they maintain is a constitutional requirement if "just compensation" is not to be afforded. It is, of course, true that the Landmarks Law has a more severe impact on some landowners than on others, but that in itself does not mean that the law effects a "taking." Legislation designed to promote the general welfare commonly burdens some more than others. The owners of the brickyard in *Hadacheck*, of the cedar trees in *Miller v. Schoene*, and of the gravel and sand mine in *Goldblatt v. Hempstead*, were uniquely burdened by the legislation sustained in those cases.[31] Similarly, zoning laws

---

a general community plan," 42 N.Y.2d 324, 330, 397 N.Y.S.2d 914, 918, 366 N.E.2d 1271, 1274 ([N.Y.]1977), it also emphasized that the implementation of the objectives of the Landmarks Law constitutes an "acceptable reason for singling out one particular parcel for different and less favorable treatment." *Ibid.*, 397 N.Y.S.2d, at 918, 366 N.E.2d, at 1275. Therefore, we do not understand the New York Court of Appeals to disagree with our characterization of the law.

30. When a property owner challenges the application of a zoning ordinance to his property, the judicial inquiry focuses upon whether the challenged restriction can reasonably be deemed to promote the objectives of the community land-use plan, and will include consideration of the treatment of similar parcels. *See generally Nectow v. Cambridge*, 277 U.S. 183, 48 S.Ct. 447, 72 L.Ed. 842 (1928). When a property owner challenges a landmark designation or restriction as arbitrary or discriminatory, a similar inquiry presumably will occur.

31. Appellants attempt to distinguish these cases on the ground that, in each, government was prohibiting a "noxious" use of land and that in the present case, in contrast, appellants' proposed construction above the Terminal would be beneficial. We observe that the uses in issue in *Hadacheck*, *Miller*, and *Goldblatt* were perfectly lawful in themselves. They involved no "blameworthiness, … moral wrongdoing or conscious act of dangerous risk-taking which induce[d society] to shift the cost to a pa[rt]icular individual." Sax, *Takings and the Police Power*, 74 Yale L. J. 36, 50 (1964). These cases are better understood as resting not on any supposed "noxious" quality of the prohibited uses but rather on the ground that the restrictions were reasonably related to the implementation of a policy—not unlike historic preservation—expected to produce a widespread public benefit and applicable to all similarly situated property. Nor, correlatively, can it be asserted that the destruction or funda-

often affect some property owners more severely than others but have not been held to be invalid on that account. For example, the property owner in *Euclid* who wished to use its property for industrial purposes was affected far more severely by the ordinance than its neighbors who wished to use their land for residences.

In any event, appellants' repeated suggestions that they are solely burdened and unbenefited is factually inaccurate. This contention overlooks the fact that the New York City law applies to vast numbers of structures in the city in addition to the Terminal—all the structures contained in the 31 historic districts and over 400 individual landmarks, many of which are close to the Terminal.[32] Unless we are to reject the judgment of the New York City Council that the preservation of landmarks benefits all New York citizens and all structures, both economically and by improving the quality of life in the city as a whole—which we are unwilling to do—we cannot conclude that the owners of the Terminal have in no sense been benefited by the Landmarks Law. Doubtless appellants believe they are more burdened than benefited by the law, but that must have been true, too, of the property owners in *Miller, Hadacheck, Euclid*, and *Goldblatt*.[33]

Appellants' final broad-based attack would have us treat the law as an instance, like that in *United States v. Causby*, in which government, acting in an enterprise capacity, has appropriated part of their property for some strictly governmental purpose. Apart from the fact that *Causby* was a case of invasion of airspace that destroyed the use of the farm beneath and this New York City law has in nowise impaired the present use of the Terminal, the Landmarks Law neither exploits appellants' parcel for city purposes nor facilitates nor arises from any entrepreneurial operations of the city. The situation is not remotely like that in *Causby* where the airspace above the property was in the flight pattern for military aircraft. The Landmarks Law's effect is simply to prohibit appellants or anyone else from occupying portions of the airspace above the Terminal, while permitting appellants to use the remainder of the parcel in a gainful fashion. This is no more an appropriation of property by government for its own uses than is a zoning law prohibiting, for "aesthetic" reasons, two or more adult theaters within a specified area, *see Young v. American Mini Theatres, Inc.*, 427 U.S. 50, 96 S.Ct. 2440, 49 L.Ed.2d 310 (1976), or a safety regulation prohibiting excavations below a certain level. *See Goldblatt v. Hempstead.*

---

mental alteration of a historic landmark is not harmful. The suggestion that the beneficial quality of appellants' proposed construction is established by the fact that the construction would have been consistent with applicable zoning laws ignores the development in sensibilities and ideals reflected in landmark legislation like New York City's. *Cf. West Bros. Brick Co. v. Alexandria*, 169 Va. 271, 282–283, 192 S.E. 881, 885–886, *appeal dismissed for want of a substantial federal question*, 302 U.S. 658, 58 S.Ct. 369, 82 L.Ed. 508 (1937).

32. There are some 53 designated landmarks and 5 historic districts or scenic landmarks in Manhattan between 14th and 59th Streets. See Landmarks Preservation Commission, Landmarks and Historic Districts (1977).

33. It is, of course, true that the fact the duties imposed by zoning and historic-district legislation apply throughout particular physical communities provides assurances against arbitrariness, but the applicability of the Landmarks Law to a large number of parcels in the city, in our view, provides comparable, if not identical, assurances.

C

Rejection of appellants' broad arguments is not, however, the end of our inquiry, for all we thus far have established is that the New York City law is not rendered invalid by its failure to provide "just compensation" whenever a landmark owner is restricted in the exploitation of property interests, such as air rights, to a greater extent than provided for under applicable zoning laws. We now must consider whether the interference with appellants' property is of such a magnitude that "there must be an exercise of eminent domain and compensation to sustain [it]." *Pennsylvania Coal Co. v. Mahon*, 260 U.S., at 413, 43 S.Ct., at 159. That inquiry may be narrowed to the question of the severity of the impact of the law on appellants' parcel, and its resolution in turn requires a careful assessment of the impact of the regulation on the Terminal site.

Unlike the governmental acts in *Goldblatt, Miller, Causby, Griggs*, and *Hadacheck*, the New York City law does not interfere in any way with the present uses of the Terminal. Its designation as a landmark not only permits but contemplates that appellants may continue to use the property precisely as it has been used for the past 65 years: as a railroad terminal containing office space and concessions. So the law does not interfere with what must be regarded as Penn Central's primary expectation concerning the use of the parcel. More importantly, on this record, we must regard the New York City law as permitting Penn Central not only to profit from the Terminal but also to obtain a "reasonable return" on its investment.

Appellants, moreover, exaggerate the effect of the law on their ability to make use of the air rights above the Terminal in two respects.[34] First, it simply cannot be maintained, on this record, that appellants have been prohibited from occupying *any* portion of the airspace above the Terminal. While the Commission's actions in denying applications to construct an office building in excess of 50 stories above the Terminal may indicate that it will refuse to issue a certificate of appropriateness for any comparably sized structure, nothing the Commission has said or done suggests an intention to prohibit *any* construction above the Terminal. The Commission's report emphasized that whether any construction would be allowed depended upon whether the proposed addition "would harmonize in scale, material and character with [the Terminal]." Record 2251. Since appellants have not sought approval for the construction of a smaller structure, we do not know that appellants will be denied any use of any portion of the airspace above the Terminal.[35]

Second, to the extent appellants have been denied the right to build above the Terminal, it is not literally accurate to say that they have been denied *all* use of even those pre-existing air rights. Their ability to use these rights has not been abrogated;

34. Appellants, of course, argue at length that the transferable development rights, while valuable, do not constitute "just compensation." Brief for Appellants 36–43.

35. Counsel for appellants admitted at oral argument that the Commission has not suggested that it would not, for example, approve a 20-story office tower along the lines of that which was part of the original plan for the Terminal. *See* Tr. of Oral Arg. 19.

they are made transferable to at least eight parcels in the vicinity of the Terminal, one or two of which have been found suitable for the construction of new office buildings. Although appellants and others have argued that New York City's transferable development-rights program is far from ideal,[36] the New York courts here supportably found that, at least in the case of the Terminal, the rights afforded are valuable. While these rights may well not have constituted "just compensation" if a "taking" had occurred, the rights nevertheless undoubtedly mitigate whatever financial burdens the law has imposed on appellants and, for that reason, are to be taken into account in considering the impact of regulation. *Cf. Goldblatt v. Hempstead*, 369 U.S., at 594 n. 3, 82 S.Ct., at 990 n. 3.

On this record, we conclude that the application of New York City's Landmarks Law has not effected a "taking" of appellants' property. The restrictions imposed are substantially related to the promotion of the general welfare and not only permit reasonable beneficial use of the landmark site but also afford appellants opportunities further to enhance not only the Terminal site proper but also other properties.[37]

Affirmed.

Mr. Justice REHNQUIST, with whom THE CHIEF JUSTICE and Mr. Justice STEVENS join, dissenting.

Of the over one million buildings and structures in the city of New York, appellees have singled out 400 for designation as official landmarks.[1] The owner of a building might initially be pleased that his property has been chosen by a distinguished committee of architects, historians, and city planners for such a singular distinction. But he may well discover, as appellant Penn Central Transportation Co. did here, that the landmark designation imposes upon him a substantial cost, with little or no offsetting benefit except for the honor of the designation. The question in this case is whether the cost associated with the city of New York's desire to preserve a limited number of "landmarks" within its borders must be borne by all of its taxpayers or whether it can instead be imposed entirely on the owners of the individual properties.

---

36. *See* Costonis, *supra* n. 2, at 585–589.

37. We emphasize that our holding today is on the present record, which in turn is based on Penn Central's present ability to use the Terminal for its intended purposes and in a gainful fashion. The city conceded at oral argument that if appellants can demonstrate at some point in the future that circumstances have so changed that the Terminal ceases to be "economically viable," appellants may obtain relief. *See* Tr. of Oral Arg. 42–43.

1. A large percentage of the designated landmarks are public structures (such as the Brooklyn Bridge, City Hall, the Statute of Liberty and the Municipal Asphalt Plant) and thus do not raise Fifth Amendment taking questions. *See* Landmarks Preservation Commission of the City of New York, Landmarks and Historic Districts (1977 and Jan. 10, 1978, Supplement). Although the Court refers to the New York ordinance as a *comprehensive* program to preserve *historic* landmarks, *ante*, at 2651, the ordinance is not limited to historic buildings and gives little guidance to the Landmarks Preservation Commission in its selection of landmark sites. Section 207-1.0(n) of the Landmarks Preservation Law, as set forth in N.Y.C. Admin. Code, ch. 8-A (1976), requires only that the selected landmark be at least 30 years old and possess "a special character or special historical or aesthetic interest or value as part of the development, heritage or cultural characteristics of the city, state or nation."

Only in the most superficial sense of the word can this case be said to involve "zoning."[2] Typical zoning restrictions may, it is true, so limit the prospective uses of a piece of property as to diminish the value of that property in the abstract because it may not be used for the forbidden purposes. But any such abstract decrease in value will more than likely be at least partially offset by an increase in value which flows from similar restrictions as to use on neighboring properties. All property owners in a designated area are placed under the same restrictions, not only for the benefit of the municipality as a whole but also for the common benefit of one another. In the words of Mr. Justice Holmes, speaking for the Court in *Pennsylvania Coal Co. v. Mahon*, 260 U.S. 393, 415, 43 S.Ct. 158, 160, 67 L.Ed. 322 (1922), there is "an average reciprocity of advantage."

Where a relatively few individual buildings, all separated from one another, are singled out and treated differently from surrounding buildings, no such reciprocity exists. The cost to the property owner which results from the imposition of restrictions applicable only to his property and not that of his neighbors may be substantial—in this case, several million dollars—with no comparable reciprocal benefits. And the cost associated with landmark legislation is likely to be of a completely different order of magnitude than that which results from the imposition of normal zoning restrictions. Unlike the regime affected by the latter, the landowner is not simply prohibited from using his property for certain purposes, while allowed to use it for all other purposes. Under the historic-landmark preservation scheme adopted by New York, the property owner is under an affirmative duty to *preserve* his property *as a landmark* at his own expense. To suggest that because traditional zoning results in some limitation of use of the property zoned, the New York City landmark preservation scheme should likewise be upheld, represents the ultimate in treating as alike things which are different. The rubric of "zoning" has not yet sufficed to avoid the well-established proposition that the Fifth Amendment bars the "Government from forcing some people alone to bear public burdens which, in all fairness and justice, should be borne by the public as a whole." *Armstrong v. United States*, 364 U.S. 40, 49, 80 S.Ct. 1563, 1569, 4 L.Ed.2d 1554 (1960). *See* discussion *infra*, at pp. 2671–2672.

---

2. Even the New York Court of Appeals conceded that "[t]his is not a zoning case.... Zoning restrictions operate to advance a comprehensive community plan for the common good. Each property owner in the zone is both benefited and restricted from exploitation, presumably without discrimination, except for permitted continuing nonconforming uses. The restrictions may be designed to maintain the general character of the area, or to assure orderly development, objectives inuring to the benefit of all, which property owners acting individually would find difficult or impossible to achieve...." Nor does this case involve landmark regulation of a historic district.... [In historic districting, as in traditional zoning,] owners although burdened by the restrictions also benefit, to some extent, from the furtherance of a general community plan.

* * *

"Restrictions on alteration of individual landmarks are not designed to further a general community plan. Landmark restrictions are designed to prevent alteration or demolition of a single piece of property. To this extent, such restrictions resemble 'discriminatory' zoning restrictions, properly condemned...." 42 N.Y.2d 324, 329–330, 397 N.Y.S.2d 914, 917–918, 366 N.E.2d 1271, 1274 ([N.Y.] 1977).

In August 1967, Grand Central Terminal was designated a landmark over the objections of its owner Penn Central. Immediately upon this designation, Penn Central, like all owners of a landmark site, was placed under an affirmative duty, backed by criminal fines and penalties, to keep "exterior portions" of the landmark "in good repair." Even more burdensome, however, were the strict limitations that were thereupon imposed on Penn Central's use of its property. At the time Grand Central was designated a landmark, Penn Central was in a precarious financial condition. In an effort to increase its sources of revenue, Penn Central had entered into a lease agreement with appellant UGP Properties, Inc., under which UGP would construct and operate a multistory office building cantilevered above the Terminal building. During the period of construction, UGP would pay Penn Central $1 million per year. Upon completion, UGP would rent the building for 50 years, with an option for another 25 years, at a guaranteed *minimum* rental of $3 million per year. The record is clear that the proposed office building was in full compliance with all New York zoning laws and height limitations. Under the Landmarks Preservation Law, however, appellants could not construct the proposed office building unless appellee Landmarks Preservation Commission issued either a "Certificate of No Exterior Effect" or a "Certificate of Appropriateness." Although appellants' architectural plan would have preserved the facade of the Terminal, the Landmarks Preservation Commission has refused to approve the construction.

I

The Fifth Amendment provides in part: "nor shall private property be taken for public use, without just compensation."[3] In a very literal sense, the actions of appellees violated this constitutional prohibition. Before the city of New York declared Grand Central Terminal to be a landmark, Penn Central could have used its "air rights" over the Terminal to build a multistory office building, at an apparent value of several million dollars per year. Today, the Terminal cannot be modified in *any* form, including the erection of additional stories, without the permission of the Landmark Preservation Commission, a permission which appellants, despite good-faith attempts, have so far been unable to obtain. Because the Taking Clause of the Fifth Amendment has not always been read literally, however, the constitutionality of appellees' actions requires a closer scrutiny of this Court's interpretation of the three key words in the Taking Clause—"property," "taken," and "just compensation."[4]

---

3. The guarantee that private property shall not be taken for public use without just compensation is applicable to the States through the Fourteenth Amendment. Although the state "legislature may prescribe a form of procedure to be observed in the taking of private property for public use, ... it is not due process of law if provision be not made for compensation." *Chicago, B. & Q. R. Co. v. Chicago*, 166 U.S. 226, 236, 17 S.Ct. 581, 584, 41 L.Ed. 979 (1897).

4. The Court's opinion touches base with, or at least attempts to touch base with, most of the major eminent domain cases decided by this Court. Its use of them, however, is anything but meticulous. In citing to *United States v. Caltex, Inc.*, 344 U.S. 149, 156, 73 S.Ct. 200, 97 L.Ed. 157 (1952), for example, *ante*, at 2659, the only language remotely applicable to eminent domain is stated in terms of "the destruction of respondents' terminals by a trained team of engineers in the face of their impending seizure by the enemy." 344 U.S., at 156, 73 S.Ct., at 203.

A

Appellees do not dispute that valuable property rights have been destroyed. And the Court has frequently emphasized that the term "property" as used in the Taking Clause includes the entire "group of rights inhering in the citizen's [ownership]." *United States v. General Motors Corp.*, 323 U.S. 373, 65 S.Ct. 357, 89 L.Ed. 311 (1945). The term is not used in the

> "vulgar and untechnical sense of the physical thing with respect to which the citizen exercises rights recognized by law. [Instead, it] ... denote [s] the *group of rights* inhering in the citizen's relation to the physical THING, *AS THE RIGHT TO POSSESS, USE AND DISPOSE OF IT....* the constitutional provision is addressed to *every sort of interest* the citizen may possess." *Id.*, at 377–378, 65 S.Ct., at 359 (emphasis added).

While neighboring landowners are free to use their land and "air rights" in any way consistent with the broad boundaries of New York zoning, Penn Central, absent the permission of appellees, must forever maintain its property in its present state.[5] The property has been thus subjected to a nonconsensual servitude not borne by any neighboring or similar properties.[6]

B

Appellees have thus destroyed—in a literal sense, "taken"—substantial property rights of Penn Central. While the term "taken" might have been narrowly interpreted to include only physical seizures of property rights, "the construction of the phrase has not been so narrow. The courts have held that the deprivation of the former owner rather than the accretion of a right or interest to the sovereign constitutes the taking." *Id.*, at 378, 65 S.Ct., at 359. *See also United States v. Lynah*, 188 U.S. 445, 469, 23 S.Ct. 349, 47 L.Ed. 539 1903);[7] *Dugan v. Rank*, 372 U.S. 609, 625, 83 S.Ct. 999, 1009, 10 L.Ed.2d 15 (1963). Because "not every destruction or injury to property by governmental action has been held to be a 'taking' in the constitutional sense,"

---

5. In particular, Penn Central cannot increase the height of the Terminal. This Court has previously held that the "air rights" over an area of land are "property" for purposes of the Fifth Amendment. See *United States v. Causby*, 328 U.S. 256, 66 S.Ct. 1062, 90 L.Ed. 1206 (1946) ("air rights" taken by low-flying airplanes); *Griggs v. Allegheny County*, 369 U.S. 84, 82 S.Ct. 531, 7 L.Ed.2d 585 (1962) (same); *Portsmouth Harbor Land & Hotel Co. v. United States*, 260 U.S. 327, 43 S.Ct. 135, 67 L.Ed. 287 (1922) (firing of projectiles over summer resort can constitute taking). *See also Butler v. Frontier Telephone Co.*, 186 N.Y. 486, 79 N.E. 716 (1906) (stringing of telephone wire across property constitutes a taking).

6. It is, of course, irrelevant that appellees interfered with or destroyed property rights that Penn Central had not yet physically used. The Fifth Amendment must be applied with "reference to the uses for which the property is suitable, having regard to the existing business or wants of the community, *or such as may be reasonably expected in the immediate future.*" *Boom Co. v. Patterson*, 98 U.S. 403, 408, 25 L.Ed. 206 (1879) (emphasis added).

7. It is, of course, irrelevant that appellees interfered with or destroyed property rights that Penn Central had not yet physically used. The Fifth Amendment must be applied with "reference to the uses for which the property is suitable, having regard to the existing business or wants of the community, *or such as may be reasonably expected in the immediate future.*" *Boom Co. v. Patterson*, 98 U.S. 403, 408, 25 L.Ed. 206 (1879) (emphasis added).

Armstrong v. United States, 364 U.S., at 48, 80 S.Ct., at 1568, however, this does not end our inquiry. But an examination of the two exceptions where the destruction of property does *not* constitute a taking demonstrates that a compensable taking has occurred here.

1

As early as 1887, the Court recognized that the government can prevent a property owner from using his property to injure others without having to compensate the owner for the value of the forbidden use.

> "A prohibition simply upon the use of property for purposes that are declared, by valid legislation, to be *injurious to the health, morals, or safety of the community*, cannot, in any just sense, be deemed a taking or an appropriation of property for the public benefit. Such legislation does not disturb the owner in the control or use of his property for lawful purposes, nor restrict his right to dispose of it, but is only a declaration by the State that its use by any one, for certain forbidden purposes, is prejudicial to the public interests.... The power which the States have of prohibiting such use by individuals of their property as will be prejudicial to the health, the morals, or the safety of the public, is not—and, consistently with the existence and safety of organized society, cannot be—burdened with the condition that the State must compensate such individual owners for pecuniary losses they may sustain, *by reason of their not being permitted, by a noxious use of their property, to inflict injury upon the community*." *Mugler v. Kansas*, 123 U.S. 623, 668–669, 8 S.Ct. 273, 301, 31 L.Ed. 205.

Thus, there is no "taking" where a city prohibits the operation of a brickyard within a residential area, *see Hadacheck v. Sebastian*, 239 U.S. 394, 36 S.Ct. 143, 60 L.Ed. 348 (1915), or forbids excavation for sand and gravel below the water line, *see Goldblatt v. Hempstead*, 369 U.S. 590, 82 S.Ct. 987, 8 L.Ed.2d 130 (1962). Nor is it relevant, where the government is merely prohibiting a noxious use of property, that the government would seem to be singling out a particular property owner. *Hadacheck, supra*, at 413, 36 S.Ct., at 146.[8]

The nuisance exception to the taking guarantee is not coterminous with the police power itself. The question is whether the forbidden use is dangerous to the safety, health, or welfare of others. Thus, in *Curtin v. Benson*, 222 U.S. 78, 32 S.Ct. 31, 56 L.Ed. 102 (1911), the Court held that the Government, in prohibiting the owner of property within the boundaries of Yosemite National Park from grazing cattle on his property, had taken the owner's property. The Court assumed that the Government could constitutionally require the owner to fence his land or take other action to prevent his cattle from straying onto others' land without compensating him.

---

8. Each of the cases cited by the Court for the proposition that legislation which severely affects some landowners but not others does not effect a "taking" involved noxious uses of property. *See Hadacheck; Miller v. Schoene*, 276 U.S. 272, 48 S.Ct. 246, 72 L.Ed. 568 (1928); *Goldblatt. See ante*, at 2660–2661, 2664.

> "Such laws might be considered as strictly regulations of the use of property, of so using it that no injury could result to others. They would have the effect of making the owner of land herd his cattle on his own land and of making him responsible for a neglect of it." *Id.*, at 86, 32 S.Ct., at 33.

The prohibition in question, however, was "not a prevention of a misuse or illegal use but the prevention of a legal and essential use, an attribute of its ownership." *Ibid.*

Appellees are not prohibiting a nuisance. The record is clear that the proposed addition to the Grand Central Terminal would be in full compliance with zoning, height limitations, and other health and safety requirements. Instead, appellees are seeking to preserve what they believe to be an outstanding example of beaux arts architecture. Penn Central is prevented from further developing its property basically because *too good* a job was done in designing and building it. The city of New York, because of its unadorned admiration for the design, has decided that the owners of the building must preserve it unchanged for the benefit of sightseeing New Yorkers and tourists.

Unlike land-use regulations, appellees' actions do not merely *prohibit* Penn Central from using its property in a narrow set of noxious ways. Instead, appellees have placed an *affirmative* duty on Penn Central to maintain the Terminal in its present state and in "good repair." Appellants are not free to use their property as they see fit within broad outer boundaries but must strictly adhere to their past use except where appellees conclude that alternative uses would not detract from the landmark. While Penn Central may continue to use the Terminal as it is presently designed, appellees otherwise "exercise complete dominion and control over the surface of the land," *United States v. Causby*, 328 U.S. 256, 262, 66 S.Ct. 1062, 1066, 90 L.Ed. 1206 (1946), and must compensate the owner for his loss. *Ibid.* "Property is taken in the constitutional sense when inroads are made upon an owner's use of it to an extent that, as between private parties, a servitude has been acquired." *United States v. Dickinson*, 331 U.S. 745, 748, 67 S.Ct. 1382, 1385, 91 L.Ed. 1789 (1947). *See also Dugan v. Rank, supra*, 372 U.S., at 625, 83 S.Ct., at 1009.[9]

2

Even where the government prohibits a noninjurious use, the Court has ruled that a taking does not take place if the prohibition applies over a broad cross section of land and thereby "secure[s] an average reciprocity of advantage." *Pennsylvania Coal*

---

9. In *Monongahela Navigation Co. v. United States*, 148 U.S. 312, 13 S.Ct. 622, 37 L.Ed. 463 (1893), the Monongahela company had expended large sums of money in improving the Monongahela River by means of locks and dams. When the United States condemned this property for its own use, the Court held that full compensation had to be awarded. "Suppose, in the improvement of a navigable stream, it was deemed essential to construct a canal with locks, in order to pass around rapids or falls. Of the power of Congress to condemn whatever land may be necessary for such canal, there can be no question; and of the equal necessity of paying full compensation for all private property taken there can be as little doubt." *Id.*, at 337, 13 S.Ct., at 630. Under the Court's rationale, however, where the Government wishes to preserve a pre-existing canal system for public use, it need not condemn the property but need merely order that it be preserved in its present form and be kept "in good repair."

Co. v. Mahon, 260 U.S., at 415, 43 S.Ct., at 160.[10] It is for this reason that zoning does not constitute a "taking." While zoning at times reduces *individual* property values, the burden is shared relatively evenly and it is reasonable to conclude that on the whole an individual who is harmed by one aspect of the zoning will be benefited by another.

Here, however, a multimillion dollar loss has been imposed on appellants; it is uniquely felt and is not offset by any benefits flowing from the preservation of some 400 other "landmarks" in New York City. Appellees have imposed a substantial cost on less than one one-tenth of one percent of the buildings in New York City for the general benefit of all its people. It is exactly this imposition of general costs on a few individuals at which the "taking" protection is directed. The Fifth Amendment

> "prevents the public from loading upon one individual more than his just share of the burdens of government, and says that when he surrenders to the public something more and different from that which is exacted from other members of the public, a full and just equivalent shall be returned to him." *Monongahela Navigation Co. v. United States*, 148 U.S. 312, 325, 13 S.Ct. 622, 626, 37 L.Ed. 463 (1893).

Less than 20 years ago, this Court reiterated that the

> "Fifth Amendment's guarantee that private property shall not be taken for a public use without just compensation was designed to bar Government from forcing some people alone to bear public burdens which, in all fairness and justice, should be borne by the public as a whole." *Armstrong v. United States*, 364 U.S., at 49, 80 S.Ct., at 1569. *Cf. Nashville, C. & St. L. R. Co. v. Walters*, 294 U.S. 405, 428–430, 55 S.Ct. 486, 494–495, 79 L.Ed. 949 (1935).[11]

As Mr. Justice Holmes pointed out in *Pennsylvania Coal Co. v. Mahon*, "the question at bottom" in an eminent domain case "is upon whom the loss of the changes desired should fall." 260 U.S., at 416, 43 S.Ct., at 160. The benefits that appellees believe will flow from preservation of the Grand Central Terminal will accrue to all the citizens of New York City. There is no reason to believe that appellants will enjoy a substantially greater share of these benefits. If the cost of preserving Grand Central Terminal were spread evenly across the entire population of the city of New York, the burden per

10. Appellants concede that the preservation of buildings of historical or aesthetic importance is a permissible objective of state action. Brief for Appellants 12. *Cf. Berman v. Parker*, 348 U.S. 26, 75 S.Ct. 98, 99 L.Ed. 27 (1954); *United States v. Gettysburg Electric R. Co.*, 160 U.S. 668, 16 S.Ct. 427, 40 L.Ed. 576 (1896). For the reasons noted in the text, historic *zoning*, as has been undertaken by cities, such as New Orleans, may well not require compensation under the Fifth Amendment.

11. "It is true that the police power embraces regulations designed to promote public convenience or the general welfare, and not merely those in the interest of public health, safety and morals.... But when particular individuals are singled out to bear the cost of advancing the public convenience, that imposition must bear some reasonable relation to the evils to be eradicated or the advantages to be secured.... While moneys raised by general taxation may constitutionally be applied to purposes from which the individual taxed may receive no benefit, and indeed, suffer serious detriment, ... so-called assessments for public improvements laid upon particular property owners are ordinarily constitutional only if based on benefits received by them." 294 U.S., at 429–430, 55 S.Ct., at 494–495.

person would be in cents per year—a minor cost appellees would surely concede for the benefit accrued. Instead, however, appellees would impose the entire cost of several million dollars per year on Penn Central. But it is precisely this sort of discrimination that the Fifth Amendment prohibits.[12]

Appellees in response would argue that a taking only occurs where a property owner is denied *all* reasonable value of his property.[13] The Court has frequently held that, even where a destruction of property rights would not *otherwise* constitute a taking, the inability of the owner to make a reasonable return on his property requires compensation under the Fifth Amendment. *See, e. g., United States v. Lynah*, 188 U.S., at 470, 23 S.Ct., at 357. But the converse is not true. A taking does not become a noncompensable exercise of police power simply because the government in its grace allows the owner to make some "reasonable" use of his property. "[I]t is the character of the invasion, not the amount of damage resulting from it, so long as the damage is substantial, that determines the question whether it is a taking." *United States v. Cress*, 243 U.S. 316, 328, 37 S.Ct. 380, 385, 61 L.Ed. 746 (1917); *United States v. Causby*, 328 U.S., at 266, 66 S.Ct., at 1068. *See also Goldblatt v. Hempstead*, 369 U.S., at 594, 82 S.Ct., at 990.

C

Appellees, apparently recognizing that the constraints imposed on a landmark site constitute a taking for Fifth Amendment purposes, do not leave the property owner empty-handed. As the Court notes, *ante*, at 2654–2655, the property owner may theoretically "transfer" his previous right to develop the landmark property to adjacent properties if they are under his control. Appellees have coined this system "Transfer Development Rights," or TDR's.

Of all the terms used in the Taking Clause, "just compensation" has the strictest meaning. The Fifth Amendment does not allow simply an approximate compensation but requires "a full and perfect equivalent for the property taken." *Monongahela Navigation Co. v. United States*, 148 U.S., at 326, 13 S.Ct., at 626.

---

12. The fact that the Landmarks Preservation Commission may have allowed additions to a relatively few landmarks is of no comfort to appellants. *Ante*, at 2656 n. 18. Nor is it of any comfort that the Commission refuses to allow appellants to construct any additional stories because of their belief that such construction would not be aesthetic. *Ante*, at 2656.

13. Difficult conceptual and legal problems are posed by a rule that a taking only occurs where the property owner is denied all reasonable return on his property. Not only must the Court define "reasonable return" for a variety of types of property (farmlands, residential properties, commercial and industrial areas), but the Court must define the particular property unit that should be examined. For example, in this case, if appellees are viewed as having restricted Penn Central's use of its "air rights," *all* return has been denied. *See Pennsylvania Coal Co. v. Mahon*, 260 U.S. 393, 43 S.Ct. 158, 67 L.Ed. 322 (1922). The Court does little to resolve these questions in its opinion. Thus, at one point, the Court implies that the question is whether the restrictions have "an unduly harsh impact upon the owner's use of the property," *ante*, at 2661; at another point, the question is phrased as whether Penn Central can obtain "a 'reasonable return' on its investment," *ante*, at 2666; and, at yet another point, the question becomes whether the landmark is "economically viable," *ante*, at 2666 n. 36.

> "[I]f the adjective 'just' had been omitted, and the provision was simply that property should not be taken without compensation, the natural import of the language would be that the compensation should be the equivalent of the property. And this is made emphatic by the adjective 'just.' There can, in view of the combination of those two words, be no doubt that the compensation must be a full and perfect equivalent for the property taken." *Ibid*

See also United States v. Lynah, supra, 188 U.S., at 465, 23 S.Ct., at 355; *United States v. Pewee Coal Co.*, 341 U.S. 114, 117, 71 S.Ct. 670, 671, 95 L.Ed. 809 (1951). And the determination of whether a "full and perfect equivalent" has been awarded is a "judicial function." *United States v. New River Collieries Co.*, 262 U.S. 341, 343–344, 43 S.Ct. 565, 566–567, 67 L.Ed. 1014 (1923). The fact that *appellees* may believe that TDR's provide full compensation is irrelevant.

> "The legislature may determine what private property is needed for public purposes—that is a question of a political and legislative character; but when the taking has been ordered, then the question of compensation is judicial. It does not rest with the public, taking the property, through Congress or the legislature, its representative, to say what compensation shall be paid, or even what shall be the rule of compensation. The Constitution has declared that just compensation shall be paid, and the ascertainment of that is a judicial inquiry." *Monongahela Navigation Co. v. United States, supra*, 148 U.S., at 327, 13 S.Ct., at 626.

Appellees contend that, even if they have "taken" appellants' property, TDR's constitute "just compensation." Appellants, of course, argue that TDR's are highly imperfect compensation. Because the lower courts held that there was no "taking," they did not have to reach the question of whether or not just compensation has already been awarded. The New York Court of Appeals' discussion of TDR's gives some support to appellants:

> "The many defects in New York City's program for development rights transfers have been detailed elsewhere.... The area to which transfer is permitted is severely limited [and] complex procedures are required to obtain a transfer permit." 42 N.Y.2d 324, 334–335, 397 N.Y.S.2d 914, 920, 366 N.E.2d 1271, 1277 ([N.Y.] 1977).

And in other cases the Court of Appeals has noted that TDR's have an "uncertain and contingent market value" and do "not adequately preserve" the value lost when a building is declared to be a landmark. *French Investing Co. v. City of New York*, 39 N.Y.2d 587, 591, 385 N.Y.S.2d 5, 7, 350 N.E.2d 381, 383, *appeal dismissed* 429 U.S. 990, 97 S.Ct. 515, 50 L.Ed.2d 602 (1976). On the other hand, there is evidence in the record that Penn Central has been offered substantial amounts for its TDR's. Because the record on appeal is relatively slim, I would remand to the Court of Appeals for a determination of whether TDR's constitute a "full and perfect equivalent for the property taken."[14]

---

14. The Court suggests, *ante*, at 2663, that if appellees are held to have "taken" property sights of landmark owners, not only the New York City Landmarks Preservation Law, but "all comparable

II

Over 50 years ago, Mr. Justice Holmes, speaking for the Court, warned that the courts were "in danger of forgetting that a strong public desire to improve the public condition is not enough to warrant achieving the desire by a shorter cut than the constitutional way of paying for the change." *Pennsylvania Coal Co. v. Mahon*, 260 U.S., at 416, 43 S.Ct., at 160. The Court's opinion in this case demonstrates that the danger thus foreseen has not abated. The city of New York is in a precarious financial state, and some may believe that the costs of landmark preservation will be more easily borne by corporations such as Penn Central than the overburdened individual taxpayers of New York. But these concerns do not allow us to ignore past precedents construing the Eminent Domain Clause to the end that the desire to improve the public condition is, indeed, achieved by a shorter cut than the constitutional way of paying for the change.

Notes and Questions

1. **The battle for Grand Central Terminal went national.** When the Penn Central Transportation Company lost the battle for Grand Central Terminal in the New York Court of Appeals, it took the war to Washington, D.C., arguing the same case, that the Landmarks Preservation Law effectuated a taking, only this time under the United States Constitution before the United States Supreme Court, although as you see, it lost there also. The grassroots effort to save the terminal, started by the Municipal Art Society ("MAS") in New York also went national, gaining support from cities across the United States. The most famous of their national exploits was the Landmarks Express, an old-fashioned whistle-stop railroad tour from New York to Washington, D.C. The train departed on April 16, 1978, the day before the Supreme Court was going to hear the case, with a televised send-off by local elected officials, including Mayor Edward Koch. On board were activist New Yorkers, members of the national news media, and many dignitaries, including of course, the face of the movement, Jacqueline Kennedy Onassis. Municipal Art Society and New York Landmarks Preservation Commission, *A Celebration of the 25th Anniversary of the Supreme Court Decision to Uphold New York City's Landmarks Law*. June 26, 2003 ("Celebration").

---

landmark legislation in the Nation" must fall. This assumes, of course, that TDR's are not "just compensation" for the property rights destroyed. It also ignores the fact that many States and cities in the Nation have chosen to preserve landmarks by purchasing or condemning restrictive easements over the facades of the landmarks and are apparently quite satisfied with the results. *See, e. g.*, Ore. Rev. Stat. §§ 271.710, 271.720 (1977); Md. Ann. Code, Art. 41, § 181A (1978); Va. Code §§ 10-145.1 and 10-138(e) (1978); Richmond, Va., City Code §§ 21–23 *et seq.* (1975). The British National Trust has effectively used restrictive easements to preserve landmarks since 1937. *See* National Trust Act, 1937, 1 Edw. 8 and 1 Geo. 6 ch. lvii, §§ 4 and 8. Other States and cities have found that tax incentives are also an effective means of encouraging the private preservation of landmark sites. *See, e. g.*, Conn. Gen. Stat. § 12-127a (1977); Ill. Rev. Stat., ch. 24, § 11-48.2-6 (1976); Va. Code § 10-139 (1978). The New York City Landmarks Preservation Law departs drastically from these traditional, and constitutional, means of preserving landmarks.

The Landmarks Express was given a hero's reception at Union Station in Washington, D.C., being met by the Vice President's wife, Joan Mondale, and Senator Daniel Patrick Moynihan. The whole event sparked a national consciousness for the preservation of historic landmarks; Grand Central Terminal was the poster child. Victory came on June 26, 1978, when Justice Brennan, writing the opinion for a majority, with a vote of 6 to 3, upheld the Landmarks Preservation Law. The microcosm of the fight for the preservation of Grand Central Terminal became a macrocosm of the fight for the preservation of national landmarks across the United States, and with it, the validity of historic preservation laws and ordinances.

2. **The social obligations of property.** Does property ownership come with a social obligation; something that begins with the duty to use property in a way that is not harmful to neighbors or society, but may be broader to encompass a sharing of some of property's surplus value for individual or societal betterment? Professor Gregory Alexander expresses the view that:

> Private ownership of those aspects of a society's infrastructure upon which the civic culture depends comes with special obligations.... Those obligations may require that an owner forego compensation, even long-term, in-kind compensation, if an urban authority legitimately invokes its power to protect private property from being altered in ways that would permanently destroy its civically unique and supportive aspects. The development of Grand Central Terminal contemplated in *Penn Central* would have inflicted on the community of New York a significant loss of cultural meaning and identity. No compensation should be constitutionally required to prevent a private owner from inflicting such a loss in the first place, a loss that is fundamentally at odds with the obligations of the owner of that property.

Gregory S. Alexander, *The Social-Obligation Norm in American Property Law*, 94 Cornell L. Rev. 745, 795–96 (2009).

3. **Grand Central Terminal's restoration.** The Supreme Court decision in *Penn Central* was only half the battle to save the historic landmark. The energy now had to shift from ensuring that the terminal was not going to be torn down, to ensuring that the terminal would not tear itself down. MAS mounted a new campaign, spurred by board member Hugh Hardy, to renovate the terminal and restore it to its former glory and significance as a modern functioning piece of history. MAS sponsored an exhibition at the New York Historical Society, published a book, and produced a nationally televised documentary, all dedicated to the grandiose structure that is the Grand Central Terminal and the need for its solidification as a New York City landmark. The Metropolitan Transit Authority ("MTA"), which was required to maintain the terminal under its lease with Penn Central, seized on the potential of this important project. The MTA'S chairman, Peter Stangl, struck a deal with Penn Central to restore the terminal and began construction on February 15, 1996. Architect John Belle was hired by the MTA to design and oversee the renovation; later on, the development team of LaSalle Partners and Williams Jackson Ewing were conscripted to head the efforts to bring restaurants and retailers to the terminal. Celebration, *supra*.

Three years after the restoration began, on Thursday, October 1, 1998, Governor George Pataki rededicated the terminal at the Rededication Celebration of Grand Central Terminal gala. The event garnered both national and international media attention, and marked the beginning of a new chapter of this venerable New York City landmark. The fight for Grand Central Terminal and its restoration has become an international illustration of a successful urban project that rejuvenated a classic, historic building, which would otherwise have been destroyed and discarded. *History: Now, The Heart of New York City*, Grand Central Terminal, http://www.gcthistory.com/ (last visited April 6, 2017). To this day, the Grand Central Terminal has become a symbol of both the historicity of New York City and its ability to adapt to a modern world using a classic framework. *See generally* J. Peter Byrne, *Historic Preservation and its Cultured Despisers: Reflections on the Contemporary Role of Preservation Law in Urban Development*, 19 Geo. Mason L. Rev. 665, 687–88 (2012) (concluding that historic preservation serves to make the modern city hospitable for contemporary life; that the role of historic preservation is not itself fixed, but has a range to grow toward new maturity).

4. **Maintenance obligations.** After the Supreme Court decision affirming the power to designate landmarks, there was the issue of the maintenance of the structure, which requires more effort than from just one entity individually; it requires a group effort collectively. In the case of Grand Central Terminal, a continuing maintenance project was agreed to by the MTA, the New York and Harlem Railroad Company, the New York Landmarks Preservation Commission, the City Planning Board, and American Premier Underwriters, Inc. American Premier, the owner of the railroad, and the Landmarks Preservation Commission agreed to maintain the structure of the terminal according to the original plan. The landmark maintenance agreement can be found on the companion website.

5. **Role of public organizations in maintaining the historic integrity.** a. What is the role of a public organization like MAS in ensuring the maintenance agreement is enforced? b. Would the public even have standing as a third-party interest? c. Would the Attorney General of New York be able to oversee the agreement? d. What should be the role of conservancy agreements or plans in reference to complex buildings?

6. **Transfer of development rights in takings analysis.** Although Chief Justice Rehnquist questioned the value of development rights, viewing them as a compensation tool by land use agencies, rather than an economic use of the land, they have been widely transferred and accepted as the norm. a. What explains the Chief Justice's position? b. What other argument could be made for opposing these rights?

7. **A land use tool.** The transfer of development rights ("TDR") is a land use tool, designed to preserve or protect natural or man-made property resources, while enabling a landowner to benefit from land ownership, although development rights are restricted. The New York State TDR enabling acts express the purpose as "to protect the natural, scenic or agricultural qualities of open lands, to enhance sites and areas of special character or special historical, cultural, aesthetic or economic interest or

Two views of Grand Central Terminal. Images by Edward Newman and Shelby D. Green with permission.

value and to enable and encourage flexibility of design and careful management of land in recognition of land as a basic and valuable natural resource." Gen. City Law § 20-f(2); Town Law § 261-a(2); Village Law § 7-701(2). Essentially, TDR programs enable landowners within valuable areas or who own property occupied by historic structures, to sell their right to develop some or all of their lands to another party who will use that right to develop somewhere else better suited for development. The development value of the receiving site is enhanced by allowing greater density or intensity, or other regulatory flexibility, otherwise not permitted without the TDR. At the same time, the land from the sending site is permanently protected through a conservation easement or use restriction. TDR programs usually contain some method of valuing the development rights that are transferred, such as by units per acre, or in square feet of floor area, or in units of height of structures. Most TDR programs are enacted as part of municipal zoning ordinances, which means that the "sending" and "receiving" zones, must be established in accordance with a comprehensive planning process. In selecting receiving sites, attention is given to the impact of greater development on infrastructure and municipal resources, such as police and fire protection, as well as on housing availability. *See generally* James A. Coon, *Transfer of Development Rights*, Local Government Technical Series A Division of the New York Department of State, Division of Local Government Services (2015); *see also Andrew J. Miller, Transferable Development Rights in the Constitutional Landscape: Has Penn Central Failed to Weather the Storm*, 39 Nat. Resources J. 459 (1999); Margaret Walls and Virginia McConnell, *Transfer of Development Rights in U.S. Communities: Evaluating Program Design, Implementation and Outcomes*, Resources for the Future, www.rff.org_rff_documents_Walls_McConnell_Sep_07_TDR_Report.pdf.

8. **A new look at a 1910 proposal for using air rights.** Looking back on the legal battle to keep developers from constructing a skyscraper in place of or on top of Grand Central Terminal, it is hard to believe that the terminal was originally meant to be a skyscraper, rising 22 stories. The original design called for pillars capable of supporting that load, but the additional stories were never built.

9. **Proposal for new East Midtown Subdistrict.** In 2017, the New York City Office of Planning adopted a plan to rezone the mid-town east section of Manhattan, among other things, creating a new East Midtown Subdistrict, which comprises the site of the terminal. The plan allows the floor to area ratios ("FARs") to increase from a base maximum of 12.0 to 15.0 to between 18.0 and 30.0, depending on location. The focus of the plan is on new development near transit stations and along wide streets, allowing the greatest as-of-right density around Grand Central Terminal and along Park Avenue. Projects that use landmarked buildings' TDRs will be required to make a contribution of the greater of 20 percent of the sale value, or a minimum contribution of $61.49 per square foot, to the Public Realm Improvement Fund. https://www1.nyc.gov/site/planning/plans/greater-east-midtown/greater-east-midtown.page?tab=7#modifications (last visited September 15, 2017).

10. **Local governments as stewards.** The *Penn Central* case confirmed the role of local governments in exercising stewardship over historic landmarks and districts. Nicholas A. Robinson, *Historic Preservation Law: The Metes & Bounds of a New Field*, 1 Pace L. Rev. 511 (1981), http://digitalcommons.pace.edu/lawfaculty/387/. It also settled the issues of facial constitutionality of preservation laws, leaving open to further litigation about how to apply preservation decisions in varied contexts. *See* Peter Byrne, *Regulatory Takings Challenges to Historic Preservation Laws After Penn Central*, 15 Fordham Envtl L. Rev. 313 (2004).

F. Subsequent Takings Jurisprudence of the U.S. Supreme Court

Following the Supreme Court's decision in *Penn Central*, the takings discussion has been reaffirmed by subsequent decisions of the Court. One such example is *Tahoe-Sierra*. While reading through the case, take note of the Court's reference to Justice O'Connor's opinion in *Palazzolo v. Rhode Island*, 533 U.S. 606 (2001).

1. The *Tahoe-Sierra* Decision

Tahoe-Sierra Preservation Council, Inc. v. Tahoe Regional Planning Agency

Supreme Court of the United States
535 U.S. 302, 122 S.Ct. 1465 (2002)

STEVENS, J. The question presented is whether a moratorium on development imposed during the process of devising a comprehensive land-use plan constitutes a *per se* taking of property requiring compensation under the Takings Clause of the United States Constitution.[1] This case actually involves two moratoria ordered by respondent Tahoe Regional Planning Agency (TRPA) to maintain the status quo while studying the impact of development on Lake Tahoe and designing a strategy for environmentally sound growth. The first, Ordinance 81-5, was effective from August 24, 1981, until August 26, 1983, whereas the second more restrictive Resolution 83-21 was in effect from August 27, 1983, until April 25, 1984. As a result of these two directives, virtually all development on a substantial portion of the property subject to TRPA's jurisdiction was prohibited for a period of 32 months. Although the question we decide relates only to that 32-month period, a brief description of the events leading up to the moratoria and a comment on the two permanent plans that TRPA adopted thereafter will clarify the narrow scope of our holding.

I

The relevant facts are undisputed. The Court of Appeals, while reversing the District Court on a question of law, accepted all of its findings of fact, and no party challenges those findings. All agree that Lake Tahoe is "uniquely beautiful," 34 F.Supp.2d 1226, 1230 (D.Nev.1999), that President Clinton was right to call it a "'national treasure that must be protected and preserved,'" *ibid.*, and that Mark Twain

1. Often referred to as the "Just Compensation Clause," the final Clause of the Fifth Amendment provides: "... nor shall private property be taken for public use without just compensation." It applies to the States as well as the Federal Government. *Chicago, B. & Q.R. Co. v. Chicago*, 166 U.S. 226, 239, 241, 17 S.Ct. 581, 41 L.Ed. 979 (1897); *Webb's Fabulous Pharmacies, Inc. v. Beckwith*, 449 U.S. 155, 160, 101 S.Ct. 446, 66 L.Ed.2d 358 (1980).

aptly described the clarity of its waters as "'not *merely* transparent, but dazzlingly, brilliantly so,'" *ibid.* (emphasis added) (quoting M. Twain, Roughing It 174–175 (1872)).

Lake Tahoe's exceptional clarity is attributed to the absence of algae that obscures the waters of most other lakes. Historically, the lack of nitrogen and phosphorous, which nourish the growth of algae, has ensured the transparency of its waters.[2] Unfortunately, the lake's pristine state has deteriorated rapidly over the past 40 years; increased land development in the Lake Tahoe Basin (Basin) has threatened the "'noble sheet of blue water'" beloved by Twain and countless others. 34 F.Supp.2d, at 1230. As the District Court found, "[d]ramatic decreases in clarity first began to be noted in the late 1950's/early 1960's, shortly after development at the lake began in earnest." *Id.,* at 1231. The lake's unsurpassed beauty, it seems, is the wellspring of its undoing.

The upsurge of development in the area has caused "increased nutrient loading of the lake largely because of the increase in impervious coverage of land in the Basin resulting from that development." *Ibid.*... Given this trend, the District Court predicted that "unless the process is stopped, the lake will lose its clarity and its trademark blue color, becoming green and opaque for eternity."[3]

Those areas in the Basin that have steeper slopes produce more runoff; therefore, they are usually considered "high hazard" lands. Moreover, certain areas near streams or wetlands known as "Stream Environment Zones" (SEZs) are especially vulnerable to the impact of development because, in their natural state, they act as filters for much of the debris that runoff carries. Because "[t]he most obvious response to this problem ... is to restrict development around the lake—especially in SEZ lands, as well as in areas already naturally prone to runoff," *id.,* at 1232, conservation efforts have focused on controlling growth in these high hazard areas.

In the 1960's, when the problems associated with the burgeoning development began to receive significant attention, jurisdiction over the Basin, which occupies 501 square miles, was shared by the States of California and Nevada, five counties, several municipalities, and the Forest Service of the Federal Government. In 1968, the legislatures of the two States adopted the Tahoe Regional Planning Compact.... The compact set goals for the protection and preservation of the lake and created TRPA as the agency assigned "to coordinate and regulate development in the Basin and to

2. According to a Senate Report: "Only two other sizable lakes in the world are of comparable quality—Crater Lake in Oregon, which is protected as part of the Crater Lake National Park, and Lake Baikal in the [former] Soviet Union. Only Lake Tahoe, however, is so readily accessible from large metropolitan centers and is so adaptable to urban development." S.Rep. No. 91-510, pp. 3–4 (1969).

3. The District Court added: "Or at least, for a very, very long time. Estimates are that, should the lake turn green, it could take over 700 years for it to return to its natural state, if that were ever possible at all." 34 F.Supp.2d, at 1231.

conserve its natural resources." *Lake Country Estates, Inc. v. Tahoe Regional Planning Agency,* 440 U.S. 391, 394, 99 S.Ct. 1171, 59 L.Ed.2d 401 (1979).

Pursuant to the compact, in 1972 TRPA adopted a Land Use Ordinance that divided the land in the Basin into seven "land capability districts," based largely on steepness but also taking into consideration other factors affecting runoff.... Unfortunately, the 1972 ordinance allowed numerous exceptions and did not significantly limit the construction of new residential housing.... The 1980 Tahoe Regional Planning Compact (Compact) redefined the structure, functions, and voting procedures of TRPA, App. 37, 94 Stat. 3235–3238; 34 F.Supp.2d, at 1233, and directed it to develop regional "environmental threshold carrying capacities"—a term that embraced "standards for air quality, water quality, soil conservation, vegetation preservation and noise." 94 Stat. 3235, 3239. The Compact provided that TRPA "shall adopt" those standards within 18 months....

During this period TRPA was also working on the development of a regional water quality plan to comply with the Clean Water Act, 33 U.S.C. § 1288 (1994 ed.). Despite the fact that TRPA performed these obligations in "good faith and to the best of its ability," 34 F.Supp.2d, at 1233, after a few months it concluded that it could not meet the deadlines in the Compact. On June 25, 1981, it therefore enacted Ordinance 81-5 imposing the first of the two moratoria on development that petitioners challenge in this proceeding. The ordinance provided that it would become effective on August 24, 1981, and remain in effect pending the adoption of the permanent plan required by the Compact. App. 159, 191.

The District Court ... construed [the ordinance] as essentially banning any construction or other activity that involved the removal of vegetation or the creation of land coverage on all SEZ lands ... It is undisputed, however, that Ordinance 81-5 prohibited the construction of any new residences on SEZ lands in either State....

Given the complexity of the task of defining "environmental threshold carrying capacities" and the division of opinion within TRPA's governing board, the District Court found that it was "unsurprising" that TRPA failed to adopt those thresholds until August 26, 1982, roughly two months after the Compact deadline. *Ibid.*... TRPA therefore adopted Resolution 83-21, "which completely suspended all project reviews and approvals, including the acceptance of new proposals," and which remained in effect until a new regional plan was adopted on April 26, 1984. Thus, Resolution 83-21 imposed an 8-month moratorium prohibiting all construction on high hazard lands in either State. In combination, Ordinance 81-5 and Resolution 83-21 effectively prohibited all construction on sensitive lands in California and on all SEZ lands in the entire Basin for 32 months, and on sensitive lands in Nevada (other than SEZ lands) for eight months. It is these two moratoria that are at issue in this case ...

II

Approximately two months after the adoption of the 1984 plan, petitioners filed parallel actions against TRPA and other defendants in federal courts in Nevada and

California that were ultimately consolidated for trial in the District of Nevada. The petitioners include the Tahoe-Sierra Preservation Council, Inc., a nonprofit membership corporation representing ... owners of both improved and unimproved parcels of real estate in the Lake Tahoe Basin.... Those individuals purchased their properties prior to the effective date of the 1980 Compact, App. 34, primarily for the purpose of constructing "at a time of their choosing" a single-family home "to serve as a permanent, retirement or vacation residence," *id.*, at 36. When they made those purchases, they did so with the understanding that such construction was authorized provided that "they complied with all reasonable requirements for building." *Ibid.*[5]

[W]e limit our discussion to the lower courts' disposition of the claims based on the 2-year moratorium (Ordinance 81-5) and the ensuing 8-month moratorium (Resolution 83-21).

The District Court began its constitutional analysis by identifying the distinction between a direct government appropriation of property without just compensation and a government regulation that imposes such a severe restriction on the owner's use of her property that it produces "nearly the same result as a direct appropriation." 34 F.Supp.2d, at 1238.... Citing our decision in *Agins v. City of Tiburon,* 447 U.S. 255, 100 S.Ct. 2138, 65 L.Ed.2d 106 (1980), it then stated that a "regulation will constitute a taking when either: (1) it does not substantially advance a legitimate state interest; or (2) it denies the owner economically viable use of her land." 34 F.Supp.2d, at 1239.... With respect to the second alternative, the court first considered whether the analysis adopted in *Penn Central Transp. Co. v. New York City,* 438 U.S. 104, 98 S.Ct. 2646, 57 L.Ed.2d 631 (1978), would lead to the conclusion that TRPA had effected a "partial taking," and then whether those actions had effected a "total taking."[10]

Emphasizing the temporary nature of the regulations, the testimony that the "average holding time of a lot in the Tahoe area between lot purchase and home construction is twenty-five years," and the failure of petitioners to offer specific evidence of harm, the District Court concluded that "consideration of the *Penn Central* factors clearly leads to the conclusion that there was no taking." 34 F.Supp.2d, at 1240....

The District Court ... found that they had been temporarily deprived of "all economically viable use of their land." *Id.*, at 1245. The court concluded that those actions therefore constituted "categorical" takings under our decision in *Lucas v. South Carolina Coastal Council,* 505 U.S. 1003, 112 S.Ct. 2886, 120 L.Ed.2d 798 (1992). It rejected TRPA's response that Ordinance 81-5 and Resolution 83-21 were "reasonable temporary planning moratoria" that should be excluded from *Lucas*' categorical approach.... [T]he

---

5. As explained *supra,* at 1471–1472, the petitioners who purchased land after the 1972 compact did so amidst a heavily regulated zoning scheme. Their property was already classified as part of land capability districts 1, 2, and 3, or SEZ land. And each land classification was subject to regulations as to the degree of artificial disturbance the land could safely sustain.

10. The *Penn Central* analysis involves "a complex of factors including the regulation's economic effect on the landowner, the extent to which the regulation interferes with reasonable investment-backed expectations, and the character of the government action." *Palazzolo v. Rhode Island,* 533 U.S. 606, 617, 121 S.Ct. 2448, 150 L.Ed.2d 592 (2001).

court concluded that TRPA's actions [effected a taking] ... partly because neither the ordinance nor the resolution, even though intended to be temporary from the beginning, contained an express termination date. 34 F.Supp.2d, at 1250–1251.[13] Accordingly, it ordered TRPA to pay damages to most petitioners for the 32-month period....

Both parties appealed. TRPA successfully challenged the District Court's takings determination, and petitioners unsuccessfully challenged the dismissal of their claims based on the 1984 and 1987 plans.... With respect to the two moratoria, the Ninth Circuit noted that petitioners had expressly disavowed an argument "that the regulations constitute a taking under the ad hoc balancing approach described in *Penn Central*" and that they did not "dispute that the restrictions imposed on their properties are appropriate means of securing the purpose set forth in the Compact."[14] ***

Contrary to the District Court, the Court of Appeals held that because the regulations had only a temporary impact on petitioners' fee interest in the properties, no categorical taking had occurred....

[T]he court read our cases involving regulatory taking claims to focus on the impact of a regulation on the parcel as a whole. In its view a "planning regulation that prevents the development of a parcel for a temporary period of time is conceptually no different than a land-use restriction that permanently denies all use on a discrete portion of property, or that permanently restricts a type of use across all of the parcel." *Id.*, at 776. In each situation, a regulation that affects only a portion of the parcel—whether limited by time, use, or space—does not deprive the owner of all economically beneficial use.[15]

---

13. Ordinance 81-5 specified that it would terminate when the regional plan became finalized. And Resolution 83-21 was limited to 90 days, but was renewed for an additional term. Nevertheless, the District Court distinguished these measures from true "temporary" moratoria because there was no fixed date for when they would terminate. 34 F.Supp.2d, at 1250–1251.

14. 216 F.3d, at 773. "Below, the district court ruled that the regulations did not constitute a taking under *Penn Central's* ad hoc approach, but that they did constitute a categorical taking under *Lucas* [*v. South Carolina Coastal Council,* 505 U.S. 1003, 112 S.Ct. 2886, 120 L.Ed.2d 798 (1992)]. *See Tahoe-Sierra Preservation Council,* 34 F.Supp.2d at 1238–1245. The defendants appealed the district court's latter holding, but the plaintiffs did not appeal the former. And even if arguments regarding the *Penn Central* test were fairly encompassed by the defendants' appeal, the plaintiffs have stated explicitly on this appeal that they do not argue that the regulations constitute a taking under the ad hoc balancing approach described in *Penn Central.*" 216 F.3d, at 773.

15. The Court of Appeals added:

"Each of these three types of regulation will have an impact on the parcel's value, because each will affect an aspect of the owner's 'use' of the property—by restricting *when* the 'use' may occur, *where* the 'use' may occur, or *how* the 'use' may occur. Prior to *Agins* [*v. City of Tiburon,* 447 U.S. 255, 100 S.Ct. 2138, 65 L.Ed.2d 106 (1980)], the Court had already rejected takings challenges to regulations eliminating all 'use' on a portion of the property, and to regulations restricting the type of 'use' across the breadth of the property. *See Penn Central,* 438 U.S. at 130–31[, 98 S.Ct. 2646] ...; *Keystone Bituminous Coal Ass'n,* 480 U.S. at 498–99[, 107 S.Ct. 1232] ...; *Village of Euclid v. Ambler Realty Co.,* 272 U.S. 365, 384, 397[, 47 S.Ct. 114, 71 L.Ed. 303] ... (1926) (75% diminution in value caused by zoning law); *see also William C. Haas & Co. v. City & County of San Francisco,* 605 F.2d 1117, 1120 (9th Cir.1979) (value reduced from $2,000,000 to $100,000). In those cases, the Court 'uniformly reject[ed] the proposition that diminution in property value, standing alone, can establish a "taking."'"

The Court of Appeals distinguished *Lucas* as applying to the " 'relatively rare' " case in which a regulation denies all productive use of an entire parcel, whereas the moratoria involve only a "temporal 'slice' " of the fee interest and a form of regulation that is widespread and well established. 216 F.3d, at 773–774.... [T]he court held that *Penn Central* was the appropriate framework for analysis. Petitioners, however, had failed to challenge the District Court's conclusion that they could not make out a taking claim under the *Penn Central* factors....

In the dissenters' opinion, the panel's holding was not faithful to this Court's decisions in *First English* and *Lucas*.... Because of the importance of the case, we granted certiorari limited to the question stated at the beginning of this opinion. 533 U.S. 948, 121 S.Ct. 2589, 150 L.Ed.2d 749 (2001). We now affirm.

III

Petitioners make only a facial attack on Ordinance 81-5 and Resolution 83-21. They contend that the mere enactment of a temporary regulation that, while in effect, denies a property owner all viable economic use of her property gives rise to an unqualified constitutional obligation to compensate her for the value of its use during that period.... Under their proposed rule, there is no need to evaluate the landowners' investment-backed expectations, the actual impact of the regulation on any individual, the importance of the public interest served by the regulation, or the reasons for imposing the temporary restriction. For petitioners, it is enough that a regulation imposes a temporary deprivation—no matter how brief—of all economically viable use to trigger a *per se* rule that a taking has occurred....

We shall first explain why our cases do not support [the petitioners] proposed categorical rule—indeed, fairly read, they implicitly reject it.... In our view the answer to the abstract question whether a temporary moratorium effects a taking is neither "yes, always" nor "no, never"; the answer depends upon the particular circumstances of the case.[16] * * * [W]e conclude that the circumstances in this case are best analyzed within the *Penn Central* framework.

IV

The text of the Fifth Amendment itself provides a basis for drawing a distinction between physical takings and regulatory takings. Its plain language requires the payment of compensation whenever the government acquires private property for a public purpose, whether the acquisition is the result of a condemnation proceeding or a physical appropriation. But the Constitution contains no comparable reference

---

Penn Central, 438 U.S. at 131[, 98 S.Ct. 2646] ...; *see also Concrete Pipe and Products, Inc. v. Construction Laborers Pension Trust,* 508 U.S. 602, 645[, 113 S.Ct. 2264, 124 L.Ed.2d 539] ... (1993). There is no plausible basis on which to distinguish a similar diminution in value that results from a temporary suspension of development." *Id.,* at 776–777.

16. Despite our clear refusal to hold that a moratorium never effects a taking, THE CHIEF JUSTICE accuses us of "allow[ing] the government to '... take private property without paying for it,' " *post,* at 1493. It may be true that under a *Penn Central* analysis petitioners' land was taken and compensation would be due. But petitioners failed to challenge the District Court's conclusion that there was no taking under *Penn Central. Supra,* at 1476, and n. 14.

to regulations that prohibit a property owner from making certain uses of her private property.[17] ... Our regulatory takings jurisprudence ... is characterized by "essentially ad hoc, factual inquiries." Penn Central, 438 U.S., at 124, 98 S.Ct. 2646, designed to allow "careful examination and weighing of all the relevant circumstances." Palazzolo, 533 U.S., at 636, 121 S. Ct. 2448 (O'CONNOR, J., concurring).

This longstanding distinction between acquisitions of property for public use, on the one hand, and regulations prohibiting private uses, on the other, makes it inappropriate to treat cases involving physical takings as controlling precedents for the evaluation of a claim that there has been a "regulatory taking,"[18] and vice versa. For the same reason that we do not ask whether a physical appropriation advances a substantial government interest or whether it deprives the owner of all economically valuable use, we do not apply our precedent from the physical takings context to regulatory takings claims. Land-use regulations are ubiquitous and most of them impact property values in some tangential way-often in completely unanticipated ways. Treating them all as *per se* takings would transform government regulation into a luxury few governments could afford. By contrast, physical appropriations are relatively rare, easily identified, and usually represent a greater affront to individual property rights.[19] "This

17. In determining whether government action affecting property is an unconstitutional deprivation of ownership rights under the Just Compensation Clause, a court must interpret the word "taken." When the government condemns or physically appropriates the property, the fact of a taking is typically obvious and undisputed. When, however, the owner contends a taking has occurred because a law or regulation imposes restrictions so severe that they are tantamount to a condemnation or appropriation, the predicate of a taking is not self-evident, and the analysis is more complex.

18. To illustrate the importance of the distinction, the Court in *Loretto,* 458 U.S., at 430, 102 S.Ct. 3164, compared two wartime takings cases, *United States v. Pewee Coal Co.,* 341 U.S. 114, 116, 71 S.Ct. 670, 95 L.Ed. 809 (1951), in which there had been an "actual taking of possession and control" of a coal mine, and *United States v. Central Eureka Mining Co.,* 357 U.S. 155, 78 S.Ct. 1097, 2 L.Ed.2d 1228 (1958), in which, "by contrast, the Court found no taking where the Government had issued a wartime order requiring nonessential gold mines to cease operations ..." 458 U.S., at 431, 102 S.Ct. 3164. *Loretto* then relied on this distinction in dismissing the argument that our discussion of the physical taking at issue in the case would affect landlord-tenant laws. "So long as these regulations do not require the landlord to suffer the physical occupation of a portion of his building by a third party, they will be analyzed under the multifactor inquiry generally applicable to nonpossessory governmental activity." *Id.,* at 440, 102 S.Ct. 3164 (citing *Penn Central*).

19. According to THE CHIEF JUSTICE's dissent, even a temporary, use-prohibiting regulation should be governed by our physical takings cases because, under *Lucas v. South Carolina Coastal Council,* 505 U.S. 1003, 1017, 112 S.Ct. 2886, 120 L.Ed.2d 798 (1992), "from the landowner's point of view," the moratorium is the functional equivalent of a forced leasehold, *post,* at 1493. Of course, from both the landowner's and the government's standpoint there are critical differences between a leasehold and a moratorium. Condemnation of a leasehold gives the government possession of the property, the right to admit and exclude others, and the right to use it for a public purpose. A regulatory taking, by contrast, does not give the government any right to use the property, nor does it dispossess the owner or affect her right to exclude others.

THE CHIEF JUSTICE stretches *Lucas'* "equivalence" language too far. For even a regulation that constitutes only a minor infringement on property may, from the landowner's perspective, be the functional equivalent of an appropriation. *Lucas* carved out a narrow exception to the rules governing regulatory takings for the "extraordinary circumstance" of a permanent deprivation of all beneficial use. The exception was only partially justified based on the "equivalence" theory cited by THE CHIEF

case does not present the 'classi[c] taking' in which the government directly appropriates private property for its own use," *Eastern Enterprises v. Apfel,* 524 U.S. 498, 522, 118 S.Ct. 2131, 141 L.Ed.2d 451 (1998); instead the interference with property rights "arises from some public program adjusting the benefits and burdens of economic life to promote the common good," *Penn Central,* 438 U.S., at 124, 98 S.Ct. 2646 ...

[The petitioners] rely principally on our decision in *Lucas v. South Carolina Coastal Council,* 505 U.S. 1003, 112 S.Ct. 2886, 120 L.Ed.2d 798 (1992)—a regulatory takings case that, nevertheless, applied a categorical rule—to argue that the *Penn Central* framework is inapplicable here....

[W]e have "generally eschewed" any set formula for determining how far is too far, choosing instead to engage in " 'essentially ad hoc, factual inquiries.' " *Lucas,* 505 U.S., at 1015, 112 S.Ct. 2886 (quoting *Penn Central,* 438 U.S., at 124, 98 S.Ct. 2646). Indeed, we still resist the temptation to adopt *per se* rules in our cases involving partial regulatory takings, preferring to examine "a number of factors" rather than a simple "mathematically precise" formula.[23] Justice Brennan's opinion for the Court in *Penn Central* did, however, make it clear that even though multiple factors are relevant in the analysis of regulatory takings claims, in such cases we must focus on "the parcel as a whole":

> " 'Taking' jurisprudence does not divide a single parcel into discrete segments and attempt to determine whether rights in a particular segment have been entirely abrogated...."

This requirement that "the aggregate must be viewed in its entirety" explains why, for example, a regulation that prohibited commercial transactions in eagle feathers, but did not bar other uses or impose any physical invasion or restraint upon them, was not a taking. *Andrus v. Allard,* 444 U.S. 51, 66, 100 S.Ct. 318, 62 L.Ed.2d 210 (1979). It also clarifies why restrictions on the use of only limited portions of the parcel, such as setback ordinances, *Gorieb v. Fox,* 274 U.S. 603, 47 S.Ct. 675, 71 L.Ed. 1228 (1927), or a requirement that coal pillars be left in place to prevent mine subsidence, *Keystone Bituminous Coal Assn. v. DeBenedictis,* 480 U.S., at 498, 107 S.Ct. 1232, were not considered regulatory takings. In each of these cases, we affirmed

---

JUSTICE's dissent. It was also justified on the theory that, in the "relatively rare situations where the government has deprived a landowner of all economically beneficial uses," it is less realistic to assume that the regulation will secure an "average reciprocity of advantage," or that government could not go on if required to pay for every such restriction. 505 U.S., at 1017–1018, 112 S.Ct. 2886. But as we explain, *infra,* at 1487–1489, these assumptions hold true in the context of a moratorium.

23. In her concurring opinion in *Palazzolo,* 533 U.S., at 633, 121 S.Ct. 2448, Justice O'CONNOR reaffirmed this approach: "Our polestar instead remains the principles set forth in *Penn Central* itself and our other cases that govern partial regulatory takings. Under these cases, interference with investment-backed expectations is one of a number of factors that a court must examine." *Ibid.* "*Penn Central* does not supply mathematically precise variables, but instead provides important guideposts that lead to the ultimate determination whether just compensation is required." *Id.,* at 634, 121 S.Ct. 2448. "The temptation to adopt what amount to *per se* rules in either direction must be resisted. The Takings Clause requires careful examination and weighing of all the relevant circumstances in this context." *Id.,* at 636, 121 S.Ct. 2448.

that "where an owner possesses a full 'bundle' of property rights, the destruction of one 'strand' of the bundle is not a taking." *Andrus,* 444 U.S., at 65–66, 100 S.Ct. 318....

In *First English,* the Court unambiguously and repeatedly characterized the issue to be decided as a "compensation question" or a "remedial question." *Id.,* at 311, 107 S.Ct. 2378 ("The disposition of the case on these grounds isolates the remedial question for our consideration").... And the Court's statement of its holding was equally unambiguous: "We merely hold that where the government's activities *have already worked a taking* of all use of property, no subsequent action by the government can relieve it of the duty to provide compensation for the period during which the taking was effective." *Id.,* at 321, 107 S.Ct. 2378 (emphasis added). In fact, *First English* expressly disavowed any ruling on the merits of the takings issue because the California courts had decided the remedial question on the assumption that a taking had been alleged. *Id.,* at 312–313, 107 S.Ct. 2378 ("We reject appellee's suggestion that ... we must independently evaluate the adequacy of the complaint and resolve the takings claim on the merits before we can reach the remedial question"). After our remand, the California courts concluded that there had not been a taking, *First English Evangelical Church of Glendale v. County of Los Angeles,* 210 Cal.App.3d 1353, 258 Cal.Rptr. 893 (1989), and we declined review of that decision, 493 U.S. 1056, 110 S.Ct. 866, 107 L.Ed.2d 950 (1990).

To the extent that the Court in *First English* referenced the antecedent takings question, we identified two reasons why a regulation temporarily denying an owner all use of her property might not constitute a taking. First, we recognized that "the county might avoid the conclusion that a compensable taking had occurred by establishing that the denial of all use was insulated as a part of the State's authority to enact safety regulations." 482 U.S., at 313, 107 S.Ct. 2378. Second, we limited our holding "to the facts presented" and recognized "the quite different questions that would arise in the case of normal delays in obtaining building permits, changes in zoning ordinances, variances, and the like which [were] not before us." *Id.,* at 321, 107 S.Ct. 2378. Thus, our decision in *First English* surely did not approve, and implicitly rejected, the categorical submission that petitioners are now advocating.

Similarly, our decision in *Lucas* is not dispositive of the question presented. Although *Lucas* endorsed and applied a categorical rule, it was not the one that petitioners propose. Lucas purchased two residential lots in 1988 for $975,000. These lots were rendered "valueless" by a statute enacted two years later. The trial court found that a taking had occurred and ordered compensation of $1,232,387.50, representing the value of the fee simple estate, plus interest. As the statute read at the time of the trial, it effected a taking that "was unconditional and permanent." 505 U.S., at 1012, 112 S.Ct. 2886. While the State's appeal was pending, the statute was amended to authorize exceptions that might have allowed Lucas to obtain a building permit. Despite the fact that the amendment gave the State Supreme Court the opportunity to dispose of the appeal on ripeness grounds, it resolved the merits of the permanent takings claim and reversed. Since "Lucas had no reason to proceed on a 'temporary taking' theory at trial," we decided the case on the permanent taking theory that both the trial court and the State Supreme Court had addressed. *Ibid.*

The categorical rule that we applied in *Lucas* states that compensation is required when a regulation deprives an owner of "*all* economically beneficial uses" of his land. *Id.*, at 1019, 112 S.Ct. 2886. Under that rule, a statute that "wholly eliminated the value" of Lucas' fee simple title clearly qualified as a taking. But our holding was limited to "the extraordinary circumstance when *no* productive or economically beneficial use of land is permitted." *Id.*, at 1017, 112 S.Ct. 2886. The emphasis on the word "no" in the text of the opinion was, in effect, reiterated in a footnote explaining that the categorical rule would not apply if the diminution in value were 95% instead of 100%. *Id.*, at 1019, n. 8, 112 S.Ct. 2886.[24] Anything less than a "complete elimination of value," or a "total loss," the Court acknowledged, would require the kind of analysis applied in *Penn Central. Lucas,* 505 U.S., at 1019–1020, n. 8, 112 S.Ct. 2886.[25]

Certainly, our holding that the permanent "obliteration of the value" of a fee simple estate constitutes a categorical taking does not answer the question whether a regulation prohibiting any economic use of land for a 32-month period has the same legal effect. Petitioners seek to bring this case under the rule announced in *Lucas* by arguing that we can effectively sever a 32-month segment from the remainder of each landowner's fee simple estate, and then ask whether that segment has been taken in its entirety by the moratoria. Of course, defining the property interest taken in terms of the very regulation being challenged is circular. With property so divided, every delay would become a total ban; the moratorium and the normal permit process alike would constitute categorical takings. Petitioners' "conceptual severance" argument is unavailing because it ignores *Penn Central's* admonition that in regulatory takings cases we must focus on "the parcel as a whole." 438 U.S., at 130–131, 98 S.Ct. 2646. We have consistently rejected such an approach to the "denominator" question.... Thus, the District Court erred when it disaggregated petitioners' property into temporal segments corresponding to the regulations at issue and then analyzed whether petitioners were deprived of all economically viable use during each period. 34 F.Supp.2d, at 1242–1245. The starting point for the court's analysis should have been to ask whether there was a total taking of the entire parcel; if not, then *Penn Central* was the proper framework.[26]

An interest in real property is defined by the metes and bounds that describe its geographic dimensions and the term of years that describes the temporal aspect of the owner's interest. *See* Restatement of Property §§ 7–9 (1936). Both dimensions must

24. Justice KENNEDY concurred in the judgment on the basis of the regulation's impact on "reasonable, investment-backed expectations." 505 U.S., at 1034, 112 S.Ct. 2886.

25. It is worth noting that *Lucas* underscores the difference between physical and regulatory takings. See *supra,* at 1478–1480. For under our physical takings cases it would be irrelevant whether a property owner maintained 5% of the value of her property so long as there was a physical appropriation of any of the parcel.

26. THE CHIEF JUSTICE's dissent makes the same mistake by carving out a 6-year interest in the property, rather than considering the parcel as a whole, and treating the regulations covering that segment as analogous to a total taking under *Lucas, post,* at 1494.

be considered if the interest is to be viewed in its entirety. Hence, a permanent deprivation of the owner's use of the entire area is a taking of "the parcel as a whole," whereas a temporary restriction that merely causes a diminution in value is not. Logically, a fee simple estate cannot be rendered valueless by a temporary prohibition on economic use, because the property will recover value as soon as the prohibition is lifted....

Neither *Lucas,* nor *First English,* nor any of our other regulatory takings cases compels us to accept petitioners' categorical submission. In fact, these cases make clear that the categorical rule in *Lucas* was carved out for the "extraordinary case" in which a regulation permanently deprives property of all value; the default rule remains that, in the regulatory taking context, we require a more fact specific inquiry. Nevertheless, we will consider whether the interest in protecting individual property owners from bearing public burdens "which, in all fairness and justice, should be borne by the public as a whole," *Armstrong v. United States,* 364 U.S., at 49, 80 S.Ct. 1563, justifies creating a new rule for these circumstances.[27]

V

Considerations of "fairness and justice" arguably could support the conclusion that TRPA's moratoria were takings of petitioners' property based on any of seven different theories. First, even though we have not previously done so, we might now announce a categorical rule that, in the interest of fairness and justice, compensation is required whenever government temporarily deprives an owner of all economically viable use of her property. Second, we could craft a narrower rule that would cover all temporary land-use restrictions except those "normal delays in obtaining building permits, changes in zoning ordinances, variances, and the like" which were put to one side in our opinion in *First English,* 482 U.S., at 321, 107 S.Ct. 2378. Third, we could adopt a rule like the one suggested by an *amicus* supporting petitioners that would "allow a short fixed period for deliberations to take place without compensation—say maximum one year—afterwhich the just compensation requirements" would "kick in."[28] Fourth, with the benefit of hindsight, we might characterize the successive actions of TRPA as a "series of rolling moratoria" that were the functional equivalent of a permanent taking.[29] Fifth, were it not for the findings of the District Court that TRPA acted diligently and in good faith, we might have concluded that the agency was stalling in order to avoid promulgating the environmental threshold carrying capacities and regional plan mandated by the 1980 Compact.... Sixth, apart from the District Court's finding that TRPA's actions represented a proportional re-

27. *Armstrong,* like *Lucas,* was a case that involved the "total destruction by the Government of all value" in a specific property interest. 364 U.S., at 48–49, 80 S.Ct. 1563. It is nevertheless perfectly clear that Justice Black's oft-quoted comment about the underlying purpose of the guarantee that private property shall not be taken for a public use without just compensation applies to partial takings as well as total takings.

28. Brief for the Institute for Justice as *Amicus Curiae* 30. Although *amicus* describes the 1-year cutoff proposal as the "better approach by far," *ibid.,* its primary argument is that *Penn Central* should be overruled, *id.,* at 20 ("*All* partial takings by way of land use restriction should be subject to the same prima facie rules for compensation as a physical occupation for a limited period of time").

29. Brief for Petitioners 44. See also Pet. for Cert. i.

sponse to a serious risk of harm to the lake, petitioners might have argued that the moratoria did not substantially advance a legitimate state interest, *see Agins* and *Monterey*. Finally, if petitioners had challenged the application of the moratoria to their individual parcels, instead of making a facial challenge, some of them might have prevailed under a *Penn Central* analysis.

As the case comes to us, however, none of the last four theories is available. The "rolling moratoria" theory was presented in the petition for certiorari, but our order granting review did not encompass that issue, 533 U.S. 948, 121 S.Ct. 2589, 150 L.Ed.2d 749 (2001); the case was tried in the District Court and reviewed in the Court of Appeals on the theory that each of the two moratoria was a separate taking, one for a 2-year period and the other for an 8-month period. 216 F.3d, at 769. And, as we have already noted, recovery on either a bad faith theory or a theory that the state interests were insubstantial is foreclosed by the District Court's unchallenged findings of fact. Recovery under a *Penn Central* analysis is also foreclosed both because petitioners expressly disavowed that theory, and because they did not appeal from the District Court's conclusion that the evidence would not support it. Nonetheless, each of the three *per se* theories is fairly encompassed within the question that we decided to answer.

With respect to these theories, the ultimate constitutional question is whether the concepts of "fairness and justice" that underlie the Takings Clause will be better served by one of these categorical rules or by a *Penn Central* inquiry into all of the relevant circumstances in particular cases. From that perspective, the extreme categorical rule that any deprivation of all economic use, no matter how brief, constitutes a compensable taking surely cannot be sustained. Petitioners' broad submission would apply to numerous "normal delays in obtaining building permits, changes in zoning ordinances, variances, and the like," 482 U.S., at 321, 107 S.Ct. 2378. Such a rule would undoubtedly require changes in numerous practices that have long been considered permissible exercises of the police power. A rule that required compensation for every delay in the use of property would render routine government processes prohibitively expensive or encourage hasty decisionmaking. Such an important change in the law should be the product of legislative rulemaking rather than adjudication.[30]

More importantly ... we are persuaded that the better approach to claims that a regulation has effected a temporary taking "requires careful examination and weighing of all the relevant circumstances." ...

A narrower rule that excluded the normal delays associated with processing permits, or that covered only delays of more than a year, would certainly have a less severe

---

30. In addition, we recognize the anomaly that would be created if we were to apply *Penn Central* when a landowner is permanently deprived of 95% of the use of her property, *Lucas,* 505 U.S., at 1019, n. 8, 112 S.Ct. 2886, and yet find a *per se* taking anytime the same property owner is deprived of all use for only five days. Such a scheme would present an odd inversion of Justice Holmes' adage: "A limit in time, to tide over a passing trouble, well may justify a law that could not be upheld as a permanent change." *Block v. Hirsh,* 256 U.S. 135, 157, 41 S.Ct. 458, 65 L.Ed. 865 (1921).

impact on prevailing practices, but it would still impose serious financial constraints on the planning process.[31] Unlike the "extraordinary circumstance" in which the government deprives a property owner of all economic use, *Lucas*, 505 U.S., at 1017, 112 S.Ct. 2886, moratoria like Ordinance 81-5 and Resolution 83-21 are used widely among land-use planners to preserve the status quo while formulating a more permanent development strategy.[32] In fact, the consensus in the planning community appears to be that moratoria, or "interim development controls" as they are often called, are an essential tool of successful development.[33] Yet even the weak version of petitioners' categorical rule would treat these interim measures as takings regardless

---

31. Petitioners fail to offer a persuasive explanation for why moratoria should be treated differently from ordinary permit delays. They contend that a permit applicant need only comply with certain specific requirements in order to receive one and can expect to develop at the end of the process, whereas there is nothing the landowner subject to a moratorium can do but wait, with no guarantee that a permit will be granted at the end of the process. Brief for Petitioners 28. Setting aside the obvious problem with basing the distinction on a course of events we can only know after the fact-in the context of a facial challenge-petitioners' argument breaks down under closer examination because there is no guarantee that a permit will be granted, or that a decision will be made within a year. See, *e.g., Dufau v. United States,* 22 Cl.Ct. 156 (1990) (holding that 16-month delay in granting a permit did not constitute a temporary taking). Moreover, under petitioners' modified categorical rule, there would be no *per se* taking if TRPA simply delayed action on all permits pending a regional plan. Fairness and justice do not require that TRPA be penalized for achieving the same result, but with full disclosure.

32. *See, e.g., Santa Fe Village Venture v. Albuquerque,* 914 F.Supp. 478, 483 (D.N.M.1995) (30-month moratorium on development of lands within the Petroglyph National Monument was not a taking); *Williams v. Central,* 907 P.2d 701, 703–706 (Colo.App.1995) (10-month moratorium on development in gaming district while studying city's ability to absorb growth was not a compensable taking); *Woodbury Place Partners v. Woodbury,* 492 N.W.2d 258 (Minn.App.1992) (moratorium pending review of plan for land adjacent to interstate highway was not a taking even though it deprived property owner of all economically viable use of its property for two years); *Zilber v. Town of Moraga,* 692 F.Supp. 1195 (N.D.Cal.1988) (18-month development moratorium during completion of a comprehensive scheme for open space did not require compensation). *See also* Wayman, Leaders Consider Options for Town Growth, Charlotte Observer, Feb. 3, 2002, p. 15M (describing 10-month building moratorium imposed "to give town leaders time to plan for development"); Wallman, City May Put Reins on Beach Projects, Sun-Sentinel, May 16, 2000, p. 1B (2-year building moratorium on beachfront property in Fort Lauderdale pending new height, width, and dispersal regulations); Foderaro, In Suburbs, They're Cracking Down on the Joneses, N.Y. Times, Mar. 19, 2001, p. A1 (describing moratorium imposed in Eastchester, New York, during a review of the town's zoning code to address the problem of oversized homes); Dawson, Commissioners recommend Aboite construction ban be lifted, Fort Wayne News Sentinel, May 4, 2001, p. 1A (3-year moratorium to allow improvements in the water and sewage treatment systems).

33. *See* J. Juergensmeyer & T. Roberts, Land Use Planning and Control Law §§5.28(G) and 9.6 (1998); Garvin & Leitner, Drafting Interim Development Ordinances: Creating Time to Plan, 48 Land Use Law & Zoning Digest 3 (June 1996) ("With the planning so protected, there is no need for hasty adoption of permanent controls in order to avoid the establishment of nonconforming uses, or to respond in an ad hoc fashion to specific problems. Instead, the planning and implementation process may be permitted to run its full and natural course with widespread citizen input and involvement, public debate, and full consideration of all issues and points of view"); Freilich, Interim Development Controls: Essential Tools for Implementing Flexible Planning and Zoning, 49 J. Urb. L. 65 (1971).

of the good faith of the planners, the reasonable expectations of the landowners, or the actual impact of the moratorium on property values.[34]

The interest in facilitating informed decisionmaking by regulatory agencies counsels against adopting a *per se* rule that would impose such severe costs on their deliberations. Otherwise, the financial constraints of compensating property owners during a moratorium may force officials to rush through the planning process or to abandon the practice altogether. To the extent that communities are forced to abandon using moratoria, landowners will have incentives to develop their property quickly before a comprehensive plan can be enacted, thereby fostering inefficient and ill-conceived growth. A finding in the 1980 Compact itself, which presumably was endorsed by all three legislative bodies that participated in its enactment, attests to the importance of that concern....

As Justice Kennedy explained in his opinion for the Court in *Palazzolo,* it is the interest in informed decisionmaking that underlies our decisions imposing a strict ripeness requirement on landowners asserting regulatory takings claims:

> "These cases stand for the important principle that a landowner may not establish a taking before a land-use authority has the opportunity, using its own reasonable procedures, to decide and explain the reach of a challenged regulation. Under our ripeness rules a takings claim based on a law or regulation which is alleged to go too far in burdening property depends upon the landowner's first having followed reasonable and necessary steps to allow regulatory agencies to exercise their full discretion in considering development plans for the property, including the opportunity to grant any variances or waivers allowed by law. As a general rule, until these ordinary processes have been followed the extent of the restriction on property is not known and a regulatory taking has not yet been established. *See Suitum* [*v. Tahoe Regional Planning Agency,* 520 U.S. 725, 736, and n. 10, 117 S.Ct. 1659, 137 L.Ed.2d 980 (1997)] (noting difficulty of demonstrating that 'mere enactment' of regulations restricting land use effects a taking)." 533 U.S., at 620–621, 121 S.Ct. 2448.

We would create a perverse system of incentives were we to hold that landowners must wait for a takings claim to ripen so that planners can make well-reasoned decisions while, at the same time, holding that those planners must compensate landowners for the delay.

Indeed, the interest in protecting the decisional process is even stronger when an agency is developing a regional plan than when it is considering a permit for a single

34. THE CHIEF JUSTICE offers another alternative, suggesting that delays of six years or more should be treated as *per se* takings. However, his dissent offers no explanation for why 6 years should be the cutoff point rather than 10 days, 10 months, or 10 years. It is worth emphasizing that we do not reject a categorical rule in this case because a 32-month moratorium is just not that harsh. Instead, we reject a categorical rule because we conclude that the *Penn Central* framework adequately directs the inquiry to the proper considerations—only one of which is the length of the delay.

parcel. In the proceedings involving the Lake Tahoe Basin, for example, the moratoria enabled TRPA to obtain the benefit of comments and criticisms from interested parties, such as the petitioners, during its deliberations.[35] Since a categorical rule tied to the length of deliberations would likely create added pressure on decisionmakers to reach a quick resolution of land-use questions, it would only serve to disadvantage those landowners and interest groups who are not as organized or familiar with the planning process. Moreover, with a temporary ban on development there is a lesser risk that individual landowners will be "singled out" to bear a special burden that should be shared by the public as a whole. *Nollan v. California Coastal Comm'n,* 483 U.S. 825, 835, 107 S.Ct. 3141, 97 L.Ed.2d 677 (1987). At least with a moratorium there is a clear "reciprocity of advantage," *Mahon,* 260 U.S., at 415, 43 S.Ct. 158, because it protects the interests of all affected landowners against immediate construction that might be inconsistent with the provisions of the plan that is ultimately adopted.... In fact, there is reason to believe property values often will continue to increase despite a moratorium.... Since in some cases a 1-year moratorium may not impose a burden at all, we should not adopt a rule that assumes moratoria always force individuals to bear a special burden that should be shared by the public as a whole.

It may well be true that any moratorium that lasts for more than one year should be viewed with special skepticism. But given the fact that the District Court found that the 32 months required by TRPA to formulate the 1984 Regional Plan was not unreasonable, we could not possibly conclude that every delay of over one year is constitutionally unacceptable.[36] Formulating a general rule of this kind is a suitable task for state legislatures.[37] In our view, the duration of the restriction is one of the important factors that a court must consider in the appraisal of a regulatory takings claim, but with respect to that factor as with respect to other factors, the "temptation

35. Petitioner Preservation Council, "through its authorized representatives, actively participated in the entire TRPA regional planning process leading to the adoption of the 1984 Regional Plan at issue in this action, and attended and expressed its views and concerns, orally and in writing, at each public hearing held by the Defendant TRPA in connection with the consideration of the 1984 Regional Plan at issue herein, as well as in connection with the adoption of Ordinance 81-5 and the Revised 1987 Regional Plan addressed herein." App. 24.

36. We note that the temporary restriction that was ultimately upheld in the *First English* case lasted for more than six years before it was replaced by a permanent regulation. *First English Evangelical Lutheran Church of Glendale v. County of Los Angeles,* 210 Cal.App.3d 1353, 258 Cal.Rptr. 893 (1989).

37. Several States already have statutes authorizing interim zoning ordinances with specific time limits. *See* Cal. Govt. Code Ann. §65858 (West Supp.2002) (authorizing interim ordinance of up to two years); Colo. Rev. Stat. §30-28-121 (2001) (six months); Ky. Rev. Stat. Ann. §100.201 (2001) (one year); Mich. Comp. Laws Ann. §125.215 (West 2001) (three years); Minn. Stat. §394.34 (2000) (two years); N.H. Rev. Stat. Ann. §674:23 (West 2001) (one year); Ore. Rev. Stat. Ann. §197.520 (1997) (10 months); S.D. Codified Laws §11-2-10 (2001) (two years); Utah Code Ann. §17-27-404 (1995) (18 months); Wash. Rev. Code §35.63.200 (2001); Wis. Stat. §62.23(7)(d) (2001) (two years). Other States, although without specific statutory authority, have recognized that reasonable interim zoning ordinances may be enacted. *See, e.g., S.E.W. Friel v. Triangle Oil Co.,* 76 Md.App. 96, 543 A.2d 863 (1988); *New Jersey Shore Builders Assn. v. Dover Twp. Comm.,* 191 N.J. Super. 627, 468 A.2d 742 (1983); *SCA Chemical Waste Servs., Inc. v. Konigsberg,* 636 S.W.2d 430 (Tenn.1982); *Sturges v. Chilmark,* 380 Mass. 246, 402 N.E.2d 1346 (1980); *Lebanon v. Woods,* 153 Conn. 182, 215 A.2d 112 (1965).

to adopt what amount to *per se* rules in either direction must be resisted." *Palazzolo,* 533 U.S., at 636, 121 S.Ct. 2448 (O'CONNOR, J., concurring). There may be moratoria that last longer than one year which interfere with reasonable investment-backed expectations, but as the District Court's opinion illustrates, petitioners' proposed rule is simply "too blunt an instrument" for identifying those cases. *Id.,* at 628, 121 S.Ct. 2448. We conclude, therefore, that the interest in "fairness and justice" will be best served by relying on the familiar *Penn Central* approach when deciding cases like this, rather than by attempting to craft a new categorical rule.

Accordingly, the judgment of the Court of Appeals is affirmed ...

Chief Justice REHNQUIST, with whom Justice SCALIA and Justice THOMAS join, dissenting.

For over half a decade petitioners were prohibited from building homes, or any other structures, on their land. Because the Takings Clause requires the government to pay compensation when it deprives owners of all economically viable use of their land, see *Lucas v. South Carolina Coastal Council,* 505 U.S. 1003, 112 S.Ct. 2886, 120 L.Ed.2d 798 (1992), and because a ban on all development lasting almost six years does not resemble any traditional land-use planning device, I dissent.

I

"A court cannot determine whether a regulation has gone 'too far' unless it knows how far the regulation goes." *MacDonald, Sommer & Frates v. Yolo County,* 477 U.S. 340, 348, 106 S.Ct. 2561, 91 L.Ed.2d 285 (1986) (citing *Pennsylvania Coal Co. v. Mahon,* 260 U.S. 393, 415, 43 S.Ct. 158, 67 L.Ed. 322 (1922)).[1] In failing to undertake this inquiry, the Court ignores much of the impact of respondent's conduct on petitioners. Instead, it relies on the flawed determination of the Court of Appeals that the relevant time period lasted only from August 1981 until April 1984. *Ante,* at 1473, 1474.... [However], [a]fter the adoption of the 1984 Plan, petitioners still could make no use of their land.

The Court of Appeals disregarded this post-April 1984 deprivation on the ground that respondent did not "cause" it. In a 42 U.S.C. § 1983 action, "the plaintiff must demonstrate that the defendant's conduct was the actionable cause of the claimed

1. We are not bound by the Court of Appeals' determination that petitioners' claim under 42 U.S.C § 1983 (1994 ed., Supp. V) permitted only challenges to Ordinance 81-5 and Regulation 83-21. Petitioners sought certiorari on the Court of Appeals' ruling that respondent Tahoe Regional Planning Agency (hereinafter respondent) did not cause petitioners' injury from 1984 to 1987. Pet. for Cert. 27–30. We did not grant certiorari on any of the petition's specific questions presented, but formulated the following question: "Whether the Court of Appeals properly determined that a temporary moratorium on land development does not constitute a taking of property requiring compensation under the Takings Clause of the United States Constitution?" 533 U.S. 948, 949, 121 S.Ct. 2589, 150 L.Ed.2d 749 (2001). This Court's Rule 14(1)(a) provides that a "question presented is deemed to comprise every subsidiary question fairly included therein." The question of how long the moratorium on land development lasted is necessarily subsumed within the question whether the moratorium constituted a taking. Petitioners did not assume otherwise. Their brief on the merits argues that respondent "effectively blocked all construction for the past two decades." Brief for Petitioners 7.

injury." 216 F.3d 764, 783 (C.A.9 2000).... The causation question is not limited to whether the 1984 Plan caused petitioners' injury; the question is whether respondent caused petitioners' injury.

We have never addressed the § 1983 causation requirement in the context of a regulatory takings claim, though language in *Penn Central Transp. Co. v. New York City*, 438 U.S. 104, 98 S.Ct. 2646, 57 L.Ed.2d 631 (1978), suggests that ordinary principles of proximate cause govern the causation inquiry for takings claims. *Id.*, at 124, 98 S.Ct. 2646. The causation standard does not require much elaboration in this case, because respondent was undoubtedly the "moving force" behind petitioners' inability to build on their land from August 1984 through 1987. *Monell v. New York City Dept. of Social Servs.*, 436 U.S. 658, 694, 98 S.Ct. 2018, 56 L.Ed.2d 611 (1978)....

Respondent is surely responsible for its own regulations, and it is also responsible for the Compact as it is the governmental agency charged with administering the Compact. Compact, Art. I (c), 94 Stat 3234. It follows that respondent was the "moving force" behind petitioners' inability to develop their land from April 1984 through the enactment of the 1987 plan. Without the environmental thresholds established by the Compact and Resolution 82-11, the 1984 Plan would have gone into effect and petitioners would have been able to build single-family residences. And it was certainly foreseeable that development projects exceeding the environmental thresholds would be prohibited; indeed, that was the very purpose of enacting the thresholds.

Because respondent caused petitioners' inability to use their land from 1981 through 1987, that is the appropriate period of time from which to consider their takings claim.

II

I now turn to determining whether a ban on all economic development lasting almost six years is a taking. *Lucas* reaffirmed our "frequently expressed" view that "when the owner of real property has been called upon to sacrifice *all* economically beneficial uses in the name of the common good, that is, to leave his property economically idle, he has suffered a taking." 505 U.S., at 1019, 112 S.Ct. 2886. The Court ... does not dispute that petitioners were forced to leave their land economically idle during this period.... [b]ut the Court refuses to apply *Lucas* on the ground that the deprivation was "temporary."

Neither the Takings Clause nor our case law supports such a distinction. For one thing, a distinction between "temporary" and "permanent" prohibitions is tenuous. The "temporary" prohibition in this case that the Court finds is not a taking lasted almost six years.[2] The "permanent" prohibition that the Court held to be a taking in *Lucas* lasted less than two years.... The "permanent" prohibition in *Lucas* lasted less than two years because the law, as it often does, changed. The South Carolina Legislature in 1990 decided to amend the 1988 Beachfront Management Act to allow the issuance of " 'special permits' for the construction or reconstruction of habitable structures seaward of the baseline." *Id.*, at 1011–1012, 112 S.Ct. 2886. Land-use reg-

2. Even under the Court's mistaken view that the ban on development lasted only 32 months, the ban in this case exceeded the ban in *Lucas*.

ulations are not irrevocable. And the government can even abandon condemned land.... Under the Court's decision today, the takings question turns entirely on the initial label given a regulation, a label that is often without much meaning. There is every incentive for government to simply label any prohibition on development "temporary," or to fix a set number of years. As in this case, this initial designation does not preclude the government from repeatedly extending the "temporary" prohibition into a long-term ban on all development. The Court now holds that such a designation by the government is conclusive even though in fact the moratorium greatly exceeds the time initially specified. Apparently, the Court would not view even a 10-year moratorium as a taking under *Lucas* because the moratorium is not "permanent." ...

More fundamentally, even if a practical distinction between temporary and permanent deprivations were plausible, to treat the two differently in terms of takings law would be at odds with the justification for the *Lucas* rule. The *Lucas* rule is derived from the fact that a "total deprivation of beneficial use is, from the landowner's point of view, the equivalent of a physical appropriation." 505 U.S., at 1017, 112 S.Ct. 2886. The regulation in *Lucas* was the "practical equivalence" of a long-term physical appropriation, *i.e.,* a condemnation, so the Fifth Amendment required compensation. The "practical equivalence," from the landowner's point of view, of a "temporary" ban on all economic use is a forced leasehold. For example, assume the following situation: Respondent is contemplating the creation of a National Park around Lake Tahoe to preserve its scenic beauty. Respondent decides to take a 6-year leasehold over petitioners' property, during which any human activity on the land would be prohibited, in order to prevent any further destruction to the area while it was deciding whether to request that the area be designated a National Park.

Surely that leasehold would require compensation. In a series of World War II-era cases in which the Government had condemned leasehold interests in order to support the war effort, the Government conceded that it was required to pay compensation for the leasehold interest.[3] *See United States v. Petty Motor Co.,* 327 U.S. 372, 66 S.Ct. 596, 90 L.Ed. 729 (1946); *United States v. General Motors Corp.,* 323 U.S. 373, 376, 65 S.Ct. 357, 89 L.Ed. 311 (1945). From petitioners' standpoint, what happened in this case is no different than if the government had taken a 6-year lease of their property. The Court ignores this "practical equivalence" between respondent's deprivation and the deprivation resulting from a leasehold. In so doing, the Court allows the government to "do by regulation what it cannot do through eminent domain—i.e., take private property without paying for it." 228 F.3d 998, 999 (C.A.9 2000) (Kozinski, J., dissenting from denial of rehearing en banc).

---

3. There was no dispute that just compensation was required in those cases. The disagreement involved how to calculate that compensation. In *United States v. General Motors Corp.,* 323 U.S. 373, 65 S.Ct. 357, 89 L.Ed. 311 (1945), for example, the issues before the Court were how to value the leasehold interest (*i.e.,* whether the "long-term rental value [should be] the sole measure of the value of such short-term occupancy," *id.,* at 380, 65 S.Ct. 357), whether the Government had to pay for the respondent's removal of personal property from the condemned warehouse, and whether the Government had to pay for the reduction in value of the respondent's equipment and fixtures left in the warehouse. *Id.,* at 380–381, 65 S.Ct. 357.

Instead of acknowledging the "practical equivalence" of this case and a condemned leasehold, the Court analogizes to other areas of takings law in which we have distinguished between regulations and physical appropriations, *see ante,* at 1478–1479. But whatever basis there is for such distinctions in those contexts does not apply when a regulation deprives a landowner of all economically beneficial use of his land. In addition to the "practical equivalence" from the landowner's perspective of such a regulation and a physical appropriation, we have held that a regulation denying all productive use of land does not implicate the traditional justification for differentiating between regulations and physical appropriations. In "the extraordinary circumstance when *no* productive or economically beneficial use of land is permitted," it is less likely that "the legislature is simply 'adjusting the benefits and burdens of economic life'... in a manner that secures an 'average reciprocity of advantage' to everyone concerned," *Lucas, supra,* at 1017–1018, 112 S.Ct. 2886 (quoting *Penn Central Transp. Co. v. New York City,* 438 U.S., at 124, 98 S.Ct. 2646, and *Pennsylvania Coal Co. v. Mahon,* 260 U.S., at 415, 43 S.Ct. 158), and more likely that the property "is being pressed into some form of public service under the guise of mitigating serious public harm," *Lucas, supra,* at 1018, 112 S.Ct. 2886.

The Court also reads *Lucas* as being fundamentally concerned with value, *ante,* at 1482–1484, rather than with the denial of "all economically beneficial or productive use of land," 505 U.S., at 1015, 112 S.Ct. 2886. But *Lucas* repeatedly discusses its holding as applying where "*no* productive or economically beneficial use of land is permitted." *Id.,* at 1017.... Moreover, the Court's position that value is the *sine qua non* of the *Lucas* rule proves too much. Surely, the land at issue in *Lucas* retained some market value based on the contingency, which soon came to fruition (see *supra,* at 1492), that the development ban would be amended.

Lucas is implicated when the government deprives a landowner of "all economically beneficial or productive use of land." 505 U.S., at 1015, 112 S.Ct. 2886. The District Court found, and the Court agrees, that the moratorium "temporarily" deprived petitioners of "'all economically viable use of their land.'" *Ante,* at 1475. Because the rationale for the *Lucas* rule applies just as strongly in this case, the "temporary" denial of all viable use of land for six years is a taking.

III

The Court worries that applying *Lucas* here compels finding that an array of traditional, short-term, land-use planning devices are takings. *Ante,* at 1485, 1486–1487. But since the beginning of our regulatory takings jurisprudence, we have recognized that property rights "are enjoyed under an implied limitation." *Mahon, supra,* at 413, 43 S.Ct. 158. Thus, in *Lucas,* after holding that the regulation prohibiting all economically beneficial use of the coastal land came within our categorical takings rule, we nonetheless inquired into whether such a result "inhere[d] in the title itself, in the restrictions that background principles of the State's law of property and nuisance already place upon land ownership." 505 U.S., at 1029, 112 S.Ct. 2886. Because the regulation at issue in *Lucas* purported to be permanent, or at least long term, we concluded that the only implied limitation of state property law that could achieve a similar long-term deprivation of all economic use would be something "achieved in the courts—by adjacent landowners (or other uniquely affected persons) under the State's law of private nuisance, or by the State under its complementary power to abate nuisances that affect the public generally, or otherwise." *Ibid.*

When a regulation merely delays a final land-use decision, we have recognized that there are other background principles of state property law that prevent the delay from being deemed a taking. We thus noted in *First English* that our discussion of temporary takings did not apply "in the case of normal delays in obtaining building permits, changes in zoning ordinances, variances, and the like." 482 U.S., at 321, 107 S.Ct. 2378. We reiterated this last Term: "The right to improve property, of course, is subject to the reasonable exercise of state authority, including the enforcement of valid zoning and land-use restrictions." *Palazzolo v. Rhode Island,* 533 U.S. 606, 627, 121 S.Ct. 2448, 150 L.Ed.2d 592 (2001).... Thus, the short-term delays attendant to zoning and permit regimes are a longstanding feature of state property law and part of a landowner's reasonable investment-backed expectations ...

But a moratorium prohibiting all economic use for a period of six years is not one of the longstanding, implied limitations of state property law.[4] Moratoria are "interim controls on the use of land that seek to maintain the status quo with respect to land development in an area by either 'freezing' existing land uses or by allowing the issuance of building permits for only certain land uses that would not be inconsistent with a contemplated zoning plan or zoning change." 1 E. Ziegler, Rathkopf's The Law of Zoning and Planning § 13:3, p. 13-6 (4th ed.2001). Typical moratoria thus prohibit only certain categories of development, such as fast-food restaurants, ... or adult businesses ... or all commercial development, ... Such moratoria do not implicate *Lucas* because they do not deprive landowners of all economically beneficial use of their land. As for moratoria that prohibit all development, these do not have the lineage of permit and zoning requirements and thus it is less certain that property is acquired under the "implied limitation" of a moratorium prohibiting all development. Moreover, unlike a permit system in which it is expected that a project will be approved so long as certain conditions are satisfied, a moratorium that prohibits all uses is by definition contemplating a new land-use plan that would prohibit all uses.

But this case does not require us to decide as a categorical matter whether moratoria prohibiting all economic use are an implied limitation of state property law, because the duration of this "moratorium" far exceeds that of ordinary moratoria. As the

---

4. Six years is not a "cutoff point," *ante,* at 1487, n. 34; it is the length involved in this case. And the "explanation" for the conclusion that there is a taking in this case is the fact that a 6-year moratorium far exceeds any moratorium authorized under background principles of state property law. *See infra,* 1495, 1496. This case does not require us to undertake a more exacting study of state property law and discern exactly how long a moratorium must last before it no longer can be considered an implied limitation of property ownership (assuming, that is, that a moratorium on all development is a background principle of state property law, *see infra,* this page).

Court recognizes, *ante,* at 1489, n. 37, state statutes authorizing the issuance of moratoria often limit the moratoria's duration....

Resolution 83-21 reflected this understanding of the limited duration of moratoria in initially limiting the moratorium in this case to 90 days. But what resulted—a "moratorium" lasting nearly six years—bears no resemblance to the short-term nature of traditional moratoria as understood from these background examples of state property law.

Because the prohibition on development of nearly six years in this case cannot be said to resemble any "implied limitation" of state property law, it is a taking that requires compensation.

* * *

Lake Tahoe is a national treasure, and I do not doubt that respondent's efforts at preventing further degradation of the lake were made in good faith in furtherance of the public interest. But, as is the case with most governmental action that furthers the public interest, the Constitution requires that the costs and burdens be borne by the public at large, not by a few targeted citizens. Justice Holmes' admonition of 80 years ago again rings true: "We are in danger of forgetting that a strong public desire to improve the public condition is not enough to warrant achieving the desire by a shorter cut than the constitutional way of paying for the change." *Mahon,* 260 U.S., at 416, 43 S.Ct. 158.

Justice THOMAS, with whom Justice SCALIA joins, dissenting.

I join THE CHIEF JUSTICE's dissent. I write separately to address the majority's conclusion that the temporary moratorium at issue here was not a taking because it was not a "taking of 'the parcel as a whole.'" *Ante,* at 1484. While this questionable rule* has been applied to various alleged regulatory takings, it was, in my view, rejected in the context of *temporal* deprivations of property by *First English Evangelical Lutheran Church of Glendale v. County of Los Angeles,* 482 U.S. 304, 318, 107 S.Ct. 2378, 96 L.Ed.2d 250 (1987), which held that temporary and permanent takings "are not different in kind" when a landowner is deprived of all beneficial use of his land. I had thought that *First English* put to rest the notion that the "relevant denominator" is land's infinite life. Consequently, a regulation effecting a total deprivation of the use of a so-called "temporal slice" of property is compensable under the Takings Clause unless background principles of state property law prevent it from being deemed a taking; "total deprivation of use is, from the landowner's point of view,

* The majority's decision to embrace the "parcel as a whole" doctrine as *settled* is puzzling. *See, e.g., Palazzolo v. Rhode Island,* 533 U.S. 606, 631, 121 S.Ct. 2448, 150 L.Ed.2d 592 (2001) (noting that the Court has "at times expressed discomfort with the logic of [the parcel as a whole] rule"); *Lucas v. South Carolina Coastal Council,* 505 U.S. 1003, 1017, n. 7, 112 S.Ct. 2886, 120 L.Ed.2d 798 (1992) (recognizing that "uncertainty regarding the composition of the denominator in [the Court's] 'deprivation' fraction has produced inconsistent pronouncements by the Court," and that the relevant calculus is a "difficult question").

the equivalent of a physical appropriation." *Lucas v. South Carolina Coastal Council,* 505 U.S. 1003, 1017, 112 S.Ct. 2886, 120 L.Ed.2d 798 (1992).

A taking is exactly what occurred in this case. No one seriously doubts that the land-use regulations at issue rendered petitioners' land unsusceptible of *any* economically beneficial use. This was true at the inception of the moratorium, and it remains true today. These individuals and families were deprived of the opportunity to build single-family homes as permanent, retirement, or vacation residences on land upon which such construction was authorized when purchased. The Court assures them that "a temporary prohibition on economic use" cannot be a taking because "[l]ogically ... the property will recover value as soon as the prohibition is lifted." *Ante,* at 1484. But the "logical" assurance that a "temporary restriction ... merely causes a diminution in value," *ibid.,* is cold comfort to the property owners in this case or any other....

I would hold that regulations prohibiting all productive uses of property are subject to *Lucas' per se* rule, regardless of whether the property so burdened retains theoretical useful life and value if, and when, the "temporary" moratorium is lifted. To my mind, such potential future value bears on the amount of compensation due and has nothing to do with the question whether there was a taking in the first place. It is regrettable that the Court has charted a markedly different path today.

Notes and Questions

1. **New line of regulatory takings jurisprudence.** a. Does *Tahoe-Sierra* establish a new line of regulatory takings jurisprudence or is it just an application of the principles laid out in *Penn Central* in a new context? b. Was rejecting a taking in the case of a temporary ban on development just another application of the parcel as whole concept, in this case, the landowner still retaining the full fee simple and the right to develop when the moratorium ends? c. Did the Court embrace the same meaning for economic impact as it did in *Penn Central*; in that case finding little economic impact because the railroad could not show that it could not continue to use the property as it had always been used and at a profit? d. How relevant was it that most owners bought their property for recreational use or for retirement homes?

2. **The values of Lake Tahoe and the imperatives of regulation.** The Court pointed out that "land use regulations are ubiquitous and most of them impact property values in some tangential way—often in completely unanticipated ways. Treating them all as *per se* takings would transform government regulation into a luxury few governments could afford." 535 U.S. at 324. Lake Tahoe is ancient, more than two million years old. It is one of the largest and deepest lakes in the world—1,645 feet deep. The early inhabitants, the Washoe Tribe, demonstrated a deep respect for the fragile environment that was their home and still revere it today. Given the unquestionable aesthetic and environmental values in Lake Tahoe, the imperatives for some form of land use regulation were great. The moratorium on development continued for nearly two decades, while the planners worked through several schemes for preservation. The most recent, the Lake Tahoe 2012 Regional Plan Update, was upheld by the Ninth Circuit in *Sierra*

Club v. Tahoe Reg'l Planning Agency, 840 F.3d 1106, 1107 (9th Cir. 2016). The opinion told the story of the lake and what led to the regulations.

> Lake Tahoe is located in the northern Sierra Nevada Mountains, and covers 191 square miles. The Lake Tahoe Region comprises 501 square miles, including the lake. The Region encompasses the Lake Tahoe basin, a watershed situated between the main crest of the Sierra Nevada and the Carson mountain ranges. The basin was acquired by the United States in the mid-1800s, but later in the century, private owners acquired much of the land and converted it to agricultural use, as well as beginning the resort industry at the south end of the lake.... In the late twentieth century, the population of the region expanded by more than 70%, with the most rapid expansion occurring in the 1970s. The attraction is the lake's size, depth, and distinctive blue color. The lake's clarity [a depth of more than 70 feet, although down from historical levels of more than 100 feet] is the result of the lack of algae.... Human activity in the late twentieth century, however, began increasing nutrients and sediments in the lake, bringing about a decline in clarity ... According to scientists, the loss of clarity was tied to nitrogen and phosphorous related to soil erosion, sewage discharge, and runoff from impervious developments. More recently, scientists added to the list of threats, atmospheric deposits caused by rain washing nitrogen from automobile exhaust down into the lake.... In addition, '[t]he Lake Tahoe Basin has also suffered from degradation of other measures of water and air quality. Many of the aesthetic and recreational values of the region have been impaired, including scenery, noise, and the ability to use the lake for recreational purposes.' These declines have been caused by onshore development, piers and other structures in the lake, and emissions from motorized watercraft.... The 2012 RPU [Regional Plan Update] was intended to 'repair damage of the past, while also promoting redevelopment of Tahoe's localized town centers to accelerate obtainment of threshold standards with more environmentally appropriate and attractive structures.'... It encouraged concentrated development by allowing TRPA itself, or local governments, through ... 'Area Plans,' to raise density, height, and coverage limits in community centers. 'Coverage' refers to the coverage of land with impervious material such as asphalt and concrete[,] emphasiz[ing] the Total Maximum Daily Load ('TMDL') model, which aims to reduce the total flow of certain pollutants into the lake.

While the water clarity of the lake has been improving since the moratorium and limits on development, it may take eons to restore it to its pristine past condition. Tahoe Regional Planning Agency, http://www.trpa.org/lake-tahoe-clarity-results-for-2015/ (last visited April 1, 2017). a. What else can be done to recapture the values of this historic lake?

3. **The *Lucas* case.** *Lucas v. South Carolina Coastal Council*, 505 U.S. 1003, 120 L. Ed. 2d 798, 112 S. Ct. 2886 (1992), was an important decision for takings jurisprudence. In that case, the Supreme Court established one of the per se rules for takings

Houses near Lake Tahoe. Carol M. Highsmith, Library of Congress.
Lake Tahoe. Julie Sims, Wikimedia Commons.

jurisprudence, namely, when all of the economically viable use of the land has been taken away by an ordinance. In 1986, the plaintiff, David Lucas, bought two residential lots on the Isle of Palms in Charleston County, in South Carolina, for $975,000, on which he intended to build single-family homes on par with the other houses in the area. In 1988, the South Carolina Legislature enacted the Beachfront Management Act, ("B.M.A."), S.C. Code Ann. § 48-39-250 *et seq.*, which amended the regulations on the use of coastal land started by South Carolina's Coastal Zone Management Act in 1976, S.C. Code Ann. § 48-39-130 *et seq.* The B.M.A. required owners of coastal land near "critical areas" to obtain permits from the South Carolina Coastal Council before engaging in any development projects on the land. The ordinances were passed as a measure to prevent the erosion of South Carolina's beaches, which were being adversely affected by the continual development of beachfront property. Unfortunately, the property that Lucas bought was just such a type of "critical area" property, effectively denying him the use of his land for what he originally intended. Lucas filed suit alleging that the restriction on his lots amounted to a taking without just compensation in violation of the Constitution. The South Carolina state trial court ruled in Lucas' favor and held that there had been a taking. The South Carolina Coastal Council appealed the decision to the South Carolina Supreme Court, which reversed the trial court's ruling. Lucas then appealed that decision to the Supreme Court of the United States.

In an opinion written by Justice Scalia, the Supreme Court held that the regulation had effected a taking without just compensation. The crux of the majority's ruling, which became known as the "total takings" test, was that when a regulation deprives an owner of all economically beneficial uses of land, it constitutes a taking. The exception to this rule, known as the nuisance exception, is when the proscribed use interests were not part of the title to begin with or are a "harmful or noxious use." For instance, if Lucas wanted to build a brewery on the property, it would not be allowed under applicable zoning laws, so it would not have mattered that the regulation prevented him from building a brewery because he could not have done so even without the regulation.

In their reasoning, the majority discussed that deprivation of all economically beneficial use of the property is effectively a deprivation of the property itself, in the eyes of the property owner. By not allowing Lucas to build single-family homes on the property, like all other plots in the area, he has been deprived of all economically beneficial use of the property. Justice Scalia, discussing the benefit and burden analysis brought forth in *Penn Central*, alluded to the idea that when all economically beneficial use is restricted, it is difficult to assume that the legislature is balancing economic benefits and burdens. The Court further reasoned that regulations that restrict all economically beneficial use of property may often be a guise for subtly forcing the property into public use, imposing the public benefit burden on a single individual, which is not allowed. Additionally, there is no way to distinguish a regulation that "prevents a harmful use" and one which bestows benefits on nearby property. Justice Kennedy, in concurrence with the majority opinion, emphasized the need to determine complete deprivation of economic benefit based on the landowner's reasonable investment-backed expectations when the property was bought.

The dissenting justices, including Justice Blackmun and Justice Stevens, took issue with the *per se* rule that the majority created. They argued that there can never be a complete deprivation of economic benefit of the property because the owner of the property can always enjoy the benefit of owning property. They also assert that the *per se* rule creates an awkward line where the entire economic benefit of the property is compromised then it is a taking, in need of compensation; however, anything short of an entire taking even 95%, would not have to be compensated.

4. **Two regimes after *Tahoe-Sierra*.** While the Court in *Tahoe-Sierra* took great pains to distinguish *Lucas*, it did not overrule it. a. What was the critical distinction? b. What is the doctrinal value of *Lucas* after *Tahoe-Sierra*? c. What are the contexts in which these respective rulings will apply? d. What do you see as the greatest difficulty in making the determination which to apply; can a moratorium, which by definition and aim is temporary, become a permanent invasion?

5. **A state court takings decision.** State courts can also make decisions on whether ordinances constitute takings. One such example is the case of *United Artists' Theater Circuit, Inc. v. City of Philadelphia*, 535 Pa. 370, 635 A.2d 612 (Pa. 1993), discussed *infra*, in Chapter 3.

6. **The future of historic preservation ordinance jurisprudence.** After constitutionality, other issues arise, such as the lawfulness of designating particular historic properties. *Estate of Tippett v. City of Miami*, 645 So.2d 533 (Fla. App. 3d Dist. 1994), is characteristic of these issues. The City of Miami, Florida adopted an Historic Preservation ordinance similar to that of New York City, MIAMI CODE §§23.1-1 to 23.1-6, which defined an historic district as "[a] geographically defined area possessing a significant concentration, linkage, or continuity of sites or structures united historically or aesthetically, by plan or physical development." MIAMI CODE, §23.1-2 *et seq.* The Bayside Historic District was designated in 1991 by the City of Miami Historic and Environmental Protection Board. The area in northeast Miami, which had been developed over a period of more than 40 years, is home to residential buildings which reflect Miami's growth from a pi-

oneer settlement to a significant metropolitan area. The Bayside area mirrored the diversity and taste of its early, fashionable residents, representing an eclectic mix of architectural styles including Frame Vernacular, Mediterranean Revival, Artes Decoratif (Art Deco), and Streamline Moderne. *See* City of Miami Planning Department, City of Miami: Historic Preservation—Bayside Historic District, http://www.historicpreservationmiami.com/bayside.html (last visited April 6, 2017). The Tippetts owned one of the houses that was to become part of the designated historic district. When the Preservation Board designated the district, the Tippets appealed the decision to the City Commission, which denied the appeal and affirmed the designation. The Tippetts then appealed the decision to the Circuit Court, Appellate Division, using the argument that the Miami Historic Preservation Ordinance used to designate their home as historic, amounted to an unlawful taking without just compensation. The Circuit Court affirmed the Preservation Board's decision.

The District Court of Appeal of the Third District dismissed the case altogether, denying certiorari. Its reasoning was based on the fact that the Tippetts had made a facial challenge to the declaration of the historic district and to the Miami Historic Preservation Ordinance under which it was created, but their case was not ripe. The Tippetts had never applied for any permits and the government entity in charge of implementing the ordinance had not reached a final decision on its implementation. Judge Gerstein, in concurrence, discussed the specifics of the ordinance, including the protocols for designation and appeal, and even exemptions, such as when the designation provides the property owner with economic hardship.

Judge Gersten then continued to discuss the other arguments against the Historic Preservation Ordinance, which no doubt may come up in future historic preservation litigation. Aside from the obvious takings argument, an argument was raised about the unlawful delegation of power by Miami's City Commission to the Preservation Board. In response, Judge Gersten reasoned that it was a legitimate delegation since "Florida's delegation doctrine [only] requires that the legislature make 'fundamental and primary policy decisions and issue some minimal standards or guidelines.'" *Estate of Tippett*, 645 So.2d at 536 (quoting *Brown v. Aualachee Regional Planning Council*, 560 So.2d 782, 784 (Fla. 1990)). Since the Miami Historic Preservation Ordinance was established by Miami's City Commission, the legislative body, the "fundamental" structure which can allow the City Commission to delegate its power was present; hence, it was not an unlawful delegation of power. Next, the Tippetts argued that the ordinance was too vague. Judge Gersten found no merit in that argument and pointed to the fact that no other court had accepted a vagueness challenge to historic preservation ordinances and that there were enough safeguards in the system to constrain the exercise of discretion. *Estate of Tippett*, 645 So.2d at 537. Finally, Judge Gersten discussed the Equal Protection challenge, for which he found no basis. In his opinion, "a rational basis exists to separate historic preservation from zoning decisions, because historic preservation decisions involve a special expertise and require considerations of criteria and purpose that differs from those of zoning." *Id.* at 538. To make his final point, Judge Gersten referenced *Penn Central* for guidance, stating the Supreme Court found that the "objective of preserving structures and areas with special historic, architectural, or cultural significance is a constitutionally permissible goal and that the ordinance method of designating specific districts and landmarks was an appropriate means to achieve this objective." *Id.* (quoting *Penn Central*, 438 U.S. at 129).

7. **Eminent domain.** Eminent domain is perhaps the first of those powers resting in the government that enables it to transfer title from private owners to itself. In the case of land use regulation and taxation, the government may accomplish this without having to pay full compensation. But, where it invokes its eminent domain powers, it is obligated to pay the private owner and the taking must be for a public use. In *Kelo v. City of New London*, 545 U.S. 469 (2005), the Supreme Court embraced an interpretation of "public use" that sparked much debate. There, the city of New London, Connecticut condemned several private homes with the immediate purpose of turning the land over to a private developer to be used for expensive waterfront development, with the long-term purpose of increasing commercial activities and tax revenues. The Court ruled that economic redevelopment "unquestionably serves a public purpose" and thus "satisf[ies] the public use requirement of the Fifth Amendment." *Kelo,* 545 U.S. at 484. The Court stated that the assertion that economic development does not qualify as public use was supported by neither precedent, nor logic. Instead, "promoting economic development is a traditional and long-accepted function of government"; and there is "no principled way of distinguishing economic development from the other public purposes that we have recognized." *Id.* While the opinion was met with much consternation by the public and legislators—many state legislatures adopted measures precluding or limiting takings for such purposes—some commentators believe the ruling reflected both pragmatism and wisdom. *See e.g.,* Abraham Bell & Gideon Parchomovsky, *The Uselessness of Public Use*, 106 Colum. L. Rev. 1412, 1412 (2006):

> Given that the government can achieve any land use goals through the powers of regulation and taxation without paying compensation to the aggrieved property owner, eminent domain is the government power least pernicious to property owners as it is the only one that guarantees them compensation. An important and counterintuitive implication of this insight is that the calls to restrict the government's ability to use eminent domain by narrowly construing public use are going to harm, rather than help, private property owners. * * * [The best solution lies] in expanding, not contracting, the number of cases in which the government can use its power of eminent domain, while limiting its ability to avoid compensation when otherwise infringing upon private property rights....

Years later, Justice John Paul Stevens, then retired, looked back, unapologetically, on *Kelo*, believing the majority rightly applied precedent. He stated that the majority wisely resisted adopting the position that would declare a substantive right against a government taking a home for economic redevelopment. 2011 Albritton Lecture at the University of Alabama School of Law, 63 Ala. L. Rev. 941–54 (2012). While regulatory takings jurisprudence continues to evolve, *Penn Central* settled for all time the issue of the legitimacy of governmental rules and limits for the protection of historic properties.

The Campaign to Preserve the Jay Heritage Estate: An Epic Battle on Many Fronts

While the "story" of Grand Central Terminal may be the most celebrated in historic preservation jurisprudence, the oft-contentious narrative of preservation continues to unfold on numerous fronts and on many societal levels. *Penn Central* set the stage for a campaign to preserve the childhood home of John Jay in the City of Rye, New York, on Long Island Sound, a contest that lasted from 1979 to 1995, and beyond. The campaign was launched by the Jay Coalition, a group of citizens and joined by some 70 civic organizations, and was fought in both state and federal arenas, as well as in the local community. In the end, the properties of the Jay Heritage Estate endure as a legacy to John Jay and as a commitment to the beauty of classic architecture, natural landscapes and vistas.

The estate is the ancestral home of John Jay, one of the nation's founders. Aside from co-authoring (with Hamilton and Madison) the Federalist Papers, the political platform for America's new government, he served in every branch of both the new federal government and that of New York State. Jay was the first Chief Justice of the U.S. Supreme Court, served as Secretary for Foreign Affairs, was the principal negotiator of both the Treaty of Paris (which recognized America's independence) and the Jay Treaty (which safeguarded the new nation's freedom), and was elected president of the Continental Congress. On the state level, he was elected governor of New York for two terms, once in his absence while abroad on State Department business. He also served as a delegate to the New York State Constitution Convention and was the first Chief Justice of the state's highest court.

While in the Jay family, the farm in Rye was known as the "Locusts." John Jay's father, Peter Jay, a successful merchant, purchased 250 acres of farmland that comprised the property. Peter Jay built a small, two-story farmhouse near the Boston Post Road in Rye, New York. Jay lived on the estate during his childhood and for most of his life, until his brother, Peter, and his family moved into the estate. Eventually, Jay retired to a farm in Bedford, New York.

When the Jay family sold the estate in 1905, it came to be known as "Alansten." Today, it consists of about 24 acres with the Greek Revival Peter Jay Mansion and Van Norden carriage house of 1912, an adjacent Westchester County Park, "Marshlands," and the Jay Family Cemetery, where Jay is buried. It is one of the County's last major undeveloped parcels on Long Island Sound. The Greek Revival mansion (pictured below) was constructed in 1838 by Jay's son, Peter Augustus Jay.

The Peter Jay Mansion. Image courtesy of Shelby D. Green.

For most of its history, the Village of Rye, like many other American villages, was configured as a small central core with an inn and a pair of churches, surrounded by scattered farms and farm houses. Throughout the 1960s and 1970s, the City of Rye and private owners helped to safeguard the Jay Estate, along with two adjacent ones, Lounsbury and the Whitby, each situated on the Boston Post Road. But in 1979, the then owner, the Methodist Church, which had used the mansion as a conference center, found that it could no longer maintain the property and decided to sell it to a developer, who planned to raze the mansion and other buildings and put up more than thirty condominiums. As part of this plan, the Methodist Church applied for approval to subdivide the property to use six acres for a religious conference center and 17 acres for development. When the application was denied, the Methodist Church contracted to sell the entire parcel to FGL&L Properties Corp. (the "developers"). The developers then applied to rezone the parcel to build more than 220,000 square feet of office space on the site.

The development proposal was met with fierce opposition from the community. While the City of Rye had a landmarks ordinance, under which changes to historic sites had to be authorized by a Certificate of Appropriateness from the City's Board of Architectural Review ("BAR"), Rye City Code, ch. 117 (1977), the ordinance required the owner to consent to designate a property as a protected landmark, which the developers were not inclined to give.

The Jay Coalition then turned to protecting the site by enfolding it within an historic district that would be listed on the National Register of Historic Places. The "Boston Post Road Historic District" included Alansten, the

Marshlands, the Jay Cemetery, and the two adjacent parcels. That status ensured that no federal project would occur in the district without an evaluation of the potential effects on the historic properties and values in the district. But this was mere procedure that did not limit what the owners could do with the property. Determined to protect the Jay Estate, in December 1983, the City Council modified the ordinance, eliminating the owner consent requirement for properties listed on the National Register of Historic Places. National Park Service and Related Programs Act, 54 U.S.C. §302101, *et. seq.*, www.nps.gov/Nr/national_register_fundamentals.htm (last visited April 1, 2017). The City Council also created a special zoning district, the "Alansten Landmark Preservation District," which covered a "view way" from the mansion to the rear property line that preserved the vista over the Marshlands to Long Island Sound, and from the Marshlands to the mansion. The ordinance also purported to protect the form of ownership of the parcel, requiring that it remain in single ownership, that all residential units be held as condominiums, and also that the owner must restore and maintain the mansion and carriage house.

In addition, the State Environmental Quality Review Act ("SEQRA"), Envtl. Conserv. Law, art. 8, applied. Among other things, SEQRA required the preparation of a statement that identified likely adverse impacts on the environment, broadly defined to include historic properties, natural areas, and even populations. In fulfilling its obligations to consider and mitigate impacts under SEQRA, as lead agency, the Rye City Council determined that it would consider only residential uses for Alansten, which effectively nullified the developers' plans.

The developers in turn went on the offensive, making claims under both state and federal law. They sued the City Council, seeking to invalidate the creation of the Alansten Landmark Preservation District, on the basis that the city exceeded its delegated powers under the state's zoning enabling act and the landmarks ordinance, when it sought to regulate the form of ownership of the property and to require rehabilitation, as opposed to maintenance, of the mansion. They also claimed that the special treatment given to National Register properties was a violation of the Equal Protection and Due Process clauses of the 14th Amendment, that there was no nexus between the ordinance and the asserted ends, and that the designation amounted to a taking of property without just compensation.

The developers both won and lost. In *FGL & L Property Corp. v. City of Rye*, 485 N.E.2d 986, 989, 991–92 (N.Y. 1985), the New York Court of Appeals agreed that the City exceeded its powers when it purported to dictate the form of ownership allowed in the Alansten Landmark Historic District, pointing out that the power to zone under the enabling act is limited to regulating land use, and does not empower a municipality to decide who may own property or how it may be owned. And, while historic preservation is a valid form of land use regulation, the court explained, it does not enable local governments to require restoration, as opposed to maintenance.

The other claims were decided by the trial courts. In a thoughtful opinion, in *DGM Partners-Rye v. City of Rye*, Index No. 4609/85 (Sup. Ct. Westchester Cnty. July 10, 1985), Judge Marbach of the Westchester County Supreme Court upheld the elimination of owner consent in the case of properties on the National Register. The court explained that the different levels of protection given to properties with potential for landmarking—including those listed on the National Register—were rationally related to the landmarks ordinance's purpose. This held true in spite of the fact that Rye's Landmarks Advisory Committee applied National Register criteria in proposing local landmarks. The court added that the National Register status was sufficiently important to merit landmark designation without requiring owner consent, and that the City Council was not obligated to landmark all National Register properties located within the City's boundaries. The court further noted that in making the final determination of local landmark designation, the City Council must use discretion and consider zoning, planning, and economics in addition to historic considerations. The court declined to rule on the takings claim, finding it unripe, since the developers had not exhausted their administrative remedies.

Having lost the challenge to the validity of the landmarks designation, the developers went on to invoke exemptions under the ordinance. They petitioned the BAR for a certificate of appropriateness to raze the structures, maintaining that they could not realize a reasonable return on the investment by selling the property. Not surprisingly, the BAR denied the request and the developers then challenged that denial in court. The appellate court affirmed the denial, noting that the entire parcel was designated as a "protected site" under the landmarks preservation ordinance, including an unobstructed public view way of the mansion from the southern property line, and that the developers failed to offer evidence that the property could not be sold at a reasonable rate of return without demolishing the buildings. *DGM Partners-Rye v. Bd. of Architectural Review*, 148 A.D.2d 608, 539 N.Y.S.2d 74, 76 (2d Dep't 1989).

Even as the developers sought demolition of the structures, they were simultaneously pursuing the subdivision application before the Planning Commission. While the Planning Commission approved the construction of 33 residential units, that approval came with a host of conditions, which the Commission believed were required for compliance with the landmark designation. More conditions were added by the BAR as part of its architectural review of the subdivision proposal.

The conditions were thought too onerous by the developers and they challenged them under the then-developing Supreme Court exactions jurisprudence, as first articulated in *Nollan v. California Coastal Comm'n*. 483 U.S. 825 (1987). In *Nollan*, the Supreme Court declared that a land use regulation, to be valid, must further the end advanced as the justification for the regulation. The developers argued that inasmuch as the public never enjoyed the view way and the Carriage House had no architectural or historic value justifying its preservation, there was no rational nexus between the preservation regulations and a legitimate governmental purpose.

The hearing officer was not persuaded. The view way area was illustrative of the landscape architecture of the colonial and early Federal periods. The mansion and carriage house were situated so as to afford a striking vista downhill toward Long Island Sound. Even though the landmark designation did not confer a right in the public to come upon the estate, the views of the mansion from the meadow of the Marshlands had been open to the public for 20 years and the construction of single-family homes in the view way would drastically change or destroy not only the traditional landscape architecture of the property, but would also deprive the public of one of the primary values of the designation. In this view, the nexus between the public good to be achieved by designation and the preservation of the view way was direct and substantial and advanced a legitimate state interest. *DGM Partners-Rye v. City of Rye*, N.Y.L.J., June 5, 1989, at 26:6 (Sup.Ct. Westchester Cnty. 1989); *DGM Partners-Rye v. Bd. of Architectural Review of City of Rye*, N.Y.L.J., Oct. 18, 1989, at 21 (Sup.Ct. Westchester Cnty. 1989); *Peter Jay Heritage Coalition v. Planning Comm'n of City of Rye*, N.Y.L.J., April 4, 1988, at 18:2 (Sup.Ct. Westchester Cnty. 1988). The appellate court affirmed the finding and rejected the developers' claim of a *per se* taking—the designation of the view way did not constitute an uncompensated sight easement and further did not amount to a physical invasion of the property. *DGM Partners-Rye v. City of Rye*, 575 N.Y.S. 2d 330 (2d Dep't 1991).

So many years of contest wore on all sides. The Jay Coalition had long believed that the best preservation for Alansten was to remove all possibility of development, by owning it. At first, the developers resisted selling the entire site, instead offering to sell a portion upon the County's assurance of subdivision approval for a smaller project on the balance of the site. This proposal was rejected because it threatened destruction of the site and would hamper the Coalition's ability to raise funds for maintenance. Thirteen years after the Methodist Church first put the property up for sale, perhaps reacting to a declining real estate market, the developers signaled that they were inclined to sell the entire parcel to the County for fair market value. The Coalition appealed to the state's Office of Parks, Recreation and Historic Preservation ("OPRHP") and the Department of Environmental Conservation ("DEC"), as well as the County, for the money to buy the estate, promising to raise funds from other sources to rehabilitate and maintain the mansion and carriage house. The OPRHP and DEC offered $4 million if the County would provide the rest. In 1993, without involving the City, the County and the developers negotiated a settlement of pending litigation and the administrative proceedings that included the purchase by the County of most of the 22.46-acre site, the remaining landscape, including historic buildings and former gardens, for $11.5 million. The agreement excepted from the purchase the Carriage House and the Mansion, as those were donated by the developer directly to the Coalition. The County had declined to take title to the two historic structures, believing that they were too costly to repair and maintain. That same year, the Jay Estate was designated a National Historic Landmark.

Even as purchase negotiations were ongoing, the developers, perhaps still smarting from the long string of defeats, hurled a final missive—a broad-based federal suit against the County, the City, and the Jay Coalition, alleging, among other things, inverse condemnation. *DGM Partners-Rye v. County of Westchester*, No. 90 Civ. 8261 (GLG) (S.D.N.Y. April 16, 1991). That suit sought over $60 million in damages. While it did not explicitly plead a conspiracy, the developers claimed the defendants took part in a scheme to render their property unmarketable through regulation and the threat of condemnation. The case was discontinued. While the complaint was not formally answered, Defendants asserted that in light of all the developers' other cases, the claims were barred by res judicata, collateral estoppel, the applicable statute of limitations, issue preclusion, abstention, or otherwise failed to state a claim. *See generally* Richard M. Gardella *The Jay Mansion: Preservation Case History*, 21 WESTCHESTER BAR J. 109 (1994); Stephen L. Kass & Michael B. Gerrard, *Preservation of the Jay Estate*, 207 N.Y.L.J. 2 (1992); WALTER STAHR, JOHN JAY: FOUNDING FATHER, https://books.google.com/books?id=a9Jm_RDtq3cC&printsec=frontcover&dq=John+Jay:+Founding+Father&hl=en&sa=X&ved=0CB0Q6AEwAGoVChMI5eGj2dXlxwIVi6KACh2WdQld#v=onepage&q&f=false (last visited April 6, 2017).

Notes and Questions

1. **Many laws at issue.** This struggle over preserving the Jay Estate, indeed epic in its length and scope, illustrates the many different types of interests that are implicated in historic preservation. Ultimately, the exercise of eminent domain, to take the property for the public purpose of preserving it, is an expression of the overarching importance of this historical association of the site with John Jay and public memory.

2. **Many fronts and impacts.** Note that this campaign was not restricted to a landmarks commission system, such as that of New York City, which the Supreme Court affirmed in the *Penn Central* case. Collateral laws and procedures were invoked by all sides. a. Do you agree with Kass & Gerrard in their assertion that preservation

law effectively merged otherwise disparate laws—land use, environmental law, historic preservation, and public land acquisition—into a set of fraternal interests "that have begun to merge into an integrated system of land-use management"? *See* Stephen L. Kass & Michael B. Gerrard, *Preservation of the Jay Estate*, 207 N.Y.L.J. 2 (1992). b. Or do you agree with Richard Gardella, the City of Rye's attorney, that "[i]t is hard to see what the City of Rye's experience means in regard to future land use regulation or broader governmental issues"? Richard Gardella, *The Jay Mansion: Preservation Case History*, 21 Westchester Bar J. 109, 129 (1994). At this stage, demolition and development of the site for housing is averted, but preservation of a decrepit mansion and carriage house are hardly assured. What must happen next?

3. **Maintenance.** Today, the premises operate under a joint cooperation and maintenance agreement between the state of New York (via the Commissioner of OPRHP), Westchester County, and the Jay Heritage Center. *See* Resolution Authorizing Cooperation and Maintenance Agreement (2012) (reproduced on casebook website).

Chapter 3

Characteristic Variations Among Historic Preservation Ordinances

A. Other Historic Preservation Ordinances for the Designation of Historic Landmarks and Districts

As noted in the previous chapter, after the decision in *Penn Central*, the number of states that adopted historic preservation legislation and local ordinances grew, and all states now have some form of historic preservation law. While most jurisdictions followed the style of the New York City ordinance in *Penn Central*, several other patterns exist, including some which predate the *Penn Central* decision.

1. Charleston, South Carolina, Historic Preservation Ordinance

The City of Charleston, South Carolina, helped paved the way for historic preservation ordinances. In 1931, Charleston became the first city to zone an historic district. As opposed to having a separate ordinance for historic preservation, the City of Charleston incorporated the aim of preserving historic structures and districts into its zoning ordinances. *See* Charleston, S.C., Zoning Ordinance, art. 2, part 6, §§ 54-230 to 54-249. Innovations in landmark preservation continue to emerge, such as under the Historic Landmark and Historic Protection Act of 1978 in the District of Columbia, D.C. Code § 6-1101, *et seq.*, which provides clever administrative procedures, such as authorizing an official, termed the "Mayor's Agent," to make final determinations on applications for alterations, demolition, new construction, and subdivisions subject to the preservation laws. *See* Georgetown University Law Library archive of Mayor's Agent decisions, https://repository.library.georgetown.edu/handle/10822/713074 (last visited February 13, 2018) (a distinguished professor of preservation law, Peter Byrne, is serving as Mayor's Agent).

Burke v. City of Charleston

United States Court of Appeals for the Fourth Circuit
139 F.3d 401 (1998)

Davis, J. Appellant Robert Burke, an artist working in South Carolina, challenges the constitutionality of a City of Charleston historic preservation ordinance that governs proposed alterations to exteriors of structures located within historic areas of the city. Burke painted a mural on the exterior wall of a restaurant located in an historic area, but the city's Board of Architectural Review invoked the ordinance and denied the restaurant owner a permit to display the mural. Burke filed suit, and the district court, after a non-jury trial, entered judgment in favor of the city. Burke appeals.

We do not reach the merits of Burke's constitutional challenge because we find that Burke lacks standing to assert a First Amendment claim. Burke relinquished his First Amendment rights when he sold his mural to the restaurant owner, who alone has the right to *display* the mural. Thus, lacking a legally cognizable interest in the *display* of his work, Burke has not suffered an injury sufficient to satisfy the constitutional requirements for standing. Moreover, even were we to conclude that Burke has suffered injury-in-fact, a decision from this Court in Burke's favor would not redress directly, if at all, the injury Burke presumably suffers. Accordingly, we vacate the judgment and remand with instructions to dismiss the complaint.

I

Ron Klenk (who is not a party to this appeal) owns a late federal style building located at 348 King Street in Charleston, South Carolina. Klenk operated a night club on the second floor of his building. Klenk decided to open a bar and grill on the first floor of the building. Impressed with the "world of creatures" Burke had created and displayed at an art show held in the night club, Klenk commissioned Burke to paint a mural depicting the creature world on the exterior masonry wall of the building, which is visible from King Street. At the time of the commission, a mural depicting a willow tree adorned the exterior wall. Burke painted over the willow tree mural with his "colorful cartoon of imaginary characters, including smiling mountains, flying creatures with impractically small wings and tiny yellow bipeds." Through the mural, Burke attempts to convey a message of tolerance for diversity by showing different creatures co-existing peacefully.

Klenk's property is located within the Old and Historic District ("District") of Charleston. The District boasts the largest collection-numbering approximately 2800—of historically significant buildings in the United States. The District is the heart of tourist interest in Charleston. In 1931, to further the establishment of an architecturally harmonious environment throughout the District, Charleston enacted its historic preservation ordinances and established its Board of Architectural Review ("BAR"). The BAR reviews all proposed exterior or fixed structural alterations, signs, murals, or other exterior changes to structures in the District before they are effected. The BAR's purpose is to ensure that alterations are complementary in style, form, color, proportion, texture, and material. Thus, those seeking to make such alterations must submit to the BAR an application for a permit and a proposal describing the work to be done.

Neither Burke nor Klenk applied for a permit before Burke began to paint the mural. The BAR discovered Burke's mural while Burke was painting it, and issued a stop work order. Subsequently, Klenk—not Burke—filed an application for a permit. The parties agreed to cover the mural with plywood pending approval of Klenk's permit application. Subsequently, they agreed to keep the mural covered for the duration of this litigation.

Burke's mural generated public controversy and extensive media attention. Many city residents opposed Burke's mural; others were favorably impressed ... Eventually, the BAR held a public hearing during which Burke, represented by counsel, submitted letters from various supporters of the mural. Others spoke against the mural at the hearing. At the conclusion of the hearing, the BAR issued a report denying Klenk's permit application. The BAR stated that the mural's size, scale, and "garish" colors did not blend with the surrounding area and that the mural was inappropriate for display in the District.

Burke, but not Klenk, filed suit in district court, alleging that the BAR's decision to deny Klenk's permit, the lack of articulable standards for approving work, and the use of a vague and overbroad ordinance, violated Burke's free speech and equal protection rights under the first and fourteenth amendments. In its answer, the city raised Burke's lack of standing as an affirmative defense. Later, however, the city voluntarily abandoned this defense. At the conclusion of a non-jury trial, the district court issued its findings of fact and conclusions of law in a thoughtful and carefully-reasoned opinion. *Burke v. City of Charleston,* 893 F.Supp. 589 (D.S.C.1995).

The district court addressed the issue of standing, noting the Second Circuit rule that an artist who sells his work to the government relinquishes his right to have his work displayed. *See Serra v. United States Gen. Serv. Admin.,* 847 F.2d 1045 (2d Cir.1988). The district court distinguished *Serra,* however, on the ground that the artist in that case was not precluded by an ordinance from displaying his expression. The court also noted that the historic preservation ordinance would operate to thwart Burke's future efforts because it would preclude him from painting another creature world mural for the interested restaurant owner whose property is also located within the District. The court concluded that Burke had standing to pursue his claims, but ultimately held that Burke failed to prove his constitutional rights were violated, and entered judgment in favor of the city as to all claims. Burke brought the present appeal, challenging only the lower court's ruling on the First Amendment issue, while abandoning his equal protection claim.

II

"'[E]very federal appellate court has a special obligation to "satisfy itself not only of its own jurisdiction, but also that of the lower courts in a cause under review," even though the parties are prepared to concede it.'" *Arizonans for Official English v. Arizona,* 520 U.S. 43, 117 S.Ct. 1055, 1071, 137 L.Ed.2d 170 (1997) (quoting *Mitchell v. Maurer,* 293 U.S. 237, 244, 55 S.Ct. 162, 165, 79 L.Ed. 338 (1934)). "And if the record discloses that the lower court was without jurisdiction [a reviewing] court will notice the defect, although the parties make no contention concerning it." 117 S.Ct. at 1072 (quoting *United States v. Corrick,* 298 U.S. 435, 440, 56 S.Ct. 829, 831, 80 L.Ed. 1263 (1936)) (brackets in original). With these guiding principles in mind, we proceed to examine the question whether Burke has standing to bring a First Amendment claim.

"Article III of the United States Constitution limits federal courts to resolving actual cases and controversies." *Finlator v. Powers,* 902 F.2d 1158, 1160 (4th Cir. 1990). A litigant does not satisfy Article III's mandate merely by "request[ing] a court of the United States to declare its legal rights" in terms "that have a familiar ring to those trained in the legal process." *Valley Forge Christian College v. Americans United for Separation of Church and State, Inc.,* 454 U.S. 464, 471, 102 S.Ct. 752, 758, 70 L.Ed.2d 700 (1982). Rather, the judicial power to pass constitutional judgment "is legitimate only in the last resort," *Chicago & Grand Trunk R. Co. v. Wellman,* 143 U.S. 339, 345, 12 S.Ct. 400, 402, 36 L.Ed. 176 (1892), and as a necessity in determining "actual cases ... involving issues that are precisely framed by their connection to specific litigants in a concrete context." *Gilles v. Torgersen,* 71 F.3d 497, 500 (4th Cir.1995).[1]

The Supreme Court has articulated various rules which govern the justiciability of disputes. The standing requirement, is "perhaps the most important" condition of justiciability, *Allen v. Wright,* 468 U.S. 737, 750, 104 S.Ct. 3315, 3324, 82 L.Ed.2d 556 (1984).... While the Supreme Court has not defined standing "with complete consistency," *Valley Forge Christian College,* 454 U.S. at 475, 102 S.Ct. at 760, the irreducible constitutional minimum of standing requires: (1) that the plaintiff personally has suffered actual or threatened injury that is concrete and particularized, not conjectural or hypothetical; (2) that the injury fairly can be traced to the challenged action; and (3) that the injury is likely to be redressed by a favorable decision from the court. *See Lujan v. Defenders of Wildlife,* 504 U.S. 555, 560–61, 112 S.Ct. 2130, 2136–37, 119 L.Ed.2d 351 (1992); *Finlator,* 902 F.2d at 1160.

Thus, "a plaintiff generally must assert his own legal rights and interests, and cannot rest his claim to relief on the legal rights or interests of third parties." *Warth v. Seldin,* 422 U.S. 490, 499, 95 S.Ct. 2197, 2205, 45 L.Ed.2d 343 (1975). Moreover, even when a plaintiff satisfies the constitutional requirements for standing, federal courts will not adjudicate a "'generalized grievance' shared in substantially equal measure by all or a large class of citizens...." *Id.* Finally, the plaintiff's complaint must fall within the zone of interests the statute or Constitution protects or regulates. *Valley Forge Christian College,* 454 U.S. at 475, 102 S.Ct. at 760; *see also Association of Data Processing Service Orgs. v. Camp,* 397 U.S. 150, 153, 90 S.Ct. 827, 829–30, 25 L.Ed.2d

1. Unquestionably, the *Wellman* rule of strict enforcement of the standing requirement has continued vitality. *Raines v. Byrd,* 117 S.Ct. 2312, 2317, 138 L.Ed.2d 849 (1997) ("We have always insisted on strict compliance with this jurisdictional standing requirement.").

184 (1970); *Branch Bank and Trust Co. v. Nat'l Credit Union Admin. Bd.*, 786 F.2d 621, 624 (4th Cir.1986).[2]

All the members of the panel agree that this is not a proper case for the application of third party standing doctrine.

III

Application of these principles to the case at hand persuades us that Burke lacks standing. The speech being regulated or infringed upon in this case is the speech of the owner of 348 King Street; only that person or entity might elect whether to "express" Burke's fantasy, as depicted in the creature world mural, by *displaying* it in the District. Burke relinquished his First Amendment rights embodied in the mural when he effectively sold it to Klenk, by creating it on Klenk's real property. *Serra*, 847 F.2d at 1049. As Burke conceded at trial, somewhat anomalously, his request for relief would be mooted should Klenk, who had at the time of trial listed the property for sale, sell his property.

Burke has failed to demonstrate injury-in-fact. *** [W]e fail to discern how the operation of the ordinance in respect to *Burke's* right to artistic expression amounts to a concrete injury, rather than a mere tangential effect, at best. Klenk commissioned Burke to create a work of art, and Klenk had little, if any input, into the creative process. Nevertheless, the legally cognizable injury arising from the Charleston ordinance falls upon the party who alone has the right to *display* the work, not the person who creates it. Put differently, as a matter of Article III standing, the ordinance must be viewed as a regulation of what is *displayed* in the District, not as a regulation of the colors or content of *unexposed* bricks and mortar. On the present record, in respect to the exterior wall of 348 King Street, that person is Klenk and only Klenk.

Thus, if we viewed the ordinance, or the Board's enforcement of it, as does the dissent, as a cause-in-fact of Burke's having to "stop work," we might well be persuaded that Burke has Article III standing to seek relief.[3] Presumably, however, Burke is not interested in continuing to work on a painting that will never be displayed. Obviously, the "mural" could as easily be created in or on a mobile medium (such as the plywood which now covers it), and Burke could work unrestrained by the ordinance in a studio

---

2. In some instances, courts will relax the prudential limitations because they are outweighed by competing considerations. Among those weightier considerations within the context of the First Amendment is the danger of chilling free speech. *Joseph H. Munson, Inc.*, 467 U.S. at 956, 104 S.Ct. at 2846–47. One who engages in protected activity regulated by statute might elect to discontinue engaging in that activity rather than launch a First Amendment attack. In such a case, society as a whole suffers a loss. *Id.* Thus, courts sometimes permit litigants to challenge a statute "not because their own rights of free expression are violated, but because of a judicial prediction or assumption that the statute's very existence may cause others not before the court to refrain from constitutionally protected speech or expression." *Broadrick v. Oklahoma*, 413 U.S. 601, 612, 93 S.Ct. 2908, 2916, 37 L.Ed.2d 830 (1973). Nevertheless, a *jus tertii* plaintiff is obligated as an initial matter to allege a distinct and palpable injury as required by Article III. *Warth*, 422 U.S. at 501, 95 S.Ct. at 2206–07; *Gilles*, 71 F.3d at 500.

3. Apparently, the mural was substantially complete when Burke ceased work on it. ***

or gallery. Upon delivery of such a composition to Klenk, however, Burke would have no basis in law to obtain a permit in Klenk's or his own name to display it upon *Klenk's* building. Similarly, he lacks standing in this case to challenge the Board's enforcement of the ordinance against *Klenk.* ***

The district court identified injury from Burke's testimony that another building owner in the District might, absent the ordinance, commission Burke to paint a mural on his exterior wall. The testimony upon which this finding was based is not included in the Appendices filed with the parties' briefs. Such a potential arrangement—a mere expectancy—does not amount to a concrete, palpable injury. Otherwise, a plaintiff could create standing through the expedience of self-serving declarations amounting to little more than argument rather than demonstrable harm.

Moreover, even assuming this testimony constitutes evidence sufficient to show injury, an order that the ordinance is unconstitutional would not likely redress Burke's grievance that the King Street mural cannot be displayed in the District. No interested building owner is obligated to commission Burke to create a mural on his exterior wall. Absent such a commission, our ruling would lie dormant. Indeed, a subsequent owner of 348 King Street, and obviously Klenk himself, would be free at any time to paint over Burke's mural, just as Klenk hired Burke to paint over the willow tree mural that adorned the exterior wall when Klenk purchased the property. Again, an injunction would lack binding or mobilizing effect upon the parties here. The result would be an inappropriate advisory opinion, a result unequivocally barred by our supreme law.[4]

The federal courts are not "publicly funded forums for the ventilation of public grievances or the refinement of jurisprudential understanding." *Valley Forge Christian College,* 454 U.S. at 473, 102 S.Ct. at 759. Rather, they are venues preserved for those who have a direct stake in the outcome of the controversy which they seek to litigate. Like the thousands upon thousands of Charlestonians and Charelston [sic] visitors who would likely take pleasure in Burke's creation were they only allowed to view it there on Klenk's wall, Burke himself, although the creator of the work, lacks such a direct stake, and as a consequence the district court lacked jurisdiction to adjudicate his claims.

IV

For the reasons discussed above, the judgment of the district court is vacated and remanded with directions to dismiss the complaint.

Wilkinson, C.J., dissenting:

The majority would deny standing to every artist whose commissioned work was suppressed by the state. I believe Burke does possess standing to challenge Charleston's

4. Indeed, for all that appears in the present record, Klenk, as a property owner in the District, might well be supportive of the *constitutionality* of the preservation ordinance, and would limit his challenge (were he to make one) to its application in a particular case. No doubt, similar real world considerations should inform interpretation of the Article III standing requirement; federal courts have no warrant, and we ought not, to adjudicate disputes resting on speculation over such matters.

historic preservation ordinance. He was commissioned to paint a mural on the exterior wall of a building in historic downtown Charleston. Charleston's Board of Architectural Review ("BAR") learned of the project and, pursuant to the preservation ordinance, directed Burke to stop work on his mural. The owner of the building applied to BAR for a permit that would allow completion of the work. Burke agreed to cover the unfinished mural with plywood pending BAR's decision. BAR eventually denied the permit application on the ground that the mural was aesthetically incompatible with Charleston's historic district. Because display is not permitted, Burke's mural remains under plywood.

*** Because of the ordinance, Burke has suffered the concrete injury of having to stop work and board up his mural, shielding it from view. An order from this court invalidating the ordinance that keeps the mural under plywood would certainly redress this injury. *** The district court even identified another concrete economic opportunity that Burke lost by virtue of the Charleston ordinance. *Burke v. City of Charleston,* 893 F.Supp. 589, 604 (D.S.C.1995). Moreover, artists receive future commissions precisely because their work is seen and displayed and admired, which Burke's cannot be so long as his mural remains under wraps.

But of course a plaintiff need not even suffer economic injury in order to protest the suppression of speech by the state. Plaintiffs protesting infringement of intellectual property interests by another private party often advance allegations of economic loss. *See* 15 U.S.C. § 1117 (trademark); 17 U.S.C. § 107 (copyright); 35 U.S.C. § 284 (patent). By contrast, plaintiffs asserting First Amendment challenges to state action have relied upon the intrinsic value of speech in countless cases where no economic interest was at stake. *See, e.g., McIntyre v. Ohio Elections Comm'n,* 514 U.S. 334, *** (1995) (invalidating ban on anonymous campaign literature as violative of First Amendment). *** Burke's standing is firmly grounded on just such an intangible, but no less legally cognizable, interest.

The majority holds that artists have no First Amendment rights once they sell their work. The majority says this is so because only the owner then has the right to display the art. Display of a piece of art may well be "speech" by its owner, as the majority suggests, but I am unwilling to hold that it wholly ceases to be speech by the artist the second it is sold. In fact, "[i]t is well settled that a speaker's rights are not lost merely because compensation is received; a speaker is no less a speaker because he or she is paid to speak." *Riley v. National Fed'n of the Blind,* 487 U.S. 781, 801, 108 S.Ct. 2667, 2680, 101 L.Ed.2d 669 (1988). In reality an audience, a paying audience, is the lifeblood of any artist, and it is the rare artist who can sustain his craft without selling many, if not most, of his works. The majority's approach thus has the practical effect of leaving most artists with little protection against government suppression of their speech. This is a sad fate for those whose creative efforts make paintings possible.

The majority makes much of the indisputable fact that the owner may freely raze the building (and the mural painted thereon) for any reason. But two critical facts distinguish the rights of the owner from the powers of the government. First, the city does not stand in the shoes of the building owner vis-à-vis the mural because the government has not bought and paid for the owner's right to dispose of the mural. * * * Second, and more fundamentally, there is a world of difference between private conduct that suppresses speech and state action that has the same effect—it is the latter that implicates the fundamental protections of the First Amendment. To equate the waiver of property rights with the waiver of constitutional rights against the government is to obliterate a critical distinction in constitutional law.

Both parties present able arguments directed at the merits of Burke's First Amendment challenge. Burke asserts a core First Amendment interest in artistic speech. Charleston counters with its interest in maintaining the aesthetic integrity of its historic district and the related interests of protecting property values and promoting tourism. Those arguments deserve to be addressed by this court just as they were by the district court. Though I express no view on the constitutionality of Charleston's historic preservation ordinance, I cannot accept the majority's denial of standing. The restrictive rule of standing imposed upon this artist ill befits the Constitution's concern for free expression and speech. *Secretary of State of Maryland v. J.H. Munson Co., Inc.*, 467 U.S. 947, 956, 104 S.Ct. 2839, 2846–47, 81 L.Ed.2d 786 (1984). This case is most straightforward—an artist is simply protesting the suppression of his work by the state. Under the majority rule, if the state boarded up the ceiling of the Sistine Chapel, Michelangelo could not contest the action in court.

Notes and Questions

1. **The relevance of copyright law.** The court did not much consider how copyright law might define the respective interests of author and building owner. This investigation could sometimes lead to a different determination of standing. Under § 106 of the Copyright Act of 1976, even after an author has transferred ownership of the physical work, he retains the exclusive intangible rights flowing from copyright: the right to reproduce, distribute, make derivative works, perform publicly and display publicly; however, the owner of a physical work has the right to display the work to viewers present where the work is kept. 17 U.S.C. §§ 106, 109(c). As to works of visual art of "recognized stature," under the Visual Artist Rights Act, ("VARA"), the author has the "moral right" to prevent destruction of the work. 17 U.S.C. § 106A. However, this right does not apply in the case of a work that is a part of a building, such as a mural, which cannot be removed from the building without the destruction, distortion, mutilation, or other modification of the work. 17 U.S.C. § 113(d)(1). While the painting here would likely fall within this exception, other kinds of works often installed in buildings—mobiles, moldings, bas reliefs—might not.

2. **Breadth of the ordinance.** The court seemed to avoid the issue of the reach of the ordinance by confining the discussion to standing. On its face, the ordinance applied to alterations of buildings, that is, to things or acts that tangibly change the physical makeup of the buildings within the district. a. Taking the court's suggestion that Burke could create his image on a mobile medium, such as a sheet of plywood or building-sized canvas, could Klenk just lean that medium depicting the same image against the building without violating the ordinance? b. Would such a display have

the same effect on the aesthetics in the district as a mural? c. How does the mural contribute to telling the story of the district?

3. **Drawing on buildings.** Drawing on three-dimensional media is ancient—Egyptian tombs and temples, the Lescaux caves, the ceiling of the Sistine Chapel. Murals have long existed in the art world. During the Great Depression, the Works Progress Administration ("WPA"), employed not only laborers to build hiking trails and bridges, but artists (some well-regarded, like Jacob Lawrence and Jackson Pollock) to paint murals in public buildings. The Federal Art Project ("FAP") was one of the divisions of the WPA. President Franklin Roosevelt had made several attempts prior to the FAP to provide employment for artists on relief, namely through the Public Works of Art Project ("PWAP"), which operated from 1933 to 1934. The Treasury Department Section of Painting and Sculpture was created in 1934 after the demise of the PWAP. However, it was the FAP which provided the widest reach, creating over 5,000 jobs for artists and producing over 225,000 works of art for the American people. In roughly the first four months of 1934, it hired 3,749 artists and produced 15,663 paintings, murals, prints, crafts, and sculptures for government buildings around the country. The only requirement imposed upon the artists was that the subject of the work somehow relate to the building in which the work would reside. Jerry Adler, 1934: The Art of the New Deal, Smithsonian Magazine, June 2009, http://www.smithsonianmag.com/arts-culture/1934-the-art-of-the-new-deal-132242698/?no-ist (last visited April 1, 2017); *see also* New Deal/WPA Art Project, http://www.wpamurals.com (last visited April 1, 2017).

European countries have long-celebrated murals in the fashion of *trompe d'oeil* (art of illusion), that use realistic imagery to create an optical illusion of depth. Graffiti art, with vernacular themes and images, on subway cars, bridges, and abandoned buildings, became both popular and menacing, starting in the late 1960s. These "aerosol artists," young people, typically, in the dark of the night, affix images on the facades of public structures. What distinguishes inspired murals from vapid graffiti may be a matter of preference. Leo Tolstoy, in his essay "What Is Art?," stated that

> Art is not, as the metaphysicians say, the manifestation of some mysterious idea of beauty or God; it is not, as the aesthetical physiologists say, a game in which man lets off his excess of stored-up energy; it is not the expression of man's emotions by external signs; it is not the production of pleasing objects; and, above all, it is not pleasure; but it is a means of union among men, joining them together in the same feelings, and indispensable for the life and progress towards well-being of individuals and of humanity. LEO TOLSTOY, WHAT IS ART 50 (Aylmer Maude trans., 1904).

By this, Tolstoy perceived both the social and political aspects of art, for it does serve to communicate perceptions of value and their fulfillment. Art, besides addressing the soul, can also be regarded as an instrument for inculcating, riling, educating, and remembering.

4. **Three regimes.** The three regimes, private property, copyright law, and historic preservation, may conflict head on: ownership confers power over the building, while Section 106A and historic preservation laws constrain that power. Do authors' moral rights preempt the authority of a local landmark commission to order erasure from a designated landmark? Local historic preservation ordinances prohibit alterations and/or destruction of a designated landmark without a certificate of appropriateness issued by the local commission. There are no absolutes in any of the regimes discussed here. Private property means the right to destroy or demolish, unless the building is a designated landmark. VARA prohibits the destruction of art on buildings, unless it cannot be removed without harm. *See Phillips v. Pembroke Real Estate, Inc.*, 459 F.3d 128 (1st Cir. 2006) (VARA does not operate to prevent removal of site-specific art). Historic preservation prohibits the alteration and/or demolition of landmarks except in cases of economic hardship. It may be that an artist forfeits her creations when she knowingly places them on other people's property or on property invested with other values, like historic buildings. But, in those cases where the artist does not know of the limits on alterations and has permission to draw, then resolution of the conflict is not easy. We could resort to property law concepts and employ the legal fiction of constructive notice of a prior interest, that is, in the public to historic buildings. But that might well entail destroying a true masterpiece, while protecting an historic landmark. How to decide which to retain? Does Banksy's image of a rat do too much violence to the beauty of an 18th century tavern? Or does it add to its value? *See Banksy graffiti of giant machine gun-toting rat doubles the value of a derelict pub,* http://www.dailymail.co.uk/news/article-1082014/Banksy-graffiti-DOUBLES-price-derelict-pub-.html (last visited September 6, 2017). We might use alternative documentation—photographs or videos of the work of art. *See Architectural Heritage Ass'n v. County of Monterey*, 122 Cal. App. 4th 1095 (2004) (finding such mitigation measures inadequate), discussed *infra*. In *Cohen v. G & M Realty L.P.*, 988 F.Supp.2d 212 (E.D.N.Y. 2013), the court thought that documenting by photos was a significant mitigation of the harm from destruction of the building. Does a photographic reproduction of a work impress and preserve in the same way as keeping the original, even if it is only visited in museums, the place where we care for artists' creations and other artifacts of life?

2. New Orleans, Louisiana, Historic Preservation Ordinance

Maher v. City of New Orleans

United States Court of Appeals for the Fifth Circuit
516 F.2d 1051, 5 ELR 20524 (1975)

Adams, C.J. The issues posed in the case at hand, although they concern a municipal ordinance, nevertheless carry implications of nationwide import.

Plaintiff Maher, on the basis of the Fifth Amendment, assails an ordinance of the City of New Orleans that regulates the preservation and maintenance of buildings in the historic Vieux Carre section of that city,[1] popularly known as the French Quarter. Maher asserts that, on its face, the Vieux Carre Ordinance affronts the due process clause, because it provides no objective criteria to guide the Commission charged with its administration. Maher also contends that the Ordinance, as applied and under the guise of regulation, constitutes a taking of his property without just compensation.[2]

After dealing with prefatory issues of res judicata and collateral estoppel, the district court reached the merits and concluded that the Ordinance was valid. [371 F. Supp. 653 (E.D.La.1974).] We affirm.

I. Factual Background.

By amendment to the Louisiana Constitution in 1936, authority was vested in the City of New Orleans to create a Commission whose purpose was stated to be:

> The preservation of such buildings in the Vieux Carre section of the City of New Orleans as, in the opinion of said Commission, shall be deemed to have architectural and historical value, and which buildings should be preserved for the benefit of the people of the City of New Orleans and the State of Louisiana, and to that end the Commission shall be given such powers and duties as the ... City of New Orleans shall deem fit and necessary.[4]

To implement the historical preservation plan, the City enacted the Vieux Carre Ordinance. That Ordinance establishes the Vieux Carre Commission and creates a framework of rules governing its powers, duties and operations. Among its other provisions, the Ordinance stipulates that, to perform construction, alteration or demolition work within the geographic boundaries controlled by the legislation, one must procure a permit approved by the Commission.[5]

---

1. New Orleans, La., Code ch. 65 (Ordinance No. 14,538) (Vieux Carre Ordinance).

2. This appears to be the first reported case in a federal court of appeals determining the constitutionality of such an enactment. *But see Whitty v. City of New Orleans*, Civ. No. 6367 (E.D.La., filed June 30, 1959) appeal dismissed, No. 18,059, 5th Cir., filed March 29, 1960 (denial of demolition permit in Vieux Carre does not offend constitution). *See also City of New Orleans v. Dukes*, 501 F.2d 706 (5th Cir. 1974), *cert. granted* 421 U.S. 908, 95 S. Ct. 1556, 43 L. Ed. 2d 773 (1975) (constitutionality of pushcart vendor regulation in Vieux Carre).

4. La. Const. Art. XIV, Sec. 22A. The same section further charges the Commission with assuring "that the quaint and distinctive character of the Vieux Carre section of the City of New Orleans may not be injuriously affected, . . . that the value to the community of those buildings having architectural and historical worth may not be impaired, and . . . that a reasonable degree of control may be exercised over the architecture of [buildings in] said Vieux Carre section . . . ."

5. Vieux Carre Ordinance § 65-8. Submission of plans for exterior changes to Commission. Before the commencement of any work in the erection of any new building or in the alteration or addition to, or painting or repainting or demolishing of any existing building, any portion of which is to front on any public street or alley in the Vieux Carre Section, application by the owner for a permit therefor shall be made to the Vieux Carre Commission, accompanied by the full plans and specifications thereof so far as they relate to the proposed appearance, color, texture of materials and architectural design of the exterior, including the front, sides, rear and roof of such building, alteration or addition or of any out building, party wall, courtyard, fence or other dependency thereof. Additional procedures are set forth at §§ 65-9, -10.

The present controversy centers on the fate of the Victorian Cottage situated at 818-22 Dumaine Street, adjacent to the Maher residence in the Vieux Carre. Mr. Maher, who owned the property until his recent death,[6] had sought since 1963 to demolish the cottage and to erect a seven-apartment complex on the site.

Following a preliminary approval of Maher's proposal by its Architectural Committee, the Commission on April 16, 1963, disapproved Maher's application to raze the cottage. Almost from the time of the original application, interested individual neighborhood owners, as well as organized groups including the Vieux Carre Property Owners and Associates, Inc., the French Quarter Residents Association and the Louisiana Council for the Vieux Carre vigorously opposed the Maher plan to tear down the cottage and to develop the property.[7]

Maher undertook a succession of attempts to secure approval of his plans from the Commission.[8] After several refusals, the Commission was finally prevailed upon to issue the permit. Ultimately, however, construction was prohibited when on August 16, 1966, the City Council for New Orleans, on the basis of an appeal, forbade the grant of a demolition permit.

While the proceedings before the Commission and City Council were pending, Maher instituted suit in the Civil District Court for Orleans Parish, Louisiana. Upon the City Council's final refusal to issue a demolition permit, the litigation in the state court was pressed. The relief requested was a declaration that the City Council's action was beyond its statutory authority and, hence, null and void. On February 26, 1968, the Civil District Court granted judgment for Maher.

The Louisiana Court of Appeal reversed, holding that the City Council's review was proper and, further, that the Ordinance was constitutional both on its face and as applied to the Maher application. [*Maher v. City of New Orleans*, 222 So.2d 608 (La.App.1969).] On appeal, the Louisiana Supreme Court affirmed the judgment of the Court of Appeals that the City Council's action lay within its authority, but held that the constitutionality of the Ordinance had not been pleaded in the trial court and consequently could not be considered on appeal.[10]

---

6. Morris Maher, original plaintiff in this dispute, died in 1973. Thereafter, his wife was substituted as plaintiff in the district court, in her capacity as administratrix of his estate. For convenience we refer to the plaintiff as Maher.

7. As intervenors, the Vieux Carre Property Owners and Associates, Inc. and the French Quarter Residents Association have filed a brief in this Court jointly with the City of New Orleans. Also participating in the brief as intervenors are the Crescent Council of Civic Associations and Louisiana Landmarks Society.

8. The route that Maher pursued through the Commission and City Council is elaborated by the district court in its opinion. 371 F.Supp. 653 (E.D.La.1974).

10. *Maher v. City of New Orleans*, 256 La. 131, 235 So.2d 402 (1970). Nonetheless, the State Supreme Court observed in dictum that in light of earlier cases where it had held the Vieux Carre Ordinance constitutional, it was "inclined to agree" with the Court of Appeal that the Ordinance on its face was not vulnerable to charges of vagueness or indefiniteness. 235 So.2d at 405, n. 3, citing *City of New Orleans v. Levy*, 223 La. 14, 64 So.2d 798 (1953); *City of New Orleans v. Pergament*, 198 La. 852, 5 So.2d 129 (1941); *City of New Orleans v. Impastato*, 198 La. 206, 3 So.2d 559 (1941).

Subsequently, in 1971, Maher filed the present federal suit under the civil rights act against the City and its agencies, seeking a declaratory judgment that the Ordinance is unconstitutional and an injunction against its enforcement.[11]

The district court held *** the Ordinance constitutional. This appeal followed. ***

III. The Vieux Carre Ordinance is a Proper Exercise of the Police Power.

The Supreme Court has erected wayposts to guide our consideration whether an enactment such as the Vieux Carre Ordinance violates due process. A legislative determination is generally accorded a presumption of constitutionality,[34] but it is nevertheless subjected to several tests before its validity is established. To be sound, the enactment must be within the perimeter of the police power, an authority residing in the law-making body to secure, preserve and promote the general health, welfare and safety. [*Berman v. Parker* 348 U.S. 26, 75 S. Ct. 98, 99 L. Ed. 27 (1959).] A regulatory ordinance, to be sustained as a suitable exercise of the police power, must bear a real and substantial relation to a legitimate state purpose.[36] The means selected must be reasonable and of general application,[37] and the law must not trench impermissibly on other constitutionally protected interests.[38]

Maher contends that, although the legislative purpose underlying the preservation of the Vieux Carre, may be unobjectionable, the general program of effectuation as well as the denial of Maher's demolition permit have inadequate standards and an arbitrary enforcement that violate due process. Furthermore, he asserts that the law is confiscatory in its operation and constitutes a taking that requires compensation.

A substantial body of precedent exists respecting the appropriate balancing of interests where an ordinance diminishes the freedom of an individual owner to dispose of his property in the name of what the lawmaker deems the greater public benefit. *** The Supreme Court has made it clear that, while the police power is not unlimited, its boundaries are both ample and protean.[41] Drawing on the rich and flexible police power, a legislature has the authority to respond to economic and cultural developments cast in a different mold, and to essay new solutions to new problems. In *Village*

11. Jurisdiction is asserted pursuant to 28 U.S.C. §§ 1331(a), 1343(3) and (4). Maher claims that the Ordinance and its enforcement deprive him of rights under 42 U.S.C. § 1983.

34. *Goldblatt v. Hempstead*, 369 U.S. 590, 82 S. Ct. 987, 8 L. Ed. 2d 130 (1962); *Village of Euclid v. Ambler Realty Co.*, 272 U.S. 365, 47 S. Ct. 114, 71 L. Ed. 303 (1926).

36. *Village of Belle Terre v. Boraas*, 416 U.S. 1, 94 S. Ct. 1536, 39 L. Ed. 2d 797 (1974) (family values); *Paris Adult Theatre I v. Slater*, 413 U.S. 49, 93 S. Ct. 2628, 37 L. Ed. 2d 446 (1973) (quality of life); *Euclid, supra* note 34 (health, traffic, safety); *Walls v. Midland Carbon Co.*, 254 U.S. 300, 41 S. Ct. 118, 65 L. Ed. 276 (1920) (preserve natural gas resource); *Lawton v. Steele*, 152 U.S. 133, 14 S. Ct. 499, 38 L. Ed. 385 (1894) (preserve fishery resource); *Mugler v. Kansas*, 123 U.S. 623, 8 S. Ct. 273, 31 L. Ed. 205 (1887) (discourage intoxication).

37. *Berman, supra* note 35; *Euclid, supra* note 34; *Reinman v. Little Rock*, 237 U.S. 171, 35 S. Ct. 511, 59 L. Ed. 900 (1915).

38. *Belle Terre, supra* note 36; *Pennsylvania Coal Co. v. Mahon*, 260 U.S. 393, 43 S. Ct. 158, 67 L. Ed. 322 (1922); *Mugler, supra* note 36.

41. *Paris Adult Theatre, supra* note 36; *Berman, supra* note 35; *Euclid, supra* note 34; *Hadacheck v. Sebastian*, 239 U.S. 394, 36 S. Ct. 143, 60 L. Ed. 348 (1915).

of Euclid v. Ambler Realty Co., the watershed case upholding the right of a municipality to enact a general zoning ordinance, the Supreme Court observed:

> [P]roblems have developed, and constantly are developing, which require, and will continue to require, additional restrictions in respect of the use and occupation of private lands in urban communities. Regulations, the wisdom, necessity and validity of which, as applied to existing conditions, are so apparent that they are now uniformly sustained, a century ago, or even half a century ago, probably would have been rejected as arbitrary and oppressive. 272 U.S. at 386–87, 47 S.Ct. at 118 [(1926)].

Accordingly, no fixed constraints may be placed on the police power for the future. Rather, each case must be evaluated as it arises, on its own facts and in light of the prevailing circumstances.[43]

A keystone of due process analysis is the determination that the state purpose to be served is legitimate. It would therefore appear beneficial to detail the substantial support that exists for a legislative determination to preserve historic landmarks and districts. *** The Ordinance in question here declares as its objective:

> The Vieux Carre shall have for its purpose the preservation of such buildings in the Vieux Carre section of the City as, in the opinion of the Commission, shall have architectural and historical value and which should be preserved for the benefit of the people of the City and State.[45]

Proper state purposes may encompass not only the goal of abating undesirable conditions, but of fostering ends the community deems worthy. In *Berman v. Parker* the Supreme Court, giving "well-nigh conclusive" effect to the legislative determination of community needs and solutions, upheld the purposes of a slum clearance program designed to "develop a more balanced, more attractive community."[46]

Nor need the values advanced be solely economic or directed at health and safety in their narrowest senses. The police power inhering in the lawmaker is more generous, comprehending more subtle and ephemeral societal interests. "The values [that the police power] represents are spiritual as well as physical, aesthetic as well as monetary. It is within the domain of the legislature to determine that the community should be beautiful as well as healthy, spacious as well as clean, well-balanced as well as carefully patrolled."[47]

43. *Berman; Euclid.*

45. Vieux Carre Ordinance §65-6. In addition to conferring cultural benefits, it is not contested that preservation of the Vieux Carre district promotes the economic welfare of the city by attracting tourists. *See also* La. Const. *supra* note 4.

46. 348 U.S. 26, 32 *** (1954). To like effect, *see Village of Belle Terre v. Boraas*, 416 U.S. 1, 9 *** (1974) ("the police power is not confined to elimination of filth, stench and unhealthy places. It is ample to lay out zones where family values ... and the blessings of quiet seclusion ... make the area a sanctuary for people."); *Euclid*[.] ***

47. *Berman*, 348 U.S. at 33 ***. *Paris Adult Theatre* *** (police power includes authority to regulate against obscenity). The Supreme Court has also affirmed the power of legislatures to enact protective

This circuit has held in *Stone v. City of Maitland* that zoning ordinances may be sustained under the police power where motivated by a desire to "enhanc(e) the aesthetic appeal of a community." [446 F.2d 83, 89 (5th Cir. 1971).] The Court noted with approbation city action to maintain "the value of scenic surroundings" and "the preservation of the quality of our environment." [Id.]

One of the nation's distinctive historic districts is found in New Orleans. The federal, *** state and local government have each ascertained that benefits would be conferred on society by preservation of the French Quarter.

Throughout the country, there appears to be a burgeoning awareness that our heritage and culture are treasured national assets. Many locales endowed with historic sites have enacted protective measures for them. The Vieux Carre Ordinance is among the earliest efforts in this regard, and has served as a prototype for similar enactments elsewhere. ***

The federal government also has acknowledged our debt to the past, in the National Historic Preservation Act of 1966:

> "The Congress finds and declares
>
> (a) that the spirit and direction of the Nation are founded upon and
>
> reflected in its historic past;
>
> (b) that the historical and cultural foundations of the Nation should be preserved as a living part of our community life and development in order to give a sense of orientation to the American people...." ***

An Advisory Committee on Historic Preservation was established, and a National Register of Historic Places was developed that included the Vieux Carre. ***

The Court is not free to reverse the considered judgment of the legislature that it is in the public interest to preserve the status quo in the Vieux Carre and to scrutinize closely any proposed change in the ambiance by private owners. Where a legislative determination is "fairly debatable, the legislative judgment must be allowed to control."[54] We thus conclude that, considering the nationwide sentiment for preserving the country's heritage and with particular regard to the context of the unique and characteristic French Quarter, the objective of the Vieux Carre Ordinance falls within the permissible scope of the police power.

Since we deal here with legislation designed to effect a legitimate economic and social policy, so long as the means chosen—a matter largely entrusted to the legislature—are reasonable and not arbitrary, due process is satisfied.[55] It is not disputed that the Vieux Carre Ordinance furthers the object of preserving the character of the district in a meaningful fashion.

---

measures regulating the use of the natural resources of the community. *Walls v. Midland Carbon Co.*, 254 U.S. 300 *** (1920) (natural gas); *Lawton v. Steele*, 152 U.S. 133 *** (1894) (fish).

54. *Euclid*, 272 U.S. at 388 ***. *See also Paris Adult Theatre* ***; *Goldblatt* ***.

55. *Berman* ***; *Euclid* ***.

The Ordinance is of general application to a well-defined geographic area. In addition, it establishes a Commission whose professional qualifications and means of selection are delineated. Within the boundaries of the French Quarter, the Commission is directed to review plans for all proposed demolition or construction and its duties and procedures are specific. After due consideration the Commission reports its recommendations to the Director of the Department of Safety and Permits, whereupon a permit for the proposed work may issue. Provision is made for review by the City Council. ***

Though generally the procedures ordained are not faulted,[57] Maher attacks the schema as violative of due process because, in his view, it provides inadequate guidance to the Commission for the exercise of its administrative judgment. The City concedes that no official objective standards have been promulgated in this regard.

To satisfy due process, guidelines to aid a commission charged with implementing a public zoning purpose need not be so rigidly drawn as to prejudge the outcome in each case, precluding reasonable administrative discretion. Because of the circumstances pertaining to the Vieux Carre, we conclude that the Ordinance provides adequate legislative direction to the Commission to enable it to perform its functions consonant with the due process clause.

While concerns of aesthetic or historical preservation do not admit to precise quantification, certain firm steps have been undertaken here to assure that the Commission would not be adrift to act without standards in an impermissible fashion. First, the Louisiana constitution,[58] the Vieux Carre Ordinance[59] and, by interpretation, the Supreme Court of Louisiana,[60] have specified their expectations for the Vieux Carre, and the values to be implemented by the legislation.

Further, the legislature exercises substantial control over the Commission's decision making in several ways. Where possible, the ordinance is precise, as for example in delineating the district,[61] defining what alterations in which locations require ap-

---

57. The suggestion was advanced that the Ordinance has been, and continues to be, enforced in an arbitrary fashion and not altogether free from influence. Evidence, including a federally funded report on the Commission's operations, was inserted in the record to support such claims. Charges that improper considerations play a role in decision making respecting the French Quarter merit serious attention by the Court. The district court decided that on balance, the allegations in this respect were not substantiated by the record. On review, we affirm the district court on the basis that its result finds support in the record and is not clearly erroneous. In so affirming, however, we pause to note that past enforcement of the Ordinance does not seem to have been uniformly predictable.

58. La. Const. Art. XIV, § 22A, urges the City to protect "the quaint and distinctive character of the area." ***

59. Vieux Carre Ordinance § 65-6 charges the Commission to "preserv[e] such buildings ... [as] shall have architectural and historical value and which should be preserved for the benefit of the people...."

60. *See, e.g., City of New Orleans v. Pergament,* 198 La. 852, 5 So.2d 129, 131 (1941), which characterized the Commission's purpose as "preserv[ing] the antiquity of the whole French and Spanish Quarter, the tout ensemble, so to speak, by defending this relic [the Vieux Carre] against iconoclasm or vandalism."

61. Vieux Carre Ordinance § 65-6.

proval,[62] and particularly regulating items of special interest, such as floodlights, overhanging balconies or signs.[63]

Another method by which the lawmaking body curbed the possibility for abuse by the Commission was by specifying the composition of that body and its manner of selection.[64] Thus, the City is assured that the Commission includes architects, historians and business persons offering complementary skills, experience and interests.

The elaborate decision-making and appeal process set forth in the ordinance creates another structural check on any potential for arbitrariness that might exist.[65] Decisions of the Commission may be reviewed ultimately by the City Council itself. Indeed, that is the procedure that was followed in the present case.[66]

It is true, as Maher observed, that no officially promulgated regulations pinpoint each decision by the Commission. Nonetheless, apart from the evident purpose of the legislation and the taut lines of review maintained by the legislature over the operation of the Commission, other fertile sources are readily available to promote a

---

62. Vieux Carre Ordinance § 65-8 (Ordinance extends to exterior work on any building that fronts on a public street or alley within the Vieux Carre). *See* note 5, *supra*.

63. Vieux Carre Ordinance §§ 56-11; -13; -17 to -33.

64. Vieux Carre Ordinance §§ 56-2 to -4. Recommendation and appointment of members. The Vieux Carre Commission shall consist of nine members, all of whom shall be citizens of the city. They shall be appointed by the Mayor with the advice and consent of the Council. The members of the Commission shall be appointed by the Mayor as follows: one from a list of two persons recommended by the Louisiana Historical Society; one from a list of two persons recommended by the Curators of the Louisiana State Museum; one from a list of two persons recommended by the Association of Commerce of the city; three qualified architects from a list of six qualified architects recommended by the New Orleans Chapter of the American Institute of Architects and three at large. § 65-3. Term; vacancies. Each of the members of the Vieux Carre Commission shall be appointed for a term of four years. Whenever the term of a member of the Commission expires the Mayor shall appoint his successor from a list selected by the body which made the original selection from which the vacancy has occurred. § 65-4. Employees and committees. The Vieux Carre Commission may select and employ such persons as may be necessary to carry out the purposes for which it is created. The City Attorney shall be ex officio the attorney for the Commission. The Commission may designate and appoint, from among its members, various committees with such powers and duties as the Commission may have and prescribe.

65. Vieux Carre Ordinance §§ 65-5; -8 to -10.

66. The Ordinance provides for review by the City Council of a disapproved petition. § 65-10. No provision expressly exists for appealing the grant of a permit, but the Louisiana Supreme Court has interpreted the Ordinance to allow such review as well. *Maher v. City of New Orleans*, 256 La. 131, 235 So.2d 402 (1970). Its determination of Louisiana law is binding on this Court. *Reinman v. City of Little Rock*, 237 U.S. 171, 35 S. Ct. 511, 59 L. Ed. 900 (1915). At oral argument it was contended that an element of arbitrariness was interjected by the right to appeal from the Commission, a body of experts, to the City Council, a legislative body responsive to the electoral process. The apparent suggestion was that the City Council does not enjoy the expert status of the Commission and, in addition, would be susceptible to political pressure in reaching its decisions. We reject such an intimation here. The expert status of the Commission members is particularly relevant to sustain its ability to function under power delegated by the legislature; the legislators themselves are the repository of public trust, and no delegation problem arises where the City Council itself decides a matter. Insofar as the suggestion is of impropriety, we affirm the district court conclusion that the proof was inadequate. *See* note 57 *supra*.

reasoned exercise of the professional and scholarly judgment of the Commission.... [I]t would seem that old city plans and historic documents, as well as photographs and contemporary writings may provide an abundant and accurate compilation of data to guide the Commission. And the district court observed,

> In this case, the meaning of a mandate to preserve the character of the Vieux Carre "takes clear meaning from the observable character of the district to which it applies." [371 F.Supp. at 664, quoting *Town of Deering ex rel. Bittenbender v. Tibbets*, 105 N.H. 481, 202 A.2d 232 (1964).]

Aside from such contemporary indicia of the nature and appearance of the French Quarter at earlier times, the Commission has the advantage at present of a recent impartial architectural and historical study of the structures in the area. The Vieux Carre Survey Advisory Committee conducted its analysis under a grant to Tulane University from the Edward G. Schleider Foundation. Building by building, the Committee assessed the merit of each structure with respect to several factors. For example, regarding the Maher cottage at issue here, the Louisiana Supreme Court noted that the Survey Committee "was of the opinion that this cottage was worthy of preservation as part of the over-all scene." [235 So.2d 402, 407, n. 4.] While the Schleider survey in no way binds the Commission, it does furnish an independent and objective judgment respecting the edifices in the area. The existence of the survey and other historical source material assist in mooring the Commission's discretion firmly to the legislative purpose.[69]

We thus conclude that the present zoning ordinance, enacted to promote the social and economic goals of preserving an historical district judged of public value, does not delegate unfettered authority to the Vieux Carre Commission. Rather, the legislature has provided adequate structure and guidelines to that administrative body[.] ***

IV. There is no Taking of the Dumaine Cottage that Would Require the Payment of Compensation.

Maher presents a twofold basis for his contention that the application of the Vieux Carre Ordinance to the cottage constitutes a taking of his property. First, he claims that unless he can build the desired apartment complex, he may not pursue the most profitable use to which his property may be put. Second, he asserts that the city may not permissibly impose an affirmative maintenance duty upon a property owner without taking the property under the power of eminent domain. We deal with these two contentions in turn.

To survive attack as a taking, the zoning regulation must as a threshold matter satisfy the due process requirements that its purpose and means are reasonable. Even if it comports with due process, a regulatory ordinance may nonetheless be a taking

---

69. In this regard, we find the present case distinguishable from *Barnes v. Merritt*, 428 F.2d 284 (5th Cir. 1970), and *Hornsby v. Allen*, 326 F.2d 605 (5th Cir. 1964). In those cases successful attacks were mounted on the denial of liquor permits, because of a total absence of proper standards to govern the administrative discretion. This circuit found that the unfettered, unreviewable power granted the agency in those situations offended due process.

if it is unduly onerous so as to be confiscatory. The Supreme Court has held that every regulation is in some sense a prohibition[75] and that whether a given regulation treads over the line of proper regulation and operates as a taking of property is a matter to be determined under all the circumstances in a specific case. Justice Holmes has remarked:

> Constitutional rights like others are matters of degree. To illustrate: Under the police power, in its strict sense, a certain limit might be set to the height of buildings without compensation; but to make that limit five feet would require compensation and a taking by eminent domain. [*Martin v. District of Columbia*, 205 U.S. 135, 139, 27 S.Ct. 440, 441, 51 L.Ed. 743 (1907).]

The Supreme Court repeatedly made clear that an ordinance within the police power does not become an unconstitutional taking merely because, as a result of its operation, property does not achieve its maximum economic potential ***[.][77] Such regulation "is not, and, consistently with the existence and safety of organized society, cannot be, burdened with the condition that the State must compensate such individual owners for pecuniary losses they may sustain...." [369 U.S. at 593, quoting *Mugler v. Kansas*, 123 U.S. 623 (1887).]

[Additionally, a]n ordinance forbidding the demolition of certain structures, if it serves a permissible goal in an otherwise reasonable fashion, does not seem on its face constitutionally distinguishable from ordinances regulating other aspects of land ownership, such as building height, set back or limitations on use. We conclude that the provision requiring a permit before demolition and the fact that in some cases permits may not be obtained does not alone make out a case of taking.

As the ordinance was applied to Maher, the denial of the permit to demolish and rebuild does not operate as a classic example of eminent domain, namely, a taking of Maher's property for government use.[82] Nor did Maher demonstrate to the satisfaction of the district court that a taking occurred because the ordinance so diminished the property value as to leave Maher, in effect, nothing.[83] In particular, Maher did not show that the sale of the property was impracticable, that commercial rental could not provide a reasonable rate of return, or that other potential use of the property was foreclosed.[84] To the extent that such is the theory underlying Maher's claim, it fails for lack of proof.

---

75. *Euclid* ***.

77. *Goldblatt v. Town of Hempstead*, 369 U.S. 590 *** (1962); *Euclid v. Ambler Realty Co.*, 272 U.S. 365 *** (1926); *Hadacheck v. Sebastian*, 239 U.S. 394 *** (1915).

82. *See United States v. Central Eureka Mining Co.*, 357 U.S. 155 *** (1958). *But see Keystone Associates v. Moerdler*, 19 N.Y.2d 78, 278 N.Y.S.2d 185, 224 N.E.2d 700 *** (Ct.Appeals 1967) (a taking of property of the old Metropolitan Opera House found where demolition was retarded and use limited severely).

83. In any case, while a substantial diminution in value may be evidence of a taking, "it is by no means conclusive." *Goldblatt v. Hempstead*, 369 U.S. at 594 ***. *See also Euclid* ***.

84. Maher objects strenuously to the district court's observation that rental values in the French Quarter are reputedly relatively high. We need not decide whether judicial notice was improperly ex-

We finally consider Maher's objection to that portion of the ordinance requiring reasonable maintenance and repair of buildings in the French Quarter.[85] By imposing an affirmative duty on property owners to prevent and correct defects, Maher claims that the City Council has overstepped permissible bounds of police power and by requiring him to make expenditures has effectively taken his property. To do this, Maher invokes the eminent domain provisions and demands just compensation.

Tests set forth by the Supreme Court again inform our analysis.[86] Once it has been determined that the purpose of the Vieux Carre legislation is a proper one, upkeep of buildings appears reasonably necessary to the accomplishment of the goals of the ordinance.[87] As noted above, the responsibility for determining the wisdom of a legislative determination is not lodged with the judiciary.

The fact that an owner may incidentally be required to make out-of-pocket expenditures in order to remain in compliance with an ordinance does not per se render that ordinance a taking. In the interest of safety, it would seem that an ordinance might reasonably require buildings to have fire sprinklers or to provide emergency facilities for exits and light. In pursuit of health, provisions for plumbing or sewage disposal might be demanded. Compliance could well require owners to spend money. Yet, if the purpose be legitimate and the means reasonably consistent with the objective, the ordinance can withstand a frontal attack of invalidity.

Our decision is narrow regarding the requirement reasonably to maintain property in the French Quarter. In holding that the ordinance provision necessitating reasonable maintenance is constitutional, we do not conclude that every application of such an ordinance would be beyond constitutional assault. For, as the Supreme Court emphasized in *Goldblatt*, even a generally constitutional regulation may become a taking in an isolated application if "unduly oppressive" to a property owner. [369 U.S. at 595, quoting *Lawton v. Steele*, 152 U.S. 133, 137 (1894).] It may be that, in some set of circumstances, the expense of maintenance under the Ordinance—were the city to exact compliance—would be so unreasonable as to constitute a taking.[89]

---

ercised in this regard, for any error that may have occurred was not reversible. We also find unpersuasive Maher's contention that a critical fact is that he inherited the property rather than purchasing it.

85. Vieux Carre Ordinance §65-36. *Preservation of existing structures by owner or person having legal custody thereof.* All buildings and structures in that section of the city known as the Vieux Carre Section ... shall be preserved against decay and deterioration and free from certain structural defects in the following manner, by the owner thereof ... [who] ... shall repair such building if it is found to have any of the following defects: There follows a list of unsafe, nonweather sound and deteriorated conditions, including falling portions of buildings, deteriorated or inadequate foundation, floors, walls, support, ceilings, roofs, chimneys, and ineffectively weathertight exterior or windows. Under Section 65-37, charges may be brought against a noncomplying owner. ***

86. *Goldblatt* ***; *Euclid* ***. In *Goldblatt*, the Supreme Court did not reach the question whether an affirmative duty to erect a fence and fill in the lake was overly burdensome and beyond the police power.

87. *Goldblatt* ***. *Euclid* ***[.]

89. *See Keystone Associates* ***.

The burden of proof as to this point falls on the party alleging the taking.[90] On the evidence presented here, the district court found that Maher had not sustained his burden of demonstrating that the upkeep provisions were inordinately burdensome.[91] We go no further than to state that we cannot find the district court determination in this regard to be erroneous.

V. Conclusion.

The Vieux Carre Ordinance was enacted to pursue the legitimate state goal of preserving the "tout ensemble" of the historic French Quarter. The provisions of the Ordinance appear to constitute permissible means adapted to secure that end. Furthermore, the operations of the Vieux Carre Commission satisfy due process standards in that they provide reasonable legislative and practical guidance to, and control over, administrative decision making.

Once the district court concluded it was at liberty, under principles of finality, to reach the merits of Maher's case, that court was not persuaded that the denial of a demolition permit was arbitrary. It did not find that the ordinance as applied to Maher constituted a taking of Maher's property for which compensation was indicated. These determinations, based on the proof proffered there, are not clearly erroneous.

An order will, therefore, be entered affirming the judgment of the district court.

Affirmed.

Notes and Questions

1. **Police powers.** In *Berman v. Parker*, 348 U.S. 26, 33 (1959), the Supreme Court recognized that the police powers of local governments extend beyond merely acting to eradicate blight, but could be used to build communities with high aesthetic values. Earlier, in *Village of Euclid v. Ambler Realty Co.*, 272 U.S. 365, 388 (1926), the Court instructed that courts should defer to the legislative body on the wisdom of an enactment, so long as the relation to the asserted ends is "fairly debatable." In upholding the ordinance in *Maher*, the court acknowledged that making administrative determinations based on aesthetics could prove troublesome, particularly where the legislative language is so lacking in standards that it could be applied in an irrational or arbitrary fashion. a. Can architectural and historical value be assessed and articulated in objective terms, such as by architectural style, type of materials, historical associations, and/or uses? b. Are such mechanisms identified by the court for cabining the administrative discretion effective?

2. **Economic hardship.** The court acknowledged that a point could be reached where the duty to maintain the historic building could become so burdensome as to constitute a taking. a. What factors would be relevant to this finding? b. Could or should standards for this determination be incorporated within the text of the ordinance? c. Recall *Penn Central Transp. Co. v. New York City*, 438 U.S. 104 (1978), dis-

90. *Goldblatt*, 369 U.S. at 596, 82 S. Ct. 987.

91. 371 F. Supp. at 662.

cussed in Chapter 2. We revisit economic hardship in the context of non-profit organizations, *infra.*

City of New Orleans v. Pergament

Supreme Court of Louisiana
198 La. 852, 5 So.2d 129 (1941)

O'Niell, C.J. The defendant has a gasoline filling station in the old section of New Orleans called the Vieux Carre. He was prosecuted in the recorder's court on a charge of violating a municipal ordinance, by displaying on his premises a large advertising sign without the permission of the Vieux Carre Commission, and contrary to the provisions of section 6 of Ordinance No. 14,538 C.C.S., as amended by Ordinance No. 15,085 C.C.S. He filed a demurrer and motion to quash the affidavit, on the ground that the ordinance if applied to his place of business would be arbitrary, unreasonable and oppressive, and would deprive him of his property without due process of law, and deny to him the equal protection of the laws. He pleaded also in his demurrer that the city had no authority to enact such an ordinance with reference to buildings like that in which he conducted his business, and particularly that such authority was not conferred by the constitutional amendment adopted pursuant to Act 139 of 1936, and designated as Section 22A of Article XIV of the Constitution. In this connection he avers that the only purpose of the amendment was to enable the municipal council to preserve for the public the architectural and historical worth of the ancient buildings in the Vieux Carre, and that his place of business, being a modern structure, having no architectural or historical worth, is not subject to the provisions of the constitutional amendment. The defendant pleaded also in his demurrer that the municipal ordinance violated the provision in section 33 of Act 136 of 1898 that "An ordinance shall not contain more than one subject."

The Recorder *** sustained the demurrer and dismissed the prosecution. The city has appealed from the decision.

The constitutional amendment which was adopted pursuant to the provisions of Act 139 of 1936, and which is Section 22A of Article XIV of the Constitution, authorized the municipal council of New Orleans to establish the commission known as the Vieux Carre Commission, the members of which are appointed by the Mayor. The purpose of the amendment is stated in these three paragraphs:

> 'The said [Vieux Carre] Commission shall have for its purpose the preservation of such buildings in the Vieux Carre section of the City of New Orleans as, in the opinion of said Commission, shall be deemed to have architectural and historical value, and which buildings should be preserved for the benefit of the people of the City of New Orleans and the State of Louisiana, and to that end the Commission shall be given such powers and duties as the Commission Council of the City of New Orleans shall deem fit and necessary.
>
> * * *

> "Hereafter and for the public welfare and in order that the quaint and distinctive character of the Vieux Carre section of the City of New Orleans may not be injuriously affected, and in order that the value to the community of those buildings having architectural and historical worth may not be impaired, and in order that a reasonable degree of control may be exercised over the architecture of private and semi-public buildings erected on or abutting the public streets of said Vieux Carre section, whenever any application is made for a permit for the erection of any new building or whenever any application is made for a permit for alterations or additions to any existing building, any portion of which is to front on any public street in the Vieux Carre section, the plans therefor, so far as they relate to the appearance, color, texture of materials and architectural design of the exterior thereof shall be submitted, by the owner, to the Vieux Carre Commission and the said Commission shall report promptly to the Commission Council its recommendations, including such changes, if any, as in its judgment are necessary, and the said Commission Council shall [sic] take such action as shall, in its judgment, effect reasonable compliance with such recommendation, or to prevent any violation thereof.
>
> 'The Commission Council of the City of New Orleans may, by ordinance or otherwise, carry the above and foregoing provisions into effect."

The Vieux Carre Commission was created by Ordinance No. 14,538 C.C.S., which was amended by Ordinance No. 15,085 C.C.S. The sixth section of the ordinance is the one which forbids the proprietor of any building in the Vieux Carre to maintain a display sign, or advertising sign, without first obtaining a permit from the Vieux Carre Commission. The ordinance prescribes the maximum size and the details of the various kinds of advertising signs which may be displayed. The maximum area of any sign or signboard allowed to be displayed in the Vieux Carre, according to the ordinance, is 8 square feet if only one side or surface of the sign is displayed, or 16 square feet if both sides are displayed. The sign or signboard which the defendant in this case is displaying in violation of the ordinance has an area of 560 square feet. The lower part of the sign measures 24 feet in width and 20 feet in height, above which is an extension 12 feet wide and having an area of 80 square feet. The size of the sign therefore is far above the ordinary, and above the maximum size allowed by the ordinance. The defendant's offense is not only that he failed to obtain or apply for permission of the Vieux Carre Commission to erect the sign but also that the size of the sign exceeds the maximum size allowed by the ordinance, and hence could not be permitted by the commission.

The ordinance might be deemed violative of the equal protection clause in the Fourteenth Amendment if the ordinance undertook to confer upon the Vieux Carre Commission the authority to grant or withhold permits arbitrarily, or without prescribing uniform requirements or standards which all persons similarly situated should be obliged to comply with. But the ordinance does prescribe such uniform requirements or standards. And there is nothing arbitrary or discriminating in forbidding the proprietor of a modern building, as well as the proprietor of one of the ancient landmarks, in the Vieux Carre to display an unusually large sign upon his premises.

The purpose of the ordinance is not only to preserve the old buildings themselves, but to preserve the antiquity of the whole French and Spanish quarter, the tout ensemble, so to speak, by defending this relic against iconoclasm or vandalism. Preventing or prohibiting eyesores in such a locality is within the police power and within the scope of this municipal ordinance. The preservation of the Vieux Carre as it was originally is a benefit to the inhabitants of New Orleans generally, not only for the sentimental value of this show place but for its commercial value as well. ***

The defendant's complaint that the municipal council did not have authority to enact the ordinance is not well founded. *** [T]he authority is embraced in the first and third paragraph which we have quoted from the constitutional amendment. *** In subsection (d) of section 1 of Act 338 of 1936, amending the city's charter, it is declared:

> "(d) The City of New Orleans shall also have all powers, privileges and functions which by or pursuant to the Constitution of this State, have been, or could be granted to, or exercised by any city, and shall have power to pass ordinances, and to exercise full police power in connection with any function of municipal government within the territorial limits of said city, including the right, power and authority, to pass ordinances on all subject matters, including subject matters which the Legislature has reserved to itself the right to regulate, but has not regulated, or has not fully regulated, on which the Legislature has reserved to itself the right to legislate, but has not legislated, or has passed general or special laws which do not cover the entire subject matter, and on any and all other subject matters without exception, regardless of whether or not the Legislature has enacted special or general laws upon the same subject matter, subject only to the limitation that the provisions of said ordinances shall not directly conflict with the provisions of any state laws upon the same subject matter."

The judgment is annulled, the defendant's demurrer is overruled, and the case is ordered remanded to the recorder's court for further proceedings consistent with the opinion which we have rendered.

City of New Orleans v. Impastato

Supreme Court of Louisiana

198 La. 206, 3 So.2d 559 (1941)

McCaleb, J. Joseph Impastato was convicted in the First Recorder's Court of New Orleans on a charge of violating Ordinance No. 14,538, Commission Council Series, as amended by Ordinance No. 15,085. Claiming that this ordinance is unconstitutional in that it is violative of the provisions of Section 22A of Article 14 of the Constitution and that the sentence imposed by the Recorder is therefore illegal and void, he has appealed directly to this Court under the authority granted by Article 7, Section 10, of the Constitution.

By Section 22A of Article 14, which was added to the Constitution by amendment adopted on November 3, 1936, the Commission Council of the City of New Orleans was authorized to create and organize a commission to be known as the Vieux Carre Commission, to be appointed by the Mayor of the City. It provides that the Commission shall have for its purpose the preservation of such buildings in the Vieux Carre section of the City of New Orleans as, in the opinion of the Commission, shall be deemed to have architectural and historical value "and which buildings should be preserved for the benefit of the people of the City of New Orleans and the State of Louisiana, and to that end the Commission shall be given such powers and duties as the Commission Council of the City of New Orleans shall deem fit and necessary...."

[The ordinances in contention,] provided for the creation of a Commission for the Vieux Carre section of the City, designated the boundaries of that section, and further provided that, before any owner of property situated within the limits of that section should erect or alter any building fronting on any public street or alley, 'application by the owner for a permit therefor shall be made to the Vieux Carre Commission, accompanied by the full plans and specifications thereof, so far as they relate to the proposed appearance, color, texture of materials and architectural design of the *exterior, including the front, sides, rear and roof*, of said building alterations or additions or of any outbuilding party wall courtyard fence or other dependency thereof ***' (italics ours) [emphasis in original].

The defendant is the owner of a certain building on the corner of Chartres and St. Louis Streets in the Vieux Carre section of the City of New Orleans known as "The Napoleon House". In the rear of this building is a patio or courtyard which is connected with Chartres and St. Louis Streets by alleyways—one of which abuts St. Louis Street and the other Chartres Street. In the latter part of 1939, the defendant undertook to enlarge and reconstruct a small lavatory attached to the rear of his building which abutted the courtyard hereinabove referred to. Upon his failure to obtain a permit from the Vieux Carre Commission to perform this work, as required by the City ordinance, he was charged by affidavit in the Recorder's Court and, after a trial, was convicted of violating the ordinance and sentenced to pay a fine.

The sole contention of the defendant is that the City ordinance under which he was prosecuted is unconstitutional because it attempts to grant to the Vieux Carre Commission much broader powers, with respect to the erection and alteration of buildings, than were delegated to it by the constitutional amendment. The precise point is that, while the Constitution authorized the City of New Orleans to assume control of the Vieux Carre section, it limited its authority over the section in regard to the erection and alteration of buildings fronting on any public street by providing that it would be necessary to obtain a permit only in cases where the exterior of the building was to be altered or rehabilitated. From this premise, it is argued that the City, in making it mandatory that a permit be applied for and obtained from the Commission before any alterations are made to the exterior, 'including the front, sides, rear and roof of said building', assumed power not authorized by the Constitution and that, therefore, the ordinance in this respect is illegal, null and void.

We are unable to discern merit in the defendant's contention. In the first place, a reading of the constitutional provision reveals a plain intention on the part of the people to delegate to the City of New Orleans, acting through a Commission to be known as the Vieux Carre Commission, full and complete authority with respect to the preservation of the architecture and the historic value of the buildings situated in the Vieux Carre section for it is declared that "to that end the Commission shall be given such powers and duties as the Commission Council of the City of New Orleans shall deem fit and necessary". This, we think, is sufficient to include all reasonable regulations made by the City respecting changes to be made to the outside of any building situated in the Vieux Carre section which fronts on a public street.

Moreover, the argument of the defendant that the alteration made by him in the rear of his building is not a change in the exterior of the structure does not impress us. The word "exterior", as applied to a building, clearly means all of the outer surfaces thereof as distinguished from its interior or the portion enclosed by the outer surfaces. The alteration made by the defendant to the lavatory situated in the rear of his building abutting the courtyard constitutes a change to the exterior or outside thereof. The word 'exterior' as used in the Constitution cannot be limited to include only the front portion of the building as contended for by defendant's counsel. Such a strained interpretation of the language employed in the constitutional amendment would merely serve to defeat the obvious intention of the people as expressed therein by rendering it impossible for the Commission to preserve the architectural design of the sides, rear and roof of any building in the Vieux Carre section.

For the reasons assigned, the conviction and sentence appealed from are affirmed.

Affirmed.

Notes and Questions

1. **"Tout ensemble."** This French term is translated to mean the total appearance or effect of something. In historic preservation districts, it refers to the complement of buildings, their styles, sizes, uses, street layout, and landscaping, that create a district whose characteristics can be discerned from a distance. It "describes an 'associational harmony,'" which places a focus "on shared human values and the community's need for cultural stability." James P. Karp, *The Evolving Meaning of Aesthetics in Land-Use Regulation*, 15 Colum. J. Envtl. L. 307, 309 (1990). The concept thus provides the predicate for regulating alterations not just on those buildings that are historic, but also to modern ones that are situated within the historic district to the extent they contribute to the overall construction of the district. The North Carolina Supreme Court, in *A-S-P Assocs. v. City of Raleigh*, 258 S.E.2d 444, 450 (N.C. 1979), stated that preservation "provides a visual, educational medium by which an understanding of our country's historic and cultural heritage may be imparted to present and future generations" and that "preservation of the historic aspects of a district requires more than simply the preservation" of buildings, but also preservation of their setting and scene; "[t]his 'tout ensemble' doctrine ... is an integral and reasonable part of effective historic district preservation." *Id.* at 451.

2. **Constraints of "tout ensemble."** a. Could "tout ensemble" achieve its purpose if, as Impastato argued, only the fronts of buildings, those parts visible from the

street, were covered by the ordinance? b. Does the concept serve to preserve the memory and landscape of the community? c. Does it allow a historic district to evolve? d. How can modern notions and concerns about community, walkability, and accessibility, for instance, be achieved at the same time?

3. **The first historic preservation ordinance focused on districts.** During the 1920s–1940s, the City of Charleston, South Carolina, began to experience increased threats to historic properties: residential and public buildings were being torn down, often to make way for new filling stations and for parking lots following the advent of automobile travel. Buildings were being dismantled for their architectural elements as art collectors purchased architectural details from residential properties to furnish their own homes or recreate period rooms in galleries and museums; and Charlestonians were selling the architectural details of their old homes for a variety of reasons, including to raise money to pay taxes, because the property was already being demolished, or because the property was located in a rundown area occupied by African-American tenants; the prices offered too tempting to resist. A public campaign for preservation began. The first movement was the establishment of the Society for the Preservation of Old Dwellings (later renamed the Preservation Society of Charleston), whose first action was to purchase the Joseph Manigault House (ca. 1803) to save it from demolition. After it became clear that preservation societies lacked the resources to buy up and maintain all the historic buildings in the city, the preservation movement focused on legislation. In 1931, the City of Charleston became the first city in the nation to adopt a zoning ordinance with provisions for the protection of historic properties. The ordinance designated part of the city as the "Old and Historic Charleston District" and established a Board of Architectural Review ("BAR"), invested with the authority to govern architectural alterations and changes made to properties located within the historic district. The BAR was to consist of five members drawn from organizations whose members might offer useful institutional expertise, including the city planning and zoning commission, the local chapters of the American Institute of Architects and the American Society of Civil Engineers, the local real estate exchange, and the Carolina Art Association. The use of a general zoning ordinance showed great vision; rather than just protecting specific buildings, it targeted entire neighborhoods for preservation. This tactic would "define the modern preservation movement." *See generally* ROBERT R. WEYENETH, HISTORIC PRESERVATION FOR A LIVING CITY, HISTORIC CHARLESTON FOUNDATION *1947–1997*, 2–3 (2000).

3. Santa Fe, New Mexico, Historic Preservation Ordinance

City of Santa Fe v. Gamble-Skogmo, Inc.

Supreme Court of New Mexico
73 N.M. 410, 389 P.2d 13 (1964)

Noble, J. This appeal requires our determination whether the historical zoning ordinance of the City of Santa Fe is ultra vires of the city's powers and whether the ordinance is valid and constitutional.

Defendants, Gamble-Skogmo, Inc. and Charles Atwell, resident manager, obtained a permit pursuant to the city building code to remodel a building within the historical zone in Santa Fe. One requirement of the plans and specifications and of the permit was that to comply with the historical zoning ordinance, the window panes not exceed thirty inches square. The window pane requirement was accomplished by installation of 'mullions' or wooden dividers back of the window panes which gave the appearance of window panes of the required size. After completion of the remodeled building, but before the city's approval, the defendants removed the dividers leaving large show windows contrary to the city ordinance and the building permit.

This appeal followed the conviction and sentence in the district court, on appeal from the city court.

We find no merit to defendants' first contention that a criminal conviction cannot be supported because the historical zoning ordinance contains no penalty clause. The historical zoning act prescribes the conditions for approval of plans and specifications upon which a building permit is issued under the building code. Defendants were charged and found guilty in city court with violation of that provision of the Uniform Building Code which requires all construction work to be according to the plans and specifications approved with the building permit. No attack was made, either in the trial court or here, upon the building code.

Santa Fe Ordinance 1957-18, adopted October 30, 1957, created an historical district and provided regulations for buildings constructed or altered therein. Its purpose is stated as:

> 'Section 2. *Purpose of Creating 'H' Historical District.*
>
> 'That in order to promote the economic, cultural and general welfare of the people of the City of Santa Fe, and to insure the harmonious, orderly and efficient growth and development of the municipality, it is deemed essential by the City Council of the City of Santa Fe, that the qualities relating to the history of Santa Fe, and a harmonious outward appearance which preserves property values and attracts tourists and residents alike, be preserved; some of these qualities being: the continued existence and preservation of historical areas and buildings; continued construction of buildings in the historic styles, and a general harmony as to style, form, color, proportion, texture and material between buildings of historic design and those of more modern design.'

Defendants next direct their attack to the historical zoning portion of the city's zoning ordinance, claiming a lack of enabling legislation authorizing such an exercise of the police power by the city.

A municipality has no inherent right to exercise police power. Its powers are derived solely from the state. *Town of Mesilla v. Mesilla Design Center & Book Store*, 71 N.M. 124, 376 P.2d 183; *Munro v. City of Albuquerque*, 48 N.M. 306, 150 P.2d 733. We, therefore, examine the statutes in force at the time the ordinance was adopted directing our inquiry to whether the grant of zoning power authorized preservation of a historical area. It is agreed that the authority, if it is to be found, must be contained in §§ 14-28-9 to 11, N.M.S.A.1953. § 14-28-10 contains a specific grant of power to regulate or restrict the erection, construction, re-construction, alteration, repair or use of buildings, structures or lands, and § 14-28-11 provides that 'such regulations and restrictions' shall be 'in accordance with a comprehensive plan *** to promote the health and the general welfare ***.' We note in passing that specific legislative authority was subsequently granted by the 'Historic District Act,' Ch. 92, Laws 1961.

Defendants assert that the enabling legislation limited a municipality's zoning power to enactment of regulations restricting the height, number of stories, and size of buildings; the size of lots and percentage thereof that may be occupied; the density of population, and the location and use of buildings for trade, industry, residence or other uses. We find no such restriction in the statute. Sec. 14-28-11, N.M.S.A.1953, grants the authority to regulate and restrict 'in accordance with a comprehensive plan ***; to promote health and the general welfare; ***.' The legislature, then, granted municipalities authority, by zoning ordinances, to restrict and regulate buildings and structures in accordance with a comprehensive plan for the general welfare of the city and its people. To be within the authorized purposes the zoning ordinance must bear some reasonable relationship to the general welfare.

The term 'general welfare' has not been exactly defined, we think, by reason of the same definitive problem expressed in *Arnold v. Board of Barber Examiners*, 45 N.M. 57, 70, 109 P.2d 779, 787, regarding the phrase 'affected with a public interest,' where it was said:

> '*** The phrase 'affected with a public interest' probably can never be given an exact definition. This is probably desirable when we reflect upon the constant and ever changing conditions of our social and economic structure. This condition clearly implies the necessity for some degree of latitude allowable for obviously necessary judicial interpretation.... '

No decisions discussing the precise question of enabling legislation have been pointed out to us nor have we found any. However, analogous questions were before the Massachusetts Supreme Court on at least two occasions. The question there was the constitutionality of proposed legislation establishing and preserving historical areas in that state. In each case the right to exercise the police power depended upon whether preservation of such an historical area and style of architecture was comprehended within the public welfare. If it was, the police power could be constitutionally exercised to preserve and protect such areas.

In the *Opinion of the Justices to the Senate*, 333 Mass. 783, 128 N.E.2d 563, 566, it was said:

> 'The announced purpose of the act is to preserve this historic section for the educational, cultural, and economic advantage of the public. If the General Court believes that this object would be attained by the restrictions which the act would place upon the introduction into the district of inappropriate forms of construction that would destroy its unique value and associations, a court can hardly take the view that such legislative determination is so arbitrary or unreasonable that it cannot be comprehended within the public welfare.'

In a second *Opinion of the Justices to the Senate*, 333 Mass. 773, 128 N.E.2d 557, 559, 561, the same question was presented regarding an act establishing historic districts known as '(1) Old and Historic Nantucket District, and (2) Old and Historic Siasconset District.' The purpose of the act was to promote the general welfare of the inhabitants of the town through "the preservation and protection of historic buildings, places and districts of historic interest; through the development of an appropriate setting for these buildings, places and districts; and through the benefits resulting to the economy of Nantucket in developing and maintaining its vacation-travel industry through the promotion of these historic associations.' ***.' The purpose was held to be for the promotion of the public welfare. We quote at some length from the Massachusetts court because of its special application to the situation presented by the instant case. In 128 N.E.2d at 561, 562, it was said:

> '*** Can it rest upon the less definite and more inclusive ground that it serves the public welfare? The term public welfare has never been and cannot be precisely defined. ***'

The court after discussing other decisions went on to say:

> '*** We may also take judicial notice that Nantucket is one of the very old towns of the Commonwealth; that for perhaps a century it was a famous seat of the whaling industry and accumulated wealth and culture which made itself manifest in some fine examples of early American architecture; and that the sedate and quaint appearance of the old island town has to a large extent still remained unspoiled and in all probability constitutes a substantial part of the appeal which has enabled it to build up its summer vacation business to take the place of its former means of livelihood. *** There has been substantial recognition by the courts of the public interest in the preservation of historic buildings, places, and districts (citing authorities).
>
> 'It is not difficult to imagine how the erection of a few wholly incongruous structures might destroy one of the principal assets of the town, ***.
>
> 'We are of opinion that in a general sense the proposed act would be an act for the promotion of the public welfare ***.'

State courts generally have held that the police power may be exercised only to protect and promote the safety, health, morals and general welfare. *** Since the legislature can preserve such historical areas by direct legislation as a measure for the general welfare, it follows that municipal ordinance protecting such areas are authorized under enabling legislation granting power to zone for the public welfare. We, therefore, hold that the purpose of the Santa Fe historical zoning ordinance is within the term 'general welfare,' as used in the municipal zoning enabling legislation.

Defendants agree that there is authority supporting the validity of ordinances enacted under legislative authority having for their purpose the preservation of historical buildings, areas or districts and limiting construction or alteration to specified historical architectural design. They, therefore, limit their challenge to the window pane restriction of the ordinance, 'single panes of glass larger than thirty inches square are not permissible except as otherwise provided,' asserting that control of buildings by regulating the size and shape of its windows has no relation to the public welfare, but on the contrary, amounts only to an aesthetic detail which they contend will not support the exercise of the police power. We find the argument to be without merit.

The cases relied upon by defendants deal with purely aesthetic regulations having no connection with preservation of an historical area or an historical style of architecture, and are, accordingly, either distinguishable upon their facts or are not persuasive under the facts of the instant case. Defendants have lifted the single architectural design from the detailed description in the ordinance of the 'Old Santa Fe Style' and say that such a minute detail of construction is only an attempt by the city to impose its idea of an aesthetic detail of architecture and is, therefore, an arbitrary and unreasonable exercise of police power. They ignore the fact that the window pane requirement is only one of very many details of the historical architectural style which it is said has evolved within the City of Santa Fe from about the year 1600 to the present, which the ordinance seeks to protect and preserve. So far as the record discloses, the window design is as much a part of the Santa Fe style as are flat roofs, projecting vigas, and wooden lintels. The announced purpose of the ordinance is to preserve the historic sections of the city and its ancient architecture for the culture and economic advantage of the people. The council has, in effect, said that to permit incongruous structures would destroy a great historic area and one of the principal assets of the city.

Since the legislative body of the city has declared that the power is being exercised for a public purpose, the role of the judiciary becomes an exceedingly narrow one. *Berman v. Parker*, 348 U.S. 26, 33, 75 S.Ct. 98, 99 L.Ed. 27; *City of Alamogordo v. McGee*, 64 N.M. 253, 327 P.2d 321.

Under the restricted attack made upon the ordinance, it seems unnecessary to decide here whether aesthetic considerations, denied under earlier decisions, furnish ground for the exercise of the police power as is increasingly held by modern authorities. *Berman v. Parker, supra*; *Opinion of the Justices*, 103 N.H. 268, 169 A.2d 762 ***. In any event, without deciding the question, such considerations cannot be entirely ignored. *People v. Stover*, 12 N.Y.2d 462, 191 N.E.2d 272. New Mexico is particularly dependent upon its scenic beauty to attract the host of visitors, the income from whose visits is a vital factor in our economy. Santa Fe is known throughout the whole country for its historic features and culture. Many of our laws have their origin in that early culture. It must be obvious that the general welfare of the community and of the State is enhanced thereby. Bearing in mind all these factors, we hold that regulation of the size of window panes in the construction or alteration of buildings within the historic area of Santa Fe, as a part of the preservation of the 'Old Santa Fe Style' of architecture, is a valid exercise of the police power granted to the city. *** In *Best v. Zoning Bd. of Adjustment of the City of Pittsburg*, 393 Pa. 106, 141 A.2d 606, 612, the court said:

> 'Not only is the preservation of the attractive characteristics of a community a proper element of the general welfare, but also the preservation of property values is a legitimate consideration ***.'

Defendants argue together their claim that the ordinance unconstitutionally delegates legislative authority to the style committee and the planning commission and that it fails to furnish adequate standards to guide the commission. It is settled that a legislative body may not vest unbridled or arbitrary power in an administrative agency but must furnish a reasonably adequate standard to guide it. *State ex rel. Holmes v. State Board of Finance*, 69 N.M. 430, 367 P.2d 925. Standards required to support a delegation of power by the local legislative body need not be specific. Most decisions hold that broad general standards are permissible 'so long as they are capable of a reasonable application and are sufficient to limit and define the Board's discretionary powers....' *See Ward v. Scott*, 11 N.J. 117, 93 A.2d 385, 387, for a full evaluation of broad standards set by various legislatures and held to be valid. In line with the foregoing, the Annotation, 58 A.L.R.2d 1083, 1087, entitled 'Attack on validity of zoning statute, ordinance, or regulation on ground of improper delegation of authority to board or officer,' points out that:

> 'In general, it may be said that there is a growing tendency to sustain delegations of zoning authority guided only by general policy standards, experience having shown that any attempt to limit the administrative decisions to matters of detail as to which precise standards can be laid down results only in creating an inflexible and unworkable zoning plan with resultant pressures on the legislative body for frequent amendments leading to the evils of spot zoning....'

Defendants argue that the exception, 'except as otherwise provided' in the 'panes of glass' provision makes the requirement meaningless. The ordinance expressly provides at least one exception to the maximum thirty-inch window pane, in permitting larger plate glass windows under portals. Applying the above principles to the terms of the ordinance under consideration, it is apparent that there has not been a grant of uncontrolled power to an administrative agency as in *State ex rel. Holmes v. State Board of Finance, supra.* As we have pointed out, the purpose of the ordinance is to preserve the historic style of architecture. To that end the 'Old Santa Fe Style' is described in great detail, including such things as roof lines, fire walls, inset and exterior portals, canales, decorative panels, etc. The functions and duties of the style committee, as provided by the ordinance, are to conform the architectural style of proposed alterations, with the description in the ordinance and the committee's determination must be based on the standard of:

> '*** harmony with adjacent buildings, preservation of historical and characteristic qualities, and conformity to the Old Santa Fe Style.'

Since the council recognized that it would be impossible to rigidly and literally set forth every detail without impairing the underlying public purpose, it adopted a policy expressed in the ordinance which enables some variances consistent with the public interest and the purpose of the overall zone plan. A reading of the entire historical section of the zoning ordinance makes it apparent the council did, however, provide specific safeguards to insure against arbitrary action or unrestricted administrative discretion. Thus, the style committee is required to report to the city planning commission and it, in turn, to the city council.

In the light of all of the foregoing, we conclude that there is no substantial basis for a claim that the ordinance vests uncontrolled discretion in an administrative body, nor does it appear that the ordinance fails to furnish the necessary standards to guide the administrative body designated by the ordinance.

Defendants assert that because other buildings in the neighborhood have display windows with panes exceeding thirty inches square, the defendants are denied the equal protection of the law by reason of failure to enforce the ordinance against others. Defendants point to five photographs of buildings which contain windows with panes in excess of thirty inches. The city has sufficiently explained that the windows complained about as unauthorized variations were exempt from the requirement for a number of reasons.

No evidence of a policy of discrimination or partiality amounting to an arbitrary or capricious administration of the ordinance has been pointed out to us. The courts will not interfere with the discretion vested in the administrative body in the absence of a showing of an abuse of its discretion. *Beirn v. Morris*, 14 N.J. 529, 537, 103 A.2d 361; *Sinclair Refining Co. v. City of Chicago*, 178 F.2d 214, 217, (7th Cir. 1949). Furthermore, it is no defense to a prosecution for violating an ordinance that others have been permitted to violate it without prosecution or punishment. *Kansas City v. Wilhoit*, 237 S.W.2d 919, 924 (Kan.City Ct.App., 1951). We find no merit to the assertion that there has been such an unequal and oppressive application of the ordinance as to amount to denial by the State of that equal protection of the laws which is secured to defendants by the Fifth Amendment to the United States Constitution.

Finding no error, the judgment and sentence appealed from are affirmed.

It is so ordered.

Compton, C. J., and Carmody, Chavez, and Moise, JJ., concur.

Notes and Questions

1. **The "Old Santa Fe Style."** The Santa Fe ordinance identifies and prescribes, in the "Downtown and Eastside" and "Historic Transition" districts, a style of architecture that has evolved within the city from the year 1600 to the present, called "Old Santa

Fe Style." This style is characterized by construction with adobe and defined as including the so-called "pueblo," "pueblo-Spanish," or "Spanish-Indian," and "territorial" styles. These structures are typically one story, long and low, with flat roofs, having a slight slope and surrounded on at least three sides by a firewall of the same color, with architraves and cornices, which, as well as doors, are frequently carved. The colors range from a light earth color to a dark earth color. The ordinance also contemplates a "Recent Santa Fe Style," a development from and an elaboration of the old Santa Fe style, also of adobe construction, but with added decorations. The Recent Santa Fe Style achieves harmony by the retention of similar materials, color, proportion, and general detail. Santa Fe Land Development Code, § 14-5.2 (E), (F), (G) Historic Districts.

2. **Harmonious but not identical.** The defendant in *Gamble-Skogmo* made an equal protection claim on the basis that there were buildings within the neighborhood that had display windows with panes exceeding thirty inches square. The court accepted the city's assertion that these "unauthorized variations" were exempt from the requirement for a number of reasons. a. What might justify such variations? b. While the court found that the ordinance provided ample guidance on the permitted features of buildings, would complete uniformity be necessary or possible in order to achieve the Old Santa Fe Style? c. Of what relevance is it that windows meeting the pane requirement might require custom manufacture? d. Could an owner meet the requirements of the ordinance by using faux materials, like fiberglass, that mimicked original materials, whose true character could only be revealed on close examination, but not at a distance? e. Would this "replica" be "historic?" f. How should the law respond to defendant's seeming attempt to circumvent the pane requirement by installing the "mullions"?

3. **Manitou Springs, Colorado.** The historic preservation ordinance in the city of Manitou Springs, Colorado, is a comprehensive plan seemingly for the entire city. The city's architecture and districts reflect its evolving history, originally a health and vacation resort built around mineral springs, and changing in response to the World Wars and the Great Depression. The many historic districts and subdistricts are defined in terms of their original and characteristic architectural structures — Cliff Dwellings, containing materials taken from the Mesa Verde Anasazi Cliff Dwellings (before the Antiquities Act of 1906); El Colorado Lodge, characterized by pueblo, revival, stucco cabins; Log Cabin, predominated by original log cabin construction; Midland, reflecting a grid pattern layout, and several districts of Victorian homes and villas, notable for the higher levels of building craftsmanship. The ordinance contains very precise guidelines on nearly every aspect of building construction — orientation, height, alignment, architectural character, roof forms and materials, even awnings in the commercial core district. New construction within historic districts is required to be compatible and to reinforce existing development, but should not imitate historic styles and construction to appear historic. Secondary structures, such as garages and shade structures are covered, requiring design integration, with free standing car ports generally prohibited. Site improvements, such as retaining walls, bridges, and stairs are required to reflect historic character. Where possible, native vegetation should be maintained,

http://www.manitouspringsgov.com/library/documents/general/historic_district_ design_guidlines.pdf (last visited April 1, 2017).

4. Early Role of Federal Government in Historic Preservation

Through warfare, our nation's sovereignty was established. Other important values—liberty, democracy, expansion and defense of territory—have all been contested in the course of so many battles over the succeeding centuries. Battlefields remind us of the great struggles and ultimate sacrifices made in the course of conflict. They are places marked by human aspiration and love of nation. While the commemoration of battlefields as hallowed grounds, is an ancient practice, it only began in the United States late in the 18th century. It was the ferocity with which the Civil War was fought and the monumental casualties, leaving deep impressions on the psyche of the country, that led to the creation of national military cemeteries and national military parks, to enable us to remember what happened there, what we gained and lost. Despite the very laudable end, there was yet opposition to Congress' plan to acquire for this purpose, nationally significant historic property from private owners, by purchase or by eminent domain. The case below illustrates what seemed the then prevailing and now enduring sentiment about preserving battlefields.

United States v. Gettysburg Electric Ry. Co. (Two Cases)[1]

Supreme Court of the United States
160 U.S. 668, 16 S. Ct. 427, 40 L. Ed. 576 (1896)

Peckham, J. The really important question to be determined in these proceedings is whether the use to which the petitioner desires to put the land described in the petitions is of that kind of public use for which the government of the United States is authorized to condemn land.

It has authority to do so whenever it is necessary or appropriate to use the land in the execution of any of the powers granted to it by the constitution. *Kohl v. United States*, 91 U.S. 367; *Cherokee Nation v. Southern Kansas Ry. Co.*, 135 U.S. 641–656, 10 S.Ct. 965; *Chappell v. United States,* 160 U.S. 499, 16 S.Ct. 397.

Is the proposed use to which this land is to be put a public use, within this limitation? The purpose of the use is stated in the first act of congress, passed on the 3d day of March, 1893 (the appropriation act of 1893), and is quoted in the above statement of facts. The appropriation act of August 18, 1894, also contained the following: 'For continuing the work of surveying, locating and preserving the lines of battle at Gettysburg, Pa., and for purchasing, opening, constructing and improving avenues along the portions occupied by the various commands of the armies of the Potomac and Northern Virginia on that field, and for fencing the same; and for the purchase,

1. The docket title of each of these cases was *United States v. A Certain Tract of Land in Cumberland Township, Adams County, State of Pennsylvania.*

at private sale or by condemnation, of such parcels of land as the secretary of war may deem necessary for the sites of tablets, and for the construction of the said avenues; for determining the leading tactical positions and properly marking the same with tablets of batteries, regiments, brigades, divisions, corps and other organizations with reference to the study and correct understanding of the battle, each tablet bearing a brief historical legend, compiled without praise and without censure; fifty thousand dollars, to be expended under the direction of the secretary of war.'

In these acts of congress, and in the joint resolution, the intended use of this land is plainly set forth. It is stated in the second volume of Judge Dillon's work on Municipal Corporations (4th Ed. §600) that, when the legislature has declared the use or purpose to be a public one, its judgment will be respected by the courts, unless the use be palpably without reasonable foundation. Many authorities are cited in the note, and, indeed, the rule commends itself as a rational and proper one.

As just compensation, which is the full value of the property taken, is to be paid, and the amount must be raised by taxation, where the land is taken by the government itself, there is not much ground to fear any abuse of the power. The responsibility of congress to the people will generally, if not always, result in a most conservative exercise of the right. It is quite a different view of the question which courts will take when this power is delegated to a private corporation. In that case the presumption that the intended use for which the corporation proposes to take the land is public is not so strong as where the government intends to use the land itself.

In examining an act of congress, it has been frequently said that every intendment is in favor of its constitutionality. Such act is presumed to be valid unless its invalidity is plain and apparent. No presumption of invalidity can be indulged in. It must be shown clearly and unmistakably. This rule has been stated and followed by this court from the foundation of the government.

Upon the question whether the proposed use of this land is public one, we think there can be no well-founded doubt. And also, in our judgment, the government has the constitutional power to condemn the land for the proposed use. It is, of course, not necessary that the power of condemnation for such purpose be expressly given by the constitution. The right to condemn at all is not so given. It results from the powers that are given, and it is implied because of its necessity, or because it is appropriate in exercising those powers. Congress *** has such other and implied ones as are necessary and appropriate for the purpose of carrying the powers expressly given into effect. Any act of congress which plainly and directly tends to enhance the respect and love of the citizen for the institutions of his country, and to quicken and strengthen his motives to defend them, and which is germane to, and intimately connected with, and appropriate to, the exercise of some one or all of the powers granted by congress, must be valid. This proposed use comes within such description. The provision comes within the rule laid down by Chief Justice Marshall in *McCulloch v. Maryland*, 4 Wheat. 421, in these words: 'Let the end be legitimate, let it be within the scope of the constitution, and all means which are appropriate, which are plainly adequate to that end, which are not prohibited but consistent with the letter and spirit of the constitution, are constitutional.'

The end to be attained, by this proposed use, as provided for by the act of congress, is legitimate, and lies within the scope of the constitution. The battle of Gettysburg was one of the great battles of the world. The numbers contained in the opposing armies were great; the sacrifice of life was dreadful; while the bravery, and, indeed, heroism, displayed by both the contending forces, rank with the highest exhibition of those qualities ever made by man. The importance of the issue involved in the contest of which this great battle was a part cannot be overestimated. The existence of the government itself, and the perpetuity of our institutions, depended upon the result. Valuable lessons in the art of war can now be learned from an examination of this great battlefield, in connection with the history of the events which there took place. Can it be that the government is without power to preserve the land, and properly mark out the various sites upon which this struggle took place? Can it not erect the monuments provided for by these acts of congress, or even take possession of the field of battle, in the name and for the benefit of all the citizens of the country, for the present and for the future? Such a use seems necessarily not only a public use, but one so closely connected with the welfare of the republic itself as to be within the powers granted congress by the constitution for the purpose of protecting and preserving the whole country. It would be a great object lesson to all who looked upon the land thus cared for, and it would show a proper recognition of the great things that were done there on those momentous days. By this use the government manifests for the benefit of all its citizens the value put upon the services and exertions of the citizen soldiers of that period. Their successful effort to preserve the integrity and solidarity of the great republic of modern times is forcibly impressed upon everyone who looks over the field. The value of the sacrifices then freely made is rendered plainer and more durable by the fact that the government of the United States, through its representatives in congress assembled, appreciates and endeavors to perpetuate it by this most suitable recognition. Such action on the part of congress touches the heart, and comes home to the imagination of every citizen, and greatly tends to enhance his love and respect for those institutions for which these heroic sacrifices were made. The greater the love of the citizen for the institutions of his country, the greater is the dependence properly to be placed upon him for their defense in time of necessity, and it is to such men that the country must look for its safety. The institutions of our country, which were saved at this enormous expenditure of life and property, ought to and will be regarded with proportionate affection. Here upon this battlefield is one of the proofs of that expenditure, and the sacrifices are rendered more obvious and more easily appreciated when such a battlefield is preserved by the government at the public expense. The right to take land for cemeteries for the burial of the deceased soldiers of the country rests on the same footing, and is connected with, and springs from, the same powers of the constitution. It seems very clear that the government has the right to bury its own soldiers, and to see to it that their graves shall not remain unknown or unhonored.

No narrow view of the character of this proposed use should be taken. Its national character and importance, we think, are plain. The power to condemn for this purpose need not be plainly and unmistakably deduced from any one of the particularly specified powers. Any number of those powers may be grouped together, and an inference from them all may be drawn that the power claimed has been conferred.

It is needless to enlarge upon the subject, and the determination is arrived at without hesitation that the use intended, as set forth in the petition in this proceeding, is of that public nature which comes within the constitutional power of congress to provide for by the condemnation of land.

It is objected that the appropriations made by the several acts of congress had been exhausted when the amended answers were put in, and that the proviso attached to the joint resolution above mentioned, prohibiting any expenditure other than such as might be appropriated in that session of congress, renders it impossible for the landowner to obtain payment, with any certainty, for his property that might be taken from him. Although it is set up in the answer of the electric company to the petition filed on the part of the United States, the fact that the fund appropriated has been exhausted does not appear by any evidence contained in either record. So far as this court can see from the record, there is an appropriation amounting to $75,000 for the purpose of obtaining land, a part of which has been found to be worth $30,000, and the other and much smaller portion is not valued. The proviso, therefore, would seem to be immaterial, as the appropriations were much larger than the value of the land to be taken. The mere fact that congress limited the amount to be appropriated for the purposes indicated does not render the law providing for the taking of the land invalid. *Shoemaker v. United States*, 147 U.S. 282–302 ***. If it appeared by proof that the appropriation for the purpose indicated had been exhausted before the proceedings had been commenced to take the land in controversy, or during the hearing, then the provision in the joint resolution directing that no obligation or liability upon the part of the government should be incurred, or any expenditure made, except out of the appropriations already made, and to be made during the then session of congress, would give rise to a very serious question. It is not now presented. Congress has the power, even now, to appropriate moneys for this purpose in addition to that which it appropriated in the two acts of 1893 and 1894. This court cannot, therefore, upon the record as it stands, give judgment for the landowner on the ground that the appropriation for the land has been exhausted in other ways, and that congress prohibited the incurring of any obligation to a greater extent than the moneys then appropriated.

Another objection taken in the court below, though not decided by that court, but which counsel for defendant in error now urges as an additional ground for the affirmance of the judgment, is that the land proposed to be taken in this proceeding was already devoted to another public use, to wit, that of the railroad company, and that it does not appear that it was the intention of congress to take land which was devoted to another public use. The defendant in error concedes, what is without doubt true, that this is a question of intention, simply. The power of congress to take land devoted to one public use for another and a different public use, upon making just compensation, cannot be disputed. Upon looking at the two acts of congress, and the joint resolution of June 6, 1894, above referred to, in the latter of which it is stated, 'There is imminent danger that portions of said battlefield may be irreparably defaced by the construction of a railway over the same, thereby making impracticable the execution of the provisions of the act of March 3, 1893,' we think it is plainly apparent that congress did intend to take this very land occupied and used by this company for its railroad. ***

It is also objected that the exception below is valid, wherein it was stated that all the land of the railroad company ought to be taken, if any were to be taken. The use for which the land is to be taken having been determined to be a public use, the quantity which should be taken is a legislative, and not a judicial, question. *Shoemaker v. United States*, 147 U.S. 282–298 ***. As to the effect of the taking upon the land remaining, that is more a question of the amount of compensation. If the part taken by the government is essential to enable the railroad corporation to perform its functions, or if the value of the remaining property is impaired, such facts might enter into the question of the amount of the compensation to be awarded. *Monongahela Nav. Co. v. United States*, 148 U.S. 312, 333, 334 ***.

It is also objected that the petition does not allege that the secretary of war has decided it to be necessary to take this land. A perusal of the petition shows that the allegation therein contained upon this subject is not very clear. It might possibly be regarded as sufficiently alleged in an argumentative kind of way, but it certainly is not as plainly alleged as it ought to be. The petition, however, can be easily amended on application to the court below before further proceedings are taken.

This, we think, completes the review of the material questions presented by the record. The first and important question in regard to whether the proposed use is public or not, having been determined in favor of the United States, we are not disposed to take any very technical view of the other questions, which might be subject to amendment or to further proof upon the hearing below.

The judgment of the Circuit Court in each case must be reversed, and the record remitted to that court with directions to grant a new trial in each.

Notes

1. **Public use.** The court provided a definition of public use that was broad and expansive, one that encompasses purposes that achieve intangible benefits, such as reverence for important monuments and events in society. It deferred to Congress on the question whether those purposes could be achieved by the establishment of the park.

2. **The story of the tower.** Less than a century later, the purpose of the battlefield would be threatened by the introduction of an overwhelming tower.

> In 1970, the National Gettysburg Tower, Inc., ("Tower Corporation") planned to build an observation tower on a site immediately adjacent to the park boundary, on the edge of the field of Pickett's Charge. Many reacted with horror. The National Park Service was opposed to the construction

Cemetery Ridge, Gettysburg National Park. National Park Service.

as planned, but negotiated an agreement with the Tower Corporation to allow the construction, but somewhere else. Under the agreement, the Tower Corporation would convey certain land to the government and agreed to abandon construction of the tower near the Gettysburg Battlefield, at the place found objectionable to the Park Service, in exchange for the government's cooperation and permission to build the tower in another area near the battlefield. The Tower Corporation also agreed to establish a charitable foundation to support the Park Service's activities at Gettysburg and at the Eisenhower Farm Historical Sight, and to construct the tower in accordance with certain specifications, with the height of the tower to be limited to 307 feet. The Park Service also conveyed a right of way for limited access to the proposed observation tower sight. The State of Pennsylvania, nonetheless, sought to enjoin the construction of the tower, relying upon a State constitutional provision, Art. I, § 27, that "[t]he people have a right to clean air, pure water, and to the preservation of the natural, scenic, historic and esthetic values of the environment." The construction of the proposed monstrosity would violate these rights. The state supreme court ruled that this provision was not self-executing, that absent a statute specifically regulating the challenged conduct, the state lacked the power of enforcement. *Commonwealth v. Nat'l Gettysburg Battlefield Tower*, 311 A. 2d 588, 589, 595 (Pa. 1973). That ruling allowed the tower to be completed and open for operation on July 29, 1974. It was not until 1987 when President Reagan ordered a boundary study of the park, was it determined that although the tower was situated outside the park, it yet visually intruded upon the entire park and that removal was the only way to restore the battlefield's integrity. In August 1990, President Bush, signed into law, "An Act to Revise the Boundary of Gettysburg National Military Park." Pursuant to the Act, a land protection plan was adopted, which among other things, included the removal of the tower as a high priority. Initial attempts to purchase the land supporting the tower were frustrated by an inability to obtain a reliable appraisal. Finally, after several efforts in Congress, funds were appropriated and a declaration of taking was implemented, which gave the National Park Service possession so that demolition of the tower could commence immediately. On July 3, 2000, after a brief ceremony, the tower was brought down by explosives. For a full account of the maneuvers, both political and opportunistic, around the life of the tower, *see* John Latschar, *The Taking of the Gettysburg Tower*, 18 The George Wright Forum 24 (2001).

3. **The Cyclorama at Gettysburg.** One of the most significant battles at Gettysburg "was the battle for defense of North Cemetery Ridge, which began in the late afternoon on July 1, 1863, and ended with Pickett's Charge on the afternoon of July 3. After pummeling Cemetery Hill and Cemetery Ridge with a grand cannonade, Confederate General Robert E. Lee sent 12,000 to 13,000 men across the exposed fields toward the Union position on North Cemetery Ridge, only to be decisively repulsed by the forces of the Union General George Meade." *Gettysburg National Military Park Final Disposition of the Gettysburg Cyclorama Building Environmental Assessment*, GETT179110 at 4 (2012). This effectively ended the battle of Gettysburg. To commemorate this event, among other things, the National Park Service ("NPS") commissioned the construction of the Cyclorama Building on the North Cemetery Ridge, taking a panoramic view of the site. Built between 1959 and 1962 and designed by architect Richard Neutra, it served as a visitor center and as a place for the display of the then 356-foot-long famous cylindrical painting created in 1884 by French artist Paul Phillippoteaux that depicted Pickett's Charge. In 1971, the NPS acquired the nearby Rosensteel's National Museum of the Civil War and began using that as the visitor center, such that the Cyclorama no longer served as the main visitor center. As part of its long-term plan to rehabilitate the North Cemetery Ridge to its historic 1863 and commemorative-era appearance, the NPS proposed to demolish the Cyclorama building, in order to restore this key battlefield site so that it could be properly interpreted. That decision was challenged by Recent Past Preservation Network, asserting that the NPS had not complied with the National Historic Preservation Act or the National Environmental Policy Act for an assessment of its impact on historic resources, including the park and the environment. In *Recent Past Pres. Network v. Latschar*, 701 F. Supp. 2d 49 (D.D.C 2010), the court agreed and the NPS was sent back to do a proper analysis of the proposal. In August 2012, the NPS issued its *Final Disposition of the Gettysburg Cyclorama Building*, GETT179110, in which it determined, after a thorough analysis of the environmental impacts and costs of the various alternative proposals, including mothballing the building, demolishing it, and removing it to another site, the building should be demolished. Removing this non-historic structure will allow us to see the field as it was during that pivotal moment in our history.

The Cyclorama Building. National Park Service.

5. Pennsylvania Historic Preservation Ordinance

The following case shows that the constitutionality of historic preservation laws may differ depending on how expansive or narrow rights are regarded under the provisions of state constitutions.

United Artists' Theater Circuit, Inc. v. City of Philadelphia

Supreme Court of Pennsylvania
535 Pa. 370, 635 A.2d 612 (1993)

Nix, C.J.

Facts

On July 10, 1991, this Court found that the Philadelphia Historic Preservation Ordinance "which authorize[d] the historic designation of private property ... without the consent of the owner, [is] unfair, unjust and amount[s] to an unconstitutional taking without just compensation in violation of Article I, Section 10 of the Pennsylvania Constitution." *United Artists' Theater Circuit, Inc. v. City of Philadelphia, Philadelphia Historical Commission,* 528 Pa. 12, 26–27, 595 A.2d 6, 13–14 (1991). *** This result stands in contrast to the result reached by the United States Supreme Court in *Penn Central Transp. Co. v. New York City,* 438 U.S. 104 *** (1978), in which that Court held that historic designation without the consent of the owner is not a "taking" under the Fifth and Fourteenth Amendments to the United States Constitution.

The City of Philadelphia filed a petition pursuant to Rule 2543 of the Pennsylvania Rules of Appellate Procedure requesting this Court to hear reargument and reconsider our July 10, 1991 ruling that the designation of a building as historic is a "taking" under our Constitution and requires "just compensation." We granted reargument on August 23, 1991, and on October 23, 1991, the parties reargued the sole issue of whether the designation of a building as historic is a "taking" under our Constitution, requiring just compensation. United Artists requests that we reaffirm our July 10, 1991 decision, and hold that a designation as historic is a taking which requires just compensation. The City of Philadelphia and the Philadelphia Historical Commission

("Commission") argue that the rights afforded by the takings provision in our Constitution mirror those of the United States Constitution; moreover, our Environmental Rights Amendment empowers the state and local governments to protect the historic resources of our Commonwealth. For the reasons that follow, we hold that under the Constitution of Pennsylvania, the designation of a building as historic without the consent of the owner is not a "taking" that requires just compensation; however, because the Commission acted outside of its statutory authority, we vacate the Commission's designation of the Boyd Theater as historic.

I. Taking

A. United States Constitution

Before we turn to the Commission's actions in this case, we must first examine the constitutionality of historic designation. The United States Supreme Court has ruled that the Fifth and Fourteenth Amendments to the United States Constitution do not prohibit a state or municipality from designating a building as "historic" and placing restrictions on the owner's use of the building. In *Penn Central Transp. Co. v. New York City*, 438 U.S. 104 *** (1978), the Supreme Court examined a claim that the New York City Landmarks Preservation Law constituted a "taking" under the Fifth and Fourteenth Amendments of the United States Constitution. The Appellants presented "a series of arguments, which, while tailored to the facts of [that] case, essentially urge[d] that any substantial restriction imposed pursuant to a landmark law must be accompanied by just compensation if it is to be constitutional." *Id.* at 128–29 ***. The Supreme Court rejected these arguments, and upheld the New York City Landmark Preservation Law. The Court found that there was no taking, that the restrictions imposed were substantially related to the general welfare, and that the regulation permitted a reasonable beneficial use of the landmark site. *Id.* at 138 ***.

The issue which confronted the United States Supreme Court mirrors the question before us today: "whether the designation of a property as historic without consent of the property owner constitutes a taking" pursuant to Article I, Section 10 of the Pennsylvania Constitution. Likewise, we are examining many of the same arguments which were raised by the Penn Central Transportation Company. It is without question that this issue, if framed as an examination under the federal Constitution, is answered by the decision of the United States Supreme Court in *Penn Central.* Here the parties urge that we examine the rights afforded to property owners under the Constitution of this Commonwealth, to determine if the rights under our Constitution are more expansive than those rights guaranteed under the federal Constitution.

B. Pennsylvania Constitution

This Court has recognized that our Constitution can provide greater rights and protection to the citizens of this Commonwealth than are provided under similar provisions of the federal Constitution. We have stated:

> [T]he federal Constitution establishes certain minimum levels which are "equally applicable to the [analogous] state constitutional provision." However,

> each state has the power to provide broader standards and go beyond the minimum floor which is established by the federal Constitution.

Commonwealth v. Edmunds, 526 Pa. 374, 388, 586 A.2d 887, 894 (1991) (quoting *Commonwealth v. Sell,* 504 Pa. 46, 63, 470 A.2d 457, 466 (1983)). In *Commonwealth v. Edmunds* ***, this Court examined the state and federal Constitutions in an appeal which challenged the acceptance of a "good faith" exception to the exclusionary rule. In *Edmunds,* we held that the Pennsylvania Constitution did not incorporate a good faith exception to the exclusionary rule for the violation of the constitutional requirement that search warrants accompany any search or seizure. * * *

II. Edmunds

A. Text

The first element [under the *Edmunds* four part analysis] to be examined is the text of the Pennsylvania Constitution. It protects the citizens of Pennsylvania from deprivations of property or takings for public use in the following provision:

> [N]or shall private property be taken or applied to public use, without authority of law and without just compensation being first made or secured.
>
> Pa. Const. art. I, § 10.

Similarly, the federal Constitution protects all citizens of the United States from deprivation of their property:

> No person ... shall be ... deprived of life, liberty, or property, without due process of law; nor shall private property be taken for public use, without just compensation.
>
> U.S. Const. amend. V.

Both provisions contain two elements. The first element is that no property may be taken without due process of law or authority of law; the second element requires that just compensation accompany any taking for public use. Therefore, the texts of both constitutional provisions are almost identical for our purposes.

B. The History Of The Provision

The second element of the *Edmunds* analysis is an examination of the history of the provision, including Pennsylvania case law.

Section 10 of Article I has its origins in Clause VIII of the Declaration of Rights in the 1776 Pennsylvania Constitution. This original clause allowed the owner's legal representative, i.e., the state legislature, to authorize the taking of property without compensation. After the federal Constitution had been ratified, Pennsylvania added a just compensation requirement to its Declaration of Rights in 1790. Since 1790, the relevant provision has remained unchanged. *See* Pa. Const. art. I, § 10 Historical Note (Purdons 1969).

An examination of our case law reveals that this Court has continually turned to federal precedent for guidance in its "taking" jurisprudence, and indeed has adopted the analysis used by the federal courts. In *Best v. Zoning Board of Adjustment,* 393 Pa.

106, 141 A.2d 606 (1958), * * *we explicitly relied upon federal precedent for two propositions. First, in examining the police powers of a state under Section 1 of Article I, we explicitly adopted the following test enunciated by Mr. Justice Harlan in *Chicago, Burlington and Quincy Railway Co. v. Illinois,* 200 U.S. 561 *** (1906): "We hold that the police power of a state *embraces regulations designed to promote the public convenience or the general prosperity,* as well as regulations designed *to promote the public health, the public morals or the public safety.*" *Id.* 393 Pa. at 114, 141 A.2d at 611 (emphasis added). Second, in response to the arguments that the denial of the most profitable use of the owner's property was an unconstitutional taking, this Court flatly rejected that proposition, citing the opinion of *Hadacheck v. Sebastian,* 239 U.S. 394 *** (1915). *Best,* 393 Pa. at 119, 141 A.2d at 613 ("Appellant's evidence on this issue amounts to no more than that she is prevented by the ordinance from putting her property to its most profitable use. This is not a constitutional objection.").

Five years later, in *Andress v. Zoning Board of Adjustment of the City of Philadelphia,* we articulated four observations regarding limitations of governmental power:

> 1) Our State and Federal Constitutions ordain, protect and guarantee *the ownership and use of private property.*
>
> 2) The Constitutionally ordained right of private property ... and other Constitutionally granted rights are not absolute. These rights and freedoms are subject to the paramount right of the Government to reasonably regulate and restrict, under a reasonable and non-discriminatory exercise of the police power, the use of property, whenever necessary for the public health, safety, morals and general welfare.
>
> 3) Neither the Executive nor the Legislature, nor any legislative body, nor any zoning or planning commission, nor any other Governmental body has the right—under the guise of the police power, or under the broad power of general welfare, or under the power of the Commander-in-Chief of the Armed Forces, or under any other express or implied power—*to take, possess or confiscate private property for public use or to completely prohibit or substantially destroy the lawful use and enjoyment of property without paying just compensation therefor.*
>
> 4) It has been difficult and at times impossible to sharply or clearly draw the dividing line between valid or constitutional zoning on the one hand and illegal or unconstitutional zoning on the other hand, *i.e.,* a taking of property with respect to the entire district zoned or with respect to a particular property.

Andress, 410 Pa. 77, 83–84, 188 A.2d 709, 712–13 (1963) (citations omitted). This Court fashioned these limitations from United States Supreme Court precedents in addition to our own jurisprudence. Analyzing the Zoning Board ruling at issue with regard to the limitations on governmental power discussed above, we explicitly relied on *United States v. Central Eureka Mining Company,* 357 U.S. 155, 168 *** (1958) for the following analysis:

> Traditionally, we have treated the issue as to whether a particular governmental restriction amounted to a constitutional taking as being a question properly turning upon the particular circumstances of each case. In doing so, we have recognized that *action in the form of regulation can so diminish the value of property as to constitute a taking.* However, the mere fact that the regulation deprives the property owner of the most profitable use of his property is not necessarily enough to establish the owner's right to compensation.

Andress, 410 Pa. at 89, 188 A.2d at 715 (quoting *United States v. Central Eureka Mining Co., supra*). This rationale formed the basis of our holding that the lower court must reevaluate the granting of a variance for the construction of an apartment building in an "A" Residential Zone.

Our reliance upon federal precedent continued in *Commonwealth v. Barnes and Tucker Co.,* 455 Pa. 392, 319 A.2d 871 (1974), where we adopted the following "classic rule" of the United States Supreme Court to determine whether state action constitutes a valid exercise of the police power or a "taking" requiring "just compensation":

> To justify the State in ... interposing its authority in behalf of the public, it must appear, first, that the interests of the public ... require such interference; and second, that the means are reasonably necessary for the accomplishment of the purpose, and not unduly oppressive upon individuals.

Id. at 418, 319 A.2d at 895 (1974) (quoting *Lawton v. Steele,* 152 U.S. 133, 137 *** (1894)). We affirmed the test when these parties returned to the Court in *Commonwealth v. Barnes and Tucker Co. (Barnes II),* 472 Pa. 115, 123, 371 A.2d 461, 465 (1977) to challenge a Commonwealth Court Order that the owners of a mine operate a facility to treat 7.2 million gallons of untreated acid mine water, 6 million gallons of which was from sources not owned by the Appellant company. We restated the classic rule of *Lawton v. Steele* to examine the parties' "taking" claim. Armed with this test, and having recognized the state's interest in protecting the Commonwealth from additional discharge of polluted water into the waters of the Commonwealth, we held that the Appellant failed to meet its burden of proving that the Order was unconstitutional. *Id.* at 123–29, 371 A.2d at 465–68.

Following the evolution of the *Lawton v. Steele* test in federal law, this Court refined its taking analysis to include a two-part analysis of the "unduly oppressive" element of the test. In *National Wood Preservers, Inc. v. Commonwealth of Pennsylvania, Dep't. of Envtl. Resources,* 489 Pa. 221, 414 A.2d 37, *appeal dismissed, National Wood Preservers, Inc. v. Pennsylvania Dep't. of Envtl. Resources,* 449 U.S. 803 *** (1980), this Court upheld Section 316 of the Clear Streams Law, 35 P.S. §691.316, as a constitutional exercise of the Legislature's police power and we held that Section 316 regulated water pollution resulting from conditions other than mine drainage. *Id.* at 225, 414 A.2d at 39. The Appellant in *Wood Preservers* focused his challenge on the requirement that the regulation not be "unduly oppressive upon individuals," the third element of the test enunciated by the United States Supreme Court in *Lawton v. Steele* and adopted by our Court in both *Barnes and Tucker* cases. In response to that challenge, a majority of this Court adopted the following two-part test for determining "unduly oppressive" regulations as enunciated in *Penn Central Transp. Co. v. New York City,* 438 U.S. 104 *** (1978):

> The first consideration is the economic impact of the regulation on the property holder. Specifically, it is relevant to compare property values before and after the regulation, though such a consideration is by no means conclusive.

The second factor identified in *Penn Central* is the character of the governmental action. The greater the extent to which governmental interference with property can be characterized as a physical intrusion, the more likely it is that such interference will be considered an unreasonable exercise of police power. *Wood Preservers,* 489 Pa. at 236–37, 414 A.2d at 45 (citations omitted). We dismissed the Appellant's claim that Appellant bore no responsibility for the condition of their land and therefore, should not bear the burden of cleaning it. *Id.* at 238–40, 414 A.2d at 46–47.

Our most recent examination of a taking claim occurred in 1991 where a majority of this Court struck down as unconstitutional an amortization provision in a zoning ordinance which placed a ninety-day expiration period on all nonconforming uses. *PA Northwestern Distributors, Inc. v. Zoning Board of the Township of Moon,* 526 Pa. 186, 584 A.2d 1372 (1991). In *PA Northwestern,* the majority of this Court did not turn to federal precedent for guidance,[2] but relied instead on the long-standing Pennsylvania law that "municipalities lack the power to compel a change in the nature of an existing lawful use of property." *Id.* at 192, 584 A.2d at 1375.

Thus, from the above case law, we glean the following three conditions for determining that state or governmental action does not constitute a taking requiring just compensation:

> 1) the interest of the general public, rather than a particular class of persons, must require governmental action;
>
> 2) the means must be necessary to effectuate that purpose;
>
> 3) the means must not be unduly oppressive upon the property holder, considering the economic impact of the regulation, and the extent to which the government physically intrudes upon the property.

The first consideration is specifically analyzed in subsection D, "Policy Considerations," *infra* at [ ]. As discussed *infra,* the citizens of Pennsylvania empowered the Commonwealth to act in areas of purely historic concern reflecting a general public interest in preserving historic landmarks which requires this type of legislation.

---

2. The majority's analysis is contrary to federal law, which allows amortization of nonconforming uses provided that the amortization schedule is reasonable with regard to the nature of the business, including any improvements, the character of the neighborhood and the harm to the property owner. *See, e.g., Major Media of the Southeast, Inc. v. City of Raleigh,* 792 F.2d 1269 (4th Cir.1986) ***.

With regard to the second element, Appellant urges that instead of historic designations, the City of Philadelphia should exercise its eminent domain powers to purchase properties it seeks to preserve. The United States Supreme Court noted a similar argument in *Penn Central,* and we find instructive its observations:

> The consensus is that widespread public ownership of historic properties in urban settings is neither feasible nor wise. Public ownership reduces the tax base, burdens the public budget with costs of acquisitions and maintenance, and results in the preservation of public buildings as museums and similar facilities, rather than as economically productive features of the urban scene.

Penn Central, 438 U.S. at 109 n. 6 ***. There is no other practical means to accomplish the public interest in preserving historic landmarks. Therefore, historic designation is essential to preserve historic landmarks.

Finally, under our last consideration, the unduly oppressive test, we review the economic impact of the regulation and the degree of physical intrusion by the government. Neither side presents specific evidence on the issue of the economic impact of the historic designation; we do note that we have upheld as constitutional regulations that prevent the most profitable use of property. Here, the regulations at issue could arguably deprive the owner of the most profitable use of his property, but this Court does not see the possibility that the owner is wholly deprived of any profitable use.[3] *See Andress,* 410 Pa. at 89, 188 A.2d at 715; *Best,* 393 Pa. at 119, 141 A.2d at 613. Nor do the parties allege that there is any physical intrusion on the property itself. Thus, the action not being "unduly oppressive," historic designation does not fulfill the elements for a "taking" requiring just compensation.

C. Related Case Law

The third factor requires an analysis of related case law from other jurisdictions. Appellees and several Amici stress that no other state has held that historic designation is a taking under its constitution, and our research confirms that point. Appellant concedes the point as well, but argues that this should not be dispositive of the issue.

The fact that no other state has broken with the *Penn Central* decision is not dispositive of the matter, but it is persuasive. In *Edmunds,* when we rejected the United States Supreme Court's recognition of a good faith exception to the exclusionary rule, we noted that the highest courts of four states had rejected the good faith exception.

---

3. There may be circumstances in which the mere designation of a property as historic would constitute a taking due to the extreme financial hardship resulting from such designation. No such facts have been presented in the instant case, nor need we decide here what level of financial hardship would meet this test. Moreover, we note that the Philadelphia Ordinance in question provides a vehicle for relief when the designation would cause a substantial hardship. The Ordinance provides relief for a party who asserts that he is deprived of "any purpose for which it is or may be reasonably adapted, or where a permit application for alteration or demolition is based, in whole or in part, on financial hardship...." Philadelphia Code § 14-2007(7)(f).

New York had rejected it in 1985, one year after the Supreme Court recognized it. By 1990, at least seven other state appellate courts had eschewed the good faith exception in *United States v. Leon*, 468 U.S. 897 *** (1984).

Conversely, in fifteen years since *Penn Central*, no other state has rejected the notion that no taking occurs when a state designates a building as historic. The decade and a half in which the *Penn Central* decision has enjoyed widespread acceptance weighs against our rejecting the *Penn Central* analysis.

D. Policy Considerations

The last prong of the *Edmunds* test is an examination of policy considerations, including unique issues of state and local concern, and their applicability within modern Pennsylvania jurisprudence. The first issue for us to examine is the issue of unique state concern.

I. State Policy

Appellant and Appellees argue that two separate sections of Article I of our Constitution ("Declaration of Rights") have bearing on the state policy regarding historic preservation. Appellant, United Artists, argues that Section 1 of our Declaration of Rights prohibits the historic designation of private property without the owner's consent or compensation. Appellees, City of Philadelphia and the Philadelphia Historical Commission, offer Section 27 of our Declaration of Rights as authority for the historic designation ordinance.

Appellant, United Artists, argues that Section 1 of Article I[4] of our Constitution provides a "direct expression ... of the inherent and fundamental nature of private property." *** Appellant argues that the lack of such direct acknowledgement of the fundamental and indefeasible right of property in the federal Constitution demonstrates that "private property occupies a more hallowed ground in our Constitution than it does under the Federal Constitution." *** Therefore, historic designation is contrary to the "inherent and fundamental nature of property." ***

This is contrary to our case law which views the scope of Section 1 of Article I in relation to its federal counterparts, the Fifth and Fourteenth Amendments. In *Best v. Zoning Board of Adjustment*, 393 Pa. 106, 110–11, 141 A.2d 606, 609 (1958) we stated:

> Section 1 of Article 1 of the Pennsylvania Constitution establishes the right of "acquiring, possessing, and protecting property...." The requirements of this *section are not distinguishable from those of section 1 of the Fourteenth Amendment to the Federal Constitution*—"nor shall any state deprive any person ... of property without due process of law...." (emphasis added) (footnotes omitted).

Therefore, Section 1 of Article I is not a source of additional rights for property owners in Pennsylvania.

4. All men are born equally free and independent, and have certain inherent and indefeasible rights, among which are those of enjoying and defending life and liberty, of acquiring, possessing and protecting property and reputation, and of pursuing their own happiness. Pa. Const. art. I, § 1.

Appellees, conversely, argue that Section 27 of Article I, the Environmental Rights Amendment,[5] establishes a state policy for the preservation of historic resources. Appellees assert that the Historic Preservation Ordinance "seeks to honor the mandate of Article 1, Section 27, that historic and aesthetic resources be preserved." *** We agree with Appellees that the Environmental Rights Amendment reflects a state policy encouraging the preservation of historic and aesthetic resources.

In 1971, the citizens of Pennsylvania adopted the Environmental Rights Amendment which recognized the "right to clean air, pure water, and to the preservation of the natural, scenic, historic and esthetic values of the environment." Pa. Const. art. 1, § 27. Using this provision of the Constitution, a group of citizens sought to block the construction of a battle tower at the site of the Battle of Gettysburg. *See Commonwealth v. Nat'l Gettysburg Battle Tower, Inc.*, 454 Pa. 193, 311 A.2d 588 (1973). In *Gettysburg*, a majority of this Court agreed that the Environmental Rights Amendment authorized the Commonwealth to act in matters of purely historic concerns. *See id.* at 201–02, 311 A.2d at 592, (O'Brien, J.) ("up until now, aesthetic or historical considerations, by themselves, have not been considered sufficient to constitute a basis for the Commonwealth's exercise of its police power"); *id.* at 207, 311 A.2d at 595, (Roberts, J., concurring) ("[p]arklands and *historical sites*, as 'natural resources' are subject to the same considerations"). Ultimately a plurality of the Court held that the Environmental Rights Amendment was not self-executing, and legislative action was necessary to accomplish the goals of that Amendment. *Id.* at 202, 311 A.2d at 592. Thus, this legislative action, the Philadelphia Historic Preservation Ordinance, is consistent with our state policy to preserve historic or aesthetic resources.

II. Local Policy

The City of Philadelphia has declared the following local policy regarding the preservation of historic resources:

> It is hereby declared as a matter of public policy that the preservation and protection of buildings, structures, sites, objects, and districts of historic, architectural, cultural, archaeological, educational and aesthetic merit are public necessities and are in the interests of the health, prosperity and welfare of the people of Philadelphia.

Philadelphia Code § 14-2007(1)(a). This policy is consistent with the Environmental Rights Amendment and is consistent with our findings in *Gettysburg Battle Tower*, 454 Pa. 193, 311 A.2d 588 (1973). Therefore, similar to the state policy, the local policy issue also weighs against our finding that historic designation is a taking.***

5. The people have a right to clean air, pure water, and to the preservation of the natural, scenic, historic and esthetic values of the environment. Pennsylvania's public natural resources are the common property of all the people, including generations yet to come. As trustee of these resources, the Commonwealth shall conserve and maintain them for the benefit of all the people. Pa. Const. art. 1, § 27 (adopted May 18, 1971).

E. Conclusion

Analysis of our case law and related case law from other jurisdictions, the texts of the constitutional provisions and policy concerns of this Commonwealth compels us to conclude that the designation of a privately owned building as historic without the consent of the owner is not a taking under the Constitution of this Commonwealth.[7]

III.

Even though the Historic Ordinance is not a taking under our Constitution, we must address the Appellant's other original claims: that the Commission exceeded its statutory authority by designating the interior of the Boyd Theater, and that the Commission's order was not supported by sufficient evidence. We find the Commission exceeded its statutory authority and thus we vacate the Commission's order designating as historical the Boyd Theater; therefore, we need not reach the issue of the sufficiency of the evidence.

The Historical Commission notified the owners of the Boyd Theater that it had determined that both the interior and exterior of the theater was historically and architecturally significant in the following notice:

> The Boyd Theater at 1908 Chestnut Street has architectural and historical significance as a magnificent and rare example of an intact Art Deco movie palace and as the finest remaining movie theater of Hoffman and Henon, the most important theater design firm in Philadelphia. The Boyd Theater which opened in 1928 is one of only two remaining first run movie palaces left in Philadelphia and the only one that is largely intact inside and out. The exteriors of the theater with its unusual curl gable and deeply recessed entryway encompassing flanking storefronts is a fine example of the Art Deco style. The interior of the Boyd through its fine detail and rarity is one of the most important Art Deco interiors left in the City. The lobbies contain magnificent etched, gilded and stained mirrors with stylized nudes and flowers, Art Deco niches and plaster elements. The auditorium retains its balcony, scalloped proscenium arch and stage, is profusely decorated and contains a mural honoring "The Modern Woman." The Boyd which had an organ and full time organist was the first theater where "Cinerama" was used in Philadelphia. The architects and engineers, Hoffman and Henon, who designed the Boyd built over 100 theaters in the Philadelphia area between 1921 and 1930 creating such theater masterpieces as The Erlanger, The Stanley and the enormous Mastbaum Theater. The Boyd, the only Art Deco theater by Hoffman and Henon serves as their finest remaining work in Philadelphia.

---

7. Both parties briefed and argued the issue of whether historic designation constitutes spot zoning. However, spot zoning is not a form of a taking which requires just compensation, it is an arbitrary exercise of police powers that is prohibited by our Constitution. *** Therefore, the spot zoning issue is wholly separate and distinct from a "taking" analysis and therefore, it is outside of the scope of this limited appeal.

*** United Artists argued that the designation of the interior of the building is outside of the scope of the ordinance.

Our review of the Philadelphia Historic Commission's determination is limited to whether the adjudication is in violation of the constitutional rights of the Appellant, or is not in accordance with law or that the provisions of subchapter B of Chapter 5 (relating to practice and procedure of local agencies) have been violated in the proceedings before the agency, or that any finding of fact made by the agency and necessary to support its adjudication is not supported by substantial evidence. If the adjudication is not affirmed, the Court may enter any order authorized by 42 Pa.C.S. §706.[8] 2 Pa.C.S. §754(b) ("Disposition of Appeal"). *See, e.g., Tegzes v. Bristol Twp.*, 504 Pa. 304, 308, 472 A.2d 1386, 1387 (1984).

The original owner, Sameric Corporation, challenged the Commission's designation of the interior of the Boyd Theater. The Commonwealth Court rejected the owner's argument, and held that the intent of the ordinance was to encompass the interior as well as the exterior of historic landmarks:

> The more perplexing problem we must resolve is whether the Commission exceeded its authority by designating as historic the *interior* of the theater. The ordinance vests the Commission with the authority to designate "buildings, structures, sites and objects." The Commission relied on the ordinance's definition of "building" as "[a] structure, its site and appurtenances created to shelter any form of human activity." On this aspect alone, we believe that in order for a building to effectuate the process of sheltering it most certainly requires an interior. Moreover, where the words of a statute or ordinance are not explicit, the intent may be ascertained by considering, among other matters, the object to be attained.

Here, without explicit reference to building *interiors,* the ordinance seeks to protect architectural styles significantly representative of historical and cultural development. Thus, we are not persuaded by [United Artists'] argument that the ordinance may legitimately preserve the theater's exterior but exclude the interior. This is so, particularly where the interior design reflects the same architectural elements. Rather, we conclude that the City Council intended "building" to include both the interior and exterior. *Sameric Corp. v. City of Philadelphia,* 125 Pa.Commw. 520, 524–25, 558 A.2d 155, 157 (1989) (citations omitted) (footnotes omitted).

The Commonwealth Court is incorrect. The Historical Commission is not explicitly authorized by statute to designate the interior of the building as historically or aesthetically significant. "[T]he power and authority to be exercised by administrative commissions must be conferred by legislative language clear and unmistakable. A

8. Section 706 provides:

An appellate court may affirm, modify, vacate, set aside or reverse any order brought before it for review, and may remand the matter and direct the entry of such appropriate order, or require such further proceedings to be had as may be just under the circumstances.

doubtful power does not exist." *Pennsylvania Human Relations Comm'n. v. St. Joe Minerals Corp.,* 476 Pa. 302, 310, 382 A.2d 731, 735–36 (1978) (quoting *Green v. Milk Control Comm'n.,* 340 Pa. 1, 3, 16 A.2d 9 (1940)). The only reference to the interior of the building is in Section 14-2007(8)(c) which places the following duty of care on the owner of a historically designated structure:

> The exterior of every historic building, structure and object and of every building, object and structure located within an historic district shall be kept in good repair *as shall the interior portions of such buildings, structures and objects, neglect of which cause or tend to cause the exterior to deteriorate, decay, become damaged or otherwise fall into disrepair* (emphasis added).

The plain meaning of this ordinance is that the interior must be maintained physically (and not aesthetically) for the express purpose of supporting the exterior of the building. However, the Commission exceeded that authority by designating the interior of the Boyd Theater. There is no "clear and unmistakable" authority to designate the interior of a building; therefore, the Commission possesses no such power. By designating the interior of the Boyd Theater, the Commission committed an error of law.

Having determined that the Commission made an error of law, we must apply the appropriate remedy. It would not be possible for us to vacate only the portion of the Order which designates the interior. We do not have before us any evidence regarding what interior portions support the exterior, nor can we separate the rationale and evidence which referred only to the exterior of the Boyd Theater from that of the interior in order to review its sufficiency. Thus, we are constrained to vacate the entire order of the Commission.

Accordingly, the Order of the Commonwealth Court is reversed, and the Order of the Commission is vacated.

Notes and Questions

1. **State versus federal constitutional protections.** The court recognized that the federal constitution specifies the minimum protections of rights, but that states may offer more expansive protections. Yet, in determining whether there has been any infringement of those rights guaranteed by the state constitution, the Pennsylvania courts have looked to federal precedent for interpretation. It seems that the analysis under the state constitution would diverge and take on an added dimension when considering articulated state and local policy. a. Were there state and local policies that argued for more expansive rights under the state's "Declaration of Rights"? b. How convincingly did the court reconcile the "Declaration of Rights" provisions with the "Environmental Rights Amendment"? c. What are the respective rights at issue under these two provisions?

2. **Exterior versus interior.** The court struck down the entire designation because it purported to cover the interior as well as the exterior. There was no clear grant of authority to regulate the interior of landmarks, except to which their use or failure to maintain impacts the exterior. However, the court seemed to accept that it was

The Ceiling in the Grand Central Terminal. Photo by Shelby D. Green.

within the powers of the legislature to grant to local governments and agencies the power to impose landmark restrictions on the interior space of buildings. In fact, many landmarks are celebrated just as much for their interior architectural and design features, such as ceilings, staircases, fireplace mantels, like the Rainbow Room in New York City, the astrological ceiling in Grand Central Terminal, the staircases in the New York Legislature building.

3. **Aftermath.** Since the decision in *United Artists' Theater Circuit, Inc.*, the Boyd Theater fell into disrepair, changing hands many times more after the decision. In 2002, when the owner of the theater, The Goldberg Group, announced that it decided to demolish the theater, a group of local preservationists and private citizens organized to create the Committee to Save the Sameric, later to become the Friends of the Boyd. Friends of the Boyd, http://www.friendsoftheboyd.com (last visited September 6, 2017). Though the theater had changed many hands after that as well, the fight to preserve it still continued until, in 2008, the Boyd Theater preservation effort was bolstered by a series of important events. In March of that year, the Preservation Alliance for Greater Philadelphia listed the Boyd Theater on its Annual Endangered Properties List, the National Trust for Historic Preservation named the Boyd Theater on its 2008 List of America's 11 Most Endangered Historic Places, and then, in August 2008, it was listed on the Philadelphia Register of Historic Places, http://cinema treasures.org/theaters/1209 (last visited September 6, 2017).

Of course, there was still some contention because the building's interior was still not eligible for historic protection under the rules for the Register as the exterior, under PHILADELPHIA CODE § 14-2007. The greatest news came in September 2008, when a Philadelphia development firm, ARC Wheeler, entered into an agreement to purchase the Boyd Theater, with plans to restore it into a live performance venue with two restaurants and for a 30-story Kimpton Hotel adjacent; the project received unanimous approval from the Historical Commission in November 2008. Friends of the Boyd, http://www.friendsoftheboyd.com (last visited March 20, 2017). Alas, those plans fell through, as well as others. The theater changed hands several more times only to meet its end in 2015, when it was demolished, a residential high rise planned

The Boyd Theater. Photo by Charmaine Zoe, Creative Commons.

to take its place, after 22 years of struggle by the Friends of the Boyd to preserve it. http://cinematreasures.org/theaters/1209 (last visited September 6, 2017). The struggle was not without lasting impact—in 2012, the city council amended the historical preservation ordinance to include interior landmarks. CITY OF PHILADELPHIA HISTORIC PRESERVATION ORDINANCE, ch. 14-1000 (2012).

District Intown Properties Limited Partnership v. District of Columbia

United States Court of Appeals, District of Columbia Circuit,
198 F.3d 874, 49 ERC 1838 (1999)

HARRY T. EDWARDS, C.J. In 1961, District Intown Limited Properties Partnership ("District Intown") purchased Cathedral Mansions South, an apartment building and landscaped lawn on Connecticut Avenue across from the National Zoo. District Intown subdivided this property into nine contiguous lots in 1988. In March 1989, all nine lots were declared historic landmarks. In July 1992, the Mayor of the District of Columbia denied District Intown's request for construction permits to build eight townhouses on eight of the nine lots, finding that the construction was incompatible with the property's landmark status. Alleging that the District of Columbia's denial constituted a taking, District Intown and its general partners sued under 42 U.S.C. § 1983 (1994) for just compensation under the Takings Clause of the Fifth Amendment.

Upon cross motions for summary judgment, the District Court granted summary judgment for the District of Columbia. *See District Intown Properties Ltd. Partnership v. District of Columbia,* 23 F.Supp.2d 30 (D.D.C.1998). The District Court held that the relevant parcel for the purposes of determining whether a taking had occurred consisted of the entire property, including the apartment building, not the eight individual lots that District Intown sought to develop. *See id.* at 35–36. The court then analyzed the alleged taking under the Supreme Court's holdings in *Lucas v. South Carolina Coastal Council,* 505 U.S. 1003 *** (1992), and *Penn Central Transportation Co. v. City of New York,* 438 U.S. 104 *** (1978). The District Court found that there was no categorical taking under *Lucas,* because District Intown had not been deprived of all economic value in the relevant parcel. The trial court further held that District Intown could not make out a claim under *Penn Central,* because its reasonable investment-backed expectations had not been disappointed and it continued to receive economic benefits from the property.

We hold that the District Court correctly found that the relevant parcel for the takings analysis consisted of the entire property held by District Intown, *i.e.,* the property as it was originally purchased in 1961 and as it was held for 27 years prior to the 1988 subdivision. All relevant objective and subjective factors support this conclusion. When the property is viewed as a single parcel, there is no doubt that it has not been rendered valueless. Indeed, even if each subdivided parcel is considered separately, District Intown has not shown a "total taking" under *Lucas.* In addition, the record here does not show that District Intown's investment-backed expectations were disappointed. This is not surprising, because District Intown could not have had any reasonable investment-backed expectations of development given the background regulatory structure at the time of subdivision. Accordingly, we hold that District Intown did not present any genuine issue of material fact in support of a takings claim under *Penn Central* or *Lucas.* We therefore affirm the District Court's judgment.

I. BACKGROUND

In 1961, District Intown purchased in fee simple Lot 1 of Subdivision Square 2106 on Connecticut Avenue, across from the National Zoo. The property was known as Cathedral Mansions South and consisted of an apartment building and adjacent landscaped lawns. District Intown made no significant changes to the property until 1988, when it subdivided Cathedral Mansions South into nine lots, designated as Lots 106 through 114. The subdivisions were recorded on June 30, 1988. Lot 106 contains the apartment building, and Lots 107 through 114 are each portions of the landscaped lawn. The record indicates that District Intown spent $2,819 to survey the parcel and to record the subdivision. The record does not reflect any other expenses.

On December 30, 1988, District Intown applied for permits to build one townhouse on each of the eight landscaped lots. The zoning and structural engineering divisions of the Department of Consumer and Regulatory Affairs approved the permits on March 7, 1989. However, because the property is located across from the National Zoo, the permits were referred to the Commission on Fine Arts. *See* D.C.CODE ANN. § 5-410 (1994) ("Shipstead-Luce Act"). The Shipstead-Luce Act, in effect since the 1930s, empowers the Commission on Fine Arts to communicate to the Mayor "recommendations, including such changes, if any, as in its judgment are necessary to prevent reasonably avoidable impairment of the public values belonging" to various buildings and parks. *Id.* On March 31, 1989, the Commission on Fine Arts recommended against construction.

Beginning in 1987, before the property was subdivided, a movement developed in the Woodley Park community in support of designating the property a historic landmark. This culminated on March 2, 1989, when the group filed a landmark designation petition. This was five days before District Intown received zoning approval for the construction. The Historic Preservation Review Board ("Review Board") approved the landmark designation on May 17, 1989. Because the landmark designation petition was pending when District Intown's permits were approved for zoning, the permits were referred to the Review Board pursuant to the District of Columbia's landmark laws, *see* D.C.CODE ANN. § 5-1001 *et seq.* ***, effective since 1979. On July 19, 1989, the Review Board recommended that the construction permits be denied. The permit applications were dismissed without prejudice on December 20, 1991.

On January 31, 1992, District Intown filed new permit applications identical in all respects to those previously dismissed. The permits were again referred to the Review Board, which recommended denial because construction on the lawn would be incompatible with its historic landmark status. Pursuant to D.C. CODE ANN. § 5-1007(e), District Intown requested a hearing before an agent designated by the Mayor. The hearing was held on July 22 and 24, 1992. The Mayor's agent agreed with the Review Board, stating that "any construction destroying the lawn" would be incompatible with its landmark status. *** In addition, the agent purported to hold that the denial of the construction permits did not work an economic hardship or constitute a taking, but the District of Columbia Court of Appeals has since declared that the agent's holding was outside his jurisdiction. *See District Intown Properties, Ltd. v. Department of Consumer and Regulatory Affairs,* 680 A.2d 1373, 1379 (D.C.1996) (decision of the Mayor's agent regarding alleged economic hardship would have no preclusive effect in any future proceeding in which District Intown might claim an uncompensated taking).

Thereafter, on March 22, 1996, District Intown filed this § 1983 action. On cross motions for summary judgment, the District Court entered summary judgment for the District of Columbia on September 25, 1998. *See District Intown Properties Ltd. Partnership,* 23 F.Supp.2d at 39. The court found that the property (*i.e.,* the "relevant parcel") for the purposes of assessing whether a taking had occurred consisted of the original Lot 1 prior to its subdivision into nine lots. *See id.* at 35–36. Because District Intown continued to receive significant economic benefits from use of the relevant parcel, the court found that appellants failed to demonstrate that their property had been rendered "valueless," and their claim to a taking under *Lucas* failed. *See id.* at 36–37. The court then turned to the *ad hoc* analysis elucidated by *Penn Central* and found that none of the *ad hoc* factors support District Intown's takings claim. *See id.* at 37–39. This appeal followed.

II. ANALYSIS

A. Standard of Review

This court reviews a grant of summary judgment *de novo. See Aka v. Washington Hosp. Ctr.,* 156 F.3d 1284, 1288 (D.C.Cir.1998) (en banc). A party is entitled to summary judgment if the record reveals that there is no genuine issue as to any material fact and that the moving party is entitled to judgment as a matter of law. *See* FED R. CIV. P. 56(c). In deciding whether there is a genuine issue of material fact, the court must assume the truth of all statements proffered by the non-movant except for conclusory allegations lacking any factual basis in the record. *See Greene v. Dalton,* 164 F.3d 671, 675 (D.C.Cir.1999). Summary judgment may be granted even if the movant has proffered no evidence, so long as the non-movant "fails to make a showing sufficient to establish the existence of an element essential to that party's case, and on which that party will bear the burden of proof at trial." *Celotex Corp. v. Catrett,* 477 U.S. 317, 322 *** (1986). As the "party challenging governmental action as an unconstitutional taking," District Intown bears a "substantial burden." *Eastern Enterprises v. Apfel,* 524 U.S. 498, 523 *** (1998).

B. The Takings Analysis

The Takings Clause of the Fifth Amendment prohibits the government from taking "private property ... for public use, without just compensation." U.S. CONST. amend. V. In a regulatory takings case, the principal focus of inquiry is whether a regulation "reaches a certain magnitude" in depriving an owner of the use of property. *Pennsylvania Coal Co. v. Mahon,* 260 U.S. 393, 413 *** (1922); *see also id.* at 415 *** (asking whether the regulation "goes too far"). The Supreme Court has indicated that most regulatory takings cases should be considered on an *ad hoc* basis, with three primary factors weighing in the balance: the regulation's economic impact on the claimant, the regulation's interference with the claimant's reasonable investment-backed expectations, and the character of the government action. *See Penn Central Transp. Co.,* 438 U.S. at 124 ***.

The meaning of the three factors identified in *Penn Central* has been amplified by the Court, both in *Penn Central* and in later cases. The *regulation's economic effect* upon the claimant may be measured in several different ways. *See Hodel v. Irving,* 481 U.S. 704, 714 *** (1987) (looking to the market value of a property); *Keystone Bituminous Coal Ass'n v. DeBenedictis,* 480 U.S. 470, 495–96 *** (1987) (looking to whether the regulation makes property owner's coal operation "commercially impracticable"); *Andrus v. Allard,* 444 U.S. 51, 66 *** (1979) (looking to the possibility of other economic use besides sale, which was prohibited by the challenged regulation); *Penn Central Transp. Co.,* 438 U.S. at 136 *** (focusing on the ability to earn a reasonable rate of return). A *reasonable investment-backed expectation* "must be more than a 'unilateral expectation or an abstract need.'" *Ruckelshaus v. Monsanto Co.,* 467 U.S. 986, 1005–06 *** (1984) (quoting *Webb's Fabulous Pharmacies, Inc. v. Beckwith,* 449 U.S. 155, 161 *** (1980)). Claimants cannot establish a takings claim "simply by showing that they have been denied the ability to exploit a property interest that they heretofore had believed was available for development." *Penn Central Transp. Co.,* 438 U.S. at 130 ***. And the *character of the governmental action* depends both on whether the government has legitimized a physical occupation of the property, *see Loretto v. Teleprompter Manhattan CATV Corp.,* 458 U.S. 419, 434–35 *** (1982), and whether the regulation has a legitimate public purpose, *see Keystone Bituminous Coal Ass'n,* 480 U.S. at 485 ***. Finally, under all three of these factors, the effect of the regulation must be measured on the "parcel as a whole." *See Penn Central Transp. Co.,* 438 U.S. at 130–31 ***.

The Supreme Court has indicated that it will find a "categorical" or *per se* taking in two circumstances. The first circumstance includes regulations that result in "permanent physical occupation of property." *Loretto,* 458 U.S. at 434–35 ***. This circumstance is not at issue in this case. The second circumstance includes regulations pursuant to which the government denies *all* economically beneficial or productive use of property. *See Lucas,* 505 U.S. at 1015 ***. This so-called "total taking" claim is at the heart of District Intown's complaint here. Unfortunately, the facial simplicity of the "total taking" standard belies the difficulty in its application. As the Court acknowledged in *Lucas,* its "rhetorical force ... is greater than its precision, since the rule does not make clear the 'property interest' against which the loss of value is to be measured." 505 U.S. at 1016 n. 7 ***.

Under both *Lucas* and *Penn Central,* then, we must first define what constitutes the relevant parcel before we can evaluate the regulation's effect on that parcel. In the instant case the question is: Does the relevant parcel consist of the property as a whole or do the eight lots for which construction permits were denied constitute the relevant parcels? This has been referred to as the "denominator problem." *E.g., Loveladies Harbor, Inc. v. United States,* 28 F.3d 1171, 1179 (Fed.Cir.1994). State law may offer some guidance on how to define the relevant parcel, but, as the Court has noted, state law is not always determinative. *Compare Lucas,* 505 U.S. at 1017 n. 7 *** (suggesting that one may look to the influence of the State's property law—whether and to what extent the State has recognized and extended legal recognition to the particular interest alleged to have been deprived of all economic value—on the claimant's reasonable expectations), *with Keystone Bituminous Coal Ass'n,* 480 U.S. at 500 *** (refusing to treat the support estate as a separate parcel of property simply because Pennsylvania law recognizes it as such and noting that "our takings jurisprudence forecloses reliance on such legalistic distinctions within a bundle of property rights").

C. The Relevant Parcel

The definition of the relevant parcel profoundly influences the outcome of a takings analysis. Above all, the parcel should be functionally coherent. In other words, more should unite the property than common ownership by the claimant. Thus, a court must also consider how both the property-owner and the government treat (and have treated) the property.

The District Court used several factors to determine the relevant parcel: the degree of contiguity, the dates of acquisition, the extent to which the parcel has been treated as a single unit, and the extent to which the restricted lots benefit the unregulated lot. *See District Intown,* 23 F.Supp.2d at 35 (citing *Ciampitti v. United States,* 22 Cl.Ct. 310, 318 (1991)). An analysis focused on these factors is eminently sound and it mirrors the approach taken by other courts in regulatory takings cases. *See Forest Properties, Inc. v. United States,* 177 F.3d 1360, 1365 (Fed.Cir.) (stressing the owner's treatment of property as a unit from the time of purchase) *** (1999); *K & K Const.,*

Inc. v. Department of Natural Resources, 456 Mich. 570, 575 N.W.2d 531, 537 (Mich.) (stressing contiguity, unity of ownership, and a common development plan) *** (1998).

Applying these factors, the District Court correctly determined that all nine lots should be treated as one parcel for the purpose of the court's takings analysis. The lots are spatially and functionally contiguous. District Intown purchased the property as a whole in 1961 and treated it as a single indivisible property for more than 25 years. District Intown presented no evidence that, even after subdivision, it treated the lawn lots separately from Lot 106, the lot that contains the apartment building, for the purposes of accounting or management. The intentional act of subdivision is the only evidence produced by District Intown that it has treated the lots as distinct units. In fact, before the Mayor's agent, District Intown did not come forward with evidence showing that it had, for accounting purposes, treated the lawn maintenance fees separately from expenses associated with maintaining the apartment building. *** While there is a dispute as to whether the adjacent landscaped lawn increases the apartment building's value, this is immaterial. Even if Lot 106 were deemed to have the same value with or without Lots 107 through 114, the application of the other three factors strongly suggests that Lots 106 through 114 are functionally part of the same property.

Appellants argue that the District Court was wrong to treat all the lots as a single parcel because it contradicts *Lucas* and two Federal Circuit cases. This argument falls flat. District Intown first argues that the *Lucas* Court termed "extreme" and "unsupportable" a similar decision by the state court in *Penn Central* to treat multiple holdings as a single parcel for takings analysis. *** This dictum, *see Lucas,* 505 U.S. at 1017 n. 7, 112 S.Ct. 2886, referred, however, only to the state court's decision to treat all of Penn Central's holdings *in the vicinity of Grand Central Station* as part of the denominator for the purposes of deciding whether plaintiffs could receive a reasonable return on their investment in Grand Central. *See Penn Central Transp. Co. v. New York,* 42 N.Y.2d 324, 397 N.Y.S.2d 914, 366 N.E.2d 1271, 1278 (N.Y.1977). The *Penn Central* Court had no need to address this holding. The *Lucas* dictum casts aspersions on the state court's elevation of one factor, unity of ownership, over other factors in determining the relevant parcel. The District Court engaged in no such "extreme" conduct here; it did not look to all of District Intown's holdings in the vicinity of Cathedral Mansions South to evaluate the economic effect of the regulation at issue here; it looked to contiguous property that was purchased and treated as a single unit by appellants.

Similarly, the two Federal Circuit cases cited by District Intown do not undermine the District Court's definition of the relevant parcel. *** Neither of these cases support appellants' position and, in fact, *Loveladies Harbor* supports the District Court's decision. In *Florida Rock Industries,* the court reviewed the Army Corps of Engineers' uncompensated rejection of the plaintiff's application to mine limestone on 98 acres of the plaintiff's wetland property. *See Florida Rock Industries,* 791 F.2d at 896. The Federal Circuit affirmed the trial court's decision to consider the 98 acres as the relevant parcel separate from the adjacent 1,462 acres of wetland. *See id.* at 904. The Federal Circuit's justification for this decision, however, was that all the evidence and the findings indicated that the Army Corps of Engineers would have rejected mining on all of the property, so there was no point to including all 1,560 acres in the relevant parcel. *See id.* at 904–05. Thus, *Florida Rock Industries* is not analogous to the instant case; there is no indication that the District of Columbia will prevent District Intown from continuing to use its property to obtain income from its apartment building.

Loveladies Harbor lends support to the District Court's decision to treat Lots 106–114 as one parcel. The plaintiff in *Loveladies Harbor* sought to develop a total of 12.5 acres of land, consisting of 11.5 acres of wetlands and one acre of filled upland. *See Loveladies Harbor,* 28 F.3d at 1180. The Army Corps of Engineers refused to grant the permit required to fill the wetlands acreage. *See id.* at 1174. In reviewing whether this denial constituted a taking the Federal Circuit found that the trial court correctly concluded that the relevant parcel was the entire 12.5 acres, not just the 11.5 acres to which the permit denial applied. *See id.* at 1181. Thus, *Loveladies Harbor* argues against treating the property burdened by the regulation separately from contiguous property.

Moreover, the *Loveladies Harbor* Court emphasized that a "flexible approach, designed to account for factual nuances," guides its analysis of the denominator problem. *Id.* These factual nuances include "whether there remained substantial economically viable uses for plaintiff's property after the regulatory imposition," *id.* (citing *Deltona Corp. v. United States,* 228 Ct.Cl. 476, 657 F.2d 1184 (Ct.Cl.1981)), and "the timing of transfers in light of the developing regulatory environment." *Id.* Both of these factors support our conclusion in the instant case that Cathedral Mansions South as a whole constitutes the relevant parcel.

Finally, *Penn Central* is instructive where, as here, appellants own a single piece of property that is divisible into several legally recognized entities. Indeed, the Court was rather blunt in saying that

> "[t]aking" jurisprudence does not divide a single parcel into discrete segments and attempt to determine whether rights in a particular segment have been entirely abrogated.

Penn Central Transp. Co., 438 U.S. at 130 ***. The Court also made it clear that a party may not "establish a 'taking' simply by showing that they have been denied the ability to exploit a property interest they heretofore had believed was available for development." *Id.* The Court found this suggestion to be "simply untenable." *Id.*

On the basis of the foregoing authority, it seems clear here that we must analyze District Intown's property not as separate, potentially divisible and transferable parcels, but as one contiguous parcel. Appellants note that the District of Columbia has taxed Lots 107 through 114 at a higher rate since subdivision, reflecting the District of Columbia's assessment that these lots are vacant developable land. They contend that it is inconsistent for the District of Columbia to speak from both sides of its mouth in this regard, claiming for tax purposes that the lots are developable, but refusing to permit development on the lots. We simply note that appellants retain the right to recombine the parcels and treat them as one property for the purposes of taxation, so no further disadvantage will befall them on this score.

We are perplexed by our concurring colleague's criticism of our approach to evaluating a takings claim. As the concurring opinion correctly notes, at bottom, the approach that we follow and the result that we reach are in accord with Supreme Court case law. Unless and until the Court instructs otherwise, we are obliged to judge within the bounds of established precedent.

D. Analysis Under Lucas

Given that Lots 106 through 114 should be treated as a single parcel, the District Court's denial of summary judgment on District Intown's *Lucas* claim is unremarkable. To come within *Lucas,* a claimant must show that its property is rendered "valueless" by a regulation. *Lucas,* 505 U.S. at 1009 ***. District Intown presented no evidence to show that the regulation deprived the property as a whole of all economically beneficial use.

Even were we to view Lot 106 as distinct from Lots 107 through 114, it seems plain that the District Court should have granted appellees' motion for summary judgment. Drawing all inferences in favor of District Intown, the record does not support the conclusion that Lots 107 through 114 are rendered "valueless" by the regulation at issue. The record contains a finding by the Mayor's agent that any construction that destroyed the lawn would be incompatible with the lawn's status as a historic landmark. ***. District Intown argues from this that its case fell on all fours within *Lucas.* District Intown seeks to extend *Lucas* beyond its reach. The *Lucas* Court consciously recognized that it was drawing an arbitrary line between total destruction of economic value and something marginally less than total destruction. *See* 505 U.S. at 1019 n. 8 *** (pointing out that while the line establishing a categorical deprivation as requiring a complete diminution in value is arbitrary as it relates to someone who only suffers a 95% deprivation in value, the person whose deprivation is "one step short of complete" may still seek compensation under the *Penn Central* balancing test). District Intown propounded no evidence that the lawns' economic value was totally destroyed as is required by *Lucas,* nor did District Intown offer evidence of the plots' fair market value after its construction permits were denied. *Cf. Florida Rock Indus.,* 791 F.2d at 905 (reversing the trial court's finding that denial of permit constituted an uncompensated taking because the court failed to consider the property's fair market value after regulation).

The concurring opinion misconstrues the opinion for the court when it suggests that, pursuant to our analysis, no compensable taking could ever be found. As noted in the foregoing discussion, we simply intend to highlight the limited nature of the *Lucas* inquiry, and note that there would be no "categorical" taking even were we to view the parcels as separate under *Lucas.* We do not pass on how the parcels would fare separately under *Penn Central*'s *ad hoc* analysis.

E. Analysis under Penn Central

There are three main factors to be considered in *Penn Central*'s *ad hoc* inquiry: the character of the government action, the regulation's economic effect on the claimant, and the effect on investment-backed expectations. District Intown does not appear to argue that the character of the governmental action counsels finding a taking; this is not a permanent invasion, but rather a general regulation with a legitimate public purpose. As to the economic effects, District Intown offered no evidence that this regulation rendered Lots 106–114 unprofitable to maintain; there is nothing in the record to suggest that the apartment building does not bring in a sufficient return for District Intown, and a claimant must put forth striking evidence of economic effects to prevail even under the *ad hoc* inquiry. *See Penn Central Transp. Co.*, 438 U.S. at 131 *** (reviewing the Court's decisions upholding regulations despite diminution in a property's value of more than 75%).

Finally, District Intown did not present sufficient evidence that it had a reasonable investment-backed expectation to develop the lawns into apartment buildings. Here, as in *Penn Central*, the regulation does not interfere with District Intown's "primary expectation" concerning the use of the parcel, because it "not only permits but contemplates that appellants may continue to use the property precisely as it has been used" for the past 28 years. *Penn Central Transp. Co.*, 438 U.S. at 136 ***.

District Intown suggested at oral argument that it has satisfied the requirement of demonstrating reasonable investment-backed expectations because it purchased property that, at the time of purchase, was subdividable. This is not sufficient to establish the existence of reasonable investment-backed expectations. In this case, where the development District Intown proposes departs from the property's traditional use, and the moment of purchase is so attenuated from the moment of subdivision, the claimant surely must point to some action beyond mere purchase to establish the reasonableness of its expectations.

Appellants also argue that their expectations of the property's use between the moment of purchase and the moment of subdivision could have reasonably changed. This may be, but when appellants subdivided they surely knew that the legal regime had changed since they first bought their property. Moreover, they knew that any subdivided parcel would be subject to that regime. *Lucas* teaches that a buyer's reasonable expectations must be put in the context of the underlying regulatory regime. *See* 505 U.S. at 1030 *** (stating that the Takings Clause does not require compensation when the restriction is proscribed by background state law rules or understandings). District Intown purchased and subdivided its property subject to an existing regulatory regime that establishes that District Intown could have had no reasonable expectations of development at the time it made its investments.

At the time of purchase, District Intown could have reasonably expected the Shipstead-Luce Act to affect its rights of development. For approximately 60 years, the Shipstead-Luce Act has restricted development on properties that, like Cathedral Mansions South, abut or border upon the National Zoo. *See* D.C. CODE ANN. § 5-410. Were that not sufficient, after 1979, D.C.'s historic landmark laws additionally limited expectations of development. *See id.* § 5-1001 *et seq.* Thus, at the time District Intown subdivided the property, it knew, or should have known, that the property was potentially subject to regulation under the landmark laws. *Cf.* Amicus Curiae Brief at 15 (pointing out that almost the entire length of Connecticut Avenue from M Street to almost a mile north of District property is either landmarked or within a historic district). Businesses that operate in an industry with a history of regulation have no reasonable expectation that regulation will not be strengthened to achieve established legislative ends. *See Concrete Pipe & Products v. Construction Laborers Pension Trust,* 508 U.S. 602 *** (1993). In this case, District Intown was in the real estate business, with a history of restriction of development for the purpose of preserving historic sites. Similarly, the Supreme Court rejected a company's claim of reasonable expectations that the Environmental Protection Agency would maintain trade secret confidentiality where the industry had long "been the focus of great public concern and significant government regulation" and the "possibility was substantial that the Federal Government ... would find disclosure [of trade secrets] to be in the public interest." *Monsanto Co.,* 467 U.S. at 1008–09 ***. Prior to and after subdivision, this particular property was the subject of increasing public activity devoted to restricting development through landmark designation. *See Good v. United States,* 189 F.3d 1355, 1361–63 (Fed.Cir.1999) (finding the claimant had no reasonable expectations where he purchased the land subject to environmental regulation and watched as public concern for the environment increased and the applicable regulations became more stringent before seeking approval for development).

District Intown also argues that the District Court's finding that the regulation did not have a significant economic impact was erroneous. District Intown bases this argument on the assertion that they presented undisputed evidence that the lawns, absent development, add nothing to the value of the apartment building. *** This argument misunderstands the substantial burden District Intown faced in District Court. District Intown had to produce evidence showing that its entire property, including Lot 106, no longer provided a reasonable rate of return given the D.C. regulation. Whether the lawns add value to the apartment building is irrelevant to whether the property as a whole can be operated at a sufficient profit even with the regulation. In short, none of the *Penn Central* factors support District Intown's claim of a compensable deprivation of property.

III. CONCLUSION

For the reasons stated above, we affirm the District Court's grant of summary judgment in favor of the District of Columbia.

So ordered.

[Concurring opinion of WILLIAMS, *J., omitted.]*

Notes and Questions

1. **Regulatory regime and landowner's investment-backed expectations.** a. Were the owner's investment-backed expectations frustrated by the landmark designation; is the owner being asked to pay "extra" to preserve what the law decrees to be the historic character of the building? b. In making this determination, how important is it that for nearly thirty years, the owner used the property for the same purposes as existed at purchase? c. In rejecting the claims, the court charged District Intown with knowledge that the property, although not landmarked at purchase, was situated in

an area where landmarking was likely; that it would have been a reasonable contemplation that the apartment building and surrounding property might be historically designated. d. Is investigating the landmark status of a property any more difficult than learning of plans for a new park or office building in the vicinity? e. Is it any less important in assessing the value of the property in deciding whether to go forward with the purchase?

2. **Notice of landmarking.** Under the New York City Landmarks Preservation Law, a designation must be recorded in the land records so as to give constructive notice to purchasers of the land. N.Y. CITY ADMIN. CODE § 25-303(k) ("Upon its designation of any improvement parcel as a landmark and of any landmark site, interior landmark, scenic landmark or historic district or any amendment of any such designation or rescission thereof, the commission shall cause to be recorded in the office of the register of the city of New York in the county in which such landmark, interior landmark, scenic landmark or district lies ..."). Would it further the cause of preservation if sellers of landmarked property were required to disclose this fact to purchasers, or is it sufficient for ordinances to provide for public recording? *See also* D.C. CODE § 6-1104(a), 1105(a), 1106(a) and 1107 (a) (requiring notice in the District of Columbia Register of applications to demolish or otherwise alter an historic property or district).

3. **Washington, D.C., historic preservation laws.** The District of Columbia has developed a mature preservation law administration scheme since enacting in 1978 its Historic Landmark and Historic Protection Act. Among other things, it contains mechanisms for the coordination of actions by the various land use agencies with respect to the same property. *See* https://planning.dc.gov/page/historic-preservation-office (last visited April 3, 2017). The application of the District's program is elaborated in *Embassy Real Estate Holdings LLC. v. District of Columbia Mayor's Agent for Historic Preservation,* 944 A. 2d 1036 (D.C. 2008). *Cf. Kalorama Heights Limited Partnership v. District of Columbia*, 655 A. 2d 865 (D.C.1994).

4. **Effect of historic districts on property values.** Economists and land use experts have concluded that preservation can increase value, both for the particular building designated and other properties in the area. *See* Vicki Been, Ingrid Gould Ellen, Michael Gedal, Edward Glaeser & Brian J. McCabe, *Preserving History or Hindering Growth? The Heterogeneous Effects of Historic Districts on Local Housing Markets in New York City*, National Bureau of Economic Research (Sept. 2014), http://www.nber.org/papers/w20446. In a comprehensive study of various historic districts, the authors report that properties located in areas that are or will become historic districts realize a 20 percent premium in value. They point out, though, these conclusions do not hold across the board—the high cost of land in Manhattan, being a particular exception.

Jay Heritage Estate Under Local and National Preservation Laws

National Historic Landmarks ("NHLs") NHLs are nationally significant historic sites, designated by the Secretary of the Interior, for their exceptional value or quality in presenting or interpreting the heritage of the United States. 54 U.S.C. §302103, 36 C.F.R. §65, https://www.nps.gov/nhl (last visited April 1, 2017). Designated in 1993, the Boston Post Road Historic District in Rye, New York, with the Jay Estate, is one of only 2,500 places across the United States designated as an NHL. https://www.nps.gov/nhl/find/statelists/ny/NY.pdf (last visited April 1, 2017). How did this come to be, and why was it important in the campaign to preserve the Jay Estate?

At the time the battle to save the Jay Estate erupted, land could be developed when the owner decided, that is, with approval of the planning commission and the board of architectural review in the case of landmarked property. That approval requirement invited community input on whether the proposed development was consistent with the public health, safety, and general welfare. At the same time, the city could not confer an historic landmark designation which might preclude development altogether, without the owner's consent.

Rye is the oldest permanent community in New York, having been first settled in 1660. *History*, City of Rye, N.Y., http://www.ryeny.gov/history.cfm (last visited Nov. 15, 2015). Originally part of Connecticut, the land was ceded (unwillingly) by King Charles II to his brother, the Duke of York, as a gift. *Id.* A royal decree in 1700 made Rye an official and permanent addition to New York. *Id.* As methods of travel improved, the Town of Rye grew in population until it became a city in 1942. *Id.*

This long history had produced many significant historic sites and structures, in addition to the Jay Heritage Estate. The Boston Post Road, which runs through the City, still features the original milestones (the 24th, 25th, and 26th from New York City) that Benjamin Franklin affixed in 1763. *Id.* A public inn known as the "Square House" hosted George Washington, John Adams, and General Lafayette; subsequently, it became Rye's first post office, served for sixty years as City Hall, and today is a museum. *Id.* Milton Road is the location of several significant buildings: The Timothy-Knapp house, the oldest house in Rye (built in the 1660s); the Milton and Purdy cemeteries, featuring centuries-old gravestones; the original Milton district school house, built in 1830 (now a private residence); and the current location of the Rye Arts Center, housed in a colonial building that was built in 1788. *Id.*

The Jay Estate is located on a busy two-lane highway, US Route 1, "The Boston Post Road." Set back from the Street, beyond an early 18th century stonewall, few residents or motorists appreciated that they drove past John Jay's resting place. Over the years, the lands south and west of the Jay Estate had been sold off for suburban home development. This historic importance of this remnant stretch of the Boston Post Road was being forgotten. In 1977, inspired by the battles to save Grand Central Terminal and other landmarks, the City of Rye adopted its landmarks preservation local law. CITY OF RYE CODE, ch. 117. Section 117-1(B) declares the intent of the ordinance, among other things, "To recognize and ensure the preservation of those elements of the City's past which represent many and varied architectural, artistic and cultural achievements which cannot be duplicated or otherwise replaced."

The Jay Coalition was aware that the federal Transportation Act of 1966 prohibited funding for federal roads in an "historic site of national, state, or local significance" unless there is no prudent and feasible alternative. 49 U.S.C. § 303(c). The limitation is explained in *Citizens to Preserve Overton Park, Inc. v. Volpe,* 401 U.S. 401 (1971). To win this protection, the Rye City Council amended the historic landmark ordinance to provide for designation without the owner's consent if the property was on the National Register of Historic Places. The Jay Coalition, with the City of Rye, successfully nominated the "Boston Post Road Historic District" to the National Register of Historic Places in 1982 (#82001275). It consisted of the Jay Family cemetery where John Jay rests, the Jay Property, known then as "Alansten," the adjacent County Park known as Marshlands Conservancy, which effectively included the 3,000 year old meadows and view shed, and the adjacent Parsons House (also an 1838 Greek Revival mansion, known as "Lounsbury," which complements the majesty of the Peter Jay Mansion. *See* PAUL DEFOREST HICKS, JOHN E. PARSONS: AN EMINENT NEW YORKER IN THE GILDED AGE (2016). Two years later, the Jay Coalition supported the decision of the City of Rye to designate as City landmarks the remaining historic parcels on the Boston Post Road: the 22.46-acre Jay Property, ("Alansten,"), the trapezoidal view way, and the Van Norden 1912 Carriage House, the neighboring Parsons House, and the 1854 Whitby castle, designed by Alexander Jackson Davis and owned by the City.

The battle over the Boston Post Road raged on. How could the historic significance of this part of Boston Post Road be definitively confirmed? The west side is the only viewshed intact, dating from the early 19th century. Post Master General Benjamin Franklin had ordered that milestones be placed along the Post Road, and one remained in the stone wall, placed opposite Jay's "Locusts."

Notes and Questions

1. **Strategies.** a. Was it a tactical mistake to the Coalition's campaign to save the Jay Estate because it was situated in the midst of other historic buildings? b. Did the landscape approach aid or hinder the preservationists' case? c. Would not the Peter

Jay Mansion, by itself, have been enough? The merits of Peter Jay's mansion were well known. William Carter Halbert, "The Jay Estate," 31 The Westchester Historian 103 (Westchester Co. Hist. Soc., 1955). d. What are the pros and cons of the Jay Coalition's strategy?

2. **Disturbances.** In 2012, a new generation of Rye citizens serving on the City's Landmarks Committee proposed moving the three existing sandstone mile markers on the Boston Post Road. Mile Marker 26 was jackhammered out of its position at Christ Church in 2012, and placed in City Hall. Mile marker 24 is at the Jay Estate on Boston Post Road. The Commission expressed concerns about the mile marker's location on this still busy U.S. route. a. Whose job is it to keep watch over the guardians? (*Quis custodiet ipsos custodes*? Juvenal, *Satire* VI, lines 347–348). b. Is preservation ever complete?

B. Not-for-Profit Owners Cases

In the Matter of the Trustees of the Sailors' Snug Harbor in the City of New York v. Platt

Supreme Court of the State of New York, Appellate Division, First Department
29 A.D.2d 376, 288 N.Y.S.2d 314 (1968)

Steuer, J. The respondent, Landmarks Preservation Commission, pursuant to chapter 8-A of the Administrative Code of the City of New York has determined that certain buildings owned by petitioner are of "a special character, special historical and aesthetic interest and value as part of the development, heritage and cultural characteristics of New York City." The result of such designation is that these buildings may not be reconstructed, altered or demolished by the petitioner without obtaining the permission of the respondent. Special Term entertained petitioner's article 78 proceeding to revoke the designation.

We deem certain of the basic questions raised to be no longer arguable. In this category is the right, within proper limitations, of the State to place restrictions on the use to be made by an owner of his own property for the cultural and aesthetic benefit of the community (*Matter of Cromwell v. Ferrier*, 19 N.Y.2d 263). It is unnecessary to trace the course of judicial thinking in this field. It is now the prerogative of the State, if not its province, to so act where the conditions exist and where constitutionally guaranteed rights are not infringed.

The situation here presented is that the petitioner, Sailors' Snug Harbor, is a charitable organization whose main activity is to provide a home for retired seafaring men beyond the age of active duty. It carries out this purpose on a tract of land 80 acres in extent located on the shore of Staten Island. These are the buildings which are the subject of the respondent's determination. These buildings were built at different times, the earliest in 1830 and the latest in 1880. Petitioner asserts that for the purpose for which these buildings are being used they have largely outlived their usefulness and they can no longer provide suitable accommodations for the elderly men quartered in them. Petitioner intends to replace them with more modern and adequate structures, and feels it would be remiss to its trust to fail to do so. In marked contrast to the accommodations provided by the interiors of the buildings is the effect produced by their exteriors. The proof showed that as a group these buildings were one of the two best examples of Greek Revival architecture in the country and, as such, part of the aesthetic heritage of the nation.

Conceding the validity of regulation, the question presented is whether in the particular instance regulation goes so far that it amounts to a taking (*Pennsylvania Coal Co. v. Mahon*, 260 U.S. 393, 415). If it does, it is constitutionally prohibited (*Vernon Park Realty v. City of Mount Vernon*, 307 N.Y. 493, 498). Chapter 8-A provides some guidelines as to what constitutes an undue burden on commercial realty and provides relief in such instances (§ 207-8.0, subd. a). However, the corresponding provisions in regard to property devoted to charitable uses are limited to the instance where the institution desires to alienate the property by sale or lease (§ 207-8.0, subd. a, par. [1], subpar. [b], cl. [2]). We agree with Special Term that this does not render the statute unconstitutional. It must be interpreted as giving power to the commission to provide relief in the situation covered by the statute, but not restricting the court from so doing in others. The criterion for commercial property is where the continuance of the landmark prevents the owner from obtaining an adequate return. *A comparable test for a charity would be where maintenance of the landmark either physically or financially prevents or seriously interferes with carrying out the charitable purpose* (emphasis added). In this instance the answer would depend on the proper resolution of subsidiary questions, namely, whether the preservation of these buildings would seriously interfere with the use of the property, whether the buildings are capable of conversion to a useful purpose without excessive cost, or whether the cost of maintaining them without use would entail serious expenditure—all in the light of the purposes and resources of the petitioner. Special Term fully appreciated these criteria of judgment but was not supplied with sufficient facts, as distinct from argument, on which to render a satisfactory determination. In the interest of justice we remand the matter for further consideration on these factual questions.

The order granting the petition should be reversed, on the law and in the exercise of discretion, and the matter remanded for the taking of further testimony, with costs to abide the event.

Botein, P. J., Stevens, McGivern and McNally, JJ., concur.

Order and judgment (one paper) unanimously reversed, on the law and in the exercise of discretion, with $50 costs and disbursements to abide the event, and the matter remanded for the taking of further testimony.

Notes and Questions

1. **Evidence and showing required.** a. Was the property owner being asked to bear the costs of maintaining a building for its historic character, even though it is un-

Music Hall at Sailors' Snug Harbor. Library of Congress.

suitable for the purposes of the organization? b. If Sailors' Snug Harbor returned to the Commission with evidence of the costs of razing and rebuilding, as opposed to renovating and maintaining, what relative weights would be assigned to historic value versus the effects on Sailors' Snug Harbor's purposes? c. Would a showing that it is simply cheaper to raze the existing structures and rebuild than to renovate be enough to tip the balance?

2. **Aftermath.** In the early 1970s, the dilapidated Sailors' Snug Harbor struggled for its survival until the Trustees announced that they would move the home to North Carolina, agreeing to sell the site to the City for market value. The first of three parcels, 14.5 acres containing the landmarked structures, were sold to the City for $1.8 million in 1972, while the remaining lands were purchased by a developer who planned a residential project. Before that happened, the City purchased the 65-acre parcel for $7.2 million. In 1976, the Snug Harbor Cultural Center, Inc. was established.

Society for Ethical Culture in the City of New York v. Spatt

Supreme Court of the State of New York, Appellate Division, First Department
68 A.D.2d 112, 416 N.Y.S.2d 246 (1979)

Sullivan, J. At issue is the propriety and constitutionality of the Landmarks Preservation Commission's designation of the Meeting House of the Society for Ethical Culture in the City of New York as a landmark.

The Society for Ethical Culture is a religious, educational and charitable organization, with tax-exempt status, founded in 1876 "to unite in one group, in one bond, those who had ... religious feeling and those who simply cared for moral betterment. [Its] ethical religion has its basis in the effort to improve the world and [its members] morally." The society is the fee owner of an entire 200-foot block front, located on Central Park West between 63rd and 64th Streets, consisting of 20,000 square feet, and the two buildings situated thereon. One building, the religious meeting house (Meeting House), serves as the society's New York headquarters; the other is the society's Ethical Culture School.

Each building is a five-story structure. The buildings are the subject of a single mortgage. They share building services, including a common boiler, interior accessways, and utilities. An auditorium occupies the first three stories of the Meeting House. The fourth and fifth floors contain administrative offices, small meeting rooms and a ceremonial hall used for meetings, weddings and other society activities. Despite the sharing of common services, the buildings are structurally independent. The school was completed in 1904, and the Meeting House was built six years later. Only the Meeting House has received landmark designation. It occupies approximately 40% of the Central Park West property, the value of which has been estimated at about $4,000,000.

The facade of the Meeting House was constructed in an architectural style known as *art nouveau*, popularized in Europe in the late 19th century. A contemporary account by a commentator in *Architecture* magazine noted that the building was "certainly quite the best piece of Art Nouveau architecture yet designed in this country, and compares well with the magnificent German department store buildings whose excellence is so great as to almost promise a future for this style." ***

The Landmarks Preservation Commission was created by the city council, *inter alia*, to protect and perpetuate "the city's cultural, social, economic, political and architectural history" by designating historic districts and landmarks. (Administrative Code of City of New York, § 205-1.0, subd b, par [a].) At the time of the designation the 11-member commission was made up of three architects, two historians, one realtor, one city planner, three businessmen, and one educator.

A landmark is defined as "[a]ny improvement, any part of which is thirty years old or older, which has a special character or special historical or aesthetic interest or value as part of the development, heritage or cultural characteristics of the city, state or nation" (Administrative Code, § 207-1.0, subd n). If, after an investigation of the premises or area under consideration, the commission is disposed to decree landmark status, it must conduct a public hearing. (Administrative Code, § 207-2.0.)

Landmark designation status subjects a property owner to an elaborate regulatory scheme which prohibits, without prior commission approval, the alteration, reconstruction, or demolition of the subject property. The statute would require the society, at its own expense, to keep the exterior of the Meeting House in good repair. (Administrative Code, §§ 207-4.0, 207-10.0.) Violations of certain of the provisions of the law would subject the society, and even its individual members, to criminal penalties. (Administrative Code, § 207-16.0.)

In the case of commercial property there is provision to alleviate financial hardship resulting from landmark designation in instances where economic return is insufficient. The property owner may seek a real estate tax exemption or remission. This countervailing compensatory provision, however, does not apply to the society, which, as a religious, educational and charitable organization is tax exempt, pursuant to section 421 of the Real Property Tax Law.

Public hearings were held on September 25 and November 27, 1973, at which the society unsuccessfully contested the proposed designation. On July 23, 1974, the commission gave the Meeting House landmark status.

Subsequently, the society commenced an article 78 proceeding to annul the commission's designation, alleging, *inter alia*, that the designation was arbitrary and capricious and that the Landmarks Preservation Law (Administrative Code, ch 8-A) as it applied to the Meeting House, was unconstitutional, because it resulted in a taking without just compensation, and violated the free exercise of religion clauses of the United States and New York State Constitutions. In ruling on a motion challenging the propriety of using an article 78 proceeding to seek a declaration of unconstitutionality, Special Term converted the proceeding to an action for declaratory judgment.

As a result of a second motion for summary judgment dismissing the petition, a trial was ordered, after which the court found that the designation was "confiscatory, unconstitutional, arbitrary and unreasonable", and enjoined the city and the commission from interfering with the society's use of the Meeting House and the land upon which it was situated. Trial Term noted that there was no substantial evidence that the Meeting House was "an architectural masterpiece, or of significant historical value", and "[t]hat the restrictions are not only a hardship but interfere with the religious, educational, and charitable purposes of the [society]." This appeal followed.

The commission argues, as it did at *nisi prius*, that the society can prevail on a theory of unjust taking only if it is able to show that the restriction prevents or seriously interferes with the accomplishment of its charitable purposes, and that any claim of hardship incurred by the society because it is required to keep the building in good repair is premature since no action has been taken against it for failure to maintain.

* * *

The Court of Appeals has noted that appellate courts may not upset the determination of an administrative tribunal, where a hearing has been held, if there is substantial evidence to support the finding. *(Matter of Pell v. Board of Educ.*, 34 N.Y.2d 222, 230 ***) The court stated that "[t]he approach is the same when the issue concerns the exercise of discretion by the administrative tribunal: The courts cannot interfere unless there is no rational basis for the exercise of discretion or the action complained of is 'arbitrary and capricious.'" *(Matter of Pell, supra*, pp. 230–231 ***) But whether dealing with a finding of fact after hearing or an exercise of discretion, "[r]ationality is what is reviewed under both the substantial evidence rule and the arbitrary and capricious standard." *(Matter of Pell*, 34 N.Y.2d 222, 231, *supra*; *see also*, *Matter of 125 Bar Corp. v. State Liq. Auth.*, 24 N.Y.2d 174, 178; *Matter of Sled Hill Cafe v. Hostetter*, 22 N.Y.2d 607, 613.) Thus, in the case at bar, our inquiry is directed to a determination of whether the commission's designation had a rational basis or, if, as the society contends, it was arbitrary and capricious. (*See Lutheran Church in Amer. v City of New York*, 35 NY2d 121, 128, n 2, 133.)

As already noted, the standard for designation is that the proposed landmark possess "a special character or special historical or aesthetic interest or value as part of the development, heritage or cultural characteristics of the city, state or nation" (Administrative Code, § 207-1.0), subd n). The panel of commission experts, among which were historians and architects, found that the Meeting House was "a rare, fine and irreplaceable example of *art nouveau* architecture in New York City, that it is one of the finest works of architect Robert D. Kohn, who had a special interest in the Ethical Movement as a leader and as President of the New York Society, and that it is both a tangible symbol of the Society's permanent social contribution and a rich architectural element of the fabric of our City." In making this finding the commission relied on the history of the society, which was founded in 1876; the architecture of the building itself; and the account in *Architecture* magazine, which referred to the building as "certainly quite the best piece of Art Nouveau architecture yet designed in this country." Thus, there was a rational basis for the finding and designation of the Meeting House as a landmark, and Trial Term's statement that "all that was shown was that it was Art Nouveau, serving a questionable environmental purpose and the history only that of the Society" was a subjective substitution of its judgment for that of the commission's historians and architects. Because the building has an architectural quality that is unique, it has a special character, and the fact that it has served as the Meeting House of the society since 1910, a period which is well over half of the society's existence, gives it an historical significance in the heritage of New York City.

The society points out that there is no evidence to suggest that the Meeting House is of extraordinary architectural distinction or that it was ever the scene of any noted historical event or the residence of any noted personage. While relevant, this is not determinative. If the preservation of landmarks were limited to only that which has extraordinary distinction or enjoys popular appeal, much of what is rare and precious in our architectural and historical heritage would soon disappear. It is the function of the Landmarks Preservation Commission to ensure the continued existence of those landmarks which lack the widespread appeal to preserve themselves.

In view of our finding that there was a rational basis for the designation, there remain for consideration only the constitutional questions raised. It has been recognized, "in a wide variety of contexts, that government may execute laws or programs that adversely affect recognized values." (*Penn Cent. Transp. Co. v. New York City*, 438 U.S. 104, 124.) ***

Merely because the State has the authority to regulate certain affairs, however, does not mean that it has the power to zone a property owner into bankruptcy or sacrifice his existence on the altar of architectural [*sic*] or historical preservation. "The general rule at least is, that while property may be regulated to a certain extent, if regulation goes too far it will be recognized as a taking." *(Pennsylvania Coal Co., supra* ***)

Although "[t]here is no set formula to determine where regulation ends and taking begins" (*Goldblatt v. Town of Hempstead*, 369 U.S. 590, 594), there are standards by which to determine whether regulation has gone too far. "The ... test for a charity would be where maintenance of the landmark either physically or financially prevents or seriously interferes with carrying out the charitable purpose." *(Matter of Sailors' Snug Harbor v. Platt*, 29 A.D.2d 376, 378; *see also, Lutheran Church in Amer. v. City of New York*, 35 N.Y.2d 121, *supra.)*

As already indicated, the society, a charitable organization, is unable to benefit from the ameliorative provisions of subdivision c of section 207-8.0 of the Administrative Code of the City of New York, which allow for a real estate tax exemption or abatement where landmark status would work a financial hardship. Hence, if the society could show that an undue financial hardship was imposed, either it must be given other financial relief or the designation must fail.

The threshold question then is whether maintenance of the Meeting House as a landmark would seriously interfere with the society carrying out its charitable purpose. The society, citing the physical inadequacy of the school building and the economic obsolescence of the turn-of-the-century Meeting House with its wasted space, argues that the designation interferes with the accomplishment of its plans for demolition of both buildings, redevelopment of the site and use of the revenues generated therefrom for its charitable purposes.

The commission characterizes the society's argument as the "highest and best use" theory, claiming that what the society seeks, in essence, is to obtain maximum economic advantage from the property, and argues that this is not a criterion in determining whether the designation of landmark status is constitutional. The society rejects this characterization and maintains that the interdependence of the two buildings renders impractical any renovation of the school building without a similar undertaking as to the Meeting House. On the other hand, if the school is to be demolished, development of only that portion—unencumbered by the designation—is not economically feasible. Thus, the society contends, to the extent that the designation prohibits demolition of the Meeting House, it is confiscatory.

Landmarks regulation inevitably has a restricting or adverse effect on property and its owner, charitable or otherwise. In *Snug Harbor* (29 A.D.2d 376, 378, *supra*), the court, in determining whether there was a taking, noted that "the answer would depend on the proper resolution of subsidiary questions, [including] ... whether the preservation of these buildings would seriously interfere with the use of the property". In *Lutheran Church in Amer. v. City of New York* (35 N.Y.2d 121, 129, *supra)*, upon which the society places great reliance, the court, in striking the designation, took note "that the use to which the property has been put for over 20 years would have to cease because of the inability under the designation to replace the building." *** [The property designated as a landmark had been used as an office, but increasing office space requirements had rendered it obsolete.]

At this juncture some factual background would be helpful in placing the matter in proper perspective. In the middle to late 1960's, the society began to explore the feasibility of developing the Central Park West property, which had become "desirable and unique" because of its proximity to Lincoln Center. Several proposals were considered. The most appealing was a plan calling for the demolition of the school and

Meeting House, high-rise development of the entire site, and lease of the property to a developer for 99 years at an annual ground rent of $175,000. According to this proposal, a high-rise, 800 unit, 240,000 square-foot luxury apartment building was to be built, in which the society would occupy 27,500 square feet on the lower floors. On the basis of the ground rent, it was estimated that the society would contemplate receipt of $2,000,000 in mortgage loan money to be applied toward "new facilities for its school on another site or toward its other charitable purposes." As envisioned by the society, the property was, in effect, to be commercially used to generate funds for its charitable purposes. Thus, it appears that the society's dominant purpose was not so much to effect improvement of inadequate or outmoded buildings as it was to exploit the development potential of the site for financial gain, albeit for charitable purposes. This is evidenced by the fact that the society is not satisfied to develop the portion of the site on which the school is situated. This part, representing 60% of the parcel, is unrestricted and can itself be further enhanced by utilization of development rights from the Meeting House site.

Although any owner is free to develop his property, all property owners, commercial or charitable, are subject to valid governmental land use regulation, including regulation which may deprive the owner of the full exploitation value of his property. Unlike *Lutheran Church in Amer. v. City of New York* (35 N.Y.2d 121, *supra)*, no interference with a hitherto existing charitable purpose or function will result from landmark designation. The designation does not deprive the society of the present use of the Meeting House, but instead would prevent it from altering or, more specifically demolishing the building, without prior commission approval, to exploit the full economic potential of the Central Park West site. The only hardship upon the society is speculative upon a prospective use of the property, i.e., large scale development and the revenues to accrue therefrom.

If, as the society contends, the buildings are outmoded and unsuitable for present needs, this was a condition which existed before it began to explore the possible avenues of site development. The society's plans had to be abandoned in 1971, at least two years before the public hearings and some three years before the landmark designation, because of the then depressed real estate market in New York City. Thus, it appears that market conditions, and not the designation, prevented the society from taking remedial action to cure the buildings' shortcomings.

The society attacks the commission's "highest and best use" characterization of its plans for the property as missing the point of its charitable purposes and concomitant freedom to pursue those purposes in whatever way it deems fit. Any regulation which frustrates the charitable purposes of the organization and imposes hardship, the society argues, is unconstitutional. However one chooses to characterize the society's plans, it is settled law that "the fact that [an ordinance] deprives ... property of its most beneficial use does not render it unconstitutional" (*Goldblatt v. Town of Hempstead*, 369 U.S. 590, 592, *supra)*, and, to our knowledge, there is no authority which excludes a charitable owner from the application of this rule. Of course, "[t]he economic impact of the regulation ... and the extent to which regulation has interfered with distinct investment-backed expectations are ... relevant considerations" in determining whether the regulation untowardly affects the anticipated use of the property. (*Penn Cent. Transp. Co. v. New York City*, 438 U.S. 104, 124, *supra.*) For over 60 years the Meeting House has served the same function for the society for which it was constructed and there is no evidence that the property was ever purchased for investment purposes.

The commission also argues that the society's claims of hardship and interference are premature since there has been no proof of the projected costs of maintenance of the Meeting House's exterior, and no action has been taken against the society for failure to maintain in good repair. The commission also notes that the maintenance required for the exterior is no more than that prudently required for the preservation of the society's interest in the building. Nonetheless, the society's rights to alienate the property are seriously constrained by the designation, since it is fairly obvious that any sale would have to be at a price substantially lower than if the property were free of the designation. As Trial Term pointed out, "permission to demolish 'quite probably would not be forthcoming'", so that any application for alteration would be futile. Consequently, to the extent that the designation impairs the value of the property, we believe that the claim of hardship is not premature. (*See Board of Coop. Educational Servs. v. Goldin*, 38 A.D.2d 267, 272.)

[T]he society also argues that the landmark designation constitutes an undue interference with the free exercise of religion in violation of the First Amendment of the United States Constitution, and section 3 of article I of the New York State Constitution. In support it cites *Matter of Westchester Reform Temple v. Brown* (22 N.Y.2d 488), which held unconstitutional, as applied, a zoning statute which would have prohibited the construction of a synagogue with adjacent parking space. Although voiding the application of the statute the court noted (p 496) that "[r]eligious structures enjoy a constitutionally protected status which severely curtails the permissible extent of governmental regulation in the name of the police powers, but the power of the regulation has not been altogether obliterated." Unlike the congregation in *Westchester*, the society does not seek simply to replace a religious facility with a new, larger facility. Instead, using the need to replace as justification, it seeks the unbridled right to develop its property as it sees fit. This is impermissible, and the restriction here involved cannot be deemed an abridgement of any First Amendment freedom, particularly when the contemplated use, or a large part of it, is wholly unrelated to the exercise of religion, except for the tangential benefit of raising revenue through development.

At this time the society has not been interfered with in the exercise of its religion. If, at some point in the future, it decides to seek permission to replace the present Meeting House with a larger one designed to meet the needs which a clearly outmoded building could not provide, and is denied permission, then perhaps a claim of unjust taking or First Amendment impairment might lie. Of course, should the society seek to replace the Meeting House to develop the property to its full economic potential, any claim of building obsolescence might be suspect. In the final analysis, obsolescence should be measured by the society's needs, not on the prospects for development of a valuable piece of property.

Accordingly, the judgment, Supreme Court, New York County (BAER, J.), entered January 15, 1976, annulling the designation of petitioner's Meeting House as a New York City landmark, should be reversed, on the law, without costs or disbursements, and the designation declared valid.

SANDLER, J. P., LANE, LUPIANO and SILVERMAN, JJ., concur.

Judgment, Supreme Court, New York, entered on January 15, 1976, reversed, on the law, without costs and without disbursements, the judgment vacated and the designation of petitioner's Meeting House as a New York City landmark declared valid.

Notes and Questions

1. **Charitable versus investment purposes.** a. The court recognizes that historic preservation laws may preempt a landowner from realizing the "highest and best use" of the property. But, is this impact any different from that of other land use regulations, like limits on uses in certain zones or height restrictions? b. In determining whether the application of the Landmarks Preservation Law to this property effects a taking, how important is it that it had never been held for its economic potential? c. When does the gap between values as limited by historic preservation laws and as potentially developed become confiscatory? d. Is the safety valve—tax exemption to charitable entities—enough to mitigate the economic impact?

1. The Marymount School Certificate of Appropriateness

Landmarks Preservation Commission
July 20, 1982
LPC Nos. 82217 and 82292

DETERMINATION OF APPLICATION FOR A CERTIFICATE OF APPROPRIATENESS TO ALTER DESIGNATED BUILDINGS INAPPROPRIATELY ON GROUNDS OF INSUFFICIENT RETURN

The Marymount School, 1026–1028 Fifth Avenue, Metropolitan Museum Historic District. Block 1495, Lots 69, 70 and 72.

Findings and Conclusions—Determinations

On the basis of the testimony presented at the Public Hearings on May 25th and June 8, 1982, the submissions of the Applicant and members of the Public, the reports from members of the staff of the Commission, and its own expertise as articulated in specific statements of several of the Commissioners, the Commission has found as follows:

A. *Proposed Alteration is Inappropriate*

The Landmarks Preservation Commission determined at a Public Meeting on April 27, 1982 which followed the Public Hearing on the application for a Certificate of Appropriateness for a rooftop addition under Section 207-6.0, that the addition was inappropriate.

B. *The appropriate standard is the one defined by the Court of Appeals in Society for Ethical Culture v. Spatt which is equivalent to the Findings Set Forth in Section 207-8.0a (2) (c) and (d).*

1. The Commission found:

   a) that the subject improvement parcels are presently and have been for more than three years exempt from real estate taxes under Section 421 (formerly 420) of the Real Property tax law and that therefore, under the provisions of Chapter 8-A the Applicant must establish the conditions set forth in Section 207-8.0a.(2).

   b) that to require the owner to sell the subject property or lease it long-term in order to enable it to establish the finding set forth in 207-8.0a.(2)(a) would seriously interfere and frustrate the purposes for which the owner holds the property and create an unconstitutional overregulation as defined in *Sailors Snug Harbor, Lutheran Church and Ethical Culture* based on the following:

      1) The subject improvements are owned by the Board of Trustees of the Marymount School of New York and the sole purpose for which it is held by them is to house the School;

      2) that the Religious of the Sacred Heart had purchased 1028 Fifth Avenue in 1926 in order to house and operate a private school for daughters of Roman Catholic families;

      3) that the Religious of the Sacred Heart had thereafter purchased 1027 Fifth Avenue in 1936, and 1026 Fifth Avenue in 1950 to expand the School;

      4) that the Religious of the Sacred Heart in 1969 had incorporated the School and transferred the land and buildings to the Board of Trustees to provide for the continued operation of the School by establishing it on a more secure financial foundation (copy of Indenture dated October 31, 1969);

      5) that the subject improvements and land were given to the School by the Order of the Sacred Heart in 1969 with the provision that the land and buildings were to revert to the Mother Order in the event the School ceased to operate at that location (Applicant's submission dated May 25, 1982); and

      6) that the applicant does not wish to sell or lease long-term the school buildings and move to another location or to close the School.

The Commission, therefore, determined that since it was bound to apply the constitutional standard set forth in *Ethical Culture, Lutheran Church* and Sailors' *Snug Harbor* and since the findings of fact the Commission must make under Section 207-8.0a (2) (3) and (d) were essentially the same ones it must make in applying that constitutional standard, in order for the Commission to make a Preliminary Determination of Insufficient Return, the applicant should establish the third and fourth conditions but would not be required to establish the first and second conditions of Section 207-8.0a(2).

C. *Findings on Applicant's Establishing that the Designated Buildings Have Ceased to be Adequate, Suitable or Appropriate for Use for Carrying Out the Purpose to Which it is and Has Been Devoted.*

1. Section 207.80a (2) (c) requires the applicant to establish that the improvement has ceased to be adequate, suitable or appropriate for use for carrying out:

    1) the purposes to which it is devoting its improvement; and

    2) those purposes to which it had devoted the improvement when acquired unless the owner is no longer engaged in pursuing such purposes.

The Commission found that the Applicant had established:

a) that the owner is a non-profit educational corporation;

b) that the purpose to which the improvement is devoted is to house the operation of an independent college preparatory day school which enrolls girls in Kindergarten through class XII and girls and boys in a preschool program and that this is the purpose to which it has been devoted since acquisition by Applicant. (Applicant's submission May 25, 1982, and statements of Applicant's representatives at Public Hearing on May 25, 1982.)

2. *Inadequacy of the Improvement for Carrying out the Owner's Purposes*

    a. *Need for the School to Offer a Full time Athletic Program*

The Commission found that the Applicant had established that it needed to offer a full time structured athletic program in order to carry out its purposes based upon the following:

1) the recommendation of the Middle States Visiting Committee, December 1971 that the School obtain a full time gymnasium and other recommendations for changes in the School's athletic program; that although non-compliance with the recommendations would not of itself lead to the loss of accreditation the import of its recommendations is to establish that the need has been identified by an organization which is independent of the Applicant and one which is expert in assessing the needs of an educational institution like the Applicant; (Enclosure Item I of Sister Kathleen Fagan's letter of June 1, 1982 to the Commission);

2) the increased willingness of Roman Catholic parents since Vatican II to send their children to non-Catholic schools has meant that Marymount is competing with a larger number of independent schools in the neighborhood for its students; Marymount's lack of

a full time structured athletic program or an on-site gymnasium program or facility might be a decisive factor on a parent's (or child's) no [sic] enlarged choice among Marymount and other independent schools. (Applicant's submission dated May 25, 1982, statements of its representatives at Public Hearing May 25, 1982, letter of Dr. Lobo to Sister Kathleen Fagan, dated May 15, 1982);

3) the increased recognition on the part of educators, parents and students of the value of intramural and extramural competitive team sports such as basketball and volleyball as an essential part of the educational development of young women, has made the present arrangements for an athletic program which can be carried out in large part within the School buildings, given their physical constraints, and Central Park, given the seasonal constraints, less acceptable than formerly. (Applicant's submissions dated May 25, 1982 and June 1982, statements of its representatives at Public Hearing May 25, 1982.);

4) after years of regularly using the gymnasium of another school, the Marymount School's confidence in its ability to provide a structured athletic program which relies in part on utilizing the gymnasium of another school or other organization has been undermined first by the fact that such usage was limited after that school became coeducational (i.e. Loyola) and second by Marymount's experience with the uncertainty of arrangements made with other schools given the fact that existing arrangements can be cancelled without adequate notice in response to last minute changes in that school's needs (i.e. P.S. 169) (Applicant's submissions of May 25, 1982 and June 1, 1982; correspondence relating to P.S. 169 in summer and fall of 1981 attached to Sister Kathleen Fagan's letter to the Commission of June 18, 1982; letter of Headmaster of Loyola School to Head of Marymount Upper School, dated August 7, 1981.); and

5) although concerted attempts have been made since the report of the Middle States Visiting Committee (December 1971) to purchase space for construction of gymnasium or to rent an outside gymnasium, they have not been successful, (Sister Kathleen Fagan's letter of June 18, 1982 with enclosures; the rental of a gymnasium in a public school located across Central Park and some distance north from Marymount for the 1981–82 school year).

b. *No Feasible Alternative Exists for an Adequate On-Site, All-Purpose Athletic Facility.*

1. *Alternative Locations*

The Commission found that the Applicant had established that there was no alternative location within the school buildings that could be used to locate an all-purpose athletic facility which would be adequate for basketball and volleyball based upon the following:

a) The Commission reviewed the plans of the existing condition of the School, and based on those plans and the staff report on minimum dimensions for a court for volleyball and basketball (Maher memorandum) found that given the floor heights and the widths of the three buildings which are separated by weight bearing walls, an on-site, all-purpose gymnasium could not be located within the buildings as presently existing without removing a ceiling or the roof, or without removing portions of the structural walls between the buildings;

b) The Commission reviewed possible alternative locations for an on-site, all-purpose athletic facility including those analyzed by Harold Buttrick & Associates, the Applicant's architects, and by James Rhodes, the architect for adjacent property owners, and found:

1. the rear cellar-first floor and the fifth floor-roof could provide alternative locations for a gymnasium which could be used for team sports including basketball and volleyball;

2. that a gymnasium in either of these locations would have a uniform height and thus would be superior in that respect to the proposed facility;

3. that either of these alternative locations would require an expenditure of two-and-a-half to four times the amount estimated for the proposed rooftop addition (Buttrick, June 18, 1982);

4. that these additional costs would, in past, result from the need to take special care to protect the designated buildings because of the extent of interference with their structure if the gymnasium were to be located in either the cellar-first floor or fifth floor-roof location, and that such resulting costs would inevitably make either alternative significantly more expensive than the rooftop addition; and

5. that the Applicant does not have either an endowment or the potential for financial assistance from the Archdiocese or the Religious of the Sacred Heart but is financially limited to contributions from its fund raising efforts and short term bank loans. (Letter of Richard Tauber, Treasurer, dated July 20, 1982. Financial Statements and Accountant's Report, Years ended June 30, 1981 and 1980.)

2. *Alternative Design for a Rooftop Addition*

The Commission reviewed the proposed designs for the rooftop addition and analyzed various alternatives and determined that there was no alternative design which would meet the requirements for an all-purpose athletic facility which would either have no or at least less adverse effects on the designated buildings based on the following:

a) that the width of the addition and the height of its west wall are the most critical factors effecting the visibility of the rooftop addition above the mansard roofs;

b) that the height and width of the addition are determined by the Applicant's identified critical need for an athletic facility which could be used for basketball and volleyball games;

c) that the proposed height of the west wall of the facility is 12 feet 8 inches which provides 11 feet 5 inches functional space (Applicant's submission May 25, 1982);

   1. which the Applicant's architects stated was the lowest height that would permit the space below to be used for basketball (statements at Public Hearing on May 25, 1982 and June 8, 1982);

   2. which is lower than the height of any of the on-site gymnasiums of the six "comparable" independent 12-grade schools (Applicant's submission dated May 25, 1982); and

   3. which is considerably lower than the 22–25 foot minimum height recommended by several persons in response to the inquiry of the Commission's staff (Maher memorandum);

d) that the proposed height at center line which has been designed to compensate for the lower west wall height although higher than that of the on-site facility of the six "comparable" independent schools, is still lower than the recommended height (statement of Applicant's architect at Public Hearing June 8, 1982); (Maher memorandum);

e) that the proposed width of the facility in 33 feet 8 inches:

   1. which the Applicant's architects stated was the narrowest width that would permit the space to be safely used for basketball (statement at Public Hearing on May 25, 1982 and June 8, 1982);

   2. which is comparable within inches to the width of the on-site gymnasium of six "comparable" independent 12-grade schools (Applicant's submissions, May 25, 1982); and

   3. which is at the narrow end of the ranges of recommended widths (Maher memorandum).

f) the increased height at the center line, the width and the length of the facility necessitates a larger and higher parapet at the south wall of 1026 Fifth Avenue which will be clearly visible but which was not found inappropriate by the Commission; and

g) that a "temporary" facility such as a "bubble" was discussed by the Commission but was considered visually inappropriate to the three designated structures and thus not a meaningful alternative.

Accordingly, having found:

1) that the purposes to which the property are now, and since acquisition, have been devoted, are to house the operation of an independent 12-grade girls school;

2) that the designated buildings have become inadequate for carrying out the owner's purpose because:

   a. the need has developed for the School to offer a full-time athletic program in order to carry out its purposes successfully;

   b. various events and changes which have occurred have caused the designated buildings to cease to be adequate for carrying out the School's purposes unless it is able to have access to a full-time athletic facility either in the improvement or in an off-site facility in the area which the School can with assurance rely on remaining available for an extended period of time; and

   c. that no alternative location within the buildings or modification of the proposed rooftop addition, in order to prevent or minimize the adverse effect to the designated property, would provide a facility that would meet the Applicant's requirements for an all-purpose athletic facility that could be used for basketball and volleyball.

The Commission found that the Applicant had established that the improvement had ceased to be adequate, suitable or appropriate for carrying out the purposes to what is not, and has, since acquisition, been devoted.

D. *Findings on Applicant's Establishing That it has Intent to Proceed Promptly With Addition*

The Commission found that the Applicant had established that it had the necessary intent to proceed promptly with construction of the inappropriate addition based on the following:

1) the Middle States Visiting Committee will be visiting again in the fall of 1982 to review the School's accreditation and the Board of Trustees has expressed the opinion that it is necessary to provide assurances to the Committee that its recommendation for a full-time athletic facility, which it made ten years ago, has been successfully addressed;

2) the Applicant's representatives have stated to the Commission that the School is under a very serious time constraint to begin construction. (Statements of Applicant's representatives at Public Hearings of May 25, 1982 and June 8, 1982, Applicant's submission, May 25, 1982; Webster & Sheffield memorandum June 7, 1982);

3) Sister Kathleen Fagan, Headmistress of the School, and Richard Tauber, Treasurer of Board of Trustees, have each written the Commission that it is the School's intent to proceed promptly with construction of the facility as soon as necessary permits have been obtained, (Fagan letter, June 22, 1982, Tauber letter, July 20, 1982); and

4) Representatives of the Applicant have stated to the Commission and Richard Tauber has informed the Commission in writing that the Applicant is in a financial position to begin work on the proposed addition as soon as it receives the necessary permits given that it has raised $400,000 to date and is able to obtain a bridge loan from a commercial bank should any obligation come due before it had raised the remaining necessary funds. (Tauber letter, July 20, 1982).

E. *Preliminary Determination of Insufficient Return*

Having found that the Applicant had established:

1) that the improvement had ceased to be adequate, suitable, or appropriate for carrying out the purposes to which it is now, and since acquisition, has been devoted and

2) that it has the necessary intent to proceed promptly with constructing the inappropriate addition,

The Commission determined that a showing of insufficient return had been established by the Applicant.

1025 Fifth Avenue, Inc. v. Marymount School of New York

Supreme Court, New York County, New York, Special Term, Part I
123 Misc.2d 756, 475 N.Y.S.2d 182, 17 Ed. Law Rep. 182 (1983)

Greenfield, J.

Motions numbered 204, 205 and 206 on the Special Term, Part I Calendar of November 10, 1983, are consolidated for disposition.

This CPLR article 78 proceeding to vacate an order and decision of the New York City Landmarks Preservation Commission which permitted the respondent Marymount School (Marymount) to construct a rooftop gymnasium on its Fifth Avenue buildings presents the court with three paradoxes:

Can a "Certificate of Appropriateness" be issued when a proposed building alteration is found to be architecturally inappropriate?

Can an exception be made for "insufficient return" in favor of a now commercial, nonprofit institution?

Can the Landmarks Preservation Commission permit alterations of a nonlandmark in an historic district when the governing statute authorizes permits only for demolition on such sites and authorizes permits for alterations only in landmark buildings?

The petitioners are two cooperative corporations which own apartment houses adjacent to Marymount. Petitioners' buildings and Marymount's town houses occupy the entire blockfront on Fifth Avenue between East 83rd and East 84th Streets facing the Metropolitan Museum of Art.

The buildings lie within the Metropolitan Museum Historic District, which was established pursuant to the authority of chapter 8-A of the Administrative Code of the City of New York (Landmark Law). The Commission has aesthetic jurisdiction over the buildings within this historic district.

Marymount is a Catholic college preparatory school with a predominately female enrollment. The three town houses which it occupies are architecturally distinguished buildings in the beaux arts style, but are not in and of themselves designated landmarks. These buildings were acquired over a span of years by the Order of the Sacred Heart of Mary (Order), which donated them to Marymount for the operation of its school. The Order retained a reversionary interest in the land and buildings in the event that Marymount ceased operation of the school on the site.

Marymount, according to its literature, prides itself on educating and challenging the whole child, intellectually, morally and physically. To the latter end, it has leased recreational and gymnastic facilities from other Catholic schools in the area when such facilities were available and has utilized other neighboring facilities on an *ad hoc* basis.

Marymount has no on-site gymnasium of its own. However, after two studies by educational evaluators and some parental complaints about the school's physical education programs, Marymount determined that it needed its own facility where instruction could be given without worrying about the vagaries of the institutions from whom it borrowed space.

It had plans drawn up for a rooftop gymnasium and then applied to the Commission for a certificate of appropriateness so that it could lawfully begin construction (Administrative Code, § 207-7.0). This was denied because the Commission found that the plans submitted clashed with and detracted from the facades of the three buildings.

Marymount then attempted to obtain a certificate of appropriateness on the ground of insufficient return. (Administrative Code, § 207-8.0.)

"Insufficient return" is almost by definition a commercial concept, and inapplicable to nonprofit institutions such as Marymount (*cf.* Administrative Code, § 207-1.0, subd v). The analogous applicable standard is that landmark-related restrictions "not physically or financially prevent, or seriously interfere with the carrying out of the charitable purpose". (*Matter of Society for Ethical Culture v. Spatt*, 51 N.Y.2d 449, 455.)

Marymount submitted a revised design which it alleges is virtually invisible from the street, except for a 15-inch span. Hearings were held on the application, and testimony taken. Staff members of the Commission were directed to study the existing Marymount structures and to determine whether the facility could be housed inside the buildings.

The Commission rendered its "Determination of Application for a Certificate of Appropriateness to alter designated buildings inappropriately on grounds of insufficient return" on July 20, 1982. This determination recorded the voluminous documentary evidence and listed persons testifying for and against the proposed addition. It then held that the proposed addition was still architecturally inappropriate, apparently without considering modifications to the original plan.

The Commission then applied the test cited above to the problem before it. It set forth in considerable detail the evidence introduced by Marymount in support of its contention that lack of the gymnasium "seriously interfered with the carrying out of the charitable purpose." This included, in addition to other factors mentioned, the growing emphasis on physical education in women's education and the decreasing availability of other facilities to the school. It found other, alternative plans for constructing the facility were not feasible. In conclusion, the determination stated:

> "Having found that the Applicant had established:
>
> "(1) that the improvement had ceased to be adequate, suitable, or appropriate for carrying out the purposes to which it is now, and, since acquisition, has been devoted and
>
> "(2) that it has the necessary intent to proceed promptly with constructing the inappropriate addition,
>
> the Commission determined that a showing of insufficient return had been established by the Applicant."
>
> The Notice to Proceed dated February 2, 1983, based upon this determination is the subject of this proceeding. Neighboring property owners, petitioners in particular, have charged that construction of the rooftop gymnasium, even as modified, would obstruct views from their apartments and lessen property values, as well as detract from the fashionable ambiance of the neighborhood.
>
> Petitioners challenge the Commission's actions on the grounds:
>
> (a) That the agency was without jurisdiction to issue the Notice to Proceed, because the relevant statute gives it authority to rule on demolition of buildings in historic districts, but not on alterations to them;
>
> (b) That assuming for argument's sake that the Commission was within its power to consider the issue, the Notice to Proceed was improperly issued because the proposed modification was not necessitated by an interference with the school's present use of its property.
>
> (c) The facts in this case plainly do not support the Commission's action; i.e., the school had demonstrated mere inconvenience, and not that its corporate purpose was being frustrated by the lack of a gymnasium.

Marymount had interposed an answer which asserts cross-claims against the co-respondent Commission in the event that the petition is granted. These include an assertion that the statute is confiscatory and therefore unconstitutional, and that the Commission erred in not considering the appropriateness of the new design.

There are procedural and ripeness deficiencies inherent in the assertion of these crossclaims. At the present time, it is sufficient to note that both the Commission and the petitioners have moved to dismiss them.

Marymount appears to have fallen into one of the many interstices in the Landmark Law. The courts have been attempting to assist the Commission in resolving problems not covered by this legislation for years. (*See e.g.*, *Lutheran Church in Amer. v. City of New York*, 35 N.Y.2d 121.)

The particular "oversight" upon which the petitioners rely occurs in the following portion of the statute: "(1) Except as otherwise provided in paragraph two of this subdivision a, in any case where an application for a permit to demolish any improvement located on a landmark site or in an historic district ... is filed with the commission, together with a request for a certificate of appropriateness authorizing such demolition, and in any case where an application for a permit to make alterations to or reconstruct any improvement on a landmark site or containing an interior landmark is filed with the commission" (Administrative Code, § 207-8.0, subd a, par [1]) (emphasis in original).

Petitioners argue that the failure to include provisions for the Commission to rule upon applications to make alterations to a *nonlandmark* building in an historic district makes the issuance of the notice to proceed an *ultra vires* act.

Petitioner relies substantially upon wording in the leading case in this area, *Matter of Trustees of Sailors' Snug Harbor v. Platt* (29 A.D.2d 376), in support of this argument. In *Snug Harbor*, the *** question presented to the court was whether denial of permission to raze these architecturally unique buildings amounted to a taking of property by the regulating authority, or confiscation without compensation. The Appellate Division commented, in considering the question:

> "Chapter 8-A [the Landmark Law] provides some guidelines as to what constitutes an undue burden on commercial realty and provides relief in such instances ... However, the corresponding provisions in regard to property devoted to charitable uses are limited to the instance where the institution desires to alienate the property by sale or lease.... We agree with Special Term that this does not render the statute unconstitutional. It must be interpreted as giving power to the commission to provide relief in the situation covered by the statute, but not restricting the court from so doing in others" (29 A.D.2d, at p 378).

Petitioners interpret *Snug Harbor* as mandating that Marymount apply first to this court, rather than to the Commission, for permission to alter its buildings, since the Commission only had jurisdiction to permit the school to demolish, as opposed to altering the building (emphasis in original).

Petitioners' interpretation of *Snug Harbor* in this context is unduly restrictive. This court believes that *Snug Harbor* gives this court the power to continue to formulate the common law which will govern in situations not foreseen in the statute. The body of case law which is of equal import and dignity with statutory law, and just as binding upon administrative agencies, will thereafter be used in the agency's determinations.

The Commission argues that this court should find that it had jurisdiction to issue the notice to proceed, and that the omission of the specific words authorizing alterations in section 207-8.0 (subd a, par [1]) was a simple oversight. The Commission urges that a review of the Landmark Law in its entirety shows that it was the legislative intent that the Commission have such jurisdiction. This court agrees. It was plainly contemplated that the Commission have jurisdiction to consider affording lesser relief to the owner of a building in a historic district than the permission to demolish, given in the subsection. *** *See generally*, Administrative Code, § 205-1.0, subd b, "Purpose and declaration of public policy"; § 207-4.0, subd a, par [1], "Regulation of construction, reconstruction, alteration and demolition."

To hold that the courts, which have limited expertise in such a specialized field, should pass *ab initio* upon the efficacy and adequacy of alterations which must be aesthetically integrated with the neighboring structures would be improper when the legislative intent to the contrary is clear (Administrative Code, § 207-2.0).

> "Statutes are presumed to have reasonable intendment. Courts are not always controlled by the literal meaning expressed in the *statute* ... "[I]f the context indicates words are inadvertently omitted, such as are necessary may be supplied by the court to complete the sense and express the legislative intent, where consideration of the whole act with reference to the subject matter to which it applies indicates the true legislative intent." (*Standard Acc. Ins. Co. v. Newman*, 2 Misc.2d 348, 359, affd 268 App.Div. 967.)["]
>
> It is not the function of any court and specifically this court to create jurisdiction by implication; however, it is the court's function to construe a statute to prevent an inconsistent and unreasonable result. (Matter of *Stockwell*, 210 App.Div. 753.) This is obviously the construction placed upon the Snug Harbor test (supra) since the Landmarks Commission has consistently applied a common-law test in these "charitable" cases not precisely covered by the statute. These cases came to the courts later, generally when the institution sought review of the Commission's decision. (See e.g., Matter of Society of E*thical Culture* [v. Spatt], 51 N.Y.2d 449, supra.) Accordingly, it is the judgment of this court that the issuance of the notice to proceed was within the Commission's jurisdiction (emphasis in original).

Petitioners go on to argue that even assuming there was jurisdiction in the Commission to entertain the matter, it misapplied the standard developed by the courts in the trilogy of cases which supply controlling precedent in this area, i.e., *Matter of Trustees of Sailors' Snug Harbor v. Platt* (29 A.D.2d 376, *supra*); *Lutheran Church in Amer. v. City of New York* (35 N.Y.2d 121, *supra*); and *Matter of Society of Ethical*

Culture v. Spatt (51 N.Y.2d 449, *supra*). The problem is that these cases arguably posit two tests: the *Snug Harbor* test, that regulation not seriously interfere with the carrying out of the charitable purpose, and a more stringent test which appears as dictum in *Ethical Culture* which explicitly reaffirmed the *Snug Harbor* test. The *Ethical Culture* test permits regulation which does not interfere with activities being carried on inside the structure. In short, if school activities were not being disrupted by the lack of a gymnasium, then the Commission should not have issued the notice to proceed.

It appears to this court that the Commission has properly applied both criteria to the problem at hand and had determined (a) that Marymount's charitable purpose of providing a well-rounded quality education is being undermined by the lack of a gymnasium, and (b) that activities within the school—the education of the students—are being hindered by the lack of a gymnasium. It is hornbook law that the court cannot substitute its opinion for that of the agency on these matters if the agency's determination has a rational basis. The court finds that the determination is supported by facts in the record and is neither arbitrary, capricious nor contrary to law. The impingement on plaintiffs and on the essential character of the historic district is minimal. A contrary determination, on the other hand, would have substantial adverse impact on the school. ***

The application is denied and the petition is dismissed. The cross motion of Marymount is denied and the cross motions of the Commission and the petitioners are denied on the ground of mootness.

Notes and Questions

1. **Value of the historic district.** a. How important in the court's gap filling efforts was the fact that the building was situated within an historic district? b. How would incompatible alterations affect the existence of the historic district? c. If petitioners' gambol that the Commission had authority to permit a demolition of, but not alterations to, a landmarked building, had been successful, would Marymount, in turn, have applied to demolish the building?

2. Mathew Brady Studio at 359 Broadway Designation Report

Introduction

In considering the following material, keep in mind that the designation is about 12 pages long and the appellate decision is only one page long. Consider whether the thoroughness of the record can make the judicial review more manageable.

The Marymount School. Photo by Downtowngal, via Wikimedia Commons.

Designation Report

Landmarks Preservation Commission
October 16, 1990; Designation List 28
LP-1758

359 BROADWAY BUILDING, Borough of Manhattan, Built 1852; architect unknown.

Landmark Site: Borough of Manhattan Tax Map Block 174, lot 33.

On December 12, 1989, the Landmarks Preservation Commission held a public hearing on the proposed designation as a Landmark of the 359 Broadway Building and the proposed designation of the related Landmark Site (Item No. 22).

DESCRIPTION AND ANALYSIS

Summary

No. 359 Broadway, on the west side of Broadway between Leonard and Franklin streets, is a distinguished early Italianate commercial building constructed in 1852, a time when this section of Broadway was the city's most prestigious shopping area, containing a number of fashionable daguerreotype studios. An important and unusual example of the Italianate style, this stone-fronted commercial building, with its distinctive and varied window openings and abundant ornament, is a blend of Italianate elements from several sources. The 359 Broadway Building has special historical significance because it was occupied by photographer Mathew B. Brady from 1853–59. Brady, one of the most important photographers in American history, was renowned for both his portraits and his numerous photographs of the Civil War which are still the primary visual document of that conflict. As the city expanded northward from the southern tip of Manhattan in the 1840s and 1850s, this area became a prosperous neighborhood of shops, saloons, and photographers devoted to serving the fashionable clientele that made Broadway the city's most distinguished promenade. Remarkably intact, No. 359 Broadway serves as a significant reminder of the area's glittering past as a premier shopping district and as a home to the studio of one of America's most noted nineteenth-century photographers, Mathew Brady.

The Commercial Transformation of Lower Broadway ***

The 359 Broadway Building was erected by owner James Thompson in 1852. Thompson, listed in New York City directories as both a saloon owner and a confectioner, operated a saloon at 359 Broadway until 1860. Thompson's Saloon at 359 Broadway, like Taylor's, served as an enticing establishment for shoppers enjoying another popular Broadway diversion, a visit: to the photographer. One of the most famous was located upstairs.

Mathew Brady's studio at 359 Broadway was one of an estimated eighty-six portrait galleries in New York City in 1853; thirty-seven of these were located on Broadway. The avenue was the favored location of Daguerreian artists because of its role as a fashionable promenade, and the prospect of a saloon and a photographer in the same building was especially inviting to passing shoppers. All of the galleries were located on upper floors of buildings and illuminated by skylights essential to indoor portraiture. Mathew Brady's studio, which occupied 359 Broadway from 1853 to 1859, was one of the most famous Broadway galleries. One of Brady's chief competitors, Martin M. Lawrence, opened a new gallery at 381 Broadway the same day that Brady opened his own studio. Another competitor, Jeremiah Gurney, had a studio located at 189 Broadway *** [189 Broadway has been demolished; 381 Broadway is extant] and was known as Broadway's oldest and most popular daguerreotypist, having founded his business in 1840. All of these studios were housed in great splendor. Brady's gallery, which occupied the upper three floors of 359 Broadway, boasted such rich furnishings as velvet tapestries and gilt chandeliers, and was typical of many of the galleries which lined this section of Broadway. In response to New York City's expanding economy and population growth, fashionable shopping areas ultimately moved further north and this section of Broadway became devoted to other commercial interests, particularly textile manufacturing. These use continue to the present day.

The changing use of the 359 Broadway Building was typical of the commercial transformation of this section of lower Broadway from the city's most prestigious shopping district to a center for manufacturing. It serves as a fitting reminder of the area's glittering past.

Mathew Brady and 359 Broadway ***

Mathew B. Brady (c. 1823–1896) was born in Warren County, New York. It appears that the unusual spelling of his first name was Brady's own invention, and that his middle initial "B." did not stand for a name but was an affectation. In

Saratoga, New York, he met portrait painter William Page, who encouraged his interest in art and later introduced him to artist and inventor Samuel F.B. Morse in New York. Brady was instructed in the daguerreotype process by Morse at age sixteen and opened his first gallery at the corner of Broadway and Fulton Street in 1844 at age twenty-one. In that same year he won the first of many prizes for his work, a premium and honorable mention from the American Institute. The following year he won first prize in two categories. In the late 1840s Brady's stated ambition became to photograph all notable Americans of the period. His *Gallery [sic] of Illustrious Americans*, published in 1850 with considerable circulation, contained portraits of an abundance of famous political and cultural figures including James K. Polk, Edgar Allan Poe, John J. Audubon, and James Fenimore Cooper.

Brady opened a new gallery at 359 Broadway on March 19, 1853, and by 1854 he had closed his gallery further downtown. Brady's gallery, occupying the upper three floors of the building, typified the luxurious standards maintained in many Broadway galleries at the time. Through an elegant street entrance flanked by display cases containing photographs, one ascended to a reception room richly furnished with satin wall hangings, gilt and enameled chandeliers, velvet tapestry carpets, and rosewood furniture. Suspended on the walls were portraits of U.S. Presidents, European nobility, generals, and cultural figures of all nations and professions. Past the reception room was an office and a ladies' parlor decorated in gold and green and furnished with rosewood furniture. Two "operating rooms"—one with a southern and one with a northern exposure—led from the reception room. Plate-cleaning and electroplating were done on the fourth floor, while the fifth floor provided storage space and a sky lit studio for special lighting effects. ***

Although Brady usually employed assistants to do the work of photographing, he was the cameraman for one special portrait taken at the time he had his Bleecker Street studio on February 27, 1860. *** On that day Abraham Lincoln arrived in New York for a campaign speech at The Cooper Union for the Advancement of Science and Art; he also agreed to sit for a portrait by Brady. Lincoln later noted that, in addition to the speech he gave that day, the tintype portrait taken by Brady (which was widely distributed as a campaign medal) was a major factor in his election to the presidency in 1860. ***

At the beginning of the Civil War Brady interested President Lincoln in a proposal to photograph battle and camp scenes. These photographs, more than 3,500 in all, contain some of Brady's best-known work and are essential documents of Civil War history. After the war he sought to recover the copies of the photographs that had passed from his hands and in 1870 he published *Brady's National Photographic Collection of War Views and Portraits of Representative Men.* In 1875 the federal government purchased from Brady a set of 2,000 of these photographs.

Brady's fortunes deteriorated rapidly with the end of the Civil War, and 'the Panic of 1873' completed his financial ruin. He continued his Photographic career in Washington, but never regained the prestige of his earlier years. In 1895 he moved back to New York where he took ill and died on January 15, 1896.

Photography in the Mid-Nineteenth Century ***

The daguerreotype was the photographic process initially used for portraiture by Mathew Brady and other artists along Broadway in the 1840s and 18 50s [sic]. It takes its name from the Frenchman Louis Jacques Mande Daguerre (1787–1851), a painter, scenic designer, and proprietor of the Diorama in Paris which was a theater without actors where enormous paintings were exhibited under changing light effects. Daguerre experimented in securing permanent images with a *camera obscure* [sic] before entering into a partnership with Joseph Nicephore Niepce (1763–1833), another important figure in the early development of photography. Daguerre perfected the method of sensitizing silver photographic plates with fumes of iodide. This involved placing the silvered side of a plate over a box containing particles of iodine. After heating, the iodine fumes produced light-sensitive silver iodide when they came in contact with silver. In 1835 Daguerre found a method of developing latent images on his photographic plates by subjecting them to mercury vapor after exposure, "fixing" the images with common salt.

In 1837 and 1838 his "daguerreotype" invention was purchased by the State of France, and within a year manuals explaining the process were published in eight languages. The "daguerreotype" served as the world's principal mode of photography for nearly two decades until it was eclipsed in the mid-1850s by the ambrotype, a less expensive variation of the daguerreotype which was printed on glass.

Because of the rapid advancement of photography in the mid-nineteenth century, the daguerreotypist became a vanishing breed. About 1854 Brady brought Alexander Gardner (1821–1882) from England, an expert in the wet-plate process, and thereafter discarded the daguerreotype. By 1861 the outmoded process, which had initially interested Brady in photography, had disappeared completely.

The Italianate Style and 359 Broadway ***

The 359 Broadway Building was one of many Italianate style commercial buildings lining Broadway in the mid-nineteenth century. Its design illustrates several influences, including that of A.T. Stewart's marble commercial palace at 280 Broadway (later known as the Sun Building, 1845–46, Joseph Trench and John B. Snook, a designated New York City Landmark). An architectural style derived from the palaces of the Italian Renaissance and introduced to London by Charles Barry with the Traveller's Club (1830–32) and to Manchester with the Athenaeum (1837), the Italianate style was distinctly urban in character; its form was cubic, flat-roofed, and nearly flat-surfaced. Alexander Turney Stewart (1803–1876), New York's wealthiest merchant, saw this style while on his annual buying trips to England, and was one of the first to bring it back to this country.

Although the overall design of the 359 Broadway Building is related to the models of the A. T. Stewart store and its English precursors, its ornament is abundant and unique. Unlike Stewart's marble palace, with its uniform square-headed window openings, 359 Broadway has a variety of openings including arched, segmentally-arched, square-arched, and unusual square-headed bays capped by triangular bell-cast arches with a suggestion of oriental inspiration. The arched window openings of the first story (now altered) and the second story suggest the rising influence of the northern Italian variety of the Italianate style, characterized by arched windows flanked by engaged columns in the manner of the Roman Colosseum, thus providing a minimum of unbroken wall surfaces. This variation in the style first appeared in the United States in 1850 when R.G. Hatfield designed the Sun Building in Baltimore. The Harper Brothers Building (1854, demolished), constructed facing Franklin Square (now occupied by footings of the Brooklyn Bridge), was an early building in this style in New York. The stacking of segmental-arched and flat-arched window openings on the third and fourth stories of 359 Broadway presages their use in cast-iron buildings in New York of the 1850s, '60s, and '70s. This variation in window openings is seen in contemporary publications devoted to cast-iron architecture, such as Daniel D. Badger's *Illustrations of Iron Architecture* published in 1865. ***

The use of a variety of bay openings suggests a blend of European influences, producing a hybrid of architectural styles and motifs within the Italianate mode. Given the great wave of immigration from many countries that hit New York in the mid-nineteenth century, it is possible that the designer of the 359 Broadway Building was a recent European immigrant. The unusual carved arches of the fifth story demonstrate an oriental or even a Gothic influence, and suggest the use of pattern books illustrating architectural details, possibly German or French. The abundance of Ornament, though innovative, is used in a rather liberal manner that suggests the involvement of a builder rather than the more deliberate hand of an architect. In any case, 359 Broadway is a precedent-setting example of the use of stacked picturesque window openings as executed in stone.

The design of the 359 Broadway Building is an unusual example of the Italianate style, illustrating the profound impact made by A.T. Stewart's marble palace and drawing on motifs from the northern Italian Renaissance, probably in combination with pattern books. It evokes these influences without being a strict imitation of any of them, and is a unique reminder of the commercial palaces that once lined Broadway when it was New York's most fashionable shopping district.

Description

This five-story Italianate style commercial building is located on the west side of Broadway approximately fifty-four feet south of Franklin Street between Leonard and Franklin Streets. It extends twenty-eight feet along Broadway. The facade displays a rich combination of Renaissance details and retains much of its original appearance.

Faced in stone, stories two through five are articulated by two bays each containing two window openings articulated by three paneled pilasters: the pilasters at the second story have a central circular motif and abstracted Corinthian capitals. The arched openings are crowned with molded archivolts and acanthus leaf keystones. The third story continues the pattern of the second story with segmentally-arched openings. Rondels contain an abstract floral motif in the northern bay and a fleur-de-lis in the southern bay and the pilasters are divided into two sections each by a square motif in the center. The third story is crowned by a projecting cornice with modillions. The fourth story has square-arched openings and pilasters divided into three sections. A projecting stringcourse at the impost level spans each bay. The fourth story is crowned by a raised frieze with semi-circular pendants. The fifth-story openings are topped by unusual triangular bell-cast arches. The pilasters are divided into two sections like those on the third story. The building is crowned by an elaborate metal cornice (with projecting elements terminating the pilasters) supported' by modillions with pendants. Metal dadoes top the cornice at each end.

The center windows of stories two through five have four-over-four double-hung wood sash and the end windows have one-over-one double-hung wood sash; an historic fire escape spans the two center bays of each story. At the second story, the southern bay is fronted by a recent addition to the fire escape. Black glass panels in the bulkheads of the southern portion of the first story support the plate glass windows of the non historic storefront. To the north paired metal doors forming a service entrance are flanked by piers faced in aluminum. The first story is surmounted by a sign covering the width of the facade.

The southern elevation, visible above neighboring buildings on Broadway, is of brick, painted beige, punctuated by two visible window openings with two-over-two aluminum sash. A chimney rises above the roofline at the center of the elevation. A painted sign reading "359/Brady's/Gallery" existed on the southern elevation until 1988 when it was painted over.

Subsequent History

Early in the history of the 359 Broadway Building, ironwork which had been installed above the center of the cornice after the building's completion was removed during the late-nineteenth century, the character of the neighborhood changed from that of the city's premier shopping district to one of mixed use, primarily textile manufacturing and wholesaling. At that time the building housed both a drygoods store and a shirt and cloak factory, and it continues to house a textile concern today. The fifth floor currently houses the Tibet Center, a cultural and religious organization.

* * *

FINDINGS AND DESIGNATION

On the basis of careful consideration of the history, the architecture and other features of this building, the Landmarks Preservation Commission finds that the 359 Broadway Building has a special character, special historical and aesthetic interest and value as part of the development, heritage and cultural characteristics of New York City.

The Commission further finds, that, among its important qualities, the 359 Broadway Building is a distinguished early Italianate stone-fronted commercial building constructed in 1852, at a time when this section of Broadway was the city's most prestigious shopping area, containing a number of fashionable daguerreotype studios; that it is an important and unusual example of the Italianate style with distinctive and varied window openings and abundant ornament blending elements from several sources; that it was occupied by noted photographer Mathew B. Brady from 1853–59, renowned for both his portraits and for his numerous photographs of the Civil War; and that, remarkably intact, it serves as a fitting reminder of the area's glittering past as an exclusive shopping district.

Accordingly, pursuant to the provisions of Chapter 74, Section 3020 (formerly Section 534 of Chapter 21), of the Charter of the City of New York and Chapter 3 of Title 25 of the Administrative Code of the City of New York, the Landmarks Preservation Commission designates as a landmark the 359 Broadway Building, 359 Broadway, Borough of Manhattan, and designates Tax Map Block 174, Lot 33, Borough of Manhattan, as its Landmark Site.

* * *

Russo v. Beckelman

Supreme Court of the State of New York, County of New York

No. 14635/91 (April 24, 1992)

Moskowitz, J. Petitioner Lena Russo invokes Article 78 of the CPLR to vacate a determination of the Landmarks Preservation Commission ("LPC"), and the City Council's affirmation of that determination that designated petitioner's building as a landmark. Petitioner also seeks a declaration that the Landmarks Law is unconstitutional and violative of due process.

Petitioner is the owner of a five story, stone commercial building located at 359 Broadway, between Franklin and Leonard Streets in Manhattan. The building was erected in 1852, at a time when this area of Lower Broadway was the city's most exclusive, prestigious and glamorous shopping area. The neighborhood was especially distinctive for its numerous daguerreotype studios, catering to the vanity of the passing crowd.

From 1853 until 1859, the top three stories of 359 Broadway housed the gallery of photographer Mathew Brady. He was feted in his own day for his society portraits in the new media of daguerreotype and photography and is respected in the present as a pioneer in the development of modern photography. Brady's reputation in this century rests mainly on his exhaustive and uncompromising photographic coverage of the Civil War. Brady's extraordinary and haunting photographs were used to compelling effect in the recent television series "The Civil War" and cannot but serve to challenge a generation who had reason to believe itself immune to the horrors of war. Brady is also remembered for his portraits of Abraham Lincoln, whose engravings still grace the penny and five dollar bill.

The LPC decided to grant landmark status to 359 Broadway, based on both its architectural merit and its connection to Mathew Brady, following a lengthy investigation, that involved considerable testimony at public hearings, as well as numerous written submissions. The LPC issued its finding on October 16, 1990 citing the buildings special character, special historical and aesthetic interest and value as part of the development, heritage and cultural characteristics of New York City.

Specifically, the LPC found that,

> [A]mong its important qualities, the 359 Broadway Building is a distinguished early Italianate stone-fronted commercial building constructed in 1852, at a time when this section of Broadway was the city's most prestigious shopping area, containing a number of fashionable daguerreotype studios; that it is an important and unusual example of the Italianate style with distinctive and varied window openings and abundant ornament blending elements from several sources; that it was occupied by noted photographer Mathew B. Brady from 1853–59, renowned for both his portraits and for his numerous photographs of the Civil War; and that, remarkably intact, it serves as a fitting reminder of the area's glittering past as an exclusive shopping district ...

In reaching its [designation] determination, the LPC adopted its staff's extensive report that details both the architectural and historic criteria for the designation.

After the City Council Zoning, Planning and Landmarks Subcommittee held additional public hearings and the City Council reviewed more written submissions overwhelmingly in favor of designation, the City Council approved the designation on February 21, 1991.

Petitioner is aggrieved by the landmarking designation of her building. Among other things, it interferes with plans for the demolition of the premises, together with two adjoining buildings petitioner also owns in order to construct a larger edifice on the site. Petitioner claims that the determination to grant landmark status to 359 Broadway is irrational and is not supported by substantial evidence. Petitioner alleges that the decision to consider 359 Broadway for landmarking was based initially only on the LPC's erroneous belief that Brady had taken a famous portrait of Lincoln at the studio at 359 Broadway. She claims that the LPC's allegedly belated recognition of the building's architectural significance was an ad hoc expedient the LPC adopted, only after the alleged collapse of the historical connection. Petitioner also argues that the Landmark Law is unconstitutionally vague.

Constitutionality of the Landmarks Law

> Section 25-302(n) of the New York City Administrative Code defines "landmark" as,
>
> [A]ny improvement, any part of which is thirty years old or older, which has a special character or special historical or aesthetic interest or value as part of the development, heritage or cultural characteristics of the city, state or nation, and which has been designated as a landmark pursuant to the provisions of this chapter.

Petitioner contends that the language employed in the statute is so broad in meaning as to be susceptible to widely differing and purely subjective interpretations. Petitioner suggests that "historical" might be read to include "virtually all of the past, however unremarkable," while a building of "aesthetic interest" might be one "marking a passing fad or ephemeral interest." Petitioner argues that the lack of definition in the statute renders it "virtually without standards," and allows the LPC to "roam at will, in purely arbitrary and capricious fashion...." Because the alleged statutory vagueness "provides no notice to the public as to those properties which may be subject to regulation under the said provisions," petitioner argues that her constitutional due process-rights have-been compromised.

The Landmarks Law has previously withstood various constitutional challenges. *Penn Central Transportation Co. v. City of New York*, 438 U.S. 104; *St. Bartholomew's Church v. City of New York*, 728 F.Supp. 958 (S.D.N.Y.) ***. In *St. Bartholomew's Church*, the District Court reasoned that, "[a]t the very least, due process requires notice and an opportunity to be heard," and that the Landmark Laws "unquestionably meet that standard in that they provide a property owner with adequate notice of the law's requirements and with the opportunity for an extensive hearing...." *Id.*, at 964. The court concluded that, "since a reasonable person can and should know what standards must be met in bringing an application for a certificate of appropriateness or in opposing a landmark designation, those statutes are not impermissibly vague." *Id.* This court agrees with the District Court's conclusion.

Statutes are endowed with an exceedingly strong presumption of constitutionality. *Lighthouse Shores, Inc. v. Town of Islip*, 41 N.Y.2d 7. In the context of criminal statutes, it has been said that laws must "give the person of ordinary intelligence a reasonable opportunity to know what is prohibited, so that he may act accordingly ..." *Grayned v. City of Rockford*, 408 U.S. 104, 108. Statutes which do not give such notice may be void for vagueness. *Id.*

Civil, as well as penal statutes, must meet the test for vagueness. *Montgomery v. Daniels*, 38 N.Y.2d 41. In either context, "the quest for definiteness does not preclude the Legislature from using ordinary terms to express ideas that find adequate interpretation in everyday usage and understanding," *People v. Illando*, 48 N.Y.2d 408, 414. Abstract words can, through daily use, disguise a "content that conveys to any interested person a sufficiently accurate concept," *Montgomery v. Daniels, supra*, at 58, citing *Kovacs v. Coope*, 336 U.S. 77, 79. If the language employed "conveys sufficiently definite warnings as to the prescribed conduct when measured by common understanding and practices," constitutional standards of due process are met. *People v. Illando, supra* at 414, citing *Miller v. California*, 413 U.S. 15, 27–28, n. 10.

This court finds that the terms employed by the Landmarks Law such as "historical" and "aesthetic interest", are ordinary terms, commonly used and understood, which convey a significantly explicit meaning allowing for application of the law in a manner not violative of due process. *** This court does not believe that a body of experts, such as the LPC is, buttressed by information supplied by historical and architectural specialists, would have any particular difficulty in appraising the value of a proposed landmark based on the alleged vagueness of the terms "historical" or "aesthetic", nor that property owners would be unaware of the standards the statute sets.

Petitioner argues that the alleged vagueness of the Landmark's [sic] Law "provides no notice to the public or the individual property owners as to those properties which may be subject to regulation," so as to allow potential purchasers forewarning of possible impediments to future development of the property. Due process does not require such notice. Petitioner has not claimed that she was unable to comprehend the historical or aesthetic criteria on which landmark designation was to be made. Rather, she merely disagrees with the designation.

Because the law, as written, permits petitioner to "know what standards must be met ... in opposing a landmark designation...," the requirements of due process have been met, and the statute is not impermissibly vague. *St. Bartholomew's Church v. City of New York*, *supra*, at 964.

The Landmark Designation

LPC determinations are subject only to the test of rationality. *Society for Ethical Culture v. Spatt*, 68 A.D.2d *aff'd*, 51 N.Y.2d 449. The court may only determine whether or not a rational basis existed for the designation and so may not substitute its judgment for that of the administrative body. *Shubert Organization v. Landmarks Preservation Committee*, 166 A.D.2d 115. The findings and determinations of the LPC are accorded considerable deference, based on the historical and architectural expertise of the LPC's members. *Id.*; *see also Committee to Save the Beacon Theatre v. City of New York*, 146 A.D.2d 397.

The evidence supporting the LPC's determination to grant landmark status to 359 Broadway is ample. The record reveals that the building first came to the LPC's attention as the result of a survey it made of the TriBeCa area in 1988 and was calendared on September 12, 1989 for the December 12 public hearing on architectural grounds. Prior to the hearing, the LPC received a letter from an organization known as The Lincoln Group of New York which informed the LPC that 359 Broadway had been one of Mathew Brady's photography studios in New York City and that steps should be taken to prevent alteration of the exterior of the building.

At the public hearing held on December 12, 1989, the LPC accepted the unusually passionate testimony of numerous witnesses attesting to the cultural and historical significance of 359 Broadway because of its connection to Brady. Oral and written testimony in favor of landmarking was offered by, among others, representatives of the Lincoln Group, the American Photographic Historical Society, the National Press Photographers, the Society for the Architecture of the City, the Municipal Arts Society, as well as by historians, writers, photographers and community groups. It was at this meeting that the representative from the Lincoln Group stated his conviction that the famous Lincoln photographs had been taken at Brady's 359 Broadway studio. After the hearing, this issue was investigated and debated by the LPC until the LPC was finally satisfied that Lincoln had probably not visited Brady's 359 Broadway studio, but had been photographed at another Brady studio located further uptown. *** [One authority, George Gilbert, Executive Director of the American Photographic Historical Society, has not admitted defeat on this issue and still argues that Brady's famous likenesses of Abraham Lincoln were created at 359 Broadway.]

The petitioner is simply wrong when she argues that the LPC only considered 359 Broadway for landmark status because of its belief in the Lincoln connection and wrong when she claims that the building's architectural significance was a contrived after-thought. It is true that most of the evidence collected by the LPC at the public hearing related to the building's connection with Mathew Brady. In fact, the LPC itself appears to have been taken aback by the volume of the evidence and the fervor of the testimony about Brady's historical significance. However, it is clear that the building was considered from the first on architectural as well as historical grounds, and that the decision to landmark the building was based on both criteria.

The architectural evidence collected throughout the landmarking process established that the building was an unusual one for its time, containing an extraordinary degree of ornamentation and attention to detail. The ornamentation, different on each floor, apparently is remarkable for its era and reflects a style that only became popular in later years. Architectural experts described the building as "unique" and "adventuresome", with a remarkable degree of exterior preserved.

Petitioner's experts, who provided the only testimony opposing landmarking, disputed the architectural worth of the building, finding it "routine" and unremarkable. Petitioner finds it significant that the building was not considered earlier for landmarking when the Tribeca Historic District was delineated, or when 359 Broadway's neighbor 361–63 Broadway was considered and approved for landmark status. Nor was 359 Broadway mentioned in Andrew S. Dolkart's *The Texture of Tribeca*. Petitioner describes 359 Broadway disparagingly as an "amalgam of several styles, designed by an unknown architect working from pattern books." On the historical side, petitioner argues that Brady's occupation of the building was "brief," and that there is "no nexus between the period in Brady's career when he performed the works" for which he is known and the building, that he occupied early in his career. Petitioner points out that virtually no trace of Brady's once opulent gallery has survived to the present day. *** [Interestingly, only recently has one such trace disappeared. For nearly 130 years the words "Brady's Gallery" appeared on the south wall of the building, on the level of the top story. The sign was painted over by petitioner in 1988, allegedly as part of the routine maintenance of the building.]

None of petitioner's contentions is sufficient to establish that the LPC's determination was irrational. The evidence supporting landmark designation is overwhelming. Commissioner Placzek stated at the public hearing, "[t]his is a case where the historic event and the architectural value join." *Records of Proceedings before the Landmarks Preservation Commission 359 Broadway*. The building had not been overlooked in earlier landmarking decisions because it was not worthy, but because it, along with many other buildings, had not yet come under scrutiny. The author of *The Texture of Tribeca* wrote to the LPC to express his admiration for 359 Broadway. Petitioner's opinion as to the architectural value of the ornamentation of 359 Broadway is a distinctly minority view.

The court does not find it significant that various LPC members voiced reservations to landmarking 359 Broadway at various times in the administrative process, or that the LPC membership discussed the question of whether or not historical significance alone would be a sufficient criterion for landmarks designation. ***

Last, the court finds nothing unreasonable in the LPC's determination that Brady's occupation of 359 Broadway is historically significant, despite the fact that it was "brief" and that, in petitioner's view, it conferred no distinction upon 359 Broadway because Brady only realized his greatest works in later years. If the historical significance of a premises depended only on whether famous deeds happened there, no historic birthplace could ever be accorded landmark status. Since the testimony amply supports the thesis that Brady's skill and technique developed, along with the fledging art and science of photography, at this studio at 359 Broadway, there is little doubt as to the property's historic significance.

There is also little doubt that the landmarking of 359 Broadway aggrieves the owner and prevents development of the site. However, the indiscriminate destruction and defacement of historically and architecturally significant properties similarly aggrieves the inhabitants of this city, depriving us of links to our own history and the lives of those who came before us. The lengthy public process required before a property is designated a landmark serves to air both individual and community concerns until a balance is struck. In the case of 359 Broadway the consensus was all but unanimous of the building's legitimate historical and architectural qualifications. Because there is a rational basis for the landmark designation, the LPC's determination and the City Council's affirmance must be upheld.

Accordingly, the petition is dismissed. ***

Russo v. Beckelman

Supreme Court of New York, Appellate Division, First Department
204 A.D.2d 160, 611 N.Y.S.2d 869 (1994)

Murphy, P.J., Carro, Wallach, Asch, Tom, JJ. Judgment, Supreme Court, New York County (Karla Moskowitz, J.), entered April 28, 1992, which denied petitioner's application to annul respondent City Counsel's approval of respondent Landmarks Preservation Commission's designation of petitioner's building as a landmark, and dismissed the petition, unanimously affirmed, without costs.

The building designated as a landmark, 359 Broadway, between Franklin and Leonard Streets, was the location of the daguerreotype gallery of Mathew Brady from 1853 until 1860. Until petitioner whitewashed the outside side wall of the building recently, one could still see a faint painted sign identifying the building as "Brady's Gallery". Brady rose to prominence in the daguerreotype trade at this location, around the time that he started to develop his business in "wet" photography. Brady also received numerous and famous personages in this gallery, although we note that the Landmarks Preservation Commission rejected any connection with the famous "Lincoln photo." While the evidence was equivocal as to which elements of the original gallery survive inside, either concealed or not, this is not an interior landmarking, and the evidence is clear that the exterior remains largely unchanged from the time of Brady's occupancy. While petitioner characterizes Brady's occupation of the building's upper floors as fleeting and insignificant, the historical evidence, consisting of numerous contemporary accounts, indicates otherwise.

The administrative record and accompanying historical materials also establish a cultural and social historical dimension to 359 Broadway that complements its association with Brady. Brady's occupancy corresponded with the period when this part of Broadway was the fulcrum of the nation's, and possibly the world's, daguerreotype trade, as well as the commercial hub of the City. This building is the sole survivor of those that housed numerous galleries, among which Brady's held prominence. This building, distinct from its specific Brady connection, was considered in its day to be an exemplar of the daguerreotypists' galleries while photography was in its genesis years. The landmarking not only preserves the building, and depicts a trade, but also provides a portrait of an era that fills a too-little appreciated niche in New York's cultural registry. The historical merits are sufficient to justify the designation regardless of the building's affiliation, if any, with the nearby Tribeca district.

The administrative record is replete with reasoned decision-making during which commissioners grappled with the different landmarking theories in light of the historical record, and we reject petitioner's contention that the final determination was a foregone conclusion. There is no compelling significance in the fact that the building was not earlier considered for landmarking in the context of the Tribeca district or neighboring structures; such determinations must be considered *ad hoc*, on their own merits (*see Matter of Doro's Rest. v. City of New York*, 179 A.D.2d 406, 578 N.Y.S.2d 163). Nor is there merit to petitioner's unconstitutional taking claim since petitioner has not been substantially deprived of the economic benefit of the property (*Penn Cent. Trans. Co. v. New York City*, 438 U.S. 104 ***), and can avail herself of transferable development rights (*Shubert Org. v. Landmarks Preservation Commn.*, 166 A.D.2d 115, 122, 570 N.Y.S.2d 504 ***), or to her claim that the relevant provisions of the Landmarks Preservation Law (Administrative Code § 25-302, 303) are unconstitutionally vague or overbroad (*Penn Cent. Transp. Co. v. New York City, supra; Rector of St. Bartholomew's Church v. City of New York*, 728 F.Supp. 958 ***). That the criteria for listing sites on the State Register of Historic Places (9 NYCRR 427.3) may be more specific does not necessarily mean that the City law is insufficiently specific.

Since the historical and cultural associations established by the record, when considered together, connote landmark worthiness to this site, we need not determine whether the association of a site with an historic personage such as Brady, as a sole criterion, would justify a designation.

We have considered petitioner's remaining contentions and find no basis for reversal.

Notes and Questions

1. **Architectural significance.** *In Society for Ethical Culture in the City of New York v. Spatt*, the charity argued that there was no evidence to suggest that the Meeting House was of extraordinary architectural distinction or that it was ever the scene of any noted historical event or the residence of any noted personage. The Landmarks

Preservation Law makes clear that designation is appropriate for buildings or districts that have a "special character or special historical or aesthetic interest or value as part of the development, heritage or cultural characteristics of the city, state or nation." The court read the ordinance to say that architectural significance alone, here, the art nouveau style, would be a sufficient basis for the designation. The building need not be the best exemplar of the architectural style, nor also be noteworthy for some historical event, to qualify for designation. a. Is the composition of the commission, being required to have architects, historians, and educators, sufficient to ensure that designations satisfy some minimum level of appreciation within the art or architecture world as to the aesthetic and/or historic character? b. Are there objective measures of architectural value that can be employed? c. What roles do the realtor, city planner, and businessmen play in the process of designation?

2. **Historical significance.** In *Russo v. Beckelman,* both the trial court and the appellate court found that the landmark designation was well-supported by the architectural features of the building alone. On the other hand, while the building's association with an historic person, the photographer, Brady, was not in doubt, it seems a particular event was in question—the making of the Lincoln photographs. a. Should a structure with no particular architectural merit be preserved merely because an important figure lived or worked there? b. Was there more here? c. Is this different from the Birmingham City Jail where the Reverend Martin Luther King, Jr. penned his famous letter? Or, the Monterey County Jail that held César Chávez?

3. Four Seasons Interior Designation

Originally, landmark ordinances protected only exteriors for public enjoyment. As the public became accustomed to being invited into the interiors, they began to raise concerns about preserving those interiors that reflected significant historic elements. Ordinances were then amended to protect interiors as well as exteriors. As you gloss over the designation consider whether there is any argument to distinguish protecting interiors from protecting exteriors.

4. Four Seasons Designation Report

Landmark's Preservation Commission
October 3, 1989; Designation List 221
IP-1666

FOUR SEASONS RESTAURANT, GROUND FLOOR INTERIOR consisting of the entrance lobby and the staircase leading from the entrance lobby to the first floor interior; FIRST FLOOR INTERIOR consisting of the restaurant lobby including the freestanding piers, the Pool Room vestibule, the Pool Room (dining room) including the marble pool, the staircase leading to the mezzanine dining room, the mezzanine dining room, the Bar Room/Grill Room vestibule, the Bar Room/Grill Room (dining room) including the bar, the staircases leading to the balcony level, and the balcony, and the balcony level dining rooms; and the fixtures and interior components of these spaces, including but not limited to, wall surfaces, floor surfaces, ceiling surfaces, doors, railings, hanging sculptures, and metal draperies; 99 East 52nd Street, Manhattan. Designed by Philip Johnson. Built 1958–59.

Landmark Site: Borough of Manhattan Tax Map Block 1307, Lot 1.

On May 17, 1988, the Landmarks Preservation Commission held a public hearing on the proposed designation as an Interior Landmark of the Four Seasons Restaurant ground floor interior consisting of the entrance lobby and the staircase leading from the entrance lobby to the first floor interior; first floor interior consisting of the restaurant lobby including the freestanding piers, the Pool Room vestibule, the Pool Room (dining room). [sic] including the marble pool, the staircase leading to the mezzanine dining room, the mezzanine dining room, the Bar Room/Grill Room, vestibule, the Bar Room/Grill Room (dining room) including the bar, the staircases leading to the balcony level, and the balcony, and the balcony level dining rooms; and the fixtures and interior components of these spaces, including but not limited to, wall surfaces, floor surfaces, ceiling surfaces, doors, railings, hanging sculptures, and metal draperies; and the proposed designation of the related Landmark Site (Item No. 3.) The hearing was continued to July 12, 1988 (Item No.1). Both hearings had been duly advertised in accordance with the provisions of law. Twenty witnesses, including the operator of the restaurant spoke in favor of designation. Three witnesses, all representatives of the owner of the Seagram Building, spoke in opposition to designation. The Commission has received many letters in favor of designation, and several letters against designation.

DESCRIPTION AND ANALYSIS

Summary

An integral component of the highly acclaimed International Style Seagram Building designed by Ludwig Mies van der Rohe (a designated New York City Landmark), the Four Seasons Restaurant Ground Floor and First Floor Interiors have been praised by architectural critics as among the finest International Style interior spaces in the United States. Designed in 1958 by celebrated architect Philip Johnson and built in 1958–59 as an innovative first-class restaurant for Restaurant Associates, it opened amid much fanfare and was at that time the costliest restaurant ever constructed. The interiors produced by Johnson and a stellar team of consultants are considered to be among Johnson's last projects to mirror the architectural theories of his mentor Mies van der Rohe. The designers used rich materials, installed with expert craftsmanship to accentuate their inherent beauty, innovative technology, and distinctive architectonic elements to shape the understated and elegantly proportioned interiors, which reflect the modular system employed in the design of the Seagram Building. The operations of the award-winning Four Seasons Restaurant were taken over in 1972 by Tom Margittai and Paul Kovi, who have kept the interior spaces in virtually intact condition and have been faithful to their original, influential design. Among the creative features of the restaurant is its seasonal theme, which inspires the meals served as well as plantings and color-coded appointments. A cultural magnet for tourists and the city's elite, it is one of New York's premier dining spaces due to the architectural preeminence of its design, the richness of its exquisite interiors, its location in the Seagram Building, and the restaurant's exceptional culinary reputation.

History of the Seagram Building ***

The Seagram Building, erected in 1956–58, is the only building in New York City designed by architectural master Ludwig Mies van der Rohe. Carefully related to the tranquil granite and marble plaza on its Park Avenue site, the elegant curtain wall of bronze and tinted glass enfolds the first fully modular modern office tower. Constructed at a time when Park Avenue was changing from an exclusive residential thoroughfare to a prestigious business address, the Seagram Building embodies the quest of a successful corporation to establish further its public image through architectural patronage. The president of Joseph E. Seagram & Sons, Samuel Bronfman, with the aid of his daughter Phyllis Lambert, carefully selected Mies, assisted by Philip Johnson, to design an office building later regarded by many, including Mies himself, as his crowning work and the apotheosis of International Style towers. The innovative, modular design of the building was a feat furthered by a coalition of talented consultants, a successful collaboration rarely realized in twentieth-century architecture, and by pioneering efforts of research and fabrication. Still virtually intact due to the foresighted maintenance plan of the Seagram Company, the building and plaza have inspired the work of many subsequent designers, affected New York's zoning regulations and real estate tax assessment, and provided a favorable environment for work and repose.

As one of the amenities of the building, the Seagram management from the beginning had the intent to provide large, elegant interior spaces with public access from the lobby. In discussions as early as 1956, several options were considered: a museum of crafts, a stylish automobile showroom (along the lines of Frank Lloyd Wright's Mercedes-Benz showroom further north on Park Avenue), and a first-class restaurant. Mies and Johnson began preliminary work on the overall design of the interior spaces prior to the selection of Restaurant Associates as the tenant. ***

Design and Construction ***

Having provided the Seagram Building with a unity between indoor and outdoor spaces, Mies carried the modular design, clearly evident on the building's exterior, into the interiors of the grand public rooms. Johnson used the structural system and generously proportioned volumes as his point of departure for the design of the restaurant interiors, substantially completed in 1958. His design took advantage of the space to create dramatic effects and elegant proportions achieved through varied ceiling heights, a controlled system of circulation through the rooms, and architectonic elements, such as the pool and the bar, which further define distinct volumes within the larger spaces. The interplay of solid and void is artfully exemplified by the sturdy bar with its delicate sculpture above. These large public spaces were conceived to have elegant interiors to complement the Seagram Building itself: walls of the spacious rooms covered with expensive wood paneling washed in light from invisible sources and floor-to-ceiling windows screened by metallic chain curtains which ripple when the ventilation system is operating. The restrained ceiling, elegant staircases, ingenious lighting scheme, sculpture, and furnishings were carefully designed to create the sophisticated simplicity associated with the International Style. Johnson's early works were noticeably indebted to Mies's architectural theories, and this design is generally regarded as Johnson's last such project.

The Four Seasons Restaurant

Five dining rooms accommodate 400 persons. Its two wine "cellars" permit the Four Seasons to boast one of the largest wine collections in the country. Upon the opening of the restaurant in July of 1959, first-class service was assured by daily indoctrination for waiters by James Beard, the famous wine and food authority. ***

The seasonal theme inspired the Four Seasons to maintain its own herb garden, an innovative venture in American restaurants. Eclectic menus combine American bounty with international culinary concepts and techniques, making the Four Seasons a pioneer of what would later be called the "New American Cuisine." These concepts are reflected visually in the restaurant's decor. Rotated seasonally, the four trees at the corners of the marble pool complement the restaurant's logo, which determines the color scheme for each season. Thus auxiliary planting as well as appointments such as uniforms, menus, and even ash trays were originally rotated every three months: pink for spring, green for summer, burnt orange for autumn, and brown for winter.[17] Establishing an optimum micro-climate for plant survival allowed the designers to integrate interior planting from the beginning of the project.[18]

Description

Located on portions of the first floor and the ground floor at the eastern end of the Seagram Building, the Four Seasons Restaurant Interiors are composed of several interior spaces, each with a distinct character and spatial quality but united by certain design elements. The Interiors of the Four Seasons Restaurant include two major dining rooms, the Pool Room at the north side of the building and the Bar/Grill Room at the south side, linked by an Entrance Corridor/Lobby which adjoins the Lobby of the Seagram Building. The East 52nd Street Entrance Lobby located at the ground floor provides access to the Bar/Grill Room by means of a broad staircase. Two small, adjoining private dining rooms are situated behind a balcony that overlooks the Bar/Grill Room. Another dining room is located at the mezzanine level of the Pool Room. The restaurant is furnished with movable custom furniture, fixtures, and accessories which still adhere to the original designs.

---

17. Today, instead of seasonal changes, the Four trees logo in four colors decorates appointments.

18. Portable mercury vapor lamps have been used to provide intense light for the trees while the restaurant is closed. *** The annual budget for planting alone was $50, 000. *** Permanent plantings include ornamental fig and fichus trees. Seasonal plantings have consisted of azaleas and white birch trees in the spring, philodendrons and cocos palmosa in the summer, burnt orange and yellow chrysanthemums and oak leaf branches in the autumn, and white chrysanthemums and white birch in the winter with red poinsettias added during the Christmas season. ***

FOUR SEASONS
Hotels and Resorts

Four Seasons Restaurant, Brilliant Pool Room. Photo by Geslin George, via Wikimedia Commons.

The Entrance Corridor/Lobby:

The entrance to the Four Seasons Restaurant Interiors from the Seagram Building Lobby (a designated New York City Interior Landmark) is reached by broad travertine steps. A glass wall provides visual continuity between the two spaces, which share certain design features: walls and floors lined in travertine, ceilings composed of gray glass mosaic set in black cement, and engaged bronze piers of the building's structural system. The bronze-framed tripartite glass wall is bisected by a central meeting rail and contains paired glass doors. A flat bronze band intersects the lower portion of the wall. Bronze piers are located near the eastern wall of the corridor, flanking Picasso's painted curtain, "The Three-Cornered Hat" (not subject to this designation). Designed to be illuminated from below, a row of raised alabaster panels, framed in bronze and protected by posts with suspended chain, is located along the floor beneath the curtain. Recessed light fixtures illuminate the space and incandescent recessed troffer lighting fixtures wash the eastern wall with light. Metal-framed glass doors at each end of the corridor lead to vestibules serving the major dining rooms. The vestibules have dropped ceilings formed by brass-colored egg-crate grids illuminated from above. The glazed eastern wall of the Pool Room vestibule reveals a wine "cellar," and the eastern wall of the Bar/Grill Room vestibule is lined in French walnut with openings to accommodate a coat-check area.

The Pool Room:

A lofty, square space with a twenty-foot high ceiling, the Pool Room is dominated at the center by a table-height twenty-foot square pool of white Carrara marble filled with continuously bubbling water. Cylindrical bronze planters holding trees sit on the floor at each of the four corners of the pool; the trees, which change seasonally, are illuminated from below with bucket lights set into the planters.

The western and northern walls are composed of continuous windows which rise above low travertine ledges. The windows are divided into vertical panels by bronze mullions; metal draperies of thin anodized aluminum chains are fitted into vertical channels in the mullions. The chains, in shades of brass, bronze, and copper, subtly ripple with the movement of air from diffusers set into the ledges below. Bronze bowl planters are suspended in front of the windows from nearly invisible wires. The southern wall, pierced by openings for the entrance and the kitchen, is lined with rectangular rawhide panels set on walnut. The bottom row of panels is gray, and those above are natural. Each wall in the room is punctuated by engaged bronze piers.

At the eastern end of the Pool Room is a rectangular mezzanine-level room reached by a broad central staircase. The base of the mezzanine is paneled in gray rawhide. The stairs and the edge of the mezzanine are lined with bronze railings composed of thin staggered rods, which, when viewed as one passes them, create the effect of movement. Panels of French walnut, designed and crafted to emphasize the prominent grain of the wood, are set behind the railings; they also pivot so that the mezzanine-level room may be either closed off or function as an extension of the Pool Room. The glazed northern wall is continued in the upper room, while the eastern wall, dominated by a large painting by James Rosenquist (not subject to this designation) and the southern wall of that room are covered in beige carpet panels.

The specially-designed ceiling is composed of square off-white panels of perforated aluminum layered over a recessed grid; the intersections of the grid are fitted with "darklites," a recessed incandescent fixture from which light is directed by bronze-finished reflectors. Recessed troffers wash the southern wall with light. The wall-to-wall carpeting has a grid pattern which echoes the overall geometry of the room. (Although not original, it was designed under the direction of Philip Johnson.)

The Bar/Grill Room:

The Bar/Grill Room is divided into several different areas. A small lounge area located at the northwest corner of the room is separated from a bar area at the southwest corner of the room by, a large, broad stairwell linking the space with the East 52nd Street Entrance Lobby. A dining area occupies the center of the room and a narrow balcony-level dining area, reached by stairs at each end, spans the eastern side of the room.

The Bar/Grill Room has some of the many architectural elements as the Pool Room; including the twenty-foot high specially-designed ceiling, window walls with metal draperies rising from travertine ledges at the west and south, French walnut paneling lining the northern and eastern walls, wall-to-wall carpet, and the balcony. The face of the balcony is now washed with light from below by a bay of incandescent lamps covered by a grid. Engaged bronze piers punctuate the walls. The carpeting is a darker version of the same design used in the Pool Room.

The stairwell between the bar and lounge areas is lined in bronze railings of thin, staggered rods. The bar area is dominated by a square walnut bar fitted with leather panels and surrounded by an ebonized oak floor. Two sculptures by Richard Lippold, composed of delicate groups of gold-dipped brass rods of varying lengths, are suspended from the ceiling by nearly invisible wires. Following his usual procedure, Lippold designed the sculptures specifically for their present locations to enhance the organization of the Bar/Grill Room. The larger sculpture contrasts dramatically with the solid walnut bar directly beneath it, creating an intimate space within the larger limits of the room. This juxtaposition is balanced by the smaller sculpture over the balcony.[20] The bar is separated from the dining area by a partition of laminated, cracked glass; this was installed in 1983 under the direction of Philip Johnson and replaced a trellis of climbing ivy. A French walnut service desk to the east of the entrance from the Corridor/Lobby and round planters (which replace the original wood planters) between the service desk and the partition also serve to define the dining area.

Two adjoining rooms are situated behind walnut-paneled doors at the northern and southern ends of the balcony; these doors have an ebonized surface on the side of the rooms. The rooms are smaller and more intimate than the large room. A vestibule behind the northern end of the balcony leads to the larger of the two rooms, which is rectangular, and joins the smaller, square room to the south by a wide doorway with a sliding ebonized door. Except for the outer wall of the southern room which has continuous windows and metal draperies, the walls are lined with rectangular panels of highly-polished hardwood set onto a dark wood surface. The ceiling is of the same grid-and-panel design used in the larger rooms, except that the surface is black and the panels are pierced with holes roughly one-inch wide and spaced apart in a random pattern, which are illuminated from above. The floors are carpeted. The vestibule at the northern end is similarly finished.

---

20. In early correspondence from Arthur S. Margolin, vice president of the Seagram Company, in a letter to Gene A. Norman, dated July 7, 1988, it states that the sculptures belong to Joseph E. Seagram & Sons, and that the company "has no intent of removing ... the Lippolds, so long as the use and character of the space ... remains substantially the same as now." Subsequently, the LPC has received a letter from Phyllis Lambert on the behalf of the Seagram Foundation, dated Sept. 29, 1989, advising the LPC that the Seagram Company has agreed that the sculptures would remain permanently on display in the Grill Room for so long as the Four Seasons remains a designated [New York City] landmark. In a letter from Richard Lippold to the LPC, dated Sept. 11, 1989, the artist states that "... my sculptures ... are built into the room and technically virtually impossible to reinstall elsewhere." He adds that the materials, proportion and scale of the sculptures are closely related to the materials, proportion and scale of the room.

The East 52nd Street Entrance Lobby:

The lower Entrance Lobby is reached at its southeastern end from East 52nd Street through two sets of glass doors separated by a vestibule with a brass-colored egg-crate grid ceiling. The outer doors are etched with vertical stripes. The floor and walls are travertine and pierced with openings along the eastern, southern, and northern walls for restrooms, an office, and a coat-check area. The space is illuminated by recessed fixtures set into a low white ceiling. Engaged bronze piers and a ceiling beam bisect the room on a north-south axis. At the western side of the lobby is a broad staircase with one landing; this links the Lobby and the Bar/Grill area. It is lined with bronze railings. The two round planters replace the original wood planters.

Subsequent History

Immediately after its opening the Four Seasons received enthusiastic reviews, both architectural and culinary; critics said that the "spectacular, modern and audacious" *** restaurant design "combines its exceptional sumptuousness with exquisite refinement." *** When it opened, the restaurant had no peer "in conception, in scale, in the wealth of talent behind it." ***

In the early 1970s, Transylvanian-born Tom Margittai, then vice-president of Restaurant Associates, was given the responsibility of selling off the business of a foundering Four Seasons Restaurant. Instead, he and the director of the Four Seasons, Hungarian-born Paul Kovi, jointly purchased it from R.A. [I]n 1972 with the goal of reviving the restaurant [t]hey hired chef Joseph Renggli, a Swiss native, and soon the restaurant became, as "one of America's leading symbols of good taste," *** extremely popular with New York's elite. A recipient of twenty-two major awards, the Four Seasons has hosted many memorable parties for national celebrities, international gourmet societies, and wine inaugurals.

Experts Ada Louise and L. Garth Huxtable, involved with the restaurant from its planning stages, have noted that the new owners "have been faithful to the [original] concept." *** The design of these famous International Style interiors has been caringly maintained. Among the handful of physical changes was the removal of an ivy-covered screen and its replacement in 1983 by a laminated, cracked glass partition designed by Johnson.

Report prepared by David M. Breiner and Elisa Urbanelli, Research Department

Report edited by Marjorie Pearson, Director of Research

FINDINGS AND DESIGNATION

On the basis of a careful consideration of the history, the architecture and other features of this building, the Landmarks Preservation Commission finds that the Four Seasons Restaurant ground floor interior consisting of the entrance lobby and the staircase leading from the entrance lobby to the first floor interior; first floor interior consisting of the restaurant lobby including the freestanding piers, the Pool Room vestibule, the Pool Room (dining room) including the marble pool, the staircase leading to the mezzanine dining room, the mezzanine dining room, the Bar Room/

Grill Room vestibule, the Bar Room/Grill Room (dining room) including the bar, the staircases leading to the balcony level, and the balcony, and the balcony level dining rooms; and the fixtures and interior components of these spaces, including but not limited to, wall surfaces, floor surfaces, ceiling surfaces, doors, railings, hanging sculptures, and metal draperies; has a special character, special historical and aesthetic interest and value as part of the development, heritage and cultural characteristics of New York City, and the Interior is one which is customarily open and accessible to the public, and to which the public is customarily invited.

The Commission further finds that, among their important qualities the Four Seasons Restaurant Interiors, integral components of the architecturally preeminent Seagram Building, are among the finest International Style interiors in the United States; that they were designed in 1958 by celebrated architect Philip Johnson and an accomplished team of consultants and built in 1958–59 for the expanding firm of Restaurant Associates as an innovative first-class restaurant; that innovative technologies and architectonic elements were incorporated to achieve the desired aesthetic and spatial effects; that the modular design of the exterior of the Seagram Building is carried into and helps to define the interior spaces; that the spacious, understated, and elegant rooms of exquisite proportions are excellently maintained; that they are outfitted with finely crafted rich materials such as bronze, white Carrara and travertine marbles, rawhide panels, French walnut and ebonized oak, and anodized aluminum; that these materials are installed with expert craftsmanship to accentuate their inherent beauty; that the distinctive design of the interior spaces and the exceptional culinary reputation of the Four Seasons make it a cultural magnet for tourists as well as New York's elite.

Accordingly, pursuant to the provisions of Chapter 21, Section 534, of the Charter of the City of New York and Chapter 3 of Title 25 of the Administrative Code of the City of New York, the Landmarks Preservation Commission designates an Interior Landmark the Four Seasons Restaurant ground floor interior.

Matter of Teachers Insurance and Annuity Association of America v. City of New York

Supreme Court of the State of New York, New York County
No. 2583/90-001 & -002; Cal. #14
(June 18, 1990) & 28 (June 25, 1990)

Shainswit, J. This case involves the Landmarks Preservation Law. The dispute-centers on the designation of the Four Seasons restaurant as an interior landmark. The parties are, as combined petitioner and plaintiff, Teachers Insurance and Annuity Association of America ("TIAA"), the present owner of the Seagram Building and the lessor of the space housing the restaurant: and, as combined defendants and respondents, the City of New York, the Board of Estimate, and the Landmarks Preservation Commission of the City of New York ("the Commission").

TIAA's pleading is an integrated petition and complaint. The petition, in its first four causes of action, seeks relief under CPLR Article 78; the ensuing fifth through ninth causes of action present a plenary suit asserting, constitutional claims that may not be raised in an Article 78 proceeding. All nine claims attack the determination of the Commission and the Board of Estimate, designating as a landmark the interior space occupied by the Four Seasons restaurant.

TIAA seeks to set aside the landmark designation, and to enjoin any enforcement of such designation. In addition, TIAA has also moved for partial summary judgment granting its constitutional claims, to the extent that they seek declaratory judgment and injunctive relief.

Respondents urge that the claims presented by way of petition should be dismissed because the landmark designation has a rational basis, finds concrete support in the record made before the Commission, and is not arbitrary or capricious. Respondents have also cross-moved to dismiss the constitutional claims, on the ground that they do not state a cause of action, and in any event are not ripe for this court's consideration. Respondents' cross-motion also seeks summary judgment, on the petitioner's complaint has no merit[sic], and that there is no material issue of fact to be tried.

We begin with what transpired before the Commission.

The Genesis of the Dispute

On December 14, 1987, TIAA proposed to the Commission that it designate the Seagram Building and its plaza as a landmark and designate the building's ground floor lobby as an interior landmark. On April 3, 1988, the Commission voted to consider the proposal, at which time it calendared a public hearing on the matter for May 17, 1988.

On April 22, 1988, the operator of the Four Seasons restaurant proposed to the Commission, without consulting TIAA, that the space that it occupies inside the Seagram Building be calendared for designation. On May 3, 1988, the Commission voted to add the possible designation of that space as an interior landmark to its agenda for the May 17 hearing. On May 17, 1988, the Commission held a public hearing on these proposed designations. Twenty-one witnesses spoke in favor of the designation of the Seagram Building and its plaza, and of the lobby. TIAA actively supported this designation. No one spoke in opposition. The matter was then laid over until July 12, 1988, for further proceedings on the proposed designation of the: restaurant space.

Thereafter, on July 12, 1988, the Commission held its public hearing with respect to the restaurant space. It heard from opponents and proponents of the proposed designation, and kept the proceedings open while it received additional written submissions from interested architects, preservation groups, and members of the art world.

On October 1, 1989, the Commission voted to designate the Seagram' Building and its plaza as a landmark, and the building's lobby and the restaurant space as interior landmarks.

TIAA continues to support the designation of the Seagram Building and its plaza, and the building's ground floor lobby as landmarks. In this litigation, TIAA challenges only the landmark designation pertaining to the Four Seasons restaurant. That interior designation, as reflected in the designation report, covers:

> *** The Four Seasons Restaurant ground floor interior consisting of the entrance lobby and the staircase leading from the entrance lobby to the first floor interior; first floor interior consisting of the restaurant lobby including the freestanding piers, the Pool Room vestibule, the Pool Room (dining room) including the marble Pool, the staircase leading to the mezzanine dining room, the mezzanine dining room, the Bar Room/Grill Room vestibule, the Bar Room/Grill Room (dining room) including the bar, the staircases leading to the balcony level dining room; and the fixtures and interior, components of these spaces, including but not limited to, wall surfaces, floor surfaces, ceiling surfaces, doors, railings, hanging sculptures, and metal draperies ***

Thereafter, on January 25, 1990, the Board of Estimate held a public hearing. After hearing various speakers in support and in opposition, the Board approved the designation. This lawsuit ensued.

The Statutory Scheme

The governing statutory framework can be concisely summarized:

Pursuant to General Municipal Law § 96-a, the State of New York has empowered the City to enact legislation "for the protection, enhancement [and] perpetuation" of "buildings and other objects having a special character or special historical or aesthetic or value," provided, however, that "such measures, if adopted in the exercise of the police power, shall be reasonable and appropriate to the purpose, or if constituting a taking of private property shall provide for due compensation[.] ***

The exercise of this power was vested in 'the Commission pursuant to City Charter Sec. 534 and the Landmarks Law, subject, however, to review by the Board of Estimate. The New York City Administrative Code § 25-301 *et seq.* declares:

> *** [A]s a matter of public policy that the protection, enhancement, perpetuation and use of the improvements and landscape features of special character or special historical or aesthetic interest or value is a public necessity and is required in the interest of the health, prosperity, safety, and welfare of the people.

Landmarks Law § 25-301(b).

The New York City Administrative Code, § 25-301, and § 534 of the New York City Charter, have collectively become known as the Landmark Law. Sec. 25-301(b)(g) specifically includes, among the public purposes of the law, the protection and the perpetuation of "interior landmarks *** for the education, pleasure, and welfare of the people of the city...."

The Commission is specifically authorized to designate Interior Landmarks:

> m. 'Interior landmark.' An interior, or part thereof, any part of which is thirty years old or older and which is customarily open or accessible to the public,

> or to which the public is customarily invited, and which has a special historical or aesthetic interest or values as part of the development, heritage or cultural characteristics of the city, state, or nation, and which has been designated as an interior landmark pursuant to the provisions of this chapter.

Landmarks Law § 25-302(m).

An Interior Landmark consists of interior architectural features:

> 1. 'Interior architectural feature.' The architectural style, design, general arrangement and components of an interior, including, but not limited to, the kind, color, and texture of the building material and the type and style of all windows, doors, lights, signs and other fixtures appurtenant to such interior.

Landmarks raw [sic] § 25-302(l).

Special Features of the Four Seasons Restaurant

The Four Seasons was designed by the noted architect, Philip Johnson, within the overall plan established by the building's architect, Mies van der Rohe. Located on portions of the ground floor and the first floor of the Seagram Building, the Four Seasons Restaurant interiors are composed of several interior spaces, each with a distinct character and spatial quality but united by certain design elements. The proportions of the rooms reflect the modular system employed in the Seagram building. The two main rooms, the pool room and the bar/grill are squares with twenty foot ceilings. The pool room is dominated by a table height twenty foot square marble pool with bubbling water with a planter at each corner. The bar/grill room is divided into a dining area and a bar area with a square walnut bar and a hanging sculpture by artist Richard Lippold above it. Both the pool and the bar/grill rooms are terraced with enclosed balconies that provide diners with a panoramic view of the restaurant spaces and urban landscape beyond. Two small dining rooms are behind the balcony in the bar/grill room. Included in the Landmark interior designation are the ground floor lobby and the first floor corridor lobby (adjacent to the Seagram lobby).

The rooms of the restaurant are finished in luxurious materials. The stairs are lined with bronze railings, composed of thin staggered rods. Metal draperies of thin anodized aluminum chains fill the floor to ceiling windows. The chains, in shades of brass, bronze, and copper, ripple with the movement of air from diffusers set into the ledges below. The artist Richard Lippold indicated to the Board of Estimate, *inter alia*, that the sculpture above the bar was designed specifically the ceiling over for the bar/grill room[sic] to create a lowering of the bar for a more intimate effect. These and other unique features of the restaurant's design and fixtures were described in detail at the proceedings before the Commission and the Board of Estimate.

The Law Governing an Article 78 Attack Upon a Landmark Designation:

In an Article 78 proceeding, where the petitioner is attempting to upset a landmark designation, the: role of the court is to review the record to see if the challenged action has a rational basis and is not arbitrary or capricious. If the record indicates a reasonable basis for the administrative determination, the court may not substitute its judgment for that of the administrative body. *Matter of Pell v. Board of Education of Union Free School Dist. No. 1 of the Towns of Scarsdale and Mamaroneck*, 34 N.Y.2d 222, 230–231 (1974); *300 Gramatan Ave. Associates v. Division of Human Rights*, 45 N.Y.2d 176 (1978).

Landmarks designations are not subject to a different standard of review. Like any other administrative determination, the test for judicial acceptance or rejection is whether the Commission's designation had a rational basis or if it was arbitrary or capricious." *Society for Ethical Culture in the City of New York v. Spatt*, 68 A.D. 2d 112 (1st Dept. 1979) *aff'd*, 51 N.Y.2d 449.

We apply this standard to this record.

The Designation of the Four Seasons as an Interior Landmark Was Supported by Individuals and Organizations with Expertise, and Paralleled Prior Designations of Interior Landmarks

Notable architects and architectural firms supported the designation.... The art world also registered its support.... Further supports included Manhattan Community Board, No. 5, the National Trust for Historic Preservation, the Fine Arts Federation of New York and the Municipal Art Society; various celebrities spanning our cultural spectrum also lent their support. The proponents greatly outnumbered the opposition, which was essentially confined to the real estate community.

The record also attests that there are scores of other interior landmark designations in New York City. These other interior designations include even courthouses: the Appellate Division, First Department; the New York County Supreme Court courthouse; and the New York Surrogates Court. Also: Grand Central Terminal; the Chrysler Building; the Empire State Building; the Woolworth Building; City Hall; the New York Public Library; the Metropolitan Museum of Art; the American Museum of Natural History; Radio City Music Hall; the Beacon Theater; Town Hall; and the interiors of 30 Broadway theatres. It is apparent that the designation of the Four Seasons falls; [sic], within the flow of interior landmark designations that the Commission has pursued in carrying out its authorized functions.

In this factual setting, the designation of the Four Seasons was a valid, proper, and reasonable exercise of the Commission's authority, which is immune from judicial erasure.

The contention of the petition that the designation of the Four Seasons is improper, because the restaurant is high priced and caters to an exclusive clientele, must be rejected by the court. The Commission's designation report was based, *inter alia*, upon a careful examination of the space and of the restaurant as operated; and the conclusion that the Four Seasons is open and accessible to the public, and the public is customarily invited to it, rests upon a rational basis.

The petitioner attacks the Commission as being subservient to "the City's elite (who have managed to protect one of its favorite watering holes at the expense of more than one million individual policy holders whose pension fund owns the building." [Petitioner/plaintiff's Memorandum of Law, p. 1.]) The short answer to petitioner/plaintiff is: the interior landmark designation is not the fruit of class warfare. It rests upon considered action by an official agency acting within clear governmental authority, and whose actions were subject to review by the Board of Estimate. Nothing in this record indicates that any segment of the administrative process was tainted by bias in favor of an "elite" group.

Interspersed in the petitioner's papers is the argument that the Commission only has jurisdiction to designate real property. Petitioner therefore claims that the bar, the Lippold sculpture the/metal chain curtains, ceiling panels, and railings are personal property, and consequently outside the jurisdiction of the Commission.

It must be observed, however, that the Landmarks Law does not make a distinction between real and personal property. As already indicated, as part of the statutory framework, the Commission's jurisdiction extends to "interior-architectural features," which include "fixtures appurtenant to such interiors [Landmarks Law, § 25-302(1))].

Interior architectural features, comparable to those identified by petitioner, have been included in other interior landmark designations. In the Appellate Divisions, First Department, Courthouse, the designation includes the main hall, the courtroom—including built-in marble benches and the judges' bench the lawyers' anteroom, the staircase to the second floor, wall and ceiling surfaces, doors, murals, chandeliers, attached light fixtures, stained glass windows, stained glass dome, freestanding wooden railings in the courtroom, wood paneling, and staircase railings. The New York County Courthouse Interior Landmark designation is of the main entrance, central rotunda, including the dome and the skylight, the five lobby hallways on the first and second floor and the fixtures and interior components of these spaces, including but not limited to the wall and ceiling surfaces, floor surfaces, lamps, chandeliers, murals and other painted decoration, balcony railings, grilles, stained glass and leaded glass, drinking fountains, mailbox, wall clocks, doors, and wrought ironwork.

It is the special aegis of the Commission to supply its own interpretation and application of the "interior architectural features", essential to an overall designation of the space, as interior landmark.

In sum, all of the causes of action presented in the Article 78 petition are without merit, and are dismissed. We now turn to the balance of the-claims, seeking relief under: the United States and New York-State-Constitutions.

The Landmark Designation of the Four Seasons Cannot be Set Aside on Constitutional Grounds

First, plaintiff urges that the designation is inconsistent with due process of law, because it does not substantially advance a legitimate governmental purpose (fifth cause of action). To support this argument, plaintiff also repeats its theme that the Four Seasons caters to an elite clientele, and highlights that the Four Seasons requires that a patron wear a jacket.

The enforcement of a[ ]dress code is not a taking of property. By no stretch of the imagination can it be converted into a violation of the lessor's interests, much less an impairment of the constitutional rights.

Further, we have passed the stage at which the concept of landmark preservation can be challenged at the threshold. Landmark preservation is now firmly rooted in our substantive law. *Pennsylvania Central Transportation Co. v. City of New York*, 438 U.S. 104 (1978).

With historic preservation now accepted as a legitimate and important government concern, the designation of the Four Seasons falls within the cultural fabric fostered by the Landmarks Preservation Law, and does not bring in its wake any due process violation.

Second: plaintiff urges that the designation forces the owner, upon expiration of the present lease,[ ] to choose between closing the space and continuing to admit restaurant operators and patrons and, therefore, takes the owner's property without compensation, in violation of the Fifth and Fourteenth Amendments and Article I, 57, of the state constitution (sixth cause of action).

The designation does not constitute a *per se* taking of property. The ruling by the United States Supreme Court in *Pennsylvania Central, supra*, that application of the Landmarks Law to Pennsylvania Central did not constitute a taking of property, is equally applicable to the landmark designation of the Four Seasons.

Further, the court need not decide whether plaintiff's "taking" claim is ripe for judicial determination. There is no occasion for the court to enter the thicket of uncertainty as to what plaintiff's economic position will be in 1999, or whether hardship provisions in the Landmarks Preservation Law can mitigate plaintiff's economic problems at that time. At this[ ] time there is no substantive support for plaintiff['s] sixth cause of action, and as a matter of law it must be dismissed for reasons already stated.

[The court went on to reject plaintiff's claims that the city wrongfully interfered with rights in personal property (two hanging Lippold sculptures and metal draperies, ceiling surfaces, doors and railings), the court finding that as to the sculpture, plaintiff had agreed to their permanent display and as to the other items, the Commission, had rationally drawn a nexus between such items and the overall cultural impact of the Four Seasons as a historic landmark that deserved full preservation]

Finally: the last claim (ninth cause of action) is that the designation violates the plaintiff-owner's right to freedom of expression and privacy. Plaintiff's memorandum (p. 67) puts this gloss upon its position: "The design and appearance of interior space is intimately associated with the owner; it is an inherently personal decision that should be left to the owner."

Any limit on freedom of expression flows from the Landmarks Preservation Law itself. Since that law has passed constitutional muster, there is no violation of any protected First Amendment right. The intent of the Landmarks Preservation Law is not to restrict free speech, but to further a substantial government interest—historic preservation. Any incidental restriction on alleged First Amendment freedoms is insubstantial; it is no greater than is essential to the furtherance of a proper and constitutional governmental interest.

Conclusion

All of the claims presented in the consolidated complaint-petition are dismissed ... [and plaintiff's] motion for partial summary judgment is in all respects denied.

Matter of Teachers Insurance and Annuity Association of America v. City of New York

Supreme Court of New York, Appellate Division, First Department
185 A.D.2d 207, 586 N.Y.S.2d 262 (1992)

SULLIVAN, J.P., AND CARRO, WALLACH AND SMITH, JJ. Order and judgment (one paper) of the Supreme Court, New York County (Beatrice SHAINSWIT, J.) entered January 17, 1991, which denied petitioner's motion for partial summary judgment on the plenary portion of this joint CPLR article 78 proceeding and plenary action and which granted respondent's cross-motion to dismiss the amended verified petition and complaint, unanimously affirmed, without costs.

Petitioner-plaintiff is the present owner of the Seagram Building located at 375 Park Avenue, Manhattan. The building is done in the international style, erected between 1956 and 1958, and is the product of the Bauhaus School architect Mies Vander Roh, [sic] and the only example of his work in New York City. The first floor lobby level contains a commercial space occupied by the Four Seasons Restaurant, the design elements of which were designed by the well known architect Philip Johnson. The Board of Estimate has adopted the recommendation of the Landmarks Preservation Commission and designated the building, its exterior plaza, interior lobby and the interior of the space occupied by the Four Seasons Restaurant as landmarks.

Designation of interior architectural features is specifically authorized under the Landmarks Preservation Law (Administrative Code of the City of New York § 25-303(a)(2). Such designation may include interior architectural features. Administrative Code § 25-302(l), (m). We have rejected challenges to designation of interior elements *per se* as well as designation of interiors when such designation was argued to restrict use of the property. *Shubert Org. v. Landmarks Preservation Commn.*, 166 A.D.2d 115, 570 N.Y.S.2d 504 *** (1991) ***. The testimony before both the Landmarks Preservation Commission and the Board of Estimate in the present case is no less compelling than the evidence adduced for those bodies with respect to the *Shubert Organization* application. Deferring as we must to the expertise of the Landmarks Preservation Commission and taking into consideration the comprehensive and voluminous record which supports the designation, we cannot conclude that the designation was arbitrary or capricious. *Matter of Gilbert v. Bd. of Estimate*, 177 A.D.2d 252, 575 N.Y.S.2d 840 (1992); *see generally Matter of Socy. for Ethical Culture v. Spatt*, 68 A.D.2d 112, 116, 416 N.Y.S.2d 246 (1979) ***.

Since petitioner is not substantially deprived of the economic benefit of this space (*Penn Cent. Transp. Co. v. New York City*, 438 U.S. 104 ***), petitioner's contention that it has suffered an unconstitutional taking is without merit. We reject petitioner's contention that the restaurant interior lacks the public character necessary for landmark designation. This restaurant is not a private club. Rather, it is an interior that is "customarily open or accessible to the public, or to which the public is customarily invited." Administrative Code § 25-302(m).

We also reject petitioner's contentions that this designation actually protects use and will unnecessarily restrict future occupancy. The fact that occupancy other than that of a restaurant might not constitute optimum commercial utilization of the space does not require a conclusion that the designation is in effect a preservation of prior use.

Furthermore, petitioner's contention that this designation inappropriately included interior features which are not fixtures is without merit. In the present case, each of the features is sufficiently connected to the restaurant interior within the definition of Administrative Code § 25-302(l) and (m). Petitioner presently does not occupy the restaurant space, which is leased now to a third-party. When petitioner regains possession, it may apply for a variance so as to remove the sculptures. Until such time as the application is denied, however, this particular claim is premature. *Church of St. Paul and St. Andrew v. Barwick*, 67 N.Y.2d 510, 518–523, 505 N.Y.S.2d 24, 496 N.E.2d 183 (1986) ***.

Finally, with respect to certain of the sculptures, the Landmarks Preservation Law in authorizing the designating of interior architectural features does not distinguish between personalty and realty.

Matter of Teachers Insurance and Annuity Association of America v. City of New York

Court of Appeals of New York

82 N.Y.2d 35, 603 N.Y.S.2d 399, 623 N.E.2d 526 (1993)

Kaye, C.J. At issue on this appeal is the statutory authority of the Landmarks Preservation Commission to landmark the interior of the Four Seasons restaurant in Manhattan.

Appellant, Teachers Insurance and Annuity Association of America (TIAA), owner of the building that houses the restaurant, argues that the Commission has exceeded its authority under the New York City Landmarks Law in that the requisite public openness is lacking; the designation impermissibly restricts future use of the space; and even if valid, the designation improperly includes certain interior furnishings. Concluding that these arguments lack merit, we affirm the Appellate Division order dismissing appellant's challenges.

I

In 1959, the Four Seasons restaurant opened on the first two floors of the newly constructed Seagram Building on Park Avenue in New York City. The building, designed by the German architectural master Ludwig Mies van der Rohe, is the sole example of his work in New York City. The celebrated American architect Philip Johnson, who assisted Mies van der Rohe in the building design, created the restaurant interior.

Both the building exterior and the restaurant interior—which reflects and complements the building's modular design and architectural innovation—have been acclaimed as quintessential expressions of the International style. No one disputes their special historical and aesthetic interest.

When TIAA purchased the building from Joseph E. Seagram & Sons in 1980, the portions of the ground and first floors occupied by the restaurant were subject to a 25-year lease that will expire in 1999. By agreement with Seagram, appellant must use its best efforts to continue to lease the space for restaurant use. If it cannot, Seagram has an option until 2025 to find a suitable restaurant tenant. TIAA also agreed to propose the building for landmarking when it became eligible.

In December 1987, appellant proposed the designation of the Seagram Building, including the building lobby and outdoor plaza. Prior to the public hearings before the Commission, and without consulting appellant, the restaurant operators themselves proposed to the Commission that the restaurant interior also be considered for landmark status. The Commission then added that proposal to the calendar and in May and July 1988 conducted public hearings.

Dozens of witnesses and letters before the Commission from prominent architects, artists, community leaders and others supported the designation of the Four Seasons interior. TIAA, several commercial real estate interests and architect Paul Byard opposed the designation.

In October 1989, the Commission unanimously landmarked the building, outdoor plaza, building lobby and the Four Seasons interior. Noting the particular architectural features of the restaurant, including its distinctive design, integral relation to the building architecture and innovative use of new technologies, the Commission found that the restaurant interior "has a special character, special historical and aesthetic interest and value as part of the development, heritage and cultural characteristics of New York City" and that "the Interior is one which is customarily open and accessible to the public, and to which the public is customarily invited." The restaurant designation accords landmark status to the entrance lobby, Grill Room, Pool Room and balcony dining rooms, and includes the marble pool, walnut bar, wall surfaces, floor surfaces, ceiling surfaces, doors, railings, metal draperies and two hanging metal sculptures commissioned by Johnson from the artist. The Board of Estimate, after its own public hearings, approved those designations.

Appellant sought to vacate the restaurant designation by a combined CPLR article 78 proceeding challenging the Commission's statutory authority and plenary action alleging an unconstitutional taking and impairment of free expression. The trial court dismissed the proceeding in its entirety, and the Appellate Division affirmed. In this Court, TIAA limits its appeal to the statutory grounds, no argument having been made regarding the dismissal of its constitutional challenges. We now affirm.

II

Responding to the loss of a number of its more significant buildings, New York City in 1965 enacted its first historic preservation statute. *** In 1973, the Landmarks

Law was amended to expand the Commission's jurisdiction by authorizing designation of interior landmarks and by charging the Commission with promoting the use of interior landmarks "for the education, pleasure and welfare of the people of the city." Administrative Code § 25-301 (b), (g). This case presents our first opportunity to review application of the Landmarks Law to an interior landmark designation, although the appeal is limited to the Commission's statutory authority, in three particular respects, to landmark the Four Seasons interior.

A landmark designation is an administrative determination, ordinarily reviewable under article 78, that must be upheld if it has support in the record, a reasonable basis in law, and is not arbitrary or capricious. *Lutheran Church v. City of New York*, 35 N.Y.2d 121, 128, n 2.

Where interpretation of statutory terms is involved, two standards of review are applicable. As the agency charged with implementing the Landmarks Law, the Commission is presumed to have developed an expertise that requires us to accept its interpretation of that law if not unreasonable. *See, Kurcsics v. Merchants Mut. Ins. Co.*, 49 N.Y.2d 451, 459. Such deference to the Commission, however, is not required where the question is one of pure legal interpretation. *See, Matter of Moran Towing & Transp. Co. v. New York State Tax Commn.*, 72 N.Y.2d 166, 173. The distinction between these standards is perhaps best understood by reference to the statutory term "special historical or aesthetic interest"—as to which courts should defer to the expertise of the Commission—and the jurisdictional predicate "customarily open or accessible to the public"—a matter of pure legal interpretation as to which no deference is required.

Public Openness Requirement

The Commission is authorized to landmark an interior 30 or more years old that is "customarily open or accessible to the public, or to which the public is customarily invited, and which has a special historical or aesthetic interest or value as part of the development, heritage or cultural characteristics of the city, state or nation." Administrative Code § 25-302(m); § 25-303(a)(2). We agree with appellant that the meaning of customary public openness—essential to the Commission's jurisdiction—is a law question for the courts rather than one of administrative expertise.

TIAA's principal argument is that the Landmarks Law must be read to require that interiors subject to landmarking have a "distinctively public character" to bring them within the Commission's jurisdiction. An "ordinary commercial space" that has not been dedicated to public use, TIAA argues, cannot be landmarked over the owner's objection.

At the outset, we note that nothing in the Landmarks Law requires an owner's consent as a prerequisite to designation. While other jurisdictions have required owner consent (*see*, 11 Boasberg, Coughlin and Miller, Historic Preservation Law and Taxation § 7.03(7)(b)(iv)), the New York City legislature, significantly, has not. Administrative Code § 25-313 (a) provides only that the owner is entitled to notice of the public hearing, and indeed, failure to give such notice does not invalidate a designation.

So long as the statutory criteria are satisfied, the Commission may make a valid designation over an owner's objection. *See,* Pyke, Landmark Preservation, at 20–22 (1969).

Underscoring the burdens a landmark designation places on property owners, (*see, e.g.,* Administrative Code §§ 25-305–25-311, 25-317; 11 Boasberg, Coughlin and Miller, Historic Preservation Law and Taxation § 7.03 (8)–(11)), and therefore urging "strict construction" of the statute, TIAA asks us to distinguish between a restaurant and "inherently" public interiors, such as railroad stations, lobbies and theaters, which are intrinsically dedicated to public use by their public assemblage purpose. Appellant asserts that the Four Seasons interior has no distinctively public purpose, pointing out that Seagram had considered such uses as an automobile showroom and art gallery before outfitting the space to accommodate the restaurant, and that permitting designations such as this will adversely impact the real estate and economy of New York City.

We reject TIAA's asserted distinction, which on its face is a difficult one. No less than a theater, which generally requires a ticket for public entry, a restaurant by the very nature of its business invites the general public to enter. *See, Weinberg v. Barry,* 634 F.Supp. 86, 93 (D DC). But even if we might agree that it would be prudent policy to adopt the distinction appellant suggests, the argument suffers a more fundamental flaw: the proffered distinction is nowhere part of the unambiguous statute we are obliged to enforce as the City legislature has written it. *See, e.g., Doctors Council v. New York City Employees' Retirement Sys.,* 71 N.Y.2d 669, 674–675.[1]

The threshold requirement prescribed by the legislature is that an interior be "customarily open or accessible to the public, or [a place] to which the public is customarily invited." The crux of this provision is *customary* openness, accessibility, invitation to the public—words that are readily understood to require usual, ordinary or habitual (rather than rare or occasional) availability to the general public. The legislature did not also specify that an interior must be intended as a place of assemblage—adding an additional dimension to customary public availability—as it might well have done if that were the intention. Consistent with the letter and purpose of the Landmarks Law, the relevant inquiry thus becomes an objective one of whether the interior is habitually open or accessible to the public at large. An interior to which the general public is usually invited, regardless of its intended purpose, falls within the ambit of the statute.

TIAA argues, additionally, that although currently open to restaurant customers, the restaurant interior should be beyond the Commission's jurisdiction because it can be adapted to private use in the future. The simple answer is that *any* structure, even a railroad station, can be converted to private use in the future; that potential cannot preclude the landmarking of appropriate interiors. *See,* Note, *American Heritage*

---

1. Appellant alternatively urges consideration of the legislative history, but points to no legislative history establishing its suggested distinction. Moreover, because the Landmarks Law is clear on its face, we need not look to the agency's prior practice in applying the statute. *See, e.g., Doctors Council,* 71 N.Y.2d, at 674–675; *see also,* McKinney's Cons Laws of N.Y., Book 1, Statutes §§ 128, 129).

at Stake: The Government's Vital Interest in Interior Landmark Designations, 25 New Eng L Rev 291, 321–322 (1990).

Applying this interpretation, unquestionably the Commission's determination that the Four Seasons "customarily" invites the public is not arbitrary or capricious. The restaurant interior having been provided for the enjoyment of New York City's residents and visitors since it opened more than three decades ago, the Commission now may seek to preserve it for others. *See,* Administrative Code § 25-301 (b).

Future Use Restriction

The Commission is expressly forbidden to use its powers "to regulate and restrict the locations of trades and industries or location of buildings designed for specific uses." Administrative Code § 25-304(a). This limitation on the Commission's jurisdiction has been read as a prohibition against the use of landmark designations for zoning purposes. *See Shubert Org. v. Landmarks Preservation Commn.,* 166 A.D.2d 115, 121 ***.

Appellant's argument for a limitation on the Commission's jurisdiction is a somewhat different one: that the Commission has violated the statutory proscription by including in the designation items that purportedly render the space unusable for any other purpose, pointing in particular to the walnut bar and marble pool.[2] Whether or not the statute should be so read, we agree with the conclusion reached by the Appellate Division that TIAA did not establish its contention that the space will be unusable for other purposes.

Designated Interior Items

Even if the designation was authorized, appellant argues, items appurtenant to the interior of the restaurant cannot properly be included in the designation. We find no such limitation in the Landmarks Law.

The City does not challenge appellant's assertion that the Commission's jurisdiction over interior landmark designations extends only to "interior architectural features," defined as the "architectural style, design, general arrangement and components of an interior, including, but not limited to, the kind, color and texture of the building material and the type and style of all windows, doors, lights, signs and other fixtures appurtenant to such interior." Administrative Code § 25-302(l). Emphasizing the word "other," appellant argues that the Commission's jurisdiction extends only to items that qualify as fixtures at common law, and it specifically challenges designation of the hanging sculptures, walnut bar, metal draperies, decorative metal railings and ceiling panels. ***

The language of the statute unambiguously states that interior architectural features are composed of the "architectural style, design, general arrangement and components of an interior." Administrative Code § 25-302(l). We agree with the Appellate Division's construction of the statute that, in authorizing the Commission to designate items

2. Appellant also protests designation of the wine cellar visible from the restaurant lobby, but the wine cellar is not included in the actual designation.

appurtenant to an interior, the legislation does not distinguish between personalty and realty.

We defer to the expertise of the Commission in its application of the provision. *See, Kurcsics,* 49 N.Y.2d, at 459.* * * The Commission found that each of the designated items was created and installed at Philip Johnson's direction as an integral element of the design of the interior. Other items specially created or chosen for the restaurant, although mentioned in the designation report, were not designated by the Commission. As demonstrated by the items chosen for designation, the Commission has drawn a rational distinction between items integral to the design of the interior space, and items that merely enhance the restaurant's ambiance. We conclude that the Commission's interpretation is not unreasonable and thus that the Commission did not exceed its authority by including the designated items. Moreover, we agree with the Appellate Division that the Commission's decision to include the designated items is supported by the record and not arbitrary or capricious and thus was within the proper exercise of the Commission's discretion. *See, Lutheran Church,* 35 N.Y.2d, at 128, n. 2.* * *

Accordingly, the order of the Appellate Division should be affirmed, with costs.

Judges SIMONS, TITONE, HANCOCK, JR., and BELLACOSA concur; Judges SMITH and LEVINE taking no part.

Notes and Questions

1. **Scope of interior landmark.** a. What makes up the interior—the design, layout, embellishments, color, wall and window coverings, moldings? b. If it also refers to overall style, like Art Deco, would the inability to change the style to one that appeals to current restaurant patrons be the kind of economic hardship that would justify alterations or abandonment of the historical features? c. What sorts of alterations might be permitted under the Landmarks Preservation Law that would preserve the historic features yet allow the property owner to appeal to patrons? d. What are the arguments for or against rescinding a designation in such cases? *See* N.Y. CITY ADMIN. CODE § 25-303[h] (Commission may rescind/modify any designation after a public hearing).

2. **Public openness requirement.** For landmarking interiors, the space must be "customarily open or accessible to the public, or to which the public is customarily invited." a. As the court pointed out, restaurants and theaters easily fall within this meaning. b. Does it also cover a lobby of an office building, that is occupied by many unrelated tenants? In *Save America's Clocks Inc. v. City of New York*, 28 N.Y.S.3d 571 (Sup. Ct. N.Y. Co. 2016), the supreme court overturned the New York City Landmarks Preservation Commission's issuance of a Certificate of Appropriateness ("COA") authorizing alterations to the interior of the famous ClockTower Suite that would all but preclude public access. In 1987, the Commission designated the former New York Life Insurance building as an historic landmark, as "[a] monumental freestanding skyscraper in the neo-Italian Renaissance style." The building was constructed between 1894 and 1898 and contains the 1897 E. Howard Watch & Clock Company's No. 4 Striking Tower Clock, one of the few remaining mechanical public tower clocks in the country (the "Clock"). The Clock is situated within a suite of rooms (the "Clock-

tower Suite") in a tower perched atop the landmark. In 1989, a Notice of Designation was recorded designating the interior portions of the property, including the Clocktower Suite. The designation stated that landmark status was warranted because the interior portions of the building have: "a special character, special historical and aesthetic interest and value as part of the development, heritage and cultural characteristics of New York City, ... and that the Interior is one which is customarily open and accessible to the public and to which the public is customarily invited." The Clocktower Suite consists of four floors, beginning at the fourteenth floor of the building. Until 2013, the fourteenth floor was used as an art gallery and contains a spiral metal staircase which leads to a landing where the pendulum of the clock is situated and continues to the fifteenth floor clocktower machinery room. The small sixteenth floor contains the clockworks and clock faces and a seventeenth floor houses the belfry, containing the Clock's 5,000-pound bell and hammer. Having fallen into disrepair, the clock was restored in 1980 by city workers working in their spare time and who rewind the clock each week. On August 14, 2014, the Landmarks Preservation Commission granted the owner's petition to make alterations to the landmark, including "a rooftop addition and bulkheads, new windows, a canopy, alterations of the facades and relocation and alteration of interior finishes" and to "electrify[] the clock operation." The owner's proposed work would convert the building from an office building to a condominium with 144 units. Most of the proposed work pertained to the 14th, 15th, and 16th floors housing the clock and its mechanism (the "Designated Interior Clock Tower Spaces"). The COA also permitted the owner to electrify the clock operations. The Commission concluded that while to be eligible for designation, an interior space must be open to the public, once landmarked, an owner was free to close the space to the public and the Commission lacked the authority to require an owner to keep a landmarked space public. The Commission also believed that as such, the Clocktower Suite would be ineligible for landmark designation. Inexplicably, the COA reserved to the Commission, the right to inspect the landmark periodically. A coalition of groups and individuals challenged the COA, asserting among other things, that it was a de facto rescission of the designation. The court rejected that assertion, since nothing in the landmark law expressly prohibited the grant of a COA where the work would essentially privatize an interior landmark. *Id.* at 581–82. But this did not end the inquiry, as the court went on to find that Commission's use of its powers arbitrary and lacked a rational basis because it acted on an erroneous interpretation of those powers. The court explained that even though the Landmarks Preservation Law does not expressly require that public access to an interior landmark be maintained, absent an express limitation to that extent, the general power to regulate interior landmarks, necessarily included the power to direct an owner to maintain public access, since public access is a specific characteristic of an interior landmark. *Id.* In fact, the work the COA allowed would render the Clocktower Suite inaccessible to the public. Moreover, even assuming *arguendo* that the Commission lacked the authority to require that it remain open to the public, there was no rational basis for allowing work that would completely eliminate public access, as this would defeat the broad purposes of the Landmarks Preservation law. *Id.* The provision in the COA allowing electrification of the clock, while otherwise within the Commission's discretion, was equally flawed because there too, the Commission didn't believe it had the power to require the clock to remain mechanical. In fact, the court pointed out, the Commission is vested with broad discretion to consider the effects of the proposed work upon its special historical or aesthetic interest value, under N.Y. City Admin. Code § 25-301[b]. *Id.* at 583. Under N.Y. City Admin. Code § 25-302(b), it is a Type A violation to "remov[e] or alter [] a significant portion of a protected feature of an interior landmark as described in the designation report." *Id.* at 584. The court stated that there was no dispute that the internal mechanism by which the Clock operates is a significant portion of the Clock itself, and if the Commission can issue a violation for its removal or alternation, the legislature intended to give the Commission the power to compel the owner to maintain the Clock's mechanical operation. *Id., aff'd* 2017 N.Y. App. Div Lexis 8517 (Nov. 30, 2017) (clock's mechanism represented an element of the designation; plain language of statute gives Commission authority to reject a COA that will cause a designated interior to be inaccessible to the public, although reasonable limits on access are permissible).

3. **Waldorf Astoria.** In March 2017, the New York City Landmarks Preservation Commission voted unanimously to designate the interior of the famed Waldorf Astoria as a historic landmark while the hotel undergoes major renovations. The hotel's exterior is already landmarked. The interior spaces open to the public include the lobby and ballroom. The renovations are expected to be completed over several years. When it reopens, the public spaces will be much smaller with much of the complex converted to condominiums. The Waldorf Astoria originally opened in 1931, and is a prime example of art deco architecture and interior design. http://www.crainsnewyork.com/article/20170307/REAL_ESTATE/170309906/city-landmarks-interior-of-waldorf-astoria-ahead-of-renovation-by-new-chinese-owners-anbang-insurance-group (last visited September 15, 2017).

4. **Art Deco.** The *Art Deco* movement was born in the 1925 Paris *Exposition Internationale des Arts Decoratifs Industriels et Moderne,* although the term did not come into common parlance until decades later. The style drew from both antiquity (Aztec and Egyptian) and nineteenth century art forms, including Cubism and Fauvisim. It was characterized by bold colors and geometric shapes and the use of unconventional materials, such as aluminum and stainless steel. The Art Deco style, widely adopted by architects and designers, started to wane in the 1940s. During the heyday, its modernism made it a popular motif for cinemas, train stations, entertainment venues, and restaurants. *See generally* Bevis Hillier and Stephen Escritt, Art Deco Style (2003). In New York City, Art Deco design is exemplified in the Chrysler Building, the Empire State Building, Radio City Music Hall, and the Rockefeller Center.

C. Regulation of Designated Historic Districts

Most historic preservation laws aim to protect not only historic buildings or structures, but also districts. A historic district is a contiguous grouping of buildings or sites that share thematic historical significance and periods of construction. They may be residential areas, commercial districts, and industrial complexes. Individually, the properties or resources in a historic district may not have particular historical, architectural, engineering, or archeological distinction, but the collection must have significance in one of these areas. Historic district ordinances strive to balance the interest in preserving the character and the integrity of the entire designated area, while also ensuring that the district thrive, embracing the new with the old, in a harmonious relationship, by controlling scale, form, and street relationships. In this vein, a certificate of appropriateness is required not only for changes to the exteriors of existing buildings, but also for the construction of new ones in the district.

Fairfield Historic District Commission v. Hall

Superior Court of Connecticut, Judicial District of Stamford-Norwalk, District at Stamford
No. X08CV030201280S (2005)

MEMORANDUM OF DECISION RE: MOTIONS FOR SUMMARY JUDGMENT

I. Background

Adams, J. The Fairfield Historic District Commission (Commission) commenced this action against Andrew and Christine Hall, who are husband and wife (Halls) seeking a declaratory judgment that the Commission has jurisdiction to require a submission by the Halls of an application for a certificate of appropriateness before placing a sculpture on the front lawn of their residence at 750 Harbor Road in the Southport area of the Town of Fairfield. The Halls deny that the Commission has jurisdiction to require or entertain any application for a certificate of appropriateness with regard to the sculpture. The Commission and the Halls have moved for summary judgment. ***

III. Facts

The following facts are not disputed. Part I of Chapter 97a of the Connecticut General Statutes, Sections 7-147a through 7-147k authorize the establishment of historic districts within the State's towns and municipalities,

> "[t]o promote the educational, cultural, economic and general welfare of the public through the preservation and protection of the distinctive characteristics of buildings and places associated with the history of or indicative of period or style of architecture of the municipality of the state or of the nation."

General Statutes § 7-147a(b). The Commission was established in the Town of Fairfield, and the Southport Historic District is one of the three historic districts created in that town. The Halls' residence and property at 750 Harbor Road is within the Southport Historic District.

In 2003 a sculpture by Anselm Kiefer, a German artist, entitled "Etroits sont les vaisseaux" (Narrow are the vessels) was apparently purchased by a corporation controlled by Mr. Hall and shipped to and placed on the lawn of the Halls' property. The sculpture is made of concrete and steel rebar. It is approximately eighty feet long and consists of seventeen variably sized wavey sections of concrete, some with protruding rebar which rest either on the ground, another section, or both. The maximum height is approximately four feet. The smallest "wave" is approximately for square feet in area and weighs 1,200 pounds. The largest is eighteen feet long and weighs approximately five and a half tons. Atop one of the "waves" is a relatively small replica of an open book made of lead. The sculpture is located entirely on the Halls' property between the house and a picket fence and bushes that front Harbor Road.

General Statutes § 7-147d(a) provides that:

> No building or structure shall be erected or altered within an historic district until after an application for a certificate of appropriateness as to exterior architectural features [has been approved by the historic district commission].

Initially, the Halls' filed an application for such a certificate, but they withdrew it prior to the Commission acting on it.

IV. Discussion

The crux of this case is whether the sculpture on the Halls' property requires a certificate of appropriateness. *** As noted in the above quoted portion of Section 7-147d(a) the Commission has jurisdiction to determine whether a certificate of appropriateness should issue in cases where a "structure" is to be "erected" within an historic district. General Statutes § 7-147a(a) defines the word "structure" as used in this statute to mean,

> ... any combination of materials, other than a building [also a defined term] which is affixed to the land and shall include, but not limited to, signs, fences and walls ...

The word "erected" is defined to mean "constructed, built, installed or enlarged." General Statutes 7-147a(a).

The Halls contend the sculpture is not a structure because it is not affixed to the land and furthermore the sculpture was not erected, as defined by the Statute. The Commission contends to the contrary.

The record reflects that the Halls leveled a portion of their sloping lawn by excavating a two foot deep trench approximately 80 feet long and four feet wide which was then filled with over 21 tons of gravel and stone to provide base for the sculpture and for additional drainage. *** The sculpture was disassembled at its former location, a storage facility in New Jersey, and transported in five large flat bed trucks to the Halls' residence and reassembled by means of a crane on the stone and gravel bed. *** This procedure of reassembly took two days and necessitated the partial closing of Harbor Drive traffic and the removal of the fence fronting the street. *** The court concludes this process falls squarely within the meaning of the word "installed." "Install" means to establish in an indicated place. *Webster's Ninth New Collegiate Dic-*

tionary (Merriam Webster, Inc. 1988). That is precisely what occurred with the sculpture at 750 Harbor Drive in August 2003. ***

A more difficult issue is whether the sculpture falls within the definition of a "structure." According to the statute a structure is any combination of materials other than a building which is affixed to the land. The Halls argue, and the Commission does not really contest, that the sculpture is not attached or secured to the property by any mechanical means. *** ([N]o "plaster, nails, bolts, rods, or screws"). Anyone with the capacity, or means, to lift the component waves could remove them. *** In fact, according to Mr. Hall the sculpture may be disassembled and donated to a museum at some time in the future. ***

Affix has been [defined] to mean to attach physically or to attach in any way. *Webster's Ninth New Collegiate Dictionary, supra.* Both parties have cited cases in the area of real property law commenting on the distinction between personal property and a "fixture" which is considered to be part of the real property it is related to. The parties correctly recognize that while these cases may be analogous they are neither directly on point nor dispositive. The case of *Capen v. Peckham*, 35 Conn. 88 ([Conn.] 1868) is illustrative[.] *** [T]he Supreme Court cites instances in which property may be considered a fixture because it is attached to the land and other instances where properties could easily be removed but are still universally conceded [sic] to the fixtures. In this case, however, there is no claim that the sculpture is anything other than personal property, not a fixture.

The required analysis in this case is broader than determining merely the meaning of the phrase "affixed to the land," because that phrase is modified and elucidated by the immediately following phrase "and shall include, but not be limited to, signs, fences and walls...." Fences are normally affixed to the land through the means of posts dug into the earth. Signs are often attached to posts or buildings, but in some cases merely lean against a structure or stand on their own legs without any attachment to the ground. Walls are sometimes built on a foundation, but in the case of traditional stone walls, demarcating fields or boundaries, they are not affixed to the ground by anything other than their own weight.

The court concludes that the sculpture at issue is a structure within the meaning of that word as defined in Section 7-147a(a). It is affixed to the land, the terrain of which was altered, leveled and transformed by a trench filled with over twenty tons of stone and gravel, by its own multi-ton weight. *See Snedeker v. Warring*, 12 N.Y. 170, 175 ([N.Y. 1854) ("A thing may be as firmly affixed to the land by gravitation as by clamps or cement"). As a work of art it is *sui generis* but the sculpture's overlapping concrete forms forming a relatively straight line of variable height is most similar in nature and form to the stone walls created by generation of farmers in New England and elsewhere a "combination of materials" which is specifically included in the statutory definition of structure.

This court's interpretation of the statute to include the Halls' sculpture within those matters requiring a certificate of appropriateness is supported by the interpretation Chapter 97a of the General Statutes in *Gentry v. City of Norwalk*, 196 Conn. 596 ([Conn. 1985). *** The Connecticut Supreme Court pointed out that Chapter 97a focuses not on people but on buildings, structures, places and surroundings and the statute is "'site' oriented." It noted that the statute provides "the bases for close control and supervision of the buildings and areas in established historic districts" and subjects property owners within an historic district to "close controls over use of their property." *Id.*, 607–8. The court is convinced that the drafters of Chapter 97a would not have intended that the placement of the sculpture on the Halls' front lawn was completely outside the jurisdiction of the Commission. By interpreting that statute, harmonious with its language, to allow the Commission to exercise its jurisdiction over the sculpture is consistent with the statute's purpose of close control enunciated in *Gentry*.

V. Conclusion

This court is not called upon to, nor does it, determine whether a certificate of appropriateness should be issued for the installation of the sculpture. At this point, having found that the sculpture is a "structure" and it has been "erected" the court holds that the Commission has the jurisdiction to make that determination.

The Commission's motion for summary judgment is granted, and the Halls' motion for summary judgment is denied.

Notes

1. **Motion to reargue.** After a timely filed motion to reargue, the Connecticut Superior Court decided on a re-argument of the Hall's case. *Fairfield Historic Dist. Comm'n v. Hall*, No. X08CV030201280S, 2005 WL 3623977 (Conn. Super. Ct. November 28, 2005). In that re-argument, the Halls asserted that, on the day of the original summary judgment decision, they had amended their answer and special answer to add that the case could not be disposed of, without an adjudication of their Free Speech claims, under Article I of the United States Constitution and sections 4 and 5 of the Connecticut Constitution. The Court recognized that the Halls were "seeking another bite of the apple." *Id.* As proof, the Court pointed out that "[w]hile the Commission's initial moving papers discussed First Amendment issues to a limited extent, in response, the Halls specifically stated '[a] First Amendment analysis is unnecessary' and further that they were presenting no First Amendment argument." *Id.* The Court also noted that while the Commission's summary judgment motion was meant to be completely inclusive of all arguments and dispositive to the case, the Halls apparently chose not to make all their arguments in support of their summary judgment motion. On this point, the Court decided that there was no legitimate reason for the Halls not to argue this point vigorously in the first instance and hence the argument brought in re-argument was rejected.

Additionally, the Court denied relief based on the constitutional argument not being ripe. In *Esposito v. Specyalski*, 268 Conn. 336, 350 (2004), the Connecticut Supreme Court had defined the ripeness requirement as "being confident that the court is not faced with a hypothetical injury or a claim dependent upon some event that has not and, in point of fact, may never occur." The Court pointed out that since the Commission had not ruled on whether the Halls could receive a certificate of appropriateness for the sculpture, there was no injury-in-fact in freedom of expression. The Commission had only brought action to require the Halls to file for a certificate of appropriateness before they began this major project, in accordance with Connecticut General Statutes § 7-147d(a), and so the Court could not grant the relief requested by the Halls.

2. **Appeal to the Connecticut Supreme Court.** The Halls appealed their case to the Supreme Court of Connecticut for a final word on the statutory interpretation of Connecticut's historic preservation statute. *Historic District Commission of Town of Fairfield v. Hall*, 282 Conn. 672, 923 A.2d 726 (Conn. 2007). The Connecticut standards for statutory interpretation are as follows: "If, after examining such text and considering such relationship, the meaning of such text is plain and unambiguous and does not yield absurd or unworkable results, extratextual evidence of the meaning of the statute shall not be considered ..." CONN. GEN. STAT. § 1-2z. "When a statute is not plain and unambiguous, [the Court] also look[s] for interpretive guidance to the legislative history and circumstances surrounding its enactment, and to its relationship to existing legislation and common law principles governing the same subject matter." 282 Conn. at 677–678, 923 A.2d at 730 (quoting *Fedus v. Planning & Zoning Commission*, 278 Conn. 751, 756, 900 A.2d 1 (2006)). Using these guidelines, the Connecticut Supreme Court determined that the term "structure" within the historic preservation statute (CONN. GEN. STAT. § 7-147d(a)), could "include heavy objects which were 'affixed' to the land by gravity and not easily moved." *Hall*, 282 Conn. at 683, 923 A.2d at 733. Accordingly, the Connecticut Supreme Court affirmed the Superior Court decision that the Hall's multi-ton sculpture on their front lawn constituted a "structure" which was subject to the jurisdiction of the Commission.

1. Denial of Certificate of Appropriateness

The following case is an example of the denial of a certificate of appropriateness for an entire district, rather than for one single historic landmark.

Figarsky v. Historic District Commission of the City of Norwich

Supreme Court of Connecticut
171 Conn. 198, 368 A.2d 163 (1976)

BARBER, J. The plaintiffs, owners of a house and lot located within the Norwich historic district, appealed to the Court of Common Pleas from a decision of the defendant commission denying their application for a certificate of appropriateness which would permit them to demolish the house. The court rendered judgment dismissing the appeal and the plaintiffs, upon the granting of certification, have appealed to this court.

The undisputed facts of the case are as follows: The Norwich historic district, established by the city of Norwich in 1967, pursuant to §§ 7-147(a) through 7-147(m) of the General Statutes, consists of the Norwichtown green, which dates back to colonial days, and about one hundred buildings and lots surrounding, or in close proximity to, the green. The plaintiffs' property, which they purchased in 1963, is a two-story building zoned for commercial uses and is located just inside the bounds of the district. The property faces the green but is bounded on two sides by a McDonald's hamburger stand and parking lot. The building is in need of some repairs, which the Norwich building inspector has ordered the plaintiffs to undertake. Rather than make the repairs, however, the plaintiffs would prefer to demolish the building. In August, 1972, the plaintiffs applied to the building inspector for a demolition permit. The building inspector informed the plaintiffs that before such a permit could be issued a certificate of appropriateness was required. The plaintiffs, therefore, applied to the defendant for a certificate, filing their application with the building inspector on November 29, 1972. The defendant held a public hearing on the application on January 25, 1973. The hearing was attended by more than 100 persons, none of whom, except for the plaintiffs and their attorney, spoke in favor of granting the application. On the following day, the commission voted unanimously to deny the plaintiffs' application.

The plaintiffs maintain that the costs of the repairs necessary for the building are prohibitive. *** At the hearing before the commission, the plaintiffs offered the testimony of a local contractor to the effect that the cost of these repairs, together with the cost of reroofing the building, would amount to between $15,000 and $18,000. The plaintiffs offered no evidence of the value of the house without repairs, its value if repaired, or the value of the lot if the building were razed. Nor did the plaintiffs disclose to the commission the use which they intended to make of the lot if the building were razed.

The commission also received numerous opinions from the plaintiffs' neighbors and from the Connecticut historical commission, the southeastern Connecticut regional planning agency, and the Connecticut society of architects *** that although the building itself is of little historic value or interest, it does, by virtue of its location, perform an important screening function, separating the green from an encroaching commercial district, and its preservation is important in maintaining the character of the historic district.[1] The commission stated its reasons for denying the application

1. A communication from the state historical commission stated, in part: 'Competent authority has placed the date of construction in or about 1760 and identified the owner at that period as keeping an inn where lawyers at the nearby Court of Norwich were accommodated. On the exterior at least, the structure has undergone considerable alteration over the years but still retains its essential form and proportions, wholly in keeping with the scale and appearance of numerous other old buildings that border the Green area. Aside from the house proper, its site is of historic interest as occupying the original home lot of the Reverend James Fitch, religious leader of the first settlers. It often happens that buildings forming a recognizable grouping, as around a green, may not individually be especially notable for architecture or historical association. But together as a unified whole they constitute a significant entity, no part of which can be removed without a definite and usually adverse effect upon the character and appearance of the entire area. This is the condition that obtains in Norwichtown. 'The commercially zoned district south and southeast of the site under consideration exhibits the unattractive characteristics of so many such areas, with disparate structures of poor design uncoordinated with one another and obtrusive advertising signs. It stands close upon the boundaries of the local historic district. If the property at 86 Town Street were demolished, it would remove the most important

as follows: 'The Commission is of the opinion that the building in question significantly contributes to the importance of the Norwichtown Green as an historic landmark, and the Commission would have violated its responsibilities as defined in §§ 7-147(a)–7-147(k), to have permitted its demolition. In weighing all the considerations concerning this Application, the Commission was cognizant of § 7-147(g) (pertaining to permissible variations), but concluded that the hardships presented by the Applicant were not of sufficient magnitude to warrant granting approval for demolition."

Procedure upon an appeal from any decision of a historic district commission is the same as that for appeals from zoning boards. General Statutes § 7-147(i). The controlling question which the trial court had to decide was whether the historic district commission had acted, as alleged in the appeal, illegally, arbitrarily and in abuse of the discretion vested in it. *Bogue v. Zoning Board of Appeals*, 165 Conn. 749, 752, 345 A.2d 9 [(Conn. 1975)]; *Byington v. Zoning Commission*, 162 Conn. 611, 613, 295 A.2d 553 [(Conn. 1971)]. Since the trial court decided the appeal solely on the record returned by the commission and made only a limited finding of facts on the issue of aggrievement, review by this court must be based on the record of the proceedings before the commission to determine whether the commission's decision is reasonably supported by the record. *Danseyar v. Zoning Board of Appeals*, 164 Conn. 325, 327, 321 A.2d 474 [(Conn. 1973)]; *Langer v. Planning & Zoning Commission*, 163 Conn. 453, 460, 313 A.2d 44 [(Conn. 1972)].

In their appeal, the plaintiffs allege that they will be forced to undergo economic hardship and loss as a result of not being permitted to demolish their building, and that the historic district commission, in denying their application for a certificate of appropriateness, acted illegally, arbitrarily and in abuse of its discretion. ***

* * *

The plaintiffs also claim that the Norwich ordinance does not vest the commission with the power to regulate the demolition of structures within the historic district. In support of this contention, the plaintiffs point out that § 14-20 of the ordinance provides that the commission 'shall administer the provisions of (the enabling act) as implemented by this article' (emphasis added), and that the ordinance itself does not mention 'demolition.' In the absence of any specific reference in the ordinance to the power to control the demolition of structures, the plaintiffs argue, no such power has been granted the commission. Section 14-17 of the ordinance, however, provides that the commission 'shall be empowered to exercise all the powers and duties and functions enumerated in such sections 7-147(a) to 7-147(k), inclusive, as

---

screening element between these evidences of low-grade commercialism and the attractiveness of the largely unspoiled Green. State recognition of the importance of this land has recently been affirmed by the erection of a historical marker under auspices of this Commission, which details the history of early years in Norwich and the central role of the Green in that history. Nomination of the entire area has been made to the National Register of Historic Places maintained by the Office of Archeology and Historic Preservation, National Park Service, United States Department of the Interior, under the National Historic Preservation Act of 1966, Public Law 89-665.'

amended, of the general statutes.' This language incorporates by reference § 7-147(d)(a) of the General Statutes which declares that '(n)o building or structure shall be ... demolished within an historic district until after an application for a certificate of appropriateness ... has been ... approved by said commission.' Furthermore, § 14-24 of the ordinances provides that '(n)o work on any type of building or structure which would change the appearance of any building or structure within the historic district when viewed from the street line shall be begun until the owner has filed an application with the building official and has received a certificate of appropriateness from the historic district commission.' Certainly the demolition of the plaintiff's building would qualify as 'work ... which would change the appearance of' a building located within the district. There is no merit to the plaintiffs' claim that the ordinance does not empower the commission to consider applications of appropriateness pertaining to the demolishing of a building or structure.

The plaintiffs' principal claim is that the Norwich historic district ordinance, implementing the state enabling act, is unconstitutional as applied to them, and that the denial of their application for a certificate of appropriateness to demolish their building amounts to a taking of their property for public use without compensation. More specifically, they contend that the ordinance is 'vague aesthetic legislation,' incapable of application in accordance with mandates of due process, and that because of the denial of their application they will be forced to expend large sums in the maintenance of their property without being able to put it to any practical use.

Neither the constitution of the United States, amendments five and fourteen, nor the constitution of Connecticut, article first, § 11, deny the state the power to regulate the uses to which an owner may devote his property.

"All property is held subject to the right of government to regulate its use in the exercise of the police power, so that it shall not be injurious to the rights of the community, or so that it may promote its health, morals, safety and welfare. The power of regulation by government is not unlimited; it cannot, as we have stated, be imposed unless it bears a rational relation to the subjects which fall fairly within the police power and unless the means used are not within constitutional inhibitions. The means used will fall within these inhibitions whenever they are destructive, confiscatory, or so unreasonable as to be arbitrary. *Euclid v. Ambler Realty Co.*, 272 U.S. 365, 47 S.Ct. 114, 71 L.Ed. 303 [(1926)]. Regulations may result to some extent, practically in the taking of property, or the restricting its uses, and yet not be deemed confiscatory or unreasonable. Courts will not substitute their judgment for the legislative judgment when these considerations are fairly debatable. They will regard their validity ... from the standpoint of existing conditions and present times.'" *State v. Hillman*, 110 Conn. 92, 105, 147 A. 294, 299 [(Conn. 1929)]. When, as here, a legislative enactment is challenged in its application as beyond the scope or as an abuse of the state's police power, two issues are raised: first, whether the object of the legislation falls within the police power; and second, whether the means by which the legislation attempts to reach that object are reasonable. *Windsor v. Whitney*, 95 Conn. 357, 369, 111 A. 354 [(Conn. 1920)].

"To be constitutionally valid, a regulation made under the police power must have a reasonable relation to the public health, safety, morality and welfare.' *State v. Gordon*, 143 Conn. 698, 703, 125 A.2d 477, 480 [(Conn. 1956)]; *DeMello v. Plainville*, 170 Conn. 675, 679, 368 A.2d 71 [(Conn. 1976)]. No contention is made that the historic district ordinance contributes to the health or safety of the public; our inquiry is limited to whether the preservation of historic areas in a static form serves the amorphous concept of 'the public welfare." *See Opinion of the Justices*, 333 Mass. 773, 778, 128 N.E.2d 557 [(Mass. 1955)]. 'The concept of the public welfare is broad and inclusive.... The values it represents are spiritual as well as physical, aesthetic as well as monetary. It is within the power of the legislature to determine that the community should be beautiful as well as healthy, spacious as well as clean, well-balanced as well as carefully patrolled.' *Berman v. Parker*, 348 U.S. 26, 33 *** [(1954)]. It is apparent from the language of the enabling statute[2] that the General Assembly, in enacting those statutes, was cognizant not only of the intangible benefits to be derived from historic districts, such as an increase in the public's awareness of its New England heritage, but of the economic benefits to be reaped as well, by augmenting the value of properties located within the old sections of the state's cities and towns, and encouraging tourism within the state. In a number of recent cases, it has been held that the preservation of a historical area or landmark as it was in the past falls within the meaning of general welfare and, consequently, the police power. *See, e.g., Maher v. New Orleans*, 516 F.2d 1051, 1060 (5th Cir. [1975]); *Annapolis v. Anne Arundel County*, 271 Md. 265, 316 A.2d 807 [(Md. 1974)]; *Lutheran Church in America v. City of New York*, 35 N.Y.2d 121, 359 N.Y.S.2d 7, 316 N.E.2d 305 [(N.Y. 1974)]; *Rebman v. Springfield*, 111 Ill.App.2d 430, 250 N.E.2d 282 [(Ill. App. Ct. 1969)]; *Opinion of the Justices, supra*, 773, 128 N.E.2d 557; *see* 1 Rathkopf, Zoning and Planning (4th Ed.), c. 15; 82 Am. Jur. 2d, *Zoning and Planning*, § 40. We cannot deny that the preservation of an area or cluster of buildings with exceptional historical and architectural significance may serve the public welfare.

The plaintiffs argue that the Norwich ordinance constitutes 'vague aesthetic legislation,' and point to our statement in *DeMaria v. Planning & Zoning Commission*, 159 Conn. 534, 541, 271 A.2d 105, 108 [(Conn. 1970)], that 'vague and undefined aesthetic considerations alone are insufficient to support the invocation of the police power,' and our dictum to the same effect. *Gionfriddo v. Windsor*, 137 Conn. 701, 704, 81 A.2d 266 [(Conn. 1951)]. The 'aesthetic considerations' involved in the Norwich ordinance are not, however, 'vague and undefined'; § 7-147(f) of the General Statutes, incorporated by reference into the ordinance, sets out with some specificity the factors to be considered by the commission in passing upon an application for a certificate of appropriateness.[3] Nor, as we pointed out in the preceding discussion,

---

2. '(General Statutes) § 7-147a. Historic districts authorized.... to promote the educational, cultural, economic and general welfare of the public through the preservation and protection of buildings, places and districts of historic interest by the maintenance of such as landmarks in the history of architecture, of the municipality, of the state or of the nation, and through the development of appropriate settings for such buildings, places and districts....'

3. '(General Statutes) § 7-147f. Considerations in determining appropriateness. If the commission determines that the proposed erection, construction, restoration, alteration, razing or parking will

do 'aesthetic considerations alone' provide the basis for the ordinance. Furthermore, as long ago as *Windsor v. Whitney*, 95 Conn. 357, 368, 111 A. 354 [(Conn. 1920)], we commented that the question of the relationship between aesthetics and the police power was not a settled question. In *State v. Kievman*, 116 Conn. 458, 465, 165 A. 601 [(Conn. 1933)], we stated that a land use regulation was not invalid simply because it was based in part on aesthetic considerations. And in *Murphy, Inc. v. Westport*, 131 Conn. 292, 302, 40 A.2d 177 [(Conn. 1944)], we indicated that aesthetic considerations may have a definite relation to the public welfare. ***

Having determined that the ordinance creating the Norwich historic district constitutes a valid exercise of the state's police power, we are left with the question of whether the application of that ordinance to the plaintiffs' property amounts to an unconstitutional deprivation of their property without compensation. *** 'A regulation which otherwise constitutes a valid exercise of the police power may, as applied to a particular parcel of property, be confiscatory in that no reasonable use may be made of the property and it becomes of little or no value to the owner.... *See, e.g., Pennsylvania Coal Co. v. Mahon*, 260 U.S. 393 [(1922)]; *Brecciaroli v. Commissioner of Environmental Protection*, 168 Conn. 349, 354, 362 A.2d 948 [(Conn. 1975)]; *Horwitz v. Waterford*, 151 Conn. 320, 323, 197 A.2d 636 [(Conn. 1964)]; *Dooley v. Town Plan & Zoning Commission*, 151 Conn. 304, 311–12, 197 A.2d 770 [(Conn. 1964)]; *Vartelas v. Water Resources Commission*, 146 Conn. 650, 657, 153 A.2d 822 [(Conn. 1959)].' *DeMello v. Plainville*, 170 Conn. 675, 679, 368 A.2d 71 [(Conn. 1976)]. *See Penn Central Transportation Co. v. City of New York*, 50 A.D.2d 265, 377 N.Y.S.2d 20 [(N.Y. App. Div. 1975)].

Whether the denial of the plaintiffs' application for a certificate of appropriateness to demolish their building has rendered the Norwich ordinance, as applied to them, confiscatory, must be determined in the light of their particular circumstances as they have been shown to exist. *Bartlett v. Zoning Commission*, 161 Conn. 24, 31, 282 A.2d 907 [(Conn. 1971)]; *Dooley v. Town Plan & Zoning Commission*, 151 Conn. 304, 311, 197 A.2d 770 [(Conn. 1964)]. In regulating the use of land under the police power, the maximum possible enrichment of a particular landowner is not a controlling purpose. *Goldblatt v. Hempstead*, 369 U.S. 590 ***[(1962)]; *Hyatt v. Zoning Board of Appeals*, 163 Conn. 379, 383, 311 A.2d 77 [(Conn. 1972)]; *Damick v. Planning & Zoning Commission*, 158 Conn. 78, 83, 256 A.2d 428 [(Conn. 1969)]. It is only when the regulation practically destroys or greatly decreases the value of a specific

---

be appropriate, it shall issue a certificate of appropriateness. In passing upon appropriateness as to exterior architectural features the commission shall consider, in addition to any other pertinent factors, the historical and architectural value and significance, architectural style, general design, arrangement, texture and material of the architectural features involved and the relationship thereof to the exterior architectural style and pertinent features of other structures in the immediate neighborhood. In passing upon appropriateness as to parking, the commission shall take into consideration the size of such parking area, the visibility of cars parked therein, the closeness of such area to adjacent buildings and other similar factors. A certificate of appropriateness may be refused for any building or structure, the erection, reconstruction, restoration, alteration or razing of which, or any parking which, in the opinion of the commission, would be detrimental to the interest of the historic district.'

piece of property that relief may be granted, provided it promotes substantial justice. *Culinary Institute of America, Inc. v. Board of Zoning Appeals*, 143 Conn. 257, 261, 121 A.2d 637 [(Conn. 1956)]. 'The extent of that deprivation must be considered in light of the evils which the regulation is designed to prevent.' *Chevron Oil Co. v. Zoning Board of Appeals*, 170 Conn. 146, 152, 365 A.2d 387, 390 [(Conn. 1976)]; *see* General Statutes § 7-147f.

The plaintiffs had the burden of proving that the historic district commission acted illegally, arbitrarily, in a confiscatory manner or in abuse of discretion. *Byington v. Zoning Commission*, 162 Conn. 611, 613, 295 A.2d 553 (Conn. 1971)]. This the plaintiffs failed to do. *** The plaintiffs went no further than to present evidence that their house was unoccupied and in need of extensive repairs. There was no evidence offered that the house, if repaired, would not be of some value, or that the proximity of the McDonald's hamburger stand rendered the property of practically no value as a part of the historic district.

The Norwich historic district commission, after a full hearing, lawfully, reasonably and honestly exercised its judgment. The trial court was correct in not substituting its own judgment for that of the commission. *Bora v. Zoning Board of Appeals*, 161 Conn. 297, 300, 288 A.2d 89 [(Conn. 1971)].

There is no error.

In this opinion the other Judges concurred.

Kalorama Heights Limited Partnership v. District of Columbia Department of Consumer and Regulatory Affairs

District of Columbia Court of Appeals
655 A.2d 865 (1994)

Ferren, J. Petitioner seeks review of an order of the Mayor's Agent under the Historic Landmark and Historic District Protection Act of 1978, D.C.Code §§ 5-1001 *et seq.* (1994 Repl.) (the Act), denying its application for a demolition permit for "Moses House," the former French Embassy in Northwest Washington. Petitioner challenges (1) the Mayor's Agent's finding that petitioner's proposed project was not one of "special merit," *id.* §§ 5-1002(10), -1002(11), -1004(e); (2) his finding that denial of the permit did not cause petitioner to suffer "unreasonable economic hardship," *id.* §§ 5-1002(14), -1004(e); and (3) the "special merit" provision of the Act itself, *id.* § 5-1002(11), as unconstitutionally vague. Finding no error and no constitutional infirmity, we affirm.

I
Facts and Proceedings

Petitioner, Kalorama Heights Limited Partnership (KHLP), purchased "Moses House," located in the Sheridan-Kalorama Area at 2129 Wyoming Avenue, N.W., for $1,045,000 in January 1989.[1] KHLP planned to demolish Moses House and to develop

1. Moses House, consisting of a main house with a smaller carriage house in the rear, was constructed in 1892 in the Queen Anne style and was redesigned in 1925 to its current neo-classical ap-

the site as a twelve-family luxury condominium apartment building with underground parking. On June 13, 1989, KHLP filed an application for a demolition permit with the Department of Consumer and Regulatory Affairs.

Meanwhile, on February 13, 1989, the Sheridan-Kalorama Historical Association (the Association) had filed an application with the Historic Preservation Review Board (the Review Board) for designation of the Sheridan-Kalorama area as an Historic District. On August 16, 1989, the area was so designated and listed on the District of Columbia Inventory of Historic Sites. Subsequently, when the National Register of Historic Places recognized the Sheridan-Kalorama Historic District, Moses House was noted as a contributing structure in that Historic District.

Before purchasing Moses House, KHLP had been aware that its proposed condominium project would require substantial zoning variances.[2] Its lawyers had advised, moreover, that there was only a fifty percent chance these variances would be granted. KHLP's lawyers also had informed KHLP that "preservationist impulses in the [Sheridan-Kalorama] area [were] quite strong."[3]

On April 25, 1990, several months after designation of the Sheridan-Kalorama area as an Historic District, KHLP's application for a demolition permit was referred to the Review Board. The Board's staff recommended denial.[4] On July 18, 1990, the Review Board held a meeting to address KHLP's application at which the Board heard oral presentations and received written submissions. The Review Board subsequently adopted the staff's recommendation against demolition.

KHLP then requested a public hearing before the Mayor's Agent. Hearings were held on October 18 and November 1, 1990, and on March 6, 1991, the Association participated as a party in opposition. *** On May 19, 1992, the Mayor's Agent issued a decision and order denying the requested [demolition] permit. In his findings of fact and conclusions of law, he noted that KHLP had not explored "alternatives other

---

pearance. Moses House served as the French Embassy and Consulate from the 1940s until 1984. It has been vacant since 1984 and has physically deteriorated.

2. KHLP's proposed development consisted of a six story, twelve unit multi-family luxury condominium building with a height of 60 feet, an underground parking garage for 26 or 27 cars, a lot occupancy of 48 percent, and a rear lot line setback of 20 feet. This development would require substantial zoning variances from regulations in the Sheridan-Kalorama area that permit development of a single family detached dwelling with a maximum height of three stories/40 feet, a maximum lot occupancy of 40 percent, and a rear lot line setback of 25 feet.

3. Since 1985, residents of the Sheridan-Kalorama district had been exploring the possibility of Historic District status for the neighborhood. In 1987, the Sheridan-Kalorama Historical Association, created as a result of many community meetings, received a grant from the District of Columbia government to undertake a comprehensive survey of Sheridan-Kalorama structures as a preliminary step towards applying for designation of the area as an Historic District. In 1988 and 1989, several public civic group and neighborhood meetings were held to discuss Historic District designation for Sheridan-Kalorama.

4. The Staff noted that KHLP's proposal would introduce "an inappropriate scale and mass" to the property that would "adversely dominate its site and surroundings." The Staff accordingly concluded that KHLP's plan was inconsistent with the Act and "would irreversibly damage the integrity of the Historic District."

than the existing residence or [KHLP's] proposed 12 unit building." He concluded that, as a consequence, KHLP had not met its burden of proving entitlement to a demolition permit as grounds of "special merit" or "unreasonable economic hardship." KHLP appeals this decision.

II
Standard of Review and Statutory Framework

We must uphold the Mayor's Agent's decision if the findings of fact are supported by substantial evidence in the record considered as a whole and the conclusions of law flow rationally from these findings. D.C.Code § 1-1510(a)(3)(E) (1992 Repl.); *District of Columbia Preservation League v. Department of Consumer & Regulatory Affairs,* 646 A.2d 984, 989 (D.C.1994); *MB Assocs. v. D.C. Dep't of Licenses, Investigation & Inspection,* 456 A.2d 344, 345 (D.C.1982); *900 G Street Assocs. v. Department of Housing & Community Dev.,* 430 A.2d 1387, 1391 (D.C.1981). Moreover, when an agency's—and, correlatively, the Mayor's Agent's—decision is based on an "interpretation of the statute and regulations it administers, that interpretation will be sustained unless shown to be unreasonable or in contravention of the language or legislative history of the statute." *Nova Univ. v. Educational Inst. Licensure Comm'n,* 483 A.2d 1172, 1190 (D.C.1984) (citation omitted), *cert. denied,* 470 U.S. 1054 *** (1985). ***

According to the Act, the Mayor's Agent may not issue a demolition permit unless he or she finds that [A] "issuance of the permit is necessary in the public interest, or that [B] failure to issue a permit will result in unreasonable economic hardship to the owner." D.C.Code § 5-1004(e). "Necessary in the public interest" is defined as "consistent with the purposes of this subchapter as set forth in § 5-1001(b)" (primarily referring to enhancement of historic landmarks and other structures in historic districts) or—of relevance to this case—"necessary to allow the construction of a project of special merit." D.C.Code § 5-1002(10). "Special merit" is defined, in turn, as "a plan or building having significant benefits to the District of Columbia or to the community by virtue of [1] exemplary architecture, [2] specific features of land planning, or [3] social or other benefits having a high priority for community services." D.C.Code § 5-1002(11). Finally, "unreasonable economic hardship" is equated with "a taking of the owner's property without just compensation." D.C.Code § 5-1002(14).

The applicant has the burden of proving entitlement to a demolition permit. *See MB Assocs.,* 456 A.2d at 345; *900 G Street Assocs.,* 430 A.2d at 1391. *** [T]he applicant must show that it considered alternatives to the total demolition of the historic building and that these alternatives were not reasonable. *See Citizens Comm. to Save Historic Rhodes Tavern v. District of Columbia Dep't of Housing & Community Dev.,* 432 A.2d 710, 718 (D.C.). ***

III
Special Merit

KHLP contends that its project "is necessary in the public interest," D.C.Code 5-1004(e), as "a project of special merit," *id.* § 5-1002(11). KHLP then stresses that the

Mayor's Agent erred in his "special merit" analysis because he failed to weigh the historical significance of Moses House against the benefits that KHLP's project would confer upon the District. ***

It is important to make clear at the outset that the Mayor's Agent is not required to carry out such a balancing analysis unless the Agent finds that the project has "special merit." *Committee of 100 on the Federal City v. District of Columbia Dep't of Consumer & Regulatory Affairs*, 571 A.2d 195, 203 (D.C.1990). *** In KHLP's case, the Mayor's Agent concluded that the proposed luxury condominium project did not have "special merit."[6] Accordingly, unless this conclusion does not flow rationally from substantial evidence of record, we cannot say that the Mayor's Agent erred in failing to undertake the balancing analysis KHLP would require.[7] *** In this case, KHLP has neither shown that its project has social or other benefits that differ from those of other condominium projects nor demonstrated that KHLP considered reasonable alternatives to complete demolition. We therefore cannot say that the Mayor's

6. In the hearings before the Mayor's Agent, KHLP contended that its proposed project would constitute a plan of "special merit" because it would confer "social or other benefits having a high priority for community services." D.C.Code § 5-1002(11). As proof of "special merit," KHLP said the condominium project would (1) generate increased tax revenues, (2) increase the stock of luxury condominiums within the District, and (3) prevent the building from being used as a diplomatic chancery. After considering all the special merit factors offered by KHLP, the Mayor's Agent concluded that KHLP had failed to satisfy its burden of proof. Specifically, the Mayor's Agent found that KHLP's projection of increased taxes was based on expected sale prices of the condominiums and that these prices were uncertain. He therefore found that KHLP had not shown with certainty that there would be an increase in tax revenues. The Mayor's Agent also noted that the prospect of increased revenues was "not in and of itself a 'special merit' within the meaning of D.C.Code § 5-1002(11)." With respect to the project's increasing the stock of luxury housing, the Mayor's Agent found that KHLP had failed to show there were no other alternatives—such as maintaining the facade of Moses House and converting the interior into a multi-family dwelling—to meet this need. In addition, the Mayor's Agent found that KHLP's argument that the condominium project would increase the housing stock did not show "special merit" because, under KHLP's reasoning, "any residential highrise with more units than the historical building it replaced would be meritorious." Finally, the Mayor's Agent found that KHLP had failed to show that the only two alternatives available for redeveloping the Moses House property were a multi-story condominium building and a chancery. The Mayor's Agent noted that, although the zoning laws of the area prohibited construction of the condominium project, the District of Columbia Comprehensive Plan Amendments of 1989, D.C. Law 8-129, cited by KHLP to support its project as having "special merit," only discouraged chanceries in residential areas; they were not prohibited. The Mayor's Agent further noted that the community had made clear it would prefer a chancery to a condominium project.

7. The Association contends that the Mayor's Agent did, in fact, weigh the historical significance of Moses House against the benefits of KHLP's project. The Association points out that before analyzing KHLP's proposed project and determining that it lacked special merit, *see supra* note 6, the Mayor's Agent had concluded from the record that "the evidence presented confirms that the history of the Building (its cultural value), including its alteration made in the 1920s, makes it an artifact of the historical period for which the Sheridan-Kalorama area was designated an Historical District" and that it "has been, and continues to be, deemed a contributing structure to the Historic District." The Association contends that, in making these two determinations, the Mayor's Agent necessarily weighed the virtues of the building against KHLP's project ...

Agent's decision finding no "special merit" is erroneous. Consequently, contrary to KHLP's contention, the Mayor's Agent was not required to weigh the historic value of Moses House against the proposed benefits of KHLP's condominium project.

IV

Unreasonable Economic Hardship

KHLP also challenges the Mayor's Agent's determination that KHLP would not suffer "unreasonable economic hardship" upon denial of the demolition permit. It contends that (1) the Mayor's Agent misapplied the law; (2) his decision was not based on substantial evidence of record; and (3) he failed to inquire into the cost of revitalizing the building.

Because "unreasonable economic hardship" is defined to mean a "taking of the owner's property without just compensation," D.C.Code § 5-1002(14), a determination of unreasonable economic hardship presupposes a finding that denial of a demolition permit would amount to a deprivation of property without due process.

We have defined the standard for "unreasonable economic hardship" in *900 G Street Assocs.* as follows:

> [I]f there is a *reasonable* alternative economic use for the property after the imposition of the restriction on that property, there is no taking, and hence no unreasonable economic hardship to the owners, no matter how diminished the property may be in cash value and no matter if "higher" or "more beneficial" uses of the property have been proscribed.

430 A.2d at 1390 (emphasis in original). The permit applicant, therefore, has the burden of proving that no reasonable alternative economic use for the property exists. *See MB Assocs.*, 456 A.2d at 345; *900 G Street Assocs.*, 430 A.2d at 1391. It follows that, to prove unreasonable economic hardship, the applicant must show that it would be deprived of "all viable economic uses of the property" without a demolition permit. *Weinberg v. Barry*, 604 F.Supp. 390, 398 (D.D.C.1985).

*** [A]lthough KHLP had demonstrated that "it would be unprofitable to renovate the property as a single family home," KHLP had not shown that other alternative uses of the property could not reasonably be found. The Mayor's Agent noted, for example, that KHLP had received unsolicited offers for Moses House from several chanceries. The Mayor's Agent also pointed out that, although KHLP had not tried to market Moses House, the latest assessed value of the property "was over a quarter of a million dollars more than the price at which it was purchased two years ago." The Mayor's Agent accordingly found that KHLP had not shown the value of Moses House had declined since KHLP purchased it. ***

[In response,] KHLP accordingly argues that the Mayor's Agent, in determining whether KHLP would suffer an unreasonable economic hardship, should have found the *900 G Street Assocs.* rule inapplicable and, instead, conducted a fact-specific inquiry focusing on the impact of the Historic District designation on KHLP's "distinct investment-backed expectations" in purchasing the property before that designation occurred. *Penn Central Trans. Co. v. City of New York*, 438 U.S. 104, 124, 98 S.Ct.

2646, 2659, 57 L.Ed.2d 631 (1978); *see also Lucas v. South Carolina Coastal Comm'n*, 505 U.S. 1003, 112 S.Ct. 2886, 120 L.Ed.2d 798 (1992).

KHLP, however, ignores the fact that the *900 G Street Assocs.* rule has been applied in cases, such as *MB Assocs.*, 456 A.2d at 345, and *Weinberg*, 604 F.Supp. at 398, where—as in this case—historical designation took place after the owner purchased the property. More significantly, and contrary to KHLP's assertions, the Mayor's Agent did address the argument that KHLP's "reasonable expectations of profit" in purchasing Moses House should be considered in determining whether denial of a demolition permit would constitute a "taking." The Mayor's Agent noted that KHLP could not reasonably have expected to construct and profit from the proposed condominium project because, before purchasing Moses House, KHLP knew that (1) there were strong preservationist trends in the area and that (2) according to KHLP's own counsel, there was only a fifty percent chance of obtaining required zoning variances to build the condominium project. The Mayor's Agent called KHLP's Moses House acquisition a "speculative investment" tantamount to a "gamble...."

The Mayor's Agent also noted, however, that KHLP had not shown it could not "sell Moses House in its current condition at a fair price" or that there was no other economically feasible use for the property than the proposed condominium project. According to the record, in fact, various chanceries had made unsolicited offers for Moses House, and a KHLP partner had testified about his personal belief that KHLP could recover its purchase price by spending "a little bit of money." The Mayor's Agent, therefore, considered whether renovation was reasonably feasible and concluded that even if it was not, KHLP had ways of avoiding loss short of obtaining a demolition permit.

In short, the record shows that KHLP failed to meet its burden of demonstrating unreasonable economic hardship, because it did not show that the value of Moses House had declined since the time of KHLP's purchase or that no other economically viable use existed. The Mayor's Agent's finding that KHLP did not show "unreasonable economic hardship," therefore, is supported by substantial evidence in the record.[10]

V

Unconstitutional Vagueness

Finally, KHLP challenges the statutory definition of "special merit," D.C.Code § 5-1002(11), claiming that the term is unconstitutionally vague and contending that its application unfairly deprived KHLP of an opportunity to know what factors the Mayor's Agent considered important in making his determination.[11] Specifically,

10. The Supreme Court's recent decision in *Lucas*, 505 U.S. at ___, 112 S.Ct. at 2896, on which KHLP heavily relies, is distinguishable. *** In this case, no such finding has been made. To the contrary, the Mayor's Agent found that KHLP received a few unsolicited offers for Moses House and that the assessed value of the property had increased since the time KHLP purchased it.

11. The Association contends that, because KHLP failed to make this argument before the Mayor's Agent, KHLP should not be allowed to make it on appeal. *See Abolaji v. D.C. Taxicab Comm'n*, 609 A.2d 671, 672 (D.C.1992) (failure to raise procedural points below left appellate court an insufficient record with which to evaluate validity of petitioner's procedural arguments). *** KHLP replies that it could not have been expected to raise a constitutional objection before the Mayor's Agent because

KHLP contends that the words comprising the third "special merit" criterion at issue here—"social and other benefits having a high priority for community services," D.C.Code § 5-1002(11)—are too imprecise to guide the Mayor's Agent in making a decision.

In a due process vagueness challenge, the inquiry is "whether the statute provides explicit standards so that the law gives 'the person of ordinary intelligence a reasonable opportunity to know what is prohibited,' and prevents 'arbitrary and discriminatory applications.'" *Nova Univ.,* 483 A.2d at 1188 (citing *Grayned v. City of Rockford,* 408 U.S. 104, 108–09 *** (1972)). Whether the statute is sufficiently precise will "depend[ ] in [large] part on the nature of the enactment." *Hoffman Estates v. Flipside, Hoffman Estates Inc.,* 455 U.S. 489, 498 *** (1982). *** Finally, the meaning of a statute can be clarified by turning to "regulations [that] amplify[ ] the statutory standard" and to "judicial and administrative interpretations [that] have elaborated its text." *LCP, Inc. v. District of Columbia Alcoholic Beverage Control Bd.,* 499 A.2d 897, 902 (D.C.1985).

The part of the "special merit" definition which KHLP challenges—namely, the alleged vagueness of the provision requiring "social or other benefits having a high priority for community services," D.C.Code § 5-1002(11)—must be viewed in the context of the Act" purposes. The Act aims at preserving historic landmarks and districts for "the health, prosperity and welfare of the people of the District of Columbia." *Id.* § 5-1001(a). Because the Act is intended to benefit the general population of the District, it follows that a project to replace an historic building must similarly offer community-wide benefits. Moreover, the phrase "high priority for community services," *id.* § 5-1002(11), makes clear that the offered benefits must be for the community at large, not primarily for a subset of privileged persons. Thus, according to reasonably clear inferences from the statutory language itself, projects such as office buildings or luxury condominiums, while generally beneficial to the community, more specifically benefit the occupants and cannot, as such, be viewed as adequate compensation for historic buildings taken away from the community as a whole; something more is required.

This court's interpretations of the "special merit" provision of the Act have enhanced understanding of the statute. These interpretations provide guidance to parties in applying for a demolition permit, and inform and assist the Mayor's Agent in deciding the case. More specifically, in *Committee of 100,* 571 A.2d at 200, we noted that, because the purpose of the statute as a whole is to preserve historic properties "as distinctive elements of the city's ... history" before "permanent loss and demolition of

---

it had no way of anticipating the need for such an argument until the Mayor's Agent issued his decision. We agree with the Association that KHLP, in recognizing the need to demonstrate it had a project of special merit, should have presented all available arguments, attacking the questionable "special merit" criterion itself in addition to attempting to demonstrate satisfaction of that criterion at the hearings or on motion for reconsideration. Thus, KHLP arguably has waived its vagueness claim. Nonetheless, we note that KHLP's challenge is not procedural, as in *Abolaji,* and is not barred by state law, as in *Jimmy Swaggart Ministries.* Accordingly, we are not precluded from considering it, and we choose to do so since the record is adequate and the parties have joined issue.

such [ ] valuable structure[s], ... the Preservation Act demands [that they] be replaced with something sufficiently 'special'" and that "[f]actors which are common to all projects are not considered special merits." *See id.* at 200–201 (new office building that merely would provide more parking than building it would replace, and would increase rent and tax revenue, is not of "special merit["] ***[12]

We do not preclude the possibility that an office building or an apartment complex may have "special merit" if it provides particular "social or other benefits" that can be said to offer "community services" for persons other than those who primarily inhabit or work in the buildings. [*See*] *Citizens Comm. to Save Historic Rhodes Tavern,* 432 A.2d at 717 n. 13. This possibility, however, does not diminish the central point applicable here: projects featuring benefits to the occupants of new buildings (such as the purchasers of KHLP's condominiums), coupled with general benefits to the District (such as increased tax revenues or increased housing stock), are not "special" enough to come within the clause identifying "special merit" as "social or other benefits having a high priority for community services."

The challenged provision of the Act is not standardless given the purposes of the Act, the context in which the Act is applied here, and the judicial decisions clarifying its meaning. Our case law, in particular, has given substantial content to the meaning of the "social or other benefits" criterion defining "special merit" under the Act. We therefore must reject KHLP's contention that the "special merit" provision of the Landmark and Historic District Protection Act is unconstitutionally vague.

VI

Conclusion

KHLP failed to meet its burden of showing that the proposed luxury condominium project had special features that distinguished it from other luxury condominium projects and that it would benefit the community in general (not merely the residents of the condominiums). KHLP also failed to consider the feasibility of reasonable alternatives to complete demolition of Moses House. * * * Furthermore, KHLP failed to meet its additional burden of showing that, without complete demolition, there could be no viable economic use for the property, or that the value of Moses House had decreased significantly from the time it was designated a contributing structure

---

12. In fact, the record shows that KHLP was aware that its proposed "special merit" factors would probably not be accepted as such under the standards established by previous court decisions. At the conclusion of the November 1, 1991 hearing the following discussion took place between the Mayor's Agent and counsel for KHLP: MAYOR'S AGENT: ... But I'm just suggesting to you at this point that I haven't heard any evidence that would meet the burden of special merit.

[KHLP'S COUNSEL]: You're rejecting the idea of additional tax revenue for the city? You're rejecting the idea of preserving the Comprehensive Plan of staying away from embassies and putting housing stock in the District of Columbia as no special merit?

MAYOR'S AGENT: ... it's a very high burden to meet when we're talking about special merit ... [y]ou would need to go back and refer me to some other cases to support your position because I'm not trying to create any new law. I'll let the courts do that....

[KHLP'S COUNSEL]: *I think this is new law.*

MAYOR'S AGENT: Well, the court will have to make new law [emphasis added].

in the Historic District. * * * Finally, as we have elaborated, the third criterion under the "special merit" provision of the statute is not unconstitutionally vague.

Affirmed.

Notes and Questions

1. **Contributing structures.** In both *Figarsky* and *Kalorama*, the subject properties were "contributing structures," which are resources that intrinsically add to the historical or architectural values for which the district is significant. In contrast, a non-contributing structure does not contribute to the significance of the district; it may be less than fifty years old or may be an older resource that has been significantly altered, or it may be a resource not associated with the historic theme or time period of the district. The properties in the cases contributed in different ways: in *Figarsky*, the building performed a screening function, separating the green from an encroaching commercial district, and in *Kalorama*, the building was originally built in a Queen Anne style, but was redesigned in a neo-classical style, and may or may not have been eligible for landmarking. Proposed changes to non-contributing structures are evaluated primarily for their impact on the historic district, while alterations to contributing structures are evaluated both for their impact on the structure and on the district. Part of the objection to the plans in *Kalorama* had to do with scale and mass, thought inappropriate for the district. a. What sorts of limits on alterations might be appropriate for non-contributing structures within an historical district?

2. **Adaptive reuse.** In both cases, the buildings had not been used for some time and had fallen into disrepair. Both owners desired to put the property to a different use, although in *Figarsky*, those plans were not laid out before the commission. a. Would adaptive reuse be an effective way of capturing unrealized value in such property? *See* Chapter 9 for a discussion of the economics of adaptive reuse.

3. **Special merit.** In *Kalorama*, the Mayor's Agent dismissed KHLP's claim that building luxury condominiums had special merit, for among other reasons, that the asserted increased tax revenues were not demonstrated with reasonable certainty. a. If instead of luxury housing, KHLP had proposed affordable housing that addressed a demonstrated housing shortage, would a balancing of the historical significance of the Moses House against the benefits of such a project be in order?

4. **Certificates of appropriateness and conditions.** A certificate of appropriateness is a document stating that proposed work is appropriate for the historic district and meets code criteria. A COA is needed when the proposed work will affect significant architectural features. Typically, applications for COA are subject to technical and design review by the agency's staff architects, whose aim is to ensure the preservation of the historical features of the exterior of structures within the historic district. Because an assessment of the existing features and the effect of the proposed changes is a fluid one, the process of obtaining a COA may resemble a form of bargaining—the historic commission granting the COA on condition that the landowner take particular measures to restore other features of the subject building or one in the district. A line of Supreme Court cases may serve to limit the kinds of conditions a city may

impose in acting on requests for a COA. First, in *Nollan v. California Coastal Comm'n*, 483 U. S. 825 (1987), the Court ruled that a government may condition approval of a permit on the dedication of property to the public only so long as there is a "nexus" between the condition and the harm sought to be remedied. In *Dolan v. City of Tigard*, 512 U. S. 374 (1994), the Court expanded on *Nollan* and ruled that there must be "rough proportionality between the property that the government demands and the social costs of the applicant's proposal." More recently in *Koontz v. St. Johns River Water Mgt. Dist.*, 133 S.Ct. 2586 (2013), the Court reiterated that *Nollan and Dolan* enable permitting authorities to insist that applicants bear the full costs of their proposals, but cautioned that the government must not make demands that would thwart the Fifth Amendment right to just compensation. The Court explained that the principles of *Nollan* and *Dolan* do not change depending on whether the government *approves* a permit on the condition that the applicant turn over property or *denies* a permit because the applicant refuses to do so. "[R]egardless of whether the government ultimately succeeds in pressuring someone into forfeiting a constitutional right, the unconstitutional conditions doctrine forbids burdening the Constitution's enumerated rights by coercively withholding benefits from those who exercise them." *Id.* at 2595.

5. **Relocating historical structures.** An owner seeking to relocate an historical structure will have the burden of demonstrating that the relocation will not affect the historical integrity or values of the property. *Farrington v. Cambridge Historical Comm'n*, 2012 Mass. LCR LEXIS 79 (Mass. Land Ct. May 18, 2012) provides an example of a successful showing for a certificate of appropriateness for a relocation. There, property owners in adjacent districts challenged a decision by Cambridge Historic Commission to grant a certificate of appropriateness to relocate an historic landmark, an antebellum church in the Greek Revival style, to the back of an adjacent vacant lot as part of a larger project for the Art Institute of Boston. The plan involved lowering the church approximately five feet to ground level, removing the existing steeple and restoring the original, the construction of a building on the former church site, and connecting the new building to the church by a glass connector. The plaintiffs challenged the decisions of both the Historic Commission and the Planning Board.

After concluding that the plaintiffs had standing to make the challenge, the court rejected the claims on the merits. The court found the Commission's decision was made on the basis of a comprehensive proposal that directly addressed each of the criteria and concerns in the landmark ordinance. In addition, the proposal was consistent with "the Landmark Study," which stated a preference for maintaining the Church in its current position, but did not prohibit or oppose relocating it. The Landmark Study stated that "relocation proposals should be evaluated in terms of a) the significance of the building on its current site and b) aspects of the development proposal that may enhance the building and/or provide significant public benefit." The relocation proposal met the requirements of the study—it was accompanied by voluminous drawings, diagrams, and renderings of the new site that showed the historic and architectural values were evaluated; the relocation of the church closer to the street would preserve the public views of the portico steeple and forward bays of the church; the restoration of the original steeple would be appropriate; and the new building would be similar in color and pattern to the Church's clapboard siding and sympathetic in mass and materials, to the landmark.

The court also upheld the Planning Board decision, finding that the statutory criteria for issuing a permit had been satisfied. Among other things, the proposal contained measures to minimize adverse impacts on abutters through setbacks, height restrictions, landscaping, limits on hours of use, and design of the structures—broken up into a series of planes for compatibility of scale and character.

* * *

Booker T. Washington House

Booker T. Washington came from the south to spend his summers on Long Island, New York. As his autobiography, *Up from Slavery*, recounts, he was born into slavery in 1856 and emancipated following the Civil War. He spent his youth working in salt furnaces and coal mines in West Virginia to put himself through school. His industry and commitment to education led to a teaching position at the Hampton Institute, then to be the first head of the newly formed Tuskegee Institute in Alabama, a position held for the rest of his life.

When he first came to the town of Huntington on Long Island in May 1907, it was to give a speech at the Huntington Opera House, entitled "Education as the Solution of the Race Problem." This was just two days after President Theodore Roosevelt had honored him with dinner at the White House, the first African-American to be so recognized. He was then regarded as one of the most influential African-Americans and considered as somewhat of an informal advisor to the president on race policies. That summer, he began looking for a summer home on Long Island, where he would be near the wealthy philanthropists who supported Tuskegee. Washington rented a farm house and planned to work on a book, *My Larger Education*, which was published in 1911. Washington reportedly told the local newspaper that he came to Huntington for two reasons: to work and to rest. He also said that he found that nature and man had worked together well to produce such a beautiful spot as Huntington.

After four summers renting, Washington decided to purchase a house. He selected a secluded spot in Fort Salonga on a bluff on Long Island Sound. The New York Times reported that the house was in "one of the finest sections of Long Island—a neighborhood where many wealthy New Yorkers have large estates." There was no opposition to Washington purchasing a summer house here, but when a rumor spread that he intended to add enough land to erect an institution similar to Tuskegee for the education of blacks, neighbors reportedly formed a syndicate and offered to buy the property from Washington for $1,500 more than he had paid for it, and to offer him another nearby tract of land.

Washington and his family enjoyed his time in Huntington—recreating on the beach, worshipping at the Bethel A.M.E. Church, where Washington taught Sunday school. In 1914, Washington sold the house to Henry Brush, not to abandon the area, but to buy another house in the area as an investment. Those plans were cut short by his untimely death a year later at the age of 59. After his death, the Fort Salonga property came to be owned by the Huntington Land Company and eventually bought by a family from Forest Hills who used it as a summer home for many years. Although unoccupied since the 1990s, the house was given local landmark designation status in 2005 and was nominated for the National Register of Historic Places. When the property was bought in 2007, the new owner, unaware of its historical status, decided to tear it down and build a new retirement home in its place. When the owner discovered the historical status, he petitioned the Town of Huntington to allow demolition. That request prompted such a public outcry, that he withdrew the application, deciding instead to relocate the house closer to the road, where it will be more visible, and to build his new house behind the relocated historic house.

Notes and Questions

1. **Loss of integrity.** Does a relocated historic structure, lose its integrity, now removed from its historic context, framing that defined it, made it understandable? See National Register Bulletin: How to Apply the National Register Criteria for Evaluation 44 (1997) ("One aspect of integrity for purposes of listing on the National Register is location, the place where the historic property was constructed or the place where the historic event occurred. The relationship between the property and its location is often important to understanding why the property was created or why something happened. The actual location of a historic property, complemented by its setting, is particularly important in recapturing the sense of historic events and persons. Except in rare cases, the relationship between a property and its historic associations is destroyed if the property is moved."). While relocation of historic property is not favored, with the Booker T. Washington house, merely refraining from tearing it down might not have been enough to preserve it, since the house was situated in an erosion zone and was in danger of falling into the water. Relocated, it survives to continue to tell the story of an American hero.

2. Hardship Applications

a. Economic Valuation

Weinberg v. City of Pittsburgh, Historic Review Commission

Commonwealth Court of Pennsylvania
651 A.2d 1182 (1994)

RODGERS, S.J. This is an appeal by the City of Pittsburgh, Historic Review Commission (Commission) from a decision of the Court of Common Pleas of Allegheny County (trial court) which reversed a decision of the Commission refusing to grant to Alvin Weinberg and Shirley Weinberg, his wife (Weinberg), a certificate of appropriateness for demolition of a designated historic structure known as Gateway House. We affirm the trial court.

Gateway House, a large two and one-half story frame dwelling, located on Fifth Avenue at Woodland Road, was built around 1860 in Gothic Revival style and is the oldest surviving element of Fifth Avenue's "millionaire row". It was not a mansion, but a gatehouse to a mansion, later replaced by the Benedum mansion. The historic significance of Gateway House is unquestioned, but is limited to the exterior, because all items of historic interest have been removed from the interior. Gateway House was designated an historic structure in April 1986 by a resolution of City Council approved by the Mayor pursuant to a city ordinance governing designation and preservation of historic structures.

Chatham College owned and used the property as a dormitory until the 1980s, and then considered using it for faculty housing, but determined the cost of renovation was too great. Gateway House has been unoccupied since 1984. In June 1985, Chatham College sold Gateway House and adjoining property to Greystone Associates, Inc., developers of a townhouse project at this location.

The City Planning Commission approved the townhouse project provided, among other things, that the developer pursue the designation of Gateway House as an historic structure. Greystone pursued the designation, but did not renovate Gateway House, and listed it for sale without success until February 1988, when Greystone sold Gateway House to Weinberg for $175,000 without a mortgage. Weinberg had previously agreed to purchase a townhouse from Greystone but, because of drainage problems at the site, desired to be released from that agreement. The developer was willing to release Weinberg if they agreed to purchase Gateway House for $175,000. In September 1986, Weinberg's son had purchased from Greystone an adjoining one-half acre lot for $188,000.

In 1989, Gateway House property was separately assessed by the City at $40,000 representing a fair market value of $160,000. Weinberg purchased Gateway House fully aware of the historic designation and the restrictions on renovations and demolition but, at the time of purchase, did not secure an estimate of the cost of renovation.

Weinberg initially intended to restore the dilapidated structure and use it for a residence. They obtained the Commission's permission to make exterior repairs and spent about $36,000. Their contractor indicated he could not guarantee the work because the house had serious structural problems. Weinberg decided to renovate the house for resale as a one or two family residence and applied for a mortgage. Pittsburgh National Bank denied the mortgage as a commercial loan because the cost of renovation would exceed the value of the renovated dwelling, but said it would consider a loan secured by other collateral.

The Weinbergs then sought a certificate from the Commission to demolish Gateway House. The Commission conducted a hearing of which no transcript was made, and denied the application. Weinberg appealed, and the trial court remanded for the making of a record. A hearing was held by the Commission on June 7, 1991. At this hearing, Michael Eversmeyer, a staff member of the Commission, submitted his report and showed slides pointing out the historic significance of Gateway House, but introduced no evidence of the fair market value of Gateway House before or after renovation, nor any evidence of the cost of renovation.

A letter dated January 4, 1990, from Rebecca Stafford, President of Chatham College, introduced at the prior hearing, was made a part of the record. In this letter, Ms. Stafford, on behalf of the College, supported demolition of Gateway House because the structure was beyond restoration and presented an attraction to vagrants, vandals and rodents. However, at the hearing on June 7, 1991, a letter from counsel for Chatham College stated that, while it believed the property continued to be an attraction to vagrants, vandals and rodents, a danger to the health and safety of its neighbors, an eyesore which adversely affected the value of neighboring properties requiring prompt remedial action, the College also believed the property was a significant historic structure and would prefer that it be renovated; but if the cost of renovation was in excess of the value of the property after renovation, the College would support demolition.

Weinberg presented the testimony of Douglas Berryman, an architect, and Lee Goldblum, a realtor. Mr. Berryman testified that, while Gateway House was in poor condition, it was not so structurally unsound to be beyond restoration. The estimated cost of such renovation was $567,000 *** Weinberg's total investment, including the initial purchase price of $175,000 and $36,000 spent for initial repairs would, therefore, exceed $850,000. ***

Mr. Goldblum, a realtor for Howard Hanna with twenty-three years experience testified that the renovated house could be marketed as two units for about $250,000 each and as a single family residence for about $500,000 to $550,000. He testified that a new home in that location would sell for about $800,000. Mr. Goldblum testified that Gateway House was on the market after 1985 and, although many people went through it, there was no real interest. He said there was little activity in purchases for renovation and not much of a market for restored homes. *** He remained of the opinion that the fair market value of Gateway House after renovation would not exceed $550,000, but when pressed conceded it was "possible" there might be someone willing to pay $800,000.

The Commission met again on August 2, 1991, in the presence of their staff and counsel for Weinberg, to consider their decision. [After considering the staff recommendations to deny the demolition permit and the Weinbergs' objections to the proposed findings, *** [t]he Commission then voted to accept the findings and recommendation of its staff denying the application for demolition.

The Commission found that the demolition of Gateway House would destroy a structure of major historical and architectural significance in the city; that Gateway House was not structurally unsound; that the owners understood the restrictions imposed upon disposition of the structure by the historic designation. *** The Commission opined the purchase price (of $175,000) should not be used as an element of the hardship argument "since a mistakenly high payment for the building was a matter under the control of the owners". *** The Commission [further] found no economic hardship because, on the basis of Mr. Goldblum's testimony, the owners could recoup their investment by selling the property as is for $200,000 to $300,000; they could renovate the property for their home, an option where economic considerations were of secondary importance; they could renovate the building for sale as a single family house and might or might not recover their costs. ***

The Commission disapproved the application to demolish Gateway House "because the building has major historic and architectural significance and because there would not be an economic hardship imposed on the owners of the property by the denial of the application." ***

On appeal by the owners, the Weinbergs, the trial court reversed because the Commission had erred in concluding that Mr. Goldblum, the owner's real estate expert, had given equivocal testimony as to the fair market value of a fully renovated Gateway House, and in finding that Mr. Goldblum had testified Gateway House could be sold as is for $200,000 to $300,000.

The Commission, joined by the *amici curiae*, the National Trust for Historic Preservation in the United States and the Pennsylvania Historical and Museum Commission, has appealed on the ground that Weinberg had failed to prove unnecessary economic hardship. * * *

Reasonable restrictions may be imposed upon private property to preserve the public interest in historic landmarks, *Penn Central Transportation Co. v. New York City,* 438 U.S. 104 *** (1978), so long as, *inter alia*, the means are not unduly oppressive upon the property holder, considering the economic impact of the regulation and the extent to which the government physically intrudes upon the property.

In *Penn Central* *** [t]he Supreme Court, review[ing] the specific economic issues, found that the historic designation allowed the owners to "continue to use the property precisely as it has been used for the past 65 years: as a railroad terminal" and found that the owners were not prevented from receiving a "reasonable return", *id.* at 136, 98 S.Ct. at 2665, even though it was not the most profitable use, particularly when the owners were entitled to off-setting benefits such as the sale of transfer development rights to the unused air space.

The *Penn Central* rationale was followed by the Pennsylvania Supreme Court in *United Artists' Theater Circuit, Inc. v. City of Philadelphia,* 535 Pa. 370, 635 A.2d 612

(1993). In *United Artists'* the court did not see the possibility that the owner was wholly deprived of any profitable use, but said:

> There may be circumstances in which the mere designation of a property as historic would constitute a taking due to the extreme financial hardship resulting from such designation....
>
> Moreover, we note that the Philadelphia Ordinance in question provides a vehicle for relief when the designation would cause a substantial hardship. The Ordinance provides relief for a party who asserts that he is deprived of 'any purpose for which it is or may be reasonably adapted, or where a permit application for alteration or demolition is based, in whole or in part, on financial hardship.'

Id. at 382, n. 3, 635 A.2d at 618, n. 3.

The Pittsburgh Ordinance, being Ordinance No. 20 of 1979, as amended, provides no such relief, but authorizes the Commission to issue a Certificate of Appropriateness of any demolition after hearing, and also provides (Subsection 513.7.1):

> The limitations upon the issuance of demolition or building permits ... for any historic structure ... shall not apply when the work involved in the permit has been ordered by the Bureau of Building Inspection or the Allegheny County Health Department for the preservation of the public health or safety.

*** The Commission argues that the owners failed to prove sufficient economic hardship to warrant the grant of a permit to demolish Gateway House. *Amici curiae* go further and argue that financial hardship should not be considered in this case because Weinberg entered upon a speculative investment with full knowledge that Gateway House was an historic structure which could not be demolished without the approval of the Commission.

However, both *Penn Central* and *United Artists'* hold that the economic impact in terms of financial hardship must be assessed in order to decide whether preservation of an historic structure continues to be a proper exercise of the police power. *** In this case, the owners argue Gateway House can no longer be used as a residence, because it must be renovated, and such renovation is not economically feasible since the cost of necessary renovation would impose a substantial financial hardship. We agree that economic hardship is a valid ground for relief, whether the private owner is a transportation company, a land developer or a home owner.

Amici curiae argue also, by analogy to the law of zoning governing the grant of variances, that an applicant who purchases an historic structure with knowledge of the restrictions, cannot claim economic hardship because he creates his own hardship. *See, e.g., McClure Appeal,* 415 Pa. 285, 203 A.2d 534 (1964). But the Commission and *amici* cite no authority applying this principle of zoning law to the law governing the designation and preservation of historic structures. *** [W]hile the rule is applicable to an applicant who knowingly assumes an unusual investment risk in hopes of a commensurate gain, it should not be invoked against a purchaser who bought at a price which assumes that zoning will permit a reasonable use of the property. *See Forest Hills Borough Appeal*, 409 Pa. 392, 187 A.2d 166 (1963).

There is no evidence in this case that the property was purchased as a speculative investment at an excessive price in hope of changing the historic structure designation in order to reap a large profit. *** In hindsight, of course, Weinberg should have engaged an architect and a contractor to get an estimate of the cost of renovation, but such oversight can hardly be equated with assuming the risk of making a highly speculative investment. In this case, we find no authority and no evidence justifying the application of the unnecessary hardship rule. ***

The record shows this property has not been maintained or occupied since 1984 except for vagrants, vandals and rodents, nor is there any requirement in the historic designation ordinance requiring maintenance or occupation. It is clear that any purchaser must renovate the property, and the Commission has accepted the necessary cost of such renovation to be $650,000 to $700,000. There is no competent evidence that the property could be sold as is for $200,000 to $300,000 because Mr. Goldblum testified there were no comparable properties upon which he could base an expert opinion. He did testify, when pressed, that the house could possibly sell for $200,000 to $300,000 but that testimony was simply a layman's guess.

Furthermore, even when seeking a zoning variance, the law does not require a property owner to attempt to sell as a prerequisite to the grant of a variance. *Valley View Civic Association v. Zoning Board of Adjustment*, 501 Pa. 550, 462 A.2d 637 (1983). In this case, it is clear that a reasonable purchaser would not buy this property if expert opinion shows he would suffer a substantial financial loss due to the cost of renovation.

The Commission's conclusion that Weinberg could borrow enough money to renovate the building as a personal residence, making the issue of economic hardship irrelevant, is without legal authority. The rights of a private property owner to use his property do not vary in this context because he is a homeowner, a transportation company or a land developer, nor on the extent of his personal wealth. *Penn Central; United Artists*'[.] ***

*** The Commission agreed that it was not economically feasible for the property to be renovated and sold as a two unit residence. It also agreed that the reasonable cost of renovation as a single family residence is $650,000 and did not disagree that Mr. Goldblum found the fair market value of such a house would not exceed $550,000, but erroneously concluded that Mr. Goldblum had equivocated in giving his opinion.

The situation was aptly summarized in the [above-mentioned] letter submitted on behalf of Chatham College dated June 7, 1991.

This Court finds there was substantial evidence supporting the conclusion of the Commission that the cost of renovation as a single family residence was about $650,000 to $700,000, and there was no substantial evidence that the cost of renovating the property would not exceed the value of the property after renovation.

On the basis of this record it is not economically feasible for the present owners, nor any subsequent owners to undertake such costly renovation. It makes little sense to allow this historic structure to remain unoccupied and to permit it to continue to deteriorate, until the Allegheny County Health Department or the Pittsburgh Bureau of Building Inspection orders it to be demolished for the preservation of the public health or safety.

Smith, J., concurs in result only.

Order

NOW, December 19, 1994, the order of the Court of Common Pleas of Allegheny County, dated November 29, 1993 *** is affirmed.

City of Pittsburgh, Historic Review Commission v. Weinberg

Supreme Court of Pennsylvania
544 Pa. 286, 676 A.2d 207 (1996)

Nix, C.J. The City of Pittsburgh, Historic Review Commission ("Commission") appeals from the Order of the Commonwealth Court which affirmed the Allegheny Court of Common Pleas' reversal of the Commission's refusal to grant a certificate of appropriateness for the demolition of a designated historic structure. We granted allocatur in order to review the standard used by the lower courts in determining that Appellees, Alvin and Shirley Weinberg, met their burden of proving that they would suffer economic hardship as a result of the Commission's action. Because we find that Appellees failed to demonstrate that they could not make any economic use of their property, we agree with the Commission's decision to deny permission to demolish the structure, and therefore, reverse the Order of the Commonwealth Court.

The structure at issue in this case is the Howe-Childs-Gateway House ("Gateway House" or "House"), which is located at the southeast corner of Fifth Avenue and Woodland Road in the City of Pittsburgh. The Gateway House was designated an historic structure in April 1986 pursuant to a Pittsburgh ordinance governing designation and preservation of historic structures and historic districts.

The Gateway House, a two and one-half story frame dwelling, was erected around 1860 in the Gothic Revival style and is a part of what was known as Fifth Avenue's Millionaire's Row. At the time of its designation as an historic structure, the Gateway House was owned by Greystone Associates ("Greystone"), the developer of a townhouse project in the area of the House. The City Planning Commission approved the Greystone project subject to conditions which, *inter alia,* required the developer to pursue designation of the Gateway House as a local historic structure and submit all plans for the renovation of the House to the Historic Review Commission for review and approval.

Greystone pursued designation but never renovated the Gateway House. In February 1988, within two years of designation of the Gateway House as an historic structure, the developer sold the property to Appellees. Appellees had entered into an agreement to purchase a new townhouse from Greystone. When Appellees became aware that there were drainage problems at the site of the townhouse, they wanted to be released from the transaction. Greystone was willing to release them if Appellees agreed to purchase the Gateway House. Greystone sold the house and lot to Appellees for $175,000. No mortgage was involved in the transaction. After Greystone sold the property to Appellees, the Gateway property was reassessed at $40,000, which represented an estimated fair market value of $160,000.

When Appellees bought the Gateway property (structure and land), they knew that the house had been designated an historic structure and would be subject to restrictions imposed by the Pittsburgh Ordinance. These restrictions included a prohibition on altering or demolishing the structure unless the owner obtained from the Commission a certificate of appropriateness allowing such action.

The Gateway House, when acquired by Appellees, was in a dilapidated condition. Because they intended to use the House as their residence, Appellees obtained the Commission's permission to have certain restoration work done. Their contractor indicated he could not guarantee the work because the House had serious structural problems. When Appellees discovered that Pittsburgh National Bank would not grant a mortgage to finance the cost of rehabilitation because the House did not meet the bank's collateral requirements,[1] Appellees sought a certificate of appropriateness from the Commission to demolish the house. It was their intention to replace it with a new brick house. None of the restrictive covenants in the deed from Greystone to Appellees would prevent Appellees from doing so.

The Commission conducted a hearing on Appellees' application for a certificate of appropriateness. No verbatim record of the testimony was made. The Commission refused to grant a certificate, and Appellees appealed to the Allegheny County Court of Common Pleas. That court remanded the matter to the Commission to make a full and complete record.

The Commission subsequently held hearings on June 7 and August 2, 1991. At the first hearing, Appellees presented the testimony of Douglas Berryman, an architect, and Lee Goldblum, a realtor. Mr. Berryman testified that the Gateway House was in poor condition but not to the point that it could not be restored. *** The contractor's estimated cost of restoring the Gateway House was $567,000.[2] *** The architect's fee for the project was estimated at $35,500. *** In order to construct a new brick house on the site following demolition of the Gateway House, Mr. Berryman estimated that it would cost in the range of $570,000 to $600,000. ***

Appellees also presented the testimony of Lee Goldblum, a realtor with the Howard Hanna Real Estate Company. Mr. Goldblum opined that a house renovated as two

1. Specifically, the Vice President of Pittsburgh National Bank indicated that the House appeared to be in rapid deterioration and the cost of the necessary renovations would exceed the fair market value of the House after those renovations were completed. *** He did, however, state that the bank would consider a commercial loan secured by other collateral. ***

2. This figure does not include an estimated $45,000 to $50,000 to construct a two-car garage for a single family.

separate units could be marketed for $250,000 each and a single family residence might sell in the range of $500,000 to $550,000. *** He further testified that a new house built on the site of the Gateway House could be worth $800,000. *** Mr. Goldblum also recounted for the Commission his experience in trying to sell the Gateway property. He stated that there were many people who expressed interest in the property during the time that it was marketed by his firm; however, no one was willing to commit the resources necessary to restore the house to a suitable condition. *** Finally, Mr. Goldblum speculated that the Gateway House could be sold in the two-hundred-thousand dollar range in unimproved condition, although he conceded that it would be impossible to know for sure "without trying to market it full tilt." ***

On August 2, 1991, the Commission reconvened in order to reach a decision on Appellees' request for a certificate of appropriateness to demolish the Gateway House. At that time, the findings and recommendation of the Commission's staff were submitted to the Commission for consideration. After deliberation, the Commission voted to accept the findings and recommendation of the staff. Specifically, the Commission found that the demolition of the Gateway House would destroy a structure of major historical and architectural significance; that the Gateway House was not structurally unsound; that Appellees knew of the historic designation of the house and the ramifications of such a designation; and that renovations would cost (excluding purchase price and interim expenses) approximately $650,000 for a single-family house with garage and $700,000 for a two-unit residence with two garages. *** The Commission also noted that "the purchase price should not be used as an element of the hardship argument, since a mistakenly high payment for the building was a matter under the control of the owners." *** The end result of the Commission's deliberations was the denial of Appellees' application for demolition of the Gateway House.

Appellees appealed the Commission's adjudication to the Court of Common Pleas of Allegheny County. The trial court reversed on the basis that the record did not support the Commission's finding that Appellees failed to meet their burden of showing that the sale of the Gateway House was impracticable. *Weinberg v. City of Pittsburgh, Historic Review Comm'n,* No. SA981 of 1990, slip op. at 28 (C.P. Allegheny County Nov. 29, 1993). The court held that the Commission erred as a matter of law in concluding that Mr. Goldblum's testimony concerning the fair market value of the house was equivocal and, thus, incompetent. *Id.* at 20. The common pleas court found nothing inherently unreliable in Mr. Goldblum's testimony that the fair market value of the house after renovation would be less than the cost of renovation. *Id.* at 24. Based on its interpretation of Mr. Goldblum's testimony, the court concluded that renovating the Gateway House was not economically feasible because the cost of renovations would be greater than the fair market value of the property after the house was renovated. *Id.* at 31.

The Commission appealed to the Commonwealth Court. In affirming the trial court's decision, the Commonwealth Court found that "there was substantial evidence supporting the conclusion of the Commission that the cost of renovation as a single family residence was about $650,000 to $700,000, and there was no substantial evidence that the cost of renovating the property would not exceed the value of the property after renovation." *Weinberg v. City of Pittsburgh, Historic Review Comm'n,* 651 A.2d 1182, 1188 (Pa.Cmwlth.1994). It agreed with the trial court that it was not economically feasible for Appellees or any subsequent owners to undertake renovation of the Gateway House. *Id.*

In reaching its determination that the Gateway House could not be renovated in an economically feasible manner, the Commonwealth Court relied on the seminal United States Supreme Court case *Penn Central Transp. Co. v. New York City,* 438 U.S. 104 *** (1978), as well as this Court's decision in *United Artists' Theater Circuit v. City of Philadelphia,* 535 Pa. 370, 635 A.2d 612 (1993). In *Penn Central,* the Landmark Preservation Commission of New York City designated Grand Central Terminal as a landmark. The owner of the terminal subsequently entered into a contract with a company to construct a multi-story office tower over the terminal. The Preservation Commission rejected the plans for the office tower construction because it believed that the terminal's historic and aesthetic features would have been adversely affected. The owner did not seek judicial review of that decision but instead filed suit in state court claiming that the historic designation constituted a taking of its property without just compensation in violation of the Fifth and Fourteenth Amendments to the United States Constitution. The trial court agreed and held that the landmarks law, as applied to the owner, was unconstitutional. The New York Court of Appeals ultimately reversed that decision. The United States Supreme Court affirmed and held that the law did not constitute a taking of the owner's property within the meaning of the Fifth Amendment as made applicable to the states through the Fourteenth Amendment. *Penn Central,* 438 U.S. at 138 ***.

The Supreme Court in *Penn Central* reaffirmed the principle that "[s]tates and cities may enact land-use restrictions or controls to enhance the quality of life by preserving the character and desirable aesthetic features of a city." 438 U.S. at 129, 98 ***. It stated, however, that the impact of such restrictions must be considered in order to determine whether the interference with the property "is of such a magnitude that 'there must be an exercise of eminent domain and compensation to sustain [it].'" *Id.* at 136 *** (quoting *Pennsylvania Coal Co. v. Mahon,* 260 U.S. 393, 413 *** (1922)). The Court thus concluded that the historic designation of Grand Central Terminal was not a taking because it did not in any way interfere with the owner's "primary expectation concerning the use of the parcel." *Id.* at 136 ***.

More recently in *United Artists' Theater Circuit v. City of Philadelphia,* 535 Pa. 370, 635 A.2d 612 (1993), this Court concluded that the designation of property as historic without the consent of the owner does not constitute a taking pursuant to Article I, Section 10 of the Pennsylvania Constitution. In so holding, we acknowledged that "this Court has continually turned to federal precedent for guidance in its 'taking' jurisprudence, and indeed has adopted the analysis used by the federal courts." *Id.* at 377, 635 A.2d at 616. After undertaking a thorough review of our past reliance on federal caselaw, we identified three conditions that determine whether governmental action constitutes a taking requiring just compensation. *Id.* at 381,

635 A.2d at 618. The condition of particular concern here is that "the means [employed by the government] must not be unduly oppressive upon the property holder, considering the economic impact of the regulation...." *Id.* To this end, we have recognized that "action in the form of regulation can so diminish the value of property as to constitute a taking." *Id.* at 379, 635 A.2d at 617 (quoting *Andress v. Zoning Bd. of Adjustment of Philadelphia,* 410 Pa. 77, 85, 188 A.2d 709, 713 (1963)) ***. "However, the mere fact that the regulation deprives the property owner of the most profitable use of his property is not necessarily enough to establish the owner's right to compensation." *Id.*

In a case factually similar to the instant case, the Commonwealth Court in *First Presbyterian Church v. City Council of York,* 25 Pa. Cmwlth. 154, 360 A.2d 257 (1976), upheld the city council's denial of a permit to demolish an historic structure known as York House. In addressing the Church's claim that the council's actions constituted a deprivation of property rights without due process, the Commonwealth Court adopted the test articulated by the Fifth Circuit in *Maher v. City of New Orleans,* 516 F.2d 1051 (5th Cir.1975), *** which required the property owner to show "that the sale of the property was impracticable, that commercial rental could not provide a reasonable rate of return, or that other potential use of the property was foreclosed." *First Presbyterian,* 25 Pa. Cmwlth. at 161, 360 A.2d at 261 (quoting *Maher,* 516 F.2d at 1066). Applying that test, the Commonwealth Court concluded that the refusal of the permit to demolish the structure did not go so far as to preclude the use of York House for any purpose for which it was reasonably adapted. *First Presbyterian,* 25 Pa. Cmwlth. at 161, 360 A.2d at 261. Accordingly, it held that the Church did not meet its burden of proving that the city council's actions constituted a taking without just compensation. *Id.* at 162, 360 A.2d at 261.

Guided by the foregoing standards and the record of the proceedings below, we must conclude that the trial court erred when it held that the evidence did not support the Commission's finding that Appellees failed to prove economic hardship. The trial court noted that at the June 7, 1991, hearing

> [Appellees] undertook their burden of proving that, if not permitted to demolish the Gateway House, they could not make any economic use of the property, by presenting evidence to show that the cost of renovating the House would be greater than the fair market value of the House after renovations were completed.

Weinberg v. City of Pittsburgh, Historic Review Comm'n, No. SA981 of 1990, slip op. at 15 (C.P. Allegheny County Nov. 29, 1993). Although the Commission determined that Appellees failed to meet their burden, the trial court disagreed insofar as the Commission's findings were based on a partial rejection of Mr. Goldblum's testimony. *Id.* at 20.

The Commonwealth Court found that there was substantial evidence to support the Commission's conclusion that the cost of renovation as a single family residence was $650,000 to $700,000. *Weinberg v. City of Pittsburgh, Historic Review Comm'n,* 651 A.2d 1182, 1187 (Pa.Cmwlth.1994). However, like the trial court, it concluded that there was insufficient evidence to support the Commission's finding that the cost of renovating the property would not exceed the value of the property after renovation. *Id.*

We disagree with the conclusion of the lower courts that the record does not support the Commission's decision to deny a certificate of appropriateness. Additionally, it is apparent that both the trial court and Commonwealth Court failed to consider the circumstances surrounding Appellees' purchase of the Gateway House in reaching their decisions. As the United States Supreme Court has observed, questions concerning the economic impact of governmental actions are essentially answered by ad hoc, factual inquiries that focus on several different factors. *Penn Central Transp. Co. v. New York City,* 438 U.S. 104, 124 *** (1978). Two important factors identified by the Court in conducting this inquiry are "[t]he economic impact of the regulation on the claimant and, particularly, the extent to which the regulation has interfered with distinct investment-backed expectations...." *Id.*

Mr. Goldblum, Appellees' real estate expert, testified that he believed the property could be sold as it exists for between $200,000 and $300,000; as a renovated single family house for $500,000 to $550,000; and as a renovated two family residence for $500,000. *** Mr. Goldblum qualified these statements by indicating that it was impossible to know the price that the property would bring until it was put on the market and promoted "full tilt." *** When questioned further by one Commission member, Mr. Goldblum expressed an opinion that a renovated, single-family residence on the site of the Gateway House could be sold for as much as $800,000. ***

Appellees assert that the present value of the property is not a relevant consideration for purposes of determining economic hardship because "any [subsequent] purchaser will be burdened with the same oppressive requirements of restoration brought about by the historic designation." *** We find this argument wholly unpersuasive. Any burden imposed on a subsequent purchaser does not affect Appellees after they receive valuable consideration for their property. Just as Greystone, the prior owner of the Gateway House, cannot now complain about the costs or complications associated with the renovation of the Gateway House, Appellees likewise cannot claim that the impediments which might confront a prospective purchaser presently impact them for purposes of proving economic hardship.

Despite the unrefuted testimony of Appellees' expert that the Gateway property could be sold as it exists for between $200,000 and $300,000, the Commonwealth Court found that "[t]here is no competent evidence that the property could be sold as is for $200,000 to $300,000 because Mr. Goldblum testified there were no comparable properties upon which he could base an expert opinion." *Weinberg v. City of Pittsburgh, Historic Review Comm'n,* 651 A.2d 1182, 1187 (Pa.Cmwlth. 1994). The Commonwealth Court is incorrect that Mr. Goldblum's estimate of the property's selling price was incompetent because of the lack of comparable properties. At the time that he testified, Mr. Goldblum had twenty-three years of experience in real estate with a particular emphasis on the area of Pittsburgh where the Gateway House is located as well as a strong interest in historic houses. *** The Commission obviously gave greater deference to Mr. Goldblum's experience than to the fact that there were no properties comparable to the Gateway House when Mr. Goldblum rendered his opinion. We thus find support for the Commission's finding that Appellees failed to prove that it would be impracticable or impossible to sell their property. *See First Presbyterian Church v. City Council of York,* 25 Pa. Cmwlth. 154, 162, 360 A.2d 257, 261 (1976).

It should also be noted that Appellees received an inducement to purchase the Gateway House in the form of a release from a preexisting obligation to buy a townhouse from Greystone. *** Appellees had concerns about the inadequate drainage of the property that they were obligated to purchase and therefore "wanted out of it." *** Although it is impossible to ascribe a monetary value to this benefit, it must nonetheless be considered when evaluating the economic impact of the Commission's actions on Appellees.

We see no reason to delve any further into the Commission's decision in this matter. Despite the thorough review by the trial court and Commonwealth Court of other testimony and evidence presented at the June 7, 1991, hearing, our inquiry need not proceed beyond the point of our determination that Appellees did not meet their burden of proving that it was impracticable or impossible to sell their property. Appellees purchased the Gateway House for $175,000 and spent approximately $36,000 on exterior repairs. The unrefuted testimony of their own expert suggests that the house could be sold for $200,000 to $300,000. That, together with the release from the obligation to purchase the townhouse from Greystone, suggests that Appellees could conceivably realize a profit if they sold the property. In any event, Appellees have not demonstrated that they have been "deprived of any profitable use" of the property. *United Artists' Theater Circuit v. City of Philadelphia,* 535 Pa. 370, 382, 635 A.2d 612, 618 (1993).

Our decision is bolstered by the fact that prior to the time of their purchase, Appellees knew that the Gateway House had been given an historic designation and were aware of the consequences of such a designation. *** The fact that they did not engage the services of an architect or contractor to estimate the cost or feasibility of restoring the Gateway House cannot serve as a basis for their claims of economic hardship after the fact.

The Order of the Commonwealth Court is reversed and the decision of the Historic Review Commission of the City of Pittsburgh to deny a certificate of appropriateness is reinstated.

Notes and Questions

1. **The owners' choices.** There were three options available to the Weinbergs: 1) sell "as is"; 2) renovate and sell; or 3) demolish and build a new home. The first course would have enabled them to be made whole. The second would have resulted in an economic loss. The third would have put them ahead. The course to which they were relegated depended in large part upon the credibility of their asserted motivations. a. Did they purchase the property for investment purposes or for their personal use? b. In any case, does an owner suffer an economic hardship merely because she cannot develop the property to realize its highest value?

2. **A property lacking economic value, but liability.** In *St. Nicholas Parish Charitable Trust v. City of Pittsburgh Historic Review Comm'n*, 2012 Pa. Dist. & Cnty. Dec. LEXIS 343 (Pa. Com. Pl. July 19, 2012), St. Nicholas Parish Charitable Trust sought a certificate of appropriateness and a certificate of economic hardship in order to demolish the 110 year old St. Nicholas Roman Catholic Church. The property, on which the historically designated church sat, was acquired between 1911 and 1956 for $59,000. Over the years the character of the area changed from a vibrant, though small, community to an industrial area. The property was only a few feet away from State Route 28, a major traffic artery. The changes in use and roadway development led to a significant decline in population that in turn eroded the congregation base. There were no homes in the area, and only one business or occupied, useable, structure along the highway. The property, including the church, was boarded up, vacant, and not open to the public. It was not accessible by sidewalk and not safely accessible by roadway.

The Trust supported its request with a verified statement that it was burdened with costs due to insurance, water bills, and electricity bills, imposing an undue hardship and an economic burden on the parish. An appraisal report placed a value of negative $670,000 on the property and stated that it had a greater value as an unimproved site (by razing the buildings). An engineer's study showed dangerous structural defects, the cost of remedying exceeding $2 million. The Trust asserted that absent the demolition of the structures on the property, including the church, it could neither put the property to any reasonable use nor expect any reasonable return from it. The Historic Review Commission ("HRC") denied the request. The Court of Common Pleas, guided by the holding in *City of Pittsburgh v. Weinberg*, reversed that decision. First, the court found that because the property was "upside down," more a liability than an asset, the Trust could not obtain any profit on its sale, modest or otherwise, whether historically designated or not. Nonetheless, the historic designation of the Church still deprived the Trust of its primary and fundamental economic interest in the property, that is, the designation prevented the Trust from "un-improving" the property, i.e. demolishing and removing the buildings. As such, the designation operated to increase the Trust's economic liability in the amount of the difference between the improved and unimproved value, anywhere from $175,704 to $301,600. The Trust would also incur ongoing "holding cost" liability of $1,800 per month merely to maintain a property for which it had no useful purpose. It was not the case that the Trust could simply walk away from the property without incurring ongoing liability in the form of taxes, utilities, insurance costs, or the risk of uninsured premises liability judgments. Instead, the Trust "was rationally and economically compelled to 'cut its losses' and relieve itself of its ongoing 'holding cost' liability by accepting a loss on the property now." *Id.* at *36. While the court noted that according to *Weinberg*, the need to respect a private property owner's primary or fundamental economic expectations to avoid a "taking" does not require ensuring the property owner's ability to secure the maximum available profit from a sale, those expectations must include the ability to divest oneself of an ongoing monetary liability at the lowest possible loss. In this case, "the historic designation, to the extent that it increased the actual economic liability of the property, constituted an impermissible taking as it deprived the Trust of its fundamental economic interest in the property." *Id.* at *38.

The court went on to explain that *Weinberg* dealt directly with only the economic expectations of the costs of a potential renovation and/or the reasonable return on a resale of the property, but did not address the question of "re-purposing" the property. While there were re-purposing proposals offered here, such as to develop the property as an immigration museum, there was "no real evidence of record to support the contention that it is possible, let alone plausible or reasonable to do so." *Id.* at *39. Two studies, an architectural feasibility study and a market study, purported to show that the property could be configured for an immigration museum, failed to contain any demonstration of the likelihood of raising the seven million dollars needed for this re-purposing, or that the market would support a revenue stream of approximately $550,000 a year that would be needed to operate the museum. The studies were also based upon a number of assumptions, which if proven untrue, could be costly—about marketable title; the possible existence of canonical restrictions on use; the soundness of the physical structure given engineer's reports finding defects and seismic issues; and ease of asbestos remediation. *Id.* at *44.

Finally, the court addressed the HRC's assertion that the economic hardship was created by the Trust by its failure to make good faith efforts to market the property for sale. The HRC's assertion in its findings that "purchasers for the property have identified and justified a re-use of the property and deemed it feasible." The court found that the record did not support a finding that the Trust either had a present, or had a recent, ability to sell the property for any positive monetary amount; instead there were several failed sales of the property, but not because the Trust rejected them. And, the language in this finding did not appear to explicitly adopt such a determination of the feasibility of such a re-use, such that the conclusion could not be accepted. In all, the "HRC's decision to deny the Applicant a Certificate of Economic Hardship [was] not supported by substantial evidence of record, and ... reversed." *Id.* at *55.

3. **If the church is demolished.** Consider these further questions: a. Once the church building is demolished, what uses of the land would be suitable? b. What scale of development will the area's real estate market support? c. In what ways, physical or otherwise, could the historic significance of this landmark structure be preserved?

D. Self-Imposed Hardships

Zaruba v. Village of Oak Park

Appellate Court of Illinois, First District, Sixth Division
296 Ill.App.3d 614, 695 N.E.2d 510, 230 Ill.Dec. 1020 (1998)

Zwick, J. The issue in this case is whether the decision of the defendant, Village of Oak Park (the Village), to deny plaintiff, John Zaruba, a Certificate of Economic

Hardship was made against the manifest weight of the evidence. The Certificate is required by a Village ordinance before a house located within an historic architectural district may be demolished. On administrative review, the circuit court reversed the Village. After reviewing the record, we find the Village's decision to deny the Certificate to have been supported by the evidence. We therefore affirm the Village's decision and reverse the circuit court.

The Village's Historic Preservation Ordinance (the Ordinance) became effective on January 1, 1994. The Ordinance prevents the demolition of landmark buildings or contributing architectural resources located within the Village's Frank Lloyd Wright Prairie School of Architecture Historic District (the District). Exceptions are made upon the granting of a Certificate of Appropriateness or Certificate of Economic Hardship.

Plaintiff purchased the property located at 616 N. Kenilworth Avenue, a lot within the District, on March 14, 1995. The property consisted of a 45-foot wide parcel containing an 86-year old single-family house. Plaintiff purchased the property for $227,500.

On June 23, 1995, plaintiff applied for a wrecking permit to demolish the building. At that time he was informed by Village staff that a wrecking permit could not be issued without the Village first issuing either a Certificate of Appropriateness or a Certificate of Economic Hardship.

Plaintiff subsequently applied for a Certificate of Appropriateness on grounds that the building was not a contributing resource to the District. The Historic Preservation Commission (the Commission) held a hearing and concluded that the building was a contributing resource. It therefore denied the plaintiff's request on July 13, 1995. Plaintiff was informed in writing of his right to challenge the decision at public hearing before the Village Board of Trustees, but elected not to pursue this remedy.

On August 1, 1995, plaintiff applied for a Certificate of Economic Hardship.

At the hearing before the Commission on September 14, 1995, plaintiff testified that he had lived for the preceding five years at 614 N. Kenilworth. For approximately 40 years prior to plaintiff's purchase of 616 N. Kenilworth, and for a short period thereafter, a man named John Glavin lived in the house at 616 N. Kenilworth. Glavin was in his early 90s at the time of the sale of his house to plaintiff.

Plaintiff testified that he had, over the years, "polite conversations" with Mr. Glavin about whether he would be willing to sell the property. In the fall prior to the hearing, the conversations became serious. Plaintiff offered Glavin $150,000 based upon a professional appraisal plaintiff commissioned showing the property was worth $165,000. Glavin was "somewhat insulted" by the offer and told plaintiff that he had already turned down a $200,000 bid for the property from a woman named Colleen Myra. Plaintiff spoke with Myra and verified her written offer to Glavin. Plaintiff eventually offered Glavin $227,500 for the property, which Glavin accepted.

Plaintiff testified that he was motivated to purchase the property because he wanted to protect his investment in his own home. *** Plaintiff stated that he believed combining the two properties would increase the value of his home, but he could not offer an estimate of by how much the properties would be worth if joined together.

He presented a detailed architectural drawing showing a proposed extension of his front porch over the existing driveway at 614 N. Kenilworth, as well as a proposed new side-facing garage which he planned to erect on the site where Glavin's house stood. The proposed garage was designed to carefully unify the two lots.

It was established at the hearing that the Glavin house had substantially deteriorated over the course of the 40 years John Glavin had lived there. There were holes in the roof where a family of raccoons had taken up residence. The furnace was seriously damaged and several radiators had been disconnected. Water was leaking into the basement through a missing door and there was exposed wiring both inside and outside the house. Mortar in the chimney had eroded and the chimney was being held together by the supports of a television antennae. Siding on the southeast corner of the house was leaking. The house's foundation required tuckpointing in three or four locations. In addition, the garage was structurally unsound and in need of demolition. Plaintiff testified that when he purchased the house it was uninsurable due to the condition of the electrical and heating systems. Glavin did not have homeowner's insurance on the property at the time of the sale to plaintiff.

After purchasing the property, plaintiff destroyed the garage and removed significant amounts of debris from the exterior of the home. He also had asbestos removed from the pipes around the furnace.

Plaintiff offered three separate and detailed estimates about what it would cost to renovate the property. *** Plaintiff reviewed the three estimates together and determined that a total "conservative estimate" of what it would cost to renovate the home would be $102,500. To this amount plaintiff added a general contractor's fee of 20% and the cost of work he had already done to the property. This brought his expected renovation sub-total to $126,997. When plaintiff added fees, taxes and the cost of borrowing, his "total estimate" for renovating the home was $141,500. ***

To establish economic hardship under the Ordinance, plaintiff offered testimony as to what the real estate market would support in the area surrounding the Glavin house. He provided "real estate comps" showing houses of a similar size and style selling at prices between $200,000 and $330,000. He noted that these figures were for houses that each had features the renovated Glavin house would not have. *** One house, just five houses away from the Glavin house, was characterized as a particularly good comparison. It included a breakfast room, a fifth bedroom, foyer, completely new master bath, a finished third floor, basement and rec room—all features the Glavin house did not have—and was listed at a selling price of $330,000. Plaintiff testified that, based on the estimated costs of renovation and the real estate market in the area, it would simply not be possible to sell the Glavin house for anything approaching $388,000.

When asked about the market value of the Glavin property as a vacant lot, plaintiff testified that he had no opinion, except to say that he was willing to pay $227,500 for it. When asked about whether he knew of the existence of the Ordinance when he purchased the property, plaintiff testified that he knew there was an ordinance, but that he was unaware of its specifics.

Several neighbors testified in favor of plaintiff's application *** that the property had been steadily deteriorating over many years. *** In opposition to the plaintiff's application, the Village presented the testimony of its Chief Building Inspector, Robert Borman. Borman testified that he had inspected the Glavin property and had given consideration to six specific areas. These were the overall condition of the building, the foundation, the heating plant, the electrical system, the plumbing system and the roof. *** Borman concluded that, "[A]lthough the house is in need of a lot of rehabilitation, my findings show that the house is structurally sound." In Borman's experience, "the building should not be considered a candidate for demolition."

Ms. Lois Merrill testified that she was an experienced licensed real estate agent doing business in Oak Park since 1974. Although Merrill was not an appraiser, she testified that part of her job was to help sellers determine what an appropriate price would be for the sale of a given home. In that context, she had prepared a market value report which showed that one property near the Glavin home had been purchased for $137,500 in 1991 and then rehabbed and sold in 1993 for $268,000. Another property had been purchased for $176,500 in 1994 and then resold for $335,000 after rehabilitation. Merrill reviewed several local properties and noted that they had been selling for between $245,000 and $330,000.

Merrill testified that she had inspected the house and determined that, if it were to be sold "as is," it would sell between $160,000 and $180,000. She stated that if the property were rehabbed, it "might sell for a range between $280,000 and $300,000." ***

A third witness for the Village was Mr. Mark Alger. He testified that he was the Construction Technologist for the Village's Single Family Homeowner Program. Mr. Alger had extensive experience in the construction and rehabilitation industry. Alger described the mission of the Single Family Home Program as bringing houses that are in the program up to Village Code and to what HUD refers to as "Housing Quality Standards." Alger used this same criteria in evaluating the Glavin home. He explained that, because of HUD's lower standards, there were disparities between what he would estimate a rehabilitation would cost and the costs plaintiff had estimated. *** In Alger's view, the cost of rehabilitating the property would be $61,350, a figure which included both a 15% contingency and general contractor's fees. He admitted that one could "easily add another $25,000" to the renovations to make the home more marketable, but that these costs were not necessary to meet HUD's Home Quality Standards.

Following the testimony plaintiff made his closing argument and the Commissioners discussed the merits of both granting and denying plaintiff's application. The Commission then voted to deny the application. Subsequently, in a written decision, the Commission found that the plaintiff had failed to establish that the house was incapable of being put to any reasonable use or that he could not obtain a reasonable economic return from the property without first demolishing the building. The Commission also found that the building was structurally sound, although in need of extensive rehabilitation costing between $60,000 and $253,000. *The Commission noted that there had been no substantial change in economic circumstances of the property since plaintiff purchased it and, therefore, any difficulty plaintiff encountered in obtaining a reasonable economic return on his purchase would be unaffected by the demolition of the building. The Commission concluded that any economic hardship placed upon the plaintiff had been brought about, at least in part, by his own actions* (emphasis added)[.]

The Village notified the plaintiff of the Commission's decision by letter dated September 26, 1995. The plaintiff timely appealed the decision to the Village Board of Trustees. Following a hearing on November 6, 1995, the Village Board adopted the Commission's findings.

On December 14, 1995, the plaintiff sought administrative review in the circuit court. On October 1, 1996, the circuit court reversed the Village and entered judgment in favor of the plaintiff. The court specifically noting that the building had been allowed to deteriorate for more than 30 years and determined that the rehabilitation of the building would cause plaintiff an economic hardship. The court also determined that the Commission should not have considered whether the plaintiff's economic hardship was self-imposed, at least absent a finding of an intent by him to circumvent the Ordinance. The Village brought this timely appeal.

As we have noted, the Ordinance precludes the issuance of a demolition permit until the issuance of a Certificate of Appropriateness or Certificate of Economic Hardship. Village of Oak Park Municipal Code, §7-9-9 (eff. January 1, 1994). A Certificate of Economic Hardship is defined by the Ordinance as:

> "A certificate issued by the Commission, after denying a certificate of appropriateness, which authorizes the performance of alterations, construction or relocation with regard to historic landmarks, or the removal or demolition of an historic landmark or a building, structure or improvement within an historic district when such historic landmarks, or properties within an historic district cannot be put to a reasonable beneficial use or the owner cannot obtain a reasonable economic return thereon without the proposed alteration, construction, relocation, removal or demolition."

We begin our analysis of the Ordinance by noting that it is the function of the appellate court to determine only whether the Commission's findings and decision which were adopted by the Board are against the manifest weight of the evidence. *Mitchell v. Sackett,* 27 Ill.App.2d 335, 343, 169 N.E.2d 833 (1960). *** Moreover, in reviewing the record, we are mindful that a Certificate of Economic Hardship is an exception to the general prohibition against demolishing contributing architectural resources located within the District. Thus, the burden at the hearing was squarely upon the plaintiff, the party seeking the certificate. *See Pontiac Lodge,* 243 Ill.App.3d at 192–93 ***, citing *Methodist Old Peoples Home v. Korzen,* 39 Ill.2d 149, 155, 233 N.E.2d 537 (1968). In determining whether property is included within the scope of an exemption, all facts are to be construed and all debatable questions resolved against granting the exemption. *See City of Chicago v. Illinois Department of Revenue,* 147 Ill.2d 484, 491–92, 168 Ill.Dec. 841, 590 N.E.2d 478 (1992).

*** [R]eversal is appropriate only when the opposite conclusion of the one reached by the Commission is "clearly evident." *Madonia v. Houston,* 125 Ill.App.3d 713, 716, 81 Ill.Dec. 62, 466 N.E.2d 648 (1984). If the record contains any evidence supporting the Commission's decision to deny the certificate, the decision must be sustained on review. *Fagiano v. Police Board,* 123 Ill.App.3d 963, 974, 79 Ill.Dec. 291, 463 N.E.2d 845 (1984).

Plaintiff argues that, under the terms of the Ordinance and with regard to the Glavin property, he "cannot obtain a reasonable economic return thereon without the proposed *** demolition." In our view, however, the evidence presented to the Commission was merely conflicting and therefore sufficient to support the Commission's ultimate determination.

The Ordinance lists five factors to be considered by the Commission in determining whether a certificate should be issued. In the context of the facts presented, where the Commission did not make any specific recommendations to the plaintiff for changes which would allow the granting of a Certificate of Appropriateness, only the following four factors are relevant:[1] (1) a substantial decrease in the fair market value of the property as a result of the denial of the certificate of appropriateness; (2) the structural soundness of any structures on the property and their suitability for rehabilitation; (3) the economic feasibility of rehabilitation or reuse of the existing structure or improvement on the property in the case of proposed demolition; and (4) the cost of the proposed construction, alteration, relocation or demolition. *See* Village of Oak Park Municipal Ordinance, §7-9-14 (eff. January 1, 1994).

Plaintiff failed to produce any evidence with regard to whether the denial of the Certificate of Appropriateness resulted in a substantial decrease in the property's fair market value. He stated repeatedly that he was not relying upon his purchase price to establish a fair market value for the Glavin property. Accordingly, this factor does not support his application.

With regard to the structural soundness of the Glavin house, all of the evidence supports the Village's decision. Robert Borman, the Village Chief Building Inspector, found that the building was deteriorating in many areas but he concluded that the building was structurally sound. The plaintiff's own evidence showed the building could be rehabilitated to Code requirements without work on the supporting structure of the house.

With regard to the feasibility of rehabilitation or use of the existing structure, we make several observations. First, plaintiff bases his entire case on a claim that the house was unmarketable at a reasonable price as a rehabilitation opportunity, yet we cannot help but note that plaintiff was unwilling to list the property so as to put his assertion of unmarketability to the test. The inference created by plaintiff's failure to list the property for sale is clearly one that must be held against his claim of unmar-

---

1. The Ordinance also states that the Commission may consider "a substantial decrease in the pre-tax or after-tax return to owners of record or other investors in the property as a result of the denial of the certificate of appropriateness."

ketability. Indeed, he admitted at the hearing that he purchased the property at what the market might consider an inflated price for rehabilitation precisely because he feared that the house would be purchased and that the new owner would expand it into the backyard. As the Village argues, if plaintiff can receive market value for the building in the same real estate market as when he purchased it, there can be no economic hardship as a result of the denial of his request to demolish the building.

Our second observation is that plaintiff only offered evidence as to what it would cost to renovate the house without adding square footage. Plaintiff's evidence leaves unresolved the question of whether the Village would have allowed a Certificate of Appropriateness for an addition to the house, as opposed to a complete tear-down *** [W]here an extension to the back of the Glavin house was proposed, it is quite possible that the plaintiff could recoup his investment.

Third, the evidence is far from clear that the house is incapable of being rehabbed and sold at a profit, at least if plaintiff had not deliberately overbid. In his brief plaintiff concedes that the property's fair market value was approximately $190,000 at the time he bought it for $227,500, but he insists that no one would willingly purchase the home as an investment at the $190,000 price. *** The fact that Colleen Myra offered to purchase the house in its dilapidated state for $200,000 is particularly damaging to plaintiff's argument. ***

Finally, with regard to the costs associated with the plaintiff's proposed renovation to the property, we note that he has failed to suggest the economic costs of leveling the Glavin house and building the new garage. These costs are important to consider because whether a Certificate of Economic Hardship should be granted under the Ordinance depends, in part, on whether demolishing the Glavin house will have the effect of lessening the economic burden of owning the property, a burden which may exist independently of whether demolition is allowed or denied. To this extent, the question is not so narrow as whether plaintiff can recover his out-of-pocket costs or make a profit by rehabilitating the Glavin property. Rather, the proper comparison must take into account all of the economic effects of plaintiff's proposal, including the net economic effect the proposed use of the Glavin lot will have on the value of plaintiff's existing home.

*** When all the costs are properly considered, it becomes clear that renovating the Glavin house for resale might be the best economic course for plaintiff *even if* a demolition permit were granted by the Commission, and *even if* renovating the property would mean plaintiff would suffer an out-of-pocket loss on his purchase of the Glavin property. *** In our view, the fact that plaintiff is willing to bear the more severe economic consequences of one course of action but not of the other is simply not relevant to an "economic" consideration of the hardship question. Assume, for example, that the house has a fair market value of $ 350,000, and that the Glavin house has a fair market value of $ 200,000. Assume further that, after buying the Glavin property for $ 200,000 and spending $ 50,000 to tear it down and erect a new garage such as the one designed by plaintiff's architect, the fair market value of the combined properties would be $ 500,000. Under this scenario, plaintiff would be proposing to spend $ 250,000 to obtain a potential economic benefit of only $ 150,000, thus causing him to suffer a $ 100,000 loss in value on the transaction. If the evidence establishes that renovating the Glavin house and selling the property to a third party would cause a loss in value to plaintiff of $ 80,000, or even one of $ 90,000, renovating the Glavin house would still make economic sense over demolishing it and erecting a garage. This is because renovating and selling the Glavin property would produce a lesser economic loss than annexing the Glavin lot, tearing down the Glavin house and building a garage. Moreover, the resale of the renovated Glavin property would have the benefit to the Village of preserving one of the District's contributing architectural resources, the central purpose of the Village's Ordinance. In our view, the fact that plaintiff is willing to bear the more severe economic consequences of one course of action but not of the other is simply not relevant to an "economic" consideration of the hardship question.

In sum, we find evidence presented to the Commission to have been sufficient to sustain the decision of the Village Board. This being the case, the Commission's refusal to grant plaintiff a Certificate of Economic Hardship is affirmed.

Circuit Court Reversed. Board of Trustees of the Village of Oak Park Affirmed.

Notes and Questions

1. **The best result.** Zaruba lost the case because he could not show that he would suffer a greater economic loss from renovating the house than from demolishing it. Were his declared reasons for purchasing the house, which was subject to the historic ordinance, but badly in need of rehabilitation, at an inflated price, relevant to his later claim of economic hardship?

2. **Market test.** The estimates of the value of the house varied widely. Why did Zaruba refuse to put the house up for sale, in its dilapidated condition?

3. **National Trust for Historic Preservation guidelines.** The National Trust has promulgated guidelines to local commissions and other regulatory agencies when assessing economic hardship claims. Assessing Economic Hardship Claims Under Historic Preservation Ordinances, NTHP PRESERVATION LAW REPORTER EDUCATIONAL MATERIALS (2005). The guidelines state that at a minimum, the following five questions should be asked:

> Is the evidence sufficient? Does the commission have all the information it needs to understand the entire picture, or is something missing. The application is not complete unless all the required information has been submitted. If additional information is needed, ask for it.
>
> Is the evidence relevant? Weed out any information that is not relevant to the issue of economic hardship in the case before you. Commissions may be given more information than they need or information on issues that are not germane to the issue, such as how much money the project could make if the historic property were demolished. The property owner is not entitled to the highest and best use of the property.

Is the evidence competent? Make an assessment as to whether the evidence establishes what it purports to show.

Is the evidence credible? Consider whether the evidence is believable. For example, ask whether the figures make sense. A commission will need to take into consideration the source of the evidence and its reliability. (If the evidence is based on expert testimony, the commission should determine whether the expert is biased or qualified on the issue being addressed. For example, it may matter whether a contractor testifying on rehabilitation expenditures actually has experience in doing historic rehabilitations.)

Is the evidence consistent? Look for inconsistencies in the testimony or the evidence submitted. Request that inconsistencies be explained. If there is contradictory evidence, the commission needs to determine which evidence is credible and why.

E. Enforcement of Designation Standards

In order for historic properties and the districts that contain them to serve the purposes of building community, making places legible, and providing a sense of place, *see* Carol Rose, *Preservation and Community*, 33 Stan. L. Rev. 473, 479–80 (1981), they must be maintained as such. All of the identified values from preservation are lost when historic properties are demolished and the entire sense of community vanishes. Demolition by neglect occurs when an owner allows his property to suffer severe deterioration, potentially beyond the point of repair. Neglect can be unintentional owing to the owner's lacking the financial means or worldly presence to maintain the property, or as an intentional strategy to evade the regulations. In the latter scenario, an owner desiring to build new developments in place of a historic building would allow the property to become severely deteriorated, then request a demolition permit on the basis that the enormous cost of repair creates an economic hardship. Historic preservation ordinances and regulations respond to both kinds of neglect and contain affirmative maintenance provisions, with specific language about required repairs and remedies with adequate means to enforce them. *See* National Trust for Historic, Preservation Law Reporter, *Educational Materials: Demolition by Neglect* (2005). To thwart intentional neglect, the ordinances look beyond a simple comparison of the cost of repairs vis-à-vis the market value of the property when considering demolition requests; but also require consideration of the historic attributes of the building and its contribution to the district as a whole.

The New York City Landmarks Preservation Law requires owners to keep the interior and exterior of their buildings in "good repair" to prevent deterioration or decay, meaning structurally sound, watertight, to ensure that significant architectural features are secure and not at risk. N.Y. City Admin. Code §§ 25-311(a), (b); 25-302(x). Any violation of this requirement can be punished by a fine of not more than $1,000 and not less than $500, or by imprisonment of not more than thirty days.

Each day that the violation persists constitutes a separate offense. *See* §§ 25-317(b) & (d). Violators may also be subject to a civil penalty which may be recovered in a civil action in any competent court or by an administrative hearing. The owner may be liable for: the fair market value of the property (with or without improvement); double the cost of replicating the features that were demolished; or an amount not more than $5,000. *See* §§ 25-317.1; 25-317.2. In the first 35 years of the Landmarks Preservation Law's existence, only one demolition by neglect case was brought, *City of New York v. 10-12 Cooper Square, Inc.*, 7 Misc.3d 253, 793 N.Y.S.2d 688 (N.Y. Supp. 2004) (discussed below). In all cases, the Landmarks Preservation Commission's approach is to work with the owner to accomplish repairs, rather than prosecute for violations. The average time-frame owners are given to make repairs after promising to do so is six months. New York has established the Historic Preservation Grant Program that provides funds up to $30,000 to not for profit and income eligible landowners for repairs to historic properties. The grants are funded by the Department of Housing and Urban Development Community Development Block Grant Program.

Notes

1. **Economic hardship to excuse maintenance.** In 1990 the City of Portland, Maine, adopted its Historic Preservation Ordinance. Under the authority of the Historic Preservation Ordinance, in February 1991, the Tracy-Causer Building was nominated as a Landmark and formally designated as one on September 4, 1991. Built around 1866 in downtown Portland, the Tracy Causer is thought to be one of the few remaining buildings in the city built immediately after the Great Fire. At the time of the designation, the building was in a decrepit condition, so the city issued an order on September 20, 1991, requiring certain repairs to be made to the building. At the time of the designation, the building was owned by the Tracy-Causer Associates ("T.C.A."). It was vacant, in an uninhabitable condition, and presented a public hazard to the extent that people were not able to enter the building and roam about within it. On October 1, 1991, the City filed a complaint in the District Court pursuant to Rule 80K to have the repair order enforced. Though T.C.A. did not originally challenge the designation, they had not made any of the requested repairs, and instead filed for a certificate of economic hardship so they would be able to demolish the building, as per the Ordinance. Subsequently, on August 26, 1992, T.C.A. withdrew the application; instead, they took issue with the enforcement of the city's repair order, requiring them to spend money on a building from which they could reap no benefit.

The repairs directed by the city were aimed at preventing the building from falling down. There were two main reasons for the order: 1) "to have the building secured against entry, to protect the public" and 2) "to stabilize the building and prevent substantial deterioration of the structure." *City of Portland v. Tracy-Causer Associates, Inc.*, Docket No. 91-LU-006, 3 (Dist. 9, Division of So. Cumberland, 1993). Without the requested repairs, the building would have continued its course of deterioration, and at least one outside structural wall was in danger of collapse, which would have effectively demolished the structure. The repairs ordered by the City would "cost the owners of the building approximately $100,000.00 to complete." *Id.* at 4. While assisting in the preservation of the building, those expenditures would not come close to returning the building to habitability. A T.C.A. estimate, found to be reasonable by the court, proved an additional $1.5 million was needed to sufficiently rehabilitate the building for occupancy. Despite this fact, the City had neither offered to help pay for the repairs, nor proposed to acquire the building from the owners, with or without compensation; though the City did not request costs, attorney's fees, or a fine assessment against the building's owners, recognizing the preservation expense.

The Maine Constitution, much like the federal Constitution, asserts that "private property shall not be taken for public uses without just compensation, nor unless the public exigencies require it." M.E. Const., art. I, § 21. T.C.A. claimed that the repair order, which required the expenditure for the preservation not for their benefit, is an unconstitutional taking under the Maine and federal Constitutions. The City took the position that "it has the authority under the Historic Preservation Ordinance to order the expenditure of funds to prevent the owners of a historic landmark from doing by lack of action that which they have received no permit to do by affirmative action, namely, demolish the building." *Tracy-Causer Associates, Inc.*, at 5.

The Maine District Court made three important findings regarding the repair order: 1) "the building in its current state [was] not commercially useful in any way," 2) "the repairs ordered by the city would bring no economic benefit whatsoever to the owners of the building," and 3) "the building owners [were] asked to expend significant funds, solely for the benefit of the public." *Tracy-Causer Associates, Inc.*, at 8. The Court further found that the property was rendered "substantially useless," *Hall v. The Board of Environmental Protection*, 528 A.2d 453, 455 (Me. 1987), and deprived the defendant of all "economically beneficial use" of its property. *Lucas v. South Carolina Coastal Council*, 505 U.S. 1003, 1007, 112 S.Ct. 2886, 2899 (1992).

For its ruling, the court cited the opinion of the Fifth Circuit in *Maher v. City of New Orleans*, 516 F.2d 1051, 1066 (5th Cir. 1975), noting that "[e]ven if it comports with due process, a regulatory ordinance may nonetheless be a taking if it is unduly onerous so as to be confiscatory." *Tracy-Causer Associates, Inc.*, at 7 (citing *Maher v. City of New Orleans*, 516 F.2d at 1065). Since the required expenditure, from the building's owners to preserve the building would not provide a premises which could be rented or inhabited, the Court found it to be "inordinately burdensome." *Tracy-Causer Associates, Inc.*, at 8. The Court further ruled that where the owner of real property is required to expend large sums on economically useless property, it has effectuated a *Lucas* style taking, depriving the owner of all economic use of the property; if the City seeks to preserve an historic building which is otherwise inhabitable, it must be prepared to compensate for such a burden. Lastly though, the Court found that the costs associated with securing the building against entry and removing vegetation did not effectuate a taking, and so T.C.A. would be required to pay for the implementation of this order.

Luckily, the Tracy-Causer building still stands today. In 1995, the building was bought by real-estate developer Stephen Goodrich for $670,000, who sold it in 2002 for $1.9 million after a $500,000 renovation. Sara Donnelly, *An Optimist Gambles*

On High-Profile Properties, Mainebiz, February, 9, 2009, http://www.mainebiz.biz/news44112.html (last visited September 7, 2017). On one of the walls of his office, Goodrich has a photograph of the Tracy-Causer building when he first bought it, a graffiti-covered, boarded-up brick edifice. *Id.* Below that photograph, is another more recent photograph that shows the boards replaced by large windows, the graffiti gone, the brick cleaned, and the trim neatly painted. *Id.* A testament to what can be accomplished through historic preservation.

See also Buttnick v. City of Seattle, 719 P.2d 93, 95 (Wash. 1986) (requiring owner to replace a defective parapet on an historic building did not result in economic hardship).

2. **Maintenance of landmark building in a state of good repair.** In *City of New York v. 10-12 Cooper Square, Inc.*, 7 Misc.3d 253, 793 N.Y.S.2d 688 (N.Y. Supp. 2004), the New York City Landmarks Preservation Commission brought an action to compel the owners of a 159-year-old Greek revival residence called the Skidmore House, to restore the building, landmarked in 1970, to "good repair." The Commission claimed that, "since acquiring the Skidmore House in 1988, the defendants have failed to maintain it and have allowed it to deteriorate to such an extent that its roof collapsed and the architectural elements that make it a landmark are at risk of being lost." *Id.* at 254. The Commission sought to compel the defendants to undertake work to preserve the landmark, including: "(1) mak[ing] the exterior of the building watertight so as to prevent deterioration, decay, damage, or disrepair; (2) maintain[ing] the significant architectural elements on the exterior to prevent deterioration, decay, damage or disrepair; and (3) maintain[ing] all of the interior of the building to avoid deterioration, decay, damage or disrepair." *Id.* In response, the owners argued that the Skidmore House was never designated as a landmark, the premises were in good repair, and that the Commission's definition of good repair is too unreasonable. *Id.*

With regard to the legality of the landmark designation, the Court ruled that although the Commission may have failed to provide public notice of the vote at the designation meeting, the amount of evidence put forth by the Commission confirms the Commission's action and the Board of Estimate's resolution. *Id.* at 255. The Commission presented to the Court "a certified copy of the minutes of the [designation meeting], dated August 18, 1970, designating the Skidmore House as a landmark, and a certified copy of the minutes of the Board of Estimate's resolution of October 8, 1970 approving the designation ... of the Skidmore House as a landmark." *Id.* at 254. The owners submitted records establishing that "there was no notice in the City Record of the calendaring of this matter before the Commission on August 18, 1970 for a vote." *Id.* at 255. Though the owners argued that the failure to give notice was fatal to the designation, because it may suggest that it was never taken, the Court noted that there is a strong presumption that "no official or person acting under oath of office will do anything contrary to his official duty, or omit anything which his official duty requires to be done." *Id.* "Substantial eviden[tiary support] is required to overcome th[is] presumption of legality." *Id.* Since the Court found that the defendants had not put forth substantial evidence of irregular conduct, the landmark designation was upheld. *Id.*

Next, turning to the landmark requirement to remain in "good repair," the court pointed out that the New York City Administrative Code § 25-311(a) specifies the requirement as keeping in good repair: "(1) all of the exterior portions of such improvement and (2) all interior portions thereof which, if not so maintained, may cause or tend to cause the exterior portions of such improvement to deteriorate, decay or become damaged or otherwise to fall into a state of disrepair." *Id.* at 255–56. Since this case was one of first impression, the Court decided that "whether or not the Skidmore House has been kept in a state of 'good repair' is ... a matter to be determined by the Commission" and that "[c]ourts will defer to a determination of an administrative agency when that decision falls under the purview of the agency's expertise." *Id.* at 257–58. The Court said it would "only intervene where an agency's determination is unreasonable..., or lacks a rational basis." Numerous inspections of the property from 1995 to 2003 had revealed the building's state of disrepair. The most recent Building Department Inspection, conducted in February 2003, found:

> ... [T]he building to be open at the roof at the front portion of the building exposing the interior to the weather, there was a beam spanning across the fireplace carrying a few floor joists (and this was typical [throughout] all floors). Due to extensive water damage this beam gave way collapsing only the floor joists in front of the fireplace at all floors. The exterior building walls and chimney show no signs of distress or cracking. There were approximately seven roof beams missing (could have been removed during construction). In conclusion, the building appeared in line and plumb, structurally sound and with proper safety measures can be repaired, renovated, and reoccupied.

Id. at 257. Though in the course of litigation, the defendants repaired the roof, the Court decided that the Commission's interpretation of the state of disrepair was "reasonable, rational, and was substantiated by the evidence presented at the hearing." *Id.* at 258. An examination of the building and examination report, conducted and written by the Director of the Historic Preservation Grant Program, set forth the steps necessary to keep the façade in "good repair." *Id.* at 257.

Lastly, the defendants argued that the obligation to preserve the building in "good repair" only applied to the building's state at the time of the designation. *Id.* at 258. In response, the Court remarked that even if they were "to accept that defendants' obligation is limited to maintaining the landmark in its condition at the time of designation, the evidence is clear that defendants have allowed the facade of the Skidmore House to deteriorate." *Id.* The Court determined that all actions by the defendants were insufficient to keep the designated Skidmore House in "good repair"; accordingly, the Court decided that the defendants would have to bring the building into "good repair" after a current inspection and assessment to be conducted by the Commission. *Id.* at 258–59.

F. State Building and Fire Codes

Some states have enacted special building codes applicable to historic properties, recognizing the unique construction issues inherent in maintaining and adaptively reusing historic buildings. Many have adopted Appendix J (regulating historic structures) of the International Building Codes, which forms the model for codes around the nation.

The California Historic Building Code ("CHBC"), HEALTH & SAFETY CODE, §§ 18950 to 18961, provides alternative building regulations for permitting repairs, alterations, and additions necessary for the preservation, rehabilitation, relocation, related construction, change of use, or continued use of a qualified historical building or structure. Among other things, the CHBC exempts historic structures from local fire standards that are more stringent than state standards; exempts them from generally applicable plumbing efficiency standards; and permits the use of wood covering materials that meet certain benchmarks. The law generally reserves to building and fire officials the power to perform their duties in the process of protecting the public health, safety, and welfare. *See also* New Jersey Rehab Subcode, N.J. ADMIN. CODE § 5:23-6 (offering guidance on the rehabilitation of historic buildings, among others, including the use of replica materials and building elements that may meet relaxed code requirements in order to preserve the historic value and integrity of an historic building); New York Uniform Fire Prevention and Building Code, 19 NYCRR Part 1219–1227, https://www.dos.ny.gov/dcea/pdf/2016%20DOS_UniformCodeSupplement_03212016.pdf (last visited April 3, 2017) (including Appendix J for special provisions for historic buildings).

Chapter 4

Federal Historic Heritage Law: Archaeology on Public Lands and in Historic Buildings

A. Antiquities Act of 1906

The Antiquities Act of 1906, 54 U.S.C. §320301, [formerly 16 U.S.C §431], signed into law by President Theodore Roosevelt, was landmark legislation because it established the mechanisms for preserving important cultural sites and natural areas on a grand scale. The President's proclamation of a national monument withdraws that area from exploration and development. Before the enactment, Congress protected such resources through the creation of national parks; Yellowstone was the first one, created in 1872 (ironically the same year as the enactment of the Mining Law of 1872 that allowed mineral exploration on federal lands). Within months of the passage of the Antiquities Act, President Roosevelt declared Devils Tower in Wyoming as a national monument, and before he left office, he had declared a total of eighteen. The case that follows reveals the interesting story behind the Act's enactment and use over its hundred-year history.

Utah Association of Counties v. Bush

United States District Court for the District of Utah, Central Division
316 F. Supp. 2d 1172, 11 A.L.R.Fed.2d 917 (2004)

Introduction

Benson, D.J. The present matter comes before the Court on defendants' Motion to Dismiss or in the alternative for Summary Judgment and plaintiffs' Motions for Summary Judgment. The motions were argued before the Court on January 15, 2004. The Court has considered the legal briefs and oral arguments of the respective parties and enters the following Opinion and Order.

Background

A. The Lawsuits and their Contentions

On September 18, 1996, President William Jefferson Clinton, invoking his authority under the Antiquities Act, designated 1.7 million acres of federal land in southeastern

Utah as the Grand Staircase-Escalante National Monument. On June 23, 1997, the Utah Association of Counties, (UAC) filed this lawsuit challenging the President's actions, naming as defendants the United States of America, William J. Clinton in his official capacity as President of the United States, Kathleen McGinty in her official capacity as chair of the Council on Environmental Quality (CEQ), Secretary of the Interior Bruce Babbitt, the United States Department of the Interior (DOI), and Patrick Shea, Director of the Bureau of Land Management (BLM).

On November 5, 1997 Mountain States Legal Foundation (MSLF) filed a similar suit against defendants Clinton, Babbitt, and the United States of America. A month later, MSLF filed an amended complaint, which added defendant McGinty. UAC's and MSLF's cases were consolidated.[1]

Plaintiffs allege:

1) The Antiquities Act is unconstitutional because it violates the delegation doctrine. Plaintiffs claim that only Congress has the authority to withdraw such lands from the federal trust.

2) By creating the Grand Staircase Monument the President acted *ultra vires* and violated the following provisions of the United States Constitution:

a) the Property Clause, U.S. Const., Art. IV, § 3, cl. 2; because the authority to manage federal lands rests exclusively with Congress; and

b) the Spending Clause, U.S. Const., Art. I, § 8, cl. 1; because only Congress has the authority to obligate money which will be drawn from the Treasury to purchase private property.

3) By creating the Grand Staircase Monument the President violated:

a) the Antiquities Act, 16 U.S.C. § 431; because he failed to designate the requisite objects of historic or scientific value and he did not limit the size of the monument to the "smallest area" necessary to preserve the objects....

c) Executive Order 10355, because the President, rather than the Secretary of the Interior, withdrew the land....

Both plaintiffs seek summary judgment as to all of the above claims.

All of the defendants seek dismissal or in the alternative summary judgment as to all claims. They challenge the Court's jurisdiction to hear the case under the doctrines of standing (as to MSLF only), ripeness and lack of judicial review authority. As to the plaintiffs' claims of violations of the United States Constitution and federal statutes, the defendants seek dismissal as a matter of law.

---

1. Pursuant to Federal Rules of Civil Procedure 25(d)(1), defendants have since been substituted to reflect a presidential and administration change. Current individual defendants are now President George W. Bush; CEQ Chair James L. Connaughton; Department of the Interior Secretary Gale Norton and Bureau of Land Management Director Kathleen Clarke.

1. The Antiquities Act

The Antiquities Act of 1906, 16 U.S.C. § 431, gives the President authority to create national monuments.[2] Since its enactment, presidents have used the Antiquities Act more than 100 times to withdraw lands from the public domain as national monuments. President Clinton's use of the Antiquities Act to create the Grand Staircase Monument in 1996 was the first use of the Antiquities Act in more than two decades. The Antiquities Act authorizes the President, "in his discretion," to establish as national monuments "objects of historic or scientific interest that are situated upon the lands owned or controlled by the government of the United States." *Id.* The Act requires the president to reserve land confined to the "smallest area compatible with the proper care and management of the objects to be protected." *Id.* For purposes of this litigation, it is helpful to look to the creation of the Act and how it has been used and interpreted since its creation in 1906.

The original purpose of the proposed Act was to protect objects of antiquity.[3] The substance of the Act, developed over a period of more than six years, was created in response to the demands of archaeological organizations. Although the scope of the archaeological organizations' proposals was limited to preservation of antiquities on federal lands, the United States Department of the Interior proposed adding the protection of scenic and scientific resources to the Act. For six years Congress rejected attempts to include the Department's proposal. It appears, however, that Congress was unable to pass the limited archaeologists' bill because of bureaucratic delays and various disagreements between museums and universities seeking authority to excavate ruins on public lands. *See* Richard M. Johannsen, *Public Land Withdrawal Policy and the Antiquities Act,* 56 Wash. L.Rev. 439, 448 (1981).

---

2. The full text of the Act reads as follows:

> The President of the United States is authorized, in his discretion, to declare by public proclamation historic landmarks, historic and prehistoric structures, and other objects of historic or scientific interest that are situated upon the lands owned or controlled by the Government of the United States to be national monuments, and may reserve as a part thereof parcels of land, the limits of which in all cases shall be confined to the smallest area compatible with the proper care and management of the objects to be protected. When such objects are situated upon a tract covered by a bona fide unperfected claim or held in private ownership, the tract, or so much thereof as may be necessary for the proper care and management of the object, may be relinquished to the Government, and the Secretary of the Interior is authorized to accept the relinquishment of such tracts in behalf of the Government of the United States.

16 U.S.C. § 431 (1976).

3. The phrase "objects of antiquity," while not in § 431 but found in § 433, has commonly been interpreted to include such items as paleontological and archaeological artifacts. When interpreting its precise meaning, however, courts have disagreed with the adequacy of the phrase. *See e.g., U.S. v. Diaz,* 499 F.2d 113, 114–5 (9th Cir.1974) (finding that the phrase "objects of antiquity" was "fatally vague in violation of the due process clause of the Constitution."); *but see U.S. v. Smyer,* 596 F.2d 939, 941 (10th Cir.1979) (holding that "when measured by common understanding and practice," the phrase was sufficiently definite to define the protected object).

Edgar Lee Hewitt, a prominent archaeologist, drafted the bill that was finally enacted in 1906. Government officials persuaded Hewitt to broaden the scope of his draft by including the phrase "other objects of historic or scientific interest." This phrase essentially allowed the Department of the Interior's proposal, which Congress had previously rejected, to be included in the final bill. In addition, while earlier proposals had limited the reservations to 320 or at the most 640 acres, Hewitt's draft allowed the limit to be set according to "the smallest area compatible with the proper care and management of the objects to be protected." Despite the presence of this broader language, there is some support for the proposition that Congress intended to limit the creation of national monuments to small land areas surrounding specific objects. Illustrative of this intent is House Report No. 2224, which states "[t]here are scattered throughout the southwest quite a large number of very interesting ruins ... [t]he bill proposes to create small reservations reserving only so much land as may be absolutely necessary for the preservation of these interesting relics." H.R. Rep. No. 2224, 59th congress, 1st sess. at 1 (1906).

Despite what may have been the intent of some members of Congress, use of the Antiquities Act has clearly expanded beyond the protection of antiquities and "small reservations" of "interesting ruins." Nothing in the language of the Act specifically authorizes the creation of national monuments for scenic purposes or for general conservation purposes. Nonetheless, several presidents have used the Act to withdraw large land areas for scenic and general conservation purposes. President Theodore Roosevelt was the first president to withdraw land under the Act, establishing a precedent other presidents later followed to create large scenic monuments. Within two years of enactment of the Act, President Roosevelt made eighteen withdrawals of land.[4]

Several monuments have been created within the general vicinity of the Grand Staircase Monument. In Utah alone, there are six such national monuments: Cedar Breaks, Hovenweep, Timpanogos Cave, Dinosaur, Rainbow Bridge, and Natural

4. The national monuments created by President Theodore Roosevelt:

9/24/06	Devils Tower, WY
12/8/06	El Morro, NM
12/8/06	Montezuma Castle, AZ
12/8/06	Petrified Forest, AZ
3/11/07	Chaco Canyon, NM
5/6/07	Cinder Cone, CA
5/6/07	Lassen Peak, CA
11/16/07	Gila Cliff Dwellings, NM
12/19/07	Tonto, AZ
1/9/08	Muir Woods, CA
1/11/08	Grand Canyon, AZ
1/16/08	Pinnacles, CA
2/7/08	Jewel Cave, SD
4/16/08	Natural Bridges, UT
5/11/08	Lewis and Clark Cavern, MT
9/15/08	Tumacacori, AZ
12/7/08	Wheeler, CO
3/2/09	Mount Olympus, WA

Bridges. Surrounding areas in Colorado and Arizona have also been designated as monuments under the Antiquities Act. Presidential proclamations creating these monuments cited geologic, paleontologic, archaeologic, and other features similar to those in the Grand Staircase Monument proclamation. Zion National Park to the west of the Grand Staircase Monument was originally Mukuntuweap National Monument, created by President Taft in 1909 to protect its "many natural features of unusual archaeologic, geologic, and geographic interest." *See* Proclamation No. 877, 36 Stat. 2498. President Wilson enlarged the boundaries of the monument in 1918 and Congress converted it to a national park in 1919.

* * *

Coincidentally, during the 1930s, the Franklin D. Roosevelt administration considered the creation of a monument in virtually the same area as the Grand Staircase Monument. President Roosevelt received a recommendation to withdraw 4.4. [M]illion acres of Utah's red rock country, creating Escalante National Monument. The Roosevelt administration ultimately rejected the idea, in large part because of local opposition. *See* James R. Rasband, *Utah's Grand Staircase: The Right Path to Wilderness Preservation?*, 70 U. Colo. L. Rev. 483, 488 (1999).

Most of the presidential withdrawals have been uncontroversial. However, there have been several legal challenges to presidential monument designations under the Antiquities Act. Every challenge to date has been unsuccessful. *See Cameron v. United States*, 252 U.S. 450, 40 S.Ct. 410, 64 L.Ed. 659 (1920) (the President's designation of the Grand Canyon as a national monument was a valid use of his authority under the Antiquities Act); *Wyoming v. Franke*, 58 F.Supp. 890 (D.Wyo.1945) (the proclamation creating the Jackson Hole National Monument complied with the standards set forth in the Antiquities Act); *Cappaert v. United States*, 426 U.S. 128, 96 S.Ct. 2062, 48 L.Ed.2d 523 (1976) (presidential proclamation withdrawing the Devil's Hole tract of land and accompanying water from the public domain and combining it with the Death Valley National Monument, explicitly reserved water rights to the federal Government and constituted a valid exercise of presidential authority under the Antiquities Act); *Anaconda Copper Co. v. Andrus*, No. A79-101 (D.Alaska, 1980); *Alaska v. Carter*, 462 F. Supp. 1155 (D.Alaska 1978) (president not subject to requirements of National Environmental Policy Act when proclaiming national monuments under the Antiquities Act).

* * *

3. *Events Leading to the Grand Staircase Proclamation*

From 1978 to 1991, the BLM conducted various studies which resulted in a recommendation that 1.9 million acres of WSAs in the state of Utah should receive wilderness designation. This recommendation, which included some of the land now part of the Grand Staircase Monument, was forwarded by then Secretary of the Interior Manuel Lujan to President George H.W. Bush in October, 1991. The recommendation was supported by a final EIS, and more than 11 years of BLM evaluation and public involvement. However, a change in presidential administrations in 1992 ended discussion about the proposed designation.

Regarding Utah wilderness, the new Secretary of the Interior, Bruce Babbitt, disagreed with the recommendations of his predecessor, believing significantly more land should be set aside.... Secretary Babbitt testified before Congress on several occasions, urging that a considerable number of additional wilderness areas should be designated in Utah. Consequently, the 104th Congress (1995–96) considered several different Utah wilderness bills, including a bill sponsored by members of Utah's congressional delegation which would designate about two million additional acres of wilderness, which was essentially the same as the previous recommendation from former Secretary Lujan. Also under consideration was a bill sponsored by Congressman Hinchey of New York and supported by national and Utah environmental groups. The Hinchey bill sought to designate 5.7 million acres of wilderness in Utah. Neither bill reached the floor of the House, and a filibuster precluded a vote in the Senate. Thereafter, Secretary Babbitt directed a second wilderness inventory, the Utah Wilderness Review, in hopes of showing that Congressman Hinchey's proposed 5.7 million acres bill warranted passage. This Utah Wilderness Review included the evaluation of the wilderness characteristics of approximately 800,000 acres of public land now part of the Grand Staircase Monument. Eventually, however, Secretary Babbitt's efforts, along with all other efforts made by those in Congress to establish wilderness in the state of Utah, were unsuccessful.

Plaintiffs contend in this litigation that the lack of success in the effort to designate additional wilderness areas in Utah was a motivating factor behind the President's decision to designate the Grand Staircase Monument. Once the proclamation was announced the affected land was preserved in much the same manner as if it had received wilderness designation.

Plaintiffs assert, and the record appears to support, that another driving force behind Secretary Babbitt's, the DOI's, and eventually the President's efforts to create the Grand Staircase Monument was to prevent the proposed Andalex Smoky Hollow coal mining operation in Kane County, Utah from coming to fruition.[5] Besides supporting Congressman Hinchey's proposed wilderness designation, which would encompass the property proposed for the Smoky Hollow Mine, Secretary Babbitt and the DOI also attacked the validity of the federal Smoky Hollow coal leases by attempting to cancel the suspension in the interest of conservation granted to the holders of the coal leases several years earlier by the Utah BLM State Director. The suspension was originally granted to allow Andalex sufficient time to secure mining permits and complete preparation of an EIS.

From the exhibits submitted by plaintiffs, the majority of which were secured by congressional subpoena, it appears that in early 1996, efforts involving various officials

---

5. The Andalex Smoky Hollow coal mine was designed as an underground mine, affecting approximately 60 acres of surface space, to be located on property that is part of the Kaiparaowits coal field. The Kaiparowits coal field is estimated by the Utah Geological Survey to contain 62.3 billion tons of coal, of which at least 11.3 billion tons could be recovered. The estimated total federal royalty payments over time from full production of Kaiparowits coal are approximately $20 billion, and the State of Utah and Utah counties would have been entitled to 50% of that amount under the Mineral Leasing Act.

within the executive branch of government began discussing the possibility of creating a national monument in Utah by way of a presidential proclamation. Internal memoranda indicate that as early as March 1996, the DOI requested that CEQ or White House officials send a letter to Secretary Babbitt under the President's signature requesting an investigation and recommendations for a Utah national monument. Plaintiffs assert that the reasoning behind the request was to enable defendants to avoid having to comply with NEPA and FLPMA, because the President is not a federal agency and not subject to either NEPA or FLPMA. An internal CEQ memorandum from Ms. McGinty to Todd Stern reveals even broader reasoning behind the request that the President sign a letter to be sent to Secretary Babbitt:

> the president will do the utah event on Aug. 17. however, we still need to get the letter (from the President to Interior Secretary Babbitt) signed asap. the reason: under the antiquities act, we need to build a credible record that will withstand legal challenge that: (1) the president asked the secretary to look into these lands to see if they are of important scientific, cultural, or historic value; (2) the secy undertook that review and presented the results to the president; (3) the president found the review compelling and therefore exercised his authority under the antiquities act. presidential actions under this act have always been challenged, they have never been struck down, however. so, letter needs to be signed asap so that secy has what looks like a credible amount of time to do his investigation of the matter. we have opened the letter with a sentence that gives us some more room by making it clear that the president and babbitt had discussed this some time ago [sic] (McGinty, e-mail to Todd Stern, July 29, 1996).

Plaintiffs allege that no such letter was sent to Secretary Babbitt.

From March 1996 to September 18, 1996, DOI officials worked closely with CEQ Director Kathleen McGinty and others to identify the lands to include in the proclamation and the actions needed to ensure that the proclamation would survive judicial scrutiny. In August 1996, the DOI conducted a database and bibliography search to prepare a record to support the proclamation. Some of the reasons for creating Grand Staircase Monument focused on the proposed Smoky Hollow coal mine and contentions that the mine would irreversibly damage the environment and Utah's public lands. These contentions, plaintiffs allege, were contradicted by the BLM's draft EIS.

Following this history, the Proclamation itself took place on September 18, 1996, when President Clinton stood at the south rim of the Grand Canyon in Arizona and announced the establishment of the 1.7 million acre Utah monument. There was virtually no advance consultation with Utah's federal or state officials, which may explain the decision to make the announcement in Arizona. The monument created a good deal of controversy, heightened even more because the presidential election was less than 8 weeks away. In making the announcement, President Clinton emphasized his "concern[ ] about a large coal mine proposed for the area" and his belief that "we shouldn't have mines that threaten our national treasures." *Remarks Announcing the*

Establishment of the Grand Staircase-Escalate National Monument, 32 Weekly Comp. Pres. Doc. 1785 (Sept. 23, 1996).

In the written Proclamation, President Clinton cited "geologic treasures" as the initial reason for creation of the monument. *See* Proclamation No. 6920, 61 Fed.Reg. 50,223 (1996). Specifically, the President noted "sedimentary rock layers ... offering a clear view to understanding the processes of the earth's formation" and "in addition to several major arches and natural bridges, vivid geological features are laid bare in narrow, serpentine canyons, where erosion has exposed sandstone and shale deposits in shades of red, maroon, chocolate, tan, gray, and white. Such diverse objects make the monument outstanding for purposes of geologic study." *Id.* Secondly, the President cited "world class paleontological sites" as grounds for the Proclamation. *Id.* According to the President, those things in need of protection consisted of "remarkable specimens of petrified wood" and "significant fossils, including marine and brackish water mollusks, turtles, crocodilians, lizards, dinosaurs, fishes, and mammals...." *Id.* Archeological interests in "Anasazi and Fremont cultures" were also said to be "of significant scientific and historic value worthy of preservation for future study." *Id.* Finally, the President mentioned the "spectacular array of unusual and diverse soils," "cryptobiotic crusts," and the "many different vegetative communities and numerous types of endemic plants and their pollinators" as warranting protection since "[m]ost of the ecological communities contained in the monument have low resistance to, and slow recovery from, disturbance." *Id.*

The President's Proclamation designating the monument required that the BLM prepare an approved Monument Management Plan no later than September 18, 1999. The approved Management Plan did not make the September deadline, but was finally approved on February 28, 2000. Since approval of the Monument Management Plan the BLM has been responsible for management of the Grand Staircase Monument.

* * *

B. *Discussion*

1. *Judicial Review*[6]

Plaintiffs seek a searching review by this court of the President's actions in creating the Grand Staircase Monument. Both plaintiffs claim the proclamation was *ultra vires* and unconstitutional. MSLF seeks a further determination that the President abused his discretion, asking in particular for a finding that the President violated the Antiquities Act by a) not properly designating objects of scientific or historic value, b)

6. With respect to the issue of standing to sue, the United States concedes that UAC has standing, but insists MSLF does not. The requirements for an initial showing sufficient to support standing in a case of this nature are relatively lenient, as set forth in *Utah v. Babbitt,* 137 F.3d 1193 (10th Cir.1998), *Colorado Environmental Coalition v. Wenker,* 353 F.3d 1221 (10th Cir.2004) and *Lujan v. Defenders of Wildlife,* 504 U.S. 555, 112 S.Ct. 2130, 119 L.Ed.2d 351 (1992). Given this relatively light burden at the present stage of the instant case and recognizing that many of the claims of UAC and MSLF are identical or similar, and in the interest of judicial economy the Court will not further address the standing question in this Opinion. While not expressly finding that MSLF has standing to sue, the Court will address all of the parties' claims, including those advanced solely by MSLF.

setting aside too much property, and c) using the Act for improper purposes, such as stopping a local coal mining operation and improperly creating wilderness areas. In conducting such a sweeping judicial review, the plaintiffs seek an interpretation of the Antiquities Act that requires a comprehensive examination of the Act's legislative history. The extensive judicial review sought by the plaintiffs is, however, not available in this case.

While there has been some debate among the United States Supreme Court justices as to whether judicial review of executive actions by the President are subject to judicial review at all,[7] recent judgments have indicated the Court's willingness to engage in a narrowly circumscribed form of judicial review. This willingness does not, however, allow judicial review of sufficient scope to assist plaintiffs' cause; long-standing United States Supreme Court precedent has clearly foreclosed the broad review for which plaintiffs contend:

> "Whenever a statute gives a discretionary power to any person, to be exercised by him upon his own opinion of certain facts, it is a sound rule of construction, that the statute constitutes him the sole and exclusive judge of the existence of those facts." For the judiciary to probe the reasoning which underlies this Proclamation would amount to a clear invasion of the legislative and executive domains.

United States v. George S. Bush & Co., 310 U.S. 371, 380, 60 S.Ct. 944, 84 L.Ed. 1259 (1940) (quoting *Martin v. Mott*, 25 U.S. 19, 12 Wheat. 19, 31–32, 6 L.Ed. 537 (1827)). A grant of discretion to the President to make particular judgments forecloses judicial review of the substance of those judgments altogether:

> [W]here a claim "concerns not a want of [Presidential] power, but a mere excess or abuse of discretion in exerting a power given, it is clear that it involves considerations which are beyond the reach of judicial power. This must be since, as this court has often pointed out, the judicial may not invade the legislative or executive departments so as to correct alleged mistakes or wrongs arising from asserted abuse of discretion."

Dalton v. Specter, 511 U.S. 462, 474, 114 S.Ct. 1719, 128 L.Ed.2d 497 (1994) (quoting *Dakota Central Telephone Co. v. South Dakota ex rel. Payne*, 250 U.S. 163, 184, 39 S.Ct. 507, 63 L.Ed. 910 (1919)).

*** Although judicial review is not available to assess a particular exercise of presidential discretion, a Court may ensure that a president was in fact exercising the authority

---

7. Justice Scalia's concurrence in *Franklin v. Massachusetts* articulates the most restrictive approach possible to the question of whether judicial review of the President's actions is permissible:

> I think we cannot issue a declaratory judgment against the President. It is incompatible with his constitutional position that he be compelled personally to defend his executive actions before a court.

505 U.S. 788, 827 (1992). In this formulation, presidential action can be reviewed by seeking an injunction against those bound to enforce a President's directive, but the possibility of direct judicial review of the President's decision, for which plaintiffs contend, is eliminated altogether as inconsistent with "the constitutional tradition of the separation of powers." *Id.* at 828, 112 S.Ct. 2767.

conferred by the act at issue. Thus ... the Court may still inquire into whether the President, when designating this Monument, acted pursuant to the Antiquities Act.

The Antiquities Act offers two principles to guide the President in making a designation under the Act:

> The President of the United States is authorized, in his discretion, to declare by public proclamation ... objects of historic or scientific interest ... to be national monuments, and may reserve as a part thereof parcels of land, the limits of which in all cases shall be confined to the smallest area compatible with the proper care and management of the objects to be protected.

16 U.S.C. §431. The Proclamation of which plaintiffs complain speaks in detail of the Monument's natural and archeological resources and indicates that the designated area is the smallest consistent with the protection of those resources. The language of the Proclamation clearly indicates that the President considered the principles that Congress required him to consider: he used his discretion in designating objects of scientific or historic value, and used his discretion in setting aside the smallest area necessary to protect those objects.

It is evident from the language of the Proclamation that the President exercised the discretion lawfully delegated to him by Congress under the Antiquities Act, and that finding demarcates the outer limit of judicial review.... This Court declines plaintiffs' invitation to substitute its judgment for that of the President, particularly in an arena in which the congressional intent most clearly manifest is an intention to delegate decision-making to the sound discretion of the President.[8]

---

8. Plaintiffs devote considerable space in their Memorandum in Support of their Motion for Summary Judgment to a discussion of congressional intent and the evidence for it. According to plaintiffs, the legislative history surrounding the passage of the Antiquities Act demonstrates that Congress intended the Act be used to protect man-made objects only, and was not intended to be available as a means for furthering presidential environmental agendas. (Plaintiffs' Combined Memo at 17 *et seq.*) Excerpts from floor debates before the Act's passage are also enlisted to prove that the Act was only intended to allow the President to withdraw very small plots of land to protect the man-made artifacts suitable for designation. *Id.* at 18. This discussion, while no doubt of interest to the historian, is irrelevant to the legal questions before the Court, since the plain language of the Antiquities Act empowers the President to set aside "objects of historic or scientific interest." 16 U.S.C. §431. The Act does not require that the objects so designated be made by man, and its strictures concerning the size of the area set aside are satisfied when the President declares that he has designated the smallest area compatible with the designated objects' protection. There is no occasion for this Court to determine whether the plaintiffs' interpretation of the congressional debates they quote is correct, since a court generally has recourse to congressional intent in the interpretation of a statute only when the language of a statute is ambiguous. *See Ardestani v. Immigration and Naturalization Service,* 502 U.S. 129, 135, 112 S.Ct. 515, 116 L.Ed.2d 496 (1991) ("The 'strong presumption' that the plain language of the statute expresses congressional intent is rebutted only in 'rare and exceptional circumstances,' when a contrary legislative intent is clearly expressed") (citations omitted).

In addition to the plain language of the statute, there is plain language on which this Court may rely in several United States Supreme Court decisions upholding particular designations of natural objects as national monuments under the Antiquities Act. In *Cameron v. United States* the Court quoted from the proclamation in which President Theodore Roosevelt designated the Grand Canyon: "The Grand Canyon, as stated in the Proclamation, 'is an object of unusual scientific interest.'" 252 U.S. 450, 455, 40 S.Ct. 410, 64 L.Ed. 659 (1920). Far from indicating that only man-made objects are suitable for designation, *Cameron* notes approvingly that the Canyon "affords an unexampled field for geologic study [and] is regarded as one of the great natural wonders." *Id.* at 456, 40 S.Ct. 410. The Court in *Cappaert v. United States* explicitly rejected the argument offered by the Plaintiffs before this Court: Petitioners ... argue ... [that] the President may reserve federal lands only to protect archeologic sites. However, the language of the Act which authorizes the President to [designate] national monuments ... is not so limited. 426 U.S. 128, 142, 96 S.Ct. 2062, 48 L.Ed.2d 523 (1976). In *Cappaert* the Court upheld a designation of a pool inhabited by "a peculiar race of desert fish ... found nowhere else in the world." *Id.* at 133, 96 S.Ct. 2062. The Court has also upheld a designation of islands notable for "fossils ... and ... noteworthy examples of ancient volcanism, deposition, and active sea erosion," rather than for human artifacts. *United States v. California* 436 U.S. 32, 34, 98 S.Ct. 1662, 56 L.Ed.2d 94 (1978).

United States v. California addresses not only the President's discretion to designate natural objects but the geographic scope of that discretion as well. Determining whether a designation had reserved only protruding rocks and islets or submerged lands and waters adjacent to them as well is "a question only of Presidential intent, not of Presidential power." *Id.* at 36, 98 S.Ct. 1662. In light of this unambiguous United States Supreme Court precedent concerning the Antiquities Act, plaintiffs' reliance on legislative history is clearly misplaced, and their arguments regarding the objects and area of designation untenable.

Even if broad judicial review of the exercise of the President's discretion is not available, plaintiffs still contend that the procedure which led to the designation fell so far afoul of the requirements of the National Environmental Policy Act (NEPA) as to warrant strip-mining the Monument.... [However,] "presidential actions under the Antiquities Act are not subject to the requirements of NEPA" ... [and regardless of where the President draws inspiration for the designation under the Antiquities Act, since it] is silent as to whether there are limitations on the sources from which the President may draw the inspiration to act, if such a limitation exists it must be found in other statutory provisions, the Constitution, or in the common law.

* * *

Assuming that plaintiffs are correct, that the original idea for the Monument was entirely the creature of the DOI, the actions of the DOI had no direct and immediate impact on the plaintiffs. It was the President's action, and not the action of the DOI, that had the legal effect of creating the Monument, and the DOI's activities therefore do not constitute final agency action reviewable under the APA.

2. *Constitutional Claims*

In contrast to the limited judicial review discussed above, judicial review to determine the constitutionality of a President's acts may be appropriate.... Plaintiffs raise three constitutional claims in this case. First, they assert that the Antiquities Act itself is unconstitutional in violation of the delegation doctrine. In addition they claim that even if the Antiquities Act is constitutional the manner in which it was utilized in creating the Grand Staircase Monument violated the Property Clause and the Spending Clause.

A. *Delegation Doctrine and Property Clause*

Plaintiffs contend that Congress violated both the delegation doctrine (or perhaps more accurately, the non-delegation doctrine) and the Property Clause by giving the President, under the Antiquities Act, virtually unfettered discretion to regulate and make rules concerning federal property. Neither contention has merit. While it is true that Congress has the express authority under the Constitution's Property Clause to "dispose of and make all needful Rules and Regulations respecting the Territory or other Property belonging to the United States," it is equally true that Congress may delegate this authority as it deems appropriate. *Yakus v. United States,* 321 U.S. 414, 64 S.Ct. 660, 88 L.Ed. 834 (1944), and any delegation is constitutionally permissible if Congress provides "standards to guide the authorized action such that one reviewing the action could recognize whether the will of Congress has been obeyed." *See Id.* at 425–26, 64 S.Ct. 660.[11]

The Antiquities Act sets forth clear standards and limitations. The Act describes the types of objects that can be included in national monuments and a limitation on the size of monuments. *See* 16 U.S.C. §431. Although the standards are general, "Congress does not violate the Constitution merely because it legislates in broad terms, leaving a certain degree of discretion to executive or judicial actors." *Touby v. United States,* 500 U.S. 160, 165, 111 S.Ct. 1752, 114 L.Ed.2d 219 (1991). Accordingly, the non-delegation doctrine is not violated, nor is the Property Clause, which has repeatedly been construed as allowing Congress to delegate its authority to the executive and judicial branches, including the power to "dispose of and make all needful Rules and Regulations respecting the Territory or other Property belonging to the United States." U.S. Const. Art. IV, §3, cl. 2....

11. The Courts have upheld virtually every congressional delegation of authority made by Congress for the last 100 years. In fact, there have only been two occasions in the 20th and 21st centuries where congressional delegations of authority were deemed unconstitutional. See *A.L.A. Schechter Poultry Corporation v. U.S.,* 295 U.S. 495, 55 S.Ct. 837, 79 L.Ed. 1570 (1935); *Panama Refining Co. v. Ryan,* 293 U.S. 388, 55 S.Ct. 241, 79 L.Ed. 446 (1935).

B. *Spending Clause*

[The court rejected plaintiff's claim that establishing the monument violated the spending clause, since the Monument pertained to government owned land and "clearly indicates that land privately owned or controlled does not pertain to the Monument, but also designates that such private land may become part of the Monument if it is acquired by future action." No federal monies were expended to acquire private land.]

3. *Statutory Claims*

* * *

C. *Executive Order 10355*

UAC next argues that the President's designation of the Grand Staircase Monument was invalid because it violated Executive Order 10355 (E.O.10355). E.O. 10355 was issued by President Harry S. Truman in 1952. It delegated to the Secretary of the Interior "the authority vested in the President by section 1 of the act of June 25, 1910 [the Pickett Act], and the authority otherwise vested in him to withdraw or reserve lands of the public domain and other lands owned or controlled by the United States ... for public purposes." 17 Fed.Reg. 4831 (May 26, 1952). The Secretary of the Interior was also authorized to "modify or revoke withdrawals and reservations of such lands heretofore or hereafter made." *Id.* The Order further directed that "[a]ll orders issued by the Secretary of the Interior under the authority of this order shall be designated as public land orders and shall be submitted to the Division of the Federal Register ... for filing and for publication in the FEDERAL REGISTER." *Id.* *** However, the President must publish such authorization in the Federal Register, but he may place terms, conditions, and limitations on the use of the delegated authority, and he may revoke the delegation "in whole or in part" at any time. *Id.*

* * *

For this argument to prevail, several prerequisites must have been fulfilled: 1) E.O. 10355 must have contemplated the transfer of the President's authority under the Antiquities Act, 2) the transfer must have been valid, that is, the underlying statute must allow such a transfer, 3) the transfer must have been complete, meaning that the President retained no authority under the Antiquities Act, and 4) E.O. 10355 must still be in force; i.e. it has not since been repealed or revoked. If any of these conditions has not been met, E.O. 10355 poses no restraint on the President's authority to designate a national monument under the Antiquities Act.

1. *Delegation of Authority under the Antiquities Act*

It is questionable whether E.O. 10355 ever delegated the authority granted to the President under the Antiquities Act. Although the language of the Order is general, to construe the Order as granting every withdrawal authority possessed by the President would, in the Court's view, be an overly broad interpretation. E.O. 10355 specifically delegates to the Secretary of the Interior the President's authority under the Pickett Act as well as "the authority otherwise vested in [the President] to withdraw and reserve lands ..."

* * *

Since E.O. 10355 was issued, land has been withdrawn on 20 different occasions to create national monuments.[15] Each of these monuments was designated by the President. No national monument has been designated by the Secretary of the Interior pursuant to E.O. 10355 since its enactment in 1952. Such action on the part of both the President and the Secretary of the Interior strongly indicates that neither interpreted E.O. 10355 to include the authority granted under the Antiquities Act. As a result, this Court will not imply such an interpretation.

* * *

2. *Validity of a Delegation of Antiquities Act Authority*

Even assuming that E.O. 10355 originally contemplated within its language delegating the authority to withdraw land for designating national monuments, "a President may only confer by Executive Order rights that Congress has authorized the President to confer." *Karuk Tribe of California v. Ammon,* 209 F.3d 1366, 1375 (Fed.Cir.2000).... The Antiquities Act provides that "[t]he President ... is authorized, *in his discretion,* to [designate national monuments]." 16 U.S.C. §431 (2000) (emphasis added). Because Congress only authorized the withdrawal of land for national monuments to be done in the President's discretion, it follows that the President is the

15. Below is a list of national monuments designated pursuant to the Antiquities Act since E.O. 10355 was issued, along with the respective President who exercised the withdrawal authority.

Dwight D. Eisenhower
7/14/56 Edison Laboratory, NJ
1/18/61 Chesapeake and Ohio Canal, MD-WV
John F. Kennedy
5/11/61 Russell Cave, AL
12/28/61 Buck Island Reef, VI
Lyndon B. Johnson
1/20/69 Marble Canyon, AZ
Jimmy Carter
12/1/78 Admiralty Island, AK (Forest Service)
12/1/78 Aniakchak, AK
12/1/78 Becharof, AK
12/1/78 Bering Land Bridge, AK
12/1/78 Cape Krusenstern, AK
12/1/78 Denali, AK
12/1/78 Gates of the Arctic, AK
12/1/78 Kenai Fjords, AK
12/1/78 Kobuk Valley, AK
12/1/78 Lake Clark, AK
12/1/78 Misty Fjords, AK (Forest Service)
12/1/78 Noatak, AK
12/1/78 Wrangell-St. Elias, AK
12/1/78 Yukon-Charley, AK
12/1/78 Yukon Flats, AK

only individual who can exercise this authority because only the President can exercise his own discretion. Discretion is defined as "[a] public official's power or right to act in certain circumstances according to personal judgment and conscience." Black's Law Dictionary 479 (7th ed.1999). It is illogical to believe that the President can delegate his personal judgment and conscience to another.

Moreover, E.O. 10355 authorizes the Secretary of the Interior to "redelegate the authority delegated to him by this order to ... the Under Secretary of the Interior and [to] the Assistant Secretaries of the Interior." If the Court were to accept UAC's argument, the unfettered discretion[16] of the President to withdraw public lands for national monuments could potentially be vested in several individuals. Such a result is untenable and clearly beyond what Congress intended when passing the Antiquities Act.

This Court is persuaded that the President, and only the President, may designate National monuments under the Antiquities Act regardless whether President Truman intended to delegate this authority by means of E.O. 10355. The Court finds support for its interpretation in *State of Alaska v. Carter,* 462 F. Supp. 1155, 1159 (D. Alaska 1978) ("The Antiquities Act authorizes the President 'in his discretion' to declare objects that have scientific interest, and are situated upon the public lands, to be national monuments. The Act authorizes only the President to declare these reservations and apparently this authority cannot be delegated." (citations omitted)).

3. *Complete Delegation of Authority*

UAC's reliance on E.O. 10355 also assumes that the delegation of authority was complete; that is, that the President relinquished all of his authority under the Antiquities Act to the Secretary of the Interior, forbidding any future action by the President himself pursuant to the Act. This interpretation is suspect where the language of E.O. 10355 does not specifically limit the President nor empower the Secretary of the Interior in such a manner. Additionally, history has shown that presidents after

---

16. Although FLPMA imposes numerous requirements on the Secretary of the Interior when withdrawing land, the Antiquities Act was specifically exempted from the reach of FLPMA. In passing FLPMA, the House stated:

> The main authority used by the Executive to make withdrawals is the 'implied' authority of the President recognized by the Supreme Court in *U.S. v. Midwest Oil Co.* (236 U.S. 459, 35 S.Ct. 309, 59 L.Ed. 673). The bill would repeal this authority and, with certain exceptions, all identified withdrawal authority granted to the President or the Secretary of the Interior. The exceptions, which are not repealed, are contained in the Antiquities Act (national monuments), Alaska Native Claims Settlement Act (native and public-interest withdrawals), the Defense Withdrawal Act of 1958, and Taylor Grazing Act (grazing districts).

H.R.Rep. No. 94-1163, 94th Cong., 2d Sess. 5 (1976), reprinted in 1976 U.S.C.C.A.N. 6175, 6203.

Therefore, when the President is creating national monuments pursuant to the Antiquities Act, his discretion would be unquestioned by Congress. If E.O. 10355 did indeed delegate to the Secretary of the Interior the President's Antiquities Act authority, it stands to reason that FLPMA would remain inapplicable to the actions of the Secretary if the Secretary designated a national monument.

Harry S. Truman continued to designate national monuments using the authority granted by the Antiquities Act.

* * *

UAC argues that the President may no longer use the authority granted to him under the Antiquities Act because of E.O. 10355. However, there is nothing in the language of the Order to indicate that, even if the authority to designate national monuments was delegated to the Secretary of the Interior—which the Court does not find—there was a complete delegation of authority. Without a specific reference to the Antiquities Act, and some indication that the President no longer intended to designate national monuments, this Court cannot conclude that E.O. 10355 constituted a complete delegation of the President's authority. On the contrary, the fact that Presidents continued to exercise Antiquities Act authority indicates that, even if E.O. 10355 was a valid delegation of authority, the authority to withdraw national monuments remained concurrently with the President and did not solely reside with the Secretary of the Interior.

* * *

Conclusion

For the foregoing reasons, defendants' Motion to Dismiss and in the alternative for Summary Judgment is granted; plaintiffs' Motions for Summary Judgment are denied in their entirety. It is so ordered.

Notes and Questions

1. **The largest national monument.** In 2006, President George W. Bush issued the proclamation establishing the Papahanaumokuakea Marine National Monument, covering 140,000 square miles, 89 million acres, around the uninhabited northern Hawaiian Islands. http://www.papahanaumokuakea.gov. *See also* Cynthia Barnett, *Hawaii is Now Home to an Ocean Reserve Twice the Size of Texas*, NATIONAL GEOGRAPHIC, Aug. 26, 2016. http://news.nationalgeographic.com/2016/08/obama-creates-world-s-largest-park-off-hawaii/. In 2016, President Barack Obama "more than quadrupled Papahanaumokuakea's size, to 582,578 square miles, an area larger than all the national parks combined." *Id.* For a look back at the Act on its hundredth anniversary, *see* David Harmon, Francis P. McManamon, Dwight T. Pitcaithley, *The Antiquities Act: The First Hundred Years of a Landmark Law*, 23 THE GEORGE WRIGHT FORUM 5 (2006).

2. **Challenges and curtailments.** The challenge to the President's powers under the Antiquities Act did not begin, nor end with President Clinton. The first curtailment of the President's authority resulted in an amendment to the Act in 1950, withdrawing the President's authority to declare monuments in the state of Wyoming without Congress's express authorization. 16 U.S.C. §431a. In 1980, following President Carter's proclamation setting aside 56 million acres in Alaska, Congress amended the

Grand Staircase Escalante National Monument. Photo by John Fowler, via Wikimedia Commons.

Alaska National Interest Land Conservation Act to require Congress's approval of any withdrawals exceeding 5,000 acres. 16 U.S.C. § 3213(a). In the 108th and 111th Congress, a variety of bills were introduced that would curtail the President's powers under the Act, some prohibiting the establishment or expansion of national monuments in particular states (Arizona, Colorado, California, Montana, Nevada, and Oregon), others setting up procedures for monument designation, and yet others requiring the President to obtain congressional approval and certify compliance with the National Environmental Protection Act before establishing a monument. Another bill purported to require the President to first propose language of proclamation to the governor of the affected area and to seek public input. *See generally* Carol Hardy Vincent and Kristina Alexander, *National Monuments and the Antiquities Act*, Cong. Res. Serv., July 20, 2010, www.crs.gov.

Bears Ears National Monument

On December 28, 2016, after months of anticipation, President Obama proclaimed 1.3 million acres of southeastern Utah as the Bears Ears National Monument. The proclamation stated that "[f]or hundreds of generations, native peoples lived in the surrounding deep sandstone canyons, desert mesas, and meadow mountaintops, which constitute one of the densest and most significant cultural landscapes in the United States." It describes the rich archeological character of the monument, revealing the historic tools and implements that tell the story of ancient peoples. The area continues to serve the cultural and ritual needs of existing Tribes, the Hopi, Zuni, and Utes, among others. The area is unsurpassed in its natural beauty, diverse geology and vegetation—from cactuses to a wide palette of wildflowers, which in turn support innumerable wildlife species. https://obamawhitehouse.archives.gov/the-press-office/2016/12/28/proclamation-establishement-bears-ears-national-monument.

3. **Angry reception.** Despite the obvious national interest in protecting this wondrous area from degradation by development, the Bears Ears proclamation was met with angry responses from Utah's Republication legislators, Sen Orrin Hatch shouted that "For Utahns in general, and for those in San Juan County in particular, this is an affront of epic proportions and an attack on an entire way of life." He added, "The President was never meant to set aside millions of acres against the express wishes of local communities and their elected representatives." Rep. Jason Chaffetz called the action a "midnight monument [which] is a slap in the face to the people of Utah ..." Stanford University, The Bill Lane Center for the American West, Debate & The West, The Bears Ears National Monument, Nov 15 2016, https://west.stanford.edu (Updated Dec. 28, 2016). Senator Hatch vowed to do everything in his power to cause the rescission of the proclamation. On December 4, 2017, President Donald Trump issued a proclamation purporting to reduce the size of Bears Ears by 85 percent and Grand Staircase Escalante by half. Presidential Executive Order on the Review of Designations under the Antiquities Act, https://www.whitehouse.gov/the-press-office/2017/04/26/presidential-executive-order-review-designations-under-antiquities-act (last visited February 3, 2018). It remains to be seen whether a successor president has such power or whether only Congress can reverse a proclamation.

B. Historic Sites Act of 1935

As the Antiquities Act gave the president power to protect archaeological sites from looting and vandalism, the Historic Sites Act of 1935, 54 U.S.C. §320101, *et seq.*, [formerly 16 U.S.C. §461] expanded upon those preservation powers by requiring the National Park Service ("NPS") to survey "historic and archaeologic sites, buildings, and objects for the purpose of determining which possess exceptional value as commemorating or illustrating the history of the United States," and to "secure, collate, and preserve drawings, plans, photographs, and other data of historic and archaeologic sites, buildings, and objects." These requirements became the basis of the Historic American Buildings Survey ("HABS") program, and later the Historic American Engineering Record ("HAER") and Historic American Landscapes Survey ("HALS"). https://www.nps.gov/hdp/hals/ (last visited April 6, 2017). The results of the survey are held in the Prints and Photographs Division of the Library of Congress. http://www.loc.gov/pictures/collection/hh/ (last visited April 6, 2017). The NPS has offered a sweeping review of the work of this survey in The Historic American Buildings Survey at Seventy Years 1933–2008.

The Historic Sites Act also requires the NPS, to "restore, reconstruct, rehabilitate, preserve, and maintain historic or prehistoric sites, buildings, objects, and properties of national historical or archaeological significance". The Jefferson National Expansion Memorial, that includes a museum and the St. Louis Gateway Arch, discussed in the case below, was the first "historic site" designated by the Historic Sites Act. https://www.nps.gov/hdp/habs (last visited April 6, 2017).

Barnidge v. United States

Circuit Court of Appeals, Eighth Circuit
101 F.2d 295 (1939)

Gardner, C.J. This is an appeal from a judgment in eminent domain proceedings, which were brought under the Act of Congress of August 21, 1935, 16 U.S.C.A. § 461 *et seq.*, known as the Historic Sites Act. The Secretary of the Interior, acting under the Historic Sites Act, determined that certain lands in the City of St. Louis, Missouri, possessed exceptional value as commemorating or illustrating the history of the United States. Thereupon, the President, by Executive Order of December 21, 1935, No. 7253, after reciting that by this Act Congress had declared a national policy to preserve for public use historic sites, buildings and objects of national significance for the inspiration and benefit of the people of the United States, and that the Secretary of the Interior had determined that certain described lands situated on the banks of the Mississippi River at and near the site of Old St. Louis, Missouri, possessed exceptional value as commemorating or illustrating the history of the United States and were a historic site, and that the City of St. Louis had agreed to contribute for the project the sum of $2,250,000, allocated to the Secretary of the Interior from the funds made available by the Emergency Relief Appropriation Act 1935, 49 Stat. 115, the sum of $4,750,000, which, with the sum of $2,250,000 to be contributed by the City of St. Louis, would make available for the said project a total sum of $9,000,000, and authorized and directed the Secretary to expend said sum in acquiring the said property and in developing and preserving it for the purposes of the Act. The City of St. Louis, pursuant to the provisions of the Act, deposited the sum of $2,250,000 to the credit of the Treasury in the Federal Reserve Bank at St. Louis. On the request of the Secretary of the Interior, this condemnation proceeding was then instituted.

The appellant filed an answer to the petition in condemnation, in which he alleged, among other things, (1) that the Historic Sites Act did not authorize condemnation of land; (2) that the use for which the land was sought was not a public use; (3) that the Historic Sites Act was an unconstitutional delegation of legislative power; and (4) that no funds were available to pay any awards in the proceeding. The Government moved to strike parts of this answer as argumentative, and as stating only erroneous conclusions of law. The appellant then made an offer of proof, purporting to sustain the issues raised by his answer, and this offer was rejected.

The lower court then appointed commissioners to view the land for the purpose of fixing the compensation to which the owners were entitled. Appellant excepted to the appointment of commissioners on substantially the same grounds which he had set out in his answer. The commissioners reported that damages and compensation for the taking of appellant's land were $13,200. Appellant filed exceptions to the commissioners' report, which were overruled. The Government also excepted to the commissioners' report on the sole ground that the award was excessive. The lower court heard the parties on the exceptions filed, and received testimony on the question of value. In the course of this hearing, appellant withdrew his exception as to the amount of the award, but proffered testimony in support of his contention that the site was not historic because the buildings on it were not historic. The lower court entered findings and judgment by which the commissioners' award was reduced to $11,000.

It has been stipulated that assignments of error based upon the action of the court in reducing the amount of the commissioners' award are withdrawn, but it is agreed that if we shall hold that the United States had the right to condemn the property, judgment should be ordered entered restoring the original commissioners' award of $13,200.

In seeking reversal, appellant in effect contends: (1) the court erred in sustaining the Government's motion to strike parts of appellant's answer; (2) there is no authority in the Historic Sites Act, or other Acts of Congress, to condemn the property of appellant for the purposes of the Historic Sites Act; (3) the use described in the Historic Sites Act is not a public one for which land may be taken by eminent domain; (4) the lands sought to be taken are not necessary for the effectuation of the purposes of the Historic Sites Act; (5) the Historic Sites Act unconstitutionally delegates legislative power.

In support of his contention that the court erred in striking parts of his answer, counsel seek to invoke the rule that all facts that were well pleaded in the answer must be accepted as true. Hence, it is urged that the allegations in the answer that there was no power in plaintiff to condemn, that no authority is vested in the Secretary of the Interior to commence proceedings, that the use is not a public one, that funds are not available, and that the Historic Sites Act is unconstitutional, must be accepted as true. But while, for the purpose of such motion, the well-pleaded facts must be accepted as true, it does not follow that conclusions of law are admitted. *Equitable Life Assur. Soc. v. Brown*, 213 U.S. 25, 29 S.Ct. 404, 53 L.Ed. 682 [(1909)]; *Pacific States Box & Basket Co. v. White*, 296 U.S. 176, 56 S.Ct. 159, 80 L.Ed. 138, 101 A.L.R. 853 [(1935)]; *Shohoney v. Quincy, O. & K.C.R. Co.*, 231 Mo. 131, 132 S.W. 1059 [(Mo. 1910)], Ann.Cas. 1912A, 1143; *Randolph v. Fricke*, 327 Mo. 130, 35 S.W.2d 912 [(Mo. 1930)].

Admitting the facts pleaded, but not appellant's conclusions of law, the court held that the parts of the answer stricken did not constitute a defense to the proceeding.

It is true that the Historic Sites Act does not purport to authorize the condemnation of property for the consummation of its purposes. However, the Act of August 1, 1888, Sec. 1, 40 U.S.C.A. § 257, contains a general grant of power or authority to prosecute condemnation proceedings where any officer of the Government is authorized to acquire real estate for public uses. Subsection (d) of Section 2 of the Historic Sites Act, 16 U.S.C.A. § 462(d), provides for authorizing the Secretary of the Interior to acquire property for the purposes of the Act "by gift, purchase, or otherwise." It has been held that the Government has the right of eminent domain as an attribute of sovereignty. *Mississippi & R. River Boom Co. v. Patterson*, 98 U.S. 403, 25 L.Ed. 206 [(1878)]; *Kohl v. United States*, 91 U.S. 367, 23 L.Ed. 449 [(1875)]; *Shoemaker v. United States*, 147 U.S. 282, 13 S.Ct. 361, 37 L.Ed. 170 [(1893)]; *United States v. Certain Lands in City of Louisville*, 78 F.2d 684 [(6 Cir. 1935)]. It is uniformly held that authority to acquire real estate conferred by the enactment of a statute after the Act of August 1, 1888, Sec. 1, 40 U.S.C.A. § 257, carries with it power to condemn. *Hanson Lumber Co. v. United States*, 261 U.S. 581, 43 S.Ct. 442, 67 L.Ed. 809 [(1923)]; *United States v. Threlkeld*, 72 F.2d 464 [(10 Cir. 1934)].

It is observed that the Historic Sites Act confers authority on the Secretary of the Interior to acquire, in the name of the United States, property for the purposes of the Act, by gift, purchase, "or otherwise." As authority had already been conferred to procure real estate for public uses by condemnation, it would seem to have been quite unnecessary to embody in this Act specific authority to acquire real estate by condemnation proceedings. We must assume that Congress had full knowledge of the Act of August 1, 1888 and of the interpretation that had been placed upon it by the courts.

* * *

It is urged that the purpose for which appellant's property is being taken is not a public purpose, for which land may be taken by eminent domain. If the Federal Government, under the Constitution, has power to embark upon the project for which the land is sought, then the use is a public one. Confessedly, the purpose cannot be a private one. Primarily, the right to determine the purpose to be a public one is in Congress. It has been held that the taking of land for commemorative purposes is for a public use. *United States v. Gettysburg Electric R. Co., supra*; *Roe v. Kansas*, 278 U.S. 191, 49 S.Ct. 160, 73 L.Ed. 259; *Old Dominion Land Co. v. United States*, 269 U.S. 55, 46 S.Ct. 39, 70 L.Ed. 162. In the last cited case, it is said (page 40): "Congress has declared the purpose to be a public use, by implication if not by express words. *** Its decision is entitled to deference until it is shown to involve an impossibility."

It appears that on the property included in this project were situated the Spanish Colonial office, where, during the administration of Thomas Jefferson, third President of the United States, all of the first territory comprised in the Upper Louisiana Purchase was transferred to the United States; the Government House at which, on March 9, 1804, Charles Dehault Delassus, the Spanish Commandant in St. Louis, transferred possession of upper Louisiana to Captain Amos Stoddard, of the United States Army, who had been delegated by France as its representative, and at which, on the morning of March 10, 1804, Captain Stoddard, as the agent of the United States, took formal possession of the Louisiana Purchase and raised the American flag, by reason of which transactions the Spanish, French, and American flags waved successively over the site within a period of twenty-four hours; the place where Laclede and Chouteau established the first civil government west of the Mississippi; the place where Lafayette was received by a grateful people; the place where the Sante Fe, the Oregon, and other trails originated; the place where Lewis and Clark prepared for their trip of discovery and exploration, and the Court House in which the Dred Scott Case was tried. We think there can be no reasonable doubt that the proposed use of this land is a public one.

It is contended by appellant that the lands sought to be taken are not necessary for the effectuation of the purposes of the Historic Sites Act. But the Secretary has determined that it is necessary and expedient to acquire these lands, and the duty of determining that fact was vested in him and not in the courts. When Congress delegates to an administrative officer the power to determine necessity, his determination, with exceptions not here important, is not subject to judicial review. *Shoemaker v. United States*, 147 U.S. 282, 13 S.Ct. 361, 37 L.Ed. 170 [(1893)].... It is argued that the act of the Secretary of the Interior in attempting to condemn the land here sought to be taken is in any event an abuse of the power granted him by the Historic Sites Act. In this connection it is urged that the sole purpose of this Act is the preservation and restoration of historic buildings, and that the condemnation of land is authorized only for that purpose. We think no such limitations can be placed upon this Act. The declared purpose of the Act is to preserve for public use historic sites, buildings, and objects of national significance.

It is finally urged that this act is violative of the Constitution because it delegates legislative power to the Secretary of the Interior. The right to delegate such power as that described in the Historic Sites Act has been quite generally upheld by the courts. *Union Bridge Co. v. United States*, 204 U.S. 364, 27 S.Ct. 367, 51 L.Ed. 523 [(1907)]; *Monongahela Bridge Co. v. United States*, 216 U.S. 177, 30 S.Ct. 356, 54 L.Ed. 435 [(1910)]; *Greenwood County v. Duke Power Co.*, 4 Cir., 81 F.2d 986, *reversed on other grounds* 299 U.S. 259, 57 S.Ct. 202, 81 L.Ed. 178 [(1936)]; *Duke Power Co. v. Greenwood County*, 91 F.2d 665 [(4th Cir. 1937)]; *Kansas Gas & Electric Co. v. City of Independence*, 79 F.2d 32, 100 A.L.R. 1479 [(10th Cir. 1935)].

We have no doubt of the power of the United States, under the Constitution, to acquire by eminent domain, or otherwise, sites of national historic significance for the purpose as declared in the Historic Sites Act and preserving them to commemorate and illustrate the nation's history.

Under the stipulation of the parties, the judgment, in the event we should hold that the United States had the right to condemn, was to be modified by restoring the original commissioners' award of $13,200. As so modified, the judgment is therefore affirmed and the cause remanded for further proceedings consistent herewith.

Notes and Questions

1. **Takings jurisprudence.** In recent years, the Supreme Court has recognized expansive eminent domain powers in state governments. In *Kelo v. New London,* 545 U.S. 469 (2005), the Court upheld the use of eminent domain powers to acquire private property for purposes of economic redevelopment, largely deferring to the state legislature as to what is a public use. Here, in *Barnidge,* the court found that the acquisition of private property in service of the Historic Sites Act was unquestionably a public use, confirming that values, other than those that are economic, are also worthy of protection.

2. **The Great Depression.** It is interesting to note that this project was undertaken in the midst of the Great Depression, usually dated from late 1929 to the eve of World War II. At its height, nearly half of the nation's banks were lost either to failure or merger, money supply shrank by a third, and unemployment reached 23%. Robert J. Samuelson, *Revisiting the Great Depression,* WILSON Q. (Winter 2012). Rather than just put out of work people on the public dole, President Franklin D. Roosevelt instead plotted economic recovery, among other things, by putting people back to work—on a wide range of public works projects, from building dams to painting murals in public buildings. *See* Bradford A. Lee, *The New Deal Reconsidered,* WILSON Q. 62 (Spring 1982). As the facts recount, the City of St. Louis shared the costs of building the arch. a. Was this just a part of its economic recovery plan to build up employment, or were there other intangible, yet equally important ends, sought? b. What events in history or what values does the arch memorialize for midwesterners?

Preserving the Jay Heritage Estate through Eminent Domain?

It is rare for an historic site to be preserved because the government seizes it from a private property owner. Westchester County, supported by the State of New York and the City of Rye, and the Jay Coalition of many civic groups and other municipalities, agreed to condemn the Jay Estate and pay just compensation for it. The New York Courts have long-confirmed that the power to take private property necessary to serve a public purpose is an inherent attribute of sovereignty. *Fifth Avenue Coach Lines v. City of New York,* 183 N.E. 2d 684 (N.Y. 1962). Condemnation for historic preservation is a public purpose. *Lubelle v. City of Rochester,* 536 N.Y.S. 2d 325 (App. Div. 1988). The state Legislature had expressly authorized Westchester County to exercise the power of eminent domain. 1948 N.Y. Laws, ch. 852; *see generally* Eminent Domain Procedure, EM. DOM. PROC. §201, *et seq.*

The owner, Diane Millstein, had acquired the site for $1 million to develop it as an investment for a law firm's pension fund. She turned down offers from the County to buy the site first for $1 million and then

$2 million. She turned down other offers, including one by citizens and the Trust for Public Land for $6.5 million. With New York State pledging $4 million, the Westchester County Board of Legislators having received appraisals of the fair market value of the Jay Estate under a subdivision plan, which the City of Rye had approved, she insisted, with an ideological fervor, that she would develop a housing complex.

In an Op-Ed published by Gannett-Westchester newspapers, she argued that "Our 23 acres are not historic, do not contain the John Jay House and are not needed for environmental purposes. Studies show that nothing remains on our 23 acres of any aspect of the original 19th century 250-acre farm ... The Jay house standing on our property was built years after John Jay died. It should not be confused with the house some miles away in Katonah [then Bedford] which John Jay did build, in which he lived and raised a family and which today is preserved by and maintained by the state." Instead of proceeding with an "as of right" residential development of 38 homes, for which her property was zoned, for years she negotiated back and forth with the City of Rye and the public, for example, proposing commercial office space developments or offering to sell six acres of the property if she could build out 84 townhouses, or 66 clustered homes, on the rest. Tom Anderson, *Developer Will Follow Plan Approved for Jay Property*, GANNETT WESTCHESTER NEWSPAPERS, June 29, 1988, at 6.

After multiple proceedings before the Rye agencies and lawsuits, public pressure mounted on Westchester County to condemn the site. The County already owned the adjacent Marshlands Conservancy County Park. The County Executive initially resisted, but agreed on condition that the Jay Coalition bear the costs of repairing the badly degraded Peter Jay Mansion and Carriage House. Tessa Melvin, *Legislators To Condemn Jay Property*, N.Y. TIMES, September 30, 1990, at 12WC. Diane Millstein filed a suit in Federal District Court, but never prosecuted it, and she and the County entered into an Agreement to Purchase on July 23, 1992. In the end, she and the five women who led the Jay Coalition (Catherine Crean, Helen Paschal, Kitty Aresty, Karen Morey Kennedy, and Rhoda Kornreich) developed a tough appreciation for the diametrically opposed, but principled positions that each side took. Diane Millstein did not respect the various government agencies which frustrated her "right to develop." In the end, she donated the Peter Jay Mansion and the Van Norden Carriage house directly to the Jay Coalition, with covenants and rights of access across the 20.5 acres she conveyed to the State and Westchester County. Like Mount Vernon, women had saved the Jay Estate. These five women incorporated the non-profit Jay Heritage Center in 1992.

C. With Heritage So Rich

After World War II, there was a prosperity boom in the United States, which led to an increase in urbanization and suburban sprawl, assisted by the federally sponsored interstate highway system started by President Dwight Eisenhower. Years later, recognizing the detrimental effect of the upheaval and landscape changing projects, First Lady Lady Bird Johnson coordinated a report which analyzed the urban renewal and its effects on the country. Robert Stipe, A Richer Heritage: Historic Preservation in 21st Century 35 (2003). The report, aptly named "With Heritage So Rich," is an accumulation of essays which created "an expansive inventory of properties reflecting the nation's heritage, a mechanism to protect those properties from unnecessary harm caused by federal activities, a program of financial incentives, and an independent federal preservation body to coordinate the actions of federal agencies affecting historic preservation." *Id.* The report called public attention to the issue and helped raise public support for further historic preservation and the passage of the National Historic Preservation Act of 1966.

Excerpt from "With Heritage So Rich"

Part I: Findings and Recommendations

Introduction

In formulating its findings and recommendations, The Special Committee on Historic Preservation has attempted to develop a program to encourage federal, state and local government, and private agencies and individuals to preserve communities, areas, structures, sites and objects significant to architectural, cultural, social, economic, political and military history and which contribute to the quality and meaning of American life.

In pursuit of this objective, the Committee, which includes representatives of all levels of government and the agencies involved, has studied problems and programs related to historic preservation in the United States and in Europe. At the request of the Committee, a number of federal agencies and the National Trust for Historic Preservation have supplied studies, reports, documents and comments on numerous historic preservation activities and accomplishments. The Committee has examined contemporary European practices in historic preservation, restoration and reconstruction. It has obtained from authoritative sources in England, France, Holland, Germany, Scandinavia, Poland, Czechoslovakia, Austria and Italy legal and administrative information which could be used to evaluate European experience in relation to American needs and proposals for improving and developing historic preservation programs in the United States.

It is clear to the committee that our own needs and the evidence of experience in Europe, where historic preservation is a major responsibility of government, suggest an expansion and development of our own programs, placing greater emphasis on government support of private efforts in historic preservation.

The Committee has been aided in its work by consultants and by the contributors whose work appears in the various chapters and photographic sections of *With Heritage So Rich*.

In accordance with this increasing desire to make historic preservation a living part of our community life and development, the Committee recommends certain new programs described in this report. Along with enlargement and enhancement of existing programs, they will broaden and deepen the scope of national historic preservation activity.

Findings

If it can be said there is a new awakening of interest in the preservation of our cultural and architectural heritage, it must be added that never was the need for it greater.

Since World War II a great wave of urbanization has been sweeping across the nation. And such is the rate of growth that in the next 40 years the United States will have to build more homes, more schools, more stores, more factories, more public facilities of all kinds than in the entire previous history of the country.

Out of the turbulence of building, tearing down and rebuilding the face of America, more and more Americans have come to realize that as the future replaces the past, it destroys much of the physical evidence of the past.

The current pace of preservation effort is not enough. It is as though the preservation movement were trying to travel up a down escalator. The time has come for bold, new measures and a national plan of action to insure that we, our children, and future generations may have a genuine opportunity to appreciate and to enjoy our rich heritage.

The United States, with a short history and an emphasis on its economic growth, has left historic preservation primarily to private interests and efforts. In the older, history-conscious countries of Europe, preservation leadership has been provided primarily by government.

At the federal level, the laws now in effect which mention preservation directly include the Antiquities Act of 1906, written to protect historic monuments on government property; an Act establishing the National Park Service in 1916; the Historic Sites Act of 1935, which defines the national policy of preservation for public use; the Act of 1949, which established and defined the powers of the National Trust for Historic Preservation; and the Housing Acts of 1961 and 1965 which gave to the Department of Housing and Urban Development powers to use federal funds to acquire open space and to move historic structures in urban renewal areas.

The following is a summary of the various federal programs which affect historic preservation.

* * *

Nearly half the buildings recorded [by the Historic American Buildings Survey] in detail in the past 30 years have already been razed or destroyed by mutilation. Yet the staff of the Historic American Buildings Survey estimates that no fewer than 90,000 additional buildings should be inventoried and that at least 18,000 of these are of such exceptional merit they should also be recorded in photographs and measure drawings. Approximately 3,000 of the 90,000 buildings are situated on federal lands and 25,000 more, located in communities throughout America, may be affected in one way or another by current federal programs and projects during the second half of the 1960's. At the current rate of progress on this Survey, it would take 75 years to accomplish its work!

The National Park Service, in cooperation with the Smithsonian Institution, coordinates the Inter-Agency Archaeological Salvage Program, involving 7 federal and many state and local agencies. This program was initiated 20 years ago to rescue irreplaceable archaeological sites destined to be permanently lost through flooding in the course of dam and reservoir construction.

* * *

While there is a growing national interest in historic preservation, it is by no means evenly distributed. In cities we find the widest discrepancies in interest and accomplishment. In cities such as New Orleans, Boston, Charleston, S.C., San Antonio, Santa Barbara, Natchez, Winston-Salem, N.C., Bethlehem, Pa. and Providence, R.I., there has been excellent and growing support by both the business community and local government. And there are others. However, there is a longer list of cities and small towns and villages where either indifference reigns or there is outright hostility. In the latter case, preservation frequently loses the battle to stronger forces. Curiously, business leaders often ignore the economic benefits of prestige values and tourist dollars.

International Cooperation

There is a growing interest in programs of international cooperation for historic preservation sponsored by the United Nations Educational, Scientific and Cultural Organization. These include the Rome International Centre for the Study of the Preservation and the Restoration of Cultural Property and the newly-established International Council on Monuments and Sites.* * *

* * *

Conclusions to the Findings

First, the preservation movement must recognize the importance of architecture, design and [a]esthetics as well as historic and cultural values. Those who treasure a building for its pleasing appearance or local sentiment do not find it less important because it lacks "proper" historic credentials.

Second, the new preservation must look beyond the individual building and individual landmark and concern itself with the historic and architecturally valued areas and districts which contain a special meaning for the community. A historic neighborhood, a fine old street of houses, a village green, a colorful marketplace, a courthouse square, an [a]esthetic quality of the townscape—all must fall within the concern of the preservation movement. It makes little sense to fight for the preservation of a historic house set between two service stations, and at the same time to ignore an entire area of special charm or importance in the community which is being nibbled away by incompatible uses or slow decay.

***

In sum, if we wish to have a future with greater meaning, we must concern ourselves not only with the historic highlights, but we must be concerned with the total heritage of the nation and all that is worth preserving from our past as a living part of the present.

Part II: Recommendations

Throughout this report the term historic preservation has been used to include the protection, rehabilitation, restoration and reconstruction of communities, areas, structures, sites and objects having historic, architectural, social or cultural significance.

To carry out the goals of historic preservation a comprehensive national plan of action is imperative. Such a plan will encourage, improve and reinforce public and private leadership.

Many individuals and private organizations have worked long and hard to preserve the physical evidences of our heritage which we are privileged to enjoy today. Public agencies have also made a substantial contribution. But to meet the current crisis and to accelerate the pace of historic preservation we need to increase the amount of government support and joint public and private efforts.

Our traditions differ from those of European countries, but we have much to learn from European experience. The weight which European governments give to historic preservation has resulted in successful programs for saving, restoring and reconstructing many different types of buildings for viable uses. There is an excellent object lesson in the European achievement in maintaining historic buildings and areas as living parts of communities and as successful economic ventures.

A national plan of action for historic preservation should include the following elements:

1) a comprehensive statement of national policy to guide the activities and programs of all federal agencies;

2) the establishment of an Advisory Council on Historic Preservation to provide leadership and guidance for the direction of inter-agency actions and to provide liaison with state and local governments, public and private groups and the general public;

3) a greatly expanded National Register program to inventory and to catalogue communities, areas, structures, sites and objects; a federal program of assistance to states and localities for companion programs; and a strong federal public information program based on the material in the Register;

4) added authority and sufficient funds for federal acquisition of threatened buildings and sites of national historic importance, and expansion of the urban renewal program

to permit local non-cash contributions to include acquisition of historic buildings on the National Register, both within and outside the project area;

5) provision for federal loans and grants and other financial aid to facilities and expansion of state and local programs of historic preservation;

6) federal financial aid to and through the National Trust for Historic Preservation to assist private interest and activity in the preservation field, for educational purposes and for direct assistance to private property holders.

***

3. Establish an adequately staffed Advisory Council on Historic Preservation, with membership representing the major federal departments and agencies involved in preservation matters, as well as state and local governments and public and private organizations interested in historic preservation and urban development. The functions of such a Council should include:

a. advising the President and the Congress on historic preservation as it affects the national welfare and providing inspiration and leadership for the implementation of the national policy

b. the development of policies, guidelines and studies for the review and resolution of conflicts between different federal and federally-aided programs affecting historic preservation

c. the encouragement, in cooperation with appropriate private organizations, of public interest and participation in historic preservation

d. supporting the National Register as an instrument of national historic preservation policy and insuring the coordination of the Register with activities of other agencies of government

e. making and publishing studies in such areas as adequacy of legislative and administrative statutes and regulations pertaining to preservation activities of state and local governments, and effects of tax policies at all levels of government on historic preservation, and

f. preparation of guidelines for assistance of state and local governments in drafting preservation legislation.

4. Provide by Internal Revenue Code amendment or clarify by regulation or published ruling the status of:

a. historic preservation as a public, exempt charitable activity, deductibility of gifts of historic easements or restrictive covenants to governmental units or exempt organizations engaged in preservation, and permissibility of revenue-producing adaptive or incidental uses

b. acceptance of a registered historic property for conveyance to the National Trust in lieu of an equivalent estate tax payment

c. income tax deductibility to private owners of registered historic properties for preservation and restoration expenditures within appropriate limitations

d. recognition of conveyances of registered historic properties to governmental units or exempt preservation organizations as present gifts, despite reserved life interests, provided the property is open to the public on a reasonable basis.

5. Make mandatory a preliminary review of the location and status of historic sites and buildings in relevant areas prior to the undertaking of federal or federally-aided programs or projects affecting plans for physical development. Where the review produces evidence of the existence of historic sites and buildings and that surveys made in accordance with the standards of the National Registry are lacking, make mandatory a historic survey prepared in accordance with such standards. * * *

6. Authorize the use of federal matching grants for acquisition by an appropriate public agency of historic structures, rehabilitation loans and grants for restoration of such structures, and recognition of public expenditures for such acquisitions as eligible non-cash contributions under urban renewal programs.* * *

7. Establish new and liberalized loan programs for private groups or individuals for acquisition and rehabilitation of historic structures and districts.

8. Enactment of a scholarship and training program for architects and technicians in the field of historic preservation, similar to the program enacted by Congress in 1964 for the field of housing and urban planning. An adequate program is of vital importance to the effective implementation of the other proposals of the Committee.

State and Local Governments (County, Town and Municipal)

1. *State*: Enact legislation establishing an appropriate state agency, and enabling and encouraging local communities to establish historic preservation districts and to acquire through eminent domain (where necessary) historic structures and sites and preservation easements and restrictive covenants, and providing special property tax treatment for historic structures and preservation and restoration expenditures.

2. *State*: Establish an organizational structure capable of:

a. providing leadership, information, standards and criteria, technical and financial assistance to local communities for preservation purposes

b. reviewing and coordinating the programs and projects of state agencies to avoid to the maximum extent conflicts with preservation objectives

c. carrying out appropriate preservation programs, plans and studies, and

d. establishing and maintaining an official state register coordinated with the National Register.

3. *State*: Enact legislation clarifying and encouraging the use of preservation easements and restrictive covenants for the benefit of governmental units and preservation organization

4. *State*: By statute or regulation, assure exemption from inheritance taxes for gifts of historic property to governmental units, the National Trust and other preservation organizations and income tax deduction for such gifts and for preservation and restoration expenditures.

5. *State and local*: Where authorized, require by legislation and appropriate notice procedures, a waiting period before demolition or significant alteration of registered historic structures, in order to provide time for acceptable alternatives and new use solutions to be worked out.

6. *Local*: Undertake a thorough and systematic survey of historic and architecturally important buildings and areas within the community, in coordination with the National Register and the State Register.

7. *Local*: Make a comprehensive study of all available legal tools for preservation purposes, including historic district zoning and formation of architectural and historic review boards. Such studies should relate to official general plans of the locality and be incorporated in Community Renewal Programs.

8. *Local*: Provide an annual budget for expenditures to preserve and maintain those historic and architectural structures and places of importance to the community.

9. The Congress should strengthen and broaden the District of Columbia historic preservation legislation.

General

1. Historic and cultural sites, structures and objects acquired with the use of federal funds and not retained by the acquiring department or agency, or not otherwise directly disposed of, should be transferable under the surplus property disposal programs to the National Trust in fee simple. The National Trust should be empowered to lodge operational responsibility for such property with local preservation groups wherever possible.

***

3. Federal authorization should be provided for matching grants to the National Trust on a two-thirds federal, one-third National Trust formula for the following purposes:

a. to provide education and clearinghouse services and financial assistance to individuals and organizations in preservation and related fields

b. to prepare information and education publications, conduct meetings and conferences, finance scholarships, develop library resources, provide technical consultation and establish award programs

c. to acquire, restore and maintain registered structures of national historic or architectural importance.

4. To assure that public funds for private historic preservation are used only for authentic needs and in accordance with established criteria, such funds should be transmitted to non-governmental organizations and private individuals only with the approval of an appropriate authority.

5. Private corporations, trade associations and labor organizations should be encouraged to identify and preserve the locations, structures and objects on which the development of their enterprise or craft has been based.

6. The great national philanthropic foundations should be urged to stimulate and assist programs for the training of architects, landscape architects, engineers, historians, designers and decorators in careers in historic preservation. In addition, they are urged to assist historic preservation research projects, publications and conference and communication media programs.

International Cooperation

The United States should provide financial support to the UNESCO historic preservation programs including the Rome Centre, and the International Council on Monuments and Sites. In addition, federal funds should be used to support international conferences and scholarships and fellowships for international study of historic preservation.

Special Committee on Historic Preservation

Albert Rains, *Chairman*

Edmund S. Muskie

William B. Widnall

Philip H. Hoff

Raymond R. Tucker

Gordon Gray

Laurance G. Henderson, *Director*

Notes and Questions

1. **With Heritage So Rich.** This report by the United States Conference of Mayors' Special Committee on Historic Preservation, was first published in 1966. The collection of essays, poetry, and photography laid a solid path for the enactment of the National Historic Preservation Act. The report has been updated several times since and continues to inspire efforts toward preservation. A 50th anniversary edition of WITH HERITAGE SO RICH is online at http://preservation50.org/about/with-heritage-so-rich (last visited April 3, 2017).

2. **New threats.** a. Consider whether the identified threats posed by increased urbanization and development have substantially abated in the fifty years since the report's publication. What new threats must we confront in the present world of conflict, shifting national fiscal priorities and climate change?

1. National Register of Historic Places

a. Criteria for Evaluation and National Park Service Guidance Documents

The Secretary of the Interior has promulgated criteria for eligibility for the National Register of Historic Places. Broadly stated, the properties that are eligible are:

> the districts, sites, buildings, structures, and objects that possess integrity of location, design, setting, materials, workmanship, feeling, and association; and
>
> (a) that are associated with events that have made a significant contribution to the broad patterns of our history; or
>
> (b) that are associated with the lives of persons significant in our past; or
>
> (c) that embody the distinctive characteristics of a type period, or method of construction, or that represent the work of a master, or that posses s high artistic values, or that represent a significant and distinguishable entity whose components may lack individual distinction; or
>
> (d) that have yielded, or may be likely to yield, information important in prehistory or history.

36 C.F.R. § 60.4. *See also* How to Apply the National Register Criteria for Evaluation, http://www.nps.gov/nr/publications/bulletins/pdfs/nrb15.pdf (last visited April 3, 2017).

Moody Hill Farms Limited Partnership v. United States Department of the Interior, National Park Service

United States Court of Appeals for the Second Circuit
205 F.3d 554 (1999)

Walker, C.J. Plaintiffs-appellees, residents of the hamlet of Coleman Station in New York state, claimed *** that the Keeper of the National Register of Historic Places, an officer of the National Park Service, acted arbitrarily and capriciously, in violation of the Administrative Procedure Act ("APA"), 5 U.S.C. § 701 *et seq.*, when she denied plaintiffs-appellees' petition to remove Coleman Station Historic District from the National Register. After the district court granted summary judgment to plaintiffs-appellees, *see Moody Hill Farms Ltd. Partnership v. United States Dep't of Interior,* 976 F.Supp. 214, 222–23 (S.D.N.Y.1997), the Park Service appealed.

At the heart of this case is a dispute between neighboring landowners about the future of Coleman Station, a hamlet in the Town of Northeast in Dutchess County, New York. Plaintiffs either are associated with Moody Hill Farms Limited Partnership, which operates a composting facility and organic farm on property within Coleman Station, or own farms within or adjacent to Coleman Station. The movement to list Coleman Station on the state and national registers of historic places was initiated by other landowners within Coleman Station who have made no secret of their opposition to Moody Hill Farms' composting activities, which they see as a threat to the district's traditional character.

In 1993, the latter group succeeded in obtaining listing for Coleman Station on the New York State Register of Historic Places. The New York State Office of Parks, Recreation and Historic Preservation ("NYHP"), pursuant to federal regulation, simultaneously nominated Coleman Station for listing on the National Register, and Coleman Station was placed on the National Register. Soon thereafter, plaintiffs challenged the New York listing on procedural grounds in state court and succeeded in having the listing removed. Plaintiffs then petitioned the Keeper to have the national listing annulled. After the Keeper denied their petition, plaintiffs filed the present suit, alleging violations of the APA and their due process rights.

With respect to the APA claim, the district court concluded that, because the criteria for the state and national registers are identical, eligibility for listing on the national register was destroyed once the state listing was voided. The district court further concluded that the procedural errors in the state listing contaminated the national nomination. Finally, the district court concluded that the Keeper erred in failing to consider an opinion by a Deputy Commissioner of the NYHP, forwarded along with plaintiffs' petition to remove Coleman Station from the National Register, that the property may lack historic integrity. The district court also denied summary judgment to defendant on plaintiffs' due process claim.

We disagree with the district court's conclusions regarding the APA claim. Because the Keeper has independent authority to determine the eligibility of properties and to add them to the National Register, the annulment of the state listing did not automatically void the national listing. Therefore, we reverse and remand for entry of judgment for defendant-appellant.

Background

The National Historic Preservation Act of 1966, 16 U.S.C. §470, *et seq.*, authorizes the Secretary of the Interior to expand and maintain a National Register of "districts, sites, buildings, structures, and objects significant in American history, architecture, archaeology, engineering and culture." *Id.* §470a(a)(1)(A). The regulations governing the procedures for listing properties on the National Register are set forth at 36 C.F.R. pt. 60. Properties may be added to the National Register in several ways, including nomination by an approved state historic preservation program, as in this case, or by a federal agency, by an individual in a state where there is no approved historic preservation program, by act of Congress or Executive Order, or by a declaration by the Secretary of the Interior. All nominations to the National Register, except those made by Act of Congress, Executive Order, or declaration by the Secretary of the Interior, must be approved by the Park Service. ***

On June 8, 1993, the New York State Review Board for Historic Preservation voted unanimously to nominate Coleman Station for listing on the state and national registers. The Review Board's decision was sent to the NYHP, New York's approved Historic Preservation Program, which, on August 12, 1993, approved the recommendation without written opinion and forwarded the nomination to the Keeper of the National Register. More than two months later, on October 25, 1993, property owners within the Coleman Station district received notification of the state listing.

On August 31, 1993, the Park Service published notice in the Federal Register that Coleman Station was under consideration for entry in the National Register. On September 30, 1993, Coleman Station was listed in the National Register, and the Park Service notified the NYHP of the national listing. Approximately one year later, on December 30, 1994, the NYHP notified property owners within the district of the national listing.

Following the state listing, plaintiffs filed an Article 78 proceeding in the New York Supreme Court in Dutchess County. They sought an annulment on various grounds, including that the state listing was accomplished in violation of the procedures set forth at N.Y.Comp.Codes R. & Regs. tit. 9, § 427.5. These regulations provide, *inter alia,* that the NYHP must notify each owner of privately owned property of a decision relating to the listing of a property on the State Register no later than 45 calendar days after the decision has been made. *** The regulations also provide that the NYHP must issue its decision in writing, setting forth the findings in support of the decision. *** [T]he state court held for plaintiffs that the NYHP's failure to comply with these procedures vitiated the state listing. *** The state court did not reach the merits of whether Coleman Station met the criteria for eligibility for listing.

Plaintiffs then petitioned the Keeper to delist Coleman Station from the National Register. In conformity with the regulations set forth at 36 C.F.R. § 60.15(c), plaintiffs filed their petition with the NYHP, which reviewed the petition and, at plaintiffs' request, forwarded it to the Keeper. In a March 9, 1995, letter to plaintiffs, which was included with the materials sent to the Keeper, the NYHP set forth its analysis of the petition. *** [T]he letter noted that questions had been raised at the meeting of the State Review Board regarding the historic integrity of the district that "should be evaluated by the Keeper of the National Register." Regarding the procedural errors in the state listing, the letter concluded that

> [t]he allegations in the petition about "procedural deficiencies" do not appear to be a basis for removal. The State Court in the proceeding referred to in the petition found that the Agency failed to follow certain procedures relating to the listing on the State Register. These procedural errors are not related to the listing of Coleman Station Historic District on the National Register. *** [T]he Agency sent out notices of the listing on the National Register on December 30, 1994, to all the property owners in the district; the federal rules do not require that notice be sent to property owners adjacent to a proposed district.

By letter dated August 18, 1995, the Keeper notified plaintiffs that their petition to remove Coleman Station from the National Register was denied. *** She explained that the district was worthy of listing according to the established criteria, and that the procedural errors in the state listing did not vitiate the national listing. Thus, although Coleman Station is no longer on the New York State Register of Historic Places, it remains on the National Register of Historic Places.

*** At stake in this litigation appears to be the risk that, if the national listing is upheld, Coleman Station's state listing will be automatically restored without any further Board action. Under New York law, any property that is listed on, or even nominated to, the National Register is deemed listed on the state register. *** Although national listing does not burden private landowners in any respect, and requires only that federal agencies take into account the effect of any proposed action on protected property, *** state listing may impose burdens on landowners within a district, such as requiring them to prepare an Environmental Impact Statement in order to obtain state approval for modifications ***.

Discussion

I. *Plaintiffs' APA Claim*

Resolution of plaintiffs' APA claim turns on a single legal question: does the Keeper have independent authority to determine whether properties are eligible for listing on the National Register and to name them to the National Register without the agreement of a State's Historic Preservation Program? We find that the Keeper does have such independent authority and that, therefore, plaintiffs' APA claim is without merit.

We begin by looking at the regulations governing the listing of properties on the National Register. These regulations establish five mechanisms for the listing of a property:

> (1) Those Acts of Congress and Executive orders which create historic areas of the National Park System administered by the National Park Service, all or portions of which may be determined to be of historic significance consistent with the intent of Congress;
>
> (2) Properties declared by the Secretary of the Interior to be of national significance and designated as National Historic Landmarks;
>
> (3) Nominations prepared under approved State Historic Preservation Programs, submitted by the State Historic Preservation Officer and *approved by the NPS;*
>
> (4) Nominations from any person or local government (only if such property is located in a State with no approved State Historic Preservation Program) *approved by the NPS* and;
>
> (5) Nominations of Federal properties prepared by Federal agencies, submitted by the Federal Preservation Officer and *approved by NPS.*

36 C.F.R. §60.1(b) (emphasis added). Where a nomination comes through a state historic preservation program, the regulations reserve final authority for the Park Service[.] ***

This reservation, combined with the Secretary of the Interior's power to name a property for listing *sua sponte,* strongly supports the inference that the Keeper has independent authority to determine whether a property should be listed, even where a nomination initially comes through a state preservation program. *** [E]ven where there is a disagreement within a state program about a property's eligibility for listing, such nominations must be forwarded to the Keeper along with an explanation of the disagreement. ***

Every circuit court to have considered the federal government's authority under the National Historic Preservation Act and related statutes to determine a property's eligibility for the National Register has concluded that the federal government is not bound by the determinations of local authorities. For example, in *Stop H-3 Association v. Coleman*, 533 F.2d 434 (9th Cir. 1976), the state of Hawaii planned to build a federally-financed highway through a valley that a private citizens' group sought to protect. The citizens' group petitioned the Secretary of the Interior to place the valley on the National Register. The Secretary determined that the valley was eligible for listing on the basis of its local historic and cultural value.

Subsequent to that determination, the Hawaii Historic Places Review Board, a state body responsible for evaluating and nominating Hawaiian properties for inclusion in the state and national registers, issued a finding that the valley was of only marginal local significance, a classification that would afford the valley no protection from destruction. *** The question presented to the Ninth Circuit was whether the Secretary of the Interior (operating through the Keeper) had the authority to deem a property worthy of listing on the National Register on account of its state or local significance despite the state authorities' determination that the property was of marginal or no local significance. ***

The Ninth Circuit upheld the authority of the Secretary. *** [T]he court noted that

> [t]he Act does not distinguish in any way between properties of "national" significance and those of "state or local" significance. There is nothing whatsoever in the Act or its legislative history to indicate that the Secretary may name some properties to the Register *** only after obtaining the concurrence of state and local authorities. *** They are all deemed significant in *American* history, and they should be. If it should be held that the Interior Secretary has no power to determine that properties have state or local historic significance, there would, in our view, be a virtual nullification of the NHPA[.] *** Such a holding would be without precedent and would completely defeat Congress's clear attempt to protect such properties by passing the NHPA....

Id. at 441 n. 13 (emphasis in original). The court concluded that

> [s]ince the Interior Secretary is the only official authorized to name properties to the National Register, *** *the Interior Secretary's determination that [a particular site] is eligible for inclusion on the National Register as a site of local historic importance is not vitiated, and cannot be vitiated, by the State Review Board's finding that the [site] has only "marginal" significance.*

Id. at 441 (emphasis added).

* * *

Plaintiffs do not cite any legal authority, contrary to *Stop H-3* *** to support the proposition that local authorities have the final word on a property's eligibility for listing on the National Register. Instead, they rely on the argument that the procedural errors that occurred in the state listing process in this case render the national listing null and void. This argument assumes that the national listing process incorporates state procedural requirements whenever a property is brought to the Keeper's attention by a state preservation program. We disagree.

Nothing in the federal regulations governing the procedural requirements concerning the listing of properties on the National Register supports plaintiffs' position that compliance with state procedural requirements is a predicate to national listing. *** [T]hese regulations establish a comprehensive set of procedural requirements that must be met for a property to be listed on the National Register upon the nomination of a state preservation program. However, nowhere in the regulations is there a requirement that state preservation programs also comply with *state* procedural requirements regarding nominations of properties for the national register. Although prejudicial error in the nomination or listing process is a ground for removal from the national register, *see* 36 C.F.R. § 60.15, we read this provision as relating to errors in the *national* nomination or listing process, not errors in the state nomination process. The effect of reading a requirement of compliance with state procedural rules into the federal scheme, it seems to us, would add unnecessary prolixity and could lead to a maze of disparate procedures for national listing from state to state. Accordingly, since there has been no allegation that the Park Service failed to comply with its own procedural requirements, plaintiffs' procedural argument must fail.

In the absence of any federal procedural failings, we do not find that the Keeper acted arbitrarily or capriciously, in violation of the APA, when she denied plaintiffs' petition to remove Coleman Station from the National Register on account of NYHP's failure to comply with state procedural requirements. Nor do we find that the Keeper failed to consider all relevant factors regarding the district's eligibility, including the purported opinion by the NYHP official who transmitted plaintiffs' removal petition to the Keeper that the district may lack historical integrity. *** Rather than expressing an independent view regarding the district's integrity, the letter sets forth concerns that had been raised before the State Preservation Review Board, and recommends that the Keeper make an independent evaluation regarding the district's eligibility.

Finally, we reject plaintiffs' contention that the state procedural flaw, even if it does not require delisting in some cases, required delisting in this case in the absence of an affirmative federal finding of eligibility for federal listing. Once the federal listing occurred, plaintiffs had the opportunity to seek to persuade the Keeper that the property does not meet the eligibility criteria, and the Keeper's obligation, as we have noted, was to consider all relevant factors bearing on eligibility. The Keeper fulfilled this obligation. ***

II. *Plaintiffs' Contention Under the Due Process Clause*

Having determined that plaintiffs' APA challenge must fail, we turn to their contention that the district court's judgment should be upheld on the alternate ground that the Keeper's action violated their rights under the Due Process Clause. We have jurisdiction to consider any contention, supported by the record, that arguably supports the judgment. In exercising that jurisdiction, we may consider the legal sufficiency of the contention.

*** "The first question in any due process inquiry is whether the plaintiff has a constitutionally protected interest." *** To succeed on a claim of a procedural due process violation, "a plaintiff must establish that state action deprived him of a protected property interest." *Sanitation & Recycling Indus., Inc. v. City of New York,* 107 F.3d 985, 995 (2d Cir. 1997).

We reject plaintiffs' due process argument because national listing on its own does not impose any burdens on plaintiffs' use of their property. National listing constrains only the ability of departments of the federal government to take action affecting a listed property without first considering the effect of that action on the property. *** Plaintiffs have not alleged that this constraint on federal action implicates their property interests.

It is, rather, the burdens associated with listing on the New York register with which plaintiffs are concerned. These burdens include those imposed by New York's SEQRA and the attendant risk that because plaintiffs' property is subject to regulation under SEQRA, it will be less valuable in securing credit from lenders. Federal law is relevant to this scheme only because New York automatically adds to its register of historic places any property nominated to or deemed eligible for listing on the National Register. ***

The fact that New York has chosen to tie its register to the national register, however, does not transform plaintiffs' due process claim—predicated on the burdens imposed by state law—into a due process claim against the National Park Service. In the absence of any allegation that national listing on its own imposes a burden that affects plaintiffs' property interests, plaintiffs' due process claim against this defendant must fail.

Conclusion

The judgment of the district court is reversed and the case is remanded for entry of judgment for defendant-appellant.

Notes and Questions

1. **Federal and state criteria.** a. When do the old ordinary, such as neighborhood historical sites or places of local folklore, become cherished heritage, entitled to legal protection? b. It was not until 1981 that the Secretary of the Interior adopted formal criteria for listing on the National Register. c. Do the criteria recognize that although historic significance may be purely local, a property is still worthy of national listing?

2. **Regulatory limitations on use or alterations.** Even though listing on the National Register does not impose any limitations on an owner's use or alteration of the property, there are yet effects. If the property is within an area of potential effects, any undertaking by a federal agency may be delayed while the Section 106 consultation takes place. This is discussed in more detail, *infra.*

2. Historic Flora and Fauna

Hatmaker v. Georgia Department of Transportation

United States District Court for the Middle District of Georgia, Albany and Americus Divisions
973 F. Supp. 1058 (1997)

Sands, D.J. Presently before the Court is Defendants' motion to dissolve and dismiss the preliminary injunction entered by the Court in the above-styled action in October 1995.

The October 1995 injunction was based upon a finding that the Secretary of the United States Department of Transportation's ("the Secretary") approval of the use of federal funds for the road widening project at issue in this litigation was given in violation of §4(f) of the Department of Transportation Act of 1966, 49 U.S.C.A. §303 (Supp.1995),[1] and §18 of the Federal-Aid Highway Act of 1968, 23 U.S.C.A. §138 (1990).[2] In reaching this decision, the Court looked to 23 C.F.R. §771.135(e), a regulation governing the applicability of the protections of §4(f) to an historic site, or questionably historic site, the integrity of which may be jeopardized by a federal-aid highway project. Section 771.135(e) states in relevant part:

> The section 4(f) requirements apply only to sites on or eligible for the National Register [of Historic Places] unless the Administration determines that the application of section 4(f) is otherwise appropriate.

At the time of the issuance of the injunction, the record clearly showed that the Friendship Oak was not listed on the National Register of Historic Places ("National Register"). However, the Court found that the state Defendants' failure to include any information regarding the Friendship Oak in their application for Federal-Aid Highway funds improperly precluded the statutorily required decision of the Secretary as to (1) the eligibility of the tree for inclusion on the National Register, and (2) whether to exercise the Administration's discretion under §771.135(e) to apply §4(f) protections to the tree. In the total absence of such decisions by the Secretary, this Court could not properly review the Secretary's ultimate determination to federally fund the road widening project that is the subject of this litigation. Accordingly, the

1. Section 4(f) of the Department of Transportation Act, 49 U.S.C.A. §1653(f), was repealed in 1983 but was recodified without substantial change at 49 U.S.C. §303.

2. Section 18 of the Federal-Aid Highway Act, 23 U.S.C.A. §138, is virtually identical to section 4(f) of the Department of Transportation Act, 49 U.S.C.A. §303. For purposes of this Order, the statutes will be referred to collectively as "§4(f)" or "section 4(f)." ***

Court remanded the case to the Secretary for a determination of whether the Friendship Oak and the surrounding area required § 4(f) protection or other regulatory action pursuant to all applicable federal laws.

On October 23, 1996, the Defendants filed a notice of compliance with the Court's injunctive order, and on December 18, 1996, the Defendants filed a supplemental notice of compliance. By these notices of compliance, the Secretary concluded:

> [T]he tree within the intersection of Philema Road and North Jefferson Street is neither on nor eligible for inclusion on the National Register of Historic Places. Consequently, the provisions of Section 4(f) are inapplicable. Additionally, we have exercised the agency's discretion under 23 C.F.R. § 771.135(e) and have declined to invoke Section 4(f).

Defendants' Notice of Compliance and Motion to Dissolve and Dismiss at 2 [hereinafter "Defendants' Motion to Dissolve and Dismiss"].

Discussion

As this Court stated in the October 1995 order granting injunctive relief: "This case is not simply about a tree. This controversy is about the integrity of the legislative process." This much has remained constant since the issuance of that order. Thus, the question presently at issue is not whether the Court believes that the protection of the Friendship Oak is favorable to the destruction of the Friendship Oak, or vice-versa. Rather, the singular purpose of judicial review in this case is to determine whether the mandates set forth by Congress to implement a policy of national concern have been adhered to by the Defendants' in the decision-making process surrounding the tree. This is both the basis and the limit of this Court's jurisdiction in this action.

In this light, the Court must presently consider two separate decisions by the Secretary. The first is the determination that the Friendship Oak is neither on nor eligible for inclusion on the National Register and thus not subject to the restrictions of § 4(f). The second is the decision not to exercise the discretion, vested with the Secretary pursuant to 23 C.F.R. § 771.135(e), to provide § 4(f) protection to the Friendship Oak for reasons other than those statutorily mandated by Congress.

A. Eligibility for § 4(f) Protection

"Section 4(f) evidences Congress' response to growing public concern over the preservation of our nation's parklands, recreation areas, wildlife and waterfowl refuges, and historic sites...." *Druid Hills Civic Association, Inc. v. Federal Highway Administration,* 772 F.2d 700, 713–14 (11th Cir. 1985). By enacting § 4(f), Congress gave a clear mandate that protection of § 4(f) properties is to be given paramount importance in the planning and execution of federally funded construction projects. *See Citizens to Preserve Overton Park v. Volpe,* 401 U.S. 402, 412, 91 S.Ct. 814, 821–22, 28 L.Ed.2d 136 [(1971)]. In fact, once a property has been designated as a § 4(f) property, the monetary expense required to protect that property in conjunction with a roadway construction project is of minimal relevance. The Secretary may only approve a transportation project that makes use of a § 4(f) property if "there is no prudent and feasible alternative to using the land...." *Id.* at 411, 91 S.Ct. at

821. "The requirements are stringent. Congress clearly reflected its intent that there shall no longer be reckless, ill-considered, wanton desecration of natural sites significantly related to our country's heritage." *Stop H-3 Association v. Coleman,* 533 F.2d 434, 438 (9th Cir. 1976).

While Congress set forth an articulate and distinct standard for the protection of §4(f) properties, it did not include a specific standard for judicial review in either the Department of Transportation Act or the Federal-Aid Highways Act. Accordingly, the Secretary's administrative decision must be reviewed pursuant to §706 of the Administrative Procedure Act. *See Citizens to Preserve Overton Park v. Volpe,* 401 U.S. 402, 413, 91 S.Ct. 814, 822, 28 L.Ed.2d 136, 5 U.S.C.A. §706 (1977).

In *Overton Park,* the Supreme Court set forth the standard of judicial review under §706 for determinations by the Secretary about the applicability of §4(f) to a particular highway project. *Druid Hills, supra,* 772 F.2d at 714. The first step in an *Overton Park* review is to determine whether the Secretary properly interpreted his authority to approve use of a §4(f) property in a Federal-Aid Highway project as limited to situations where no feasible and prudent alternatives exist. *Overton Park, supra,* 401 U.S. at 415–16, 91 S.Ct. at 823–24; *Druid Hills, supra* 772 F.2d at 714. In the present case, however, the Secretary found that the Friendship Oak is not a §4(f) property. Therefore, the first phase of review under *Overton Park* is inapplicable to the current analysis.

The second step is to determine whether the Secretary's ultimate decision—in this case, the finding that the Friendship Oak is not a §4(f) property—was "arbitrary, capricious or an abuse of discretion." *Overton Park, supra,* 401 U.S. at 416, 91 S.Ct. at 817; *Druid Hills, supra,* 772 F.2d at 714 5 U.S.C.A. §706(2)(A). "This assessment requires an evaluation of whether 'the decision was based on a consideration of the relevant factors and whether there has been a clear error in judgment.'" *Druid Hills, supra,* 772 F.2d at 714 (quoting *Overton Park, supra,* 401 U.S. at 416, 91 S.Ct. at 823–24). "Although the judicial inquiry should be penetrating, the court is not empowered to substitute its judgment for that of the Secretary." *Druid Hills, supra,* 772 F.2d at 714.

Finally, the Court must determine whether the Secretary's action followed the necessary procedural requirements. *Overton Park, supra,* 401 U.S. at 417, 91 S.Ct. at 824; *Druid Hills, supra,* 772 F.2d at 714.

For each of these inquiries, "the focal point for judicial review should be the administrative record already in existence [on the basis of which the administrator's determination was made], not some new record made initially in the reviewing court." *Druid Hills, supra,* 772 F.2d at 714 (quoting *Camp v. Pitts,* 411 U.S. 138, 142, 93 S.Ct. 1241, 1243–44, 36 L.Ed.2d 106, 111 (1973)).

As stated above, in deciding whether the Friendship Oak *requires* §4(f) status, the Secretary must determine whether the tree is on or eligible for the National Historic Register. *See* 23 C.F.R. §771.135(e). To be considered for the National Register a property or site must meet the regulatory requirements promulgated pursuant to the

National Historic Preservation Act (NHPA). 16 U.S.C.A. §470a. [54 U.S.C. §306108] The criteria for evaluation under NHPA are set forth in 36 C.F.R. §60.4, which provides, in pertinent part:

> The quality of significance in American history, architecture, archeology, engineering, and culture is present in districts, sites, buildings, structures, and objects that possess integrity of location, design, setting, materials, workmanship, feeling, and association and
>
> (a) that are associated with events that have made a significant contribution to the broad patterns of our history; or
>
> (b) that are associated with the lives of persons significant in our past; or
>
> (c) that embody the distinctive characteristics of a type, period, or method of construction, or that represent the work of a master, or that possess high artistic values, or that represent a significant and distinguishable entity whose components may lack individual distinction; or
>
> (d) that have yielded, or may likely yield, information important in prehistory or history.

Pursuant to the Court's October 1995 order, the Georgia Department of Transportation ("GDOT") conducted an extensive study of the historic value of the Friendship Oak in light of the criteria for eligibility on the National Register. *** Upon completion of this historic evaluation, GDOT submitted its evidence and conclusions to the Secretary. The Secretary then conducted an independent review and reached an independent determination that the Friendship Oak is not eligible for inclusion on the National Register.

In conducting their evaluation, GDOT researched the historic associations of the Friendship Oak in several contexts, including: Native Americans; early trails and roads; land surveys; the Civil War; lynchings; landmark tree registers; the Spanish-American War; and general local significance. As to all but the final three categories, the administrative record is generally uncontroverted. It is with respect to the latter three categories that the Plaintiffs most strongly object to the Secretary's determination not to protect the Friendship Oak under §(4)(f).

1. Uncontroverted Areas in the Administrative Record

The GDOT study found that until the early nineteenth century Native Americans populated what is now Dougherty County. However, the study could not find evidence of any association between the Friendship Oak, or the immediately surrounding area, and significant activities in Native American history. Nor did the study find a significant relationship between the tree and any continuing activities of Native American culture.

The study also found that many historic trails, roads, and stage coach routes passed through the Albany area during the nineteenth and early twentieth centuries. Again, however, no evidence indicated that these routes were marked by, or even located near, the Friendship Oak. Similarly, an examination of survey maps and notes, made when the region was platted for distribution to white settlers, failed to show any specific identification of an oak tree at the site of the Friendship Oak, either as a boundary tree or as a local landmark.

The GDOT study also incorporated reviews of Civil War reports and maps. Such reviews failed to produce evidence supporting a finding that the Friendship Oak served as a military landmark or stood at the site of any significant event during the Civil War.

In addition, GDOT studied information compiled by the American Civil Liberties Union relating to lynchings in Georgia. Although this information revealed the dark and all too prevalent history of lynchings in southwestern Georgia, the evidence did not connect these lynchings with any tree in the immediate area of the Friendship Oak.

As to all of these areas of historic review, the Plaintiffs have failed to show any issues that are in serious dispute *within* the administrative record. Nor have the Plaintiffs revealed that the administrative record ignored any significant pieces of data in these areas such that the Secretary's ultimate determination could only be construed as clearly erroneous or an abuse of discretion. With regard to these areas of historic study, the Plaintiffs have generally relied upon the bare assertions of historic significance set forth in their complaint. The Secretary was not required to give great weight to such assertions in the face of the contrary evidence within the administrative record.

As to the remaining areas of historic review discussed above, the Plaintiffs' arguments in opposition to the motion to dissolve the October 1995 injunction are based more directly upon the findings and conclusions within the administrative record.

2. Inclusion on Landmark Tree Registers and Guide Books

The administrative record included a review of several landmark tree registers. One such register, the Georgia Urban Forest Council, Georgia Landmark and Historic Tree Register (the "Urban Forest Council Register"), listed the Friendship Oak as an historic live oak. In order to determine whether inclusion of the Friendship Oak on the Urban Forest Council Register triggered §4(f), the GDOT study compared the requirements for registration on that list with those of the National Register. The study concluded that the requirements for inclusion on the two registers are not equivalent, with the National Register's standards requiring greater scrutiny.

In order to determine the actual basis for inclusion of the Friendship Oak on the Urban Forest Council Register, the GDOT study examined the application to the Council, which coincidentally was submitted by the Plaintiffs, for consideration of the tree as an historic live oak. The GDOT study concluded that the application was comprised of assertions based wholly, or in large part, on unsubstantiated hearsay. In fact, the application was based upon the same claims of historic significance as argued by the Plaintiffs in the course of this litigation. Thus, the GDOT study made pursuant to the October 1995 injunction addressed each of these contentions. As discussed herein, the GDOT study revealed little, if any, factual support for the claims of historicity set forth in the application to the Georgia Urban Forest

Council. Thus, the Court cannot say that the Secretary was clearly erroneous or abused his discretion in deciding to rely on the entirety of factual evidence within the administrative record rather than the simple inclusion of the Friendship Oak on the Urban Forest Council Register in determining that the tree is not subject to § 4(f).

* * *

3. The Spanish American War—Camp Churchman

The GDOT study found that the area surrounding the Friendship Oak served as "Camp Churchman," a stopping ground for American soldiers to muster out of service from the Spanish American War. The study further found that the establishment of the camp itself, as well as certain of the events transpiring there, were of some local significance at the time. However, no evidence in the administrative record indicated that any particular oak tree in the area served as a significant landscape feature of the encampment.[3] In addition, the study concluded that the area as a whole had lost its integrity as a site of historic significance due to subsequent development of the land, including the construction of a golf course, a subdivision, and commercial development, as well as the impoundment of the two creeks that apparently formed the boundaries of the camp. Based on the lack of evidence of the tree itself having played a significant role in the history of Camp Churchman and the general loss of integrity of the surrounding area, the GDOT study concluded that the Friendship Oak could not convey a sufficient association to Camp Churchman, or the Spanish-American War, to be considered eligible for inclusion on the national register.

The requirements of integrity for eligibility for inclusion on the National Register are set forth in 36 C.F.R. § 60.4. *See supra.* In addition to meeting the requirements of one of the four general categories of historic sites enumerated in that regulation, a site must possess integrity of location, design, setting, materials, workmanship, feeling, and association. A detailed analysis of the integrity of the Friendship Oak and the surrounding area as they relate to Camp Churchman, is set out at pages 43 to 47 of the "Philema Road Oak Tree—Historic Narrative and National Register Eligibility Discussion" attached to Defendants' motion to dissolve and dismiss. A detailed review of this analysis is unnecessary, as the administrative record leaves no questions

3. On May 19, 1997, the Plaintiffs sought to supplement the record with the affidavit of Owen D. Winters. Mr. Winters' affidavit states that as a young boy he heard stories from his grandfather about the elder's service in the Spanish-American War. Mr. Winters recalls being told of a winter spent with the troops at a camp "in Georgia." His grandfather told him that a large tree stood by the commander's tent, and that the tree was remarkable because very few trees populated the immediate area. Mr. Winters recalls being told that the tree was so large that it served as a landmark for the encampment and a point of reference when giving directions. Having learned about the instant litigation, Mr. Winters believes that the encampment spoken of by his grandfather was Camp Churchman, and that the large tree must be the Friendship Oak. ***

about whether the area that comprised Camp Churchman has been completely altered by commercial development. *** [T]he Defendants have from the beginning of this litigation maintained the position that a single tree, standing alone and without human alteration cannot convey historic value and thus cannot qualify for the National Register. The Court rejected this argument in the October 1995 injunctive order, but the administrative record presently before the Court is replete with comments by various officials to the effect that a single, unaltered tree cannot qualify for the National Register. In support of this position, the Defendants conducted a survey of all "tree" listings currently on the National Register. Only four of the approximately 65,000 listings reviewed were determined to be single trees, and two of them had been altered in some fashion by humans. The other two trees, while unmarked by humans, had a well documented history of direct and significant involvement in the ceremonial and/or judicial practices of two separate Native American societies. The inclusion of these two trees appears to preclude the argument that single, unaltered trees cannot qualify for the National Register, and there are a litany of hypotheticals that could easily test the Defendants' position on this issue. However, it suffices to say that the relevant statutory language does not even suggest that a single tree cannot qualify for the National Register, and the Court does not accept the Defendants' arguments in this regard.

On the other hand, a tree, like any other site or object, must inhere the appropriate historic characteristics and associations, defined in 36 C.F.R. §60.4, to qualify for inclusion on the National Register. As with the Native American tribal trees discussed above, these historic qualities must, to some degree, be verifiable. As previously discussed, the Defendants undertook an extensive study in this regard and were unable to find evidence of any direct association between the Friendship Oak and Camp Churchman. *** On the one hand, the tree is all that remains of Camp Churchman. On the other hand, the tree does not appear to have played any more significant role in the events at Camp Churchman than did the dirt on the ground or the air in the sky. *** While the Court cannot say that the Secretary's decision in this case was wise, it also cannot find that the decision was illegal on the basis of the tree's relationship to Camp Churchman. Without any direct association between the tree and the camp, the law does not *require* a finding of eligibility for the National Register under 36 C.F.R. §60.4.

4. Present Day Local Significance

To a small degree the GDOT study examined the local significance of the tree to area residents. GDOT discovered that at least some residents agree that the tree that is the subject of this litigation is not the true "Friendship Oak." According to such residents, the true Friendship Oak was located in the same vicinity but was either destroyed by fire in the 1960s or cut down during the construction of the Liberty Expressway in the 1970s. The GDOT study also found that while there is significant local sentiment for the tree, as evidenced by the intense, local debate that has surrounded this litigation, the City Commissioners have refused to designate the tree as a site of local historic significance. Thus, the conclusion of the GDOT study is that the current popularity of the Friendship Oak among many members of the local community is not dispositive on the issue of historic preservation as the tree has neither been officially recognized as a site of local historic value nor acknowledged by an extended *history* of local public support.

*** [T]he Plaintiffs contend that the failure of the Albany City Commissioners to designate the tree as a site of local, historic significance is not dispositive on the issue of the applicability of §4(f). The Plaintiffs conversely argue that the Secretary was *required* to apply §4(f) to the Friendship Oak due to the passage of a resolution by the Dougherty County Board of Commissioners recognizing the value of the tree to local citizens.

In support of each of these arguments, the Plaintiffs look to *Stop H-3 Association v. Coleman*, 533 F.2d 434 (1976). In *Stop H-3*, the State of Hawaii planned to build a Federal-Aid Highway through the Moanalua Valley. *Id.* at 436. A private group petitioned the Secretary of the Interior to have the valley placed on the National Register. *Id.* at 439. Although the Secretary of the Interior found that the valley "had not been conclusively demonstrated to be of *national* historic significance," he nevertheless found the valley eligible for inclusion on the National Register due to the valley's *local* historic and cultural value. *Id.* (emphasis added). Subsequent to the Secretary of the Interior's determination, the Hawaii Historic Places Review Board issued a finding that the valley was only of "marginal" local significance and undeserving of protection. *Id.* at 439–440. The Court of Appeals for the Ninth Circuit held that the jurisdiction of the Secretary of the Interior under §4(f) was not limited to sites of national historic significance, but rather that it extended to sites of state or local significance as well:

> If it should be held that the Interior Secretary has no power to determine that properties have state or local historic significance, there would, in our view, be a virtual nullification of the NHPA and Section 4(f).... Whenever a city or state preferred a federally-funded highway to an historic site, the local body could simply declare the site insignificant. Such a holding would be without precedent and would completely defeat Congress's clear attempt to protect such properties by passing NHPA and 4(f).

Id. 441 n. 13. *** Thus, the Plaintiffs in the present case are correct in arguing that the refusal of the Albany City Commissioners to designate the Friendship Oak as a sight of local historic significance is not dispositive on the question of whether the tree merits §4(f) protection on the basis of local historic significance.

The Plaintiffs conversely argue that the resolution of the Dougherty County Commissioners, identifying the Friendship Oak as a site of "significant value" to the community, triggers the protections of §4(f). In *Stop H-3*, the Ninth Circuit explained that *** "if *any* of the officials having jurisdiction to determine that a site has national, State, or *local* historic significance, so decides then section 4(f) applies." *Stop H-3, supra*, 533 F.2d at 441 (emphasis added). ***

*** While the [Commissioners'] resolution states that the tree has "significant value," nowhere does the resolution refer to the Friendship Oak as a site of such significant local historic value as to warrant any type preservation effort. In fact, the very purpose of the resolution was to place a dollar value ($61,156.00) on the tree and to request that GDOT fund half of the tree's "replacement cost." To construe such a resolution as establishing that the Friendship Oak holds the type of irreplaceable historic and cultural values that § 4(f) seeks to protect is illogical and runs squarely in the face of the resolution's plain language and intent. Therefore, the Secretary is not bound by virtue of the Dougherty County Commissioners' Resolution to provide § 4(f) protections to the Friendship Oak. ***

It is of course ironic that if the Friendship Oak were preserved as a result of this litigation, even without a finding of National Register eligibility, the very nature of the community's fight to save the tree and the surrounding media coverage of the same could perhaps sufficiently enhance the tree's local historic status to the level required for National Register eligibility. However, the purpose of § 4(f) is to protect, among other things, those sites and objects that have achieved a requisite level of historic significance and integrity at the time that a relevant, federally-funded project is presented for administrative review. Section 4(f) is not to a tool to be used to create historic significance.

For the foregoing reasons, the Court finds that the Secretary's decision that the Friendship Oak is not eligible for the National Register was not arbitrary, capricious or an abuse of discretion.

* * *

C. Procedure Was Properly Followed

The procedure for identifying historic properties is set forth at 36 C.F.R. § 800.4. This regulation states in relevant part:

> (c) Evaluating historical significance.
>
> (1) In consultation with the State Historic Preservation Officer and following the Secretary's Standards and Guidelines for Evaluation [48 FR 44716], the Agency Official shall apply the National Register Criteria to properties that may be affected by the undertaking and that have not been previously evaluated for National Register eligibility. The passage of time or changing perceptions of significance may justify reevaluation of properties that were previously determined to be eligible or ineligible.
>
> (3) If the Agency Official and the State Historic Preservation Officer agree that the criteria are not met, the property shall be considered not eligible for the National Register....

In the present case, GDOT provided the U.S. Department of Transportation, Federal Highway Administration with an extensive review of the historicity of the Friendship Oak. The USDOT then conducted an independent review of this information, and USDOT also forwarded the information to the State Historic Preservation Division of the Georgia Department of Natural Resources. Both USDOT and the State Historic Preservation Division independently concluded that the Friendship

Oak is not eligible for the National Register. Upon these findings, the Secretary has made an independent judgment that the Friendship Oak is not eligible for the National Register, and concurrently declined to exercise his discretion under 23 C.F.R. § 771.135(e) to provide § 4(f) protection for the tree. *See Defendants' Motion to Dissolve and Dismiss* at 3–4.

Accordingly, the Defendants have properly followed the procedures set forth for identification and protection of historic properties pursuant § 4(f) and all applicable regulations.

D. Conclusion

As stated, the role of the Court in this action is to ensure that the procedures set forth by Congress for implementing a policy of national concern have been properly followed by the Defendants. For the foregoing reasons, the Court finds (1) that the Defendants properly followed the procedures for evaluating the historicity of the Friendship Oak, (2) that the Secretary's determination that the Friendship Oak is not eligible for inclusion on the National Register was not arbitrary, capricious, or an abuse of discretion, and (3) that the Secretary's decision not to exercise his unfettered discretion under 23 C.F.R. § 771.135(e) to provide § 4(f) protection for the Friendship Oak is not properly reviewable by this Court.

While the Court finds that the decision made by the Secretary was legal, it is not for this Court to determine if that decision was wise in the face of local public interest in preservation. Clearly, the Secretary was not powerless to leave the Friendship Oak standing despite a finding that its historicity was insignificant. How to respond to the efforts of local citizens and interested parties to save the tree in the face of commercial development was a choice for the Secretary and locally elected officials. They have made their decision. The wisdom of that decision is ultimately left to the consideration, observation and evaluation of present and future generations in the absence of the shade of the Friendship Oak.

Accordingly, Defendants' motion to dissolve and dismiss should be, and hereby is, GRANTED. The preliminary injunction entered by the Court on October 26, 1995 in the above-styled action is DISSOLVED as of June 12th, 1997 at 10:50 a.m. It is FURTHER ORDERED that the above-styled action is hereby DISMISSED.

Historic Tree Stories

Historic trees and their stories abound. There is "Survivor Tree," over 90 years old, located in downtown Oklahoma City that survived the 1995 bombing of the Alfred P. Murrah Federal Building. Before the bombing, the tree was the only place for shade in the building's parking lot. After the bombing, investigators considered chopping it down to recover evidence embedded in it from the blast. The tree was spared this fate when investigators were able to recover evidence from the tree's trunk and branches. The Oklahoma City National Memorial and Museum was created to honor "those who were killed, those who survived, and those changed forever" by the 1995 bombing and it was agreed that "one of the components of the Memorial must be the Survivor Tree," as a symbol of human resilience. http://www.americanforests.org/blog/the-survivor-tree/ (last visited April 6, 2017).

The Angel Oak in John's Island, South Carolina, is thought to be more than 1,400 years old, without doubt, one of the oldest living things east of the Mississippi River. Originally, it was a part of a land grant that remained in the same family for four generations, then became a part of a marriage settlement. Not only old, the tree is gargantuan, standing 65 feet tall, 160 feet in diameter, with a trunk of 25-feet in circumference, and an overall spread of 17,100 square feet.

The Gettysburg Address Honey Locust stood quietly on a hilltop behind President Abraham Lincoln on November 19, 1863 when he gave the Gettysburg Address, that so impressed upon the nation the ultimate sacrifices of the many who had fallen there. Historic Tree Stories, American Forests, http://www.cintas.com/customer_applications/Documen Tree/files/Historic-Tress.pdf (last visited April 6, 2017).

Some trees have a more infamous history, such as those used for the lynching of black people. "The lynching tree is the most potent symbol of the trouble nobody knows that blacks have seen but do not talk about because of the pain of remembering—visions of black bodies dangling from Southern trees, surrounded by jeering white mobs—is almost too excruciating to recall." James H. Cone, The Cross and the Lynching Tree 3 (2011). Should these trees be preserved as historic monuments? As reminders of an ugly past?

* * *

What Is A Tree Worth?
Jill Jonnes, The Wilson Q. (Winter 2011)

"Trees brighten city streets and delight nature-starved urbanites. Now scientists are learning that they also play a crucial role in the green infrastructure of America's cities."

*** In 2006, [the renowned environmental scientist] Gregory McPherson and his colleagues were adding Queens as a reference city when the New York Parks Department asked them to value all of New York City's 592,000 street trees. With the advances made over the preceding dozen years, McPherson could deliver a far more sophisticated report than he had for Chicago. Energy savings: New York City's trees annually saved roughly $28 million, or $47.63 per tree. Air pollution: Each street tree removed an average of 1.73 pounds of air pollutants per year (a benefit of $9.02 per tree), for a total of more than $5 million. The report also calculated that street trees reduced stormwater runoff by nearly 900 million gallons each year, saving the city $35.6 million it would have had to spend to improve its stormwater systems. The average street tree intercepted 1,432 gallons, a service worth $61, a figure large enough to impress cost-conscious city managers.

McPherson and his colleagues were also able to tally various benefits associated with aesthetics, increased property values and economic activity, reduced human stress, and improved public health, which were estimated at $52.5, or $90 a tree. These drew on straight-up economic studies of real estate prices as well as social science research, which showed, for example that hospital patients who could see a tree out the window of their room were discharged a day earlier than those without such a view. Other studies showed that shopping destinations with trees had more customers than those that didn't, and leafy public-housing projects experienced less violence than barren ones. All these data led to the finding that each year New York City's street trees delivered $122 million in benefits, or about $209 a tree. As New York City's parks and forestry officials well knew, they received $8 million a year to plant and tend street trees, and spent another $6.3 million to pay personnel. The net benefit they were getting for all these trees was an impressive $100 million. For the first time, urban forestry science had a dramatic effect on public policy. In 2008, Mayor Michael Bloomberg quadrupled the city's forestry budget, from $8 million to $31 million (down last year to $27 million), when he launched Million Trees NYC, a partnership with entertainer Bette Midler's nonprofit New York Restoration Project. McPherson was thrilled to see science elevate urban forestry above the level of "a kumbaya idea." The million trees (350,000 are in the ground so far) planted by 2018 will transform the Big Apple, and those lush, tree-lined streets and shaded parks may well become Bloomberg's most visible legacy.***"

* * *

Dugong v. Rumsfeld

United States District Court of the Northern District of California
No. C 03-4350 MHP, 2005 WL 522106 (March 2, 2005)

Patel, J. Plaintiffs, consisting of the Okinawa dugong, American and Japanese environmental groups, and three individual Japanese citizens, brought this action against defendants Donald H. Rumsfeld, Secretary of Defense, and the United States Department of Defense, alleging that defendants failed to comply with the requirements of the National Historic Preservation Act ("NHPA"), 16 U.S.C. § 470a-2, [54 U.S.C. § 307101] and the Administrative Procedure Act ("APA"), 5 U.S.C. §§ 701–706. Now before the court is defendants' motion to dismiss for failure to state a claim and for lack of subject matter jurisdiction. Having considered the arguments of the parties and for the reasons set forth below, the court enters the following memorandum and order.

Background

I. *United States Military Bases and Okinawa*

The United States has maintained military bases on Okinawa since 1945. ***

The United States Department of Defense maintains and controls a number of military bases on Okinawa, including the Marine Corps Air Station Futenma, which operates facilities and provides services and materials to support Marine Corps aircraft operations. *** In November 1995, the United States and the government of Japan established the Special Action Committee on Okinawa ("SACO"), a bilateral committee with the primary purpose of reducing the burden of the United States military presence on the Okinawans. *** SACO recommended that Marine Corps Air Station Futenma be replaced by a sea-based facility, and in [a] Final Report, issued by the SCC on December 2, 1996, … created the Futenma Implementation Group ("FIG"), a bilateral Japan-United States committee under the supervision of the SCC. *** The implementation group was charged with formulating a "detailed implementation plan" by December, 1997, encompassing "concept development and definition of operational requirements, technology performance specifications and construction method, site survey, environmental analysis, and final concept and site selection." ***

On September 29, 1997, the United States Department of Defense released a document entitled "Operational Requirements and Concept of Operations for Marine Corps Air Station Futenma Relocation, Okinawa, Japan," ("1997 Operational Requirements") which outlined the Department of Defense's "functional requirements and concept of operations" for the replacement facility *** [at] Henoko Bay, adjacent to Camp Schwab. *** This document was updated and superceded by the 2001 Preliminary Operational Requirements dated February 15, 2001. ***

*** In August, 2000, the Consultative Body of Futenma Relocation, composed exclusively of local and national officials from the Government of Japan, was established in order to produce a "Basic Plan" that identified the "location, size, construction method and runway orientation of the Futenma Replacement Facility." *** The Basic Plan issued by this body in July, 2002, approved the Governor of Okinawa's decision to relocate Marine Corps Air Station Futenma to Nago City's Henoko District, immediately offshore from the Marine Corps' Camp Schwab[, satisfying] the locational requirements announced in the 1997 Operational Requirements. ***

The Naha Defense Facility Administration, a department of the Japanese Defense Agency, has, with the approval of the United States Department of Defense, constructed an office building within Camp Schwab to manage its on-site work relating to construction of the new facility. *** In addition, the facility is planning to carry out a technical survey that will include the boring of approximately 63 holes into Henoko Bay's coral reef and ocean floor. ***

II. *The Okinawa Dugong*

The dugong is an herbivorous marine mammal that inhabits tropical and subtropical coastal and island waters in the Indo-Pacific from East Africa to Vanuatu. *** The Okinawa dugong (*Dugong dugon*) is a small, isolated population of the Dugong species found in the waters off the eastern coast of Okinawa. *** One of the smallest known populations of dugong, it is thought to comprise "about 50 individuals," which feed on the "few remaining sea grass beds in that area," one of which is off the Henoko coast. *** The animal is central to the creation mythology, folklore, and rituals of traditional Okinawan culture. ***

According to a 2002 United Nations Environmental Programme report, the construction of a military base near Henoko could "destroy some of the most important known remaining dugong habitat in Japan," with "potentially serious" repercussions for such a small population. *** The report predicts that "unless measures are undertaken to protect dugongs in the Okinawan region they will soon be extinct in Japanese waters." *** The dugong is listed as "endangered" under the United States Endangered Species Act. 16 U.S.C. § 1531 *et seq.;* 50 C.F.R. § 17.11. The patterns of dugong feeding activity and the range of its active habitat are in dispute, but it is agreed that Henoko Bay provides "viable sea grass areas" which are "potential dugong feeding areas." *** In Japan, the Okinawa dugong is a protected "natural monument" under that country's "Law for the Protection of Cultural Properties." *** Henoko Bay has not been designated for cultural protection nor listed as a natural monument. ***

* * *

Legal Standard

* * *

II. *The National Historic Preservation Act*

Congress enacted the NHPA in 1966 with the goal of preserving the "historical and cultural foundations of the Nation ... in order to give a sense of orientation to the American People." 16 U.S.C. § 470(b)(2)[54 U.S.C. § 307701]. The Act establishes that "[i]t shall be the policy of the Federal Government, in cooperation with other nations and in partnership with the States, local governments, Indian tribes, and private organizations and individuals ... [to] provide leadership in the preservation of the prehistoric and historic resources of the United States and of the international community of nations." 16 U.S.C. §470-1(2). The NHPA authorizes the Secretary of the Interior to maintain a National Register of Historic Places "composed of districts, sites, buildings, structures, and objects significant in American history, architecture, archeology, engineering, and culture." 16 U.S.C. §470a(1)(A). *** [S]ection 470f of the Act, *** imposes a dual obligation on federal agencies: the substantive duty to "weigh effects" in deciding whether to undertake the federal action and the procedural duty to consult with the Advisory Council. ***

In 1980, Congress amended the NHPA to implement the United States' participation in the Convention Concerning the Protection of the World Cultural and National Heritage. The amendment includes section 470a-2, which provides that:

> Prior to the approval of any Federal undertaking outside the United States which may directly and adversely affect a property which is on the World Heritage List or on the applicable country's equivalent of the National Register, the head of a Federal agency having direct or indirect jurisdiction over such undertaking shall take into account the effect of the undertaking on such property for purposes of avoiding or mitigating any adverse effects.

16 U.S.C. §470a-2. In 1998, the Secretary of the Interior published suggested guidelines for federal agency responsibilities under the amended Act[, which specify that] "efforts to identify and consider effects on historic properties in other countries should be carried out in consultation with the host country's historic preservation authorities, with affected communities and groups, and with relevant professional organizations." 63 Fed.Reg. 20,496 and 20,504 (April 24, 1998). Such consultation "should be undertaken early in the planning stage of any Federal action that might affect historic properties." *Id.* Therefore, *** federal agencies are obligated under section 470a-2 to consider adverse effects, and they are guided by Secretary of the Interior guidelines to consult with foreign bodies.

III. *Administrative Procedures Act*

The NHPA does not provide an independent basis for judicial review of agency actions. However, the Administrative Procedures Act ("APA") authorizes judicial review of final agency actions "for which there is no other adequate remedy in a court." 5 U.S.C. §704. Final agency actions are defined as actions which "mark the consummation of the agency's decisionmaking process," defined as not "merely tentative or interlocutory [sic] nature," and which determine "rights or obligations" or from which "legal consequences will flow." *** An agency action or decision may be set aside if the court finds it to be "arbitrary, capricious, an abuse of discretion, or otherwise not in accordance with law." 5 U.S.C. §706(2). ***

Discussion

I. *The National Historic Preservation Act*

Defendants assert that the NHPA does not apply to the circumstances of the present action. The language of section 470a-2 stipulates that the statute applies to "any federal undertaking" affecting "a property" that is "on the applicable country's equivalent of the National Register." 16 U.S.C. §470a-2. Defendants contend that the Japanese Law for the Protection of Cultural Properties is not "equivalent" to the National Register of Historic Places, the dugong cannot constitute "property," and the United States Department of Defense has taken no action that could be considered a "federal undertaking." The court considers these issues in turn.

A. The Equivalence of Japan's Law for the Protection of Cultural Properties and the National Register

Section 470a-2 applies to properties which are included on the UNESCO World Heritage List or on "the applicable country's equivalent of the National Register." 16 U.S.C. §470a-2. The applicability of the NHPA to the Okinawa dugong thus turns on whether the Japanese law which designates it for preservation, the Law for the Protection of Cultural Properties, is Japan's "equivalent" of the National Register.

According to the language of the Japanese act itself, the Law for the Protection of Cultural Properties was motivated by an awareness that "the cultural properties of the country are indispensable to the correct understanding of its history, culture, etc., and that they form a foundation for its cultural development for the future." Art. VIII, Law for the Protection of Cultural Properties ***. The law seeks to "preserve and utilize cultural properties, so that the culture of the Japanese people may be furthered and a contribution ... made to the evolution of world culture." *** Similarly, the NHPA was motivated by the belief that "the historical and cultural foundations of the Nation should be preserved as a living part of our community life and development in order to give a sense of orientation to the American people." 16 U.S.C. §470(b)(2). The Law for the Protection of Cultural Properties is the only law concerned with the protection of cultural properties in Japan, just as the NHPA is the chief American law governing the issue in this country. *** And like the NHPA, with its expansive scope, the plain language of the Japanese law covers a broad range of properties[, which] stipulates that "cultural properties" may include historic buildings, works of art, archeological sites, gardens, places of scenic beauty, and other "natural monuments." *** The National Register and the Law for the Protection of Cultural Properties thus reflect similar motives, share similar goals, and generally pertain to similar types of property.

Defendants argue that the Japanese law which protects the dugong as a "national monument" is not "equivalent" to the National Register because the former includes "both inanimate and animate things," whereas the latter "provides no legal recognition or protection whatever for any animal species." *** First of all, by employing the word "equivalent," section 470a-2 does not require that the National Register and the foreign list in question be identical. *** [T]he court interprets the section as requiring that the foreign list be "corresponding or virtually identical especially in effect or function." Both registers have corresponding and indeed virtually identical effects (to designate the cultural and historical heritage of the nation for special protections) and the same function (using the mechanism of a cultural protection register). An interpretation of section 470a-2 requiring that the foreign list be "identical" to the American one would, like the use of the NHPA's definition of "historic property" discussed below, contradict the international aspect of the section. To require that foreign lists include only those types of resources which are of cultural significance in the United States would defy the basic proposition that just as cultures vary, so too will their equivalent legislative efforts to preserve their culture. *** To require identical definitions of culture would eviscerate section 470a-2's explicit recognition of "equivalent" foreign lists.

The National Register and the Japanese Register are also equivalent because their authorizing statutes serve parallel roles in each nation's statutory scheme for the protection of human and natural resources. The Law for the Protection of Cultural Properties developed independently from Japan's laws protecting wild animals for their biological value. *** For an animal species to be listed under the Cultural Properties law, it must possess sufficient cultural value; whether or not it is endangered or biologically valuable is irrelevant *** The Cultural Properties law is the only cultural protection law of its kind in Japan. *** Similarly, the NHPA is the United States' cultural protection legislation, existing apart from other statutes protecting endangered species. *Compare* 16 U.S.C. § 470 et seq. *with* 16 U.S.C. § 1531 et seq. Both statutes have evolved in a similar direction towards greater inclusiveness of natural, as well as cultural, places and things. ***

Lastly, the statutes demonstrate an equivalent commitment to protecting significant bridges between human culture and history, on the one hand, and wildlife, on the other. The presence of culturally significant animals has been the basis of many listings and determinations of eligibility for the National Register, including several animal habitats important in Native American tribal histories. *** The fact that the National Register classifies these listings using the name of a site, rather than the name of the culturally-significant animal species present there, does not undermine an argument for equivalence with the Japanese List. On the contrary, both lists have the same effect—the protection of animals in specific settings of cultural importance—rendering their different nomenclatures merely incidental. The dugong is protected in an equivalent way: the Law for the Cultural Protection of Properties lists one particular population, the Okinawa dugong, for protection because the animal has special importance in native Okinawan mythology and culture. ***

Indeed, this line of reasoning explaining the statutes' equivalence arguably reaches even further, as both the National Register and the Japanese Register list properties of biological value, without an explicit cultural dimension. Defendants argue that nature per se is not protected under the NHPA, absent some historical dimension. Yet in fact, wildlife refuges are included on the National Register without any cultural or historical links. *** In addition, the UNESCO World Heritage List, which is expressly referenced as a benchmark for the coverage of section 470a-2, also lists marine wildlife habitat and sanctuaries for protection. *** This is "equivalent" to the category of "natural monuments" under the Japanese law, which permits animals to be designated as cultural properties if they are "of great scientific-historic value" and "commemorate Japan's natural environment." ***

In light of the many similarities between the lists generated by the Law for the Protection of Cultural Properties and by the NHPA, the Japanese law is an "equivalent of the National Register" within the meaning of section 470a-2.

B. The Dugong as "Property"

This court's inquiry could justifiably end with the finding of equivalence between the two lists at issue in this case, as well as the conceded fact that the Okinawa dugong is protected on the Japanese list. The language of section 470a-2 applies to "propert[ies]" which are "on the World Heritage List or on the applicable country's equivalent of the National Register." While reasonable jurists might dispute the degree to which "property" is intended as a restrictive term in the amendment, it will nevertheless pursue defendants' argument that section 470a-2 can only apply if the Okinawa dugong can be understood as property within the NHPA statutory scheme.

The term "property" is not defined in the NHPA. However, the statute defines the phrase "historic property" as "any prehistoric or historic district, site, building, structure, or object included in, or eligible for inclusion on the National Register, including artifacts, records, and material remains related to such a property or resource." 16 U.S.C. § 470w(5). *** [But requiring] that a foreign property meet the NHPA's definition of "historic property" would conflict with the statute's explicit reference to foreign law, refocusing the analysis on domestic considerations and criteria. Congress clearly intended a different standard to govern the eligibility of properties for protection under section 470a-2, as demonstrated by the wording of the section itself[,] *** utilizing the term "property" rather than the domestically-defined "historic property[.]" [Additionally,] the section sets out a foreign standard for determining those properties to which it applies, requiring that properties be on UNESCO's World Heritage List or on the foreign country's "equivalent of the National Register." *** Thus, the focus is on the property's actual inclusion on a foreign list, rather than whether a particular property would be eligible under National Register criteria.

Congress's intention to set this different standard for historically significant properties under section 470a-2 is also supported by the legislative history. The section was enacted to provide "legislative implementation for United States participation in the [UNESCO-sponsored] Convention Concerning the Protection of the World Cultural and Natural Heritage." *** Congress acknowledged that the Convention, "leaves it to each participating nation to identify and delineate the meritorious heritage properties situated in its own territory." *** In light of these considerations, the definition of "historic property" set out in the NHPA cannot be controlling in the section 470a-2 context. Accordingly, plaintiffs need only prove that the dugong is a "property."

It remains for the court to interpret the parameters of the term "property" as utilized in section 470a-2. Here, the NHPA and the federal regulations still provide guidance. Without the untenable focus on significance in American history, "property" becomes simply a "district, site, building, structure, or object." An "object" is defined as "a material thing of functional, aesthetic, cultural, historical or scientific value that may be, by nature or design, movable yet related to a specific setting or environment." 36 C.F.R. § 60.3(j). Plaintiffs have satisfied their burden to show that the dugong fulfills each element of the CFR's definition. The dugong is indisputably a "material thing," as opposed to something of a spiritual or intellectual nature. The plaintiffs have provided evidence that the dugong possesses "functional, aesthetic, cultural, historical or scientific value," particularly a special cultural significance in Okinawa. *** Plaintiffs have provided uncontroverted evidence that in Okinawan creation mythology, the dugong is considered the ancestor of human beings, and that in traditional Okinawan folklore and ritual, the dugong is revered as a "female mermaid spirit," worshiped at special shrines as a deity responsible for successful fishing expeditions, and feared as an "ocean spirit" capable of creating tsunamis. *** Songs concerning the dugong are "regularly sung" by shamans and residents of the Henoko Bay area, further suggesting a contemporary cultural value beyond the dugong's status as a "wild animal." *** Finally, there can be no dispute that the Okinawa dugong is "movable yet related to a specific setting or environment," namely, Henoko Bay, which is in the "middle" of the offshore area where "the dugongs and the seabeds they use for feeding and habitat are located." ***

Defendants contend that a wild animal cannot qualify as "property," and that there is no indication in the NHPA and its amendments, the accompanying legislative history, the implementing regulations and guidelines, or case law that Congress "sought to expand the NHPA's statutory coverage in order to protect or preserve wild animals." *** [Though] very little precedent exists governing the question of whether a living thing can constitute a property eligible for the National Register[, the] decision of the one district court that has dealt with the issue undermines defendants' argument that the dugong is automatically disqualified. In *Hatmaker v. Georgia Department of Transportation,* 973 F.Supp. 1047 (M.D.Ga. 1995), plaintiffs sought a preliminary injunction against continued construction of a federally-funded road widening project that involved destruction of an oak tree of significance in Native American history. The court held that the tree was at least potentially eligible for placement on the National Register and granted the preliminary injunction. *Id.* at 1056–57. In a subsequent case, *** the court again rejected the defense's argument that an unaltered tree could not qualify for the National Register. *** In assessing the applicability of the statute, the court emphasized the verifiable nature of the contested object's historic qualities. *Id.* at 1067.

Hatmaker is analogous to the present case. While animals obviously differ from trees, their distinguishing qualities are not significant under the plain language of the statute. The dugong may, like a tree, fall under the category of "object," as "a material thing of functional, aesthetic, cultural, historical or scientific value that may be, by nature or design, movable yet related to a specific setting or environment." 36 C.F.R. §60.3(j).

Defendants' remaining arguments against the dugong's status as property are equally unavailing. Defendants argue that the Ninth Circuit has held that the state and federal governments cannot "own" wild animals, and therefore that such animals cannot be property. *** [But w]hether the government owns the property is irrelevant to a determination of eligibility for the National Register[,] *** a mere lack of ownership or possibility of ownership does not disqualify a thing from constituting property. As the Tenth Circuit has noted, while it is "well settled that wild animals are not the *private* property of those whose land they occupy," they "are instead a sort of *common* property whose control and regulation are to be exercised [by the government] 'as a trust for the benefit of the people."' *Mountain States Legal Foundation v. Hodel,* 799 F.2d 1423, 1426 (10th Cir. 1986) (emphasis added) ***.

* * *

The Okinawa dugong is movable, yet related to a specific setting or environment. It is protected under Japanese law on the basis of its cultural and historical importance to the Okinawan people. Therefore, section 470a-2 of the NHPA can apply to the Okinawa dugong, an animal protected for cultural, historical reasons under a foreign country's equivalent statutory scheme for cultural preservation.

C. *The Marine Corps Air Station Futenma Relocation As a "Federal Undertaking"*

Section 470a-2 applies to "any Federal undertaking outside the United States." 16 U.S.C. §470a-2. *** To this court's knowledge, no case law specifically interprets the NHPA definition of "undertaking" in the context of section 470a-2. However, precedent interpreting "undertaking" in the domestic application of NHPA provides an important guide in the present action. The two statutes are governed by the same definition of "undertakings" under the NHPA. *** The one notable difference between the provisions governing federal undertakings conducted domestically and those that are undertaken abroad is that "undertakings" in the domestic context are triggered by the more restrictive event of "the approval of the expenditure of any Federal funds ... or the issuance of any license" rather than, in the case of section 470a-2, "the approval of any Federal undertaking." *Compare* 16 U.S.C. §470f, *with* 16 U.S.C. §470a-2. The triggering clause for section 470a-2 is thus more broad, indicating that Congress may have intended a less restrictive definition of undertakings to apply to federal projects abroad.

The standards for identifying "undertakings" under the NHPA have been widely held to be "similar" to those for identifying "major federal actions" under the National Environmental Protection Act. *** Factors to consider in evaluating major federal actions include: (1) the agency's degree of discretion over the federal aspects of the project, (2) whether federal aid has been given, and (3) whether the overall level of federal involvement is sufficient to transform "essentially private action into federal action." *** Courts have construed the NHPA's broad definition of "undertakings" to include a wide range of direct and indirect means of federal support, such as financing, licensing, construction, land grants, and project supervision.

* * *

Beyond the operational requirements planning stages, disputed issues of material fact also remain as to whether the Department of Defense has engaged in subsequent and on-going federal undertakings relating to the military base. While plaintiffs have not yet engaged in discovery to investigate their allegation that defendants are involved in supervising the design and construction of the replacement air base, they have produced several recent documents demonstrating that the United States has exercised regulatory oversight of the planning and construction of the new military base, including granting approval for preliminary engineering and environmental surveys. *** [T]he question of whether the "undertakings" alleged by plaintiffs "may directly and adversely affect" the dugong, as also required under section 470a-2, is outside the scope of the present pre-discovery motion. *** Therefore, [while] section 470a-2 can, as a matter of law, apply to the federal undertakings alleged in this case. However, disputed issues of material fact remain regarding the scope and contours of these undertakings, as well as the nature of defendants' on-going influence on the location, survey methods, design, and construction of the replacement facility. Defendants will be permitted to renew their motion for summary judgment on these factual issues following the close of discovery.

* * *

Conclusion

Defendants' motion to dismiss, converted into a motion for summary judgment on the issue of the applicability of the NHPA to the circumstances of the present action is DENIED.

IT IS SO ORDERED.

Notes and Questions

1. **Cultural references.** a. Should it ever matter that the "historic property" protected in the other country is not something that would appear on our national or any state registers of historic places; instead, is it always sufficient that the other country celebrates and protects it? b. Is the result a *de facto* extension of the NHPA, at least as it operates in the other country? c. Are our interests in living things better served by specific protective legislation, such as the Endangered Species Act of 1973, 16 U.S.C. § 1531 (protecting all endangered species and the ecosystems on which they depend)?

2. **International Protection for Dugong Migratory Habitat.** The international community has come together to protect the Dugong. Apart from the Convention on Migratory Species, a Memorandum of Understanding on the Conservation and Management of Dugongs and their Habitats Throughout Their Range ("UNEP/CMS Dugong MoU") was entered into on October 31 2007. So far, there are twenty-six signatories, including Australia, Eritrea, France, Madagascar, Myanmar, the United Arab Emirates, the United Republic of Tanzania, India, the Comoros, Kenya, Japan, Iran, and the Philippines. The MoU and the associated Conservation and Management

Plan ("CMP") provides a platform for preserving the Dugong by coordinating conservation and management activities throughout their migratory range. The CMP provides the basis for focused species and habitat-specific activities, such as studying the causes of Dugong mortality; conserving, improving, and managing habitats; raising public awareness of Dugong conservation; improving legal protection of Dugongs and their habitats; and enhancing cooperation among nations and regions. Memorandum of Understanding on the Convention on the Conservation of Migratory Species of Wild Animals, http://www.cms.int/dugong (last visited April 6, 2017).

3. When Does NHPA Apply?

Section 306108 [formerly § 106] of NHPA provides:

> The head of any Federal agency having direct or indirect jurisdiction over a proposed Federal or federally assisted undertaking in any State and the head of any Federal department or independent agency having authority to license any undertaking, prior to the approval of the expenditure of any Federal funds on the undertaking or prior to the issuance of any license, shall take into account the effect of the undertaking on any historic property. The head of the Federal agency shall afford the Council a reasonable opportunity to comment with regard to the undertaking.[1]

* * *

The cases that follow make clear that while Section 106 is procedural by its terms, those procedures must be followed nonetheless toward the end of substantive protection of historic properties.

WATCH v. Harris

United States Court of Appeals for the Second Circuit
603 F.2d 310 (1979)

Oakes, C.J. An ongoing urban renewal project in the heart of a small New England city has evidently awakened in the minds and hearts of local citizens concern about

1. Section 106 read:

> The head of any Federal agency having direct or indirect jurisdiction over a proposed Federal or federally assisted undertaking in any State and the head of any Federal department or independent agency having authority to license any undertaking shall, prior to the approval of the expenditure of any Federal funds on the undertaking or prior to the issuance of any license, as the case may be, take into account the effect of the undertaking on any district, site, building, structure, or object that is included in or eligible for inclusion in the National Register. The head of any such Federal agency shall afford the Advisory Council on Historic Preservation established under title II of this Act a reasonable opportunity to comment with regard to such undertaking.

Under § 306108, historic property is defined in § 300308 to include "any prehistoric or historic district, site, building, structure, or object included on, or eligible for inclusion on, the National Register, including artifacts, records, and material remains relating to the district, site, building, structure, or object."

the historical heritage that the project impinges upon. The citizens formed the plaintiff organization by the acronym WATCH, Waterbury Action to Conserve Our Heritage, Inc., and the organization brought suit against three individual federal officials, the Secretary, Regional Administrator, and Area Director of the United States Department of Housing and Urban Development, hereinafter collectively called HUD, and against the Waterbury Urban Renewal Agency (WURA), defendant below and appellant here. The Central Business District Renewal Project No. Conn. R-107 (the Project) contemplated the demolition of a number of buildings in a twenty-acre area. In seeking to stop that demolition WATCH below urged that defendants had not complied with the requirements of the National Environmental Policy Act (NEPA), 42 U.S.C. §4321 *et seq.*, the National Historic Preservation Act (NHPA), 16 U.S.C. §470 [54 U.S.C. §306108] *et seq.*, and certain regulations of HUD and of the Advisory Council on Historic Preservation.[1] In a careful and comprehensive opinion, the United States District Court for the District of Connecticut, T. Emmet CLAIRE, Chief Judge, held that NEPA was applicable but that, because the loan and capital grant contract was executed before any affected properties were listed in the National Register, NHPA was not. He also held that subsequent regulations of the Advisory Council on Historic Preservation *** could not apply because they would be "inconsistent" with NHPA, the underlying statute. Accordingly, the court granted WATCH's motion for a preliminary injunction to restrain the defendants from proceeding with the Project.

* * *

WURA appeals from the grant of the preliminary injunction [and WATCH] cross-appeals and urges that NHPA is applicable to the Project.

Background

The City of Waterbury, after workshop sessions, meetings, public hearings, and the like, adopted an urban renewal plan to rehabilitate an area of 20.6 acres in downtown Waterbury north of Interstate 84. On May 11, 1973, WURA and HUD executed a Loan and Capital Grant Contract (the Contract), pursuant to which HUD was to give WURA project loans aggregating in excess of $12,800,000 and a capital grant in excess of $11,500,000. The plan calls for demolition of 83 of some 113 buildings in the project area and for the construction of high rise, high density commercial and office space. The project is still far from completion. As of January 28, 1977, 55% of the land had been acquired; 35% of the buildings had been demolished; although no land had been disposed of, project improvements were 25% complete; and relocation was 45% complete. As of November 28, 1978, 27 of the

---

1. The HUD Handbook of Departmental Policies, Responsibilities and Procedures for Protection and Enhancement of Environmental Quality 1390.1, 38 Fed.Reg. 19182, 19185 (1973), provides:

> Any HUD action or undertaking which has an effect on a property listed on, or nominated to, the National Register of Historic Places will require Special Environmental Clearance and must comply with section 106 of the National Historic Preservation Act of 1966 and implementing procedures.

buildings scheduled for demolition remained standing. WURA's executive director testified that as of November 1978, WURA had spent only $12 million of the total cost of the project; that WURA has not disposed of or agreed to convey some of the real estate on which the remaining buildings scheduled for demolition sit; that WURA has not even acquired certain property from private owners; and that a number of the remaining buildings scheduled for demolition are occupied by tenants of WURA.

It is of some importance to the resolution of this case that under the Contract the work is done in phases, each of which requires HUD's permission. Under Section 108(A) of the Contract, WURA is required promptly to submit to HUD documentary data with respect to any action that WURA proposes to take in carrying out the Project. ***

*** [T]he acquisition of properties, the demolition of buildings, and changes in the urban renewal plan all require HUD's on-going permission. Section 108(B) explains that this permission is necessary to insure that the "Agency (WURA) shall not take any step which might, in the opinion of the Secretary (of HUD), violate applicable Federal laws or regulations ..."

In the eyes of WATCH, the buildings in the project area possess historical interest because they are "of a classic turn-of-the-century main street type," representing an eclectic collection of architectural styles including Renaissance revival, Richardsonian romanesque, Greek revival, and Italianate. The cultural, social, architectural, and historic significance of the neighborhood escaped the attention of the local citizenry[,] at least they were not moved by the writings of Ada Louise Huxtable until December 1, 1976, when the Waterbury Commission on Aging suggested to the State Historic Preservation office that the H. H. Peck carriage house, located within the Project area, be considered for listing on the National Register of historic places. When on May 6, 1976, WURA forwarded to HUD's area office HUD Form ECO-1 setting forth the applicant's environmental information with respect to the project area, WURA stated that "(t)here are no known significant historic, archaeological, or architectural sites or properties listed on, or being considered for nomination to, the National Register of Historic Places." Similarly there were no responses to HUD's legal advertisements on January 5, 1977, in two Waterbury newspapers that HUD was performing an environmental assessment of the Project and was inviting comment by January 20.

On January 28, 1977, HUD completed its Special Environmental Clearance for the Project, observing that "(t)here are no properties listed or nominated to the National Register of historical places." Based on this Clearance, HUD concluded that there was no significant environmental impact and that the processing of the Project could proceed. But HUD did not consult with the State Historic Preservation office (SHPO) about eligible properties before preparing the Clearance, and there was disputed testimony that it also did not consult about listed or nominated properties. Neither the ECO-1 nor the Clearance expressly considered alternatives to demolition of buildings designated for demolition in the Project area. HUD did not prepare an environmental impact statement for the Project area and did not consult with the national Advisory Council on Historic Preservation.

However, on April 21, 1977, WURA did transmit information to HUD about the potential eligibility of the carriage house. On December 29, 1977, HUD wrote to the Department of Interior and expressed its finding that the house was not eligible but requested a determination from the Department. The Keeper of the National Register determined that the house was eligible on February 7, 1978. In late December, 1977, attorneys for members of WATCH who owned property in the Project area wrote to HUD demanding National Register eligibility determinations with respect to all the commercial buildings in the Project area. On January 18, 1978, HUD ordered a "freeze," [i]. e., that no federally assisted acquisition, disposition, renovation, or demolition be conducted on any structure within the Project area until the area office had made a Register eligibility determination. The Advisory Council on Historic Preservation subsequently informed the HUD area office that it had become aware of the Project and requested an evaluation of the significance of the central business district. The State Historic Preservation officer on March 22, 1978, also wrote to the HUD area office stating that he had made a field inspection in February and concluding that several portions of the area were eligible for inclusion, because the area was "a substantially intact 19th century commercial district," one of the more complete 19th century downtown areas in Connecticut, and some of the buildings were "outstanding examples of their types."

The "freeze" lasted from January 18, 1978, to August 31, 1978, while HUD inspected the project and gathered data. In September, 1978, HUD terminated its attempts to obtain Register eligibility determinations and recommenced demolition. At this point SHPO informed the Deputy Assistant Secretary of HUD that it had not been consulted and suggested an immediate review of HUD's decision not to seek an eligibility determination. WURA has evidently entered into a contract for the demolition of the remaining buildings scheduled for demolition. WATCH brought suit in October, 1978, and the district court granted a preliminary injunction on December 22, 1978.

The Decision of the Court Below and Contentions of the Parties

Judge Clarie held that NHPA was inapplicable, that Advisory Council and HUD regulations, *** were either inapplicable or invalid, but that NEPA did apply.

Judge Clarie concluded the NHPA was inapplicable because in 1973, when the contract here was executed, Section 106, 16 U.S.C. § 470f, provided that "(t) he head of any Federal agency ... shall, prior to the approval of the expenditure of any Federal funds on the undertaking ... take into account the effect of the undertaking on any district, site, building, structure or object that is included in the National Register." Although the statute was amended in 1976 to refer to property "including in or eligible for inclusion in the National Register" (emphasis added), the language "prior to the approval of the expenditure of any Federal funds" remained. As Judge Clarie duly noted, a number of federal courts, in reviewing NHPA challenges to federally assisted urban renewal projects, have interpreted the "approval" language to mean the time when a grant and loan contract is executed. Because no properties in the Project area were listed when the Contract was signed, Judge Clarie reasoned, NHPA imposes no present duty upon HUD to consider the effect of the Project on eligible properties or properties listed after 1973.

The court next addressed the applicability of HUD regulations. Pursuant to Executive Order 11593, 36 Fed. Reg. 8921 (1971), directing federal agencies to adopt procedures to assure that federal programs contribute to historic preservation, HUD incorporated by reference the guidelines which the Advisory Council on Historic Preservation had promulgated. *** Under the authority of NHPA, these guidelines originally established procedures for determining whether a federally assisted undertaking had an effect on a listed property. 38 Fed. Reg. 5388 (1973). Under the authority of Executive Order 11593 and NEPA as well as NHPA, the Advisory Council revised the regulations effective January 25, 1974. 39 Fed. Reg. 3366. The guidelines, which have not been subsequently amended, are published at 36 C.F.R. § 800.

The district court noted that these revised guidelines differ from NHPA in two important respects. First, even prior to the 1976 amendment to § 470f, the Guidelines directed that the federal agency consider the effect of any proposed undertaking on properties "that are included in [o]r eligible for inclusion in the National Register." 36 C.F.R. § 800.4 (emphasis supplied). Second, the Guidelines mandate continuing compliance with the Act, even after the date of signing the Loan and Capital Grant Contract, as long as the federal agency retains any authority to make changes in the project which could alter its impact on historical and cultural properties. 36 C.F.R. § 800.3(c) and (g).

* * *

Judge Clarie went on to find, however, that NEPA did apply. He reasoned that the granting of approval for acquisition or demolition of any property was a "major federal action" within the meaning of 42 U.S.C. § 4332 and pointed out that the courts have construed this language and that of 42 U.S.C. § 4331(b) to mean that a federal agency must comply with NEPA so long as it retains, as HUD did here, significant control over the project. The judge noted that HUD recognized its continuing responsibility when it imposed a "freeze" on the Project. He found that once new information (the potential eligibility of several structures for listing) was made available, HUD should have conducted a new "threshold" determination as to whether an environmental impact statement was required. If as a result of this threshold determination HUD had decided that Register-eligible properties would be affected, then a detailed environmental impact statement would be required under the case law. ***

WATCH seeks to uphold the district court decision in respect to NEPA but contends in respect to NHPA that the cases construing Section 106 to call for a cut-off date as of the date of the loan and capital grant agreement, *** have been erroneously decided. In the view of WATCH, Section 106 "applies to require Advisory Council review as long as HUD retains the control to make approvals pursuant to the grant-loan Contract." WATCH also argues that the guidelines of the Advisory Council do apply because they are procedural, irrespective of any construction of the Act itself; because they were promulgated before HUD made its environmental assessment in 1977; and because the Handbook was adopted pursuant to NEPA and Executive Order 11593 as well as NHPA.

In this appeal, *** WURA argues, [that] if NHPA is inapplicable, NEPA must also be inapplicable, for several reasons. First, notwithstanding the specific language in Section 101(b) of NEPA, *** WURA asserts that NHPA is the only federal statute applicable to historic preservation. Second, WURA relies upon a series of cases involving the air and water pollution acts and stating that where an act is the "functional equivalent" of NEPA, NEPA is not applicable. Third, WURA argues that if an environmental impact statement is required, NEPA is in conflict with NHPA and thus should not be enforced, under the Supreme Court decision in *Flint Ridge Development Co. v. Scenic Rivers Association*, 426 U.S. 776, 96 S.Ct. 2430, 99 L.Ed.2d 205 (1976) (holding that the Interstate Land Sales Full Disclosure Act, 15 U.S.C. § 1701, displaces NEPA where they are in direct conflict).

WURA also argues that even if NEPA applies, HUD followed its own regulations; thus HUD's determination that an environmental impact statement did not have to be prepared was not arbitrary, capricious, or otherwise not in accordance with law.

On this appeal HUD now takes a position contrary to WURA, arguing that Congress has incorporated considerations of historic preservation into NEPA, that NHPA is not the functional equivalent of NEPA, and finally that there is no irreconcilable conflict between NHPA and NEPA that would justify exempting from the operation of Section 102(2)(C) of NEPA an urban renewal project which might have a significant effect on historic resources.

Discussion

We take up the NHPA question first because if WATCH is correct that NHPA has been erroneously construed, both the supposed conflict that the court found between the statute and regulations and the supposed conflict that WURA urges between NHPA and NEPA disappear. We do this in recognition of the principle of statutory construction that "when two statutes are capable of co-existence, it is the duty of the courts, absent a clearly expressed congressional intention to the contrary, to regard each as effective." *Morton v. Mancari*, 417 U.S. 535, 551, 94 S.Ct. 2474, 2483, 41 L.Ed.2d 290 (1974).

A. NHPA

Whether NHPA § 106, 16 U.S.C. § 470f, is applicable here depends upon whether the court below was correct in holding that the execution of the loan and grant contract was, within the meaning of the statute, "the approval of the expenditure of any federal funds on the undertaking...." and the [o]nly such approval. If it were, then the "cut-off" date for compliance with NHPA was the time of the execution of the loan and grant contract; and because no properties were nominated to, or even considered eligible for listing on, much less listed on, the National Register as of that date, NHPA would clearly not apply. *** We conclude, however, that the provisions of NHPA do not cease to apply simply because an agency has preliminarily approved expenditures. Those provisions should apply until the agency has finally approved the expenditure of funds at each stage of the undertaking. Because our conclusion differs from that of most courts that have addressed the question, our reasoning must be stated with care.

We begin with the language of the statute. The clues to its meaning, unfortunately, are few and ambiguous. Some do suggest that even a preliminary authorization amounts to a cut-off. Thus the first sentence of § 106 states that a federal agency having jurisdiction over a "Proposed Federal or federally assisted undertaking" (emphasis added) shall consider its effect on listed properties. And the language "any" in the phrase "prior to the approval of the expenditure of any Federal funds" might refer to the initial funding only. On the other hand, the language also supports the interpretation that the preliminary approval is not a cut-off. The term "proposed" might simply be shorthand for "proposed or continuing," and "any" might mean any expenditure of federal funds, not the expenditure of initial funds. Moreover, if the statute intended to establish a cut-off once an agency gave preliminary approval to expenditures, one might expect it to read "prior to the approval of the undertaking," rather than "prior to the approval of the expenditure of any Federal funds on the undertaking." Finally, it is possible to interpret the term "undertaking" as referring not simply to an urban renewal project but to each of the project's several phases.

Because we believe that the words of the statute are susceptible to either reading, we must look to other guides to ascertain the true congressional intent. In doing so, we must be cognizant of the principle that although legislative history may serve as a guide to the actual purpose of Congress in enacting a law, it is that purpose which we must keep uppermost in mind.

Congress never explicitly considered the specific problem before us, so far as the recorded legislative history of the initial National Historic Preservation Act shows. *** Nevertheless the legislative history does shed light on the underlying problems that Congress attempted to meet and its method of meeting them; the history therefore helps "to manifest (congressional) purposes in their completeness...."

Congressional interest in historic preservation has been longstanding. *** But it was not until a United States Conference of Mayors study by a special committee on historic preservation, entitled "With Heritage So Rich," that Congress, in enacting NHPA, took the key step of protecting not only "nationally significant" properties but also properties of "historical, architectural, or cultural significance at the community, State or regional level ... against the force of the wrecking ball." H.R.Rep.No.1916, *Supra*, 1966 U.S.Code Cong. & Admin.News at p. 3309. The House Report emphasized the importance of focusing attention on the significance of such community, state or regional properties, specifically in "the urban renewal field," and of striking a "meaningful balance ... between preservation of these important elements of our heritage and new construction...." *Id.* The proposed NHPA had a threefold purpose, according to the House Report:

> (1) to strengthen and expand the work being done under section 2(b) of the act of August 21, 1935 ... and to establish a national register of sites, structures, and the like which are significant in American history, architecture, archeology,

> and culture; (2) to encourage local, regional, State, and National interest in the protection of such properties; and (3) to establish an Advisory Council on Historic Preservation charged with the duties of advising the President and the Congress on matters relating to preservation of such properties, recommending measures to coordinate public and private preservation efforts, and reviewing plans for Federal undertakings and the undertakings of others involving Federal assistance or requiring a Federal license which affect sites, structures, and the like listed in the national register referred to above.

H.R.Rep.No.1916, *Supra*, 1966 U.S.Code Cong. & Admin.News at pp. 3307–08.

The legislative history of § 106 begins with S.3098 *** [s]ection 202 of that bill provided:

> The head of any Federal agency having direct or indirect jurisdiction over a proposed Federal or federally assisted project in any State shall, prior to the approval of the expenditure of any Federal funds on the project, take into account the effect of the project on any site, building, or object of national significance that is included in the national register established under section 101(a) of this Act.

The executive branch secured the introduction of S.3035 on March 2, 1966, but the bill contained no comparable provision. In a letter of June 7, 1966, to the Chairman of the Senate Committee on Interior and Insular Affairs, the Deputy Assistant Secretary of the Interior recommended that S.3035 be enacted in lieu of S.3098. He also recommended, however, the adoption of some of the provisions of S.3098, including Section 202, suggesting that the section be expanded to include All [sic] structures of historic significance that are included on the national register, not simply structures of national significance.

After brief hearings on the bills, the Senate Committee on Interior and Insular Affairs reported out S.3035 with amendments. Section 106 of the reported bill repeated the language "prior to the approval of the expenditure of any Federal funds on the project," expanded the protection to all historic properties, required the federal agency to report any effect on a listed property to the Advisory Council on Historic Preservation, and provided for a sixty-day waiting period, beginning at the time the report is made to the Advisory Council, "before Federal funds may be expended for the project concerned." The Committee Report explained that Section 106 "is intended to insure that the Federal agencies will not work at cross purposes with the goals of historic preservation and provides for a meaningful review of Federal or federally assisted projects which affect historic properties identified on a national register." S.Rep.No.1363, 89th Cong., 2d Sess. 8 (1966). With little general discussion and no discussion of § 106, the Senate passed the bill on July 11, *** and referred it to the House Committee on Interior and Insular Affairs.

The House Committee Report contains some language that buttresses the strict cut-off interpretation of § 106. One of the responsibilities of the Advisory Council, the Report stated, was "reviewing Plans for Federal undertakings and the undertakings of others," H.R.Rep.No.1916, *supra*, 1966 U.S.Code Cong. & Admin.News, p. 3308 (emphasis added). The Report further explained that the bill "requires ... agencies (whose undertakings affect listed properties) to afford the Advisory Council an ample, fair, and reasonable opportunity to comment with regard to such Proposed undertakings before they are commenced." *Id.*, 1966 U.S.Code Cong. & Admin.News, p. 3310 (emphasis added). But although this "proposal" language demonstrates a congressional commitment to delaying the initial federal funding of a program until the effect on listed properties has been assessed, it hardly demonstrates a converse commitment to rushing forward with the program once initial funding has been approved. *** On a more sensitive analysis, the legislative history reveals a determination to protect historic properties at every stage where the federal agency approves funding.

The House considered the bill on September 19 and October 10 and passed it by voice vote on the latter date. The Senate agreed to the House amendments on the following day without discussion, and the President signed the bill into law on October 15, 1966. *** Representative Leo O'Brien, after explaining that the first purpose of the bill was to provide federal funds for local preservation, stated: "Second, the program would be reinforced by providing that no Federal agency may make money available under other Federal programs, such as urban renewal, which will affect a historically significant structure until account has been taken of these effects and until opportunity has been given to the Advisory Council ... to comment on the plan." 112 Cong.Rec. 25940 (1966). WURA contends that O'Brien's comment suggests that the accounting and notice requirements do not apply when "the federal money has already been appropriated." But we find the comment more ambiguous; indeed, the omission of any reference to "approval" and the emphasis on expenditures militate somewhat in favor of the view that the accounting and notice requirements do apply to each approval of funding in a continuing program.

Thus the direct legislative history of § 106 is inconclusive. Apparently Congress never explicitly considered the specific issue before us, whether "approval" and "undertaking" in § 106 should be interpreted as imposing that section's accounting and notice requirements on funding approvals that occur after an initial approval of funding for a continuing program.

* * *

[A]lthough Congress did not consider the narrow issue before us in 1966, it did intend in § 106 to provide "a meaningful review" of federally assisted projects which affect historic properties, S.Rep.No.1363, *supra*. We believe that our interpretation of § 106 provides a far more meaningful review than the strict cut-off interpretation.

It is not without significance that the Advisory Committee [sic] itself came to interpret the Act as applying on a stage-by-stage basis. *** Generally speaking, an agency's own interpretation of an act that it is charged with executing is entitled to some weight, provided that the interpretation does not directly conflict with the intent of Congress. An administrative construction is particularly persuasive if Congress considers but fails to change it. ***

The 1976 amendments greatly increased the federal funding of historic preservation, gave the Advisory Council on Historic Preservation independent agency status, and somewhat incidentally extended the protection of § 106 to eligible as well as listed properties. It may be significant that the Senate Report treated this extension as simply a "housekeeping" amendment, and hence of not overwhelming substantive importance. *** Such a characterization is consistent with our interpretation of § 106. For if "approval" of expenditures may occur in the several stages of a project, it is somewhat less important whether a property is included or eligible. Even if the property must be included on the Register before § 106 applies, a phase-by-phase interpretation ensures that the impact on many eligible properties will be considered once they are listed.

* * *

The sum and substance of all this is, we think, a congressional purpose, expanding over the years, to make certain that federal agencies give weight to the impact of their activities on historic preservation. Throughout Congress has recognized that it is necessary to identify the properties that are of state, community, or local significance, and this was one of the major purposes of the 1966 Act itself. The problems of identification were and remain considerable, as the 1976 legislative history recognizes. One would suppose that Congress, having these problems in mind, did not intend to adopt a strict cut-off date, at least as to grant and loan contracts such as this one where the federal agency gives its final approval to the expenditure of federal funds only in stages. And § 108(B) of the contract explains that one of the purposes of phased approval is to ensure that the local agency does not take any step which, in HUD's opinion, might violate federal law.

Such an interpretation of NHPA is entirely consistent with the regulations of the Advisory Council, the agency charged by NHPA to act; with Executive Order 11593; and with NEPA. The regulations we have already described. The Executive Order, promulgated in 1971, directed federal agencies, in consultation with the Advisory Council, to "institute procedures to assure that Federal plans and programs contribute to the preservation and enhancement of non-federally owned sites, structures and objects of historical, architectural or archaeological significance." 36 Fed.Reg. 8921 (May 15, 1971), 1971 U.S.Code Cong. & Admin.News, p. 2545. And NEPA, as we have pointed out, *** explicitly includes historic preservation as an environmental objective and imposes a continuing responsibility of compliance.

We are not persuaded by the cases, *** which have interpreted Section 106 of NHPA as imposing a "cut-off." None of the cases carefully considered the distinction between initial approval and additional approvals in an ongoing undertaking. Nor is there any indication that either Congress or the Advisory Council believes that these cases supply a binding interpretation. Certainly the Advisory Council regulations, *** do not so indicate. And there is no reference in the legislative history of the 1976 amendments to the decided cases in the lower federal courts ***. Thus it would be very difficult to argue that Congress by silence adopted any judicial interpretation of the cut-off rule.

Moreover, the mandate of NHPA as enacted in 1966 is quite broad, 16 U.S.C. § 470. We are no more willing to give a "crabbed interpretation" to Section 106 of the Act than the courts have been in respect to NEPA. *Calvert Cliffs' Coordinating Committee v. United States Atomic Energy Commission*, 146 U.S.App.D.C. 33, 41, 449 F.2d 1109, 1117 (1971); *** *See also Penn Central Transportation Co. v. New York City*, 438 U.S. 104, 131, 98 S.Ct. 2646, 57 L.Ed.2d 631 (1978) (recognizing that the promotion of the general public welfare by historic preservation in the form of landmarks regulation is a legitimate exercise of the state police power and holding that such regulation is not necessarily an unlawful taking requiring the award of compensation)[.] *** We conclude that Section 106 as amended applies to require HUD and Advisory Council review as long as HUD retains the authority to make funding approvals pursuant to the grant and loan contract.

Here, there is no question that HUD had not approved all stages of the funding in 1976, when the amendment to § 106 requiring consideration of Eligible properties became effective, or in 1978, when the Keeper of the National Register determined that the H. H. Peck carriage house was eligible. Nor is there any question that HUD did not comply with § 106 if it was applicable, for even after the "freeze," HUD did not consider the effect of the project on the carriage house and did not solicit the Advisory Council's advice. We therefore hold that HUD's conduct violated § 106 of NHPA.

* * *

Notes and Questions

1. **Statutory analysis.** This was an urban renewal project on a huge scale, one that continued to develop well after initial conception. Finding the text of the NHPA silent on the question of the relevant cut-off point for a § 106 review, whether it is the approval of the expenditures or the actual expenditure of funds, the court looked to legislative history. a. How much did the broad purposes of the Act weigh in the court's conclusions on the congressional intent? b. How would those purposes be defeated if the court had accepted WURA's assertion? c. Did WURA's position reflect sound land redevelopment practices?

2. **Applying the logic.** In *Save the Courthouse Committee v. Lynn*, 408 F. Supp. 1323 (S.D.N.Y. 1979), the District Court for the Southern District of New York reached a different conclusion than the court in *WATCH v. Harris*, despite the factual similarity between the cases. In *Save the Courthouse*, the plaintiffs claimed violations of NHPA and NEPA by HUD and the White Plains Urban Renewal Agency (the "Agency") in planning to destroy the Westchester County Courthouse in White Plains, New York, for the purposes of urban renewal. On December 31, 1974, the court issued a temporary restraining order enjoining the demolition of the Courthouse.

When the merits of the issue reached the District Court in 1979, the court noted that the words of Section 106 of NHPA clearly state that "the property which is affected by the undertaking must be included in the National Register at the time that the approval of the expenditure of Federal funds is being considered." *Id.* at 1335. "The Courthouse was not listed in the National Register until January 16, 1975 and therefore HUD had no responsibilities under § 106 with respect to the Courthouse prior to that time." *Id.* The court was therefore of the opinion that the registration of the Courthouse did not impose a requirement on HUD to submit the proposed demolition to the Advisory Council for comment pursuant to Section 106. The court took note of the fact that the project was already substantially under way, and that stopping the demolition and renovation project would impose an unduly burdensome restriction of the project. The court asserted that:

> At this point of the project development the overall federal financial commitment has already been made. HUD may not unilaterally choose to reassess its overall approval of the expenditures of federal funds for the urban renewal project. Consequently, in this Court's view, it is highly unlikely under the circumstances presented here that HUD need comply with § 106 of NHPA.

Id. at 1336.

Turning to the issue of the applicability of NEPA to the case, the District Court stated that "[w]hile enacted on January 1, 1970, it is clear that NEPA may be applicable to projects on-going at the time of its enactment provided the Federal agency thereafter has remained meaningfully involved in its implementation." *Id.* at 1340. Though HUD argued that no federal action had occurred since 1965 in regard to the Courthouse, the court pointed out that this argument overlooked the fact that the demolition, which was financially supported by the federal government, was an integral part of a large urban renewal plan. "To view the proposed demolition as an isolated act independent of the broader context in which this action is being taken would appear to be an unsatisfactory method of determining the presence of federal involvement." *Id.*

The court next discussed Section 102 of NEPA, which requires in part "that before taking 'major Federal actions significantly affecting the quality of the human environment,' all federal agencies must, 'to the fullest extent possible' prepare a 'detailed statement' (environmental impact statement) (EIS) which shall analyze, inter alia, the environmental impact of the proposed action and alternatives to such action." 42 U.S.C. § 4332. The federal agency involved in the project is the initial party authorized to make the "threshold determination" of whether there is major federal action significantly affecting the quality of the human environment. Looking at the EIS attempt made by HUD, the court found that the effort put forth by the agency was inadequate. The report contained no "meaningful discussion" of legitimate alternatives to demolition. Instead of holding a meeting to hear or soliciting other alternatives from local interest groups such as the plaintiffs, HUD adopted a "hands off" approach and allowed the local officials and agencies to decide the fate of the Courthouse. The court focused on these two main points when it concluded that "the plaintiffs ha[d] made the necessary showing sufficient to support the granting of preliminary relief with respect to the inadequacy of the 'threshold determination' made by the federal agency." *Id.* at 1343.

The opinion in *Save the Courthouse* contrasts sharply with *WATCH v. Harris* and that opinion's failure to address NHPA with the appropriate depth. Instead of attempting to create the necessary injunction through NHPA, the court in *Save the Courthouse* focused on NEPA, a proposition that Justice Lumbard's concurrence asserted in the *WATCH v. Harris* decision.

3. **Revisiting the Section 106 process.** The Advisory Council on Historic Preservation ("ACHP") regulations, 36 C.F. R. § 800.2(o), include within the definition of "undertaking," "new and continuing projects, activities, or programs and any of their elements not previously considered under Section 106." When is this further review required? The courts have held that "where the project's Section 106 review has already been completed, and no new elements have been added to the project, it does not amount to an undertaking." *See, e.g., McMillan Park Committee v. National Capital Planning Comm'n,* 968 F. 2d 1283 (D.C. Cir. 1992) (Planning Commission's review of an amendment to the project did not constitute an undertaking); *Battle Mt. Band v. United States BLM,* 2016 U.S. Dist. LEXIS 115093 (D. Nev. August 26, 2016) (commencement of construction of power line pursuant to agency notice to proceed which was reviewed in the original Section 106 review was not an undertaking requiring new review).

4. **The requirement to consult.** While the NHPA does not prohibit changes, nor even the destruction of historic properties, it does require that before any federal undertaking that might adversely impact properties either listed on the National Register or eligible to be listed, the federal agency first consult with ACHP and any State Historic Preservation Officer ("SHPO") before commencing any activity. Even though the agency might earnestly believe that its proposed action poses no threat to the historic property, consulting with the ACHP and the SHPO allows an independent assessment of likely impacts and possible ways that the agency could avoid them. In the cases that follow, the courts find that in order for the consultation requirement to serve its intended purposes, it must be more than merely salutary.

Committee to Save Cleveland's Huletts v. U.S. Army Corps of Engineers

United States District Court of the Northern District of Ohio, Eastern Division
163 F. Supp. 2d 776 (2001)

O'Malley, D.J. Plaintiffs, the Committee to Save Cleveland's Huletts, Edward J. Hauser, James H. Korecko, Jerry C. Mann, Stephen L. Merkel, and Rimantas Saikus (collectively the "Committee"), seek declaratory and injunctive relief against defendants, the U.S. Army Corps of Engineers, Chief of Engineers Lt. General Joe N. Ballard and District Engineer Mark D. Feirstein, (comprising "the Corps"). Plaintiffs *** are primarily interested in (1) a declaration that the defendants acted improperly when they authorized the Cleveland-Cuyahoga Port Authority (the "Port Authority") to dredge an area of Lake Erie near Whiskey Island and (2) an order revoking or voiding that authority. The parties have filed cross-motions for summary judgment, each asserting they are entitled to judgment as a matter of law with respect to plaintiffs' claims.

*** The Court finds that plaintiffs' claim that the Port Authority "segmented" its application, pursuant to the National Historic Preservation Act (the "NHPA"), 16 U.S.C. § 470h-2(k), is not ripe, and thus grants summary judgment to the Corps on this claim and dismisses it. The Court further finds, however, that the Corps violated the NHPA by issuing a permit without awaiting comment from the Ohio State Historic Preservation Office (the "Ohio SHPO") or the Advisory Council on Historic Preservation (the "ACHP"). As explained below, a finding that the Corps issued the permit in violation of the NHPA entitles plaintiffs to all the relief the Court finds it is able to grant; the Court, accordingly, declines to reach the plaintiffs' remaining claims....

The Court hereby Orders the Corps to revoke the Letter of Permission, permit no. 1999-01471(0), issued to the Port Authority on May 14, 1999.... If the Port Authority requires any further dredging in the area covered by that permit, it must reapply for authority to do so. If a new application is made, defendants must comply with all requirements of the NHPA, including those mandating formal notice to the Ohio SHPO and ACHP and contemplating a waiting period after such notice prior to the issuance of a permit. The Corps must also consider whether the scope of any new permit sought implicates 16 U.S.C. § 470h-2(k). The Corps may then determine whether and under what conditions to reissue the permit. ***

I. Background

The Hulett Iron Ore Unloaders ("Huletts") at issue in this suit were enormous ore unloading machines, about ten stories tall, that stood near where the Cuyahoga River flows into Lake Erie on the Pennsylvania Railway Ore Dock (the "Ore Dock"), located on Whiskey Island. George Hulett invented these imposing machines in the late 1800's. At one time, seventy-five Huletts unloaded ore from boats in the Great Lakes. Virtually all of the Huletts have now been dismantled or destroyed and none are currently in operation.[4] The four Huletts located on Cleveland's waterfront operated continuously from 1912 to 1992. After 1992, the Huletts were rendered obsolete by more modern methods of unloading bulk cargo from Lake Erie vessels. In 1993, the Huletts were designated a Cleveland Historic Landmark. In 1997, the Ore Dock was listed in the National Register of Historic Places; the primary historic aspect of the Ore Dock prompting that designation was the presence of the Huletts.[5] The Committee, which counts a relative of George Hulett among its members, was formed for the purpose of attempting to preserve the Huletts.

The Cleveland Bulk Terminals (the "CBT"), located adjacent to the Ore Dock on Whiskey Island, are used for processing and handling of bulk cargo, including ore,

---

4. There are currently four Huletts in existence. Two are located on the shores of Lake Michigan in Chicago, Illinois. As will be discussed below, the other two are in storage here in Cleveland, after having been removed from the Ore Dock.

5. The Huletts have not been designated a National Historic Landmark.

which comes to Cleveland by boat and is then transported throughout the area and beyond by rail and truck. In 1997, the Port Authority entered into a lease agreement with Oglebay Norton Terminals, Inc., granting Oglebay Norton the authority to use the CBT and surrounding areas for the receipt, storage, processing, loading and unloading of waterborne cargo and to operate the Ore Dock as an industrial dock to facilitate that transfer process. The Port Authority agreed to maintain and oversee the docking facilities themselves and the lease agreement expressly recited that, although the Huletts were located on the leased premises, the Port Authority would retain all authority over and responsibility for them. The lease agreement also contained the parties' acknowledgment that the Huletts were not, as of that point in time, operational.

At about this same time, the Port Authority commissioned an architectural and engineering study of all the Cleveland-area port facilities, including those on Whiskey Island. The study concluded *** that the continued presence of the Huletts on the Ore Dock limited the operations of the CBT "by restricting cargo transfer activities and ... inhibiting any type of transhipment vessel to vessel cargo transfer." The study concluded that the "model" use of the facility was a use which allowed for full dockside access in front of the CBT—i.e., a use with the Huletts no longer in their then-current location.

In 1998, the Port Authority adopted a Master Plan contemplating long-term improvements to its facilities. The Master Plan essentially endorsed the recommendations of the previously-commissioned study of the Port Authority facilities, including those relating to the CBT and the Huletts. Thereafter, the Port Authority embarked on an improvement project for Whiskey Island whose stated objective was to "increase the capacity and operational flexibility of the bulk handling facility" and to "increase the economic development and job creation potential of the [CBT's] facility." The project contemplated the removal of the Huletts from the dock facilities and the destruction of certain other structures which had been used primarily as support facilities for the Huletts when the Huletts were in operation.

In the fall of 1998, the Port Authority commissioned a "Historic Preservation Mitigation Plan" to assess ways to mitigate the effects of its proposed improvement project on the historic structures on Whiskey Island, including the Huletts. The Committee was invited to participate in this study and to provide comments regarding its recommendations. The Port Authority then submitted its mitigation plan to the Cleveland Landmarks Commission, along with a request that the Commission approve renovation of the dock facilities, including the destruction of three of the four Huletts. The Port Authority proposed the dismantling of the last of the Huletts for relocation to another site and the expenditure of funds for education programs regarding the Huletts and their historical significance.

After public comment and a hearing, the Landmarks Commission granted the Port Authority's request, subject to an agreement that the Port Authority would dismantle two, not one, of the Huletts and store those machines for future reassembly by historic preservationist or educational groups. Although the Committee appealed this decision to Cleveland's Board of Zoning Appeals, after a hearing, the decision of the Landmarks Commission was affirmed.

While this process was ongoing, the Ore dock and CBT remained in use and continued to serve as a transfer point for moving bulk goods from vessels to railcars and trucks for shipment. Boats, accordingly, continued to dock at and unload from an area in front of the CBT and adjacent to the portion of the Ore Dock on which the Huletts were located. *** To carry out its responsibilities, the Port Authority, among other things, historically has conducted maintenance dredging of the area alongside the Ore Docks, so as to sustain the draft depth necessary for vessel traffic, and historically has been granted the authority to do so by the Corps.

In March of 1999, the Port Authority submitted an application to the Corps, seeking a permit to again conduct dredging alongside the Ore Dock. It is this permit which is at the heart of this litigation. *** In describing its permit request, the Port Authority said it was seeking authority to conduct maintenance dredging only. The Port Authority asserted that its request was "not part of the proposed expansion" and, instead, was intended to allow for maintenance of "previously approved draft depth." *** The Port Authority did not, however, initially limit its permit request to that area where dredging previously had been conducted. Rather than seek a permit for the 600 foot area traditionally dredged, the Port Authority sought permission to dredge a 2000 foot area along the dock.... And, the Port Authority indicated its belief that future actions under its Master Plan would require additional permits from the Corps. ***

The Corps submitted the Port Authority's permit request to various agencies for review. While those environmental agencies to whom the permit was submitted expressed no concern, various agencies with oversight over historic preservation questions did do so, as did the plaintiffs in this case. Thus, the Corps' administrative record reflects substantial contact during the months of March, April and May of 1999 with plaintiffs and the Ohio State Historic Preservation Office (the "Ohio SHPO").... The concerns expressed by these individuals and entities all centered on the impact this proposed dredging permit might have on the Huletts; if the purpose or effect of the dredging was to ready the Ore Dock for anticipated expansion, the plaintiffs and the Ohio SHPO believed that a full assessment of the effect of the expansion would be required under the NHPA.

*** The Corps told the Port Authority that an application requesting dredging for only those areas historically dredged likely would not require § 106 review before a permit could issue, because such a request would not further or facilitate *expansion,* as distinct from maintenance, of the CBT. The Corps also emphasized, however, that if any additional dredging or bulkhead work was necessary, in areas beyond those historically dredged, the Port Authority was required to include it in its initial application and to submit to a § 106 review before any further work could be conducted on its improvement project. The Corps pointed out that permits subsequently requested could be rejected on grounds of anticipatory demolition under § 470h-2(k) of the NHPA.

In early May, 1999, the Port Authority responded to the Corps' concerns by indicating that it intended to scale-back its permit request to cover only the 600 foot area historically dredged[.] *** On May 13, 1999, the Port Authority revised its permit application in writing and scaled back its request from a 2000 by 60 foot area to a 600 by 25 foot area. The Port Authority formally assured the Corps that no additional dredging or bulkhead work was anticipated. ***

On May 14, 1999, the day after the revised permit application was received, the Corps issued a Letter of Permission (1999-01471(0)) to the Port Authority authorizing dredging in the 600 by 25 foot area. The Letter of Permission remains in effect through May 14, 2004.

*** [O]n September 28, 1999, the ACHP wrote a letter to the Corps, stating that it believed the Corps had violated § 106 of the NHPA, because it issued the Letter of Permission without waiting fifteen days for comment from the Ohio SHPO. The ACHP further noted that it appeared that the Corps allowed the Port Authority to "segment" the project by only allowing dredging of part of the originally requested dredging area, leading the ACHP to conclude that the Port Authority would request the remainder of the dredging after the Huletts and other historic structures had been demolished. As the Huletts would already be destroyed at the time of any future request, the ACHP feared it would be foreclosed from commenting on any future projects at the CBT. There is no record of any response by the Corps to this letter. *** In late November of 1999, the Port Authority and Oglebay Norton contracted with Signature Services to demolish two of the Huletts and to dismantle and store the other two. As mentioned earlier, this contract was approved by the Cleveland Landmarks Commission. It was, moreover, entered into pursuant to demolition permits issued by the City of Cleveland and the State of Ohio.

It was not until December 13, 1999, more than six months after the dredging permit had issued, the Ohio SHPO and ACHP had objected, and the dredging had been completed, that plaintiffs sought a remedy in this Court [having lost challenges in state court]. As described below, plaintiffs' primary objective in filing suit here, like its state court and local administrative efforts, was to stop the Port Authority from demolishing or displacing the Huletts.

II. Procedural History

On December 13, 1999, plaintiffs initiated this action by filing a Motion for a Temporary Restraining Order, asking the Court to enjoin the Port Authority, Oglebay Norton Co., and Signature Services, Inc. (the "private party defendants") from destroying the Huletts. Plaintiffs premised this request on their contention that the dredging permit was issued in violation of the NHPA. While the plaintiffs named the U.S. Army Corps of Engineers, Lt. General Joe Ballard, and District Engineer Mark Fierstein (the "federal defendants") in their original complaint, they did not seek any injunctive relief against these federal defendants. Indeed, plaintiffs complaint did not seek any relief whatsoever, injunctive or otherwise, against the federal defendants.

On December 15, 1999, two days later, the Court held a hearing on plaintiffs' Motion for a Temporary Restraining Order. The Court found that it could not enjoin the private party defendants under the authority of a federal statute that only applied to federal entities absent a showing of substantial federal involvement in the activity of those private parties. *** The Court concluded that, even if it were true that the dredging permit impacted the Huletts, because all of the dredging contemplated under the permit had been completed over six months before, there was no continuing federal involvement in the dredging project. The Court also found that, as of December 1999, there was no federal involvement, *i.e.* no federal money, no federal permit, etc., that was necessary for or contemplated in connection with any aspect of the Whiskey Island improvement project. The Court, therefore, denied the Temporary Restraining Order.

* * *

On January 19, 2000, the Court received a Motion from the National Historic Trust asking leave to participate in the proceedings as Amicus Curiae. The Court granted that motion at the preliminary injunction hearing.

[Plaintiffs' motion for preliminary injunction was denied on account of the absence of continuing federal involvement.]

* * *

After the preliminary injunction hearing, plaintiffs finally amended their complaint. In their amended complaint, plaintiffs allege that the Corps violated its own regulations when it issued a Letter of Permission allowing the Port Authority to dredge the area in front of the Huletts. Plaintiffs also allege that they were harmed by being denied their right, under the ACHP's and the Corps' regulations, to participate in the § 106 review and the Corps' permitting process. The plaintiffs, therefore, added to their prayers for relief requests that the Court declare that the Corps violated the NHPA, revoke the permit and force the Corps to undergo a § 106 review process and allow public participation in that process....

On May 3, 2000, plaintiffs filed a second Motion for a Temporary Restraining Order, this time asking the Court to order the Corps to suspend immediately all unexpired permits issued to the Port Authority, to withhold the issuance of any new permits requested by the Port Authority, and to refrain from funding, performing, or allowing to be performed, any dredging, repairs, or any other work on behalf of the Port Authority *at any site in the Cleveland area.* The Court held a hearing on May 9, 2000, and determined that there were no exigent circumstances and no irreparable injury to the plaintiffs which would allow the Court to issue a temporary restraining order at that time. The Huletts had already been taken down and the Court had already determined that, given the nature and timing of the claims plaintiffs asserted in this action, it did not have the authority to stop their destruction. There was, moreover, unrebutted evidence in the record that no further dredging was contemplated under the permit plaintiffs contend was issued in violation of the NHPA. Thus, to the extent the Court could grant any relief for the plaintiffs' loss of their right to public comment under the NHPA or the Corps' own regulations, that relief could be granted after a full trial, allowing time for adequate preparation by all parties. ***

Plaintiffs currently bring three claims against the Corps. Plaintiffs allege: (1) the Corps violated the National Historic Preservation Act ("NHPA"), 16 U.S.C. § 470f, and Advisory Council on Historic Preservation Regulations at 36 C.F.R. Part 800, by granting a dredging permit to the Port Authority to dredge Lake Erie in front of the four Hulett Ore Unloaders without conducting a § 106 review to determine whether issuing the permit would affect the preservation of the Huletts; (2) the Corps violated § 470h-2(k) of the NHPA by allowing the Port Authority to unlawfully "segment" its application for dredging by only asking for part of the dredging it contemplated under its "Master Plan;" and (3) the Corps violated its own regulations by not allowing public comment during the permitting process, by issuing a permit through the abbreviated process of a "Letter of Permission," and by granting the Port Authority a permit pursuant to an incomplete application.

III. Law and Argument

* * *

A.

The facts in this case merit a threshold inquiry into the question of mootness. [The court concluded that the suit was not moot inasmuch as further dredging theoretically could occur, in which case, the court could grant relief.] * * *

B.

Under the NHPA, it is the policy of the federal government to "foster conditions under which our modern society and our prehistoric and historic resources can exist in productive harmony and fulfill the social, economic, and other requirements of present and future generations." 16 U.S.C. § 470-1(1). *** Section 106 of the NHPA requires that, whenever a federal agency has "direct or indirect jurisdiction" over a project or program that could affect historic properties, the federal agency must study ways to avoid or mitigate any adverse impacts to those properties and afford the ACHP a "reasonable opportunity to comment." 16 U.S.C. § 470f. The NHPA is, thus, a precatory statute; the federal agency authorizing the undertaking has the ultimate authority to decide whether or not to proceed with the undertaking. The NHPA forces an agency, however, to stop and consider the consequences of its undertakings on any historic property, and assures that the agency does so by requiring it to receive comment from the ACHP, or agencies acting in its stead, and from the public before proceeding with any such undertaking.

* * *

1.

In order to comply with the NHPA, a federal agency considering an undertaking must go through the process outlined in the ACHP's regulations. *** First, the regulations require a federal agency to consult with the State Historic Preservation Office ("SHPO") of the State in which the undertaking is to occur to: (a) determine and document the area of potential effect; (b) identify historic properties within the scope of potential effects; and (c) determine whether those properties are listed in or eligible for listing in the National Register of Historic Places. ***

There is no dispute that the Huletts have been on the National Register of Historic Places since 1997. There is also no dispute that the Corps contacted the Ohio SHPO to discuss whether the Huletts would be in the area of "potential effect" if the Corps were to issue the dredging permit originally requested by the Port Authority. And, it is clear from the administrative record that the Corps received and responded to public input regarding the impact of the permit on the Huletts from, among others, the plaintiffs themselves. The dispute in this matter centers on what the Corps did, and what it did not do, next. After identifying the issue—i.e., the presence of the Huletts in an area upland of that to be dredged—and consulting interested parties, the Corps concluded that the dredging activity would have "no effect" on the Huletts. ***

The Corps may be correct that the dredging under the permit at issue here had no effect on the ultimate removal of the Huletts from Whiskey Island. The Corps is also correct that the ultimate decision whether to issue a permit lay with the Corps, and not the ACHP. The Corps is not correct, however, that it was free to reach those conclusions without further, and more formal, dialogue with the Ohio SHPO, the ACHP and the public.

An agency's obligations do not end with its own conclusion of no effect, even if that finding is made after "consultation" with the SHPO and the public. If a federal agency proposes a finding of no effect, it must document its findings in publicly available materials, notify the relevant SHPO and allow fifteen days for a response. Only if the SHPO fails to object within that time frame may the agency proceed to act without further consultation under the NHPA. If the SHPO does object, additional steps in the § 106 process must be taken, including, at minimum, submission of the issue to the ACHP, either in the form of an agreement with the SHPO of no adverse effect, or in the form of a request for a full thirty (30) day review by the ACHP.

None of these formal notification procedures occurred prior to issuance of the Port Authority permit. Indeed, as plaintiffs point out, the Corps issued the dredging permit (1) before formally notifying the Ohio SHPO or the Council of its proposed finding of "no effect" (2) before properly documenting its findings, and (3) without waiting the necessary fifteen (15) days for the Ohio SHPO to respond to the finding of "no effect." Having taken this precipitous action, moreover, the Corps then ignored both the Ohio SHPO's and the ACHP's objections to the Corps' finding of "no effect," even though those objections were timely made and were received by the Corps before any work under the permit had been performed.

* * *

The Corps argues that it made a finding of "no effect," that is, that the dredging in the historically dredged area would not affect the demolition of the Huletts, after consulting with the Ohio SHPO and, thus, was free to proceed with the permitting process. The Corps is mistaken, however; [t]he regulations contemplate a far more formal procedure, which includes, at minimum, written notification to the relevant SHPO accompanied by documentation supporting the agency's finding, followed by a waiting period of fifteen (15) days. Quite simply, while the Corps may have thought its decision was both a considered and correct one, it was one which impermissibly truncated the consultation process mandated by the NHPA and the regulations promulgated thereunder. After having circumvented the process, moreover, the Corps failed to revoke the permit once formal objections were received from both the Ohio SHPO and the ACHP. The Court is compelled to conclude, accordingly, that the Corps violated the ACHP regulations, and hence the NHPA, when it issued the dredging permit to the Port Authority which is the subject of this action.

2.

The Corps contends that the Court is *not* compelled to conclude that it violated the NHPA merely because the Court finds that the Corps failed to comply with the ACHP regulations set forth at 36 CFR § 800.1 *et seq.* *** Because the Corps has adopted regulations governing its own authority and obligations, including those under the NHPA, the Corps contends it is against these regulations which its actions should be judged. The Corps asserts, *** that, when the Court assesses the Corps' actions in light of its own regulations, set forth at 36 C.F.R. § 325 Appendix C., the Court must apply the deferential standard of review dictated by the Administrative Procedures Act. ***

The Corps contends that it was authorized by its own regulations to interpret the "permit area" narrowly when considering the impact of the permitted activity on historic properties and that it was justified in issuing the permit without "formal" notification of its intention to do so to the Ohio SHPO. The Corps argues that, given the nature of the permit ultimately sought and the Corps' extensive consultation with all relevant agencies and interested parties, its decision to issue the permit was, even if not in technical compliance with the ACHP regulations, not arbitrary and capricious under its own.

The Corps is correct that the NHPA permits agencies to promulgate regulations governing their own programs and to set forth in those regulations methods for compliance with the NHPA. The NHPA commands that such regulations be "consistent" with those issued by the ACHP, however, which is expressly authorized to promulgate comprehensive regulations under the Act. *** The ACHP regulations themselves also authorize the issuance of counterpart regulations. Again, however, that authority is limited to regulations which are adopted in consultation with *and are approved by* the ACHP....

All parties agree that there is no record of the ACHP ever approving or concurring in the Corps' regulations. The Court has already found, moreover, that, to the extent the Corps' regulations allow it to issue a permit in the absence of the formal consultation, notification and objection procedures outlined in the ACHP regulations, the Corps' procedures are inconsistent with, and indeed, in derogation of those ACHP regulations. The Corps, accordingly, cannot rely on its own regulations to define the scope of its notice obligations or to define the "permit area" governing the circumstances giving rise to those obligations. *** Because the Corps cannot rely on its own regulations to determine compliance with the NHPA in the circumstances at issue in this case, moreover, the Corps' argument that it did not arbitrarily and capriciously violate its own regulations does not affect the Court's determination that the Corps violated the NHPA.

C.

Plaintiffs also allege that the Corps violated §470h-2(k) of the NHPA because it issued a permit to the Port Authority for only part of the dredging originally requested. Plaintiffs assert that the Port Authority needed a permit for the rest of the originally requested dredging area to complete the CBT improvement project, but only asked for part of the dredging it required in order to avoid the § 106 review process. Plaintiffs believe that, now that the Huletts have been demolished and § 106 review is less meaningful, the Port Authority will apply to the Corps for additional permits. Plaintiffs contend that the Corps knew or should have known that the Port Authority was attempting to skirt the § 106 review process when it reduced its application from a 2000 foot area to a 600 foot area and that the Corps should have refused to issue a permit for that reduced area without going through the full § 106 process.

The plaintiffs, however, misread §470h-2(k). *** This section provides only that a federal agency may not grant a permit to an applicant who has *already* adversely affected historic property—i.e., it is a prohibition against granting permits to applicants who have committed anticipatory demolition. Section 470h-2(k) works to punish those who would seek to manipulate the § 106 process by denying them access to post-demolition permits. It does not, as plaintiffs contend, require agencies to presage whether an applicant will ask for permits at some unspecified time in the future. And, it does not authorize denial of a current permit based on *suspicions* that additional permits may be sought.

The record in this case clearly evidences why plaintiffs' interpretation of §470h-2(k) would be unworkable. *** It would place an unreasonable burden upon federal agencies to require them to second-guess an applicant's stated intentions, as plaintiffs assert the Corps should have done here. It could, moreover, result in the denial of legitimately sought permits on grounds that amount to mere speculation regarding future intentions. *** Quite simply, plaintiffs' claim asserting anticipatory demolition under §470h-2(k) is not yet ripe because the factual predicate to such a claim does not exist....

* * *

The Port Authority sought its original permit when the Huletts were intact. The permit was issued and the work was done without any change in the character of surrounding historic properties. The Corps and the Port Authority have both told this Court, moreover, that no more work is planned under the existing permit, and that the Port Authority will not require any further permits relating to its improvement of the CBT. There is, accordingly, no basis upon which the Court can declare that the Port Authority engaged in anticipatory demolition under the NHPA prior to issuance of any permit. And, on the record before the Court, there may never be any basis to do so. *** If the Port Authority were now to request dredging in areas beyond that encompassed by the permit, plaintiffs could seek to invoke §470h-2(k) to stop the Corps from granting another permit to the Port Authority. Until that occurs, however, plaintiffs' claim under 16 U.S.C. §470h-2(k) is not ripe.... The Court, therefore, will dismiss those claims.

D.

As the Court explained above, because it has found that the Corps issued the dredging permit in violation of the NHPA by failing to wait for comments from the Ohio SHPO or the ACHP, and then failing to continue to pursue the § 106 process after those entities objected, there is no need to reach the plaintiffs' alternate arguments that the Corps violated the Corps' own regulations. The Court can provide no additional relief to the plaintiffs for those alternate claims, and sees no need to go through the exercise of determining those claims when a decision either way would have no effect. ***

IV. Conclusion

* * *

Because the plaintiffs have shown that the Corps issued the permit prematurely under the NHPA, the Court grants plaintiffs the following relief: (1) the Corps must immediately revoke the Letter of Permission (No.1999-01471(0)) that it issued to the Port Authority allowing dredging in 600 by 25 foot area on May 14, 1999.***

Pueblo of Sandia v. United States

United States Court of Appeals, Tenth Circuit
50 F.3d 856 (1995)

Seymour, C.J. The Pueblo of Sandia and various environmental groups brought suit for declaratory and injunctive relief against the United States and a National Forest Service supervisor, alleging that the Forest Service failed to comply with the National Historic Preservation Act (NHPA), 16 U.S.C. §§ 470 *et seq.*, in its evaluation of Las Huertas Canyon in the Cibola National Forest. The Pueblo asserts that the New Mexico canyon contains numerous sites of religious and cultural significance to the tribe, qualifying the canyon as a "traditional cultural property" eligible for inclusion in the National Register of Historic Places. The Forest Service, however, concluded that the canyon did not constitute a traditional cultural property and instituted a new management strategy for it. The district court granted summary judgment for the Forest Service, finding that it had made a reasonable and good faith effort to identify historic properties. Because we conclude that the Forest Service's efforts were neither reasonable nor in good faith, we reverse and remand.

I.

Las Huertas Canyon is located in the Sandia Mountains northeast of Albuquerque, New Mexico. Lying within the Cibola National Forest, the canyon is under the supervision of the Forest Service. The Sandia Pueblo reservation is nearby, and tribal members visit the canyon to gather evergreen boughs for use in significant private and public cultural ceremonies. *** They also harvest herbs and plants along the Las Huertas Creek which are important for traditional healing practices. *** The canyon contains many shrines and ceremonial paths of religious and cultural significance to the Pueblo. ***

In July 1988, the Forest Service released a Draft Environmental Impact Statement (DEIS) detailing eight alternative management strategies for Las Huertas Canyon.

After an extended comment period, the Forest Service selected a ninth alternative, Alternative I, as the preferred strategy. Alternative I required the realignment and reconstruction of the Las Huertas Canyon Road and additional improvements to the area, including the rehabilitation and expansion of several picnic grounds and the installation of sanitary facilities at other locations. ***

Voicing concerns that the strategy would adversely impact traditional cultural properties and practices in the canyon by encouraging additional traffic and visitation to the area, the Pueblo filed an administrative appeal of the decision. The Deputy Regional Forester affirmed the decision, altering the snow plowing and road closure provisions of Alternative I in response to complaints from other appellants. The decision became administratively final in January 1990 when the Chief of the Forest Service declined to review it.

The Pueblo filed this suit in federal court, alleging numerous statutory violations.[1] The Pueblo subsequently amended the complaint to plead a violation of the NHPA, 16 U.S.C. 470 *et seq.* The Pueblo alleged that the Forest Service failed to comply with section 106 of the NHPA when it refused to evaluate the canyon as a traditional cultural property eligible for inclusion on the National Register.

The parties filed cross motions for summary judgment on the issue of NHPA compliance. By the time the district court heard the motions, the State Historic Preservation Officer (SHPO) had concurred in the Forest Service's conclusion that certain specific sites near the roadway and picnic grounds were not eligible for the National Register. In a Memorandum Opinion and Order entered April 30, 1993, the district court noted that "[t]he administrative record is silent as to whether any of the sites found were evaluated [by the Forest Service] against the National Register Criteria as required by [the NHPA], and whether the sites met the criteria." *** The court accepted the SHPO's concurrence as "evidence that the Forest Service met the substantive requirements with respect to the roadway and the picnic area." ***

Although concerned that the Forest Service "does not appear to have taken the requirements of [the NHPA] very seriously," the court relied on the agency's assertion that it would diligently pursue information on the potential historic value of other individual sites within the canyon. *** On that basis, the court granted summary judgment for defendants, and plaintiffs filed this appeal.*** Significantly, nine months later the SHPO withdrew his concurrence upon receiving evidence suggesting that traditional cultural properties existed in Las Huertas Canyon. *** The SHPO concluded

1. Sandia Pueblo alleged that the Forest Service's approval of the Final Environmental Impact Statement (FEIS) violated the National Environmental Policy Act, 42 U.S.C. 4321, et seq. (NEPA); the National Forest Management Act, 16 U.S.C. 1600 et seq. (NFMA); the Clean Water Act, 33 U.S.C. 1251 et seq. (CWA); the American Indian Religious Freedom Act, 42 U.S.C. 1996 (AIRFA); and the Administrative Procedures Act, 5 U.S.C. 701 et seq. (APA). The Pueblo abandoned the NFMA, AIRFA, and CWA claims and does not appeal the district court's grant of summary judgment for defendants on the NEPA and APA claims.

that the withheld information had a substantial impact on the inquiry into the canyon's eligibility for the Historic Register. He wrote:

> Much of our consultation, dating back to September of 1992, concentrated on determining what would represent a "reasonable" attempt to identify [Traditional Cultural Properties] that may be affected by the project. *Bulletin 38* ... states that "a 'reasonable' effort depends in part on the likelihood that such properties may be present." Mr. Lauriano's statement, supported by the ethnographic overview provided by Dr. Brandt, indicates that Las Huertas Canyon is used for ceremonial purposes, contains plants and soils used in traditional ceremonies and contains traditional trails that lead to other [traditional cultural properties] [, *** suggesting] that properties that may be eligible to the National Register of Historic Places may be affected by the proposed improvements[.] ***
>
> *** Consequently, the SHPO recommended an ethnographic analysis of the canyon to further evaluate the possibility that it contained traditional cultural properties.
>
> Consistent with *Bulletin 38,* this analysis should include interviews with appropriate pueblo representatives, field inspections and documentation. I recommend that the Forest Service hire a professional ethnographer to conduct this analysis. An independent professional is most likely to be able to work out any impasse that may have developed between the pueblos and the Forest Service. I also believe that this procedure will give the Pueblos a reasonable opportunity to provide us with enough documentation to conduct a formal determination of eligibility as outlined in *Bulletin 38.* ***

We review the district court's summary judgment de novo. *Housing Authority v. United States,* 980 F.2d 624, 628 (10th Cir. 1992).

II.

The NHPA requires the Forest Service to "take into account the effect of [any] undertaking on any district, site, building, structure, or object that is included in or eligible for inclusion in the National Register." NHPA, § 106, 16 U.S.C. § 470f (1993). Section 106 also mandates that the agency afford the Advisory Council on Historic Preservation "a reasonable opportunity to comment" on the undertaking. *Id.* *** The Advisory Council has established regulations for federal agencies to follow in complying with section 106. *** The process is designed to foster communication and consultation between agency officials, the SHPO, and other interested parties such as Indian tribes, local governments, and the general public.

First, the Agency Official must review all existing information on the site, request the SHPO's views on ways to identify historic properties, and seek information from interested parties likely to have knowledge about historic properties in the area. 36 C.F.R. § 800.4(a). In light of this information, the agency determines any need for further investigation.

In consultation with the SHPO, the agency then must make a "reasonable and good faith effort to identify historic properties that may be affected by the undertaking and gather sufficient information to evaluate the eligibility of these properties for the National Register." 36 C.F.R. § 800.4(b). Finally, for each property identified, the agency official and the SHPO must evaluate the property on the basis of the National Register criteria to determine its eligibility for inclusion. 36 C.F.R. § 800.4(c).

The Pueblo claims that the sites within the Las Huertas Canyon are traditional cultural properties which are thus eligible for inclusion in the National Register.... The Pueblo asserts that the Forest Service's conclusion to the contrary stems from that agency's failure to make a "reasonable and good faith effort" to identify historical properties.

A. *Reasonable Effort*

The Forest Service contends that it engaged in reasonable efforts to identify historic properties in Las Huertas Canyon. The record reveals that the Forest Service did request information from the Sandia Pueblo and other local Indian tribes, but a mere request for information is not necessarily sufficient to constitute the "reasonable effort" section 106 requires. Because communications from the tribes indicated the existence of traditional cultural properties and because the Forest Service should have known that tribal customs might restrict the ready disclosure of specific information, we hold that the agency did not reasonably pursue the information necessary to evaluate the canyon's eligibility for inclusion in the National Register.

During the assessment phase of the section 106 process, the Forest Service mailed letters to local Indian tribes, including the Sandia Pueblo, and individual tribal members who were known to be familiar with traditional cultural properties. *** The letters requested detailed information describing the location of the sites, activities conducted there, and the frequency of the activities. *** They also asked tribes to provide maps of the sites, drawn at a scale of 1:24,000 or better, as well as documentation of the historic nature of the property. *** Forest Service officials also addressed meetings of the All Indian Pueblo Council and the San Felipe Pueblo. *** The officials informed the groups that traditional cultural properties are eligible for inclusion in the National Register and requested the same specific information required in the letters. ***

None of the tribes or individuals provided the Forest Service with the type of information requested in the letters and meetings. We conclude, however, that the information the tribes did communicate to the agency was sufficient to require the Forest Service to engage in further investigations, especially in light of regulations warning that tribes might be hesitant to divulge the type of information sought.

Prior to its final determination on April 29, 1993 that Las Huertas Canyon contained no traditional cultural properties, the Forest Service was aware of numerous claims to the contrary. As early as January 5, 1987, the Governor of the Sandia Pueblo informed the Forest Service that the Las Huertas Canyon was an area "of great religious and traditional importance to the people of Sandia Pueblo." *** The minutes of a Las Huertas Canyon Work Group meeting on March 10, 1987 reveal that the group knew that Native Americans used the canyon area for a number of ceremonial, religious, and medicinal purposes. *** During the period of public comment on the eight alternatives, the Sandia Pueblo supported alternative C, which it believed would be most likely "to permit the Sandia members to perform secret, traditional activities in more seclusion." ***

On August 9, 1989, the Regional Forester took the affidavit of Philip Lauriano, an elder and religious leader of the Sandia Pueblo. Mr. Lauriano listed several "long-standing religious and traditional practices" which take place in the canyon and alluded to sacred sites which it contains. *** In 1992, Dr. Elizabeth Brandt, a highly qualified anthropologist who is an expert on the Sandia Pueblo, provided a detailed ethnographic overview of the tribe's religious and cultural connections to the canyon.... Dr. Brandt noted the canyon's significance to the Pueblo as a source of herbs and evergreen boughs, which have been an integral part of certain Pueblo ceremonies for at least 60 years.[4] She also described certain ceremonial paths and sites in the canyon which "serve as gateways for access to the spirit world," concluding that

> [t]hese sites and their functions would be significantly impaired if not totally destroyed as a result of the planned development of the Canyon, thus cutting off spiritual access for religious leaders and those responsible for the actions which occur at these shrines. These sites are critical to the religious practice, cultural identity, and overall well-being of the Pueblo. *** Based on these factors, she concluded that "Las Huertas Canyon constitutes a Traditional Cultural District with multiple Sites for the Sandia Tribe." ***

Furthermore, the Forest Service received communications clearly indicating why more specific responses were not forthcoming. At the meeting with the San Felipe Pueblo, tribal members indicated that "[t]hey did not want to disclose any specific details of site locations or activities." *** A representative of the Sandia Pueblo made the same claim at the All Indian Pueblo Council meeting. *** Brandt also commented upon the Pueblo people's general unwillingness "to divulge any information regarding their religious practices." *** This reticence to disclose details of their cultural and religious practices was not unexpected. National Register Bulletin 38 warns that "knowledge of traditional cultural values may not be shared readily with outsiders" as such information is "regarded as powerful, even dangerous" in some societies. *** Joseph Tainter, an archeologist for the Forest Service, "acknowledged that [P]ueblos are often reluctant to provide such information" and promised confidential treatment of any communications. ***

*** Based on the information contained in the Lauriano and Brandt affidavits, the SHPO ultimately concluded that the "properties [ ] may be eligible to the National Register of Historic Places" but "we do not have enough information to make a determination of eligibility." *** We agree. The information communicated to the Forest Service as well as the reasons articulated for the lack of more specific information

4. Oral testimony establishes that the Pueblo have gathered evergreen boughs in Las Huertas Canyon for at least 60 years. Dr. Brandt notes, however, that the canyon has probably played a role in tribal religious and cultural practices for centuries as archeological evidence reveals that the Pueblo village has remained at essentially the same site since the 1300s.

clearly suggest that there is a sufficient likelihood that the canyon contains traditional cultural properties to warrant further investigation. We thus hold that the Forest Service did not make a reasonable effort to identify historic properties. *** Consistent with *Bulletin 38*, this analysis should include interviews with appropriate Pueblo representatives, field inspections and documentation.... An independent professional [ethnographer] is most likely to be able to work out any impasse that may have developed between the Pueblos and the Forest Service. ***

B. Good Faith Effort

The Pueblo also claims that the Forest Service failed to make the requisite good faith effort to identify traditional cultural properties in Las Huertas Canyon. It bases this assertion on the fact that the Forest Service withheld relevant information from the SHPO during the required consultation process. The district court expressed concern about the Forest Service's commitment to the section 106 process and placed great weight upon the SHPO's concurrence in granting summary judgment. Thus, the withdrawal of that concurrence upon discovery of the withheld information suggests that the Forest Service did not put forth a good faith effort to identify historic properties.

The regulations require that "[i]n consultation with the [SHPO], the Agency Official shall make a reasonable and good faith effort to identify historic properties." 36 C.F.R. § 800.4(b). Indeed, consultation with the SHPO is an integral part of the section 106 process. *** Affording the SHPO an opportunity to offer input on potential historic properties would be meaningless unless the SHPO has access to available, relevant information. Thus, "consultation" with the SHPO mandates an informed consultation.

The Forest Service did not provide the SHPO copies of the Lauriano and Brandt affidavits until after the consultation was complete and the SHPO had concurred. *** In fact, the Forest Service informed the SHPO during consultation that "[c]onsultations with pueblo officials and elders, and other users of the Las Huertas Canyon area, disclosed no evidence that the ... area contains traditional cultural properties." *** The SHPO's initial concurrence was based on this report. *** Once the SHPO acquired access to the withheld information, he withdrew his concurrence, noting the relevance of the documents and his concern that "our not having received [them] has affected our ability to consult appropriately under Section 106 of the [NHPA]." ***

Moreover, the regulations require that once the agency concludes that no historic properties are present, it must provide the SHPO documentation of that finding. 36 C.F.R. § 800.4(d). The Forest Service rendered its final decision that no traditional cultural properties exist in Las Huertas Canyon on April 29, 1993. *** The report was sent to the SHPO on May 4, 1993, prompting the SHPO's concurrence nine days later. The relevant documents, i.e., the Lauriano and Brandt affidavits, were not communicated to the SHPO until January 14, 1994. *** Thus, the Forest Service failed to provide documentation of its decision to the SHPO in a timely manner.

Prior to the SHPO's letter revealing that the Forest Service withheld relevant information, the district court expressed reservations about the Forest Service's approach to the section 106 process. The court noted its concern "that the Forest Service does not appear to have taken the requirements of this Act very seriously." *** Those reservations were partially alleviated by the fact that the SHPO had concurred, at that time, with part of the Forest Service's new management plan. *** By withholding relevant information from the SHPO during the consultation process, however, the Forest Service further undermined any argument that it had engaged in a good faith effort. We thus hold that the Forest Service did not make a good faith effort to identify historic properties in Las Huertas Canyon.

Because we conclude that the Forest Service did not make a reasonable and good faith effort in its evaluation of Las Huertas Canyon, we REVERSE the judgment of the district court and REMAND for further proceedings in accordance with this opinion.

Notes and Questions

1. **Advisory Council.** The National Historic Preservation Act established the Advisory Council on Historic Preservation ("ACHP"), an independent agency. It is comprised of twenty-three members: A chair appointed by the President selected from the general public, the Secretary of the Interior, the Architect of the Capitol, the Secretary of Agriculture, the heads of seven other federal agencies whose activities affect historic preservation, one governor appointed by the President, one mayor appointed by the President, the president of the National Conference of State Historic Preservation Officers, the Chairman of the National Trust, four experts in the field of historic preservation appointed by the President from architecture, history, archeology, and other appropriate disciplines, three members from the general public, appointed by the President, one member of an Indian tribe or Native Hawaiian organization who represents the interests of the Indian tribe or Native Hawaiian organization of which he or she is a member, appointed by the President. 54 U.S.C. § 304101. In addition to its role in the Section 106 process, the ACHP is charged with advising the President and Congress on matters relating to historic preservation and recommending measures and guidelines to facilitate the purposes of the Act. 54 U.S.C. § 304102(a).

2. **ACHP's advice.** In *Committee to Save Cleveland's Huletts*, the Corps correctly pointed out that the decision to issue a permit was theirs alone, perhaps with the belief that it had the expertise to make that decision, but the ACHP did not. a. If that is the case, what could the ACHP have added to the review? b. Could it have urged the agency to see the Hulett not simply as an obsolete tool, but as an engineering monument and an historic structure that could tell us about the burdens and effects of industry of the past, the shaping of the dock, and the toils of men?

3. **Advisory nature of review.** In both of the preceding cases, the courts overruled the agency decisions that were taken in violation of the consultation requirement. a. What should happen on remand? b. If after listening to the ACHP and the SHPO, the agencies do not follow their advice, on what basis, if any, can anyone challenge decisions that are certain to harm an historic property? c. Are there laws or principles that could be invoked to require avoidance of harm?

4. **Cultural divide.** *Pueblo of Sandia* may reveal a seemingly insurmountable cultural divide; an instance of cultural myopia on the agency's part. a. Why didn't *National*

Register Bulletin 38: Guidelines for Evaluating and Documenting Traditional Cultural Properties, https://www.nps.gov/nr/publications/bulletins/nrb38) (last visited April 6, 2017), inform the agency's assessment in the first instance as to differing cultural rules, norms, and concerns? b. What must the agency do to discover and protect traditional cultural property where traditional cultural norms protect that property by not revealing its location?

* * *

Slave Graves

In May 1991, during the construction of a 34-story $276 million federal building in New York City, a remarkable discovery happened—more than 400 skeletal remains of slaves—men, women, and children. Because the project was a federal undertaking, NEPA and NHPA required a cultural resource survey, including archeological field testing to determine whether any historic resources might be impacted by the construction. Upon learning of the discovery, the African-American community, the mayor, and other public officials demanded a halt to the construction to ensure proper handling of the find. The Cobb Laboratory at Howard University offered a research plan for the interdisciplinary archeological, bio-anthropological, and historical study of the remains, and with the U.S. General Services Administration ("GSA") and the U.S. Army Corps of Engineers Center of Expertise for the Curation and Management of Archaeological Collections, produced a comprehensive report. The study provided invaluable evidence of the life and culture of New York's seventeenth and eighteenth-century Africans—about their health, diet, physical condition, and causes of death. http://www.mvs.usace.army.mil/Missions/Centers-of-Expertise/Curation-Mgmt-of-Archaeological-Collections/Reports/(last visited February 13, 2018). In 1993, the burial site was designated a National Historic Landmark and in 2006, President Bush declared it a National Monument under the Antiquities Act.

* * *

Proclamation 7984—Establishment of the African Burial Ground National Monument

February 27, 2006

By the President of the United States of America

A Proclamation

In Lower Manhattan, at the corners of Duane and Elk Streets, lies an undeveloped parcel of approximately 15,000 square feet that constitutes a remaining portion of New York City's early African Burial Ground. The site is part of an approximately 7-acre National Historic Landmark established on April 19, 1993. From the 1690s to the 1790s, the African Burial Ground served as the final resting place of enslaved and free

Africans in New York City, New York. It contains the remains of those interred, as well as the archeological resources and artifacts associated with their burials. Prior to the date of this proclamation, the site was administered by the General Services Administration (GSA), and it will be the location of a memorial, to be constructed soon according to a design selected on April 29, 2005, through a competition conducted by the GSA with the participation of the National Park Service (NPS) and other interested parties.

Whereas the African Burial Ground National Monument will promote understanding of related resources, encourage continuing research, and present interpretive opportunities and programs for visitors to better understand and honor the culture and vital contributions of generations of Africans and Americans of African descent to our Nation;

Whereas section 2 of the Act of June 8, 1906 (34 Stat. 225, 16 U.S.C. 431) (the "Antiquities Act") authorizes the President, in his discretion, to declare by public proclamation historic landmarks, historic and prehistoric structures, and other objects of historic or scientific interest that are situated upon lands owned or controlled by the Government of the United States to be national monuments, and to reserve as a part thereof parcels of land, the limits of which in all cases shall be confined to the smallest area compatible with the proper care and management of the objects to be protected;

Whereas it would be in the public interest to preserve the portion of the African Burial Ground at the corner of Duane and Elk Streets in New York City, and certain lands as necessary for the care and management of the historic and scientific objects therein, as the African Burial Ground National Monument;

Now, Therefore, I, George W. Bush, President of the United States of America, by the authority vested in me by section 2 of the Act of June 8, 1906 (34 Stat. 225, 16 U.S.C. 431), do proclaim that there are hereby set apart and reserved as the African Burial Ground National Monument for the purpose of protecting the objects described above, all lands and interests in lands owned or controlled by the Government of the United States with the boundaries described on the accompanying land description, which is attached and forms a part of this proclamation. The Federal land and interests in land reserved consist of approximately 15,000 square feet, which is the smallest area compatible with the proper care and management of the objects to be protected.

All Federal lands and interests of lands within the boundaries of this monument are hereby appropriated and withdrawn from all forms of entry, location, selection, sale, or leasing or other disposition under the public land laws, including, but not limited to, withdrawal from location, entry, and patent under mining laws, and from disposition under all laws relating to mineral and geothermal leasing.

* * *

The establishment of this monument is subject to valid existing rights.

Nothing in this proclamation shall be deemed to revoke any existing withdrawal, reservation, or appropriation; however, the national monument shall be the dominant reservation.

Warning is hereby given to all unauthorized persons not to appropriate, injure, destroy, or remove any feature of this monument and not to locate or settle upon any lands thereof.

In Witness Whereof, I have hereunto set my hand this twenty-seventh day of February, in the year of our Lord two thousand six, and of the Independence of the United States of America the two hundred and thirtieth.

George W. Bush

http://www.nps.gov/afbg/learn/management/presidential-proclamation.htm (last visited February 13, 2018).

African Burial Grounds. Photo by Chris Light, via Wikimedia Commons.

* * *

5. Historic Preservation Aided by Environmental Review

Muckleshoot Indian Tribe v. U.S. Forest Service

United States Court of Appeals, Ninth Circuit
177 F.3d 800 (1999)

Per Curiam. Plaintiffs Muckleshoot Indian Tribe, Pilchuck Audubon Society, and Huckleberry Mountain Protection Society appeal the district court's grant of summary judgment on consolidated challenges to a land exchange between the United States Forest Service and Weyerhaeuser Company. Plaintiffs contend that the Forest Service violated the National Environmental Policy Act ("NEPA"), 42 U.S.C. § 4332, and the National Historic Preservation Act ("NHPA"), 16 U.S.C. §§ 470–470w. We have jurisdiction pursuant to 28 U.S.C. § 1291, and we reverse.

I. *Background*

Huckleberry Mountain, the land subject to the dispute in this case, is located in the Green River watershed in the Mt. Baker-Snoqualmie National Forest ("the Forest") in the state of Washington. The Forest contains sixteen percent of the wilderness in the Pacific Northwest. Thirteen percent (259,545 acres) of the 1,983,774 acres within the National Forest boundary are privately owned, primarily by Weyerhaeuser and other large corporations. Most of the privately-owned lands are in the southern portion of the Forest, and are intermingled with federal lands in a checkerboard pattern of ownership that remains from the federal land grants to railroads a century ago.

Motivated in large part by a desire to unify land ownership, the United States Forest Service ("the Forest Service") and Weyerhaeuser Company ("Weyerhaeuser") began negotiations for a series of land exchanges pursuant to 43 U.S.C. § 1716, which authorizes the exchange of public lands within the National Forest system where "the public interest will be well served" by the exchange. In the 1980s, the Forest Service negotiated a land exchange[,] *** the Alpine Lakes Exchange, as it became known, [where] the United States conveyed a total of 21,676 acres of federally-owned Forest land to Weyerhaeuser and Burlington Northern in exchange for other property owned by the two companies. In the present appeal, plaintiffs challenge another land exchange between Weyerhaeuser and the Forest Service, the Huckleberry Mountain Exchange ("the Exchange"), in which the Forest Service again traded old growth forest lands in the Huckleberry Mountain area. Many of the parcels conveyed by the Forest Service in the Alpine Lakes Exchange are near or contiguous to federal lands that are part of the Exchange at issue in this appeal.

Although land within the Huckleberry Mountain Exchange Area had been tentatively identified during the Alpine Lakes Exchange negotiations between 1984 and 1987, negotiations began anew in 1988 with a revised list of federal land under consideration for exchange. In July 1991, Weyerhaeuser and the Forest Service signed a Statement of Intent to enter into an exchange, which identified the parcels to be included in the exchange. Between 1992 and 1994, the Forest Service conducted surveys regarding wetlands, wildlife, rare plants, hazardous waste, cultural resources and other matters, and subsequently reduced the federal acreage proposed for transfer.

The Forest Service initiated public consultation and comment and developed a list of six exchange alternatives. In July 1996, the Forest Service released a draft Environmental Impact Statement ("EIS"), pursuant to NEPA, 42 U.S.C. § 4332(2)(C), and mailed over 300 copies to interested parties. It then conducted three open meetings in communities near the Forest. Among those who provided comments on the Draft EIS was the Muckleshoot Indian Tribe (the "Tribe").

On November 26, 1996, the Forest Service issued a final EIS after receiving comments on the draft EIS. The EIS considered three alternatives.[1] Concurrently, the Forest Service issued a Record of Decision that called for an implementation of the Exchange through a modification of "Alternative No. 3" as evaluated in the EIS.[2]

The Pilchuck Audubon Society and the Huckleberry Mountain Protection Society (collectively "the Societies") and the Tribe lodged separate appeals of the EIS and the ROD with the Office of the Regional Forester. These appeals were denied on March 7, 1997. On March 28, 1997, pursuant to the ROD, Weyerhaeuser and the Forest Service executed an exchange agreement under which Weyerhaeuser conveyed to the United States 30,253 acres of land in and around Mt. Baker National Forest in return for 4,362 acres of land in the Huckleberry Mountain area.[3] In addition, Weyerhaeuser donated to the United States 962 acres to the Alpine Lakes Wilderness and 1,034 acres for Forest Service management. The National Forest lands that Weyerhaeuser received included old growth, commercial grade timber. The Forest Service also exchanged to Weyerhaeuser intact portions of the Huckleberry Divide Trail, a site important to the Tribe and that the Forest Service found eligible for inclusion in the National Register for Historic Preservation. Weyerhaeuser gave the Forest Service lands that were, for the most part, heavily logged and roaded. Weyerhaeuser intends to log the lands it received in the Exchange.

In the spring of 1997, the Tribe and the Societies commenced separate actions in the district court seeking declaratory and injunctive relief to halt the Huckleberry Mountain Exchange. The district court consolidated the two actions and granted Weyerhaeuser's motion to intervene because it was party to the Exchange. The com-

---

1. Alternative two proposed an exchange of up to 6,273 acres of Forest Service lands for up to 32,010 acres of Weyerhauser lands. Alternative three would remove 1,885 acres from the exchange. That acreage, and an additional 141 acres, would be donated by Weyerhaeuser to the Forest Service contingent on the implementation of that alternative. Nine hundred sixty two acres of the donated parcel would be donated for inclusion in the Alpine Lakes Wilderness Area and 1,034 acres would be proposed for management without timber harvest emphasis. Under that alternative, Weyerhaeuser would also retain title to the subsurface mineral estates on lands transferred to the Forest Service.

2. The modifications removed 1,280 acres of federal lands located near the town of Greenwater and 320 acres of federal land around Mule Springs, an important Tribal site; retained a cost-share status between the Forest Service and Weyerhaeuser for Forest Service Road 7125 to ensure continued tribal access to the site; and modified the terms of the mineral rights that Weyerhaeuser received.

3. Weyerhaeuser did not retain title to certain subsurface mineral estates as described in the EIS. Instead, it retained the rights to a portion of the royalties from any minerals leased or sold by the Forest Service on those lands.

bined action, brought pursuant to the Administrative Procedures Act, 5 U.S.C. §§701–06, alleged violations of the Federal Lands Policy and Management Act, 43 U.S.C. §1701 *et seq.*, the General Exchange Act, 16 U.S.C. §485; the Weeks Act, 16 U.S.C. §516; the National Forest Management Act, 16 U.S.C. 1600 *et seq.;* NHPA, 16 U.S.C. §470 *et seq.*, and NEPA, 42 U.S.C. 4321 *et seq.* The Tribe also asserted that the government breached its duty of trust to the Tribe. The district court denied all of these claims. *** Plaintiffs appeal only their claims under NHPA and NEPA. The plaintiffs did not seek a stay of the district court's order pending appeal. The Exchange was finalized on March 12, 1998.

*** Because the district court decided the case on a motion for summary judgment, we review that determination de novo. *Neighbors of Cuddy Mountain v. United States Forest Service*, 137 F.3d 1372, 1376 (9th Cir. 1998). An agency's factual findings should be "overturned only if they are arbitrary and capricious." *Sierra Club v. Clark*, 756 F.2d 686, 691 (9th Cir. 1985).

II. The National Historic Preservation Act Claims

The Muckleshoot Tribe is made up principally of descendants of tribes or bands that were parties to the Treaty of Point Elliott and the Treaty of Medicine Creek. The Tribe was organized pursuant to the Indian Reorganization Act of June 18, 1934. *** The United States, acting by and through the Secretary of the Interior and his duly authorized delegatees, has consistently recognized the Muckleshoot Tribe as the political successor in interest to certain of the Indian tribes, bands and villages that were parties to the Treaty of Point Elliott or the Treaty of Medicine Creek. ***

The Indian ancestors to the present Muckleshoot Tribe included people from villages on the Green and White Rivers that form part of the drainage for Huckleberry Mountain. The Tribe alleges that for thousands of years, the ancestors of present tribal members used Huckleberry Mountain for cultural, religious, and resource purposes—uses that continue to the present day. The Forest Service lands exchanged to Weyerhaeuser were part of the Tribe's ancestral grounds.

Section 10 of NHPA requires that, prior to any federal undertaking, the relevant federal agency "take into account the effect of the undertaking on any district, site, building, structure, or object that is included in or eligible for inclusion in the National Register" and "afford the Advisory Council on Historic Preservation ... a reasonable opportunity to comment with regard to such undertaking." 16 U.S.C. §470f ***

We have held that Section 106 of NHPA is a "stop, look, and listen" provision that requires each federal agency to consider the effects of its programs. *** The Forest Service must confer with the State Historic Preservation Officer ("SHPO") and seek the approval of the Advisory Council on Historic Preservation ("Council").

Additional NHPA provisions apply to Indian tribes.

> (A) Properties of traditional religious and cultural importance to an Indian tribe ... may be determined to be eligible for inclusion in the National Register.

> (B) In carrying out its responsibilities under Section 106, a Federal Agency shall consult with any Indian Tribe ... that attaches religious and cultural significance to properties described in Subparagraph (A).

16 U.S.C. §470a(d)(6). *** The Tribe's claims under NHPA can be divided into three categories. The Tribe first contends that the Forest Service failed to consult adequately with it regarding the identification of traditional cultural properties. The Tribe also contends that the Forest Service inadequately mitigated the harmful impact of the exchange on sites of cultural significance. Finally, the Tribe argues that the Forest Service violated NHPA by failing to nominate certain sites to the National Register. We conclude that the Forest Service has not satisfied NHPA's mitigation requirements.

A. *Identification of Traditional Cultural Properties*

This Court has not yet had the opportunity to interpret the specific consultation requirements of NHPA. *** Although we confront somewhat different issues, *Pueblo of Sandia v. United States,* 50 F.3d 856, 860 (10th Cir. 1995) is instructive. The Tenth Circuit *** found that although none of the tribes provided the information specifically solicited by the letters and presentation, the statements of the Governor of the Sandia Pueblo, a religious leader, and a highly qualified anthropologist, all indicating that the land was sacred, and that the tribes were unlikely to reveal information on the use of these lands, were sufficient to require the agency to evaluate the property for inclusion in the National Register. *Id.* at 861. The court also determined that the agency had failed to perform the required "good faith consultation" with the State Historic Preservation Office, and reversed the district court order approving the federal action. *Id.* at 862.

In the case before us, the record shows that the Forest Service researched historic sites in the Exchange area and communicated several times after the commencement of the public comment period with Tribal officials regarding the identification and protection of cultural resources that might be affected by the Exchange. The Forest Service initially identified only Mule Springs as eligible for listing in the National Register, and concluded that any adverse effect "may be negated through appropriately conducted data recovery." Two years later, after considering the concerns of the Tribe, the Forest Service excluded Mule Springs from the Exchange and retained the Forest Service access road in a cost-share status. Because this site was excluded from the Exchange, the district court correctly concluded that the Tribe suffered no injury. The Forest Service initially concluded that the Huckleberry Divide Trail ("Divide Trail") was ineligible for listing. After the SHPO suggested otherwise, the Forest Service reconsidered and found it eligible for listing but nonetheless included it in the lands exchanged to Weyerhaeuser. We discuss the Divide Trail in more detail below.

The Tribe also contends that the Forest Service ignored its claims that numerous other places of historical importance were situated on the portions of Huckleberry Mountain proposed for exchange. The Tribe requested a study of its historical places and trails, but in response, the Forest Service, which had already carried out research in the area, simply requested the immediate disclosure of any information the Tribe possessed about those sites. The Tribe was unable, or unwilling, to provide information sufficient to persuade the Agency that it should reconsider its decisions.

The Forest Service's action is in tension with the recommendations of the *National Register Bulletin 38: Guidelines for Evaluating and Documenting Traditional Cultural Properties* ("Bulletin 38"). Bulletin 38 provides the recognized criteria for the Forest Service's identification and assessment of places of cultural significance. In *Sandia,* the Tenth Circuit's finding that the agency had violated NHPA rested in part upon its finding that the agency failed to adhere to that document. 50 F.3d at 861. The Tribe urges us to find a comparable violation in this case.

While the deviations from Bulletin 38 policies in this case are similar to those in *Sandia,* they appear not to be as egregious, and probably do not provide sufficient grounds to conclude that the Forest Service failed to comply with NHPA identification and consultation requirements. First, Bulletin 38 does not impose a mandatory procedure, but merely establishes guidelines. Contravention of those recommendations, standing alone, probably does not constitute a violation of NHPA. Second, in this case, unlike *Sandia,* the Forest Service continued to seek the requested information over a period of time, *** and the Forest Service had previously conducted research of its own to identify relevant traditional cultural properties.

Unlike in *Sandia,* there is no evidence that the Forest Service withheld information from the SHPO pertaining to historic sites, or failed to engage in good faith negotiations with SHPO. *** The record shows that the Forest Service resisted the Tribe's requests for a formal study of cultural properties because it would impede the finalization of the Exchange. Given more time or a more thorough exploration, the Forest Service might have discovered more eligible sites. However, the record also shows that the Tribe had many opportunities to reveal more information to the Forest Service. Although the Forest Service could have been more sensitive to the needs of the Tribe, we are unable to conclude that the Forest Service failed to make a reasonable and good faith effort to identify historic properties. ***

* * *

B. *The Effects of the Exchange*

The Tribe also claims that the Forest Service's attempt to mitigate the adverse effect of transferring a portion of the Divide Trail, an important tribal ancestral transportation route, was inadequate. We agree.

When an agency determines that a property is eligible for listing, it must assess the effects of any proposed undertaking on the eligible property, 36 C.F.R. § 800.4(e), "giving consideration to the views ... of interested persons." 36 C.F.R. § 800.5(a). Interested persons include tribes. 36 C.F.R. § 800.1(c)(2).

An undertaking has an "effect" when the undertaking "may alter characteristics of the property that may qualify the property for inclusion in the National Register ... [including] alteration to features of a property's location, setting, or use...." 36 C.F.R. § 800.9(a). An "effect" is "adverse" when it may "diminish the integrity of the property's location, ... setting..., feeling, or association." 36 C.F.R. § 800.9(b). ***

In 1995, the Forest Service re-evaluated the eligibility of the Divide Trail for listing. The Divide Trail is a 17.5 mile historic aboriginal transportation route. The Forest Service found that portions of the trail possessed "adequate integrity of location, setting and feeling" to satisfy the eligibility criteria of 36 C.F.R. § 60.4. In the proposed Exchange, a portion of the intact trail would be transferred to Weyerhaeuser, where it would likely be logged and rendered ineligible for listing. Transfer and destruction of historic property are "adverse" effects. ***

The regulations offer three options to mitigate an otherwise adverse effect so that it is "considered as being not adverse," two of which are implicated here. 36 C.F.R. § 800.9(c). First, an agency may conduct appropriate research "[w]hen the historic property is of value *only for* its potential contribution to archeological, historical, or architectural research, *and* when such value can be substantially preserved through the conduct of appropriate research...." 36 C.F.R. § 800.9(c)(1) (emphasis added). Second, an adverse effect becomes "not adverse" when the undertaking is limited to the "transfer, lease, or sale of a historic property, *and adequate restrictions or conditions are included* to ensure preservation of the property's significant historic features." 36 C.F.R. § 800.9(c)(3) (emphasis added). The Tribe insists that the Forest Service elected the wrong remedy. We agree.

To mitigate the adverse effect of the Exchange, the Forest Service proposed to map the trail using a global positioning system and to photograph significant features along the trail. It rejected an easement or covenant because it concluded that it was too expensive and impractical to monitor Weyerhaeuser's land practices, and because "only" 25 percent of the eligible miles of trail would be transferred out of federal ownership. It also rejected the imposition of conditions to prevent logging and other degradation. *** [P]hotographing and mapping the trail are not "adequate restrictions or conditions" that "ensure preservation of the property's significant historic features." ***[5] The parties agree that the trail is likely to be logged if it is transferred, *** previously logged and "obliterated" portions of the trail are ineligible for listing.

The district court determined erroneously that the Forest Service had proceeded under (c)(1) and concluded that the agency acted properly because any adverse effect may be "negated" if the historical and archeological value of the property can be preserved by conducting research on the site. The Forest Service did not, and could not, proceed under (c)(1). Under 36 C.F.R. § 800.9(c)(1), research is appropriate mitigation where the historic property is of value *only* for "its potential contribution to archeological, historical, or architectural research." The Muckleshoots value the Divide Trail for more than its "potential contribution to ... research."

* * *

5. We note that, in proposing this mitigation, the Forest Service claimed that transferring a property "may be determined to have no adverse effect if conditions are included to ensure preservation of the property's *historic values*" (emphasis added). It misunderstands its obligations. Preserving a property's historic values is not the same as preserving its "significant historic features."

While we do not decide whether the Forest Service's reasons for rejecting deed restrictions were valid, we note that it could have removed the trail from the Exchange as it did with Mule Springs. We conclude that documenting the trail did not satisfy the Forest Service's obligations to minimize the adverse effect of transferring the intact portions of the trail.

* * *

III. *National Environmental Policy Act*

NEPA requires federal agencies such as the Forest Service to prepare a detailed environmental impact statement ("EIS") for "all major actions significantly affecting the quality of the human environment." 42 U.S.C. §4332(2)(C). An EIS must address the cumulative impacts of a project and consider adequate alternatives. *** In evaluating whether an agency's EIS complies with NEPA's requirements, we must determine whether it contains "a reasonably thorough discussion of the significant aspects of the probable environmental consequences." *** We review for an abuse of discretion. ***

*** The Tribe contends that the identification and analysis of cumulative environmental impacts in the Forest Service's EIS did not meet the requirements of NEPA. The Societies contend that the EIS inadequately defined the purpose and need for the Huckleberry Land Exchange as required by NEPA, and did not identify or evaluate sufficient alternatives for the exchange. We consider each of these issues in turn.

A. *Assessment of Cumulative Impacts under NEPA*

We first address the Tribe's contention that the Forest Service failed to consider the cumulative impact of the exchange. *** Regulations implementing NEPA require that a federal agency consider "[c]umulative actions, which when viewed with other proposed actions have cumulatively significant impacts and should therefore be discussed in the same impact statement." 40 C.F.R. §1508.25(a)(2).

In *City of Carmel-By-The-Sea v. U.S. Dept. of Transp.*, 123 F.3d 1142 (9th Cir. 1997), we noted that an EIS must *** include a "useful analysis of the cumulative impacts of past, present and future projects." *Id.* at 1160. This requires "discussion of how [future] projects together with the proposed ... project will affect [the environment]." *Id.* The EIS must analyze the combined effects of the actions in sufficient detail to be "useful to the decisionmaker in deciding whether, or how, to alter the program to lessen cumulative impacts." *Id.* at 1160 (internal citations omitted). Detail is therefore required in describing the cumulative effects of a proposed action with other proposed actions. ***

The Tribe contends that the EIS gives inadequate consideration to the cumulative impacts of logging on the 1984 Alpine Lakes Exchange lands, of existing logging and other disturbances in the Green River watershed, and of a future land exchange with the Plum Creek Timber Company that involves lands in the same vicinity as the Huckleberry Mountain Exchange. The district court held that the Forest Service did not need to consider the 1984 Alpine Lake Exchange because it was part of the baseline environment and, as such, was considered in the EIS for the Mt. Baker Snoqualmie National Forest Land and Resource Management Plan, *** ("LRMP"). The district court also held that the Plum Creek exchange was "too uncertain" to require a discussion of cumulative effects. We do not agree with those conclusions.

Appellees urge that because the final EIS for the Huckleberry Exchange is tiered to the LRMP, it sufficiently analyzes the cumulative impacts of the Exchange.

"Tiering" is defined as:

> [T]he coverage of general matters in broader environmental impact statements (such as national program or policy statements) with subsequent narrower statements or environmental analyses (such as regional or basinwide program statements or ultimately site-specific statements) incorporating by reference the general discussions and concentrating solely on the issues specific to the statement subsequently prepared.

40 C.F.R. § 1508.28[.] *** We have previously interpreted the regulations to allow tiering only to another environmental impact statement. *** The Huckleberry Exchange EIS is tiered erroneously to the Forest Plan, not the EIS for the Forest Plan. Our review of the Forest Plan and its accompanying EIS reveals that those documents do not account for the specific impacts of the Exchange and do not remedy the Forest Service's failure to account for the impacts of the Exchange in the Huckleberry Exchange EIS. ***

The LRMP EIS, prepared in 1990, was prepared before the Huckleberry Exchange lands were identified with any certainty. The concept of the Huckleberry exchange was mentioned only in a pool of possible projects that would help meet the goals of the Forest Plan. There was no detail concerning those projects and their impacts. The proposed Exchange simply was not concrete enough to allow for adequate analysis. Moreover, the LRMP EIS did not analyze the impact of increased logging on the parcels that had been transferred out of federal ownership in the 1984 Alpine Lakes Exchange. Many of those parcels are in the same vicinity as the old growth forest lands the Forest Service transferred to Weyerhaeuser. If we were to adopt the Forest Service's approach, the cumulative impacts of land exchanges would escape environmental review.

The problem is compounded by the very general and one-sided analysis of the cumulative impact information that the Huckleberry Exchange EIS does contain. While the district court was correct in observing that there are "twelve sections entitled 'cumulative effects,'" these sections merely provide very broad and general statements devoid of specific, reasoned conclusions.

* * *

The statement notably contains no evaluation whatsoever of the impact on natural resources of timber harvesting on the lands transferred to Weyerhaeuser, nor does it assess the possible impacts that such harvesting could have upon surrounding areas. The statement focuses solely on the beneficial impact the exchange will have on lands received by the Forest Service. All of those described benefits are contingent on appropriate Forest Service action and funds to promote the recovery of the harvested lands that it will acquire. This lopsided analysis is repeated in virtually every cumulative impact statement ***

We hold that the cumulative impact statements that are provided in the EIS are far too general and one-sided to meet the NEPA requirements. *** The statements fall far short of a "useful analysis" as required by *City of Carmel,* 123 F.3d at 1160. ***

The appellees also attempt to tier the Exchange EIS to the Green River Watershed Report to cure the deficiencies of the cumulative impact analysis of the Exchange EIS. Such reliance is impermissible under the NEPA regulations, which only permit tiering to prior EIS's. 40 C.F.R. §§ 1502.20 and 1508.28. *** The analysis in the Green River Watershed Report, even if appropriately allowed as a tiering document, demonstrates the need for a more thorough cumulative impact analysis. ***

Plaintiffs also contend that the EIS failed to analyze adequately the cumulative effects of a future land exchange involving Plum Creek Timber Company that, according to plaintiffs, was "reasonably foreseeable" at the time the Exchange EIS was prepared. An agency must analyze the incremental impact of the action "when added to other past, present, and *reasonably foreseeable* future actions...." 40 C.F.R. § 1508.7 (emphasis added). The district court determined that the Plum Creek Exchange was too speculative to require analysis.*** Our review of the record suggests that the Plum Creek transaction was not remote or highly speculative. Rather, it was reasonably foreseeable and it should have been considered in the EIS. A summary of the proposed Plum Creek transaction already had been prepared by the Forest Service by 1995. ***

Moreover, the record reflects that the Forest Service was all but certain that the National Forest lands in the upper Green River Basin would be included in the Plum Creek exchange. The Huckleberry Exchange EIS was issued in November 1996. In July 1996, the Green River Watershed plan described the Plum Creek exchange, and in January 1997, two months after the Huckleberry Exchange EIS issued, a revised map showing lands to be exchanged in the Plum Creek Exchange was published. The Plum Creek Exchange was not too speculative in November, 1996, to be analyzed in the Huckleberry Exchange EIS. *** Given the virtual certainty of the transaction and its scope, the Forest Service was required under NEPA to evaluate the cumulative impacts of the Plum Creek transaction. *** In the absence of an EIS that takes into consideration the cumulative effects of the planned land sales and resultant environmental impacts, we cannot conclude that the Forest Service took the necessary "hard look" at the cumulative environmental impacts of the Huckleberry Exchange. ***

B. *Failure to Consider an Adequate Range of Alternatives*

We also agree with the Societies' contention that the Forest Service violated NEPA by failing to consider a range of appropriate alternatives to the proposed exchange. *** The Societies first contend that the EIS fails to properly specify the underlying purpose and need to which the proposal is responding as required by NEPA regulations. ***

The EIS states that the purpose and need for the proposal is to "consolidate ownership and enhance future resource conservation and management by exchanging parcels of National Forest System and Weyerhaeuser land." The Societies argue that this narrowly stated purpose fails to meet the requirements of section 1502.13 as it was interpreted in *City of Carmel,* where we held that "[t]he stated goal of a project necessarily dictates the range of reasonable alternatives and an agency cannot define its objectives in unreasonably narrow terms." 123 F.3d at 1155.

*** [I]n the course of evaluating the options that would best achieve the stated purpose of the proposed action, the Forest Service failed to consider an adequate range of alternatives. The EIS considered only a no action alternative along with two virtually identical alternatives. The selected alternative, Alternative 3, differed from Alternative 2 only in that it re-labeled a portion of the lands Weyerhaeuser transferred to the Forest Service a donation rather than an exchange, and added 141 acres of donated land.

In addressing the claims that the Forest Service erred in failing to mitigate the possible harms of the exchange, the district court concluded that there was no evidence that Weyerhaeuser would agree to plaintiffs' proposed alternative of the Forest Service purchasing the Weyerhaeuser land rather than exchanging for it and that there was no evidence that the agency failed to consider, as required by *Resources Ltd., Inc. v. Robertson,* 35 F.3d 1300, 1305 (9th Cir. 1994), "a reasonably full range of alternatives." *** Our review of the record, *** compel us to reach the opposite conclusion.

* * *

Although NEPA does not require the Forest Service to "consider every possible alternative to a proposed action, nor must it consider alternatives that are unlikely to be implemented or those inconsistent with its basic policy objectives," *Seattle Audubon Society v. Moseley,* 80 F.3d 1401, 1404 (9th Cir. 1996), we are troubled that in this case, the Forest Service failed to consider an alternative that was more consistent with its basic policy objectives than the alternatives that were the subject of final consideration. In this case, the applicable regulation controlling implementation of the Federal Land Policy Management Act, 43 U.S.C. § 1701 *et seq.,* pursuant to which the Exchange was transacted, dictates that the agency officer authorized to conduct a land exchange "shall reserve such rights or retain such interests as are needed to protect the public interest or shall otherwise restrict the use of Federal lands to be exchanged, as appropriate." 36 C.F.R. 254.3(h). A detailed consideration of a trade involving deed restrictions or other modifications to the acreage involved is in the public interest and should have been considered.

We also recognize that an agency's discussion of alternatives must be "bounded by some notion of feasibility." *** Counsel for Weyerhaeuser conceded at oral argument that the imposition of deed restrictions was a viable alternative to the Exchange Agreement of March 28, 1997. A "viable but unexamined alternative renders [the] environmental impact statement inadequate." *** Imposition of deed restrictions was a feasible alternative that could not be ignored.

The plaintiffs also argue that the land could have been purchased outright with funds from the Federal Land and Water Conservation Fund. While the Forest Service itself cannot appropriate these funds, it can request them. The record reflects that such a request was never made, and indeed, this option was not even considered.

The appellees respond that, because it was not clear that the funds would be available for such a purchase, the Forest Service had no obligation to consider it, as it constituted a "remote and speculative" alternative. *** However, NEPA regulations state that agencies shall "include reasonable alternatives not within the jurisdiction of the lead agency." 40 C.F.R. § 1502.14(c). This alternative clearly falls within the range of such reasonable alternatives, and should have been considered. ***

The Forest Service also contends that because the purpose of the transaction was to carry out an "exchange" and not a purchase, it was not required to consider this alternative. *** To the extent that Weyerhaeuser would have been exchanging its lands for federal monies rather than federal lands, we do not recognize such an inconsistency.

NEPA "does not mandate particular results," but "simply provides the necessary process" to ensure that federal agencies take a "hard look" at the environmental consequences of their actions. *Robertson v. Methow Valley Citizens Council,* 490 U.S. 332, 350, 109 S.Ct. 1835, 104 L.Ed.2d 351 (1989). We conclude that in this case, the Forest Service failed to take the necessary hard look at the environmental impacts of the exchange and similarly failed to consider adequate alternatives to the proposed exchange.

V. *Conclusion*

We hold that the Forest Service failed to meet the requirements of NHPA and NEPA. Its attempt to mitigate the adverse effect of transferring portions of the Divide Trail by documenting the trail did not comport with the regulations. It did not adequately consider the cumulative impacts of the Huckleberry Exchange in conjunction with past or reasonably certain future transactions. To the extent it attempted an analysis of cumulative impacts, the analysis was one-sided. Finally, it did not consider adequate alternatives to implement the Exchange.

* * *

We REVERSE and REMAND to the district court with directions that it remand to the Forest Service for further proceedings consistent with this opinion. Given Weyerhaeuser's representations that it has destroyed approximately ten percent of the property, and will continue to do so, we also enjoin any further activities on the land such as would be undertaken pursuant to the Huckleberry Mountain Exchange Agreement as executed on March 28, 1997 until such time as the Forest Service satisfies its NHPA and NEPA obligations. ***

Notes and Questions

1. **Traditional cultural properties.** Properties of cultural and religious importance ("PCRI"), also called traditional cultural property ("TCP"), are eligible for inclusion in the National Register. They include sacred places that figure in traditional belief systems and that are used for prayer, along with their associated implements. Their protection may be difficult because of the same belief system sought to be protected—native peoples often refuse to disclose their location. The NHPA still requires the agency to make reasonable and good faith effort to identify such property despite the attitude of the native people. In *Te-Moak Tribe of Western Shoshone of Nevada v. United States Dep't of Interior*, 608 F.3d 592 (9th Cir. 2010), the Ninth Circuit

ruled that efforts of the Bureau of Land Management ("BLM") to locate and identify TCPs were sufficient. There, the BLM was considering mineral exploration around Horse Canyon in Nevada, near Mt. Tenabo, considered a locus of power and source of life for the Western Shoshone. The mountain figured in creation stories and world renewal, was a place for prayer, and a burial ground for the Shoshone. Even though there had been extensive documentation of TCPs from an earlier project, the BLM sent a description of the proposed project and a letter to the Tribe asking for help identifying any additional concerns and in developing alternatives to reduce potential impacts. The Tribe did not respond to this letter, nor to telephone calls from the BLM. The BLM nevertheless conditioned the project on the requirement to take specific avoidance measures to protect TCPs. The Ninth Circuit upheld the BLM's determination that no adverse effects would occur to TCPs, and also that the exclusion zone protocol was adequate to protect the discrete features that make the designated TCPs eligible for the National Register—the top of the mountain, the caves, and burial grounds, but not the general landscape.

2. **Duty to consult.** The regulations promulgated by the Advisory Council on Historic Preservation ("ACHP") state that the Tribal Historic Preservation Officer ("THPO") is the official representative for purposes of Section 106 consultation. 36 C.F.R. §§800.2(c)(2)(i)(A), 800.3(c)(1). "Consultation with an Indian tribe must recognize the government-to-government relationship between the Federal government and Indian tribes," and the consultation should be conducted in a manner "sensitive to the concerns and needs of the Indian tribe ..." 36 C.F.R.§800.2(c)(2)(ii)(C). Consultation should provide the tribe with "a reasonable opportunity to identify its concerns about historic properties, advise on the identification and evaluation of historic properties, including those of traditional religious and cultural importance, articulate its views on the undertaking's effects on such properties, and participate in the resolution of adverse effects." 36 C.F.R.§800.2(c)(2)(ii)(A). In *San Juan Citizens Alliance v. Norton*, 586 F. Supp. 2d 1270 (D. New Mex. 2008), the court found that obligation was met when the BLM held public meetings, sent letters to 24 Native American Tribes and 27 Navajo Chapters, used a consulting firm to conduct interviews with rural Navajo residents, and held face-to-face meetings with tribal leaders. The court ruled that the agency was not required to consult with every individual tribal chapter, but only with the THPO. *See also Standing Rock Sioux Tribe v. U.S. Army Corps of Eng'rs*, 205 F. Supp. 3d 4 (D.D.C. 2016) (agency made dozens of attempts to engage thetribe, while the tribe largely refused).

3. **Post review discoveries.** New discoveries of historical properties during a project are governed by 36 C.F.R. §800.13. That section lays out specific obligations for a federal agency upon discovery of new historical properties after completion of a Section 106 review, but before project completion. The required measures include taking actions to avoid, minimize, or mitigate any adverse effects, care for the property if relevant under the Archeological Resource Protection Act, 16 U.S.C. §§470aa– 470mm, and notify the THPO in the case of TCPs. Parties to a project can develop a programmatic agreement to govern the actions to be taken in such cases, which will be controlling.

4. **Photographic documentation as mitigation.** a. Did the court read the mitigation language in the regulations to require the Forest Service to choose the route with the least amount of impact on the historic property? b. If that were the case, would photographic documentation ever meet this standard? c. Or, did the regulations say only that the Forest Service could avoid the characterization of the effect as adverse by implementing the mitigation measures, thereby limiting ACHP review? d. Could the Forest Service, having identified the historic property and the adverse effects, decide to proceed nonetheless?

5. **Revised regulations.** In 2000 the regulations were revised. Section 800.9 was redesignated 800.5, and the new section does not prescribe mitigation measures, but only defines an adverse effect to include "transfer, sale or lease ... without adequate or legally enforceable restrictions or conditions to ensure long-term preservation of the property's historical significance." 36 C.F.R. § 800.5. Does the revised regulation achieve the same object as the earlier version?

6. **Overarching policies and goals.** The Federal Land Policy Management Act of 1976 ("FLPMA"), 43 U.S.C. §§ 1701–1787, is a sweeping mandate to land management agencies to engage in comprehensive planning toward the preservation of public lands. Among other things, FLPMA requires "public lands be managed in a manner that will protect the quality of scientific, scenic, historical, ecological, environmental, air and atmospheric, water resource, and archeological values ..." 43 U.S.C. § 1701(a)(8). a. Was the Forest Service overly concerned about efficient management, and not so much with preserving the resources—the TCPs, the old growth timber? b. Who benefitted most from this land exchange? BLM regulations on land exchanges require that exchanges must be in the public interest and the exchanged lands have relatively equal value and the regulations state that the agency can protect the public interest by reserving rights on or retaining interests in the lands exchanged. 36 C.F.R. § 254.3(a), (b), (h).

Hoonah Indian Association v. Morrison

United States Court of Appeals, Ninth Circuit
170 F.3d 1223 (1999)

Kleinfeld, C.J. These appeals relate to two timber sales, and raise questions under the Alaska National Interest Lands Conservation Act (ANILCA), and the National Historic Preservation Act (NHPA).

Facts

The Forest Service gave notice of its intent to conduct timber sales in the Tongass National Forest in Southeast Alaska. 58 Fed.Reg. 21559-01, 37458-01 (1993). Two sales were proposed, called the Northwest Baranof and Eight Fathom, on Baranof Island north of Sitka, and on Chichagof Island around Hoonah. *** The timber sales were planned pursuant to the Tongass Timber Reform Act, 16 U.S.C. § 539d. This federal law speaks not to all national forests but only to one, the Tongass National Forest in Southeast Alaska. It commands the Secretary of Agriculture to sell enough wood from the Tongass National Forest, subject to certain qualifications, to satisfy market demand:

> **a. Tongass National Forest timber supply; satisfaction of certain market demands**
>
> Subject to appropriations, other applicable law, and the requirements of the National Forest Management Act of 1976 (Public Law 94-588), except as provided in subsection (d) of this section, the Secretary shall, to the extent consistent with providing for the multiple use and sustained yield of all renewable forest resources, seek to provide a supply of timber from the Tongass National Forest which (1) meets the annual market demand for timber from such forest and (2) meets the market demand from such forest for each planning cycle.

16 U.S.C. § 539d(a). *** Final Environmental Impact Statements were published in February, 1996 for the Northwest Baranof project, and in May, 1996 for the Eight Fathom project.

Hoonah Indian Association and Sitka Tribe brought this lawsuit and now appeal. Hoonah is among Alaska's larger villages, about 800 people, and Sitka is among its largest cities (by Alaska standards), close to 9,000 people. The Native community in each town has a tribal government. Both towns are in Southeast Alaska. Though the towns are distinct from the tribal governments (Sitka is largely non-Native, with a substantial Tlingit minority), the tribal governments are referred to herein for convenience as Hoonah and Sitka. Sitka and Hoonah both argue that the timber sales would violate [the Alaska National Interest Land Conservation Act's, ("ANILCA")] 16 U.S.C. § 3120, limitation on dispositions affecting subsistence uses of public land. Sitka also argues that the Northwest Baranof sales would violate the National Historic Preservation Act, 16 U.S.C. § 470f.

The tribal governments moved for summary judgment, which was denied. They sought injunctions, which were denied as well. *** The Tribes appeal. *** We have jurisdiction to review denial of the injunction under 28 U.S.C. § 1292(a)(1).

Analysis

[The court rejected the tribes' clam is under ANILCA, finding that ANILCA contemplated restrictions on subsistence uses not only as might be required by law, but also as consistent with sound management principles for the utilization of the public lands. A significant restriction of subsistence uses might not be necessary to achieve compliance with the Tongass Timber Reform Act, yet necessary to conform to sound management principles for such "utilization" under ANILCA. The forest supervisor determined that timber sales was consistent with sound management practices—that a substantial component of the economy of Southeast Alaska depended on a viable timber industry; the timbering aimed to meet the industry's three-year supply of timber; and clearcutting would help to prevent the reinfection of the dwarf mistletoe. These findings were not arbitrary and capricious.]

II. *National Historic Preservation Act*

This issue affects only the Northwest Baranof sale on Baranof Island outside of Sitka, not the Eight Fathom sale on Chichagof Island near Hoonah. ***

The National Historic Preservation Act issue has to do with whether the route or routes one clan of the Tlingits, the Kiks.adi, took should have been designated a cultural site and the timber sale should have been enjoined while the process for listing it proceeded. The Tlingit fort is a historic site in present-day Sitka, but the route or routes of the march were not designated.

The applicable procedure under the Act, 16 U.S.C. §§ 470 et seq., is for State Historic Preservation Officers to identify and nominate properties for the National Register. 16 U.S.C. 470a(b)(3). The Act requires agencies, prior to undertaking projects on federal land, to "take into account the effect of the undertaking on any district, site, building, structure, or object that is included in or eligible for inclusion in the National Register." 16 U.S.C. § 470f. ***

In preparing the Environmental Impact Statement for the Northwest Baranof timber sales, Forest Service archaeologists identified 45 historic properties, and determined that 39 were eligible for inclusion in the National Register. The State Historic Preservation Office, charged with administering the NHPA, agreed with the Forest Service's findings. The Forest Service, with the Tribe's agreement, decided the 39 designated sites would not be affected by the timber sale. The route of the retreat after the Russian reconquest, called in the record the Kiks.adi Survival March, was not among the sites listed as eligible. The Sitka Tribe contends that the Forest Service's procedure regarding identification of the "Kiks.adi Survival March" violated the National Historic Preservation Act.

The Forest Service early in the process decided that the route of the survival march might be eligible for inclusion because of its cultural importance. The reason that it was ultimately not designated as a cultural site is that the Forest Service was unable to determine just where the Kiks.adi Survival March went. The Tribe argues that this was an arbitrary and capricious failure to designate, because oral history suggested multiple routes, at least one for the strong men and another for the women, children, and old people, and because it was arbitrary to require a site with observable physical identification.

The regulations say that if the relevant agency official and state historic preservation officer "agree that the criteria are not met, the property shall be considered not eligible." 36 C.F.R. § 800.4(c)(3). The Alaska State Historic Preservation Officer determined that the Survival March Trail was not eligible because it did not meet established criteria that "it have identified physical features" and that it be "a location where the people regularly returned to." Her determination was based upon review of the materials submitted to her by a panel of experts. The Tribe did not appeal the State Historic Preservation Officer's decision. It could have under 36 C.F.R. § 60.12. Failure to do so makes that decision unchallengeable for failure to exhaust administrative remedies, under 36 C.F.R. § 60.12(e).

The Tribe did challenge the Forest Service's environmental impact statement on the ground that the Forest Service did not recommend listing the Kiks.adi Survival March trail. Our review of that decision is limited to whether it was arbitrary or capricious. ***

The statute defines "historic property" and "historic resource" as "any prehistoric or historic district, site, building, structure, or object included in, or eligible for inclusion on the National Register...." 16 U.S.C. §470w(5). The words "district, site, building, structure or object" all connote something more concretely bounded and defined than a general area over which a group of people passed.

The Tribe notes that 36 C.F.R. §800.4(c)(1) requires agencies to "apply the National Register Criteria to properties that may be affected by the undertaking and have not been previously evaluated for National Register eligibility," and argues that the Forest Service never applied the National Register Criteria to the Survival March routes. But the record shows that it did. The Forest Service made extensive efforts for close to three years to identify the Kiks.adi Survival March routes, by consulting with experts and considering tribal traditions and individuals' recollections of what relatives had told them. There was no physical marking, no documentation, and no well established tribal consensus, to establish exactly what bear and deer trails, beaches, and other paths the retreating Kiks.adi had taken.

The regulations require the agency official to "[s]eek information in accordance with agency planning processes from ... Indian tribes." 36 C.F.R. 800.4(a)(iii). He did. The tribe could not tell him just where the retreating Kiks.adi passed. *** The Forest Service followed the regulations and used the National Register criteria, as the Tribe says it should have. Those criteria do not support the Tribe's position. *** There was no original source documentation, and all the materials available were carefully evaluated, and did not confirm the accuracy of any suggested path. The criteria say that "[t]he actual location of a historic property, complemented by its setting, is particularly important in recapturing the sense of historic events and persons." *** The "actual location" of the Kiks.adi route is unknown, and the Tribe's own submission called it a "symbolic" location as opposed to an "actual" one.

* * *

That important things happened in a general area is not enough to make the area a "site." There has to be some good evidence of just where the site is and what its boundaries are, for it to qualify for federal designation as a historical site. The Historian of the National Register of Historic Places wrote, in opposition to listing the Kiks.adi route, that his staff consistently rejected "nominating such a wide swath of land with little if any identified physical features." The Historian noted that when trails had been designated, such as the Lewis and Clark Trail, only those particular rock formations, ruts, and other identified physical features where the trail was "confined to a very narrow corridor" were listed. That a general unbounded and imprecisely located area has important cultural significance is not enough. Abraham's tomb is an identifiable site, but the wanderings of the Jews in the Sinai Desert after the Exodus did not leave any accurately identifiable path that could be a "site."

The Forest Service did not act arbitrarily and capriciously, on this record, in concluding that it could not identify a "site" as the Kiks.adi Survival March.

Conclusion

The district judge correctly determined that because the Tribe could not prevail on the merits, and the Forest Service determinations were not arbitrary or capricious, the Tribe's prayer for an injunction against the timber sales should be denied. The judgment of the district court is AFFIRMED.

Notes and Questions

1. **Conserving Alaskan lands.** In November 1980, Congress passed the Alaska National Interest Lands Conservation Act ("ANILCA"). It called for major conservation all across the state of Alaska, moving 104 million acres into national parks and preserves, forests, or fish and wildlife preserves. In addition, another 50 million acres were identified as wilderness. It is sometimes described as the most important environmental legislation in the history of the nation. 93 Stat. 2371, 16 U.S.C. §§ 3101–3233.

2. **Ancient paths.** a. Should this place, the "route of the survival," with no historic markers remaining extant, be preserved because it was once there? b. Should we preserve a place simply because of memory? c. Is it enough that some people remember its location, even if little to nothing is known about it? d. Is the fact that human activity once or still occurs on the path be sufficient to deem it worthy of historic recognition and legal protection? e. Should this undefined, yet remembered place, be protected as such? f. Is this any different than the place of a long buried colonial encampment or battlefield? Compare the undertakings in Australia to map the song lines (or dreaming tracks) of that continent's Aboriginal People. *See Ancient Origins*, at http://www.ancient-origins.net/history-ancient-traditions/songlines-mapping-journeys-creation-ancestors-australia-005398 (last visited April 1, 2017).

3. **An undefined place as a National Monument.** On March 25, 2013, President Barack Obama declared the Harriet Tubman Underground Railroad National Monument. Proclaiming this "landscape" a National Monument makes the point that remembrance need not be confined to a particular place on the ground, but embraces associations, movement, and communication. The Monument protects this landscape to honor Harriet Tubman, who born into slavery, liberated herself, and returned to the place of her birth many times to conduct family, friends, and others north to freedom. The National Park Service concluded that the landscape to be nationally significant because of its deep association with Tubman and the Underground Railroad. The area includes open fields, marsh, and thick woodlands of Dorchester County, Maryland, where Tubman lived. An 8-mile long waterway, completed in the 1830s, connects Parsons Creek and Blackwater River with Madison Bay and opens up some of Dorchester's more remote territory. The Jacob Jackson Home Site, 480 acres of flat farmland, woodland, and wetland is nearby and was the site of one of the first safe houses along the Underground Railroad. In the same area is the farm that belonged to the man who owned Tubman's mother and her children. A few miles

away is the Bucktown Crossroads, where a slave overseer struck the 13-year-old Tubman with a heavy iron as she tried to protect a young fleeing slave, leaving a lifelong injury. A quarter mile to the north are Scotts Chapel, founded in 1812, and the associated African-American graveyard. Across from Scotts Chapel is another African-American graveyard with headstones dating to 1792. Bazel Church, on a one-acre clearing edged by the road and enveloped by cultivated fields and forest, is the place where slaves worshipped outdoors during Tubman's time.

The landscape is representative of those existing in the early- and mid-19th century when enslavers and enslaved worked the farms and forests. It is the place where the enslaved and free worked to find freedom for all. It was the means for communication and the path to freedom. "The Underground Railroad was everywhere within it." https://obamawhitehouse.archives.gov/the-press-office/2013/03/25/presidential-proclamation-harriet-tubman-underground-railroad-national-m (last visited March 25, 2017).

6. Who Has Standing to Assert Section 106? What Injuries Are Cognizable?

Pye v. United States

United States Court of Appeals, Fourth Circuit
269 F.3d 459 (2001)

Widener, C.J. This is a suit brought by Russ and Lee Pye, seeking to require the Corps of Engineers to conform to statutory and regulatory requirements before issuing a permit to construct a road crossing within the waters of the United States. The Pyes own adjoining land to the land on which the road crossing is constructed. Their land also adjoins what is known as Tract M of the Sheppard Tract on which an eighteenth century plantation house connected to the Hayne family is situated and is near to, a matter of several hundred feet, the site of an African American cemetery owned by Westvaco. The cemetery itself adjoins the Pyes' land and is probably partly on the Pyes' land. The old plantation house is eligible for the National Register of Historic Places, as is the African-American cemetery.

The district court dismissed the Pyes' complaint for lack of standing. We are of opinion such dismissal was error, and we vacate and remand for consideration of the merits of the Pyes' complaint.

I.

The series of events giving rise to this litigation stems from the County's proposal to improve an existing dirt access road (the road) leading from United States Highway 17 ... to the southwest corner of an approximately 750-acre tract of the County's land called the Sheppard Tract. *** The improvements affect all of the access road, which is owned by the County and open to private use only with County permission. A .23-acre segment of the road is covered by waters of the United States. The road runs along the west side of the Sheppard Tract and cuts through it at its southwest corner, northwest corner, and northern end. The road leads directly from U.S. Highway 17 to a 33-acre field, designated Area M, at the southwest corner of the Sheppard Tract. Area M contains the remains of an eighteenth century plantation home site. The Pyes' property is adjacent to Area M and contains part of an historic African American cemetery. Both the plantation home site and that of the cemetery have been declared eligible for entry on the National Register of Historic Places. The Sheppard Tract, the Pyes' property, and other adjacent property are all part of a larger area known as Encampment Plantation. Encampment Plantation has historic significance because in addition to containing the eighteenth century plantation home remains, the graveyard, and other historic sites, it may have been the location where troops were stationed during the Revolutionary War to guard South Carolina's state government which met across the Edisto River during the British occupation of Charleston.

In order to improve access to Area M, the County proposed to fill the 0.23 acres of wetland occupied by the road, to grade the road, and to install a culvert to permit drainage under the improved road. Because the project involved filling wetlands, the County had to obtain a permit from the Corps under section 404 of the Clean Water Act, 33 U.S.C. § 1344....

*** On January 24, 1995, the County applied for a Nationwide Permit 14 under section 404 of the Clean Water Act to improve the road, indicating that it now planned to use the land at the end of the road for a dirt borrow pit [(A dirt borrow pit is a pit used to supply earth for filling or embanking projects.)] and, later, for training police dogs. On April 20, 1995, the Advisory Council on Historic Preservation (the Advisory Council) notified the Corps that the road improvement might have an effect on Encampment Planation [sic], which would include the eighteenth century plantation home remains, a site that was either included in, or eligible for, the National Register of Historic Places. Additionally, the County had commissioned a cultural resource survey of the Sheppard Tract, obviously to determine the historical value of the area. The survey revealed that the eighteenth century plantation home site could be eligible for listing in the National Register of Historic Places, along with other sites in the area. After receiving the results of the survey in May 1996, the County abandoned its plans to create the dirt borrow pit. As of July 1996, the County intended to use the road to access Area M only for conducting routine maintenance of the land and for training police dogs.

The Corps forwarded the County's permit application on July 31, 1996 to *** [various government agencies]. Both the National Marine Fisheries Service and the Fish and Wildlife service responded to the Corps concerning the project's effects, as required under section 7 of the Endangered Species Act. 16 U.S.C. §§ 1531–43. The Deputy State Historic Preservation Officer also responded and indicated that the eighteenth century plantation home site was eligible for listing on the National Register of Historic Places. On January 23, 1997, the United States Department of the Interior, National Parks Service, found the Hayne Plantation site and the African American cemetery site eligible for listing on the National Register of Historic Places and informed the

Corps of that decision by copy of that letter. The letter indicated that the Service did not find that the area was eligible for listing as a rural historic district.

The Pyes filed a complaint in the United States District Court, District of South Carolina on February 19, 1997 alleging that the Corps failed to complete all the required steps under federal law prior to granting the County the Nationwide Permit 14. They asserted federal question jurisdiction under 28 U.S.C. § 1331 and because the United States was a defendant. They sued under the Administrative Procedure Act, 5 U.S.C. § 702; The Clean Water Act, 33 U.S.C. § 1251, *et seq.*; The National Historic Preservation Act, 16 U.S.C. § 470. The National Environmental Policy Act, 42 U.S.C. § 4321, *et seq.*; and The Endangered Species Act, 16 U.S.C. § 1531, *et seq.* The Corps answered the complaint on April 25, 1997. In response to the litigation, the Corps suspended the permit on May 13, 1997 to confirm that it was properly authorized.

Under this further review, the Corps notified the Fish and Wildlife Service to confine its analysis concerning endangered species to Area M. The Fish and Wildlife Service, later that month, answered that it could not discern any adverse impact on Area M. On November 19, 1997, the Corps reinstated the County's Nationwide Permit 14, allowing it to complete the road improvement project. In reinstating the permit, the Corps did not consider the impact of the improvement on the historic site in Area M, or any other area, instead, confining its analysis to the "footprint" [consisting only of the actual 100 foot stretch of road containing wetlands] of the roadway area to be filled, which did not contain any historically relevant sites.

After reinstatement of the permit, the Corps moved for summary judgment on February 10, 1998. The district court granted summary judgment in favor of the Corps and dismissed the complaint, finding that the Pyes did not have standing to bring this action because they did not demonstrate either an injury in fact, causation of an injury by the Corps, or the ability of the court to redress an injury. *Pye v. United States, Army Corps of Eng'rs,* No. 2:97-00431-2 (D.S.C. July 24, 1998). The County advises us that it has completed the road improvement project, however the Corps freely admits that the wetland fill is easily removed. Having considered the record, and after oral argument, we are of opinion that the Pyes have standing to bring their suit, and we vacate and remand.

Before discussing the question of standing, it is well that we recount some principal facts.

* * *

The ante-bellum plantation site and the African-American cemetery site are both within a few hundred feet of the road which is the issue here. There was evidence aplenty in the district court, in the Garrow Report, that a significant part of the historical value of both the African-American cemetery and the Hayne plantation site was that neither, because of their location, had been subject to marauders:

> *Feeling* [in finding a rural historic landscape] incorporates all of the above attributes. A general test for feeling is whether the site or district could serve as a teaching example, without the need to ignore major post-occupational

> changes. The feeling of the proposed district is very strong; it is one of the few tracts in the county with well-preserved remains from the planter's house, slave settlement, upland fields, rice fields, and associated infrastructure without alteration by post-bellum or modern occupation or use. ***
>
> The cemetery also is a good example of a distinctive, regionally important type of cemetery. The African American tradition of grave decorations/grave goods was strongly followed, and most of these goods have been preserved beneath recently developed topsoil. The site has not undergone the disturbance or removal of grave goods that commonly occurs as part of a misguided effort to "clean up" a burial ground. The cemetery can serve as a well-preserved example of a community cemetery of rural African Americans who followed a well-entrenched set of rules regarding burial customs. The cemetery was apparently not linked to a specific church, as were many later African American cemeteries, and it was not a single-family cemetery. Rural African American cemeteries of the antebellum and postbellum periods were once a common element of the Southern landscape, but many have been lost from memory, removed, or impacted by development or logging. As a cemetery that embodies the distinctive characteristics of the Sea Coast African American type, site 38CH1590 is recommended as eligible under Criterion C.***

We also note that the County commenced with proposing Area M for an ash dump and both improving and paving the road to U.S. 17. As opposition developed, it changed the proposed use to a dirt mine and later changed the proposed use to a dog-training facility. The degree of improvement of the road was changed from a paved road merely to an improved road. The Corps has described the project as "to improve an existing roadway and to make it an all-weather road."

Despite the fact of objections to the Corps' lack of addressing the impact of the road on the wetlands of the entire Sheppard tract and the effect of improved and easier access to the historical sites, the Corps addressed neither prior to issuing the permit, choosing instead to confine its consideration to what it calls "the footprint," which is the actual fill of the wetland area, only without regard to any of the surrounding countryside, except, perhaps, Area M.

II.

We review the district court's grant of summary judgment *de novo.* *** Standing is a threshold jurisdictional question which ensures that a suit is a case or controversy appropriate for the exercise of the courts' judicial powers under the Constitution of the United States. *** The core goal of the standing inquiry is to ensure that a plaintiff bringing an action has enough of a stake in the case to litigate it properly. ***

A.

To demonstrate standing at the summary judgment stage, a plaintiff must set forth evidence of an injury in fact in addition to that provided in the complaint, which will be taken as true for purposes of deciding the motion. *Lujan v. Defenders of Wildlife,* 504 U.S. 555, 561, 112 S.Ct. 2130, 119 L.Ed.2d 351 (1992). *** A part of the Pyes' support for their allegations of standing were the affidavits of Mrs. Lee Pye and Dr. Michael Trinkley, a professional archaeologist. These documents, together with other documents in the record, explain that the Pyes own land next to, and probably including, an area containing designated historic sites and allege that the road improvements authorized by the Corps' permit will adversely affect that historic area. Dr. Trinkley asserted that the improved road will affect the historic cohesiveness of the area and will, by providing better access, result in the presence of more looters at the historic sites. Additionally, the Pyes have alleged that their interests in the cohesiveness and integrity of the historical sites were further impaired by the Corps' failure to consider the effect on the sites of the issuance of the permit, and the failure of the Corps to allow public participation and commentary by the Advisory Council as mandated by the Act and the Corps' own regulations.

In this context, *** adjacent landowners often have standing to challenge the government's failure to follow statutorily prescribed procedures so long as this failure impairs a separate concrete interest of the plaintiff. *** Indeed, in such cases standing to sue is so self-evident that the Supreme Court often has dispensed with the inquiry altogether. *** Likewise, in *Waterford Citizens' Assn. v. Reilly,* 970 F.2d 1287 (4th Cir. 1992), we held that nearby plaintiffs have standing to challenge failures of agencies to comply with the National Historic Preservation Act. *Waterford* involved an organization of citizens concerned about the effect of an EPA decision to allow a developer of townhouses outside of the town of Waterford to hook into Waterford's sewer system. In permitting the hook-up, the EPA failed to comply with a Memorandum of Agreement it had voluntarily made with various historic preservation agencies. *Waterford,* 970 F.2d at 1289. The Memorandum of Agreement essentially reopened the Section 470f consultation process, the same process at issue in the instant case. In *Waterford,* we held that the plaintiffs "clearly [had] standing to bring this issue to court." 970 F.2d at 1288 n. 1, 1290. We did not require that the residents demonstrate that they lived in the vicinity of the project at issue.

* * *

We think the Pyes have demonstrated an injury comparable to the injuries demonstrated by the Waterford *** plaintiffs. The Pyes are not only in the vicinity of the proposed action, but are adjacent landowners. The Keeper has designated adjoining and what is probably a portion of their land as eligible for listing on the National Register along with the individual site contained in the Sheppard Tract. Most importantly, however, the eligible African American cemetery abuts directly the Pyes' land, and probably overlaps it. Therefore, the challenged action may lead to trespassing, vandalism, and looting of historic sites not only on the Sheppard Tract, but also to the historic site on the Pye property. The Pyes are the people most directly affected by the challenged action, and if they do not have standing, to see that the government complies with the regulatory provisions, then the National Historic Preservation Act's requirement for consideration of the effect of federal permits on historic places is merely a "procedural calisthenic." We decline to so hold.

The Corps endeavors to undermine the concreteness of the Pyes' injury by arguing that any development by the County is speculative and that the construction project itself will not actually destroy any of these historic sites. The Corps' arguments in this regard are unavailing, however. It is abundantly clear from the record that the county wishes to use this 750 acre parcel for something. *** No reason is advanced that this road will remain a road to nowhere for long. We cannot say that future development enabled by the Corps' permit is so speculative as to render the Pyes' allegations of injury abstract.

Similarly, that the proposed project will not actually touch any of the historic sites on either the Sheppard Tract or the Pyes' property is of no moment. *** The plaintiffs in *Waterford* alleged that the actions would physically destroy historic sites. 970 F.2d at 1289. *** Even if no shovels or backhoes will touch either historic area, damage to historic areas can occur in less direct ways. Indeed, the Corps' own regulations embrace this by mandating consideration of "the effects of undertakings on any known historic properties that may occur outside the permit area." *** Directness, while it may be relevant to causation and to extent of damages, is irrelevant to the presence of injury-in-fact. While at first blush the project here may appear to be trivial, the smallest of endeavors can have enormous consequences if undertaken improvidently. ***

Finally, the fact that the Pyes' aesthetic concerns pertaining to the integrity and cohesiveness of the historic district and individual sites are also widely held by the populace of the County does not render them any less concrete and particularized as to the Pyes. The Supreme Court has held that aesthetic and environmental injuries can constitute an injury in fact sufficient to support a plaintiff's standing. *** While it is true that the Court has stressed that a generalized grievance shared by the population at large cannot be a basis for standing, *** it is equally true that merely because an injury is widely held does not necessarily render it abstract and thus not judicially cognizable. *** So long as the plaintiff himself has a concrete and particularized injury, it does not matter that legions of other persons have the same injury. *** In short, the Pyes' injuries do not stem from a "common concern for obedience to law," *** but from individual concerns about the integrity and cohesiveness of historical sites in their own backyard. *** In light of the foregoing, we are of opinion that the Pyes have alleged sufficiently concrete injuries to establish the first prong of the standing inquiry....

B.

Because the Pyes established an injury in fact, we turn to a prudential inquiry to determine whether their injury is within the zone of interests targeted by the National Historic Preservation Act. The zone of interests test consists of a two part inquiry: first, determining which interests the statute at issue arguably protects and second, determining whether the agency action affects those interests. *TAP Pharm. v. United States Dep't of Health and Human Servs.*, 163 F.3d 199, 203 (4th Cir. 1998) ***. The National Historic Preservation Act is a relevant statute under the Administrative Procedure Act for the purposes of applying the zone of interests test. ***

The purpose of the National Historic Preservation Act is to remedy the dilemma that "historic properties significant to the Nation's heritage are being lost or substantially altered, often inadvertently, with increasing frequency." 16 U.S.C. § 470(b)(3). To remedy this problem, the Act prescribes the section 470f process, which requires federal agencies with the authority to license an undertaking "to take into account the effect of the undertaking on any ... site ... that is ... eligible for inclusion in the National Register" prior to issuing the license. 16 U.S.C. § 470f. *** The Corps' own regulations pursuant to the National Historic Preservation Act require it to "take into account the effects, if any, of proposed undertakings on the historic properties both within *and beyond* the waters of the U.S." 33 C.F.R. pt. 325 app. C(2)(a) (emphasis added). And we note that that regulation just mentioned authorizes the Corps to condition the permit so as to minimize harm to the historic sites, which seems to have been overlooked in this case.

In this case, the Pyes have asserted an interest directly targeted by the National Historic Preservation Act and its regulations. As adjacent, and probably actual, property owners, they are members of the public concerned with the impact of the Nationwide Permit 14 on a historic site next to and on their property and want to ensure that the Corps takes into account the effects of the improved road on that site. *** [T]he National Historic Preservation Act is aimed at the preservation of areas like the sites here, the African-American cemetery and the Hayne plantation, and expressly provides for interested members of the public to participate in the permitting process when those areas may be affected by agency action. As such, we conclude that the Pyes' claims are within the zone of interests protected by the National Historic Preservation Act.

C.

Plaintiffs must also show that their injury is fairly traceable to the defendant's conduct. ***. The district court found that the Pyes failed to demonstrate the causation element because they did not present evidence indicating the extent to which looting would increase once the county improved the road. We disagree with this analysis of the causation requirement.

Plaintiffs' injury is caused by the improved road, not the existing road, and but for the improvements on the road authorized by the Corps' permit, the injuries the Pyes complain of, an increased probability of looting and destruction of cohesion in the area, have less probability of occurring. The improvements must facilitate access, otherwise the County would not want them. If access is facilitated for the County, it will also facilitate access for other persons, including looters. The Trinkley affidavit provided evidence that linked looting with access to historic sites. While this evidence itself is sufficient to establish causation, the Pyes' injury is also directly traceable to the Corps' conduct because the Corps failed to consider the Pyes' input on the road improvements as required by the National Historic Preservation Act. ***

D.

Lastly, the Pyes must also show that the court can redress their injury with the requested relief in this case. *** However, where the plaintiffs validly assert a procedural injury, they need not meet "the normal standards for redressability and immediacy."

Lujan, 504 U.S. at 572 n. 7, 112 S.Ct. 2130. That is to say, the Pyes need not establish that their cohesiveness and integrity injuries will be fully remedied by a favorable decision by the court below, only that there is a procedural remedy by which the plaintiffs' concerns may be aired before the agency.

The National Historic Preservation Act Section 470f regulations give the Pyes an affirmative right to participate in the permitting process as consulting parties. 36 C.F.R. § 800.2(c)(6), (d)(1). The Army Corps is required to "take into account" the effects of the issuance of the permit on historic sites prior to making its final decision. 16 U.S.C. § 470f. In evaluating these effects, the Corps must seek the views of interested parties, including the Pyes and the Advisory Council, in (1) identifying historic properties potentially affected by granting the permit, (2) assessing whether those resources will be adversely affected by granting the permit, and (3) seeking ways to avoid and reduce harm to the affected resources. 36 C.F.R. §§ 800.4(a)(3), 800.5(a)(1–2)(vii), 800.5(d)(2). While the Pyes allege concerns about future development, they also raise concerns about the effect of the *improved* road itself, including the looting and destruction of the area's cohesiveness that would be considered if the Corps followed the National Historic Preservation Act's mandates. Thus, we may redress the Pyes' injury by requiring the Corps to comply with the procedures required by the National Historic Preservation Act.*** We therefore conclude that the Pyes have established the redressability requirement for standing.

* * *

IV.

The Pyes have adequately and amply established that they have been injured by the actions of the Corps in a concrete and particular way, that they are within the zone of interests served by the National Historic Preservation Act, and that their grievances are likely to be redressed by a favorable decision in this case. Therefore, the Pyes have demonstrated standing to bring the underlying suit, and we so hold.

The judgment of the district court is vacated and the case remanded for proceedings not inconsistent with this opinion.

VACATED AND REMANDED.

Notes and Questions

1. **Private right of action and standing.** Unlike almost every environmental protection statute, except NEPA, the NHPA does not expressly provide for a private right of action for citizens and most courts have ruled that there is none. *See San Carlos Apache Tribe v. United States,* 417 F.3d 1091 (9th Cir. 2005). No matter, the courts generally recognize the Administrative Procedure Act ("APA"), 5 U.S.C. § 702, as the ready vehicle to challenge the actions of federal agencies as they fulfill their statutory duties. *See, e.g., Citizens to Preserve Overton Park, Inc. v. Volpe,* 401 U.S. 402, 91 S.Ct. 814 (1971) (reviewing Department of Transportation action under the APA). Still, even where there is a statutory cause of action, a citizen plaintiff must establish standing to sue. As the case explains, the Supreme Court has imposed both Constitutional (requiring showing of injury in fact, causation, and redressability) and prudential

(requiring that plaintiff be within the zone of interests protected by the statute) limits on standing. *Lujan v. Defenders of Wildlife*, 504 U.S. 555, 560–61 (1992); *see also Lexmark v. Static Control*, 134 S.Ct. 1377, 1388, 188 L.Ed. 2d 392, 405 (2014) ("prudential standing" is a misnomer, instead Court presumes that a statutory cause of action extends only to plaintiffs whose interests "fall within the zone of interests protected by the law invoked;" "zone of interests" serves as a limitation on the cause of action for judicial review conferred by the Administrative Procedure Act (APA) and applies to all statutorily created causes of action). However, a further articulation of the standing requirement makes it fairly easy for a citizen to show standing. In *Friends of the Earth, Inc v. Laidlaw Envtl.Svces., Inc.*, 528 U.S. 167, 181 (2001), the Court ruled that a citizen plaintiff need not show environmental harm to establish standing, a technical violation of the law suffices, so long as the plaintiff suffers some injury, even if only hypothetical. *See generally* Jonathan H. Adler, *Stand or Deliver: Citizen Suits, Standing, & Environmental Protection*, 12 DUKE ENVIR. L & POL'Y FORUM 39 (2001) (questioning whether liberalized standing can be taken to enhance environmental quality). The Pyes were able to show more than a technical violation of the NHPA and their injuries were more than hypothetical.

2. **Alternatives.** a. Why did the Corps proceed despite indications from the SHPO and the National Park Service that the site was eligible for the National Register? b. Was there no other route available?

3. **Relative importance of the interests.** a. How do the respective interests at issue—the site of a slave plantation and a project to improve road conditions—compare in terms of importance? b. What sort of accommodation can possibly be reached between the Pyes and the Corps?

John Jay and the Abolition of Slavery

How can broad societal movements find expression in a place? How can a single landmark, like the Jay Estate in Rye, N.Y., shed light on the vast injustice of slavery? New York State's approach to abolishing slavery owes much to John Jay and his children. Jay founded the Manumission Society of New York, and against opposition advocated for gradual emancipation of enslaved African-Americans. Free blacks could vote in New York, and supported Federalists like Jay. Slaves lived, worked, and retired on the Jay Estate. On visiting the Jay Estate, Tony Hiss has observed that the Jay Heritage Center hopes to be "a national focal point for a continuing conversation about the two greatest pieces of unfinished American business—race and land; meaning how we treat each other and how we treat the rest of God's creation." The Jay Estate is an historic site along the *African-American Heritage Trail.* https://parks.ny.gov/historic-sites/39/details.aspx (last visited April 6, 2017).

Understanding Jay's Manumission Society sheds light on the intergenerational struggle to abolish slavery. Time erased evidence of slavery from the Jay Estate. Archaeology reveals only traces. This intangible past is recalled at the Jay Estate by linking the deeds of the Jays and the Manumission Society to the land. The Jay Heritage Center presents "Striving for Freedom" as a living tableau of the struggle against slavery at the Jay Estate in Rye. www.youtube.com/watch?v=Asc83-leask. Jay's values were proclaimed with the founding of the Society: "It is our duty, therefore, both as free Citizens and Christians, not only to regard with compassion, the injustice done to those among us who are held as slaves; but to endeavor, by lawful ways and means, to enable them to share equally with us in that civil and religious Liberty, with which an indulgent providence has blessed these states, and to which these our brethren are, by nature, as much entitled to as ourselves." AMERICAN MERCURY (1785), reported in the Hudson Gazette (JHC Archives). *See also* DAVID N. GELLMAN, EMANCIPATING NEW YORK: THE POLITICS OF SLAVERY AND FREEDOM (2008).

Professor Paul Finkelman delivered the 2012 John Jay Lecture, "Jay is for Justice: From Slaveholders to Abolitionists, the Jay Family and Racial Justice" at the Jay Heritage Center. His ENCYCLOPEDIA OF AFRICAN AMERICAN HISTORY 1619–1895 (2006) documents this era. Archival records inform a living re-imagination in places where Jay and his servants and compatriots anguished about injustice. In Finkelman's estimation, Jay's founding of the New York Manumission Society in 1785 was critical for ending slavery in New York and advancing civil rights. The Society organized boycotts of merchants and newspapers whose owners were involved in the slave trade. It founded the African Free School for the poor and orphaned children of slaves and free African Americans. Jay's son, William Jay, and his son, John Jay II, carried onward the Jay Family commitment to abolishing slavery.

In 1777, John Jay drafted a state law to abolish slavery, which like his second in 1785, failed to win adoption. In 1785, all but one State legislator voted in favor of gradual emancipation, but could not agree on what civil rights should be granted once slaves were freed. Finally, in 1799, as Governor, Jay signed into law the Gradual Emancipation Act that freed slave children born after July 4, 1799, but indentured them until they were young adults. The emancipation of slaves by the Quakers had been legalized in 1798. At that date, there were still 33,000 slaves statewide. In 1817, a new law passed that would free slaves born before 1799, but not until 1827. By the 1830 census there were only 75 slaves in New York and the 1840 census listed no slaves in New York City. EDGAR J. MCMANUS, HISTORY OF NEGRO SLAVERY IN NEW YORK (1968); JAKE SUDDERTH, JOHN JAY AND SLAVERY (2002). In 1854, when Horace Greeley honored William Jay, he reflected "To Chief Justice Jay may be attributed, more than any other man, the abolition of Negro bondage in this state."

D. Department of Transportation Act of 1966, Section 4(f)

Citizens to Preserve Overton Park, Inc. v. Volpe

Supreme Court of the United States
401 U.S. 402, 91 S.Ct. 814 (1971)

MARSHALL, J. The growing public concern about the quality of our natural environment has prompted Congress in recent years to enact legislation[1] designed to curb the accelerating destruction of our country's natural beauty. We are concerned in this case with § 4(f) of the Department of Transportation Act of 1966, as amended,[2] and § 18(a) of the Federal-Aid Highway Act of 1968, 82 Stat. 823, 23 U.S.C. § 138 (1964 ed., Supp. V) (hereafter § 138).[3] These statutes prohibit the Secretary of Transportation from authorizing the use of federal funds to finance the construction of highways through public parks if a "feasible and prudent"[4] alternative route exists. If no such route is available, the statutes allow him to approve construction through parks only if there has been "all possible planning to minimize harm" to the park.[5]

---

1. *See, e.g.*, The National Environmental Policy Act of 1969, 83 Stat. 852, 42 U.S.C. § 4321 *et seq.* (1964 ed., Supp. V); Environmental Education Act, 84 Stat. 1312, 20 U.S.C. § 1531 *et seq.* (1970 ed.); Air Quality Act of 1967, 81 Stat. 485, 42 U.S.C. § 1857 *et seq.* (1964 ed., Supp. V); Environmental Quality Improvement Act of 1970, 84 Stat. 114, 42 U.S.C. §§ 4371–4374 (1970 ed.).

2. "It is hereby declared to be the national policy that special effort should be made to preserve the natural beauty of the countryside and public park and recreation lands, wildlife and waterfowl refuges, and historic sites. The Secretary of Transportation shall cooperate and consult with the Secretaries of the Interior, Housing and Urban Development, and Agriculture, and with the States in developing transportation plans and programs that include measures to maintain or enhance the natural beauty of the lands traversed. After August 23, 1968, the Secretary shall not approve any program or project which requires the use of any publicly owned land from a public park, recreation area, or wildlife and waterfowl refuge of national, State, or local significance as determined by the Federal, State, or local officials having jurisdiction thereof, or any land from an historic site of national, State, or local significance as so determined by such officials unless (1) there is no feasible and prudent alternative to the use of such land, and (2) such program includes all possible planning to minimize harm to such park, recreational area, wildlife and waterfowl refuge, or historic site resulting from such use." 82 Stat. 824, 49 U. S. C. § 1653 (f) (1964 ed., Supp. V).

3. "It is hereby declared to be the national policy that special effort should be made to preserve the natural beauty of the countryside and public park and recreation lands, wildlife and waterfowl refuges, and historic sites. The Secretary of Transportation shall cooperate and consult with the Secretaries of the Interior, Housing and Urban Development, and Agriculture, and with the States in developing transportation plans and programs that include measures to maintain or enhance the natural beauty of the lands traversed. After the effective date of the Federal-Aid Highway Act of 1968, the Secretary shall not approve any program or project which requires the use of any publicly owned land from a public park, recreation area, or wildlife and waterfowl refuge of national, State, or local significance as determined by the Federal, State, or local officials having jurisdiction thereof, or any land from an historic site of national, State, or local significance as so determined by such officials unless (1) there is no feasible and prudent alternative to the use of such land, and (2) such program includes all possible planning to minimize harm to such park, recreational area, wildlife and waterfowl refuge, or historic site resulting from such use." 23 U.S.C. § 138 (1964 ed., Supp. V).

4. 49 U.S.C. § 1653 (f) (1964 ed., Supp. V); 23 U.S.C. § 138 (1964 ed., Supp. V).

5. *Ibid.*

Petitioners, private citizens as well as local and national conservation organizations, contend that the Secretary has violated these statutes by authorizing the expenditure of federal funds[6] for the construction of a six-lane interstate highway through a public park in Memphis, Tennessee. Their claim was rejected by the District Court,[7] which granted the Secretary's motion for summary judgment, and the Court of Appeals for the Sixth Circuit affirmed.[8] After oral argument, this Court granted a stay that halted construction and, treating the application for the stay as a petition for certiorari, granted review.[9] 400 U.S. 939 91 S.Ct. 246, 27 L.Ed.2d 262. We now reverse the judgment below and remand for further proceedings in the District Court.

Overton Park is 342-acre city park located near the center of Memphis. The park contains a zoo, a nine-hole municipal golf course, an outdoor theater, nature trails, a bridle path, an art academy, picnic areas, and 170 acres of forest. The proposed highway, which is to be a sixlane, high-speed, expressway,[10] will sever the zoo from the rest of the park. Although the roadway will be depressed below ground level except where it crosses a small creek, 26 acres of the park will be destroyed. The highway is to be a segment of Interstate Highway I-40, part of the National System of Interstate and Defense Highways.[11] I-40 will provide Memphis with a major east-west expressway which will allow easier access to downtown Memphis from the residential areas on the eastern edge of the city.[12]

Although the route through the park was approved by the Bureau of Public Roads in 1956[13] and by the Federal Highway Administrator in 1966, the enactment of § 4(f) of the Department of Transportation Act prevented distribution of federal funds for the section of the highway designated to go through Overton Park until the Secretary of Transportation determined whether the requirements of § 4(f) had been met. Federal funding for the rest of the project was, however, available; and the state acquired a right-of-way on both sides of the park.[14] In April 1968, the Secretary announced that he concurred in the judgment of local officials that I-40 should be built through the park. And in September 1969 the State acquired the

6. *See* 23 U.S.C. § 103.

7. The case originated in the United States District Court for the District of Columbia. On application of the Secretary of Transportation it was transferred to the United States District Court for the Western District of Tennessee, which entered the summary judgment.

8. 432 F.2d 1307 (CA6 1970).

9. This Court ordered the case to be heard on an expedited schedule.

10. The proposed right-of-way will be 250 to 450 feet wide and will follow the route of a presently existing, nonaccess bus route, which carries occasional bus traffic along a 40- to 50-foot right-of-way.

11. *See* 23 U.S.C. § 103 (d) (1964 ed., Supp. V).

12. The proposed right-of-way will be 250 to 450 feet wide and will follow the route of a presently existing, nonaccess bus route, which carries occasional bus traffic along a 40- to 50-foot right-of-way. 432 F.2d 1307 (CA6 1970).

13. At that time the Bureau of Public Roads was a part of the Department of Commerce. The Department of Transportation Act, 49 U.S.C. § 1651 et seq. (1964 ed., Supp. V), which became effective on April 1, 1967, transferred the Bureau to the new Department of Transportation.

14. The Secretary approved these acquisitions in 1967 shortly after the effective date of § 4 (f).

right-of-way inside Overton Park from the city.[15] Final approval for the project—the route as well as the design—was not announced until November 1969, after Congress had reiterated in § 138 of the Federal-Aid Highway Act that highway construction through public parks was to be restricted. Neither announcement approving the route and design of I-40 was accompanied by a statement of the Secretary's factual findings. He did not indicate why he believed there were no feasible and prudent alternative routes or why design changes could not be made to reduce the harm to the park.

Petitioners contend that the Secretary's action is invalid without such formal findings[16] and that the Secretary did not make an independent determination but merely relied on the judgment of the Memphis City Council.[17] They also contend that it would be "feasible and prudent" to route I-40 around Overton Park either to the north or to the south. And they argue that if these alternative routes are not "feasible and prudent," the present plan does not include "all possible" methods for reducing harm to the park. Petitioners claim that I-40 could be built under the park by using either of two possible tunneling methods,[18] and they claim that, at a minimum, by using advanced drainage techniques[19] the expressway could be depressed below ground level along the entire route through the park including the section that crosses the small creek.

Respondents argue that it was unnecessary for the Secretary to make formal findings, and that he did, in fact, exercise his own independent judgment which was supported by the facts. In the District Court, respondents introduced affidavits, prepared specifically for this litigation[, w]hich indicated that the Secretary had made the decision and that the decision was supportable. These affidavits were contradicted by affidavits introduced by petitioners, who also sought to take the deposition of a former

---

15. The State paid the City $ 2,000,000 for the 26-acre right-of-way and $ 206,000 to the Memphis Park Commission to replace park facilities that were to be destroyed by the highway. The city of Memphis has used $ 1,000,000 of these funds to pay for a new 160-acre park and it is anticipated that additional parkland will be acquired with the remaining money.

16. Respondents argue that the only issue raised by petitioners' pleadings is the failure of the Secretary to make formal findings. But when petitioners' complaint is read in the revealing light of *Conley v. Gibson*, 355 U.S. 41 (1957), it is clear that petitioners have also challenged the merits of the Secretary's decision.

17. Petitioners contend that former Federal Highway Administrator Bridwell's account of an April 3, 1968, meeting with the Memphis City Council given to the Senate Subcommittee on Roads of the Senate Committee on Public Works supports this charge. See Hearings on Urban Highway Planning, Location, and Design before the Subcommittee on Roads of the Senate Committee on Public Works, 90th Cong., 1st and 2d Sess., pt. 2, pp. 478–480 (1968).

18. Petitioners argue that either a bored tunnel or a cut-and-cover tunnel, which is a fully depressed route covered after construction, could be built. Respondents contend that the construction of a tunnel by either method would greatly increase the cost of the project, would create safety hazards, and because of increases in air pollution would not reduce harm to the park.

19. Petitioners contend that adequate drainage could be provided by using mechanical pumps or some form of inverted siphon. They claim that such devices are often used in expressway construction.

Federal Highway Administrator[20] who had participated in the decision to route I-40 through Overton Park.

The District Court and the Court of Appeals found that formal findings by the Secretary were not necessary and refused to order the deposition of the former Federal Highway Administrator because those courts believed that probing of the mental processes of an administrative decisionmaker was prohibited. And, believing that the Secretary's authority was wide and reviewing courts' authority narrow in the approval of highway routes, the lower courts held that the affidavits contained no basis for a determination that the Secretary had exceeded his authority.

We agree that formal findings were not required. But we do not believe that in this case judicial review based solely on litigation affidavits was adequate.

A threshold question—whether petitioners are entitled to any judicial review—is easily answered. Section 701 of the Administrative Procedure Act, 5 U.S.C. § 701 (1964 ed., Supp. V), provides that the action of "each authority of the Government of the United States," which includes the Department of Transportation,[21] is subject to judicial review except where there is a statutory prohibition on review or where "agency action is committed to agency discretion by law." In this case, there is no indication that Congress sought to prohibit judicial review and there is most certainly no "showing of 'clear and convincing evidence' of a *** legislative intent" to restrict access to judicial review. *Abbott Laboratories v. Gardner*, 387 U.S. 136, 141, 87 S.Ct. 1507, 1511, 18 L.Ed.2d 681 (1967) ***[22]

Similarly, the Secretary's decision here does not fall within the exception for action "committed to agency discretion." This is a very narrow exception.[23] Berger, *Administrative Arbitrariness and Judicial Review*, 65 Col. L. Rev. 55 (1965). The legislative history of the Administrative Procedure Act indicates that it is applicable in those rare instances where 'statutes are drawn in such broad terms that in a given case there is no law to apply.' S.Rep. No. 752, 79th Cong., 1st Sess., 26 (1945).

Section 4(f) of the Department of Transportation Act and § 138 of the Federal-Aid Highway Act are clear and specific directives. Both the Department of Transportation Act and the Federal-Aid to Highway Act provide that the Secretary "shall not approve any program or project" that requires the use of any public parkland "unless (1) there is no feasible and prudent alternative to the use of such land, and (2) such program includes all possible planning to minimize harm to such park ***."

20. Petitioners wanted to question former Highway Administrator Bridwell. See n. 17, *supra*.

21. In addition, the Department of Transportation Act makes the Administrative Procedure Act applicable to proceedings of the Department of Transportation. 49 U. S. C. § 1655 (h) (1964 ed., Supp. V).

22. See also *Rusk v. Cort*, 369 U.S. 367, 379–380 (1962).

23. The scope of this exception has been the subject of extensive commentary. See, *e. g.*, Berger, Administrative Arbitrariness: A Synthesis, 78 Yale L. J. 965 (1969); Saferstein, Nonreviewability: A Functional Analysis of "Committed to Agency Discretion," 82 Harv. L. Rev. 367 (1968); Davis, Administrative Arbitrariness is Not Always Reviewable, 51 Minn. L. Rev. 643 (1967); Berger, Administrative Arbitrariness: A Sequel, 51 Minn. L. Rev. 601 (1967).

23 U.S.C. § 138 (1964 ed., Supp. V); 49 U.S.C. § 1653(f) (1964 ed., Supp. V). This language is a plain and explicit bar to the use of federal funds for construction of highways through parks—only the most unusual situations are exempted.

*** For this exemption to apply the Secretary must find that as a matter of sound engineering it would not be feasible to build the highway along any other route.[24] Respondents argue, however, that the requirement that there be no other "prudent" route requires the Secretary to engage in a wide-ranging balancing of competing interests. They contend that the Secretary should weigh the detriment resulting from the destruction of parkland against the cost of other routes, safety considerations, and other factors, and determine on the basis of the importance that he attaches to these other factors whether, on balance, alternative feasible routes would be "prudent."

But no such wide-ranging endeavor was intended. It is obvious that in most cases considerations of cost, directness of route, and community disruption will indicate that parkland should be used for highway construction whenever possible. ***

Congress clearly did not intend that cost and disruption of the community were to be ignored[27] by the Secretary.[28] But the very existence of the statutes[29] indicates that protection of parkland was to be given paramount importance. The few green havens that are public parks were not to be lost unless there were truly unusual factors present in a particular case or the cost or community disruption resulting from alternative routes reached extraordinary magnitudes. If the statutes are to have any meaning, the Secretary cannot approve the destruction of parkland unless he finds that alternative routes present unique problems.

Plainly, there is "law to apply" and thus the exemption for action "committed to agency discretion" is inapplicable. But the existence of judicial review is only the start: the standard for review must also be determined. For that we must look to § 706 of

---

24. See 114 Cong. Rec. 19915 (statement by Rep. Holifield).

27. See, *e. g.*, S. Rep. No. 1340, 90th Cong., 2d Sess., 18–19; H. R. Rep. No. 1584, 90th Cong., 2d Sess., 12.

28. The legislative history indicates that the Secretary is not to limit his consideration to information supplied by state and local officials but is to go beyond this information and reach his own independent decision. 114 Cong. Rec. 24036–24037.

29. The legislative history of both § 4 (f) of the Department of Transportation Act, 49 U.S.C. § 1653 (f) (1964 ed., Supp. V), and § 138 of the Federal-Aid Highway Act, 23 U.S.C. § 138 (1964 ed., Supp. V), is ambiguous. The legislative committee reports tend to support respondents' view that the statutes are merely general directives to the Secretary requiring him to consider the importance of parkland as well as cost, community disruption, and other factors. See, e. g., S. Rep. No. 1340, 90th Cong., 2d Sess., 19; H. R. Rep. No. 1584, 90th Cong., 2d Sess., 12. Statements by proponents of the statutes as well as the Senate committee report on § 4 (f) indicate, however, that the Secretary was to have limited authority. See, *e. g.*, 114 Cong. Rec. 24033–24037; S. Rep. No. 1659, 89th Cong., 2d Sess., 22. See also H. R. Conf. Rep. No. 2236, 89th Cong., 2d Sess., 25. Because of this ambiguity it is clear that we must look primarily to the statutes themselves to find the legislative intent.

the Administrative Procedure Act, 5 U.S.C. §706 (1964 ed., Supp. V), which provides that a "reviewing court shall *** hold unlawful and set aside agency action, findings, and conclusions found" not to meet six separate standards.[30] In all cases agency action must be set aside if the action was "arbitrary, capricious, an abuse of discretion, or otherwise not in accordance with law" or if the action failed to meet statutory, procedural, or constitutional requirements. 5 U.S.C. §§706(2) (A), (B), (C), (D) (1964 ed., Supp. V). In certain narrow, specifically limited situations, the agency action is to be set aside if the action was not supported by "substantial evidence." And in other equally narrow circumstances the reviewing court is to engage in a de novo review of the action and set it aside if it was "unwarranted by the facts." 5 U.S.C. §§706(2)(E), (F) (1964 ed., Supp. V).

Petitioners argue that the Secretary's approval of the construction of I-40 through Overton Park is subject to one or the other of these latter two standards of limited applicability. First, they contend that the "substantial evidence" standard of §706(2)(E) must be applied. In the alternative, they claim that §706(2)(F) applies and that there must be a *de novo* review to determine if the Secretary's action was "unwarranted by the facts." Neither of these standards is, however, applicable.

Review under the substantial-evidence test is authorized only when the agency action is taken pursuant to a rulemaking provision of the Administrative Procedure Act itself, 5 U.S.C. §553 (1964 ed., Supp. V), or when the agency action is based on a public adjudicatory hearing. *See* 5 U.S.C. §§556, 557 (1964 ed., Supp. V). The Secretary's decision to allow the expenditure of federal funds to build I-40 through Overton Park was plainly not an exercise of a rulemaking function. *** And the only hearing that is required by either the Administrative Procedure Act or the statutes regulating the distribution of federal funds for highway construction is a public hearing conducted by local officials for the purpose of informing the community about the proposed project and eliciting community views on the design and route. 23 U.S.C.

30. "To the extent necessary to decision and when presented, the reviewing court shall decide all relevant questions of law, interpret constitutional and statutory provisions, and determine the meaning or applicability of the terms of an agency action. The reviewing court shall—

"(1) compel agency action unlawfully withheld or unreasonably delayed; and

"(2) hold unlawful and set aside agency action, findings, and conclusions found to be—

"(A) arbitrary, capricious, an abuse of discretion, or otherwise not in accordance with law;

"(B) contrary to constitutional right, power, privilege, or immunity;

"(C) in excess of statutory jurisdiction, authority, or limitations, or short of statutory right;

"(D) without observance of procedure required by law;

"(E) unsupported by substantial evidence in a case subject to sections 556 and 557 of this title or otherwise reviewed on the record of an agency hearing provided by statute; or

"(F) unwarranted by the facts to the extent that the facts are subject to trial de novo by the reviewing court.

"In making the foregoing determinations, the court shall review the whole record or those parts of it cited by a party, and due account shall be taken of the rule of prejudicial error." 5 U. S. C. §706 (1964 ed., Supp. V)

§ 128 (1964 ed., Supp. V). The hearing is nonadjudicatory, quasi-legislative in nature. It is not designed to produce a record that is to be the basis of agency action—the basic requirement for substantial-evidence review. *See* H.R.Rep.No.1980, 79th Cong., 2d Sess.

Petitioners' alternative argument also fails. *De novo* review of whether the Secretary's decision was 'unwarranted by the facts' is authorized by § 706(2)(F) in only two circumstances. *** Neither situation exists here.

Even though there is no *de novo* review in this case and the Secretary's approval of the route of I-40 does not have ultimately to meet the substantial-evidence test, the generally applicable standards of § 706 require the reviewing court to engage in a substantial inquiry. Certainly, the Secretary's decision is entitled to a presumption of regularity. *** But that presumption is not to shield his action from a thorough, probing, in-depth review.

The court is first required to decide whether the Secretary acted within the scope of his authority. *Schilling v. Rogers*, 363 U.S. 666, 676–677, 80 S.Ct. 1288, 1295–1296, 4 L.Ed.2d 1478 (1960). This determination naturally begins with a delineation of the scope of the Secretary's authority and discretion.*** As has been shown, Congress has specified only a small range of choices that the Secretary can make. *** The reviewing court must consider whether the Secretary properly construed his authority to approve the use of parkland as limited to situations where there are no feasible alternative routes or where feasible alternative routes involve uniquely difficult problems. And the reviewing court must be able to find that the Secretary could have reasonably believed that in this case there are no feasible alternatives or that alternatives do involve unique problems.

[Additionally, §] 706(2)(A) requires a finding that the actual choice made was not "arbitrary, capricious, an abuse of discretion, or otherwise not in accordance with law." 5 U.S.C. § 706(2)(A) (1964 ed., Supp. V). To make this finding the court must consider whether the decision was based on a consideration of the relevant factors and whether there has been a clear error of judgment. *** Although this inquiry into the facts is to be searching and careful, the ultimate standard of review is a narrow one. The court is not empowered to substitute its judgment for that of the agency.

The final inquiry is whether the Secretary's action followed the necessary procedural requirements. Here the only procedural error alleged is the failure of the Secretary to make formal findings and state his reason for allowing the highway to be built through the park.

Undoubtedly, review of the Secretary's action is hampered by his failure to make such findings, but the absence of formal findings does not necessarily require that the case be remanded to the Secretary. Neither the Department of Transportation Act nor the Federal-Aid Highway Act requires such formal findings. Moreover, the Administrative Procedure Act requirements that there be formal findings in certain rulemaking and adjudicatory proceedings do not apply to the Secretary's action here. See 5 U.S.C. §§ 553(a)(2), 554(a) (1964 ed., Supp. V). *** Plainly, there is no ambiguity here; the Secretary has approved the construction of I-40 through Overton Park and has approved a specific design for the project.

Petitioners contend that although there may not be a statutory requirement that the Secretary make formal findings and even though this may not be a case for the reviewing court to impose a requirement that findings be made, Department of Transportation regulations require them. This argument is based on DOT Order 5610.1,[31] which requires the Secretary to make formal findings when he approves the use of parkland for highway construction but which was issued after the route for I-40 was approved.[32] Petitioners argue that even though the order was not in effect at the time approval was given to the Overton Park project and even though the order was not intended to have retrospective effect the order represents the law at the time of this Court's decision and under *Thorpe v. Housing Authority*, 393 U.S. 268, 281–282, 89 S.Ct. 518, 525–526, 21 L.Ed.2d 474 (1969)["an appellate court must apply the law in effect at the time it renders its decision"], should be applied to this case.

* * *

While we do not question that DOT Order 5610.1 constitutes the law in effect at the time of our decision, we do not believe that Thorpe compels us to remand for the Secretary to make formal findings.[33] Here, unlike the situation in Thorpe, there has been a change in circumstances—additional right-of-way has been cleared and the 26-acre right-of-way inside Overton Park has been purchased by the State. Moreover, there is an administrative record that allows the full, prompt review of the Secretary's action that is sought without additional delay which would result from having a remand to the Secretary.

* * *

Thus it is necessary to remand this case to the District Court for plenary review of the Secretary's decision. That review is to be based on the full administrative record that was before the Secretary at the time he made his decision.[34] But since the bare record may not disclose the factors that were considered or the Secretary's construction of the evidence it may be necessary for the District Court to require some explanation in order to determine if the Secretary acted within the scope of his authority and if the Secretary's action was justifiable under the applicable standard.

---

31. The regulation was promulgated pursuant to Executive Order 11514, dated March 5, 1970, 35 Fed. Reg. 4247, which instructed all federal agencies to initiate procedures needed to direct their policies and programs toward meeting national environmental goals.

32. DOT Order 5610.1 was issued on October 7, 1970.

33. Even if formal findings by the Secretary were mandatory, the proper course would be to remand the case to the District Court directing that court to order the Secretary to make formal findings. See R. Robertson & F. Kirkham, Jurisdiction of the Supreme Court of the United States §446, p. 929 (R. Wolfson & P. Kurland ed. 1951). Of course, the District Court is not prohibited from remanding the case to the Secretary. See *infra*, at 420.

34. The Solicitor General now urges that in order to avoid additional delay the proper course is to remand the case to the District Court for review of the full administrative record.

The court may require the administrative officials who participated in the decision to give testimony explaining their action. Of course, such inquiry into the mental processes of administrative decisionmakers is usually to be avoided. *United States v. Morgan*, 313 U.S. 409, 422, 61 S.Ct. 999, 1004–1005, 85 L.Ed. 1429 (1941). And where there are administrative findings that were made at the same time as the decision *** there must be a strong showing of bad faith or improper behavior before such inquiry may be made. But here there are no such formal findings and it may be that the only way there can be effective judicial review is by examining the decisionmakers themselves. ***

The District Court is not, however, required to make such an inquiry. It may be that the Secretary can prepare formal findings including the information required by DOT Order 5610.1 that will provide an adequate explanation for his action. Such an explanation will, to some extent, be a '*post hoc* rationalization' and thus must be viewed critically. If the District Court decides that additional explanation is necessary, that court should consider which method will prove the most expeditious so that full review may be had as soon as possible.

Reversed and remanded.

Separate opinion of Mr. Justice Black, with whom Mr. Justice Brennan joins.

I agree with the Court that the judgment of the Court of Appeals is wrong and that its action should be reversed. I do not agree that the whole matter should be remanded to the District Court. I think the case should be sent back to the Secretary of Transportation. It is apparent from the Court's opinion today that the Secretary of Transportation completely failed to comply with the duty imposed upon him by Congress not to permit a federally financed public highway to run through a public park "unless (1) there is no feasible and prudent alternative to the use of such land, and (2) such program includes all possible planning to minimize harm to such park ***." 23 U.S.C. § 138 (1964 ed., Supp. V); 49 U.S.C. § 1653(f) (1964 ed., Supp. V). That congressional command should not be taken lightly by the Secretary or by this Court. It represents a solemn determination of the highest law-making body of this Nation that the beauty and health-giving facilities of our parks are not to be taken away for public roads without hearings, factfindings, and policy determinations under the supervision of a Cabinet officer—the Secretary of Transportation. The Act of Congress in connection with other federal highway aid legislation,[1] it seems to me, calls for hearings—hearing that a court can review, hearings that demonstrate more than mere arbitrary defiance by the Secretary. *** [T]his record contains not one word to indicate that the Secretary raised even a finger to comply with the command of Congress. It is our duty, I believe, to remand this whole matter back to the Secretary of Transportation for him to give this matter the hearing it deserves in full good-faith obedience to the Act of Congress. That Act was obviously passed to protect our public parks from forays by road builders except in the most extraordinary and imperative

1. See 23 U. S. C. § 128 (1964 ed., Supp. V) and regulations promulgated thereunder, 34 Fed. Reg. 727–730 (1969).

circumstances.[2] *** I dissent from the Court's failure to send the case back to the Secretary, whose duty has not yet been performed.

Mr. Justice BLACKMUN.

I fully join the Court in its opinion and in its judgment. I merely wish to state the obvious: (1) The case comes to this Court as the end product of more than a decade of endeavor to solve the interstate highway problem at Memphis. (2) The administrative decisions under attack here are not those of a single Secretary; some were made by the present Secretary's predecessor and, before him, by the Department of Commerce's Bureau of Public Roads. (3) The 1966 Act and the 1968 Act have cut across former methods and here have imposed new standards and conditions upon a situation that already was largely developed.

This undoubtedly is why the record is sketchy and less than one would expect if the project were one which had been instituted after the passage of the 1966 Act.

Notes

1. **Section 4(f).** The Department of Transportation Act of 1966, Pub.L. 89-670, § 4(f), although re-codified as 49 U.S.C. § 303, is still referred to as Section 4(f) in most, if not all, court opinions. Additionally, Congress has amended Section 4(f) to permit a land manager to consent to alteration of a historic landmark or site, even with a feasible alternative when there is only a *de minimis* adverse impact on the historic site. *See* 49 U.S.C. § 303(d).

2. **On remand.** On remand to the District Court for the Western District of Tennessee, *Citizens to Preserve Overton Park, Inc. v. Volpe*, 335 F. Supp. 873 (W.D. Tenn. 1972), the court conducted a full hearing and probed the prior administrative proceedings, finding that the Secretary had made a proper decision as to the design of the proposed route and had only to determine whether the Overton Park route was the sole feasible and prudent route. Accordingly, the court remanded the case to the Secretary "only for the purpose of making a route determination in compliance with section 4(f) of the Department of Transportation Act of 1966 as that provision has been construed by the Supreme Court." *Id.* at 885.

Secretary Volpe, after a searching administrative review of the matter, refused to approve the Overton Park route on January 18, 1973. Citing the onerous standards set forth by the NEPA and the Federal-Aid Highway Act, the Federal Highway Administration's noise standards, and the Supreme Court's interpretation of Section 4(f), Volpe reconsidered his original opinion:

> On the basis of the record before me and in light of guidance provided by the Supreme Court, I find that an Interstate highway as proposed by the State through Overton Park cannot be approved. On that record I cannot find, as the Statute requires, and as interpreted by the courts, that there are no prudent

---

2. See also *Named Individual Members of the San Antonio Conservation Society v. Texas Highway Department*, 400 U.S. 968, 972 (1970) (dissents from the denial of certiorari).

> and feasible alternatives to the use of parkland nor that the broader environmental protection objectives of the NEPA, and the Federal-Aid Highway Act have been met, nor that the existing proposal would comply with FHWA standards on noise.

Citizens to Preserve Overton Park, Inc. v. Brinegar, 494 F.2d 1212, 1213–1214 (6th Cir. 1974). The Secretary emphasized his willingness to reconsider alternative avenues for the project. Based on the Secretary's new position, the Sixth Circuit determined that the Secretary was relieved of the burden of explaining himself until the state approved a new proposal. Over the next ten years, the City of Memphis and the Department of Transportation ("DOT) explored various alternatives for Interstate 40, including a two-level tunnel under the park and building the highway in a deep trench, along the original route through the Park. All were rejected by the Federal Highway Administration. On January 26, 1981, DOT finally removed the Midtown Memphis segment of Interstate 40 from the federal interstate highway plan, owing in no small measure to the cost (estimated as high as $300 million). Also, Interstate 240, a loop around Midtown Memphis, had been constructed and provided a feasible alternative route. In 1987, the State of Tennessee deeded the 26 acres of Overton Park back to the City of Memphis. Citizens to Preserve Overton Park, http://www.overtonparkforever.org/2011/03/fortyyearsago.

3. **The unflattering history of Overton Park.** On November 14, 1901, the City of Memphis purchased the 342-acre tract of land from Nashville residents Ella and Overton Lea (for $110,000) and "Lea's Woods" became Overton Park. The Park was officially named after John Overton, a co-founder of Memphis, on July 25, 1902. The Park was designed by landscape architect George Kessler and is now a part of a comprehensive plan that also includes Martin Luther King Riverside Park and the Memphis Parkway System. Overton Park Conservancy, http://www.overtonpark.org/history (last visited March 15, 2017). However, it was not until the mid-1960s that black citizens were given unrestricted access to the Park. Before that, they could enter only on Thursday afternoons to visit the Memphis Zoo and Aquarium. The only other park facilities available to blacks in the city for most of the 20th century were Church Park on Beale Street and Douglass Park, which was specifically developed for their use in 1914. John Linn Hopkins, *Overton Park: The Evolution Of A Public Space*, Memphis Park, City Of Memphis, Public Commission Construction Office, Prepared For Ritchie Smith Associates Overton Park Master Plan September 1, 1987.

4. **Corridor H. Alternatives.** In *Corridor H. Alternatives, Inc. v. Slater*, 166 F.3d 368 (D.C. Cir. 1999), environmental and public interest groups (collectively referred to as "CHA") brought an action against various government agencies in opposition to a proposed highway project that was part of the Appalachian Highway Development System, alleging violations of NEPA and the Department of Transportation Act §4(f)). CHA asserted that the Federal Highway Administration ("FHWA") violated Section 4(f) by "failing to identify all the historic sites it was charged with protecting prior to its decision approving the route of the proposed highway and by erroneously concluding that the highway would not 'use' two of the sites it did identify." *Id.* at 369. CHA also charged

FHWA with violating NEPA by "failing to give adequate consideration to the improvement of existing roads as an alternative to the construction of the new highway." *Id.* FHWA had chosen the parcel in accordance with its powers under the Appalachian Regional Development Act of 1965, 40 U.S.C. app. §§1 *et seq.*, which Congress enacted for the very purpose of creating an Appalachian highway system. *Id.* at §2(a).

The court explained that the U.S. Department of Transportation regulations implementing Section 106 of NHPA require three steps to be taken for compliance:

> "First, the agency must identify the properties that are listed or eligible for listing in the National Register. 36 C.F.R. §800.4. Next, it must evaluate the effects of the proposed undertaking on those properties. *Id.* at §800.5. Finally, if the agency determines that the project would have an adverse effect on a historic property, it must consider measures to mitigate the potential damage."

Corridor H., 166 F.3d at 370.

FHWA, along with other government agencies, began planning for the Corridor H project in the late 1970s. A draft Environmental Impact Statement ("EIS") was produced in 1981, but work on the project was suspended until 1990. Instead, they decided to proceed with the environmental review in two stages, each of which resulted in the issuance of a draft EIS. These deliberations culminated in 1996 with the issuance of the Record of Decision ("ROD") for the Corridor H project. The ROD approved the four-lane Build Alternative as the preferred basis for the project as well as its adoption of the modified corridor route and highway alignments so as to avoid the constructive use (indirect impacts from the proximity of a proposed project adjacent to, or nearby, a Section 4(f) property that results in substantial impairment to the property's activities, features, or attributes) of the Corricks Ford and Moorefield Civil War battlefields. FHWA concluded that, by virtue of these modifications, the highway would not "substantially impair" the battlefields. The ROD also incorporated a segment-by-segment approach to compliance with Section 106, whereby the project was split into sections to assess the impact on historic places as the construction progressed. Additionally, "in recognition of the fact that the Section 4(f) process could not be completed prior to the identification of the protected historic sites pursuant to Section 106, the ROD specified that its approval of the project was conditional only and would not become final as to any section of the corridor 'until the section 106 process has been completed for that section and for any immediately adjacent section(s).'" *Corridor H.*, 166 F.3d at 372.

CHA challenged the approval of the Corridor H project in district court. The District Court granted summary judgment in favor of FHWA, even though both parties advanced reasonable arguments, because they had to "give deference to agency decisions that are not arbitrary or capricious." *Corridor H Alternatives, Inc. v. Slater*, 982 F. Supp. 24, 35 (D.D.C. 1997). CHA appealed the decision to the D.C. Circuit, which affirmed in part and reversed in part.

The Circuit Court decided that the plain language of Section 4(f)—that "any use of lands from a section 4(f) property shall be evaluated early in the development of the action when alternatives to the proposed action are under study," 23 C.F.R. §771.135(b) (1998)—requires the agencies to complete the section 4(f) process before issuing the ROD fixing the proposed four-lane highway route. In regard to NEPA, the Circuit Court agreed with the District Court that the agencies complied with the NEPA "hard look" requirement for the environmental impact assessment and weighed it against their responsibilities in accordance with the Appalachian Regional Development Act. Accordingly, they found that FHWA and the agencies had reasonably contemplated alternative routes and decided on the four-lane highway proposal in a way that was not "arbitrary or capricious." As such, the Circuit Court directed the agencies to "complete the section 4(f) process before proceeding further with the Corridor H project." *Corridor H.*, 166 F.3d at 374.

5. **I-Care Case.** In *Citizen Advocates for Responsible Expansion, Inc. (I-CARE) v. Dole*, 770 F.2d 423 (5th Cir. 1985), I-CARE, a group of citizens, community leaders, and business persons, challenged the planned expansion of a segment of an interstate highway in downtown Fort Worth, Texas, on environmental grounds. The project centered on the intersection of I-30 and I-35W, known by local commuters as the "Mixmaster"—a "complicated maze of highways, access roads, ramps, and merging lanes," *id.* at 426, located close to the central business district of the city. The area immediately west of the Mixmaster is a four-lane section of a thirty-foot high elevated east-west highway called the Overhead, which extends westward passing over a public park known as the Water Garden, one of the most popular park facilities in Fort Worth. *Id.* "The Water Garden is comprised of terraced plantings and a series of waterfalls and pools surrounding a large stone plaza. It has received national acclaim for its unique design and the recreational opportunities it affords in an urban, downtown environment." *Id.* at 427. Had the project been completed, the Overhead's distance from the park would have decreased from forty-five to nine feet. The Overhead also overlooked several buildings that are either on or are eligible for inclusion in the National Register of Historic Places. "The buildings, constructed in the 1930s, represent the craft and special design found in excellent architecture of that period and symbolize the early development of modern Fort Worth." *Id.* at 427. According to the proposal, some of these buildings were to be demolished outright while others would be drastically affected. For example:

> [T]he Post Office would be affected most dramatically by the proposed project. The facade of the front of the Post Office features sixteen impressive turned limestone columns that are topped with Corinthian-style capitals manifesting carved cattle heads. The entire building is veneered with cut limestone and is punctuated with numerous stone carvings and bronzed embossed medallions. The original project plans placed the expanded Overhead twenty feet from the front of the Post Office, rather than eighty feet as the existing Overhead is. Because the height of the expanded Overhead would be approximately that of the Post Office Building, the Overhead would create an awning-like effect on the front of the building, shading the building during parts of the day, obscuring practically any view of the sky, obstructing a view of the facade for

> all but close passers-by, and giving people standing on the steps of the Post Office a view of the numerous and rather unattractive Overhead support columns.

Id. at 427. The crux of I-CARE's argument concerned the inadequacies and fallacies of the agencies' environmental impact statement, which the Circuit Court described as "a bizarre pattern of administrative indecision and/or confusion at best, or perhaps even public deception at worst." *Id.* at 428.

The respondents, various federal and state government agencies, had conducted environmental impact reviews and held public meetings to discuss the expansions. Even though the I-30 plan included the Overhead, the agencies did not notify those whom the project would affect since they included the notice in their I-35 expansion plan. The Overhead is located on I-30. Despite these facts, the District Court had found that the agencies' environmental review process was sufficient and upheld their conclusion that adverse environmental effects of the project would be minimal. *See I-CARE v. Dole*, 586 F. Supp. 1094 (N.D. Tex. 1984).

In contrast, on appeal, the Fifth Circuit held that: 1) the state and federal agencies failed to compile a sufficient, reviewable, administrative record in support of their determination that the quality of the human environment would not be significantly affected by the proposed expansion project; 2) an Environmental Impact Statement ("EIS"), under § 102(2)(C) of the National Environmental Policy Act of 1969 ("NEPA"), 42 U.S.C. § 4332(2)(c), should have been prepared for all projects including the Overhead; 3) the District Court erroneously found that the Overhead expansion would not adversely affect a state park and historical buildings protected by the Department of Transportation Act; and 4) the state and federal agencies violated the notice and hearing requirements of the Federal-Aid Highway Act by failing to reach out to all those affected by the proposed project. Accordingly, holding that the agencies "failed to carry out procedures required by law," the Circuit Court remanded the matter for further proceedings concerning the Overhead expansion in accordance with federal law. It also suggested that the agencies separate the Overhead project from the I-35 project to avoid completing an EIS for the entire project. *I-CARE v. Dole*, 770 F.2d at 443.

Druid Hills Civic Association, Inc. v. Federal Highway Administration

United States Court of Appeals for the Eleventh Circuit
772 F.2d 700 (1985)

Henderson, C.J. Druid Hills Civic Association, Inc., *et al* *** and National Trust For Historic Preservation in the United States *** appeal the November 14, 1984 order of the United States District Court for the Northern District of Georgia denying their motions to enjoin construction of the Presidential Parkway (Parkway), a proposed 2.4 mile highway running east from the I-75/I-85 stub in downtown Atlanta to Ponce de Leon Avenue, an east-west arterial that is part of the Olmsted Park network in Atlanta's Druid Hills Historic District. On appeal, the appellants contend that the district court erred in finding that the named appellees complied with the requirements of the National Environmental Policy Act of 1969 (NEPA), 42 U.S.C. §§4321–4347 (1982), section 4(f) of the Department of Transportation Act of 1966, 49 U.S.C. §303 (1982),[1] and section 18 of the Federal-Aid Highway Act of 1968, 23 U.S.C. §138 (1982).[2]

Facts and Historical Background[3]

For a better understanding of the current litigation, it is necessary to detail the history of the tract comprising the proposed Parkway. In the late 1960s and early 1970s, the Georgia Department of Transportation (GDOT) acquired approximately 219 acres as right-of-way for two multi-lane highways, one oriented north-south (I-485) and one extending east-west (Stone Mountain Tollway). The land, known locally as the Great Park, was cleared of dwellings and other structures and has been vacant ever since. In 1971, the United States District Court for the Northern District of Georgia enjoined construction of I-485 pending completion of an environmental impact statement (EIS) by the GDOT and the Federal Highway Administration (FHWA).[4] The GDOT prepared an EIS which was approved by the FHWA. The Secretary of the United States Department of Transportation (USDOT) nevertheless rejected the EIS in 1973 because it did not satisfy the requirements of section 4(f).

As a result of strong opposition to the Stone Mountain Tollway, Governor Jimmy Carter appointed a commission to examine the project and make recommendations. The commission recommended against building the Tollway until an assessment could

---

1. Section 4(f) of the Department of Transportation Act, 49 U.S.C. §1653(f), was repealed in 1983 but was recodified without substantial change at 49 U.S.C. §303.

2. Section 18 of the Federal-Aid Highway Act, 23 U.S.C. §138, is virtually identical to section 4(f) of the Department of Transportation Act, 49 U.S.C. §303. For purposes of this appeal, the statutes will be referred to collectively as "section 4(f)."

Section 4(f) states:

> (a) It is the policy of the United States Government that special effort should be made to preserve the natural beauty of the country-side and public park and recreation lands, wildlife and waterfowl refuges, and historic sites.
>
> (b) The Secretary of Transportation shall cooperate and consult with the Secretaries of the Interior, Housing and Urban Development, and Agriculture, and with the States, in developing transportation plans and programs that include measures to maintain or enhance the natural beauty of lands crossed by transportation activities or facilities.
>
> (c) The Secretary may approve a transportation program or project requiring the use of publicly owned land of a public park, recreation area, or wildlife and waterfowl refuge of national, State, or local significance, or land of an historic site of national, State, or local significance (as determined by the Federal, State, or local officials having jurisdiction over the park, area, refuge, or site) only if—
>
> (1) there is no prudent and feasible alternative to using that land; and
>
> (2) the program or project includes all possible planning to minimize harm to the park, recreation area, wildlife and waterfowl refuge, or historic site resulting from the use.

49 U.S.C. §303 (1982).

3. This section is taken substantially from the district court opinion and from the purpose and need section of the environmental impact statement.

4. *Morningside-Lenox Park Association, Inc. v. Volpe*, 334 F. Supp. 132 (N.D.Ga.1971).

be made on the effect of the impending construction of the MARTA[5] east rail line. Governor Carter accepted the commission's recommendation in December, 1972.

In 1973, the City of Atlanta withdrew its support for I-485 and the Atlanta Regional Commission (ARC) deleted the project from its Regional Transportation Plan in 1974. The State Transportation Board removed I-485 from the interstate highway system plan in 1974, which action was approved by the FHWA in 1975. In 1977, the GDOT began to dispose of all I-485 properties north of St. Charles Avenue but retained all the right-of-way south of that point for future transportation improvements in the east-west corridor.

Over the succeeding years, numerous alternatives for the use of the Great Park were developed. In 1974, Atlanta Mayor Maynard Jackson proposed the "Great Park" concept, a plan that included a variety of recreational and cultural facilities. In 1975, the City of Atlanta retained Arkhora Associates to prepare a reuse planning study for the Great Park. Arkhora's conceptual plan advocated a passive open space consisting of recreation areas, cultural facilities and housing. To meet transportation needs, the Arkhora proposal recommended that the I-75/I-85 stub be connected to DeKalb Avenue. The GDOT opposed the recommended action because it did not use the existing right-of-way to meet transportation needs and thereby failed to address the legal consequences of using the land for a non-transportation purpose. In 1977, the ARC adopted the Decatur Parkway Connector and Decatur Parkway, a road connecting the I-75/I-85 stub to an improved DeKalb Avenue, as part of its Regional Transportation Plan.

Atlanta Great Park Planning, Inc. (AGPP), a public nonprofit corporation, was formed in 1975 to study and plan for reuse of the property. AGPP's board of directors included representatives of ten neighborhoods, the Cities of Atlanta and Decatur, DeKalb County and the State of Georgia. A report published in 1977 acknowledged that the Great Park could serve not only as a major recreational area but also as a stimulus for economic development and cultural revitalization but withheld recommendation pending further study. In 1978, AGPP retained H. Randall Roark to study housing opportunities in the right-of-way. In addition to its housing proposals, Roark's study, published in 1979, adopted the transportation, open space and economic development recommendations contained in the Arkhora plan and the AGPP's 1977 report. The GDOT did not support the Roark plan for the same reasons that it opposed the earlier Arkhora proposal.

* * *

The current design came into existence in the early 1980s. After leaving office in 1981, President Jimmy Carter began to formulate plans for a presidential library, museum and policy center (the Complex). President Carter regarded the Great Park property as an ideal location for the Complex because of its proximity to the central business district and metropolitan Atlanta universities, its relative seclusion and its accessibility to the interstate highway network.

---

5. The Metropolitan Atlanta Rapid Transit Authority.

In 1981, Andrew Young sought election as mayor of Atlanta. He ran in part on a platform of opposition to any roadway through the Great Park. After his election, Mayor Young reversed his position and in 1982 supported the so-called Mayor's Plan, the basic proposal sought to be enjoined in this litigation. The Mayor's Plan includes the Jimmy Carter Complex, a thirty-acre park surrounding the Complex, and a 2.4 mile highway consisting of a pair of two-lane roadways, one eastbound and one westbound, which circumscribe the Complex and park. In addition, the City of Atlanta is developing a housing plan for use of the remaining acreage. The Complex and roadside park would be located on existing right-of-way but further land acquisition would be necessary to build the highway.

* * *

In August, 1982, the FHWA placed a notice of intent to prepare an EIS in the *Federal Register.* On April 21, 1983, the FHWA, the lead agency for the Parkway project, signed the draft EIS, *** copies of the draft statement were distributed to agencies, organizations and individuals. The draft EIS allocated four pages to a discussion of the building of the Parkway, but only two sentences to the alternative of not building it. Other alternatives, including previous plans for the area, a road extending only to the presidential library, a road terminating at Moreland Avenue, intersection improvements on existing streets, a two-lane Parkway and traffic improvements in the Ponce de Leon Avenue/Scott Boulevard corridor were discussed in four pages of text. Additional discussion of alternatives, including the proposed Decatur Parkway, was incorporated into the section addressing impacts on properties protected by section 4(f).

The GDOT and the FHWA conducted three informal public information meetings between May 31 and June 2, 1983 in neighborhoods adjacent to the project and a fourth public information meeting at the Atlanta Civic Center on June 7, 1983, [at which [a]pproximately 1,500 to 3,000 people attended.]

Several federal agencies commented on the draft EIS, including the Department of the Interior (DOI), the Environmental Protection Agency (EPA), the General Services Administration and the USDOT. DOI first recommended that the final EIS give consideration to whether the proposed Parkway would meet transportation needs. The comments noted that it was not clear that termination of the Parkway at Ponce de Leon Avenue, an east-west arterial, would substantially relieve traffic congestion and provide for future transportation needs in the east-west corridor. In addition, the DOI stated that discussion of alternatives in the draft EIS was inadequate and recommended that the final statement contain a more extensive discourse of the no-build and Moreland Avenue termination alternatives. Given these deficiencies, the DOI felt that the draft EIS failed to adequately address section 4(f) considerations. The EPA found that the draft statement did not adequately evaluate the impact on air quality. The USDOT took the position that the draft EIS adequately addressed the effects of the project and measures to minimize harm. The department's comments further stated, however, that the draft EIS did not contain sufficient information to support a determination that there was no feasible and prudent alternative to the use of lands protected by section 4(f). Furthermore, the draft statement did not demonstrate a need for the Parkway as opposed to improvements to existing facilities. Therefore, the USDOT suggested a more thorough investigation of the Decatur Parkway alternative. The department concluded that it appeared that the proposed project would aggravate, rather than alleviate, traffic conditions on Ponce de Leon Avenue. The FHWA and the GDOT held meetings with the various agencies to evaluate their comments.

On August 4, 1983, ten days after the expiration of the period for comment on the draft EIS, the GDOT made the decision to proceed with preparation of the final EIS around the build, i.e., Parkway, option. The GDOT and FHWA also began preparation of a Preliminary Case Report (PCR) pursuant to section 106 of the National Historic Preservation Act of 1966, 16 U.S.C. § 470f [54 U.S.C. § 306108], and 36 C.F.R. § 800 to evaluate the impact of the project on historic and archaeological resources. The PCR was forwarded to the Georgia Department of Natural Resources on October 25, 1983 and to the United States Advisory Council on Historic Preservation (ACHP) on November 3, 1983. Copies of the PCR were made available to the public for comment....

* * *

On May 22, 1984, the FHWA approved the final EIS. Copies of the statement were distributed to interested parties and notice of the approval was published in the *Federal Register*. In addition to alternatives raised in the draft EIS, the final EIS discussed MARTA, a light rail proposal, one-way pairings of streets, staggered work hours, and toll charges and provided a more detailed discussion of the Decatur Parkway alternative.

The DOI, EPA, individuals and organizations submitted comments on the final EIS. The DOI decided that the statement did not adequately respond to the department's comments on the draft EIS and was not responsive to the requirements of section 4(f). Accordingly, the department objected to section 4(f) approval of the project.

On June 25, 1984, the chairman of the ACHP filed a formal notice of referral with the Council on Environmental Quality (CEQ). The CEQ solicited written comments from the public on the national importance of the Parkway and held a public meeting on July 17, 1984. On September 20, 1984, the CEQ determined that the proposed Parkway was not of national importance and declined to further review the project. The CEQ requested the FHWA to resume its normal decision-making process. On September 21, 1984, the FHWA, acting through William Van Luchene, the designee of the Secretary of the USDOT, approved and executed a record of decision.

These actions for declaratory and injunctive relief were initiated on September 24 and September 28, 1984.... Carter Library, Inc., the entity responsible for developing the Carter Complex, obtained title to the 3.2 acres on which the Complex would be built via a landswap with the GDOT on October 2, 1984. Construction commenced the same day.

I. NEPA

* * *

II. *Section 4(f)*

A. *Standard of Review*

*** The Supreme Court enunciated the standard of judicial review of the Secretary's section 4(f) determination in *Overton Park*. While the Secretary's decision is entitled to a presumption of regularity, that presumption does not "shield his action from a thorough, probing, in-depth review." 401 U.S. at 415, 91 S.Ct. at 823, 28 L.Ed.2d at 153. *** In reviewing the district court's decision affirming the Secretary's section 4(f) action, "'the focal point for judicial review should be the administrative record already in existence [on the basis of which the administrator's determination was made], not some new record made initially in the reviewing court.'" *** Since the appellate court applies the same standard of review as the district court, we need accord no particular deference to the district court's conclusions as to whether the administrative record supports the Secretary's decision. *Id.* If the record fails to show a sufficient basis for the administrative decision, the 4(f) determination must be overturned. ***

B. *Analysis*

***

(1) *Section 4(f)(1)*

Section 4(f)(1) requires a finding of no feasible or prudent alternatives to the use of parklands and historic sites before the Secretary can approve the use of such property for highway purposes. An alternate route that also impacts upon parks and historic sites is not an "alternative to the use" of such property. *Louisiana Environmental Society, Inc. v. Coleman*, 537 F.2d 79, 85 (5th Cir. 1976) (*LES II*). Thus, in making the section 4(f)(1) assessment, the Secretary is concerned with those alternatives that do not also impact on parks and historic sites.

* * *

The section 4(f) statement contained in the EIS [] discussed five alternatives to the Parkway project: the no-build option, the Decatur Parkway, two plans for roads terminating at Moreland Avenue and widening of Ponce de Leon Avenue with improved signalization. Of these, the no-build option is the only alternative to the use of section 4(f) areas because the other proposals contemplated the "use" of parklands and/or historic districts to some degree. *** The district court examined the consequences of not building the highway and found that the Secretary could reasonably have concluded that the no-build option was not prudent because it failed to meet the need which the project was designed to address and because it might have resulted in loss of the Carter Complex or reduction in its scope.

[T]he district court properly interpreted *LES II* [*Louisiana Environmental Soc., Inc. v. Dole*, 707 F.2d 116 (5th Cir. 1983)] to provide support for its conclusion that the

Secretary could reasonably have rejected the no-build option as imprudent for failure to fulfill the need for a highway in Atlanta's east-west corridor. ***. Accordingly, since the no-build alternative could reasonably have been found imprudent, we affirm this portion of the district court's order.[19]

(2) *Section 4(f)(2)*

Section 4(f)(2) imposes the duty to utilize all possible planning to minimize harm to parks and historic sites before the Secretary can approve a route using section 4(f) property. Relocation of the highway through another portion of the section 4(f) area or through other section 4(f) properties must be considered as a means of minimizing harm[.] *** [S]ection 4(f)(2) requires a simple balancing process which totals the harm caused by each alternate route to section 4(f) areas and selects the option which does the least harm. *** The only relevant factor in making a determination whether an alternative route minimizes harm is the quantum of harm to the park or historic site caused by the alternative. *** The Secretary is free to choose among alternatives which cause substantially equal damage to parks or historic sites. ***

The court in *LES II* made it clear that the Secretary does not have to accept an alternate route which causes less harm to parks and historic sites. Rather, the court construed section 4(f)(2) to mean that the route must also be feasible and prudent. *** The determination whether the route is infeasible or imprudent is based on factors other than the route's impact on section 4(f) areas. *Id.*

Applying this legal standard to the proposed *** alternatives, the district court found that the Secretary's determination that the alternatives either did not minimize harm or were imprudent was reasonable. *** With the present record, it is difficult to see how the Secretary could have made the proper evaluation mandated by section 4(f)(2) of the harm caused by each of these options. A meaningful balancing of the damage done by the preferred route with that caused by the alternatives was therefore impossible. Accordingly, we are unable to review the correctness of the district court's findings as to the Decatur Parkway and Moreland Avenue plans because we conclude that the Secretary did not make the requisite findings necessary for an informed comparison of

19. The district court concluded that loss of the Complex could constitute a truly unique or unusual factor. The court continued with the statement, "Thus, even if No-Build were prudent, the magnitude and uniqueness of the Carter Complex could justify an exception to the prudent requirement." Given our disposition of the section 4(f)(1) claim, it is not necessary that we determine whether possible loss of the Complex or reduction in its scope is enough to render the no-build option imprudent. Indeed, it is not certain that such an occurrence would come to pass. *See* Final EIS, Vol. I, at 85 ("There would also be a possibility that the no-build might include a presidential library and policy center at or near its presently proposed location."). We do note, however, that Congress enacted no exceptions to the requirement that there be no prudent alternatives to the use of parks and historic sites before the Secretary can approve a project using protected properties. As such, possible loss of the Complex would be a factor to consider in determining whether no-build was imprudent, not an event warranting an exception to the prudence requirement.

the relative harms anticipated by the construction of the various routes. It is the deficiency in this "testing" process that afflicts the integrity of the EIS. *Id.* at 86.[20] ***

* * *

In summary, the case must be remanded to the Secretary for adequate findings of the impact on 4(f) properties caused by the Decatur Parkway and the two Moreland Avenue plans. This review should encompass an accurate assessment of the characteristics of the property that will be affected by the alternative[.] *** The Secretary's review must also address the quantity of harm that will accrue to the park or historic site and the nature of that harm, e.g., visual impact or physical taking. It will not suffice to simply state that an alternative route would affect 4(f) properties without providing some rational, documented basis for such a conclusion. In short, the same consideration must be given to whether these alternative routes would minimize harm to the section 4(f) properties as was accorded the adopted route.

After reviewing the voluminous record in this case, we are mindful of the tremendous task confronting the Secretary in resolving these difficult issues. However, the magnitude of the problem does not diminish the need to follow the stringent requirements of section 4(f)(2). All of the proposed routes involved in this litigation will affect parklands and historic sites to some degree. It is important then that all of these options be carefully examined in an effort to minimize the damage to section 4(f) lands. ***

For the foregoing reasons, we AFFIRM in part, REVERSE in part, and REMAND to the district court for proceedings consistent with this opinion.

Notes and Questions

1. **Substantive requirements.** Unlike NEPA, Section 4(f) by its terms, does impose substantive requirements upon the agency, indeed an affirmative duty to minimize harm to parkland or historic properties.

2. **Relevant harm.** a. What kind of harm is relevant in this calculation? Physical destruction of structures or places? Increased noise? More high speed traffic? Impairment of view? b. Can the different harms be measured with the same yardstick? c. What if the chosen route was the site of an important event? d. How important is it to select the most direct route to make automobile travel more efficient and less polluting even where historic properties are present?

---

20. It is not entirely clear whether the Secretary rejected the various alternatives because they failed to minimize harm or because they were imprudent. The EIS states that the various alternatives are not feasible and prudent but then proceeds to list reasons that largely relate to the alternatives' impacts on parks and historic sites. As cautioned by the court in *LES II*, a route that minimizes harm may be rejected as imprudent only for reasons other than its impact on 4(f) properties. 537 F.2d at 86. On the remand, the Secretary must furnish a more specific analysis of the impact on 4(f) areas occasioned by the various alternatives. If this review results in the conclusion that the harm caused by an alternative is substantially equal to that caused by the preferred route, the Secretary is free to choose among the routes. If the alternative does minimize harm, however, it can be rejected as imprudent only for truly unusual reasons other than its impact on parks and historic sites.

3. **Deference to the agency.** a. How much deference is appropriate to give to the agency making the determination of feasibility? b. Is feasibility measured only by technological concerns? Economic? c. Or, can it encompass the larger goals of environmental protection and historical preservation?

Merritt Parkway Conservancy v. Mineta

United States District Court for the District of Connecticut
424 F.Supp.2d 396 (2006)

Kravitz, D.J. In this lawsuit, Plaintiffs Merritt Parkway Conservancy, [et al.,] challenge the decision of Defendants Secretary of Transportation and the Federal Highway Administration ("FHWA") to approve a highway construction project (the "Interchange Project") that was designed and will be managed by Defendant Commissioner of the Connecticut Department of Transportation ("ConnDOT"). The Interchange Project *** will reconstruct and substantially enlarge the interchange between U.S. Route 7, Main Avenue, and the Merritt Parkway (U.S. Rt. 15) in Norwalk, Connecticut.

The Merritt Parkway is a scenic road familiar to all citizens of Connecticut. The Parkway, which was designed and built in the 1930s, is listed in the National Register of Historic Places and has been designated a National Scenic Byway and State Scenic Road. ***

It is clear that the Interchange Project, as currently designed, will have a significant impact on many of the aesthetic and historic features of the Merritt Parkway, including its historic bridges, ramps, ornamental parapets, and piers, as well as its park-like landscape and vistas. But it is equally clear that changes to the Merritt Parkway / Rt. 7 interchange to make it fully directional and to ease the significant traffic congestion in the Main Avenue area are needed. The difficulty is in reconciling the public interest in safety and convenience with the public interest in preservation of an important historic resource.

Congress undoubtedly thought it had provided an answer to this recurrent problem when it enacted Section 4(f) of the Department of Transportation Act[.] *** In enacting Section 4(f), Congress required FHWA to engage in planning and substantive analysis before FHWA approves a project so as to lessen the likelihood of disruption once a project is approved. Plaintiffs maintain that FHWA has failed to comply with this congressional mandate and, despite repeated encouragement from the Court, the parties have been unwilling or unable to reach a negotiated settlement of their differences. The Court is therefore confronted with a truly regrettable situation. The Interchange Project has already been approved by FHWA and, in reliance on that approval, ConnDOT has awarded costly bids for the project and has even begun preliminary construction. If the Interchange Project proceeds, Plaintiffs assert that irreparable harm to historic and natural resources will occur; if it does not proceed, taxpayers will foot the bill for increased costs in completing a highway project that is undoubtedly long overdue and important to the State of Connecticut. Either way, the citizenry is disserved.

*** The Court's role is properly limited to assuring itself and the public, by means of what the Supreme Court has termed a "thorough, probing, in-depth review" of the administrative record, *Citizens To Preserve Overton Park, Inc. v. Volpe,* 401 U.S. 402, 415, 91 S.Ct. 814, 28 L.Ed.2d 136 (1971), that the Interchange Project was designed and approved by FHWA in accordance with Congress's substantive instruction that the FHWA engage in "all possible planning to minimize harm" to the Merritt Parkway.

Unfortunately, the administrative record, which this Court has reviewed in depth, does not adequately demonstrate that FHWA satisfied the requirements of Section 4(f)(2). The Court emphasizes that this conclusion does not mean that the current Interchange Project design fails to minimize harm to the Merritt Parkway. All it means is that the administrative record before this Court does not demonstrate that FHWA made such a finding or upon what reasoned basis it did so ***. But FHWA is not the only party at fault in this case *** Had Plaintiffs pressed their objections sooner, it is possible that disruption of the Interchange Project might have been avoided. ConnDOT is not blameless either. It has been well aware of Plaintiffs' concerns since at least 2004. Yet *** ConnDOT consciously chose to proceed without making changes to the Interchange Project, knowing full well that litigation would likely ensue and that the project might be delayed as a result. ***

Because the administrative record is inadequate to show that FHWA satisfied the stringent substantive mandate of Section 4(f), the Court concludes that the matter must be remanded to FHWA to cure the defects in its compliance with Section 4(f). *** In view of the voluntary moratorium of construction activity that has been and, at this time, remains in place, the Court will defer entry of an order on injunctive relief for one week, pending input from the parties on whether continuation of the voluntary moratorium is possible (which is the Court's preference), or if not, the appropriate scope and duration of carefully tailored injunctive relief.

I. Procedural History

In this action, commenced on May 31, 2005, Plaintiffs claim that in designing and approving the Interchange Project, Defendants failed to abide by the requirements of Section 4(f)(2) of the Department of Transportation Act, 49 U.S.C. § 303, as well as the National Environmental Policy Act ("NEPA"), 42 U.S.C. § 4332(2)(C) and (E), and the National Historic Preservation Act ("NHPA"), 16 U.S.C. § 470. Specifically, Count I alleges that the FHWA's approval of the Interchange Project was arbitrary and capricious and contrary to the requirements of Section 4(f). Counts II and III claim that the determination that the Interchange Project would not have a significant impact on the environment was arbitrary and capricious and contrary to NEPA. Finally, Count IV asserts that the failure to consider alternative designs to reduce or minimize harm to the Merritt Parkway and other historic and natural resources violated NHPA and a Memorandum of Agreement ("MOA") executed between FHWA, the State Historic Preservation Officer, and ConnDOT.

* * *

II. The Administrative Record

The parties agree that this Court's review of FHWA's actions is limited to the administrative record that was before the agency at the time it approved the Interchange Project. *See Overton Park,* 401 U.S. at 420, 91 S.Ct. 814 ("[R]eview is to be based on the full administrative record that was before the Secretary at the time he made his [Section 4(f)] decision."). *** After the Court identified several troubling gaps in the administrative record at oral argument—gaps acknowledged by FHWA—Defendants moved to supplement the record with *** files *** inadvertently omitted from the initial designation of the record. ***

Courts considering the appropriate scope of an administrative record must strike a balance between two often competing interests. On the one hand, *** "[t]he focal point for judicial review should be the administrative record already in existence, not some new record made initially in the reviewing court." *Camp v. Pitts,* 411 U.S. 138, 142, 93 S.Ct. 1241, 36 L.Ed.2d 106 (1973). On the other hand, courts must protect the public interest in ensuring that agencies do not ignore inconvenient information or "skew the record ... by excluding pertinent but unfavorable information," *Fund for Animals v. Williams,* 391 F.Supp.2d 191, 197 (D.D.C.2005) ***. These interests are both satisfied by holding that "[t]he complete administrative record consists of all documents and materials directly or indirectly considered by the agency," *Bar MK Ranches v. Yuetter,* 994 F.2d 735, 739 (10th Cir.1993) (emphasis added)[.] *** Applying this approach to the lengthy collaboration between FHWA and ConnDOT on the Interchange Project, the Court concludes that all ConnDOT records relating to the joint federal-state Interchange Project should be considered part of the administrative record before the FHWA.

Unfortunately, it appears that a number of pertinent documents in ConnDOT's custody were omitted from the record as originally submitted to the Court, and Defendants have requested that they be allowed to supplement the record to make good this oversight. *** To be clear, FHWA and ConnDOT seek only to add documents created contemporaneously with the development of the Interchange Project and kept in ConnDOT's files. There is no request to introduce extra-record evidence such as technical reports that ConnDOT and FHWA should have considered but did not, or post-hoc justifications for inadequately reasoned past decisions. ***

As Plaintiffs concede, "[t]he designation of the Administrative Record ... is entitled to a presumption of administrative regularity ... absent clear evidence to the contrary." *Overton Park,* 401 U.S. at 416, 91 S.Ct. 814. *** Defendants in their papers have expressly represented to the Court that "the records sought to be added were all in existence prior to this suit and among the documents reviewed by [Conn]DOT and FHWA when they were performing their Environmental Assessment and Section 4(f) Evaluation." *** In view of the presumption of regularity that attaches to this explanation, and the Court's prior conclusion that all ConnDOT documents relating to the Interchange Project are properly considered part of the administrative record, the Court GRANTS Defendants' Joint Motion to Supplement Administrative Record ***

III. Findings of Fact

* * *

A. The Merritt Parkway

The Merritt Parkway is a thirty-eight mile stretch of scenic highway running east from the New York State line in Greenwich, Connecticut, to the Housatonic River. As a result of a variety of unique architectural, engineering, and historic features, including seventy-two bridges in a variety of modern architectural styles (sixty-five of which are formally listed as "contributing factors" to the historic significance of the Parkway), the Merritt Parkway was listed on the National Register of Historic Places in 1991. That designation brought the Merritt Parkway within the protective ambit of Section 106 of National Historic Preservation Act, 16 U.S.C. §470f, and hence Section 4(f) of the Department of Transportation Act. Of the numerous bridges on the Merritt Parkway, three are located within the area of the Interchange Project: the Main Avenue Bridge, a classical revival, rustic design stone arch bridge over Main Avenue that was listed as a contributing element to the historic value of the Merritt Parkway in the 1991 nomination of the Parkway for the National Register; the Norwalk River Bridge, a triple-arched concrete bridge across the Norwalk River; and a concrete skew-span bridge over the Metro North right of way, west of the Norwalk River. All three of these bridges date to between 1936 and 1938. In addition, the Interchange Project will also affect the stone-arched Glover Avenue Bridge, which is not on the Parkway but is independently eligible for listing on the National Register of Historic Places and therefore is subject to the requirements of Section 4(f).

In 1994, ConnDOT developed comprehensive planning, maintenance, and landscaping specifications for the Parkway, namely the Merritt Parkway Landscape Master Plan and the Merritt Parkway Guidelines for General Maintenance and Transportation Improvements. These were followed at some point before 1999 by the Merritt Parkway Conservation and Restoration Plan: Bridge Restoration Guide. *** In order to monitor compliance with the Merritt Parkway Guidelines, ConnDOT also created the Merritt Parkway Advisory Committee ("MPAC")[.] ***

B. The Interchange Project

The current controversy arises from ConnDOT's plans to improve traffic flow and safety by reconstructing the interchange between the Merritt Parkway and Main Avenue in Norwalk, and by creating in the same area what the FHWA described at oral argument as a "massive interchange" providing full access from all directions between the Merritt Parkway and U.S. Route 7. The Interchange Project has a lengthy history dating back over thirty years, to a time when the Merritt Parkway was not listed on the National Register of Historic Places, and when design plans were not subject to review for compliance with Section 4(f) or the Guidelines.

* * *

F. The Final [Environmental Assessment (EA)]

In December 2000, two-and-a-half years after publication of the Draft EA, and one year after execution of the MOA, FHWA released its Final EA / Section 4(f) Evaluation for the Interchange Project ("Final EA"). The Final EA acknowledged ConnDOT's decision not to move forward with the Freeway Extension project. Instead, ConnDOT would proceed with a so-called Widening Alternative, which "represent[ed] a substantial reduction in environmental impacts compared with the Freeway [Extension] Alternative ... [and] the best balance of transportation service, protection of sensitive environmental resources, and cost." ***

The Final EA again explicitly pointed out that the Glover Avenue Bridge would be replaced. It also noted that "[i]mpacts to other bridges cannot be avoided *** because the project includes the construction of new ramps ***." *Id.* at 23. However, as in the Draft EA and the Section 106 documentation, and by contrast with the discussion of the Glover Avenue Bridge, the Final EA never mentioned the fact that the plans for the Interchange Project required the demolition of the Main Avenue Bridge, that the Project had rejected a five-lane alternative in favor of a six-lane alternative for Main Street, or why.

Like the Draft EA and the Section 106 documentation, the Final EA contained no description of any efforts the parties had already undertaken to minimize or mitigate harm to the Merritt Parkway. Instead, the Final EA again deferred assessment of the likely impacts and the appropriate mitigation pending final design detailing. *Id.* at 21. Accordingly, the Final EA stated that "modifications to the Merritt Parkway *will be evaluated for consistency with* the Merritt Parkway Master Landscape Plan ... and the Merritt Parkway Guidelines for General Maintenance and Transportation Improvements," *id.* at 28 (italics in original omitted; emphasis added), that "*[d]uring development of the build alternatives,* measures to avoid impacts to existing cultural and natural resources ... *will be investigated,*" *id.* ***

On January 30, 2001, just six weeks after the Final EA had asserted that final design detailing had not been completed and had stated that "development of the build alternatives" would be "investigated," ConnDOT wrote to FHWA requesting approval for the design of the Interchange Project. During that six-week period there is nothing in the administrative record that shows that any build alternatives were being developed, let alone investigated for compliance with the Merritt Parkway Guidelines. Nevertheless, the Division Administrator of FHWA signed his concurrence to the design plan on February 1, 2001. ***

Plaintiffs assert that this action by the Division Administrator constituted final approval of the Interchange Project for purposes of Section 4(f) analysis. However, FHWA points out that ConnDOT-requested exceptions to the design standards for the project as late as November 2001, *** and only submitted plans characterized as 90% final in December 2001[.] *** As a result, FHWA insists that its approval of the final design of the Interchange Project did not occur until December 2001. *** The Court regrets the lack of clarity on this critical issue of the date of final design approval given how important that date is to the Section 4(f) process. Nonetheless, a presumption of regularity attaches to agency representations and decisions. *** Therefore, in view of this presumption of regularity, the Court is willing to give Defendants the benefit of the doubt and accept their contention that the final design approval came in December 2001, not in February.

* * *

IV. Summary Judgment

* * *

As explained below, because the record does not demonstrate that FHWA ever determined that the Interchange Project, as finally designed and approved, complied with Section 4(f), nor ever ensured that the commitments it had made in the MOA had been fulfilled, the Court concludes that a remand is appropriate on the Section 4(f) claim. With respect to Plaintiffs' remaining claims the Court concludes that it need not, and accordingly does not, reach Plaintiffs' alternative grounds for the identical relief under NEPA and NHPA. ***

A. Section 4(f) of the Department of Transportation Act ***

Notably, whereas "Section 106, like NEPA, is essentially a procedural statute," "section 4(f) … imposes a substantive mandate on the Administration: It prohibits the agency from taking an action that 'uses' a historic resource unless there is 'no prudent and feasible alternative to using that land' and the agency engages in 'all possible planning' to 'minimize harm' to the sites." *City of Alexandria v. Slater,* 198 F.3d 862, 871 (D.C.Cir. 1999). Furthermore, the "substantive mandate," *id.,* imposed by Section 4(f) is "stringent," *Stop H-3 Ass'n v. Dole,* 740 F.2d 1442, 1447 (9th Cir. 1984).

Plaintiffs concede that there is no prudent and feasible alternative that avoids all impact to the Merritt Parkway, so their challenge is not mounted under Section 4(f)(1). Instead, Plaintiffs allege that FHWA violated the Section 4(f)(2) requirement to ensure that the Project included all possible planning to minimize harm to protected historic resources. The Second Circuit has held that "[t]he affirmative duty to minimize the damage to [historic resources] is a condition precedent to approval for such a taking for highway purposes where federal funds are involved; and the Secretary must withhold his approval unless and until he is satisfied that there has been, in the words of the statute, 'all possible planning to minimize harm.'" *Monroe County Conservation Council v. Volpe,* 472 F.2d 693, 700–01 (2d Cir. 1972). Thus, to satisfy the substantive mandate of Section 4(f)(2), the record must indicate that FHWA ensured that the Interchange Project "minimized harm" to the Merritt Parkway prior to final approval.

Section 4(f)(2) itself does not elaborate on what constitutes "all possible planning to minimize harm." However, case law and FHWA publications indicate that the duty to minimize harm has two components. First, harm minimization requires FHWA to consider alternatives that result in less or less-drastic use of a Section 4(f) resource. *** This does not mean that FHWA must choose the alternative that does the least harm to protected areas using any means technically possible. "Although there is no express feasible and prudent exception to subsection (2), the act clearly implies that one is present." *** Thus, an alternative that minimizes harm can still be rejected if it is infeasible or imprudent. ***

Second, harm minimization requires "mitigation measures that compensate for residual impacts." *** In other words, whatever harm cannot be avoided by choosing between construction alternatives should be mitigated by design choices within the chosen construction option. Thus, if the only feasible construction plan requires removal of historic features, mitigation measures should be considered. Both aspects of FHWA's duty under Section 4(f)(2)—assessment of alternatives and consideration of minimization measures—are reflected in the commitments FHWA made in the MOA and the Final EA to investigate build alternatives to avoid impact to existing resources, to evaluate modifications for consistency with the Merritt Parkway Guidelines, and to ensure compliance with the Guidelines to the extent feasible.

FHWA's determination that the approved Interchange Project included all possible planning to minimize harm is reviewable under the arbitrary and capricious standard of the Administrative Procedure Act ("APA"), 5 U.S.C. §706(2)(A). *** Under this standard, "the power of a court in effectuating the purpose of judicial review ... is narrowly drawn. Courts must defer to the action taken by the agency, which is presumed to be valid." *** [A]lthough "the Secretary's decision [to approve highway route] is entitled to a presumption of regularity ... that presumption is not to shield his action from a thorough, probing, in-depth review ... consider[ing] whether the decision was based on a consideration of the relevant factors." *Overton Park,* 401 U.S. at 415–16, 91 S.Ct. 814 (internal citations omitted). Although FHWA need not have "consider[ed] in detail each and every conceivable variation of the alternatives stated," *** FHWA must set forth alternatives "sufficient[ly] to permit a reasoned choice," ***. So long as the record is adequate to "insure that there was consideration of the relevant factors and [no] clear error of judgment," in FHWA's decision, *** FHWA's "determination[ ] that a particular plan minimizes harm ... deserves even greater deference than [an] agency determination concerning practicable alternatives," *Conservation Law Foundation v. Federal Highway Administration,* 24 F.3d 1465, 1476–77 (1st Cir. 1994).

B.

Under the deferential standard of review and legal principles that guide this Court's review, FHWA needed only to present the Court with an administrative record tying its decision to approve the final design of the Interchange Project to facts indicating: (1) that the feasibility and prudence of alternative construction designs with less impact on the Merritt Parkway had been evaluated; and (2) that mitigation measures compensating for residual impacts had been complied with to the extent feasible. Unfortunately, the administrative record supplied to the Court does not show that FHWA complied with these requirements.

With respect to the requirement that alternative designs be considered as a means of minimizing harm, neither the Draft nor Final EA set forth any alternative ways of building the Interchange Project. To the contrary, the Draft and Final EA both candidly admit that, by contrast with the Freeway Extension, the only options considered for the Interchange Project were Build and No-Build. ***

Second, the Court notes that although Section 4(f) itself does not provide for written documentation of the basis for FHWA's conclusion that Section 4(f) has been satisfied, FHWA's Section 4(f) implementing regulations require that "evaluations of alternatives to avoid the use of section 4(f) land and of possible measures to minimize harm to such lands shall be developed by the applicant in cooperation with the Administration … *[and] presented in the draft EIS [or] EA.*" 23 C.F.R. § 771.135(i) (emphasis added). ***

The mere presence in the record of documents from which FHWA *might* have concluded that the requirements of Section 4(f)(2) had been met does not allow the Court to infer that FHWA in fact so concluded. Quite simply, this Court "is not empowered to substitute its judgment for that of the agency." *SPARC,* 352 F.3d at 558. *** But before the Court can defer to the agency, "the agency must provide an adequate explanation for its actions, … [and] the explanation must show a rational connection between the facts found and the choice made," and "the required explanation must be articulated by the agency at the time of its action." *Inova Alexandria Hosp. v. Shalala,* 244 F.3d 342, 350 (4th Cir. 2001). ***

Section 4(f)(2) requires FHWA to have considered alternative ways of constructing the Interchange Project that would minimize harm to the Merritt Parkway. It may be that all such designs would have been extraordinarily expensive or utterly inadequate to meet traffic flow and safety needs, and thus infeasible and imprudent under Section 4(f)(1), but nothing in the record tells the Court whether FHWA in fact reached such a conclusion, or on what basis, and the Court may not scour the record to reach conclusions that FHWA itself may or may not have made.

* * *

What we know, I think, from the record is this: … the Guidelines were considered at meetings … there's a final design and we know that the final design, at least in certain respects, doesn't comply with the Guidelines, but the piece that's missing … is the piece that shows that there was an informed decision that [we] cannot comply with this guideline because it's infeasible for these reasons.

* * *

In the end, the best that can be said is that the administrative record demonstrates—as FHWA's counsel so commendably and candidly acknowledged at oral argument—"a not-so-good compliance" with Congress's directions in Section 4(f). While FHWA gamely suggested that even "not-so-good compliance" would satisfy its obligations, the Court cannot agree. Unlike the procedural focus of NEPA, Section 4(f) imposes important substantive requirements. *** As the Supreme Court explained in *Overton Park,* Section 4(f) embodies the determination of Congress that a "special effort" be made, that "protection of parkland [and historic resources] … be given paramount importance … [and not] lost unless there were truly unusual factors present in a particular case or the cost or community disruption resulting from alternative [designs] reached extraordinary magnitudes." *Overton Park,* 401 U.S. at 413–14, 91

S.Ct. 814. Where the administrative record contains no evidence that FHWA, after considering all relevant factors, concluded that the feasibility of less harmful construction options had been evaluated and that the commitment to comply with the Guidelines to the extent feasible had been fulfilled, the Court simply cannot conclude, as it must, that FHWA "acted with [its] thumb on the scale, conscious of the importance of protecting the lands listed in the statute." *Eagle Foundation, Inc. v. Dole,* 813 F.2d 798, 803 (7th Cir. 1987).

Accordingly, the Court concludes that FHWA has not met its Section 4(f)(2) obligation to ensure that all possible planning was done to minimize harm prior to approving the Interchange Project. ***

V. Remedy

Because it is not for the Court to substitute its judgment for that of FHWA, or "infring[e] upon the agency's decisions in areas where it has expertise," *National Audubon Society v. Hoffman,* 132 F.3d 7, 19 (2d Cir. 1997), "the appropriate remedy is to remand the case to the agency to correct the deficiencies in the record and in its analysis," *id.* at 18. ***

*** If preparation of an adequate Section 4(f) evaluation in accordance with the will of Congress is not to be "a hollow exercise," *Chelsea Neighbor. Ass'n. v. U.S. Postal Service,* 389 F.Supp. 1171, 1186 (S.D.N.Y. 1975), construction should not proceed until FHWA has had an opportunity to assess whether the current design of the Interchange Project embodies all possible planning to minimize harm to the Merritt Parkway and that the Merritt Parkway Guidelines have been complied with to the extent feasible. *** Construction may go forward as soon as FHWA cures the defects in its compliance with Section 4(f)(2). ***

Notes and Questions

1. **Scope of review issues.** The Court, while deferential to the responsibilities of the FHWA, finds against the agency. a. Why was the ruling restrained? b. Given such a glaring failure to comply with the requirements of Section 4(f), would a stern chastisement likely lead to better compliance on remand? The court explained that what was missing was evidence that the agency consciously considered alternatives and designs for mitigation. c. What must such an evaluation include? What sorts of harms besides destruction of the historic bridges must be considered?

2. **Value of documenting review.** In *Citizens to Preserve Overton Park, Inc.*, the Supreme Court ruled that Section 4(f) did not require any particular written findings. Do the challenges and ruling in this case argue for documenting the Section 4(f) review, not only to ensure agency compliance, but also for meaningful court review?

3. **Rethinking designs.** Since this decision, the CDOT has considered no fewer than 15 different designs. In 2015, Governor Dannel Malloy announced a plan calling for $200 million to overhaul the Merritt Parkway/Route 7 interchange, including among other things building final connections to and from the Route 7 connector and enhancing the Main Avenue/Merritt Parkway interchange.

River Fields, Inc. v. Mary Peters

United States District Court, W.D. Kentucky
2009 U.S. Dist. LEXIS 63620 (July 23, 2009)

Charles R. Simpson III, J. [Various homeowners associations challenged a decision by the U.S. Department of Transportation and local governments to widen to two-lanes the historic Harrods Creek Bridge, a one-lane bridge carrying the River Road Scenic Byway over Harrods Creek in the Upper River Road area of Louisville, Kentucky ("Harrods Creek Bridge Project," or the "Project"). The Bridge was both individually eligible for listing in the National Register of Historic Places ("National Register"), and also as a contributing element to the National Register-eligible River Road Historic District, nestled within a collection of other National Register-listed historic districts, and adjacent to several individually listed National Register historic properties. The plaintiffs maintained that the government (the Secretary of Transportation and the Federal Highway Administration) failed to comply with, among other things, Section 4(f) of the Department of Transportation Act ("Section 4(f)"), 23 U.S.C. § 138, 49 U.S.C. § 303 when it executed a programmatic Section 4(f) approval in lieu of preparing an individual Section 4(f) evaluation.]

* * *

Section 4(f) provides, in pertinent part:

> [T]he Secretary may approve a transportation program or project ... requiring the use of publicly owned land of a public park, recreation area, or wildlife and waterfowl refuge of national, State, or local significance, or land of an historic site of national, State, or local significance (as determined by the Federal, State, or local officials having jurisdiction over the park, area, refuge, or site) only if—(1) there is no prudent and feasible alternative to using that land; and (2) the program or project includes all possible planning to minimize harm to the park, recreation area, wildlife and waterfowl refuge, or historic site resulting from the use. 49 U.S.C. § 303; 23 U.S.C. § 138. Under FHWA regulations, determinations approving the use of Section 4(f) property "shall include sufficient supporting documentation to demonstrate why there is no feasible and prudent avoidance alternative and shall summarize the results of all possible planning to minimize harm to the Section 4(f) property." 23 C.F.R. § 774.7(a). * * *

The FHWA has adopted several "[p]rogrammatic Section 4(f) evaluations ... a time-saving procedural alternative to preparing individual Section 4(f) evaluations under [23 C.F.R. § 774.7(a)] for certain minor uses of Section 4(f) property." 23 C.F.R. § 774.7(d). The programmatic Section 4(f) evaluations implicated here are the "Historic Bridges" and "Minor Involvement with Historic Sites" Programmatic Section 4(f) Evaluations.[9] "The determination whether a programmatic Section

9. Historic Bridges; Programmatic Section 4(f) Evaluation and Approval, 48 Fed. Reg. 38,135 (Aug. 22, 1983); Nationwide Section 4(f) Evaluations and Approvals for Federally-Aided Highway

4(f) evaluation applies to the use of a specific Section 4(f) property shall be documented as specified in the applicable programmatic Section 4(f) evaluation." 23 C.F.R. § 774.3(d)(1). Both the Historic Bridges and Minor Involvement with Historic Sites Programmatic Section 4(f) Evaluations make clear that "[t]he programmatic Section 4(f) evaluation does not apply if a reasonable alternative is identified that is not discussed in this document." Historic Bridges Programmatic Section 4(f) Evaluation at 38,139. "If the project facts do not fall within the applicability criteria of the programmatic evaluation or if any of the conditions of the programmatic evaluation are not met, then an individual Section 4(f) evaluation is required." Minor Involvement with Historic Sites Programmatic Section 4(f) Evaluation at 31,111.

The FHWA utilized the Historic Bridges and Minor Involvement with Historic Sites Programmatic Section 4(f) Evaluations to determine approval for the use of historic sites for the Harrods Creek Bridge Project. Plaintiffs allege that the FHWA failed to consider their reasonable "Enhanced One-Lane Bridge Alternative," and that the impact of the Project on historic sites is not minor. Therefore, Plaintiffs assert that the FHWA is required to prepare an individual Section 4(f) evaluation for the Project. Defendants assert that they have fully complied with the requirements of Section 4(f).* * *

DISCUSSION

Standards of Review

The ... decision[] made by the FHWA challenged by Plaintiffs here [is] subject to judicial review pursuant to the Administrative Procedure Act, 5 U.S.C. § 704, et seq. The standard of review is whether the agency decisions are "arbitrary, capricious, an abuse of discretion, or otherwise not in accordance with law." *Camp v. Pitts*, 411 U.S. 138, 142, 93 S. Ct. 1241, 36 L. Ed. 2d 106 (1973).* * *

In reviewing the FHWA's Section 4(f) decision, the court's role is to decide: (1) Whether the FHWA acted within the scope of its authority; (2) Whether the FHWA's decision was based on a consideration of the relevant factors and whether there has been a clear error of judgment; and (3) Whether the FHWA's action followed the necessary procedural requirements. *Citizens to Preserve Overton Park, Inc. v. Volpe*, 401 U.S. 402, 415–17, 91 S. Ct. 814, 28 L. Ed. 2d 136 (1971).

The court "is not to determine the *correctness*, in some ultimate sense, of an agency's actions. A reviewing court is limited to determining only the *legality* of the challenged action." *Di Vosta Rentals, Inc. v. Lee*, 488 F.2d 674, 678 (5th Cir. 1973) (emphasis in original). The court may not substitute its judgment for that of the agency. *Vermont Yankee Nuclear Power Corp. v. Natural Res. Def. Council*, 435 U.S. 519, 98 S. Ct. 1197, 55 L. Ed. 2d 460 (1978); *Overton Park*, 401 U.S. 402, 91 S. Ct. 814, 28 L. Ed. 2d 136 (1971).

Projects With Minor Involvement With Public Parks, Recreation Lands, Wildlife and Waterfowl Refuges, and Historic Sites, 52 Fed. Reg. 31,111 (Aug. 19, 1987).

Section 4(f)

Plaintiffs allege that the FHWA violated Section 4(f) by approving the use of historic sites for the Project based on programmatic Section 4(f) evaluations, which Plaintiffs argue do not apply. Plaintiffs argue that the Historic Bridges Programmatic Section 4(f) Evaluation does not apply because the FHWA failed to consider Plaintiffs' Enhanced One-Lane Bridge Alternative. Plaintiffs argue that the Enhanced One-Lane Bridge Alternative is a reasonable alternative to the widening of the Bridge and therefore an individual Section 4(f) evaluation is required to determine whether the Enhanced One-Lane Bridge Alternative is feasible and prudent. 23 C.F.R. §§774.3(a), (d). The Enhanced One-Lane Bridge Alternative would include the following elements: (1) rehabilitation of the Bridge as a one-lane bridge in accordance with the U.S. Secretary of the Interior Standards; (2) resurfacing and other measures to extend the useful life of the Bridge; (3) repair of guardrails and implementation of other measures such as appropriate signage and roadway markings to enhance the safety of the Bridge; and (4) only if demonstrably necessary, traffic control devices and/or illumination to reduce the chance of accidents on the Bridge.

Defendants assert that the Enhanced One-Lane Bridge Alternative is no different from the one-lane rehabilitation option that Plaintiffs previously advocated and therefore offers nothing new. Defendants rejected the one-lane rehabilitation alternative during the [the National Historic Preservation Act] Section 106 process because it would not improve safety. Defendants explain that, for example, any rehabilitation of the Bridge, whether one-lane or two, would necessarily include appropriate signage and roadway markings consistent with state and federal safety and design standards. *See* 23 C.F.R. §650.405(b)(2).

Whether the Enhanced One-Lane Bridge Alternative is "new" or not, Plaintiffs argue that the FHWA's rejection of a one-lane alternative was arbitrary and capricious. Plaintiffs argue that the FHWA rejected their one-lane bridge alternative based solely on Defendants' unfounded assertion that one-lane bridges are inherently unsafe. Plaintiffs also argue that Defendants' own traffic accident information for the Bridge belies the contention that one-lane bridges are unsafe. In fact, Defendants' data shows that traffic accidents on the Bridge have not only been historically few and far between but minor, as well. Plaintiffs argue that the data demonstrates that the traffic-calming effect of the one-lane Bridge is integral to safety. Plaintiffs further argue that Defendants' own consultant report supports the one-lane rehabilitation option. Defendants' One-Lane Bridge Safety Report states that "The use of standard traffic control devices in a uniform manner, based on an analysis of the driver's task at the specific bridge location, is the proper means for restructuring driver expectancies and is the best solution short of reconstruction."

One-lane bridges may not be inherently unsafe and traffic control devices may improve safety on them. However, the issue here is not, as Plaintiffs suggest, "whether an acceptable degree of public safety on a one-lane bridge can be achieved utilizing measures such as lane marking, signage, lighting and traffic control devices." The only issue here is whether the FHWA abused its discretion by finding that a one-lane rehabilitation of the Harrods Creek Bridge was not a reasonable alternative to the Project. The court concludes that the FHWA did not abuse its discretion in so finding.

Defendants previously rejected the one-lane bridge alternative for the straightforward reason that it would not improve safety. Despite the summary appearance of various conclusions in the CE Checklist, there is ample evidence in the administrative record to support the FHWA's conclusion that the one-lane bridge alternative would not improve safety. It is evident that the FHWA relied on Defendants' traffic studies and reports. Most notably, the One-Lane Bridge Safety Report unambiguously concluded that while traffic control devices can improve safety on a narrow bridge, they are only the best solution in instances short of reconstruction.

Plaintiffs focus on the finding that traffic control devices can improve safety on narrow bridges. However, the report states that this means of safety improvement is "the best solution short of (thus, meaning alternative to) reconstruction." The FHWA determined that reconstruction to widen the bridge deck to two-lanes was the preferred alternative for the Bridge because the current structure with two-lane approaches at both ends creates a likelihood of collision, noting that:

> The western approach has a horizontal curve with insufficient sight distance which increase [sic] the likelihood of rear end collisions. For the period April 2000 to March 2003 there were 7 rear end collisions. In addition because the approach roadway is two-lanes there is the potential for head-on collision. There was one documented head on collision on the bridge in August 2002.

The conclusion that the preferred alternative is reconstruction to widen the deck is supported by the One-Lane Bridge Safety Report, which included data showing that "one-lane bridges, where the bridge is more narrow than the approach roadway, create an unsafe condition with potential hazardous consequences for motorists using River Road." Therefore, no one-lane bridge alternative solves the safety concerns found by the FHWA. The preferred alternative of reconstruction is fully supported in the record. * * *

The FHWA acted within the scope of its authority in executing the programmatic Section 4(f) approvals because there was no prudent and feasible alternative to the Project and the Project includes all possible planning to minimize harm to historic sites resulting from the Project. The FHWA's decision was based on a consideration of the relevant factors and was neither arbitrary nor capricious. The FHWA followed the necessary procedural requirements. Accordingly, Plaintiffs have failed to show any valid reason why the Harrods Creek Bridge Project should not proceed. * * *

Notes and Questions

1. **Historic bridges and highways.** Bridges are integral elements of the transportation system and historic bridges raise special issues in the fulfillment of our transportation needs. The most significant challenge is striking a balance between preserving excep-

tional examples of our historic infrastructure while meeting modern engineering standards. Historic bridge research has focused on: "historic context development, historic bridge inventories, management and preservation plans, and rehabilitation practices." Antony F. Opperman, Hope E. Luhman, Emily Pettis, and Stephanie Stoermer, *Transportation and Historic Preservation: Progress and Research*, 262 TR News 25, 27 (May–June 2009). A recent survey of states revealed the most common obstacle to accommodation to be the inflexibility of the American Association of State Highway and Transportation Officials standards, while adhering to the Secretary of the Interior's *Standards for Treatment of Historic Properties*. Parsons-Brinckerhoff and Engineering and Industrial Heritage: A Context for Common Historic Bridge Types. Final Report, NCHRP Project 25-25, Task 15, Transportation Research Board of the National Academies, 2005, www.trb.org/NotesDocs/25-25%2815%29_FR.pdf (last visited March 25, 2017).

Among other things, historic bridges often have existing conditions, such as substandard bridge width or sidewalk width, that if updated to meet modern engineering standards, and vehicular load capacity, may result in an adverse effect on their historic features. Bridge design features like metal trusses and masonry arches cannot be widened or rehabilitated for higher load capacity without adversely affecting the bridge. In some cases, reconstruction of stone masonry, reinforcement of cores, and replacing girder connections may be employed to achieve safety requirements while preserving aesthetics. Sometimes, exceptions or variances can be employed for preservation outcomes that avoid adverse effects. Many states have executed Programmatic Agreements that outline the process for complying with federal regulations for cultural resources and implementation of the Federal-Aid Highway Program. *See* Historic Bridge Rehabilitation and Approaches to Programmatic Agreements, Summary and Analysis of Current Practices Nationwide 2014, www.meadhunt.com/data/publications/HistoricBridgeRehabandPACurrentPracticesNationwide.pdf (last visited March 25, 2017).

The strong interest in the rehabilitation of bridges is reflected in *Guidelines for Rehabilitation and Replacement.* Final Report NCHRP Project 25-25, Task 19, Transportation Research Board of the National Academies, 2007. What is emerging is the "awareness that the aesthetics of new bridges in historic areas can benefit from context-sensitive solutions," as well as a willingness of engineers to engage in a dialogue with historic preservation professionals. *Id.* at 27.

2. **Deference to the agency.** This case shows the considerable degree of deference courts give to the agency decision; that it is largely irrelevant if opponents have developed a far better plan, so long as the one chosen is not arbitrary.

3. **Mimicking.** Among the measures the FHWA determined to employ to minimize the impact on the historic values at risk was to "mimic the original in appearance and materials and vegetation that [would be] removed [and would] be replaced in accordance with a landscape plan." a. Will the recreated bridge be historic? b. Will it serve to remind us of olden times when travel was of a wholly different kind—slower and not mechanical?

4. **Programmatic evaluations.** While they aim to streamline and make more predictable the outcomes in the evaluation, there is also a likelihood that some things might be left out. The *Programmatic Section 4(f) Evaluation and Approval for FHWA Projects that Necessitate the Use of Historic Bridges* states that it is applicable in cases where the "FHWA Division Administrator determines that the facts of the project match those set forth in the sections of this document labeled Alternatives, Findings, and Mitigation," which includes:

1. Do nothing;
2. Build a new structure at a different location without affecting the historic integrity of the old bridge, as determined by procedures implementing the NHPA;
3. Rehabilitate the historic bridge without affecting the historic integrity of the structure, as determined by procedures implementing the NHPA.

And

1. For bridges that are to be rehabilitated, the historic integrity of the bridge is preserved, to the greatest extent possible, consistent with unavoidable transportation needs, safety, and load requirements;
2. For bridges that are to be rehabilitated to the point that the historic integrity is affected or that are to be moved or demolished, the FHWA ensures that, in accordance with the Historic American Engineering Record (HAER) standards, or other suitable means developed through consultation, fully adequate records are made of the bridge;
3. For bridges that are to be replaced, the existing bridge is made available for an alternative use, provided a responsible party agrees to maintain and preserve the bridge; and
4. For bridges that are adversely affected, agreement among the SHPO, ACHP, and FHWA is reached through the Section 106 process of the NHPA on measures to minimize harm and those measures are incorporated into the project. This programmatic Section 4(f) evaluation does not apply to projects where such an agreement cannot be reached.

5. **Suitability of programmatic agreement.** a. Does the peculiar configuration of the bridge here suggest that it might not be appropriate for the programmatic evaluation? b. Should the court rule on the determination to use the programmatic evaluation, as well as the general Section 4(f) analysis? c. Would the outcome have been any different?

6. **Recording engineering landmarks.** Engineering landmarks are recorded by the American Society of Mechanical Engineers ("ASME"). https://www.asme.org/about-asme/engineering-history/landmarks (last visited March 31, 2017). The American Society of Civil Engineers ("ASCE") designates Historic Civil Engineering Landmarks. http://www.asce.org/landmarks/#/e6ea0cd2d528ba2f3cdec3a624404fef (last visited March 30, 2017). These important specialized landmarks registries are not congruent with the National Register of Historic Places. a. Should they be? Grand Central Terminal is listed by the ASCE for its integration of roads and rails, which since 1913

continues to work smoothly. *See* http://www.asce.org/project/grand-central-terminal/ (last visited March 30, 2017). b. Should technological excellence be a factor for bridges listed on the National Register?

E. Native American Graves Protection and Repatriation Act

Bonnichsen v. United States (The Kennewick Man Case)

United States Court of Appeals, Ninth Circuit
367 F.3d 864, 04 Cal.Daily.Op.Serv. 3365 (2004)

Gould, C.J. This is a case about the ancient human remains of a man who hunted and lived, or at least journeyed, in the Columbia Plateau an estimated 8340 to 9200 years ago, a time predating all recorded history from any place in the world, a time before the oldest cities of our world had been founded, a time so ancient that the pristine and untouched land and the primitive cultures that may have lived on it are not deeply understood by even the most well-informed men and women of our age. Seeking the opportunity of study, a group of scientists as Plaintiffs[1] in this case brought an action against, *inter alia*, the United States Department of the Interior, challenging various Indian tribes'[2] claim to one of the most important American anthropological and archaeological discoveries of the late twentieth century, and challenging the Interior Department's decision honoring the tribes' claim. The discovery that launched this contest was that of a human skeleton, estimated by carbon dating to be 8340 to 9200 years old, known popularly and commonly as "Kennewick Man," but known as "the Ancient One" to some American Indians[3] who now inhabit regions in Washington, Idaho, and Oregon, roughly proximate to the site on the Columbia River at Kennewick, Washington, where the bones were found. From the perspective of the scientists Plaintiffs, this skeleton is an irreplaceable source of information about early New World populations that warrants careful scientific inquiry to advance knowledge of distant times. Yet, from the perspective of the intervenor-Indian tribes the skeleton is that of an ancestor who, according to the tribes' religious and social traditions, should be buried immediately without further testing.

1. Plaintiffs are experts in their respective fields. Plaintiff Bonnichsen is Director of the Center for the Study of the First Americans at Oregon State University. Plaintiff Brace is Curator of Biological Anthropology at the University of Michigan Museum of Anthropology. Plaintiffs Gill, Haynes, Jantz, and Steele are anthropology professors. Plaintiff Owsley is division head for physical anthropology at the Smithsonian Institution's National Museum of Natural History. Plaintiff Stanford is Director of the Smithsonian's Paleo Indian Program.

2. The Tribal Claimants—present in this appeal as intervenors—are the Confederated Tribes & Bands of the Yakama Indian Nation, the Nez Perce Tribe of Idaho, the Confederated Tribes of the Umatilla Indian Reservation, and the Confederated Tribes of the Colville Reservation.

3. We use the term "American Indian" because the definition of "Native American," as used in Native American Graves Protection and Repatriation Act, is a disputed issue in this appeal.

Plaintiffs filed this lawsuit seeking to stop the transfer of the skeleton by the government to the tribes for burial, and the district court held in favor of the scientists—Plaintiffs.... The Secretary of the Interior and the intervenor-Indian tribes appeal. We have jurisdiction under 28 U.S.C. § 1291 and affirm the judgment of the district court barring the transfer of the skeleton for immediate burial and instead permitting scientific study of the skeleton.

In July 1996, teenagers going to a boat race discovered a human skull and bones near the shore of the Columbia River just outside Kennewick, Washington ... The remains were found on federal property under the management of the United States Army Corps of Engineers ("Corps") and, at the request of the county coroner, were removed for analysis by an anthropologist, Dr. James Chatters, pursuant to an Archaeological Resources Protection Act of 1979 ("ARPA"), 16 U.S.C. §§ 470aa–470mm, permit. Because of physical features such as the shape of the skull and facial bones, anthropologists at first thought the remains were those of an early European settler. But the anthropologists then found a stone projectile point embedded in the skeleton's upper hip bone. The object's design, when viewed with x-rays and CT scans of the hip, resembled a style that was common before the documented arrival of Europeans in the region. Further study of the remains revealed characteristics unlike those of a European settler, yet also inconsistent with any American Indian remains previously documented in the region. A minute quantity of metacarpal bone was radiocarbon dated. The laboratory estimated the age of the bones to be between 8340 and 9200 years old.[6]

Human skeletons this old are rare in the Western Hemisphere, and most found have consisted of only fragmented remains. *** Dr. Chatters testified in an affidavit: "The Kennewick Man skeleton is virtually intact. It lacks only the sternum and a few small nondiagnostic bones of the hands and the feet. Although some of the ribs and other long bones are fragmented, they can be reconstructed. The skull and the lower jaw are complete and are not deformed. The bones of the skeleton are extremely well preserved, with only minor surface mineralization and little if any evidence of decay."

The skeleton attracted attention because some of its physical features, such as the shape of the face and skull, differed from those of modern American Indians. Many scientists believed the discovery might shed light on the origins of humanity in the Americas. On August 31, 1996, Dr. Douglas Owsley, Division Head for Physical Anthropology at the Smithsonian Institution in Washington, D.C., made arrangements

---

6. Human skeletons this old are rare in the Western Hemisphere, and most found have consisted of only fragmented remains. The record indicates that less than twelve securely dated human crania older than 8000 years have been found in the United States. By contrast, about 90 percent of this skeleton was recovered in good condition. Dr. Chatters testified in an affidavit: "The Kennewick Man skeleton is virtually intact. It lacks only the sternum and a few small nondiagnostic bones of the hands and the feet. Although some of the ribs and other long bones are fragmented, they can be reconstructed. The skull and the lower jaw are complete and are not deformed. The bones of the skeleton are extremely well preserved, with only minor surface mineralization and little if any evidence of decay."

for Dr. Chatters to bring this important find to the Smithsonian's National Museum of Natural History for further study....

Indian tribes from the area of the Columbia River opposed scientific study of the remains on religious and social grounds.[8] Four Indian groups (the "Tribal Claimants") demanded that the remains be turned over to them for immediate burial. The Tribal Claimants based their demand on the Native American Graves Protection and Repatriation Act ("NAGPRA"), 25 U.S.C. § 3001 *et seq.* The Corps agreed with the Tribal Claimants and, citing NAGPRA, seized the remains on September 10, 1996, shortly before they could be transported to the Smithsonian. The Corps also ordered an immediate halt to DNA testing, which was being done using the remainder of the bone sample that had been submitted earlier for radiocarbon dating. After investigation, the Corps decided to give the remains to the Tribal Claimants for burial. As required by NAGPRA, the Corps published a "Notice of Intent to Repatriate Human Remains" in a local newspaper on September 17, 1996, and September 24, 1996.

The scientists and others, including the Smithsonian Institution, objected to the Corps' decision, arguing that the remains were a rare discovery of national and international significance. In late September and early October 1996, several scientists asked Major General Ernest J. Herrell, Commander of the Corps' North Pacific Division, to allow qualified scientists to study the remains.

The scientists did not convince the Corps to permit them to study the remains, and commenced this litigation on October 16, 1996, in the United States District Court for the District of Oregon. In an opinion issued June 27, 1997, the district court denied the Corps' motion for summary judgment, finding that the Corps had "acted before it had all of the evidence," "did not fully consider or resolve certain difficult legal questions," and "assumed facts that proved to be erroneous." *Bonnichsen II,* 969 F.Supp. 628, 645 (D.Or.1997). The district court vacated the Corps' earlier decision on disposition of the remains and remanded the case to the Corps for further proceedings. *Id.* at 644–45. The district court also denied, without prejudice, Plaintiffs' motion to study the remains and directed the Corps to consider, on remand, "whether to grant [P]laintiffs' request [under ARPA] for permission to study the remains." *Id.* at 632, 651.

On March 24, 1998, the Corps and the Secretary of the Interior entered into an agreement that effectively assigned to the Secretary responsibility to decide whether

8. For example, the Tribal Claimants urged that "when a body goes into the ground, it is meant to stay there until the end of time. When remains are disturbed and remain above the ground, their spirits are at unrest.... To put these spirits at ease, the remains must be returned to the ground as soon as possible." *Bonnichsen III*, 217 F. Supp. 2d at 1121 (quoting Joint Tribal Amici Memorandum (1997) at 4–5). We note that the Ethnic Minority Council of America, in its *amicus* brief, urges that: "Potential descendants [of Kennewick Man] may not be members of the Joint Tribal Claimants or believe in the expressed 'Indian' religious interpretations made by the political leaders of the tribes." Further, as suggested by *amicus* Ohio Archaeological Council, in the absence of a conclusive determination of cultural affiliation, the Tribal Claimants cannot establish that permitting Plaintiffs-scientists to study the Kennewick Man's remains offends their religious views or customs.

the remains were "Native American" under NAGPRA, and to determine their proper disposition. The Department of the Interior then assumed the role of lead agency on this case.

Almost two years after this matter was remanded, the Secretary's experts began to examine the remains in detail. The experts estimated that Kennewick Man was 5'9" to 5'10" tall, 45 to 50 years of age when he died, and 15 to 20 years old when the projectile point became embedded in his hip. The experts could not determine, from non-destructive examination of the skeleton alone, when Kennewick Man lived. However, analysis of sediment layers where the skeleton was found supported the hypothesis that the remains dated back not less than 7600 years ago and Kennewick Man could have lived more than 9000 years ago (the date indicated by the initial radiocarbon dating of the skeleton). Further study of the sediment was recommended, but the Corps' decision to bury the discovery site in April 1998 prevented completion of those studies.[10]

The experts compared the physical characteristics of the remains—e.g., measurements of the skull, teeth, and bones—with corresponding measurements from other skeletons. They concluded that Kennewick Man's remains were unlike those of any known present-day population, American Indian or otherwise.

The Secretary's experts cautioned, however, that an apparent lack of physical resemblance between the Kennewick Man's remains and present-day American Indians did not completely rule out the possibility that the remains might be biologically ancestral to modern American Indians. Moreover, although Kennewick Man's morphological traits did not closely resemble those of modern American Indian populations, the Secretary's experts noted that Kennewick Man's physical attributes are generally consistent with the very small number of human remains from this period that have been found in North America.

Relying solely on the age of the remains and the fact that the remains were found within the United States, on January 13, 2000, the Secretary pronounced Kennewick Man's remains "Native American" within NAGPRA's meaning. And on September 25, 2000, the Secretary determined that a preponderance of the evidence supported the conclusion that the Kennewick remains were culturally affiliated with present-day Indian tribes. For this reason, the Secretary announced his final decision to award

10. The Corps buried the discovery site of the remains under approximately two million pounds of rubble and dirt, topped with 3700 willow, dogwood, and cottonwood plants. The lengthy administrative record that Defendants filed with the district court documents only a portion of the process by which the decision to bury the site was made. Nevertheless, that record suggested to the district court that the Corps' primary objective in covering the site was to prevent additional remains or artifacts from being discovered, not to "preserve" the site's archaeological value or to remedy a severe erosion control problem as Defendants represented. *Bonnichsen III*, 217 F. Supp. 2d at 1125. Burial of the discovery site hindered efforts to verify the age of Kennewick Man's remains, and effectively ended efforts to determine whether other artifacts are present at the site which might shed light on the relationship between the remains and contemporary American Indians. *Id.* at 1126.

Kennewick Man's remains to a coalition of the Tribal Claimants. The Corps and the Secretary also denied Plaintiffs' request to study the remains.

Plaintiffs filed an amended complaint in the district court challenging the Secretary's decisions. The district court again ruled in Plaintiffs' favor. As pertinent to this appeal, the district court vacated the Secretary's decisions as contrary to the Administrative Procedure Act, 5 U.S.C. § 706(2)(A) ("APA"), on the ground that the Secretary improperly concluded that NAGPRA applies ... *Bonnichsen III,* 217 F.Supp.2d at 1138–39. The district court also held that, because NAGPRA did not apply, Plaintiffs should have the opportunity to study Kennewick Man's remains under ARPA. Defendants and the Tribal Claimants appealed, and we stayed the district court's order granting Plaintiffs—scientists' study of the remains pending our decision herein....

II

We first address an issue of jurisdiction. The Tribal Claimants argue that we lack jurisdiction because: (1) Plaintiffs' alleged injuries are not "redressable" by court action, and (2) Plaintiffs lack standing to bring claims alleging violations of NAGPRA because Plaintiffs do not seek to invoke interests within the "zone of interests" protected by NAGPRA.

A

As a general rule, the three constitutional standing requirements are imposed by the "case" or "controversy" provision of Article III:

> (1) that the plaintiff have suffered an "injury in fact" ...; (2) that there be a causal connection between the injury and the conduct complained of ...; and (3) that it be likely, as opposed to merely speculative, that the injury will be redressed by a favorable decision.

Bennett v. Spear, 520 U.S. 154, 167, 117 S.Ct. 1154, 137 L.Ed.2d 281 (1997). The Tribal Claimants do not dispute that Plaintiffs meet the first two constitutional standing requirements, and we so hold. But the Tribal Claimants argue that Plaintiffs do not meet the third requirement.

* * *

[Even] if NAGPRA does not apply (as we must assume in determining whether Plaintiffs have standing), ARPA applies. Kennewick Man's remains are of archaeological significance and were collected pursuant to an ARPA permit. Neither Appellant disputes that ARPA gives Plaintiffs the opportunity to study Kennewick Man's remains if NAGPRA does not apply. We conclude that it is likely that Plaintiffs' injury will be redressed by a favorable decision on the NAGPRA issue, and thus Plaintiffs have constitutional standing.

B

Second, the Tribal Claimants argue that Plaintiffs lack standing to bring claims alleging violations of NAGPRA because Plaintiffs do not seek to invoke interests within the "zone of interests" that NAGPRA protects. The Tribal Claimants urge that Congress enacted NAGPRA only with the interests of American Indians in mind, so only American Indians or Indian tribes can file suit alleging violations of NAGPRA. We reject this argument.

The "zone of interests" test invoked by the Tribal Claimants is a judge-made "prudential standing requirement," independent of the three immutable constitutional standing requirements of Article III. *** Congress can modify or abrogate the zone of interests test *** and Congress did exactly that in NAGPRA's broadly worded "enforcement" section. That statute, 25 U.S.C. § 3013, provides that "[t]he United States district courts shall have jurisdiction over any action brought by any person alleging a violation of this chapter." Section 3013 by its terms broadly confers jurisdiction on the courts to hear "*any action*" brought by "*any person alleging a violation.*" *Id.* (emphasis added).

The Supreme Court has held that such broad statutory language effectively negates the prudential zone of interests test *** § 3013 of NAGPRA contains the broad "any person" formulation and includes no textual limitation on federal court jurisdiction. Moreover, § 3013 does not contain the more restrictive formulations Congress sometimes uses to limit standing. *** We hold that § 3013 does not limit jurisdiction to suits brought by American Indians or Indian tribes. "Any person" means exactly that, and may not be interpreted restrictively to mean only "any *American Indian* person" or "any Indian Tribe." …

III

Our review of the Secretary's decision to transfer Kennewick Man to the Tribal Claimants is governed by the APA, which instructs courts to "hold unlawful and set aside agency action, findings, and conclusions found to be … arbitrary, capricious, an abuse of discretion, or otherwise not in accordance with law." 5 U.S.C. § 706(2)(A).

NAGPRA vests "ownership or control" of newly discovered Native American human remains in the decedent's lineal descendants or, if lineal descendants cannot be ascertained, in a tribe "affiliated" with the remains. 25 U.S.C. § 3002(a). NAGPRA mandates a two-part analysis. The first inquiry is whether human remains are Native American within the statute's meaning. If the remains *are not* Native American, then NAGPRA does not apply. However, if the remains *are* Native American, then NAGPRA applies, triggering the second inquiry of determining which persons or tribes are most closely affiliated with the remains.

The parties dispute whether the remains of Kennewick Man constitute Native American remains within NAGPRA's meaning. NAGPRA defines human remains as "Native American" if the remains are "of, or relating to, a tribe, people, or culture *that is* indigenous to the United States." 25 U.S.C. § 3001(9) [(emphasis added)]. The text of the relevant statutory clause is written in the present tense *** [t]hus the statute unambiguously requires that human remains bear some relationship to a *presently existing* tribe, people, or culture to be considered Native American.

* * *

In the context of NAGPRA, we conclude that Congress's use of the present tense is significant. *** Congress, by using the phrase "is indigenous" in the present tense, referred to presently existing tribes, peoples, or cultures. We must presume that Congress gave the phrase "is indigenous" its ordinary or natural meaning. *** We conclude that Congress was referring to *presently existing* Indian tribes when it referred to "a tribe, people, or culture *that is* indigenous to the United States." 25 U.S.C. § 3001(9) (emphasis added).

NAGPRA also protects graves of persons not shown to be of current tribes in that it protects disjunctively remains "of, or relating to" current indigenous tribes. Thus, NAGPRA extends to all remains that relate to a tribe, people, or culture that is indigenous to the United States, *see* 25 U.S.C. § 3001(9) (defining human remains as Native American if they are "of, *or relating to,* a tribe, people, or culture that is indigenous to the United States") (emphasis added).

Our conclusion that NAGPRA's language requires that human remains, to be considered Native American, bear some relationship to a presently existing tribe, people, or culture accords with NAGPRA's purposes. As regards newly discovered human remains, NAGPRA was enacted with two main goals: to respect the burial traditions of modern-day American Indians and to protect the dignity of the human body after death. NAGPRA was intended to benefit modern American Indians by sparing them the indignity and resentment that would be aroused by the despoiling of their ancestors' graves and the study or the display of their ancestors' remains. ***

Congress's purposes would not be served by requiring the transfer to modern American Indians of human remains that bear no relationship to them. Yet, that would be the result under the Secretary's construction of the statute, which would give Native American status to any remains found within the United States regardless of age and regardless of lack of connection to existing indigenous tribes.[17] The exhumation, study, and display of ancient human remains that are unrelated to modern American Indians was not a target of Congress's aim, nor was it precluded by NAGPRA.

NAGPRA was also intended to protect the dignity of the human body after death by ensuring that Native American graves and remains be treated with respect. Congress's purpose is served by requiring the return to modern-day American Indians of human remains that bear some significant relationship to them.

---

17. At oral argument, the government urged that its interpretation of remains as Native American when found within the United States would apply even to remains as old as 100,000 or 150,000 years, close to the dawn of *homo sapiens.* Indeed, the government at oral argument even said that if remains of a mythical first man and woman, an "Adam and Eve," were found in the United States, those remains would be "Native American" under the government's interpretation of NAGPRA. Thus the government's unrestricted interpretation based solely on geography, calling any ancient remains found in the United States "Native American" if they pre-date the arrival of Europeans has no principle of limitation beyond geography. This does not appear to us to be what Congress had in mind. Nor does the legislative history support NAGPRA coverage of bones of such great antiquity.

*** Though NAGPRA's two inquiries have some commonality in that both focus on the relationship between human remains and present-day Indians, the two inquiries differ significantly. The first inquiry requires only a general finding that remains have a significant relationship to a presently existing "tribe, people, or culture," a relationship that goes beyond features common to all humanity. The second inquiry requires a more specific finding that remains are most closely affiliated to specific lineal descendants or to a specific Indian tribe. The district court's interpretation of NAGPRA preserves the statute's two distinct inquiries. Because the record shows no relationship of Kennewick Man to the Tribal Claimants, the district court was correct in holding that NAGPRA has no application.

The Secretary finally argues that, under *Chevron U.S.A. v. Natural Res. Def. Council,* 467 U.S. 837, 104 S.Ct. 2778, 81 L.Ed.2d 694 (1984), we must defer to the Secretary's interpretation of "Native American." The Secretary by regulation has defined "Native American" to mean "of, or relating to, a tribe, people, or culture indigenous to the United States." 43 C.F.R. § 10.2(d). The Secretary's regulation, enacted through notice and comment rulemaking, defines Native American exactly as NAGPRA defines it, with one critical exception: the regulation omits the present-tense phrase "that is." *** We hold, for the reasons discussed above, that NAGPRA's requirement that Native American remains bear some relationship to a *presently existing* tribe, people, or culture is unambiguous, and that the Secretary's contrary interpretation therefore is not owed *Chevron* deference. *** Moreover, the Secretary's regulation conflicts with NAGPRA's plain language and so is invalid for that reason. *** Finally, the common maxim of statutory construction that we must give effect, if possible, to every word Congress used is fatal to the Secretary's attempt to amend NAGPRA by removing the phrase "that is." *** We hold that, notwithstanding 43 C.F.R. § 10.2(d), NAGPRA requires that human remains bear a significant relationship to a *presently existing* tribe, people, or culture to be considered Native American. The district court did not err in reaching that conclusion.

*** If accepted, the Secretary's interpretation would mean that the finding of any remains in the United States *in and of itself* would automatically render these remains "Native American." This interpretation would leave no meaning for the "relating to" clause, unless we were to interpret the clause to cover remains found outside the United States. But we cannot conclude that Congress intended an absurd result[.] *** By reading NAGPRA's definition of "Native American" literally, meaning is given to each of its terms. Some remains may be covered because they are remains of a tribe, people, or culture that is indigenous, while other remains may be covered because they are "related to" a currently existing indigenous tribe, people, or culture.

* * *

Although NAGPRA does not specify precisely what *kind* of a relationship or precisely *how strong* a relationship ancient human remains must bear to modern Indian groups to qualify as Native American, NAGPRA's legislative history provides some guidance on what type of relationship may suffice. The House Committee on Interior and Insular Affairs emphasized in its report on NAGPRA that the statute was being enacted with modern-day American Indians' identifiable *ancestors* in mind. *** Human remains that are 8340 to 9200 years old and that bear only incidental genetic resemblance to modern-day American Indians, along with incidental genetic resemblance to other peoples, cannot be said to be the Indians' "ancestors" within Congress's meaning. Congress enacted NAGPRA to give American Indians control over the remains of their genetic and cultural forbearers, not over the remains of people bearing no special and significant genetic or cultural relationship to some presently existing indigenous tribe, people, or culture.

The age of Kennewick Man's remains, given the limited studies to date, makes it almost impossible to establish *any* relationship between the remains and presently existing American Indians. At least no significant relationship has yet been shown. We cannot give credence to an interpretation of NAGPRA advanced by the government and the Tribal Claimants that would apply its provisions to remains that have at most a tenuous, unknown, and unproven connection, asserted solely because of the geographical location of the find.

IV

Finally, we address the Secretary's determination that Kennewick Man's remains are Native American, as defined by NAGPRA. We must set aside the Secretary's decision if it was "arbitrary" or "capricious" because the decision was based on inadequate factual support. *** We review the full agency record to determine whether substantial evidence supports the agency's decision that Kennewick Man is "Native American" within NAGPRA's meaning. Here, after reviewing the record, we conclude that the record does not contain substantial evidence that Kennewick Man's remains are Native American within NAGPRA's meaning.

The administrative record contains no evidence—let alone substantial evidence—that Kennewick Man's remains are connected by some special or significant genetic or cultural relationship to any presently existing indigenous tribe, people, or culture. An examination of the record demonstrates the absence of evidence that Kennewick Man and modern tribes share significant genetic or cultural features. *** As pointed out by *amici* Texas Historical Commission, under the framework proposed by the government and the Tribal Claimants, as soon as any remains are determined to be pre-Columbian, *any* study or testing of such remains would have to stop. This blanket prohibition could result in improper disposition of remains to parties wholly unrelated to the remains.

No cognizable link exists between Kennewick Man and modern Columbia Plateau Indians. When Kennewick Man's remains were discovered, local coroners initially believed the remains were those of a European, not a Native American, because of their appearance. Later testing by scientists demonstrated that the cranial measurements and features of Kennewick Man most closely resemble those of Polynesians and southern Asians, and that Kennewick Man's measurements and features differ significantly from those of any modern Indian group living in North America....

Scant or no evidence of cultural similarities between Kennewick Man and modern Indians exists. *** [A]vailable evidence is insufficient either to prove or disprove cultural or group continuity dating back earlier than 5000 B.C., which is the case with regard to the Kennewick Man's remains, and that there is evidence that substantial changes occurred in settlement, housing, diet, trade, subsistence patterns, technology, projectile point styles, raw materials, and mortuary rituals at various times between the estimated date when Kennewick Man lived and the beginning of the "Plateau Culture" some 2000 to 3000 years ago.*** [I]t was not until 2000 to 3000 years ago that populations began to settle into the villages and bands that may have been the antecedents of modern Indian tribes something like those encountered by European settlers and colonists. As the Secretary summarized, "[c]ultural discontinuities are suggested by evidence that the cultural group existing 8500–9500 years ago was likely small in size and highly mobile while the Plateau culture consisted o[f] larger, more sedentary groups."*** [E]ven if we assume that Kennewick Man was part of a stable social group living in the area, it still would be impossible to say whether his group's burial practices were related to modern tribes' burial practices. The Secretary also noted that "the linguistic analysis was unable to provide reliable evidence for the 8500–9500 period."

The Secretary's only evidence, perhaps, of a possible cultural relationship between Kennewick Man and modern-day American Indians comes in the form of oral histories. *** [O]ral traditions showed no necessary tale of a superseding migration with newer peoples displacing older ones. *** [But,] because oral accounts have been inevitably changed in context of transmission, because the traditions include myths that cannot be considered as if factual histories, because the value of such accounts is limited by concerns of authenticity, reliability, and accuracy, and because the record as a whole does not show where historical fact ends and mythic tale begins, we do not think that the oral traditions *** were adequate to show the required significant relationship of the Kennewick Man's remains to the Tribal Claimants. As the district court observed, 8340 to 9200 years between the life of Kennewick Man and the present is too long a time to bridge merely with evidence of oral traditions.

Considered as a whole, the administrative record might permit the Secretary to conclude reasonably that the Tribal Claimants' ancestors have lived in the region for a very long time. However, because Kennewick Man's remains are *so* old and the information about his era is *so* limited, the record does not permit the Secretary to conclude reasonably that Kennewick Man shares special and significant genetic or cultural features with presently existing indigenous tribes, people, or cultures. We thus hold that Kennewick Man's remains are not Native American human remains within the meaning of NAGPRA and that NAGPRA does not apply to them. Studies of the Kennewick Man's remains by Plaintiffs—scientists may proceed pursuant to ARPA.

We remand to the district court for further proceedings consistent with this opinion.

AFFIRMED.

Notes and Questions

1. **Oral traditions.** The United Nations Educational, Scientific, and Cultural Organization ("UNESCO") Programs on Intangible Cultural Heritage affirms that "oral traditions and expressions are used to pass on knowledge, cultural and social values and collective memory. They play a crucial part in keeping cultures alive." Some types of oral expression are common and can be used by entire communities while others are limited to particular social groups. It may take many forms, including proverbs, riddles, tales, nursery rhymes, legends, myths, epic songs and poems, charms, prayers, chants, songs, dramatic performances, and more. Because they are passed on by word of mouth, oral traditions and expressions often vary significantly in their telling. Stories are a combination—differing from genre to genre, from context to context, and from performer to performer—of reproduction, improvisation and creation. http://www.unesco.org/culture/ich/en/oraltraditionsandexpressions00053 (last visited March 15, 2017).

2. **Cultural lens.** a. Did the court's dismissal of oral tradition reveal a misunderstanding of the nature of that evidence? By definition, it is not fixed, but may have evolved over time. b. If there is a kernel of truth in it, should not that be enough? c. Who should determine what part of indigenous culture is entitled to preservation? d. Who is the rightful stakeholder of relics of the past once re-discovered? *See generally* Rebecca Tsosie, *Repatriation Symposium: NAGPRA and The Problem Of "Culturally Unidentifiable" Remains: The Argument For A Human Rights Framework*, 44 Ariz. St. L.J. 809 (Summer 2012) (examining whether NAGPRA and related United States laws are consistent with emerging human rights norms, in particular those embraced by the U.N. Declaration on the Rights of Indigenous Peoples, G.A. Res. 61/295, U.N. Doc. A/RES/61/295 (Oct. 2, 2007)).

3. **Aftermath.** a. In 2016 the Army Corps of Engineers confirmed that Kennewick Man was Native American. A group of scientists based in Denmark were able to recover DNA from a fragment of hand bone and used it to map his genetic code. Comparing it to peoples around the world, they concluded that the closest match was to modern Native Americans. The Army Corps of Engineers was able to independently verify these results. This finding means that Kennewick Man is covered by NAGPRA.

4. **Preservation of prehistoric relics.** It seems that both sides of this dispute regarded the remains of Kennewick Man with reverence, but held different notions about how to protect them. a. How should the prehistoric relic, whose connections with modern peoples is tenuous, be preserved?

5. **Database.** The National Park Service maintains a database of "Culturally Unidentifiable Native Americans" and "Culturally Affiliated Native Americans." www.nps.gov/nagpra (last visited March 1, 2017).

Statement on the Repatriation of The Ancient One

February 20, 2017

On Friday, February 17, 2017, the remains of The Ancient One, otherwise known as Kennewick Man, were returned to the tribes who claim him as their ancestor.

The Burke Museum provided secure and respectful curation of The Ancient One from 1998–2017, under contract to the US Army Corps of Engineers, the government agency that controlled the remains until they were repatriated.

The return of the Ancient One to the tribes is the right decision and was long overdue. It is consistent with the Burke's commitment to both the legal and the ethical principles of NAGPRA—federal law that allows tribes to reclaim human remains and cultural items from museums and other institutions.

* * *

After DNA findings confirmed The Ancient One was Native American, the tribes who claim him as their ancestor could begin the process of reclaiming his remains under NAGPRA.

Simultaneously, U.S. Senator Patty Murray and Congressman Denny Heck sponsored legislation (S. 1979 and H.R. 4131) to expedite his return to the tribes. Language from these bills was added to the Water Infrastructure Improvements Act for the Nation (WIIN), which was signed by President Obama on Friday, December 16, 2016.

The WIIN Act superseded the NAGPRA process and prompted the Army Corps of Engineers to transfer control of the remains to the Washington State Department of Archaeology and Historic Preservation (DAHP), on the condition that DAHP return the remains to the claimant tribes.

* * *

The remains were reburied in a private ceremony and location, according to the traditions of the tribes.

* * *

While the remains were cared for by the Burke Museum, the Museum was not involved in research conducted on the remains. *** The Ancient One was never displayed. The remains were kept in a private, secure location at the Burke Museum, http://www.burkemuseum.org/blog/kennewick-man-ancient-one.

6. **Compliance with NAGPRA.** Under NAGPRA, federal agencies and federally-funded museums (except the Smithsonian) must also repatriate sacred objects, cultural patrimony and funerary objects. 25 U.S.C. § 3005. The Act also prohibits the unauthorized excavation and trafficking in such artifacts found on federal or tribal lands. *See generally*, Steven J. Gunn, *The Native American Graves Protection and Repatriation Act at Twenty: Reaching the Limits of Our National Consensus*, 36 Wm. Mitchell L. Rev. 503 (2010). In 2010, the General Accounting Office reported that after almost 20 years since enactment, "key federal agencies still have not fully complied with the act for their historical collections acquired on or before NAGPRA's enactment." Overall, the Army Corps of Engineers, the Forest Service, and the National Park Service did the most work to identify their NAGPRA items, but the Bureau of Land Management, among others, had done the least. Up through 2009, only 55 percent of the human remains and 68 percent of the associated funerary objects that had been published in notices in the Federal Register of inventory completion had been repatriated. "As a result, policymakers, Indian tribes, and Native Hawaiians organizations do not have access to readily available information about culturally affiliated NAGPRA items that have not been repatriated." GAO Highlights, *Native American Graves Protection And Repatriation Act, After Almost 20 Years, Key Federal Agencies Still Have Not Fully Complied with the Act*, http://www.gao.gov/products/GAO-10-768 (last visited March 1, 2017).

F. National Environmental Policy Act

Robertson v. Methow Valley Citizens Council

Supreme Court of the United States
490 U.S. 332, 109 S.Ct. 1835 (1989)

Stevens, J. [Writing a unanimous opinion.] We granted certiorari to decide two questions of law.... As framed by petitioners, they are:

> "1. Whether the National Environmental Policy Act requires federal agencies to include in each environmental impact statement: (a) a fully developed plan to mitigate environmental harm; and (b) a 'worst case' analysis of potential environmental harm if relevant information concerning significant environmental effects is unavailable or too costly to obtain.
>
> "2. Whether the Forest Service may issue a special use permit for recreational use of national forest land in the absence of a fully developed plan to mitigate environmental harm." ***

Concluding that the Court of Appeals for the Ninth Circuit misapplied the National Environmental Policy Act of 1969 (NEPA), 83 Stat. 852, 42 U.S.C. § 4321 *et seq.*, and gave inadequate deference to the Forest Service's interpretation of its own regulations, we reverse and remand for further proceedings.

I

The Forest Service is authorized by statute to manage the national forests for "outdoor recreation, range, timber, watershed, and wildlife and fish purposes." 74 Stat. 215, 16 U.S.C. § 528. *** Pursuant to that authorization, the Forest Service has issued "special use" permits for the operation of approximately 170 Alpine and Nordic ski areas on federal lands. ***

The Forest Service permit process involves three separate stages. The Forest Service first examines the general environmental and financial feasibility of a proposed project and decides whether to issue a special use permit. *** Because that decision is a "major Federal action" within the meaning of NEPA, it must be preceded by the preparation of an Environmental Impact Statement (EIS). 42 U.S.C. § 4332. If the Service decides to issue a permit, it then proceeds to select a developer, formulate the basic terms of the arrangement with the selected party, and issue the permit. *** In a final stage of review, the Service evaluates the permittee's "master plan" for development, construction, and operation of the project. Construction may begin only after an additional environmental analysis *** and final approval of the developer's master plan. This case arises out of the Forest Service's decision to issue a special use permit authorizing the development of a major destination Alpine ski resort at Sandy Butte in the North Cascade Mountains.

Sandy Butte is a 6,000-foot mountain located in the Okanogan National Forest in Okanogan County, Washington. At present Sandy Butte, like the Methow Valley it overlooks, is an unspoiled, sparsely populated area that the District Court characterized as "pristine." *** In 1968, Congress established the North Cascades National Park and directed the Secretaries of the Interior and Agriculture to agree on the designation of areas within, and adjacent to, the park for public uses, including ski areas. 82 Stat. 926, 930, 16 U.S.C. §§ 90, 90d-3. A 1970 study conducted by the Forest Service pursuant to this congressional directive identified Sandy Butte as having the highest potential of any site in the State of Washington for development as a major downhill ski resort.***

In 1978, Methow Recreation, Inc. (MRI), applied for a special use permit to develop and operate its proposed "Early Winters Ski Resort" on Sandy Butte and an 1,165-acre parcel of land it had acquired adjacent to the National Forest. The proposed development would make use of approximately 3,900 acres of Sandy Butte *** and would stimulate extensive commercial and residential growth in the vicinity to accommodate both vacationers and staff.

In response to MRI's application, the Forest Service, in cooperation with state and county officials, prepared an EIS known as the Early Winters Alpine Winter Sports Study (Early Winters Study or Study). The stated purpose of the EIS was "to provide the information required to evaluate the potential for skiing at Early Winters" and "to assist in making a decision whether to issue a Special Use Permit for downhill skiing on all or a portion of approximately 3900 acres of National Forest System land." *** A draft of the Study was completed and circulated in 1982, but release of the final EIS was delayed as Congress considered including Sandy Butte in a proposed wilderness area. *** When the Washington State Wilderness Act of 1984 was passed, however, Sandy Butte was excluded from the wilderness designation, and the EIS was released.

The Early Winters Study *** evaluated five alternative levels of development of Sandy Butte that might be authorized, the lowest being a "no action" alternative and the highest being development of a 16-lift ski area able to accommodate 10,500 skiers at one time. The Study considered the effect of each level of development on water resources, soil, wildlife, air quality, vegetation, and visual quality, as well as land use and transportation in the Methow Valley, probable demographic shifts, the economic market for skiing and other summer and winter recreational activities in the Valley, and the energy requirements for the ski area and related developments. The Study's discussion of possible impacts was not limited to on-site effects, but also, as required by Council on Environmental Quality (CEQ) regulations, *see* 40 CFR § 1502.16(b) (1987), addressed "off-site impacts that each alternative might have on community facilities, socio-economic and other environmental conditions in the Upper Methow Valley." *** As to off-site effects, the Study explained that "due to the uncertainty of where other public and private lands may become developed," it is difficult to evaluate off-site impacts, *** and thus the document's analysis is necessarily "not site-specific," ***. Finally, the Study outlined certain steps that might be taken to mitigate adverse effects, both on Sandy Butte and in the neighboring Methow Valley, but indicated that these proposed steps are merely conceptual and "will be made more specific as part of the design and implementation stages of the planning process." ***

The effects of the proposed development on air quality and wildlife received particular attention in the Study. In the chapter on "Environmental Consequences," the first subject discussed is air quality. *** [T]he discussion included an analysis of cumulative impacts over several years resulting from actions on other lands as well as from the development of Sandy Butte itself. The Study concluded that although the construction, maintenance, and operation of the proposed ski area "will not have a measurable effect on existing or future air quality," the off-site development of private land under all five alternatives—including the "no action" alternative—"will have a significant effect on air quality during severe meteorological inversion periods." *** The burning of wood for space heat, the Study explained, would constitute the primary cause of diminished air quality, and the damage would increase incrementally with each of the successive levels of proposed development. *** The Study cautioned that without efforts to mitigate these effects, even under the "no action" alternative, the increase in automobile, fireplace, and wood stove use would reduce air quality below state standards, but added that "[t]he numerous mitigation measures discussed" in the Study "will greatly reduce the impacts presented by the model." ***

In its discussion of air-quality mitigation measures, the *** Study suggested that Okanogan County develop an air quality management plan, requiring weatherization of new buildings, limiting the number of wood stoves and fireplaces, and adopting monitoring and enforcement measures.[5] In addition, the Study suggested that the Forest Service require that the master plan include procedures to control dust and to comply with smoke management practices.[6]

In its discussion of adverse effects on area wildlife, the EIS concluded that no endangered or threatened species would be affected by the proposed development and that the only impact on sensitive species was the probable loss of a pair of spotted owls and their progeny. *** With regard to other wildlife, the Study considered the impact on 75 different indigenous species and predicted that within a decade after development vegetational change and increased human activity would lead to a decrease in population for 31 species, while causing an increase in population for another 24 species on Sandy Butte. *** Two species, the pine marten and nesting goshawk, would be eliminated altogether from the area of development. ***

In a comment in response to the draft EIS, the Washington Department of Game voiced a special concern about potential losses to the State's largest migratory deer herd, which uses the Methow Valley as a critical winter range and as its migration route. *** The state agency estimated that *** "the ultimate impact on the Methow deer herd could exceed a 50 percent reduction in numbers." *** The agency asserted that "Okanogan County residents place a great deal of importance on the area's

---

5. The Study recommended the following action:

"1. The County will initiate the formation of an Air Quality Control Authority or similar administrative structure pursuant to Washington State statutes.

"2. The County will develop an airshed management plan that incorporates strategies which will result in ambient air quality standards for the Methow Valley that are stricter than existing State standards. As part of the airshed management plan, the following mitigation measures will be considered:

"—Development of land use codes specifically addressing site development and project design directed at energy efficiency and air pollution control.

"—Requiring all new construction to be fully weatherized to reduce the need for supplemental heating sources (i. e., wood) beyond the central facilities heating needs.

"—Restricting the number of fireplaces and wood stoves. At a minimum, few fireplaces should be allowed in accommodations constructed for tourist use.

"—Encouraging the use of alternative, non-polluting energy sources.

"—Establishing a certification mechanism for wood stoves and fireplace inserts.

"—Establishing an air pollution monitoring system specifically designed to alert local residents to impending pollution episodes and to record long term changes in air quality levels. Such long term data will be used to evaluate the success or failure of the mitigation and impose more stringent measures if standards are violated.

"—Development of enforcement measures to assure that standards will be met." Early Winters Study 68–69.

6. The Study recommended the following on-site, air-quality mitigation measures:

"1. The Master Plan will require prompt revegetation of all disturbed areas and the mandatory application of dust control measures (e. g., rocking and oiling) on unpaved construction roads.

"2. The construction phase will follow established Forest Service/State of Washington smoke management practices identified in the Washington State Smoke Management Plan. The Master Plan will identify opportunities for utilization of waste wood, generated by the project, thereby minimizing open burning." *Id.*, at 69.

deer herd." *** Because the deer harvest is apparently proportional to the size of the herd, the state agency predicted that "Washington business can expect to lose over $3 million annually from reduced recreational opportunity." *** The Forest Service's own analysis of the impact on the deer herd was more modest. *** Although its estimate indicated a possible 15 percent decrease in the size of the herd, it summarized the State's contrary view in the text of the EIS, and stressed that off-site effects are difficult to estimate due to uncertainty concerning private development. ***

As was true of its discussion of air quality, the EIS also described both on-site and off-site mitigation measures. Among possible on-site mitigation possibilities, the Study recommended locating runs, ski lifts, and roads so as to minimize interference with wildlife, restricting access to selected roads during fawning season, and further examination of the effect of the development on mule deer migration routes.... Off-site options discussed in the Study included the use of zoning and tax incentives to limit development on deer winter range and migration routes, encouragement of conservation easements, and acquisition and management by local government of critical tracts of land. *** [Again,] the proposed options were primarily directed to steps that might be taken by state and local government.

Ultimately, the Early Winters Study recommended the issuance of a permit for development at the second highest level considered—a 16-lift ski area able to accommodate 8,200 skiers at one time. On July 5, 1984, the Regional Forester decided to issue a special use permit as recommended by the Study[, saying,] that no major adverse effects would result directly from the federal action, but that secondary effects could include a degradation of existing air quality and a reduction of mule deer winter range. *** He therefore directed the supervisor of the Okanogan National Forest, both independently and in cooperation with local officials, to identify and implement certain mitigating measures. ***

Four organizations (respondents)[11] opposing the decision to issue a permit appealed the Regional Forester's decision to the Chief of the Forest Service. *** After a hearing, he affirmed the Regional Forester's decision. Stressing that the decision, which simply approved the general concept of issuing a 30-year special use permit for development of Sandy Butte, did not authorize construction of a particular ski area and, in fact, did not even act on MRI specific permit application, he concluded that the EIS's discussion of mitigation was "adequate for this stage in the review process."***

11. The four organizations were Methow Valley Citizens Council, Washington State Sportsmen's Council, Washington Environmental Council, and the Cascade Chapter, Sierra Club. These organizations, with the exception of Washington State Sportsmen's Council, are respondents herein. MRI, the permittee, is also a respondent in this Court, but since it supports the Government's action, we shall use the term "respondents" to refer only to the opponents of the Early Winters proposal.

Thereafter, respondents brought this action under the Administrative Procedure Act, 5 U.S.C. §§701–706, to obtain judicial review of the Forest Service's decision. Their principal claim was that the Early Winters Study did not satisfy the requirements of NEPA, 42 U.S.C. §4332.... With the consent of the parties, the case was assigned to a United States Magistrate. [T]he Magistrate filed a comprehensive written opinion and concluded that the EIS was adequate *** [in disclosing] the adverse impacts on the mule deer herd and on air quality and that there was no duty to prepare a "worst case analysis" because the relevant information essential to a reasoned decision was available. *** [T]he Magistrate [further] stressed that courts apply a "rule of reason" in evaluating the adequacy of an EIS and "take the uncertainty and speculation involved with secondary impacts into account in passing on the adequacy of the discussion of secondary impacts." *** On the subject of mitigation, he explained that "[m]ere listing ... is generally inadequate to satisfy the CEQ regulations," but found that "in this EIS there is more—not much more—but more than a mere listing of mitigation measures." ***

Concluding that the Early Winters Study was inadequate as a matter of law, the Court of Appeals reversed. *Methow Valley Citizens Council v. Regional Forester,* 833 F.2d 810 [(9th Cir. 1987). The court held that the Forest Service could not rely on "'the implementation of mitigation measures'" to support its conclusion that the impact on the mule deer would be minor, "since not only has the effectiveness of these mitigation measures not yet been assessed, but the mitigation measures themselves have yet to be developed." *Id.*, at 817. It then added that if the agency had difficulty obtaining adequate information to make a reasoned assessment of the environmental impact on the herd, it had a duty to make a so-called "worst case analysis." ***

The court found a similar defect in the EIS' treatment of air quality. Since the EIS made it clear that commercial development in the Methow Valley will result in violations of state air-quality standards unless effective mitigation measures are put in place by the local governments and the private developer, the Court of Appeals concluded that the Forest Service had an affirmative duty to "develop the necessary mitigation measures *before* the permit is granted." *** The court held that this duty was imposed by both the Forest Service's own regulations and § 102 of NEPA[;] *** a substantive requirement that "'action be taken to mitigate the adverse effects of major federal actions.'" *Ibid.* *** For this reason, it concluded that "an EIS must include a thorough discussion of measures to mitigate the adverse environmental impacts of a proposed action." 833 F.2d, at 819. The Court of Appeals concluded by *** [stressing that] "[t]he importance of the mitigation plan cannot be overestimated. It is a determinative factor in evaluating the adequacy of an environmental impact statement. Without a complete mitigation plan, the decisionmaker is unable to make an informed judgment as to the environmental impact of the project-one of the main purposes of an environmental impact statement." *Id.*, at 820 ***

II

Section 101 of NEPA declares a broad national commitment to protecting and promoting environmental quality. 83 Stat. 852, 42 U.S.C. §4331. To ensure that this commitment is "infused into the ongoing programs and actions of the Federal Government, the act also establishes some important 'action-forcing' procedures." 115 Cong.Rec. 40416 (remarks of Sen. Jackson). *** Section 102 thus, among other measures

> "directs that, to the fullest extent possible ... all agencies of the Federal Government shall—
>
> * * *
>
> "(C) include in every recommendation or report on proposals for legislation and other major Federal actions significantly affecting the quality of the human environment, a detailed statement by the responsible official on—
>
> "(i) the environmental impact of the proposed action,
>
> "(ii) any adverse environmental effects which cannot be avoided should the proposal be implemented,
>
> "(iii) alternatives to the proposed action,
>
> "(iv) the relationship between local short-term uses of man's environment and the maintenance and enhancement of long-term productivity, and
>
> "(v) any irreversible and irretrievable commitments of resources which would be involved in the proposed action should it be implemented." 83 Stat. 853, 42 U.S.C. §4332.

The statutory requirement that a federal agency contemplating a major action prepare such an environmental impact statement serves NEPA's "action-forcing" purpose in two important respects. *** It ensures that the agency, in reaching its decision, will have available, and will carefully consider, detailed information concerning significant environmental impacts; it also guarantees that the relevant information will be made available to the larger audience that may also play a role in both the decisionmaking process and the implementation of that decision.*** [T]he strong precatory language of § 101 of the Act and the requirement that agencies prepare detailed impact statements inevitably bring pressure to bear on agencies "to respond to the needs of environmental quality." 115 Cong.Rec. 40425 (1969) (remarks of Sen. Muskie).

Publication of an EIS, both in draft and final form, *** gives the public the assurance that the agency "has indeed considered environmental concerns in its decision-making process," *** and, perhaps more significantly, provides a springboard for public comment, ***. Thus, in this case the final draft of the Early Winters Study reflects not only the work of the Forest Service itself, but also the critical views of the Washington State Department of Game, the Methow Valley Citizens Council, and Friends of the Earth, as well as many others, to whom copies of the draft Study were circulated.*** Moreover, with respect to *** the adverse effects on air quality and the mule deer herd[,] *** the EIS serves the function of offering those bodies adequate notice of the expected consequences and the opportunity to plan and implement corrective measures in a timely manner.

The sweeping policy goals announced in § 101 of NEPA are thus realized through a set of "action-forcing" procedures that require that agencies take a " 'hard look' at environmental consequences," *** and that provide for broad dissemination of relevant environmental information. Although these procedures are almost certain to affect the agency's substantive decision, it is now well settled that NEPA itself does not mandate particular results, but simply prescribes the necessary process. *** If the adverse environmental effects of the proposed action are adequately identified and evaluated, the agency is not constrained by NEPA from deciding that other values outweigh the environmental costs. *** Other statutes may impose substantive environmental obligations on federal agencies, but NEPA merely prohibits uninformed—rather than unwise—agency action.

*** [O]ne important ingredient of an EIS is the discussion of steps that can be taken to mitigate adverse environmental consequences. *** Implicit in NEPA's demand that an agency prepare a detailed statement on "any adverse environmental effects which cannot be avoided should the proposal be implemented," 42 U.S.C. § 4332(C)(ii), is an understanding that the EIS will discuss the extent to which adverse effects can be avoided. [O]mission of a reasonably complete discussion of possible mitigation measures would undermine the "action-forcing" function of NEPA. Without such a discussion, neither the agency nor other interested groups and individuals can properly evaluate the severity of the adverse effects. *** Recognizing the importance of such a discussion in guaranteeing that the agency has taken a "hard look" at the environmental consequences of proposed federal action, CEQ regulations require that the agency discuss possible mitigation measures in defining the scope of the EIS, 40 CFR § 1508.25(b) (1987), in discussing alternatives to the proposed action, § 1502.14(f), and consequences of that action, § 1502.16(h), and in explaining its ultimate decision, § 1505.2(c).

*** In this case, the off-site effects on air quality and on the mule deer herd cannot be mitigated unless nonfederal government agencies take appropriate action. Since it is those state and local governmental bodies that have jurisdiction over the area in which the adverse effects need be addressed and since they have the authority to mitigate them, it would be incongruous to conclude that the Forest Service has no power to act until the local agencies have reached a final conclusion on what mitigating measures they consider necessary.... Even more significantly, it would be inconsistent with NEPA's reliance on procedural mechanisms—as opposed to substantive, result-based standards—to demand the presence of a fully developed plan that will mitigate environmental harm before an agency can act. ***

We thus conclude that the Court of Appeals erred, first, in assuming that "NEPA requires that 'action be taken to mitigate the adverse effects of major federal actions,' " 833 F.2d, at 819 ***, and, second, in finding that this substantive requirement entails the further duty to include in every EIS "a detailed explanation of specific measures which *will* be employed to mitigate the adverse impacts of a proposed action," 833 F.2d, at 819 (emphasis supplied).

III

The Court of Appeals also concluded that the Forest Service had an obligation to make a "worst case analysis" if it could not make a reasoned assessment of the impact of the Early Winters project on the mule deer herd. Such a "worst case analysis" was required at one time by CEQ regulations, but those regulations have since been amended. Moreover, although the prior regulations may well have expressed a permissible application of NEPA, the Act itself does not mandate that uncertainty in predicting environmental harms be addressed exclusively in this manner. Accordingly, we conclude that the Court of Appeals also erred in requiring the "worst case" study.

* * *

The Court of Appeals recognized that the "worst case analysis" regulation has been superseded, yet held that "[t]his rescission ... does not nullify the requirement ... since the regulation was merely a codification of prior NEPA case law." 833 F.2d, at 817, n. 11. This conclusion *** is erroneous in a number of respects. Most notably, review of NEPA case law reveals that the regulation, in fact, was not a codification of prior judicial decisions. *** The cases cited by the Court of Appeals ultimately rely on the Fifth Circuit's decision in *Sierra Club v. Sigler,* 695 F.2d 957 (1983). *Sigler,* however, simply recognized that the "worst case analysis" regulation codified the "judicially created principl[e]" that an EIS must "consider the probabilities of the occurrence of any environmental effects it discusses." *Id.,* at 970–971. As CEQ recognized at the time it superseded the regulation, case law prior to the adoption of the "worst case analysis" provision did require agencies to describe environmental impacts even in the face of substantial uncertainty, but did not require that this obligation necessarily be met through the mechanism of a "worst case analysis." *** CEQ's abandonment of the "worst case analysis" provision, therefore, is not inconsistent with any previously established judicial interpretation of the statute.

Nor are we convinced that the new CEQ regulation is not controlling simply because it was preceded by a rule that was in some respects more demanding. In *Andrus v. Sierra Club,* 442 U.S., at 358, 99 S.Ct., at 2341, we held that CEQ regulations are entitled to substantial deference. In that case we recognized that although less deference may be in order in some cases in which the "'administrative guidelines'" conflict "'with earlier pronouncements of the agency,'" ***, substantial deference is nonetheless appropriate if there appears to have been good reason for the change, 442 U.S., at 358, 99 S.Ct., at 2341. Here, *** the amendment was designed to better serve the twin functions of an EIS-requiring agencies to take a "hard look" at the consequences of the proposed action and providing important information to other groups and individuals. CEQ explained that by requiring that an EIS focus on reasonably foreseeable impacts, the new regulation "will generate information and discussion on those consequences of greatest concern to the public and of greatest relevance to the agency's decision," 50 Fed.Reg. 32237 (1985), rather than distorting the decisionmaking process by overemphasizing highly speculative harms, 51 Fed.Reg. 15624–15625

(1986); 50 Fed.Reg. 32236 (1985). In light of this well-considered basis for the change, the new regulation is entitled to substantial deference. Accordingly, the Court of Appeals erred in concluding that the Early Winters Study is inadequate because it failed to include a "worst case analysis."

IV

The Court of Appeals also held that the Forest Service's failure to develop a complete mitigation plan violated the agency's own regulations. 833 F.2d, at 814, n. 3, 819, and n. 14. Those regulations require that an application for a special use permit include "measures and plans for the protection and rehabilitation of the environment during construction, operation, maintenance, and termination of the project," 36 CFR § 251.54(e)(4) (1988), and that "[e]ach special use authorization ... contain ... [t]erms and conditions which will ... minimize damage to scenic and esthetic values and fish and wildlife habitat and otherwise protect the environment," § 251.56(a)(1)(ii). *** [T]he Court of Appeals concluded that "[s]ince the mitigation 'plan' here at issue is so vague and undeveloped as to be wholly inadequate, ... the Regional Forester's decision to grant the special use permit could be none other than arbitrary, capricious and an abuse of discretion." 833 F.2d, at 814, n. 3. We disagree.

The Early Winters Study made clear that on-site effects of the development will be minimal and will be easily mitigated. *** Given the limited on-site effects of the proposed development, the recommended ameliorative steps—which, for example, called for "prompt revegetation of all disturbed areas," ... cannot be deemed overly vague or underdeveloped.

The Court of Appeals' conclusion that the Early Winters Study's treatment of possible mitigation measures is inadequate apparently turns on the court's review of the proposed off-site measures. Although NEPA and CEQ regulations require detailed analysis of both on-site and off-site mitigation measures, *** there is no basis for concluding that the Forest Service's own regulations must also be read in all cases to condition issuance of a special use permit on consideration (and implementation) of off-site mitigation measures. The Forest Service regulations were promulgated pursuant to a broad grant of authority "to permit the use and occupancy of suitable areas of land within the national forests ... for the purpose of constructing or maintaining hotels, resorts, and any other structures or facilities necessary or desirable for recreation, public convenience, or safety," 16 U.S.C. § 497, and were not based on the more direct congressional concern for environmental quality embodied in NEPA. *** As is clear from the text of the permit issued to MRI, the Forest Service has decided to implement its mitigation regulations by imposing appropriate controls over MRI's actual development and operation during the term of the permit. It was surely not unreasonable for the Forest Service in this case to have construed those regulations as not extending to actions that might be taken by Okanogan County or the State of Washington to ameliorate the off-site effects of the Early Winters project on air quality and the mule deer herd. This interpretation of the agency's own regulation is not "plainly erroneous or inconsistent with the regulation," and is thus controlling. ***

V

In sum, we conclude that NEPA does not require a fully developed plan detailing what steps *will* be taken to mitigate adverse environmental impacts and does not require a "worst case analysis." In addition, we hold that the Forest Service has adopted a permissible interpretation of its own regulations. The judgment of the Court of Appeals is accordingly reversed, and the case is remanded for further proceedings consistent with this opinion.

It is so ordered.

Justice BRENNAN, concurring.

I write separately to highlight the Court's observation that "one important ingredient of an EIS is the discussion of steps that can be taken to mitigate adverse environmental consequences." *Ante,* at 1846.

Notes and Questions

1. **Environmental Impact Statement ("EIS").** It is important to note that the EIS is generally not of great concern to a reviewing court. Here, however, the Supreme Court turned the EIS into a focal point and set forth guidelines for future court decisions in assessing the adequacy of an EIS. In fact, the EIS was so important in this instance that Justice Brennan wrote a separate concurrence solely to make note of an integral aspect of the EIS.

2. **Procedural and not substantive burdens.** The EIS does not compel the agency to take any of the measures to mitigate the environmental effects likely to result from the proposed action, only that the agency identify potential harm and consider them before proceeding. a. What then are some of the salutary effects of an EIS? b. How is the cause of environmental protection furthered by requiring a thoughtful report, but no action to be taken pursuant to it?

3. **Deference to the quality of the environmental study.** The Court did not venture to question the quality of the environmental study. But how can a plan to use approximately 3,900 acres of what was described as a pristine area, that would stimulate extensive commercial and residential growth in the vicinity by vacationers and staff, not be identified as an adverse impact?

G. Intersection of Environmental and Historic Issues

Greene County Planning Board v. Federal Power Commission

United States Court of Appeals for the Second Circuit
94 P.U.R.3d 51, 455 F.2d 412 (1972)

KAUFMAN, C.J. We are called upon to assess the licensing procedures of the Federal Power Commission in a proceeding upon the application[1] of the Power Authority of the State of New York (PASNY) for authorization to construct a high-voltage transmission line. Although the petitioners—Greene County Planning Board, the Town of Durham, New York, and the Association for the Preservation of Durham Valley—raise several interesting arguments, the dispute centers on compliance with the procedural mandates of Section 102(2) (C) of the National Environmental Policy Act of 1969 (NEPA), 42 U.S.C.A. §4332(2) (C), which requires all federal agencies to issue a "detailed statement" on the environmental impact of all "major Federal actions significantly affecting the quality of the human environment ..." This section is an essential "action forcing" provision ... in legislation designed "[t]o declare a national policy which will encourage productive harmony between man and his environment; to promote efforts which will prevent or eliminate damage to the environment and biosphere and stimulate the health and welfare of man; to enrich the understanding of the ecological systems and natural resources important to the Nation; and to establish a Council on Environmental Quality."[3] NEPA §2, 42 U.S.C.A. §4321. *** We find that the Commission has not complied with NEPA and remand for further proceedings ***

A brief statement of the proceedings thus far will aid in comprehending the arguments advanced. On August 15, 1968, PASNY filed an application to construct, operate and maintain a 1,000,000 kilowatt pumped storage power project ... along the middle reaches of Schoharie Creek in the towns of Blenheim and Gilboa, New York, some forty miles southwest of Albany. The project as proposed, inter alia, con-

---

1. Application was made pursuant to Section 4(e) of the Federal Power Act, 16 U.S.C. §797(e), which provides in pertinent part:

> The Commission is hereby authorized and empowered—
>
> *****
>
> (e) To issue licenses to citizens of the United States, or to any association of such citizens, or to any corporation organized under the laws of the United States or any State thereof, *** for the purpose of constructing, operating, and maintaining dams, water conduits, reservoirs, power houses, transmission lines, or other project works necessary or convenient for the development and improvement of navigation and for the development, transmission, and utilization of power across, along, from, or in any of the streams or other bodies of water over which Congress has jurisdiction under its authority to regulate commerce ***

3. *See generally* Hanks & Hanks, An Environmental Bill of Rights: The Citizen Suit and the National Environmental Policy Act of 1969, 24 Rutgers L.Rev. 230 (1970); Peterson, An Analysis of Title I of the National Environmental Policy Act of 1969, 1 Environmental L.Rep. 50035.

sisted of: (1) an upper reservoir; (2) a lower reservoir (including a dam across Schoharie Creek); (3) an outdoor powerhouse and (4) three 345 kilovolt transmission lines—one from the switchyard adjacent to the powerhouse to a substation at New Scotland, one to a substation at Fraser and the last to a substation at Leeds.... [After consulting with several federal agencies, the Commission granted the license.] ***

* * *

NEPA became effective on January 1, 1970, after PASNY applied for the transmission line permits, but before the permits were issued for the Gilboa-New Scotland and Gilboa-Fraser lines. It was not until almost a year later, on December 2, 1970, that the Commission issued Order No. 415 to implement procedures in accord with NEPA. 18 C.F.R. §§2.80–.82 (January 1, 1971). Section 2.81 (b) of the regulations required each applicant for a license for a "major project" to file its own detailed statement of environmental impact developing fully the five factors listed in section 102(2)(C) of NEPA.[9] Although the regulations required the Commission staff to prepare a detailed statement in the case of all uncontested applications, no such statement was required where applications were contested.[10] ***

In accordance with Commission regulations, PASNY filed its impact statement on March 26, 1971, covering the proposed Gilboa-Leeds line and two alternative routings. The Commission reviewed the statement as to sufficiency of form, *** and then circulated it for comment to agencies with "special expertise with respect to any environmental impact involved." ***

Finally, by order issued May 4, 1971, the Commission ordered a hearing on PASNY's proposals and set a prehearing conference for June 22, 1971. At this conference, Durham and Greene County *** requested the Presiding Examiner to set a date for the Commission to file its own impact statement pursuant to NEPA. Then, by motions filed July 6 and July 12, 1971, the intervenors moved for an order vacating, rescinding or suspending the June 6, 1969, license of the entire project and enjoining further construction, alleging that the Commission did not comply with the notice requirements of the Federal Power Act and the mandates of NEPA. *** The Presiding Examiner denied each of the motions, and the movants filed timely notices of appeal to the Commission. *** [T]he Commission granted rehearings and by orders dated

---

9. The five factors are:

(i) the environmental impact of the proposed action.

(ii) any adverse environmental effects which cannot be avoided should the proposal be implemented.

(iii) alternatives to the proposed action.

(iv) the relationship between local short-term uses of man's environment and the maintenance and enhancement of long-term productivity, and

(v) any irreversible and irretrievable commitments of resources which would be involved in the proposed action should it be implemented.

10. ... The Commission revised its rules by Order No. 415-B, issued November 19, 1971. 36 Fed.Reg. 22738 (Nov. 30, 1971). Section 2.81 no longer requires the Commission to prepare its own statement in uncontested proceedings.

October 28 and 29, 1971, it formally denied the appeals. Petitioners ask us to review those orders. ***

* * *

I. *Compliance with NEPA*

A. *Gilboa-Leeds Transmission Line*

Section 102(2) (C) of NEPA, as we stated at the outset, requires every federal agency to "include in every recommendation or report on proposals for ... major Federal actions significantly affecting the quality of the human environment" a detailed environmental impact statement. Prior to making the statement, the agency must "consult with and obtain the comments of any Federal agency which has jurisdiction by law or special expertise with respect to any environmental impact involved." The detailed statement, however, "*must accompany the proposal through the existing agency review processes....*"

It is conceded that authorization of the Gilboa-Leeds line, an integral part of the Blenheim-Gilboa Project, would constitute a major federal action. The parties, however, are in vigorous disagreement over when the Commission must make its impact statement. The Commission argues that PASNY's statement, reviewed as to form by the Commission and circulated by it, suffices for the purposes of Section 102(2) (C) and that the Commission is not required to make its own statement until it files its final decision. Petitioners argue that the Commission must issue its statement prior to any formal hearings. PASNY, perhaps recognizing that the Commission's position is untenable, but nevertheless anxious to expedite the proceedings, proposes a third course of action. It urges that the Commission can draft its statement on the basis of the hearings, but to be circulated by it for comment before its final decision. It is clear to us that petitioners offer the correct interpretation.

Section 101(a) of NEPA, 42 U.S.C.A. §4331(a), declares that "it is the continuing policy of the Federal Government ... to use all practicable means and measures ... in a manner calculated to foster and promote the general welfare, to create and maintain conditions under which man and nature can exist in productive harmony, and fulfill the social, economic, and other requirements of present and future generations of Americans." To this end the government must "coordinate Federal plans, functions, programs, and resources...." NEPA §101(b), 42 U.S.C.A. §4331(b). As long as six years ago, this Court remanded a case to the Commission because, in granting a license for the construction of a similar pumped storage power project at Storm King Mountain on the Hudson River, it had failed to weigh the factors of "the conservation of natural resources, the maintenance of natural beauty, and the preservation of historic sites." ... *Scenic Hudson Preservation Conference v. Federal Power Commission* [Scenic Hudson I], 354 F.2d 608, 614 (1965), cert. denied *sub nom. Consolidated Edison Co. of New York v. Scenic Hudson Preservation Conference*, 384 U.S. 941, 86 S.Ct. 1462, 16 L.Ed.2d 540 (1966). We commented there: "In this case, as in many others, the Commission has claimed to be the representative of the public interest. This role does not permit it to act as an umpire blandly calling balls and strikes for adversaries appearing before it; the right of the public must receive active and affirmative protection at the hands of the Commission." *Id.* at 620. But NEPA, which was a response to the urgent need for a similar approach in all federal agencies, ... went far beyond the requirement that the agency merely consider environmental factors and include those factors in the record subject to review by the courts.

In addition to the environmental impact statement, Section 102(2) requires the agency, inter alia, to:

> (A) utilize a systematic, interdisciplinary approach which will insure the integrated use of the natural and social sciences and the environmental design arts in planing and in decisionmaking which may have an impact on man's environment;
>
> * * *
>
> (D) study, develop, and describe appropriate alternatives to recommended courses of action in any proposal which involves unresolved conflicts concerning alternative uses of available resources;
>
> * * *
>
> (E) recognize the worldwide and long range character of environmental problems....

We view this section as did the District of Columbia Circuit. It is a mandate to consider environmental values "at every distinctive and comprehensive stage of the [agency's] process." The primary and nondelegable responsibility for fulfilling that function lies with the Commission. *Calbert Cliffs' Coordinating Committee, Inc. v. United States Atomic Energy Commission*, 449 F.2d 1109, 1119 (D.C. Cir. 1971) ***

The Federal Power Commission has abdicated a significant part of its responsibility by substituting the statement of PASNY for its own. The Commission appears to be content to collate the comments of other federal agencies, its own staff and the intervenors and once again to act as an umpire.... The danger of this procedure, and one obvious shortcoming, is the potential, if not likelihood, that the applicant's statement will be based upon self-serving assumptions.... In fact, PASNY's statement begins: "Neither the construction nor the operation of the Gilboa-Leeds transmission line will have any significant adverse impact on the environment." But, the Gilboa-Leeds line, if constructed as proposed, will cut a swath approximately 35 miles long and 150 feet wide across the face of Greene and Schoharie Counties. It is small consolation that the line will not scar either existing historical sites or designated park land.*** [I]ntervenors generally have limited resources, both in terms of money and technical expertise, and thus may not be able to provide an effective analysis of environmental factors. It was in part for this reason that Congress has compelled agencies to seek the aid of all available expertise and formulate their own position early in the review process. ***

* * *

Though we conclude that the Commission was in violation of NEPA by conducting hearings prior to the preparation by its staff of its own impact statement, we are of the view that it did not seek improperly the advice of other agencies on the basis of PASNY's application. Section 102(2) (C) compels the agency to seek this advice before preparing its statement. Section 102(1), however, directs that "to the fullest extent possible" regulations should be interpreted and administered in accordance with the policies of NEPA *** Then, on the basis of comments received from these agencies and all interested parties, it prepares its final detailed statement, which is offered in evidence at a contested hearing.

* * *

Fully recognizing that delay unfortunately is incident to our mandate and PASNY's claim that the Blenheim-Gilboa Project is a vitally needed power facility, we can only add our voice to that of the District of Columbia Circuit in *Calvert Cliffs'*: Delay is a concomitant of the implementation of the procedures prescribed by NEPA, and the spectre of a power crisis "must not be used to create a blackout of environmental consideration in the agency review process." 449 F.2d at 1122. "It is far more consistent with the purposes of the Act to delay operation at a stage where real environmental protection may come about than at a stage where corrective action may be so costly as to be impossible." *Id.* at 1128.

* * *

[Furthermore, i]n an effort to avoid any confusion or misunderstanding on remand, we are constrained to comment on the Commission's planning responsibility. Under Section 10(a) of the Federal Power Act, the Commission cannot issue a license unless the project is "best adapted to a comprehensive plan ... for the improvement and utilization of waterpower development and for other beneficial public uses, including recreational purposes; ..." In *Scenic Hudson* I we commented that the Commission's failure to inform itself of Consolidated Edison's future interconnection plans "cannot be reconciled with its planning responsibility under the Federal Power Act." 354 F.2d at 622. ***

* * *

B. *Blenheim-Gilboa Project and Approved Transmission Lines*

Petitioners ask us to stay construction of the pumped storage facility and the two approved transmission lines, now 80% complete, pending compliance with NEPA. Although there can be no question that the Act applies to all major federal actions taken after January 1, 1970, despite the fact that construction of the project under consideration may have commenced prior to that date, *** we see no basis for applying NEPA retroactively to the licensing of the basic project which became final nearly six months prior to the effective date of the Act. ***

With respect to the Gilboa-New Scotland and Gilboa-Fraser lines, however, there can be no question that the Commission failed to comply with NEPA. The lines were approved on April 10, 1970, but the Commission failed to issue the requisite detailed environmental statement. Nevertheless, we find no compelling basis for halting construction of the lines so far advanced and decline to reopen the authorization proceedings. *** Although we might arrive at a different conclusion if there were significant potential for subversion of the substantive policies expressed in NEPA, *** the Commission did require PASNY in submitting its plans to "give appropriate consideration to recognized guidelines for protecting the environment"[31] and also conducted its own independent investigation of alternative routings. Moreover, it would be unreasonable to expect instant compliance with all of the Act's procedural requirements, *** and there is no indication (as there is with respect to the Gilboa-Leeds line) of obstinate refusal to comply with NEPA. ***

* * *

The petitions for review are granted in part and denied in part, and the case is remanded for further proceedings in accordance with this opinion.

Notes and Questions

1. **Calculated or oversight.** a. Were you convinced that the agency's approval of the lines without compliance with NEPA was not intentional based on what it viewed as the exigencies of a looming power crisis? b. The agency proceeded in this fashion despite all the legislative and regulatory calls for deliberative action. Given this, what kinds of remedies or sanctions might be appropriate?

2. **Value of statement *before* hearings.** Environmental impact statements, in the first instance, serve to define the issues, although those issues may be either broadened or narrowed during the public hearing. In this view, consider whether it is possible to have meaningful public hearings on possible environmental impacts of a project without first having identified and studied those impacts?

3. **Council on Environmental Quality guidelines for coordination.** Recognizing that NEPA and Section 106 of NHPA might operate in parallel, though related, regimes, NEPA being broadly concerned with adverse impacts on the human environment and Section 106 being more narrowly focused on historic properties within the area of potential effects, the timing and order of assessing the impacts diverging, the Council on Environmental Quality ("CEQ"), promulgated Regulations for Implementing the Procedural Provisions of the National Environmental Policy Act, 40 C.F.R. Parts 1500–1508, to encourage integration of the NEPA process with other planning and environmental reviews, such as Section 106. In March 2013, the CEQ released a *NEPA and NHPA Handbook for Integrating NEPA and Section 106.* Council on Environmental Quality, Executive Office of the President & Advisory Council on Historic Preservation, *NEPA and NHPA: A Handbook for Integrating NEPA and Section 106* (2013), *available at* http://www.achp.gov/docs/NEPA_NHPA_Section_106_Handbook_Mar2013.pdf. The Handbook provides advice on implementing the CEQ's regulations that require agencies to "integrate the NEPA process with other planning at the earliest possible time to ensure that planning and decisions reflect environmental

31. *See, e. g.*, Guidelines for the Protection of Natural, Historic, Scenic, and Recreational Values in the Design and Location of Right-of-Way and Transmission Facilities, Report of the Working Committee on Utilities of the President's Council on Recreation and Natural Beauty (Dec. 27, 1968), reprinted in Commissioner Bagge's concurrence in the June 6, 1969, license. 41 F.P.C. at 725.

values, to avoid delays in the process, and to head off potential conflicts." The Handbook is a joint effort between the CEQ and the Advisory Council on Historic Preservation. The goals and benefits of the coordination include the facilitation of broad discussion of the environmental effects, the development of a comprehensive review schedule to timely meet regulatory requirements, and time savings. The Handbook also expects that integration will enhance public engagement where interested parties are involved under both statutes at the same time; avoid the duplication of time consuming processes; and promote transparency and accountability through better, more informed decisions.

The key concepts covered in the Handbook are:

- Beginning integration as early as possible
- Educating stakeholders on the benefits of coordination
- Developing comprehensive planning schedules and comprehensive communication plans
- Using NEPA documents to facilitate Section 106 consultation and vice versa
- Completing both reviews before issuing final agency decision

Significantly, coordination will mean a single identification and assessment of effects to historic properties and an opportunity for incorporating Section 106 factors in the scoping requirements for NEPA assessments. Recognizing differences in statutory terminology that might operate to impede coordination, for example, "context" under NEPA refers to geographic, biophysical, and social context, but means "historic significance" under NHPA, the Handbook contains a comprehensive comparison of the meanings of terms.

The Handbook also aims to help parties determine early in the project planning when they might benefit from the NEPA § 106 substitution process, that is, using NEPA to comply with Section 106, including a "roadmap," with relevant factors, such as the degree of agency involvement in the development of the NEPA documents and the degree of the delegation of authority to staff to implement the process.

4. **Intersection of alternative energy sources and natural and cultural resources.** While off-shore wind energy projects are now recognized as important sources of clean renewable energy, they are not without impact on the environment and other cultural resources. The Cape Wind Project proposed for Nantucket was met with many objections, including that it threatened the habitats of wildlife (foraging ducks, terns) and would interfere with the sacred sun-greeting ritual of the Mashpee Wampanoag. In *Public Emples. for Envtl. Responsibility v. Hopper*, 827 F. 3d 1077, 1083 (D.C. Cir. 2016), the District of Columbia Circuit Court of Appeals, ruled that the agency's environmental evaluation of the proposed energy station was flawed because, among other things, it failed to obtain sufficient site-specific data on seafloor and subsurface hazards; it did not "take a 'hard look' at the geological and geophysical environment."

H. Protections for National Historic Landmarks

Presidio Historical Ass'n v. Presidio

United States Court of Appeals for the Ninth Circuit
811 F.3d 1154 (2016)

McKEOWN, Circuit Judge. This appeal calls upon us to address the future development footprint of the historical heart of the Presidio of San Francisco ("Presidio")—a former military base that is now a National Park and a National Historic Landmark. Like the city in which it sits, the Presidio is caught in the middle of competing forces: on the one hand, a strong commitment to preservation, and on the other, the inexorable tide of change, development, and economic pressures.

The area of the Presidio at issue—the Main Post, sometimes referred to as the focal point of the Presidio—is managed by the Presidio Trust (the "Trust"), a wholly-owned government corporation created by the Presidio Trust Act. Omnibus Parks and Public Lands Management Act of 1996, Pub. L. No. 104-333, 110 Stat. 4097 (codified at 16 U.S.C. §460bb app.) ("Presidio Trust Act" or "PTA"). The Trust is governed by both the Presidio Trust Act and the National Historic Preservation Act ("NHPA"). 54 U.S.C.A. §300101 et seq. (West 2015).[1]

Under the Presidio Trust Act, the Trust must fulfill the dual statutory purposes of preserving the historic and natural character of the Presidio and making the Presidio financially self-sustaining. PTA §§101(5), (6), (7). To meet those directives, the Trust in 2002 adopted the Presidio Trust Management Plan (the "Plan"). The Trust amended the Plan for the Main Post district in 2011 (the "Update"). Among other things, the Update provided for extensive demolition and new construction on the Presidio's Main Post, including a new lodge, an expansion of the Presidio Theatre, an addition to the Presidio Chapel, and an archaeology lab.

This appeal is limited to the Update's proposed new lodge adjacent to the Presidio's Main Parade Ground. Labeling it as a "lodge" is something of a misnomer, because it is not a single, unitary structure. Instead, the design envisions twelve buildings totaling 70,000 square feet at a "maximum height of 30 feet above existing grade," with each building connected by "open-air porches" and styled after the historic, Civil War-era Graham Street barracks that once stood in roughly the same location. For simplicity, we refer to this proposed development as "the lodge." While the Trust envisioned the lodge as opening the park to more cultural, educational, and public uses and contributing to financial sustainability, critics allege the project contributes to commercialization of the park and undermines the Main Post's historic character.

Central to the appeal is whether the construction of a new lodge (70,000 square feet), offset by demolition of other buildings (94,000 square feet) in the Main Post, constitutes "replacement of existing structures of similar size in existing areas of de-

---

1. Unless otherwise noted, all citations to 54 U.S.C.A are drawn from West's annotated 2015 edition of the United States Code.

velopment" under the Presidio Trust Act. PTA § 104(c)(3). We also address whether, in settling on the lodge location and design, the Trust complied with Section 110(f) of the NHPA, which requires that the Trust "to the maximum extent possible ... undertake such planning and actions as may be necessary to minimize harm to the landmark." 54 U.S.C.A. § 306107. Because the Trust complied with its obligations under both statutes, we affirm the district court's grant of summary judgment in favor of the Trust.

Background

The Presidio has been described as the birthplace of San Francisco and is noted for its diverse architectural styles and formal landscapes that illustrate the complex layering of construction over time. In the mid-twentieth century, the Presidio began a transition from a fully-functioning military base to the recreational preserve that it is today, starting with its designation as a National Historic Landmark District in1962. In 1994, the National Park Service ("Park Service") assumed control of the Presidio from the Army and managed the property under the Golden Gate National Recreation Area Act ("Golden Gate Act"), 16 U.S.C. § 460bb et seq. The Golden Gate Act sought to "preserve for public use and enjoyment certain areas of Marin and San Francisco Counties, California, possessing outstanding natural, historic, scenic, and recreational values, and ... to provide for the maintenance of needed recreational open space necessary to urban environment and planning." Id. § 460bb. The Act limited new construction within covered lands to "reconstruc[tion]," and specifically provided that "[a]ny ... structure which is demolished may be replaced with an improvement of similar size...." *Id.* § 460bb-2(i).

Not long after, Congress revisited the Park Service's responsibility for the entirety of the Presidio, in part out of a desire to reduce the government's financial responsibility for maintaining the park. The result was the 1996 Presidio Trust Act, which divided the Presidio into two areas (Area A and Area B) and gave the newly formed Presidio Trust the authority to oversee, manage, and develop Area B of the park, roughly eighty percent of the area. PTA § 104(a).[2] Specifically, the Trust is required to manage Area B in accordance with the Golden Gate Act and the Park Service's "General Management Plan" for the Presidio, both of which require protecting the historic character and predominantly natural setting of the Presidio. *Id.* At the same time, the Trust Act imposed a duty to develop a management plan "designed to reduce expenditures ... and increase revenues to the Federal Government to the maximum extent possible." *Id.* § 104(c). To incentivize the Trust to fulfill this latter goal, the Trust Act called for a fifteen-year phase-out of budgetary support, leaving the Trust responsible for making the Presidio financially self-sustainable. *Id.* § 105(b). As of 2013, the Presidio had achieved financial self-sustainability and no longer required subsidies from the federal government.

In 2002, the Trust adopted a Plan to fulfill the directives of the Trust Act. For management purposes the Plan created seven planning districts. These districts adapted

2. The Park Service retained the remaining twenty percent of the park, denominated Area A, which runs along the coastline.

the earlier planning districts established by the Park Service, and were "based on each area's historic uses; jurisdictional boundaries; human-made features such as roads, fences, and walls; and natural features and demarcations, including topography and vegetation." Each district had a designated "planning concept" that would guide "future planning and building use decisions." Like any part of the Trust's Plan, these planning districts and their applicable planning concepts may be altered at a later date. Amendments to the Plan, however, are subject to statutory and administrative limitations and may require, for example, administrative review, public comment, or consultation with government agencies. PTA §§ 103(c)(6), 104(c).

The Main Post district, number 1, was designated as "Mixed-Use/Visitor & Community Focus,"[3] with a vision that it would be "the heart of the Presidio" and a "focal point for visitor orientation." The Plan capped total building area in the Main Post district at 1,240,000 square feet. It also capped lodging space in the park at 2 51,000 square feet.

This map outlines Areas A and B (including the seven planning districts): [Map omitted and can be viewed in the website materials. Eds.].

Frustrated with the persistent "empty and uninviting" feel of the Main Post and its failure to achieve anticipated public visitation, the Trust began to consider a revision to the Plan as early as 2005. Because the Trust was interested in larger lodging options than anticipated in the original Plan, the Update required a formal amendment process, including an environmental review under the National Environmental Policy Act ("NEPA"), 42 U.S.C. § 4332, and a formal consultation under Section 106 of the NHPA.

After several years and multiple iterations of environmental review, consultation, and public comment, the Trust released its Update in 2010. The following year, the Trust documented its decision-making process in a Record of Decision, and formally adopted the Update on February 23, 2011. The centerpiece of the Update—and the only component challenged in this appeal—is the lodge proposal. The proposal ultimately reflected a scaled-back approach that the Trust adopted after consultation with interested parties, including the Park Service, the California State Historic Preservation Officer, and the Advisory Council on Historic Preservation.

The twelve small buildings of the lodge, which are aesthetically modeled after the historic Graham Street barracks, would be located on and adjacent to the footprint of Building 34 (a 31,824-square-foot, modern, non-historical building on the Main Parade that is slated for demolition under the Update). This parcel is adjacent to the Main Parade Ground, which the Trust converted from a parking lot to grassy, open space years ago. This setup is depicted in the following schematic: [schematic omitted and can be viewed in the website materials. Eds.].

According to the Trust, this mitigated design concept would greatly increase the public amenities in the Main Post area while also "strengthen[ing] the articulation

3. The two adjacent planning districts—the Crissy Field district, number 2, and the Letterman district, number 3—were designated as "Mixed-Use/Visitor & Cultural Focus" and "Mixed-Use/Office & Residential," respectively.

of historic open spaces." Compared with the Trust's plans for the lodge before the proposal went through NEPA and NHPA consultation, the modified lodge design also does more to ensure that the "scale, massing, height, and design" are "compatible with the surrounding historic environment."

The lodge proposal was part of a more extensive plan within the Update, which contemplated approximately 146,500 square feet of construction: 24,000 square feet of already completed construction plus 122,500 square feet of new construction. The new construction included the 70,000 square feet for the lodge buildings, as well as additions to the Presidio Theatre, additions to the Presidio Chapel, an archaeology lab, and incidental new construction.

In its final form, the Update slated approximately 148,010 square feet of buildings for demolition. Of those, 94,000 square feet are in the Main Post planning district.[4] As part of the Doyle Drive Project, the Trust also included another 54,071 square feet of demolition from the nearby Crissy Field planning district (Buildings 605 and 606) and Letterman planning district (Building 1158) in its demolition calculations. This project will be a "partially tunneled and covered parkway that reestablishes a connection between Crissy Field and the Main Post."

The proposed construction and demolition projects in the Update netted out to a negative 1,510 square feet. The mathematical maneuver of totaling square footage from the Main Post planning district plus the nearby Crissy Field and Letterman planning districts meant that the Trust could say that the Update as a whole led to a net square footage decrease. Thus, according to the Trust, it met its statutory obligation because the new buildings would replace existing buildings of similar square footage.

The Trust rooted its approach in what is termed the "banking" interpretation of Section 104(c)(3), under which the Trust could undertake new construction ("replacement") so long as the square footage ("similar size") of the new construction was offset by aggregate demolition from any developed part of Area B ("existing areas of development"). The Trust explicitly relied on the banking interpretation in adopting both the Plan and the Update, and it has been the Trust's operative theory of new construction authority until the current litigation. After the Trust finalized the Update, the Presidio Historical Association and the Sierra Club (the "Associations") filed suit, challenging the Update on the grounds that the new lodge violated applicable statutes.

On cross-motions for summary judgment, the district court granted summary judgment to the Trust. The district court specifically disclaimed any reliance on the Trust's banking interpretation of Section 104(c)(3) of the Presidio Trust Act: "In reaching a conclusion that the Trust acted within its statutory authority, the court need not decide (and does not hold) that the Trust can 'bank' square footage from any area of development or one planning district and use it as it chooses in another area or district."

---

4. This number includes 59,417 square feet of new demolition plans; 32,259 square feet of new demolition (Buildings 204, 231, and 230) attributable to a related project renovating Doyle Drive; and 2,263 square feet of already completed demolition.

Instead, the district court found Section 104(c)(3) ambiguous and held that the lodge proposal was well within any reasonable interpretation permitted by the statute.

The district court also held that, whether Section 110(f) of the NHPA imposes procedural or substantive obligations on agencies, it could not "see what else the Trust could have done besides not build the hotel at all." Finally, the district court concluded that the Trust complied with NEPA and was not required to re-circulate its Final Supplemental Environmental Impact Statement for public comment after making relatively modest changes to the lodge proposal.

On appeal, the Associations raise claims only under the Presidio Trust Act and the NHPA—not NEPA—and have framed the questions on appeal as limited to the lodge construction.[5] ***We review de novo the district court's decision on the motion for summary judgment. *Turtle Island Restoration Network v. NMFS*, 340 F.3d 969, 973 (9th Cir. 2003).

Analysis

I. The Presidio Trust Act

At the center of the dispute over the lodge proposal is interpretation of Section 104(c) of the Presidio Trust Act. This section requires the Trust to "develop a comprehensive program for management of those lands and facilities within the Presidio which are transferred to the administrative jurisdiction of the Trust.... Such program shall consist of—

> (1) demolition of structures which in the opinion of the Trust, cannot be cost-effectively rehabilitated, and which are identified in the management plan for demolition,
>
> ...
>
> (3) new construction limited to replacement of existing structures of similar size in existing areas of development ..."

PTA § 104(c).

The Trust reads Section 104(c)(3) to permit new construction in any existing area of development so long as the new construction is offset by demolition in any existing area of development throughout the park—i.e., the banking interpretation. In the course of litigation, the Trust also advanced a narrower interpretation of the statute that would permit new construction so long as it is offset by demolition in the same existing area of development—*i.e.*, what the Associations term the "banking lite" interpretation. The Associations take the position that Section 104(c)(3) limits new

---

5. The key issue on appeal is posed as follows: "Does the Presidio Trust's 2010 management plan violate Section 104(c)(3) of the Presidio Trust Act ... by authorizing approximately 70,000 square feet of new construction on existing open space in the Main Post?" The second issue under the *NHPA* is likewise framed around the legality of the "plan to construct a new commercial hotel on the Main Post."

construction to replacement of demolished structures with "buildings of roughly the same size in roughly the same place"—essentially a building-by-building, or one-up, one-down, approach.

We reject the Trust's broader banking theory, but agree that the statute supports a variant of its narrower interpretation. The buildings scheduled for demolition within the same Main Post planning district (94,000 square feet) offset the lodge's 70,000 square feet of new construction within close proximity to the demolished structures. We therefore hold that the lodge proposal qualifies as a "replacement of existing structures of similar size in [an] existing area[] of development." PTA § 104(c)(3). Because the lodge is the only new construction at issue in this appeal, we need not concern ourselves with the calculations related to the remaining demolition and new construction contained within the Update. Nor do we explore the outer limits of what is permissible under the statute.

Our reasoning rests on the familiar Chevron analysis because the Trust is a government entity with statutory authority to make binding policy regarding Area B of the Presidio. *Chevron, U.S.A., Inc. v. Nat. Res. Def. Council, Inc.*, 467 U.S. 837, 842–43, 104 S. Ct. 2778, 81 L. Ed. 2d 694 (1984); *High Sierra Hikers Ass'n v. Blackwell*, 390 F.3d 630, 648 (9th Cir. 2004) (treating the precedential value of an agency's statutory authority as determinative of whether Chevron applies). Under Chevron, we look first to the text of the statute to determine whether "Congress has directly spoken to the precise question at issue." *Chevron*, 467 U.S. at 842. "If the intent of Congress is clear, that is the end of the matter; for the court, as well as the agency, must give effect to the unambiguously expressed intent of Congress." Id. at 842–43. If the intent of Congress is not clear, then we consider whether the Trust's interpretation is "based on a permissible construction of the statute." Id. at 843.

In reaching their preferred, albeit divergent, readings of "replacement of existing structures of similar size," both sides start with the proposition that the statute is unambiguous. Yet the seemingly simple statute raises more questions than it answers and we conclude that it is ambiguous with respect to the scope of the Trust's authority to undertake new construction. A dizzying array of square footage figures offered by the parties hints at deep underlying ambiguity, and nothing in the plain text of the statute—the common denominator for the purposes of our analysis—adds any clarity. See *United States v. Ermoian*, 752 F.3d 1165, 1168 (9th Cir. 2013) We begin, as any effort to interpret a statute must, with the text.").

We first consider the Associations' position that the statute unambiguously mandates a rough one-up, one-down principle. This argument fails on a plain language reading of the statute. The Associations largely assume that the word size refers to square footage, but we note that size might also refer to a building's volume, height, footprint, scale, massing, or some combination of factors that are simply not delineated by the statute and thus inevitably require interpretation and judgment calls on the part of both the Trust and this court. Additionally, the term similar, particularly as part of the phrase "similar size," itself evokes a qualitative judgment, which is anathema to the notion of clarity at Chevron step one.

The purported plain meaning of the word replacement does not fare any better. To be sure, the contours of its accepted meaning limit the realm of possibilities, requiring that there be a plausible connection between the replacement and its predecessor. See Oxford English Dictionary (3d ed. 2009) (defining replace as "to provide a substitute for" or "put an equivalent in place of"). But whatever inherent limiting effect the word replacement might impart, the narrow meaning is lost when the word is read in context. The statute refers to replacement of "existing structures" rather than an "existing structure." PTA § 104(c)(3). Thus, this language does not preclude a building or groups of buildings from replacing other groups of buildings, making it increasingly difficult to be sure what must be compared for similarity, let alone how to compare it.

The ambiguity of this phrase stands out in contrast with the Golden Gate Act, which employed similar, but far clearer, language limiting new construction. See 16 U.S.C. § 460bb-2(i) (prohibiting new construction generally but allowing "[a]ny ... structure which is demolished" to be "replaced with an improvement of similar size" (emphasis added)). Had Congress intended the Trust Act to maintain the same strictures that governed new construction in the Presidio under the Golden Gate Act, it presumably would have kept the singular form, which better supports a one-up, one-down principle. *Schwenk v. Hartford*, 204 F.3d 1187, 1201 n.12 (9th Cir. 2000). Where limiting language present in earlier statutes is not included in later legislation, it can be presumed that the omission was intentional.").

The Associations acknowledge that the phrase "replacement of existing structures of similar size" does not bind the Trust to put new construction in exactly the same place and make it exactly the same in appearance or even footprint as the prior structures. They assert only that the Trust must put new construction "roughly" in the same location as the demolished building and make it "roughly" the same size. The Associations further acknowledge that it might be possible under their interpretation to remove several buildings and replace them with one new building of similar aggregate size. This common-sense concession certainly embraces one plausible reading of the statute, but one can posit both narrower and more expansive definitions of the provision's operative terms, which are inherently abstract and imprecise. The specificity that Chevron step one demands is simply lacking here.

The statute also states that the new construction may only replace existing structures in "existing areas of development." PTA § 104(c)(3) (emphasis added). The reference to "existing areas" would be rendered superfluous if the provision required the Trust to proceed on a building-by-building basis, since the building being replaced would necessarily have been in an existing area of development. *See Marx v. Gen. Revenue Corp.*, 133 S. Ct. 1166, 1177–78, 185 L. Ed. 2d 242 (2013) (noting that a statutory interpretation that renders other statutory language superfluous is generally disfavored, particularly if there is another interpretation that gives effect to every clause and word of a statute). Reading the phrase "replacement of existing structures of similar size" in light of the phrase "existing areas of development" compounds the ambiguity of PTA § 104(c)(3). In sum, we are unconvinced by the Associations' reading of the statute.

Nor are we persuaded that the Trust's banking interpretation passes the test at *Chevron* step one. *** At Chevron step one, we determine whether Congress has spoken to the "precise question at issue." *Chevron*, 467 U.S. at 842. The answer here is no. The statute is unclear. Notably, neither side presents a compelling argument for any definitive, unambiguous definition of what is required of the Trust. In the end, the most that can be said of the statute is that it grants some unspecified discretion to the Trust to undertake new construction projects within certain obscure strictures.

In the face of an ambiguous statute, under the second step of the Chevron analysis, we defer to the Trust's interpretation so long as it is "based on a permissible construction of the statute." *Chevron*, 467 U.S. at 843. We hold that the Trust's expansive banking interpretation is impermissible because it is "manifestly contrary to the statute." *Household Credit Servs., Inc. v. Pfennig*, 541 U.S. 232, 239, 124 S. Ct. 1741, 158 L. Ed. 2d 450 (2004) (citation omitted).

While the new construction authority granted by the Presidio Trust Act is indeed capacious, there are nevertheless limits to what the Trust can read into the Act's delegation of authority. *Util. Air Regulatory Grp. v. E.P.A.*, 134 S. Ct. 2427, 2442–43, 189 L. Ed. 2d 372 (2014) ("Even under Chevron's deferential framework, agencies must operate 'within the bounds of reasonable interpretation.'" (quoting *City of Arlington v. F.C.C.*, 133 S. Ct. 1863, 1868, 185 L. Ed. 2d 941 (2013)). The key infirmity of the banking interpretation is that it imposes no discernible limits on the Trust's development authority across the Presidio, and thus would lead to an "enormous and transformative expansion" of the Trust's "regulatory authority without clear congressional authorization." *Id.* at 2444. *** Taken at face value, the Trust's theory would render the entire Area B of the Presidio subject to unspecified development under the Trust Act, so long as square footage from somewhere (or multiple somewheres) was replaced with square footage anywhere else in the Presidio.

That the banking interpretation would permit unlimited authority puts it at odds with a major purpose of the Trust Act—i.e., to implement "sound principles of land use planning" and "protect[] the Presidio from development and uses which would destroy the scenic beauty and historic and natural character of the area and cultural and recreational resources[.]" PTA § 101(5). That is reason enough to conclude that the banking interpretation is impermissible. *See Chem. Mfrs. Ass'n v. E.P.A.*, 217 F.3d 861, 867, 342 U.S. App. D.C. 355 (D.C. Cir. 2000) (holding EPA's interpretation of an ambiguous statutory provision unreasonable where it was inconsistent with the Clean Air Act's purpose).

* * * If nothing else, Section 104(c)(3) was designed to prohibit the wholesale repurposing of remote corners of the Presidio that currently feature vastly different characteristics and disparate levels of development. Yet the banking interpretation permits just that—the Trust offers no effective limiting interpretation that would account for the Trust's duty to preserve the existing architectural and natural diversity of the Presidio. The Trust's banking interpretation cannot pass muster because it "entirely fail[s] to consider an important aspect of the problem" at hand. *Michigan v.*

E.P.A., 135 S. Ct. 2699, 2707, 192 L. Ed. 2d 674 (2015) (quoting *Motor Vehicle Mfrs. Ass'n of United States, Inc. v. State Farm Mut. Auto. Ins. Co.*, 463 U.S. 29, 43, 103 S. Ct. 2856, 77 L. Ed. 2d 443 (1983)). * * *

The ultimate question is whether the lodge proposal falls within the statutory mandate that new construction projects are limited to "replacement of existing structures of similar size in existing areas of development...." PTA § 104(c)(3). *See also* 5 U.S.C. § 706(2). We conclude that it does. The new lodge construction is projected for 70,000 square feet, while the physically proximate planned demolition within the Main Post planning district alone amounts to over 90,000 square feet.[8]

As already explained, the term "replacement" is not confined to a one-for-one demolition/new construction meaning. Instead, replacement can include, collectively, construction of more than one structure offset by demolition of more than one structure, thus giving meaning to the plural language of "existing structures." PTA § 104(c)(3) (emphasis added). Further, treating the "similar size" restriction as encompassing at least a comparison of the square footage of the relevant demolished buildings, without necessarily cabining its meaning to that unit of analysis, ties the statutory requirements together in a manner consistent with the statute's language and purpose. *Id.* Finally, the phrase "existing areas of development" should be limited to development in areas physically proximate to the location of the building being replaced.[9] *Id.* This interpretation harmonizes all of the elements of the statute. *See Boise Cascade Corp. v. E.P.A.*, 942 F.2d 1427, 1432 (9th Cir. 1991) ("Under accepted canons of statutory interpretation, we must interpret statutes as a whole....").

We conclude that the Trust's Update with respect to the proposed lodge and the offsetting demolition in the Main Post area is consistent with Section 104(c)(3). Without doubt, the proposed lodge is physically proximate to the other Main Post demolition sites. Each of the buildings being "replace[d]" is within several hundred yards of the proposed lodge and falls within a similarly developed area of the Presidio. It does not matter that there may be more structures than before: the new buildings still replace the other buildings within the Main Post planning district. To be sure, there remains some leeway as to how far the statute extends, especially with respect

8. The Trust left open the question of whether it will follow through in demolishing Buildings 40 and 41, which are located in the Main Post planning district and were counted in its 94,000 square feet demolition calculation. Even without these two buildings, which total 16,514 square feet, the rest of the planned demolition in the Main Post planning district would still exceed the 70,000 square feet of new lodge construction.

9. Unlike the more sweeping banking theory, this interpretation also imposes some foreseeable limits on the Trust's new construction authority that are more in keeping with the purposes of the Presidio Trust Act. The Trust could not, for instance, undertake isolated new construction in a remote corner of the park, because it would need to establish physical proximity to an existing area of development in which the purported "replacement" was located. This interpretation further reinforces the purposes of the Presidio Trust Act by allowing the Trust to draw new construction authority from physically proximate parcels that are already likely similar in character. It therefore prevents the Trust from fundamentally re-purposing certain areas of the part in one fell swoop, and generally preserves the architectural, historic and natural diversity of the Presidio as a whole.

to the requirement of physical proximity. But we need not delineate the outer limits of that extension nor consider whether proximity is defined by the boundaries of the planning districts. * * *

II. The National Historic Preservation Act

Because the Presidio is a National Historic Landmark District, any project that alters the Presidio's structures is subject to the provisions of the NHPA. 54 U.S.C.A. § 306101. The NHPA imposes two sets of obligations on federal agencies, depending on the features of the historic site at issue.

To begin, requires an agency undertaking a project expected to adversely affect a public or private site listed on the National Register of Historic Places to "take into account the effect of the undertaking on any historic property." 54 U.S.C.A. § 306108. Congress created the Advisory Council on Historic Preservation ("Advisory Council") to aid in the implementation of this task and to "recommend measures to coordinate activities of Federal, State, and local agencies and private institutions and individuals relating to historic preservation[.]" *Id.* § 304102(a)(1). The Advisory Council has promulgated extensive regulations governing Section 106 consultation. See 36 C.F.R. §§ 800 et seq. These regulations require the undertaking agency to consult with other parties regarding whether the project poses any identifiable adverse effects, *id.* § 800.5, and to "seek ways to avoid, minimize or mitigate the adverse effects," *id.* § 800.6(b)(1)(i).

A second requirement is that projects affecting government-owned sites and National Historic Landmarks, such as the Presidio, trigger the additional statutory requirements of Section 110, which was added to the statute in 1980. Pub. L. No. 96-515, 94 Stat. 2987 (1980) (codified as amended at 54 U.S.C.A. § 306101 et seq.). Section 110 sought to "clarif[y] and codif[y] the minimum responsibilities expected of federal agencies in carrying out the purposes of the [NHPA][.]" H.R. Rep. No. 96-1457, at 36 (1980). For instance, agencies must seek to use historic properties available to them before embarking on construction or acquisition, 54 U.S.C.A. § 306101(a)(2), and must develop a preservation program for federally-owned properties, id. § 306102. National Historic Landmarks are subject to the specific requirements of Section 110(f), which reads, in relevant part: "Prior to the approval of any Federal undertaking that may directly and adversely affect any National Historic Landmark, the head of the responsible Federal agency shall to the maximum extent possible undertake such planning and actions as may be necessary to minimize harm to the landmark." *Id.* § 306107.

In discharging its obligations under the NHPA, the Trust engaged in extensive Section 106 consultation with multiple parties, including state historical preservation officers, the Advisory Council, and the public. Ultimately, the Trust adopted recommendations made by the Park Service and interested entities to address and mitigate any adverse effects of the lodge. The Advisory Council and other consulting parties signed a memorandum of agreement confirming compliance with the required planning processes. See 36 C.F.R. § 800.6(c).

In light of the extensive compliance efforts under Section 106, the Associations, not surprisingly, do not challenge that aspect of the Trust's planning. However, they argue that the Trust failed to comply with the additional requirements of Section 110(f). According to the Associations, the Section 110(f) language relating to a) "minimiz[ing] harm to the landmark" and b) "to the maximum extent possible," imposes a heightened substantive standard against which the Trust's final decision must be judged.[10]

We disagree. Our court has consistently held that "the NHPA, like NEPA, is a procedural statute requiring government agencies to 'stop, look, and listen' before proceeding" when their action will affect national historical assets. *Te-Moak Tribe of Western Shoshone of Nev. v. United States DOI*, 608 F.3d 592, 607, 610 (9th Cir. 2010) (*quoting Muckleshoot Indian Tribe v. U.S. Forest Serv.*, 177 F.3d 800, 805 (9th Cir. 1999)); *see also Lee v. Thornburgh*, 877 F.2d 1053, 1056, 278 U.S. App. D.C. 265 (D.C. Cir. 1989) ("Our review of the statutory text [of the NHPA] persuades us that Congress intended these provisions to have a limited reach; they are aimed solely at discouraging federal agencies from ignoring preservation values in projects they initiate, approve funds for or otherwise control."). Although these cases do not reference Section 110(f) specifically, they do post-date adoption of the section.

Section 110(f) cannot be read in a vacuum. It builds on the general consultation process set out in Section 106, which the Associations acknowledge is a procedural "stop, look, and listen" requirement, but sets out a heightened procedural standard for National Historic Landmarks, calling for "planning and actions as may be necessary to minimize harm to the landmark." 54 U.S.C.A. § 306107. The obligation referred to is the requirement to "undertake such planning and actions," and to do so to the "maximum extent possible." Id.

Congress often requires agencies to consider a variety of alternatives on the theory that such consideration makes it more likely substantive results will follow. See Joseph L. Sax, *The (Unhappy) Truth About NEPA*, 26 Okla. L. Rev. 239, 240 (1973) ("NEPA's obvious, if unstated, assumption was that by requiring the agencies to explore, consider, and publicly describe the adverse environmental effects of their programs, those programs would undergo revision in favor of less environmentally damaging activities."). Thus, Congress may mix substantive language with purely procedural constraints. Such is the case here: the directive "minimizing harm to the landmark" to the "maximum extent possible" reflects what Congress apparently hoped would result from heightened analysis.

The only other circuit to confront the issue is in accord that Section 110(f) is not a substantive mandate. In addressing Section 4(f) of the Department of Transportation Act, 49 U.S.C. § 303(c), the First Circuit held that "Section 4(f), unlike sections 106 and 110(f) [of the NHPA], imposes a substantive mandate." *Neighbor-*

10. Section 110(f) goes on to say that the responsible agency "shall afford the [Advisory] Council a reasonable opportunity to comment with regard to the undertaking." 54 U.S.C.A. § 306107. The Associations do not assert that this portion of Section 110(f) is substantive, and the Advisory Council's affirmation in the memorandum of agreement that the Trust had afforded it an "opportunity to comment on the Undertaking" is in any event sufficient to satisfy this obligation.

hood Ass'n of the Back Bay, Inc. v. Fed. Transit. Admin., 463 F.3d 50, 64 (1st Cir. 2006).[11]

The legislative history confirms that Congress intended to impose only a "higher standard for agency planning in relationship to landmarks before the agency brings the matter to the council." H.R. Rep. No. 96-1457, at 38 (1980) (emphasis added). Indeed, the legislative committee noted that, "[a]lthough [it] deleted a mandatory requirement that an agency first determine that 'no prudent and feasible alternative to such undertaking exists,' [it] [did] intend for agencies to consider prudent and feasible alternatives." *Id.* (emphasis added). As with NEPA, it would be difficult to interpret this history as suggesting anything other than an intent to require agencies to canvass their options with a keen eye.

We are not persuaded by the argument of amicus curiae National Trust for Historic Preservation that Congress clearly intended to model Section 110(f) on another statute that the courts have interpreted as substantive—Section 4(f) of the Department of Transportation Act. 49 U.S.C. § 303(c). Notably, Section 4(f), while including nearly identical language about minimizing harm, also includes a very important qualifier not present in the NHPA, namely that historic sites may be approved "only if ... there is no prudent and feasible alternative to using that land[.]" 49 U.S.C. § 303(c) (emphasis added). The First Circuit recognized this critical difference in declaring Section 4(f) to be a substantive mandate, in contrast to Section 110(f). *Neighborhood Ass'n*, 463 F.3d at 64. If anything, Congress's decision to strip the mandatory language about exhausting prudent and feasible alternatives from the bill that eventually became Section 110(f), see H.R. Rep. 96-1457, at 38, is evidence of Congress's intent to distinguish Section 110(f) from Section 4(f) of the transportation legislation. *Schwenk*, 204 F.3d at 1201 n.12.

Although court decisions interpreting other, similar statutes can be persuasive, our best guide to what this statute means is the text. The legislative history of Section 110(f) is icing on the cake. *See City & Cnty. of S.F. v. U.S. Dep't of Transp.*, 796 F.3d 993, 998 (9th Cir. 2015) (noting that the first source to examine is the "plain words of the statute" and the last is "similar provisions within the statute as a whole and the language of related or similar statutes" (citations omitted)); *Negusie v. Holder*, 555 U.S. 511, 519–20, 129 S. Ct. 1159, 173 L. Ed. 2d 20 (2009) (rejecting an analogy to a holding in a case interpreting another, similar statute where the language and design of the statute in the case at hand were distinguishable).

In holding that Section 110(f) does not impose a substantive obligation, we do not mean that Congress failed to heighten the procedural hurdles an agency must satisfy with respect to projects affecting National Historic Landmarks. The Trust cannot rest

11. The Fifth Circuit has also held generally that NHPA is a procedural statute. *See Coliseum Square Ass'n, Inc. v. Jackson*, 465 F.3d 215, 225 (5th Cir. 2006). Although it went on to note that Section 110(f) "imposes an affirmative duty on federal agencies to minimize harm to National Historic Landmarks where it finds that a project will adversely affect such landmarks," the court did not reach that specific question because there was no adverse effect. *Id.* at 243–44.

on the fact that, by all indications, it complied with the letter of Section 106. Something more was required under Section 110(f). The best indication of what else was required can be found in the legislative history, which says that the agency should at least "consider prudent and feasible alternatives" to avoid adverse effects. H.R. Rep. No. 96-1457, at 38; see also 63 Fed. Reg. 20,495, 20,503 (Apr. 24, 1998). This obligation stands on top of the more general duty in the Section 106 consultation process to "seek ways to avoid, minimize or mitigate ... adverse effects." 36 C.F.R. § 800.6(b). In short, the Trust was required to thoroughly consider—rather than simply identify and catalog—prudent and feasible alternatives to its proposed lodge design and in its planning process.

We are satisfied that the Trust met this heightened standard within the planning process. The original lodge proposal changed dramatically over time, from a behemoth building to a smaller, historically appropriate collection of buildings. In its 2009 response to the Trust's plans, the Park Service recommended that the Trust "[r]educe the footprint, scale, massing, and height of the proposed lodge; break up the mass into separate buildings ... or remove the lodge from the Main Post." In response, the Trust broke the lodge into twelve separate buildings with spaces of ten to twenty feet between them to preserve visual continuity between the Old and Main Parade Grounds, reduced the total square footage from its earlier proposals, and adopted at least a partially historically integrated design concept.

The Trust also gave consideration to possible lodging in the existing Montgomery Street Barracks buildings, but found that the project was not feasible at the time. As late as 2010, in the final stages of its deliberation, the Trust gave extensive consideration to at least three lodging alternatives in its Final Supplemental Environmental Impact Statement, none of which included any new lodge construction.[12] In the Trust's judgment, arrived at through extensive public engagement, these no-lodge alternatives were insufficient for the purposes of the Main Post Update. Altogether, the Trust's thorough consideration of lodging options in available existing properties was sufficient to satisfy its obligation to "use, to the maximum extent feasible, historic property available to the agency[.]" 54 U.S.C.A. § 306101(a)(2); see also 63 Fed. Reg. at 20,500 ("An agency] has an affirmative responsibility to seek and use historic properties to the maximum extent feasible in carrying out its activities."). Nothing in the record suggests that the Trust "relied on factors Congress did not intend it to consider, entirely failed to consider an important aspect of the problem, or offered an explanation that runs counter to the evidence before the agency or is so implausible that it could not be ascribed to a difference in view or the product of agency expertise." *Cascadia Wildlands v. Bureau of Indian Affairs*, 801 F.3d 1105, 1110 (9th Cir. 2015) (*quoting Ecology Ctr. v. Castaneda*, 574 F.3d 652, 656 (9th Cir. 2009)).

12. These included: 1) "Lodging in Pershing Hall (Building 42) and dormitory rooms for visitors in Buildings 40 and 41"; 2) "Lodging in Pershing Hall and B&Bs in upper Funston Avenue Officers' Quarters (Buildings 11–16)"; and 3) "Residences in Pershing Hall and dormitory rooms for visitors in Buildings 40 and 41."

The Park Service and the Trust disagreed about whether the goals of the Update could be accomplished without a new lodge. The Park Service concluded that a "new lodge at the Main Post is not the only means to 'welcome visitors and animate the Main Parade'" and that "there are other ways to achieve this goal, such as through rehabilitation of existing buildings at the Main Post, the establishment of a Visitor Center, and programs." Likewise, the Presidio Historical Association stated that its problems with the Update stemmed not from a lack of "hard work and creativity," but from problems "at the level of the concepts themselves." But under the terms of Section 110(f), the Trust was not obligated to agree with the Park Service's or the Presidio Historical Association's views—it had to give them full and reasoned consideration, which it did. Indeed, the Trust "incorporate[d] the majority of the recommendations outlined in the [Park Service's] report," and offered reasoned explanations where it deviated from the Park Service's preferred result. The Trust's procedural undertakings surely meet the heightened standard of care imposed by Section 110(f) to undertake "to the maximum extent possible ... such planning and actions as may be necessary to minimize harm to the landmark." 54 U.S.C.A. § 306107.

Conclusion

Because the Trust complied with the Presidio Trust Act and the NHPA, we affirm the district court's grant of summary judgment to the Trust with respect to the proposed 70,000 square feet of new lodge construction on the Main Post of the Presidio. We do not consider the Trust's proposed replacement construction other than the lodge.

AFFIRMED.

Notes and Questions

1. **New designs, construction, and features.** a. How is adaptive reuse to be designed for a project area as extensive as the Presidio? b. What are some of the environmental impacts when new construction is to sit on an old site? c. What new uses are appropriate? Consider Deborah Bardwick, *From Post to Pond: How the Public Created the Presidio's Crissy Field Marsh,* 6 Golden Gate U. Envtl. L. J. 7 (2012), available at http://digitalcommons.law.ggu.edu/cgi/viewcontent.cgi?article=1090&context=gguelj (last visited April 5, 2017).

2. **The restored fort.** The Presidio was Imperial Spain's most northern government seat in California, which had been under continuing demolition and development until conveyed to the National Park Service to be part of the Gateway Recreation Area. a. Finding that Section 110(f) merely imposes procedural requirements on the agency, even in the case of National Historic Landmarks, a status conferred because of their "exceptional values," 36 C.F.R. Part 65, is the court saying that the Trust could demolish all the historic buildings to put up ones that are modern and do not recall the past? b. How will the imperative to become self-sustaining lead to development that affects its historic integrity?

I. Historic Structures within Parks

Historic structures situated within parks and wilderness areas raise issues about how to reconcile protection of the built environment with conservation of nature. New York State's Adirondack Park, where the Forest Preserve is established as "forever wild" by Article XIV of the State Constitution, has struggled to save grand sites, such as Sagamore or other "Great Camps" or iconic small lookout towers once used for spotting forest fires. A Conference on "Cultural Heritage in the Wilds" at Camp Top Ridge (May 1978) explored these issues. The Workshop Report presented below explores ways to accommodate both sets of values. Since 1990 Adirondack Architectural Heritage (AARCH) has campaigned to design historic preservation measures into wilderness stewardship. *See* http://www.aarch.org.

1. Cultural Heritage in the Wilds: Conference Report

Camp Topridge, New York

May 25 and 26, 1978

The issue of creating a state register for historic and cultural resources and the ramifications of creating such a register were not fully explored. Should New York State compile and administer a State Register of Historic Places? Pending state legislation, if enacted, will create such a state register. With its creation will come many new compliance responsibilities for state and local governments.

A final issue which future discussion should address is the development of criteria to judge the adequacy of an inventory. Questions such as "What constitutes a good inventory?" and "To what extent are present inventories deficient and how should they be augmented?" remain to be further explored.

—George Nagle

WORKSHOP II: LEGAL/JURISDICTIONAL/POLICY:
ISSUES AND ALTERNATIVES

*** The workshop instinctively focused upon Article XIV, which seemed to be the most important element in the equation for the preservation of historic structures associated with state Forest Preserve lands.

The most important portion of Article XIV for this discussion is the first section:

> The lands of the state, now owned or hereafter acquired, constituting the Forest Preserve as now fixed by law, shall be forever kept as wild forest lands. They shall not be leased, sold, or exchanged, or be taken by any cor-

---

* *** This designation refers not only to those acres which are currently owned by the State of New York and managed by the Department of Environmental Conservation. It will also refer to lands, in private ownership, which may be candidates for acquisition and inclusion in the "wild forest lands" of the state. The "wild forest land" designation was chosen as a generic description for Adirondack open space property in preference to the more technical, though commonly used "wilderness" designation.

poration, public or private, nor shall the timber thereon be sold, removed or destroyed.

*** The Forest Preserve is defined in Sec. 9-0101 of the Environmental Conservation Law as including "the lands owned or hereafter acquired by the state" within twelve Adirondack counties and four Catskill counties, with certain specified exceptions. It includes approximately 2.6 million acres of land in the Adirondack Park. The state is required to manage this enormous landmass as "wild forest land."*

It is certain that when the Forest Preserve as created in 1885, no one then living considered the possibility that one day the Great Camps and their lands would be ripe for inclusion within the Forest Preserve. No one contemplated the prospect that the structures, then new or under construction, would one day become an issue in the preservation and use of the Forest Preserve.

* * *

The public concern for the Forest Preserve, frequently reiterated in constitutional amendments and in rejection of proposed amendments, has led the managers of the Forest Preserve to be conservative in their management and use of this resource. *** Such traditional conservation is perhaps the rationale underlying the view that "forever wild" means that any structure on land in the Adirondack or Catskill Park which becomes state owned is inconsistent with the concept of wild forest land and must be removed, torn down, or destroyed.

The immediate effects of this view are striking when one considers the necessary fate of the estate buildings in the Santanoni Preserve and the farm outbuildings on the state land which was associated with the Sagamore property. These buildings are on presently owned state land. The issue assumes even more importance when one considers that as a result of present land acquisition monies made available through the Environmental Quality Bond Act of 1972, many of the existing Great Camps may be candidates for state ownership in the near future.

The days for the traditionally conservative land management policies may have passed. The reluctance of the State of New York, through its Department of Conservation and since 1970 its Department of Environmental Conservation, to purchase wild forest lands with associated structures may have been appropriate in a time before the recognition of the unique cultural value of such historic places. *** However, the State of New York is the only entity in a position to purchase large tracts of wild forest land for preservation purposes. Some significant tracts of wild forest lands are associated with the architecturally and culturally significant Great Camps. The traditional state policy of avoiding or destroying buildings may, therefore, no longer be appropriate.

The workshop addressed the following range of possibilities for future state policies with reference to the Great Camps of the Adirondack Park and the relevant constitutional provisions. These possibilities are presented below in reverse order to the amount of time which the workshop devoted to the various strategies.

We can maintain the status quo.

This would involve a variety of possible actions.

a. Private organizations, such as the Preservation League of New York State, the Adirondack Conservancy Committee of The Nature Conservancy, and others, may serve as either holders of property or brokers to find other purchasers or users of historic structures which have existed with large acreages of potential Forest Preserve lands.

* * *

There are a variety of problems, present and potential, with the private mechanisms for historic preservation. First is the availability of private groups willing and able to so serve. In addition, one must consider the desirability of creating private in-holdings and a patchwork of ownership in Forest Preserve areas.

Private ownership may prove only a short-term solution to the ownership of the great estates, *** [but t]he private ownership pattern does not allow for comprehensive management of these special sites. Inconsistent plans and different levels of economic resources may result in changes to the historic structures which are not in the best interest of the historic integrity of these properties.

* * *

The Natural Heritage Trust (Public Authorities Law, § 2000 *et seq.*) is a public benefit corporation created to receive and administer private gifts and bequests of real and personal property donated to the state for conservation, outdoor recreation, and historic preservation.

* * *

There are certain legal difficulties in continuing the status quo for historic structures presently or hereafter owned on Forest Preserve lands. Most prominently, there is a continuing legal uncertainty as to the propriety of the management solutions undertaken. This uncertainty has existed at least since the 1930's when the People rejected the so-called "recreational amendment" to Article XIV. The Department of Environmental Conservation and its predecessor agency have been forced to make management decisions in the face of this legal uncertainty.

* * *

Recognizing the necessity for state ownership of non-Forest Preserve parcels of land within the Adirondack and Catskill blue lines, but concerned for the apparently inclusive language of Article XIV, the "other than conservation purposes" doctrine has been developed. The regional headquarters for the Departments of Transportation and Environmental Conservation and other similar properties are owned for state purposes not specifically associated with the Forest Preserve. Such ownership and use has been justified on the theory that, in protecting Forest Preserve lands from economic exploitation or sale, the constitutional drafters did not intend to prohibit legitimate state ownership of properties for purposes other than Forest Preserve protection. Therefore, since the state ownership of these parcels is for non-Forest Preserve functions, these properties arguably do not come within the Forest Preserve protections of Article XIV.

* * *

No one is particularly comfortable with the "other purposes" doctrine. None of the lawyers attending the workshop expressed any enthusiasm for testing the constitutional limits of this manufactured solution to the problem of state property ownership in the Adirondack Park.

We can seek legislation to clarify the cultural preservation issues.

*** Two variations were identified[.] ***

a. A special state corporation, similar to the Natural Heritage Trust, could be created to serve as a holding entity or a management device for cultural and other historic properties which might come into state ownership in the Adirondack Park. The Urban Development Corporation (UDC) was suggested as a possible model. Just as the UDC was designed to allow circumvention of the constitutional debt limitation of the state, this special state corporation could be utilized as a management tool for clarifying the limits of Article XIV with relation to historic properties.

b. An amendment to the legislative definition of the "Forest Preserve" in the Environmental Conservation Law was suggested. Such an amendment, to be added as a fourth exception to the list of property within the Adirondack Park counties [Environmental Conservation Law § 9-0101], which is not considered part of the Forest Preserve, might read as follows:

6. The 'Forest Preserve' shall include the lands owned or hereafter acquired by the state … except:

d. Lands, not wild lands, containing historic sites or structures.

The workshop was concerned to indicate that the above remarks are the most preliminary exploration of these issues. Further consideration of any proposed legislation should include assessment of the tax consequences of any decision for the state and Adirondack localities; the availability of resources to carry out any such legislative solution; and the propriety of controlling the intensity of use in such specially vulnerable sites as historic structures.

A constitutional amendment may be proposed.

This was the area in which the bulk of the workshop discussion was focused. The following resolution was proposed.

We recommend a constitutional amendment as a long-range solution to the problems of management of historic structures in state ownership in the Adirondack Park.

*** A discussion of the possible content of such an amendment yielded the following suggestions. One proposal was language to the effect that historic buildings may be preserved on lands which come into state hands within the Adirondack Park. A second alternative would be the identification of specific sites which should be preserved. Such identification would come through a comprehensive survey of historic Adirondack Park resources.

A third alternative would create a land bank similar to that allowed the Department of Transportation (DOT) at the same time that the People of the State authorized the

Adirondack Northway Amendment to Article XIV. A small quantity of land, not to exceed 500–1,000 acres, would be made available for historic preservation on state land without the necessity for a constitutional amendment to approve each acquisition.

*** Some of the lawyers in the workshop raised as an issue the possible legal effect which such an amendment, or proposal for such amendment, might have upon the existing management policies in the Adirondack Park. Such a proposal, carrying the implication that a constitutional amendment is necessary to achieve its ends, would cast doubt upon DEC management policies with respect to historic preservation during the pendency of the amendment. If the amendment failed, this failure must add an interpretation to the existing case law and policy to the effect that DEC's status quo policies for these historic structures are not constitutionally acceptable.

Among the several constitutional possibilities, the land bank idea captured the imagination of the workshop participants. However, many issues still remain to be resolved. Should this be a positive or a negative bank? The DOT bank is basically negative in type, allowing withdrawals from the land bank up to a specified amount.

* * *

*** Quoting Commissioner of Environmental Conservation Peter A. A. Berle introducing and co-sponsoring this conference, a long list of legal questions remain.

> ... (b) the legality of alternative use (e.g., recreational or educational) of such structures; (c) the need for statutory clarification of the right of governmental and private bodies to acquire conservation easements; (d) the need to amend the State Land Master Plan in order to provide greater protection for historic sites and structures; (d) the need to amend the State Land Master Plan in order to provide greater protection for historic sites and structures; (e) the legal implications of the Comprehensive Statewide Historic Preservation Act of 1978; (f) the legal implications of designating the Forest Preserve as a National Historic Landmark; and (g) the legal implications of placing a structure on the National Register of Historic Places.

Continued discussion of these issues must precede any resolution of them.

* * *

2. A Proposal for a Comprehensive Policy for Historic Preservation in the Adirondack and Catskill Parks

Honorable Maurice Hinchey

Chairman, Environmental Conservation Committee
New York State Assembly

*** Article 14 of our State Constitution which acted to keep our Forest Preserve forever wild also acted to create some thorny legal problems with which the State has had to grapple over the years. The Conference at Camp Topridge in 1978 represented a concerted attempt on the part of public officials, environmentalists and preservationists to come to grips with the difficult questions proposed by the apparent conflict between Article 14 and the preservation of historical resources in the Forest Preserve. When Senator Dunn and I introduced, and our respective Houses passed last session, legislation calling for a Constitutional amendment to exchange 10 acres of Forest Preserve land containing the caretaker buildings at Sagamore, for 200 acres of wild forest land within the Adirondack Park, some groups criticized the bill as a piecemeal approach and demanded a comprehensive solution. Today, after many months of discussion and the thorough review of the various proposals which have been made in the past, we are submitting a proposal for a comprehensive approach to historic preservation in the Adirondack and Catskill Parks.*** Its particular merit is that it will provide a prescription for action and pull together those elements in a program that will not only be consistent with, but we believe also will reinforce Article 14. However, before discussing the proposal, I would like to share with you my thoughts regarding one of the alternative proposals which has advanced and received some considerable amount of attention, and that is the establishment of a land bank. I have a number of specific criticisms *** The amendment would provide that a specified amount of acreage in the Adirondack Park now part of the Forest Preserve or to be acquired by the State, be dedicated and administered to preserve its historic character. This would establish a classification of State land use (the State Nature and Historical Preserve) within the Adirondack Park separate from the Forest Preserve classification. Proponents of this approach argue that it will provide the State with the necessary discretion to accommodate preservation by State ownership in years to come. They point to the Highway Land Bank which permits up to 400 acres of Forest Preserve to be used for highway improvements. My specific criticisms are as follows: First, the criteria in land bank proposals to date, for determining the historic significance of property, and this of course is the sole basis for removing property from the Forest Preserve protection. Such criteria, however, is vague and will understandably create confusion and disagreement on individual sites. Secondly, the amount of acreage to be set in the bank would necessarily be arbitrary. Thirdly, I don't believe the need for the land bank has been fully demonstrated. And unless the State is to pursue a policy of preservation through State ownership, there seems to be no need for a land bank. Fourthly, the bank would establish a floating spot zone without consideration of compatibility with adjoining land. Fifthly, we might ask what superior rationale can be argued for an historic preservation land bank as compared with, let us say, a bank for wildlife habitat management, scientific forestry, recreational facilities, for campgrounds, for municipal facilities or land exchanges. The preservation bank would also differ in character from other Adirondack banks which were for public utility purposes. Well, I think that it is obvious that if there were a proliferation of Adirondack banks, it would reduce the wild forest classification to being just one of many competing State land classifications in the Adirondack Park rather than the exclusive criterion for State lands. Sixthly, it would generate pressure for the State to establish a system of historic sites in the Adirondack Park, a program frankly that the State is in no position to finance. To sum up, I believe the land bank proposal would undermine the intent of Article 14, and because of this, I am leery of introducing a proposal which might weaken the mechanism which has been so successfully protecting our Forest Preserve.

The Sagamore proposal, which I mentioned earlier, becomes part of what I would propose as a comprehensive approach. This proposal, which has been supported as a fair and equitable exchange, is in keeping with the tradition of Constitutional exchanges over the last century. If I may quote from the State Land Use Master Plan as follows: "Between 1895 and 1978, there were 130 proposed amendments introduced in the State Legislature to exchange Article 14, but only 17 have been successful in passing both the Legislature and public referendum. In each of the 17 successful measures, the Forest Preserve lands involved were restricted to small acreages and were quite precisely delineated." *** [T]his is also true of the Sagamore amendment. It will allow the preservation under a single ownership for the complete complex of the historic Sagamore Great Camp, and it will provide for an increase in wild forest land within the preserve. It attacks a unique situation with a site specific amendment, and it represents a carefully delineated exchange of small acreage. At our workshop session of the 1978 Topridge conference, a resolution was adopted proposing a Constitutional amendment as a long-range solution to the problem of management of the historic structures in the Adirondack Park. It was agreed that it would have to be narrowly drawn so as to be clearly explainable to the general public and to avoid any unnecessary threat to the wild forest character of the Forest Preserve. *** One proposal was language to the effect that historic buildings may be preserved on lands which come into State hands within the Adirondack State Park. A second alternative would be the identification of specific sites which should be preserved by comprehensive survey of historic Adirondack Park resources. One of the objections raised at the workshop was that a comprehensive inventory of historic preservation sites would take possibly two to three years, and that passage of a Constitutional amendment would require three to four years. I need not remind you *** that if action were taken then, the Constitutional amendment might have been in position to be put in place today. *** [F]inally a quote from the legislative proposal that we have drafted *** goes as follows: "The Legislature finds that the potential exists for conflict between the policies of protecting the wild forest character of public lands and preserving significant historic resources of the Adirondack and Catskill Parks. Such conflicts may exist upon State acquisition of historic sites that thereupon would be subject to the forever wild restrictions of the Constitution. The Legislature further finds that protection of wild forest character of public lands and protection of historic resources in the Adirondack and Catskill Parks can be compatible goals for facilitating and supporting historic preservation in the private land areas of the parks." The legislation would accomplish this in several ways. First, by creating an advisory committee of the historic resources of the parks, with governmental and private sector representatives, this committee would cause to be prepared within two years of the effective date, a comprehensive inventory of historical, archaeological, architectural and cultural resources of the two parks. The commission would also recommend administrative actions and, if necessary, legislation, including any assistance that can be offered private owners of historic resources, to assure preservation of such resources. It would also publish guidelines for attracting private purchases. Second, unless required in order to protect the public safety, or deemed necessary for the conservation of critical and unique natural areas, the State would not acquire or accept ownership of structures or improvements in the parks listed on the State Register of Historic Sites or the State inventory. Third, if such improvements or structures are offered for purchase by the State, it would be the responsibility of the appropriate State official, in consultation with the advisory committee, to seek a private purchaser who would preserve such historic resources.

*** [A]dditional Constitutional amendments might be necessary in the future *** if the State continues to purchase properties containing historic structures in the Adirondack and Catskill Parks. The Department of Environmental Conservation is not in a position to bear the financial burden of maintaining [these] historic structures. Nor is it likely that in these stringent economic times the State will be able to do much in that direction even in the future. We must turn, I believe, to the private sector for support for these historic landmarks. The legislation we are proposing has the virtue of being both pragmatic and, I think, entirely consistent with the spirit of Article14. It does not violate the integrity of the forever wild concept, and it provides an efficient program for furthering our desire to preserve the historical and architectural heritage of the Adirondack and Catskill Parks.

Notes and Questions

1. **Great Camp Sagamore.** As mentioned in this proposal, concern for historic and archaeological resources was not a central concern in creating a New York State Park in the Adirondacks to be kept "Forever Wild" under Article XIV of the New York State Constitution. As such, issues arose concerning a supposed conflict of interest in keeping the Adirondack Park Forever Wild while preserving historic structures within the Park's wilderness. Great Camp Sagamore is the most pertinent example of the conflict between these two competing ideas.

During the Gilded Age, great robber barons built palatial mansions in the Adirondacks to escape the drudgeries of city life as well as the masses that stayed at public hotels within the Adirondack Park. "The grand camps look rather like millionaires' pioneer villages, clusters of large and small log buildings set in a clearing carved out of the primeval Adirondack forest." Michael deCourcy Hinds, Adirondack Survivors: Rustic Grand Camps, N.Y. Times, August 27, 1981. http://query.nytimes.com/gst/fullpage.html?res=9904EFD7123BF934A1575BC0A967948260&pagewanted=1 (last visited April 7, 2017). The similarity of appearance amongst these "camps" is due to the actions of William West Durant, who designed and built many of them from 1876 to 1901, intending to sell them to powerful and socially prominent figures and enhancing the image of the Adirondacks as a chic vacation destination. *See id.*

Camp Sagamore was built from 1885 to 1897 at Blue Mountain Lake. It is an amazing example of characteristic Durant design:

Camp Sagamore. Photo by Mwanner, via Wikimedia Commons.

> [L]og houses, artfully woven, with rough bark exteriors and paneled interiors; stonework, jigsaw-puzzle-perfect, in fireplaces and chimneys; walkways connecting many buildings, and the most up-to-date mechanical equipment then available. These rustic camps in the wilderness were meant to house up to 100 guests and had hot running water, gas illumination and flush toilets—conveniences that were just being introduced in the cities.

Id. After construction was completed, Durant lived in the Camp from 1897 until Alfred G. Vanderbilt bought the Camp for his family to use for recreation during the summer months. http://greatcampsagamore.org/overview/ (last visited April 6, 2017). When Alfred died in 1915 on the Lusitania, his widow Margaret Emerson took up residence on the property until 1954, when she gave the Camp to Syracuse University. In 1974 much of the vast acreage surrounding these camps was bought by the State of New York and added to the Adirondack Park. In 1983 the State acquired the structures themselves. *Id.; see also* Beverly Bridger, Great Camp Sagamore: The Vanderbilts' Adirondack Retreat (2000).

Preserving Great Camp Sagamore *in situ* within the Adirondack Park—a wilderness to be kept "Forever Wild"—required a constitutional amendment. On November 8, 1983, citizens of the State of New York voted to amend Article XIV § 1 of the New York State Constitution to "facilitate the preservation of historic buildings listed on the national register of historic places *** [by conveying] to Sagamore Institute, Inc., a not-for-profit educational organization, approximately ten acres of land and buildings thereon *** located on Sagamore Road *** within the Adirondack Park ***." The amendment was passed "[n]otwithstanding the foregoing provisions," which included the "Forever Wild" clause. In this way, the State of New York was able to circumvent the possible contradiction between preserving an historic building *in situ* within a Park meant to remain "Forever Wild."

2. **Fire towers in the Adirondack Park.** Recently, historic preservation issues regarding fire towers within the Adirondack Park have arisen. These towers were strategically placed throughout the Park to help spot and respond to forest fires within the great wilderness. Once an extremely important feature of Park protection, these towers became obsolete with the development of helicopters and airplanes, which can easily fly over the Park in search of fires. One general belief resulting from the "Forever Wild" provision in the New York State Constitution is that structures within the Park should either be allowed to deteriorate or be dismantled when no longer necessary. Despite this general interpretation, many local Adirondack residents have shown public support for saving the fire towers for their historic significance. http://www.dec.ny.gov/outdoor/100900.html (last visited April 6, 2017). The Department of Environmental Conservation ("DEC") regarded the towers as inconsistent with the State Land Master Plan, and in February 2010, it released a study recommending that the St. Regis and Hurricane Mountain fire towers be removed. New York State Department of Environmental Conservation, FIRE TOWER STUDY FOR THE ADIRONDACK PARK 5 (2010), *available at* http://www.dec.ny.gov/docs/lands_forests_pdf/ftowerstudy.pdf (last visited April 6, 2017). The Adirondack Park Agency's ("APA") State Lands Committee agreed with the DEC recommendation and decided on October 17, 2010 to recommend the dismantling of these fire towers and the designation of the land surrounding them as "primitive land." This designation meant that the towers would not be restored and would ultimately have to be removed if they became too unsafe. This was an attempt to balance the concept of wilderness with historic preservation. Many alternatives to the APA's proposed plan existed, including funding by local residents to restore the fire towers or removal of the fire towers for display in local towns. Under the State Land Master Plan, there was another recourse for preserving the towers as historic with little change needed to the actual plan, by simply reclassifying the area as historic. *See* New York State Executive Law, EXEC. LAW, art. 27, § 816. Responding to mounting pleas by the public, in October 2014, the APA adopted the St. Regis Mountain Fire Tower Historic District, Unit Management Plan, http://www.dec.ny.gov/docs/lands_forests_pdf/srmfthafina1.pdf (last visited April 6, 2017) and the Hurricane Mountain Fire Tower Historic District Unit Management Plan, http://www.dec.ny.gov/docs/lands_forests_pdf/hmfthafinal1.pdf (last visited April 6, 2017), both of which preserve the fire towers and open them up to the public. This outcome was an interesting test of the role of historic preservation within designated wilderness areas.

3. **Forever Wild forever.** a. Examining these two situations along with the "Forever Wild" provision of the New York Constitution, do you think that the interests in historic preservation and keeping the Adirondack Park as wilderness can ever be reconciled? b. If so, how? (Consider the New York State Land Master Plan, EXEC. LAW, art. 27, § 816). c. New York State allows for a reconsideration of its Constitution every 20 years. If there is a constitutional convention, should Article XIV § 1 be changed to allow for historic preservation within the Adirondack Park? d. If so, what change(s) would you prescribe?

Olympic Park Associates v. Mainella

United States District Court for the Western District of Washington
2005 WL 1871114, No. C04-5732FDB (August 1, 2005)

Burgess, J. Plaintiffs Olympic Park Associates and Wilderness Watch, joined by Plaintiff Public Employees for Environmental Responsibility, move for summary judgment on their claims that the National Park Service (NPS) has violated the Wilderness Act and the National Environmental Policy Act (NEPA) in deciding to replace two collapsed shelters within Olympic National Park (ONP) with new structures that were built off-site, and which would be placed in the locations of the collapsed shelters after being transported to the former sites by helicopter.

The United States of America, on behalf of the named officials of the National Park Service, cross-moves for summary judgment and opposes Plaintiff's motion for summary judgment.

Background

The following summarized chronological information is taken from the parties' memoranda[.] *** In 1938, Congress designated Olympic National Park on the Olympic peninsula. In 1974 the Wilderness Act was enacted, and NPS proposed that Congress designate the Olympic Wilderness Area (approximately 96% of the total acres) within Olympic National Park. At that time, the Park Service began internal deliberations about the appropriateness of shelters in ONP in conjunction with the Park Service's public evaluation of the eligibility of ONP lands for wilderness designation under the Wilderness Act. Also, in 1974, the Park Service prepared an Environmental Impact Statement (EIS) pursuant to the National Environmental Policy Act of 1969 (NEPA), which proposed to establish 826,139 acres of wilderness in ONP. The EIS called for the removal of a majority of shelters, but also provided for the retention of a number of shelters for health and safety purposes. Included in the list of those shelters previously and subsequently chosen for retention for health and safety purposes were Home Sweet Home and Low Divide, the shelters at issue herein. (*See* AR 5792 (ONP Shelter List, 2003).)

The 1974 EIS also determined that historic properties were not to be affected by the creation of the wilderness designation. In 1984, the Park undertook an historical structure evaluation of park properties under the National Historic Preservation Act, which determined that a number of shelters were eligible for listing in the National Register of Historic Places, and which were placed on the Park's List of Classified Structures (LCS) and set aside for historic retention. The Home Sweet Home and Low Divide shelters were not on this list as set aside for historic retention pursuant to this evaluation, citing that the structures were not yet 50 years old and that both had sustained a "considerable loss of physical integrity." *** In 1988 the Olympic Wilderness was formally designated.

* * *

Ultimately, on January 11, 2001, the Washington State Office of Archaeology and Historic Preservation found the two shelters to be eligible for placement in the National

Historic Register following clarification that the structures were over fifty years old. Notwithstanding the fact that the shelters had collapsed under snow loads from storms during the winter of 1998, both shelters were deemed eligible for the National Historic Register because

> [i]n spite of collapse, the shelter[s] (prior to [collapse]) contributed to the important historic pattern of shelter construction and recreational use. This location, the setting, association, and feeling are significant aspects of historic use within the park....

(AR 416-17.) With the shelters deemed eligible for listing as historic, the Park proposed to the State a plan to rebuild the shelters as contribution to the Park's broader efforts "to maintain the historic feeling and appearance of portions of the park trail system." (AR 462-63.)

The two shelters were constructed in a Park maintenance yard and completed in February 2002. The Park then considered options for replacing the shelters at their historic locations[.] *** Following a public comment period and review the Park Service chose the alternative of transporting the shelters by helicopter *** to the respective historic sites with a finding that this alternative would pose no significant environmental impact (FONSI). This alternative was selected because it preserved "important historic aspects of ONP's heritage through reconstruction of the Low Divide and Home Sweet Home trail shelters"; it "would aid in reducing risk to visitor health and safety by providing shelter in times of emergency"; it "would limit the amount of time spent reconstructing structures in wilderness (using mechanized equipment during breeding season), and flights would occur after breeding seasons for Northern spotted owl and marbled murrelets"; and it used a combination of materials, including "reused materials from the once-standing shelters." (AR 476.)

Standard of Review

* * *

Judicial review of federal agency actions under NEPA and the Wilderness Act is governed by the Administrative Procedures Act (APA), 5 U.S.C. § 701 *et seq. The Wilderness Society v. U.S. Fish & Wildlife Service,* 353 F.3d 1051, 1059 (9th Cir.2003) (en banc) (amended 360 F.3d 1374 (9th Cir.2004)). Under the APA, a district court may set aside an agency action only if that action is "arbitrary, capricious, an abuse of discretion, or otherwise not in accordance with law." 5 U.S.C. § 706(2)(A) *** A district court may not substitute its judgment for that of the agency, *** and the court's review is limited to the administrative record at the time the agency made its decision. *Camp v. Pitts,* 411 U.S. 138, 142, 93 S.Ct. 1241, 36 L.Ed.2d 106 (1973) ***

Discussion

Both parties to this action acknowledge the beauty and wildness of the Olympic Wilderness Area within Olympic National Park. The value of preserving such land was recognized as early as 1897 when President Grover Cleveland set aside over two million acres of the peninsula's mountains and forests as the Olympic Forest Reserve. The Park Service recognizes that there has been an ongoing tension between people's use and enjoyment of the Park and the need to preserve the Park's wildness for future generations. In the 1930s, tourism was emphasized, and by 1933, hundreds of miles of trails and an estimated 90 trail shelters were installed. (AR 6005.) The shelters at issue in this case—Home Sweet Home and Low Divide—joined the trail system by 1935. (AR 5499, 5502.)

With the advent of the proposal to designate the Olympic Wilderness Area within the park, the NPS prepared an EIS in 1974. In the EIS, the environmental impacts associated with shelters was discussed, and, among other things it was noted:

> *** [W]ith greatly expanding backcountry use, the demand for shelter use has exceeded the supply, and the impact has spread beyond and between the structures with numerous campsites and fire rings appearing, especially in the heavily used lowland valleys.

(AR 3151-52.) Both shelters at issue were located in subalpine meadow terrain. (AR 513.) *** [T]he EIS called for the removal of the majority of shelters, but called for retention of Home Sweet Home and Low Divide for health and safety reasons. *** In 1998, these shelters collapsed under heavy snow. *** Therefore, the situation from the time of the 1974 EIS until the Olympic Wilderness was formally designated in 1988, the Home Sweet Home and Low Divide shelters were designated under the EIS for health and safety retention, but were not listed for historic retention.

When the shelters were reconsidered in 1996 for historic preservation, they meanwhile collapsed in 1998. Following the January 11, 2001 determination that Home Sweet Home and Low Divide were eligible for historic preservation, an Environmental Assessment (EA) was issued in January 2004. The EA points to the historic preservation designation for the shelters in spite of their collapse, indicates that it has already been decided that the shelters will be rebuilt (they had already been completed in February 2002), and that the EA addresses "decision of how to restore two historic shelters to their original locations," and, specifically, the proposal to airlift the two shelters from the Elwha utility yard to their original locations. (AR 497, 497A.)

The Wilderness Act of 1964 was enacted to "secure for the American people of present and future generations the benefits of an enduring resource of wilderness." *** 16 U.S.C. §§ 1131–34. The Act required that wilderness areas

> shall be administered for the use and enjoyment of the American people in such manner as will leave them unimpaired for future use and enjoyment as wilderness, and so as to provide for the protection of these areas, the preservation of their wilderness character, and for the gathering and dissemination of information regarding their use and enjoyment as wilderness.

16 U.S.C. § 1131(a). "Wilderness" is defined as follows:

> A wilderness *** is hereby recognized as an area where the earth and its community of life are untrammeled by man, where man himself is a visitor who does not remain. An area of wilderness is further defined to mean in this chapter an area of undeveloped Federal land retaining its primitive character

> and influence, without permanent improvements or human habitation, which is protected and managed so as to preserve its natural conditions and which (1) generally appears to have been affected by the forces of nature, with the imprint of man's work substantially unnoticeable; (2) has outstanding opportunities for solitude or a primitive and unconfined type of recreation; (3) has at least five thousand acres of land or is of sufficient size as to make practicable its preservation and use in an unimpaired condition; (4) may also contain ecological, geological, or other features of scientific, educational, scenic, or historical value.

16 U.S.C. § 1131(c). The Wilderness Act prohibits certain activities and structures, except for measures required in emergencies, in any wilderness area:

> *** [T]here shall be no commercial enterprise and no permanent road within any wilderness area designated by this Chapter and, except as necessary to meet minimum requirements for the purpose of this Chapter (including measures required in emergencies involving the health and safety of persons within the area), there shall be no temporary road, no use of motor vehicles, motorized equipment or motorboats, no landing of aircraft, no other form of mechanical transport, and no structure or installation within any such area.

16 U.S.C. § 1133(c). *** The Environmental Assessment (EA) concerning the proposal "to use a Heavy Lift Type 1 Chinook Boeing 234 Helicopter to airlift two pre-framed shelters" into the sites of the former Home Sweet Home and Low Divide shelters nevertheless recognizes that the values changed as to shelters when the Olympic National Park's Olympic Wilderness was designated[.]

*** In spite of recognizing the shift in values upon the designation of the Olympic Wilderness, because the two structures had been determined eligible for the National register of Historic Places in 1998, even though a combination of deferred maintenance on these structures and heavy snow (greater than 18 feet) in 1998–99 led to their destruction, the decision was made to reconstruct them. (AR 497.) Thus, the National Park Service concluded in the EA, which was prepared to satisfy the requirements of the National Environmental Policy Act (NEPA, 1969 as amended), that airlifting the structures into the Wilderness was the best choice[.] *** This decision of the National Park Service to airlift the reconstructed shelters into the Olympic Wilderness brings the values of historic preservation and wilderness preservation into conflict with each other. How to resolve the conflict between these two concepts is the issue presented in this case.

There is no specific provision for maintaining and/or replacing shelters within the Olympic Wilderness; the law creating the Olympic Wilderness Area specifically allowed the National Park Service to "upgrade maintain and replace" only one structure—an underground powerline—as long as the maintenance and operation was "consistent with wilderness management." P.L. 100-688, § 102, 102 Stat. 3961 (November 16, 1988).

The emergency exception of Section 16 U.S.C. § 1133(c) of the Wilderness Act referenced earlier herein *** most logically refers to matters of urgent necessity rather than to conveniences for use in an emergency. As the National Park Service itself has recognized in the context of the EA for the proposal to airlift the structures into the wilderness:

> The Wilderness Act and current NPS Management Policies encourage wilderness users to prepare for, and encounter the wilderness on its own terms, striving to provide "primitive and unconfined" recreation opportunities, complete with the risks that arise from wildlife, weather conditions, etc. NPS wilderness management policies do not support the provision of facilities in wilderness specifically to eliminate these risks.

(AR 497, emphasis added.) Moreover, the definition of "wilderness" is an area "retaining its primitive character and influence, without permanent improvements or human habitation." 16 U.S.C. § 1131(c). The emergency exception cannot support the insertion of the shelters into the Olympic Wilderness.

*** The National Historic Preservation Act's (NHPA) effect in the context of the Wilderness Act was addressed in *Wilderness Watch and Public Employees for Environmental Responsibility v. Mainella*, 375 F.3d 1085 (11th Cir.2004):

> As an initial matter, we cannot agree with the Park Service that the preservation of historical structures furthers the goals of the Wilderness Act. *** The NHPA requires agencies to "assume responsibility for the preservation of historic properties" they control.
>
> * * *
>
> The agency's obligations under the Wilderness Act are quite different. The Wilderness Act [states that a] wilderness area should "generally appear [ ] to have been affected primarily by the forces of nature, with the imprint of man's work substantially unnoticeable." *** Another section of the Act explicitly states that, except as necessary for minimal administrative needs that require occasional vehicle use," there shall be ... no structure or installation within any such [wilderness] area." 16 U.S.C. § 1133(c). As the Park Service notes, Section 1133(b) mentions "historical use" along with "recreational, scenic, scientific, educational, [and] conservation" uses. However, this list tracks the definition of wilderness areas in § 1131(c), which describes" a primitive and unconfined type of recreation" and "ecological, geological, or other features of scientific, educational, scenic, or historical value." 16 U.S.C. § 1131(c). Given the consistent evocation of "untrammeled" and "natural" areas, the previous pairing of "historical" with "ecological" and "geological" features, and the explicit prohibition on structures, the only reasonable reading of "historical use" in the Wilderness Act refers to natural, rather than man-made features.

375 F.3d 1085, 1091–92[.] *** The Court's reasoning in *Wilderness Watch v. Mainella* is persuasive. *** Once the Olympic Wilderness was designated, a different perspective

on the land is required. Regarding the Olympic Wilderness, that perspective means "land retaining its primitive character and influence, without permanent improvements or human habitation, which is protected and managed so as to preserve its natural conditions." 16 U.S.C. § 1131(c). If under NPS wilderness management policies wilderness users are to be encouraged "to prepare for, and encounter the wilderness on its own terms, complete with the risks that arise from wildlife, weather conditions, etc." *** for a wilderness user to come across a brand new structure in a subalpine meadow would surely be disconcerting and obviously detract from experiencing, in the Park Service's words, "wilderness on its own terms" *** in a land of "primeval character and influence, without permanent improvements or human habitation." 16 U.S.C. § 1131(c). *** If the reconstructed shelters were placed in the Olympic Wilderness, regardless of whether they were placed in the locations of the former shelters, the National Park Service would not be administering the area in accordance with its mandate under the Wilderness Act[.]

Furthermore, the NHPA's goal of preserving historic structures allows for "rehabilitation, restoration, stabilization, maintenance," (16 U.S.C. § 470w(8)), among other things, but it does not require reconstruction. Thus, where the former shelters at issue here have been destroyed by natural forces, NHPA does not require reconstruction. ***

The National Park Service argues that the Historic Sites Act of 1935 at section 462(f) "requir[es] NPS to restore, reconstruct, rehabilitate, preserve and maintain *historic property*," (emphasis in original), but Section 466(a) of that Act provides that no funds may be expended for the purposes of Section 462(f) unless and until Congress specifically authorizes such an appropriation. There is no assertion that Congress has authorized the appropriation of funds to NPS to build the new shelters at issue here and to place them in the Olympic Wilderness.

The National Park Service points to the Organic Act of 1916 as requiring it "to conserve *historic objects*," citing 16 U.S.C. § 1, where there is a general description of why Congress created the National Park System: "to conserve the scenery and the natural and historic objects and the wild life therein...." *Id.* Even so, the NPS also interprets the Wilderness Act to require greater protection than the Organic Act would require. "The effect of the Wilderness Act is to unambiguously place an additional layer of protection on wilderness areas within the National Park System."*** NPS Reference Manual 41 at p. 8. The Organic Act cannot be interpreted to require replacement of collapsed shelters with new reconstructions to be placed in the wilderness by helicopter where the Wilderness Act is a specific, protective statute militating against such intrusions.

The Wilderness Act provides that an agency utilizing its authority under other laws in ways that affect the wilderness must do so pursuant to the requirements of the Wilderness Act as a whole[.] *** A long established rule of statutory construction is that where there is a specific provision that governs an issue, it takes superiority over any general provision. Here, the Wilderness Act under which the Olympic Wilderness was designated, is the specific provision, while the National Historic Preservation Act, among others earlier mentioned, is the general. This rule allows the NPS to administer the Olympic Wilderness for other purposes only insofar as to also preserve its wilderness character.

Conclusion

The National Park Service has not considered its shelter replacement proposal giving proper deference to the mandates of the Wilderness Act. *** There has been a clear error of judgment in this case because although the NPS, *arguendo,* may have proceeded appropriately under the operative historic preservation laws to determine whether the shelters were historic, the subsequent decision concerning whether to place reconstructed shelters in the former locations of Home Sweet Home and Low Divide failed to properly reconcile doing so with the mandate to preserve the wild and primitive character of the Olympic Wilderness. The Home Sweet Home and Low Divide shelters have collapsed under the natural effects of weather and time, and to reconstruct the shelters and place the replicas on the sites of the original shelters by means of a helicopter is in direct contradiction of the mandate to preserve the wilderness character of the Olympic Wilderness. *** Rather than emphasizing tourism and providing hundreds of miles of trails and approximately 90 shelters, a different "feeling" of wilderness is sought to be preserved for future generations to enjoy, a place "where the earth and its community of life are untrammeled by man" and which retains "its primitive character and influence, without permanent improvements." 16 U.S.C. § 1131(c). The Park Service need not build replica shelters to be airlifted into locations where the original shelters once stood in order to preserve history. It is apparent from the record that photographs and other chronicles document the history of the usage of Olympic National Park before the Olympic Wilderness was designated.

NOW, THEREFORE, IT IS ORDERED:

1. Plaintiffs' Motion for Summary Judgment is GRANTED;
2. Defendants' Motion for Summary Judgment is DENIED;
3. This cause of action is DISMISSED and the Clerk of the Court is directed to enter judgment for Plaintiffs.

Notes and Questions

1. **Purposes of structures.** a. Do structures perform a function other than shelter? b. What might the collapsed shelters tell us about the past? c. About how we built things? d. What building materials were available? e. What we lived to do? f. How the climate has changed? g. Would the reconstructed shelters serve the same function? h. Would they remind us of the originals?

2. **Specific versus general provision.** In the end, the court resolved what seemed a direct conflict between the NHPA (to preserve historic structures *in situ*) and the Wilderness Act (to keep out traces of man) by relying upon a rule of statutory construction: that where there is a specific provision that governs the issue, it takes priority over a general provision. a. Isn't the NHPA specific as to historic properties? b. Could the conflict have been resolved based on how the NPS aimed to preserve history?

Chapter 5

Emergent Parallel State and Federal Procedures

A. State Historic Preservation Acts

State historic preservation programs are necessary complements and integral components of federal historic preservation programs. Every state maintains an historic preservation office, a consulting party under the National Historic Preservation Act. States assist the federal government with the identification of properties for listing on the National Register of Historic Places and help review applications for federal rehabilitation tax credits. In other respects, states pursue their own discrete interests, operating in parallel with the federal scheme. State laws preserve public buildings and state-specific cultural heritage; protect private properties from effects of government projects; and authorize the adoption of local preservation ordinances and easement programs that prevent alteration and/or destruction of historic properties and resources. *See generally* Georgetown University Library, Historic Preservation Resources, https://repository.library.georgetown.edu/handle/10822/761776 (last visited July 20, 2017) (for links to the historic preservation programs among the states). The cases below demonstrate the limits of state historic preservation acts and how they sometimes intersect with other state and local laws.

1. Consultation Requirements

Sierra Club v. Board of Education of City of Buffalo

Supreme Court of New York, Appellate Division, Fourth Department
127 A.D.2d 1007, 512 N.Y.S.2d 954 (1987)

DENMAN, J.P., BOOMER, BALIO, LAWTON and DAVIS, JJ. *** Judgment affirmed without costs.

Martin Luther King, Jr. Park, a part of the Olmsted Park System in Buffalo, is listed on the National Register of Historic Places. In 1983, the City Board of Education selected a portion of the park adjacent to the Buffalo Museum of Science as the site for its science magnet school and in 1985, the State Department of Education approved the proposed site. Petitioners now appeal from the dismissal of this C.P.L.R. article 78 proceeding to annul the approval and enjoin construction of the school claiming that there was no statutory authority for the alienation of park lands and that respondents failed to comply with the requirements of P.R.H.P.L. 14.09.

In 1916, the State Legislature amended the Buffalo City Charter specifically to empower the city to discontinue its parks and other stated improvements (L 1916, ch 260). We cannot conclude, as does the dissent, that in conferring the power of discontinuance, the Legislature intended this amendment to have no effect ***. The 1916 special act unambiguously sanctions the city's discontinuance of park lands held in public trust *** and is ample authority for the city's approval of use of its park lands for a public school. Subsequent legislation authorizing the construction and maintenance of the Buffalo Museum of Science and approving its use and occupation by the Buffalo Society of Natural Science does not indicate that the city lacked the power to discontinue park lands. In 1922 the Legislature amended the Buffalo City Charter by adding a new section, 5-a, to provide in part: "The council of the city of Buffalo shall have discretionary authority to provide a site and furnish money for the construction and equipment in whole or in part, of a building for the use and occupation of the Buffalo Society of Natural Sciences *** either by setting apart for such purpose land owned or acquired by such city for park or playground purposes, or by purchasing or otherwise acquiring land or property not previously devoted to a public use" (L 1922, ch 524).

The purpose of this legislation was to empower the city to provide a site and public funds for the construction and financing of a museum to be occupied and operated by a *private* organization. *** The 1928 enactment (L 1928, ch 530) merely approved use of city funds for support of the Society and maintenance of the museum. It did not authorize or approve discontinuance of park lands.

In selecting and approving the park as a site for the school, respondents fully complied with the mandates of P.R.H.P.L. 14.09. All feasible and prudent alternatives were explored, and proposals for avoiding or mitigating adverse impacts upon this historic site were considered. The Office of Parks, Recreation and Historic Preservation (OPR) was consulted in the early stages of project development. OPR fully reviewed the proposed plan as well as draft and final environmental impact statements. It suggested several alternative and mitigating factors, all of which were considered. Nearly all of the suggested proposals for mitigating adverse impacts were adopted as part of the plan. Ultimately OPR concluded that locating the school next to the museum was necessary for the programmatic educational needs of the students. There is no requirement that respondents do everything possible to preserve the historic site. The statute requires consideration of feasible and prudent alternatives and mitigation of adverse impacts to the fullest extent practicable. *Matter of Ebert v. New York State Off. of Parks, Recreation & Historic Preservation*, 119 A.D.2d 62, 66, *lv. denied* 68 N.Y.2d 612. That duty was met here, and this record fails to suggest that the determination of OPR or the State Education Department was irrational.

* * *

All concur, except Lawton, J., who dissents and votes to reverse and grant the petition, in accordance with the following memorandum.

Lawton, J. (Dissenting).

I dissent. Since this park property is impressed with a public trust, its "use for other than park purposes requires the direct and specific approval of the State Legislature, plainly conferred." *Stephenson v. County of Monroe*, 43 A.D.2d 897. The majority finds such specific authority in Laws of 1916 (ch 260, § 1), wherein the Buffalo City Charter, as part of a general revision, was amended in part to authorize the city to "discontinue streets, alleys and highways, parks, markets". However, this amendment did not modify the charter's specific limitation that the city's authority over its parks was "except as otherwise provided by law". Subdivision (2) of section 20 of the General City Law provides that the city's title to its parks is inalienable. Buffalo's authority to discontinue its parks is, therefore, limited by the provisions of the General City Law and its use of this property for other than park purposes requires a special act of the Legislature ***. Indeed, the City of Buffalo has previously sought and obtained such specific Legislative authority prior to alienating a part of this very same park property ***.

No plainly conferred specific approval for such alienation being provided by Laws of 1916 (ch 260), Buffalo's action in discontinuing its park without prior legislative approval is an unauthorized violation of the sanctity of this long-recognized public trust[.] ***

Notes and Questions

1. **The relevance of the public trust.** a. Should a property covered by the public trust be entitled to greater protection (if only procedural) than one that is merely an historic site? In *Comparative Guide to the Western States' Public Trust Doctrine: Public Values, Private Rights, and the Evolution Toward an Ecological Public Trust*, 37 Ecology L.Q. 53 (2010), Professor Robin Craig urges us to conceive of the public trust doctrine as any other common law principle—one that expands and adjusts in response to an evolving and changing society. While once largely concerned with the right to traverse navigable waters, the doctrine is now applied to a range of other limited resources, including rural park lands, the dry sand area of the beach, and wildlife. *See also* Shelby D. Green, *No Entry to the Public Lands: Towards a Theory of a Public Trust Servitude for a Way Over Abutting Private Land*, 14 Wyo. L. Rev. 19 (2014). b. Should national monuments proclaimed under the Antiquities Act be protected under the public trust doctrine? The seminal work making the case for preserving historic properties, With Heritage So Rich, seems to cast heritage as an essential component of civilization. "It is these things ... that we want to keep before our eyes as part of our lived life as a people and as connective links between a past which millions of Americans helped to make and a future which we must continue to make." *Id.* at 24.

Ebert v. New York State Office of Parks, Recreation & Historic Preservation

Supreme Court of New York, Appellate Division, Third Department
119 A.D.2d 62, 505 N.Y.S.2d 470 (1986)

Casey, J. We hold that the State University Construction Fund (Fund) is not required to comply with a local historical preservation ordinance before it can demolish an existing structure on a State college campus as part of a construction project.

In 1982, the trustees of Cornell University submitted a proposal for the demolition of Stone Hall, a building owned by the State and formerly used by the State College of Agriculture and Life Sciences at Cornell University, and for the construction of a considerably larger educational facility in its place. The proposal received the approval of the trustees of the State University of New York, and budget requests for the project were approved by the Governor and the Legislature. The Fund followed certain procedures preliminary to the actual demolition and construction, including consultation with the State Commissioner of Parks, Recreation and Historic Preservation (State Commissioner) pursuant to P.R.H.P.L. 14.09, and the preparation of draft and final environmental impact statements pursuant to the State Environmental Quality Review Act (SEQRA; ECL art. 8).

In 1984, Stone Hall and several adjacent buildings were listed in the State and national historic preservation registers, and the following year the City of Ithaca Landmark Preservation Commission (local agency) designated Stone Hall as a local landmark. Pursuant to a City of Ithaca ordinance, no building so designated could be demolished without a permit issued by the local agency. The Fund refused to comply with this permit requirement, contending that its project was exempt from regulation by the local agency. The demolition of Stone Hall began on February 10, 1986.

Within hours of the commencement of the demolition work, petitioners, as advocates of historic preservation, commenced a C.P.L.R. article 78 proceeding by service of a petition and an order to show cause, which contained a temporary restraining order enjoining the Fund from demolishing Stone Hall. Petitioners alleged that the Fund and the State Commissioner had failed to explore alternatives and to mitigate the adverse impact of demolishing Stone Hall, as required by P.R.H.P.L. 14.09, that the environmental impact statements prepared by the Fund pursuant to SEQRA (ECL 8-0109) were inadequate and that the Fund was required to obtain a permit from the local agency. Plaintiff, the City of Ithaca, commenced an action for a permanent injunction based upon the permit requirement and moved for a preliminary injunction.

Special Term held that the Fund was required to obtain a permit from the local agency before Stone Hall could be demolished, and granted injunctive relief to petitioners and plaintiff. As to petitioners' claims that there was a lack of compliance with the requirements of P.R.H.P.L. 14.09 and SEQRA, Special Term dismissed that portion of the petition. The Fund and petitioners have appealed from the adverse portions of the resulting judgment and order.

The State adopted a comprehensive statutory framework for historic preservation in 1980 (L 1980, ch 354). Known as the New York State Historic Preservation Act of 1980, the legislation provided that its purpose is: "to continue and advance the state's historic preservation programs and activities, to continue the responsibility for the coordination of such programs and activities with the commissioner of parks and recreation, to foster consistency of state activities with historic preservation policy, to encourage and assist local governments in local preservation programs and activities and to encourage and assist private agencies and individuals undertaking preservation by private means" (L 1980, ch 354, § 1). To this end, the act added historic preservation articles to the General Municipal Law (General Municipal Law art 5-K), the Public Buildings Law (Public Buildings Law art 4-B) and the Parks, Recreation and Historic Preservation Law (P.R.H.P.L. art. 14).

The framework provided by General Municipal Law article 5-K is "intended to maintain and encourage the opportunity and flexibility for the counties, cities, towns and villages of the state to manage the historic and cultural properties *under their jurisdiction* in a spirit of stewardship and trusteeship for future generations." General Municipal Law § 119-aa (emphasis supplied). Thus, local governments are empowered to "[p]rovide by regulations, special conditions and restrictions for the protection, enhancement, perpetuation and use of places, districts, sites, buildings, structures, works of art and other objects having a special character or special historical, cultural or aesthetic interest or value." General Municipal Law § 119-dd (1). Local governments are also authorized to establish landmark or historical preservation boards or commissions to carry out the local historic preservation programs. General Municipal Law § 119-dd (2).

Public Buildings Law article 4-B provides that its purpose is "to provide that the instrumentalities of the state administer the historic and cultural properties *under their control* in a spirit of stewardship and trusteeship for the future generations" Public Buildings Law § 60 (emphasis supplied). To achieve this purpose, the Commissioner of the Office of General Services or the chief executive officer of any State agency is required to consult with the State Commissioner "as early in the planning process as may be practicable when planning to demolish, alter or transfer any property *under their jurisdiction* listed on the state or national register

> *** for the purpose of exploring alternatives to demolition, alteration or transfer." Public Buildings Law § 63 (1) (emphasis supplied). P.R.H.P.L. 14.09 contains more procedural and substantive detail as to the consultation process when State agency activity might affect historical or cultural property. ***

Construing the act as a whole and considering its various provisions together and with reference to each other ***, and taking into account the legislative history of the act and the statutes of which it is made a part ***, we conclude that the authority granted to local governments to regulate properties under their jurisdiction for historical preservation purposes does not include the power to regulate the activity of a State agency which might affect historical or cultural property under the control and jurisdiction of the State agency. The act contains a comprehensive review process at the State level for such State agency activity. *See*, Public Buildings Law § 63 (1);

P.R.H.P.L. 14.09. Had the Legislature intended the review process for such activity to occur at both the State and local levels, it would have so provided; its failure to include such a provision is significant[.] *** Rather than establishing duplicative review procedures, the act calls for coordination and cooperation ***. With respect to State agency activities, P.R.H.P.L. 14.09 (2) expressly seeks "to avoid inconsistency or duplication in review functions", and the Governor's memorandum of approval states that his concerns about duplication in the review process and delay of State projects had been satisfied ***. Thus, we conclude that State agency projects, such as that at issue herein, are subject to historical preservation review only at the State level, as detailed in P.R.H.P.L. 14.09 and 9 N.Y.C.R.R. part 428.

Turning to the question of whether there was compliance in this case with the requirements of P.R.H.P.L. 14.09, we agree with Special Term that petitioners' claim must fail. The record firmly establishes that the Fund fully explored all feasible and prudent alternatives and gave due consideration to feasible and prudent plans which would avoid or mitigate adverse impacts, as required by P.R.H.P.L. 14.09 (1). The thrust of petitioners' argument is that the act requires that all *possible* measures be taken to preserve historic structures, but P.R.H.P.L. 14.09 is written in terms of "feasible and prudent" plans and alternatives ***, and a State agency must avoid or mitigate adverse impacts only "[t]o the fullest extent practicable" ***. The decision to demolish Stone Hall was based upon a determination that it was not feasible, prudent or practicable to preserve the structure, and our review of the record reveals nothing irrational in such a determination. ***. We also find lacking in merit petitioners' claim that the "hard look" required under SEQRA was not undertaken by the responsible State agencies.

Having concluded that the requirements of the State-level historic review process under P.R.H.P.L. 14.09 were complied with and that the proposed project is not subject to an additional historical preservation review at the local level, we further conclude that Special Term erred in granting injunctive relief to petitioners and plaintiff.

Mahoney, P. J., Kane, Mikoll and Levine, JJ., concur.

Judgment modified, on the law, without costs, by reversing so much thereof as granted petitioners' relief on their third cause of action; said cause of action dismissed; and, as so modified, affirmed.

Order modified, on the law, without costs, by reversing so much thereof as granted plaintiff's motion for a preliminary injunction; motion denied; and, as so modified, affirmed.

Notes and Questions

1. **Apparent or real conflict.** a. Might local historical values be overlooked if review occurs only on the state level? b. Can the site of an old mill or the grange only have meaning for those locals? c. Should there be mechanisms requiring and weighing local input?

* * *

2. State Registers

Many states maintain official lists of inventories or registers of historic and cultural resources. Listing properties on the state registers not only celebrates the state's history, but also identifies those properties deserving protection against harm from governmental projects and for financial support (rehabilitation grants and tax incentives) for their preservation. Listing on a state register may also trigger special consideration under environmental protection laws. While state registers tend to include properties of state or local significance, the criteria for listing mirrors that for the National Register. A wide range of properties are eligible—sites, buildings, districts, and objects—and significance may relate to events or persons, architecture, or knowledge of important historical or prehistorical issues. The New York state register uses the same eligibility criteria as for the National Register. *See* N.Y. P. R.H.P.L. § 14.07. Historic properties are included in a state register pursuant to four types of actions: comprehensive surveys, (*see, e.g.*, R.I. Gen Laws § 42-45-5); the nomination for listing in the National Register (*see, e.g.*, Md. Code Ann. § 5A-323(b)(1); at the request of individuals or organizations (*see, e.g.*, Ill. Admin. Code § 4140.10); and through a state agency inventorying process (*see, e.g.*, Cal. Pub. Res. Code § 5024).

3. Agency Stewardship Obligations

Successful state historic preservation programs depend not solely on laws preventing harm to historic resources, but significantly on agency stewardship. Stewardship signifies an affirmative duty to oversee and take care of something valuable. Many states have adopted stewardship programs patterned after Section 110 of the National Historic Preservation Act. One good example is that adopted by the state of Georgia. Ga. Code §§ 12-3-55 directs the "heads of all state agencies" to "assume responsibility for the preservation of historic properties" under their ownership. In addition, before "acquiring, constructing, or leasing buildings for purposes of carrying out agency responsibilities," each state agency is required to "use, to the maximum extent, and as operationally appropriate and economically feasible, historic properties available to the agency." Each agency is to maintain a program under which historic properties are "managed and maintained in a way that considers the preservation of their historic, archaeological, architectural and cultural values" and "give [ ] special consideration to the preservation of such values in the case of properties designated as having historic significance to this state." Each agency program must include a process for the identification and evaluation of historic properties, as well as the development and implementation of agreements "regarding the means by [which] such adverse effects on such properties will be considered."

Just as under Section 110(f) of the NHPA, the Georgia statute contains requirements for considering effects of an undertaking affecting National Historic Landmarks and to undertake planning and actions to minimize harm. Agencies are also required to ensure that no loans, permits, licenses or other form of assistance is provided to applicants who have "intentionally and adversely affected a historic property" unless

By 1986, Montgomery Ward Company ceased operations on the site and vacated the building. It has since fallen into severe disrepair, with peeling paint, broken windows, graffiti, and numerous code violations, including the presence of asbestos-containing materials. The building sustained slight damage in the 1989 Loma Prieta earthquake, but has suffered no structural degradation.

Acting in response to public objections to the continuing deterioration of the Montgomery Ward Building, on October 17, 1995, the Oakland City Council directed the office of economic development and employment to formulate a plan for redevelopment of the property as a community shopping center. The City of Oakland (City) subsequently entered into an agreement with Montgomery Ward Company *** to demolish the building [and] jointly redevelop the property[.] ***

An initial study was conducted and a mitigated negative declaration for the proposed Montgomery Ward redevelopment project was prepared and released for public review in December of 1995. The initial study indicated that the Montgomery Ward Building had been "preliminarily designated as 'B+a3'" by the Oakland Cultural Heritage Survey (OCHS) in a report issued in September of 1995, and was "also considered to be eligible for the National Register of Historic Places. According to this report, the Montgomery Ward store and warehouse ... is an outstanding example of an early 20th century utilitarian-Arts and Crafts warehouse with Gothic revival overtones." ***

A component of the City's general plan is the historic preservation element which was promulgated to "encourage preservation of significant older properties and areas which have been designated as Landmarks, Preservation Districts, or Heritage Properties." *** Any structure receiving at least a "B" rating, such as the Montgomery Ward Building, is considered of "*major historical* or architectural value," with most individually eligible for the National Register and all "eligible for City landmark designation" (italics added).

The OCHS rating of B+a3 was assigned to the Montgomery Ward Building "particularly for its design quality and type/style and historical associations." The OCHS indicates that the "Survey rating makes it a historic property under Oakland's Historic Preservation Element. It meets the definition of a Historic Structure in the Oakland Unreinforced Masonry (URM) ordinance. This building appears individually eligible for the National Register of Historic Places in the context of masonry buildings (commercial) in Oakland."

The technical report which accompanies the historic preservation element also states that "for CEQA purposes" any facilities rated "either 'A' or 'B'" by the OCHS are "considered 'historic'" in the City of Oakland.[3] The technical report adds that during

---

3. According to the technical report, all of the following facilities are considered "historic" UNDER CEQA: "(a) City landmarks, (b) State Historical Landmarks and State Points of Historical Interest, (c) facilities contributing to an S-7 Preservation Combining Zone, (d) facilities on or eligible for the National Register of Historic Places, (e) facilities rated either 'A' or 'B' by either the City's Cultural Heritage Survey or the Citywide Preliminary Historical and Architectural Inventory, and (f) facilities contributing to Areas of Primary or Secondary Importance (APIs and ASIs) identified by either the Survey or Inventory."

CEQA Initial Studies, any "significant effects on these properties" must be identified, "and either the effects are mitigated to a nonsignificant level or an EIR is required."

Upon noting the B+a3 rating given to the Montgomery Ward Building by the OCHS, the initial study proposed five mitigation measures: (1) preparation of an "historic resources documentation report" to provide historic material for City archives; (2) a historical building survey to "further document this historic structure"; (3) design of the proposed shopping center to "reflect elements of the Montgomery Ward building's original architecture"; (4) display on the site of a plaque or marker commemorating the building; and (5) consultation with a qualified archeologist to monitor excavation for discovery of any possible cultural resources. The initial study concluded that "With these mitigation measures, the project will result in less than significant impacts to cultural resources." The proposed mitigated negative declaration was subsequently circulated for public review and comment.

An appeal of the proposed mitigated negative declaration was filed on January 11, 1996, by the Oakland Heritage Alliance (OHA), a group of more than 800 members which monitors projects with potential impacts upon cultural and architectural resources in the City. In the administrative appeal and subsequent public hearing before the City Planning Commission, the OHA protested the lack of an EIR and the inadequacy of the mitigation measures. Alternatives to demolition were mentioned, including concepts presented by two local architects to preserve, renovate and remodel the building into an office, retail and condominium complex. The OHA also submitted a letter from State Historic Preservation Officer ... Cherilyn Widell, who offered her opinion that the building "appears eligible for listing in the National Register of Historic Places ..." as "one of the city's most important examples of early twentieth century industrial architecture."

The City Landmarks Preservation Advisory Board agreed in a letter to the City Office of Planning and Building Environmental Review coordinator dated January 11, 1996, that the Montgomery Ward Building, although "not a City landmark ... does appear eligible for listing on the National Register and received a B+a3 rating," but supported the proposed negative declaration with two minor changes to the mitigation measures.

A staff report to the City Planning Commission in response to the OHA appeal also mentioned *** [that] "*** the building has not been nominated or placed on the National Register of Historic Places, is not a City Landmark, is not on the City's Historic Preservation Study List, and is not subject to either the Unreinforced Masonry Ordinance or Earthquake Repair Ordinance regulations and related definitions of 'Historic Properties.'" *** "[B]ased on the lack of landmark identification or study list placement of the subject property, the existence of numerous additions over the years to the building which have degraded the visual quality of the structure and resulted in a questionable eligibility status for National Register placement, and the incorporation of several mitigation measures included in the Negative Declaration to offset the impacts associated with demolition of the structure, the proposed project does not warrant a 'yes' on the Initial Study checklist, nor does it create an unmitigatable significant environmental impact."

Following the hearing, the City Planning Commission rejected the OHA appeal and approved the negative declaration on February 7, 1996. Appellant filed a petition for writ of mandate on March 11, 1996, and sought a temporary restraining order to prevent demolition of the building. Meanwhile, the City purchased the building from Montgomery Ward Company and entered into an agreement to proceed with asbestos abatement and demolition work. The temporary restraining order was denied, and the parking structure of the building was subsequently demolished. The petition for writ relief was also denied after a hearing, and this appeal followed. We granted appellant's petition for writ of supersedeas to stay further demolition activities.

Discussion

* * *

I. *The CEQA Standards.*

Under section 21168.5, our review of respondents' efforts to comply with CEQA "'shall extend only to whether there was a prejudicial abuse of discretion. Abuse of discretion is established if the agency has not proceeded in a manner required by law or if the determination or decision is not supported by substantial evidence.'" *** Our limited function is to determine "'... whether policymakers have been adequately informed of the consequences of their decisions, and whether the public has sufficient information to evaluate the performance of their elected officials.' [Citation.]" ***

Sections 21100 and 21151 require that all lead and local agencies prepare, or cause to be prepared by contract and certify the completion of an EIR on any project they intend to carry out or approve which may have a significant effect on the environment. If a lead agency determines: "There is no substantial evidence, in light of the whole record" that the project may have a significant effect on the environment or if it identifies potentially significant effects on the environment but revises the project through mitigation measures so that the effects are insignificant, it shall then adopt a negative declaration and no EIR is then required. §§ 21080, subd. (c), 21064. "However, the Supreme Court has recognized that CEQA requires the preparation of an EIR 'whenever it can be fairly argued on the basis of substantial evidence that the project may have significant environmental impact.' *** Thus, if substantial evidence in the record supports a 'fair argument' significant impacts or effects may occur, an EIR is required and a negative declaration cannot be certified." *Quail Botanical Gardens Foundation, Inc. v. City of Encinitas* 29 Cal.App.4th 1597, 1602 (1994). The burden is on the petitioner to demonstrate by citation to the record the existence of substantial evidence supporting a fair argument of significant environmental impact. ***

"*** If there is substantial evidence of such impact, contrary evidence is not adequate to support a decision to dispense with an EIR. ***" *Sierra Club v. County of Sonoma* 6 Cal.App.4th 1307, 1316–1317 (1992). "Restated, when the reviewing court: 'perceives substantial evidence that the project might have such an impact, but the agency failed to secure preparation of the required EIR, the agency's action is to be set aside because the agency abused its discretion by failing to proceed "in a manner required by law."' ..." (*Quail Botanical Gardens Foundation, Inc. v. City of Encinitas,* *supra*, 29 Cal. App. 4th at p. 1602.) Under the Guidelines, '"[s]ubstantial evidence'"' is 'enough relevant information and reasonable inferences from this information that a fair argument can be made to support a conclusion, even though other conclusions might also be reached.'" (Cal. Code Regs., tit. 14, § 15384, subd. (a).)" ***

*** "A court reviewing an agency's decision not to prepare an EIR in the first instance must set aside the decision if the administrative record contains substantial evidence that a proposed project might have a significant environmental impact; in such a case, the agency has not proceeded as required by law. ***" Under this standard, deference to the agency's determination is not appropriate. * * *

Section 21060.5 defines the "environment" to include "historic" conditions within an area which will be affected by a proposed project. *** According to section 21084.1, a "project that may cause substantial adverse change in the significance of a *historical resource* is a project that may have a significant effect on the environment" ([emphasis] added). "'A project will normally have a significant effect on the environment if it will *** [d]isrupt or adversely affect ... a property of *historic or cultural significance to a community* or ethnic or social group' (Guidelines, appen. G, subd. (j).) [(emphasis added)]." *** Thus, the significant impacts of a discretionary project upon a historic building must be considered in an EIR. *** The crucial issue, then, is whether the Montgomery Ward Building qualifies as a historical resource for purposes of CEQA.

II. *The Definition of a Historical Resource under CEQA.*

According to section 21084.1, a "historical resource" is "a resource listed in, or determined to be eligible for listing in, the California Register of Historical Resources. Historical resources included in a local register of historical resources, as defined in subdivision (k) of Section 5020.1, or deemed significant pursuant to criteria set forth in subdivision (g) of Section 5024.1, are presumed to be historically or culturally significant for purposes of this section, unless the preponderance of the evidence demonstrates that the resource is not historically or culturally significant. The fact that a resource is not listed in, or determined to be eligible for listing in, the California Register of Historical Resources, not included in a local register of historical resources, or not deemed significant pursuant to criteria set forth in subdivision (g) of Section 5024.1 shall not preclude a lead agency from determining whether the resource may be an historical resource for purposes of this section."

Thus, as we read the statute, three categories of historical resources have been created by section 21084.1. First, the mandatory provision of the statute specifies that buildings "listed in, or determined to be eligible for listing in, the California Register of Historical Resources" ... must in all cases be granted status as historical resources. Second, buildings "included in a local register of historical resources, as defined in subdivision (k) of Section 5020.1, or deemed significant pursuant to criteria set forth in subdivision (g) of Section 5024.1," are presumptively historical resources unless the preponderance of the evidence demonstrates otherwise. Third, buildings which do not fall within the mandatory or presumptive categories may still be deemed historical resources at the discretion of the lead agency.

* * * The language of sections 21084.1 and 5020.1 does not demand formal listing of a resource in a national, state or local register as a prerequisite to "historical" status. The statutory language is more expansive and flexible.

Section 21084.1 includes within the mandatory definition of historical resources all buildings either "listed in, *or determined to be eligible for* listing" in the California Register. Section 5020.1, subdivision (k), defines presumptively historic buildings in similarly disjunctive language by stating that a " '[l]ocal register of historical resources' means a list of properties officially designated *or* recognized as historically significant by a local government pursuant to local ordinance or resolution" (italics added). The California Register description of historical resources also encompasses eligibility in addition to listing; it provides that "historical resources" shall include "California properties formally determined *eligible for, or listed* in, the National Register of Historic Places" (§ 5024.1, subd. (d)(1), italics added). *** [F]inally, if historical resources were limited to properties actually listed, owner resistance to inclusion or mere government inaction might forestall preparation of an EIR for a worthy structure, a result certainly not sanctioned by CEQA. ***

III. *The Montgomery Ward Building as a Historical Resource.*

The evidence amassed in the initial study persuades us that the low threshold of a "fair argument" of significant impacts upon a historical resource has been met. Upon review of the record we find that the Montgomery Ward Building must be placed within the category of resources *presumed* to be historical within the meaning of sections 21084.1 and 5020.1, subdivision (k).

The City's own internal documentation consistently recognized the historical significance of the Montgomery Ward Building. It was described in the official City historical survey as at least arguably, if not definitively, eligible for inclusion in the National Register of Historic Places. The OCHS was an elaborate, comprehensive survey authorized and conducted by the City as part of the general plan for purposes of "environmental review" and definitive classification of buildings as historic landmarks. It was not merely an information gathering endeavor for general classification and inventory purposes. The City Landmarks Preservation Advisory Board agreed with the OCHS that the building appears "eligible for listing on the National Register," as did the State Historic Preservation Officer. The "B+a3" rating given to the building by the City placed it within the category of "major" historical importance, which rendered it "an historic property under Oakland's Historic Preservation Element" of the City's general plan and "eligible for City landmark designation." The Historic Preservation Element of the City's general plan adds that "for CEQA purposes" the building is "considered historic." In the accompanying technical report, the necessity of an EIR absent mitigation of impacts to the building to insignificant levels was noted. Under the particular circumstances presented to us, we regard the authoritative "historic" designation of the property in the City's general plan as equivalent to recognition of it "as historically significant" by local ordinance or resolution under section 5020.1, subdivision (k).

We accordingly conclude that the Montgomery Ward Building must be classified as a presumptively "historical resource" within the meaning of section 21084.1. We further conclude that the presumption of historic status has not been rebutted by any evidence in the record....

The proposed demolition of the building can hardly be considered anything less than a significant effect. In a related context, subdivision (q) of section 5020.1 specifies that "'[s]ubstantial adverse change' means *demolition, destruction*, relocation, or alteration such that the significance of an historical resource would be impaired" (italics added). We *** conclude that unless the mitigation measures proposed by the City reduce the effects of the demolition of the building to less than significant levels, an EIR is mandatory. ***

IV. *The Mitigation Measures.*

The approved mitigation measures essentially include documentation of the structure in a report and survey, display of a commemorative plaque, and a new shopping center with design features which reflect architectural elements of the demolished building. Documentation of the historical features of the building and exhibition of a plaque do not reasonably begin to alleviate the impacts of its destruction. A large historical structure, once demolished, normally cannot be adequately replaced by reports and commemorative markers. Nor, we think, are the effects of the demolition reduced to a level of insignificance by a proposed new building with unspecified design elements which may incorporate features of the original architecture into an entirely different shopping center. This is so particularly where, as here, the plans for the substitute building remain tentative and vague. We conclude that the stated mitigation measures do not reduce the effects of the demolition to less than a level of significance. ***

*** [S]ubstantial evidence supports a fair argument that significant impacts may occur. An EIR is required to identify and examine the full range of feasible mitigation measures and alternatives to demolition. *** Accordingly, the City failed to proceed in the manner required by law by certifying the mitigated negative declaration. ***

Notes and Questions

1. **Attempts at appeal.** The Court of Appeal denied a petition for rehearing on March 6, 1997. The California Supreme Court denied defendants' and respondents' petition for review May 14, 1997. 1997 Cal. LEXIS 2600.

2. **Mitigation measures.** The city proposed to mitigate the substantial adverse effects on the historical resource by, among other things, a "'documentation report' to provide historic material for City archives" and "an historical building survey to 'further document this historic structure.'" a. What would such documentation involve? Photographs? An architect's narrative or monograph? Maintaining the architectural blueprints? b. Would they be sufficient to reduce the effects of the demolition to less than significant level? c. Can such measures ever be adequate mitigation against a proposed demolition of a historic resource?

From a "Brownfield" to a New Preservation Model at Jay Heritage

How did the Jay Property, once "preserved," become contaminated with hazardous materials? What happens when nature conservation in parklands appears to compete with cultural heritage preservation? How do competing visions of public programs become reconciled?

After 1992, when Westchester County took possession of the 21.5 acres of the Jay Property surrounding the Peter Jay Mansion and the Van Norden Carriage House, the State of New York and the County entered into a Cooperative Agreement (July 7, 1997) by which the County agreed to take full responsibility to manage the parcel, while maintaining existing significant landscape features and restoring certain buildings. Despite this undertaking, the County did not announce public plans to restore the Jay Property in its Parks Master Plans, but planned to move the Marshland's environment center into the former "Zebra Barn." The County appeared to be merging its Jay Property into Marshlands Conservancy, without making a public decision to do so.

The County Parks Department, always underfunded, had not welcomed the Westchester County Board of Legislators' decision to acquire the property by eminent domain, arguing the funds for the purchase price could have been better spent on existing parklands, not acquiring new property. For several years, while the Jay Heritage Center ("JHC") raised $8 million, invested it and worked at stabilizing and restoring the Peter Jay Mansion and Van Norden Carriage House, the County Parks Department left the County's acreage alone. The County regularly referred to the Jay Property as if it were part of Marshlands Conservancy Park. Vegetation flourished, including invasive vines and brambles. In passively managing natural parklands, there is a logic to allowing nature to function on its own. This is how the County Parks Department largely managed the wood of the County's adjacent 150 acre Marshlands Conservancy park. In the case of a cultural property, however, this meant that trees grew up in areas that were once formal gardens, and several outbuildings deteriorated rapidly because the County Parks Department had no plan or funds for their care or restoration.

In retrospect, it appears that Westchester County considered the Jay site as a kind of surplus land. The Parks staff decided to transport waste to the property from other county parks. They filled the estate's former swimming pool with solid fill removed from the County's Edith Read Sanctuary and Playland Park nearby, and added discarded containers of crankcase oil, pesticides, and various kinds of solid waste. The Country claimed filling the pool was part of the cultural site planning. When the pool was full, however, another area of the property was also used as a dumping ground. None of these practices was disclosed or permitted.

In 2010, the JHC discovered the growing cache of wastes, and demanded that the dumping stop. It formally complained to the state Department of Environmental Conservation ("DEC") that the County Parks Department was in violation of state and federal environmental laws banning dumping of both hazardous and solid wastes. The JHC requested that the County fulfill its obligations under the 1997 Cooperative Agreement with New York State, and demanded that County trucks cease driving over and compacting presumed archaeological sites, such as the places where it appeared housing for slaves once existed on the property. Theresa Juva, *Jay Heritage President Upset by County Work*, THE JOURNAL NEWS, Jan. 26, 2010, at 3A.

After an investigation, the DEC ordered the County Parks Department to remove the fill within 30 days and [be taken] to a "permitted landfill." In April 2010, *MyRye.Com* reported that "while most of the solid waste being removed was placed illegally by the County Parks Department this spring, at least one of the piles of waste the DEC is requiring be removed was placed—according to the DEC letter—'between 1983 and 1993.'" JHC President Suzanne Clary stated that: "JHC was obviously distressed that County Parks brought new waste to the Jay Property in January and that past County administrations had failed for nearly 2 decades to clean up the waste left on the site by the former developer and prior owners. But following constructive and positive talks with the new County administration this week, JHC is optimistic that there will be no repetitions of such violations in the future. Furthermore, we are hopeful that this incident has prompted County Parks to establish new protocols for the use and screening of fill used at all the parks and historic sites in its care." *See* http://www.myrye.com/my_weblog/2010/04/state-dec-to-county-parks-clean-up-jay-house-mess-or-we-pursue-legal-action.html.

Beyond the clean up of the site, Westchester County's failure to comply with its 1997 agreement with the State, or adhere to the Secretary of the Interior's Standards for Historic Places, led the JHC to initiate legal action in state court against the County for tortious interference with the JHC in frustrating the historic preservation of the Jay Property. In settlement of that action, the County agreed to turn the 21.5 acres of the Jay Property to the JHC to preserve as steward. "Landmark Agreement Ensures Preservation of Historic Jay Property in Rye," Westchester County Executive Press Release *at* http://www3.westchestergov.com/news/all-press-releases/4358-astorino-announces-landmark-agreement-that-ensures-preservation-of-historic-jay-property-in-rye (last visited April 6, 2017).

The main terms are:

- The county and state, as owners, will grant a 10-year license, which is renewable after the initial term, to the JHC for the use of the property. This will give the JHC the ability to raise funds to operate the park and make improvements.
- The county and state will have the right to approve or disapprove any physical alterations to the property.
- The property will continue to be operated and maintained as state and county parkland and will be accessible to the general public. The JHC may establish admission fees, subject to approval by the state and the county consistent with county fee structures.
- JHC will create and pay for a specific maintenance and restoration by a schedule detailed in the agreement, dealing with landscape, invasive plant removal and restoration of historic structures, among other things.
- The county will continue to police the property.
- The county will no longer spend approximately $25,000 annually to maintain the property, and JHC will be responsible for ongoing maintenance and the capital improvements that the property requires.
- The county will remain responsible for the costs of any environmental remediation that may be required on the property for conditions that existed prior to the license agreement. Any environmental remediation required as a result of JHC's restoration work will be the responsibility of JHC.

Notes and Questions

1. **Forging relations for stewardship.** a. What does this settlement, which was forged in 2013 and investing the stewardship for all the Jay Property in the Jay Heritage Center, suggest about the relative merits of government agency preservation versus preservation by citizen non-profit organizations? b. Or is this an example of a public-private partnership being shaped over time? The state and county, after four decades of struggle, are now aligned with the Jay Heritage Center in stewardship of the Jay Estate, https://parks.ny.gov/historic-sites/39/details.aspx (last visited April 6, 2017). c. What does this saga suggest about how we define historic significance and agree on memory?

Architectural Heritage Association v. County of Monterey

California State Court of Appeal, Sixth District
122 Cal.App.4th 1095, 19 Cal.Rptr.3d 469 (2004)

McAdams, J. This appeal presents a challenge to the adoption of a mitigated negative declaration under CEQA, the California Environmental Quality Act.[1] Under the standard that governs our review here, we conclude that the challenge has merit. We therefore reverse the judgment.

Introduction

This dispute involves Monterey County's Old Jail, located in Salinas, California. The County of Monterey (County) intends to demolish the Old Jail. Acting through its board of supervisors, the County decided to proceed under CEQA by way of a mitigated negative declaration. Plaintiffs Architectural Heritage Association and Mark Norris challenge that decision. According to plaintiffs, there is evidence supporting a fair argument that the planned demolition will result in loss of the jail's historic value and that the proposed mitigation measures are inadequate. Plaintiffs have pressed their claims both administratively and judicially.

To provide perspective for the procedural and substantive aspects of this dispute, we begin with an overview of CEQA.

Statutory Background

CEQA embodies our state's policy that "the long-term protection of the environment ... shall be the guiding criterion in public decisions." (§ 21001, subd. (d)[.] *** As this court recently noted, "the overriding purpose of CEQA is to ensure that agencies regulating activities that may affect the quality of the environment give primary consideration to preventing environmental damage. [Citation.]" *Save Our Peninsula Committee v. Monterey County Bd. of Supervisors,* 87 Cal.App.4th 99, 117 (2001). As an aid to carrying out the statute, the State Resources Agency has issued a set of regulations, called Guidelines for the California Environmental Quality Act (Guidelines).[2] Together, CEQA and the Guidelines protect a variety of environmental values. Historic resources are among them. ***

Consistent with California's strong environmental policy, the statute and regulations "have established a three-tiered process to ensure that public agencies inform their decisions with environmental considerations." *** "The first tier is jurisdictional, requiring that an agency conduct a preliminary review in order to determine whether CEQA applies to a proposed activity. (Guidelines, §§ 15060, 15061.)" *** "If, however, the project does not fall within any [CEQA] exemption,

---

1. CEQA is codified in the Public Resources Code, starting at section 21000. Further unspecified section references are to that code.

2. The Guidelines are located at title 14 of the California Code of Regulations, starting at section 15000. Further unspecified guideline references are to those regulations.

the agency must proceed with the second tier and conduct an initial study. (Guidelines, § 15063.)" ***

The second tier of the process, the initial study, serves several purposes. Guidelines, § 15063, subd. (c). One purpose is to inform the choice between a negative declaration and an environmental impact report (EIR). *Id.*, subd. (c)(1)[.] *** Another of the initial study's purposes is to eliminate unnecessary environmental impact reports. Guidelines, § 15063, subd. (c)(7).

"CEQA excuses the preparation of an EIR and allows the use of a negative declaration when an initial study shows that there is no substantial evidence that the project may have a significant effect on the environment." *** In certain situations where a straightforward negative declaration is not appropriate, the agency may permit use of a mitigated negative declaration (MND)[,] "[i]f the initial study identifies potentially significant effects on the environment but revisions in the project plans 'would avoid the effects or mitigate the effects to a point where clearly no significant effect on the environment would occur' ***"[.] *** If the project does not qualify for a negative declaration of either type, "the third step in the process is to prepare a full environmental impact report...." ***

The California Supreme Court has "repeatedly recognized that the EIR is the 'heart of CEQA.' *** "[S]ince the preparation of an EIR is the key to environmental protection under CEQA, accomplishment of the high objectives of that act requires the preparation of an EIR whenever it can be fairly argued on the basis of substantial evidence that the project may have significant environmental impact." *No Oil, Inc. v. City of Los Angeles* 13 Cal.3d 68, 75, 118 Cal.Rptr. 34, 529 P.2d 66 (1974). The court stressed "the importance of preparing an EIR in cases ... in which the determination of a project's environmental effect turns upon the resolution of controverted issues of fact and forms the subject of intense public concern." ***

With that overview of CEQA in mind, we now turn to the facts underlying this proceeding.

Factual and Procedural Background

At the heart of this dispute is the County's Old Jail, built in 1931 in the Gothic Revival style. The three-story structure was designed by Reed & Corlett, an architectural and engineering firm "responsible for numerous buildings in the San Francisco Bay Area from 1912 to 1933, many of which are still standing." The jail is located directly adjacent to the Monterey County courthouse, at 142 West Alisal Street in Salinas. The building is approximately 40 feet tall, with some 19,000 square feet of floor space. It consists of two primary wings, which are separated by a secured passageway. The original blueprints for the jail provided for a number of uses, some quite outmoded under current penal practices. The plans thus included a boys' department, vagrants' quarters, an insane cell, a padded cell, a delousing room, a darkroom, and a room for liquor storage. Some of the jail cells "contain detailed and artistic graffiti done by prisoners."

In December 1970, César Chávez was incarcerated in the Old Jail for approximately two weeks, for refusing to obey a court order to halt the United Farm Workers' lettuce boycott. His incarceration drew international attention, prompted visits from Coretta Scott King and Ethel Kennedy, and galvanized the burgeoning farm worker movement.

By the 1980s, the County had ceased using the structure as a jail. Since then, it has been used for records storage and as a temporary holding facility for prisoners appearing in court.

In December 1999, by unanimous vote of its Board of Supervisors, the County directed its staff "to take necessary actions to provide for demolition of [the] old jail facility in Salinas."

Various assessments of the jail preceded and followed the County's decision to demolish the structure.

Assessments of the Old Jail

1. Physical Condition

Several reports commissioned by the County evaluated the jail's physical condition. A 1998 report noted the presence of asbestos and lead-based paint at the Old Jail. In August 2000, a property condition report on the Old Jail was prepared by Professional Service Industries, Inc. (PSI). Among other things, PSI's property condition report concluded that the roofs were in poor condition and that the building did not comply with the Americans with Disabilities Act. In September 2000, an indoor air quality evaluation revealed high levels of mold spores and lead dust in most locations in the building.

2. Historic Status

The County also commissioned an assessment of the Old Jail as a cultural and historic resource. Dr. Robert Cartier of Archaeological Resource Management undertook that assessment, which was completed in July 2000. *** In a section of the report detailing the jail's factual history, Cartier noted that it "was visited by some notable historical figures" and he specifically mentioned the 1970 jailing of César Chávez.

In his evaluation of the jail's cultural significance, Cartier stated: "A cultural resource is considered 'significant' if it qualifies as eligible for listing in the California Register of Historic Resources (CRHR). Properties that are eligible for listing in the CRHR must meet one or more" of four criteria, which he set forth in the report. [*See* section 5024.1, subdivision (c); Guidelines, section 15064.5, subdivision (a)(3).] The second factor (criterion 2) is particularly relevant here: "Association with the lives of persons important to local, California, or national history." Cartier observed that the Old Jail "is not currently listed on the California Register of Historic Resources. The jail structure does appear, however, to qualify as potentially eligible for listing on the CRHR under criterion 2...."

The Cartier report also set forth the four parallel criteria for listing on the National Register of Historic Places (NRHP). [*See* 36 C.F.R. Part 60.4.] Again, the second criterion is most pertinent here. That factor, criterion b, applies to places "associated with the lives of persons significant in our past." As with the state registry, Cartier observed, the Old Jail "is not currently listed on the National Register of Historic Places. However, this structure does appear to qualify ***"

Near the end of his report, Cartier stated: "Due to the historic significance of the structure, several alternative mitigations are outlined below." The listed mitigations include: (1) retention and adaptation of the structure, though that "may be impractical due to its age and condition"; (2) photographic documentation to historic survey standards; [those of the Historic American Building Survey.] (3) preparation of a historic monograph; (4) reuse of architectural elements from the building; and (5) maintaining the architectural blueprints at the local historical society.

In September 2000, County staff submitted the reports to the County Board of Supervisors.

Administrative Proceedings under CEQA

In November 2000, the County's Office of Capital Projects applied for a demolition permit for the Old Jail. Application was made to the County's Planning and Building Inspection Department (Department). Although the Department's director believed that issuance of the demolition permit was exempt under CEQA, the Department nevertheless reviewed and processed the application under the Act "out of an abundance of caution and in order to be responsive to concerns that the jail is an historic resource."

1. *The Initial Study*

The initial study [, completed on June 1, 2001,] identified several environmental factors potentially affected by demolition of the Old Jail, including cultural resources. With respect to that aspect, the research underlying the initial study "focused on the structure's characteristics and its contribution to the historic fabric of the City of Salinas and the County of Monterey." The initial study noted Cartier's conclusion that the Old Jail "qualifies as potentially eligible for listing on both the CRHR and the National Register." The initial study then concluded: "Consequently, the old jailhouse is a significant historical resource as defined by CEQA [Guidelines] Section 15064.5."

The initial study stated: "Without appropriate and extensive mitigation, the proposed demolition will cause a substantial adverse change to an historic resource." But it also noted that "the architectural integrity of the resource has been diminished by the deteriorated physical condition of the structure and the hazardous materials that are found extensively within" its components. Based on those factors, the initial study stated, "renovation or reuse of the structure is not feasible. However, the demolition of the building represents an incremental loss of both the architectural style of 1930s jail construction and an historic resource potentially eligible for listing on both the California Register of Historic Resources and the National Register of Historic Places. Without appropriate mitigation, the demolition would have impacts that are cumulatively considerable when viewed in connection with the effects of past demolitions of architecturally significant and historically significant structures within the state. ***." [T]he listed mitigations mirror those in Cartier's report. ***

Ultimately, the initial study concluded, with the proposed mitigations, the adverse environmental effects on cultural resources from demolition of the Old Jail will be less than significant. Based on that conclusion, the initial study called for preparation of a mitigated negative declaration.

2. *The Mitigated Negative Declaration*

On June 14, 2001, the County gave notice of its intent to adopt a mitigated negative declaration. *** Public comments were received in response. One was from the County's Historic Resources Review Board (Historic Board). The members of the Historic Board were "unanimous in their opinion that the draft Initial Study is insufficient upon which to address mitigation measures and recommend the County undertake a more extensive [EIR]." *** The comment period on the mitigated negative declaration ended on July 16, 2001.

A public hearing followed nearly a year later. ***. Those opposed to issuance of the demolition permit argued for preparation of an EIR, based on claims that the Old Jail is a cultural and historic resource. *** At the conclusion of the hearing, the Department adopted the mitigated negative declaration, together with a mitigation monitoring and reporting program, and it issued the demolition permit for the Old Jail. In order to mitigate the demolition's impact on the jail's value as an historic resource, the following conditions were imposed: photographic documentation to HABS standards; preparation of an historic monograph, including detailed descriptions of the jail's construction, the social environment in which it was built, its association with local, state, and national history, and jail culture; reuse or duplication of architectural elements from the building, with certain salvage details called out; and maintaining a complete set of the architectural and engineering blueprints at various agencies, including the local historical society.

3. *Plaintiffs' Administrative Appeal*

On July 12, 2002, plaintiff Architectural Heritage Association filed an appeal of the decision with the County's Board of Supervisors. As one of the grounds for its administrative appeal, Architectural Heritage Association argued that the mitigated negative declaration did not reduce the environmental impacts of demolishing the Old Jail to a level of insignificance. *** At the conclusion of that hearing, County's Board of Supervisors denied the appeal and affirmed the Department's decision adopting the mitigated negative declaration.

Judicial Proceedings

On August 27, 2002, plaintiffs Architectural Heritage Association and Mark Edwin Norris filed a petition for writ of mandate, naming as respondents the County of Monterey and its board of supervisors [challenging the] ... decision to certify the MND. constituted a violation of CEQA. *** [T]he court [rejected the challenge finding that] "the mitigation measures adopted by [the County] will appropriately preserve the historic attributes of that two week period of César Chávez's life" [spent in the jail]."

Issues

* * *

Questions Presented

As distilled by the parties' briefs, the substantive issues presented are (1) whether the Old Jail is an historic resource, (2) whether its demolition will have a significant environmental impact, and (3) whether the proposed mitigation measures are adequate to reduce that impact to insignificance. ***

Discussion

Before addressing the substantive questions presented, we first discuss three threshold issues that frame and govern our analysis.

I. Threshold Issues

* * *

Summarizing the three threshold issues, (A) we apply the fair argument standard to all three substantive issues presented—historicity, impact, and mitigation; (B) we limit our review to the administrative record; and (C) we consider whether plaintiffs have carried their burden. With the foregoing principles in mind, we turn to the substantive issues presented by this appeal.

II. Analysis

As we explain below, we conclude that plaintiffs have carried their burden of showing substantial evidence in the administrative record supporting a fair argument (A) that the Old Jail is an historic resource, (B) that its demolition will have a significant environmental impact, and (C) that the proposed mitigation measures are inadequate to reduce that impact to insignificance. In light of those conclusions, we do not reach the question of segmentation.

A. Historic Status

According to plaintiffs, there is adequate evidence supporting a fair argument of historicity in the initial study alone. But they also cite other evidence, including the Cartier report, the Historic Board recommendation for a full EIR, and comments by speakers at the public hearings. The County discounts the substantiality of the cited evidence to support plaintiffs' historic status claim. *** Our examination of the record persuades us that the "fair argument" test is satisfied here.

*** In the words of the initial study, "the old jailhouse is a significant historical resource as defined by CEQA [Guidelines] Section 15064.5." *** The County attempts to discount that conclusion. It urges that "the sole basis" for the determination "is the same portion of the Cartier Report that places a heavy reliance on the Jail's association with César Chávez as a ground for deeming the Jail a historic resource." *** We are not persuaded by the County's attempts to minimize the evidentiary force of the initial study. Under the low threshold that governs our review, the initial study incorporates "enough relevant information and reasonable inferences from this information that a fair argument can be made" that the Old Jail is an historic resource. *** Here, that information includes the initial study's nod to "the architectural style of 1930s jail construction" as well as its adoption of Cartier's conclusion that the structure is "potentially eligible" for listing on both the NRHP and the CRHR based on its social or cultural significance. *** Based on those observations alone, there is a fair argument that the Old Jail is historic.

*** [T]he County challenges the evidentiary value of Cartier's assessment of NRHP eligibility to the extent it is based on association with César Chávez. As before, however, we find that challenge unavailing. Eligibility for inclusion on the National Register is not determinative. The governing statute "does not demand formal listing of a resource in a national, state or local register as a prerequisite to 'historical' status. The statutory language is more expansive and flexible." ***

In July 2001, by unanimous vote following a scheduled public meeting, the Historic Board submitted the subcommittee's recommendation to the Department, thereby endorsing the view that the jail is an historic resource. In doing so, the Historic Board rejected the Department's recommendation that it adopt the mitigated negative declaration and approve the demolition permit.

The County attempts to minimize the finding of historic status by the Historic Board[. T]he County characterizes the Historic Board's finding as a "gratuitous conclusion" that carries no evidentiary weight, because it was made without conducting the specific type of public hearing envisioned by the Monterey County Code for the designation of historic resources. *** As to the County's *** point, we note that the Historic Board determination *was* made at a public hearing, at which review of the proposed MND was on the agenda—apparently at the request of the Department itself. Under the circumstances, we find nothing in the hearing process that diminishes the evidentiary force of the Historic Board's finding. *** [W]e find the Historic Board's determination to be fact based and *** constitutes substantial evidence that the jail is historic.

4. Speakers

At the public hearing held by the Department in June and July 2002, a number of citizens voiced their opposition to the proposed mitigated negative declaration. *** [O]ne of the speakers, *** is a certified historian; she linked the jail with "the perilous labor unrest in the Salinas Valley." *** [This] and other speakers' remarks represent fact-based observations by people apparently qualified to speak to the question of the jail's historic status. That testimony constitutes substantial evidence, because it consists of "facts, reasonable assumptions predicated upon facts, and expert opinion supported by facts." ***

* * *

B. Demolition as a Significant Impact

Having concluded that there is a fair argument supporting the jail's status as an historic resource, we next consider the effect of its proposed demolition.

*** "A project that may cause a substantial adverse change in the significance of an historical resource is a project that may have a significant effect on the environment." Guidelines, § 15064.5, subd. (b). "Substantial adverse change in the significance of an historical resource means physical demolition" or other adverse effects, such that the significance of the historic resource "would be materially impaired." Guidelines, § 15064.5, subd. (b)(1). *** Material impairment occurs when a project alters or destroys "those physical characteristics of an historical resource that convey its historical significance and that justify its inclusion" in a state or local historic registry. ***

Based on substantial evidence in the administrative record in this case, there can be little doubt that demolition will result in a substantial adverse impact on the jail. The initial study flatly states: "Without appropriate and extensive mitigation, the proposed demolition will cause a substantial adverse change to an historic resource." *** The County does not contend otherwise. Rather, it simply progresses to the next step in the analysis, the adequacy of the mitigation measures.

C. Mitigation

*** By statutory definition, a mitigated negative declaration is one in which (1) the proposed conditions "avoid the effects or mitigate the effects to a point where *clearly* no significant effect on the environment would occur, *and* (2) there is *no substantial evidence* in light of the whole record before the public agency that the project, as revised, may have a significant effect on the environment." § 21064.5 (italics added).

Here, to mitigate the impact of demolition on the jail's historic significance, the County imposed the following conditions: (1) photographic documentation; (2) preparation of an historic monograph; (3) salvage of certain architectural elements; and (4) maintenance of a set of blueprints.

Plaintiffs contend that the proposed mitigation measures are not adequate. They assert: "As drawing a chalk mark around a dead body is not mitigation, so archival documentation cannot normally reduce destruction of an historic resource to an insignificant level." As support for that assertion, plaintiffs rely on *City of Oakland, supra,* 52 Cal.App.4th 896, 60 Cal.Rptr.2d 821. *** Countering plaintiffs' assertion of inadequate mitigation, the County cites three grounds for distinguishing *City of Oakland.* We are not persuaded by any of them. *** [W]e find no basis on which to distinguish *City of Oakland.* The analysis in that case is sound, and we apply it here. *** On this record, we find substantial evidence supporting a fair argument that the proposed mitigation measures are inadequate, in that they fail to reduce the environmental detriment "to a point where clearly no significant effect" will result. § 21064.5.

D. Need for an EIR

Without undertaking a full EIR, the County determined that the jail could not be saved, finding that "its preservation or adaptive reuse is impractical due to its age, design, and deteriorating condition, and opening up the building for more usable spaces would seriously degrade the structural integrity of the building and pose a safety hazard to its occupants and neighbors."

We find this determination insupportable, both factually and legally.

As a factual matter, the administrative record discloses mixed conclusions concerning the physical condition of the structure, as well as an incomplete investigation both of the jail's condition and of alternatives to demolition. *** In determining that preservation of the jail was impractical, the County relied on Cartier's report for evidentiary support. Cartier's report mentions retention and adaptation as an alternative mitigation. But it notes that such a course for the jail "may be impractical due to its age and condition (e.g., its roof problems, deterioration of the concrete construction, specific design for secured incarceration, and its lack of compliance with current building codes)." The apparent basis for Cartier's assessment of the jail's condition is PSI's report. But as we explained above, that report is not definitive on the question of the jail's structural condition, much less on the need for demolition.

At the public hearings, several speakers urged the County to further explore alternatives to demolition, such as adaptive reuse. [One speaker] asserted that "a qualified historic architecture engineer needs to be brought in to assess the potential for remodeling the structural reinforcement." [Another] observed that "an EIR will require that viable reuse be examined." That refrain is repeated in the final addendum to Carey & Company's historic monograph, which states: "A question has arisen as to whether the existing building can be rehabilitated. It is Carey & Co.'s opinion that a study of this nature would involve reopening the environmental review process *** analysis under CEQA [and] would probably be considered an alternatives analysis. Such an analysis would involve not only the feasibility of rehabilitating the existing building, but also other options such as moving the building, rehabilitating and adding on to the building, and doing nothing. One of the alternatives would probably have to be one that is environmentally superior to the proposed project. In this case that would be preserving and rehabilitating the building as a jail or for a new use, such as county offices." *** The foregoing evidence discloses the need for further investigation of alternatives to demolition.

As a legal matter, the County erred in proceeding without benefit of a full environmental impact report. One function of an EIR is to address the adequacy of proposed mitigation measures. Guidelines, § 15126.4. Another function is to consider alternatives to the project. Guidelines, § 15126.4. Neither was fully explored here. *** By instead certifying the mitigated negative declaration, the County failed to proceed in the manner required by law. ***

Conclusion

Based on our independent review of the entire administrative record, we find that plaintiffs have carried their burden of citing to substantial evidence that supports a fair argument that the Old Jail is an historic resource, that its demolition will have a significant environmental impact, and that the proposed mitigation measures are inadequate to reduce that impact to insignificance. Based on that finding, and given the low threshold required for initial preparation of an EIR and the legislative preference for resolving doubts in favor of full environmental review, we conclude that this case must be remanded for preparation of an environmental impact report. ***

Notes and Questions

1. **Historical significance.** a. Should the Monterey County Jail with no particular architectural merit be preserved merely because it once held César Chávez? b. Does it serve to remind us of his fight to improve the lot of the migrant workers who toiled in the fields? c. Does the Birmingham County Jail where the Reverend Martin Luther King, Jr. penned his famous letter have a greater claim to preservation?

2. **Attempted end run around an EIR.** a. Did the County attempt to avoid mitigation based on the poor condition of the historical resource? b. How did the court block this convenient maneuver?

3. **César Chávez National Monument.** On October 8, 2012, President Obama proclaimed the César Chávez National Monument, Nuestra Senora Reine de la Paz (Our Lady Queen of Peace). La Paz, in Keene, California, had served as the national headquarters of the United Farm Workers and the home and workplace of Chávez. It was the place where thousands of farm workers came for support, training and to negotiate contracts. César Chávez was the symbol of the farmworker movement and served as its national leader for most of his life. La Paz is the gravesite of Chávez. La Paz was already listed on the National Register of Historic Places and a National Historic Landmark, CECH_Establishment.pdf, https://obamawhitehouse.archives.gov/the-press-office/2012/10/01/president-obama-establish-c-sar-e-ch-vez-national-monument (last visited March 4, 2017).

4. **California acts to streamline approval of development projects but preserves protections for historic and cultural resources.** As under most state environmental protection laws, the California Environmental Quality Act ("CEQA") requires that the environmental impacts of development projects be identified and mitigated. In October 2013, the legislature enacted amendments to the law designed to make the approval process less time consuming and less costly. The legislation drew a new line in the balance between economic stimulation through development and environmental protection from the effects of development. Bill Text-SB-743 Environmental quality: transit oriented infill projects, judicial review streamlining for environmental leadership development projects, and entertainment and sports center in the City of Sacramento, leginfo.legislature.ca.gov/faces/billNavClient.xhtml?bill_id=201320140SB743; *see generally*, Legislative Changes to California Environmental Quality Act Ease Requirements for Urban Infill Projects, http://www.mondaq.com/unitedstates/x/266582/real+estate/Legislative+Changes+To+Californias+CEQA+Ease+Requirements+For+Urban+Infill+Projects (last visited April 5, 2017). Among other things, the amendments ease the requirements for certain classes of urban infill projects (residential, mixed-use residential, or employment center projects) within a transit priority area, by removing

from consideration a number of impacts, including inadequate parking and aesthetic impacts. Cal Pub Resources Code § 21099(d)(1). This was not a wholesale elimination of non-physical impacts from consideration. The amendments state that the new provision does not "affect, change or modify the authority of a lead agency to consider aesthetic impacts pursuant to local design review ordinances or other discretionary powers under other laws," *id.* at § 21099(d)(2)(A), and it expressly excludes from the meaning of aesthetic impacts, those on historical or cultural resources. *Id.* at § 21099 (d)(2)(B). They also preserve the authority of a public agency to establish or adopt thresholds of significance that are more protective of the environment. *Id.* at § 21099(e). The provisos and reservations of authority to the lead agency significantly curtail the reach of the amendments. There are further CEQA exemptions identified, including residential, employment center or mixed use development projects in a specific plan area in which a prior environmental impact report was prepared, provided that the project is in a "transit priority area," the proposed project is consistent with a sustainable communities strategy or an alternative planning strategy for which the State Air Resources Board has accepted a metropolitan planning organization's determination that greenhouse gas emissions targets will be achieved. *Id.* at § 21155.4(a). The amendments provide that level of service standards shall not apply to the streets and highways within an infill opportunity zone. Cal Govt Code § 65088.4(b). Instead, the Office of Planning and Research is directed to adopt new guidelines to determine the significance of transportation impacts of projects in transit priority areas, with the aim of promoting the reduction of greenhouse gas emissions, the development of multimodal transportation networks, and a diversity of land uses. Cal Pub Resources Code § 21099(b)(1). In accomplishing these ends, the legislation directs that new metrics must be adopted that move away from the frequently used "level of service" standards, instead focusing on the vehicle miles traveled, vehicle miles traveled per capita, automobile trip generation rates, or automobile trips generated. *Id.* The "level of service" metric was thought to prioritize autos over pedestrians, transit riders, and bikers. It had been criticized because of the perverse effects generated, that is, by measuring transportation impacts on car congestion alone, and ignoring other factors, such as the number of additional car trips generated by a project, or the number of pedestrians using an intersection, that might trigger time-consuming and costly CEQA review. For example, a project to build a new sidewalk that facilitated the walkability of a street and discouraged car use, if that sidewalk replaced a car lane causing more traffic congestion, environmental review and mitigation might be required. In this way, the CEQA became "a barrier to promoting walking." Zoe Loftus-Farren, *Reform of California Environmental Quality Act Has Greens Split,* http://www.earthisland.org/journal/index.php/elist/eListRead/reform_of_californias_environmental_quality_act_has_greens_split/ October 1, 2013 (*quoting* Amanda Eaken, deputy director of NRDC's Sustainable Communities, Energy and Transportation Program). Another example is if a project promised to concentrate workers, but in the short term, increased commuter traffic, although with a long term increase in the viability of mass transit, the CEQA might yet require the developer to expand local roads to mitigate traffic impacts. *Id.* With the revisions, planners can consider multi-modal travel and greenhouse gas emissions in infill areas. Upon the certification of new guidelines, automobile delay, as described solely by "level of service" or similar measures of vehicle capacity or traffic congestion, shall not be considered a significant impact under the law. CAL PUB RESOURCES CODE §21099(b)(1). In the case of leadership projects that promise the creation of high-wage, highly skilled jobs, a streamlining process may be available. *Id.* at §21183. The project must not result in additional emission of greenhouse gases and must have entered into a binding and enforceable agreement that all mitigation measures required shall be conditions of approval of the project. *Id.* Despite the express retention of protection for historic and cultural resources, the amendments will challenge courts and administrators to read the provisions, not discretely, but as a whole, for coherence in policy. This means that some impacts, though eliminated in other contexts, may have to be considered to protect historic or cultural resources that are located in the vicinity of a project.

2. New York's Historic Preservation Act

a. Applicant's Guide to the State Historic Preservation Act

New York State Department of Environmental Conservation

New York State Department of Environmental Conservation has published a handy guide to historic preservation measures in the state. Among other things, the guide provides a definition of historic and cultural resources and advises on the kind of assessment that may be in order to determine whether protective actions are required. *See* http://www1.dec.state.ny.us/docs/permits_ej_operations_pdf/shpaappl guide.pdf (last visited April 6, 2017).

Dunk v. City of Watertown

Supreme Court of New York, Appellate Division, Fourth Department
11 A.D.3d 1024, 764 N.Y.S.2d 753 (2004)

GREEN, J.P., PINE, SCUDDER, MARTOCHE and HAYES, JJ. Appeal from a judgment (denominated order) of the Supreme Court, Jefferson County (Hugh A. GILBERT, J.), entered April 15, 2004 in a proceeding pursuant to C.P.L.R. article 78. The judgment dismissed the petition.

It is hereby ordered that the judgment so appealed from be and the same hereby is unanimously affirmed without costs.

Memorandum:

Petitioner commenced this C.P.L.R. article 78 proceeding to annul respondent's determination relating to the proposed demolition of three buildings. Petitioner contends that Supreme Court should have determined that the City Council's issuance of a negative declaration pursuant to article 8 of the Environmental Conservation Law (State Environmental Quality Review Act (SEQRA)) was arbitrary and capricious because the proposed action was the total demolition of three buildings listed on the State and National Registers of Historic Places. We reject that contention.

In reviewing whether a determination was made in accordance with SEQRA and its implementing regulations, the court is "limited to reviewing whether the determination was made in violation of lawful procedure, was affected by an error of law or was arbitrary and capricious or an abuse of discretion[.]" *Matter of Gernatt Asphalt Prods. v. Town of Sardinia,* 87 N.Y.2d 668, 688 (1996). The court's role is not "to weigh the desirability of any proposed actions or choose among alternatives but only to insure that the agency has satisfied the substantive and procedural requirements of SEQRA and of the regulations implementing it[.]" *Matter of Village of Westbury v. Department of Transp. of State of N.Y.,* 75 N.Y.2d 62, 66 (1989). The court should review the record to determine "whether the agency identified the relevant areas of environmental concern, took a 'hard look' at them, and made a 'reasoned elaboration' of the basis for its determination[.]" *Matter of Jackson v. New York State Urban Dev. Corp.,* 67 N.Y.2d 400, 417 (1986). *** An agency must prepare an environmental impact statement (EIS) if it determines that a proposed action "may have a significant effect on the environment[.]" ECL 8-0109 (2). *** The proposed project here was classified as a Type I action, which "carries with it the presumption that it is likely to have a significant adverse impact on the environment and may require an EIS" (6 N.Y.C.R.R. 617.4 (a)(1)), but an EIS is not a per se requirement for a Type I action ***. "Although the threshold triggering an EIS is relatively low, a 'negative declaration is properly issued when the agenc[y] ha[s] made a thorough investigation of the problems involved and reasonably exercised [its] discretion[.]'" *Matter of Spitzer v. Farrell,* 100 N.Y.2d 186, 190 (2003).

Here, the City Council, as lead agency, completed a full environmental assessment form and made the requisite determination that the identified adverse environmental impacts would not be significant. The City Council thus issued a negative declaration, thereby obviating the need for an EIS ***. Contrary to petitioner's contention, the City Council identified the relevant areas of environmental concern, took the requisite hard look at them, and in its negative declaration set forth a reasoned elaboration of the basis for its determination of no environmental significance ***. The City Council determined that the demolition of the buildings did not have environmental significance because, although they were historic buildings, they were only a relatively small part of the Historic District in the City. The City Council further elaborated that the buildings were unsafe and an "eyesore" and that there was little opportunity for rehabilitation. The record establishes that the City Council complied both procedurally and substantively with SEQRA. The City Council's determination to issue a negative declaration was neither arbitrary and capricious nor an abuse of discretion ***.

We reject petitioner's further contention that the demolition should be considered with the Streetscape Enhancement Project (Streetscape Project) for purposes of SEQRA review and that there was improper segmentation of environmental review in this case ***. Segmentation is "the division of the environmental review of an action such that various activities or stages are addressed under (part 617) as though they were independent, unrelated activities, needing individual determinations of significance[.]" 6 N.Y.C.R.R. 617.2 (ag). The proposed demolition and the Streetscape Project were not in any way related, other than with respect to their general locations. The Streetscape Project involved sidewalk, road, and utility improvements and had nothing to do with the buildings in the area. The projects were planned separately and are independent of each other ***.

Notes and Questions

1. **Different results.** a. Can the different results in *Dunk* and *Architectural Heritage Association* be explained by the different statutory schemes or by different factual showings by the agencies? In both cases, the buildings had fallen into disrepair and renovation would have been challenging. b. What compelling evidence might have been presented in *Dunk* for a different result?

2. **Streetscapes.** The Watertown Streetscape Enhancement Project was funded by a grant from the New York State Department of Transportation's Transportation Enhancement Program (since superseded by the Transportation Alternatives Program). The city's project involved streetscape improvements, street reconstruction, sidewalk vault infilling and repair, sidewalk replacement, and utility replacement throughout the district. Other improvements included new streets, curbing, brick pavers, street trees, tree grates, landscaping, ornamental streetlights, kiosks, and street furniture. http://www.citywatertown.org/index.asp?NID=275 (last visited February 20, 2017). a. In this light, consider whether the effects on historical resources from streetscape alterations and demolition of buildings are reciprocal and intertwined? b. Is the historic character of the district defined to a significant extent by its surroundings, including natural and man-made landscapes? c. Like New York City's colonial Dutch street patterns, do streetscapes tell us whether the design was dictated by geography or defense or commerce or livability?

Complementary State Laws Helped to Save the Jay Heritage Estate

When the struggle to preserve the Jay Estate began, the existing legal regime offered little more than formal recognition of its importance, but no protection against destruction. The National Register for Historic Places imposed only procedural limits against actions that promised adverse effects on historic properties and only in the case of a federal undertaking. National Park Service and Related Programs Act, 54 U.S.C. § 306108. At the same time, the local ordinance required owner consent for landmark designation. The advocates for preservation looked to other laws for protections of this historic site; in particular, the New York State Environmental Quality Review Act ("SEQRA"), ENVTL. CONSERV. LAW, Art. 8.

SEQRA was adopted in the wake of our nation's burgeoning awareness of the need to act aggressively and with foresight to protect the environment. While on the surface it is the state analog to the federal National Environmental Policy Act ("NEPA"), 42 U.S.C. §4321, SEQRA is far more comprehensive. NEPA is largely procedural, requiring only an identification of adverse environmental impacts from major federal projects, and does not require any measures at mitigation. SEQRA, on the other hand, is more substantive, as among other things, it requires more than a mere "consideration" of the potential adverse environmental impacts of a project. Rather, the law goes further and requires the lead agency to take a "hard look" at the potential adverse impacts of a project, and if such impacts are found, imposes an affirmative duty to mitigate those impacts. N.Y.C.R.R. tit. 6, §§617.2(1); 617.9 ("environment" includes resources of "historic or aesthetic significance", so that a local agency must determine the impacts of any proposed action on such impacts, and, choose the alternatives which avoid or minimize adverse effects on such resources); *H.O.M.E.S. v. N.Y.S. Urban Development Corporation*, 69 A.D. 2d 222, 418 N.Y.S. 2d 287 (4th Dept. 1979) (agencies must take a "hard look" at the project). It was SEQRA's requirement of an environmental impact statement ("EIS") and the obligation to mitigate discovered adverse impacts that led the City of Rye to scale back and condition the proposed development of the Jay Estate. Eventually, those conditions proved too burdensome to the developers, leading to the purchase of the property by the County.

In later years, state and local environmental laws have proven pivotal in protecting the estate against deliberate and harmful activities by the County. As stated above, in 2010, it was discovered that for two decades, the County had been unlawfully dumping construction debris and fill that contained arsenic, pesticides, and other pollutants on the edge of the estate and in the drained swimming pool. The Jay Heritage Center ("JHC") appealed to the state Department of Environmental Conservation to issue a cease and desist order and to remedy the damage. After several rounds of litigation in the courts, the parties reached an agreement under which the County transferred oversight for the upkeep of the estate to the JHC. Suzanne Clary, *The Jay Property Threatened by Erasure*, http://tclf.org/landslides/the-jay-property-threatened-by-erasure (last visited April 6, 2017); *see also*, Theresa Juva, *Jay Center Claims Neglect by County, Moves to Sue*, The Journal News, May 20, 2010, at 4a.

Chapter 6

Regulation of Archaeological Resources

The protection of archeological resources occurs on both the federal and state levels. On the federal level are the Archeological and Historic Protection Act of 1974, as amended, 54 U.S.C. §§312501–312508, and the Archaeological Resource Protection Act of 1979, 16 U.S.C. §470aa-mm. Following suit, state, local, and tribal governments have developed policies on archeological resources located on their lands; more than two-thirds of state historic preservation laws include curatorial issues and at least 20 states have curation policies and guidelines. These non-federal laws and policies tend to mirror the federal laws and regulations (at 36 C.F.R. 79). National Park Service, Archeology Program, https://www.nps.gov/history/archeology////collections/Laws_06.htm; *see also* Carol L. Carnett, A Survey of State Statutes Protecting Archeological Resources. Archeological Assistance Study No. 3, Archeological Assistance Division. Washington DC: National Park Service (1995).

A. State Archaeological Statutes

Whitacre v. Indiana

Court of Appeals of Indiana, Fifth District
619 N.E.2d 605 (1993)

Barteau, J. Whitacre appeals the trial court's judgment in favor of the Indiana Department of Natural Resources (IDNR) on Whitacre's petition for declaratory judgment. The sole issue on appeal is whether Indiana Code 14-3-3.4, the Indiana Historic Preservation and Archeology Act (the "Act"), is applicable to privately owned property. We conclude that it is and affirm the trial court.

Facts

The facts are straightforward. Whitacre and his wife are amateur archeologists. In 1982, they discovered a Hopewell Indian site with artifacts dating to *circa* 150 A.D. on a 40-acre farm in Dearborn County, Indiana. With permission from the property owner, they began excavating areas of the site and removing artifacts. In 1987, the Whitacres purchased the farm and continued excavating and conducting investigations. In July, 1989, after hearing that a new law had been passed, Whitacre inquired of an archeologist at IDNR about the necessity of a permit for conducting investigations on his own property. Whitacre was informed that he would need a permit. After investigating the law on his own, Whitacre determined that he did not need a permit and filed this declaratory judgment action.

The trial court concluded that Ind. Code [(I.C.)] 14-3-3.4 was applicable to private property and not just property owned or leased by the State of Indiana.

Discussion

The thrust of this appeal is whether a person needs to have an archeological plan approved by the Indiana Department of Natural Resources before that person may disturb *private* property for the purpose of discovering artifacts or burial objects.

The Historic Preservation and Archeology Act, I.C. 14-3-3.4, established the division of historic preservation and archeology within the IDNR to administer and develop the programs and policies of the Act. I.C. 14-3-3.4-2. *** [T]he policies to be furthered by the Division include encouraging the continuous maintenance and integrity of historic sites and structures and coordinating the activities of local historical associations, commissions and private individuals and organizations interested in the historic culture of Indiana. It has been stated that protecting our national and state heritage through the preservation of archeological sites is included in the broad spectrum of legitimate interests of government. *Indiana Dept. of Natural Resources v. Indiana Coal Council, Inc.*, 542 N.E.2d 1000, 1005 (Ind. 1989). "The information in these sites expands our knowledge of human history and prehistory and thus enriches us as a state, nation and as human beings." *Id.*

When construing a statute, this court is guided by several rules of statutory construction. First, it must be noted that when a statute is clear and unambiguous on its face, the court need not, and indeed may not, interpret the statute. *** When a statute is ambiguous, the court must ascertain the intent of the legislature and interpret the statute *** as a whole and attempt to give effect to all provisions. *** A statutory amendment changing a prior statute indicates a legislative intention that the meaning of the prior statute has been changed. *Wright v. Fowler*, 459 N.E.2d 386 (Ind.App. 1984). Another consideration in construing a statute is to give effect to the purpose of the statute. *State v. Adams*, 583 N.E.2d 799 (Ind.App. 1992), *trans. denied.*

With these guidelines in mind, we conclude that private property is included within the scope of I.C. 14-3-3.4 as amended. Unless the legislature intended to give the state the power to oversee and regulate the treatment of historical and archeological findings on private property, section 15 of the amended act is virtually meaningless, as a review of the old and new statutes shows. Prior to 1989, I.C. 14-3-3.4 restricted activities that affected historic sites or structures only within the boundaries of property owned or leased by the state. Indiana Code 14-3-3.4-7 provided:

> A person who knowingly, without a permit, conducts a field investigation or alters historic property within the boundaries of property owned or leased by the state commits a Class B misdemeanor.

Thus, prior to 1989, Whitacre was not required to have an archeological plan approved by the state in order to conduct archeological investigations and excavations on his own property.

In 1989, the legislature amended I.C. 14-3-3.4. Specifically, I.C. 14-3-3.4-7 was amended to provide:

> Except as provided in sections 14 through 16 (I.C. 14-3-3.4-14-14-3-3.4-16) of this chapter, a person who knowingly, without a permit, conducts a field investigation or alters historic property within the boundaries of property owned or leased by the state commits a Class A misdemeanor.

Sections 14 through 16 are new sections that provide for (1) the adoption of rules establishing standards for plans, I.C. 14-3-3.4-14, (2) the necessity of a plan, I.C. 14-3-3.4-15, and (3) steps to take when buried human remains are disturbed, I.C. 14-3-3.4-16. Of particular relevance to this appeal is section 15, which provides:

> (a) A person who disturbs the ground for the purpose of discovering artifacts or burial objects must do so in accordance with a plan approved by the department under section 14 (I.C. 14-3-3.4-14) of this chapter.
>
> (b) A person who recklessly, knowingly, or intentionally violates this section commits a Class A misdemeanor.

I.C. 14-3-3.4-15. "Plan" is defined as "an archeological plan for the systematic recovery, analysis, and disposition by scientific methods of material evidence and information about the life and culture in past ages." I.C. 14-3-3.4-1.

Nothing in chapter 3.4 explicitly states that the chapter applies only to property owned or leased by the state or that it applies to private property. However, section 13 does provide that the requirement of a plan when disturbing ground does not apply to (1) surface coal mining regulated under I.C. 13-4.1, (2) cemeteries and human remains subject to I.C. 23-14, (3) disturbing the earth for an agricultural purpose, and (4) collecting any object (other than human remains) that is visible on the surface of the ground. These activities are typically conducted on private property, not state owned or leased property; thus, section 13 is superfluous if the chapter applies only to state owned or leased property.

Further, prior to the amendments, I.C. 14-3-3.4-7 prohibited conducting field investigations or *altering historic property* within the bounds of property owned or leased by the state without a permit. *** Thus, in effect, I.C. 14-3-3.4-7 already prohibited disturbing the ground of state owned or leased property without a permit if anything of historic significance was on the property. The new section 15 adds nothing to the chapter unless it is interpreted as expanding the scope of coverage by prohibiting the disturbance of *any* "ground" for purposes of discovering artifacts or burial objects without an approved plan. I.C. 14-3-3.4-15. The legislature specifically did not restrict this section to only "the ground" of state owned or leased property as it did in section 7. Thus, we conclude that the legislature intended to mean any ground within the State of Indiana, whether owned by the state or privately owned.

*** The purpose of the Historical Preservation and Archeology Act is to further our understanding of the state's heritage and historical culture by preserving and studying what has been left behind. Obviously, not all sites of historical or archeological significance are located on property owned or leased by the state. *** The legislature, through the 1989 amendments, expanded the scope of the Act to include not only "historic sites" and "historic structures," as defined in I.C. 14-3-3.4-1, and located on state owned or leased property, but also to include any property where a person discovers or tries to discover "artifacts" or "burial objects," as defined in I.C. 14-3-3.4-1. Through the amendments, the state may regulate activities on private property that affect our historical and archeological culture; thus, the state is better able to discover and preserve more of our heritage. This is *** best effectuated by construing the Act to include private, as well as state owned, property.

We also find support for interpreting the statute to protect private as well as state owned property in a recent opinion from the Seventh Circuit Court of Appeals. In *United States of America v. Gerber*, 999 F.2d 1112 (7th Cir. 1993), the Seventh Circuit had to decide if a conviction pursuant to the federal Archaeological Resources Protection Act of 1979 was valid where the Indian artifacts had come from privately owned land in Indiana. The Court interpreted the Act as applying to artifacts found on privately owned property as well as property owned by the federal government or by Indian tribes, even though the Act explicitly refers only to property owned by the federal government or by Indian tribes. The Court concluded that such an interpretation best furthered the purposes of the Act "to secure, for the present and future benefit of the American people, the protection of archaeological resources and sites...." *Gerber*, 999 F.2d at 1114. It is also interesting to note that the Court assumed the amended Indiana statute at issue in our case applied to privately owned land. 999 F.2d at 1116[.] *** Consistent with the interpretation of the federal Act, we interpret the Indiana Act as applying to privately owned property.

The trial court's judgment is affirmed.

Notes

1. **Indiana Supreme Court.** On appeal, the Indiana Supreme Court affirmed what it called the "well-reasoned opinion of Judge Barteau," holding that the Act applied to privately-owned land. *Whitacre v. Indiana*, 629 N.E.2d 1236 (Ind. 1994). The court only added an observation from the Attorney General for the Department of Natural Resources' brief "that the statute works for the benefit of people like Whitacre interested in archaeology by preserving for their study Indiana's archaeological treasures." *Id.* at 1237.

B. Archaeological Resources Protection Act of 1979

United States v. Gerber

United States Court of Appeals for the Seventh Circuit
999 F.2d 1112 (1993)

Posner, J. Arthur Joseph Gerber pleaded guilty to misdemeanor violations of the Archaeological Resources Protection Act of 1979, 16 U.S.C. §§470aa *et seq.*, and was sentenced to twelve months in prison, reserving however his right to appeal on the ground that the Act is inapplicable to his offense. What he had done was to transport in interstate commerce Indian artifacts* that he had stolen from a burial mound on privately owned land in violation of Indiana's criminal laws of trespass and conversion. The section of the Archaeological Resources Protection Act under which he was convicted provides that "no person may sell, purchase, exchange, transport, receive, or offer to sell, purchase, or exchange, in interstate or foreign commerce, any archaeological resource excavated, removed, sold, purchased, exchanged, transported, or received in violation of any provision, rule, regulation, ordinance, or permit in effect under State or local law." 16 U.S.C. §470ee(c). Gerber argues that despite the references in this section to state and local law, the Act is inapplicable to archaeological objects removed from lands not owned either by the federal government or by Indian tribes. His back-up argument is that the provisions, rules, regulations, and so forth of state or local law to which the Act refers are limited to provisions expressly protecting archaeological objects or sites, as distinct from laws of general application such as those forbidding trespass and theft. The issues are novel because this is the first prosecution under the Act of someone who trafficked in archaeological objects removed from lands other than either federal or Indian lands.

More than fifteen hundred years ago in the American midwest Indians built a series of large earthen mounds over prepared mound floors containing human remains plus numerous ceremonial artifacts and grave goods made of silver, copper, wood, cloth, leather, obsidian, flint, mica, quartz, pearl, shells, and drilled, carved, or inlaid human and bear teeth. This mound culture, the product of a civilization that included the beginnings of settled agriculture, an elaborate ceremonialism, and far-flung trading networks, has been dubbed the "Hopewell phenomenon." *** In 1985 farmers sold General Electric a piece of untillable land in southwestern Indiana adjacent to one of its factories. The land contained a prominent knob on top of a ridge. Unbeknownst to anyone this knob was a Hopewell burial mound ***. The mound and its contents (which included two human skeletons) were intact—even the perishable materials such as wood and leather artifacts were well preserved—and when discovered it would prove to be one of the five largest Hopewell burial mounds known.

A highway was planned to run through the ridge on which the knob was located. In the course of construction, in 1988, earth was removed from the knob to stabilize the roadbed. Workmen engaged in this removal discovered in the knob curious objects—turtleback-shaped rocks—which they showed to a heavy-equipment operator on the project, named Bill Way, who happened to be a collector of Indian artifacts. Recognizing the significance of the find, Way nosed his bulldozer into the knob and quickly discovered hundreds of artifacts, including copper axeheads, inlaid bear canines, and tooled leather. He loaded these items into his pickup truck and covered up the excavation he had made. An acquaintance put him in touch with Arthur Joseph Gerber, a well-known collector of Indian artifacts and promoter of annual Indian "relic shows." Gerber paid Way $6,000 for the artifacts and for revealing to

* We are mindful that "Native American" is the term preferred by most members of the American Indian community. Since, however, the statute and both of the parties use the term "Indian," we have decided to do likewise.

Gerber the location of the mound. Way took Gerber to the site the same night, encountering other people digging for Indian artifacts. Gerber returned to the site several more times, excavating and removing hundreds of additional artifacts, including silver earspools, copper axeheads, pieces of worked leather, and rare silver musical instruments, some with the original reeds preserved. On Gerber's last visit to the site he was detected by a General Electric security guard and ejected. Shortly afterward Gerber sold some of the artifacts at his annual "Indian Relic Show of Shows" in Kentucky. He acknowledges that in entering upon General Electric's land without the company's permission and in removing, again without its permission, Indian artifacts buried there, he committed criminal trespass and conversion in violation of Indiana law. He also acknowledges having transported some of the stolen artifacts in interstate commerce.

The preamble of the Archaeological Resources Protection Act of 1979 states that "archaeological resources on public lands [defined elsewhere in the Act as *federal* public lands] and Indian lands are an accessible and irreplaceable part of the Nation's heritage" and that the purpose of the Act is "to secure, for the present and future benefit of the American people, the protection of archaeological and sites which are on public lands and Indian lands." 16 U.S.C. §§470aa(a)(1), (b). Consistent with this preamble, most of the Act is given over to the regulation, in the form of civil and criminal penalties, permit requirements, forfeiture provisions, and other regulatory devices, of archaeological activities *on federal and Indian lands.* The criminal penalties are for archaeological activities conducted on those lands without a permit and for trafficking in archaeological objects that have been removed from them in violation either of the Act's permit requirements or of any other federal law. §§470ee(a), (b). Gerber did not remove Indian artifacts from federal or Indian lands, however, and was therefore prosecuted under the third criminal provision (§470ee(c), quoted earlier), which is not in terms limited to such lands.

The omission of any reference in subsection (c) to federal and Indian lands was, Gerber argues, inadvertent. Not only the preamble of the Act, but its legislative history, shows that all that Congress was concerned with was protecting archaeological sites and objects on federal and Indian lands. This is indeed all that the preamble mentions; and a principal sponsor of the Act said that "it does not affect any lands other than the public lands of the United States and [Indian] lands." 125 Cong.Rec. 17,394 (1979) (remarks of Congressman Udall). The legislative history contains no reference to archaeological sites or objects on state or private lands. *** [I]f the Act applies to nonfederal, non-Indian lands, its provisions are at once overinclusive and underinclusive: overinclusive because the Act authorizes the federal court in which a defendant is prosecuted to order, in its discretion, the forfeiture of the archaeological objects involved in the violation *to the United States* (unless they were removed from Indian lands), §§470gg(b), (c); underinclusive because the provisions authorizing civil penalties and the payment of rewards to informers out of fines collected in criminal prosecutions under the Act are administered by officials who lack jurisdiction over nonfederal, non-Indian lands. §§470bb(2), 470ff, 470gg(a). *** Most scholarly commentators on the Act assume that it is limited to federal and Indian lands. *** Gerber reminds us of the rule of lenity in interpreting criminal statutes and of the implied constitutional prohibition against excessively vague criminal statutes. He adds that subsection (c) of section 470ee would not be a nullity if the Act were held to be limited to sites and objects on federal and Indian lands. A number of state laws prohibit trafficking in stolen Indian artifacts regardless of their origin, and it has not been suggested that these statutes are preempted by the federal Act even with respect to artifacts stolen from federal or Indian lands. A person who trafficked in Indian artifacts in violation of state law would be subject to federal prosecution only under subsection (c) even if the artifacts had been removed from federal or Indian lands, if the removal happened not to violate federal law.

We are not persuaded by these arguments. *** Subsection (c) appears to be a catch-all provision designed to back up state and local laws protecting archaeological sites and objects wherever located. *** The reference to interstate commerce would be superfluous if the subsection were limited to artifacts taken from federal or Indian lands, since either source would establish federal jurisdiction with no need to require proof that the artifacts were transported in interstate commerce. Probably the subsection was added as an afterthought, so one is not surprised that it does not jibe perfectly with the surrounding provisions; but that does not make it invalid, and it certainly is not vague. And we cannot see how the purposes of the Act would be undermined by our giving subsection (c) the interpretation that its words invite.

An amicus brief filed by several associations of amateur archaeologists claims that such an interpretation will infringe their liberty to seek to enlarge archaeological knowledge by excavating private lands. But there is no right to go upon another person's land, without his permission, to look for valuable objects buried in the land and take them if you find them. At common law General Electric would have been the owner of the mound and its contents regardless of the fact that it was unaware of them. *** Although we have found no Indiana cases, we are given no reason to suppose that the Indiana courts would adopt a different rule. It would make no difference if they would. Whatever the rightful ownership of the mound and its contents under current American law, no one suggests that Way or Gerber obtained any rights to the artifacts in question. No doubt, theft is at the root of many titles; and priceless archaeological artifacts obtained in violation of local law are to be found in reputable museums all over the world. But it is almost inconceivable that Congress would have wanted to encourage amateur archaeologists to violate state laws in order to amass valuable collections of Indian artifacts ***. It is also unlikely that a Congress sufficiently interested in archaeology to impose substantial criminal penalties for the violation of archaeological regulations (the maximum criminal penalty under the Act is five years in prison plus a $100,000 fine, § 470ee(d)) would be so parochial as to confine its interests to archaeological sites and artifacts on federal and Indian lands merely because that is where most of them are.

We conclude that section 470ee(c) is not limited to objects removed from federal and Indian lands, but we must consider Gerber's alternative argument, that the section is limited to removals in violation of state and local laws explicitly concerned with the protection of *archaeological* sites or objects. Gerber argues that if it is not so limited all sorts of anomalies are created. ***

*** [W]e agree with the general point, that the Act is limited to cases in which the violation of state law is related to the protection of archaeological sites or objects. A broader interpretation would carry the Act far beyond the objectives of its framers and create pitfalls for the unwary. But we do not think that to be deemed related to the protection of archaeological resources a state or local law must be *limited* to that protection. A law that forbade the theft of Indian artifacts "and any other objects having historical or artistic value" could not reasonably be thought a law unrelated to the protection of such artifacts merely because it had broader objectives. That is essentially what Indiana's laws forbidding trespass and conversion have: objectives that include but are not exhausted in the protection of Indian artifacts and other antiquities. A law that comprehensively protects the owner of land from unauthorized incursions, spoliations, and theft could well be thought to give all the protection to buried antiquities that they need, making the passage of a law specially protecting buried antiquities redundant—and the passage of new laws is never costless and rarely easy. The interpretation urged by Gerber would if accepted compel states desiring federal assistance in protecting Indian artifacts in nonfederal, non-Indian lands within their borders to pass laws that might duplicate protections already adequate conferred on landowners sitting atop undiscovered archaeological sites by existing laws of general applicability. ***

We conclude that Gerber's conduct was forbidden by the Act. ***

Affirmed.

Notes and Questions

1. **State versus federal law.** Gerber was liable because of the underlying trespass under state law. a. Does ARPA prohibit a landowner from selling or otherwise trafficking in Indian artifacts found on his private lands? b. Can or should Congress declare all such artifacts as belonging to the state, to be held for the public benefit, much like resources held under the public trust? c. Compare the *Abandoned Shipwrecks Act* of 1987, 43 U.S.C. § 2101 (establishing federal government ownership of the majority of abandoned shipwrecks located in national waters; vesting in State governments the authority to claim and manage abandoned shipwrecks on State submerged lands; and making the laws of salvage and finds not applicable to any shipwreck covered under the Act).

2. **Finding the past.** Should the prospect of finding the past in places where prehistoric life is revealed through archaeology be a sufficient basis for restricting the excavation or building on such sites?

3. **Extending the prohibitions.** On July 14, 2016, Congress adopted a joint resolution, S.Con. Res. 49, 114th Congress, 2015–2016, supporting efforts to stop the theft, illegal possession, sale, transfer, and export of tribal cultural items of Indians,

Alaska Natives, and Native Hawaiians in the United States and internationally. It calls on the Secretaries of Interior, Homeland Security, State, and Commerce to take affirmative action to stop the practice of trafficking in tribal cultural items. It directs the Comptroller to conduct a study of trafficking. Companion bills, later introduced in both houses, H.R. 5854 and S. 3127, Safeguard Tribal Objects of Patrimony, have not advanced out of Committee.

United States v. Shivers

United States Court of Appeals for the Fifth Circuit
96 F.3d 120 (1996)

Jones, C.J. Billy Ray Shivers found buried treasure at the site of an abandoned lumber mill company town. Unfortunately for Shivers, the site is located in the Angelina National Forest, and the federal government claimed ownership of and seized from Shivers some 50–70 metal tokens he uncovered with a metal detector. The district court denied his Fed. Rule Crim. Proc. 41(e) motion seeking return of the tokens, as it concluded Shivers did not own them pursuant to either the Archeological Resources Protection Act ("ARPA"), 16 U.S.C. §470ee, or the common law of finds. This court approves the district court's conclusion and therefore affirms.

Background

The tokens that Shivers excavated from the Aldridge Lumber Company mill site were used by the saw mill as payment for workers 50–100 years ago. The tokens and other items were seized pursuant to a search warrant from Shivers's home when the government came to believe he had obtained them in violation of ARPA, which forbids the un-permitted excavation of archeological resources from federal lands.

When the government chose not to pursue criminal charges against Shivers, it eventually gave back the rest of the seized property, but refused to return the tokens to him. The district court's rebuff of Shivers's Fed.R.Crim.Proc. 41(e) motion for return of seized property gives rise to this appeal.

Discussion

* * *

B. *Ownership under the ARPA: 16 U.S.C. §470kk*

Shivers argues that the plain language of ARPA §470kk vests him with ownership of the Aldridge tokens because he is a private collector of coins and other artifacts not defined by the ARPA as archaeological resources.

*** An "archaeological resource" is statutorily defined as

> any material remains of past human life or activities which are of archeological interest, as determined under uniform regulations promulgated pursuant to this chapter.... No item shall be treated as an archaeological resource under regulations under this paragraph *unless such item is at least 100 years of age.*

16 U.S.C. § 470bb(1) (emphasis added). "Archaeological resources" so defined remain property of the United States if removed from public lands. *** Since the Aldridge tokens are between 50 and 100 years old, however, they are not "archaeological resources" for purposes of the ARPA.

Shivers's principal argument rests on a facile premise: because the tokens are not "archaeological resources," § 470kk of the ARPA conveys an ownership interest to him as a private collector of coins. Section 470kk provides that

> [n]othing in this chapter applies to, or requires a permit for, the collection for private purposes of any rock, coin, bullet, or mineral which is not an archaeological resource, as determined under uniform regulations promulgated under section 470bb(1) of this title.

16 U.S.C. § 470kk(b). From this provision, Shivers infers that private individuals *are* authorized by ARPA to remove coins less than 100 years old from public land and to retain ownership.

Shivers also suggests that the purpose and policy of the ARPA support his conclusion. By encouraging private collection of non-"archaeological resources", the ARPA may actually help safeguard these resources, protecting them from further dislocation caused by either human or natural disturbances. *** Shivers urges that the asserted failure to retain ownership over non-"archaeological resources" evinces congressional intent to cede their ownership to private collectors.

But the premise on which Shivers's argument rests is a faulty one, belied by the very passage on which he relies. Section 470kk(b) provides that "*[n]othing in this chapter applies to … the collection for private purposes* of any rock, coin, bullet, or mineral which is not an archaeological resource…." (emphasis added). Because the ARPA does not apply to artifacts less than 100 years old, it does not regulate the private collection of such non-"archaeological resources". This statute cannot vest Shivers with an ownership interest in the tokens because it neither divests ownership interest from the United States or, indeed, says anything at all about "archaeological resources" it does not cover.

*** The statute merely provides that private collectors need not obtain a permit for the collection of certain artifacts. Shivers implies a transfer of property rights from this provision, arguing that since the statute allows for the private collection of non-"archaeological resources," it necessarily entitles the collector to retain or own what he has collected. This conclusion, however, is neither supported by the text of the statute nor is it a necessary implication of the right to collect non-"archaeological resources." Admittedly, the express statutory authorization to collect non-"archaeological resources" without a permit is much less valuable to a private collector if he may not retain what he collects; unless the collector enjoys collection for its own sake, ARPA furnishes little incentive to discover and gather non-"archaeological resources." But it would not be absurd to conclude that Congress dispensed with the cumbersome process of requiring permits for gathering non-"archaeological resources," even though it refused to transfer ownership of these less ancient artifacts.

Further, the ARPA is concerned with protecting the integrity of archaeological sites, presumably even more so if they are located in national forests. *See, e.g.*, 16 U.S.C. § 470cc(b)(1)-(b)(2) (requiring that those who apply for a permit to excavate archaeological resources be "qualified to carry out the permitted activity.") ***. The record suggests that several hundred shovel holes found at the Aldridge site were attributed to Shivers's excavation activities.... Considering the resulting landscape alteration, Congress's intent to regulate digging or excavating on public archaeological sites is easy to understand, while Shivers's contrary position in favor of encouraging unregulated amateur collection is virtually incomprehensible.

Finally, the "arrowhead exception" to the ARPA discussed by Shivers is inapposite and irrelevant. This exception is not intended to encourage removal of arrowheads from public lands, but rather to exempt such removal from the civil and criminal penalty provisions of the ARPA. *** Unlike the tokens excavated by Shivers, the arrowhead exception is limited to those found on the surface of public lands. ***. Also, the ARPA expressly provides that the removal of arrowheads can be penalized under other regulations or statutes. *** No inferences or implications helpful to Shivers are found in these provisions.

* * *

C. *Ownership and the Federal Common Law of Finds*

The district court concluded not only that the ARPA did not convey to Shivers an ownership interest in the Aldridge tokens, but also that in the absence of express or statutory title transfer, the federal common law of finds dictates that the United States, not Shivers, owns the tokens.

The federal common law of finds, including certain critical exceptions, is pertinent to this case. As the Eleventh Circuit explained,

> [t]he common law of finds generally assigns ownership of the abandoned property without regard to where the property is found. Two exceptions to the rule are recognized: *First, when the abandoned property is embedded in the soil, it belongs to the owner of the soil;* Second, when the owner of the land where the property is found (whether on or embedded in the soil) has constructive possession of the property such that the property is not 'lost,' it belongs to the owner of the land.

Klein v. Unidentified Wrecked & Abandoned Sailing Vessel, 758 F.2d 1511, 1514 (11th Cir.1985) (emphasis added). *** [T]he Aldridge tokens excavated by Shivers were buried in the soil of the Angelina National Forest. *** [T]his soil belongs to the United States, and with it the embedded tokens under the first exception to the federal common law of finds discussed in *Klein*.[2]

2. Analyzing the ARPA, Judge Posner has also explained that "there is no right to go upon another person's land, without his permission, to look for valuable objects buried in the land and take them if you find them." *United States v. Gerber*, 999 F.2d 1112, 1114–15 (7th Cir. 1993), *cert. denied*, 510 U.S. 1071, 114 S. Ct. 878, 127 L. Ed. 2d 74 (1994).

Shivers['] ... only retort is that the common law of finds is inapplicable because Congress expressly provided in § 470kk(b) of the ARPA that private collectors enjoy ownership of the non-archaeological resources that they discover on public lands. As already discussed, this contention is indefensible. The district court correctly held that the United States owns the tokens that Shivers discovered.

Conclusion

For the foregoing reasons, the judgment of the district court denying Shivers's 41(e) motion for the return of the Aldridge tokens is AFFIRMED.

Notes and Questions

1. **Competing interests.** a. How does one know what the site will produce? b. If the concern is for protecting the site from the degradation of digging, then does the exception make sense, other than that Congress meant to claim only "archaeological resources" as defined by the statute? c. Should Congress amend the statute to state clearly the two interests contemplated: protecting the site and retaining ownership of things discovered? d. Will the ruling discourage amateur archeologists? e. Would this be a good thing? *See generally* Sherry Hutt, *The Archaeological Resources Protection Act At 30: Permits For Data Recovery On Federal Lands, A Law And Policy Analysis*, 13 Great Plains Nat. Resources J. 12 (2010).

* * *

Willamette Meteorite Agreement

* * *

New York, New York—June 22, 2000—The American Museum of Natural History and the Confederated Tribes of the Grand Ronde Community of Oregon today signed a historic agreement that ensures access to the Willamette Meteorite, a world famous scientific specimen at the Museum, by the Grand Ronde for religious, historical, and cultural purposes while maintaining its continued presence at the Museum for scientific and educational purposes. The agreement recognizes the Museum's tradition of displaying and studying the Meteorite for almost a century, while also enabling the Grand Ronde to re-establish its relationship with the Meteorite with an annual ceremonial visit to the Meteorite.

The agreement reflects mutual recognition of and respect for the traditions of both the Tribe and the Museum. As part of the agreement, the Tribe agrees to drop its claim for repatriation of the Willamette Meteorite and not to contest the Museum's ownership of it. However, the agreement also stipulates the Meteorite would be conveyed to the Tribe if the Museum failed to publicly display it, except for temporary periods for preservation, safety, construction and reasons beyond the reasonable control of the Museum. Also in keeping with the agreement, the Museum will place a description of the Meteorite's significance to the Clackamas in the Hall of the Universe, alongside a description of the Meteorite's scientific importance.

* * *

"I can't begin to tell you how much this means to us," said Kathryn Harrison, Grand Ronde Tribal Council chair. "Since the termination of our tribe by the federal government in 1954, we have worked hard to gather our people together to share our unique and important past. This agreement goes even further because it looks towards our future. I consider it one of the outstanding milestones we've reached for our tribal members."

"It is an honor to sign this historic agreement with the Confederated Tribes of the Grand Ronde," said Ellen V. Futter, president of the Museum. "This constructive resolution demonstrates the Tribe's and the Museum's enlightened and progressive approach to discovering the opportunities that lie within our traditions. Our agreement reflects mutual respect and understanding and signals new possibilities for an ongoing and fruitful relationship, and I am pleased to announce that the Museum will establish a new internship program for Native American young people with tribal members of the Grand Ronde as its first participants. It has been a privilege and pleasure to work with our friends in the Grand Ronde."

The largest meteorite ever found in the United States, the Willamette is believed by scientists to be the iron core of a planet that was shattered in a stellar collision billions of years ago. The Meteorite crashed into Earth's surface thousands of years ago traveling at more than 40,000 miles per hour. The Museum purchased the Willamette Meteorite in 1906 and since then the unique scientific specimen has been on almost continuous display at the Museum and viewed by millions of visitors from around the world. The Willamette Meteorite is the centerpiece of the Cullman Hall of the Universe in the Museum's recently opened Rose Center of Earth and Space.

Known as "Tomanowos" to the Clackamas, who lived in the Willamette Valley before the arrival of European settlers, the Meteorite is revered by the Clackamas and their descendants. According to the tradition of the Clackamas, Tomanowos has healed and empowered people in the Willamette Valley since the beginning of time. The Clackamas believe that Tomanowos came to the valley as a representative of the Sky People and that a union occurred between the sky, earth, and water when it rested in the ground and collected rainwater in its basins. The rainwater served as a powerful purifying, cleansing, and healing source for the Clackamas and their neighbors. Tribal hunters, seeking power, dipped their arrowheads in the water collected in the Meteorite's crevices. These traditions and the spiritual link with Tomanowos are preserved today through the ceremonies and songs of the descendants of the Clackamas. Beginning in the 1850s, the Clackamas, along with more than 20 other tribes and bands from western Oregon and northern California, were relocated to the Grand Ronde Reservation in Oregon. Today, the Confederated Tribes of the Grand Ronde, a federally recognized tribe, is the successor to the Clackamas Tribe.

Growing out of discussions with the Grand Ronde, but separate from the agreement, the Museum also proposes, in keeping with its mission of scientific and cultural education, to establish an internship program for Native American young people. Such a program, which the Museum anticipates developing in consultation with the Grand Ronde and others, would facilitate an open and reciprocal exchange of information and expertise between Native Americans and the Museum and would have the following general purposes:

- to foster Native Americans' sharing a deeper understanding and appreciation of their customs, traditions, and history with the Museum community and the general public;
- to share with Native Americans information from Museum collections and research about their history, and help to restore their ancestral traditions;
- to share Museum expertise in archaeology and anthropology to advance ongoing study by Native Americans of their culture and traditions;
- to cultivate scientific knowledge and appreciation of the local environments of Native American tribes; and
- to assist in the dissemination of learning on these and related matters between and among Native Americans, museums, and the general public.

The Museum's internship program is expected to have tribal members from the Grand Ronde as its first participants.

* * *

Over one million people from around the world have already visited the Rose Center for Earth and Space, universally hailed as an architectural, scientific, and educational triumph since it opened to the public on February 19, 2000. The Rose Center comprises the Cullman Hall of the Universe, the Hayden Planetarium, and the Gottesman Hall of

Planet Earth. The American Museum of Natural History, since its founding in 1869, has been one of the world's preeminent institutions of scientific and cultural research and education.

The Confederated Tribes of Grand Ronde was formed in 1856 when the federal government forced member tribes to cede their ancestral lands in the valleys of Western Oregon and relocate to a reservation in Oregon's Coast Range. Member tribes included the Kalapuya, Molalla, Chasta, Umpqua, Rogue River and Clackamas, as well as other smaller bands and tribes. Grand Ronde leaders are committed to building self-sufficiency and turning things around for tribal members and the Oregon communities in which they live. The Grand Ronde own and operate Spirit Mountain Casino, the most successful casino in the Pacific Northwest, and have developed other tribal enterprises in construction and environmental management, real estate investment and inventory logistics services. Its Spirit Mountain Community Fund has given more than $9 million to non-profit organizations since 1997, making it Oregon's eighth largest charitable foundation. http://www.amnh.org/exhibitions/permanent-exhibitions/rose-center-for-earth-and-space/dorothy-and-lewis-b.-cullman-hall-of-the-universe/willamette-meteorite-agreement (last visited April 6, 2017).

The Willamette Meteorite. Photo by Loadmaster (David Tribble), via Wikimedia Commons.

Jay Heritage Pre-History and Archaeology

Should stewardship of archaeological sites be required by law? Is this dimension of historical memory "significant"? The Jay Estate holds the promise of new knowledge being produced on the site through archaeology, proving a 3000 year of habitation by indigenous peoples, the colonial and post-colonial land uses. On federal lands, the Historic Sites Act of 1935, 54 U.S.C. § 320101, the Archaeological and Historic Preservation Act of 1974, 54 U.S.C. § 312502, or the environmental impact assessment procedures and duties under the National Environmental Policy Act, 42 U.S.C. § 4321, mandate the study and conservation of artifacts of antiquity. Under the National Historic Preservation Act of 1966, 54 U.S.C. § 300101, states have cooperated with the Advisory Council on Historic preservation and the National Park Service to prepare archaeological surveys of federal lands. But what duties with respect to prehistoric sites exist under state or local law for private property stewards?

The Jay Heritage Center ("JHC") voluntarily has explored the archaeological heritage of its site, and within its means begun to explore this dimension of cultural heritage. Does it have any legal duty to do so? Does the City of Rye or the State of New York?

The original Peter Jay Mansion had a kitchen building directly to the south of the mansion. It posed a great danger of fire that could engulf the 1838 house. That structure was removed. The JHC arranged to have an archaeological excavation to ascertain the location of the kitchen. John Clarkson Jay, Jr., a descendent of John Jay, donated to the JHC from the Jay family collections, a water color and pencil sketch of the Locusts (c. 1745) in 2009. They depict the kitchen wing, and other structures that since have been lost. These historic works of art were the basis for depicting the Locusts on a mural by Guy Pene du Bois (1884–1958), which was painted as a Works Progress Administration project on the walls of the Rye Post Office in 1938. Is the memory preserved in the mural sufficient, or should it inspire archaeological digs?

The JHC has commissioned the preparation of initial reports about archaeological investigations of the Jay Estate, and has done small-scale excavations. JHC is aware of the approximate possible locations of other buildings on the property including those lived in by enslaved African-Americans. Numerous Indian relics have been found on the property. The artifacts emerge mixed together across different periods of time, for example a 4000 year old golden quartz projectile point discovered next to a Paleo Indian pottery shard and a later kaolin clay pipe favored by Jay. Local historical societies hold collections of Indian artifacts gathered from the Jay property and other sites in the area. JHC reports that artifacts have been found from Archaic and Woodland periods, as well as more recent colonial times and John Jay's own period of occupation of the Rye estate.

Promising as it may be, archaeology takes a secondary role to other stewardship priorities. Like many historic site managers, the JHC lacks the funds to undertake archaeological exploration of different periods of human activity on the property, from the Paleo-Indian to the Federalist period. Why preserve a 3,000 year old ethnographic living meadow, and not address the record of the indigenous people who first created the meadow? What is its duty to protect and preserve prehistory? Why is archaeology often a secondary priority in the interpretation and study of landmark sites? Why do local governments and state agencies neglect stewardship of prehistory? Why should JHC voluntarily address archaeological issues on the Jay Property?

In New York, only the procedural obligation for environmental impact assessment obliges a local government, state agency, or private party to assess archaeological resources located on privately held land. State Environmental Quality Review Act ("SEQRA"), ENVTL. CONSERV. LAW, Art. 8. New York, like other states, has not substantively enhanced the duty for pre-history since first enacting laws in the early 20th century. New York State established the nation's first state sponsored archaeological program, granting permits for persons to conduct excavations. N.Y. EDUC. LAW §§ 2323–2234, and requiring consideration of cultural assets in highway planning. N.Y. TRANSP. LAW § 14-a. Most states in the eastern United States have similar laws; Pennsylvania, which as the second oldest state regime, was second. PA. STAT. ANN., Title 71, § 1042. In most cases, archaeological assets on private lands are not expressly protected by law. While not mandating protection, a handful of states urge owners to protect cultural sites. *See e.g.*, ARK. STAT. ANN. § 801 and N.C. GEN. STAT. § 70-1.

C. Indian Tucker Act

United States v. White Mountain Apache Tribe

Supreme Court of the United States
537 U.S. 465, 123 S.Ct. 1126 (2003)

Souter, J. The question in this case arises under the Indian Tucker Act: does the Court of Federal Claims have jurisdiction over the White Mountain Apache Tribe's suit against the United States for breach of fiduciary duty to manage land and improvements held in trust for the Tribe but occupied by the Government. We hold that it does.

I

The former military post of Fort Apache dates back to 1870 when the United States established the fort within territory that became the Tribe's reservation in 1877. In 1922, Congress transferred control of the fort to the Secretary of the Interior (Secretary) and, in 1923, set aside about 400 acres, out of some 7,000, for use as the Theodore Roosevelt Indian School. Act of Jan. 24, 1923, ch. 42, 42 Stat. 1187. Congress attended to the fort again in 1960, when it provided by statute that "former Fort Apache Military Reservation" would be "held by the United States in trust for the White Mountain Apache Tribe, subject to the right of the Secretary of the Interior to use any part of the land and improvements for administrative or school purposes for as long as they are needed for the purpose." Pub.L. 86-392, 74 Stat. 8 (1960 Act). The Secretary exercised that right, and although the record does not catalog the uses made by the Department of the Interior, they extended to about 30 of the post's buildings and appurtenances, a few of which had been built when the Government first occupied the land. Although the National Park Service listed the fort as a national historical site in 1976, the recognition was no augury of fortune, for just over 20 years later the World Monuments Watch placed the fort on its 1998 List of 100 Most Endangered Monuments. ***

In 1993, the Tribe commissioned an engineering assessment of the property, resulting in a finding that as of 1998 it would cost about $14 million to rehabilitate the property occupied by the Government in accordance with standards for historic preservation. This is the amount the Tribe sought in 1999, when it sued the United States in the Court of Federal Claims, citing the terms of the 1960 Act, among others,[1] and alleging breach of fiduciary duty to "maintain, protect, repair and preserve" the trust property. ***

The United States moved to dismiss for failure to state a claim upon which relief might be granted and for lack of subject-matter jurisdiction. While the Government acknowledged that the Indian Tucker Act, 28 U.S.C. §1505, invested the Court of Federal Claims with jurisdiction to render judgments in certain claims by Indian tribes against the United States, including claims based on an Act of Congress, it stressed that the waiver operated only when underlying substantive law could fairly

1. These included the Snyder Act, 42 Stat. 208, as amended, 25 U.S.C. §13, the National Historic Preservation Act, 80 Stat. 915, 16 U.S.C. §470, *et seq.*

be interpreted as giving rise to a particular duty, breach of which should be compensable in money damages. The Government contended that jurisdiction was lacking here because no statute or regulation cited by the Tribe could fairly be read as imposing a legal obligation on the Government to maintain or restore the trust property, let alone authorizing compensation for breach.[2]

The Court of Federal Claims agreed with the United States and dismissed the complaint for lack of jurisdiction, relying primarily on the two seminal cases of tribal trust claims for damages, *United States v. Mitchell,* 445 U.S. 535, 100 S.Ct. 1349, 63 L.Ed.2d 607 (1980) *(Mitchell I),* and *United States v. Mitchell,* 463 U.S. 206, 103 S.Ct. 2961, 77 L.Ed.2d 580 (1983) *(Mitchell II). Mitchell I* held that the Indian General Allotment Act (Allotment Act), 24 Stat. 388, as amended, 25 U.S.C. § 331 *et seq.* (1976 ed.) (§§ 331–333 repealed 2000), providing that "the United States does and will hold the land thus allotted ... in trust for the sole use and benefit of the Indian," § 348; *Mitchell I, supra,* at 541, 100 S.Ct. 1349, established nothing more than a "bare trust" for the benefit of tribal members. *Mitchell II, supra,* at 224, 103 S.Ct. 2961. The general trust provision established no duty of the United States to manage timber resources, tribal members, rather, being "responsible for using the land," "occupy[ing] the land," and "manag[ing] the land." 445 U.S., at 542–543, 100 S.Ct. 1349. The opposite result [was] obtained in *Mitchell II,* however, based on timber management statutes, 25 U.S.C. §§ 406–407, 466, and regulations, 25 CFR pt. 163 (1983), under which the United States assumed "elaborate control" over the tribal forests. 463 U.S., at 209, 225, 103 S.Ct. 2961. *Mitchell II* identified a specific trust relationship enforceable by award of damages for breach. *Id.* at 225–226, 103 S.Ct. 2961.

Here, the Court of Federal Claims compared the 1960 Act to the Allotment Act in *Mitchell I,* as creating nothing more than a "bare trust." It saw in the 1960 Act no mandate that the United States manage the site on behalf of the Tribe, and thus no predicate in the statutes and regulations identified by the Tribe for finding a fiduciary obligation enforceable by monetary relief.

The Court of Appeals for the Federal Circuit reversed and remanded, on the understanding that the United States' use of property under the proviso of the 1960 Act triggered the duty of a common law trustee to act reasonably to preserve any property the Secretary had chosen to utilize, an obligation fairly interpreted as supporting a claim for money damages. The Court of Appeals held that the provision for the Government's exclusive control over the building actually occupied raised the trust to the level of *Mitchell II,* in which the trust relationship together with Government's control over the property triggered a specific responsibility.

Chief Judge Mayer dissented on the understanding that the 1960 Act "carve[d] out" from the trust the portions of the property that the Government is entitled to

2. Although it appears that the United States has not yet relinquished control of any of the buildings, the United States concedes that "some buildings have fallen into varying states of disrepair, and a few structures have been condemned or demolished." Brief for United States 4. For present purposes we need not address whether or how this affects the Tribe's claims.

use for its own benefit, with the consequence that the Tribe held only a contingent future interest in the property, insufficient to support even a common law action for permissive waste. 249 F.3d 1364, 1384 (2001).

We granted certiorari to decide whether the 1960 Act gives rise to jurisdiction over suits for money damages against the United States, 535 U.S. 1016, 122 S.Ct. 1604, 152 L.Ed.2d 619 (2002), and now affirm.

II

A

Jurisdiction over any suit against the Government requires a clear statement from the United States waiving sovereign immunity, *Mitchell I, supra,* at 538–539, 100 S.Ct. 1349, together with a claim falling within the terms of the waiver, *Mitchell II, supra,* at 216–217, 103 S.Ct. 2961. The terms of consent to be sued may not be inferred, but must be "unequivocally expressed," *** in order to "define [a] court's jurisdiction," *Mitchell I, supra,* at 538, 100 S.Ct. 1349 ***. The Tucker Act contains such a waiver, *Mitchell II, supra,* at 212, 103 S.Ct. 2961, giving the Court of Federal Claims jurisdiction to award damages upon proof of "any claim against the United States founded either upon the Constitution, or any Act of Congress," 28 U.S.C. § 1491(a)(1), and its companion statute, the Indian Tucker Act, confers a like waiver for Indian tribal claims that "otherwise would be cognizable in the Court of Federal Claims if the claimant were not an Indian tribe," § 1505.

Neither Act, however, creates a substantive right enforceable against the Government by a claim for money damages. *Mitchell I, supra,* at 538–540, 100 S.Ct. 1349; *Mitchell II, supra,* at 216, 103 S.Ct. 2961. As we said in *Mitchell II,* a statute creates a right capable of grounding a claim within the waiver of sovereign immunity if, but only if, it "can fairly be interpreted as mandating compensation by the Federal Government for the damage sustained." 463 U.S., at 217, 103 S.Ct. 2961 (quoting *United States v. Testan,* 424 U.S. 392, 400, 96 S.Ct. 948, 47 L.Ed.2d 114 (1976)) (internal quotation marks omitted).

This "fair interpretation" rule demands a showing demonstrably lower than the standard for the initial waiver of sovereign immunity. "Because the Tucker Act supplies a waiver of immunity for claims of this nature, the separate statutes and regulations need not provide a second waiver of sovereign immunity, nor need they be construed in the manner appropriate to waivers of sovereign immunity." *Mitchell II, supra,* at 218–219, 103 S.Ct. 2961. It is enough, then, that a statute creating a Tucker Act right be reasonably amenable to the reading that it mandates a right of recovery in damages. ***

B

The two *Mitchell* cases give a sense of when it is fair to infer a fiduciary duty qualifying under the Indian Tucker Act and when it is not. The characterizations of the trust as "limited," *Mitchell I,* 445 U.S., at 542, 100 S.Ct. 1349, or "bare," *Mitchell II, supra,* at 224, 103 S.Ct. 2961, distinguish the Allotment Act's trust-in-name from one with hallmarks of a more conventional fiduciary relationship. *** Although in form the United

States "h[e]ld the land ... in trust for the sole use and benefit of the Indian," 25 U.S.C. § 348, the statute gave the United States no functional obligations to manage timber; on the contrary, it established that "the Indian allottee, and not a representative of the United States, is responsible for using the land," that "the allottee would occupy the land," and that "the allottee, and not the United States, was to manage the land." *Mitchell I,* 445 U.S., at 542–543, 100 S.Ct. 1349. Thus, we found that Congress did not intend to "impose any duty" on the Government to manage resources, *** and we made sense of the trust language, considered without reference to any statute beyond the Allotment Act, as intended "to prevent alienation of the land" and to guarantee that the Indian allottees were "immune from state taxation," *Mitchell I, supra,* at 544, 100 S.Ct. 1349.

The subsequent case of *Mitchell II* arose on a claim that did look beyond the Allotment Act, and we found that statutes and regulations specifically addressing the management of timber on allotted lands raised the fair implication that the substantive obligations imposed on the United States by those statutes and regulations were enforceable by damages. The Department of the Interior possessed "comprehensive control over the harvesting of Indian timber" and "exercise[d] literally daily supervision over [its] harvesting and management," *Mitchell II, supra,* at 209, 222, 103 S.Ct. 2961 ***, giving it a "pervasive" role in the sale of timber from Indian lands under regulations addressing "virtually every aspect of forest management," *Mitchell II, supra,* at 219, 220, 103 S.Ct. 2961. As the statutes and regulations gave the United States "full responsibility to manage Indian resources and land for the benefit of the Indians," we held that they "define[d] ... contours of the United States' fiduciary responsibilities" beyond the "bare" or minimal level, and thus could "fairly be interpreted as mandating compensation" through money damages if the Government faltered in its responsibility. 463 U.S., at 224–226, 103 S.Ct. 2961.

III

A

The 1960 Act goes beyond a bare trust and permits a fair inference that the Government is subject to duties as a trustee and liable in damages for breach. The statutory language, of course, expressly defines a fiduciary relationship[3] in the provision that Fort Apache be "held by the United States in trust for the White Mountain Apache Tribe." 74 Stat. 8. Unlike the Allotment Act, however, the statute proceeds to invest the United States with discretionary authority to make direct use of portions of the trust corpus. The trust property is "subject to the right of the Secretary of the Interior to use any part of the land and improvements for administrative or school purposes for as long as they are needed for the purpose," *ibid.,* and it is undis-

3. Where, as in *Mitchell II,* 463 U.S. 206, 225, 77 L. Ed. 2d 580, 103 S. Ct. 2961 (1983), the relevant sources of substantive law create "all of the necessary elements of a common-law trust," there is no need to look elsewhere for the source of a trust relationship. We have recognized a general trust relationship since 1831. *Cherokee Nation v. Georgia,* 5 Pet. 1, 16, 30 U.S. 1, 8 L. Ed. 25 (1831) (characterizing the relationship between Indian tribes and the United States as "a ward to his guardian"); *Mitchell II, supra,* at 225 (discussing "the undisputed existence of a general trust relationship between the United States and the Indian people").

puted that the Government has to this day availed itself of its option. As to the property subject to the Government's actual use, then, the United States has not merely exercised daily supervision but has enjoyed daily occupation, and so has obtained control at least as plenary as its authority over the timber in *Mitchell II*. While it is true that the 1960 Act does not, like the statutes cited in that case, expressly subject the Government to duties of management and conservation, the fact that the property occupied by the United States is expressly subject to a trust supports a fair inference that an obligation to preserve the property improvements was incumbent on the United States as trustee. This is so because elementary trust law, after all, confirms the commonsense assumption that a fiduciary actually administering trust property may not allow it to fall into ruin on his watch. "One of the fundamental common-law duties of a trustee is to preserve and maintain trust assets," *Central States, Southeast & Southwest Areas Pension Fund v. Central Transport, Inc.*, 472 U.S. 559, 572, 105 S.Ct. 2833, 86 L.Ed.2d 447 (1985) ***. Given this duty on the part of the trustee to preserve corpus, "it naturally follows that the Government should be liable in damages for the breach of its fiduciary duties." ... *Mitchell II, supra,* at 226, 103 S.Ct. 2961.

B

The United States raises three defenses against this conclusion, the first being that the property occupied by the Government is not trust corpus at all. It asserts that in the 1960 Act Congress specifically "carve[d] out of the trust" the right of the Federal Government to use the property for the Government's own purposes. *** [T]his position is at odds with a natural reading of the 1960 Act. It provided that "Fort Apache" was subject to the trust; it did not read that the trust consisted of only the property not used by the Secretary. Nor is there any apparent reason to strain to avoid the straightforward reading; it makes sense to treat even the property used by the Government as trust property, since any use the Secretary would make of it would presumably be intended to redound to the benefit of the Tribe in some way.

Next, the Government contends that no intent to provide a damages remedy is fairly inferable, for the reason that "[t]here is not a word in the 1960 Act—the only substantive source of law on which the Tribe relies—that suggests the existence of such a mandate." *** To the extent that the Government would demand an explicit provision for money damages to support every claim that might be brought under the Tucker Act, it would substitute a plain and explicit statement standard for the less demanding requirement of fair inference that the law was meant to provide a damages remedy for breach of a duty.*** [The] fundamental objection to the Government's position is that, if carried to its conclusion, it would read the trust relation out of Indian Tucker Act analysis; if a specific provision for damages is needed, a trust obligation and trust law are not. And this likewise would ignore *Mitchell I,* where the trust relationship was considered when inferring that the trust obligation was enforceable by damages. To be sure, the fact of the trust alone in *Mitchell I* did not imply a remedy in damages or even the duty claimed, since the Allotment Act failed to place the United States in a position to discharge the management responsibility asserted. To find a specific duty, a further source of law was needed to provide focus for the trust relationship. But once that focus was provided, general trust law was considered in drawing the inference that Congress intended damages to remedy a breach of obligation.

* * *

Finally, the Government argues that the inference of a damages remedy is unsound simply because damages are inappropriate as a remedy for failures of maintenance, prospective injunctive relief being the sole relief tailored to the situation. *** We think this is clearly wrong. If the Government is suggesting that the recompense for run-down buildings should be an affirmative order to repair them, it is merely proposing the economic (but perhaps cumbersome) equivalent of damages. But if it is suggesting that relief must be limited to an injunction to toe the fiduciary mark in the future, it would bar the courts from making the Tribe whole for deterioration already suffered, and shield the Government against the remedy whose very availability would deter it from wasting trust property in the period before a Tribe has gone to court for injunctive relief. *Mitchell II,* 463 U.S., at 227, 103 S.Ct. 2961 ***.

IV

The judgment of the Court of Appeals for the Federal Circuit is affirmed, and the case is remanded to the Court of Federal Claims for further proceedings consistent with this opinion.

It is so ordered.

Justice GINSBURG, with whom Justice BREYER joins, concurring.

I join the Court's opinion, satisfied that it is not inconsistent with the opinion I wrote for the Court in *United States v. Navajo Nation, ante,* 537 U.S. 488, 123 S.Ct. 1079, 155 L.Ed.2d 60 (2003).

Both *Navajo* and the instant case are guided by *** *(Mitchell I),* and *** *(Mitchell II).* *** *Mitchell I* and *Mitchell II,* as *Navajo* explains, instruct that "[t]o state a claim cognizable under the Indian Tucker Act..., a Tribe must identify a substantive source of law that establishes specific fiduciary or other duties, and allege that the Government has failed faithfully to perform those duties." *Navajo, ante,* 537 U.S., at 506, 123 S.Ct. 1079. If the Tribe satisfies that threshold, "the court must then determine whether the relevant source of substantive law 'can fairly be interpreted as mandating compensation for damages sustained as a result of a breach of the duties [the governing law] impose[s].'" *Ibid.* (quoting *Mitchell II,* 463 U.S., at 219, 103 S.Ct. 2961).

In this case, the threshold set by the *Mitchell* cases is met. The 1960 Act, Pub. L. 86-392, 74 Stat. 8, provides that Fort Apache shall be "held by the United States in trust for the White Mountain Apache Tribe" and, at the same time, authorizes the Government to use and occupy the fort. *Ante,* at 1130. Thus, as the Court here observes, the Act expressly and without qualification employs a term of art ("trust") commonly understood to entail certain fiduciary obligations, *** and "invest[s] the United States with discretionary authority to make direct use of portions of the trust corpus," *ante*, at 1133 ***. Further, as the Court describes, the Tribe tenably maintains that the Government has "availed itself of its option" to "exercis[e] daily supervision ... [and] enjo[y] daily occupation" of the trust corpus, *ante*, at 1133, but has done so in a manner irreconcilable with its caretaker obligations. The dispositive question, accordingly, is whether the 1960 measure, in placing property in trust and simultaneously providing for the Government-trustee's use and occupancy, is fairly interpreted to mandate compensation for the harm caused by maladministration of the property.

[In] *Navajo*, *** [t]he coal-leasing provisions of the IMLA and its allied regulations, *** lacked the characteristics that typify a genuine trust relationship: Those provisions assigned the Secretary of the Interior no managerial role over coal leasing; they did not even establish the "limited trust relationship" that existed under the law at issue in *Mitchell I*. *** In the instant case, as the Court's opinion develops, the 1960 Act in fact created a trust not fairly characterized as "bare," given the trustee's authorized use and management. The plenary control the United States exercises under the Act as sole manager and trustee, I agree, places this case within *Mitchell II's* governance.* To the extent that the Government allowed trust property "to fall into ruin," *ante*, at 1133, I further agree, a damages remedy is fairly inferable.

Justice Thomas, with whom The Chief Justice, Justice Scalia, and Justice Kennedy join, dissenting.

The majority's conclusion that the Court of Federal Claims has jurisdiction over this matter finds support in neither the text of the 1960 Act, *** nor our case law. As the Court has repeatedly held, the test to determine if Congress has conferred a substantive right enforceable against the Government in a suit for money damages is whether an Act "can fairly be *interpreted* as mandating compensation by the Federal Government for the damage sustained." *United States v. Testan*, 424 U.S. 392, 400, 96 S.Ct. 948, 47 L.Ed.2d 114 (1976) *** (emphasis added). Instead of faithfully applying this test, however, the Court engages in a new inquiry, asking whether common-law trust principles permit a "fair inference" that money damages are available, that finds no support in existing law. *Ante*, at 1132. But even under the majority's newly devised approach, there is no basis for finding that Congress intended to create anything other than a "bare trust," which we have found insufficient to confer jurisdiction on the Court of Federal Claims in *** *(Mitchell I)*. Because the 1960 Act "can[not] fairly be interpreted as mandating compensation by the Federal Government for damage sustained" by the White Mountain Apache Tribe (Tribe), *Testan, supra*, at 400, 96 S.Ct. 948, I respectfully dissent.

I

In *United States v. Testan, supra*, at 400, 96 S.Ct. 948, the Court stated that a "grant of a right of action [for money damages against the United States] must be made

* *** Occupation of the trust corpus by the trustee is a common feature of trusteeship, and does not itself alter the fiduciary obligations that an expressly created trust ordinarily entails. ***

with specificity." *** The majority agrees that the 1960 Act does not specifically authorize the award of money damages; indeed, the Act does not even "spea[k] in terms of money damages or of a money claim against the United States." *** Instead, the Court holds that the use of the word "trust" in the 1960 Act creates a "fair inference" that there is a cause of action for money damages in favor of the Tribe. ***

But the Court made clear in *Mitchell I* that the existence of a trust relationship does not itself create a claim for money damages. The General Allotment Act, the statute at issue in *Mitchell I,* expressly placed responsibility on the United States to hold lands "in trust for the sole use and benefit of the Indian...." 445 U.S., at 541, 100 S.Ct. 1349 (quoting 24 Stat. 389, as amended, 25 U.S.C. § 348). Despite this language, the Court concluded that the congressional intent necessary to render the United States liable for money damages was lacking. The Court reasoned that the General Allotment Act created only a "bare trust" because Congress did "not *unambiguously* provide that the United States ha[d] undertaken full fiduciary responsibilities as to the management of allotted lands."[1] 445 U.S., at 542, 100 S.Ct. 1349.

The statute under review here provides no more evidence of congressional intent to authorize a suit for money damages than the General Allotment Act did in *Mitchell I.* The Tribe itself acknowledges that the 1960 Act is "silen[t]" not only with respect to money damages, but also with regard to any underlying "maintenance and protection duties" that can fairly be construed as creating a fiduciary relationship. *** Indeed, unlike the statutes and regulations at issue in *** *(Mitchell II),* the 1960 Act does not "establish ... 'comprehensive' responsibilities of the Federal Government in managing the" Fort Apache property. *** Because there is nothing in the statute that "clearly establish[es] fiduciary obligations of the Government in the management and operation of Indian lands," the 1960 Act creates only a "bare trust." ***

In addition, unlike the statutes and regulations at issue in *Mitchell I* and *Mitchell II,* "[n]othing in the 1960 Act imposes a fiduciary responsibility to manage the fort for the benefit of the Tribe and, in fact, it specifically carves the government's right to unrestricted use for the specified purposes out of the trust." *** The 1960 Act authorizes the "Secretary of the Interior to use any part of the land and improvements for administrative or school purposes for as long as they are needed for that purpose." 74 Stat. 8. The Government's use of the land does not have to inure to the benefit of the Indians. Nor is there any requirement that the United States cede control over the property now or in the future. *** If Congress intended to create a compensable

1. The Court of Claims has observed that the relationship between the United States and Indians is not governed by ordinary trust principles: "The general relationship between the United States and the Indian tribes is not comparable to a private trust relationship. When the source of substantive law intended and recognized only the general, or bare, trust relationship, fiduciary obligations applicable to private trustees are not imposed on the United States. Rather, the general relationship between Indian tribes and [the United States] traditionally has been understood to be in the nature of a guardian-ward relationship. A guardianship is not a trust. The duties of a trustee are more intensive than the duties of some other fiduciaries." *Cherokee Nation of Oklahoma v. United States,* 21 Cl. Ct. 565, 573 (1990) (citations and internal quotation marks omitted).

trust relationship between the United States and the Tribe with respect to the Fort Apache property, it provided no indication to this effect in the text of the 1960 Act. Accordingly, I would hold that the 1960 Act created only a "bare trust" between the United States and the Tribe.

II

In concluding otherwise, the majority gives far too much weight to the Government's factual "control" over the Fort Apache property, which is all that distinguishes this case from *Mitchell I.* The majority holds that the United States "has obtained control at least as plenary as its authority over the timber in *Mitchell II.*" *Ante,* at 1133. This analysis, however, "misconstrues ... *Mitchell II* by focusing on the extent rather than the nature of control necessary to establish a fiduciary relationship." 46 Fed.Cl. 20, 27 (1999). *** [U]ntil now, the Court has never held the United States liable for money damages under the Tucker Act or Indian Tucker Act based on notions of factual control that have no foundation in the actual text of the relevant statutes.

Respondent argues that *Mitchell II* raised control to talismanic significance in our Indian Tucker Act jurisprudence. To be sure, the Court did state:

> "[A] fiduciary relationship necessarily arises when the Government assumes such elaborate control over forests and properties belonging to the Indians.... '[W]here the Federal Government takes on or has control or supervision over tribal monies or properties ... (unless Congress has provided otherwise) even though nothing is said expressly in the authorizing or underlying statute (or other fundamental document) about a trust fund, or a trust or fiduciary connection.'" *Id.,* at 225, 103 S.Ct. 2961 (quoting *Navajo Tribe v. United States,* 224 Ct.Cl. 171, 183, 624 F.2d 981, 987 (1980)).

However, this case does not involve the level of "*elaborate* control over" the Tribe's property that the Court found sufficient to create a compensable trust duty in *Mitchell II. Mitchell II* involved a "comprehensive" regulatory scheme that "addressed virtually every aspect of forest management," and under which the United States assumed "*full* responsibility to manage Indian resources and land for the benefit of the Indians." 463 U.S., at 220, 222, 224, 103 S.Ct. 2961 (emphasis added). Here, by contrast, there are no management duties set forth in any "fundamental document," and thus the United States has the barest degree of control over the Tribe's property. ***

Moreover, even assuming that *Mitchell II* can be read to support the proposition that mere factual control over property is sufficient to create compensable trust duties (which it cannot), the Court has never provided any guidance on the nature and scope of such duties. And, in any event, the Court has never before held that "control" alone can give rise to, as the majority puts it, the specific duty to "preserve the property." *Ante,* at 1133. Indeed, had Congress wished to create such a duty, it could have done so expressly in the 1960 Act. Its failure to follow that course strongly suggests that Congress did not intend to create a compensable trust relationship between the United States and the Tribe.

* * *

The Court today fashions a new test to determine whether Congress has conferred a substantive right enforceable against the United States in a suit for money damages. In doing so, the Court radically alters the relevant inquiry from one focused on the actual fiduciary duties created by statute or regulation to one divining fiduciary duties out of the use of the word "trust" and notions of factual control. *** Because I find no basis for this approach in our case law or in the language of the Indian Tucker Act, I respectfully dissent.

Notes and Questions

1. **The historic properties.** a. Why would the Indians care about preserving Fort Apache? b. Were there other historic values at risk in this case? c. How will a monetary award help to preserve these values?

2. **Liability of the federal government.** a. Because the federal government holds sovereign immunity, it can be sued only when it waives that immunity. Here, the Indian Tucker Act, the companion to the Tucker Act, waives that immunity in the case of claims brought by native tribes. However, what must be shown is that there was some other law imposing a duty on the federal government, the breach of which could fairly be read to mandate compensation. In his dissent, Justice Thomas, did not read the trust duties imposed on the federal government under the Fort Apache Act, as such a law, describing the relationship as a "bare trust." What, if any, burdens or responsibilities would flow from such a device? If none, what would be its purpose? b. What obligations exist, or should exist, in preservation law to act as trustees for the legacy of cultural heritage for peoples who no longer exist in an historic place? c. Would an affirmative injunction compelling the government to fulfill its fiduciary duties adequately redress the neglect of traditional trust duties? d. Would it ensure prospective compliance? *See Cobell v. Salazar*, 679 F.3d 905 (D.C. Cir. 2012) (approving settlement of claims for breach of trust in managing Indian lands and ordering an accounting for more than $1.4 billon), *cert. denied*, 133 S.Ct. 543, 184 L.Ed. 2d 370 (2012).

D. 36 C.F.R. Part 79: Curation of Federally-Owned and -Administered Archaeological Collections

One recent development, being studied by the National Park Service, is the handling of archaeological and historic resources excavated from federal, public lands. Title 36, Chapter 1, Part 79 of the Code of Federal Regulations (36 C.F.R. Part 79), was passed to address the issue of the archaeological collections which had been collected through the systematic excavation of public land for various public works projects. The stated purpose of the regulation is to "*** establish definitions, standards, procedures and guidelines to be followed by Federal agencies to preserve collections of prehistoric and historic material remains, and associated records, recovered under the authority of the Antiquities Act, [54 U.S.C. §320301], the Reservoir Salvage Act [54 U.S.C. §312507], section 110 of the National Historic Preservation Act, [54 U.S.C. §306101] or the Archaeological Resources Protection Act (16 U.S.C. 470aa–mm)." 36 C.F.R. Part 79.1. As the following article discusses, this regulation has taken a toll on the both the federal organizations which do the excavations, in addition to those institutions which house them; causing both to scrounge for funds to adhere to the regulation. Last, but certainly not least, the archaeological collections themselves have been affected, with much underfunding for the Curation of the collections in accordance with 36 C.F.R. Part 79, many of the artifact collections have begun to deteriorate, basically erasing them from the archaeological record.

One glaring question, for future discussion, would be whether an archaeologist would have standing to bring suit against the government for archaeological collections that are not kept in good repair. Considering the mandate of the preceding acts concerning the federal government's responsibility to care for archaeological and historical collections, would it be actionable if they failed to do so?

1. A Decade of Study into Repository Fees for Archaeological Curation

S. Terry Childs & Seth Kagan, National Park Service, Archaeology Program

(Washington, D.C. 2008)

Many [archaeological] repositories *** have a long history of providing curatorial services at no cost to the collection owners to manage, store, and care for archeological collections created during projects on federal, state, local, and private lands. At least two factors were involved in the development of this relationship. One was the enactment of the Antiquities Act in 1906. It required that "the gatherings" from an archeological investigation on federal land be placed "... for permanent preservation in public museums" [54 U.S.C. §320302], such as university and state museums. The second factor was that university faculty and students were often involved in the archeological projects [on public lands] that created the collections of artifacts, ecofacts, and associated records. The resulting collections were then stored in their affiliated university museums, and the ensuing curatorial services were often provided to the federal or state agency collection owners in an informal exchange for access to and use of the collections in university research and education. This worked out well for both the museums and government, especially federal agencies that did not have repositories or adequate staff to catalog, store, and manage these collections. At the state level, some state-funded repositories, especially museums, existed and curated archeological collections from state lands.

The enactment of additional historic preservation laws, including the National Historic Preservation Act of 1966 (NHPA), the Archeological and Historic Preservation Act of 1974 (AHPA), and the Archaeological Resources Protection Act of 1979 (ARPA), and their implementing regulations initiated changes in that relationship. Several things happened. First, a sharp increase in the number of federal- and state-mandated archeological projects resulting from those laws yielded an equally sharp rise in the number of collections being sent to repositories for curation. Although repositories might have had room to store new collections in those years, they did not have adequate staff to catalog, conserve, box, and provide access to the sudden influx of collections. Nor did they have proper security and fire prevention systems in place (Ford 1977; Lindsay et al. 1979, 1980; Marquardt 1977; General Accounting Office 1987). [Yes, that's right; treasure hunters do not stop their hunt when it leaves the site.]

Second, the regulations "Curation of Federally-Owned and Administered Archeological Collections" (36 C.F.R. Part 79) were issued in 1990. These regulations clearly state that federal agencies own the new and existing collections resulting from publicly-supported projects on federal lands or from federal undertakings under their control, and are responsible for the long-term curation and care of these collections. The regulations also establish procedures and standards for the proper curation of federal collections, which include many potentially costly storage and housekeeping requirements that most repositories did not have in place. A number of state and local governments adapted these regulations into state and local regulations and policies, which affected an even broader range of repositories.

Finally, the archeological community has long recognized that archeological collections are irreplaceable, non-renewable resources. However, it is relatively recent that its members have come to appreciate just what it means to preserve archeological artifacts, records, and reports in perpetuity for research, education, and heritage uses (Marquardt et al. 1982; also see Sullivan and Childs 2003 for a history of the plight of archeological collections in the 20th century.) This involves a significant commitment by archeologists to properly budget for collections recovery and care as they develop each project scope of work.

All of these factors increased costs for those repositories accepting archeological collections for curation. Who is responsible for covering these costs? From where will the necessary funding come? Although 36 C.F.R. Part 79 identified federal agencies as responsible for the costs of collections from federal lands, this would not cover collections from state, local, and private lands. Repositories began to react. By 1975, at least one repository implemented a fee for the long-term curation of collections and, by 1985, over 30 repositories across the U.S. were charging curation fees. The days of curatorial services for archeological collections at no cost to their owners were coming to an end.

[Those which had already been charging fees for curation have begun to increase their fees to meet the actual costs of curation in perpetuity. Repositories in states which have larger swaths of public land tend to charge more, as development of the public lands continues as the amount of collections increases and the repositories try to meet the needs of all of them.]

This is a key issue that requires careful dialogue between the repositories and the federal government agencies, in particular, that own and are responsible for the collections. This is because many collections are the result of compliance activities, often by a third party permittee, for a land-use action that requires mitigation (e.g., cell tower construction, oil pipeline). The permittee or proponent of the action pays for the curation fees out of the project budget, which ends when the project ends. There is no funding for continuing annual fees. Furthermore, many government agencies fund development projects, such as the construction of irrigation systems or highways, and lack appropriated funds for ongoing programs to pay for annual fees.

* * *

There continues to be inadequate funding available to support the long-term care and management of archeological collections. This includes the professional staff to provide the necessary services, and the space to house the collections and make them accessible across the United States. Therefore, both the collection owners and the repositories benefit when an appropriate fee is charged and paid for curation services. The public, including researchers, educators, students, and culturally-affiliated people, also benefit when the collections are in good condition and are curated in a protected place for ongoing access and use. [But as posited before, if the collections are not kept in accordance with 36 C.F.R. Part 79, who, if anyone, would have the legal right to bring action for this deficiency?]

Notes and Questions

1. **Objects from archaeological collections.** Can objects from archaeological collections be independently listed on the National Register of Historic Places? As the name suggests, the National Register of Historic Places is focused on the protection of *places*. In reality, there are very few archaeological objects that have been listed independently in the National Register. Since archaeological collections are moveable, they generally are not listed. However, the art collection contained in the Frick Art Reference Library Building in New York City has been listed based on its relationship to the building; the removal of the collection from the *place* would compromise its integrity. *See* National Park Service, *National Historic Landmark Nomination, The Frick Collection and Frick Art Reference Library Building*, https://www.nps.gov/nhl/find/statelists/ny/Frick.pdf (last visited April 6, 2017).

The following are independent objects that are listed on the National Register of Historic Places, several of which are more like structures (e.g., tombs and large rocks):

1. Name and Number: Pohaku ka luahine, 73002273
   State and County: HAWAII, Honolulu County
   Location: Address Restricted, Kanehoe vicinity
   Date Registered: July 23, 1973
2. Name and Number: Dighton Rock, 80000438
   State and County: MASSACHUSETTS, Bristol County

Location: Across the Taunton River from Dighton in Dighton Rock State Park, Dighton vicinity
Date Registered: July 1, 1980

3. Name and Number: Inscription Rock, 73001432
State and County: OHIO, Erie County
Location: Kelleys Island, Kelleys Island vicinity
Date Registered: June 18, 1973

4. Name and Number: Nancy Ward Tomb, 73001815
State and County: TENNESSEE, Polk County
Location: South of Benton on U.S. 411, Benton vicinity
Date Registered: April 11, 1973

Chapter 7

Landscapes under Several Points of Use

A. Urban Parks

Urban parks are important in our social lives and the environment. Open spaces are places for physical activity and for community, drawing together diverse human cultures. Trees cleanse the air and their beauty encourages mental balance. As America became an urban nation, urban planners were prescient when they enlisted the aid of architects like Frederick Law Olmsted to design major city parks, such as New York City's Central Park and San Francisco's Golden Gate Park, setting aside land to be forever public and open. Urban parks can also tell stories—about the history of the city, how it came to be settled and the paths of development. Once defined, urban parks become places for protest, celebration, competition, and tragedy. In the past couple of decades, urban parks programs have become creative, embracing organic notions of space, including greenways along rivers, converted abandoned railroad lines, and community gardens in vacant lots.

1. Olmsted Parks

Frederick Law Olmsted, who lived mostly during the nineteenth century, is generally considered as America's pioneering landscape architect. Born in Hartford, Connecticut in 1822, his philosophy embraced both a sense of rural life and of the technical and modern worlds. His professional work began during the mid-nineteenth century, a period of great transformation in society—from agricultural and rural to urban and industrial pursuits. The imperatives of a ready labor force caused sharp increases in urban populations, which pressed the need for natural, open areas for health and recreation. In 1853, the New York State Legislature approved the establishment of Central Park and Olmsted was named Superintendent of Construction of Central Park in 1857. He designed the park along with the English architect, Calvert Vaux, to whom he had been introduced by the proponent of the park, Andrew Jackson Downing. Their plan, called the Greensward Plan, was notable for its combination of the formal and naturalistic settings with artistic embellishments like terraces and ornate bridges. The design was such that pedestrians and carriages could use the park without interfering with the other, and the roads allowed direct, but unobtrusive, vehicular through-traffic. After the Greensward Plan was adopted, Olmsted was appointed Chief Architect of Central Park.

Olmsted and Vaux went on to design several other New York City parks, including Prospect Park in Brooklyn and Morningside Park in Manhattan. Vaux came to have a distinguished career in the city, designing private homes, public institutions such as the American Museum of Natural History and the Metropolitan Museum of Art, and many other parks in the city's parks system. Olmsted went on to leave his mark worldwide—the United States Capitol grounds, the 1893 Columbian Exposition grounds in Chicago, and Mont Royal Park in Montreal, Canada. His legacy is unrivaled and enduring. *See generally Olmsted-Designed New York City Parks*, http://www.nycgov parks.org/about/history/olmsted-parks (last visited April 6, 2017).

Notes and Questions

1. **Peace Bridge Park.** In 2004, residents in the neighborhood of the Peace Bridge that crosses the Niagara River connecting Interstate I-90 in Buffalo, New York, with the Queen Elizabeth Way in Fort Erie, Ontario, Canada, challenged a proposal to build a new bridge south of the existing bridge and to make improvements to the Peace Bridge Plaza. The historic Peace Bridge was built to commemorate a century of peace between Canada and the U.S. The multiple-arch and steel-plated girder bridge, built from 1925–1927, is recognized for the association to this event and its engineering. The proposed project threatened effects on a number of resources, including the existing Peace Bridge and Prospect Park, designed by Frederick Law Olmsted, the Hutchinson Memorial Chapel, as well as the Prospect Hill Historic District. In addition, thirteen residences eligible for the National Register, but located outside the historic district would have been removed. It was also anticipated that archeological remains would be discovered in the construction area. The opponents to the plan asserted that the new design of the plaza would isolate the park system, diminish the visitor experience, and overwhelm the historic district. After ten years of planning, the parties finally executed a Memorandum of Agreement that significantly scaled back the plans to minimize the impact on the park and the historic resources. www.achp.gov/docs/CaseDigestAug2010.pdf (last visited April 7, 2017). But in 2011, the ACHP reported that due to budgetary issues, it appeared unlikely that the project would be completed. *See* www.achp.gov/docs/CaseDigestFall2011.pdf (last visited April 7, 2017); *see generally Mitskovski v. Buffalo And Fort Erie Public Bridge Authority*, 689 F.Supp.2d 483 (W.D.NY. (2010).

B. Viewsheds

1. The Olana Viewshed: Objection to Consistency Certification Letter to Mr. David Loomes, Director of the Greenport Project, St. Lawrence Cement Company, LLC

Randy A. Daniels, Secretary of State, New York State Department of State
Re: F-2004-0863; Army Corps of Engineers/New York District Permit Application #2000-00943-Y; St. Lawrence Cement Company, LLC—Greenport Project—Hudson River Town of Greenport/City of Hudson, Columbia County and Town of Catskill, Greene County; DEC #4-1040-000011 (April 19, 2005)

In April 2005, the New York Department of State ("DOS") filed an objection to a proposal by the St. Lawrence Cement Corporation to operate a cement factory along the Hudson River in the Town of Greenport. In a thorough and comprehensive report, the DOS concluded that the proposal failed to demonstrate consistency with the state Coastal Management Program. Among other things, the scale and intensity of the proposed factory, occupying more than 500 acres, 14 of which were on the riverfront and operating around the clock, would generate noise and particulate matter; its siting would impede access to the scenic and water resources and significantly impede the town's revitalization program, which contemplated a movement away from industrial activities in the area toward residential, tourist, and recreational uses. Because the negative effects from the plant's operation would make the area less desirable for these other purposes, it would, despite offering employment and tax benefits, have a negative economic impact on the town overall, threatening its sustainability. Significantly, the proposed operation would intrude on the viewshed of the wondrous Olana, the state historic site built by the Hudson River School artist, Frederic Church. The full report is found on the companion website.

Notes and Questions

1. **Athens, New York, and the gas-fired power plant.** In September 1997, a battle similar to the one discussed above, erupted across the Hudson River in Athens, New York. *See Pogliani v. United States Army Corps of Engineers*, 166 F. Supp. 2d 673 (N.D.N.Y. March 28, 2007). Athens Generating, a subsidiary of Pacific Gas & Electric Corporation, submitted a preliminary proposal required for a Certificate of Environmental Compatibility and Public Need under Article X of the New York Public Service Law to the New York State Board on Electric Generation Siting and the Environment ("Siting Board"). N.Y. Pub. Ser. § 121. The company proposed to use federal waters and wetlands for the construction and operation of a new gas-fired power plant in the Village of Athens. Athens Generating completed its final proposal on October 22, 1998. In 1999, after lengthy public hearings on the proposed project, the Hearing Examiners from the New York State Department of Environmental Conservation ("DEC") and the New York State Department of Public Service ("DPS") rec-

Olana. Photo by Daderot, via Wikimedia Commons.

ommended that the Siting Board grant the Certification with specified terms and conditions.

Private citizens, along with the support of Citizens for the Hudson Valley, Inc., concerned about the adverse environmental effects of the power plant originally brought suit in New York State Court under Article 78 of the New York Civil Practice Law and Rules ("CPLR") and Article X, seeking the nullification of the Siting Board's decision as "arbitrary and capricious." 166 F. Supp. 2d 678. They also pointed to the fact that the Hudson River and Hudson Valley are designated as National Heritage Areas due to their historic and economic significance; thus, the state and federal governments must be aware of and sensitive to the impact of industrial construction in the area. In particular, the plaintiffs discussed the degradation of "undisturbed vistas or 'viewsheds' from historic homes such as the Olana Mansion." *Id.* However, the New York State Supreme Court, Appellate Division, Third Department unanimously upheld the Siting Board's decision. *See Citizens for the Hudson Valley v. N.Y. State Bd. On Elec. Generation Siting and the Env't*, 281 A.D.2d 89 (N.Y. App. Div. 2001). The court found substantial evidence in the record to support the decision that construction of the power plant was in the public interest despite the environmental impacts. The court reasoned that the proposed plant would "contribute to competition, thereby lowering electricity prices." 166 F. Supp. 2d 680.

Concurrent with this proceeding, Athens Generating had submitted a proposal to the U.S. Army Corps of Engineers ("Corps") for a permit to undertake certain construction activities in Corps jurisdictional areas. On August 4, 1999, the Corps issued a public notice describing the project and requested public comment. The Corps also conducted a review of the potential impacts on the historic properties in conjunction with the New York State Historic Preservation Officer ("SHPO") and the Advisory Council on Historic Preservation ("ACHP"). After revisions by Athens Generating, the SHPO decided that the project complied with restrictions. Regardless, the Corps issued a letter to ACHP, which, pursuant to Section 106 of the National Historic Preservation Act ("NHPA"), stated that the project would have an adverse visual effect on the historic properties including Olana. Therefore, it requested a Section 106 review proceeding on the effects. The Corps held a hearing and issued a final Memorandum of Agreement for a conditional permit based on Athens Generating's obligation to avoid, mitigate and/or minimize the project's potential adverse effects. *Id.* at 682. The Corps also put forth an Environmental Assessment ("EA") pursuant to the National Environmental Policy Act ("NEPA"), concluding that the project qualified as "major Federal action significantly affect[ing] the quality of the human environment." 42 U.S.C. §4332(C). The EA discussed various environmental, health, safety, and historic concerns raised by the public. In the end, the Corps issued the permit to Athens Generating; it had determined that the negative effects were not significant enough to affect the quality of the human environment. 166 F. Supp. 2d at 686.

In a federal action, private citizens with the help of the organization Stand Together Oppose Power Plant ("S.T.O.P.P.") requested declaratory and injunctive relief under NEPA and NHPA to enjoin the Corps from issuing the permit and to declare that the Corps had violated various substantive and procedural aspects of those two Acts. The District Court for the Northern District of New York ruled for the defendant in its motion for summary judgment. It found that the Corps had sufficiently addressed the environmental issues in its reports and that no further analysis was needed for an official Environmental Impact Statement ("EIS") because the project's scale was not large enough to trigger that requirement. The court pointed to the fact that the permit given to Athens Generating was conditioned upon continued monitoring of all environmental impacts identified in the EA which were to be eliminated or minimized by various mitigation measures. *Id.* at *682, 686. The court also found that the Corps had sufficiently considered the comments of all interested parties and the feasibility of alternative sites. *Id.* at 698.

2. **The Hudson River Valley Greenway: New York State's viewshed.** On December 31, 1991, New York Governor Mario Cuomo signed into law the Hudson River Valley Greenway Act. *See* Envtl. Conserv. Law §§44-0101, *et seq.* The Act amended portions of the Environmental Conservation Law, the Navigation Law, and the State Finance Law. In the memorandum from the Governor's office accompanying the approval of the Act, Governor Cuomo stressed the Act's importance in the protection and enhancement of the "aesthetic, environmental and recreational resources of the Hudson River Valley." The Act's stated objective is to "advance the state's commitment

to the preservation, enhancement and development of the world-renowned scenic, natural, historic, cultural and recreational resources of the Hudson river valley while continuing to emphasize economic development activities and remaining consistent with the tradition of municipal home rule." *Id.* at §44-0101. To accomplish these goals, the Act includes many benefits for municipalities participating in Greenway protection, and created a process for regional decision-making for the Hudson River Valley. For instance, the Act created a Hudson River Valley Greenway Communities Council to assist municipalities with preservation, growth and development. The Council is responsible for "prepar[ing] objectives to advance each of the five greenway criteria: natural and cultural resources protection, regional planning, economic development including agriculture and urban development, public access and heritage education." *Id.* at §44-0107(8). The Council is also charged with conducting periodic studies related to the greenway criteria, participating in the environmental review process for proposed actions within the greenway, encouraging individuals and entities to preserve the greenway and "designat[ing] multi-county planning districts ... based on environmental, economic and social factors linking counties, cities, towns and villages...." *Id.* at §44-0107(7)–(16).

The Act also created the Greenway Heritage Conservancy for the Hudson River Valley to help communities plan for economic development consistent with Greenway objectives and to implement programs to ensure public access to the Hudson River. The Conservancy provides technical assistance to state, county, and local officials to facilitate the development and implementation of programs designed to promote resource protection, conservation, and management. *Id.* at §44-0113(15). The Conservancy is even authorized to purchase interests or rights (i.e., conservation easements) in real property within the Greenway, to be held by the state, for the purposes of a riverside park, the greenway trail, or preservation as open space. *Id.* at §44-0113(10). Aside from this aid to participating municipalities, the Act also provided for the creation of a Hudson River Trail, which would run along both sides of the River, including riverfront trails, scenic highways, urban cultural park trails, and railroad beds throughout. In all, the Greenway spans ten counties, including Albany, Rensselaer, Columbia, Greene, Ulster, Dutchess, Orange, Putnam, Rockland, and Westchester, and the Town and Village of Waterford in Saratoga County. It does not include the lands within the blue line of the Catskill Park. Municipalities are not penalized for failing to participate in the Greenway effort. However, benefits like state assistance for economic development and park and municipal land management make it difficult to understand why a municipality would refrain from joining the program. As discussed in the above cases, many of the towns along the Hudson River rely on the River as an essential ingredient of economic growth—the River's aesthetic beauty attracts urbanites and their expendable income.

3. **Different results.** a. Now that you have been introduced to the Hudson River Valley Greenway Act, why do you think that the above cases had to be decided under other environmental laws and regulations? Both cases concern towns bordering the Hudson River. b. Would the use of the Greenway Act be a benefit or a hindrance to

those towns? c. Think back to *Greene County Planning Board v. Federal Power Comm'n*, 455 F.2d 412 (2d Cir. 1972), concerning the construction of the high voltage power line along the Hudson River. d. How would the decision turn out under the Hudson River Valley Greenway Act, if it could be decided under that statute?

4. **Hudson River School.** The Hudson River School describes the group of American landscape painters during the 1820s to 1870s who drew inspiration from the picturesque wilderness of the Catskill region, through which the Hudson River flows. Known as America's first true artistic fraternity, the school was an outgrowth of the Romantic movement that celebrated the natural beauty of the American landscape and reflected a departure from European schools of painting. Thomas Cole, the English émigré, regarded as the founder of the movement, was followed to the region and style by such painters as Thomas Doughty, Albert Bierstadt, Asher Durand, and Frederic Church. The School flourished until about the time of the centennial. Frederic Church is also known for building Olana, the renowned and beautiful estate, celebrated not only for its architectural values, but also for the beauty of its surrounding views, which Church often included in his paintings. The site is considered one of the finest designed landscapes and a masterpiece of American landscape design. *See* The Hudson River School | Essay | Heilbrunn Timeline of Art History | The Metropolitan Museum of Art, http://www.metmuseum.org/toah/hd/hurs/hd_hurs.htm (last visited April 7, 2017).

Columbia River Gorge United-Protecting People and Property v. Yeutter

United States Court of Appeals for the Ninth Circuit
960 F.2d 110 (1992)

Schroeder, C.J. This is an action challenging the constitutionality of the Columbia River Gorge National Scenic Area Act, 16 U.S.C. §§ 544–544p which was enacted in 1986. Its purposes were to protect the economy and enhance the scenic, cultural, recreational and natural resources of the Columbia River Gorge. The Gorge occupies a uniquely beautiful and rich area in Oregon and Washington bordering the Columbia River. The Act contemplated interim management of the area by the Secretary of Agriculture and long-term management by the Columbia Gorge Commission, an agency to be established by a compact between the two states. 16 U.S.C. § 544c. The Act set forth in some detail the manner in which the Commission was to function and conditioned Congress' consent to the Compact upon compliance with those conditions. The Compact has now been entered into and the Commission is functioning according to the plan outlined in the Act.

The plaintiffs in this action, individual property owners, an organization called the "Columbia Gorge United-Protecting People and Property," and members of that organization, claimed they were adversely affected by the operation of the Commission. They sued both the Secretary of Agriculture and the Commission alleging that the Act violated both the Federal and State Constitutions. Following a hearing on the merits, the district court granted summary judgment in a thoughtful opinion rejecting all of the plaintiffs' claims. Columbia River Gorge United is the sole appellant in this action[.] *** In this appeal Columbia River Gorge United renews its contentions that the Act violates the United States Constitution, alleging specifically that the Act violates the Tenth Amendment, the Commerce, Property and Compact Clauses and the Fifth Amendment entitlement to equal protection.

Underlying all of appellant's contentions is the recurring theme that the Act and the Compact are contrary to the true wishes of the states of Oregon and Washington, and that the states were coerced into accepting conditions laid down by Congress. The Commission in this case is represented by the Attorneys General of both states who vigorously maintain that both the Act and the Compact were a product of mutual cooperation between federal and state governments to achieve a result satisfactory to both states. To the extent that appellant's arguments rest upon issues of fact with respect to coercion, they have been resolved against the plaintiffs by the district court in findings which are not clearly erroneous. We therefore deal only with issues of law.

Operation of the Act

The Act establishes a "partnership between the Federal Government, the States of Oregon and Washington, and the nearly 50 units of local government within the Columbia River Gorge for the purpose of protecting and enhancing" property and resources within the Gorge. 132 Cong.Rec. 29496 (Oct. 8, 1986) (remarks of Senator Hatfield). The Act accomplishes this goal by creating the Columbia River Gorge National Scenic Area and ratifying an interstate compact between Washington and Oregon which regulates land use and development activities within the Scenic Area.

The Act calls for the creation of a thirteen member Commission composed of three residents appointed by the three Oregon Gorge counties, three residents appointed by the three Washington Gorge counties, three members appointed by each state governor and one non-voting Forest Service employee appointed by the Secretary of Agriculture. 16 U.S.C. § 544c. Once created, the Commission is charged with the development of a management plan that regulates, through land use ordinances, the development and use of various categories of land within the Scenic Area. In furtherance of this purpose, the Commission is, within the first year of its establishment, to complete a resource inventory, an economic opportunity study, and a recreational assessment of the Scenic Area. 16 U.S.C. § 544d(a). Within two years the Commission is to complete land use designations for privately owned land within the Scenic Area. 16 U.S.C. § 544d(b). The Secretary of Agriculture will, during this same period, take corresponding steps with respect to federally owned land within the Scenic Area. 16 U.S.C. § 544f.

Once these tasks are accomplished, the Commission is to develop and adopt a management plan for the Scenic Area. Under the Act, the Plan must include land use designations, management direction for the use of federal land, and guidelines for adoption of land use ordinances. After the Plan is approved by the Secretary of Agriculture, counties will be instructed to submit land use ordinances to the Commission for approval.

If a county fails to submit an acceptable plan, the Commission is authorized to develop and implement a county plan that is consistent with the overall management plan.

Under the Act, and the resulting Compact, all land use within the Columbia River Gorge Scenic Area, whether private, federal or local, will be consistent with the management plan developed by the Commission. Congressional consent to this interstate compact is expressly contingent upon inclusion in the Compact of all powers and responsibilities assigned to the Commission under the Act. 16 U.S.C. § 544 *o*(d).

The Columbia River Gorge Compact was ratified by Oregon and Washington in 1987. The Compact incorporated the Gorge Act and established the Commission in accordance with the federal statute. Or.Rev.Stat. § 196.150 (1987); Wash.Rev.Code § 43.97.020 (1987).

Discussion

We deal first with the appellant's contentions that the Act violates the authority granted to Congress in both the Commerce and Property Clauses of the Constitution and is therefore outside the scope of the legislative power granted to Congress by the United States Constitution.

The Commerce Clause, Article I, section 8, of the Constitution provides that Congress "shall have Power ... to regulate Commerce with foreign Nations and among the several States." The Clause has, of course, been interpreted expansively to authorize regulation not only of channels and instrumentalities of interstate commerce but of "activities affecting commerce." *** Similarly, activity that is seemingly insignificant may be regulated where one individual's "contribution, taken together with that of many others similarly situated, is far from trivial." *Wickard v. Filburn,* 317 U.S. 111, 127–28, 63 S.Ct. 82, 90–91, 87 L.Ed. 122 (1942). The district court correctly disposed of appellant's contention that the Act goes beyond this expansive power.

The district court found, and appellant does not dispute, that among Congress' concerns was a desire to preserve the beauty of the area for those who would travel to use the rivers and mountains in it for recreation, thus directly causing interstate travel. Congress also intended to regulate competing economic activities within the scenic area that are activities directly affecting interstate commerce. These activities include logging and fishing. Moreover, and perhaps most important, the area itself is unique in that it consists of portions of two states bisected by a navigable waterway. In such an area, virtually all activities affecting the land, the economy, the environment, or the resources have interstate ramifications. *** Interstate bodies of water are frequently the subject of interstate compacts. *** There is thus no merit to the appellant's claim on appeal that by upholding the constitutionality of the Compact, we are upholding the authority of Congress to impose zoning regulations throughout the country. As the district court noted, Congress found this area to be one of critical national significance.

Appellant also contends that the Act goes beyond the grant of authority to Congress under the Property Clause of the Constitution which provides that Congress has power "to dispose of and make all needful Rules and Regulations respecting the Territory or other Property belonging to the United States." U.S. Const., art. IV, § 3, cl. 2. Appellant argues that even though some seventeen percent of the land in the affected area is federally owned, Congress may not regulate development in the entire area. *** We need not determine, however, whether all or a portion of the Act would go beyond the reach of Congress' power under the Property Clause. We have already determined that the Act is within Congress' power under the Commerce Clause. *** For a similar reason, the Act cannot be a violation of the Tenth Amendment. Since the Act is within the powers granted to Congress under the Commerce Clause, it cannot constitute an exercise of a power reserved to the states. We therefore need not address the federal government's position that the appellant lacks standing to assert the rights of the states under the Tenth Amendment.

We then turn to the appellant's contention that the regulatory system is a product of a compact that is not valid under the Compact Clause. Under the Compact Clause, U.S. Const., art. I, § 10, cl. 3, any interstate agreement that increases the political power of states must be approved by Congress. "The relevant inquiry must be one of impact on [the] federal structure." *United States Steel Corp. v. Multistate Tax Comm'n.*, 434 U.S. 452, 471, 98 S.Ct. 799, 812, 54 L.Ed.2d 682 (1978). All parties to this appeal agree that the Compact between Washington and Oregon, pursuant to which the Commission was established to oversee the Columbia River Gorge Area, is one which requires such congressional consent. Through the Act, Congress consented in advance to this Compact on the condition that the Compact contain certain specific provisions. Advance consent with requirements attached is itself perfectly valid, as the Supreme Court has held. *Cuyler v. Adams*, 449 U.S. 433, 440–41, 101 S.Ct. 703, 707–08, 66 L.Ed.2d 641 (1981). This court has *** [affirmed] that Congress may condition consent upon a compact containing specific terms, including the creation of a compact agency. ***

*** [T]here are distinct benefits from the kind of detailed advance planning between states and the federal government that led to this Compact. Such planning is fully consistent with the purpose of the Compact Clause. Regional arrangements may represent a necessary method for handling problems, such as transportation, waste disposal and environmental preservation, which because of their interstate nature cannot be handled by individual states acting alone. Professors Landis and Frankfurter, in their seminal article on the Compact Clause, strongly recommended the Compact device for "fashioning new instruments adapted to new situations." Frankfurter & Landis, *The Compact Clause of the Constitution—A Study in Interstate Adjustments*, 34 Yale L.J. 685, 688 (1925). Foresighted in their thinking, the authors understood that "imaginative adaptation of the compact idea should add considerably to resources available to statesmen in the solution of problems presented by ... growing interdependence." *Id.* at 729. *** [T]he compact has been used in a variety of unique situations to promote both state and federal interests: "An unusual feature of a compact does not make it invalid." *** The Columbia River Gorge Compact is just such an innovative solution to a difficult interstate land preservation problem.

The appellant finally contends that the Act violates the Fifth Amendment entitlement to equal protection because Gorge area residents must submit to local land use decisions made by non-elected officials, while state residents outside the Gorge area are subject to land use regulation only by elected officials. Insofar as the appellant argues that the Act violates electoral rights guaranteed by the state constitutions or local laws, this challenge fails. When Congress, acting within constitutional limits, creates federal law, state law is nullified to the extent that compliance with both the federal and the state law would be a physical impossibility. *Hillsborough County, Fla. v. Auto Med. Labs.,* 471 U.S. 707, 713, 105 S.Ct. 2371, 2375, 85 L.Ed.2d 714 (1985).

The equal protection challenge lodged by the appellant is based upon geographic discrimination. Residents outside the Gorge area get to vote for their land-use planners, while those inside the Gorge area do not. The equal protection clause, however, is not violated when a geographic area is singled out for different treatment. The Supreme Court has held that "there is no rule that counties, as counties, must be treated alike; the Equal Protection Clause relates to equal protection of the laws 'between persons as such rather than between areas.'" *Griffin v. County School Bd. of Prince Edward County,* 377 U.S. 218, 230, 84 S.Ct. 1226, 1233, 12 L.Ed.2d 256 (1964) ***. Different treatment of different areas is permissible, provided there are reasons for such treatment that do not reflect unconstitutional motivations. *Griffin,* 377 U.S. at 231, 84 S.Ct. at 1233. Preservation of the Columbia River Gorge Area is a permissible Congressional objective and a valid exercise of the power delegated to Congress under the Commerce Clause of the Constitution.

AFFIRMED.

Notes and Questions

1. **The Columbia River Gorge National Scenic Area Act.** Lawrence Watters, counsel for the Columbia River Gorge Commission, wrote an article concerning the Columbia River Gorge National Scenic Area Act's constitutionality, its jurisdiction, and issues concerning inverse condemnation under the Act. *See* Lawrence Watters, *The Columbia River Gorge Scenic Area Act,* 23 Envtl. L. 1127 (1993). The article primarily discusses Ninth Circuit cases and reasoning that determined these federal issues. In those cases, Watters notes, the Ninth Circuit established a "framework for the interpretation of the Act and the Compact." *Id.* at 1128. The Compact is an agreement between the federal government, the states of Oregon and Washington, six counties, and four Native American tribes that contains a "comprehensive structure for the management of the Gorge as a region," including the protection of natural resources and economic sustainability along both sides of the river. *Id.* Watters points out *Yeutter*'s importance in establishing both the state and federal constitutionality of the Act. *Id.* at 1129.

Next, Watters discusses another case that concerned an application to develop property near the Columbia River Gorge, *Broughton Lumber Co. v. Columbia River Gorge Commission,* 975 F.2d 616 (9th Cir. 1992). In that case, Broughton Lumber Co. ("Broughton") wished to split a tract of land it owned into residential developments along the bluff of the River. The executive director of the Columbia River Gorge Commission denied the application for the project. In response, Broughton filed suit in federal court, arguing that the Act had essentially taken its land through inverse condemnation. *See* Watters, 23 Envtl. L. at 1137 (citing *Broughton Lumber*, 975 F.2d at 618). After the District Court dismissed the inverse condemnation suit for lack of subject matter jurisdiction, the Ninth Circuit reviewed the matter *de novo* on appeal.

Broughton argued that federal court jurisdiction was proper because Congress "abrogated the states' immunity under the Eleventh Amendment to the U.S. Constitution." *Id.* at 1137. The court decided that the National Scenic Area Act did not abrogate the immunity of the states from suit in federal courts because that intent was not revealed in clear language. Broughton also argued that the Act and the Compact had also provided a waiver of sovereign immunity for the Gorge Commission that was imputed to the states, but the court rejected this notion. The Ninth Circuit reasoned that the Gorge Commission, as an interstate agency, had not explicitly consented to the suit in federal court. As set forth in 16 U.S.C. §544(b)(6), "[t]he State court of the State of Oregon and Washington shall have jurisdiction *** over any civil action brought *** against the Commission, a State, or a county *** [citizen suits]." The Ninth Circuit continued to stress that the Gorge Commission's waiver of immunity in state court does not act as a waiver of immunity in the federal courts. *Id.* at 1139. The Ninth Circuit therefore held that the inverse condemnation action had been properly dismissed. *Id.*

Finally, Watters' discusses the Ninth Circuit's reasoning that even if there was jurisdiction based on a waiver of sovereign immunity, Broughton's case for inverse condemnation was not ripe for adjudication, because 1) there must have been a "final and authoritative determination of the type and intensity of development legally permitted on the subject property," *Broughton Lumber*, 975 F.2d at 622; and 2) " 'if a State provides for an adequate procedure for seeking just compensation,' plaintiffs may not bring as-applied claims to federal court until they have 'used the procedure and been denied just compensation.' " *Id.* at 622. Broughton failed to utilize the procedure provided for in each state that afforded compensation for inverse condemnation. Therefore, it failed the second prong of the Ninth Circuit's ripeness requirements. 23 Envtl. L. at 1141.

In conclusion, Watters stresses the importance of these two Ninth Circuit opinions, *Yeutter* and *Broughton Lumber*, in establishing a uniform set of legal standards for litigation under the Act. *Yeutter* held that the U.S. Constitution gave Congress the power to preserve the Gorge through the interstate Compact. *Broughton Lumber* held that the state courts of Oregon and Washington have exclusive jurisdiction over litigation concerning the Act.

2. **Prevention of significant deterioration requirements.** The prevention of significant deterioration ("PSD") requirements of the Clean Air Act, 42 U.S.C. §7401, are designed to protect the views of vast landscapes from air pollution, including

smoke plumes and smog. Such vast landscapes include the Columbia River Gorge, as well as views of the Grand Canyon. Congress expressly enacted these requirements to protect views and public welfare, not just public health. *See* 42 U.S.C. §§4791, 4292 (concerning the importance of the imposition of these requirements for visibility). The concerns with the air pollution around viewsheds, on the other hand, are not general PSD visibility issues for the Clean Air Act. Viewshed visibility deals with the same issue, but it is more site specific for an important viewshed. For example, steam is not a pollutant, so the Clean Air Act at the federal level cannot handle the issue. But a site specific ordinance or Compact, such as the Columbia River Gorge National Scenic Area Act, would be able to do so. How analogous would the Clean Air Act be on a larger scale?

3. **Urban development and urban viewsheds.** The Grand Canyon is not listed on the National Register of Historic Places. However, it is a National Park and it is home to many National Register Sites within the Park area. The Park is also subject to the requirements of the Clean Air Act. If there were a site within or near a city that suffered from air pollution due to facility siting, should visibility be considered as a basis for restricting emissions? For urban areas, this presents a whole different issue. A dispute between Fordham University and the New York Botanical Garden concerned such an issue. *New York Botanical Garden v. Bd. of Stds. & Appeals of City of N.Y.*, 91 N.Y.2d 413 (N.Y. 1998). Built in 1896, the New York Botanical Garden ("NYBG") is a National Historic Landmark and is listed on the National Register of Historic Places. Fordham University originally owned the land on which both the Botanical Garden and the Bronx Zoo are situated, but later sold the land to the City of New York for use as a zoo and garden. In 1993, Fordham applied to the New York City Department of Buildings ("DOB") for a permit to build a 480-foot-tall radio broadcasting tower on its campus next to NYBG, which the DOB issued without reservation. *Id.* at 416–17. After construction began and the detrimental effect of the tower's skyline surrounding the Garden became obvious, the NYBG voiced its objection to the issuance of the permit. Under section 12-10 of the New York City Zoning Resolution, "use conduct on the same zoning lot as the principal use to which it is related," is a legitimate accessory use of the property. The DOB Commissioner determined that the radio tower was an accessory use within the meaning of section 12-10 and confirmed the permit. NYBG appealed the decision to the Board of Standards and Appeals ("BSA"), but it too unanimously agreed with the Commissioner's decision as it saw the tower as "clearly incidental to the educational mission for the University" because Fordham has a radio broadcasting educational program. *Id.* at 418. The BSA determined that the only issue was whether the proposed tower was "incidental" and/or "customarily found" in connection with a university, which it is because other universities in the area operate similar stations and towers. *Id.*

The NYBG subsequently filed suit to annul the BSA's decision, under New York C.P.L.R. Article 78. *Id.* The trial court dismissed the petition, finding the BSA's decision neither arbitrary nor capricious. The BSA reasoned that the NYBG's main argument was the detrimental impact on the aesthetics of the area, which it did not find convincing. *Id.* The Appellate Division unanimously affirmed, pointing to the BSA's reasoning that this type of tower is commonplace among local universities. *Id.* On appeal, the New York Court of Appeals determined that "when applying its expertise in a particular field to interpret statutory language, an agency's rational construction is entitled to deference." *Id.* at 419. Since the BSA is comprised of experts of land use and planning, its determination that the radio tower was an accessory use within the meaning of the statute should receive court deference.

Concerning the NYBG's argument against the BSA's decision that the size of the tower was "customarily found" to be used in similar university settings, the Court of Appeals determined that the BSA's decision was "supported by substantial evidence." *Id.* at 421. Interestingly, the Court also refused to address the NYBG's argument that the BSA had abrogated its "obligation to consider the environmental impact of the tower on an adjoining property," *i.e.*, the NYBG. *Id.* at 422. The court reasoned that since section 12-10 makes no reference to environmental considerations and since the NYBG has already raised a claim under the NHPA with the Federal Communications Commission, which was still pending, it was not a "part of the legal equation" before the court. *Id.* at 423. This case is a poignant example of how historic preservation must rely on local legal authority in urban settings, sometimes without the desired outcome. Does this case suggest that in urban settings historic and viewshed preservation will tend to take a back seat to the local needs for the future?

4. **Cultural landscapes.** Over the past century, our perception of the surrounding environment has been radically altered by the concept of "cultural landscape." In THE BEHOLDING EYE: TEN VERSIONS OF THE SAME SCENE, D.W. Meinig (1979) defined "landscape" as a dynamic, hybrid medium that links various human and non-human entities." Carl Sauer, a "founding father" of American cultural geography, studied landscapes from a different perspective and introduced the term "cultural landscape." He understood "landscape" to be "an area made up of a distinct association of forms, both physical and cultural," while the cultural landscape was something "fashioned from a natural landscape by a culture group. Culture is the agent, the natural area is the medium, the cultural landscape the result." Carl Sauer, *The Morphology of Landscape*, 2.2 GEOGRAPHY 19–54 (1925). Sauer's point was that culture shaped nature as much as the nature shaped culture, nature determining only the outer contours of cultural choices. In this way, the history of the "cultural landscapes" can be seen as an examination of how spaces evolve, are constructed, and lived in. It is infused with both aesthetic choices and political decisions. J.B. Jackson, who wrote much on everyday American landscapes, stressed the merits of discerning symbolism in culture that lies invested in the morphology of landscapes. J.B. JACKSON, DISCOVERING THE VERNACULAR LANDSCAPE: THE WORD ITSELF (1984) (founder, editor, and publisher of *Landscape*, a magazine that aimed to change the way scholars, designers, and planners understand the everyday places, which yet affect us in deep ways).

Cultural landscape can refer to a variety of areas or constructs, from grand estates, farmlands, public gardens and parks, college campuses, and cemeteries, to scenic highways, industrial sites, city streets, and even works of art, narratives of cultures, and expressions of regional identity. The history of the cultural landscape then is "the story of how places are planned, designed, built, inhabited, appropriated, celebrated, despoiled, and discarded"; it is the story of "the ditchdiggers and piledrivers, the streetcar workers and the railroad mechanics, the canal drivers and crane operators who represent class, ethnic, and gender history shaping the landscape in ways that have barely been studied." Alice E. Ingerson, What are cultural landscapes?, quoting the urban historian, Dolores Hayden, 1996, pp. 15, 21, 43, http://www.docsford.com/document/1142600 (last visited September 9, 2017).

While the idea of "landscape preservation" may seem an oxymoron, the act of preserving landscapes tending to prevent them from transforming over time, thus being opposed to their inherent dynamic nature, during the past two decades, a variety of policy frameworks have been designed worldwide for the protection and stewardship of cultural landscapes. Besides working to reveal beauty, aesthetics, and history, the conception of cultural landscapes has served to cause municipalities to broaden the focus of preservation from singular buildings to entire districts and rural areas. Local historic preservation ordinances specifically include "landscapes" as protected property. *See e.g.,* City of Eureka, California (defining cultural landscape "as a geographic area that (1) has been used, shaped, or modified by human activity, occupation, intervention; or (2) possesses significant value in the belief system of a culture or society" and including protections for designed and rural landscapes). Eureka, California, Code of Ordinances, Title XV, Land Usage, Ch. 157, Historic Preservation; *see also* Rocky Hill, N.J., Developmental Regulations Ordinance, §704F(8), 713; Texas Historical Commission, Preservation Connection, http://www.thc.texas.gov/public/upload/forms/Texas%20Statewide%20Preservation%20Plan%202011_2020.pdf.

5. **Landscapes on the National Register of Historic Places.** The National Register of Historic Places recognizes historically significant cultural landscapes. *See General Guidelines for Identifying and Evaluating Historic Landscapes February* 1999. The National Mall, between the Washington and Lincoln Memorials in Washington, D.C., is listed in the National Register as an example of "Landscape Architecture." Designed by Pierre Charles L'Enfant in 1791, the Mall has remained a central focal point in Washington, D.C. It was built as a major crossroads through the City, creating a central boulevard connecting the inner city to other roads emanating from its central location. Designated as a "landscape architecture" site on October 15, 1966, the National Mall is truly a landscape to behold, and one that most visitors make a point of visiting due to its location among so many great monuments and museums. The full designation report, as well as other information concerning the site is available on the National Park Service website, in the National Register database, http://nrhp.focus.nps.gov/natregsearchresult.do?fullresult=true&recordid=0 (last visited April 6, 2017).

6. **Cultural landscapes and the National Park Service.** The National Park Service ("NPS") has been the most active catalyst in the emerging cultural landscape preservation movement in the United States. Landscape architect Charles A. Birnbaum, of the NPS, stated in 1994 that "[i]n landscapes ... more than any other type of historic

resource, communities rightly presume a sense of stewardship.... Wise stewardship protects the character or spirit of a place by recognizing history as change over time.... Landscapes ... help us understand ourselves as individuals, communities and as a nation. Their ongoing preservation can yield ... above all, a sense of place or identity for future generations." Charles A. Birnbaum, *Protecting Cultural Landscapes: Planning, Treatment and Management of Historic Landscapes* (Washington, DC: National Park Service, 1994), Preservation Brief 36, National Park Service, U.S. Department of the Interior, https://www.nps.gov/tps/how-to-preserve/briefs/36-cultural-landscapes.htm (last visited April 6, 2017).

The NPS defines "cultural landscape" "as a geographic area, including both cultural and natural resources and the wildlife or domestic animals therein, associated with a historic event, activity, or person, or that exhibit other cultural or aesthetic values." Four categories of cultural landscapes are recognized:

- designed landscape: a landscape that was consciously designed or laid out by a landscape architect, master gardener, architect or horticulturist according to design principles or an amateur gardener working in a recognized style or tradition.
- vernacular landscape: a landscape that evolved through use by the people whose activities or occupancy shaped that landscape. Through social or cultural attitudes of an individual, family or a community, the landscape reflects the physical, biological, and cultural character of those everyday lives.
- historic site: a landscape significant for its association with a historic event, activity or person.
- ethnographic landscape: a landscape containing a variety of natural and cultural resources that the associated people define as heritage resources.

Secretary of the Interior's Guidelines for the Treatment of Cultural Landscapes, https://www.nps.gov/tps/standards/four-treatments/landscape-guidelines/index.htm (last visited April 6, 2017).

7. **Rural historic landscapes.** The National Register of Historic Places defines "rural historic landscape" as "a geographical area that has historically been used by people, or shaped or modified by human activity, occupancy, or intervention, and that possesses a significant concentration, linkage, or continuity of areas of land use, vegetation, buildings and structures, roads and waterways, and natural features." National Park Service, U.S. Dep't of Interior, *Guidelines for Evaluating and Documenting Rural Historic Landscapes* (1989, Revised 1999). The Guidelines list a number of factors to consider in determining whether a landscape meets the criteria for inclusion on the register, including land uses and activities; patterns of spatial organization; response to the natural environment; cultural traditions; circulation networks; boundary demarcations; vegetation related to land use; buildings, structures, and objects; clusters; archeological sites; and small-scale elements. *Bulletin: How to Evaluate and Nominate Designed Historic Landscapes,* https://www.nps.gov/nr/publications/bulletins/nrb18/ (last visited April 6, 2017).

Jay Heritage Landscape Stewardship

The Peter Jay Mansion entails preservation on several different planes. The great meadow flowing east from the mansion to Long Island Sound offers a commanding view from the mansion, and in turn from the Sound back toward to the mansion. Historic views were of and from the America Yacht Club sailing races on the Sound in the 19th century. John Clarkson Jay was a co-founder of one of America's earliest yacht clubs. The street-scape of the Boston Post Road Historic District is a National Historic Landmark in its own right. Looking north along and over the 18th century stone walls along this highway from the Jay Estate to the Parsons Estate, the views are unchanged since the 1840s. Within the landscape, the Jay Heritage Center ("JHC") is restoring the 20th century formal gardens installed by owners after the Jays, and before their neglect and destruction. From the air, the great meadow and Marshlands Conservancy park appear as the only remnant, intact natural landscape along the western Long Island Sound coast in New York State.

Does historic preservation protect landscapes at all these different scales? Should it? WILLIAM H. WHYTE, THE LAST LANDSCAPE (1968) describes the politics of open space, and identifies many of the legal policing tools now used to protect historic properties. He urged not saving isolated cultural sites, but also the spaces around and connecting them. Why does the Jay Estate exist apart from protections under the New York coastal zone management program ("CZM"), N.Y. EXEC. LAW. §§ 910–923, enacted under the federal Coastal Zone Management Act, 16 U.S.C. 1451? Should inter-municipal and state coastal zone planning link the Jay Estate and adjacent Marshlands Conservancy to the wider regional space of Long Island Sound?

Between 2000–2002 the JHC completed a cultural landscape report for its 21.5 acre property and the Marshlands Conservancy 150 acres of parklands. For several years, the Friends of Marshlands opposed restoration of the Jay Estate for fear that doing so would diminish the wildlife habitat. How could use of CZM planning mediate such policy disputes? After 1927, the great meadow itself became much contracted from its area in 1858 or 1906. As vegetation encroaches on it, what should be done? Should its widest landscape scale be restored? How do perspectives of ecology and culture shape the answer?

The Jay Estate was also home to one of America's first women landscape architects, Mary Rutherfurd Jay (1872–1953), who was John Jay's great, great granddaughter. From her third year, she grew up on the Jay Estate. Her archives feature a photograph of her at the Peter Jay Mansion.

http://archives.ced.berkeley.edu/collections/jay-mary-rutherfurd (last visited April1, 2017); *see also* her obituary: "Miss Mary Rutherfurd Jay, Garden Authority—Landscape Architect, 81, Who Wrote and Lectured, Dies—Descendant of Chief Justice," N. Y. TIMES, (October 5, 1953). The Jay Estate's landscape was a major influence on Mary Rutherfurd Jay's career. Is the historical significance of the Jay Estate derived in part from the landscape of its gardens and plantings? Suzanne Clary, "The Jay Property Threatened by Erasure," The Cultural Landscape Foundation (2010), http://tclf.org/landslides/the-jay-property-threatened-by-erasure (last visited April 6, 2017).

Notes and Questions

1. **Outside the Greenway.** Although not situated in the Hudson River Valley, Westchester County is included within the Hudson River Valley Greenway, the nation's first statutory greenway, enacted to keep the viewsheds of the entire Hudson Valley intact. http://www.hudsongreenway.ny.gov/home.aspx (last visited April 6, 2017). a. Is it coincidence that the Jay Estate preserves a viewshed on the eastern edge of Westchester County, in ways emblematic of the Hudson River Valley Greenway? b. Why is it difficult for preservation law to function at a landscape level scale? Europe has a treaty to encourage stewardship of landscapes ("Landscape means an area, as perceived by people, whose character is the result of the action and interaction of natural and/or human factors"). European Landscape Convention (Council of Europe, at http://www.coe.int/en/web/landscape (last visited April 6, 2017). c. Do you agree with William Whyte, when he writes "The less of our landscape there is to save, … the better our chance of saving it"?

Chapter 8

Accommodating Cultural Heritage Legal Obligations with Competing Public Policies

A. Landmark Designation and the Regulation of Religious Buildings and Sites

Over time the architecture of religious buildings has been most admired, with features—arches, spires, and naves—designed to inspire reverence, devotion, contemplation, and awe. Religious buildings perform many community functions: they make local history legible, they reflect artistic patrimony, and they lend themselves to many social and religious services. In recent times, urban religious institutions have had to confront growing social and demographic pressures, ranging from a migration of people and wealth to the suburbs and declining numbers of clergy and congregations. These trends in turn have led to decreased revenue and, consequently, deferred maintenance of buildings. In their search for sources of revenue to sustain their missions, religious institutions have considered demolition of deteriorating or unproductive buildings, reconfiguring structures for different uses, as well as sale of land to commercial developers. These choices, however, may be precluded by local preservation ordinances. While religious institutions and their property have special protections against unreasonable economic hardship and substantial burdens, under the First and Fifth Amendments of the Constitution and the Religious Land Use and Institutionalized Persons Act of 2000 ("RLUIPA"), 42 U.S.C. § 2000cc, the cases and notes that follow consider how these laws work to balance the larger societal interests in preserving these historic edifices against the particular economic imperatives of religious institutions.

1. St. Bartholomew's Church in New York City

a. Letter to Reverend Thomas H. Bowers Concerning the Certificate of Appropriateness for St. Bartholomew's Church

New York Historic Preservation Commission Chairman Gene Norman
LPC 84-0828 (Demolition of Community House), LPC 84-0829 (New Building), LPC 84-0830 (Modification of Zoning Resolution), St. Bartholomew's Church (LP-0275) (June 21, 1984)

Pursuant to Section 207-6.0 of the Administrative Code of the City of New York, the Landmarks Preservation Commission, at the Executive Session of June 12, 1984, following the Public Hearing of January 31, 1984, and subsequent Executive Sessions of May 22, 1984 and June 5, 1984, voted not to grant a Certificate of Appropriateness for demolition of the Community House at the subject property and the construction on its site of a new 60-story office tower, as put forward in your application completed on January 9, 1984. At the request of the applicant, the Landmarks Commission held open the record on the Public Hearing to April 16, 1984, and the applicant accordingly agreed to extend the Commission's time to reach a determination to June 21, 1984.

The application was docketed as three calendar items: 1) a request for a Certificate of Appropriateness for demolition of the Community House and the terraces and gardens to the south of the church; 2) a request for a Certificate of Appropriateness for the construction of a new 60-story office tower to be located on the site of the Community House and above the rear of the church, which would incorporate original material salvaged from the Community House and reconstructed as a portion of the proposed office tower, and the reconstruction of portions of the terraces and gardens; and 3) a request that the Landmarks Preservation Commission apply on behalf of the applicant to the City Planning Commission for a special permit pursuant to Section 74-711 of the Zoning Resolution, for modification of bulk requirements for zoning lots divided by district boundaries, height and setback, urban plaza and pedestrian circulation space. *** The portion of the application requesting that the Commission apply for a special permit includes a proposed preservation program for the church.

The proposed 60-story office tower would provide six floors of space to be utilized as a new Community House; four above the lobby space and two below. The construction of the new facility would require the excavation of the site to 40 feet below the level of the existing church foundation footings along the south wall of the church.

The new building, which has a stepped plan, cantilevers progressively towards St. Bartholomew's Church at its base to overhang the rear portion of the church, coming to within approximately 15 feet of its dome. It then rises sheer from the 10th floor to the 50th floor, stepping back from that point in a series of setbacks to the roof. The new tower would be clad in reflective glass, with minimized horizontal and vertical joints. The lobby of the new building would be located at the present basement level of the Community House, and would be entered via a sunken terrace leading from Park Avenue. The sunken terrace would replace the raised terrace currently providing access to the Community House.

The Commission noted that the designation report for St. Bartholomew's Church and Community House states that construction on the church was begun in 1917. Designed by Bertram Goodhue in a style based on Byzantine precedents, the church is built on a latin cross plan. One of the most striking features of St. Bartholomew's is its polychromy, produced by the blending of salmon colored brick with grayish limestone, marble and tiles of various hues. The design for the church incorporates a Romanesque style porch designed by McKim Mead and White, which was part of the earlier St. Bartholomew's Church at Madison Avenue and 44th Street.

Over the crossing of the church, atop a high drum, sits an octagonal dome sheathed with tile and marble in highly colored and intricate designs. A large rose window with intricate tracery lights the south wall of the shallow transcept. The transcept adjoins a cloister situated between the church and the Community House which is attached to the south wall of the church. The Community House, designed by Mayers, Murray and Phillip, associates of B.G. Goodhue, was completed in 1928. Faced in the same salmon colored brick as the church, the Community House features limestone band courses continued from the church as well as decorative details similar in character and scale to those used in the church.

The location of the Community House at the rear of the lot affords a large open space in the southwest sector of the lot, in the ell formed by the church and the Community House. *** The materials of the terraces and gardens continue to repeat those of the church.

The report further states that the church complex, imposing in mass and striking in appearance and in form, occupies a prominent site, which include the entire Park Avenue blockfront and extends more than halfway into the block towards Lexington Avenue.

With regard to the application, the Commission found that the proposed new building fails to relate in texture, material, style or proportion to the landmark; that the cantilevering of the new building over a portion of the rear of the church brings it into such close proximity to that building as to cause it to visually suppress the church and be at odds with the volumetric quality of the building's design, which requires a sense of open space around it to allow for the rounded, compounded forms of the Byzantine-inspired dome to be perceived; that the angular, harp, metallic vocabulary of the new building creates a totally incompatible contrast to the polychromed, ornamented and plastic forms of the church; that the highly reflective and faceted cladding of the new building has negative impact on the church in that it draws attention to the new building and away from the church; that the new building diminishes the visibility of the rose window in the south transcept of the church, one of its distinctive architectural features; that the depression of the south terrace to provide access to the new building destroys the upward processional movement of the present design relationship between the terrace and the church; and that the proximity of the tower to the church gives the visual appearance of piercing the dome.

In summary, the Commission found that the proposed new building, competes with, minimizes and trivializes the landmark through its massing, size, and location relative to the church, by its lack of harmony in terms of materials, and through its destruction of the relationship between the church, the Community House and the terraces and gardens. The Commission also found that the proposed design for the new building does not protect or enhance the exterior architectural features which cause the landmark to possess a special aesthetic and historic interest and value. The Commission, therefore, determined the proposal to be inappropriate. Accordingly, the Commission determined that, in this instance, the proposed demolition of the Community House was also inappropriate. Having voted not to grant Certificates of Appropriateness for the demolition of the Community House and for the construction of the proposed new building, the applicant's request for the Commission to apply [sic] the City Planning Commission for a special permit was moot.

The Commission noted in its discussion that it did not consider either the Community House or the south terrace and gardens to be inviolate or inalterable and stressed that a design for a new building in this location could be found to be appropriate.

The Commission also discussed the offer to modify the design which was set forth in the letter dated May 16, 1984, from your counsel, John Zuccotti, to the Commission. *** The Commissioners determined that the magnitude of the inappropriateness of the proposed design was such that no meaningful modification could be made without a major redesign, which would require a new public hearing, and thus the offer could not be accepted.

Finally, the Commission discussed several procedural issues which had been raised by your legal representatives in the submissions with the application, at the Public Hearing of January 31, 1984, and in the letter of Paul Windels, Esq., of Windels, Marx, Davies and Ives, of February 21, 1984. This supplementary material included a request for "Certificate of Appropriateness and Relief Incidental Thereto." It further requested that should the Commission deny the Certificate of Appropriateness, the Commission should either rescind the designation of the Church and Community House or make a hardship determination under either Section 207-8.0 of the Administrative Code or under the judicial test of *Sailors' Snug Harbor* and *Lutheran Church.*

As to the request that the Commission rescind the designation of St. Bartholomew's Church and Community House, the Landmarks' Law does not provide a formal procedure for application to the Commission either for designation or rescission of a designation. The Commission calendars a public hearing on a proposed rescission based on information either of possible error of significant fact in the designation determination or subsequent events which have affected a designated building so as to destroy or cause the loss of significant features or characteristics thereby causing the structure to lose its significance under the criteria for designation of the Landmarks Law. *** The Commission has not had any information presented to it on error of fact in its initial designation determination or loss of significant features that would cause it to calendar a public hearing on the proposed rescission of the designation.

Another procedural issue considered by the Commission was the relevance of the material submitted on the financial status of the Church and the physical condition of the designated buildings. This information would have been relevant to the Commission in making its determination on whether to apply to the City Planning Commission pursuant to Section 74-711 for a modification of the bulk requirements of the Zoning Resolution in order to further the preservation of the Landmark Church. As was previously stated, the Commission's determination that the proposed design was inappropriate and the vote to deny the Certificate of Appropriateness rendered the determination on the special permit application moot.

As to the request that the Commission make a hardship determination, such a determination would be contrary to established procedures of the Commission, to the published notice of the items scheduled for consideration at the Public Hearing, and the expressed statements of the Chairman and Counsel at the Public Hearing.

In the several meetings of the Commission staff with representatives of Tufo & Zuccotti, in the two years proceeding the filing of the applications, the Commission's procedures for applications for demolition and alteration of a landmark and for new construction on a landmark site under the appropriateness provisions of Section 207-6.0 and under the hardship provisions of Section 207-8.0 were fully discussed. The established procedures of the Commission with separate hearings, held sequentially, for the separate determinations of appropriateness and hardship were not questioned. As reiterated at the January 31, 1984 Public Hearing, the findings for a determination that a particular proposal is an appropriate alteration of a landmark are different and separate from those that would be made to determine that a hardship resulting from the landmark designation had been established. Only in the instance of a request for a permit for total demolition of an individual landmark would a separate determination of inappropriateness be unnecessary. In addition, in this instance the request for the special permit application made a preliminary finding of appropriateness clearly necessary. The Commission can, and has, calendared the two public hearings for the same day when the applicant claimed that time was an element of the hardship; it was not so asserted for this application.

Contrary to statements made in the supplementary materials *** and at the public hearing, the courts in interpreting the Landmarks Law so as to fulfill constitutional requirements have never held that the specific provisions and criteria of Section 207-8.0 "are inapplicable" to religious organizations; *Society of Ethical Culture v. Spatt* is clear authority in support of the Commission's position. Now that the Commission has determined that the proposal is inappropriate, the hardship procedures of Section 207-8.0 a(2) for a property exempt from real estate taxes are fully available. Furthermore, as was also explained in the discussions with your legal representatives and at the Public Hearing, when a charitable organization makes an application for a Certificate of Appropriateness on ground of insufficient return, the Commission will make the preliminary finding of insufficient return if the applicant establishes either the statutory findings of Section 207-8.0 or meets the judicial test for hardship set forth in *Sailors' Snug Harbor* and cited by the courts in *Lutheran Church*, *Ethical Culture* and *1025 Fifth Avenue v. Marymount School of New York*.

In conclusion, as stated in the designation report for St. Bartholomew's Church, the Commission believes "it has the obligation and it has the desire to co-operate with owners of Landmarks." The Commission remains willing to work with representatives of the Church either on an application for a Certificate of Appropriateness for a new proposal or for an application under the hardship provisions for tax exempt properties. The Commission also remains committed to "give due consideration and act promptly in accordance with the provisions of the Landmarks Preservation Law" on any application which may be filed for the Landmark Site.

Rector, Wardens, and Members of the Vestry of St. Bartholomew's Church v. City of New York

United States District Court for the Southern District of New York
728 F. Supp. 958 (1989) (Amended 1990)

Sprizzo, D.J. Plaintiff, the Rector, Wardens and Members of the Vestry of St. Bartholomew's Church bring this action pursuant to 42 U.S.C. § 1983, for declaratory and injunctive relief and for damages. Plaintiff contends that defendants, City of New York and the Landmarks Preservation Commission of the City of New York ("Commission"), have violated its rights under the First, Fifth and Fourteenth Amendments to the United States Constitution, and under the laws of the State of New York. The Court has, by agreement of the parties, held a bench trial on the evidence previously submitted to the Commission in 1985 and 1986. After reviewing that evidence *de novo* and considering the law applicable thereto, the Court makes the following findings of fact and conclusions of law pursuant to Fed.R.Civ.P. 52(a)....

Background

St. Bartholomew's Church is a Protestant Episcopal Church organized under the laws of the State of New York as a non-profit religious corporation. The Church building, designed by Bertram Goodhue, was completed in 1919, and is located on the east side of Park Avenue between East 50th and East 51st Streets in the City of New York. *** Next to the church building is a seven floor community house constructed by Goodhue's successor firm during the years 1926–28. *** The community house provides, in combination with the church building, a home for a variety of social and religious activities in which the Church is engaged.[2] In addition to the two structures, the Church's Park Avenue property is improved by a garden and terrace area. ***

---

2. Among other things, the community house provides athletic facilities, including a pool and basketball court, a theatre, a pre-school for sixty students, meeting rooms, kitchen and dining facilities and office space. The church building, in conjunction with the community house, provides clothing, meals and sleeping quarters for the homeless....

In March of 1967, the church, the exterior of the community house and the surrounding property were designated as landmarks by the Commission, a designation plaintiff did not then oppose.*** Subsequently, however, plaintiff filed two applications with the Commission seeking a Certificate of Appropriateness under what is now N.Y. City Admin.Code § 25-307.*** The first such application, *** sought permission to tear down the community house and erect in its place a fifty-nine story office tower[; it] was denied as an inappropriate alteration on June 21, 1984. *** The second application, *** sought to demolish the community house in favor of a forty-seven story office tower[;] it was also denied as inappropriate on August 26, 1985. *** After the denial of plaintiff's second application, a further application to build the forty-seven story tower was made on September 3, 1985, on grounds of insufficient return pursuant to sections 207-4.0 and 207-8.0 of the New York City Administrative Code.[5]

The Commission held public hearings on plaintiff's third application on October 29, 1985, December 3, 1985, and January 21, 1986. *** At those hearings the Commission heard testimony from all interested parties, including expert witnesses who testified regarding the suitability of the community house to its charitable purpose, the extent and cost of necessary structural and mechanical repairs for both the church and community house, and the state of the Church's finances. In addition, the Commission received many reports from the testifying experts and other submissions. After the close of the last public hearing, *** considering all of the evidence submitted, the Commission voted on February 25, 1986, to deny plaintiff's application. *** On October 10, 1986, the Commission issued its written determination denying the application. ***

Thereafter, plaintiff brought the instant action alleging the following constitutional claims: 1) that the landmark laws are facially unconstitutional to the extent they impact the property of any church because they interfere with the free exercise of religion in violation of the First Amendment; 2) that the landmark laws are facially unconstitutional because they treat charitable and commercial institutions differently in violation of the equal protection clause of the Fourteenth Amendment; 3) that the landmark laws are unconstitutional as applied to St. Bartholomew's as a consequence of the Commission's denial of their applications for a certificate of appropriateness, because that denial interfered with the free exercise of religion and because the denials constitute a taking of property without compensation; 4) that the landmark laws both facially and as applied to St. Bartholomew's violate the establishment clause by

5. Section 207-8.0(2)(c), now found at § 25-309(a)(2)(c), provides that a certificate of appropriateness on the ground of insufficient return shall be granted when the applicant shows, *inter alia*, that: "such improvement has ceased to be adequate, suitable or appropriate for use for carrying out both (1) the purposes of such owner to which it is devoted and (2) those purposes to which it had been devoted when acquired unless such owner is no longer engaged in pursuing such purposes." In addition, New York law requires that a certificate of appropriateness be granted where failure to do so would "prevent or seriously interfere" with the applicant's ability to carry out its charitable purpose. *See Society for Ethical Culture v. Spatt,* 51 N.Y.2d 449, 454–55, 415 N.E.2d 922, 925, 434 N.Y.S.2d 932, 935 (1980); *Lutheran Church in America v. City of New York,* 35 N.Y.2d 121, 131, 316 N.E.2d 305, 311, 359 N.Y.S.2d 7, 16 (1974).

requiring an intrusive examination of the church's internal affairs in the hardship application process; 5) that the landmark laws both facially and as applied violate the doctrine of substantive due process by depriving the Church of its property's reasonable income production without a compelling state interest; 6) that the legal standards for designation of a landmark and for granting a certificate of appropriateness are impermissibly vague in violation of the due process clause of the Fourteenth Amendment; 7) that the lack of cross-examination of witnesses in the certificate of appropriateness procedure, the vagueness of the Commission's first two denial letters, the Commission's failure to consider economic hardship in the second application and the Commission's failure to allow plaintiff to submit responses to the Commission's witnesses all constitute due process violations. In addition, plaintiff brought state law claims for Article 78 relief alleging that the Church should have been granted a certificate of appropriateness under New York law....

Plaintiff then moved for partial summary judgment on its claims of facial unconstitutionality, and defendant cross-moved for summary judgment.... These motions were later supplemented to add the issue of whether plaintiff's Article 78 claims were justiciable in a federal forum. ***

Discussion

I. *Plaintiff's Claims of Facial Unconstitutionality*

A. *First Amendment Claims*

The Court rejects plaintiff's contention that the landmark laws unconstitutionally interfere with the free exercise of the religious beliefs of any church that is designated a landmark. The gravamen of plaintiff's free exercise claim is that by restricting a church's ability to use its property as it wishes in support of its religious or charitable mission, the landmark laws impermissibly burden the exercise of religious belief.

That claim lacks merit. A statute abridges the free exercise of religion when it coerces the affected individuals into violating their religious beliefs or when "[it] penalize[s] religious activity by denying any person an equal share of the rights, benefits and privileges enjoyed by other citizens." *Lyng v. Northwest Indian Cemetery Protective Ass'n.*, 485 U.S. 439, 449, 108 S.Ct. 1319, 1325, 99 L.Ed.2d 534 (1988) *** A substantial interference with the free exercise of religion may also occur where church property is taken, even by condemnation, for state purposes. *** However, the mere possibility that a church may at some time want to make a different use of its landmarked property creates no more than an incidental burden on the practice of religion that does not "require the state to come forward with a compelling reason justifying its actions." *** Therefore, the designation of church buildings as landmarks does not in and of itself violate the free exercise clause.... This is especially true since the landmark designation does not deprive the Church of the right to seek a certificate of appropriateness to alter its property if the nature of that property is such that it no longer can be used to carry out its religious or charitable mission.

Plaintiff also contends that because the New York statutory and judicial tests for determining when a certificate of appropriateness may be granted on the grounds of hardship require an intrusive examination into the finances and internal workings of the Church, those tests, both on their face and as applied to St. Bartholomew's, result in an excessive entanglement between government and religion in violation of the establishment clause. *** [T]hat doctrine has normally been applied in factual situations in which state aid to religious institutions requires extensive and continuous monitoring of church activities to ensure that government financing is being used solely for secular purposes. [It] has no applicability where, as here, the government must make an inquiry into church finances for the limited purpose of determining the validity of a church's claim of financial hardship.

B. *Equal Protection Claims*

Plaintiff alleges that because the landmark laws provide different hardship tests for commercial and charitable entities including religious institutions, they violate the equal protection clause. Because the Court has already found that the laws do not on their face impermissibly burden religion, any differences in treatment need only be justified by a rational basis....

* * *

Since the hardship test for commercial enterprises is based upon the ability to earn a reasonable return from its property, it is obvious that a similar standard could not be applied to an entity which exists for charitable and not commercial purposes.... Indeed, it would make little sense, and might in fact be irrational, to apply the charitable test to a commercial property or the commercial test to a charitable property. It follows that the so called disparity in treatment is nothing more than a reasonable effort by the state to afford hardship relief to both classes of entities based upon criteria specifically tailored to the nature of each.

C. *Due Process Claims*

Plaintiff also argues that the legal standards for designating a landmark and for granting a certificate of appropriateness are impermissibly vague and give the Commission virtually unfettered discretion in making its decisions. Therefore plaintiff argues the laws do not comport with the minimum requirements of procedural due process.

At the very least, due process requires notice and an opportunity to be heard. *** The landmark laws unquestionably meet that standard in that they provide a property owner with adequate notice of the law's requirements and with the opportunity for an extensive hearing, especially in view of the interpretation placed upon those laws by the courts of New York. *** While it is true that the procedures available at a landmark hearing are not the same as those available at a civil trial, that is not what due process requires. *** Moreover, under New York law there is a right to judicial review of Commission decisions in the state court system, *** a circumstance that further supports the rejection of plaintiff's due process claims. ***

In sum, the Court rejects plaintiff's contentions that the landmark laws are unconstitutional on their face as to all churches, and grants summary judgment for defendants as to those claims.

II. *The Trial of this Action*

*** [T]he Court held a trial with respect to plaintiff's claim that the landmark laws were unconstitutional as applied. Plaintiff's contentions in that regard are twofold: (1) that because it could no longer carry out its religious mission in its existing facilities the denial of its hardship application constituted a taking of its property without just compensation; and (2) the denial of that application constituted an impermissible burden on the exercise of its religious beliefs.

Initially, the Court was of the view that it could have a trial *de novo*[. On reconsideration,] the Court *** concluded that it would be inappropriate to predicate a finding of unconstitutionality on facts which the Commission never had an opportunity to consider, especially since under the statutory scheme, a new application for hardship exemption can be made at any time based upon additional facts.... Therefore, the Court *** will evaluate this claim solely on the basis of the record before the Commission.... However, since the Court is presented with a claim of constitutional deprivation, it must make a *de novo* review of that evidence. ***

III. *Plaintiff's Unconstitutional As Applied Claims*

A. *Just Compensation Claims*

Plaintiff's claim of unconstitutionality as applied depends upon plaintiff's ability to prove that it can no longer carry out its religious mission and charitable purpose in its existing facilities because those facilities are inadequate and because it cannot afford to expend the sums necessary to make those facilities adequate. It is that circumstance that underlies plaintiff's contention that the denial of its hardship application deprived it of its property without just compensation in violation of the Fifth Amendment and abridged its right to freely exercise its religious belief in violation of the First Amendment.

At the outset it should be noted that the Supreme Court has never passed upon the constitutionality of a regulation, such as the landmark laws, as applied to the property of a charitable or religious institution. However, in dealing with commercial property, the Supreme Court has recognized that there is no magic formula for determining when a taking has occurred. *See Penn Central*[.] *** Factors of particular significance, however, are the economic impact of the government action, *i.e.*, its interference with legitimate investment expectations, and the character of the government action, *e.g.*, is the action a physical taking or a land use regulation. *** These factors must be evaluated in light of the overriding rule that the Fifth Amendment contemplates continued use of a property as it was used in the past, and thus permits no substantial interference with the property owner's primary investment expectations or reasonable beneficial use. ***

While the concept of legitimate investment expectation is not directly transferable to a charitable or religious institution, the concepts of reasonable beneficial use and the owner's primary expectations are equally applicable to both. Moreover, the New York Courts have developed a takings standard for charitable institutions embodying these concepts that is a constitutionally acceptable standard for determining when there has been a taking of charitable property, *i.e.*, where the landmark designation would prevent or seriously interfere with the carrying out of the charitable purpose of the institution [in *Ethical Culture* and *Lutheran Church*.] *** Therefore, the Court adopts this test to determine whether plaintiff's Fifth Amendment rights were violated as a consequence of the denial of its hardship application.

B. *Free Exercise Claim*

Assuming *arguendo* that plaintiff's charitable work is the exercise of religion for First Amendment purposes, plaintiff must prove that it can no longer carry out this work in its existing facilities to sustain its free exercise claim. *** Thus, in this case, the First Amendment inquiry is identical in scope to the Fifth Amendment inquiry, since to prevail on either claim plaintiff must prove that it can no longer carry out its religious mission in its existing facilities.*** For the reasons that follow, the Court finds that plaintiff has failed to carry that burden, and that judgment must be entered for the defendant.

C. *Findings of Fact*

Plaintiff contends that the community house is an inadequate structure for carrying out the Church's religious mission and charitable purpose. Plaintiff further alleges that both the community house and the church are in an advanced state of disrepair and cannot be rehabilitated for less than $11 million. Thus, plaintiff argues it can only rehabilitate the Church and carry out its charitable purpose if it is allowed to demolish the community house, build the office tower in its place, and reap the revenues therefrom. Finally, plaintiff contends that its finances are in such a deplorable state that even if the two buildings could be rehabilitated for less than $11 million, it cannot afford to spend more than a minimal sum upon such work. ***

1. *Adequacy of Community House Space*

*** Plaintiff contends that the evidence shows that: the usable space available in the community house is insufficient to accomodate [sic] the variety of activities that compete for the space; that it wishes to expand its existing programs but cannot do so given those space constraints; that it is forced to conduct activities in spaces that are inappropriate for those activities;[17] and that renovation of the interior of the community house is impractical and not feasible. *** Plaintiff relies primarily upon an analysis of the use and configuration of the community house space undertaken at plaintiff's request by Walker Associates, an interior design firm. In addition to the testimony of its president, Keith Keppler[.] *** In those reports and testimony, *** Walker found that the community house lacked sufficient usable space, that the ex-

17. A focal point of plaintiff's contention in this regard is its claim that it is forced to carry out its feeding program for the homeless from the church mortuary chapel, and thus must carry food from the community house kitchen downstairs and the length of an entire city block to reach the church. In addition, the Church contends that it cannot continue to provide shelter for the homeless in the church narthex because that space is inappropriate, and because it can only provide shelter for ten persons per night in that area....

isting usable space was inefficiently designed and poorly distributed, and that the multiplicity of uses of that space created scheduling conflicts.[18] In sum, Walker found that the Church could only continue to successfully carry out its charitable and social activities by moving to another more suitable facility, and that the proposed forty-seven story office tower was such a facility. ***

However, the Court, based upon flaws in Walker's methodology and upon conflicting evidence, finds that Walker's conclusions are incorrect, and that plaintiff has failed to prove by a preponderance of the evidence that the community house is unsuitable for its current use. *** First, it is clear that Walker did not attempt to examine the building plans of the community house before it determined that the building could not be easily altered. *** If it had done so, it would have found that in fact the building does not contain massive load bearing walls, but instead is a light steel frame structure that is easily susceptible to alteration.[19] Second, Walker based its finding of inadequate usable space upon calculations appropriate to a commercial office building, the area of Walker's expertise, and not upon calculations appropriate to plaintiff's facility. *** Third, measuring the adequacy of space in an existing building was an unusual task for Walker, which was used to projecting space for designs of proposed buildings. *** Furthermore, Walker presented no evidence of objective observations of how the facility is actually used over time. The Court finds therefore that Walker's conclusions are without adequate factual support.

Moreover, other evidence demonstrates that the community house is adequate for the purposes to which it is devoted. Weekly building activity schedules, if anything, supported the conclusion that the community house's space was in fact underutilized, that many of the rooms were not used at all during the day, or were used by very few, and that no scheduling conflicts were apparent. *** In fact, the Church was able to rent out some of its space to area businesses, and has formed a special committee to increase those rentals. *** Moreover, although plaintiff complained that it could accommodate only sixty pupils in its preschool, it has an occupancy permit for one hundred pupils, and therefore underutilizes the capacity of even its preschool facilities. ***

* * *

The credibility of plaintiff's evidence is further undercut by the fact that its proposed new building, which reverses the proportion of space above and below ground in the existing facility, would be only marginally better, if at all, in terms of usable space, *** and significantly inferior in many other respects such as the quality of the below

18. Specifically, Walker found that the community house contained a net usable area of approximately 38,000 sq. ft., that the Church programs required a usable area of approximately 46,000 sq. ft., leaving a space deficit of approximately 8,000 sq. ft....

19. For this reason, and because it was unsupported by any evidence, the Court also rejects Walker's contention that interior renovation of the community house would cost approximately $ 3.4 million.

ground environment, the choked single access point of the office building lobby, ... and the absence of any plan to encompass the ministry to the homeless in the new structure, which oddly enough is a program that plaintiff asserts it does not have adequate space for in the present structure.[22] In sum, plaintiff's reliance upon the Walker report and the Court's rejection of that report supports the conclusion that plaintiff has failed to show by a preponderance of the evidence that the community house is an inadequate structure for conducting its activities....

2. *Required Exterior and Mechanical Repairs*

Plaintiff's second major factual contention is that the community house and the church building both require a complete overhaul and replacement of existing mechanical systems, and substantial repair and replacement of exterior structural systems at a cost of approximately $11 million. Plaintiff's sole support for this proposition is a study of the mechanical systems and the building exteriors undertaken in 1985 by O'Brien, Krietzburg and Associates ("OKA"), a firm of professional construction managers, submitted through two reports, *** and the testimony of OKA's president, James O'Brien ***. In formulating its recommendations, OKA relied upon the report of Edwards & Zuck, P.C., who evaluated the plumbing, mechanical and electrical systems, *** the report of Caine, Farrell & Bell, architects, who examined the exteriors, *** and the report of Barr & Barr, Inc., builders, who provided cost estimates of the repairs. ***

Based upon these three reports, OKA concluded that poor maintenance programs in the past have caused the overall exterior physical condition of the buildings to seriously deteriorate, and that the buildings' mechanical systems were outdated and in some cases inoperative. *** The Court does not find OKA's assessment persuasive for the following reasons. First, it is clear from the testimony of Ronald Alexander, a former vestryman in charge of the Church's building committee, that OKA was told to maximize the cost of estimates to the greatest defensible extent, and that OKA undertook to do just that by advocating replacement over rehabilitation wherever possible. *** Moreover, OKA admitted a bias in favor of replacement, ... and indeed had little experience in rehabilitating older buildings. In addition, OKA did not rely on a full set of plans and specifications in evaluating necessary repairs. *** Instead, OKA relied solely on the reports of other firms who were not called to testify before the Commission.

These reasons would be a sufficient basis to reject OKA's conclusions. There is, however, ample additional evidence to show that not only did OKA grossly overestimate the amount of work required, but that its method for allocating costs to that

22. In addition, plaintiff has failed to show why the existing community house dining facilities, or even the auditorium, could not replace the church mortuary chapel as the site of the breakfast feeding program for the homeless. Both of those facilities are much closer to the kitchen and are never used in the morning.

work is seriously flawed. For example, OKA recommended wholesale replacement of the church's front steps and the blue stone steps leading from Park Avenue to the terrace. *** However, other evidence showed that only the top platform of the church steps and one of the blue stone steps required replacement. *** Similarly, OKA advocated replacement of all of the sidewalk when only part of the sidewalk was cracked and in need of repair.

* * *

In sum, it is clear from OKA's report that their object was not to determine what repairs were truly necessary or required, but to maximize the amount of work and the cost of that work. There is simply no other explanation, and none has been offered, for OKA's wholesale reliance upon replacement and complete rejection of rehabilitation, especially since there is abundant evidence that many of the systems examined could in fact be rehabilitated.

* * *

4. *The Church's Financial Condition*

Plaintiff contends that even if it could put the church and the community house in good working order for $3 million, its financial circumstances do not permit it to expend that amount of money while it continues to run its other programs. The Court rejects this contention as unsupported by the evidence produced before the Commission.

There is little disagreement in the record over the size of the Church's endowment. Although subject to fluctuations in the stock market, the market value of the Church's portfolio stood in excess of $12.5 million at the end of 1985. *** Its total funding for 1984 was $14,355,000, including other operating revenues. *** While this sizeable endowment would appear on its face to be capable of supporting a capital expenditure of $3 million, plaintiff contends that much of that endowment cannot be expended under New York law, and much of the rest of the endowment is restricted for specific purposes....

Although this contention may be true in a general sense, plaintiff has failed to recognize that some of the restrictions permit the use of these funds to support of the church building and the community house. These funds could therefore be used for necessary capital expenditures. Moreover, these funds if used for this purpose could free up unrestricted funds that have been designated by the vestry for the same purpose.

One witness before the Commission estimated that as much as $6 million of the endowment could be used for capital expenditure purposes. *** Of that $6 million, $2.9 million is expendable for specific purposes, and $3.1 million at the discretion of the vestry. *** Plaintiff's own accountants reported that of the Church's $12 million endowment, $2.7 million was expendable for designated purposes, $4.5 million was unrestricted and $4.8 million was restricted as to principal. *** Thus, the Court finds plaintiff's claim that because parts of the endowment are restricted it cannot use some of them for capital projects to be incredible and unsupported by the evidence.

The Church also contends that if it takes $3 million out of its endowment, it will be unable to operate its other programs due to loss of income from the endowment. While it is true that income from the endowment makes up a significant portion of the Church's $3 million annual operating revenue, *** that claim is unpersuasive for the following reasons.

First, the Church does not have to remove $3 million from the endowment all at once. The endowment could be depleted gradually over a period of years as the work on the church and the community house is performed.... Gradual depletion would not only lessen operating revenue lost due to lower dividend and interest income, but would also allow capital appreciation to offset the yearly withdrawals. Second, the Church has, over the last ten years operated at close to a break even level, showing surpluses in some years and losses in others. *** Moreover, it has done so while spending more than $1.6 million on expenses related to the development of the office tower. *** These facts not only show that the Church is able to make use of large amounts of endowment income for discretionary spending, but also constrain the Court to reject plaintiff's contention that it has been forced to make drastic cutbacks in operating expenses because current revenues from endowment income are insufficient to fund the Church's programs.

Finally, the Church has presented no evidence to show what effect withdrawals from the endowment would have on its operating budget. In fact, it did not provide the Commission with any financial projections that would enable this Court to determine its future financial prospects. This failure is fatal to plaintiff's claim of prospective financial hardship. *** Not only has the Church failed to provide such financial projections, it has failed to consider either the possibility of a capital fund raising project or the possible sale of the Church's air rights to a nearby building. *** The Court finds, therefore, that fund raising is at least a reasonable alternative that must be explored before plaintiff's claim of financial hardship can be accepted as credible.

Similarly, plaintiff denies that there is any possibility of selling its air rights to raise revenue. Plaintiff relies primarily on the assertion that it has not had any offers to buy those rights. In fact, interest in purchasing those rights was expressed in a written submission to the Commission. *** It also appears that interest in the development rights was expressed in the past, but was not pursued by the Church. *** Thus, the Court finds that sale of the Church's air rights presents a reasonable method of alternative fund raising that must be explored before a claim of financial hardship can be supported....

In sum, the Court finds that the Church has failed to show that it cannot afford to pay for the cost of necessary repairs to the church and the community house. It follows that plaintiff has failed to show that its financial situation precludes it from restoring its property and carrying out its religious mission and charitable purpose. Therefore the Court finds, as a matter of fact, that the Church has failed to prove that its community house is inadequate for the purposes to which it is devoted, that the Church has failed to prove that it is incapable of carrying out its charitable purpose within those facilities, and that although those facilities do require some repair and rehabilitation, the Church has failed to show that it cannot afford to pay for those necessary repairs and rehabilitation.

Conclusion

Since plaintiff has failed to show by a preponderance of the evidence that it can no longer conduct its charitable activities or carry out its religious mission in its existing facilities, plaintiff's First and Fifth Amendment claims must be rejected. The clerk is directed to enter judgment for the defendants and close the above-captioned action.

It is SO ORDERED.

Rector, Wardens, and Members of the Vestry of St. Bartholomew's Church v. City of New York

United States Court of Appeals for the Second Circuit
914 F.2d 348 (1990)

Winter, C.J. This appeal poses the question of whether a church may be prevented by New York City's Landmarks Law, now codified at New York City Administrative Code Sections 25-301 to 25-321 (1986), from replacing a church-owned building with an office tower. The question implicates both First and Fifth Amendment issues. Specifically, the Rector, Wardens, and Members of the Vestry of St. Bartholomew's Church ("the Church") appeal from Judge Sprizzo's decision that the New York City Landmarks Law, as applied to an auxiliary structure next to the Church's main house of worship, did not impose an unconstitutional burden on the free exercise of religion or effect a taking of property without just compensation.

The district court grounded its decision on its finding that the Church had failed to prove that the landmark regulation prevented the Church from carrying out its religious and charitable mission in its current buildings. We agree that this is the legal standard established by Supreme Court precedent governing both free exercise and takings claims. Moreover, we find no clear error in the district court's factual determinations. We therefore affirm. We also affirm the denial of a motion to intervene by a group of persons opposed to the Church's plans to develop its property.

* * *

On appeal, the Church renews its free exercise and takings claims and argues that the district court's factual findings were clearly erroneous.

In the course of proceedings, the district court denied a motion to intervene on the side of defendants made by several individual parishioners and the Committee to Oppose the Sale of St. Bartholomew's Church Incorporated, a group of St. Bartholomew's members and others opposed to commercial development of the Church's property. It held that the proposed intervenors had no ownership interest in the property at issue and that their participation would interfere with the efficient administration of the litigation. *** A year later, after the parties agreed that the trial in the instant action should be conducted solely on the record before the Commission, the proposed intervenors renewed their motion, which was again denied. *** The proposed intervenors appeal from this ruling.

Discussion

Sections 1 and 2 of this portion of the opinion reject the Church's free exercise and takings claims. Our discussion assumes the affirmance of the district court's factual findings as detailed in section 3.

1. *The Free Exercise Claim*

The Church argues that the Landmarks Law substantially burdens religion in violation of the First Amendment as applied to the states through the Fourteenth Amendment. In particular, the Church contends that by denying its application to erect a commercial office tower on its property, the City of New York and the Landmarks Commission (collectively, "the City") have impaired the Church's ability to carry on and expand the ministerial and charitable activities that are central to its religious mission. It argues that the Community House is no longer a sufficient facility for its activities, and that the Church's financial base has eroded. The construction of an office tower similar to those that now surround St. Bartholomew's in midtown Manhattan, the Church asserts, is a means to provide better space for some of the Church's programs and income to support and expand its various ministerial and community activities. The Church thus argues that even if the proposed office tower will not house all of the Church's programs, the revenue generated by renting commercial office space will enable the Church to move some of its programs—such as sheltering the homeless-off-site. The Church concludes that the Landmarks Law unconstitutionally denies it the opportunity to exploit this means of carrying out its religious mission. Although the Landmarks Law substantially limits the options of the Church to raise revenue for purposes of expanding religious charitable activities, we believe the Church's claims are precluded by Supreme Court precedent.

As the Court recently stated in *Employment Division v. Smith,* 494 U.S. 872, 110 S.Ct. 1595, 108 L.Ed.2d 876 (1990), the free exercise clause prohibits above all "'governmental regulation of religious *beliefs* as such.'" *** No one seriously contends that the Landmarks Law interferes with substantive religious views. However, apart from impinging on religious beliefs, governmental regulation may affect conduct or behavior associated with those beliefs. Supreme Court decisions indicate that while the government may not coerce an individual to adopt a certain belief or punish him for his religious views, it may restrict certain activities associated with the practice of religion pursuant to its general regulatory powers. ***

The synthesis of this caselaw has been stated as follows: "[T]he right of free exercise does not relieve an individual of the obligation to comply with a 'valid and neutral law of general applicability on the ground that the law proscribes (or prescribes) conduct that his religion prescribes (or proscribes).'" *** The critical distinction is thus between a neutral, generally applicable law that happens to bear on religiously motivated action, and a regulation that restricts certain conduct because it is religiously oriented. ***

The Landmarks Law is a facially neutral regulation of general applicability within the meaning of Supreme Court decisions. It thus applies to "[a]ny improvement, any part of which is thirty years old or older, which has a special character or special historical or aesthetic interest or value." N.Y.C. Admin. Code § 25-302(n) (1986).

It is true that the Landmarks Law affects many religious buildings. The Church thus asserts that of the six hundred landmarked sites, over fifteen percent are religious properties and over five percent are Episcopal churches. Nevertheless, we do not understand those facts to demonstrate a lack of neutrality or general applicability. Because of the importance of religion, and of particular churches, in our social and cultural history, and because many churches are designed to be architecturally attractive, many religious structures are likely to fall within the neutral criteria — having "special character or special historical or aesthetic interest or value" — set forth by the Landmarks Law. N.Y.C. Admin. Code § 25-302(n) (1986). This, however, is not evidence of an intent to discriminate against, or impinge on, religious belief in the designation of landmark sites.

The Church's brief cites commentators, including a former chair of the Commission, who are highly critical of the Landmarks Law on grounds that it accords great discretion to the Commission and that persons who have interests other than the preservation of historic sites or aesthetic structures may influence Commission decisions.... Nevertheless, absent proof of the discriminatory exercise of discretion, there is no constitutional relevance to these observations. Zoning similarly regulates land use but it is hardly a process in which the exercise of discretion is constrained by scientific principles or unaffected by selfish or political interests, yet it passes constitutional muster. ***

The Church argues that landmarking and zoning differ in that landmarking targets only individual parcels while zoning affects larger segments. However, the Landmarks Law permits the designation of historic districts, *** while all zoning laws provide for variances for individual sites. Even if the two forms of regulation bear the different characteristics asserted by the Church, those differences are of no consequence in light of *Penn Central Transportation Company v. New York City,* 438 U.S. 104, 98 S.Ct. 2646, 57 L.Ed.2d 631 (1978). There, the Court stated:

> [L]andmark laws are not like discriminatory, or 'reverse spot,' zoning: that is, a land-use decision which arbitrarily singles out a particular parcel for different, less favorable treatment than the neighboring ones. In contrast to discriminatory zoning, *** the New York City law embodies a comprehensive plan to preserve structures of historic or aesthetic interest ***

Id. at 132, 98 S.Ct. at 2663 (citation omitted). *** It is obvious that the Landmarks Law has drastically restricted the Church's ability to raise revenues to carry out its various charitable and ministerial programs. In this particular case, the revenues involved are very large because the Community House is on land that would be extremely valuable if put to commercial uses. Nevertheless, we understand Supreme Court decisions to indicate that neutral regulations that diminish the income of a religious organization do not implicate the free exercise clause. *** The central question in identifying an unconstitutional burden is whether the claimant has been denied the ability to practice his religion or coerced in the nature of those practices. ***

We agree with the district court that no First Amendment violation has occurred absent a showing of discriminatory motive, coercion in religious practice or the Church's inability to carry out its religious mission in its existing facilities. *** In sum, the Landmarks Law is a valid, neutral regulation of general applicability, and as explained below, we agree with the district court that the Church has failed to prove that it cannot continue its religious practice in its existing facilities....

2. *The Takings Claim*

The Church also claims that the Landmarks Law so severely restricts its ability to use its property that it constitutes confiscation of property without just compensation in violation of the Fifth and Fourteenth Amendments.... However, the Supreme Court's decision in *Penn Central* compels us to hold otherwise.

* * *

Applying the *Penn Central* standard to property used for charitable purposes, the constitutional question is whether the land-use regulation impairs the continued operation of the property in its originally expected use. We conclude that the Landmarks Law does not effect an unconstitutional taking because the Church can continue its existing charitable and religious activities in its current facilities. Although the regulation may "freeze" the Church's property in its existing use and prevent the Church from expanding or altering its activities, *Penn Central* explicitly permits this. In that case, the Landmarks Law diminished the opportunity for Penn Central to earn what might have been substantial amounts by preventing it from building a skyscraper atop the [Grand Central] Terminal. Here it prevents a similar development by the Church—one that, in contrast to the proposal to build an office tower over Grand Central Terminal, would involve the razing of a landmarked building—at least so long as the Church is able to continue its present activities in the existing buildings. In both cases, the deprivation of commercial value is palpable, but as we understand *Penn Central,* it does not constitute a taking so long as continued use for present activities is viable.

The Church offers several arguments to distinguish *Penn Central,* but we find them unavailing. First, it argues that while Penn Central stipulated that it was able to earn a "reasonable return" on the Terminal even under the regulation, *** in this case, the use of the Community House for commercial purposes would yield an estimated return of only six percent. Even if true, this fact is irrelevant. "Reasonable return" analysis was appropriate to determine the viability of the existing commercial use of the Terminal but has no bearing on the instant matter because the existing use of the Community House is for charitable rather than commercial purposes. So long as the Church can continue to use its property in the way that it has been using it—to house its charitable and religious activity—there is no unconstitutional taking.

Second, the Church notes that it presented a second proposal for a smaller building to the Commission, but Penn Central did not. This hardly makes any difference. Just as the Commission in *Penn Central* remained open to a building addition that "'would harmonize in scale, material and character,'" *** with the Terminal, it invited appellant to propose an addition to the Community House in the instant matter. Finally, we reject as unsupported appellant's argument that in *Penn Central* the property owner continued to enjoy valuable, transferrable rights to develop the airspace above the Terminal, *** while the Church's development rights have little value. ***

3. *Findings of the District Court*

The principal factual finding of the district court—one central to its rejection of the Church's free exercise and takings claims—was that the Church "failed to show by a preponderance of the evidence that it can no longer conduct its charitable activities or carry out its religious mission in its existing facilities." *St. Bartholomew's Church v. City of New York,* 728 F.Supp. 958, 974–75 (S.D.N.Y.1989) (opinion and order).

The Church claims that the Community House is an inadequate facility in which to carry out the various activities that presently comprise the Church's religious mission and charitable purpose. It further claims that it cannot afford to make the needed repairs and renovations to the Community House and Church building. It concludes that it must be allowed to replace the Community House with a revenue-generating office tower. The district court was unconvinced. It found that the Church failed to prove that the Community House is fundamentally unsuitable for its current use and that the cost of repair and rehabilitation is beyond the financial means of the Church. Appellant argues on appeal that these findings were clearly erroneous. *** We disagree.

a. *Adequacy of the Community House*

The Church claims that the amount and configuration of usable space in the Community House is insufficient to accommodate the Church's various programs. It relies principally upon an analysis of space in the Community House by Walker Associates, an interior design firm hired by the Church. Presented to the Commission in three written reports and related oral testimony (collectively, "the Walker Report"), this study concluded that the demands for space by the Church's various programs exceeded the capacity of the Community House. Additionally, the Walker Report stated that renovation or expansion was impractical due to the structural inflexibility of the building.

The district court discredited the Walker Report. With regard to space, there is no dispute that the Community House currently is too small. The Walker Report found that 8000 square feet of extra space is needed. The Commission placed the deficiency at about 4500 square feet. *** Fatal, however, to the Church's claim is the absence of any showing that the space deficiency in the Community House cannot be remedied by a reconfiguration or expansion that is consistent with the purposes of the Landmarks Law. The Walker Report assumed that the Community House had an outmoded structure that precluded such an option. In fact, the building has a modern, light steel frame structure and was designed so that two additional floors could easily be added. Moreover, the Commission has indicated that it would be receptive to a proposal from the Church for such an addition. While expanding the amount of available space in the Community House may not provide ideal facilities for the Church's expanded programs, ... it does offer a means of continuing those programs in the existing building. Certainly the intermediate option of limited expansion must be thoroughly explored before jumping to replacement with a forty-seven story office building.

b. *Cost of Repair and Rehabilitation*

The Church also argues that the necessary repairs to the physically deteriorating Church building and Community House would be prohibitively expensive. It relies on a study of the mechanical systems and exteriors of those buildings prepared by O'Brien, Krietzburg and Associates, a construction management firm, and submitted to the Commission through written reports and oral testimony (collectively, "the OKA Report"). The OKA Report estimated that it would cost approximately $11 million over two years to bring the buildings' mechanical, electrical, and plumbing systems into proper working order and to repair the buildings' exteriors.

The district court also rejected this conclusion, faulting the OKA Report for being biased in favor of replacement over rehabilitation, ignoring actual conditions at the property site, and using an inappropriate method of estimating costs. Further, the district court pointed to contradictory evidence presented to the Commission, both by persons opposing the proposed development and by neutral consultants. Based on this information, the court found $3 million "phased in over a period of several years" to be a reasonable estimate for repairs and replacement.

On appeal, the Church does not seriously defend the $11 million estimate contained in the OKA Report. Instead, it accepts the $3 million estimate for the work that it covers, but argues that this figure disregards certain "major elements of cost." In particular, the Church asserts that an additional $500,000 is necessary for life safety measures, $647,000 for repair of the church organ, and $360,000 for architectural and engineering fees. The City counters that the life safety additions would unnecessarily exceed building code requirements, that organ repair is not a proper expense for this proceeding, and that design fees would be negligible. *** We need not rule on this dispute[. *** E]ven if the potential cost of repairs totaled $4.5 million, the Church has not adequately demonstrated that it is unable to meet this expense. Thus, the district court's central finding that the Church had failed to prove that it cannot continue in its existing facilities does not hinge on whether any portion of this $1.5 million was excluded from its estimate of repair costs.

c. *The Church's Finances*

As a corollary to its claim that repair and rehabilitation of the Church building and Community House would be too costly, the Church argues that its financial condition does not allow it to make the necessary improvements and also continue its other programs. The district court, however, found that appellant had failed adequately to prove this assertion, a finding that is not clearly erroneous.

The Church has three primary sources of support and revenue: contributions in the form of pledges and offerings collected at worship services, income earned on investments, and fees charged for participation in activities conducted under its sponsorship. *** Over the decade preceding 1985, the Church's sources of revenue have sporadically kept pace with expenses, exceeding them in 1975, 1977, 1980, 1983 and 1984, and falling behind in 1976, 1978, 1979, 1981, and 1982. On the whole, the Church had only a slight net deficit over this period. *** The Church's principal argument is that a major improvement expenditure of the type required to repair and renovate the Church building and Community House would severely damage this "precarious" balance of revenues and expenses. Because such an expenditure would come from endowment funds, the Church contends, future investment income will inevitably decline as the result of a depleted portfolio. Such a decrease in future revenues, it concludes, will produce "severe deficits."

While a reduced principal will yield less investment income, the Church has not demonstrated that its budget cannot withstand building improvement expenditures under a reasonable financing procedure. *** Appellant has offered no financial projections or cash flow analyses to prove that these financing methods are not feasible. Without such data, the district court's finding that the Church failed to prove prospective financial hardship is not clearly erroneous.

We also cannot ignore the paucity of evidence offered by the Church to show that other forms of revenue are not available. Its claim that a capital fundraising drive already has been exhausted as a financing possibility is undercut by evidence that longtime members of the congregation cannot recall any such drive. Also, evidence before the Commission indicated that the transferrable development rights for the airspace above the Church property are, contrary to the Church's claim, not worthless.

Finally, the Church argues that even if its endowment could withstand a building project, it is not at liberty to withdraw large sums for that purpose because of legal restrictions on the use of its investment funds. In particular, it urges that Section 717 of the New York Not-For-Profit Corporation Law prohibits the Church from expending the sums necessary to undergo a building project. That provision, however, does no more than impose upon the Church a fiduciary duty of care to manage the congregation's money in a prudent and responsible fashion, *see* N.Y. Not-for-Profit Corp. Law §§ 513, 717 (McKinney Supp.1990), and would be implicated only if the expenditures in question would unacceptably impair the Church's financial condition....

4. *The Motion to Intervene*

The proposed intervenors argue that the district court should have granted their motion to intervene on the side of the defendants at trial. We may reverse the denial of a motion to intervene only for "abuse of discretion." *** No such abuse is present

St. Bartholomew's Episcopal Church. Photo by Štěpán Roh, Creative Commons.

here. The district court properly denied intervention as of right under Fed. R. Civ. P. 24(a)(2) because the proposed intervenors lack any legally protectable interest in this matter. Under New York law, as a Protestant Episcopal Church, St. Bartholomew's is a corporate body placed in the trusteeship of its church wardens and vestrymen. *** To the extent that the proposed intervenors are members of the parish, they enjoy only the right to vote in the election of the church wardens and vestrymen. *** Thus, the Rector, Wardens and Members of the Vestry is the proper party to litigate the constitutionality of encumbrances placed on Church property.

* * *

Conclusion

For the reasons stated above, we affirm both the judgment of the district court in favor of the defendants-appellees and the order of that court denying the motion to intervene.

Notes and Questions

1. **Three questions.** How well do the cases address these questions: a. When can the government require the preservation of a religious site without there being an interference with the free exercise of religion? b. Should religious property be treated differently than property not devoted to religious practices? c. To what extent can or should public funds be invested in preserving them?

2. **Takings.** Under the court's analysis, it seems that so long as there are creative options available to the institution for meeting its financial needs, there will be no taking. a. Would this hold true if the cost of renovations had equaled or exceeded all the Church's resources? b. Would the court still have insisted that it use one of the

creative options? c. Did the court apply the same takings analysis used for for-profit entities with the necessary showing the same? d. Is the evaluation of hardship in the context of obtaining a certificate of appropriateness better at accommodating the particular circumstances of an ailing religious institution? *See* N.Y.C. Admin. Code § 25–309.

3. **Other approaches to economic hardship.** The District of Columbia historic preservation law defines "unreasonable economic hardship" to mean "that failure to issue a permit would amount to a taking of the owner's property without just compensation or, in the case of low-income owner(s) ... would place an onerous and excessive financial burden upon such owner(s). D.C. Code § 6-1102(14). The Pennsylvania courts seem to treat non-profits as any other commercial owner, requiring a showing that "the ordinance went so far as to preclude the use of the property for any purpose for which it was reasonably adapted," and that "sale of the property was impracticable, that commercial rental could not provide a reasonable rate of return, or that other potential use of the property was foreclosed. *First Presbyterian Church of York v. City Council of York*, 360 A.2d 257 (Pa. Commw. Ct. 1976), *citing Maher v. City of New Orleans*, 371 F. Supp. 653 (E.D. La. 1974); *see also Park v. City of Williamsport*, 680 A.2d 835, 837 (Pa. 1996). *See generally* Christine Faller, *Economic Hardship and Historic Preservation of Non-Profits: Balancing Individual Burden with Community Benefit*, http://scholarship.law.georgetown.edu/hpps_papers/28 (last visited April 7, 2017).

4. **Test for determining constitutionality of landmark designation ordinance as it applies to religious property.** The Second Circuit interpreted *Employment Division, Dep't. of Human Resources of Oregon v. Smith* to ask "is the law a neutral and generally applicable law or does the law restrict conduct because it is religiously oriented?" Finding the New York ordinance falling in the former category, it upheld the application to the church. a. Do you agree with the court's application of the rule? b. Is the line articulated so clearly discernable? c. Embracing the Second Circuit's interpretation, the Tenth Circuit, in *Grace United Methodist Church v. City of Cheyenne*, 451 F.3d 643 (10th Cir. 2006), has stated that "[n]eutral rules of general applicability normally do not raise free exercise concerns even if they incidentally burden a particular religious practice or belief." A law is neutral if the law's purpose is not to infringe on or restrict religious practices. The court went on to conclude that land use regulations are neutral and generally applicable laws if they are motivated by secular purposes and impact all land owners equally, stating:

> [S]everal federal courts have held that land use regulations ... are neutral and generally applicable notwithstanding that they may have individualized procedures for obtaining special use permits or variances.... According to these courts ... [zoning laws] are generally applicable if they are motivated by secular purposes and impact equally all land owners in the city seeking variances.

Id. at 649–50. To establish a substantial burden on the free exercise of religion, the religious property owner will have to show a burden beyond the historic designation.

5. **Religious property exemption from historic preservation laws.** Most preservation ordinances at the state and local levels do not provide exemptions for religious property, but a few do. *See, e.g.*, MUN. CODE OF CHICAGO, ILL., ch. 2-120, § 660 and CODE OF ORDINANCES, PITTSBURGH, PA. tit 11, 1101.03(a)(7) ("nomination of a religious structure shall only be made by the owner(s) of record of the religious structure"). Some of these ordinances are narrowly tailored to apply only to places of worship, but not to property merely because it is owned by a religious institution, like schools or community centers. California allows religious property owners to exempt themselves from historic preservation if they can demonstrate a "substantial hardship ... likely to deprive the [institution] of economic return on its property, the reasonable use of its property, or the appropriate use of its property in the furtherance of its religious mission." CAL GOVT CODE §§ 25373(c), (d). What are the pros and cons of such exemptions?

2. First Covenant Church in Seattle, Washington

While the Second and Tenth Circuits found the rationale in *Employment Division, Dep't. of Human Resources of Oregon v. Smith* to be coherent and sound, the cases that follow thought otherwise.

First Covenant Church of Seattle v. City of Seattle

Supreme Court of Washington
114 Wash.2d 392, 787 P.2d 1352 (1990)

DORE, J. (En banc). This is a case of first impression.

First Covenant Church challenges the constitutionality of two separate but interrelated ordinances, the Seattle Landmarks Preservation Ordinance 106348 [(now codified as Seattle Municipal Code 25.12.)] and Seattle ordinance 112425 designating First Covenant Church a landmark. The Church brought a declaratory judgment action seeking declaration that the Seattle ordinance designating the church a landmark and the Seattle Landmarks Preservation Ordinance as applied to churches were unconstitutional and void. The trial court held that the Church's claim was premature and entered summary judgment in favor of the City. We hold that this case presents a justiciable issue properly presented for declaratory judgment and that the designation ordinance and the Landmarks Preservation Ordinance as applied to churches are unconstitutional as they violate the right of free exercise of religion as guaranteed by the United States and Washington State Constitutions. We reverse.

Facts

First Covenant Church of Seattle is a nonprofit Washington corporation. The Church owns and operates the church located at Pike and Bellevue in Seattle which is used exclusively for religious purposes.

In 1977, the City of Seattle adopted the Seattle Landmarks Preservation Ordinance to, *inter alia*,

> designate, preserve, protect, enhance and perpetuate those sites, improvements and objects which reflect significant elements of the City's cultural, aesthetic, social, economic, political, architectural, engineering, historic or other heritage ...

SMC 25.12.020(B) (1977). Pursuant to that ordinance, the Landmarks Preservation Board nominated First Covenant Church as a landmark on October 15, 1980. A public hearing was held on January 7, 1981, at which the Church objected to the nomination. Following the hearing, the board voted to approve the designation of the church as a landmark. On April 22, 1981, the board voted to adopt controls to preserve the exterior of the church and recommended to the Seattle City Council that it approve those controls.

The Church and the City were unable to come to an agreement regarding application of the controls and the matter was referred to a hearing examiner. A public hearing was held before an examiner on June 3, 1981, at which the Church objected to designation of the church as a landmark building. On July 2, 1981, the hearing examiner recommended that the city council approve the controls proposed by the board for the preservation of the church facade.

Over 4 years later, September 17, 1985, the city council adopted ordinance 112425 formally designating the church a landmark and placing specific controls upon the Church's ability to alter the structure's exterior. More than 5 years elapsed from the date the board nominated the church for landmark status until the city council passed the designating ordinance. Throughout that entire period the Church remained subject to the controls proposed by the board and the landmarks ordinance's provisions requiring the landmark owner to obtain a Certificate of Approval for structural changes necessitating a building permit.[2]

The Church brought a declaratory judgment action against the City in January 1986, seeking declaration that application of the Seattle Landmarks Preservation Ordinance to churches was unconstitutional and that the ordinance designating First Covenant Church a landmark was void. *** The trial court held that the landmarks ordinance properly applied to churches and that until the City applied the landmarks ordinance in a manner that impinged upon the Church's constitutional rights to operate its religious property without interference from the City, the Church's claim that the landmarks ordinance violated its rights of religious freedom was premature.

Prior to trial, the City filed a motion for summary judgment seeking dismissal of all of the Church's remaining causes of action. The trial court granted summary judgment and dismissed the Church's complaint in its entirety with prejudice. *** The Church appealed both summary judgment orders. The Court of Appeals certified the appeal here.

---

2. Under the Landmarks Preservation Ordinance, once the board designates a landmark the provisions of the landmarks ordinance requiring a Certificate of Approval for alterations or significant changes to the landmark apply to the property owner. SMC 25.12.390 (1977).

Issues

Two issues are presented:

(1) Is a constitutional challenge to the Seattle Landmarks Preservation Ordinance by the Church premature until the ordinance is enforced?

(2) Is the Seattle Landmarks Preservation Ordinance as applied to churches unconstitutional under the free exercise of religion provisions of the United States and Washington State Constitutions?

Analysis

The issue of whether the Church's cause of action is premature requires a determination of whether there exists a justiciable controversy and whether the Church's challenge satisfies the ripeness doctrine. We find that a justiciable controversy exists and that the Church's claims are ripe for judicial determination.

The Church brought its action for declaratory judgment pursuant to the Uniform Declaratory Judgments Act, RCW 7.24.020, and applicable court rules. In order for a court to rule on a declaratory judgment, the case must present a justiciable controversy. *State ex rel. Graham v. Northshore Sch. Dist. 417,* 99 Wash.2d 232, 246, 662 P.2d 38 (1983). This court established that a justiciable controversy exists under the Act if the controversy presents:

> (1) ... an actual, present and existing dispute, or the mature seeds of one, as distinguished from a possible, dormant, hypothetical, speculative, or moot disagreement, (2) between parties having genuine and opposing interests, (3) which involves interests that must be direct and substantial, rather than potential, theoretical, abstract or academic, and (4) a judicial determination of which will be final and conclusive.

Diversified Indus. Dev. Corp. v. Ripley, 82 Wash.2d 811, 815, 514 P.2d 137 (1973) ***. All four elements must be satisfied or the court must dismiss the case; otherwise, the court enters into the prohibited area of advisory opinions. *** This case satisfies all four elements and, therefore, presents this court with a justiciable controversy.

The Church argued that the designation of the church structure as a landmark and the imposition of controls constituted substantial interference by the City with the Church's religious freedom. According to the Church, several impacts occurred immediately upon the board's designation of the church as a landmark. Those impacts included: interference with the Church's freedom to alter the exterior of the church structure; necessary secular approval of any proposed alteration of the facade requiring additional paperwork, negotiations and hearings; a limitation on the Church's ability to sell its property; and uncertainty of discretionary approval confronting the Church in its planning of any exterior change. In addition, an uncontroverted affidavit stated that landmark designation of the church resulted in a depreciation of the market value of the property from $700,000 to $400,000. ***

The City contends that, absent the submission of a proposal for alteration, the Church's claim is speculative and premature. The trial court agreed and granted the City's motion for summary judgment.

The Church's challenge to the constitutionality of the landmarks ordinance as applied to church property and the designation of the church as a landmark satisfies the justiciable controversy test. The dispute involves a present controversy between parties with opposing interests. The landmarks board designated First Covenant Church a landmark and the city council formalized that designation by passing ordinance 112425. The Church asserts that landmark designation of churches violates the constitutional guaranty of freedom of religious expression. The interests of the City and the Church are substantial and a determination by this court as to the constitutionality of the landmarks ordinance will clarify valuable property rights of churches and their freedom to practice religion. A decision here will be welcomed throughout the United States, as this is a case of first impression on this constitutional challenge. ***

The Ordinances Create an Unconstitutional Infringement Upon the Church's Right of Free Exercise of Religion

The issue is whether the law should prefer religious freedom or an exercise of the police power to maintain the architectural and cultural interests associated with landmark preservation. Although First Amendment rights are not absolute, "freedom of religion [is] in a preferred position." *Murdock v. Pennsylvania,* 319 U.S. 105, 115, 63 S.Ct. 870, 876, 63 S.Ct. 891, 87 L.Ed. 1292 (1943). ***

The separation between Church and State is rooted in the historical foundations of this nation. *** While recognizing instances where the compelling interests of the government outweigh its citizens' right to freely pursue their religious beliefs, the judiciary in this nation consistently prohibits unjustified governmental interference with an individual's constitutional right of free exercise of religion.

The Church contends that the Landmarks Preservation Ordinance, as applied to church property, and the designating ordinance are unconstitutional as they violate the Church's right of free exercise of religion guaranteed by the first amendment to the United States Constitution … and Washington's Const. art. 1, § 11 (amend. 34)….

To establish a violation of free exercise, the complaining party must show "the coercive effect of the enactment as it operates against him in the practice of his religion." *** If such an infringement is established, the court subjects the challenged legislation to strict scrutiny analysis requiring the governmental body to prove that (1) a compelling state interest exists to justify the regulation and (2) the regulation constitutes the least restrictive means to achieve the government's objective. *Sherbert v. Verner,* 374 U.S. 398, 83 S.Ct. 1790, 10 L.Ed.2d 965 (1963) ***.

* * *

The ordinances at issue require the Church to seek secular approval of any proposed change to the church's facade requiring a building permit. SMC 25.12.670 (1977); Seattle city ordinance 112425 (1985) app. B, at 226. The landmarks ordinance requires that once the landmarks board files an approval of a nomination of a landmark, the landmark owner must obtain a Certificate of Approval from the board before the owner may make alterations or significant changes to the designated features or characteristics of the landmark or make significant changes or alterations which would violate any control imposed by the designating ordinance. SMC 25.12.670 (1977).... A control set forth in the designating ordinance specifically requires the Church to obtain a Certificate of Approval for any alteration to the exterior of the church structure requiring a building permit. *** The practical effect of the provisions is to require a religious organization to seek secular approval of matters potentially affecting the Church's practice of its religion.

The City claims that the designating ordinance's exemption for changes based upon liturgy precludes any interference by the City with the Church's practice of religion. The designating ordinance provides:

Section 2. The following controls upon alteration of the landmark are hereby imposed:

> A Certificate of Approval must be obtained or the time for denying a Certificate of Approval must have expired before the owner may make any alteration which requires a building permit, to any portion of the exterior of the building; *** Provided further that *nothing herein shall prevent any alteration of the exterior when such alterations are necessitated by changes in liturgy,* it being understood that the owner is the exclusive authority on liturgy and is the decisive party in determining what architectural changes are appropriate to the liturgy. *When alterations necessitated by changes in liturgy are proposed, the owner shall advise the Landmarks Preservation Board in writing of the nature of the proposed alterations and, the Board shall issue a Certificate of Approval. Prior to the issuance of any Certificate, however, the Board and owner shall jointly explore such possible alternative design solutions as may be appropriate or necessary to preserve the designated features of the landmark.*

*** Seattle city ordinance 112425 (1985). We find that the liturgy exception does not mitigate the City's infringement upon the Church's right of free exercise. The liturgy exception establishes a vague standard which does not withstand close scrutiny.

The designating ordinance contains no definition of "liturgy". Absent a contrary definition provided in the ordinance, words of an ordinance are to be given their usual and ordinary meaning. *** *Webster's Third New International Dictionary* (1971) at page 1323 defines liturgy as "a rite or series of rites, observances, or procedures prescribed for public worship in the Christian church in accordance with authorized or standard form". According to that definition, liturgy essentially refers to the religious activity occurring within a church as part of the religious ritual. It provides a vague criterion for the Church to rely upon when planning alterations to the church exterior. *** The anomalies created by the liturgy exception are cumbersome and would result in numerous delays in carrying out routine church work. We find that the liturgy exception constitutes a vague and unworkable criterion that fails to accommodate the constitutional rights of the Church and infringes on the Church membership's ability to freely practice its religion.

Even if the liturgy exception represented an appropriate criterion, the requirements of the designating ordinance still violate the Church's right of free exercise. The controls placed upon the Church require that if the Church proposes a change based upon liturgy, prior to the issuance of a Certificate of Approval "the Board and owner shall jointly explore such possible alternative design solutions as may be appropriate or necessary to preserve the designated features of the landmark." App. B at 226. Seattle city ordinance 112425 (1985). Regardless of the religious nature of the proposed alteration, the Church must submit its plans to the board, a secular body, and negotiate possible alternatives. That requirement creates unjustified governmental interference in religious matters of the Church and thereby creates an infringement on the Church's constitutional right of free exercise. Furthermore, the parallel provisions of the landmarks ordinance requiring a landmark owner to obtain a Certificate of Approval prior to making structural changes to the landmark also infringe upon the Church's religious freedom.

A substantial infringement of a First Amendment right can be justified only by proof of a compelling governmental interest. *** The United States Supreme Court found that landmark preservation represented an important state interest but did not express the view that it constituted a compelling interest. *Penn Cent. Transp. Co. v. New York City,* 438 U.S. 104, 98 S.Ct. 2646, 57 L.Ed.2d 631 (1978).

In *Penn Central,* the Supreme Court addressed the validity of the application of New York City's Landmarks Preservation Law to a commercial building. *** The appellants did not allege any violation of a fundamental right. Absent such a claim, the Court was able to employ minimal scrutiny in its analysis of New York City's Landmarks Preservation Law. Although the Court held that the landmarks law satisfied the limited inquiry of minimal scrutiny, it seems most likely the Court would not have reached the same result had it analyzed the law under strict scrutiny.

We hold that the preservation of historical landmarks is not a compelling state interest. Balancing the right of free exercise with the aesthetic and community values associated with landmark preservation, we find that the latter is clearly outweighed by the constitutional protection of free exercise of religion and the public benefits associated with the practice of religious worship within the community. ***

Conclusion

We hold that the Seattle Landmarks Preservation Ordinance 106348 and Seattle ordinance 112425 designating First Covenant Church a landmark violate the Church's First Amendment rights under the United States Constitution and Washington's Const. art. 1, § 11 (amend. 34).

We reverse the City's summary judgment and grant summary judgment of dismissal to the Church.

UTTER, J. [along with CALLOW, C.J., DURHAM, J., and PEARSON, J. Pro Tem.] (concurring).

I agree with the majority's conclusion that this declaratory judgment action is ripe for decision and that the landmark preservation ordinance cannot be applied to the

First Covenant Church. I write separately to emphasize the facts which require this decision in this case and to indicate the legal standards which should govern such cases in the future.

I

As the majority points out, the landmark designation has reduced the value of the church's property, its most valuable asset. Since the landmark designation is complete and has had an impact on the church, consideration of this case is not premature.

The dissent argues correctly that we should dispose of the question of whether state regulation of the church's building modifications violates the church's free exercise rights by adopting the defendant's interpretation of the ordinance. This would make any changes to the church's structure for religious purposes exempt from the ordinance's review procedures.

In order to do that, however, we have to reach the issue. Because the case presents a ripe justiciable controversy, we should reach this issue.

The dissent cites two cases to support its view that this case is neither ripe nor justiciable. *** In both these cases the court found that the matter before it was justiciable. ***

The dissent complicates the inquiry into justiciability greatly by introducing the concept of ripeness as articulated by the United States Supreme Court in *Abbott Laboratories v. Gardner, supra* 387 U.S. at 148–49, 87 S.Ct. at 1515–16. None of our prior cases have cited *Gardner* or approved of its characterization of the ripeness doctrine.

More importantly, *Gardner* supports finding that this case is ripe. *Gardner* involved a preenforcement challenge to Food and Drug Administration regulations. *Gardner,* 387 U.S. at 138–39, 87 S.Ct. at 1509–10. The *Gardner* Court held that the challenge was ripe and remanded to the Court of Appeals for the Third Circuit for a ruling on the merits. 387 U.S. at 156, 87 S.Ct. at 1519. Although the government had not yet enforced the regulations against the drug companies, the Court held that the impact of the regulations "is sufficiently direct and immediate as to render the issue appropriate for judicial review at this stage." *Gardner,* 387 U.S. at 152, 87 S.Ct. at 1517. The Court noted that the purpose of the declaratory judgment act required judicial review. *** Similarly, the church has been designated a landmark; like the drug companies, it must obey the challenged law if constitutional. It need not await the application of each individual restriction of the act before challenging its constitutionality. It has a right to the declaratory judgment it seeks.

Washington precedent on ripeness in land use cases does not allow us to delay a decision just because the litigant has not suffered enough injury to satisfy the court. In our previous cases we have decided whether claims were ripe on the basis of whether the administrative action was final, not on the intensity of the litigant's complaint. ***

II

The majority's conclusion that application of this ordinance to this church constitutes a free exercise violation is correct because the church has shown that application of the ordinance to it greatly diminishes the value of its principal asset. As the dissent states, adopting the City's construction of its own ordinance will avoid the necessity of deciding the question of whether state approval of the church's modification of its building violates the First Amendment. But the issue of whether the ordinance violates the constitution because of its impact on church finances requires a constitutional decision.

Prior to the United States Supreme Court's decision in *Jimmy Swaggart Ministries v. Board of Equalization,* 493 U.S. 378, 110 S.Ct. 688, 107 L.Ed.2d 796 (1990), Supreme Court precedent seemed to prohibit the imposition of a financial burden on the practice of religion. *** Because of this it appeared that a land use restriction imposed specifically on a church causing gross diminution in the value of its principal asset might violate the free exercise clause....

Our precedent and the precedent of the New York Court of Appeals provides useful guidance to the proper evaluation of the effects of financial burdens imposed by land-use restrictions on the free exercise of religion. This topic necessarily requires development by state courts because the United States Supreme Court has never decided a land use case involving a church's free exercise claim.... Indeed, until recently the Court had decided few cases involving burdens upon churches as institutions as opposed to burdens on individuals. ***

In *Sumner v. First Baptist Church, supra,* this court held that the application of a building code ordinance to a church school presented a free exercise claim. The plurality stated that the practical effect of uncompromising application of the building code would be to close down the church operated school. *** *Sumner* supports the proposition, *** that regulations imposing financial burdens on churches can create a free exercise claim. Because the burden created in this case is so much greater than the burden imposed in *Sumner,* we must sustain the church's challenge in this case.

* * *

Although I think that our decision in *Sumner* compels us to rule in First Covenant's favor in the instant case, I write separately to urge that we apply a different approach in future cases *** [W]e ought to require a very specific showing of hardship to justify exemption from land-use restrictions in the future.

New York's courts require that landmark designation not prevent or seriously interfere with the carrying out of a church's religious and charitable purposes. *See Lutheran Church in Am. v. New York,* 35 N.Y.2d 121, 131, 316 N.E.2d 305, 359 N.Y.S.2d 7 (1974) ***. We should adopt the New York test as the means of evaluating free exercise claims in land use. While imposition of a financial burden does not per se create a free exercise problem, the free exercise clause does not allow the state to impose financial burdens throttling religious practice. ***

The New York cases have not outlawed the application of land use restrictions to churches. Instead, the cases permit relief from the strictures of ordinances when they genuinely interfere with a church's ability to perform its mission. For example, in *In re Westchester Reform Temple v. Brown,* 22 N.Y.2d 488, 239 N.E.2d 891, 293 N.Y.S.2d 297 (1968), the New York Court of Appeals required the zoning authorities to modify a setback requirement interfering with a needed expansion of a synagogue. The court relied heavily on the "undisputed fact ... that the present facilities must be expanded to meet the increasing needs of the congregation." *** It rested its opinion on First Amendment grounds. ***

On the other hand, the New York Court of Appeals rejected the argument that a decline in market value alone constituted a free exercise violation in *In re Society for Ethical Culture v. Spatt,* 51 N.Y.2d 449, 456, 415 N.E.2d 922, 434 N.Y.S.2d 932 (1980) ***. Nevertheless, a landmark ordinance cannot be applied to prohibit a church from realizing sufficient profits to move or replace its building if it becomes unsuitable to its needs. ***

Our decision in *Sumner* and the uncontested gross diminution of the value of its property justify the majority's decision in this case. [But,] we should apply the New York approach to future cases.

Dolliver, J. (dissenting).

The issue before the court is whether the Seattle landmarks preservation ordinance 106348 (Seattle Municipal Code 25.12), under the authority of which the church building owned by and housing the plaintiff has been declared a landmark ***, unconstitutionally impinges upon plaintiff's right to its free exercise of religion. U.S. Const. amend. 1; *see also* Const. art. 1, § 11 (amend. 34). I would hold that it does not.

In contrast to the extended analysis of the majority, I believe the case can be decided easily and summarily. Particularly in cases of this nature the court should render a decision only on those issues necessary to decide the case.

* * *

In its motion for summary judgment, defendant stated:

> Any changes that First Covenant chooses to make to the exterior of the structure *for religious purposes* are exempted from the normal landmarks review and approval requirement. As written, therefore, the imposed controls cannot interfere with First Covenant's free exercise of religion. ***

By this statement, which is surely in the interest of the plaintiff, the City has given its interpretation of the term "liturgical exception" in the ordinance designating the First Covenant Church as a landmark. Thus, all this court need do is confirm the interpretation of the City, and the City will be bound to that position. If this is done, the ordinance on its face would not threaten the use made of the building by the congregation or changes made in the exterior of the building so long as any uses or changes are for religious purposes. Since this, as I understand it, is the real concern of the plaintiff, if this approach were adopted, the case of the plaintiff would collapse.

As to other questions which plaintiff may have as to the validity of the ordinance, there is neither a justiciable controversy *** nor is the matter ripe for litigation ***. Finally, to suggest that the requirement the church and landmarks board "shall jointly explore such possible alternative design solutions as may be appropriate or necessary to preserve the designated features of the landmark" (majority, at 1360) is an excessive burden on the "free exercise of religion" is to trivialize the great protections of the First Amendment.

I would affirm the trial court. This court should by its opinion confirm the interpretation by the City of Seattle landmarks preservation ordinance 106348 and hold the ordinance does not apply to any changes made to the First Covenant Church for "religious purposes". The discussion of other issues raised by the landmarks preservation ordinance, including the effect of a decision by plaintiff to use or sell its property for "nonreligious purposes", should wait until another day.

Smith and Brachtenbach, JJ., and Baker, J. Pro Tem., concur.

First Covenant Church of Seattle v. City of Seattle

Supreme Court of Washington
120 Wash.2d 203, 840 P.2d 174 (1992)

Dore, C.J. (En banc)[.] We reinstate our holding in *First Covenant Church v. Seattle*, [114 Wash.2d 392, 787 P.2d 1352 (1990), *cert. granted, judgment vacated and remanded*, 499 U.S. 901, 111 S.Ct. 1097, 113 L.Ed.2d 208 (1991),] that applying the City's ordinances to the church violates the free exercise guaranties of the First Amendment to the federal constitution and article 1, Section 11 of the state constitution. We have fully considered the Supreme Court's holding in *Employment Div., Dep't of Human Resources v. Smith*, [494 U.S. 872, 110 S.Ct. 1595, 108 L.Ed.2d 876 (1990),] and we conclude that *Smith* is distinguishable from this case and does not compel a different result.

Issue

Whether applying Seattle's Landmarks Preservation Ordinance to First Covenant violated the church's right to free exercise under the state and the federal constitutions?

Facts

*** A majority of this court concluded, in *First Covenant*, that First Covenant's claims that the Landmarks Preservation and designation ordinances violated the free exercise of religion were not premature. *First Covenant Church v. Seattle, supra* 114 Wash.2d at 398–400, 787 P.2d 1352. A majority, for different reasons, also concluded that applying the City's ordinances to First Covenant burdened the Church's right of free exercise of religion under the federal and state constitutions. *** And the majority, again for different reasons, concluded that the liturgy exemption did not mitigate the burden on free exercise. ***

The majority applied the strict scrutiny analysis of *Sherbert v. Verner*, 374 U.S. 398, 83 S.Ct. 1790, 10 L.Ed.2d 965 (1963), when assessing the free exercise claim. It concluded that landmark preservation was not a "compelling interest" that justified the burden on First Covenant's right to free exercise and, therefore, that applying the City's ordinances to First Covenant violated First Covenant's free exercise rights under the state and federal constitutions. *First Covenant Church v. Seattle, supra* 114 Wash.2d at 408, 787 P.2d 1352.

The City appealed. The United States Supreme Court vacated the judgment and remanded it to us for "further consideration in light of *Employment Division, Department of Human Resources of Oregon v. Smith* ..."[499 U.S. 901 (1991)]. The Christian Legal Society (CLS), as *amicus curiae*, supports First Covenant. The Municipal Art Society of New York and the National Trust for Historic Preservation in the United States filed briefs supporting the City of Seattle.

Analysis

The Supreme Court remanded *First Covenant* to this court, for "further consideration in light of" *Employment Div., Dep't of Human Resources v. Smith, supra.* * * *

The First Amendment provides that "Congress shall make no law respecting an establishment of religion, or prohibiting the free exercise thereof...." The First Amendment absolutely prohibits the regulation of beliefs "as such" and the government may not compel or punish the expression of religious belief. *Employment Div., Dep't of Human Resources v. Smith*, 494 U.S. 872, 876–77, 110 S.Ct. 1595, 1599, 108 L.Ed.2d 876, 884 (1990) (*Smith* II). Justice Scalia presumes that the First Amendment prohibits a law that bans conduct only when the conduct is engaged in for religious purposes or because of the religious belief it displays. *Smith* II, at 876–77, 110 S.Ct. at 1599.

The Court warns that religious motivation does not place conduct "beyond the reach of a criminal law that is not specifically directed at [the] religious practice". *Smith* II at 878, 110 S.Ct. at 1599. *** Justice Scalia suggests that the First Amendment does not bar application of a neutral, generally applicable law to religiously motivated conduct unless the conduct involves "[T]he Free Exercise Clause in conjunction with other constitutional protections", such as freedom of speech, the press, or the right of parents to educate their children. *Smith* II, at 881, 110 S.Ct. at 1601. The *Smith* II case does not present a "hybrid situation", in which the free exercise claim is "connected to" a communicative activity or parental right. The Court, therefore, concludes that applying Oregon's criminal law to the counselors does not violate the First Amendment. ***

The Court next considers whether it must evaluate the claim for exemption from Oregon's criminal law under the "compelling interest" test set forth in *Sherbert v. Verner.* [374 U.S. 398 (1963)] Justice Scalia states that the *Sherbert* test does not require an exemption "from a generally applicable criminal law." *Smith* II, at 884, 110 S.Ct. at 1603. *** Justice Scalia opines that applying the *Sherbert* test broadly will "court anarchy" because "people of almost every conceivable religious preference" could demand exemptions from "civic obligations of almost every conceivable kind" based on their right to freely exercise religion. *Smith* II, at 888, 110 S.Ct. at 1605. Justice Scalia concludes "we cannot afford the luxury of deeming *presumptively invalid, ...* every regulation of conduct that does not protect an interest of the highest order." *Smith* II, at 888, 110 S.Ct. at 1605. ***

Language in the *Smith* I and *Smith* II opinions suggests that the *Smith* II rule applies only to free exercise challenges to criminal prohibitions. Other federal and state courts, however, have specifically rejected this argument and concluded that the *Smith* II holding is not limited to criminal cases.[7] The rule of *Smith* II applies in both civil and criminal cases and may apply in this case if the City's preservation ordinances are neutral and generally applicable.

Smith II states that the "right of free exercise does not relieve an individual of the obligation to comply with a 'valid and neutral law of general applicability....'" *Smith* II, 494 U.S. at 879, 110 S.Ct. at 1600. First Covenant and the CLS contend that the City's Landmarks Preservation Ordinances are not neutral or generally applicable because the sites, improvements, and objects they govern are arbitrarily selected, and the selection process requires individual evaluation of each building, site, or improvement....

The designation criteria of SMC 25.12 is neutral. It applies to "[a]n object, site or improvement which is more than twenty-five (25) years old" and meets the designation criteria. SMC 25.12.350. The definitions of "object" and "improvement" are also facially neutral. SMC 25.12.190, .140. *** Designation ordinance 112425, however, is not neutral. It alludes to religious facilities in the two references to "liturgy". Because the Landmarks Preservation Ordinances specifically refer to religious facilities, they are not "neutral". ***

The landmark ordinances must also be "generally applicable" laws. Justice Scalia contrasted "generally applicable" tax laws with statutes that contain "a system of individualized exceptions", that "create[ ] a mechanism for individualized exemptions" or that lend themselves to "individualized governmental assessment" of the conduct governed. *Smith* II, 494 U.S. at 884, 110 S.Ct. at 1603. *** The landmark ordinances at issue here are unlike a general tax law because they invite individualized assessments of the subject property and the owner's use of such property, and contain mechanisms for individualized exceptions. *** The City's Landmarks Preservation Ordinance is not generally applicable. ***

---

7. *Rector, Wardens, & Members of Vestry of St. Bartholomew's Church v. New York*, 914 F.2d 348, 354 (2d Cir. 1990) (Second Circuit applies *Smith* II reasoning to a free exercise challenge to landmarks preservation ordinance), *cert. denied*, 499 U.S. 905 (1991); *Salvation Army v. Department of Comm'ty Affairs*, 919 F.2d 183, 194–96 (3d Cir. 1990) (Third Circuit applies *Smith* II in a free exercise/zoning case); *Vandiver v. Hardin Cy. Bd. of Educ.*, 925 F.2d 927, 932 (6th Cir. 1991) (Sixth Circuit applies *Smith* II rule when parents allege Kentucky's equivalency exams law violates free exercise); *Health Servs. Div., Health & Env't Dep't v. Temple Baptist Church*, 112 N.M. 262, 814 P.2d 130 (Ct. App.) (New Mexico court applies *Smith* II when church contends day-care license law violates free exercise), *cert. denied*, 112 N.M. 235 (1991); *Black v. Snyder*, 471 N.W.2d 715 (Minn. Ct. App. 1991) (*Smith* II standard applies to civil claims, including breach of contract, defamation, and harassment).

The City and the National Trust for Historic Preservation (National Trust) insist that *Rector, Wardens, & Members of Vestry of St. Bartholomew's Church v. New York,* [*supra*] compels a different result. *** The court concluded that the landmark law did not "demonstrate a lack of neutrality or general applicability" and that, absent proof that the Commission exercised its discretion in a discriminatory way, "there [was] no constitutional relevance" to the church's claim. *St. Bartholomew's Church,* at 354–55.

St. Bartholomew's is distinguishable from this case. St. Bartholomew's accepted designation as a landmark, without objection. First Covenant has objected continuously to designation. St. Bartholomew's sought an exception for an adjunct building, not its church building. First Covenant seeks an exception for its church building. St. Bartholomew's sought an exception to use its property for commercial purposes. First Covenant seeks an exemption so that it may continue to use its church for exclusively religious purposes. St. Bartholomew's did not allege that designation reduced its principal asset, only that it impeded its ability to generate additional revenue to expand its programs. Uncontroverted evidence supports First Covenant's claim that designation reduces the values of its principal asset by almost one-half. Finally, the parties in *St. Bartholomew's* did not challenge the effect of the religious exemption on the New York law's constitutionality, and the religious exemption in the New York law is not "liturgy" based, as is Seattle's. *St. Bartholomew's* is factually distinguishable and does not control this case.

The rule in *Smith* II also does not apply because First Covenant's claim presents a "hybrid situation". The cases upon which the Supreme Court relied when it formulated the "hybrid claim" exception, as well as other authority, support the view that a "hybrid" case is one in which a single claim encompasses several protected interests.[9] The Church's claim is "hybrid" because designation not only violates First Covenant's right to freely exercise religion, it infringes on First Covenant's rights to free speech.

"Speech" includes nonverbal conduct if the conduct is "sufficiently imbued with elements of communication". *Spence v. Washington,* 418 U.S. 405, 409, 94 S.Ct. 2727, 2730, 41 L.Ed.2d 842 (1974). Whether conduct constitutes speech depends on the nature of the activity, combined with the factual context and environment in which the activity is undertaken. *Spence v. Washington, supra.* There must be "[an] intent to convey a particularized message" and a great "likelihood ... that the message would be understood by those who view it". ***

First Covenant claims, and no one disputes, that its church building itself "is an expression of Christian belief and message" and that conveying religious beliefs is part of the building's function. First Covenant reasons that when the State controls the architectural "proclamation" of religious belief inherent in its church's exterior it effectively burdens religious speech. We agree with First Covenant's reasoning. The relationship between theological doctrine and architectural design is well recognized.

---

9. See cases collected in *Smith II, 494 U.S. at 881–82. See also American Friends Serv. Comm'ty Corp.,* 941 F.2d at 810–11; *Health Servs. Div., Health & Env't Dep't v. Temple Baptist Church, supra* at 265–66; *State v. Hershberger,* 462 N.W.2d 393, 396 (Minn. 1990).

*** The exterior and the interior of the structure are inextricably related. When, as in this case, both are "freighted with religious meaning" that would be understood by those who view it, then the regulation of the church's exterior impermissibly infringes on the religious organization's right to free exercise and free speech. ***

In summary, *** First Covenant's case is distinguishable from *Smith* II because *Smith* II is a police power case and this case is not. The less protective free exercise standard set forth in *Smith* II, therefore, does not apply to First Covenant's claim. The City's preservation ordinances, unlike the statutes in *Smith* II, are not neutral and generally applicable. Further, *Smith* II does not apply because the case presents a "hybrid situation": First Covenant's claim involves the free exercise clause in conjunction with free speech. The *Sherbert* Court's "compelling interest" test, therefore, applies to the justiciable controversy before us.

Applying the *Sherbert* "compelling interest" test, we address the church's contention that subjecting it to the controls of the Landmarks Preservation Ordinance burdens its right to freely exercise religion *** in two ways. The ordinances burden free exercise "administratively" because they require that First Covenant seek the approval of a government body before it alter the exterior of its house of worship, whether or not the alteration is for a religious reason. *** Further, they burden First Covenant financially, because they reduce the value of the Church's property by almost half....

The City alleges that financial burdens do not violate the First Amendment, under *Jimmy Swaggart Ministries v. Board of Equalization,* 493 U.S. 378, 110 S.Ct. 688, 107 L.Ed.2d 796 (1990). The City is mistaken: *Swaggart* does not control this case. *Swaggart* held that imposition of California's sales and use tax on the in-state sales of Jimmy Swaggart Ministries did not violate the free exercise clause because the sales tax was not a "precondition to the exercise of evangelistic activity" and was more "akin to a generally applicable income or property tax". *** The Court warned, however, "a more onerous tax rate, even if generally applicable" might violate the constitution if it too severely impeded religious activity. ***

After *Swaggart,* the State may impose on religious activity a neutral, generally applicable tax that does not act as a prior restraint on religious conduct. *** It is clear, however, that a financial burden on religious activity, if too gross, may unconstitutionally infringe on free exercise *** Designation of First Covenant's church so grossly diminishes the value of the Church's principal asset that it impermissibly burdens First Covenant's right to free exercise of religion.

The City urges that the "liturgy exemption" alleviates any burden on the exercise of religion. We do not believe that the exemption cures either the "administrative" or the financial infringements of First Covenant's right to free exercise.

First, the plain and ordinary meaning of the term "liturgy", which we employ absent a statutory definition of that term, ... does not provide a workable standard that protects the constitutional rights of the church. *** Secondly, adopting the City's interpretation of the phrase "necessitated by changes in liturgy" as meaning "for religious purposes" does not resolve the ambiguity. *First Covenant, supra* at 406, 787

P.2d 1352. The City still has the right to determine what is or what is not for a religious purpose and it acknowledged at argument that it reserved the right to determine if the "religious purpose" claim was "bona fide". ***

Ordinance 112425 also requires that First Covenant seek the City's approval before it alters its church, even for presumptively valid "liturgical" purposes. The exemption states that if the Church proposes an alteration "necessitated by changes in liturgy", "the Board and owner shall jointly explore such possible alternative design solutions as may be appropriate or necessary to preserve the designated features of the landmark." The requirement that the Church negotiate with the City constitutes unjustified governmental interference in religious matters and infringes First Covenant's right to free exercise.

Finally, the liturgy exemption does not mitigate the financial burden that designation imposes on First Covenant. Regardless of how the exemption is construed, the Church suffers the same dramatic depreciation in the value of its property and principal asset. In sum, the liturgy exemption does not cure the infringement of free exercise by the Landmarks Preservation Ordinance.

If government action burdens the exercise of religion, but the State demonstrates that it has a compelling interest in enforcing its enactment, that interest will justify the infringement of First Amendment rights. *Sherbert,* 374 U.S. at 406–07, 83 S.Ct. at 1795–96. *** We hold that the City's interest in preservation of esthetic and historic structures is not compelling and it does not justify the infringement of First Covenant's right to freely exercise religion. The possible loss of significant architectural elements is a price we must accept to guarantee the paramount right of religious freedom.

Upon further consideration, in light of *Smith* II, we conclude that applying the City's preservation ordinances to First Covenant's church violates the church's right to freely exercise religion under the First Amendment.

Although we might distinguish this case from *Smith* II, and base our decision solely on federal grounds, we decline to do so. Like the *State v. Hershberger,* 462 N.W.2d 393 (Minn.1990) court, we eschew the "uncertainty" of *Smith* II and rest our decision also on independent grounds under the Washington constitution. *** Washington, like all the states, may provide greater protection for individual rights, based on its " 'sovereign right to adopt in its own Constitution individual liberties more expansive than those conferred by the Federal Constitution.' " *State v. Gunwall,* 106 Wash.2d 54, 59, 720 P.2d 808, 76 A.L.R.4th 517 (1986). Six nonexclusive factors, set forth in *State v. Gunwall, supra,* are relevant in determining whether the Washington State Constitution extends broader rights to citizens than the federal constitution:

1. The textual language of the state constitution;
2. Significant differences in the texts of parallel provisions of the federal and state constitutions;
3. State constitutional and common-law history;

4. Preexisting bodies of state law, including statutory law;
5. Differences in structure between the federal and the state constitutions; and
6. Matters of particular state interest or local concern.

Gunwall, at 61–62, 720 P.2d 808. *** The criteria suggests to counsel where briefing might appropriately be directed and helps insure that, if this court uses independent state constitutional grounds, it considers these criteria. *State v. Gunwall, supra* at 61–62, 720 P.2d 808. *** First Covenant cites *Gunwall,* and its argument is complete enough that we will address the state free exercise claim.

Article 1, section 11, of the Washington State Constitution provides that:

> Absolute freedom of conscience in all matters of religious sentiment, belief, and worship, shall be guaranteed to every individual, and no one shall be molested or disturbed in person or property on account of religion; but the liberty of conscience hereby secured shall not be so construed as to excuse acts of licentiousness or justify practices inconsistent with the peace and safety of the state.

* * *

The text of the state constitution focuses both on belief and on conduct, as evidenced in the terms "worship", "acts", and "practices". Article 1 clearly protects both belief and conduct. *** The language of our state constitution is significantly different and stronger than the federal constitution. The First Amendment limits government action that "prohibits" free exercise. Our state provision "absolutely" protects freedom of worship and bars conduct that merely "disturbs" another on the basis of religion. Any action that is not licentious or inconsistent with the "peace and safety" of the state is "guaranteed" protection.* * *

The United States Constitution is a grant of limited power, authorizing the federal government to exercise only those constitutionally enumerated powers that the States expressly delegate to it. Our state constitution imposes limitations on the otherwise plenary power of the State to do anything not expressly forbidden by the state constitution or federal law. *Gunwall,* 106 Wash.2d at 66, 67, 720 P.2d 808. This also supports construing article 1, section 11, more broadly, to protect free exercise.

Finally, recalling that the *Gunwall* factors are not exclusive, resort to independent state law is appropriate because *Smith* II is "uncertain". The majority's analysis in *Smith* II departs from a long history of established law and adopts a test that places free exercise in a subordinate, instead of preferred, position. *** Finally, the majority in *Smith* II accepts the fact that its rule places minority religions at a disadvantage. Our court, conversely, has rejected the idea that a political majority may control a minority's right of free exercise through the political process. *** Analysis based on the *Gunwall* factors clearly demonstrates that resort to independent state grounds is warranted in this case.

Article 1, section 11 of the state constitution absolutely protects "freedom of conscience in all matters of religious sentiment, belief, and worship" and guarantees that "no one shall be molested or disturbed in person or property on account of religion". This constitutional guaranty of free exercise is "of vital importance." *** State action is constitutional under the free exercise clause of article 1 if the action results in no infringement of a citizen's right or if a compelling state interest justifies any burden on the free exercise of religion. *** The State also must demonstrate that the means chosen to achieve its compelling interest are necessary and the least restrictive available. ***

Seattle's ordinances, as discussed fully in our First Amendment analysis, impose unconstitutional administrative and financial burdens on First Covenant's free exercise of religion. The "liturgy exception" in the designation ordinance does not alleviate the harm. As detailed in our analysis of First Covenant's federal right to free exercise, the exemption standard is vague, the exemption still requires that the Church seek secular approval before making religiously motivated changes to its facade, and the exemption does not alleviate the adverse financial impact of designation on First Covenant. *** Finally, a compelling state interest does not justify the impermissible burden. Application of the Landmarks Preservation Ordinance is not necessary to prevent a grave danger to the public health, peace, or welfare[.] *** Interests, such as preservation of significant structures, are not "of sufficient magnitude to outweigh" the free exercise of religion.

We conclude that imposing the City's Landmarks Preservation Ordinance on First Covenant's church violates First Covenant's right to free exercise of religion under article 1, section 11 of our state constitution. * * *

Conclusion

1. Imposing the City's Landmarks Preservation Ordinance on First Covenant's church violates First Covenant's right to free exercise of religion under the First Amendment.

2. The Supreme Court's decision in *Smith* II does not compel a different result. *Smith* II considered the application of neutral, generally applicable criminal laws to religious conduct. Seattle's Landmarks Preservation Ordinances are not neutral or generally applicable. The First Amendment freedom of religion claim in *Smith* II did not include other protected rights, like freedom of speech. First Covenant's First Amendment claim joins both a protected interest in the free exercise of religion and in free speech. *Smith* II is distinguishable from this case.

3. *St. Bartholomew's* does not control our First Amendment analysis. St. Bartholomew's embraced designation as a landmark building without objection; did not seek an exception for its house of worship, but an adjacent building; did not allege that designation reduced its principal asset; and *St. Bartholomew's* did not consider the constitutionality of a liturgy-based religious exemption. First Covenant, conversely, objected continuously to designation; sought an exception for its house of worship; demonstrated that designation grossly reduced the value of the church's principal asset; and First Covenant challenged the constitutionality of a liturgy-based religious exception.

4. Article 1, section 11, of our state constitution, which absolutely protects the free exercise of religion, extends broader protection than the First Amendment of the federal constitution and precludes the City from imposing its Landmarks Preservation Ordinance on First Covenant's church.***

UTTER, J. [with whom DURHAM, GUY and JOHNSON, JJ. Join] (concurring).

I agree with the majority's conclusion that application of the Seattle Landmarks Preservation Ordinance *** to the First Covenant Church of Seattle violates the First Amendment of the United States Constitution and article 1, § 11 of the Washington State Constitution. The majority persuasively demonstrates that the United States Supreme Court's opinion in *Employment Div., Dep't of Human Resources v. Smith,* 494 U.S. 872, 110 S.Ct. 1595, 108 L.Ed.2d 876 (1990), does not compel a different result. Nonetheless, I write separately to emphasize certain facts which require this result and to set forth federal and state constitutional standards we should apply in future cases.

II

The application of the Ordinance to First Covenant's church is unconstitutional for two reasons. First, as indicated by the majority, it impacts the expression of religious beliefs. *** Second, it substantially interferes with the carrying out of the Church's religious or charitable purpose by substantially diminishing the value of its principal asset.

Although financial burdens on religious entities do not constitute a per se free exercise violation, the United States Supreme Court has indicated that an onerous financial burden can violate the First Amendment. *** [Additionally, w]e have previously found financial burdens on churches may raise free exercise issues. In *Sumner v. First Baptist Church,* 97 Wash.2d 1, 639 P.2d 1358 (1982), we held that the application of a building code ordinance to a church school presented a free exercise claim. Here the magnitude of the financial burden is severe enough to persuade me that landmark designation violates the church's right to free exercise. *** For future cases, I still believe we should require a specific showing of hardship to justify exemption from land use restrictions. We should follow New York's courts by requiring a landmark designation not prevent or seriously interfere with the carrying out of a church's religious and charitable purposes. ***

III

The factors we outlined in *State v. Gunwall,* 106 Wash.2d 54, 59, 720 P.2d 808 (1986), support the majority's conclusion that Const. art. 1, § 11 guarantees greater religious freedom than its federal counterpart. *** Unlike the majority, I would devote more attention to the rich language of Const. art. 1, § 11. A truly independent state constitutional discourse cannot occur if we resort solely to federal jurisprudence in defining rights protected under our state constitution. *** Accordingly, I offer an alternative to the majority's analysis of Const. art. 1, § 11 which focuses on the unique text of that provision.

The majority correctly notes that words such as worship, acts, and practices indicate both belief and religiously motivated conduct are protected under our state constitution. *** The language of Const. art. 1, § 11 indicates the drafters considered religious belief and practice to be closely related. *** For two additional reasons, protection of religious liberty is stronger under Const. art. 1, § 11 than under the free exercise clause of the First Amendment. First, Const. art. 1, § 11 grants Washington citizens affirmative rights that are absolute. The free exercise clause of the First Amendment only limits government action at the point of prohibiting the exercise of religion. It provides that "Congress shall make no law respecting an establishment of religion, or *prohibiting* the free exercise thereof; ..." *** U.S. Const. amend. 1. Thus, the text of Const. art. 1, § 11 indicates we should start with the assumption that government may not interfere with sincerely held religious belief and religious practice.

Second, Const. art. 1, § 11 expressly limits the governmental interests that may outweigh the otherwise absolute right to religious liberty. Only the government's interest in peace and safety or in preventing licentious acts can excuse an imposition on religious liberty. ***

> Conversely, the free exercise clause of the first amendment has been interpreted to allow varied government interests to justify such an imposition. *** Therefore, landmark designation of the church is only valid if it furthers one of the limited, countervailing governmental interests listed in Const. art. 1, § 11: preventing licentious practices or acts that are inconsistent with peace and safety in our state.

*** Historic preservation does not prevent licentious behavior, or ensure peace or safety. While the Ordinance has a very noble aim, it simply does not further one of the limited governmental interests that the drafters of our state constitution thought important enough to infringe on religious liberty. ***

DOLLIVER, J. (dissenting).

I cannot agree with the majority's conclusions that *Employment Div., Dep't of Human Resources v. Smith,* (*Smith II*) 494 U.S. 872, 110 S.Ct. 1595, 108 L.Ed.2d 876 (1990) does not apply to this case and that the Landmarks Preservation Ordinance *** and the implementing ordinance *** violate First Covenant's right of free exercise under the federal constitution and article 1, section 11 of the state constitution. Therefore, I dissent.

In *Smith II,* the court held the First Amendment did not place the religiously motivated use of peyote beyond the reach of a criminal law which was not specifically directed at that religious practice. To do so would be contrary to First Amendment jurisprudence which has never "relieved the individual from obedience to a general law not aimed at the promotion or restriction of religious beliefs." *Smith II,* 494 U.S. at 879, 110 S.Ct. 1595 ***. The First Amendment is not offended "if prohibiting the exercise of religion ... is not the *object* of the [regulation] but merely the incidental effect of a generally applicable and otherwise valid provision ..." *** *Smith II,* 494

U.S. at 878, 110 S.Ct. at 1600. Thus, the Court held neutral, generally applicable laws which only incidentally affect religiously motivated action and which do not involve other constitutional protections, do not offend the free exercise of religion. ***

The Landmarks Preservation Ordinance and its implementing ordinance, like the criminal prohibition against peyote use in *Smith II,* are neutral, generally applicable laws which do not involve other constitutional protections. The ordinances apply neutrally and generally to protect an object, site or improvement which is more than 25 years old and which "has significant character, interest or value, as part of the development, heritage or cultural characteristics of the City, state, or nation". SMC 25.12.350. While the landmark ordinances will affect many religious buildings because of their social and cultural importance, this does not demonstrate a lack of neutrality or general applicability. *** Indeed, the majority admits the designation criteria in the Landmarks Preservation Ordinance are neutral. Majority, at 180.

The majority, however, asserts the implementing ordinance's two references to "liturgy", which provide an *exemption* for religiously motivated exterior changes, transform the otherwise neutral ordinance into a non-neutral one. *** The irony, even the perversity, of this position is apparent. The Court in *Smith II* recognized the role the political process could and has played by providing exemptions in generally applicable laws for religiously motivated practices. *Smith II,* 494 U.S. at 890, 110 S.Ct. at 1606. Particularly, the Court endorsed legislatures which had made, even though it was not constitutionally required, "nondiscriminatory religious-practice exemption[s]" in their criminal drug laws for "sacramental peyote use". *Smith II,* 494 U.S. at 890, 110 S.Ct. at 1606. In this case, the Landmarks Preservation Ordinance makes no reference to religious facilities. Only the implementing ordinance, which must necessarily focus on the designated church site, is deemed not neutral because of its exception for liturgically required exterior changes. Yet, the majority uses this exemption as the reason the landmark ordinances fail the neutrality test! Incredible. This is bootstrapping of the most egregious nature.

Next, the majority contends the Seattle landmark ordinances are not generally applicable and characterize them as being similar to laws in the unemployment compensation field, which remains the only context in which the Court has invalidated laws under the compelling governmental interest test set forth in *Sherbert v. Verner,* 374 U.S. 398, 83 S.Ct. 1790, 10 L.Ed.2d 965 (1963) (*Sherbert* test). Majority, at 181. This majority position sweeps broader than *Smith II* justifies, is contrary to the application of *Smith II* by other courts in land use cases, and misconstrues the landmark ordinances as involving a system of individualized exemptions.

In *Smith II,* the court attempted to create a cohesive context of free exercise jurisprudence. *** In so doing, the Court stated the *Sherbert* test had been used in the past to invalidate laws only in the unemployment compensation field but that "[i]n recent years we have abstained from applying the *Sherbert* test (outside the unemployment compensation field) at all." *Smith II,* 494 U.S. at 883, 110 S.Ct. at 1602 (test not used in social security, governmental logging and construction, military dress, and prison contexts). *** Although *Smith II* concerned a challenge to a criminal prohibition, the majority recognizes that *Smith II* applies in both civil and criminal cases. *See* majority, at 180 n. 7. Because this case does not involve unemployment compensation and does involve the City's ability to carry out its public policy, the majority's assumption that the *Sherbert* test even applies in this context is erroneous. ***

The legal issue in *St. Bartholomew's* is virtually identical to that presented here. In *St. Bartholomew's,* the New York City Landmarks Preservation Commission denied the church's application to demolish a building designated as a landmark to construct a commercial office tower in its place. The building was designated a landmark pursuant to religion-neutral designation criteria similar to the ordinance in this case. *** Once designated, the Commission had to approve any alteration or demolition of the building designated as a landmark. *** The court held *Smith II* applied, noted the landmark law would affect many religious buildings, but concluded the law was a valid, neutral regulation of general applicability because there was no "evidence of an intent to discriminate against, or impinge on, religious belief in the designation of landmark sites." *St. Bartholomew's,* 914 F.2d at 354. Similarly, First Covenant has presented no evidence of such discriminatory intent.

The majority's attempt to distinguish *St. Bartholomew's* on the facts is unconvincing. Free exercise, if applicable at all in the landmark preservation arena, should not depend on when a church objects to a regulation, whether the affected building is an adjunct or a main church building, or whether the claimed financial restrictions are characterized as a reduction in market value or revenue generation. Majority, at 181. These matters are simply irrelevant under the *Smith II* analysis. Moreover, the landmark law in *St. Bartholomew's* did not have an exception for alterations required by liturgy, which is present here. *** Even assuming secular design regulation of the exterior of a church violates free speech, which I am far from convinced it does, the landmark ordinances cannot restrict the church's expression of religious belief because the City has agreed that exterior changes required by liturgy are removed from the landmark regulations.

The church has also failed to show how the Seattle ordinances burden their free exercise, either administratively or financially. The administrative burden the majority asserts impermissibly burdens free exercise boils down to the City's ability to "bring the Church and the religious question [whether the exterior change has a bona fide liturgical base] before the courts". Majority, at 184. This results because the exception endorses liturgically based exterior changes and places exclusive authority in the church to determine when changes are required by liturgy. *** The City has agreed that exterior changes necessitated by liturgy are exempted from normal landmark regulations. ***

Once the true nature of the majority's purported "administrative burden" is properly understood, it is apparent that it is not the type of burden which is protected by the First Amendment. Although, clearly, courts will not presume "to question the *centrality* of particular beliefs or practices to a faith" ***, no court has stretched the free exercise clause to the point where establishing *the fact of religious motivation* for conduct, or, in this case, a liturgical base for an exterior change, is considered, by itself, a religious hardship. Those wishing to shield their conduct under the First Amendment from otherwise valid governmental regulation must first show they merit its broad protections. *** To hold otherwise, as does the majority, would indeed "permit every citizen to become a law unto himself." ***

The church has also failed to show an unconstitutional financial burden. First, the alleged reduction in market value caused by the designation is a disputed fact in this case. The reduction is based upon one appraisal, which is disputed by the City, and which was never the subject of fact finding by the trial court. Even if the reduction is taken as fact, the church has not shown the alleged reduction prohibits or interferes with religious practice. ***

Lastly, I would find no violation of article 1, section 11 of the Washington State Constitution. As discussed above, the administrative burden of showing that an exterior change has, in fact, a liturgical base is not a burden which the First Amendment or article 1, section 11 of the Washington State Constitution can protect. The church must be required to show that its conduct falls within the protections afforded by the First Amendment and article 1, section 11 of the Washington State Constitution. *** In addition, the church has failed to show the Seattle landmark ordinances create an impermissible financial burden under Const. art. 1, § 11; the reduction in market value is a disputed fact and the church has presented no evidence the alleged reduction interferes with its religious practice. ***

I would hold the landmark ordinances are neutral, generally applicable laws which neither implicate the free exercise clause of the First Amendment nor violate article 1, section 11 of the Washington State Constitution. The protections afforded by the federal and state religion clauses are not properly invoked when a claimant has not been denied the ability to practice his religion or coerced in the nature of those practices. To hold the religion clauses applicable in this context denigrates their true meaning and unjustifiably limits the City's efforts to preserve the cultural assets of the City in the interest of the general welfare. ***

Smith and Brachtenbach, JJ., concur.

Notes and Questions

1. **Character of historic preservation laws.** Rather than apply *Smith* categorically, the court found grounds on which to distinguish it, as well as grounds under state law to invalidate the historic preservation laws as they applied to religious property. a. Is the court's characterization of historic preservation laws correct? b. While not every property contains the general historical merit to warrant designation, for those that do, are the rules the same? c. Are these ordinances any different from those specifying minimum square footage or limiting particular uses in specific zones, that would apply to religious and secular property alike?

2. **Compelling governmental interest.** Whether the governmental objective is compelling, so as to allow some incursion into fundamental rights, does not derive from some fixed list of interests. Rather, it is determined on a case by case basis. Long ago,

Justice Rehnquist acknowledged that there is no constitutional guide to the derivation of compelling interests. *Weber v. Aetna Casualty and Surety Co.*, 406 U.S. 164, 181 (1972) (Rehnquist, J., dissenting). The Court has recognized a range of interests as compelling, including national security, *Haig v. Agee*, 453 U.S. 280 (1981) (outweighing right to travel), avoiding appearances of corruption, *Buckley v. Valeo*, 424 U.S. 1 (1976) (outweighing first amendment rights), interests in health, *Roe v. Wade*, 410 U.S. 113 (1973) (outweighing unrestricted right to abortion), protection of children, *Prince v. Massachusetts*, 321 U.S. 158, 166–67 (1944) (outweighing religious liberty), labor relations, *United Mine Workers v. Gibbs*, 383 U.S. 715 (1966) (interest in avoiding labor violence outweighing freedom of association). In *Nixon v. Administrator of Gen. Servs.*, 433 U.S. 425, 452–54 (1977), the Court recognized the interest in the preservation of historic materials for policy evaluation, litigation, and public confidence that overrode the interest in private property and privacy. In another instance, the Court has also found the interest in eradicating the continuing effects of past discrimination as a compelling governmental interest. *Fullilove v. Klutznick*, 448 U.S. 448, 496 (1980) (Powell, J., concurring) (resting on the due process and equal protection clauses of the Fifth and Fourteenth Amendments); *Regents of the Univ. of Cal. v. Bakke*, 438 U.S. 265, 311–15 (1978) (Powell, J.) (resting on the First Amendment as well as the equal protection clause). *See generally*, Stephen E. Gottlieb, *Compelling Governmental Interests: An Essential But Unanalyzed Term In Constitutional Adjudication*, 68 B.U.L. Rev. 917 (1988).

3. **Special values in religious structures.** a. What are the particular historic values in religious structures whose protection should be viewed as compelling? b. How do these weigh against any religious injunctions on the use and care of the property of these institutions? c. What other kinds of accommodations between the religious institution and the city might be worked out to facilitate protection?

Keeler v. Mayor & City of Cumberland

United States District Court for the District of Maryland

940 F. Supp. 879 (1996)

Smalkin, D.J. This action is before the Court on the plaintiffs' motion for summary judgment on Counts II, III, VI, VII and IX of their amended complaint. The defendants have opposed the motion. The issues having been fully briefed, no oral hearing is necessary. Local Rule 105.6 (D.Md.).

Factual and Procedural Background

The plaintiffs in this action, Cardinal William H. Keeler, Roman Catholic Archbishop of Baltimore, and Sts. Peter and Paul's Roman Catholic Congregation, Inc. (collectively "the Church"), sue the City of Cumberland for permission to demolish a monastery and a chapel which the plaintiffs deem to be "a draining financial liability." *** The Church seeks to replace the old monastery and chapel, both of which are in disrepair, with smaller, modern facilities, and to add gardens and a parking lot. Because the church buildings are part of Cumberland's Washington Street Historic District, however, the Church cannot demolish them without first securing a Certificate of Appropriateness from the Cumberland Historic Preservation Commission. The Church applied to the Commission for such a certificate but its application was denied. This litigation followed.

In a ten-count complaint filed on January 18, 1996, the Church alleged that the City's refusal to issue the Certificate of Appropriateness violated its rights under the First, Fifth and Fourteenth Amendments to the United States Constitution and under corresponding provisions of the Maryland Declaration of Rights. In Count I of the complaint, the Church also alleged a cause of action arising under the Religious Freedom Restoration Act of 1993, 42 U.S.C. § 2000bb (RFRA). The City moved to dismiss the complaint in its entirety. On June 10, 1996, this Court granted the City's motion with respect to Count I because RFRA, which forms the basis of the Church's cause of action in that Count, violates the constitutional principle of separation of powers. *Keeler v. Mayor & City Council of Cumberland,* 928 F.Supp. 591 (D.Md. 1996). The Court denied the City's motion with respect to the remaining counts.

The Church now seeks summary judgment on the following counts of the complaint: Counts II and III, which allege violations of Free Exercise Rights protected by the Constitution of the United States and by the Maryland Declaration of Rights; Counts VI and VII, which allege that the City took the Church's property without just compensation, in violation of the state and federal constitutions; and Count IX, which alleges that the Historic Preservation Committee's actions violated state statutory law. [Additionally,] the Church seeks an order directing the City to issue a Certificate of Appropriateness for the demolition of the monastery, a declaratory judgment, money damages, its attorney's fees, and other proper relief.

* * *

Count—X—Violations of the Enabling Statute

The Church contends that Cumberland's historic zoning ordinances violate Maryland law because they grant to the City of Cumberland authority which exceeds that contemplated by the enabling statute, Md.Ann.Code art. 66B, §§ 8.01 *et seq*. Because "[a] fundamental and longstanding principle of judicial restraint requires that courts avoid reaching constitutional questions in advance of the necessity of deciding them," *** and because a decision favorable to the Church on the statutory issue would render consideration of the constitutional claims unnecessary, this Court must first address the Church's arguments under Count IX.

According to the Church, "the very part of the [Cumberland] Ordinance relied on by Defendants to reject Plaintiffs' application was different than [sic] and contrary to the relevant state enabling statute." *** The Church refers to section 7.c. of Ordinance No. 2970, which addresses those situations in which, because a building is deemed to be of particular historical importance, the Historic Preservation Commission is authorized to negotiate with the owners to formulate an economically feasible use for the property. *** Section 7.c. provides, in part, as follows:

> In the event that the commission and the owner are unable to reach either an economically feasible plan for preservation or any other means of preserving the building, and unless in these circumstances the commission is satisfied that the proposed ... alteration ... will not materially impair the historic value of the structure, the commission shall reject the application.

Applying §7.c. in the present case, the Commission denied the Church's application for permission to demolish the Monastery after the Commission had "concluded that the structures at issue are of unusual importance and no economically feasible plan can be formulated for their preservation." ***

*** Specifically, the Church argues that Article 66B, §8.09 of the Maryland Code, which pertains to buildings deemed to be of unusual importance, precludes the City from rejecting applications for demolition where there is no economically feasible plan to preserve the property. The statute provides, in pertinent part, as follows:

> (a) If an application is submitted for reconstruction or alterations affecting the exterior appearance of a structure ... the preservation of which the commission deems of unusual importance..., the commission shall attempt with the owner of the structure to formulate an economically feasible plan for the preservation of the structure. Unless in these circumstances the commission is satisfied that the proposed [alteration] will not materially impair the historic value of the structure, the commission shall reject the application....
>
> (b) If an application is submitted for reconstruction, alteration, or for moving or demolition of a structure that the commission deems of unusual importance and no economically feasible plan can be formulated, the commission shall have ninety days ... to negotiate with the owner and other parties in an effort to find a means of preserving the building.

Md.Ann.Code art. 66B, §8.09. According to the Church, §8.09 treats buildings for which there is no economically feasible means of preservation quite differently from buildings which can feasibly be preserved. The Church argues that the statute must be read to grant local commissions the authority to reject applications only if there is an economically feasible way to preserve the property. According to the Church, §8.09 requires local commissions to grant such applications if there is no economically feasible preservation plan. *** The enabling statute, however, does not so provide, whether expressly or by necessary implication**

Contrary to the Church's contentions, the statute simply does not provide that applications must be granted at the end of the ninety-day period if no plan is formulated. Neither is such a gloss on the statute "the only reasonable interpretation of the law," as the Church suggests. *** In sharp contrast to the General Assembly's explicit command that applications to make alterations must be denied if an economically feasible means of preserving the building can be found, the legislature is silent with regard to a local commission's choice of outcome when no such plan can be made. ***

The issue before the Court is whether Cumberland's zoning ordinances are illegal because the City has exceeded the legislative authority granted to it in Article 66B. The Cumberland Ordinance is consistent with the plain language of the enabling statute. Although the Church has identified some ambiguity in § 8.09 of Article 66B, the statute is silent on the precise point at issue. This Court therefore declines to hold, as a matter of law, that the City of Cumberland violated Maryland law when it enacted Ordinance 2970. Accordingly, the Church's motion for summary judgment on Count IX will be denied.

Count II—Free Exercise under the First Amendment

The Church contends that the City of Cumberland's refusal to permit demolition of the Monastery impermissibly infringes upon its parishioners' right to the free exercise of the Catholic religion. Specifically, the Church argues[, that they "have a religious obligation to place the spiritual needs of the faithful entrusted to their care above concern for the preservation of a dilapidated building[.] *** Demolition of the Monastery is the cornerstone of the Parish's plans to improve worship at the Parish, to increase accessibility to worship and other religious services for the handicapped, elderly and other parishioners, and to use its property as an expression of religious belief."

*** In support of this position, the Church has submitted affidavits from several of its officials. *** The City characterizes the Church's evidentiary support as "a number of self-serving affidavits from various individuals as to the perceived impact upon them of the Historic Commission's decision to deny the certificate." *** The City seems to suggest that this Court should regard the affidavits with suspicion, in part because they represent a subjective belief that there is a religious aspect to the Church's decision to demolish the Monastery.

Under the circumstances of this case, however, this Court has no authority to disregard the affiants' declaration of their beliefs. After all, what is the First Amendment about if not about one's subjective beliefs? (This Court has yet to encounter any objective beliefs.)

As the Supreme Court emphatically stated in *Employment Division, Dept. of Human Resources of Oregon v. Smith,* 494 U.S. 872, 110 S.Ct. 1595, 108 L.Ed.2d 876 (1990) ("*Smith II*"), "[r]epeatedly and in many different contexts, we have warned that courts must not presume to determine the place of a particular belief in a religion or the plausibility of a religious claim." 494 U.S. at 887, 110 S.Ct. at 1604 (collecting Supreme Court cases). *** In a free exercise case that raises questions about the content of individuals' religious beliefs, therefore, a court may assess only the sincerity of the professed beliefs, and must leave aside the question of their truth. *** The City does not contend that the views expressed in the affidavits of the clergy and the parishioners are anything but sincere. Indeed, the record is entirely devoid of evidence that might support any such allegation. Consequently, the City's denial of the Certificate of Appropriateness infringes upon the Church's free exercise rights if the affidavits, taken as true, reveal that the demolition of the Monastery implicates elements of the Roman Catholic religion.

The Church in the present case asserts that Roman Catholic law, teaching and tradition require it to replace the old Monastery with facilities more appropriate to its liturgical needs. Msgr. Schleupner, who holds a graduate degree in Canon Law, states in his affidavit that "the Monastery is ecclesiastical property that must be administered in pursuit of the proper ends of the Church." *** Because of Cumberland's refusal to issue the Certificate of Appropriateness, however, the Church cannot choose to demolish the Monastery and to release funds for the construction of more modern facilities. According to Msgr. Schleupner, "to be denied the capacity of making the concrete, practical choices that will most appropriately reflect the community's discernment of God's will is to be substantially burdened in the free exercise of an incarnational and sacramental religion" such as Catholicism. ***

In a similar vein, *** Cardinal Keeler stated that "the construction and renovation plans for the Sts. Peter and Paul Parish are motivated by our sincerely-held Catholic beliefs regarding worship, ministry, association, education, expression and church administration." *** Numerous parishioners also submitted affidavits explaining that the existing buildings fail to satisfy the needs of the congregation, and that the new construction is crucial to the spiritual growth of the parish. ***

The affidavits clearly describe a sincerely-held belief that the Monastery must be demolished and replaced as part of the Church's Roman Catholic mission. This Court is not empowered to question the validity of that belief. Under the circumstances, the Church has established, as a matter of law, that its decision to demolish the Monastery involves the exercise of the Roman Catholic faith and implicates First Amendment free exercise principles.

The First Amendment to the United States Constitution prohibits the government from legislating "an establishment of religion or prohibiting the free exercise thereof." U.S. Const. amend. I. The constitutionality of government regulation that burdens religious practice depends to a large extent upon the neutrality of the regulation with respect to religion, and upon the state's commitment to uniform enforcement of its law. Thus, "a law that is neutral and of general applicability need not be justified by a compelling governmental interest even if the law has the incidental effect of burdening a particular religious practice." *Church of the Lukumi Babalu Aye, Inc. v. City of Hialeah,* 508 U.S. 520, 531, 113 S.Ct. 2217, 2226, 124 L.Ed.2d 472 (1993) (citing *Smith II*). By contrast,

> [a] law burdening religious practice that is not neutral or not of general application must undergo the most rigorous of scrutiny. To satisfy the commands of the First Amendment, a law restrictive of religious practice must advance "'interests of the highest order'" and must be narrowly tailored in pursuit of those interests.

Church of the Lukumi Babalu Aye, 508 U.S. at 546, 113 S.Ct. at 2233. *** In the present action, the City contends that, under the principles set forth in *Smith II,* it has no obligation to treat the Church differently from any other owner of property when enforcing its historic preservation regulations. By contrast, the Church alleges that *Smith II* does not govern this case, because Cumberland's historic preservation ordinance is not a "neutral, generally applicable regulatory law." *Smith II,* 494 U.S. at 880, 110 S.Ct. at 1601. Consequently, according to the Church, Cumberland must invoke a compelling governmental interest to justify its refusal to issue the Certificate of Appropriateness.

In *Smith II,* the Supreme Court held that Oregon could give effect in unemployment compensation proceedings to its criminal law prohibiting the possession of controlled substances, despite that law's effect on individuals' free exercise rights. *** The Supreme Court, however, declined to follow *Sherbert v. Verner,* 374 U.S. 398, 83 S.Ct. 1790, 10 L.Ed.2d 965 (1963), *** which had held a compelling interest standard applicable to government regulation that infringed upon free exercise rights. *** Concluding that the *Sherbert* compelling interest test had been "developed in a context that lent itself to individualized governmental assessment of the reasons for the relevant conduct," the Court in *Smith II* distinguished the prior unemployment cases[.] *** The Court held that where a state uniformly enforces a neutral law of general applicability, the state need not identify a compelling interest served by its legislation. By contrast, "where the State has in place a system of individualized exemptions, it may not refuse to extend that system to cases of 'religious hardship' without compelling reason." *** Consequently, to the extent that Cumberland's historic zoning laws provide for a "system" of exemptions and exceptions, the free exercise analysis requires application of principles other than those set forth in *Smith II.*

Cumberland City ordinance No. 2970 provides for the establishment of a Historic Preservation Commission. Ordinance 2970, § 3. The Commission is empowered to designate historic districts. *Id.,* § 5. In addition, a Certificate of Appropriateness must be sought and received from the Commission before any person may "commence[ ] any reconstruction, alteration or removal of any exterior feature, or commence[ ] any change in the exterior color ... or commence[ ] the demolition of any structures ... in any Architectural and Historic Preservation District." *Id.,* § 6.a. If the application for alteration or demolition involves "a structure, the preservation of which the commission deems of unusual importance to the City, State or nation," and if no economically feasible plan can be formulated for preservation, then the Commission is empowered to negotiate with the property owners and others in an attempt to preserve the building. *Id.,* § 7.b. Should no such agreement be reached, the Commission must reject the application. *Id.,* § 7.c. Section 7.d., however, lists several circumstances which may suspend the Commission's obligation to reject a § 7.b. application [if]:

> (1) The structure is a deterrent to a major improvement program which will be of substantial benefit to the City of Cumberland;
>
> (2) Retention of the structure would cause undue financial hardship to the owner; or
>
> (3) The retention of the structure would not be to the best interest of a majority of persons in the community.

Ordinance 2970, §7.d. *** Clearly, Cumberland's Historic Preservation Ordinance is significantly different from the "across-the-board criminal prohibition on a particular form of conduct" sustained in *Smith II.* Rather, like the unemployment compensation programs at issue in *Sherbert,* *** the ordinance "has in place a system of individual exemptions." *Smith II,* 494 U.S. at 884, 110 S.Ct. at 1603. *** *Smith II* recognized that where the government enacts a system of exemptions, and thereby acknowledges that its interest in enforcement is not paramount, then the government "may not refuse to extend that system [of exemptions] to cases of 'religious hardship' without compelling reason." 494 U.S. at 884, 110 S.Ct. at 1603 ***. Accordingly, the City's zoning regulation is not entitled to enforcement under the principles set forth in *Smith II.* As a "law restrictive of religious practice," the City of Cumberland's Historic Preservation Ordinance must instead " 'advance interests of the highest order' and be narrowly tailored in pursuit of those interests." *Church of Lukumi Babalu Aye,* 508 U.S. at 546, 113 S.Ct. at 2233.

The City of Cumberland's purposes in enacting Ordinance No. 2970 are stated to be "safeguarding the heritage of the City ...; stabilizing and improving property values ...; fostering civic beauty; strengthening the local economy; and promoting the use and preservation of historic districts and/or sites for the education, welfare and pleasure of the residents of the City." Ord. No. 2970, §1.a. In its opposition to the Church's summary judgment motion, the City nowhere asserts that historic preservation is a compelling interest of government. Courts and commentators are apparently unanimous in opining that it is not. *** In light of these authorities, this Court holds that the City of Cumberland has failed to assert a compelling state interest in support of its Historic Preservation Ordinance.

Accordingly, the Court holds, as a matter of law, that the City's refusal to grant the Church a Certificate of Appropriateness for the demolition of its monastery impermissibly violates the Church's right to the free exercise of religion protected by the First Amendment. The Church is therefore entitled to summary judgment on Count II of the complaint.

*Count—I—Free Exercise under the Maryland Declaration of Rights***

In light of this Court's disposition of the Church's cause of action under the First Amendment, it is unnecessary for the Court to determine the relationship between the First Amendment, as interpreted by *Smith II,* and Article 36 of the Maryland Declaration of Rights. Because the holding of *Smith II* does not directly govern this action, the City must assert a compelling governmental interest for its restriction of the plaintiffs' free exercise rights regardless of whether Article 36 is to be read *in pari materia* with the First Amendment or whether it independently requires strict scrutiny of government action. Because the compelling interest test applies under either view of Maryland law, it would be inappropriate for this Court to decide whether, or to what extent, the Court of Appeals of Maryland would find *Smith II* pertinent to the construction of Article 36 of the Maryland Declaration of Rights. "It is axiomatic that questions of state constitutional law are to be answered by state courts, rather than by the federal judiciary." *Green v. Zendrian,* 916 F.Supp. 493, 498 (D.Md.1996).

Because the City's infringement of the plaintiffs' free exercise rights is prohibited by Article 36 of the Maryland Declaration of Rights unless it is justified by a compelling governmental interest, and because the City has failed to allege such a compelling interest, the plaintiffs are entitled to summary judgment on Count III of their complaint.

Counts VI and VII—Takings under the Fifth & Fourteenth Amendments and under Article III, § 40 of the Constitution of Maryland

The Church alleges that the City's refusal to issue the Certificate of Appropriateness for the demolition of the Monastery requires it to preserve and maintain the Monastery, amounting to an unconstitutional taking of property without just compensation. The Church alleges violations of both the Fifth Amendment to the United States Constitution, as incorporated against the states through the Fourteenth Amendment, and of Articles 19 and 24 of the Maryland Declaration of Rights, the state due process clauses. *** Although the Church does not allude to it. Article III, § 40 of the Maryland Constitution specifically prohibits the enactment of state legislation "authorizing private property[ ] to be taken for public use, without just compensation … being first paid or tendered to the party entitled to such compensation." The Court of Appeals of Maryland has long held that the federal and state takings clauses "have the same meaning and effect in reference to an exaction of property, and that the decisions of the Supreme Court on the Fourteenth Amendment are practically direct authorities" for the construction of state takings claims. *Bureau of Mines of Maryland v. George's Creek Coal & Land Co.,* 272 Md. 143, 156, 321 A.2d 748 (1974). *** Accordingly, the same body of law governs both Count VI and Count VII.

State regulation of property amounts to a taking "where regulation denies all economically beneficial or productive use of land." *Lucas v. South Carolina Coastal Council,* 505 U.S. 1003, 1015, 112 S.Ct. 2886, 2893, 120 L.Ed.2d 798 (1992). *** To amount to a taking, the challenged state regulation must do more than place an economic strain on the landowner; it must "leave his property economically idle," *** or render the property "essentially valueless by government action," ***. The City's refusal to grant the Church a Certificate of Appropriateness for the demolition of the Monastery requires the Church to maintain the Monastery at a safe standard of repair. *** The buildings are undoubtedly in a state of serious disrepair. *** The cost of complete renovation of the Monastery and other buildings was estimated by the Church at "$2,000,000 plus dollars[.]" *** In light of the high cost of all proposed renovations, the City has stipulated that "no economically feasible plan can be formulated" for the preservation of the Church buildings. Under these circumstances, there is no doubt that the application of Cumberland Historic Zoning Ordinances to the Church has rendered the Church property economically useless, and has worked a regulatory taking. Consequently, the Church is entitled to a declaratory judgment that the City's refusal to issue the Certificate of Appropriateness is unconstitutional.

The Fifth Amendment, however, "is designed not to limit the governmental interference with property rights *per se,* but rather to secure *compensation* in the event of otherwise proper interference amounting to a taking." *** Accordingly, the proper remedy for an unconstitutional taking is not an injunction against the government or an order seeking relief from the regulation, but damages. *** In addition to requesting both a declaratory judgment and an order directing the City to issue the Certificate of Appropriateness, the Church has asked for damages "in an amount to be determined." ***

In its complaint the Church made a general request for relief in the form of damages, but it did not ask for damages in its summary judgment motion. Furthermore, the Church's proposed "Order" submitted in connection with the summary judgment motion only requires the City to issue the Certificate of Appropriateness and to pay attorneys' fees. No mention is made of money damages. Nevertheless, the Church has not expressly disavowed its earlier request for damages, and this Court must give it the opportunity to establish its right to compensatory relief, should it so desire. Of course, damages may only be calculated with respect to the actual loss of use experienced by the Church. *** Any issue of future damages is mooted by this Court's finding that the defendants cannot constitutionally continue to require the Church to maintain the property. Because the Church has not presented any evidence that it has yet suffered any provable or compensable economic loss, this Court's Order will offer the Church an opportunity to establish a right to money damages if it elects to do so.

Notes and Questions

1. **The Religious Freedom Restoration Act of 1993.** In response to the Supreme Court's decision in *Employment Division, Dep't. of Human Resources of Oregon v. Smith*, 494 U.S. 872, 110 S.Ct. 1595, 108 L.Ed.2d 876 (1990), Congress passed the Religious Freedom Restoration Act, 42 U.S.C. § 2000bb ("RFRA"). RFRA, as its name suggests, was aimed at preventing laws from substantially burdening the free exercise of religion. Congress became alarmed at the Supreme Court's decision in *Smith* not to apply the strict scrutiny standard of *Sherbert v. Verner*, 374 U.S. 398, 83 S.Ct. 1790 (1963) to any law which adversely effects free exercise of religion. Strict scrutiny would have required that any law hampering the free exercise of religion be justified by a "compelling governmental interest." RFRA purported to require the Supreme Court to apply the strict scrutiny standard in such free exercise cases. That vindication of the religious groups was short-lived because in the landmark decision of *City of Boerne v. Flores*, 521 U.S. 507, 117 S.Ct. 2157 (1997), the Supreme Court invalidated RFRA.

There, Catholic Archbishop Flores of San Antonio, Texas applied for a permit to expand the St. Peter Catholic Church, in Boerne, Texas. *Id.* at 512. The Boerne City Council had passed an ordinance authorizing the Boerne Historic Preservation Commission to designate historic sites and historic districts within the city and to review applications to modify sites within these districts. *Id.* When the Archbishop applied for such a permit, the Commission denied the application, relying on the ordinance and the fact that the Church was located in an historic district. *Id.* In response, the Archbishop filed suit in federal court claiming the denial of the permit ran afoul of RFRA. The District Court found that RFRA was an unconstitutional extension of Congress' § 5 powers under the

Fourteenth Amendment of the Constitution. *City of Boerne v. Flores*, 877 F. Supp. 355 (W.D. Tex. 1995). On interlocutory appeal, the Fifth Circuit Court of Appeals reversed, finding RFRA constitutional. 73 F.3d 1352 (5th Cir. 1996). The Supreme Court reversed the Fifth Circuit decision. 521 U.S. 507 (1997). The Court ruled that Congress had exceeded its powers under the enforcement clause of the Fourteenth Amendment, as it pertained to state and local governments, to the extent that RFRA purported to define rights rather than simply enforce those rights already existing under the Constitution. RFRA aimed to protect churches against the application of laws of general application, a right that does not exist under the Constitution. *Id.* at 519. Also, RFRA swept too broadly, applying to every agency and official, to laws of every description, imposing a tremendous burden on governmental functions. *Id.* at 534–35.

In declaring RFRA unconstitutional, the Court relaxed the scrutiny required of local land use laws, including local historic preservation ordinances, thereby making it easier for local governments to prohibit religious institutions from altering historic buildings for religious purposes, on a national scale. A few years later, however, the situation would change.

2. **The Religious Land Use and Institutionalized Persons Act of 2000.** Shortly after *City of Boerne*, Congress took up the matter of religious freedom in the context of government regulation once more and passed the Religious Land Use and Institutionalized Persons Act of 2000, 42 U.S.C. § 2000 cc-1 ("RLUIPA"). RLUIPA essentially reinstated RFRA in a different guise, using the Spending Clause to require local municipalities to accommodate religious freedom in land use laws in order to receive federal funds. Again, the Act established that for a local government to pass a "land use regulation in a manner that imposes a substantial burden" on religious exercise, there must be a "compelling governmental interest" and the law must use the "least restrictive means" to accomplish its purpose. 42 U.S.C. § 2000 cc-5(a). This applies whenever a "substantial burden is imposed in a program or activity that receives Federal financial assistance." *Id.*

There have been many challenges to the constitutionality of RLUIPA in the district and circuit courts, but all have upheld it. *See* Shelby D. Green, *Zoning In and Out Churches: Limits On Municipal Zoning Powers By The Religious Land Use And Institutionalized Persons Act*, 37 Real Est. L.J. 163 (2008) (discussing how local governments are working around RLUIPA). Even when an historic preservation or zoning law is completely devoid of any discriminatory intent, some courts apply strict scrutiny upon judicial review. In some cases, the ordinances have survived this stringent level of review. One such example is the case of *Episcopal Student Foundation v. City of Ann Arbor*, 341 F. Supp. 2d 691 (E.D. Mich. 2004). There, Canterbury House—a non-profit corporation and instrumentality of the Episcopal Church—filed suit in federal court alleging that the City of Ann Arbor violated RLUIPA by denying a permit to demolish and rebuild Canterbury House because it was located in the Old Fourth Ward Historic District. The religious mission of Canterbury House is to attract members through communal participation in activities; however, its building was not large enough to accommodate the activities of the group. At a public hearing on March 12,

2002, the Historic Commission rejected the permit because "(a) the current building was in good repair, (b) its proposed demolition did not meet the Historic Commission's criteria for granting such permits, and (c) the proposed new building altered the character of the neighborhood, which the Commission believed should be historically preserved." *Id.* at 694–95.

In determining whether this finding violated RLUIPA, the District Court assessed the extent of the "substantial burden" on religious exercise alleged by Canterbury House. The court broke down the jurisprudence concerning the infringement on the free exercise of religion into two categories: 1) "where compliance with the statute itself violates the individual's religious beliefs and non-compliance may subject him to criminal sanctions or the loss of a significant government privilege or benefit," and 2) "where compliance with the challenged regulation makes the practice of one's religion more difficult or expensive, but the regulation is not inherently inconsistent with the litigant's beliefs." *Id.* at 701–02. The District Court found that the burden on Canterbury House (namely not being able to provide a "multi-faceted" facility to fulfill "all of its religious needs") did not rise to the level of the first category of infringements on free exercise of religion. *Id.* at 704. Nothing prevented it from pursuing its religious beliefs, coerced its members into abandoning or violating those beliefs or dissuaded members from practicing their faith. *Id.* Said the court "there is no indication that Canterbury House is precluded from fulfilling its religious mission through worship as a whole, or through its various other activities, in other locations throughout the city." *Id.* The court said that if Canterbury House wanted to expand its activities, it could look toward other real estate in the city. As to the second category, the court found that "although Canterbury House may incur additional financial burdens, such as rental spaces to accommodate its entire congregation, or if it seeks additional growth, such financial burdens are not 'substantial' under RLUIPA." *Id.* at 706. The court granted summary judgment for the city.

3. **Facial challenge to RUILPA.** In *Roman Catholic Bishop of Springfield v. City of Springfield*, 724 F.3d 78 (1st Cir. 2013), the First Circuit rejected a facial challenge under RUILPA on the creation of a single-parcel historic district that encompassed a church that the archdiocese was considering for deconsecration. In 2004, the Roman Catholic Bishop of Springfield ("RCB") began a process of "pastoral planning" to assess the Diocese's financial and human resources on account of declining numbers of clergy and parishioners. The planning included the discontinuation of services at Our Lady of Hope ("Church"), an Italian Renaissance structure built in 1925. Discontinuance would have required the removal of religious ornamentation and perhaps even destruction of the church to prevent their use for "profane" purposes. On news of the pastoral planning process, the historical commission created the single-parcel historical district. The RCB challenged the ordinance on the ground that it interfered with its free speech and religion rights and violated RLUIPA, by intruding on its pastoral planning process, inhibiting future sale, the proceeds of which would benefit the parish, and by imposing continued costs of maintenance, insurance, and security for the church.

The First Circuit rejected the challenges in their entirety. While the ordinance was a "land use regulation" and the deconsecration process, a "religious exercise" within the meaning of RLUIPA, 42 U.S.C. § 2000cc-5(7)(A), the court explained that the mere enactment of the ordinance did not impose a substantial burden on the RCB. *Id.* at 97. The court reviewed the question of whether the ordinance imposed a "substantial burden" *de novo.* While RLUIPA does not define "substantial burden," the background of the statute's enactment provides some indication of Congress's intended meaning. The determination rested upon a number of factors, including whether the regulation appears to target a religion, religious practice, or members of a religious organization because of hostility to that religion itself; whether local regulators have subjected the religious organization to a process that may appear neutral on its face, but in practice is designed to reach a predetermined outcome contrary to the group's requests; whether the land use restriction was "imposed on the religious institution arbitrarily, capriciously, or unlawfully," such as where, for instance, local regulators disregard objective criteria and instead act adversely to a religious organization based on the objections of a "small but influential" group in the community or where local regulators base their decisions on misunderstandings of legal principles. *Id.* at 97–98. Essentially, the court explained, RLUIPA aims to prohibit an ordinance where the context raises an "inference" of hostility to a religious organization, even when the evidence does not necessarily show the explicit discrimination "on the basis of religion" contemplated by subsection (b). No facts here showed such hostility. It did not single out or otherwise target religion, religious practice, or members of the RCB, nor was it imposed on the RCB arbitrarily, capriciously, or unlawfully. Even though the ordinance was not a neutral law of general applicability, because historic districts are specially created and pertain only to particular property in limited areas, it did not single out for special benefit or burden the RCB solely because of its religious beliefs. The ordinance did not target deconsecration as such, but merely required RCB to delay its decisions while the historical commission evaluated its application, a process that would ordinarily take no more than sixty days. *Id.*

The RCB failed to show that the costs of maintaining the church imposed "substantial pressure on [RCB] to modify its behavior" or that any financial burdens were fairly traceable to the Ordinance, since it did not submit evidence of the degree of these expenses, nor of the Church's value before or after passage of the Ordinance.

While the court found troubling circumstances surrounding the enactment of the ordinance—it was proposed only after the news of plans to close the Church, urged by parishioners opposed to the closing decision, and completed in a matter of weeks without fully considering the objections of the church—they were not enough to establish that the ordinance was motivated by religious hostility. Instead, the facts showed that the City's intent in creating the district was to prevent the RCB from following the same path it had taken with another local church, which had been closed, deconsecrated, and sold to a developer who demolished it. It was arguably because the RCB might conclude that demolition of the Church was required that the City chose to intervene. In any event, designating the Church as a single-parcel historic

Chabad Lubavitch Community Center. Photo by Lily Adler, used with permission.

district did not establish a process, apparently neutral, that in fact would result in the denial of any request that the RCB may make to the SHC. *Id.* at 99.

Finally, the court found that that the district was a single-parcel did not mean that the ordinance treated the RCB on less than equal terms with a nonreligious assembly or institution, as proscribed by 42 U.S.C. § 2000cc(b)(1), because the City had over the years enacted a number of historic districts of varying sizes, that often included both secular and religious buildings. *Id.* at 100. The court noted that in *Penn Central Transp. Co. v. New York City*, 438 U.S. 104 (1978), the Supreme Court remarked that landmark laws are not necessarily operating in a discriminatory manner when they single out particular parcels for special treatment. For all the same reasons, the First Amendment challenges were dismissed.

The Second Circuit also found RUILPA was triggered by historic preservation laws in *Chabad Lubavitch of Litchfield Cnty., Inc. v. Litchfield*, 768 F.3d 183 (2d Cir. 2014). Chabad Lubavitch purchased a building in a residential historic district and proposed to modify it for religious and other services. The proposal called for a 17,000 square-foot addition, hanging a double door on the front of the house, and adding a clock tower featuring a Star of David. The historic preservation commission denied Chabad Lubavitch's application for a certificate of appropriateness. Chabad Lubavitch sued, alleging a violation of RLUIPA. The Court of Appeals ruled that the application of the historic preservation law triggered RLUIPA's substantial burdens analysis because the commission applied loosely defined, subjective standards, such as "historical and architectural value and significance."

B. The First Amendment's Freedom of Speech Clause

Globe Newspaper Company v. Beacon Hill Architectural Commission

United States Court of Appeals for the First Circuit
100 F.3d 175 (1996)

TORRUELLA, C.J. *** WE ARE LEFT TO DECIDE IMPORTANT ISSUES THAT REQUIRE A BALANCING BETWEEN FIRST AMENDMENT RIGHTS AND GOVERNMENTAL INTERESTS.

Defendant-Appellant Beacon Hill Architectural Commission (the "Commission") enacted a regulation, the Street Furniture Guideline, which effectively bans newspaper distribution boxes from the public streets of the Historic Beacon Hill District in Boston, Massachusetts (the "District"). The validity of this regulation was challenged in a suit filed in district court by Plaintiffs-Appellees, a group of newspaper publishers (the "Newspapers"). The district court held that the Commission lacked the authority to adopt the regulation and also that it violated rights guaranteed by the First Amendment. *See Globe Newspaper Co. v. Beacon Hill Architectural Comm'n,* 847 F.Supp. 178 (D.Mass. 1994).

In the ensuing appeal by the Commission, we concluded that the appropriate course of action was to certify the dispositive issue of state law to the Supreme Judicial Court of Massachusetts (the "SJC") and so proceeded. To the question

> Did the Beacon Hill Architectural Commission have the authority under 1955 Massachusetts Act Chapter 616 (as amended) to adopt the "Street Furniture Guideline"?

[T]he SJC answered in the affirmative. *See Globe Newspaper Co. v. Beacon Hill Architectural Comm'n,* 421 Mass. 570, 659 N.E.2d 710 (1996). In its response, the SJC held that the Commission had authority to regulate newsracks and other "street furniture" through rulemaking and to completely ban entire classes of structures such as newsracks. *Id.* at 590–91, 659 N.E.2d 710. Specifically, it said:

> *** Regulation of the sidewalks is rationally related to the goal of preserving the Historic Beacon Hill District. *** We conclude that, apart from constitutional considerations, outright bans on certain classes of structures are merely a practical consequence of the [C]ommission's ability to proscribe inappropriate exterior architectural features within the [D]istrict.

Id. We thus focus our attention on the constitutional issue, which requires us to determine whether the Street Furniture Guideline violates rights guaranteed by the First Amendment to the Newspapers. We conclude that it does not and reverse the decision of the district court.

Background

The Historic Beacon Hill District was created by an act of the Massachusetts General Court in 1955 *** ("the Act") ***. The Act is intended to

> promote the educational, cultural, economic and general welfare of the public through the preservation of the historic Beacon Hill district, and to maintain said district as a landmark in the history of architecture and as a tangible reminder of old Boston as it existed in the early days of the commonwealth.

1955 Mass. Acts ch. 616, § 2. The District's historical significance can hardly be doubted. *** Indeed, it was listed in the National Register of Historic Places and designated a National Historic Landmark on October 15, 1966, pursuant to the National Historic Preservation Act of 1966, 16 U.S.C. § 470 *et seq.*

The Commission was created to review proposed changes to the "exterior architectural feature[s]" of "structures" within the District. *** Anyone wishing to construct, reconstruct or alter an exterior architectural feature is required to apply to the Commission for a certificate of appropriateness. The Commission, "[i]n passing upon appropriateness," shall consider, *inter alia,* "the historical and architectural value and significance, architectural style, general design, arrangement, texture, material and color of the exterior architectural feature involved and the relationship thereof to the exterior architectural features of other structures in the immediate neighborhood." 1955 Mass. Acts ch. 616, § 7. Furthermore, the Commission must "spread upon its records the reasons for [its] determination" that a certificate of appropriateness should not issue. *Id.* An aggrieved party may appeal the Commission's decision to the Superior Court for Suffolk County, which "shall annul the determination of the [C]ommission" if it is "unwarranted by the evidence" or "insufficient in law." *Id.* at § 10.

*** "[G]iven the stream of applications for certificates of appropriateness, the Commission developed uniform policies toward certain recurring types of proposed alterations." *Globe Newspaper,* 40 F.3d at 20. Specifically, in 1981, it formally adopted the policies as "guidelines." These guidelines regulate exterior architectural features such as masonry, roofs, windows, sash and shutters, doors, trim, paint, and ironwork. One of the guidelines states that "[f]reestanding signs are not permitted."

In the District, the Newspapers distribute their publications via home delivery, mail, store sales, street vendors, and "newsracks." … Newsracks, we explained, are newspaper distribution boxes painted in various colors and featuring the name of the newspaper and other advertising logos, which are commonly anchored to lampposts, signposts, or fixtures on the sidewalk. The plaintiffs maintain a total of thirty-nine newsracks in the district.… Within the District, there are eleven stores that distribute, or are available to distribute, the Newspapers' publications. Outside the District, but within one block of the District's boundaries, the Newspapers' publications are sold through stores and newsracks.… It is undisputed that no point within the District is more than 1,000 feet (approximately 1/5 of a mile) from a source of the Newspapers' publications.

Newsracks were first introduced to the District in the early 1980s, and by 1983, Beacon Hill residents had begun to complain of the "unsightliness, congestion and inconvenience associated with the vending machines." The Commission believed that the newsracks violated the guideline prohibiting free-standing signs. It took no enforcement action, however, because a city-wide regulation of newsracks was being discussed in the early 1980s.

In 1990, no regulation having been adopted, the Beacon Hill Civic Association petitioned the Commission for a guideline to exclude newsracks from the District. After holding a public meeting regarding the petition, ... the Commission conducted a survey and completed, in January, 1991, a study entitled the "Publication Distribution Box Report" (the "Report"). *** Soon thereafter, on February 21, 1991, the Commission held a public hearing on the proposal ... to adopt guidelines for newsracks and, ultimately, adopted the following guideline:

> Publication distribution boxes (any boxes placed on the sidewalks to distribute publications, whether for charge or not) visible from a public way are not allowed within the District.

In its decision, the Commission indicated that the publication distribution guideline ("PDG") was consistent with its guideline banning freestanding signs and the Commission's decisions denying the installation of traffic signal control boxes on the sidewalks, and the regulation of the installation of a cable television system in the District.

A few months later, on April 1, 1991, the Commission notified the Newspapers of the new guideline. One month later, it requested that the Newspapers remove their newsracks by June 1, 1991. Then, after the Newspapers requested that the Commission reconsider its decision to adopt its regulation, the Commission heard testimony from the Newspapers in July, 1991. After voting to deny reconsideration, the Commission extended the removal deadline until October 1, 1991. Within a month, the Newspapers brought suit in district court seeking declaratory relief, damages, and preliminary and permanent injunctive relief from the regulation, on the grounds that it violated their First Amendment right to distribute newspapers in the District.

After a bench trial on stipulated facts, the court ruled from the bench that the regulation offended the First Amendment[. ***] "instead of being narrowly tailored with respect to the limitation on speech[, the PDG] is narrowly tailored to focus only on speech. It applies to no form of visual clutter other than public[ation] distribution boxes ***"[.] [The trial judge] did not decide the case on state law grounds, however, because "the questions about the Architectural Commission's authority are at least debatable on the present record ... and perhaps would require some supplementation of the record in order for the Court to resolve them...." *** *Globe Newspaper,* 40 F.3d at 20 (quoting bench trial transcript).

After the bench ruling but before judgment had entered, the Commission adopted a new guideline—the present Street Furniture Guideline—that bans all "street furniture," not just newsracks, from the District:

> *** Street furniture is defined as any structure erected or placed in the public or private ways on a temporary or permanent basis. *** Authorized public safety/public welfare street furniture includes, but is not limited to, such

> structures as street lights, traffic lights, mail boxes, fire hydrants, street trees, and trash receptacles. Any such authorized public safety/public welfare street furniture or approved store-front merchandise stands shall be subject to Commission review and shall be in keeping with the architectural and historic character of the District and the criteria for exterior architectural features as specified in Chapter 616 of the Acts of 1955 as amended.

Having done so, the Commission moved for reconsideration of the judgment, arguing that the new guideline was free from the constitutional defects of the old. This time, the district judge not only held that the new guideline fared no better under the First Amendment, but also that the Commission lacked authority under Massachusetts law to adopt the new regulation. ***

Discussion

I. *The First Amendment and the Street Furniture Guideline*

A. *Standard of Review*

*** [W]e review *de novo* the district court's legal determinations, according a significant amount of deference to the court's factual determinations and to most of its resolutions of mixed fact/law issues, letting them stand unless they are clearly erroneous. *** In a case such as this one, however, "where the trial court is called upon to resolve a number of mixed fact/law matters which implicate core First Amendment concerns, our review, at least on these matters, is plenary so that we may reduce the likelihood of '"a forbidden intrusion on the field of free expression.'" ***.

B. *Legal Framework*

The First Amendment states that "Congress shall make no law ... abridging the freedom of speech, or of the press." U.S. Const. amend. I. It is beyond dispute that the right to distribute newspapers is protected under the First Amendment. *** Here, *** the Street Furniture Guideline effectively bans the use of newsracks as a method of distributing newspaper in the District. The issue, of course, is whether under the circumstances of the case, the Newspapers' First Amendment rights are impinged. We know that few constitutional rights, if any, are absolute, and in most constitutional litigation what courts are called upon to do is to balance competing fundamental rights. *** Such is the present situation.

It is by now axiomatic that the degree of protection provided by the Constitution depends "on the character of the property at issue." *Perry Educ. Ass'n v. Perry Local Educators' Ass'n*, 460 U.S. 37, 44, 103 S.Ct. 948, 954, 74 L.Ed.2d 794 (1983).... In the instant case, the "property at issue" is the District's streets and sidewalks. The Supreme Court has repeatedly recognized public streets "as the archetype of a traditional public forum." *** In these traditional public fora, "places which by long tradition or by government fiat have been devoted to assembly and debate," *Perry*, 460 U.S. at 45, 103 S.Ct. at 954, government's authority to restrict speech is "sharply circumscribed." *Id.* As the Court in *Perry* explained,

> [f]or the state to enforce a content-based exclusion it must show that its regulation is necessary to serve a compelling state interest and that it is narrowly drawn to achieve that end.

Id. In traditional public fora, content-based restrictions are presumptively invalid and subject to "strict" scrutiny. *** The Court in *Perry* made clear, however, that in traditional public fora

> [t]he state may also enforce regulations of the time, place, and manner of expression which are content-neutral, are narrowly tailored to serve a significant government interest, and leave open ample alternative channels of communication.

Perry, 460 U.S. at 45, 103 S.Ct. at 955. Such time, place, and manner regulations are subject to "intermediate" scrutiny. ***

*** The key issue is thus determining whether the Street Furniture Guideline is content-based or otherwise has a content-based impact in which publications, particularly newspapers, are singled out for negative treatment, as is claimed by the Newspapers, or is content neutral on its face and application, as is alleged by the Commission. ***

C. *Content-Neutrality and Content-Based Impact*

As this circuit has noted, ... the "'principal inquiry in determining content neutrality, in speech cases generally and in time, place, or manner cases in particular, is whether the government has adopted a regulation of speech because of disagreement with the message it conveys.'" *** (quoting *Ward v. Rock Against Racism,* 491 U.S. 781, 791, 109 S.Ct. 2746, 2754, 105 L.Ed.2d 661 (1989)). "A regulation that serves purposes unrelated to the content of expression is deemed neutral, even if it has an incidental effect on some speakers or messages but not others." *Ward,* 491 U.S. at 791, 109 S.Ct. at 2754.

Under this test, the Street Furniture Guideline seems to be the very model of a content-neutral regulation. It does not make or otherwise demand reference to the content of the affected speech, either in its plain language or in its application. Indeed, as applied to newsracks, it operates as a complete ban without any reference to the content of a given publication whatsoever[.] *** Furthermore, like the ban on posted signs which the Court upheld in *Members of City Council of City of Los Angeles v. Taxpayers for Vincent,* 466 U.S. 789, 804–05, 104 S.Ct. 2118, 2128–29, 80 L.Ed.2d 772 (1984), the Street Furniture Guideline is directed at aesthetic concerns and is unrelated to the suppression of ideas[.] *** That the Street Furniture Guideline results in a total ban on newsracks is nothing more than an incidental effect of its stated aesthetic goal of enhancing the historic architecture of the District by reducing visual clutter: there is nothing in the record to contradict this.

The Newspapers contend, however, that this directive has a content-based impact, because it singles out publishers, and most significantly daily newspapers, serving Boston for special, negative treatment. *** The district court, in their view, correctly concluded that because the regulation exempts store-front merchandise and public safety/welfare structures, it singles the press for special treatment and, thus, raises "similar concerns … of 'censorial effects'" ***.

We disagree. *** We note first that, to the extent the Newspapers' "targeting" and "differential treatment" arguments essentially rest upon the notion that strict scrutiny is always justified when the practical effect of a regulation is to regulate the First Amendment rights of a select group, this notion is misguided. *National Amusements*, 43 F.3d at 739. Simply put, this notion

> flies in the teeth of the secondary effects doctrine. Under [this] formulation, any regulation that has an effect on fewer than all First Amendment speakers or messages could be deemed to be a form of targeting and thus subjected to strict scrutiny. Yet the Supreme Court has recognized that a municipality lawfully may enact a regulation that "serves purposes unrelated to the content of expression … even if it has an incidental effect on some speakers or messages but not others."

Id. at 740 (quoting *Ward*, 491 U.S. at 791, 109 S.Ct. at 2754). *** Most relevant to the instant case, … "[s]econdary effects can comprise a special characteristic of a particular speaker or group of speakers," *** "an exception to the prohibition on differential treatment for regulations aimed at secondary effects, so long as the disparity is reasonably related to a legitimate government interest." *National Amusements*, 43 F.3d at 740.

The Street Furniture Guideline falls within that exception. As an initial matter, we note that there is no indication that the Commission's alleged "targeting" or "differential treatment" was done in a purposeful attempt to interfere with the Newspapers' First Amendment activities: while it clearly takes away one method of distribution, other methods are left untouched. ***

More importantly, "street furniture" can obviously create or add to visual clutter in different ways such that solutions calling for differential treatment might be warranted. *** ***Contrary to the Newspapers' contentions, that exempt street furniture, store-front signs, or other tangible signs of modern life may also constitute or add to "visual clutter" does not necessarily render the differential treatment unjustified[,] *** [T]he Newspapers' argument also seems to ignore practical and historical differences between merchants' on-site signs and bulky newsracks anchored along the sidewalks. It is safe to assume, at least in the absence of record evidence to the contrary, that the newsracks' overall bulky structure is reasonably predictable as compared to store-front signs, which lend themselves more readily to case-by-case review ***.

Finally, we are unpersuaded by the Newspapers claim that, because the regulation deprives publishers of an already significant and still growing percentage of their readers, its impact is hardly "incidental." *** [Instead] ample alternative channels exist for the Newspapers to reach even these accidental transients passing through the District as well as those readers with more frequent ties to the District.

In sum, we find no cognizable basis for invoking strict scrutiny and, thus, apply an intermediate level of scrutiny.

D. *The Street Furniture Guideline Under Intermediate Scrutiny*

Strict scrutiny aside, restrictions on the time, place and manner of protected expression in a public forum—and the Street Furniture Guideline's effective ban on newsracks upon the District's public and private ways certainly qualifies as such a restriction—should be upheld so long as they are "content-neutral, ... narrowly tailored to serve a significant governmental interest, and allow for reasonable alternative channels of communication." *Perry,* 460 U.S. at 45, 103 S.Ct. at 955[.] *** As we have already discussed, the Street Furniture Guideline is content-neutral. We turn, thus, to the remainder of the analysis.

Aesthetics: A Significant Government Interest?

Pointing to the fact that preservation of the District "as a landmark" is mandated by state law, *see* Acts of 1955, ch. 616, § 12, the Commission contends that its interest in preserving the District's historic and architectural character is a substantial government interest that justifies a narrowly tailored restriction. The Newspapers roundly disagree, arguing that the Commission's invocation of its statutory purpose cannot justify a ban of newsracks in a public forum. ***

The Commission has certainly met the "significant governmental interest" prong. *** Although there is no need to accord the Commission a greater than average interest in aesthetics, it would not be unreasonable to do so given its statutory mandate as well as the District's significance to both Massachusetts and the nation as a whole, as evidenced by its designation as a National Historic Landmark. *** Indeed, ... there is abundant authority for the proposition that aesthetic interests constitute a significant government interest justifying content neutral, narrowly tailored regulations of a public forum that leave open ample alternative channels. *** Our conclusion that the Commission's specified interests are "significant" does not end the inquiry. As "[i]n most cases, the outcome [of this prong] turns not on whether the specified interests are significant, but rather on whether the regulation is narrowly tailored to serve those interests." *Gold Coast,* 42 F.3d at 1345.

Is the Street Furniture Guideline Narrowly Tailored?

As the district court correctly set forth, the Court in *Ward* "explained that the narrow tailoring requirement *** is satisfied so long as the ... regulation promotes a substantial government interest that would be achieved less effectively absent the regulation.'" *National Amusements,* 43 F.3d at 744 (quoting *Ward,* 491 U.S. at 799, 109 S.Ct. at 2758). The regulation will be valid if it does not burden "substantially more" speech than is necessary to further the government interest. *Ward,* 491 U.S. at 799, 109 S. Ct. at 2758 *** Where aesthetic interests are at play, the challenged regulation must be judged by overall context: the government must show that the regulation of the feature at issue "would have more than a negligible impact on aesthetics," which generally requires that the government be making a *bona fide* or "comprehensive coordinated effort" to address aesthetic concerns in the affected community. ***

*** We ... conclude that the regulation is narrowly tailored. First, and without a doubt, it promotes the Commission's significant or substantial ... government interest in preserving the District's aesthetics: as the SJC observed, "the [C]ommission has determined that [newsracks] are inappropriate, in part because they did not exist at the time with which the [C]ommission's preservation efforts are concerned." *Globe Newspaper,* 421 Mass. at 590, 659 N.E.2d 710. Second, as the Report's review of the five available alternatives ... indicate, the Commission's aesthetic interest in preserving the District's historic and architectural character would not be achieved as effectively, absent the regulation.... *** Finally, it does so without burdening "substantially more" speech than is necessary: it does not burden, or otherwise adversely affect, any other means of distribution, including the use of street vendors in the public forum. *** Significantly, we note that the district court acknowledged, albeit implicitly, that the challenged regulation meets this test: nowhere in its opinion did the district court conclude that the Street Furniture Guideline would fail to advance the Commission's interest or that its interest would be achieved as effectively absent the regulation.***

*** As the Court made clear in *Ward:*

> So long as the means chosen are not substantially broader than necessary to achieve the government's interest, however, the regulation will not be invalid simply because a court concludes that the government's interest could be adequately served by some less-speech-restrictive alternative. "The validity of [time, place, and manner] regulations does not turn on a judge's agreement with the responsible decisionmaker concerning the most appropriate method for promoting significant government interests" or the degree to which those interests should be promoted.

Ward, 491 U.S. at 800, 109 S.Ct. at 2758 ***. As the Sixth Circuit observed, the Court "has repeatedly deferred to the aesthetic judgments of municipalities and other government bodies when evaluating restrictions on protected expression." *Gold Coast,* 42 F.3d at 1346 ***. Of course, *** courts are not merely to defer to the government's subjective judgment; instead, aesthetic considerations must be judged by overall context and the government must make its requisite showing. ***

*** [T]he Commission's actions since newsracks became a subject of concern in the early 1980s—including survey, report and public hearings—demonstrate that it carefully calculated the costs and benefits. The path it chose to follow—eliminating the newsracks altogether—is the most effective solution aimed at reducing visual clutter and preserving the District's historic character. Designing the newsracks to better "blend in" and conform with the District's architectural and historic character by having, say, an "old-fashioned" or colonial "look," would promote the Commission's interest by reducing their "unsightliness." It would not achieve, however, as effective a reduction in "the visual clutter created by their presence on the sidewalks [which] clearly detracts from the historic and architectural character of the [D]istrict," ... or, for that matter, the long-standing concerns regarding "congestion and inconvenience."

*** [Additionally,] contrary to the Newspapers' suggestion, that the Street Furniture Guideline operates as a complete ban does not, by itself, mean that it is not "narrowly tailored." While the Court has clearly "voiced particular concern with laws that foreclose an entire medium of expression," *** bans on the use of privately owned structures or displays on public property have been upheld. ***

* * *

Moreover, unlike cases where the medium of expression involves the exercise of speech by an individual or where the medium is a uniquely valuable mode of expression, *** the medium of expression here is the use of a privately owned structure placed on public property for which, as we discuss below, there are ample alternative channels available for the distribution of the Newspapers' publications.

In sum, we conclude—contrary to the district court—that the Street Furniture Guideline is narrowly tailored.

The Final Hurdle: Ample Alternative Channels?

The district court did not reach this final prong, but we must before the full First Amendment ... analysis is completed.

Below, and on appeal, the Commission claims that ample alternative channels exist. The challenged regulation, it points out, leaves unaffected the Newspapers' primary means of distribution within the District: home delivery, sales by stores, street vendors, and mail. *** Even without newsracks, the Commission highlights, the Newspapers' publications are available within the District 24-hours a day, seven days a week, through private stores. Further still, it is undisputed that no point within the District is more than 1,000 feet (approximately 1/5 of a mile) from a source of publications and that adjacent to the District numerous additional sources exist, including newsracks[.] ***

Here, it is undisputed that the Street Furniture Guideline does not affect the Newspapers' freedom to exercise their right to distribute publications through street vendors in the very public forum—the District's sidewalks—from which the newsracks are banned. [W]e conclude that the Street Furniture Guideline satisfies this last prong. *** In reaching this conclusion we reject as essentially irrelevant the contention that the cost of street vendors, let alone 24-hour street vending, is substantially more costly than placing a stationary newsrack. The First Amendment does not guarantee a right to the most cost-effective means of distribution or the rent-free use of public property. ***

* * *

In short, ... "'That the city's limitations on volume may reduce to some degree the potential audience for respondent's speech is of no consequence, for there has been no showing that the remaining avenues of communication are inadequate.'" *National Amusements,* 43 F.3d at 745 (quoting *Ward,* 491 U.S. at 802, 109 S.Ct. at 2760). Here, because the SFG leaves intact an alternative means of distribution within the public forum, *** we conclude that the Street Furniture Guideline's effective ban on newsracks in no way runs afoul of the Newspapers' First Amendment right to distribute their publications. Accordingly, with this last prong satisfied, we find that the challenged guideline passes muster under the First Amendment: it is a reasonable, content-neutral time, place and manner restriction on the Newspapers' right to distribute their publications in the District.

* * *

Last, but not least: We also dismiss as irrelevant their claim that the SJC's decision signals a danger for newsracks in all historic districts[.] *** What the Newspapers fail to appreciate is that newsracks are nothing more than structures occupying, if not monopolizing, public space on the sidewalks, which—with or without publications within—simply are not immunized from regulations passing muster under the First Amendment.

In sum, our opinion today stands unaffected by the clatter of these alarmist claims. Without more ado, we reverse the district court's decision.

* * *

Conclusion

For the foregoing reasons, the district court's decision is reversed, the award of attorneys' fees is vacated, and the case is remanded to the district court for entry of judgment in favor of the Commission, and for such further necessary and appropriate proceedings and orders as are consistent with this decision.

Costs are granted to Appellant.

CYR, C.J. (DISSENTING).

As I agree with the district court, *see Globe Newspaper,* 847 F.Supp. at 193–95, that the Commission has yet to establish, *inter alia,* that its Street Furniture Guideline is "narrowly tailored," *Perry,* 460 U.S. at 45, 103 S.Ct. at 955 ***, I respectfully dissent.

This case turns on whether the Commission established that its outright ban on all newsracks within the District represents a reasonable means to its concededly legitimate regulatory end, in the sense that the ban "is in proportion to the interest served"; that is to say, "not necessarily the least restrictive means," but one which is "narrowly tailored to achieve the desired objective." *** The Commission is specifically charged with preserving the District as a unique "old Boston" community and the importance of preserving the architectural and historical esthetics within the District, for the benefit of the community, the Commonwealth, and the Nation, is not in question. *** Nonetheless, the sweeping presumption indulged by the Commission—that the nonconforming nature of all newsracks represents an esthetic blight only an outright ban can remedy—is not entitled to deference in the First Amendment context. The Commission is required first to demonstrate that it carefully considered obvious alternative regulatory means before imposing its outright ban against all newsracks within the District. *** The record does not demonstrate that the Commission has met its burden.

By the same token, the unquestionable efficiency of a *total ban* on all newsracks does not satisfy the "narrow tailoring" requirement. Otherwise, there would be virtually no role left to be served by the requirement that governmental entities "carefully calculate" the burdens their regulatory actions impose on protected expressive activity, *** since an outright ban will almost invariably prove most efficient in rooting out unbecoming appurtenances. Moreover, ***, esthetics-based regulations often stem from subjective assessments not readily amenable either to objective measurement or empirical refutation, thereby warranting careful judicial scrutiny. ***

The historical basis for the Commission ban against all newsracks within the District is incontestable: newsracks "did not exist at the time with which the [C]ommission's efforts are concerned." While the District is "a tangible reminder of old Boston," however, it nonetheless remains a contemporary residential and commercial community. *** [N]otwithstanding the Commission mandate to preserve the District's colonial and post-colonial characteristics, residents rely upon (or at least tolerate) many uncharacteristic obtrusions, at least one of which (cable television boxes) presumably was introduced after the Commission came into existence in 1955. *** Even though many of these nonconforming modernities are *regulated* by the Commission—often robustly—rather *than banned outright,* the Commission concedes that newsracks are the only "street furniture" it subjects to an outright ban.

As the district court correctly noted, there can be no question that an outright ban on all nonconforming modernities *** offers the most efficient approach to restoring historical and architectural integrity. Where the First Amendment is implicated, however, efficient governmental regulation must be "narrowly tailored." Yet the Commission neither demonstrates that "obvious less-burdensome alternatives" are unavailable, *** nor explains why the *ad hoc* permitting process it uses to regulate anachronous utilities such as cable television boxes should not be enlisted for newsrack regulation. ***

Furthermore, the Commission has not explained its rationale for concluding *** that a permissible basis exists for *assuming* that newsracks, without regard to size, signage, design, color, location or number, cannot comport with its esthetic standards. ***[26] Nor has the Commission shown that any perceived "visual clutter" could

---

26. In its Staff Report, the Commission cites its 1983 and 1990 surveys of the District's newsracks, and identifies five alternatives: (1) an outright ban on all newsracks; (2) an outright ban on all newsracks, except those distributing non-"commercial" speech, whose design and placement would be regulated; (3) an outright ban on all newsracks in District residential areas, with design and placement regulations for non-"commercial" newsracks on Charles Street; (4) no outright ban on any newsrack, but general regulation of their size, design, color, location, and attachment; and (5) delaying any District regulation pending the City's decision whether to regulate newsracks city-wide. The Staff Report fails to demonstrate the required "narrow tailoring," for three reasons. First, the Report was based solely on surveys of *then-existing* newsracks, *see* Commission Staff Report, at 65 ("None of the distribution box designs can be said to be architecturally appropriate"), and does not consider the feasibility of a different newsrack design more consonant with the desired esthetics. Indeed, the analysis of Alternative # 4 merely states that any such design criteria would have "to be drafted" at some later time. *See id.* at 68. This plainly does not amount to "careful calculation."

Second, the Commission points to no other record evidence that it ever actively considered alternative newsrack design proposals. Even though the Commission now acknowledges that it *failed to send notice* of its November 15, 1990, public hearing to plaintiffs' respective circulation departments, the Staff Report touts the fact that, after years of public opposition to a newsrack ban, plaintiffs had

not be addressed by restricting, severely *if necessary,* the location (*e.g.,* within the Charles Street "commercial" zone) and the number of newsracks within the District. Plainly, these obvious alternatives, if efficacious, would be much less burdensome on the important First Amendment expressive activity the Commission proposes to ban outright.

As the court appropriately acknowledges, of course, considerable deference is due the Commission. *** Nevertheless, deference to an outright ban on protected expressive activity cannot be predicated on anything less than a reasoned showing that the Commission "carefully calculated" alternative means with a view to their suitability to address legitimate regulatory interests *proportionate* to the resulting burdens on any protected First Amendment activity. ***

The failure to make such a showing is especially flagrant in the present context, since the Commission settled on a total ban because newsracks were unknown in post-colonial times, yet it continues to regulate, rather than prohibit outright, numerous post-colonial appurtenances, without explaining why a newsrack need inevitably be more unbecoming historically and architecturally than a trash receptacle or a streetlight pole. If its response is merely that the trash receptacle or streetlight pole serves a more useful purpose which must somehow be tolerated, then the Commission seriously undervalues both the utility of expressive activity (*i.e.,* newspaper distribution) and the First Amendment protection to which it is entitled. As the failure to demonstrate the required "narrow tailoring" undermines the challenged Street Furniture Guideline under the three-part *Perry* test, I would affirm the district court judgment.

One World One Family Now v. Miami Beach

United States Court of Appeals for the Eleventh Circuit
175 F.3d 1282 (1999)

Barkett, C.J. One World One Family Now, a California nonprofit corporation dedicated to educating the public about spiritual ecology, Bhaktivedanta Mission, Ltd., a Hawaii nonprofit corporation dedicated to the dissemination of its religion, and Gregory Scharf, an individual (collectively "One World"), appeal from a final judgment in favor of the city of Miami Beach, Florida and chief of police Richard

---

lodged no comments at the public hearing. In a letter to the Commission shortly after the first guideline was promulgated, however, the Boston Globe not only objected to the "notice" provided by the Commission, but reminded the Commission of the Globe's "historical willingness" throughout the preceding eight-year period to negotiate a mutually agreeable newsrack guideline short of a total ban. Finally, the Report rejects Alternatives 2–4 on the ground that they would tax the Commission's limited enforcement resources. Administrative burden is an appropriate consideration in the "careful calculation" inquiry. Yet even accepting the Commission's uncorroborated reference to its limited administrative resources, it fails because it simply presumes, *sub silentio,* that the expressive activity here involved is somehow due less protection than the anachronous appurtenances the Commission has decided to regulate, but not to ban, and therefore that it is less deserving of individualized treatment under the Commission's *ad hoc* permitting process. Nor does the Report attempt a comprehensive overview of current Commission administrative enforcement expenditures relating to its regulation of these other unhistorical appurtenances.

Barreto (collectively "the city"). One World sought declaratory and injunctive relief under 42 U.S.C. § 1983 alleging that a Miami Beach ordinance restricting the sale of message-bearing t-shirts from tables on the public walkways of Miami Beach's commercial district violated the First Amendment. The district court denied relief. We affirm.

Background

This case involves a city ordinance affecting Ocean Drive, a main tourist attraction because of its large concentration of nightclubs and popular restaurants on an oceanfront strip in the historic Art Deco district of Miami Beach. The Art Deco district encompasses a significant portion of the southern end of the city. Because the area has been designated as part of the National Registry of Historic Places, the city has heavily regulated the district to protect its unique aesthetics and ambience. Within the district, vending from streets and sidewalks is prohibited. The only exception to this general prohibition is that full-service restaurants operating from an enclosed structure may serve food on outdoor tables. [*Miami Beach, Fla., Zoning Ordinance* 89-2665, §§ 5–7, 18, 19 (1996).]

In September 1997, the city enacted the Nonprofit Vending and Distribution Ordinance ("ordinance") [*Miami Beach, Fla., City Code* ch.25, art. 25-66.1 (1997)], which added another exception to the general ban on portable tables: allowing nonprofit groups the limited use of tables for solicitation and vending at five locations on the east side of the street in Miami Beach's commercial district. The ordinance provided for a restricted number of such tables by nonprofit groups, for which interested eligible parties can apply by lottery.... The ordinance only permits nonprofit organizations to use the tables from 8 a.m. to one half hour after sunset. [*Miami Beach, Fla., City Code* ch.25, art. 25-66.1 (1997).]

As soon as the ordinance became effective, One World filed this action seeking declaratory and injunctive relief, as well as an order temporarily restraining enforcement of the ordinance. One World claimed that because the west side of the street provides better opportunities to reach people, and the ordinance limits its activity to the east side before sunset, the ordinance has a chilling effect on speech. The city countered that the ordinance helps to maintain smooth pedestrian traffic flow as well as the aesthetic beauty and character of the district, and also helps prevent crime at nighttime. After a non-jury trial, the district court denied One World's motion for injunctive relief and entered judgment on the merits in favor of Miami Beach, finding the ordinance to be a valid time, place, and manner restriction. This appeal followed....

Discussion

The First Amendment protects the communication of ideas. We have recognized that ideas may be communicated through pure speech, expressive conduct, or the use of various media that facilitate the communication of ideas. This case does not involve pure speech or expressive conduct, ... but rather a medium used to facilitate communication, specifically the use of portable tables on a public sidewalk.... A public sidewalk is a "quintessential public forum[ ]." *Perry Educ. Ass'n v. Perry Local Educators' Ass'n*, 460 U.S. 37, 45, 103 S.Ct. 948, 74 L.Ed.2d 794 (1983). The question presented here is whether the city can constitutionally permit only eating establishments to place tables on a public sidewalk *** while prohibiting all other commercial establishments ... and nonprofit groups from placing tables on those same sidewalks.

I

In determining whether the government has violated free speech rights, the initial inquiry is whether the speech or conduct affected by the government action comes within the ambit of the First Amendment. In this case, the initial question is whether using tables to assist in the sale of the t-shirts is protected activity. We find that, under the law of this Circuit, that question has been answered in the affirmative. In *International Caucus of Labor Committees v. Montgomery,* 111 F.3d 1548 (11th Cir. 1997), we characterized a ban on tables on city sidewalks as one "regulating expressive activity in a public forum" and upheld the ordinance only after concluding that it met the standards for a valid time, place, and manner regulation of speech in a public forum. *Id.* at 1550, 1551–53 ***. Thus, our precedent establishes that tables used to distribute protected literature come within the protection of the First Amendment.

II

After determining that the activity in question is protected by the First Amendment, we must next determine whether the relevant government conduct is content neutral or content based. If it is content based, we never reach the time, place, and manner analysis, applying instead the strict scrutiny test which requires the government entity to show that the action is narrowly tailored and serves a compelling state interest. *Perry Educ. Ass'n,* 460 U.S. at 45, 103 S.Ct. 948. It is only if we find the governmental action content neutral that we examine whether the action is a permissible time, place, and manner regulation. *Metromedia, Inc. v. City of San Diego,* 453 U.S. 490, 518, 101 S.Ct. 2882, 69 L.Ed.2d 800 (1981) ***.

In this case, One World argues that because the city permits an exception to the general ban on all tables on the west side of the street for restaurants but not for nonprofit organizations, the ordinance at issue discriminates based on content. As support for this proposition, One World directs us to *Metromedia,* 453 U.S. at 503, 101 S.Ct. 2882, where the Court considered a city ordinance which permitted on-site billboards with commercial messages specifically related to the commercial use of the premises, but prohibited the use of the on-site billboards to carry both commercial messages not related to the site and also some noncommercial messages.... The Court upheld the ordinance insofar as it regulated commercial speech, permitting the distinction between commercial speech related to the site and commercial speech that did not have a connection to the billboard premises. However, the Court found that limiting the content of the billboards to commercial speech while not permitting all noncommercial messages "effectively inverts" the law by affording greater protection to commercial than to noncommercial speech. *Id.* at 513, 101 S.Ct. 2882.

We find *Metromedia* inapposite to the instant case. The prohibition in the San Diego ordinance was directed at billboards, a well-established medium of communication used only to convey messages. That ordinance specifically differentiated between messages on the basis of content, permitting on-site advertisers to display commercial messages but prohibiting these same advertisers from displaying other commercial messages. It likewise permitted some non-commercial messages [e.g., signs with religious symbols, but not other types of ideological signs] and prohibited others.... Because the ordinance was specifically directed to the subject matter of the billboards, it was content based in its intended purpose and effect.

In contrast, the Miami Beach ordinance does not address the subject matter of any message, but only the placement of physical structures on the public walkways intended for pedestrian traffic. Indeed, One World does not contest the city's stated intent, that it has imposed the regulation for purposes of traffic and aesthetics and not to control any particular message. One World argues that the ordinance is content based because while the city tolerates tables for restaurants on the west side of Ocean Drive, it does not allow nonprofit groups the same privilege. We find this argument without merit. Although there is differential treatment ***, such a distinction between nonprofit and commercial tables does not turn the ordinance into a content-based one[.] ***

III

*** [W]e now move to the question of whether the regulation passes the time, place, and manner test. The Supreme Court has held that even in a public forum, the government may impose reasonable restrictions on the time, place, and manner of protected speech, provided the restrictions "[1] are justified without reference to the content of the regulated speech, [2] that they are narrowly tailored to serve a significant government interest, and [3] that they leave open ample alternative channels for communication of the information." *Ward v. Rock Against Racism*, 491 U.S. 781, 791, 109 S.Ct. 2746, *** (1989).

First, for the reasons previously stated, we find the ordinance to be content neutral in purpose and effect. Second, to meet the narrow tailoring requirement, the ordinance "need not be the least restrictive or least intrusive means of doing so. Rather, the requirement of narrow tailoring is satisfied so long as the regulation ... promotes a substantial government interest which would be achieved less effectively absent the regulation." *Ward*, 491 U.S. at 781, 109 S.Ct. 2746 ***. However, as *Ward* makes clear, this "does not mean that a time, place, or manner regulation may burden substantially more speech than is necessary to further the government's legitimate interests." ***

The city is entitled to make a judgment that removing tables from the west side of Ocean Drive, which is more crowded because it serves the popular outdoor cafés, serves the city's interest in eliminating obstacles to pedestrian flow. The Supreme Court has held that pedestrian traffic regulation is one of the more specialized and intensely local types of problems. *** Whereas an array of café tables adjacent to a restaurant is designed to let pedestrians stroll by while customers dine undisturbed, a single table staffed by an organization vending for profit or nonprofit goods and distributing information aims at causing people to stop, loiter, perhaps bargain, engage in dialogue, or obtain the correct change, all of which potentially impedes the efficiency of the pedestrian path ***.

There is also no question that the city's further interest in creating an aesthetic ambiance which will attract tourists to the historic Art Deco district—which it considers "the economic lifeblood of the city"—is a substantial government interest, especially where, as here, a designated historic area is at issue. *** It is well within the city's discretion to decide tables not related to a restaurant would interfere with the city's style and ambience which the city seeks to preserve on the west side of Ocean Drive. We are satisfied that the city's exception for restaurant tables and for no others on the west side of the street is dictated by the city's interest in regulating traffic and in the special aesthetic concerns of the historic district advanced by permitting diners to sit outside and take advantage of the area's warm weather and ocean air. Although there may be other ways to accomplish the city's goals, we find that in this case the narrow-tailoring requirement has been met.

Third, we are similarly satisfied that there are alternative channels for nonprofit groups to communicate their message. Since the ordinance does not regulate solicitation or vending or other First Amendment activity without the use of a table, One World can speak, communicate and sell its merchandise freely on the west side of the street. *** The only activity prohibited under the ordinance is the use of portable tables on the west side of Ocean Drive. That the city's limitations may reduce the potential audience to some degree is of no consequence, for there has been no showing that the remaining avenues are inadequate. Because this regulation of physical structures on the public walkways is content neutral, narrowly tailored, and leaves open alternative channels of communication, we find that it does not present an unreasonable restriction on the time, place, and manner of protected speech.

* * *

Finally, One World argues briefly that the ordinance also violates the Equal Protection clause. We reject this argument because this issue was never presented to the trial court. For all of the foregoing reasons, the judgment of the district court is AFFIRMED.

Notes and Questions

1. **Regulating aesthetics to preserve the historic character of the district.** In both *Globe Newspaper Co.* and *One World One Family*, the challenged regulation did not pertain to an historic structure, rather other structures and activities within an historic district. a. Can you see why historic preservation ordinances must embrace aesthetics in order to achieve their ends? b. Is there a greater need for criteria for evaluating aesthetics than for historic character? c. Do you agree with the dissent in *Globe Newspaper Co.*, that the city should be required to show that it considered alternatives to an outright ban on newspaper boxes?

2. **Alternative focus.** While both courts upheld the ordinances against First Amendment challenges, they seemed to identify different cognizable effects; in *Globe Newspaper Co.*, the court evaluated the effect of the ban on newspaper boxes on access by the public to newspapers, and in *One World One Family*, the court focused on the ability of the vendors to market their goods at a different location within the district. How are these concerns relevant to the challenges?

C. Access to Landmarks and the Americans with Disabilities Act

The Department of Justice's revised regulations for Titles II and III of the Americans with Disabilities Act of 1990 ("ADA"), 42 U.S.C. § 12101, were published in the Federal Register on September 15, 2010. These regulations adopted revised, enforceable accessibility standards called the 2010 ADA Standards for Accessible Design. ("2010 Standards"). The compliance date for using the 2010 Standards for program accessibility and barrier removal was March 15, 2012. The 1991 ADA Standards for Accessible Design, printed as Appendix A of the Title III regulation in the Code of Federal Regulations, July 1, 1994, could be used for new construction and alterations under Titles II and III until March 14, 2012, https://www.ada.gov/2010ADAstandards_index.htm.

As a general rule, alterations to qualified historic buildings—that is, historic buildings listed on either the National Register for Historic Places, or a state's equivalent—must comply with the alterations requirements of the ADA just as any other building would. 28 C.F.R. § 36.405(b) (requiring compliance with the historic property provisions of ADA Accessibility Guidelines for Buildings and Facilities ("ADAAG") to the maximum extent feasible); *see also* United States Access Board Guide to ADA Standards, § 202.5, www.access-board.gov/. However, exceptions are made for qualified historic buildings where providing access under the ADA would threaten or destroy the historic significance of the building or facility. 28 C.F.R. § 35.151(b)(3)(ii). In such cases, alternative methods of access should be provided as described under 28 C.F.R. § 35.150. Under § 35.150(b)(3), alternative methods of achieving program accessibility include using audio-visual materials and devices to depict those portions of a historic property that cannot otherwise be made accessible; assigning persons to guide individuals with handicaps into or through portions of historic properties that cannot otherwise be made accessible; or relocating programs and services to accessible locations. Alternative requirements also pertain to accessible routes, entrances and toilet rooms, and allow an accessible route which is only required from one site access point (such as the parking lot); a steeper ramp than is ordinarily permitted; an accessible entrance, not necessarily the one used by the general public; only one accessible toilet, which may be unisex; and accessible routes required only on the level of the accessible entrance. ADA Title III Technical Assistance Manual § III-6.4000. The decision to use alternative standards must be made in consultation with the appropriate advisory body (the state historic preservation officer or Advisory Council on Historic Preservation) and interested persons should be invited to participate in the decision-making process.

Neighborhood Association of the Back Bay, Inc. v. Federal Transit Administration

United States Court of Appeals for the First Circuit
463 F.3d 50 (2006)

Dyk, J. The Neighborhood Association of the Back Bay, Inc. ("NABB") and the Boston Preservation Alliance ("BPA") (collectively "Plaintiffs") brought suit against the Federal Transit Authority ("FTA") and Massachusetts Bay Transportation Authority ("MBTA"), asserting that planned modifications to the Copley Square transit station violated historical preservation statutes. The United States District Court for the District of Massachusetts denied preliminary and final injunctive relief. Because we conclude that the plaintiffs have not established a violation of applicable federal or state statutes, we affirm.

Background

This case primarily presents questions as to whether the FTA, in providing funding to the MBTA to make the Copley Square station compliant with the Americans with Disabilities Act ("ADA"), 42 U.S.C. §§ 12101–12213 (2000), has violated various federal statutes designed to preserve historic properties.

I.

Under Title II of the ADA, 42 U.S.C. §§ 12131–12165 (2000), and its implementing regulations, 49 C.F.R. §§ 37.47–51, public transit authorities receiving federal funds are required to identify "key stations" in their transit stations and then make those stations accessible to wheelchair users. 42 U.S.C. § 12147. *** In 1992 the Copley Square station was identified by the MBTA as a key station, and plans were made to modify the station to make it wheelchair accessible. To make the station wheelchair accessible would require installation of new inbound and outbound elevators to transport wheelchair users. *** Under 49 U.S.C. § 5310, the FTA provides federal funds to state entities such as the MBTA to assist them in achieving compliance with the ADA. However, in providing funding, the FTA, like other federal agencies, must ensure that the funded projects comply with various federal statutes dealing with historic preservation, including two sections of the National Historic Preservation Act ("NHPA")-16 U.S.C. § 470f ("section 106"), and 16 U.S.C. § 470h-2(f) ("section 110(f)"). The FTA must also comply with Section 4(f) of the Department of Transportation Act of 1966 ("DOTA"), 49 U.S.C. § 303 ("section 4(f)").

The problem with the planned modifications to the Copley Square station lies in the fact that the station is adjacent to the Boston Public Library ("the Library") and the Old South Church ("the Church"), both of which are designated as National Landmarks and are listed on the National Register of Historic Places. The Library and Church are located within the Back Bay Historic District, which is itself on the National Register of Historic Places, as is the existing inbound entrance headhouse to Copley station. The proposed modifications to the station would require use of part of the Library steps for the inbound elevator and construction of an outbound elevator adjacent to the Church. The plaintiffs contend that the proposed modifications would violate sections 106, 110 and section 4(f). Understanding plaintiffs' contentions requires a description of these statutes, and the process by which the FTA sought to achieve compliance with their requirements.

Section 106 of the NHPA requires federal agencies, "prior to the approval of the expenditure of any Federal funds on the undertaking" to "take into account the effect" a federal undertaking will have on "any district, site, building, structure, or object that is included in or eligible for inclusion in the National Register" and to "afford the Advisory Council on Historic Preservation ... a reasonable opportunity to comment with regard to such undertaking." The regulations under this section make clear that section 106 is applicable only when the proposed action would have an "adverse effect" on an historic property such as the Library and the Church. 36 C.F.R. § 800.5.

Section 110(f) of NHPA provides that "[p]rior to the approval of any Federal undertaking which may directly and adversely affect any National Historic Landmark" the agency "shall, to the maximum extent possible, undertake such planning and actions as may be necessary to minimize harm to such landmark, and shall afford the Advisory Council on Historic Preservation a reasonable opportunity to comment on the undertaking." A precondition to the application of section 110(f) is an action that "may directly and adversely affect" a Landmark property, such as the Church or Library.

Section 4(f) provides that the Secretary of Transportation may approve a transportation project "requiring the use of ... land of an historic site ... only if: (1) there is no prudent and feasible alternative to using that land; and (2) the ... project includes all possible planning to minimize harm to the ... historic site...." 49 U.S.C. § 303(c) ("Section 4(f)"). The provision applies only if there is a "use" of an historic site.

To comply with these statutes, the FTA must find that the state entity complies with each statute before disbursing federal funds for any transportation project, including an ADA accessibility project. But the FTA need not undertake separate reviews under each statute. 36 C.F.R. § 800.3(b). Furthermore, in determining compliance with these statutes a federal agency such as the FTA can rely on state agencies such as the MBTA, and on consultants. 36 C.F.R. § 800.2(a)(3). Here, the FTA, in concluding that the Copley Station project complied with all these statutes, relied on "information, analyses and recommendations" prepared by the MBTA. The MBTA, in turn, relied on consultants.

II

The MBTA initially addressed the requirements of the ADA in 1995. The MBTA commissioned a consultant to perform a study, the "Schematic Design Report" (the "1995 Report"), that explored options for making these key stations accessible. The 1995 Report identified several options for locating elevators at the Copley Square station, and listed advantages and disadvantages of each. It identified four options for locating the outbound elevator: option A located the elevator in front of the Church, and options B, C, and D located it across the street from the Church. The report noted that option A "has the most serious historic adjacency issues" with respect to the Church, but that it created "[n]o major impacts on streetscape elements and infrastructure," required little construction work, and was "[l]ocate[d] along the main path of access."

The report identified two potential locations for the inbound elevator: option E located the elevator adjacent to the existing historic wrought iron subway entrance on the Library steps, and option F located it about 150 feet away from the existing entrance without using the Library steps. Option E called for the construction of a matching structure on the other side of the existing entrance. The 1995 Report concluded that failure to build this matching structure would "seriously compromise the explicit symmetry of the [historic landmark] composition." It also stated that option E "is problematic because it not only creates the very difficult task of imposing new structures along side the intricately detailed wrought iron headhouse, but also creates many interface problems with the Boston Public Library." As for option F, the report noted that it had a lesser "streetscape and urban impact" than option E, "but place[d] the entrance in a remote location from the main entry to the station," which raised questions of ADA compliance and also posed a number of engineering difficulties.

At some point before May 28, 2002, the MBTA settled on option E (library steps), minus the matching structure, for the inbound elevator, and option A for the outbound elevator, locating the elevator in front of the Church. The matching structure for the inbound elevator was rejected because it would have been positioned above the Library's basement, making it impractical to anchor. Meetings were held with representatives of the Library and the Church; no objection was raised to the locations of the elevators. However, on August 22, 2003, plaintiff NABB by letter requested various changes to the project, including the locations for both inbound and outbound elevators. The letter requested that the inbound elevator be placed 150 feet away from the existing Library entrance (option F), rather than on the Library steps, and that the outbound elevator be placed across the street from the Church rather than directly in front of it. NABB did not then assert that the placement of the elevators violated federal statutory requirements.

The MBTA first addressed the requirements of the various federal historical preservation statutes when it requested that its preservation consultant prepare a report (the "Carolan Report"). *** [T]he Carolan Report only discussed section 106 and did not mention section 4(f) at all. Nor did the report address the requirements of section 110(f). The report described the project, including the planned elevator locations, and explained the effects of the project. The report concluded that "the primary effect of [the project] would be a visual one," and that the selected designs "will not interfere with existing historic architectural structures." The report did not discuss the alternative locations, but concluded that the planned locations and designs for the inbound and outbound elevators would not have an "adverse effect" within the meaning of section 106. *** On August 29, 2003, based on the Carolan Report, the MBTA sent a letter to the FTA stating that "[i]n view of these facts, it is our opinion that the project will have 'No Adverse Effect' on any historic resources." The MBTA "request[ed] a determination of No Adverse Effect by FTA."

As the regulations require, ... the FTA by letter formally advised the Massachusetts Historic Commission ("MHC") of the Copley Station improvement on January 23, 2004, and requested "[the MHC's] concurrence in [the FTA's] determination that this project will have no adverse effect on historic resources." The parties appear to agree that this letter constitutes the FTA's finding of "no adverse effect" under section 106. The MHC concurred in the FTA's finding of "no adverse effect" on January 29, 2004.

As required by section 4(f) regulations, in a February 5, 2004, letter to the Department of the Interior ("DOI"), the FTA addressed the requirements of section 4(f); found that the project complied with section 4(f); and requested the DOI's concurrence in that finding. The FTA found that "[b]ased on our review of the attached documentation [including the Carolan Report, renderings and schematics] as well as consultation with the Massachusetts State Historic Preservation Officer *** we have determined that [in the language of section 4(f)] there is no prudent and feasible alternative to the proposed project and that all possible measures to minimize harm have been included in the project planning." The DOI concurred on May 10, 2004.

In connection with an environmental assessment required by the National Environmental Policy Act ("NEPA"),[2] the FTA on December 30, 2004, issued a "Finding of No Significant Impact" ("FONSI") as required by NEPA. As part of this document the FTA further explained its conclusions with regard to 4(f). The FTA acknowledged that "[a]n element of the proposed project [the inbound elevator] ... will use land from the [Library]," and that the alternative of placing the elevator 150 feet away had not been presented in the [MBTA's] earlier 4(f) evaluation [the Carolan Report]. However, the report concluded that this alternative was not "prudent and feasible" within the meaning of section 4(f) because it would not coincide with the circulation path of the public to the maximum extent practicable, as required by the ADA.[3] The

2. NEPA requires federal agencies to consider the environmental impacts of agency decisions. 42 U.S.C. §§4321–4370(e); 40 C.F.R. §1500-1518 (2004). Federal agencies are required to prepare an Environmental Impact Statement ("EIS") for any action that could significantly affect the quality of the human environment. 42 U.S.C. §4332(2)(C); 40 C.F.R. §1508.27. Agencies file an Environmental Assessment ("EA") in order to determine whether an EIS is required. 40 C.F.R. §1501.4. If on the basis of the EA the agency determines an EIS is not required, the agency publishes a "Finding of No Significant Impact," or "FONSI." 40 C.F.R. §1501.4(e). Here, the FTA prepared an EA and a FONSI. The FONSI found that "the proposed project will have no significant adverse impacts on the environment," and thus that an EIS was not required.

3. In particular, the EA stated that option F (placing the inbound elevator 150 feet away from the existing entrance) was not "appropriate or feasible" because it created a segregated entrance for handicapped individuals, and would require the construction of a tunnel linking the passengers to the fare collection area, or the implementation of a "caged gate" system, which would require an MBTA station operator to periodically release batches of individuals from a caged area at the base of the elevator. The EA noted that eliminating the matching headhouse from option E increased the impact of the headhouse, but explained that retaining the headhouse was "infeasible from an engineering perspective."

alternatives for the outbound elevator were rejected for engineering and passenger-flow reasons.

III

Plaintiffs NABB and BPA filed suit under the APA on June 9, 2005, alleging that the FTA and MBTA violated sections 106 and 110(f) of NHPA, and section 4(f) of DOTA in approving the project. The plaintiffs also alleged that the MBTA had violated Massachusetts General Laws Chapter 161A, Section 5(k), which required the MBTA to afford parties a "timely opportunity" to participate in the development of "major transportation projects."

Following a hearing, the district court denied plaintiffs' request for injunctive relief on November 8, 2005. On November 23, 2005, plaintiffs timely appealed. On December 28, 2005, the district court issued a Memorandum and Order setting forth its reasoning.

* * *

Addressing the likelihood of success, the district court rejected the plaintiffs' argument that the FTA violated the procedural requirements of the section 106 regulations by failing adequately to document its "no adverse effect" finding, by failing to independently review the project, or by failing to consult with the requisite "consulting parties" in reaching the conclusion that there would be no adverse effect. The district court also concluded that plaintiffs had not established that the no adverse effect finding was arbitrary and capricious.

Next, the district court rejected plaintiffs' argument that section 110(f) was violated. The court held that section 110(f), which is triggered when an undertaking "may directly and adversely affect" a National Historic Landmark, does not apply when an agency properly determines a project has no adverse effect. *** The court then rejected plaintiffs' contention that section 4(f) was violated. The court first addressed the proposed inbound elevator, and held that although the inbound elevator would "use" a historic landmark, the plaintiffs had failed to establish "prudent and feasible" alternatives to that use because the proposed alternatives failed to achieve the project's purpose of complying with ADA requirements. As for the outbound elevator, the district court sustained the agency's conclusion that the planned construction would not directly or constructively "use" a historic landmark, and thus section 4(f) did not apply.

Finally, the court addressed the plaintiffs' state law claim, and held that the MBTA had not violated section 5(k) because the MBTA had afforded the plaintiffs a timely opportunity to participate in the design process. *** Proceeding with the remaining "preliminary injunction" factors, the district court found that there was no risk of irreparable harm because the project would have no adverse effect on the properties; that the public interest would best be served by making the stations ADA accessible as soon as possible; and that the balance of hardships favored the MBTA and the public because further delays would be expensive and could disrupt the MBTA's ADA accessibility plans.

We have jurisdiction pursuant to 28 U.S.C. § 1291.

Discussion

Judicial review here is governed by the Administrative Procedure Act, 5 U.S.C. §706, which requires that agency action be set aside if the action was "arbitrary, capricious, an abuse of discretion, or otherwise not in accordance with law" or if the action failed to meet statutory, procedural, or constitutional requirements.

Precision of expression is not the hallmark of either the historic preservation statutes involved here or the regulations promulgated to implement those statutes. *** Under the *Chevron* doctrine, an agency's interpretation of a statute is entitled to weight when the statute is silent or ambiguous. *See Chevron, U.S.A., Inc. v. Natural Resources Defense Council, Inc.*, 467 U.S. 837, 842–43, *** (1984). We also owe deference to an agency's interpretation of its own regulations. ***

Here, we owe *Chevron* deference to the statutory interpretations reflected in the regulations promulgated by the Advisory Council on Historic Preservation ("ACHP") under sections 106 and 110, and promulgated by DOTA under section 4f. We also owe deference to the decision of the FTA interpreting the DOTA regulations, because the FTA is an agency within the DOT. *** We do not owe deference to the FTA's interpretation of regulations promulgated by other agencies, such as the section 106 and 110(f) regulations. Nonetheless, we owe deference to the FTA's no adverse effect finding under sections 106 and 110, since the FTA has jurisdiction to make the finding, even though it does not have interpretive authority. ***

Underlying deference to agency action are assumptions that the agencies are better able to articulate the pertinent policies, and to reconcile the policies of potentially conflicting statutes. An equally important assumption is that the agencies will, in fact, carefully consider the policy issues and articulate their resolution with clarity. Here the goals of the historic preservation statutes potentially conflict with the mandates of the ADA. *** Of even greater concern, the agencies (ACHP, DOTA, ATBCB) charged with promulgating regulations interpreting the historic preservation statutes and reconciling them with the ADA have issued regulations that are in some respects cryptic and confusing. While we have been able to construe those regulations in the present case so as to resolve the matter at hand, the deficiencies in the existing regulations likely invite further litigation as to future projects.

I. *Compliance with Section 106 of NHPA*

The National Historic Preservation Act of 1966, 16 U.S.C. §470 *et seq.*, "requires each federal agency to take responsibility for the impact that its activities may have upon historic resources, and establishes the Advisory Council on Historic Preservation ["ACHP"] ... to administer the Act." *City of Grapevine v. Dep't of Transp.*, 17 F.3d 1502, 1508 (D.C.Cir. 1994).

Section 106 of the NHPA requires that the FTA or any other federal agency, in funding a project,

> take into account the effect of the undertaking [project] on any district, site, building, structure, or object that is included in or eligible for inclusion in the National Register. The head of any such Federal agency shall afford the

> Advisory Council on Historic Preservation *** a reasonable opportunity to comment with regard to such undertaking.

The Library and Church are included in the National Register. Under such circumstances, the ACHP regulations require the FTA to determine whether the project will have an "adverse effect" on the historic properties. 36 C.F.R. § 800.5. If the agency finds an adverse effect, then the agency must follow procedures under section 800.6 designed to avoid or mitigate the adverse effects. 36 C.F.R. §§ 800.5(d)(2); 800.6(a),(b); 800.7[.] *** Section 106 is a procedural statute that requires agency decisionmakers to "stop, look, and listen," but not to reach particular outcomes. *Narragansett Indian Tribe v. Warwick Sewer Authority*, 334 F.3d 161, 166 (1st Cir. 2003).

Plaintiffs argue that for various reasons the requirements of section 106 were not met. Plaintiffs first contend that the FTA committed procedural error during the process leading up to the "no adverse effect" finding. Plaintiffs complain that the FTA did not conduct an independent analysis of historical impacts of the undertaking and instead improperly relied on the determination of the Carolan Report and the MBTA. However, the regulations expressly permit an agency to "use the services of applicants, consultants, or designees to prepare information, analysis and recommendations," 36 C.F.R. § 800.2(a)(3) ***.

Although the plaintiffs urge that there is no indication that the FTA made the required independent determination, there is no specific requirement in the statute, the regulations or the APA that the FTA provide detailed explanations for its decision or use any particular form of words signifying that it made an independent determination.... Moreover, we are required to presume that the FTA abided by the statutory requirements in the absence of any showing that it did not do so. *** As the district court found here, "[p]laintiffs offer no credible evidence indicating that the FTA did not conduct an independent review, or that it 'rubber stamped' the MBTA's conclusion of 'no adverse effects.'"

We also see no merit in plaintiffs' contention that the documentation provided to the MHC by the FTA did not adequately explain the basis of the no adverse effect finding. *** The plaintiffs' primary contention is that the underlying documentation did not address alternative locations for the elevators, but there is nothing in the statute or regulations that requires the consideration of alternatives in making the no adverse effect determination. Plaintiffs' fallback position is that the document did not consider elevator location at all in reaching the no adverse effects finding. This is not correct. The documents, including the Carolan Report, described in detail the basis for the finding and considered the location of the elevators in making the finding....

Turning to the merits, the plaintiffs also contend that the no adverse effect finding is not sustainable. Again, we disagree.

Plaintiffs argue that the regulations promulgated under section 106 compel a finding of "adverse effect." Their principal contention is that locating the inbound elevator on the Library steps will have an adverse effect on the Library.

The section 106 regulations, 36 C.F.R. § 800.5 ("Assessment of adverse effects"), set forth the criteria for determining whether an action will have an adverse effect. Section 800.5(a) provides that the "agency official shall apply the criteria of adverse effect to historic properties within the area of potential adverse effects." Section 800.5(a)(1) ("Criteria of adverse effect") provides:

> An adverse effect is found when an undertaking may alter, directly or indirectly, any of the characteristics of a historic property that qualify the property for inclusion in the National Register in a manner that would *diminish the integrity* of the property's location, design, setting, materials, workmanship, feeling or association.... (emphasis added).

The FTA relied on various documents to support its no adverse effect finding, including its implicit conclusion that the integrity of the Library was not compromised. The plaintiffs argue that the 1995 Report would only support a finding of no diminishment if the original option E had been adopted (using matching headhouses on either side of the library) and that the report did not support such a finding with respect to the final plan that eliminated the matching headhouse. Plaintiffs correctly point out that the 1995 Report concluded that the elimination of the matching headhouse would "*seriously compromise the explicit symmetry of the composition*" (emphasis added).... However, the 1995 Report was not addressed to federal statutory requirements, and the FTA primarily relied on the later Carolan report, which was prepared after the elimination of the matching headhouse, for this purpose. The Carolan Report described the historic setting of Copley Station at length, and concluded that the selected designs "will not interfere with existing historic architectural structures." *** The plaintiffs have failed to show that this finding, on which the FTA relied, was arbitrary or capricious.

Plaintiffs also urge that, even if the FTA['s decision] was not arbitrary and capricious ***, section 800.5(a)(2), which lists specific examples of adverse effects, compels an adverse effect finding. This section provides that:

> [a]dverse effects on historic properties include, but are not limited to:
>
> (i) Physical destruction of or damage to all or part of the property;
>
> (ii) Alteration of a property, including restoration, rehabilitation, repair, maintenance, stabilization, hazardous material remediation, and provision of handicapped access, that is not consistent with the Secretary's standards for the treatment of historic properties (36 CFR part 68) and applicable guidelines....

Plaintiffs argue that locating the inbound elevator on the Library steps has an adverse effect on the Library because disturbing the Library steps constitutes "[p]hysical destruction of or damage to all or part of the property" under subpart (i). *** This interpretation is inconsistent with the structure of the regulations. Under subpart (ii) adverse effects include "[a]lteration of a property, including ... provision of handicapped access ... that is not consistent with the Secretary [of the Interior's] standards for the treatment of historic properties (36 C.F.R. part 68) and applicable guidelines."

800.5(a)(2)(ii) (emphasis added). Thus, subpart (ii) effectively recognizes that alterations consistent with the Secretary's regulations will not create an adverse effect if they are designed to secure handicapped access. In this respect the regulations are evidently designed to avoid potential conflicts with the requirements of the ADA. If subpart (ii) is to be given its full effect, subpart (i) cannot compel an adverse effect finding when a property is physically altered to secure handicapped access in a manner that could be said to "damage" the property. Rather, subpart (i) must be read to refer only to "damage" that does not come within the purposes enumerated in subpart (ii). In other words, alterations for the provision of handicapped access are governed exclusively by subpart (ii).

We similarly reject the plaintiffs' contentions that the placement of the inbound elevator could violate subsection (iv) ("[c]hange of the character of the property's use or of physical features within the property's setting that contribute to its historic significance") and subsection (v) ("[i]ntroduction of visual, atmospheric or audible elements that diminish the integrity of the property's significant historic features")[, *** since] the project complied with subsection (ii) ***. We [also] find no merit in plaintiffs' confusing contention that there was an adverse effect within the meaning of subpart (ii) itself[, since p]laintiffs have not shown that the alterations to the Library steps are inconsistent with the Secretary of the Interior's standards for the treatment of historic properties set out in 36 C.F.R. part 68.

We finally reject plaintiffs' argument that the placement of the *outbound* elevator would have an adverse effect on Old South Church; and that placement of both elevators would have an adverse effect on the design of the Back Bay region of the city, which itself appears in the National Register of Historic Places; and that the rehabilitation of the existing wrought iron entrance would constitute an adverse effect under subpart (ii). The FTA's finding of no adverse effect encompassed the project as a whole, including both the inbound and the outbound elevator. The plaintiffs have failed to show that this finding was arbitrary or capricious. *** [Therefore w]e conclude that the agency's finding of "no adverse effect" must be sustained.

II. *Compliance with Section 110(f)*

Plaintiffs next argue that even if the "no adverse effect" finding was proper under section 106, section 110(f) was violated. Section 110 of the NHPA imposes more stringent procedural requirements when National Historic Landmarks are involved, *** [like] the Library and the Church [here involved]. Section 110(f) provides:

> Prior to the approval of any Federal undertaking which may directly and adversely affect any National Historic Landmark, the head of the responsible Federal agency shall, to the maximum extent possible, undertake such planning and actions as may be necessary to minimize harm to such landmark, and shall afford the Advisory Council on Historic Preservation a reasonable opportunity to comment on the undertaking.

The implementing regulation for section 110(f), 36 C.F.R. § 800.10, calls for the same procedures as section 106[,] *** requiring consultation with the ACHP, but further requires that the agency "invite the Secretary [of the Interior] to participate in the consultation where there may be an adverse effect" and requires that the ACHP "report the outcome of the section 106 process ... to the Secretary [of the Interior]...." 36 C.F.R. §§ 800.10(c), (d).

Unfortunately, in the course of the lengthy review process, the FTA did not directly address section 110(f). On appeal the FTA and MBTA urge that, nonetheless, the district court's decision may be affirmed because section 110(f), like section 106, is only triggered when there has been an "adverse effect," and that the section 106 "no adverse effect" finding (that we have already sustained) means that section 110(f) is inapplicable.

Plaintiffs disagree. They point out that the heightened planning and consultation requirements of section 110 are triggered when an undertaking "*may* directly and adversely affect" a historic landmark. Plaintiffs urge *** that a no adverse effect finding is not the same as a finding that there is no possible adverse effect.

We think the language of section 110(f) is ambiguous and that this ambiguity is not resolved by the legislative history speaking of the "higher standards" for compliance with section 110. That committee report language was not referring to a stricter standard for a section 110 adverse effect finding, but rather to the higher standard imposed once an adverse effect finding has been made. H.R.Rep. No. 1457, 96th Cong., 2d. Sess. 36–38, *reprinted in* U.S.C.C.A.N. 6378, 6399–6401 ***.

* * *

Because we conclude section 110(f) is not implicated when there is no adverse effect, and the FTA properly concluded that the project would have no adverse effects, we reject plaintiffs' argument that 110(f) was violated.

III. *Compliance with Section 4(f)*

Next, we turn to plaintiffs' claim that the FTA's approval of the Copley Station improvements violated section 4(f). *** Section 4(f), unlike sections 106 and 110(f), *** imposes a dual requirement, providing that the Secretary of Transportation may approve a project "requiring the use of land of an historic site only if: (1) there is no prudent and feasible alternative to using that land; and (2) the project includes all possible planning to minimize harm to the ... historic site resulting from the use." 49 U.S.C. § 303(c). The Supreme Court's decision in *Overton Park* requires courts reviewing agency action under the APA for compliance with 4(f) to follow the traditional approach to review of administrative action. *Citizens to Preserve Overton Park, Inc. v. Volpe*, 401 U.S. 402, 414, 91 S.Ct. 814, 28 L.Ed.2d 136 (1971) (citing 5 U.S.C. § 706(2)(A), (B), (C), (D) (1964 ed., Supp. V))....

Plaintiffs argue that the FTA's approval of the inbound and outbound elevator locations for the Copley Station project violates both sections 4(f)(1) and 4(f)(2).

A. *The Inbound Elevator*

1. *Section 4(f)(1)*

Plaintiffs first argue that the placement of the inbound elevator on the steps in front of the Library constitutes a direct "use" of an historic site for which there is a "prudent and feasible" alternative under section 4(f)(1). Since the defendants agree that the elevator "uses" the historic site, the only issue is whether there is a "prudent and feasible alternative."

In *Overton Park,* the Supreme Court drew a distinction between feasibility and prudence. A feasible alternative is one that can be built as a matter of sound engineering. 401 U.S. at 411, 91 S.Ct. 814 ***. Here, appellees do not contend that the alternative location, away from the library steps, could not be built. Rather, they maintain that that alternative is not "prudent." ...

It is well settled that an alternative is not prudent if it does not meet the transportation needs of a project.[10] The transportation needs of the project include ADA compliance. The FTA determined that placing the handicap accessible elevator entrance 150 feet from the main entrance would create a segregated handicap entrance and violate ADA regulations.[11] The FTA's conclusion in this respect is not arbitrary or capricious. Guidelines promulgated under the ADA require that "accessible route[s] shall, to the maximum extent feasible, coincide with the route for the general public." 49 C.F.R. pt. 37, app. A 4.3.2(1). With respect to "Key Stations" (such as Copley) "[t]he circulation path, including an accessible entrance and an accessible route, for persons with disabilities shall, to the maximum extent practicable, coincide with the circulation path for the general public." 49 C.F.R. pt. 37, app. A 10.3.1(1), 10.3.2(2).[12] While plaintiffs correctly point out that the regulations thus only require that the path coincide with that of the general public to the extent that this is "feasible" and "practicable," we read those qualifications as directed only to engineering and cost considerations and not to concerns of historic preservation. ***

*** It is sufficient for present purposes to conclude that a project that will not have an "adverse effect" under sections 106 and 110 cannot "threaten or destroy" the historic significance of the project for purposes of section 504 of the ADA. This is a situation in which the historic preservation statutes have spoken "more specifically to the topic at hand" than the ADA. *** There is no suggestion here, and it is indeed inconceivable, that the ADA was designed to be more protective of historical properties than the primary historical preservationist statutes themselves (sections 106 and 110).

---

10. *City of Bridgeton v. FAA,* 212 F.3d 448, 461 (8th Cir. 2000) an alternative "that does not effectuate the project's purposes is, by definition, unreasonable, and need not be evaluated in detail under 4(f)"); *Citizens against Burlington, Inc. v. Busey,* 290 U.S. App. D.C. 371, 938 F.2d 190, 203 (D.C. Cir. 1991); *Hickory Neighborhood Defense League v. Skinner,* 910 F.2d 159, 164 (4th Cir. 1990) (in approving highway project, Secretary may reject as imprudent alternatives that will not solve or reduce existing traffic problems); *Druid Hills,* 772 F.2d at 715; *Arizona Past & Future Found. v. Dole,* 722 F.2d 1423, 1428–29 (9th Cir. 1983).

11. The FONSI explained that the "FTA did not consider this alternative to be prudent and feasible since it would not coincide with the circulation path of the general public [and thus would not comply with the ADA]." The attached Environmental Assessment, and the 1995 Report reached the same conclusion.

12. They also require that handicap entrances be situated to "minimize the distance which wheelchair users and other persons who cannot negotiate steps may have to travel compared to the general public." 49 C.F.R. pt. 37, app. A, 10.3.1(1).

2. *Section 4(f)(2)*

We also reject plaintiffs' contention that the FTA violated the requirement of section 4(f)(2) that it undertake "all possible planning to minimize harm to the ... historic site...." *** Although the language of 4(f) does not define the set of alternatives that must be considered when performing a 4(f)(2) balancing, we agree with our sister circuits that have held that an agency need only consider alternatives that are feasible and prudent.... Here, as we have already discussed, plaintiffs have failed to establish that the agency failed to consider a prudent alternative to placing the inbound elevator on the Library steps (*i.e.* an alternative that would achieve ADA compliance)....

B. *The Outbound Elevator*

We also reject plaintiffs' argument that placement of the outbound elevator on the Church sidewalk triggers section 4(f). Section 4(f) is not triggered unless a project "uses" a historical site. Here, the parties appear to agree that the outbound elevator does not directly use a historic site. Plaintiffs nonetheless contend that placing the outbound elevator on the Church sidewalk constitutes a "constructive" use of an historic site.

Under the regulations, a "constructive" use occurs if the impact of locating the project near the site is "so severe that the protected activities, features, or attributes that qualify [it] for protection under 4(f) are substantially impaired." 23 C.F.R. §771.135(p)(2). The regulations are ambiguous as to what constitutes a constructive use. However, the regulations provide that a constructive use does not occur when there is a finding of 'no effect' or 'no adverse effect' under section 106. 23 C.F.R §771.135(p)(5)(i). Here, the FTA's 'no adverse effect' finding related to the project as a whole, including the outbound elevator. In light of our conclusion that the "no adverse effect" finding was proper, the FTA's finding that placement of the elevator on the Church sidewalk did not constitute a "use" of a historic site was not erroneous. ***

* * *

Conclusion

Having determined that neither the FTA nor the MBTA acted unlawfully, we conclude that the district court properly denied preliminary and final injunctive relief. For the foregoing reasons, we therefore affirm the district court's judgment.

Affirmed.

Garthright-Dietrich v. Atlanta Landmarks, Inc.

United States Court of Appeals for the Eleventh Circuit
452 F.3d 1269 (2006)

Dubina, C.J. Appellants, Margo Gathright-Dietrich and Bonnie Bonham, appeal the district court's order granting summary judgment to appellee, Atlanta Landmarks, Inc., on their claim pursuant to Title III of the Americans with Disabilities Act ("ADA"), 42 U.S.C. §12182, *et seq.* For the reasons that follow, we affirm.

I. *Background*

The venue at issue in this appeal is The Fox Theatre ("The Fox") in Atlanta, Georgia, which was designed in the late 1920's. The Fox serves the Atlanta area as a unique and opulent entertainment center. The Fox is owned and operated by Atlanta Landmarks, Inc., a non-profit organization that led a successful community-wide effort to "Save The Fox" in the 1970's. The Fox contains significant historic features ranging from its seating configuration, to its simulated night-sky ceiling, to its faux painting techniques, to its original DC current-run elevators with AC converters. Because of these unique features, in 1974, the National Register of Historic Places added The Fox to its list. In 1976, the United States Department of the Interior designated The Fox a National Historic Landmark. Additionally, in 1991, due to its architectural and historical significance, The Fox became one of only nine buildings in the State of Georgia to be designated a Landmark Museum Building by the State Historic Preservation Officer of the Georgia Department of Natural Resources.

Prior to the passage of the ADA, The Fox installed removable theater seats to accommodate individuals in wheelchairs and created wheelchair-accessible restrooms. From the mid-1980's and throughout the 1990's, The Fox continued its efforts to make the theater more disabled-accessible, including (1) the installation of an elevator to give disabled patrons access to the theater's ballrooms; (2) the installation of a wheelchair-accessible box office; (3) the installation of a wheelchair-accessible telephone; (4) the addition of four new wheelchair-accessible restrooms; (5) the addition of a wheelchair-accessible concession area on the mezzanine level of the theater; and (6) the installation of a ramp to give performers, patrons, and visitors in wheelchairs access to the stage.

*** The Fox's current amenities and policies include between 19 and 25 wheelchair-accessible seating positions with companion seats located throughout the orchestra level; nine aisle seats with removable armrests at various locations on the orchestra level; a ticket-pricing policy that includes the option of paying the lowest ticket price for every show if you are a disabled patron; seven wheelchair-accessible restrooms; wheelchair-accessible concession areas; wheelchair-accessible drinking fountains; a wheelchair ramp to enable patrons who use wheelchairs to utilize the south exit of the theater; and many more "disabled-friendly" policies.

Appellants, undisputed patrons of the arts, have attended numerous events at The Fox. They filed suit under Title III of the ADA alleging that they and other wheelchair patrons are denied access to events at The Fox comparable to the access given to non-wheelchair patrons. Specifically, the appellants asserted that certain areas designated for wheelchair patrons are physically inaccessible to them; that the quality of their access is inferior; and that barriers exist in connection with ticket pricing and sales at The Fox. Following discovery, The Fox filed a motion for summary judgment, contending that the ADA did not mandate removal of any alleged architectural barriers. The district court granted The Fox's motion, finding that although the appellants proved that there were seating barriers, they failed to meet their burden of production to demonstrate that removal of those barriers was "readily achievable." In so ruling, the district court adopted the approach followed by the Tenth Circuit in *Colorado Cross Disability Coalition v. Hermanson Family Limited Partnership I,* 264 F.3d 999 (10th Cir. 2001), the only appellate decision addressing the issue. The district court also found that the changes that The Fox had already made to accommodate wheelchair patrons at the theater were sufficient to satisfy the ADA. Appellants filed a timely appeal.

II. *Issue*

Whether the district court erred in granting summary judgment to The Fox because it determined that appellants could not meet their burden of production on the issue of whether their proposed modifications relating to wheelchair seating at The Fox were "readily achievable" under Title III of the ADA.

* * *

IV. *Discussion*

A. *Title III of the ADA*

The ADA is comprehensive legislation that addresses discrimination against disabled individuals. *** Title III applies to the present case and provides:

> No individual shall be discriminated against on the basis of disability in the full and equal enjoyment of the goods, services, facilities, privileges, advantages, or accommodations of any place of public accommodation by any person who owns, leases (or leases to), or operates a place of public accommodation.

42 U.S.C. § 12182(a). Congress enacted the ADA on January 25, 1993. *** The ADA imposes different requirements on the owners and operators of facilities that existed prior to its enactment date. For those facilities, the ADA states that discrimination includes a private entity's "failure to remove architectural barriers ... where such removal is readily achievable." 42 U.S.C. § 12182(b)(2)(A)(iv). Where removal is not "readily achievable," failure of the entity to make goods, services and facilities "available through alternative methods if such methods are readily achievable," may constitute discrimination under the ADA. 42 U.S.C. § 12182(b)(2)(A)(v).

The ADA defines "readily achievable" as "easily accomplishable and able to be carried out without much difficulty or expense." 42 U.S.C. § 12181(9). Congress included in the ADA factors to be considered in evaluating whether removal of a barrier is "readily achievable." These factors are (1) nature and cost of the action; (2) overall financial resources of the facility or facilities involved; (3) number of persons employed at such facility; (4) effect on expenses and resources; (5) impact of such action upon the operation of the facility; (6) overall financial resources of the covered entity; (7) overall size of the business of a covered entity; (8) the number, type, and location of its facilities; (9) type of operation or operations of the covered entity, including composition, structure, and functions of the workforce of such entity; and (10) geographic separateness, administrative or fiscal relationship of the facility or facilities in question to the covered entity. *Id.*

"The Department of Justice [ ] has interpreted the ADA's barrier removal and alteration requirements in accordance with the Congressional desire to take into account the national interest in preserving significant historical buildings." *** Thus, in the context of an historic building, "barrier removal would not be considered 'readily achievable' if it would threaten or destroy the historic significance of [the] building." *** ADA Title III DOJ Technical Assistance Manual § III-4.4200. The alterations to the historic building need only comply with the accessibility standards "to the maximum extent feasible." 28 C.F.R. § 36.405(a). The ADA's implementing regulations provide specific procedures for determining feasibility, and the regulations state that "[i]f it is *** not feasible to provide physical access to an historic property ... in a manner that will not threaten or destroy the historic significance of the building or facility, alternative methods of access shall be provided...." 28 C.F.R. § 36.405(b).

B. *Application of Standard*

Appellants argue on appeal that the district court erred in applying the burden of proof established in *Colorado Cross.* Under this approach, the plaintiff has the initial burden of production to show (1) that an architectural barrier exists; and (2) that the proposed method of architectural barrier removal is "readily achievable," i.e., "easily accomplishable and able to be carried out without much difficulty or expense[.]" *** *Colorado Cross,* 264 F.3d at 1007. If the plaintiff meets this burden, the defendant then bears the ultimate burden of persuasion that barrier removal is not "readily achievable." *Id.* at 1002–03 ***.

Appellants *** object to the amount and specificity of evidence required to meet their burden of showing that barrier removal was "readily achievable." Appellants contend that in order to meet their burden of production on this issue, the district court held that they must present evidence of "(1) a specific design to remove the barriers alleged; (2) the cost of removal or of the proposed remedy; and (3) the effect on the finances and operation of the facility." *** Because of the expense involved in drafting what amounts to a "pre-approved construction contract for a sum certain which includes detailed plans, impact statements, engineering studies, and permits," the appellants argue that this standard guarantees that "virtually no plaintiff could afford to bring an architectural barrier removal claim." *** We disagree.

The district court did not err in following the burden of proof enunciated in *Colorado Cross,* and *** did not impose too heavy a burden on appellants to show that barrier removal was "readily achievable." The appellants did not satisfy their burden of production to show that a vast majority of the alleged conditions they cited, *** constituted barriers to access for wheelchair patrons under the ADA. As for the alleged seat-number barrier, the appellants could not meet their burden of showing that the barrier removal was "readily achievable." Under the standard enunciated in *Colorado Cross,* a plaintiff must present sufficient evidence so that a defendant can evaluate the proposed solution to a barrier, the difficulty of accomplishing it, the cost implementation, and the economic operation of the facility. Without evidence on these issues, a defendant cannot determine if it can meet its subsequent burden of persuasion.

In this case, appellants submitted three proposed options relating to wheelchair seating, but they failed to produce any reliable evidence that those proposals were "readily achievable." Appellants' seating proposals involved the addition of at least 27 wheelchair seating positions, as well as modification of the existing wheelchair locations. *** However, these proposals were non-specific, conceptual proposals that did not provide any detailed cost analysis. Appellants did not provide any evidence of the number of seats lost, the number of wheelchair and companion seats gained, where they could be located, what it would cost to implement them, or what effect they could have economically or operationally on the theater. Appellants also failed to provide expert testimony to assure the feasibility of their proposed seating modifications and did not *** address the engineering and structural concerns associated with their proposals or the effect that those proposals would have on the historic features of the theater.

Additionally, appellants failed to show that their proposed modifications were inexpensive. Not only did appellants fail to produce a financial expert to link the estimated costs of their proposals with The Fox's ability to pay for them, they failed to take even the rudimentary steps of formulating what those estimated costs might be or providing any evidence of The Fox's financial position and ability to pay those costs. *** Accordingly, we conclude that the district court did not err in finding that the appellants could not meet their burden of production for barrier removal.

*** The Fox rebutted any showing by establishing that removal of the alleged barriers could not be accomplished without much difficulty or expense. The Fox presented undisputed evidence that lowering a portion of the floor, as appellants proposed, would directly affect the historic nature of the theater; the actual seating configuration in the theater is a character-defining feature of The Fox, and the permanent removal of seats would require the approval of the State Historic Preservation Officer; the floor that would be affected by appellants' proposals is historically significant; the implementation of certain of appellants' proposals would involve closing the theater for a period of time; the appellants' proposals would result in the elimination of seats belonging to season ticket holders; and a decrease in the number of regular theater seats would directly impact The Fox's ability to compete with other venues, possibly resulting in lost revenue. Therefore, The Fox satisfied its burden of persuasion, proving that barrier removal was not "readily achievable."

V. *Conclusion*

*** [W]e conclude that the district court properly applied the *** standard enunciated in *Colorado Cross* to the particular facts of this case, we affirm the district court's order granting summary judgment to The Fox.

Notes and Questions

1. **Conflict between laws.** In both *Neighborhood Ass'n of the Back Bay, Inc.,* and *Garthright-Dietrich*, the courts recognized conflicts between the requirements of the ADA and historic preservation. a. In dismissing a claim of adverse effect by finding that the proposed alterations were consistent with the Secretary of Interior's Standards on the Treatment of Historic Properties, did the courts ignore other kinds of adverse

U.S. Supreme Court Building.

effects? b. Did the court in *Neighborhood Ass'n of the Back Bay, Inc.*, treat Section 805.5(a)(2)(ii) as a safe harbor, rather than one of a list of types of adverse effects to consider? c. In *Garthright-Dietrich*, the court ruled that historic character was an element in determining whether alterations under the ADA were readily achievable. How much weight should this factor be given? Was this ruling consistent or inconsistent with *Neighborhood Ass'n of the Back Bay?*

2. **Access as a fundamental right.** In *Tennessee v. Lane*, 541 U.S. 509 (2004), the Supreme Court ruled that physical access to court was a fundamental right. It explained that the duty to accommodate the handicapped was entirely consistent with well-established due process principles that "'within the limits of practicability, a state must afford to all individuals a meaningful opportunity to be heard' in the courts," *id.* at 532, and "ordinary considerations of cost and convenience alone cannot justify a State's failure to provide individuals with a meaningful right of access to the courts." *Id.* at 532–33. a. How does this imperative change the considerations as they pertain to courthouses that are historic properties, often built atop a steep set of steps?

1. Americans with Disabilities Act Historic Sites Compliance

Molski v. Foley Estates Vineyard and Winery, LLC

United States Court of Appeals for the Ninth Circuit
531 F.3d 1043 (2008)

NELSON, S.C.J. This case involves a paraplegic who encountered discriminatory barriers to access when he visited a winery with his grandmother. Unwilling to remove barriers to the historic wine-tasting room, Foley Estates Vineyard and Winery ("Foley") began providing services on a gazebo with a "big bell" where individuals barred from the wine-tasting room could ring for service. Jarek Molski and Disability Rights Enforcement, Education, Services ("DREES") sued Foley for injunctive relief and damages to redress physical barriers to wheelchair accessibility. The district court ordered barrier removal within the building, but determined that it would not be readily achievable to make an accessible ramp to the entrance. We affirm the injunction requiring barrier removal within the building and we remand for the district court to apply 28 C.F.R. §36.405 and the Americans with Disabilities Act Accessibility Guidelines for Buildings and Facilities, 28 C.F.R. §36 app. A §4.1.7 ("ADAAG §4.1.7" or "§4.1.7") when evaluating whether an accessible ramp would be readily achievable.

Factual and Procedural Background

On January 18, 2003, Jarek Molski[, a paraplegic who requires a wheelchair for mobility,] visited the Foley Estates Winery with his grandmother. While attending a wine-tasting, Molski encountered multiple physical barriers to entry with his wheelchair. An accessibility expert, Rick Sarantschin, conducted a *sub rosa* [(private)] investigation of the property on October 12, 2003. Sarantschin confirmed the existence of barriers to entry including a ramp with a slope that varies between 6% and 20%; a raised threshold measuring 4.5"; a round door knob; a rear door width of only 30"; another door width of 31.25"; and a wine-tasting counter height of 42". Jarek Molski and DREES filed suit against Foley on December 22, 2003.

Prior to the commencement of litigation, Foley undertook $23,994 in renovations to provide all services on a wheelchair-accessible gazebo. Renovations included an accessible ramp from the parking lot and a "big bell" to summon for service. Nearly two years into the court proceedings, the Santa Barbara County Historic Landmarks Advisory Commission declared Foley Estates a "Place of Historical Merit" by way of resolution No. 2005-01.

At trial, the court heard expert testimony regarding proposed methods of barrier removal and associated costs. The court also heard testimony from Foley's architectural historian, who opined that an access ramp would have a severe impact on the historical nature of the cottage. The judge determined that it would cost $34,074 to construct an access ramp to the rear of the building, and it would cost $5,130 to remove all physical access barriers inside the building. The judge found that removal of interior barriers would be readily achievable, but removal of exterior barriers would not be readily achievable because it would threaten the architectural significance of the property. In reaching this finding, the judge held that 28 C.F.R. §36.405 and ADAAG §4.1.7 do not apply to barrier removal for existing facilities. Thus, the judge allocated the burden of production to the plaintiff to show that the proposed alteration would not threaten the historic significance of the building. The trial judge issued a permanent injunction requiring barrier removal inside the cottage.

DREES timely appeals the district court's findings regarding the applicability of 28 C.F.R. §36.405 and ADAAG §4.1.7, and the ready achievability of constructing an accessible ramp. Foley cross-appeals and challenges the permanent injunction requiring removal of interior physical barriers.

Jurisdiction and Standard of Review

DREES filed the underlying action for violations of the Americans with Disabilities Act of 1990, 42 U.S.C. §§ 12101–12300, in federal court pursuant to 28 U.S.C. § 1331. We exercise jurisdiction over the appeal pursuant to 28 U.S.C. § 1291. *** "The interpretation of [the ADA] is a question of law subject to *de novo* review." *** We also review the district court's allocation of the burden of proof *de novo*. *** We review the court's decision whether to grant equitable relief under the ADA for an abuse of discretion. ***

Discussion

I. *Exterior Ramp*

A. *Applicable Regulations*

On appeal, we are asked to decide whether 28 C.F.R. § 36.405 and ADAAG § 4.1.7 apply to barrier removal in existing facilities. By their terms, these regulations apply to "alterations;" however, 28 C.F.R. § 36.304(d)(1) extends their application to readily achievable barrier removal in existing facilities. Despite this regulatory directive, the district court declined to apply § 36.405 and § 4.1.7. We reverse and remand.

Our analysis begins with 28 C.F.R. § 36.304, which regulates barrier removal in existing facilities of public accommodation. That section requires "[a] public accommodation [to] remove architectural barriers in existing facilities ... where such removal is readily achievable."*** 28 C.F.R. § 36.304(a) [The ADA defines readily achievable as "easily accomplishable and able to be carried out without much difficulty or expense." 42 U.S.C. § 12181(9). Factors to consider include the costs of the project, the resources of the facility and entity, and the nature of the entity and its operations. *Id.*]. The regulation goes on to specify that, "measures taken to comply with the barrier removal requirements of this section shall comply with the applicable requirements for *alterations* in § 36.402 and §§ 36.404–36.406. ..." 28 C.F.R. § 36.304(d)(1) (emphasis added). If compliance under those additional regulations would not be readily achievable, "a public accommodation may take other readily achievable measures to remove the barrier that do not fully comply with the specified requirements." 28 C.F.R. § 36.304(d)(2).

In this case, we look to the regulations governing historic buildings because the Santa Barbara County Historic Landmarks Advisory Commission designated the building as a place of local historic merit. Through its plain language, 28 C.F.R. § 36.304(d)(1) directs vendors to comply with 28 C.F.R. § 36.405[3] when making readily achievable accommodations. Section 36.405 requires qualified historic buildings to "comply to the maximum extent feasible with [ADAAG § 4.1.7]." 28 C.F.R. § 36.405(a). Under § 4.1.7, "if the entity undertaking the alterations believes that compliance with

3. Section 36.405 applies to "facilities that are eligible for listing in the National Register of Historic Places ... or are designated as historic under State or local law."

the requirements ... would threaten or destroy the historic significance of the building ... the entity should consult with the State Historic Preservation Officer." ADAAG § 4.1.7(2)(b). "If the State Historic Preservation Officer agrees that compliance with the accessibility requirements for accessible routes (exterior and interior), ramps, entrances or toilets would threaten or destroy the historical significance of the building or facility, the alternative requirements in 4.1.7(3) may be used." *Id.* Under our reading, 28 C.F.R. § 36.304(d)(1) requires compliance with § 36.405, which incorporates § 4.1.7(2)(b) and provides a procedure for businesses to seek alternative requirements for historic properties.

Our reading of 28 C.F.R. § 36.304 preserves the leniency allocated to existing facilities under Title III of the Americans with Disabilities Act. The ADA only requires barrier removal in existing facilities "where such removal is readily achievable." 42 U.S.C. § 12182(b)(2)(A)(iv). Section 36.304 integrates the "readily achievable" standard into both § 36.304(a) and § 36.304(d)(2). Section 36.304(a) ensures that only readily achievable barrier removal triggers the incorporation of § 36.405 and § 4.1.7, and § 36.304(d)(2) allows for partial compliance if full compliance with those regulations would not be readily achievable. Thus 28 C.F.R. § 36.304 incorporates § 36.405 and § 4.1.7 into the ready achievability framework, and retains the flexible standard reserved for existing facilities.

Additionally, § 4.1.7 establishes a procedure for determining whether barrier removal in existing facilities will be readily achievable. According to the ADA Title III Technical Assistance Manual ("ADA Manual") § III-4.4200, "[b]arrier removal would not be considered 'readily achievable' if it would threaten or destroy the historic significance of a building or facility that is ... designated as historic under State or local law." The standard set in § 4.1.7 is identical to the standard of ready achievability proffered by the ADA Manual. This similarity between the language suggests that application of § 4.1.7 is consistent with the standard for existing historic facilities. Therefore, the procedure set forth in § 4.1.7 may be used to determine what is readily achievable in existing historic facilities.

For the foregoing reasons, we find that the district court erred when it refused to apply § 36.405 and § 4.1.7 to readily achievable barrier removal in existing facilities. We acknowledge that three courts have considered historical significance as a factor for determining ready achievability without invoking 28 C.F.R. § 36.405 or ADAAG § 4.1.7.[4] However, we find the explicit regulatory language to be more persuasive than the absence of discussion of these regulations in our sister circuits. Therefore, we remand to the district court to apply § 36.405 and § 4.1.7 when determining whether an exterior ramp would be readily achievable.

---

4. In, *Gathright-Dietrich v. Atlanta Landmarks, Inc.*, 452 F.3d 1269, 1275 (11th Cir. 2006), *Colorado Cross Disability Coalition v. Hermanson Family Ltd.*, 264 F.3d 999, 1007 (10th Cir. 2001), and *Speciner v. Nations-Bank, N.A.*, 215 F. Supp. 2d 622, 631 (D. Md. 2002), courts have considered historical significance as a factor for determining ready achievability without invoking 28 C.F.R. § 36.405 or ADAAG § 4.1.7. Notably, none of these cases rejects the application of 28 C.F.R. § 36.405 and ADAAG § 4.1.7; they simply proceed without analyzing those authorities.

B. *Burden of Production*

At trial, the judge relied on *Colorado Cross Disability Coalition v. Hermanson Family Ltd.*[, 264 F.3d 999, 1007 (10th Cir. 2001),] to find that DREES bore the initial burden of production for the question of ready achievability. *** *Colorado Cross* failed to address § 36.405 and § 4.1.7. This omission tainted the inquiry into who bears the burden of production for the ready achievability of barrier removal in historic facilities. We reverse and remand because we find that § 4.1.7 counsels in favor of placing the burden of production on the defendant.

*** Under § 4.1.7(2)(b), "if the entity undertaking alterations believes that compliance with the requirements ... would threaten or destroy the historic significance of the building ... the entity should consult with the State Historic Preservation Officer." Although this clause uses permissive language, it calls upon the party who believes that compliance would threaten the historical significance of the building to consult the appropriate agency. It does not place that burden on the party advocating for remedial measures. Thus, the language of § 4.1.7(2)(b) counsels in favor of placing the burden of production upon the defendant. *** By placing the burden of production on the defendant, we place the burden on the party with the best access to information regarding the historical significance of the building. The defendant sought the historical designation in this case. Thus, the defendant possesses the best understanding of the circumstances under which that designation might be threatened. The defendant is also in the best position to discuss the matter with the Santa Barbara County Historic Landmarks Advisory Commission and to request an opinion on proposed methods of barrier removal. As a result, the defendant is in a better position to introduce, as part of its affirmative defense, detailed evidence and expert testimony concerning whether the historic significance of a structure would be threatened or destroyed by the proposed barrier removal plan.

As the dissent reasoned in *Colorado Cross*, "[i]f plaintiffs must all but present the court with a pre-approved construction contract for a sum certain which includes detailed plans, impact statements, engineering studies, and permits to meet their threshold burden, virtually no plaintiff could afford to bring an architectural barrier removal claim under 42 U.S.C. § 12182(b)(2)(A)(iv)." *Colorado Cross*, 264 F.3d at 1011 (Lucero, J., dissenting). We need not require an ADA plaintiff to undertake such heroic measures. Congress relies on private actors, i.e., disabled individuals, to enforce the ADA by filing lawsuits. Thus plaintiffs should not be deterred from filing meritorious claims by an inappropriate allocation of the burden of production.

We find that the language of § 4.1.7, the access to information, and the congressional intent behind the ADA support placing the burden of production on the defendant. Thus, we reverse and remand for the district court to assign the burden of production to the defendant on the issue of whether barrier removal would threaten the historical significance of the building.

II. *Duty to Remove Interior Barriers*

When the district court ordered removal of interior barriers to the building, the court arguably enhanced the probability that persons with disabilities would attempt to traverse the non-compliant ramp to access the building. *** We *** affirm the district court's injunction requiring barrier removal inside the building.

Both parties find support for their positions in 28 C.F.R. § 36.304(d)(2). According to this regulation:

> If ... the measures required to remove a barrier would not be readily achievable, a public accommodation may take other readily achievable measures to remove the barrier that do not fully comply with the specified requirements. Such measures include, for example, providing a ramp with a steeper slope.... No measure shall be taken, however, that poses a significant risk to the health or safety of individuals with disabilities or others.

28 C.F.R. § 36.304(d)(2). DREES relies on the provision for partial accommodation wherever complete accommodation is not readily achievable. Foley relies on the caution against partial accommodations where they pose a significant risk to health and safety. We find that partial accommodation was appropriate in this case.

First, § 36.304(d)(2) expressly contemplates that a venue may provide a ramp with a steeper slope. The provision of such a ramp does not excuse the facility from otherwise making readily achievable accommodations to the maximum extent feasible. Therefore, the fact that there is an *existing* ramp with a steeper slope also does not excuse the facility from making readily achievable accommodations to the maximum extent feasible. Second, the inaccessibility of entry to one group of individuals does not justify retaining barriers to access inside the building for all others who may safely gain entry. Where readily achievable, the interior of the building must be made accessible for all ***.

Foley argues that removing barriers to the interior of the building might tempt people with disabilities to traverse a ramp that is nearly twelve percent steeper at points than ADA Guidelines recommend. According to Foley, this temptation implicates 28 C.F.R. § 36.304(d)(2) because it "poses a significant risk to the health or safety of individuals with disabilities." When weighing this consideration, we recognize the diversity in the population of persons with disabilities who might seek to use this ramp. People using canes, walkers, braces, and powered chairs can often navigate a steeper ramp than people using manual chairs, so safety risks vary with the nature of the disability and adaptive equipment. Notably, the only evidence that Foley cites to support its theory of a health and safety risk is the pleading of a manual wheelchair user who complained of trauma to his upper extremities[; but,] the ramp might not cause injury to people using different adaptive equipment. Because safe access is possible for many persons who might need or use the ramp, the district court did not abuse its discretion by ordering readily achievable accommodations to the interior of the wine-tasting room.

III. *Alternative Gazebo*

Foley argues that the provision of all relevant services on the wheelchair-accessible gazebo was legally adequate as a means of barrier removal. We reject this argument and affirm the district court's imposition of readily achievable barrier removal inside the building.

As a threshold matter, a facility may only substitute alternatives to barrier removal where "as a result of compliance with the alterations requirements specified in paragraph (d)(1) of this section, the measures required to remove a barrier would not be readily achievable." 28 C.F.R. § 36.304(d)(2). As noted above, the district court did not abuse its discretion in determining that barrier removal inside the building was readily achievable. In light of this holding, no alternative accommodations can supplant the legally required barrier removal.

*** We acknowledge Foley's efforts to serve this community; however, these efforts do not change Foley's obligation to make readily available changes to enable the maximum participation possible for those who are able to access the interior of the wine-tasting room. The gazebo places those who could otherwise access the wine-tasting room at a disadvantage that the ADA seeks to remove. Thus, the Gazebo is not an appropriate alternative accommodation.

Conclusion

We REVERSE and REMAND for the district court to apply § 36.405 and § 4.1.7 and place the burden of production on the defendant. Additionally, we AFFIRM the district court's permanent injunction requiring removal of interior barriers to wheelchair access.

REVERSED AND REMANDED IN PART AND AFFIRMED IN PART

FERNANDEZ, C.J., concurring and dissenting:

I concur in the majority's determination that the district court did not err when it required Foley Estates Vineyard and Winery, LLC, to make changes to the interior of its building pursuant to the Americans with Disabilities Act, 42 U.S.C. § 12181–12189 ("ADA"). However, I dissent from the majority's reversal of the district court's order denying a demand that Foley make the proposed exterior changes.

It is important to note that this is not a case where Foley sought to construct a new facility. *** Nor is it a case where Foley sought to alter an old facility. *** It is, instead, a case where Foley was not seeking to make any change, but Disability Rights Enforcement Education Services: Helping You Help Others (hereafter "Disability Rights") demanded that changes be made because the failure to do so would be discriminatory. *** However, a mere failure to remove an architectural barrier is discriminatory only "where such removal is readily achievable." *** In other words, the mere existence of the barrier *** only becomes wrongful if removal can be readily achieved.

Barrier removal is readily achievable when it is "easily accomplishable and able to be carried out without much difficulty or expense." *** That definition *** imposes a much less stringent standard upon owners of existing properties than that imposed upon owners who undertake new construction and are required to show structural impracticability in order to avoid violating the ADA. *** It is also less stringent than the "maximum extent feasible" standard imposed upon owners who seek to alter their facilities. ***

In determining ready achievability, "the nature and cost of the action needed" must be taken into account. *** Furthermore, because it was never intended that the nation's architectural heritage be destroyed under the banner of readily achievable accessibility, special consideration is given to buildings that "are designated as historic under State or local law." 28 C.F.R. § 36.405(a). As to those, it is important to avoid changes that would "threaten or destroy the historic significance of the building...." *Id.* § 36.405(b). *** "Barrier removal would not be considered 'readily achievable' if it would threaten or destroy the historic significance of a building or facility that is ... designated as historic under State or local law." Dep't of Justice, ADA Title III Technical Assistance Manual: Covering Pub. Accommodations & Commercial Facilities, § III-4.4200[.] *** It is through that lens that we must review the district court's decision in this case because the Foley building in question is a Craftsman house which has been designated as a Place of Historic Merit by the Santa Barbara County Historic Landmark Commission. Nobody doubts that.

When that proper method of examining the district court's determination is used, it is apparent that the district court did not clearly err ... when, based on the record before it, the court determined that the changes suggested by Disability Rights would, in fact, severely impact or destroy the historic significance of Foley's building. In reaching that conclusion, the court relied upon the unrebutted evidence from an expert architectural historian, Dr. Pamela Post, who testified to that effect and added that if the suggested changes had been made previously, they would have made the designation of the house as a Place of Historic Merit problematic. She, by the way, is the person who presented the initial report that supported the designation of the property in the first place.

But, argues Disability Rights, the district court was not permitted to make that finding. Why? Well, Disability Rights points to the fact that the regulation on removal of barriers states that when measures *are* taken to comply with readily achievable barrier removal requirements, any alterations made are to comply with 28 C.F.R. § 36.405(a) "for the element being altered." 28 C.F.R. § 36.304(d)(1). Of course, that is no surprise because if a change is made, it becomes an alteration and ought to then make the property accessible. But, to state that the intent of the regulation is to make barrier removal essentially the same as voluntary alteration is to conflate those two different concepts by making the very threshold for removability the same as the standard for alteration. That cannot have been the intent of the regulation.

*** Disability Rights' second step is even more problematic. Having been referred to 28 C.F.R. § 36.405, we should, says Disability Rights, then note that § 36.405 further refers to 28 C.F.R. Pt. 36, app. A (hereafter "Appendix A"). And, notes Disability Rights, § 4.17(2)(b) of Appendix A states that when making alterations to historic buildings the entity (here Foley) "should consult with the State Historic Preservation Officer." What Disability Rights bypasses is the clear definition of "should" as used in Appendix A. As opposed to "may" and "shall," the word "should" by definition "[d]enotes an advisory specification or recommendation." *See* Appendix A § 3.4. I fail to see how or why the existence of that recommendation of a possible course of action would preclude a district court from taking direct expert testimony and making a finding on the effect of a proposed change on the historic significance of the property in question. Thus, the claim that the district court could not make a finding on the issue must fail.

Disability Rights also raises questions about whether it had any burden to propound a prima facie case that included an element regarding the effect of its proposed changes on the historic significance of the property. Other courts have indicated that plaintiffs, like Disability Rights, do have that obligation. *See, e.g., Gathright-Dietrich v. Atlanta Landmarks, Inc.,* 452 F.3d 1269, 1273–75 (11th Cir. 2006)[.] *** However, I see no need to resolve that issue in this case. The district court decided the question of ready achievability after a trial. *** Here the district court received all evidence that the parties chose to put forward, and made a finding that there would be a deleterious impact upon the historic significance of the property. No more was needed, and the fact that Disability Rights did not put forth any historic significance evidence of its own, expert or otherwise, is fatal to its position. *See, e.g., Gathright-Dietrich,* 452 F.3d at 1275; *Colorado Cross,* 264 F.3d at 1009.

In short, as I see it, the district court's perspicacity and care led it to the correct result in this case. Its decision should be affirmed.

Thus, I concur in part and respectfully dissent in part.

Notes and Questions

1. **Burden of production.** This court placed the burden of production on whether alterations are readily achievable on the property owner, whereas in *Gathright-Dietrich*, the court expressly faulted the plaintiff for failing to offer concrete alterations plans that showed the mechanics, but also that analyzed the economics of the alterations. *In Molski*, the court believed that the property owner was best placed to determine the effect on the historic character by proposed changes, because of its ability to engage preservation officials. a. But, without specifics from a plaintiff, will the property owner be able to have meaningful discussions? b. Will the property owner have to develop all the various scenarios for change and offer a case for rejecting each one?

2. **Cobblestones and accessibility.** Cobblestone streets and ways contributed to the charm of early New York City. But after centuries of wear by carriages, pedestrians, and bicycles, the once vibrant and sturdy cobblestones are worn and graying. A controversial proposal to replace them in the Dumbo and Vinegar Hill sections of the New York City Borough of Brooklyn, sparked a heated controversy. The initial proposal contemplated uniform stones, some cut with machines and lasers, whereas the original stones were rounded and irregular. The objection by preservationists and residents caused the Department of Transportation to offer to install new cobblestones that are aged artificially—like stonewashed jeans, to appear more worn—and in varying shades of tans, beiges, browns, and grays. Some decried this plan as "phony urbanism." While the Department promised to save as many of the old cobblestones as possible,

it maintained that the stones must be replaced in order to comply with the Americans with Disabilities Act. Stones on a crosswalk or sidewalk cannot vary in height by more than a quarter of an inch, a much smaller difference than exists in some parts of the area. The project would "restore the street's historical elegance while removing stumbling blocks for the thousands of people walking and biking in the neighborhood daily." Matt Flegenheimer, *Time Is Past for Many of City's Old Cobblestones*, http://www.nytimes.com/2013/03/30/nyregion/time-is-past-for-many-of-citys-old-cobblestones.html?_r=0 (last visited April 6, 2017).

Chapter 9

Adaptive Reuse and Economic Development of Historic Structures

A. Adaptive Reuse

1. New Uses for the Historic

Adaptive reuse means repurposing an existing building, while retaining and restoring as much of the original structural and passive aspects as possible. The notion of repurposing old, decaying, structures is not new, but in recent years, adaptive reuse has experienced somewhat of a rebirth after losing popularity following World War II, when tax policies favored demolishing, rather than rehabilitating buildings. In the 1950s and 1960s, planners and government officials came to see the failures of urban renewal programs, as slum clearance was indiscriminate; that it destroyed all that was valuable and could be renewed, along with all that was ugly. The policy was to tear down old buildings and replace them. *See, e.g., WATCH v. Harris* (in Chapter 4). This assessment, along with the steep new construction and demolition costs, led planners and developers with the creative vision of architects, to turn to rehabilitation in search of new, commercially viable use for old structures. Some of the first commercial "rehabs" are recorded in the continuing legal education course books of the Practicing Law Institute in New York. N. A. Robinson, Historic Preservation Law 1979–1984, #168, 185, 202, 222, 253.

Ever since Ghiradelli Square in San Francisco was converted from a factory complex in 1962–65 into an upscale restaurant and tourist attraction on San Francisco Bay (listed on the National Register of Historic Places in 1982 as Pioneer Woolen Mills and D. Ghiradelli Company), or Boston made Faneuil Hall and Quincy Market in 1969 into the magnet for remaking Boston's harborfront, http://lostnewengland.com/tag/quincy-market/ (last visited September 10, 2017), and Society Hill in Philadelphia went from being a slum in the 1950s to being recognized in 2008 by the American Planning Federation commendation for excellence, https://www.planning.org/greatplaces/neighborhoods/2008/societyhill.htm (last visited April 1, 2017), it has become fashionable to repurpose buildings, which are no longer serving their original purpose. Schools become apartment buildings. Storefronts become pubs. Factories become office- or mixed-use complexes. Rundown waterfronts become gateways to harbors and riverfronts. Examples of successful commercial redevelopment of historic structures are diverse.

As an alternative to new construction, adaptive reuse serves the twin goals of historic preservation by revitalizing landmarks and reducing greenhouse gas emissions. Preserving an historic structure saves embodied energy, consumes less energy, and produces less waste than new construction. Recycled projects are less costly, require less capital to start, and take less time to complete. *See* Sheila Conejos, Craig Langston, Jim Smith, *Improving the Implementation of Adaptive Reuse Strategies for Historic Buildings*, http://epublications.bond.edu.au/sustainable_development (last visited April 5, 2017) (describing an Adaptive Reuse Potential Model for ranking adaptive reuse according to reuse potential that predicts useful life); Sara E. Sharpe, *Revitalizing Cities: Adaptive Reuse of Historic Structures*, http://digitalcommons.wayne.edu/macaa2012scholarship/18 (last visited April 5, 2017) (describing case studies on successful adaptive reuse projects, including Ghirardelli Square in San Francisco, Baltimore Harbor, and Pittsburgh Station Square).

Adapting historic structures for commercially viable new uses fulfills one of the fundamental objectives of historic preservation. As Ada Louise Huxtable expressed it before adaptive reuse become popular, "What we need is continuity ... historic preservation is not sentimentality but a psychological necessity. We must learn to cherish history and to preserve worthy old buildings ... we must learn how to preserve them, not as pathetic museum pieces, but by giving them new uses." Huxtable, *Lessons in How To Heal the City's Scars*, N.Y. Times, May 27, 1973, at 111, http://query.nytimes.com/mem/archive-free/pdf?res=9E05E3DD123DE63ABC4F51DFB3668388669EDE (last visited April 5, 2017); *See generally,* James Marston Fitch, Historic Preservation—Curatorial Management of the Built World (1990).

The adaptive reuse of historic structures is today expected. "Rehabbed" historic sites have character and unique attributes that make them appealing to a wide range of owners, renters, or patrons. It is popular, and there is a caché, which brings added market value to a well-restored old building made new. This is the dimension of preservation law in which one can do well by doing good. Local governments deploy adaptive reuse as part of their urban revitalization programs. Real estate developers appreciate the incentives and clear paths laid out for their redevelopment of existing buildings. Although Congress has changed the income tax and other tax incentives often, and doubtless will again, the patterns of adaptive reuse are well established. This chapter introduces now familiar patterns of economic redevelopment of historic structures.

2. Regulatory Guidance and Support

At their core, adaptive reuse projects have in common a local ordinance that designates buildings in historic districts or individual landmark buildings, and standards for how to retain the historic characteristics of the buildings while adapting it to a new purpose, rapid federal and state tax write-offs or other incentives, such as special bulk or density development provisions for owners who preserve while they rehabilitate historic buildings. They add value to the community. *See* Donovan Rypkema and Caroline Cheong, *Measuring Economic Impacts of Historic Preservation, A Report to the Advisory Council on Historic Preservation* (2011), http://www.placeeconomics.com/wp-content/uploads/2012/02/economic-impacts-of-hp.pdf (last visited March 15, 2017) (reporting on comprehensive study of the positive values from historic preservation, including small business incubation, affordable housing, sustainable development, neighborhood stabilization, center city revitalization, job creation, promotion of the arts and culture, small town renewal, heritage tourism, and economic development).

Many of the common obstacles, such as building codes, environmental review, and zoning ordinances are being removed in recognition of the great public benefit of preservation; some cities have enacted special ordinances and regulations aiming to make rehabilitation more attractive and feasible. Los Angeles has an Adaptive Resource Ordinance designed to facilitate the conversion of historic and underutilized structures into new housing units, by providing expedited approval and exemption from the zoning and code requirements that apply to new construction. www.preservation.lacity.org/incentives/adaptive-reuse-ordinances (last visited April 2, 2017).

San Francisco has a comprehensive adaptive reuse policy that has resulted in many successful projects, like the Ferry Building, built in 1892 as a terminus for ferries traversing the bay, now a bustling marketplace. The Clocktower Building, formerly a factory, is now used as New York loft-style apartments. The city policy employs both incorporation and juxtaposition techniques. With incorporation, elements of old buildings are incorporated into new buildings. Bits and pieces of buildings, called spolia, as well as facades are preserved. Sometimes, a historic building is kept in its original location, but surrounded on all sides with newer, different construction. Some recent examples include the former Union Square's City of Paris, where the rotunda and glass dome were retained and incorporated into a Neiman Marcus department store. Juxtaposition involves creating something new that responds, but does not mimic the old; instead amplifying each other. This is exemplified by additions to existing buildings and infill construction, and by the relation of new to older forms, such as alleys or piers. Some examples include the former Jessie Street Substation, now the Contemporary Jewish Museum, which presents a brilliant blue, steel cubic structure against an historic brick façade, and the 178 Townsend, that displays the addition of four stories, containing 94 rental housing units, behind the edifice of the former Arc Light Company Station B building, a sleek glass structure inserted into the original masonry building. "Adaptive reuse enables buildings with great bones to enjoy new life." Adapt, Transform, Reuse, *Spur and San Francisco Architectural Heritage*, (July 4, 2013), www.spur.org/publications/library/articles/adapt-transform-reuse (last visited April 1, 2017).

The National Trust for Historic Preservation has consistently championed legislation for adaptive reuse of historic buildings in the commercial setting, in addition to advancing the stewardship of public buildings and structures preserved by non-profit associations. Elizabeth D. Malloy, The History Of The National Trust For Historic Preservation (1976). As early as 1973, the National Trust pioneered adaptive reuse of sites such as the 10-story Wainwright office building in St. Louis, an early skyscraper designed by Dankmar Adler and Louis Sullivan in 1890. The Trust presented the case for the feasibility of tax credits for historic preservation in 1972. The Trust was instrumental in the adoption of the National Historic Preservation Act, which established firm foundations for encouraging preservation of historic structures in all federal agencies and for deployment of the federal government's economic incentives for preservation.

The Secretary of the Interior has promulgated standards for historic structures, which guide the application of tax credits. Historic Preservation Certifications Under the Internal Revenue Code, 36 C.F.R. § 67. There are also state and non-governmental guidelines for "rehabs." Energy efficiency certification standards have been prepared by the U.S. Green Building Council for historic resource preservation and adaptive reuse of buildings. http://www.usgbc.org/articles/preserving-historic-green-neighborhoods (last visited April 5, 2017).

The Jay Heritage Estate:
A Case Study in Adaptive Reuse and Sustainability

Historic buildings are inherently sustainable, as they were designed with many sustainability features that respond to climate and site—windows designed for natural light, orientation for shade and air flow. Thus, sustainability begins with preservation. When effectively restored and reused, these features can produce substantial energy savings; the use of existing materials and infrastructure minimizes the environmental impacts and preserves the historic character of older towns and cities.

Two buildings on the Jay Estate are being carefully and responsibly restored to preserve their historic and aesthetic values and for sustainability. The Jay Heritage Center ("JHC") has developed a restoration plan for the 1838 Greek Revival mansion, the centerpiece of the Jay Estate, and the 1907 Van Norden Carriage House, which serves as the Visitor and Education Center, not only to achieve the ends of preservation and sustainability, but also to educate the public about that process. Under the plan, each room or area in the mansion will be restored to only 25%–90% of period finish. This is a deliberate choice made by the JHC, working closely with its architects not to completely finish any one space, so as to better illustrate the preservation and restoration processes undertaken as if caught mid-act. With this premise, the 21st century challenges that were posed by restoring 19th century elements will be graphically revealed.

Construction of Peter Jay's 1838 mansion reflects the frugal practices of that era. Beams, nails, fixtures, and any other reusable parts of the Jay's "Locusts" farmhouse were recycled and used in constructing the new mansion. CHARLES WASHINGTON BAIRD, CHRONICLES OF A BORDER TOWN (1871). The building is sited atop a rise, receiving cooling winds from Long Island Sound through wide windows; it enjoys natural "air conditioning' in the summers. In the 20th century, a furnace and piping for heating the building was installed. During the period when the real estate developer, DMG Partners, sought to demolish the building, it suffered a period of deliberate neglect. Its external pillars rotted, and its front door and interior fireplaces and piping systems were looted.

When in 1992 the JHC came to own the building, its board decided to present the mansion as a restoration workshop, to teach about how to apply the Secretary of the Interior's standards and guidelines, 36 C.F.R. § 67, and educate about the difficulties and opportunities of restoring old buildings. All in the same building, the Peter Jay Mansion presents instances of preservation, rehabilitation, restoration, and reconstruction (see the definitions of these terms in 36 C.F.R. § 68.2). Stewardship of the Peter Jay Mansion necessitates continuous consultations with experts and artisans about repair of foundation stonework, the classic Greek Revival pillars, windows, studies of layers of paint and wall papers, and replacement of lost or damaged wooden features.

Yet what about energy? The U.S. Green Building Council has standards for a rating system to evaluate green buildings, Leadership in Energy and Environmental Design ("LEED"). Could LEED standards guide stewardship of the work on the Peter Jay Mansion? LEED standards do not give credit for Peter Jay's reuse of materials from 1838, nor give credit for such energy *inefficient* measures as retaining historic walls without insulation or single pane glazing of windows. *See* "The Greening of Historic Properties" (2006), at http://www.ncshpo.org/PDFs/2007AM/LEED/GreeningNationalSummitWhitePaper2006.pdf (last visited April 1, 2017). To preserve the historic fabric of the site, the JHC decided to adapt LEED standards to the unique conditions of its site, design its own energy efficiency goals, and measure its progress in attaining them. Drawing on advice in programs such as the City of Boulder's "*Making Your Historic Building Energy Efficient: Volume 1 Principles and Approaches*" (2007), https://www-static.bouldercolorado.gov/docs/making-your-historic-building-efficient-volume-1-principles-approaches-1-201305201348.pdf (last visited April 5, 2017), and working with Consolidated Edison Company of New York, geothermal water-source heat pumps were installed under estate roadways for heating and cooling, adapting the existing 20th century piping in the mansion. All HVAC equipment is highly efficient. In sourcing materials for restoring woodwork, only wood certified as being from sustainable sources is used. The rehabilitation will maintain over 90% of the existing material fabric of the building, including irreplaceable resources, such as original structural timbers, teak flooring, and marble tiles. Exterior and interior ornamental elements have been salvaged and restored. New construction elements utilize recycled materials wherever possible; new structural beams and columns in the building incorporate 98% recycled steel, and new structural concrete in the building incorporates 21% post-industrial blast furnace slag by dry weight. All exterior lights are minimized to avoid light pollution, and the most regularly used building spaces have large windows that let in light and provide pleasant views of the surrounding landscape. *See* Jay Heritage Center, "Stewardship Through Smart Choices" (2017).

Notes and Questions

1. **Need for dialogue.** The JHC is determined to achieve as many points in the LEED system as possible while keeping its commitment to retaining the historic fabric (like older windows and brick noggin) and restoring authentic finishes (with period appropriate materials), which might not be compatible with attaining a full LEED certificate. Do these twin objectives serve to highlight the need for a dialogue on the creation of a different LEED category for historic buildings, one that fully recognizes the value of the embodied energy of the structure and the preservation of its original materials, one that recognizes the quaint energy efficiency tools in the original structure?

2. **Conflicting policies.** After taking the Jay Property in Rye, N.Y. by eminent domain, for historic preservation public purposes, Westchester County's Parks Department incrementally sought to merge the Jay landscape into the adjacent Marshlands Conservancy County Park, without engaging in any public decision-making to that effect. This led to repeated controversies between the County and the Jay Heritage Center ("JHC"), in which the JHC eventually prevailed. a. However, as an example of competing public policies, what measures do you recommend to identify such potential conflicts at the outset and establish means to avert them? b. Or do you see any benefits to the continued existence of competing public policies attached to the same historic place?

3. Economic Successes of Adaptive Reuse

The best evidence of the economic and cultural success of rehabilitation of historic structures is the record of awards in which independent juries recognize the distinction as adaptively redeploying historic structures. For example, consider the National Housing and Rehabilitation Association's "Timmy" Awards for Excellence in Historic Rehabilitation, which are named after Boston University Professor J. Timothy Anderson, who pioneered an early conversion of an old school into residential housing. These awards cover buildings in 5 categories: (a) Best Commercial/Retail/NonResidential Project; (b) Best Historic Rehab Utilizing Low Income Housing Tax Credits (LIHTC); (c) Small—Best Historic Rehab Utilizing LIHTCs; (d) Large—Best Historic Rehab Utilizing New

Markets Tax Credits; and (e) Best Market-Rate or Mixed Income Residential. The criteria applied are the following: Overall design and quality; Interpretation and respect of historic elements; Market/financial success; Innovative approach to construction and use of building materials; Community impact; and Sustainability. See https://betterbuildingssolutioncenter.energy.gov/sites/default/files/Thurs%20-%20Adaptive%20Reuse%20Reimagining%20Existing%20Buildings.pdf (last visited April 5, 2017).

4. Market Dynamics

Communities that have adopted a municipal ordinance for landmarks or historic districts have signaled their readiness to accommodate adaptive reuse of designated buildings. An owner of a site not yet on the National Register of Historic Places, or designated under the local ordinance, will want to secure such an official finding of historic significance, since this qualifies the property for economic incentives that help preserve the structures. Older cities that have lost their industrial base, or were formerly important because of geography or transportation advantages, have an abundance of well-built old structures of that by-gone age. Vacant or distressed real estate is available for purchase at favorable prices, making the basis for redevelopment commercially attractive. Like any commercial venture, the market for the product needs to be identified and cultivated.

Strategies for commercial rehabilitation of historic structures involve the interplay of preservation law, taxation of income and real property, real estate development financing aspects, along with zoning and other land use considerations. Stephen L. Kass, Judith M. LaBelle And David A. Hansell, Rehabilitating Older And Historic Buildings (1985, with 1991 Supplement). Adapting and rehabilitating historic structures into new developments is estimated to reduce construction time by up to 18% and can save 12+/–% over comparable new development. National Trust for Historic Preservation Information Series No. 53 (1991). Real estate is a capital asset that produces a net income for its owner or investors over prolonged periods of ownership. Its profitability is a factor of: (a) money received (annual net proceeds after paying rents, taxes, and paying principal and interest on mortgages or loans); (b) appreciation (the value recognized in a sale of the property for an amount greater than was paid to acquire it); (c) amortization (the increase in the equity as rents or income reduce outstanding indebtedness); and (d) tax savings (federal or state income tax deductions allowed for depreciation; preservation tax credits, which reduce an owner's taxable income without any expenditure in cash; and real property tax reductions, which diminish the taxes paid to state or local governments). The relative importance of these four general categories will differ significantly depending on where the property is located and what laws govern at any point in time.

The rehabilitation of an historic structure also entails an assessment of how the community and real estate market value historic amenities. If financing is sought from syndicating the investment, the project competes with other opportunities for investors to produce income. A realistic evaluation of the project's ability to produce an attractive return is needed, although increasingly investors with a commitment also to community historic preservation will back a rehab project at somewhat lesser financial returns because they value a social investment.

The capital costs of historic preservation "rehab" projects are the acquisition of the land and buildings, the costs of adaptive remodeling or demolition of parts of the site as allowed by the municipality's certificate of appropriateness, and the cost of new construction. Design, legal, and labor costs are a part of this equation. The physical construction-related costs can be 60–80% of the total costs, and the associated "soft costs" for services, 20–40%. Estimates of income depend on market conditions for rentals once a project has been completed. Operating income must appear to be realizable from the initial plans. Market conditions can reveal occupancy and vacancy rates in an area. Lease provisions (length of the term and share in tax payments, costs passed through to tenants, etc.) determine income. An historic building is often regarded as prestigious and can command a high rent. Operating expenses must also be estimated realistically, and energy efficiency designs can reduce the cost of utilities, while making the site attractive to tenants. Because all real estate projects are initially expensive, the terms on which capital are raised is a very important factor in any project.

For many years, the National Trust Community Investment Corporation, as a subsidiary of the National Trust, has advanced the use of the federal 20% Historic Tax Credit ("HTC") for preservation, as for example in advising on partnership structures that raised funds to finance rehabilitations by allocating HTCs to investors. The Trust, with partners such as the Historic Tax Credit Coalition, has provided education and support to maintain the HTC. *See* www.SaveHistoricCredit.org (last visited April 5, 2017). The Trust documents that every $1 of HTC leverages more than $4 in private investment. It states that "$200,000 in historic tax credits spurs $800,000 in private dollars, creating $1 million in investment. For everyone $1 million in historic property investment 16 jobs are created and $2.1 million in economic activity is catalyzed." National Trust, "Catalyst for Change" (June 2014) at 20, http://www.placeeconomics.com/resources/catalyst-for-change-the-federal-historic-tax-credit-transforming-communities/ (last visited September 14, 2017).

The HTC support for commercial preservation rehabilitation is complemented by how federal buildings and sites are managed. The year 2016 was the 50th anniversary of the National Historic Preservation Act. Under Section 2 of Executive Order 13287, issued by President George W. Bush, http://www.preserveamerica.gov/EOtext.html (last visited April 5, 2017), since 2004 "federal agencies have been [required] to examine its policies, procedures, and capabilities to ensure that its actions encourage, support, and foster public-private initiatives and investment in the use, reuse, and rehabilitation of historic properties, to the extent such support is not inconsistent with other provisions of law, the Secretary of the Interior's Standards for Archeology and Historic Preservation, and essential national department and agency mission requirements." This has produced leasing and cost sharing approaches for federal historic structures. Advisory Council on Historic Preservation, *In A Spirit of Stewardship: A Report on Federal Historic Property Management* (2015), http://www.trb.org/Main/Blurbs/172122.aspx (last visited April 7, 2017).

B. Federal Tax Incentives for Rehabilitation

Federal Tax Incentives for Rehabilitating Historic Buildings

National Park Service
U.S. Department of the Interior
Statistical Report and Analysis
for Fiscal Year 2016
https://www.nps.gov/tps/tax-incentives/taxdocs/tax-incentives-2016statistical.pdf

The Federal Historic Preservation Tax Incentives Program, administered by the National Park Service in partnership with the State Historic Preservation Offices, is the nation's most effective Federal program to promote community revitalization and encourage private investment through historic building rehabilitation. Since the program's inception in 1976, the tax incentives have spurred the rehabilitation of historic structures of every period, size, style, and type. The incentives have been instrumental in preserving the historic places that give our cities, towns, and rural areas their special character and have attracted new private investment to our Main Streets and historic cores of our urban areas alike. The tax incentives also generate jobs, enhance property values, create affordable housing, and augment revenues for Federal, state, and local governments. Through this program, vacant or underutilized schools, warehouses, factories, apartments, churches, retail stores, hotels, houses, farms, and offices throughout the country have been restored to life in a manner that maintains their historic character.

* * *

The historic preservation tax credit applies specifically to income-producing historic properties and investors in a rehabilitation project must have a meaningful stake in the success or failure of the project. *Historic Boardwalk Hall v. Commissioner*, 694 F. 3d 425 (3rd Cir. 2012) (explaining that the investor must have something at risk); *see also* Rev. Proc. 2014-12 (December 2013). The current tax incentives for preservation, established by the Tax Reform Act of 1986 (Pub. Law 99-514; 26 U.S.C. § 47 [formerly Section 48(g)]), include a 20% tax credit for the *certified rehabilitation expenditures* of *certified historic structures* and a 10% tax credit for the rehabilitation expenditures of *nonhistoric, non-residential buildings* built before 1936. A building must be individually listed in the National Register of Historic Places or be certified as contributing to a registered historic district in order to qualify for the 20% credit. *Federal Tax Incentives for Rehabilitating Historic Buildings* Statistical Report and Analysis for Fiscal Year 2016 ("Incentives"), https://www.nps.gov/tps/tax-incentives/taxdocs/tax-incentives-2016statistical.pdf at 6. The HTC program is jointly administered by the National Park

Service and the Internal Revenue Service. In all cases the rehabilitation must be a substantial one and must involve a depreciable building. The State Historic Preservation Officer is the first point of contact for property owners seeking the rehabilitation tax credit. *Id.* The Secretary of the Interior has promulgated Standards for Rehabilitation, 36 C.F.R. § 67, as a guide for determining whether a rehabilitation qualifies as a certified rehabilitation for tax purposes, https://www.nps.gov/tps/standards/rehabilitation/rehab/stand.htm (last visited March 28, 2017).

From time to time, Congress has increased these credits for limited periods for the rehabilitation of buildings located in areas affected by natural disasters. On February 16, 2017, reconciled House and Senate versions of the *Historic Tax Credit Improvement Act of 2017* were introduced in Congress in the Senate by Ben Cardin (D. Md.) and Susan Collins (R. Maine) and in the House by Mike Kelly (R. Pa.) and Earl Blumenauer (D. Oregon). Among other things, the bills would increase the rehabilitation credit for certain small projects to 30%, to make sure the rural west and non-urban areas have the same ability to take advantage of the credit. This increased small deal credit would be capped at qualified rehabilitation expenses of $2.5 million, approximately $750,000 in credits. The bills also would allow rehabilitation expenditures not exceeding $2.5 million to be transferred as a tax certificate. Significantly, the bills redefine "substantial rehabilitation" by changing the threshold to qualify for the credit to 50% of adjusted basis instead of 100% of adjusted basis as the program currently requires. Another provision reduces the amount of the depreciable basis adjustment from 100% to 50% of the amount of the historic tax credit. Finally, the bills modify the disqualified lease rules to limit the definition of a "disqualified lease" to those leases that are part of a sale leaseback arrangement involving a nonprofit that has used the property before certification as a historic rehabilitation and eliminates from that rule other types of leases that inhibit the rehabilitation of these buildings, such as those with purchase options, leases in excess of 20 years, and leases in buildings that use tax-exempt financing. H.R. 1158, S. 425, 115th Cong. 2017–2018.

1. Economic Effects of Historic Tax Credits

Annually, the National Park Service, Technical Preservation Services releases a report on the impacts of the historic tax credit, and in 2016, working with the Rutgers University Edward J. Bloustein School of Planning and Public Policy (ejb@policy.rutgers.edu), it employed an analytic new model for an assessment of the effects of the credit over its entire period of use. *Annual Report on the Economic Impact of the Federal Historic Tax Credit for FY 2016*, https://www.nps.gov/tps/tax incentives/taxdocs/economic-impact-2016.pdf. The results were remarkable. The NPS reports that there were 1,039 completed historic rehabilitation projects certified by the NPS, for which rehabilitation costs of $5.85 billion qualified for the 20% historic tax credit. Many were for buildings that stood abandoned or under-utilized. Their restoration revitalized communities, with 55% of them located in low- and moderate-income census tracks. Inflation-adjusted for 2016 dollars, the credit-assisted cumulative national economic figures indicate that the $131.8 billion in historic rehabilitation expenditures produced substantial economic benefits.

FYs 1978-2016	$131.8bn	FY 2016 $6.5bn
Jobs (persons/years)	2,441,000	109,000
Income	$106.6bn	$4.6bn
Output	$297.7bn	$12.3bn
GDP	$144.9bn	$6.2bn
Taxes	$41.7bn	$1.7bn

Thirty percent of the jobs (727,000) and $42.3bn in GDP were in the construction sector. There were further historic tax credit contributions to jobs (447,000) and GDP ($19.2bn) in the service sector, with similar results for the manufacturing sector (508,000 jobs and $37.9bn in GDP) and retail trade sector (356,000 jobs and 10.5bn GDP). Overall the historic tax credit produced nearly 2.5 million new jobs. The tax credit's cost of $25.2bn stimulated investments more than five times greater ($131.8bn). Significantly also, the cumulative benefits for the national economy far outweighed the costs of the historic tax credit—the credit costs the U.S. Treasury $25.2bn over the period 1978-2016, and cost the National Park Service $1.2bn for its certification services. These were off-set by the new tax revenues for the U.S. Treasury of $29.8bn in federal tax receipts compared with the $25.2bn in credits allocated. Thus, on the narrow issue of recouping the 20% historic tax credit, the record is positive. The historic tax credit generates income that covers its costs and makes money for the federal government.

In addition, the historic tax credit has had a significant impact on housing. Since the inception of the program, over 520,000 housing units have been rehabilitated or created. *Incentives*, *supra*, at 12. In Fiscal Year 2016, there were more than 21,000 (6,500 rehabilitated and 14,000 new units). *Id.* Of the total housing units rehabilitated or created, 153,255 have been low- and moderate-income housing units. *Id.* Various Department of Housing and Urban Development ("HUD") programs, such as the low-income housing tax credits, have been used by private investors in conjunction with preservation tax credits to achieve this goal. *Id.* In particular, the federal Low-Income Housing Tax Credit Program, 26 U.S.C. § 42, provides a tax credit on returns for investments in low-income housing, either new construction or rehabilitation of existing structures. The credit is approximately 9% per year for 10 years or 4% for property subsidized by tax-exempt bonds.

* * *

2. Repeal or Revision of the Historic Tax Credit, the 115th Congress, 1st Session

None of these social and economic benefits mattered when on November 2, 2017, the House of Representatives, without holding hearings, adopted H.R. 1, "Tax Cuts and Jobs Act," amendments to the Internal Revenue Code, within the procedures to adopt the nation's budget. The House bill entirely repealed the historic tax credit.

When the Senate's Committee on Finance released its version of this tax reform legislation on November 11, 2017, it reduced the credit from 20% to 10% and eliminated entirely the 10% tax credit for buildings built before 1936 which have not sought certification as historic. If, however, the Historic Tax Credit Improvements Act of 2017 (S.425, H. 1158) (discussed above) had been allowed to advance to adoption in each House, it would have reinstated and strengthened the historic tax credit. The sponsors of this bill cited the National Park Service/Rutgers Annual Report to make the case for the historic tax credit. *See* https://www.cardin.senate.gov/newsroom/press/release/cardin-and-collins-kelly-and-blumenauer-introduce-bipartisan-bicameral-bill-to-stimulate-infrastructure-development-through-the-preservation-of-historic-properties (last visited November 27, 2017).

In December 2017, at the last moment, Congress voted to preserve the tax credit, but with changes. The 20% credit must now be taken over five years, instead of in its entirety in the year the rehabilitation is completed. To be sure, this was not the first time that historic tax credits had been threatened, most recently, on December 11, 2014. Rep. Dave Camp (R. Mi.) introduced H.R. 1, "Tax Reform Act of 2014," which included the repeal of the credit. The present controversy in Congress is yet a distressing illustration of how hard it has been to create and keep the historic tax credit over the years, despite its positive fiscal history and brilliant adaptive reuse record. *See generally*, Stephanie Meeks and Kevin C. Murphy, The Past and Future City: How Historic Preservation is Reviving America's Communities (2016)(discussing the critical role that historic tax credits play in this revival).

3. Historic Preservation Easements

An historic preservation easement is a voluntary legal agreement, usually in the form of a deed, that protects a significant historic property in perpetuity, through restrictions on the development of or changes to the property. It may be designed to preserve lands around a historic site, or to protect the exterior appearance of a historic structure under state property law for protecting the façade of a building. State laws that permit easements in gross enable a charitable organization to receive and hold the easement, and apply the rights granted under the easement to protect the historic site. The receiving organizations need to be recognized as qualified under § 501(c)(3) of the Internal Revenue Code.

The donation of an historic preservation easement may be eligible for tax benefits. In particular, under 26 U.S.C. § 170(h), the value of the easement protecting a certified historic structure or an historically important land area, can be claimed as a charitable deduction from federal income tax. For purposes of adjusting the cost basis of a property, to make a rehabilitation project more cost-effective and profitable, it is important to appraise the value of the easement in terms of actual market conditions. The Treasury Department's regulations interpreting § 170(h) are found at Treas. Reg. 1.170A-14. The IRS has issued a "Conservation Easements Audit Techniques Guide" (2016) at https://www.irs.gov/businesses/small-businesses-self-employed/conservation-easement-audit-techniques-guide (last visited March 15, 2017). The organization holding the easement is obliged to report the status of the easement annually (Schedule D, IRS Form 990). Donors of a conservation easement must file IRS Form 8283 documenting the preservation terms in the charitable contribution. Easements of religious sites enable a community to enjoy the façades of important churches for their historic value. *See* Jess R. Phelps, *Scarcely A Vestige of Antiquity Remains: Evaluating the Role of Preservation Easements in Protecting Historic Religious Architecture*, 44 Envtl. Law Rep. 10808 (2014).

4. Tax Incentives at Work

Most states have enacted a range of tax incentives to facilitate the rehabilitation of historic buildings and other structures. Those in New Jersey, http://www.nj.gov/dep/hpo/3preserve/preserve.htm (last visited April 5, 2017), North Carolina, https://www.presnc.org/get-help/tax-credits/ (last visited April 5, 2017), and Connecticut, http://www.cultureandtourism.org/cct/cwp/view.asp?a=3933&q=430786 (last visited April 5, 2017) are characteristic of state programs that have been designed to be integrated with the federal programs. Maine makes available a 25% rehabilitation tax credit for small historic preservation projects, http://www.maine.gov/mhpc/tax_incentives/small_project_rehabilitation_credit.html (last visited April 5, 2017); *see generally* State Tax Credits for Historic Preservation A Policy Report, Produced by the National Trust for Historic Preservation, http://www.preservationnation.org/information-center/economics-of-revitalization/rehabilitation-tax-credits/additional-eesources/nthp_state_tax_credits_model_policy.pdf (last visited April 5, 2017); Novogradac, Historic Tax Credit Resource Center, http://www.novoco.com/historic/htc/state_programs.php (last visited March 28, 2017).

a. Annex — The Mills at High Falls Project: Federal and State Programs

In New York State, the State Preservation League plays a role analogous to the National Trust for Historic Preservation, working with state agencies and local governments and local historic societies and preservation non-governmental organizations. The League also makes its own grants available. http://www.preservenys.org/ (last visited September 10, 2017). The Commissioner of the New York State Office of Parks, Recreation and Historic Preservation (OPRHP) is the State Historic Preservation Officer and maintains the State Register of Historic Places. https://parks.ny.gov/shpo/ (last visited April 5, 2017). The Mills at High Falls in Rochester, New York, illustrates a successful historic rehabilitation in New York.

Annex—The Mills at High Falls: A Textbook Case in Preservation Finance

The buildings in the Annex Project were formerly industrial mill buildings, constructed in 1855. They are situated in the Teoronto Block Historic District, in the city of Rochester, New York. They consist of a row of three-story, five-bay brick structures, for historically mixed-use (boarding rooms, church meeting place, hotels and taverns) and were constructed with stone, glass, and cast-iron commercial storefronts. In 2005, the Eastman Kodak Company donated the buildings to the local urban league, which decided to rehabilitate them. The site qualified for federal historic tax credits because the district was listed on the National Register. It also qualified for low income housing tax credits because of the proposed use for low-income housing. Other state and local funding sources were available, including from New York State's Homes and Community Renewal Agency ("HCR") and local tax exemptions. In all, for a total qualified rehabilitation expenditure of $6.7 million, the project received a 20% federal tax credit of $1.3 million and a matching 20% state tax credit of $1.3 million. The project created 64 direct and indirect/induced jobs, generated $3.3 million in household income and $102,000 in state tax revenue, adding $4.7 million to total gross state product. The Annex was rehabilitated to offer modern affordable housing on every floor, even on the first floor which was originally used for commercial activities, but the rehabilitation left in place the exterior mid-19th century vernacular design of industrial buildings. The rehabilitation project of Annex—The Mills at High Falls transformed a group of vacant and hazardous historic commercial buildings into a fine exemplar for affordable urban rental housing. *See* The Preservation League of New York State, http://www.preservenys.org/uploads/3/1/6/2/31626961/23537_annex_the_mills_at_high_falls_tax_credit_case_study_-_rochester.pdf (last visited September 14, 2017).

Test your grasp on the economics of adaptive reuse of historic structures

Every community has old buildings that have a story to tell. Consider the economics of identifying a small structure to rehabilitate for residential housing. A vacant building, or one in a transitional neighborhood which supports only low rents, could be rehabilitated and placed on the rental market in shape to command higher rents. If the building is a row house, or could be one of several buildings rehabilitated at the same time, there are economies of scale to be realized.

What would be the advantage of researching the historic significance of the buildings or the neighborhood or setting in which they are located? Would they qualify for landmark status or could the area be a historic district under a local historic preservation ordinance? Would a nomination to the state and federal Registers of Historic Places be worthwhile? What federal or state tax incentives might be available to enhance the economic attractiveness of the project? How would it be financed?

Here is a *pro forma* for a rehabilitation years ago, of an older building, before using any façade easements or tax incentives. Why would a project developer want to employ historic incentives? How does local urban redevelopment planning facilitate local governmental approvals for building rehabilitations? Assume the local government seeks housing rehabs with a community development loan program, but does not yet have a local historic preservation program and the Owner obliges the lessee to pay electrical utility bills for the rental unit.

Exurbia or *Inurbia*: The Neglected Small Building

That neglected, small 19th century residence or overlooked building from the 1920s, or the single home from the post-World War II building boom, may appear to be of little value or promise. Would this rental rehabilitation project's acquisition/rehabilitation budget for a site in an inner city or remote township be attractive? The local land use laws place it already in a residential zone.

Development Budget

Development Costs	Budget
Rehabilitation	$17,000
Contingency	3,000
Bank fee (2%)	1,520
Legal Services	3,000
Bank Application fee	150
Title Insurance	200
Recording	70

Total Development Cost	$24,940
Acquisition Price	85,000
Total Financing Requirement	$109,940
Financing:	
Bank Mortgage 9%—30 yrs	$78,000
Community Dev't Forbearance Loan—10 yrs	10,000
Owner's cash investment	21,940
Total Financing:	$109,940
Operating Budget	
Rental Income	*Budget*
1 bedroom $390/month	$4,680
3 bedroom $560/month	$6,720
2% Vacancy loss	– *$228*
Net rental income	$11,172
Operating Expenses:	
Debt Service ($78,000 at 9% for 30 yrs)	$7,531
Real Property Taxes	985
Insurance	500
Utilities (water/sewer)	250
Maintenance	425
Total Operating Expenses	$9,691
Profit—6.7% return (cash on cash)	$1,481
Tax Benefit (cash value of Depreciation)	1,300
Annual Loan Forgiveness (10 yrs)	1,000
Return after taxes (17.2%)	3,781
Post rehab bank appraisal of value	$168,000
Post rehab equity gain	73,000
Capital gain return on investment	333%

Notes and Questions

1. **Small projects.** a. How do you critique this prosaic example of a small rehab project? b. What options does a small village or inner city community have? c. What perils do an owner/redeveloper/landlord face? d. Should she live in the neighborhood, or nearby, to undertake this sort of rehab? e. If rehabs are slow in the area, what would make the "first" rehab realistic? f. Can the caché of history make a difference if no one remembers the historic past of this little neighborhood? g. Does preservation law have the bandwidth to worry about small projects?

Financing the Jay Estate's Restoration

The economics of preserving a non-profit site present a different story from a commercial rehabilitation. The restoration and adaptive reuse of the Jay Estate illustrate the four key sources of financing for non-profit preservation projects: (a) fund-raising from the public to a non-profit corporation, which has been qualified with the Internal Revenue Service under INT. REV. CODE, 26 U.S.C. § 102(2)(c) to receive contributions for which the donors may claim a charitable deduction on their own income tax returns; (b) donations of time and services from individuals, who work to raise funds, provide professional services, conduct education programs or maintain the grounds; (c) contributions by companies of grants or services; and (d) grants from government agencies, at local, state or national levels. Gifts from the private sector are needed to persuade governmental agencies that the grantee is a viable organization, and often are needed to match government grants. A strategy for continuous fund-raising is essential for a non-profit organization like the Jay Heritage Center ("JHC").

After the success of the Jay Coalition's campaign to save the Jay Estate, the JHC received title to 1.5 acres containing the Peter Jay Mansion and the estate's later added Van Norden Carriage House, but the stabilization and restoration of the site was a daunting challenge. Both the State of New York and County of Westchester had refused to take title to those two buildings, because they were in decrepit conditions. From 1979 to 1992, the real estate developer who owned the site had done nothing to maintain the buildings. She sought permission to demolish them. This is an example of "demolition by neglect." Both had been vandalized, and the developer allowed anyone to remove fixtures and piping. The interior was used for filming a B-rated horror movie, and the walls spray-painted and distressed. The City of Rye had tepidly enforced its building code standards, but both structures were uninhabited (and uninhabitable).

The first challenge was to announce publicly that the JHC would restore the property. This resulted in persons returning, voluntarily, the carved Mahogany front door of the mansion and the Carriage House's clock. Once repairs were made to shore up the building foundations and close roof leaks, the JHC focused on the front façade of the mansion, which the public viewed from the Boston Post Road. Expert reports were commissioned, successively, on each stage of the restoration. Replacement pillars and shutters were created, windows restored, and paints mixed to replicate original colors. Volunteer architects and lawyers served on the board, contributing their expertise to oversee the work. Restoration was painstakingly slow, both to adhere to the Secretary of the Interior's Standards for Rehabilitation and because the pace of donations was slow as the JHC Board conducted fund-raising events, sought grants, and enlisted volunteers. Jay descendants and activists from the Jay Coalition raised funds each year, as they had earlier for the battle to save the site. The first big breakthrough was a gift of $3 million from one of the Jay Coalition's founders, Catherine (Kitty) Aresty. A building restoration fund could be established, with a capital budget. Specific discrete restoration projects were identified and new donors sought for these. By 2009, the annual operating revenues to pay for insurance, maintenance, utilities, research, annual audit fees, printing, educational programs, set-asides for a reserve fund, and site preservation activities, was $200,000 per year, much of this raised by fund-raising events organized by volunteers. Without volunteers leading and staffing much of this effort, the JHC could not have raised and spent the more than $7 million to meet restoration costs for the buildings and grounds.

The JHC's commitment has been to celebrate the life and contributions of John Jay nationally, and to restore and exhibit all periods of the history of the estate in Rye. Suzanne Clary was elected JHC's president in 1991, and launched an inspired strategic plan and projects. In 2013, Westchester County turned over to the JHC stewardship of the 21 acres, which the County had neglected; parks officials had little interest in historic restoration and informally were preparing for the day when they could annex the acres to the adjacent Marshlands Conservancy Park. Suzanne Clary and her Board could now turn to restoring the entire landscape. The JHC had discovered landscape designs for the 20th century estate gardens in an archive in New Jersey, and had commissioned new studies on the historic landscape from prehistoric to contemporary periods. A cultural landscape plan was prepared for the entire 23 acre Jay Estate. The estate is being returned to a dignified setting, befitting the adjacent Jay Family Cemetery, where John Jay rests. Begun in 2016, the historical restoration of the estate's gardens is estimated to cost $1.5 million; $500,000 came from private donations to match a New York State "Empire Development" grant of $500,000. The success inspired two families to donate another $350.000. Douglas P. Clement, *Of (Founding) Fathers and Sons*, N.Y. Times, WE, March 13, 2016 at 10.

4. Grants

Grants for the rehabilitation and preservation of historic properties are available from government and non-government agencies. Among federal agencies, HUD offers a number of grant programs. *See* Community Development Block Grant Program, Preserving America, https://portal.hud.gov/hudportal/documents/huddoc?id=DOC_14211.pdf (last visited September 15, 2017). The National Trust for Historic Preservation offers small grants to non-profits and public agencies, for among other things, main street development and preservation. https://savingplaces.org/stories/how-to-apply-for-grants-from-the-national-trust-preservation-fund#.Wbv2zch942w (last visited September 15, 2017). For a comprehensive guide to historic preservation funding, *see* U.S. Senator Kirsten E. Gillibrand, A Guide to Historic Preservation, Arts, & Cultural Institutions, & Tourism Funding Opportunities and Incentives: How to Navigate the Funding Process (2015), https://www.gillibrand.senate.gov/imo/media/doc/Gillibrand%20Historic%20Preservation,%20Arts%20&%20Cultural%20Institutions,%20&%20Tourism%20Funding%20Opportunities%20and%20Incentives%202015.pdf. This guide can be found on the companion website.

Chapter 10

International Stewardship of Cultural Heritage

Cultural heritage is a universal concept, although the degree of importance attributed to its protection may vary among nations. Nevertheless, notions on what is and what kind of protections should be afforded cultural heritage are often evaluated through comparative law analysis. *See* INTERNATIONAL ENCYCLOPEDIA OF COMPARATIVE LAW, vol. 5, § v, Para 128 at 32 (1983) ("Basis for Liability"). The United States has long viewed cultural heritage as possessing international dimensions and consequences; from the beginning of the formal historic preservation movement, the National Trust for Historic Preservation had advanced efforts for the United States to cooperate with other nations in historic preservation, including for the protection of monuments in times of armed conflict. The Trust saw no difference between the destruction of monuments in World War II and the wanton bulldozers destroying monuments in peace time, both equally demoralizing to civilization. ELIZABETH D, MULLOY, NATIONAL TRUST FOR HISTORIC PRESERVATION 32–35 (1976).

Many international environmental agreements directly or indirectly cover historic sites and specify how nations should cooperate to care for historic monuments and sites in both wartime and in peace. These directives have been restated and succinctly presented, primarily for government officials who require ready access to this body of international law, in L. KURUKULASURIYA AND NICHOLAS A. ROBINSON, MANUAL ON INTERNATIONAL ENVIRONMENTAL LAW (UN Environment Programme, 2006), which is accessible at http://digitalcommons.pace.edu/lawfaculty/791/ (last visited April 5, 2017). The United States has otherwise agreed with other nations on norms and standards for stewardship of cultural heritage through its joinder of various pacts and conventions, some of which we discuss here.

A. United Nations Educational, Scientific, and Cultural Organization ("UNESCO")

The United Nations Educational, Scientific, and Cultural Organization ("UNESCO") was formed in 1946 to establish peace "upon the intellectual and moral solidarity of mankind" and "to contribute to peace and security by promoting collaboration among nations through education, science and culture." http://www.un.org/en/sections/history/history-united-nations/ (last visited April 5, 2017). This goal would be accomplished in part, by assuring the protection of the world's cultural property.

1. The International Council of Monuments and Sites ("ICOMOS")

In 1964, the International Council of Monuments and Sites ("ICOMOS") was founded by the Venice Charter for the Conservation and Restoration of Monuments and Sites to act as a primary advisor to UNESCO on the conservation and preservation of architecture and monuments. https://www.icomos.org/charters/venice_e.pdf (last visited March 5, 2017). Monuments are structures that are valued for their "historical, artistic, architectural, scientific or ethnological point of view" and groups of buildings are defined to include "all groups of separate or connected buildings and their surroundings, whether urban or rural, based on their architecture, their homogeneity or their place in the landscape. *See* ICOMOS, http://www.icomos.org/en/. In its advisory capacity, ICOMOS has adopted standards for historic sites and monuments through formal charters and principles, works to formulate proactive plans for the rehabilitation and preservation of sites, and develops links between public authorities and conservationists to coordinate and synthesize efforts. *Id.* at ICOMOS Statutes, Articles 3, 4.

The guidelines established by the Charter were prepared by a group of conservation professionals. ICOMOS is composed of some 10,000 individual expert members in 144 countries, and works through 110 national committees and 28 international scientific committees. Its membership encompasses fields such as architecture, archaeology, anthropology, and history. http://www.icomos.org (last visited March 20, 2017). The United States Committee for ICOMOS facilitates participation by American preservation law specialists in ICOMOS.

2. The Convention Concerning the Protection of World Cultural and Natural Heritage

In 1972, UNESCO adopted the Convention Concerning the Protection of World Cultural and Natural Heritage ("World Heritage Convention"). The World Heritage Convention serves as one of the most important global instruments for conserving natural and cultural heritage. http://whc.unesco.org/en/about (last visited April 5, 2017). Its mission is to identify objects and places recognized as possessing "outstanding universal values." The World Heritage Convention expressed the conviction of the States Parties "that deterioration or disappearance of any item of the cultural ... heritage constitutes a harmful impoverishment of the heritage of all the nations of the world." *WHC, Preamble, Second Recital.* It speaks of the recognized "importance, for all the peoples of the world, of safeguarding this unique and irreplaceable property, to whatever people it may belong," *WHC, Preamble, Fifth Recital,* and declares "that parts of the cultural ... heritage ... of outstanding interest ... need to be preserved as part of the world heritage of mankind as a whole." *WHC, Preamble, Second Recital.* These objects and places are inscribed on the World Heritage List.

The kinds of natural or cultural sites that can be considered for inscription on the World Heritage List include monuments (architectural works, sculpture and painting, elements or structures of an archaeological nature), cave dwellings, buildings, groups of buildings because of their architecture, their homogeneity, or their place in the landscape; sites, natural and man-made; archeological areas; physical and biological formations; and geological and physiographical formations that constitute the habitat of threatened species of animals and plants, which are of outstanding universal value from the point of view of history, art or science, archeology, conservation or natural beauty.

Cultural and natural property that forms part of the world heritage remains subject to the legislation of the state where it is located. Thus, territorial sovereignty and property rights over elements of the world's natural heritage are respected by the World Heritage Convention. However, the country hosting a heritage site has both rights and duties. Article 4 requires each party to ensure the identification, protection, conservation, presentation, and transmission of heritage to future generations, and States Parties must cooperate in the protection of the world cultural and natural heritage. This duty includes an obligation not to take any deliberate measures that might damage directly or indirectly the cultural or natural heritage. Parties periodically have to submit reports to a specially created committee on the measures that they have taken to implement the Convention.

The Convention establishes a World Heritage Committee to apply these provisions. This "Intergovernmental Committee for the Protection of the Cultural and Natural Heritage of Outstanding Universal Value," consists of twenty-one members elected by the General Assembly of States Parties during the General Conference of UNESCO. Representatives of international intergovernmental and Non-Governmental Organizations may attend the meetings in an advisory capacity and be invited to participate in particular discussions and problems.

The World Heritage Committee also has the power to remove properties from the World Heritage List if the property has deteriorated to the extent that it has lost those characteristics which determined its inclusion in the World Heritage List, where the intrinsic qualities of a World Heritage site were already threatened at the time of its nomination by actions of man, and where the necessary corrective measures as outlined by the State Party at the time, have not been taken within the time proposed. The possibility of deletion from the List acts as an incentive on States Parties to comply with the Convention's requirements.

The World Heritage Convention has so far been ratified by 183 States Parties, and 1052 sites have been inscribed on the World Heritage List in 165 countries. For inscription of any site on the List, a site must meet one or more of the ten criteria contained in the Operational Guidelines for the Implementation of the World Heritage Convention and their related conditions of integrity. *Operational Guidelines for the Implementation of the World Heritage Convention,* 77, U.N. Doc. WHC. 17/01 (July 12, 2017), UNESCO, Intergov't Comm. for Prot. of World Cultural & Nat. Heritage. The sites on the list reflect different values: 814 are related to outstanding cultural values, 203 have extraordinary natural values, and 35 reflect both cultural and natural values.

Notes and Questions

1. **When is a monument historically significant?** Preserving cultural monuments can involve nations in a range of international disputes. The sites in the Holy City of Jerusalem are symptomatic of this problem. *See* 2016 UNESCO Draft Decision (UNESCO Doc. 200 EX/PX/DR.25.2 Rev. PARIS, 12 October 2016); https://www.theatlantic.com/news/archive/2016/10/unesco-controversy-over-jerusalems-holy-sites/504149/ (last visited April 6, 2017). How political are decisions over monuments? Consider this English journalist's analysis:

> Well, just nine per cent of the world heritage sites are in Africa and seven per cent in Arab countries, compared with 50 per cent in Europe and North America. This does suggest a certain cultural bias, but there are other political considerations. The US, whose government saw UNESCO as a stalking horse for Communist and Third World countries to attack the West throughout the 1980s and 1990s, has refused to propose any new heritage sites since 1995. In that year, plans to open a gold mine near Yellowstone Park in Wyoming got the area placed on UNESCO's "world heritage in danger" list. Conservatives in Washington decided that the scheme was an undercover attempt to subvert America's rights to govern itself and to destroy the fabric of US sovereignty.

Paul Vallely, *The Big Question: What is a World Heritage Site, and does the accolade make a difference?* The Independent (November 78, 2008) at http://www.independent.co.uk/news/world/politics/the-big-question-what-is-a-world-heritage-site-and-does-the-accolade-make-a-difference-997955.html (last visited April 6, 2017).

2. **Threats from all directions.** Threats to listed monuments come from many directions. When the preservation of a World Heritage site is in doubt, actions are taken to address the threats to the site. Deliberate destruction of a monument is an extreme example. Consider the "Old Bridge" (*Stari Most*), which spanned the Neretva river in the old town of Mostar. The original bridge was built by Suleiman the Magnificent in 1557 to replace an older wooden suspension bridge. The arch of the Old Bridge stood for 427 years, until it was destroyed during armed conflict between Bosnia and Herzegovina in the former Yugoslavia in 1993. After its destruction, a temporary cable bridge was erected in its place. Not essential as a military target, its destruction has been termed by Andras Riedlmayer as an act for "killing memory," aiming to erase evidence of a shared cultural heritage and peaceful co-existence. Martin Coward, Urbicide: The Politics of Urban Destruction 1–7 (2009). Reconstruction commenced in 2001, and a reconstructed bridge opened on July 23, 2004, after an estimated cost of $15.5 million paid for by UNESCO and several nations. a. What should nations do when confronted with the destruction of world heritage by belligerents that are not part of the United Nations systems? Consider the Bamiyan Valley cultural assets.

Archeological Remains of the Bamiyan Valley:
The WHC Findings for Inscription and the Aftermath

Brief Description

The cultural landscape and archaeological remains of the Bamiyan Valley represent the artistic and religious developments which from the 1st to the 13th centuries characterized ancient Bakhtria, integrating various cultural influences into the Gandhara school of Buddhist art. The area contains numerous Buddhist monastic ensembles and sanctuaries, as well as fortified edifices from the Islamic period. The site is also testimony to the tragic destruction by the Taliban of the two standing Buddha statues, which shook the world in March 2001.

* * *

General view of the Bamiyan Valley

"Outstanding Universal Value"

* * *

Enclosed between the high mountains of the Hindu Kush in the central highlands of Afghanistan, the Bamiyan Valley opens out into a large basin bordered to the north by a long, high stretch of rocky cliffs. The Cultural Landscape and Archaeological Remains of the Bamiyan Valley comprise a serial property consisting of eight separate sites within the Valley and its tributaries. Carved into the *Bamiyan Cliffs* are the two niches of the giant Buddha statues (55m and 38m high) destroyed by the Taliban in 2001, and numerous caves forming a large ensemble of Buddhist monasteries, chapels and sanctuaries along the foothills of the valley dating from the 3rd to the 5th century C.E. In several of the caves and niches, [are] remains of wall paintings and seated Buddha figures. * * * The numerous Buddhist monastic ensembles and sanctuaries, as well as fortified structures from the Islamic period, testify to the interchange of Indian, Hellenistic, Roman, Sasanian and Islamic influences.

The site is also testimony to recurring reactions to iconic art, the most recent being the internationally condemned deliberate destruction of the two standing Buddha statues in March 2001.

Criterion (i): The Buddha statues and the cave art in Bamiyan Valley are an outstanding representation of the Gandharan school in Buddhist art in the Central Asian region.

Criterion (ii): The artistic and architectural remains of Bamiyan Valley, an important Buddhist centre on the Silk Road, are an exceptional testimony to the interchange of Indian, Hellenistic, Roman and Sasanian influences as the basis for the development of a particular artistic expression in the Gandharan school. To this can be added the Islamic influence in a later period.

Criterion (iii): The Bamiyan Valley bears an exceptional testimony to a cultural tradition in the Central Asian region, which has disappeared.

Criterion (iv): The Bamiyan Valley is an outstanding example of a cultural landscape which illustrates a significant period in Buddhism.

Criterion (vi): The Bamiyan Valley is the most monumental expression of the western Buddhism. It was an important centre of pilgrimage over many centuries. Due to their symbolic values, the monuments have suffered at different times of their existence, including the deliberate destruction in 2001, which shook the whole world.

Integrity (2011)

The heritage resources in Bamiyan Valley have suffered from various disasters and some parts are in a fragile state. A major loss to the integrity of the site was the destruction of the large Buddha statues in 2001. However, a significant proportion of all the attributes that express the Outstanding Universal Value of the site, such as Buddhist and Islamic architectural forms and their setting in the Bamiyan landscape, remain intact at all 8 sites within the boundaries, including the vast Buddhist monastery in the Bamiyan Cliffs which contained the two colossal sculptures of the Buddha.

Authenticity (2003)

The ... remains of the Bamiyan Valley continue to testify to the different cultural phases of its history. Seen as a cultural landscape, the Bamiyan Valley, ... continues to express its Outstanding Universal Value in terms of form and materials, location and setting, but may be vulnerable in the face of development and requires careful conservation and management.

Protection and management requirements (2011)

The monuments and archaeological remains of the Bamiyan Valley are public property, owned by the State of Afghanistan. However, large parts of the buffer zone are in private ownership.... The State *Law on the Protection of Historical and Cultural Properties* (Ministry of Justice, May 21st 2004) is in force and provides the basis for financial and technical resources. The management of the serial property is under the authority of the Ministry of Information and Culture ("MoIC") and its relevant departments.... At present, the management system is provisional with help from the international community for the appropriate administrative, scientific and technical resources. Since 2003, UNESCO has been leading a three-phase safe-guarding plan for the property. Its focus has been to consolidate the Buddha niches, to safeguard the artefacts that survived the destruction of the Buddha statues and to render the site safe, notably by pursuing the complex de-mining operations at the site. A Management Plan for the property is under preparation with the objective to prepare and implement a programme for the protection, conservation and presentation of the Bamiyan Valley, to undertake exploration and excavation of the archaeological remains, and to prepare and implement a programme for sustainable cultural tourism in the Valley.... In March 2011, it was concluded by Afghan officials and international experts at a meeting of the 9th Bamiyan Expert Working Group hosted by UNESCO that the World Heritage site is potentially ready to be removed from the List of World Heritage in Danger by 2013, pending continued progress in addressing security risks, the structural stability of the remains of the two giant Buddha sculptures and their niches, the conservation of the archaeological remains and mural paintings and implementation of the Management Plan.

Justification for Inscription Document

Long Description

* * * The nominated site consists of eight separate core zones, each with its buffer zone: the Bamiyan Cliffs on the north side of the valley include the two colossal niches that contained the large standing Buddha figures. The Kakrak Valley caves, some 3 km south-east of the Bamiyan cliffs, date from the 6th to 13th centuries. The two main important groups of the Fuladi Valley caves ... which have important decorative features, ... consist[ing] of fortification walls, towers, and citadels of earthen structures dating from the 6th to 8th centuries. * * *

Historical Description

Afghanistan was the ancient Bactria, one of the provinces of the Persian Empire under the Achaemenids[, under the rule of] Alexander the Great, the Seleucid dynasty, and the Maurya dynasty of northern India. [From the 2d Century, there was a succession of rulers, t]he Kushans, a group of nomadic tribes, [to the Sasanians in the] mid-3rd century, [to central Asian nomads] ... in the 5th century; [to] a coalition of Sasanians and Western Turks ... mid-6th century. The Silk Roads passed through Afghanistan, and contributed to the diffusion of Buddhism from India in this region in the 1st century CE. The Kushans were patrons of the arts and religion, and were responsible for the introduction of Buddhist art in the Bactrian style, which was influenced by Hellenistic art, and the Sasanians. Islamic art and architecture were introduced to Bamiyan in the 11th century CE.... The town of Bamiyan was designed on the model of the Khorassan region of Iran.... [T]he development included the fortified settlements.... The army of Genghis Khan ruined the town of Bamiyan and looted the Buddhist monasteries in the early 13th century. The Mughal emperor Aurangzeb (1618–1707) ordered his army to shoot off the legs of the large Buddha. The valley was abandoned for a long period, but at the end of the 19th century, the caves were inhabited and used as shelters for domestic animals.

In 1979, there were over 7,000 inhabitants in the Bamiyan town. From the 1970s, the area was used by the military. In the 1990s, it was exposed to armed conflicts. In 2001, the large Buddha statues were destroyed by the Taliban.

Cultural Landscape and Archaeological Remains of the Bamiyan Valley—UNESCO World Heritage Centre, whc.unesco.org/en/list/208/ (last visited Feb. 8, 2018).

3. **Recourses for deliberate destruction.** Despite the declaration in the World Heritage Convention preamble that cultural property is "the world heritage of mankind as a whole," and must be protected and preserved, if those bent on destruction are not inclined to embrace this position, such as when the Taliban destroyed the statues of Bamiyan, the recourses available to the international community may be very limited. a. Will close scrutiny, comment, and criticism of the acts be effective or will otherwise peace-seeking nations have to resort to military strategies to protect the heritage that sustains us all? *See* Roger O'Keefe, *World Cultural Heritage Obligations to the International Community As a Whole?*, 53 Int'l Comparative L. Q. 189 (2004) (discussing the problem of achieving adherence to the principles espoused in the Convention). For a comprehensive description of the protections for cultural property, *see* Roger W. Mastalir, *A Proposal for Protecting the "Cultural" and "Property" Aspects of Cultural Property Under International Law*, 16 Fordham Int'l L. J. 1033 (1992–93).

B. Inscription on the List of World Heritage in Danger

The World Heritage Convention maintains a "List of World Heritage in Danger." WHC, Article 11, paragraph 4; *World Heritage in Danger: A Compendium Of Key Decisions On The Conservation Of Natural World Heritage Properties Via The List Of World Heritage in Danger* (IUCN, 2009). Danger is ascertained by referring to specific and proven imminent or potential threats that could have a negative effect on a property's World Heritage values. http://whc.unesco.org/en/Committee (last visited April 6, 2017). States Parties are eligible for financial assistance from the World Heritage Fund, annually about $4 million to assist them in identifying, preserving, and promoting World Heritage sites. There is also available emergency assistance for urgent action to repair damage caused by human-made or natural disasters.

C. Helping Nations to Protect Monuments

UNESCO was instrumental in cooperating with Egypt to save monuments from the era of the Pharoahs in the Nile River valley when the High Aswan Dam was constructed.

UNESCO's Rescue of the Abu Simbel Temple

While the international movement for protecting heritage coalesced after the world wars, one event that aroused particular international concern during peacetime was the decision to build the Aswan High Dam in Egypt, which promised to flood the valley containing ancient treasures, the Abu Simbel temples. In 1959, UNESCO made an appeal to the governments of Egypt and Sudan to save the temples, then launched an international campaign which involved dismantling and moving the temples to dry ground. The campaign cost about $80 million, half of which was donated by some fifty countries.

In 1954, an international committee of experts determined that a new dam over the Nile River was necessary to facilitate greater farm operations in order to produce sufficient food for the growing Egyptian population. Before dams, farmers could plant but once per year after the Nile had flooded and left behind its rich silt. A new dam would enable farmers to plant three crops instead of just one. The old dam had ceased to be effective in controlling the flooding. A new dam would also generate electricity to support industrial activity in the nation. Kanchana Wangkeo, *Monumental Challenges: The Lawfulness of Destroying Cultural Heritage During Peacetime*, 28 Yale J. Int'l L. 183 (2003); *see also* Lucia Allais, *Integrities: The Salvage of Abu Simbel*, 50 Grey Room 6 (Winter 2013).

Construction on the Aswan High Dam started in 1960 and was completed after eleven years in 1971. It is 3600 meters long and 111 meters high. It has 12 turbines, which generate over 10 billion kilowatts of electricity every year. Thirty thousand Egyptian people were involved in building the dam, working day and night to complete it.

When the new dam was proposed, experts predicted that the dam would back up the Nile for more than 400 miles into Egypt and over 300 miles into Sudan, covering the area known as lower Nubia. Nubia had been the site of at least six different civilizations between 3800 B.C. and 600 A.D. The dam threatened the site and the numerous artifacts found there, including the famous temples of Abu Simbel and Philae Island, situated in the Nile River. These temples were culturally significant because of their historical method of construction and their detailed artistic features. They were hewn into the side of a mountain. One chamber reached as far as 61 meters.

Historical Relics and Sovereignty

Egypt's motivation for the dam was economic necessity. A dramatic rise in population pressed for increased food production and abundant electricity. President Nasser determined that land reclamation was an integral part of the nation's agronomic policy. That same economic necessity meant the destruction of the historic relics. As no state objected to the construction of the dam, it took an appeal from the affected nations, Egypt and Sudan, to enlist international involvement to protect historic relics. While the norms of state sovereignty prevailed over international reactions to cultural heritage, there might also have been a norm against destroying cultural heritage. Political concerns seem to have operated to prevent nations from attempting to block the construction of the dam, instead choosing to work with Egypt to preserve those monuments in the dam's way. Wangkeo, 28 YALE J. INT'L L. at 210–212.

International Efforts

Before construction of the dam began, an international mission was launched to save the temples. In 1959, the Egyptian and the Sudanese Governments requested independently from each other, UNESCO's assistance to save the sites and monuments threatened by submergence by the dam. UNESCO appealed for international cooperation to assist these governments and authorized studies preparatory to the work of safeguarding Abu Simbel and archaeological investigations of the sites in Sudanese Nubia to be undertaken as a matter of urgency. To encourage nations to participate in these efforts, Egypt offered to allow the removal of six temples and half of artifacts discovered, with some exceptions. *Id.* at 206.

The international rescue efforts saved the temples of Abu Simbel and Philae Island as well as twenty other Nubian temples. *Id.* at 208. In order to relocate the temples, they had to be cut into pieces and put together again on new sites. Twenty-six countries participated directly in the excavation and preservation efforts and forty-seven countries contributed a total of $25.5 million, while private individuals and groups donated $7.5 million. *Id.* at 208. President Kennedy asked Congress for $10,000,000 to join in the effort. His goals were twofold—preserve priceless historical monuments, but also to establish ties in the Middle East and North Africa as a counterbalance to the influence of the Soviet Union, which had financed the construction of the dam. Congress appropriated $16 million. In appreciation for its efforts in the rescue, Egypt presented the United States the Temple of Dendur, built around 15 B.C. by the Roman governor of Egypt and dedicated to Isis and Osiris. Weighing over 800 tons, the temple was transported in 661 pieces on the United

States freighter Concordia Star in 1965. To select the site for the temple, the government set up bidding contest. The Metropolitan Museum of Art in New York City won the contest and displays the temple in the Sackler Wing, where the scenery and lighting of Nubia are recreated, alongside a reflecting pool. www.ilsussidiario.net/News/English-Spoken-Here/2011/4/6/PHOTO-50-years-since-JFK-helped-save-Egyptian-monuments/165305 (last visited April 6, 2017).

Removal and Reassembly

Abu Simbel, one of six temples erected in Nubia during the reign of Ramses II, is comprised of two massive rock temples — the larger one in honor of Egypt's then three state deities and features four large statues of Ramses and the smaller, dedicated to the goddess Hathor, as personified by Nefertari, Ramses' wife. The temples are believed to have been carved out of the mountainside during 13th century B.C., as a lasting monument to Ramses and his queen and to intimidate his Nubian neighbors. Because they were hewn out of single pieces of stone, the temples had to be sawed into more than 3,000 ten to forty ton blocks. The reassembled monument is 65 meters higher and 200 meters back from the river on an artificial hill made from a domed structure. The removal and reassembly of the temple is considered by many to be one of the most remarkable feats of archaeological engineering. Allais, 50 Grey Room at 20–21.

The success of this campaign led to others — Venice, Italy and its Lagoon and the Archaeological Ruins at Moenjodaro in Pakistan, and restoration of the Borobodur Temple Compounds in Indonesia. http://whc.unesco.org/en/about.

Abu Simbel, Egypt. Photo by David Mateos Garcia, Wikimedia Commons.

D. Protections for Cultural Resources during Times of Armed Conflict

1. Conventions, Pacts, and Protocols

Although concern for the protection of cultural artifacts dates back to ancient times and legislation for the protection of monuments and works of art appeared in Europe as early as the 15th century, the first international convention on the issue was the 1899 Hague Convention with Respect to the Laws and Customs of War on Land. *See* B.G. Trigger, A History of Archeological Thought 29–30, 36 (1994); L.V. Prott and P.J. O'Keefe, Law and the Cultural Heritage 34 (1984). Among other things, the Convention prohibited the pillaging of towns and the destruction or intentional damage to religious, charitable and educational institutions, historical monuments, and works of art or science. Articles 23, 27, 28, 56.

The 1907 Hague Convention annexed many of the articles and provisions of the 1899 version, but stressed the necessity of giving notice to the enemy of protected properties by marking the buildings with distinctive particular and visible signs, so that troops and military activities could avoid them. Convention (IV) Respecting the Laws and Customs of War on Land and its Annex: Regulations Concerning the Laws and Customs of War on Land, The Hague, 18 Oct. 1907, www.archive.org/stream/hagueconventions00inteuoft/hagueconventions00inteuoft_djvu.txt, Articles 27, 56.

The Roerich Pact, sangha.net/roerich/roerich-pact.html, was signed into effect in Washington, D.C., in 1935, largely as a Pan-American rather than an international treaty. The pact purported to adopt a universal flag to be used in times of danger to preserve national and private immovable monuments during times of war and during peace. http://www.cprinst.org/Home/cultural-property-laws/1935-roerich-pact (last visited April 6, 2017). It specified that historic monuments, museums, scientific, artistic, educational, and cultural institutions so marked, should be considered as neutral and thus respected and protected by belligerents. *Id.* at Article 1.

While the terms of the Conventions and the Roerich Pact were hopeful, warring nations in their aggression did not heed the interdictions on injury to property of cultural and historical significance. The historian, Robert Bevan, comments that the destruction of buildings—historic, symbolic, or merely utilitarian, "is often the result of political imperatives rather than simply military necessity." Architecture, he maintains, "is not just maimed in the crossfire; it is targeted for assassination or mass murder." Culturally significant buildings are destroyed as a part of genocide, as political propaganda, to demoralize an enemy. The fire-bombing of Dresden and the wholesale cultural annihilation of Warsaw by Nazi occupiers are cases in point. The Destruction Of Memory: Architecture at War 271–72 (2006).

The haunting atrocities and excesses of war led to the 1949 Geneva Convention, which aimed to redress war crimes against nations and people, but it did not expressly cover destruction of cultural property—those things that yet define and sustain a people. *Fourth Geneva Convention of August 12, 1949 Relative to the Protection of Civil-*

ian Persons in Time of War. Some limited protection for historic references and monuments came in the 1977 Protocols I and II, additions to the Convention adopted to protect cultural property. Article 53 of Protocol I, pertaining to international armed conflict and Article 16 of Protocol II, pertaining to non-international armed conflict, both prohibit acts of hostility directed against historic monuments, works of art, or places of worship, and the use of such property for military purposes. Article 53 of Protocol I also prohibits reprisals against such property.

The 1954 Hague Convention deals exclusively with cultural property. *The Convention for the Protection of Cultural Property in the Event of Armed Conflict,* portal.UNESCO.org/culture/en/ev.php-RL_ID=8450&URL_D0=D0_TOPIC &URL_SECTION=201.html) (last visited April 6, 2017). The United States Senate ratified the 1954 Hague Convention in 2008. The Convention commands that cultural property, both movable and immovable, must be safeguarded and respected as the common heritage of humankind; that cultural heritage is the property of all mankind regardless of its location; and "damage to cultural property belonging to any people whatsoever means damage to the cultural heritage of all mankind, since each people makes its contribution to the culture of the whole world." *Id.*

Article 1 of the 1954 Hague Convention provides a non-exhaustive list of "cultural property" that includes significant architectural monuments, art works, whether religious or secular, books or manuscripts of artistic or historical significance, museums, large libraries, archives, archaeological sites, historic buildings, and other objects of artistic, historical, or archaeological interest, as well as scientific collections and refuges created specifically to shelter cultural property during hostilities.

Under Article 4, nations are obligated to take measures during peacetime and during war to safeguard and respect such property. They must refrain from locating strategic or military equipment near cultural property and the targeting of cultural property, except in cases of military necessity, and must prohibit and prevent theft, pillage, or misappropriation of, and any acts of vandalism directed against cultural property.

The protections of the 1954 Hague Convention were strengthened by two additional Protocols. The First Protocol, written at the same time as the Convention, prohibits the exportation of cultural objects from occupied territory, and requires the return at the end of hostilities of any cultural objects illegally removed from occupied territory or placed in the territory of another State Party for safekeeping during armed conflict. *Protocol to the Convention for the Protection of Cultural Property in the Event of Armed Conflict,* portal.UNESCO.org/culture/en/ev.php-RL_ID=8450&URL_D0=D0_TOPIC &URL_SECTION=201.html) (last visited April 6, 2017).

The Second Protocol of 1999 deals with the issue of responsibility for prohibited acts, clarifying that each State Party has an obligation to create a criminal offense under its domestic law and to extend jurisdiction to non-nationals for certain offenses. *Id.* Articles 16, 17 (extradition). It narrows the military necessity waiver, requiring a Nation to ascertain whether a military objective includes cultural property, to avoid and minimize incidental damage to cultural property, and refrain from undertaking an attack that will cause harm to cultural property that is disproportionately excessive in comparison to the expected military advantage. Articles 6, 7.

The Second Protocol also provides enhanced protection to cultural property in the case of cultural heritage of the "greatest importance for humanity"; which property is not to be used for military purposes or to shield military sites. Any cultural property under enhanced protection is entitled to absolute immunity from attack, except under narrow circumstances. Articles 10, 11, 12. The Second Protocol further provides for the sheltering of movable cultural property in times of conflict, establishes centers for property of very great importance, Article 8, and provides protections for such property in transport. Articles 12, 13, 14.

Also of note, the Second Protocol prohibits the carrying out of archaeological excavation, except where "strictly required to safeguard, record or preserve cultural property" and prohibits "any alteration to, or change of use of, cultural property which is intended to conceal or destroy cultural, historical or scientific evidence." Article 9.

Notes

1. **The problem of enforcement.** As with all treaties and pacts, enforcement of the Hague Convention and Protocols (against both signatories and non-signatories) has proven to be the greatest obstacle toward the realization of their provisions. The desire for rude martial advantage will often prevail over sentimental and pacific concerns, as shown by the unwarranted destruction of the Mostar Bridge in Yugoslavia, in 1993. The monument had for many decades served as the literal and metaphoric bridge between the two cultures (Muslim and Christian) on either side of it. The 2015 wanton destruction of the 2000 year-old Tempel of Bel, in Palmyra, Syria, with its colonnaded avenues and many stone carved temples, by the Islamist military group ISIS, left only the "ruins of memory." Heidi Stalla, *What We Lost in Palmyra*, Wilson Q. 3 (Fall 2015). The destruction was part of a propaganda campaign. http://news.nationalgeographic.com/ 2015/09/150901-isis-destruction-looting-ancient-sites-iraq-syria-archaeology/ (last visited April 2, 2017). As it stands, only international customary law, to the extent that it can be shown that the destruction of cultural property is prohibited by principles of universal recognition, may provide a basis for actions against non-signatories.

2. **Criminal conviction in the Hague.** In September 2016, Ahmad al Faqi al Mahdi was convicted of war crimes for destroying historic shrines, nine mausoleums, and a mosque, at the world heritage site of Timbuktu, Mali in 2012. Article 8(2)(e)(iv) of the Rome Statute punishes the "intentional ... attacks against buildings dedicated to religion, education, art, science or charitable purposes, historic monuments, hospitals and places where the sick and wounded are collected, provided they are not military objectives." Rome Statute of the International Criminal Court, U.N. Doc. A/Conf. 183/9. It was the first time that the court in The Hague had tried a case of cultural destruction. Mahdi was a member of Ansar Dine, an Islamist group that occupied Timbuktu for months. The Ansar Dine regarded the shrines and the city's ancient manuscripts, covering everything from history to astronomy, as heretical. Mahdi,

a religious scholar, directed fighters to wreck several sites with pickaxes and chisels after failing to deter locals from praying at them. He was sentenced to nine years imprisonment. *Situation in the Republic Of Mali, In The Case of the Prosecutor v. Ahmad Al Faqi Al Mahdi,* No. ICC-01/12-01/15 27 September 2016. Timbuktu is famous for its distinctive mud and wood architecture. It was a center of Islamic learning between the 13th and 17th centuries and was added to the UNESCO world heritage list in 1988. More than 700,000 manuscripts had survived in public libraries and private collections, as well as books on religion, law, literature and science.

3. **Additional reading.** For additional coverage of the international regime for protecting cultural property, consider the following sources: Patty Gerstenblith, *The Destruction of Cultural Heritage: A Crime Against Property or A Crime Against People?,* 15 J. Marshall Rev. Intell. Prop. L. 336 (2015); Patty Gerstenblith, *From Bamiyan to Baghdad: The Conduct of Warfare and the Preservation of Cultural Heritage at the Beginning of the Twenty-First Century,* 37 Geo. J. Int'l L. 245 (2006); Cherif Bassiouni, *Reflections on Criminal Jurisdiction in International Protection of Cultural Property,* 10 Syracuse J. Int'l L. & Com. 281 (1983); Roger O'Keefe, The Protection of Cultural Property in Armed Conflict (2006); Kevin Chamberlain, War and Cultural Heritage 3 (2004); Jiri Toman, The Protection of Cultural Property in the Event of Armed Conflict 3 (1996); War and Occupation in Iraq, *Chapter 2, Destruction of Cultural Heritage,* Global Policy Forum, www.globalpolicy.org/component/content/article/168/37146.html (last visited April 6, 2017); Sabine von Schorlemer, Cultural Heritage Law: Recent Developments of the Laws of War and Occupation (2009).

2. The Blue Shield

The problems of applying international laws to protect monuments in times of armed conflict gave rise to the establishment of the International Committee of the Blue Shield ("ICBS") in 1954, as an analogous effort to that of the Red Cross. http://www.ancbs.org/cms/en/about-us (last visited March 16, 2017). ICOMOS is an advisor to "Blue Shield International." After reading the description of Blue Shield International below, reflect on the reasons why the protection of monuments in times of armed conflict continues to be so problematic.

The International Committee of the Blue Shield (ICBS)

A Professional Committee, an International and Independent Organization

It covers museums and archives, audiovisual supports, libraries, and monuments and sites. It brings together the knowledge, experience and international networks of the following non-governmental organizations dealing with cultural heritage:

-ICA: International Council on Archives
-ICOM: International Council of Museums
-IFLA: International Federation of Library Associations and Institutions
-ICOMOS: International Council on Monuments and Sites
-CCAAA: Coordinating Council of Audiovisual Archives Associations

Increasing awareness, Training, Intervention

ICBS works for the protection of the world cultural heritage by co-ordinating preparations to meet and respond to emergency situations as well as post-crisis support.

ICBS promotes good standards through risk management training and awareness-raising campaigns for professionals and the general public. Its unrivalled body of expertise allows the Organisation to collect and share information on threats to cultural property worldwide, thus helping international players to take the appropriate measures in case of armed conflict or disaster. ICBS intervenes as an advisor and cooperates with other bodies including UNESCO, ICCROM and the International Committee of the Red Cross (ICEC). Finally in emergency situations, ICBS encourages the safeguarding and the restoration of cultural property, the protection of threatened goods, and helps the professionals from the affected countries to recover from disasters.

International Recognition

The Second Protocol to the Hague Convention agreed in April 1999 gave a new impetus to ICBS's role and that of its associated organizations. Indeed, ICBS is recognized as an advisory international organization to the inter-governmental Committee for the Protection of Cultural Property in the Event of Armed Conflict.

A National Committee Structure

The international initiative of ICBS is taken up and supported by local initiatives. Blue Shield Committees were set up in 20 countries and are being formed in 19 other countries. They bring together the various professions, local and national government, the emergency services and the armed forces. They also provide a forum for them to improve emergency preparedness by sharing experiences and exchanging information. They supply a focus for raising national awareness of the threats to cultural heritage. These Committees promote the ratification and implementation by national governments of the Hague Convention. The Association of National Committees of the Blue Shield (ANCBS) has its headquarters in The Hague, Netherlands. It was founded in December 2008 to coordinate the efforts made by all the National Committees regarding the strategic and operational guidelines adopted by ICBS.

3. Protections for Cultural Property during the Civil War: The Lieber Code

Originally published as General Orders No. 100, by the War Department in 1863, the Lieber Code was the result of an initiative urged by Francis Lieber to the commander of the Union forces during the Civil War. The aim was to summarize the laws of war and to identify and highlight those humane aspects. Lieber was born in Berlin and, as a youth, fought in his native country's wars against France. While he was a scholar of history and political science, Lieber had more than an academic interest in the subject of war: three sons fought in the Civil War, two on the Union side and the third, fighting for the South, was killed. Theodor Meron, *Francis Lieber's Code and Principles of Humanity*, 36 COLUM. J. TRANSNAT'L L. 269, 271 (1997).

Lieber believed in a harsh and violent war on the theory that the harsher the war, the shorter the war; that "[t]he more vigorously wars are pursued, the better it is for humanity." *Id.* at 271; *see, e.g.,* Lieber Code Art. 15 (military necessity admits of destruction of life and limb of armed enemies; Art. 17 (starving the enemy permitted). Paradoxically, in Lieber's mind, a harsh war did not entail the wanton infliction of cruelties, *see, e.g.,* Lieber Code, Art. 11 (no extortions or revenge); Art. 16 (no cruelty); Art. 28 (no retaliation); Art. 68 (no unnecessary and revengeful destruction of life); Art. 71 (no infliction of additional wounds on the injured), nor the total annihilation of all that is precious in the conquered nation. Even though ownership of the cultural resources is said to belong to the conquering nation, the Code nonetheless requires protection of these resources. It starts with the proposition that "[a] victorious army appropriates all public money, seizes all public movable property ... and sequesters for its own benefit or of that of its government all the revenues of real property belonging to the hostile government or nation. The title to such real property remains in abeyance during military occupation, and until the conquest is made complete." *Id.* at Art. 31. But, then goes on to exempt certain property from the meaning of "public property," including that belonging to "churches, hospitals, or other establishments of an exclusively charitable character, to establishments of education, or foundations for the promotion of knowledge, whether public schools, universities, academies of learning or observatories, museums of the fine arts, or of a scientific character." *Id.* at Art. 34. At the same time, the Code prescribes care for those resources taken by the conquering nation.

First, "[c]lassical works of art, libraries, scientific collections, or precious instruments, such as astronomical telescopes, as well as hospitals, must be secured against all avoidable injury, even when they are contained in fortified places whilst besieged or bombarded." *Id.* at Art. 35. Then, only "if such works of art, libraries, collections, or instruments belonging to a hostile nation or government, can be removed without injury, the ruler of the conquering state or nation may order them to be seized and removed for the benefit of the said nation. The ultimate ownership is to be settled by the ensuing treaty of peace." *Id.* at Art 36. The Code goes on to provide that "[i]n no case shall they be sold or given away, if captured by the armies of the United States, nor shall they ever be privately appropriated, or wantonly destroyed or injured." *Id.*

The code can be found at Yale Law School, Lillian Goldman Law Library, The Avalon Project, Documents in Law, History, Diplomacy, http://avalon.law.yale.edu/19th_century/lieber.asp (last visited April 6, 2017).

* * *

E. Return of Stolen Cultural Property

The strong injunctions against destruction of cultural property notwithstanding, during and post wartime, many cultural objects, particularly art works, were routinely and wrongfully removed from their countries of origin. Whether an object could be recovered depended upon the vagaries of the applicable domestic law. In 1970, a UNESCO Special Committee meeting in Paris adopted the *Convention on the Means of Prohibiting and Preventing the Illicit Import, Export and Transfer of Ownership of Cultural Property.* 823 U.N.T.S. 231 (1972), TIAS 7008. The United States joined the Convention in 1983 when Congress passed the Convention on Cultural Property Implementation Act (the "CCPIA"), 19 U.S.C. §2601. The Convention provides for the recovery and return of objects stolen from museums, shrines, and public monuments, and a concerted international effort to thwart the pillage of cultural patrimony.

Museums have changed acquisition standards—backing off from works unless provenance research substantiates that a work was removed from the probable country of modern discovery before 1970 or was legally exported from that country after 1970. *Report Of The AAMD Task Force On The Acquisition Of Archeological Material And Ancient Art, June 4, 2008.*

The National Stolen Property Act, 18 U.S.C. §§371, 2314, 2315, was adopted to enforce foreign laws claiming State title to cultural property, including archeological material. Violation of the Act carries stiff prison terms (up to 10 years). *See United States v. McClain*, 545 F.2d 988 (5th Cir. 1977) and 593 F.2d 658 (5th Cir. 1979) (prosecution for importing Mexican cultural property).

In 1995, the International Institute for the Unification of Private Law, ("UNIDROIT") adopted the Convention on Stolen or Illegally Exported Cultural Objects. The Convention aimed to reduce the illicit trafficking in cultural heritage property under a unified international law that would "gradually, but profoundly, change ... the conduct of the actors in the art market and of all buyers," by requiring the return of a cultural object that has been stolen. The Convention defines cultural objects as those which, on religious or secular grounds, are of importance for archaeology, prehistory, history, literature, art or science. http://www.unidroit.org/instruments/cultural-property/1995-convention (last visited April 1, 2017). *See generally* Carol A. Roehrenbeck, *Repatriation of Cultural Property—Who Owns the Past? An Introduction to Approaches and to Selected Statutory Instruments*, 38 Int'l J. Legal Info. Issue 2, Article 11, available at http://scholarship.law.cornell.edu/ijli/vol38/iss2/11 (last visited March 31, 2017). The Convention does not protect a possessor who is a good faith purchaser; instead, the burden rests with purchasers to inquire into and be certain that the object is being lawfully traded before agreeing to purchase. *Id.*

* * *

Notes

1. **Monuments men.** During World War II, President Franklin Roosevelt authorized the cooperation of academic institutions with the Joint Chiefs of Staff and directed the creation of the "American Commission for the Protection and Salvage of Artistic and Historic Monuments in War Areas," the "Roberts Commission," in August 1943. This led the military to create the "Monuments, Fine Arts and Archives Service (MFA&A)", from which the Monuments Men emerged. The Monuments Men was incorporated as a section of the Supreme Headquarters of the Allied Expeditionary Force commanded by Dwight D. Eisenhower. While the Monuments Men was a collaborative effort of Allied nations, the majority of their members were Americans, comprised of civilians, officers, and enlisted men (and women) from the Army, Navy, and Marine Corps. This rag tag group was able to recover thousands of pieces of art stolen by the Germans and to repatriate the works after the war. *See generally*, James B. Cogbill, *Protection of Arts and Antiquities during Wartime: Examining the Past and Preparing for the Future,* Military Review (Jan./Feb. 2008); Ilaria Dagnini Frey, *How the Monuments Men Saved Italy's Treasures*, Smithsonian Magazine (Jan. 2014); Lynn H. Nicholas, *What the Monuments Men Wrought*, The Wall Street Journal, January 29, 2014, at D5; Tom Mashberg, *Not All Monuments Men Were Men*, The New York Times, February 2, 2014, at 19.

* * *

F. Protecting Landscapes as Historic Architecture and Monuments

1. International Landscape Protection Programs

In 1992 the World Heritage Committee agreed that cultural landscapes could meet the criteria of "outstanding universal value" for inscription on the list of World Heritage

Sites and revised the Convention's guidelines accordingly. The Committee recognized that cultural landscapes have "values in their own right that are different from the scientific and the perceptually based scenic qualities of properties valued for their natural characteristics." The term "cultural landscape" is understood to refer to the intersection of humankind and the natural environment and represent the "combined works of nature and of man" designated in Article 1 of the Convention. "They are illustrative of the evolution of human society and settlement over time, under the influence of the physical constraints and/or opportunities presented by their natural environment and of successive social, economic and cultural forces, both external and internal." Section 36 of the Guidelines, http://whc.unesco.org/en/culturallandscape (last visited September 11, 2017).

The protection of cultural landscapes works to spur modern techniques of sustainable land-use and enhance natural values in the landscape, which are helpful in maintaining biological diversity. *Id.* at Section 38. The World Heritage Convention has divided cultural landscapes into three main categories:

1. Clearly defined landscape designed and created intentionally by man. The most easily identifiable, this category embraces garden and parkland landscapes constructed for aesthetic reasons which are often (but not always) associated with religious or other monumental buildings and ensembles. Examples include Cultural Landscape of Sintra in Portugal and the Lednice-Valtice Cultural Landscape in the Czech Republic, whose primary values are expressed in their design, but also reflect particular cultural responses to the natural environment.
2. Organically evolved landscape. This results from an initial social, economic, administrative, and/or religious imperative, and has developed its present form by association with and in response to its natural environment. Such landscapes reflect that process of evolution in their form and component features. Examples include the Rice Terraces of the Philippine Cordilleras and the Hallstatt-Dachstein Salzkammergut Cultural Landscape in Austria, both of which are traditional settlements that reflect cultural adaptations to their particular natural environments.

   These fall into two sub-categories:

   a. a relict (or fossil) landscape is one in which an evolutionary process came to an end at some time in the past, either abruptly or over a period. Its significant distinguishing features are, however, still visible in material form.
   b. continuing landscape is one which retains an active social role in contemporary society closely associated with the traditional way of life, and in which the evolutionary process is still in progress. At the same time it exhibits significant material evidence of its evolution over time.
3. Associative cultural landscape. The inclusion of such landscapes on the World Heritage List is justifiable by virtue of the powerful religious, artistic, or cultural associations of the natural element, rather than material cultural evidence, which may be insignificant or even absent. The Tongariro National Park in

> New Zealand and Ulur u-Kata Tjuta National Park in Australia, are good examples because they are traditional homelands of indigenous peoples who have deep spiritual associations with these places.

http://whc.unesco.org/documents/publi_wh_papers_26_en.pdf (last visited April 6, 2017); *see generally*, Nora Mitchell and Susan Buggey, *Protected Landscapes and Cultural Landscapes: Taking Advantage of Diverse Approaches*, the George Wright Forum 17(1) 35 (2000); Arnold R. Alanen and Robert Z. Melnick, Preserving Cultural Landscapes in America (2000).

2. European Landscape Convention

The European Landscape Convention, adopted by the Committee of Ministers of the Council of Europe in 2000 in Strasbourg, aims to promote European landscape protection, management, and planning. www.coe.int/europeanlandscapeconvention (last visited April 6, 2017). The convention covers natural, rural, urban, and periurban areas and is concerned with landscapes that might be considered outstanding, as well as everyday or degraded landscapes. "Landscape" is defined as "an area, as perceived by people, whose character is the result of the action and interaction of natural and/or human factors."

The Council expressed the view that landscapes are an integral factor in furtherance of the well-being of individuals and the community, helping to shape a European identity. The preservation of landscapes also serves to stimulate public interest in cultural, ecological, environmental, and social aspects of communities, and provides a resource favorable to economic activity, particularly to tourism. The concern for protecting landscapes was a response to technological advances in agriculture and industry and other commercial activity that had led to degradation of the natural aspects of landscapes. The Convention articulates general legal principles to guide the adoption of national and community landscape policies and the establishment of international co-operation in this field.

Each member state is obligated to undertake programs to protect, manage and/or plan their landscapes through general and specific measures, with the participation of the public and of local and regional authorities. The four general measures at the national level are: 1) the legal recognition of landscape as an essential component of cultural identity; 2) the adoption of policies to protect, manage, and plan landscapes; 3) creation of procedures to include the general public, local and regional authorities in the formulation and implementation of landscape policies; and 4) the integration of landscape policy into regional and town planning policies, cultural, environmental, agricultural, social and economic policies, and any other policies, which may impact the landscape.

The five specific measures at the national level are: 1) raising awareness; 2) training and education on landscape policy, protection, management, and planning; 3) identifying and evaluating, mobilizing efforts and visions; 4) setting landscape quality objectives; and 5) implementing policies, through various instruments for the protection, management and/or planning of landscapes. www.coe.int/europeanlandscape convention (last visited September 11, 2017).

3. Urban Landscapes

The urban landscape is the basis for social cohesion, diversity, and innovation. It enhances livability and encourages regeneration. Every American city and town contains traces of its history in the landscapes, which ought to be preserved as a source of understanding of how a city or town has developed over time. Unfortunately, care is often not taken to protect the larger panorama of history; instead the early historic preservation efforts focused on a few architectural monuments that tended to celebrate a few great men and not the laborers, the service workers, or ethnic communities.

In November 2011, UNESCO adopted a recommendation on the Historic Urban Landscape, http://portal.unesco.org/en/ev.php-URL_ID=48857&URL_DO=DO_TOPIC&URL_SECTION=201.html (last visited April 6, 2017). The recommendation was meant to move the efforts "beyond the preservation of the physical environment, and focuses on the entire human environment with all of its tangible and intangible qualities" and to "increase the sustainability of planning and design interventions by taking into account the existing built environment, intangible heritage, cultural diversity, socio-economic and environmental factors along with local community values." *See New Life for Historic Cites: The Historic Urban Landscape Approach Explained*, http://whc.unesco.org/uploads/news/documents/news-1026-1.pdf (last visited April 6, 2017). UNESCO views the city as a continuum in time and space and a key asset for human, social, and economic development. Preserving the urban landscape is "an alternative method to cutting the city up through 'zoning' into separate conservation areas, which thereby become ghettos of historic preservation." Instead, UNESCO urges cities to support "the integration of environmental, social and cultural concerns into the planning, design and implementation of urban development" toward achieving a balance between "preservation and protection of urban heritage, economic development, functionality and livability of a city." *Id.* at 9. The approach outlined consists of several components, including assessing the city's natural, cultural, and human resources, considering their vulnerability from socio-economic pressures and climate change; using participatory planning and stakeholder consultations to decide on conservation aims and actions; integrating urban heritage values into a wider framework of city development; and establishing priorities for actions and policies for conservation and development, including good stewardship. *Id.* at 16. One recent successful urban landscape project noted is the High Line in New York City. It is a linear public park built on an historic freight rail line elevated above the streets on Manhattan's West Side. It is celebrated for its creative selection and arrangement of plants and park amenities, while revealing the original purposes of the property. More than 3 million people visit the High Line annually. *Id.* at 21.

The High Line, New York City. Photo by Shelby D. Green.

Notes

1. **Systematizing landscape protection regimes.** Despite what seems to be a growing recognition of the importance of protecting cultural landscapes, there are yet many issues still in debate, such as whether it is possible to systemize or codify landscape preservation and to maintain historic or cultural landscapes in the face of ongoing cultural and social changes; how the effort should respond to the threat posed by climate change; and improvements in building materials and design technologies. Significantly, because the emergence of a landscape is fluid and in flux, it is difficult to know when to draw, protect, or ignore boundaries. Questions about who decides cultural significance and how this process plays out through appropriate methods of use, presentation, and interpretation have become critical issues. Charges of eurocentrism being the lens used by the World Heritage Committee in inscribing cultural landscapes on the List cannot be ignored. *See Exploring the Boundaries of Historic Landscape Preservation*, Proceedings of the Twenty-ninth Annual Meeting of the Alliance for Historic Landscape Preservation 2007, https://cup.sites.clemson.edu/pubs/alliance/alliance-book.pdf (last visited April 6, 2017) (scholars debating the larger policy and practical issues of landscape preservation).

G. Social and Economic Benefits of International Protections for Cultural Heritage

Most seem to agree that belonging to an international community of appreciation and concern for cultural heritage that reflects the most inspired acts of humankind, serves to protect and inculcate an appreciation of the values inhering in these properties. Having sites inscribed on the World Heritage List works to elevate the importance of heritage preservation in the consciousness of communities. Sites inscribed on the World Heritage List also benefit from the comprehensive management plans developed by experts for adequate preservation measures and monitoring mechanisms. When these sites are well-planned for and organized respecting sustainable tourism principles, they can bring important funds to the site and to the local economy. UNESCO World Heritage Centre—The World Heritage Convention, http://whc.unesco.org/en/convention (last visited September 11, 2017).

According to a recent study by the Directorate for Cultural Heritage, Norway, the protections afforded to cultural heritage are value generators in a post-industrial economy. https://brage.bibsys.no/xmlui/discover (last visited April 6, 2017). The report found that cultural landscapes, townscapes, and individual buildings are used as input or a backdrop for many electronic games, film and television industry, and by businesses in their marketing and customer relations activities. According to Norway's report, "[c]ultural heritage is a major contributor to the income from tourism, which stands for 5.5% of the European Union GDP, generates more than 30% of its revenues from trade in external services, and employs 6% of the EU workforce." *Id.* at 3. In fact, visits to castles and abbeys in France represented 15% of foreign income. *Id.* at 12.

Recent data shows that the daily spending of the cultural heritage tourist is 60% higher than other tourists/travelers. As Norway's report documents, cultural heritage increases the need for employment in the hotels, restaurants, and in the transport sector. Outside of tourism, the report found evidence of significant job creation from cultural heritage protection, starting with those involved in the rehabilitation and repairs and maintenance of cultural heritage property, having a multiplier effect, creating additional employment from every direct one created. The positive economic and non-economic effects include such benefits as: reducing poverty, raising national employment and total outputs from industrial and service industries; foreign exchange earnings; as well as raising educational levels, identity and cultural, social cohesion and inclusion. *Id.* at 6–7.

* * *

John Jay and International Law

John Jay was the most important diplomat of the 18th century in America. The Continental Congress chose Jay to represent the American States in Madrid in 1779. Spain held lands along the Mississippi River, even then an important trade corridor for the new nation, and was a counterweight to Great Britain during the Revolutionary War. In 1782, Benjamin Franklin summoned him to Paris for the peace negotiations with Great Britain. At Jay's insistence, the three American commissioners refused to commence negotiations until Britain acknowledged them as representatives of the United States of America. Britain had to begin the negotiations by recognizing the independence of the new nation. A plaque commemorates the site of the negotiations in Paris.

Jay returned to Rye, N.Y. from Paris in 1784, but while at sea, the Congress elected Jay to serve as Secretary of Foreign Affairs. He effectively became America's first Secretary of State when he took his oath of office on December 21, 1784. He served for five years, turning over his records to Thomas Jefferson, who was the first Secretary of State under the new United States Constitution. Jay established America's first consular posts in China and elsewhere.

Jay wrote the Federalist Papers that addressed foreign affairs (numbers 2, 3, 4, 5, and 64), and was instrumental in New York's ratification of the new federal Constitution. While serving as United States Supreme Court Chief Justice, George Washington recalled him to diplomatic service, as America's Minister Plenipotentiary to London in 1794. In what history recalls as the "Jay Treaty," Great Britain agreed to leave its forts on America's western frontier, and in a diplomatic innovation, an arbitration procedure was agreed to settle claims still outstanding after the Revolutionary War. This treaty secured American shipping from British harassment and averted renewed war, but it was unpopular with sectors of the American public. Nonetheless, while on this mission, New York voters elected him to be the second Governor of the State of New York, and he left the Supreme Court to take up this post.

In many cities, buildings carry plaques that recall historic events that transpired therein. London's Blue Plaques commemorate John F. Kennedy, but not John Jay. http://www.english-heritage.org.uk/visit/blue-plaques/about-blue-plaques/ (last visited April 6, 2017). When should building plaques be placed? Who should place them? Should they be mounted for an event or persons at a site where the original building no longer exists? What memories are captured by a building plaque, such as the one in Paris for John Jay? New York City was the capital of the United States where Jay led America's crucial foreign diplomacy. Why is this dimension of his legacy not recalled?

Plaque Celebrating John Jay. Photo by Jayapura, Free Art License, via Wikimedia Commons.

Chapter 11

Historic Preservation and Impacts of Climate Change

A. Anticipating Impacts

The five Assessment Reports of the Intergovernmental Panel on Climate Change (IPCC) have described the current and anticipated impacts of climate change, https://www.ipcc.ch/report/ar5/ (last visited April 1, 2017), the more recent of which includes predictions of remarkable increases in the measures of climate change: carbon dioxide concentration levels greater than any time in the last 650,000 years; significant rises in global average temperatures; substantial rises in global ocean heat content and consequently sea levels. www.ippc.ch/pub/pub.htm (last visited March 31, 2017). It is expected that changes in extreme and/or severe weather events such as heat waves, droughts, extreme precipitations, severe tropical cyclones, will also occur. *Climate Change 2014, Synthesis, Summary of Policy Makers*, https://www.ipcc.ch/pdf/assessment-report/ar5/syr/AR5_SYR_FINAL_SPM.pdf at 7–11 (last visited March 20, 2017). Historic sites are vulnerable to the effects of intense weather conditions, sea level rise and storm surges on coastal areas, and this vulnerability is increased by a lack of resources to maintain or restore them. "[C]limate change will constitute one of the major challenges of the 21st century" to the preservation of historic properties. Director-General of UNESCO, Koïchiro Matsuura. Case Studies on Climate Change and Cultural Heritage, http://unesdoc.unesco.org/images/0015/001506/150600e.pdf (last visited April 6, 2017) ("Case Studies"). Many sites on the World Heritage List, designated because they are irreplaceable sources and reflections of human existence and inspiration, may be threatened by impacts of climate change. In 2007, the World Heritage Committee published a paper addressing the issues relating to climate change and world heritage properties. *Issues Related To The State Of Conservation Of Properties Inscribed On The World Heritage List*, (WHC-06/30.COM/7.1, p. 22), The Impacts Of Climate Change On World Heritage Properties (activity-393-1.doc.) ("Impacts"). The projected impacts from climate change described in that paper, are both physical and social—ranging from erosion of physical structures to the break-up and even abandonment of the societies and communities supporting World Heritage Sites, with the eventual loss of cultural memory. Impacts at § V(H), ¶ 120. Independent assessments concur with UNESCO's findings. *See e.g.*, Monica Contestibile, "Cultural World Heritage At Risk," *Nature Climate Change* 4, 243 (2014), http://www.nature.com/nclimate/journal/v4/n4/full/nclimate2189.html (last visited April 6, 2017).

Climate change threatens the physical integrity of historic sites in myriad ways:

- Rising air temperatures accelerate the melting of glaciers, destroying the extraordinary aesthetic beauty of mountainous regions and destroying the habitat of rare wildlife species such as the snow leopard. Melting glaciers portend flooding from glacial lake outbursts, putting human settlements and landmarks in danger.
- Increased ocean temperatures and acidification produce bleaching events that impede conservation and lead to death of tropical reefs, putting hundreds of thousands of fish species, who find habitat in the reefs at risk.
- Increased air temperatures threaten hydrological cycles and terrestrial biodiversity, causing migration of pests and invasive species that lead to infestation of timber and other organic building materials. There is also the threat of disruption of the timing of biological events, such as flowering, and the relationships between predator and prey, parasite and host, plant and pollinator.
- Increased floods, changes in precipitation, melting permafrost and changes in soil composition threaten the loss of buried archaeological evidence and compromise the integrity of ancient buildings designed in a specific climate.
- Sea level rise and coastal erosion threaten to inundate coastal areas and historic and all other structures located in coastal lowlands.

See UNESCO's Case Studies, which note impacts of climate change on specific heritage sites, such as in the City of London and Venice (effects of high tides, storm surges). *See also* SUSAN SHEARING, HERE TODAY, GONE TOMORROW? CLIMATE CHANGE AND WORLD HERITAGE 9 (2007); Caithleen Daly, *Climate Change and the Conservation of Sites*, REVIEW OF IMPACTS THEORY CONSERVATION AND MANAGEMENT OF ARCHAEOLOGICAL SITES, 293–310, Vol. 13 (no. 4) (2011); NICHOLAS ROBINSON, DAVID HODAS, JAMES GUSTAVE SPETH, CLIMATE CHANGE LAW: MITIGATION AND ADAPTATION (2009); WORLD HERITAGE IN DANGER: A COMPENDIUM OF KEY DECISIONS ON THE CONSERVATION OF NATURAL WORLD HERITAGE PROPERTIES VIA THE LIST OF WORLD HERITAGE IN DANGER (IUCN, 2008); May Cassar, "Climate Change and the Historic Environment, http://discovery.ucl.ac.uk/2082/1/2082.pdf (2005) (last visited April 1, 2017).

Climate change impacts will disrupt human settlements in predictable ways. Flood and storm surges and intense winds from extreme weather effects are already evident. Recovery from "Super Storm Sandy" in New York has taken years. Local governments need to rethink how planning and development policies and laws prioritize their historic and cultural heritage. *See* John Travis Marshall and Ryan Max Rowberry, *Urban Wreckage and Resilience: Articulating A Practical Framework for Preserving, Reconstructing and Building Cities*, 50 IDAHO LAW REV. 50–84 (2014). Cities that enjoy significant tourism because of being home to historic landmarks and monuments will find their revenues at risk. *See* "World Heritage and Tourism in a Changing Climate," (UNESCO, UNEP and UCS 2016) at http://www.ucsusa.org/global-warming/global-warming-impacts/world-heritage-tourism-sites-climate-change-risks#.WOBjeiMrK8o (last visited April 6, 2017).

Responding to impacts of climate change on landmarks and cultural landscapes will require strategic and integrated planning. Cultural heritage will need to be singled out as a priority in land use planning at the landscape scale. Because this is not done now, communities are likely to fail to observe change caused by climate change that is outside normal ranges before the damage is irreparable. Cultural landscapes will likely find increased extremes of wetting and drying, increased risk of subsidence and decay of stonework and erosion, and losses of indigenous vegetation. For example, mature trees lost to extreme weather cannot be replaced with trees of equal age. Even so, what trees should be replanted? Are trees that are more resilient to new temperature or rainfall conditions more suitable? Cultural landscapes require assessments in different time periods, both long and short term views. *See generally* Robert Z. Melnick, *Climate Change and Landscape Preservation: A Twenty-First Century Conundrum*, APT Bulletin: Journal of Preservation Technology, 40:3–4 (2009).

1. United States Historic Properties and Preparedness

The Union of Concerned Scientists issued a report in 2014 on "National Landmarks At Risk." http://www.ucsusa.org/global_warming/science_and_impacts/impacts/national-landmarks-at-risk-from-climate-change.html#.WOBhPyMrK8o (last visited March 31, 2017). They provide case studies of sites with known records of damage and predictable risks, from Boston Harbor's landmarks to those at Ellis Island and Cape Canaveral. What should property managers of these historic sites be doing to anticipate and prevent harm? Is insurance enough? Many government-owned sites are "self-insured" and expect taxpayers to respond if damage occurs, but will this approach be adequate in the future given the magnitude of impacts expected?

The National Park Service ("NPS") is monitoring the effects of climate change on the nation's protected resources. At Joshua Tree National Park, changes in climate are making the park inhospitable to its namesake species. The melting of glaciers is occurring in both Glacier National Park and Mount Rainier National Park, threatening permanent loss of cultural and natural resources and causing downstream runoffs in the waterways alongside the historic roads. Rising sea levels and intensifying storms are feared to alter the landscape at Assateague Island National Seashore and affect the access and experience of visitors. Climate Change Response Strategy and Climate Change Action Plan, http://www.nps.gov/subjects/climatechange/index.htm (last visited April 1, 2017).

The NPS believes that tackling climate change depends on well-developed practices, reinforced by federal mandates and NPS initiatives, such as the *Green Parks Plan* and *Climate Change Action Plan*, that require agencies to become more sustainable and to track and mitigate greenhouse gas emissions. These initiatives require that parks consider the effects of climate change before building, renovating, or making significant capital investments into NPS facilities and to make educated and calculated adaptation, siting, construction, repair, and rehabilitation decisions. www.nps.gov/orgs/socc/mitigation and adaptation.htm (last visited April 1, 2017).

The NPS has provided some guidance on preparing for the impacts of climate change on historic and cultural properties. *See* https://www.nps.gov/subjects/climatechange/adaptationforculturalresources.htm (last visited April 1, 2017).

> Unlike natural systems, cultural resources are utterly dependent upon people to help them withstand climate change. The adaptation strategy for cultural resources considers climate change impacts to specific locations, materials, and significance of these resources and the sustainability and feasibility of potential responses. An adaptive framework for cultural resource management includes the following steps:
>
> 1. Inventory: What resources exist within areas of concern? What is their character? How and to whom are they significant?
> 2. Vulnerability assessment: What are the threats to identified resources and to areas awaiting inventory?
> 3. Development of adaptation options: How do we define the universe of potential responses? Which ones are feasible? Which ones are sustainable? How do we engage stakeholders to choose among them?
> 4. Implementation: Ongoing action to undertake resource- and threat-appropriate responses or mitigate predicted losses.
>
> The adaptation options step is the most common point of discussion in adaptation planning, but it cannot function well without the other steps in the framework. While options can take many forms, a general list includes: (1) No action, determine need for monitoring; (2) Deflect or remove environmental stressor; (3) Modify resource to better withstand environmental stressor; (4) Movement, either through relocation of a stationary resource or enabling migration of a biotic resource; (5) Document comprehensively, allow location to be lost; (6) Document briefly, allow location to be lost; and (7) Interpret the change, as climate change is the heritage of the future.

* * *

2. Sea Level Rise and Coastal Historic Sites: Venice, New Orleans, & New York

Relative sea levels are rising world-wide. The New York State Department of Environmental Conservation has officially determined that by 2100, sea levels on the State's Atlantic coast could rise 75 inches (6.2 feet). 6 NYCRR Part 490 (2017). By the 2020s, the New York City area is expected to experience a ten-inch rise, and 30 inches by the 2050s. Promulgation of these projections was required by the State's Community Risk and Resiliency Act. ENVTL CONSERV. LAW § 3-0319. They will be used in land use planning and in preparing environmental impact assessments. These sea level projections present challenges to a large number of coastal landmarks in New York City. The same problems exist for cities such as Venice, which is subsiding while sea levels gradually rise. http://www.livescience.com/19195-venice-sinking-slowly.html (last visited September 11, 2017), and for New Orleans (Drew Broach, "New Orleans Area Sea Rise to be among world's highest," *Times-Picayune,* Nov. 28, 2016, at http://www.nola.com/environment/index.ssf/2016/11/new_orleans_sea_level_rise_amo.html). Maps of projected sea levels are increasingly available. *See e.g.*, http://geology.com/sea-level-rise/venice.shtml (last visited April 6, 2017).

How do these three cities reflect comparable issues confronting landmarks in all coastal regions?

Three Cities Threatened by the Seas:
Three Approaches to their Protection and Preservation

(1) *Venice*

The "Most Serene Republic of Venice," is threatened by the confluence of man-made and natural circumstances. Poorly developed infrastructure, poorly constructed buildings (many of wood and reed) and poorly defended shores, have left the city vulnerable to devastation through flooding and fire. As the city sits in a lagoon, the peril of flooding is ever-present. Yet, over the centuries, the Venetian Republic pursued development over conservation. It was only in the 19th century that the notion of restoration and protection took hold. Though the tension between conservation and modernization persisted, today conservation laws exist to the point that over ninety-five percent of buildings in Venice are listed as historical monuments. Venice: Myth and Reality—The Future Cities project, futurecities.org.uk/2012/11/02/venice-myth-and-reality.

While the ancient Venetians resorted to rituals, ceremonies and myths in response to the forces of the sea, the increasing numbers of high water events from climate change and the toll exacted by the millions of tourists upon the fragile historic monuments, has led the country to appreciate that spiritual measures would not be enough to hold back the insistent sea. *See id.* The dramatic flood of November 1966 when Venice and other areas in the lagoon were completely submerged, was the great impetus for national legislation to safeguard Venice. Recent observations about climate change and the resulting sea level rise portend two great threats to the viability of the city—the lessening of the city's capacity to "float" in the lagoon and the loss of land to subsidence by eustasy. Since 1900, the average number of flooding events has risen by some four hundred times and the number of occurrences of tides equal to or greater than 80 cm have increased by some six times. In the past 100 years, Venice has sunk resulting in an althimetric loss of 23 cm, 12 cm from sea level rise and eustasy accounting for the remaining 11 cm of this change. This loss of land and rising of seas mean greater intensity and frequency of flooding events. *Integrated System for the Safeguard of Venice and its Lagoon from Flooding (MOSE) 2014*, http://climate-adapt.eea.europa.eu/metadata/case-studies/integrated-system-for-the-safeguard-of-venice-and-its-lagoon-against-flooding-mose (last visited April 6, 2017).

Technological Responses

The most recent effort in managing the sea is the Mose (Modulo Sperimentale Elettromeccanicoor or Experimental Electromechanical Module), flood defense system. The system consists of a series of mobile barriers, made up of lines of flap-gates built into the inlet canal beds, designed to isolate the lagoon from the sea in the case of tides higher than the pre-established height, +110 cm. The system limits the closure of the inlets up to three to five times per year, with the current sea level, by this assuring water quality, safeguarding the morphology and landscape and facilitating port activities. The system (with the reinforcement of the coastal strip) was designed on the basis of a precautionary criterion to cope with an increase of up to 60 cm in sea level, that is, higher even than the latest estimates from the IPCC which predict an increase in sea level of between 18 and 59 cm during the next 100 years. *Id.*

The Forecast

In 2011, UNESCO convened a workshop on the ecological implications of climate change on the Venice Lagoon. The aim of the workshop was to develop a basis for a better understanding of the vulnerability of the Venice Lagoon in relation to climate change mechanisms and to contribute to the development of appropriate responses. The challenges for the city were identified as re-establishing an average sea level that allows full, urban and social functions without disturbing the physical structure of the City—world renowned as an irreplaceable socio-cultural ecosystem. The report of the Workshop, *The Future of Venice and Its Lagoon in the Context of Global Climate Change: The Ecological Implications of Climate Change on the Lagoon in Venice*, www.unesco.org/venice (last visited April 6, 2017), identified both global responses (including changes in the water column, river hydrology and a northward shift of bioclimatic regions) and site-specific effects. In particular, the report concludes that the Lagoon in Venice will be affected and driven mainly by a combination of rising air and sea temperatures (by 3.5°C and 3.0°C, respectively), that result in increased salinity and inadequate filtration due to an increasing number of flooding events that disturb the desirable hydrological balance necessary for a healthy lagoon, in turn giving rise to migration of species and the introduction of invasive species. As rainy seasons become more intense and short-term, with flash floods, there will be less soil infiltration into groundwater. The loss of sediment on the lagoon floor will affect nutrient levels and composition, disturbing habitats for species of plant and animal life. These physical effects will in turn inflict stress upon the foundations and walls of the city's fabric, undermining the physical structure. The forecast "implies a drastic change in land use in the watershed, a change in the use of the lagoon and a change in the City's infrastructures ..." *Id.* at 28.

The Death of a Jewel

UNESCO's overall assessment is that the predictions are for sea level rises to points that cannot be tolerated by the city. Some frightening scenarios are suggested. A partial closing of the lagoon as planned to be accomplished by the MOSE system, will prevent surges of the sea, but only for so long. A gradual complete closing of the lagoon will mean its death, as all the negative effects of climate change, especially species impoverishment and risk of further entrophication, will be accelerated in a lagoon without water exchange, leading to ecological collapse. This may mean that the world may have to choose between closure of the entire lagoon or enucleation of Venice and the islands. *Id.* at 8.

(2) *New Orleans*

The city had not suffered flooding from the Mississippi River since 1895; instead, the most damaging floods have come from hurricane surge off of Lake Pontchartrain. Since 1559, there have been 177 hurricanes along Louisiana's coastline. J. D. Rogers, M.ASCE, *Development of the New Orleans Flood Protection System prior to Hurricane Katrina,* J. of Geotechnical And Geoenvironmental Eng'g (May 2008). Before Hurricane Katrina in 2005, the threat of inundation from the river and hurricanes was addressed by a system of pump stations that pumped water into the river, the lake, and adjacent bayous. Concrete flood walls along the subsiding drainage canals were constructed in the 1990s, although some transition elements remained incomplete when Hurricane Katrina struck. *Id.* at 1.

Hurricane Katrina accelerated what had been a gradual, yet inexorable, movement. Like Venice, Louisiana has been experiencing land loss at an alarming rate—more than 1,880 square miles since the 1930s, http://www.coastalmasterplan.louisiana.gov/whats-at-stake/overview (last visited April 3, 2017).

The storm was historic in the historic city of New Orleans. About one-fifth of New Orleans' urban area is in an historic district listed on the National Register of Historic Places. The rage of the storm caused the levee/floodwall breaches, leading to widespread flood damage to residential neighborhoods throughout the New Orleans area. Scores of people died and tens of thousands of historic homes throughout the city were destroyed. It was the single largest disaster for cultural resources in the United States since the National Historic Preservation Act of 1966 (NHPA) was enacted. Hurricane Katrina in the Gulf Coast Mitigation Assessment Team Report ("Assessment Team Report"), http://www.fema.gov/media-library-data/20130726-1520-20490-4521/549_ch8.pdf (last visited April 6, 2017).

The parts of New Orleans that were destroyed were the low rent districts. The depth of the waters ranged from one foot in the Jefferson Parish in the west, up to 8 feet on the lower Ninth ward. Juliette Landphair, "*The Forgotten People of New Orleans*": *Community, Vulnerability, and the Lower Ninth Ward,* 94 J. of Am. His. 837–45 (Dec. 2007). The high ground along Lake Pontchartrain between the 17th Street Canal and the Industrial Canal were essentially free of flooding. These relatively elevated land areas that formed parts of the rim of the New Orleans "bowl" suffered the least amount of flooding from Hurricane Katrina. Structural damage to the majority of buildings in New Orleans came from high velocity floodwaters and strong winds that produced waves that dislodged buildings from their foundations and took down load-bearing walls. Residential buildings sited immediately behind failed sections of levees or other flood control structures were the most vulnerable.

As the Federal Emergency Management Agency (FEMA) arrived on the scene, it discovered that the task of removing damaged structures would be complicated by obligations under Section 106 of NHPA, 54 U.S.C. § 306108, that requires in a federal undertaking, the agency consider the effects of the project on historic properties and consult with applicable state, tribal, and local parties to develop ways of mitigating any effects. The first task facing FEMA was to identify historic properties. To meet its obligation under NHPA while quickly carrying outs its own functions, FEMA employed the National Park Service's Cultural Resource GIS Facility, that enabled the assessment of more than 40,000 structures in a fraction of the time it would have taken using other data collection methods. *GPS and GIS Technologies Speed Assessment of Historic Sites in Post-Katrina New Orleans*, http://www.gislounge.com/gps-historic-sites-katrina (last visited April 6, 2017). The NPS system collects locational data to establish a baseline of inventory information. Each resource was mapped as a point, line, or polygon, which enabled expert historians to record features and attributes data in a GIS with geospatial location as the common element, making it possible to share the data among many different systems. A data dictionary ensured consistent collection and recording of a structure's architectural style using local terms, while also assessing its structural integrity relating to flood damage. Using the integrated "Trimble GPS" handheld device, the assessor made entries describing more than 40 architectural details of the roof, exterior, windows and foundation. As FEMA crews assessed buildings on five aspects of structural integrity, a surveyor filled out the data collection menu, and a photographer used a digital camera to take photos from different vantages. *Id.*

Technological Responses

Following Hurricane Katrina, the State of Louisiana adopted what had been described as a ground breaking planning effort by the state's Coastal Protection and Restoration Authority ("CPRA"). The 2012 Coastal Master Plan, http://www.coastalmasterplan.louisiana.gov/2012-master-plan/elements-of-the-plan (last visited April 5, 2017), casts the calamity as an opportunity to take bold action to save the coast and secure south Louisiana's future. The CPRA's plan was based on a two-year analysis involving some of the state's best scientists as well as national and international specialists. The state used this analysis to select more than one hundred high performing projects, which if fully implemented, could substantially increase flood protection for communities and create a sustainable coast. The prominent components of the master plan are: 1) protection—use of a combination of restoration, nonstructural, and targeted structural measures to provide increased flood protection for all communities and 2) restoration—use of an integrated and synergistic approach to ensure a sustainable and resilient coastal landscape. Structural measures include levees, flood walls, and pumps that protect large areas, including restoring barrier islands, headlands and shorelines. Nonstructural measures include risk reduction actions that homeowners and businesses can individually take, such as elevating or floodproofing.

In 2017, the state published Louisiana's Comprehensive Master Plan for a Sustainable Coast, coastal.la.gov/wp-content/uploads/2016/08/2017-MP_Book_Single_Combined-01.05.2017.pdf, which by it terms, "set[ ] an ambitious path to respond to the loss of coastal land and the threats from storm surge events." The plan embraces the key components of the 2012 plan and aims to achieve these goals through restoration and structural risk reduction measures.

The Forecast

Given the importance of so many of south Louisiana's natural assets—its waterways, natural resources, unique culture, and wetlands—the land loss crisis was identified as nothing short of a national emergency. Both plans contained expressed provisions for the improvement of flood risk protection for archaeological sites and historic properties, historic sites, and historic districts. But given the very ominous threats from climate change, it remains to see how well the projects reduce flood risk and how well they build new land or sustain the land existing. Both plans expressed the belief that it was possible to halt in a significant way, the net loss of land that had been accelerating over the last several decades. Rebuilding of the coast would mean new habitats for wildlife, improved storm buffering capacity, and greater protection for coastal residents and businesses.

Inevitability and Folly of Rebuilding

While the CPRA plans seemed visionary, its hopefulness might be too high. As in the case of Venice, the first response to disasters through its history was to rebuild, although with prophylactic measures incorporated. But, is this the best vision? Can human structures be constructed to resist the ravages of another Katrina or should humans just yield and set up elsewhere? One researcher conceived of two plans for rebuilding a safer, more sustainable New Orleans. One is to create a delta for the river in a location away from the city and the other is to move the working class out of the city into a new, New Orleans and leave the old city as a tourist destination. As its history has shown, the Mississippi Delta is a dynamic event and not a static landmark. This means that any long term plan for the delta must embrace working with the river instead of against it. Reclaiming soil by building up the delta, seems a natural and safer alternative to allowing the river to continue to run straight into the gulf. David P. Muth, *The Once and Future Delta*, in PERSPECTIVES ON THE RESTORATION OF THE MISSISSIPPI DELTA: THE ONCE AND FUTURE DELTA, J. DAY, G.P. KEMP, A.FREEMAN, D.P. MUTH, eds 8–10 (2014).

(3) *New York*

In October 2012, Hurricane Sandy, dubbed a "superstorm," attacked the North Atlantic shore. Its tropical force winds extended more than 1000 miles, making it three times the size of Hurricane Katrina. The mean high tide was more than fourteen feet, exceeding by four feet all events that came before. Sandy caused a sea surge of large volumes of water as well as powerful waves that wreaked havoc on buildings and infrastructure. Record ocean waves of over thirty feet were measured in the ocean southeast of the Rockaway Peninsula. Hundreds of homes and buildings were destroyed and scores of people died or suffered serious injury. A staggering 51 square miles of New York City flooded—17 percent of the city's total land mass. Scores of historic monuments were damaged by the storm, starting with the most prominent, Ellis Island, where the Immigration Museum sits, and Liberty Island, a 12 acre island located a mile south of lower Manhattan on which the Statue of Liberty sits. Normally, Liberty Island is protected from extreme weather by the New York Harbor, but stood in the direct path of Hurricane Sandy and the massive storm surge. The hurricane covered 75% of Liberty Island

and almost all of Ellis Island, flooding the basements of all buildings, destroying electric, water, sewer, HVAC, phone systems, and security systems, as well as radio equipment. Two piers and the perimeter walkway and railings around the island were severely damaged. The 126 year old iron statue, however, withstood the storm's fierce winds and kept its stature as a beacon of liberty. *Hurricane Sandy Recovery*, http://www.nps.gov/stli/after-hurricane-sandy.htm (last visited April 6, 2017).

At another part of the coast, Sandy put the South Street Seaport Museum under several feet of water. The Police Museum, the Italian renaissance style First Precinct Police Station, that was built on a landfill in what had been a boat slip, suffered extensive flood damage. The wooden floors of the Robbin's Reef Lighthouse were destroyed. The grounds of the Alice Austen House, Staten Island, home of one of America's earliest and most prolific female photographers, a Gothic Revival style cottage now a museum, were soaked, causing moisture in the basement where important photography and paper collections are stored. The Jewish Center of Brighton Beach, Brooklyn, a 1931 Mediterranean Revival synagogue, suffered extensive flood damage to its basement and first floor.

Other monuments felt the ravages of Sandy's winds. At the Woodlawn Cemetery in the Bronx, many large trees were toppled, damaging historic monuments and gravestones. So too was the Sailors' Snug Harbor Cultural Center on Staten Island, that had several windows and doors blown out by the storm. The 1799 stone building, Mt. Vernon Hotel Museum, converted to a hotel in 1826, now a museum run by the Colonial Dames of America, had the exterior wooden shutters ripped from their hinges. The effects of the storm also fell upon Prospect Park, Brooklyn, The Cemetery of the Evergreens, and the Garibaldi-Meucci Museum on Staten Island dedicated to Italian American heritage in America, where trees were toppled and exteriors damaged. New York Landmarks Conservancy, Preservation Issues, Sandy Assistance Update October 29, 2013—A Year After Sandy, http://www.nylandmarks.org/advocacy/preservation_issues/sandy_assistance_update_90_days_later (last visited April 6, 2017).

Technological Responses

The city adopted an ambitious plan for defending the city from climate change—to make it tougher. Rejecting the impossible notion of walling off the city, the plan describes a resilient city—not one that is shielded from climate change all of the time, but one that is protected by effective defenses and adapted to mitigate most climate impacts; capable of springing back quickly when those defenses are breached by severe events. Recommendations range from installing removable flood walls in lower Manhattan to restoring marshes in Jamaica Bay in Queens, including flood proofing on homes and setting repair timeframe standards for phone and internet service providers. In lower Manhattan, a removable system of posts and slats is contemplated to be deployed to form temporary flood walls. Projects also include a 15-to-20-foot levee to guard part of Staten Island, building dunes in the Rockaways, building barrier systems of levees and gates to bar one creek from carrying floodwaters inland, and possibly creating a levee and a sizeable new "Seaport City" development in lower Manhattan.

The measures also contemplate increasing coastal edge elevation, installing structures to minimize upland wave zones and protect against storm surges, and improving coastal design and governance. Rebuilding would include resiliency features (such as locating electrical power mechanisms atop buildings) and new zoning ordinances that encourage retrofitting buildings to the same extent, as well as authorizing cost-effective housing types that are resilient. *After Sandy*, http://uli.org/wp-content/uploads/ULI-Documents/AfterSandy.pdf (last visited April 6, 2017).

The Forecast

Although FEMA's flood maps in effect when Sandy hit indicated that 33 square miles of New York City might be inundated during a "100-year" flood, that is, the kind of flood estimated to have only a one percent chance of occurring in any given year, Sandy's storm tide caused flooding that exceeded the 100-year floodplain boundaries by 53 percent citywide. The predictions of the New York City Panel on Climate Change (NPCC) are dire: more intense storms by the 2050s and more intense storm impacts as the rise in sea levels raise the base level of water around the five boroughs.

The Imperatives of a New Land Use Philosophy

No doubt the rhythms and monotony of the ocean waves can be contemplative, hypnotic, soothing, enrapturing, but these feelings cannot justify the placement of structures at the striking point of the next Hurricane Sandy. Indeed, rebuilding at the edge of the sea, even with resiliency, may reflect a naiveté as to the ways of nature, too costly for society to indulge. The very evident effects of climate change may call us to embrace further limits on where we are allowed to settle. For those historic structures and valuable cultural resources already in place, the task of fortifying them will be a great one.

Notes and Questions

1. **Governmental responses.** In the wake of recent severe weather events, many municipalities and state governments are taking pro-active measures against loss and destruction, including requiring fortifications (against wind and tremors) and elevation of structures and infrastructure, removing populations from coasts, increasing required setbacks for building at the shoreline, and making some areas undevelopable. *See* Shelby D. Green, *Building Resilient Communities While Keeping Housing Safe from Sea Changes in Nature and Policy*, 54 Washburn L.J. 527 (2015).

2. **Protocols and gaps.** The federal Advisory Council on Historic Preservation and the Federal Emergency Management Agency have developed a "Model Statewide Programmatic Agreement" for local governments to prepare to protect historic properties from the adverse impacts of climate change events? *See* www.achp.gov/fema-pa.html (last visited September 11, 2017). a. Are such measures adequate? b. Should nations demand that environmental impact assessments as required under Principle 17 of the Rio Declaration on Environment and Development be prepared to assess risks to historic sites and cultural heritage and be protected to the fullest extent possible? c. Why does NEPA not yet require such a measure? *See* NEPA and NHPA, A Handbook for Integrating NEPA and Section 106 (Council on Environmental Quality and the Advisory Council on Historic Preservation, March 2013), at www.achp.gov/docs/NEPA_NHPA_Sectipon_106_Handbook_Mar2013.pdf.

3. Moving Monuments from Harm's Way

The preference for historic preservation is to maintain a landmark *in situ*, where it has integrity of place. When this location is subject to extreme flooding conditions, or is subject to erosion, or in an area where rising sea levels will inundate the area, the issue arises about moving the landmark to a safe location. This was done with the Roman Temple of Dendur, which in 1965 was moved from the rising waters caused by the construction of the Aswan High Dam in Egypt to the Metropolitan Museum of Art in New York. The sandstone of the Temple of Dendur is preserved from the elements of weather by being rebuilt in a climate controlled interior building. In the United States, lighthouses are also being moved. The complications associated with such moves are cautionary tales.

George Washington commissioned the first lighthouse in America in 1797, the Highland Light in Truro, Massachusetts. In the 1830s, a sturdy brick lighthouse replaced the original wooden structure. Edward Hopper's iconic painting of the Highland Light, in Harvard University's Art Museum, is widely reproduced. As the Atlantic Ocean's waves eroded the bluffs on which the lighthouse stood, its site was in danger, and in 1996 it was moved 450 feet to the west. The Coast Guard had turned the Highland Light over to the National Park Service. The move, which was funded both by government grants and the Truro Historical Society, was delicately and successfully undertaken by the International Chimney Corporation of Buffalo, New York and Expert House Movers of Maryland. In 2014, however, cracks and broken bricks appeared.

A $50,000 NPS study determined that a ventilation shaft within the brick walls had been blocked when the lighthouse was moved, and the top ventilation vents painted over, so that moisture condensed within the walls. Rehabilitation of the ventilation shaft and repairs to the brickwork will require $1.5 million starting in 2018. Ben Gagnon, *Highland Light Scheduled for Repairs*, The Cape Codder, p. A12 (March 24, 2017).

Notes and Questions

1. **Removal of structures in wake of rising seas.** a. Should a structure be moved or relocated in order to preserve it, for instance, a lighthouse away from the encroaching seas? b. When a structure is moved from its original site, has it lost its historic integrity?

2. **Preserving by moving.** a. What generic issues arise from moving landmarks? b. How can the original site be documented and interpreted? c. Must the new site be nearby? d. Is the new site historic because it now hosts the landmark structure? Consider the case of the Gay Head lighthouse.

Gay Head Lighthouse

"Perched atop multi-colored cliffs at the western end of Martha's Vineyard, Gay Head Lighthouse occupies a picture-perfect location. The cliffs exhibit vivid hues of green, yellow, black, brown, red, and white and attract visitors from all over the world. The first European to name this natural feature was explorer Bartholomew Gosnold, who ... in 1602, called them Dover Cliffs after the famous chalky landmark along the English Channel.... By the 1660s, the area became ... known as Gay Head because of the gaily-colored cliffs. In 1998 the town nearest the lighthouse changed its name from Gay Head to Aquinnah, which is Wampanoag for 'end of the island.'

In December 2012, it was reported 'The land on which the light tower is situated is eroding at a rate of nearly two feet per year and only 50 feet now remain between the tower and the approaching cliffs,' that 'If the Gay Head Light is not relocated, Martha's Vineyard will undoubtedly lose a historic emblem within just a few short years.' A buffer of thirty feet was needed to move the lighthouse, so the relocation had to occur before 2022.... On February 5, 2013, residents voted to acquire the lighthouse and appropriated $5,000 from the town's Community Preservation Act (CPA) funds for a feasibility and planning study for saving the lighthouse.... In September 2014, the Town of Aquinnah's application to take ownership of the lighthouse was approved, and the structure was officially awarded to the town on February 20, 2015.... Relocation of the tower was carried out over a three-day period in May 2015, after a concrete pad at the new site had been prepared. The lighthouse came to rest atop its new foundation at 11:10 a.m. on May 30, and a champagne bottle was smashed against the lighthouse to celebrate the end of its 175-foot journey. International Chimney Corporation, which moved Sankaty Head Lighthouse on Nantucket in 2007 and Highland Lighthouse and Nauset Lighthouse on Cape Cod in 1996, supervised the relocation and employed the services of Expert House Movers." Gay Head Lighthouse, Massachusetts at Lighthousefriends.com, http://www.lighthousefriends.com/light.asp?ID=627 (last visited April 6, 2017).

3. **Preserving Light: Historic Lighthouses.** Lighthouses have played a vital role in America's history, serving as beacons to sea-farers and traders and sentinels for our coastlines, as well as symbols of our rich cultural past. In 2000, Congress passed the National Historic Lighthouse Preservation Act (NHLPA), Pub. L. 106-355, 54 U.S.C. § 305101, *et seq.*, as an amendment to the National Historic Preservation Act, to establish a lighthouse preservation program that recognizes the cultural, recreational, and educational value of these heroic properties, especially for local coastal communities and nonprofit organizations. Under the NHLPA, historic lighthouses and light stations ("lights") are made available for transfer at no cost to federal agencies, state and local governments, and non-profit organizations, as stewards of maritime history, for park and recreation, cultural and historic, and educational uses. While serving to preserve maritime heritage, the program also provides substantial cost savings to the United States Coast Guard (USCG) since the historic structures, expensive to repair and maintain, are no longer needed by the USCG to meet its mission as aids to navigation.

Under the act, non-profit entities stand on equal footing with federal agencies and other public bodies to obtain historic lighthouse properties. Non-profit organizations are encouraged to organize and incorporate prior to the official notice of available lights being issued. A group must demonstrate its financial ability to maintain the historic light station and commitment to adhering to historic covenants and other terms and conditions of the transfer.

Since the NHLPA program's inception in 2000, 120 lights (including the GayHead Lighthouse) have been transferred to eligible entities. Sixty-four percent of the transferred lights (74 lights) have been conveyed through stewardship transfers to interested government or not-for-profit organizations, while 36 percent (46 lights) have been conveyed through public sales, generating over $6.3 million dollars.

The General Services Administration (GSA), USCG, and National Park Service (NPS) work jointly to ensure that the government finds suitable new stewards for available historic light stations. Initially, USCG identifies lights that are no longer needed for mission purposes at the beginning of the government's fiscal year (October–December). The three partner agencies work together to develop an annual list of lights that will become available to new stewards. Eligible lighthouses and stations

Fort Point Lighthouse, San Francisco, California. Photo by Shelby D. Green.

are announced through a Notice of Availability (NOA). If interested parties submit an Expression of Interest (EOI), they are sent an application and those that respond are provided the opportunity to inspect the properties during an open house session. USCG and NPS assess the submitted applications on the merits of the preservation, the reuse plan, financial viability, and how the light will be managed. If there are no interested parties or suitable applicants, the light is recommended by the Department of Interior (DOI) for a public sale. GSA will then schedule and hold a public auction for the light. Conveyance documents include covenants for historic preservation and public access. Stewardship transfers also require that public access to the light be maintained. The USCG retains a right for access and to service aids to navigation equipment for any active lights.

In order to be eligible for the NHLPA program, light stations must receive a "historic" designation through a listing on the National Register of Historic Places or be formally determined eligible for listing by NPS's Keeper of the National Register. *See generally,* GSA Office of Real Property Utilization and Disposal, 2015 Program Highlights Report, National Historic Lighthouse Preservation Act, https://www.nps.gov/maritime/nhlpa/reports/2015NHLPAReport.pdf.

Table of Cases

Index